Business and Administrative Communication

NINTH EDITION

Business and Administrative Communication

KITTY O. LOCKER
The Ohio State University

DONNA S. KIENZLER
Iowa State University

McGraw-Hill Irwin

McGraw-Hill
Irwin

BUSINESS AND ADMINISTRATIVE COMMUNICATION

Published by McGraw-Hill/Irwin, a business unit of The McGraw-Hill Companies, Inc., 1221 Avenue of the Americas, New York, NY, 10020. Copyright © 2010, 2008, 2006, 2003, 2000, 1998, 1995, 1992, 1989 by The McGraw-Hill Companies, Inc. All rights reserved. No part of this publication may be reproduced or distributed in any form or by any means, or stored in a database or retrieval system, without the prior written consent of The McGraw-Hill Companies, Inc., including, but not limited to, in any network or other electronic storage or transmission, or broadcast for distance learning.

Some ancillaries, including electronic and print components, may not be available to customers outside the United States.

This book is printed on acid-free paper.

1 2 3 4 5 6 7 8 9 0 DOW/DOW 0 9

ISBN   978-0-07-016718-6

MHID   0-07-016718-4

To my beloved husband Jim and closest friend Kitty.

Kitty O. Locker was an Associate Professor of English at The Ohio State University in Columbus, Ohio, where she coordinated the Writing Center and taught courses in business and technical discourse and in research methods. She also taught as Assistant Professor at Texas A&M University and the University of Illinois.

She also wrote *The Irwin Business Communication Handbook: Writing and Speaking in Business Classes* (1993), coauthored *Business Writing Cases and Problems* (1980, 1984, 1987), and coedited *Conducting Research in Business Communication* (1988). She twice received the Alpha Kappa Psi award for Distinguished Publication in Business Communication for her article "'Sir, This Will Never Do': Model Dunning Letters 1592–1873" and for her article "'As Per Your Request': A History of Business Jargon." In 1992 she received the Association for Business Communication's Outstanding Researcher Award.

Her research included work on collaborative writing in the classroom and the workplace, and the emergence of bureaucratic writing in the correspondence of the British East India Company from 1600 to 1800.

Her consulting work included conducting tutorials and short courses in business, technical, and administrative writing for employees of URS Greiner, Ross Products Division of Abbott Laboratories, Franklin County, the Ohio Civil Service Employees Association, AT&T, the American Medical Association, Western Electric, the Illinois Department of Central Management Services, the Illinois Department of Transportation, the A. E. Staley Company, Flo-Con, the Police Executive Leadership College, and the Firemen's Institute. She developed a complete writing improvement program for Joseph T. Ryerson, the nation's largest steel materials service center.

She served as the Interim Editor of *The Bulletin of the Association for Business Communication* and, in 1994–95, as President of the Association for Business Communication (ABC). She edited ABC's *Journal of Business Communication* from 1998 to 2000.

In 1998, she received ABC's Meada Gibbs Outstanding Teacher Award.

Kitty O. Locker passed away in 2005.

Donna S. Kienzler is a Professor of English at Iowa State University in Ames, Iowa, where she teaches in the Rhetoric and Professional Communication program. She is the Director of Advanced Communication and oversees more that 120 sections of business and technical communication annually. She is also an Assistant Director of the university's Center for Excellence in Learning and Teaching, where she teaches classes, seminars, and workshops on pedagogy; directs graduate student programming; and directs the Preparing Future Faculty program.

Her research focuses on pedagogy and ethics. Her article with Helen Ewald, "Speech Act Theory and Business Communication Conventions," won an Association for Business Communication (ABC) Alpha Kappa Psi Foundation Award for distinguished publication in business communication. Her article with Carol David, "Towards an Emancipatory Pedagogy in Service Courses and User Departments" was part of a collection that won a National Council of Teachers of English (NCTE) Award for Excellence in Technical and Scientific Communication: Best Collection of Essays in Technical or Scientific Communication.

She has done consulting work for the Air Force, Tracor Consulting, Green Engineering, Northwestern Bell, Iowa Merit Employment, the Iowa Department of Transportation, the University of Missouri, and her local school district.

She is active in the Association for Business Communication (ABC), where she currently serves on the Business Practices and the Teaching Practices

Committees. She also served on ABC's Ad Hoc Committee on Professional Ethics, which developed a Professional Ethics Statement for the national organization.

In 2002, she received ABC's Meada Gibbs Outstanding Teacher Award.

Donna and Kitty became close friends in graduate school at the University of Illinois, Urbana–Champaign, where they shared the same major professor. They remained close friends, and indeed considered each other family, until Kitty's death. During those wonderful years, their favorite topic of conversation was *Business and Administrative Communication;* they discussed content for the original book proposal, content for the first edition, changes for subsequent editions, and future plans for the book. Everything from new sidebars and footnotes to major organizational changes made its way into those long, frequent conversations. These conversations have helped Donna carry on Kitty's tradition of excellence.

Welcome to *Business and Administrative Communication* (BAC). This textbook can make learning about business communication easier and more enjoyable.

You'll find that this edition of BAC is as flexible, specific, interesting, comprehensive, and up-to-date as its predecessors. The features users particularly like have been retained: the anecdotes and examples, the easy-to-follow lists, the integrated coverage of ethics and international business communication, the analyses of sample problems, the wealth of exercises and assignments. But a good book has become even better. This edition of BAC includes major changes.

Major Changes to the Ninth Edition

Major changes make the ninth edition even better:

- New chapter on the business environment, including sections on topics such as
  - Ethics.
  - Interpersonal communication.
  - Networking.
  - Time management, including multitasking.
- Separate chapter on proposals, with expanded coverage of both proposals and business plans.
- Expanded coverage of electronic communication including new topics such as instant messaging, social networks, electronic privacy, and Word 2007.
- New material in the job chapters such as the new section on application essays for students applying for internships, fellowships, and graduate and professional schools.
  - New material on the job search such as the use of keywords, safety considerations with online ads and job sites, online job fairs, altruistic job opportunities, and the role of networking in the job search process.
  - New material on interviewing such as meal etiquette, hidden negatives, employment history gaps, poor questions for interviewees to ask, and group interviews.
- New material on teamwork such as consensus building, crisis leadership, and 360-degree feedback.
- New material on researching including the use and misuse of Wikipedia and focus groups.
- Expanded material on topics such as PowerPoint, Web site design, social networks, layoffs, and performance appraisals.
- More emphasis on choosing and using conventions (checklists, patterns of organization) within the individual context of a specific writing task and audience.

Content Updates

In addition to the major changes, the ninth edition has new material throughout to keep it up-to-date for instructors and interesting for students:

- Current content such as
  - President Obama keeping his BlackBerry.
  - Incomprehensible documents as part of the financial meltdown of 2008.

- Definitions of torture with respect to waterboarding by two different attorneys general.
- Tips for handling a layoff in both job search documents and interviews.
- Bank scripts for leery customers after the September 2008 meltdown.
- Sexting.
- Speedo's high-tech swimsuit that helped swimmers win in the Olympics.
- New material from business best sellers:
  - Patrick Lencioni, *The Five Dysfunctions of a Team*
  - Bill Walsh, *The Elephants of Style: A Trunkload of Tips on the Big Issues and Gray Areas of Contemporary American English*
  - Geoff Smart and Randy Street, *Who: The A Method for Hiring*
  - Randy Pausch, *The Last Lecture*
- Interesting new examples:
  - Dilbert May Get You Fired.
  - Intern Queen.
  - Outlandish debt collection.
  - Tiger Woods and April bond performance.
  - Toy safety recall notices.
  - Doomsday clock.
- New exercises based on current events.

Features Retained

BAC retains the features that have made it a top textbook in business communication:

- **BAC is flexible.** Choose the chapters and exercises that best fit your needs. Choose from in-class exercises, messages to revise, problems with hints, and cases presented as they'd arise in the workplace. Many problems offer several options: small group discussions, individual writing, group writing, or oral presentations.
- **BAC is specific.** BAC provides specific strategies, specific guidelines, and specific examples. BAC takes the mystery out of creating effective messages.
- **BAC is interesting.** Anecdotes from a variety of fields show business communication at work. The lively side columns from the *Wall Street Journal* and a host of other sources provide insights into the workplace.
- **BAC is comprehensive.** BAC includes international communication, communicating across cultures in this country, ethics, collaborative writing, organizational cultures, graphs, and technology as well as traditional concerns such as style and organization. Assignments offer practice dealing with international audiences or coping with ethical dilemmas.
- **BAC is up-to-date.** The ninth edition of BAC incorporates the latest research and practice so that you stay on the cutting edge.

Supplements

The stimulating, user-friendly supplements package has been one of the major reasons that BAC is so popular. All of the supplements are available on the book's Web site.

1. The **Instructor's Resource Manual** contains
   - **Answers to all exercises,** an overview and difficulty rating for each problem, and, for several of the problems in the book, a detailed analysis, discussion questions, and a good solution.
   - **Additional exercises and cases for** diagnostic and readiness tests, grammar and style, and for letters, memos, and reports.
   - **Lesson plans and class activities for each chapter.** You'll find discussion guides, activities to reinforce chapter materials and prepare students for assignments, and handouts for group work, peer editing, and other activities.
   - **Sample syllabi** for courses with different emphases and approaches.

2. The **Test Bank** contains approximately 2,000 test items with answers. Each is tagged with learning objective, level of difficulty (corresponding to Bloom's taxonomy of educational objectives), AACSB standards, and page number.

   AACSB Statement. The McGraw-Hill Companies is a proud corporate member of AACSB International. Understanding the importance and value of AACSB accreditation, *Business and Administrative Communication,* 9e, has sought to recognize the curricula guidelines detailed in the AACSB standards for business accreditation by connecting selected questions in the Test Bank to the general knowledge and skill guidelines found in the AACSB standards.

   The statements contained in *Business and Administrative Communication,* 9e, are provided only as a guide for the users of this text. The AACSB leaves content coverage and assessment within the purview of individual schools, the mission of the school, and the faculty. While *Business and Administrative Communication,* 9e, and the teaching package make no claim of any specific AACSB qualification or evaluation, we have, within *Business and Administrative Communication,* 9e, labeled selected questions according to the six general knowledge and skills areas.

3. A **Computerized Test Bank** is available to qualified adopters in both Macintosh and Windows formats, and allows professors to generate and edit their own test questions.

4. The **BAC Web site** at www.mhhe.com/locker9e identifies sites for business, research, ethics, and job hunting. The Instructor's Manual, Test Bank, and PowerPoints are available to instructors. Additional exercises, quizzes, student PowerPoints, and iPod content are available to help students improve their writing and communication skills.

Continuing the Conversation

This edition incorporates the feedback I've received from instructors who used earlier editions. Tell me about your own success stories teaching *Business and Administrative Communication.* I look forward to hearing from you!

Donna S. Kienzler

All writing is in some sense collaborative. This book in particular builds upon the ideas and advice of teachers, students, and researchers. The people who share their ideas in conferences and publications enrich not only this book but also business communication as a field.

Many people reviewed the 8th edition, suggesting what to change and what to keep. Additional reviewers commented on drafts of the 9th edition or completed in-depth surveys, helping to further improve the book. We thank all of these reviewers for their attention to detail and their promptness!

Mark Alexander, *Indiana Wesleyan University*

Jean Baird, *Brigham Young University—Idaho*

Michael Benton, *Bluegrass Community and Technology College*

Yvonne Block, *College of Lake County*

Maureen Bogdanowicz, *Kapiolani Community College*

Paula Brown, *Northern Illinois University*

Trudy Burge, *University of Nebraska—Lincoln*

Nicole Buzzetto-More, *University of Maryland—East Shore*

Peter Cardon, *University of South Carolina*

Kelly Chaney, *Southern Illinois University—Carbondale*

Andrea Compton, *St. Charles Community College*

Linda Di Desidero, *University of Maryland—University College*

Veronica Dufresne, *Finger Lakes Community College*

Donna Everett, *Morehead State University*

Joyce Ezrow, *Ann Arundel Community College*

Bartlett Finney, *Park University—Parkville*

Lynda Fuller, *Wilmington University*

Mark Hama, *Angelo State University*

Tanya Henderson, *Howard University*

Beth Hoger, *Western Michigan University—Kalamazoo*

Carolyn Jewell, *Fayetteville State University*

Jamie Strauss Larsen, *North Carolina State University*

Sally Lawrence, *East Carolina University*

Paul Lewellan, *Augustana College*

Bobbi Looney, *Black Hills State University*

Catherine Macdermott, *Saint Edwards University*

Kelly McCormick–Sullivan, *Saint John Fisher College*

Julianne Michalenko, *Robert Morris University*

Gregory Morin, *University of Nebraska—Omaha*

Andrea Muldoon, *University of Wisconsin—Stout*

Anne Nail, *Amarillo College*

Melinda Phillabaum, *IUPUI—Indianapolis*

Greg Rapp, *Portland Community College*

Betty Jane Robbins, *University of Oklahoma*

Deborah Roper, *California State University—Dominguez Hills*

Helen W. Spain, *Wake Technical Community College*

Jane Starnes, *University of Texas—Austin*

Natalie Stillman-Webb, *University of Utah—Salt Lake City*

Lori Townsend, *Niagara County Community College—Sanborn*

Jie Wang, *University of Illinois—Chicago*

Craig Warren, *Pennsylvania State—Erie Behrend College*

Rebecca Wiggenhorn, *Clark State Community College*

Paula Williams, *Arkansas Northeastern College*

Annette Wyandotte, *Indiana University Southeast*

In addition, the book continues to benefit from people who advised me on earlier editions:

Bill Allen, *University of LaVerne*

Vanessa Arnold, *University of Mississippi*

Lynn Ashford, *Alabama State University*

Lenette Baker, *Valencia Community College*

Dennis Barbour, *Purdue University—Calumet*

Laura Barelman, *Wayne State College*

Fiona Barnes, *University of Florida*

Jan Barton-Zimerman, *University of Nebraska—Kearney*

Jaye Bausser, *Indiana University—Purdue University at Fort Wayne*

Sallye Benoit, *Nicholls State University*

Raymond W. Beswick, *formerly of Synerude, Ltd.*

Carole Bhakar, *The University of Manitoba*

Cathie Bishop, *Parkland College*

Randi Meryl Blank, *Indiana University*

Bennis Blue

John Boehm, *Iowa State University*

Maureen S. Bogdanowicz, *Kapi'olani Community College*

Kendra S. Boggess, *Concord College*

Melanie Bookout, *Greenville Technical College*

Christy Ann Borack, *California State University, Fullerton; Orange Coast College—Costa Mesa*

Charles P. Bretan, *Northwood University*

Vincent Brown, *Battelle Memorial Institute*

John Bryan, *University of Cincinnati*

Phyllis Bunn, *Delta State University*

Janice Burke, *South Suburban College of Cook County*

Robert Callahan—*The University of Texas—San Antonio*

Andrew Cantrell, *University of Illinois*

Danny Cantrell, *West Virginia State College*

Susan Carlson

John Carr, *The Ohio State University*

Kathy Casto

Jay Christiansen, *California State University—Northridge*

Lynda Clark, *Maple Woods Community College*

Brendan G. Coleman, *Mankato State University*

John Cooper, *University of Kentucky*

Donna Cox, *Monroe Community College*

Christine Leigh Cranford, *East Carolina University*

Tena Crews, *State University of West Georgia*

Carla Dando, *Idaho State University*

Susan H. Delagrange, *The Ohio State University*

Mark DelMaramo, *Thiel College*

Moira E. W. Dempsey, *Oregon State University*

Gladys DeVane, *Indiana University*

Jose A. Duran, *Riverside Community College*

Dorothy J. Dykman, *Point Loma Nazarene College*

Marilyn Easter, *San Jose State University*

Anna Easton, *Indiana University*

Susan Fiechtner, *Texas A&M University*

Susan Finnerty, *John Carroll University*

Mary Ann Firmin, *Oregon State University*

Melissa Fish, *American River College*

W. Clark Ford, *Middle Tennessee State University*

Louisa Fordyce, *Westmoreland County Community College*

Paula J. Foster, *Foster Communication*

Mildred Franceschi, *Valencia Community College—West Camp*

Linda Fraser, *California State University, Fullerton*

Silvia Fuduric, *Wayne State University*

Robert D. Gieselman, *University of Illinois*

Cheryl Glenn, *Pennsylvania State University*

Mary Greene, *Prince George's Community College*

Jane Greer

Daryl Grider, *West Virginia State College*

Peter Hadorn, *Virginia Commonwealth University*

Ed Hagar, *Belhaven College*

Elaine Hage, *Forsythe Technical Community College*

Barbara Hagler, *Southern Illinois University*

Robert Haight, *Kalamazoo Valley Community College*

Les Hanson, *Red River Community College, Canada*

Kathy Harris, *Northwestern State University*

Mark Harstein, *University of Illinois*

Maxine Hart, *Baylor University*

Vincent Hartigan, *New Mexico State University*

David Hawes, *Owens Community College*

Charles Hebert, *The University of South Carolina*

Ruth Ann Hendrickson

Paulette Henry, *Howard University*

Deborah Herz, *Salve Regina University*

Robert Hill, *University of LaVerne*

Kenneth Hoffman, *Emporia State University*

Elizabeth Hoger, *Western Michigan University*

Carole A. Holden, *County College of Morris*

Carlton Holte, *California State University, Sacramento*

Glenda Hudson, *California State University, Bakersfield*

Elizabeth Huettman, *Cornell University*

Melissa Ianetta, *University of Southern Indiana*

Susan Isaacs, *Community College of Philadelphia*

Daphne A. Jameson, *Cornell University*

Elizabeth Jenkins, *Pennsylvania State University*

Lee Jones, *Shorter College*

Paula R. Kaiser, *University of North Carolina—Greensboro*

Jeremy Kemp, *San Jose State University*

Robert W. Key, *University of Phoenix*

Joy Kidwell, *Oregon State University*

Susan E. Kiner, *Cornell University*

Lisa Klein, *The Ohio State University*

Gary Kohut, *University of North Carolina, Charlotte*

Sarah McClure Kolk, *Hope College*

Keith Kroll, *Kalamazoo Valley Community College*

Milton Kukon, *Southern Vermont College*

Linda M. LaDuc, *University of Massachusetts—Amherst*

Suzanne Lambert, *Broward Community College*

Newton Lassiter, *Florida Atlantic University*

Barry Lawler, *Oregon State University*

Cheryl Ann Laws, *City University*

Gordon Lee, *University of Tennessee*

Kathy Lewis-Adler, *University of North Alabama*

Luchen Li, *Iowa State University*

Dana Loewy, *California State University—Fullerton*

Andrea A. Lunsford, *Stanford University*

Elizabeth Macdonald, *Thunderbird Graduate School of International Management*

John T. Maguire, *University of Illinois*

Michael D. Mahler, *Montana State University*

Margaret Mahoney, *Iowa State University*

Gianna Marsella

Pamela L. Martin, *The Ohio State University*

Iris Washburn Mauney, *High Point College*

Patricia McClure, *West Virginia State College*

Nancie McCoy-Burns, *University of Idaho*

Brian R. McGee, *Texas Tech University*

Virginia Melvin, *Southwest Tennessee Community College*

Yvonne Merrill, *University of Arizona*

Julia R. Meyers, *North Carolina State University*

Paul Miller, *Davidson College*

Scott Miller

Jayne Moneysmith, *Kent State University—Stark*

Josef Moorehead, *California State University—Sacramento*

Evelyn Morris, *Mesa Community College*

Frederick K. Moss, *University of Wisconsin—Waukesha*

Frank P. Nemecek, Jr., *Wayne State University*

Cheryl Noll, *Eastern Illinois University*

Nancy Nygaard, *University of Wisconsin—Milwaukee*

Robert Von der Osten, *Ferris State University*

Carole Clark Papper

Greg Pauley, *Moberly Area Community College*

Jean E. Perry, *University of Southern California*

Linda N. Peters, *University of West Florida*

Florence M. Petrofes, *University of Texas—El Paso*

Evelyn M. Pierce, *Carnegie Mellon University*

Cathy Pleska, *West Virginia State College*

Susan Plutsky, *California State University—Northridge*

Virginia Polanski, *Stonehill College*

Janet Kay Porter, *Leeward Community College*

Susan Prenzlow, *Minnesota State University—Mankato*

Brenda Price, *Bucks County Community College*

Brenner Pugh, *Virginia Commonwealth University*

David Ramsey, *Southeastern Louisiana University*

Kathryn C. Rentz, *University of Cincinnati*

Janetta Ritter, *Garland County Community College*

Naomi Ritter, *Indiana University*

Jeanette Ritzenthaler, *New Hampshire College*

Ralph Roberts, *University of West Florida*

Carol Roever, *Missouri Western State College*

Alisha Rohde

Mary Jane Ryals, *Florida State University*

Mary Saga, *University of Alaska—Fairbanks*

Betty Schroeder, *Northern Illinois University*

Nancy Schullery, *Western Michigan University*

Kelly Searsmith, *University of Illinois*

Sherry Sherrill, *Forsythe Technical Community College*

Frank Smith, *Harper College*

Pamela Smith, *Florida Atlantic University*

Don Soucy

Janet Starnes, *University of Texas—Austin*

Ron Stone, *DeVry University*

Bruce Todd Strom, *University of Indianapolis*

Judith A. Swartley, *Lehigh University*

Christine Tachick, *University of Wisconsin—Milwaukee*

Mel Tarnowski, *Macomb Community College*

Bette Tetreault, *Dalhousie University*

Barbara Z. Thaden, *St. Augustine's College*

Linda Travis, *Ferris State University*

Lisa Tyler, *Sinclair Community College*

Donna Vasa, *University of Nebraska—Lincoln*

David A. Victor, *Eastern Michigan University*

Catherine Waitinas, *University of Illinois—Champaign-Urbana*

Vicky Waldroupe, *Tusculum College*

Randall Waller, *Baylor University*

George Walters, *Emporia State University*

Linda Weavil, *Elon College*

Judy West, *University of Tennessee—Chattanooga*

Paula Weston

Gail S. Widner, *University of South Carolina*

Andrea Williams

Marsha Daigle Williamson, *Spring Arbor University*

Bennie Wilson, *University of Texas—San Antonio*

Rosemary Wilson, *Washtenaw Community College*

Janet Winter, *Central Missouri State University*

Bonnie Thames Yarbrough, *University of North Carolina—Greensboro*

Sherilyn K. Zeigler, *Hawaii Pacific University*

I'm pleased to know that the book has worked so well for so many people and appreciative of suggestions for ways to make it even more useful in this edition. I especially want to thank the students who have allowed me to use their letters and memos, whether or not they allowed me to use their real names in the text.

I am grateful to all the business people who have contributed. The companies where I have done research and consulting work have given me insights into the problems and procedures of business and administrative communication. Special acknowledgment is due Joseph T. Ryerson & Son, Inc., where Kitty created the Writing Skills program that ultimately became the first draft of this book. And I thank the organizations that permitted McGraw-Hill/Irwin to reproduce their documents in this book and in the ancillaries.

Many thanks to Teamkitty—the six graduate students and one honors student who helped with the ninth edition: Karen Bovenmyer, Lisa Brus, Anish Dave, Abhigit Rao, Matthew Search, Christopher Toth, and Rachel Wolford. They helped find new material, update sidebars and footnotes, and add new exercises. Special thanks go to Karen, who performed research wonders and checked all citations; Anish, who wrote the All-Weather case; Matt, who sorted reams of materials into useful bundles; and Chris, who provided updates for the visual and technology components, served as a sounding board for new ideas, and also sorted reams of materials.

More thanks for Christopher Toth, who prepared the Instructor's Manual and the PowerPoint slides, and Christine Jonick, who prepared the Test Bank.

The publisher, McGraw-Hill/Irwin, provided strong editorial and staff support. I am particularly grateful to Dana Woo for providing extra support, Kelly Pekelder for answering innumerable questions, and Sarah Evertson for finding such wonderful photos.

I also wish to thank Susanne Riedell, Michelle Gardner, Matt Diamond, and Sue Lombardi for the appearance of the book and Web site. Further thanks go to Michelle for her good humor, enormous patience, gentle nudges, and great problem-solving abilities.

And, finally, I thank my husband Jim, who provided support, research, editorial assistance, and wifely duties.

A Guided Tour

Business and Administrative Communication, by Kitty O. Locker and Donna S. Kienzler, is a true leader in the business communications field. The 9th edition is designed to teach students how to think critically, communicate effectively, and improve written and oral business communication skills. These skills will successfully prepare students to meet a variety of challenges they may face in their future careers.

Beyond covering the broad scope of topics in both oral and written business communication, this text uses a student-friendly writing style and strong design element to hold student attention. In addition, real-world examples and real business applications underscore key material within the text.

We invite you to learn about this new edition and its features by paging through this visual guide.

CHAPTER PEDAGOGY

CHAPTER OUTLINE AND LEARNING OBJECTIVES

Each chapter begins with a chapter outline and learning objectives to guide students as they study. The first exercise for each chapter, Reviewing the Chapter, poses questions specifically linked to the chapter's learning objectives.

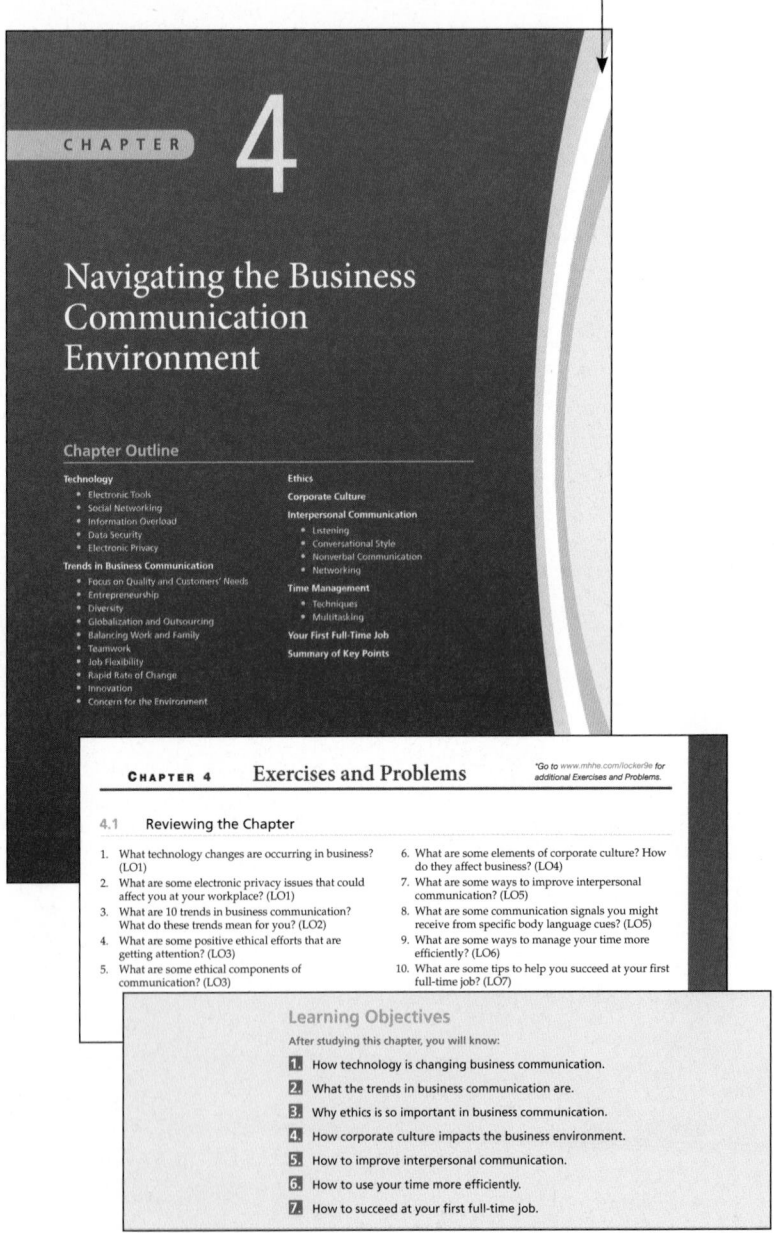

CHAPTER 4

Navigating the Business Communication Environment

Chapter Outline

Technology
- Electronic Tools
- Social Networking
- Information Overload
- Data Security
- Electronic Privacy

Trends in Business Communication
- Focus on Quality and Customers' Needs
- Entrepreneurship
- Diversity
- Globalization and Outsourcing
- Balancing Work and Family
- Teamwork
- Job Flexibility
- Rapid Rate of Change
- Innovation
- Concern for the Environment

Ethics

Corporate Culture

Interpersonal Communication
- Listening
- Conversational Style
- Nonverbal Communication
- Networking

Time Management
- Techniques
- Multitasking

Your First Full-Time Job

Summary of Key Points

CHAPTER 4   Exercises and Problems   *Go to www.mhhe.com/locker9e for additional Exercises and Problems.*

4.1 Reviewing the Chapter

1. What technology changes are occurring in business? (LO1)
2. What are some electronic privacy issues that could affect you at your workplace? (LO1)
3. What are 10 trends in business communication? What do these trends mean for you? (LO2)
4. What are some positive ethical efforts that are getting attention? (LO3)
5. What are some ethical components of communication? (LO3)
6. What are some elements of corporate culture? How do they affect business? (LO4)
7. What are some ways to improve interpersonal communication? (LO5)
8. What are some communication signals you might receive from specific body language cues? (LO5)
9. What are some ways to manage your time more efficiently? (LO6)
10. What are some tips to help you succeed at your first full-time job? (LO7)

Learning Objectives

After studying this chapter, you will know:

1. How technology is changing business communication.
2. What the trends in business communication are.
3. Why ethics is so important in business communication.
4. How corporate culture impacts the business environment.
5. How to improve interpersonal communication.
6. How to use your time more efficiently.
7. How to succeed at your first full-time job.

AN INSIDE PERSPECTIVE

Each chapter is introduced with current news articles relevant to the chapter's concepts. These opening articles set the stage for the chapter's content and allow students a glimpse at how the material applies in the business world.

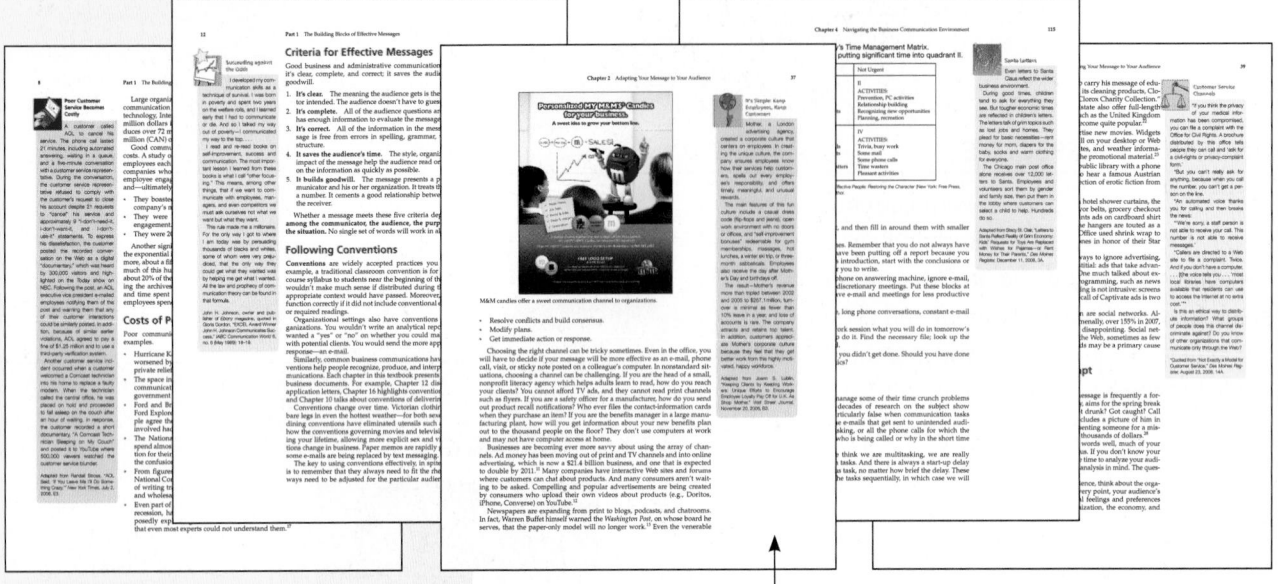

SIDEBARS

These novel and interesting examples effectively enhance student understanding of key concepts. Featured in the margins of every chapter, these sidebars cover topic areas that include International, Legal/Ethical, Just for Fun, Technology, and On the Job. In addition, gold stars identify "classic" sidebars.

INSITE LINKS

These helpful URLs point to Web sites that include organizations and resources of effective business communication. These examples underscore the role of the Web in business communication and serve to motivate and enrich the student learning experience. These Web sites cover a wide range of reference sources, including corporate, small business, nonprofit, and government Web sites.

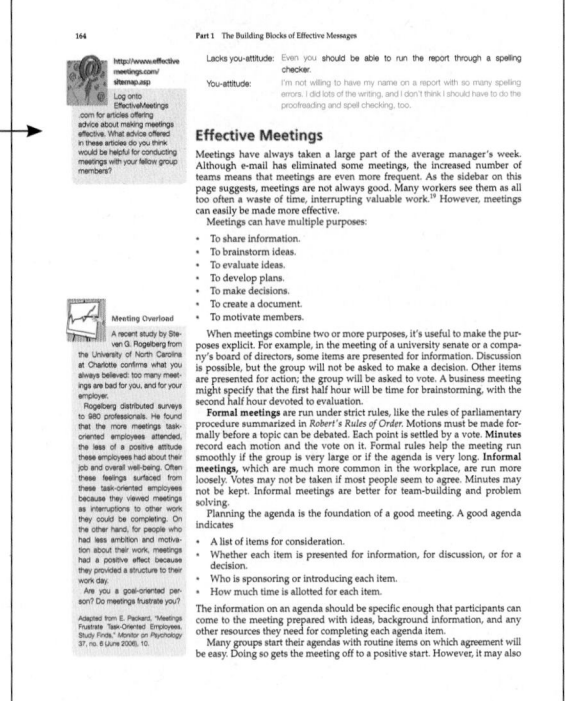

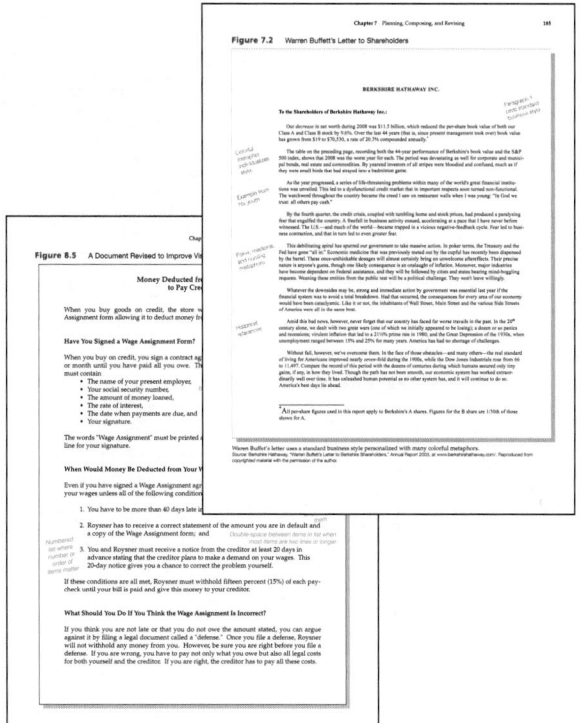

FULL-PAGE EXAMPLES

A variety of visual examples featuring full-sized letters, memos, e-mails, reports, and résumés are presented in the text. These examples include the authors' "handwritten" annotations, explaining communication miscues while offering suggestions for improvement.

GOOD AND BAD EXAMPLES

Paired effective and ineffective communication examples are presented so students can pinpoint problematic ways to phrase messages to help improve their communication skills. Commentaries in red and blue inks indicate poor or good methods of message communication and allow for easy comparison.

CHECKLISTS

Checklists for important messages appear throughout the book. These helpful lists serve as a handy reference guide of items to keep in mind when composing and editing messages.

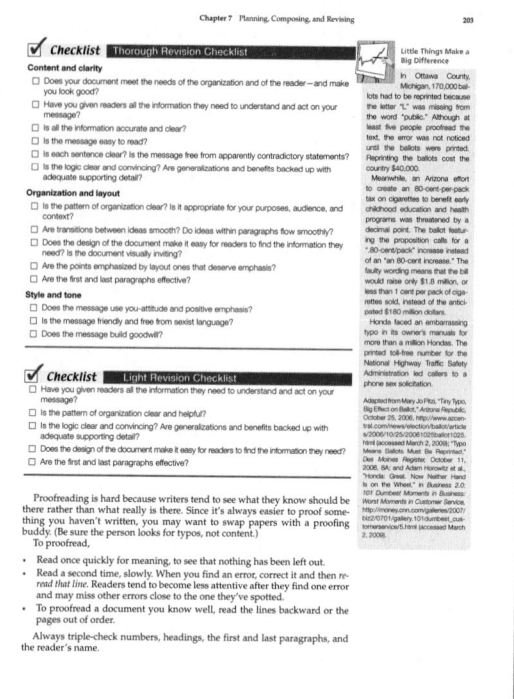

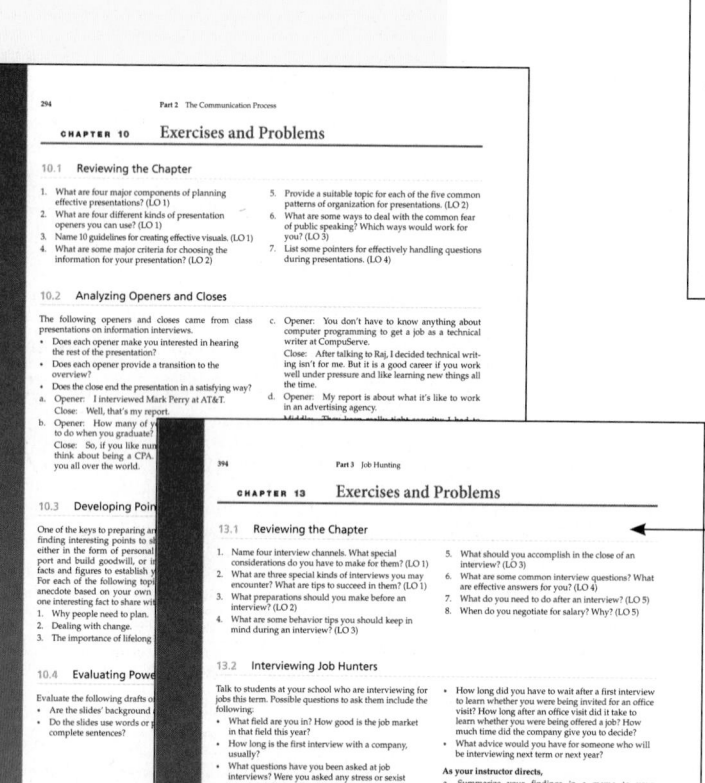

EXERCISES AND PROBLEMS

These hands-on exercises are flexible and can be used as in-class discussions or as individual and group assignments. These workplace exercises allow students to assume a role or perform a task in a variety of realistic business scenarios. Helpful "hints" provide structure and guidance to students for them to complete the exercises.

The first exercise is always a collection of chapter review questions connected to the learning objectives. The last exercise is always part of the ongoing All-Weather case, offering students a rich business scenario, complete with daily complications.

A WEALTH OF SUPPLEMENTS
IN THE NEW ONLINE LEARNING CENTER

NEW ONLINE LEARNING CENTER

Numerous resources available for both instructors and students are online at www.mhhe.com/locker9e. Instructor resources include downloadable versions of the

- Instructor's Manual
- Test Bank
- PowerPoint.

Student resources include

- Practice exercises
- Quizzes
- Student PowerPoint
- iPod content
- Memo, letter, and résumé templates
- Links to business communication resources.

CONTENTS

PART ONE The Building Blocks of Effective Messages

1 Succeeding in Business Communication 2

In the News 3
Communication Ability = Promotability 4
"I'll Never Have to Write Because . . ." 5
Communicating on the Job 6
The Cost of Communication 6
Costs of Poor Communication 8
Benefits of Improving Communication 11
Criteria for Effective Messages 12
Following Conventions 12
Understanding and Analyzing Business Communication Situations 13
How to Solve Business Communication Problems 13
How to Use This Book 17
Ongoing Case 18
Summary of Key Points 19
Exercises and Problems for Chapter 1 20

2 Adapting Your Message to Your Audience 28

In the News 29
Identifying Your Audiences 30
Ways to Analyze Your Audience 31
Choosing Channels to Reach Your Audience 36
Using Audience Analysis to Adapt Your Message 39
Audience Analysis Works 44
Audience Benefits 45
Writing or Speaking to Multiple Audiences with Different Needs 50
Summary of Key Points 51
Exercises and Problems for Chapter 2 52

3 Building Goodwill 60

In the News 61
You-Attitude 62
Positive Emphasis 66
Tone, Power, and Politeness 72
Reducing Bias in Business Communication 74
Summary of Key Points 79
Exercises and Problems for Chapter 3 80

4 Navigating the Business Communication Environment 88

In the News 89
Technology 90
Trends in Business Communication 98
Ethics 104
Corporate Culture 106
Interpersonal Communication 108
Time Management 114
Your First Full-Time Job 116
Summary of Key Points 117
Exercises and Problems for Chapter 4 117

5   Communicating across
Cultures   124

In the News   125

Global Business   126

Diversity in North America   128

Ways to Look at Culture   129

Values, Beliefs, and
Practices   130

Nonverbal Communication   132

Oral Communication   137

Writing to International
Audiences   138

Learning More about International
Business Communication   140

Summary of Key Points   140

Exercises and Problems for
Chapter 5   141

6   Working and Writing
in Teams   150

In the News   151

Team Interactions   152

Working on Diverse Teams   158

Conflict Resolution   160

Effective Meetings   164

Collaborative Writing   165

Summary of Key Points   169

Exercises and Problems for
Chapter 6   170

PART TWO   The Communication Process

7 Planning, Composing, and Revising 178

In the News 179

The Ways Good Writers Write 180

Activities in the Composing Process 180

Using Your Time Effectively 182

Brainstorming, Planning, and Organizing Business Documents 182

Writing Good Business and Administrative Documents 183

Half-Truths about Style 184

Ten Ways to Make Your Writing Easier to Read 187

Organizational Preferences for Style 199

Revising, Editing, and Proofreading 200

Getting and Using Feedback 204

Using Boilerplate 204

Readability Formulas 205

Summary of Key Points 206

Exercises and Problems for Chapter 7 207

8 Designing Documents 216

In the News 217

The Importance of Effective Design 218

Design as Part of Your Writing Process(es) 218

Design and Conventions 219

Levels of Design 219

Guidelines for Page Design 220

Designing Brochures 227

Designing Web Pages 229

Testing the Design for Usability 231

Summary of Key Points 231

Exercises and Problems for Chapter 8 232

9 Creating Visuals and Data Displays 240

In the News 241

When to Use Visuals 242

Guidelines for Visual Design 243

Integrating Visuals in Your Text 250

Designing Data Displays and Images 251

Summary of Key Points 257

Exercises and Problems for Chapter 9 257

10 Making Oral Presentations 274

In the News 275

Identifying Purposes in Oral Presentations 276

Comparing Written and Oral Messages 277

Planning a Strategy for Your Presentation 278

Planning PowerPoint Slides 282

Choosing Information to Include in a Presentation 284

Organizing Your Information 286

Delivering an Effective Presentation 288

Handling Questions 291

Making Group Presentations 292

Summary of Key Points 292

Exercises and Problems for Chapter 10 294

PART THREE   Job Hunting

11 Building Résumés   300

In the News   301
A Time Line for Job
Hunting   302
Evaluating Your Strengths and
Interests   303
Using the Internet in Your Job
Search   304
How Employers Use
Résumés   305
Guidelines for Résumés   306
Kinds of Résumés   308
What to Include in a
Résumé   310
References   319
What Not to Include in a
Résumé   322
Dealing with Difficulties   323
Electronic Résumés   325
A Caution about Blogs and Social
Networking Sites   328
Honesty   329
Summary of Key Points   330
Exercises and Problems for
Chapter 11   331

12 Writing Job Application
Letters   340

In the News   341
How Job Letters Differ from
Résumés   342
How to Find Out about Employers
and Jobs   342
Content and Organization for Job
Application Letters   346
E-Mail Application Letters   355
Creating a Professional
Image   357
Application Essays   360
Summary of Key Points   361
Exercises and Problems for
Chapter 12   362

13 Interviewing for a
Job   370

In the News   371
21st Century Interviews   372
Interview Strategy   373
Interview Preparation   373
Interview Channels   376
Interview Practice   377
Interview Customs   378
Traditional Interview Questions
and Answers   380
Kinds of Interviews   386
Final Steps for a Successful Job
Search   389
Summary of Key Points   393
Exercises and Problems for
Chapter 13   394

PART FOUR   Basic Business Messages

14 Sharing Informative and Positive Messages   398

In the News   399

Information Overload   400

Common Media   401

Organizing Informative and Positive Messages   404

Subject Lines for Informative and Positive Messages   407

Managing the Information in Your Messages   408

Using Benefits in Informative and Positive Messages   409

Ending Informative and Positive Messages   410

Humor in Informative Messages   411

Varieties of Informative and Positive Messages   411

Solving a Sample Problem   416

Summary of Key Points   419

Exercises and Problems for Chapter 14   420

15 Delivering Negative Messages   434

In the News   435

Organizing Negative Messages   437

The Parts of a Negative Message   441

Apologies   445

Tone in Negative Messages   447

Alternative Strategies for Negative Situations   448

Varieties of Negative Messages   450

Solving a Sample Problem   452

Summary of Key Points   456

Exercises and Problems for Chapter 15   457

16 Crafting Persuasive Messages   470

In the News   471

Analyzing Persuasive Situations   472

Choosing a Persuasive Strategy   476

Why Threats Are Less Effective than Persuasion   476

Making Persuasive Direct Requests   477

Writing Persuasive Problem-Solving Messages   479

Tone in Persuasive Messages   489

Varieties of Persuasive Messages   489

Sales and Fund-Raising Messages   491

Solving a Sample Problem   504

Summary of Key Points   508

Exercises and Problems for Chapter 16   509

PART FIVE   Proposals and Reports

17 Planning and
    Researching
    Reports   526

    In the News   527
    Varieties of Reports   528
    The Report Production
    Process   529
    Report Topics   530
    Research Strategies for
    Reports   532
    Source Citation and
    Documentation   547
    Summary of Key Points   554
    Exercises and Problems for
    Chapter 17   555

18 Writing Proposals and
    Progress Reports   562

    In the News   563
    Writing Proposals   564
    Writing Progress Reports   574
    Summary of Key Points   578
    Exercises and Problems for
    Chapter 18   578

19 Analyzing Information
    and Writing
    Reports   582

    In the News   583
    Using Your Time Efficiently   584
    Analyzing Data and Information for
    Reports   585
    Choosing Information for
    Reports   593
    Organizing Information in
    Reports   594
    Presenting Information Effectively
    in Reports   602
    Writing Formal Reports   607
    Summary of Key Points   627
    Exercises and Problems for
    Chapter 19   628

A Formats for Letters, Memos, and E-Mail Messages 636

Formats for Letters 637

Formats for Envelopes 643

Formats for Memos 647

Formats for E-Mail Messages 647

State and Province Abbreviations 653

B Writing Correctly 654

Using Grammar 655

Understanding Punctuation 659

Punctuating Sentences 660

Punctuation within Sentences 662

Special Punctuation Marks 666

Writing Numbers and Dates 667

Words That Are Often Confused 668

Proofreading Symbols 673

Exercises and Problems for Appendix B 675

Glossary 680

Notes 689

Photo Credits 703

Name Index 704

Company Index 708

Subject Index 711

Business and Administrative Communication

Succeeding in Business Communication

Chapter Outline

Communication Ability = Promotability

"I'll Never Have to Write Because . . ."

Communicating on the Job

The Cost of Communication

Costs of Poor Communication

- Wasted Time
- Wasted Efforts
- Lost Goodwill
- Legal Problems

Benefits of Improving Communication

Criteria for Effective Messages

Following Conventions

Understanding and Analyzing Business Communication Situations

How to Solve Business Communication Problems

- Answer the Six Questions for Analysis.

- Organize Your Information to Fit Your Audiences, Your Purposes, and the Situation.
- Make Your Document Visually Inviting.
- Revise Your Draft to Create a Friendly, Businesslike, Positive Style.
- Edit Your Draft for Standard English; Double-Check Names and Numbers.
- Use the Response You Get to Plan Future Messages.

How to Use This Book

Ongoing Case

Summary of Key Points

Hurricane Katrina Storms Communication Lines

On August 29, 2005, Hurricane Katrina swept through Mississippi and Louisiana leaving massive destruction. During the storm, communication failures among local, state, and federal officials left their own harm.

The main communication problems included these issues:

• Lack of communication among responding organizations: FEMA claimed it was days before they knew about the thousands of people in the New Orleans Convention Center.

• Incompatible communication systems: The lack of coordination and communication caused by these systems put even more lives at risk by delaying assistance where it was most needed. Some rescuers in helicopters were unable to communicate with rescuers in boats. Some units of the National Guard actually used runners to communicate.

• Inconsistent messages: State and local agency teams received conflicting messages which led to confusion.

> *"During the storm, communication failures among local, state, and federal officials left their own harm."*

• Inaccurate communication:

  • Media reports about violence in the Superdome scared people already in the building, who heard the reports on radios, and frightened away drivers of trucks carrying critical supplies.

  • Exaggerated reports of looting convinced some residents to stay to protect their property instead of evacuating.

  • False reports of shooting at helicopters resulted in some agencies in other states refusing to send trained emergency workers.

  • The National Guard delayed assistance at the Convention Center while it waited to assemble enough personnel to deal with security problems—problems which turned out to be grossly overstated.

• Missing information: Public officials lacked facts to address media inaccuracies.

The massive communication problems led to an entire chapter on communication in the U.S. House of Representatives report on the Hurricane Katrina disaster.

Source: U. S. House of Representatives, "A Failure of Initiative: Final Report of the Select Bipartisan Committee to Investigate the Preparation for and Response to Hurricane Katrina," in *GPO Access: Legislative Resources: Congressional Committee Materials Online via GPO Access,* www.gpoaccess.gov/congress/index.html (accessed January 15, 2009).

Learning Objectives

After studying this chapter, you will know:

1 Why you need to be able to communicate well.

2 What the costs of communication are.

3 What the costs of poor communication are.

4 What role conventions play in business communication.

5 How to solve business communication problems.

Communication Is Key to Pay

How can you make more money at your job? The number one way, according to the *Wall Street Journal*, is to "listen to your boss." Specifically, do the work your boss wants done, follow directions, work hard, and let your boss know what you have accomplished. Employees who follow this method collect raises at a rate of 9.9%, while average performers receive 3.6% and poor performers get 1.3%, according to one survey.

Just as important is to make sure you ask your manager to define expectations. Don't assume you know what your manager wants. Make sure you understand what your manager considers an outstanding performance in your position.

Adapted from Perri Capell, "10 Ways to Get the Most Pay out of Your Job," *Wall Street Journal*, September 18, 2006, R1.

Business depends on communication. People must communicate to plan products and services; hire, train, and motivate workers; coordinate manufacturing and delivery; persuade customers to buy; and bill them for the sale. Indeed, for many businesses and nonprofit and government organizations, the "product" is information or services rather than something tangible. Information and services are created and delivered by communication. In every organization, communication is the way people get their points across and get work done.

Communication takes many forms: face-to-face or phone conversations, informal meetings, presentations, e-mail messages, letters, memos, reports, blogs, text messaging, and Web sites. All of these methods are forms of **verbal communication**, or communication that uses words. **Nonverbal communication** does not use words. Pictures, computer graphics, and company logos are nonverbal. Interpersonal nonverbal signals include how people sit at meetings, how large offices are, and how long someone keeps a visitor waiting.

Communication Ability = Promotability

Even in your first job, you'll communicate. You'll listen to instructions; you'll ask questions; you may solve problems with other workers in teams. In a manufacturing company, workers may be updating assembly or safety procedures. In an insurance company, clerks answer customers' letters. Even "entry-level" jobs require high-level skills in reasoning, mathematics, and communicating. As a result, communication ability consistently ranks first among the qualities that employers look for in college graduates.[1]

The advantage of communication skills became acutely important in this decade, after the booming economy of the 1990s and the expansion of Internet technology gave way to a more sober business environment. Robert O. Best, Chief Information Officer of UNUMProvident, an insurance corporation, cautions, "You used to be able to get away with being a technical nerd. . . . Those days are over."[2] As more people compete for fewer jobs, the ones who will build successful careers are those who can communicate well with customers and colleagues—using words to teach, motivate, and build positive business relationships.

The National Commission on Writing surveyed 120 major corporations, employing nearly 8 million workers. Almost 70% of respondents said that at least two-thirds of their employees have writing responsibilities included in their position descriptions. E-mail and presentations with visuals (such as PowerPoint slides) were universal. Over half the respondents also reported other forms of communication as frequently required: memos and correspondence, 70%; formal reports, 62%; and technical reports, 59%. Respondents also noted that communication functions were least likely to be outsourced.[3]

Because communication skills are so important, good communicators earn more. Research has shown that among people with two- or four-year degrees, workers in the top 20% of writing ability earn, on average, more than three times as much as workers whose writing falls into the worst 20%.[4] Jeffrey Gitomer, business consultant and author of best-selling business books, says there are three secrets to getting known in the business world; all of them are communication skills:

1. Writing: "Writing leads to wealth."
2. E-zining: "I reach more than 130,000 subscribers each week."
3. Speaking: "The secret is being prepared."[5]

In spite of the frequency of on-the-job writing and the importance of overall communication skills, employers do not find college students well skilled in writing. A recent survey of employers conducted on behalf of the Association of American Colleges and Universities found that writing was one of the weakest skills of college graduates.[6] In another large survey, respondents noted that a lack of "effective business communication skills appears to be a major stumbling block among new [job] entrants—even at the college level. Spelling errors, improper use of grammar, and the misuse of words were common in written reports, PowerPoint presentations, and e-mail messages."[7]

"I'll Never Have to Write Because . . ."

Some students think that a secretary will do their writing, that they can use form letters if they do have to write, that only technical skills matter, or that they'll call rather than write. Each of these claims is fundamentally flawed.

Claim 1: Secretaries will do all my writing.

Reality: Because of automation and restructuring, job responsibilities in offices have changed. Today, most secretaries have become administrative assistants with their own complex tasks such as training, research, and database management for several managers. Managers are likely to take care of their own writing, data entry, and phone calls.

Claim 2: I'll use form letters or templates when I need to write.

Reality: A **form letter** is a prewritten, fill-in-the-blank letter designed to fit standard situations. Using a form letter is OK if it's a good letter. But form letters cover only routine situations. The higher you rise, the more frequently you'll face situations that aren't routine, that demand creative solutions.

Claim 3: I'm being hired as an accountant, not a writer.

Reality: Almost every entry-level professional or managerial job requires you to write e-mail messages, speak to small groups, write documents, and present your work for annual reviews. People who do these things well are likely to be promoted beyond the entry level. Employees in jobs as diverse as firefighters, security professionals, and construction project managers are all being told to polish their writing and speaking skills.[8]

Claim 4: I'll just pick up the phone.

Reality: Important phone calls require follow-up letters, memos, or e-mail messages. People in organizations put things in writing to make themselves visible, to create a record, to convey complex data, to make things convenient for the reader, to save money, and to convey their own messages more effectively. "If it isn't in writing," says a manager at one company, "it didn't happen." Writing is an essential way to make yourself visible, to let your accomplishments be known.

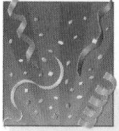

Communicating on the Job

Communication—oral, nonverbal, and written—goes to both internal and external audiences. **Internal audiences** are other people in the same organization: subordinates, superiors, peers. **External audiences** are people outside the organization: customers, suppliers, distributors, unions, stockholders, potential employees, trade associations, special interest groups, government agencies, the press, and the general public.

People in organizations produce a large variety of documents. Figures 1.1 and 1.2 list a few of the specific documents produced at Ryerson Tull. The company, which fabricates and sells steel, aluminum, other metals, and plastics to a wide variety of industrial clients, has processing centers and sales offices across the United States and Canada.

All of the documents in Figures 1.1 and 1.2 have one or more of the **three basic purposes of organizational writing:** to inform, to request or persuade, and to build goodwill. When you **inform,** you explain something or tell readers something. When you request or **persuade,** you want the reader to act. The word *request* suggests that the action will be easy or routine; *persuade* suggests that you will have to motivate and convince the reader to act. When you **build goodwill,** you create a good image of yourself and of your organization—the kind of image that makes people want to do business with you.

Most messages have multiple purposes. When you answer a question, you're informing, but you also want to build goodwill by suggesting that you're competent and perceptive and that your answer is correct and complete.

The Cost of Communication

Writing costs money. Besides the cost of computers, software, printers, paper, and sometimes postage, there is the major expense: employees' time. Even short e-mails take time, especially now that employees write so many of them.

Business communication involves paper documents, electronic communications, but most of all, interpersonal abilities.

Figure 1.1   Internal Documents Produced in One Organization

Document	Description of document	Purpose(s) of document
Transmittal	Memo accompanying document, telling why it's being forwarded to the receiver	Inform; persuade reader to read document; build image and goodwill
Monthly or quarterly report	Report summarizing profitability, productivity, and problems during period. Used to plan activity for next month or quarter	Inform; build image and goodwill (report is accurate, complete; writer understands company)
Policy and procedure bulletin	Statement of company policies and instructions (e.g., how to enter orders, how to run fire drills)	Inform; build image and goodwill (procedures are reasonable)
Request to deviate from policy and procedure bulletin	Persuasive memo arguing that another approach is better for a specific situation than the standard approach	Persuade; build image and goodwill (request is reasonable; writer seeks good of company)
Performance appraisal	Evaluation of an employee's performance, with recommended areas for improvement or recommendation for promotion	Inform; persuade employee to improve
Memo of congratulations	Congratulations to employees who have won awards, been promoted, or earned community recognition	Build goodwill

The letter sent to taxpayers by the Internal Revenue Service announcing that rebate checks would be coming cost $41.8 million. Even with huge economies of scale, the letters cost about 32 cents to print, process, and mail. The cost does not include employee time in the writing and processing.[9]

Document cycling processes also increase costs. In many organizations, all external documents must be approved before they go out. A major document may **cycle** from writer to superior to writer to another superior to writer again 10 or more times before final approval.

Longer documents can involve large teams of people and take months to write. An engineering firm that relies on military contracts for its business calculates that it spends $500,000 to put together an average proposal and $1 million to write a large proposal.[10]

Figure 1.2   External Documents Produced in One Organization

Document	Description of document	Purpose(s) of document
Quotation	Letter giving price for a specific product, fabrication, or service	Inform; build goodwill (price is reasonable)
Claims adjustment	Letter granting or denying customer request to be given credit for defective goods	Inform; build goodwill
Job description	Description of qualifications and duties of each job. Used for performance appraisals, setting salaries, and hiring	Inform; persuade good candidates to apply; build goodwill (job duties match level, pay)
10-K report	Report filed with the Securities and Exchange Commission detailing financial information	Inform
Annual report	Report to stockholders summarizing financial information for year	Inform; persuade stockholders to retain stock and others to buy; build goodwill (company is a good corporate citizen)
Thank-you letter	Letter to suppliers, customers, or other people who have helped individuals or the company	Build goodwill

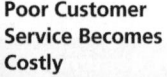

Poor Customer Service Becomes Costly

A customer called AOL to cancel his service. The phone call lasted 21 minutes, including automated answering, waiting in a queue, and a five-minute conversation with a customer service representative. During the conversation, the customer service representative refused to comply with the customer's request to close his account despite 21 requests to "cancel" his service and approximately 9 "I-don't-need-it, I-don't-want-it, and I-don't-use-it" statements. To express his dissatisfaction, the customer posted the recorded conversation on the Web as a digital "documentary," which was heard by 300,000 visitors and highlighted on the *Today* show on NBC. Following the post, an AOL executive vice president e-mailed employees notifying them of the post and warning them that any of their customer interactions could be similarly posted. In addition, because of similar earlier violations, AOL agreed to pay a fine of $1.25 million and to use a third-party verification system.

Another customer service incident occurred when a customer welcomed a Comcast technician into his home to replace a faulty modem. When the technician called the central office, he was placed on hold and proceeded to fall asleep on the couch after an hour of waiting. In response, the customer recorded a short documentary, "A Comcast Technician Sleeping on My Couch" and posted it to YouTube where 500,000 viewers watched the customer service blunder.

Adapted from Randall Stross, "AOL Said, 'If You Leave Me I'll Do Something Crazy,'" *New York Times*, July 2, 2006, E3.

Large organizations handle so much paper that even small changes to their communication practices amount to millions of dollars. Through better use of technology, InterContinental Hotels Group cut communications costs by $2.6 million dollars in two years. Similarly, the University of Calgary, which produces over 72 million documents a year, is expecting to reduce costs by $13.8 million (CAN) over seven years.[11]

Good communication is worth every minute it takes and every penny it costs. A study of 335 US and Canadian companies with an average of 13,000 employees each and median annual revenues of $1.8 billion found that those companies who best communicated with their employees enjoyed "greater employee engagement and commitment, higher retention and productivity, and—ultimately—better financial performance. . . .

- They boasted a 19.4% higher market premium (the degree to which the company's market value exceeds the cost of its assets).
- They were 4.5 times more likely to report high levels of employee engagement.
- They were 20% more likely to report lower turnover rates."[12]

Another significant cost of communication is e-mail storage. In addition to the exponential increase in frequency, e-mails are also growing in size. Furthermore, about a fifth of them come with attachments. And businesses are storing much of this huge load on their servers. But the cost of the hardware is only about 20% of the storage cost; the remainder is for administering and maintaining the archives. These costs include downtime when storage systems crash and time spent retrieving lost or corrupted messages. Chevron estimates its employees spend 1½ to 3 days a month searching for needed information.[13]

Costs of Poor Communication

Poor communication can cost billions of dollars. We all can think of examples.

- Hurricane Katrina caused billions of dollars of damage—damage that was worsened by horrendous miscommunications between federal, state, and private relief organizations (see In the News on page 3).
- The space industry has had billion-dollar mistakes—mistakes where miscommunications were major contributing factors as confirmed by official government investigations (see sidebars on pages 9 and 11).
- Ford and Bridgestone Firestone's failure to coordinate the design of the Ford Explorer and its tires cost them billions of dollars. In hindsight, people agree the mistakes could have been prevented if the different teams involved had communicated more effectively with each other.[14]
- The National Commission on Writing reported to Congress that states spend almost a quarter billion dollars annually on remedial writing instruction for their employees, and that indirect costs of that poor writing—from the confusions and errors caused—are probably even higher.[15]
- From figures provided by the members of the Business Roundtable, the National Commission on Writing calculated the annual private sector costs of writing training at $3.1 billion.[16] These figures do not include the retail and wholesale trade businesses.
- Even part of the subprime mortgage collapse, which helped spark a global recession, has been connected to poor communication. Documents supposedly explaining some of the riskier investments were so convoluted that even most experts could not understand them.[17]

Not all communication costs are so dramatic. When communication isn't as good as it could be, you and your organization pay a price in wasted time, wasted effort, lost goodwill, and legal problems.

Wasted Time

Bad writing takes longer to read as we struggle to understand what we're reading. How quickly we can do this is determined by the difficulty of the subject matter and by the document's organization and writing style.

Second, bad writing may need to be rewritten. Poorly written documents frequently cycle to other people for help.

Third, ineffective communication may obscure ideas so that discussions and decisions are needlessly drawn out.

Fourth, unclear or incomplete messages may require the receiver to gather more information and some receivers may not bother to do so; they may make a wrong decision or refuse to act.

Wasted Efforts

Ineffective messages don't get results. A receiver who has to guess what the sender means may guess wrong. A reader who finds a letter or memo unconvincing or insulting simply won't do what the message asks.

One company sent out past-due bills with the following language:

> Per our conversation, enclosed are two copies of the above-mentioned invoice. Please review and advise. Sincerely, . . .

The company wanted money, not advice, but it didn't say so. The company had to write third and fourth reminders. It waited for its money, lost interest on it—and kept writing letters.

Lost Goodwill

Whatever the literal content of the words, every letter, e-mail, or report serves either to build or to undermine the image the reader has of the writer.

Part of building a good image is taking the time to write correctly. Even organizations that have adopted casual dress still expect writing to appear professional and to be free from typos and grammatical errors.

Messages can also create a poor image because of poor audience analysis and inappropriate style. The form letter printed in Figure 1.3 failed because it was stuffy and selfish. The comments in red show specific problems with the letter.

1. **The language is stiff and legalistic.**   Note the sexist "Gentlemen:" and obsolete "Please be advised," "herein," and "expedite."
2. **The tone is selfish.**   The letter is written from the writer's point of view; there are no benefits for the reader. (The writer says there are, but without a shred of evidence, the claim isn't convincing.)
3. **The main point is buried** in the middle of the long first paragraph. The middle is the least emphatic part of a paragraph.
4. **The request is vague.**   How many references does the supplier want? Are only vendor references OK, or would other credit references, like banks, work too? Is the name of the reference enough, or is it necessary also to specify the line of credit, the average balance, the current balance, the years

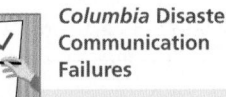

Columbia **Disaster Communication Failures**

In 2003, the *Columbia* space shuttle disintegrated on re-entry, resulting in the deaths of all seven crew members. The independent research team investigating the disaster found communication problems to be the root cause of the accident. The researchers concluded that organizational barriers prevented effective communication of critical safety information and restrained communication of professionals.

The report identified the following communication problems:

- Communication flow between managers and subordinates: Managers did not heed the concerns of the engineers regarding debris impacts on the shuttle. Throughout the project, communication did not flow effectively up to or down from program managers.

- Circulation of information among teams: Although engineers were concerned about landing problems and therefore conducted experiments on landing procedures, the concerns were not relayed to managers or to system and technology experts who could have addressed the concerns.

- Communication sources: Managers received a large amount of their information from informal channels, which blocked relevant opinions and conclusions from engineers.

Source: *Columbia* Accident Investigation Board, "Report of *Columbia* Accident Investigation Board, Volume I," in *NASA Home, Mission Sections, Space Shuttle, Columbia,* http://www.nasa.gov/columbia/home/CAIB_Vol1.html (accessed June 8, 2009).

Figure 1.3   A Form Letter That Annoyed Customers

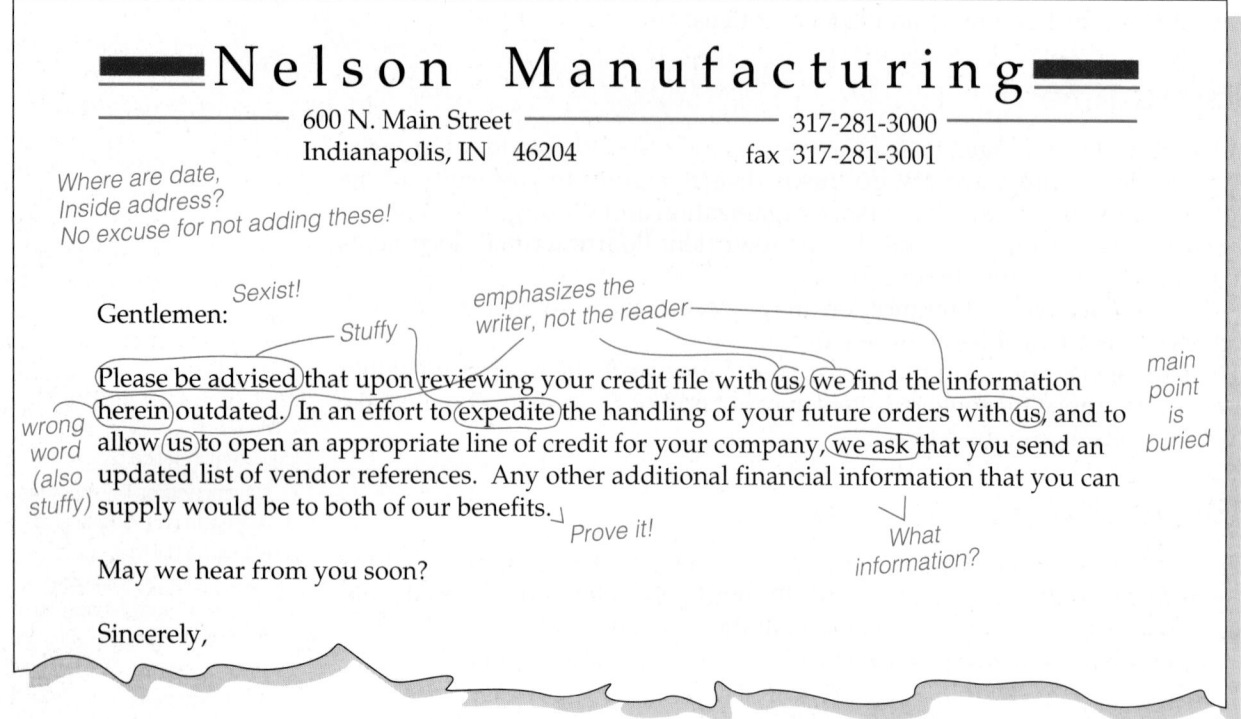

credit has been established, or other information? What "additional financial information" does the supplier want? Annual reports? Bank balance? Tax returns? The request sounds like an invasion of privacy, not a reasonable business practice.

5. **Words are misused** (*herein for therein*), suggesting either an ignorant writer or one who doesn't care enough about the subject and the reader to use the right word.

Legal Problems

Poor communication choices can lead to legal problems for individuals and organizations. The news is full of examples. Domino's pizza, which promised to deliver pizza to your door in 30 minutes, dropped that promise after a lawsuit, involving an accident with a Domino's delivery person, claimed that the pledge led to accidents. Domino's settled for a sum in the seven-figure range, but dropped the promise because the company feared other lawsuits.[18]

Individual communications can also have legal consequences. Steamy text messages revealed an affair between Detroit mayor Kwame Kilpatrick and one of his aides; both the messages and the affair contradicted testimony the mayor had given under oath. Consequences included loss of office, jail time, and a $1 million fine.

US Representative Mark Foley resigned after his instant messages to House pages were published. E-mails helped bring about the fall of senior Enron executives, Boeing CEO Harry Stonecipher, Credit Suisse First Boston banker Frank Quattrone, Merrill Lynch analyst Henry M. Blodgett, Hewlett-Packard Chairperson Patricia Dunn, and Wal-Mart Vice Presidents Julie Roehm and Sean Womack. One San Francisco law firm says that 70% of their routine evidence now comes from e-mails.[19]

In particular, letters, memos, e-mails, and instant messages create legal obligations for organizations. When a lawsuit is filed against an organization, the lawyers for the plaintiffs have the right to subpoena documents written by employees of the organization. These documents may then be used as evidence, for instance, that an employer fired an employee without adequate notice or that a company knew about a safety defect but did nothing to correct it.

These documents may also be used as evidence in contexts the writer did not intend. This means that a careless writer can create obligations that the organization does not mean to assume. For instance, a letter from a manager telling a scout troop they may not visit a factory floor because it is too dangerous could be used in a worker's compensation suit.[20]

Careful writers and speakers think about the larger social context in which their words may appear. What might those words mean to other people in the field? What might they mean to a judge and jury?

Benefits of Improving Communication

Better communication helps you to

- **Save time.** Eliminate the time now taken to rewrite badly written materials. Reduce reading time, since comprehension is easier. Reduce the time taken asking, "What did you mean?"

- **Make your efforts more effective.** Increase the number of requests that are answered positively and promptly—on the first request. Present your points—to other people in your organization; to clients, customers, and suppliers; to government agencies; to the public—more forcefully.

- **Communicate your points more clearly.** Reduce the misunderstandings that occur when the audience has to supply missing or unclear information. Make the issues clear, so that disagreements can surface and be resolved more quickly.

- **Build goodwill.** Build a positive image of your organization. Build an image of yourself as a knowledgeable, intelligent, capable person.

Business Communication Lessons from Mars

The *Mars Climate Orbiter* spacecraft lost contact with NASA mission control just after it arrived at Mars. A subsequent investigation revealed that the main problem was a minor software programming error caused by communication errors.

Like many business projects, the *Mars Climate Orbiter* involved a wide range of people in a range of locations. The programmers who wrote the software that controlled the spacecraft's engines worked in Great Britain, and used metric measurements in their calculations, while the engineers who made the satellite's engines worked in the United States, and used English measurements. Both teams assumed that they were using the same measurement standards, neither team made any attempt to check, and no one else caught the error. With that failure, NASA lost a $125 million satellite and years of effort, while gaining a major public embarrassment.

Adapted from NASA MCO Mission Failure Mishap Investigation Board, "Mars Climate Orbiter Mishap Investigation Board Phase I Report," ftp://ftp.hq.nasa.gov/pub/pao/reports/1999/MCO_report.pdf (accessed January 16, 2009).

When the *Mars Climate Orbiter* spacecraft crashed as a result of poor communication, the United States lost a $125 million satellite and years of effort.

Criteria for Effective Messages

Good business and administrative communication meets five basic criteria: it's clear, complete, and correct; it saves the audience's time; and it builds goodwill.

1. **It's clear.**   The meaning the audience gets is the meaning the communicator intended. The audience doesn't have to guess.
2. **It's complete.**   All of the audience questions are answered. The audience has enough information to evaluate the message and act on it.
3. **It's correct.**   All of the information in the message is accurate. The message is free from errors in spelling, grammar, word order, and sentence structure.
4. **It saves the audience's time.**   The style, organization, and visual or aural impact of the message help the audience read or hear, understand, and act on the information as quickly as possible.
5. **It builds goodwill.**   The message presents a positive image of the communicator and his or her organization. It treats the receiver as a person, not a number. It cements a good relationship between the communicator and the receiver.

Whether a message meets these five criteria depends on **the interactions among the communicator, the audience, the purposes of the message, and the situation.** No single set of words will work in all possible situations.

Following Conventions

Conventions are widely accepted practices you routinely encounter. For example, a traditional classroom convention is for instructors to distribute a course syllabus to students near the beginning of the semester. The document wouldn't make much sense if distributed during the final week because the appropriate context would have passed. Moreover, the document would not function correctly if it did not include conventional elements such as due dates or required readings.

Organizational settings also have conventions particular to specific organizations. You wouldn't write an analytical report to your boss who only wanted a "yes" or "no" on whether you could make the scheduled meeting with potential clients. You would send the more appropriate and conventional response—an e-mail.

Similarly, common business communications have conventions. These conventions help people recognize, produce, and interpret different kinds of communications. Each chapter in this textbook presents conventions of traditional business documents. For example, Chapter 12 discusses conventions of job application letters, Chapter 16 highlights conventions of persuasive messages, and Chapter 10 talks about conventions of delivering oral presentations.

Conventions change over time. Victorian clothing conventions prohibited bare legs in even the hottest weather—for both sexes. For most of us, shifting dining conventions have eliminated utensils such as shrimp forks. Consider how the conventions governing movies and television have changed just during your lifetime, allowing more explicit sex and violence. Similarly, conventions change in business. Paper memos are rapidly giving way to e-mails, and some e-mails are being replaced by text messaging.

The key to using conventions effectively, in spite of their changing nature, is to remember that they always need to fit the rhetorical situation—they always need to be adjusted for the particular audience, context, and purpose.

For instance, Chapter 15 provides guidelines on constructing negative messages. However, you will need to adapt these guidelines based on the way your organization presents their negative messages. Some organizations will use a more formal tone than others; some present negative news bluntly, while others ease into it more gently.

Since every organization will be unique in the conventions they follow, the information presented in this text will provide a basic understanding of common elements for particular genres. You will always need to adjust the basics for your particular needs.

The best way to learn conventions in a particular workplace is to see what other workers are doing. How do they communicate with each other? Do their practices change when they communicate with superiors? What kinds of letters and memos do they send? How much do they e-mail? What tone is preferred? Close observation will help your communications fit in with the conventions of your employer.

Understanding and Analyzing Business Communication Situations

The best communicators are conscious of the context in which they communicate; they're aware of options.

Ask yourself the following questions:

- **What's at stake—to whom?** Think not only about your own needs but also about the concerns your boss and your audience will have. Your message will be most effective if you think of the entire organizational context— and the larger context of shareholders, customers, and regulators. When the stakes are high, you'll need to take into account people's feelings as well as objective facts.
- **Should you send a message?** Sometimes, especially when you're new on the job, silence is the most tactful response. But be alert for opportunities to learn, to influence, to make your case.
- **What channel should you use?** Paper documents and presentations are formal and give you considerable control over the message. E-mail, phone calls, and stopping by someone's office are less formal. Oral channels are better for group decision making, allow misunderstandings to be cleared up more quickly, and seem more personal. Sometimes you may need more than one message, in more than one channel.
- **What should you say?** Content for a message may not be obvious. How detailed should you be? Should you repeat information that the audience already knows? The answers will depend on the kind of message, your purposes, audiences, and the corporate culture. And you'll have to figure these things out for yourself, without detailed instructions.
- **How should you say it?** How you arrange your ideas—what comes first, second, and last—and the words you use shape the audience's response to what you say.

How to Solve Business Communication Problems

When you're faced with a business communication problem, you need to develop a solution that will both solve the organization's problem and meet the psychological needs of the people involved. The strategies in this section will help you solve the problems in this book. Almost all of these strategies can also be applied to problems you encounter on the job.

- **Gather knowledge.**   What are the facts? What can you infer from the information you're given? What additional information might be helpful? Where could you get it? What emotional complexities are involved?
- **Use the six questions for analysis in Figure 1.4 to analyze your audience, your purposes, and the situation.**   Try to imagine yourself in the situation, just as you might use the script of a play to imagine what kind of people the characters are. The fuller an image you can create, the better.
- **Brainstorm solutions.**   In all but the very simplest problems, there are *several* possible solutions. The first one you think of may not be best. Consciously develop several solutions. Then measure them against your audience and purposes: Which solution is likely to work best?
- **If you want to add or change information, get permission first.**   You can add facts or information to the problems in this book only if the information (1) is realistic, (2) is consistent with the way real organizations work, and (3) does not change the point of the problem. If you have any questions about ideas you want to use, *ask your instructor.* He or she can tell you *before* you write the message.

Use this process to create good messages:

- Answer the six questions for analysis in Figure 1.4.
- Organize your information to fit your audiences, your purposes, and the context.
- Make your document visually inviting.
- Revise your draft to create a friendly, businesslike, positive style.
- Edit your draft for standard spelling, punctuation, and grammar; double-check names and numbers.
- Use the response you get to plan future messages.

Answer the Six Questions for Analysis.

The six questions in Figure 1.4 help you analyze your audience(s), purpose(s), and the organizational context.

1. **Who is (are) your audience(s)? What audience characteristics are relevant for this particular message? If you are writing or speaking to more than one person, how do the people in your audience differ?**

    How much does your audience know about your topic? How will they respond to your message? Some characteristics of your audience will be

Figure 1.4   Questions for Analysis

---

1. Who is (are) your audience(s)? What audience characteristics are relevant for this particular message? If you are writing or speaking to more than one person, how do the people in your audience differ?
2. What are your purposes in communicating?
3. What information must your message include?
4. How can you build support for your position? What reasons or benefits will your audience find convincing?
5. What objection(s) can you expect your audience to have? What negative elements of your message must you de-emphasize or overcome?
6. What aspects of the total situation may affect the audience's response? The economy? The time of year? Morale in the organization? The relationship between the audience and the communicator? Any special circumstances?

irrelevant; focus on ones that matter *for this message.* Whenever you address several people or a group, try to identify the economic, cultural, or situational differences that may affect how various subgroups may respond to what you have to say.

2. **What are your purposes in communicating?**

    What must this message do to solve the organization's problem? What must it do to meet your own needs? What do you want your audience to do? To think or feel? List all your purposes, major and minor.

    Even in a simple message, you may have several related purposes: to announce a new policy, to make the audience aware of the policy's provisions and requirements, and to have them feel that the policy is a good one, that the organization cares about its employees, and that you are a competent communicator and manager.

3. **What information must your message include?**

    Make a list of the points that must be included; check your draft to make sure you include them all. To include information without emphasizing it, put it in the middle of a paragraph or document and present it as briefly as possible.

4. **How can you build support for your position? What reasons or benefits will your audience find convincing?**

    Brainstorm to develop reasons for your decision, the logic behind your argument, and possible benefits to the audience if they do as you ask. Reasons and audience benefits do not have to be monetary. Making the audience's job easier or more pleasant is a good benefit. In an informative or persuasive message, identify multiple audience benefits. In your message, use those that you can develop most easily and most effectively.

    Be sure the benefits are adapted to your audience. Many people do not identify closely with their organizations; the fact that the organization benefits from a policy will help the individual only if the saving or profit is passed directly on to the employees. Instead, savings and profits are often eaten up by returns to stockholders, bonuses to executives, and investments in plants and equipment or in research and development.

5. **What objection(s) can you expect your audience to have? What negative elements of your message must you de-emphasize or overcome?**

    Some negative elements can only be de-emphasized. Others can be overcome. Be creative: Is there any advantage associated with (even though not caused by) the negative? Can you rephrase or redefine the negative to make the audience see it differently?

6. **What aspects of the total situation may affect audience response? The economy? The time of year? Morale in the organization? The relationship between the audience and the communicator? Any special circumstances?**

    Audiences may like you or resent you. The organization may be prosperous or going through hard times; it may have just been reorganized or may be stable. All these different situations will affect what you say and how you say it.

    Think about the news, the economy, the weather. Think about the general business and regulatory climate, especially as it affects the organization specified in the problem. Use the real world as much as possible. Think about interest rates, business conditions, and the economy. Is the industry in which the problem is set doing well? Is the government agency in which the problem is set enjoying general support? Think about the time of year. If it's fall when you write, is your business in a seasonal slowdown after

Just a Deadline. No Directions

School assignments are spelled out, sometimes even in writing. In the workplace, workers are less likely to get details about what a document should include. The transition can be disorienting. One intern reported, "I was less prepared than I thought. . . . I was so used to professors basically telling you what they want from you that I expected to be, if not taught, then told, what exactly it was that they wanted these brochures to accomplish. . . . They have not taken the time to discuss it—they just put things on my desk with only a short note telling me when they needed it done. No directions or comments were included."

Intern's quotation from Chris M. Anson and L. Lee Forsberg, "Moving Beyond the Academic Community," *Written Communication* 7, no. 3 (April 1990): 211.

Classroom versus Workplace Contexts

Professors Aviva Freedman and Christine Adam found in a research study that students have to relearn ways to acquire basic knowledge when trying to mesh with their employer's organization once they enter the workforce.

School is structured to help students learn. On the other hand, the workplace is structured to get results, not help the learner/new employee. New college graduate hires frequently don't understand the context of communications. For example, new employees have to figure out which coworkers are trustworthy and can be a guide while not pushing away others.

Moreover, the roles of participants in each situation are different. While school settings have an instructor as the voice of authority, workplace settings are comprised of people with varying degrees of relevant and useful knowledge.

What has been your experience with internships? Have you noticed other ways in which workplace settings differ from classroom expectations?

Adapted from Aviva Freedman and Christine Adam, "Learning to Write Professionally: 'Situated Learning' and the Transition from University to Professional Discourse," *Journal of Business and Technical Communication* 10, no. 4 (October 1996): 395–427.

a busy summer? Gearing up for the Christmas shopping rush? Or going along at a steady pace unaffected by seasons?

To answer these questions, draw on your experience, your courses, and your common sense. Read the *Wall Street Journal* or look at a company's Web site. Sometimes you may even want to phone a local business person to get information. For instance, if you needed more information to think of audience benefits for a problem set in a bank, you could call a local bank to find out what services it offers customers and what its rates are for loans.

Organize Your Information to Fit Your Audiences, Your Purposes, and the Situation.

You'll learn several different psychological patterns of organization later in this book. For now, remember these three basic principles:

1. Put good news first.
2. In general, put the main point or question first. In the subject line or first paragraph, make it clear that you're writing about something that is important to the reader.
3. Disregard point 2 and approach the subject indirectly when you must persuade a reluctant audience.

Make Your Document Visually Inviting.

A well-designed document is easier to read and builds goodwill. To make a document visually attractive

- Use subject lines to orient the reader quickly.
- Use headings to group related ideas.
- Use lists and indented sections to emphasize subpoints and examples.
- Number points that must be followed in sequence.
- Use short paragraphs—usually six typed lines or fewer.

If you plan these design elements before you begin composing, you'll save time and the final document will probably be better.

The best medium for a document depends on how it will be used. For example, a document that will be updated frequently may need to be on a Web site so the reader can easily obtain the most current information.

Revise Your Draft to Create a Friendly, Businesslike, Positive Style.

In addition to being an organizational member or a consumer, your reader has feelings just as you do. Writing that keeps the reader in mind uses **you-attitude**. Read your message as if you were in your reader's shoes. How would you feel if *you* received it?

Good business and administrative writing is both friendly and businesslike. If you're too stiff, you put extra distance between your reader and yourself. If you try to be too chummy, you'll sound unprofessional. When you write to strangers, use simple, everyday words and make your message as personal and friendly as possible. When you write to friends, remember that your message may be read by people you've never even heard of: avoid slang, clichés, and "in" jokes.

Sometimes you must mention limitations, drawbacks, or other negative elements, but don't dwell on them. People will respond better to you and your organization if you seem confident. Expect success, not failure. If you don't believe that what you're writing about is a good idea, why should they?

You emphasize the positive when you

- Put positive information first, give it more space, or set it off visually in an indented list.
- Eliminate negative words whenever possible.
- Focus on what is possible, not what is impossible.

Edit Your Draft for Standard English; Double-Check Names and Numbers.

Business people care about correctness in spelling, grammar, and punctuation. If your grasp of mechanics is fuzzy, if standard English is not your native dialect, or if English is not your native language, you'll need to memorize rules and perhaps find a good book or a tutor to help you. Even software spelling and grammar checkers require the writer to make decisions. If you know how to write correctly but rarely take the time to do so, now is the time to begin to edit and proofread to eliminate careless errors. Correctness in usage, punctuation, and grammar is covered in Appendix B.

Always proofread your document before you send it out. Double-check the reader's name, any numbers, and the first and last paragraphs.

Use the Response You Get to Plan Future Messages.

Evaluate the **feedback**, or response, you get. The real test of any message is "Did you get what you wanted, when you wanted it?" If the answer is *no*, then the message has failed—even if the grammar is perfect, the words elegant, the approach creative, the document stunningly attractive. If the message fails, you need to find out why.

Analyze your successes, too. You want to know *why* your message worked. There has to be a reason, and if you can find what it is, you'll be more successful more often.

How to Use This Book

This book has many aids to help you learn the material.

- Chapter outlines, learning objectives, and headings all provide previews of the contents. They can give you hooks on which to hang the information you are reading.
- Examples of written documents provide illustrations of effective and ineffective communications. Comments in red ink highlight problems; those in blue ink note effective practices.
- Words and phrases in bold are defined in the glossary at the end of the book.
- Sidebars provide workplace examples of ideas discussed in the text. They are categorized for you by the icons that appear beside them. A gold star with any icon signifies a classic example.
  - On-the-job examples have flip chart icons.
  - Ethics and legal examples have scale icons.

Help Your Customers (to) Fish

Fish, a business best seller for over a decade, presents the Fish philosophy. Under this philosophy, managers and employees use a friendly, businesslike, positive style with these basic elements:

- **Choose your attitude.** Employees at any job can choose the attitude toward the work they perform. Not all jobs are glamorous: the work of a fish seller is difficult, but the employees at Pike Place Fish choose to have "playful, cheerful" attitudes toward work. Choose your responses to the work you perform.

- **Play.** Work is serious business, but you can have fun while you work. At Pike Place Fish, employees throw fish. At First Guaranteed, employees turn on small lights when they have a good idea. The benefits to playing at work are low turnover, pride in the work, increased sales, and energy toward the work.

- **Make their day.** Customers should be included in the fun. Pike Place Fish selects customers to help catch the thrown fish. Respectfully engage customers to create positive energy and goodwill.

- **Be present.** Employees should be focused and engaged at work so they can help their colleagues and customers.

How can you adapt the Fish philosophy in your workplace and life?

Adapted from Stephen C. Lundin, Harry Paul, and John Christensen, *Fish: A Remarkable Way to Boost Morale and Improve Results* (New York: Hyperion, 2000), 78.

• Web sites have a hand holding an @ sign.
• Technology examples have laptop icons.
• International examples have globe icons.
• Fun examples have confetti icons.

• Chapter summaries at the end of each chapter, and review questions at the beginning of each set of chapter exercises, help you review the chapters for retention.

Ongoing Case

The last problem in each set of chapter exercises is an ongoing case to provide you with a richer context for problem solving. It involves the company All-Weather, Inc., and various characters.

All-Weather, Inc., is a midwestern company manufacturing vinyl, wood, aluminum, steel, and fiberglass composite windows and doors. All-Weather's window offerings include single- and double-hung windows, casement windows, awning windows, geometrical windows, picture windows, basement windows, bow and bay windows, sliding windows, and fixed windows. Its door offerings include interior doors, exterior doors, swinging and sliding patio doors, and garage doors. All-Weather's products are certified by the American Architectural Manufacturers Association and the Window and Door Manufacturers Association. In 2007, its net revenues and net profits amounted to approximately $150 million and $25 million, respectively. Headquartered in St. Paul, MN, it operates from 32 offices and five plants across the United States and six offices internationally, employing close to 900 personnel in the United States and 18 personnel outside the United States.

Based in the company headquarters, the Human Resources Department looks after recruitment, selection, orientation, training, promotion, performance appraisal, compensation, termination, safety, environment, and other personnel-related matters. In terms of communication activities, the department prepares memos, letters, forms, policy statements, presentations, job descriptions and advertisements, contract documents, and reports, advising upper management and working with other departments and stakeholders on issues related to human resources. The department also has a Web site on the company Intranet.

As Vice President of Human Resources, Doug leads a team of three managers—Caleb, Miguel, and Erin, each of whom has an executive reporting to him or her. Caleb's responsibilities include training, safety, environment, employee relations, and stakeholder response. Miguel is responsible for performance appraisal, promotion, benefits, and compensation. Erin is responsible for recruitment, selection, orientation, and termination. The department also has a secretary, an assistant, and a programmer. Recently, a student-intern—Kioni, an MBA student from Kenya—joined the department. Here is a complete list of personnel working in All-Weather's HR Department:

• Doug: Vice President
• Caleb, Miguel, Erin: Managers
• Tanner: Executive reporting to Caleb
• Linda: Executive reporting to Miguel
• Rudy: Executive reporting to Erin
• Staff: May (Secretary), Paul (Assistant), Jim (Programmer)
• Kioni (Student-Intern)

Summary of Key Points

- Communication helps organizations and the people in them achieve their goals. The ability to write and speak well becomes increasingly important as you rise in an organization.
- People put things in writing to create a record, to convey complex data, to make things convenient for the reader, to save money, and to convey their own messages more effectively.
- **Internal documents** go to people inside the organization. **External documents** go to audiences outside: clients, customers, suppliers, stockholders, the government, the media, and the general public.
- The three basic purposes of business and administrative communication are to inform, to request or persuade, and to build goodwill. Most messages have more than one purpose.
- Poor writing wastes time, wastes effort, and jeopardizes goodwill.
- Good business and administrative writing meets five basic criteria: it's clear, complete, and correct; it saves the reader's time; and it builds goodwill.
- To evaluate a specific document, we must know the interactions among the writer, the reader(s), the purposes of the message, and the content. No single set of words will work for all readers in all situations.
- Common business communications have conventions, as do organizations. Business communicators need to follow conventions appropriate for their needs.
- To understand business communication situations, ask the following questions:
  - What's at stake—to whom?
  - Should you send a message?
  - What channel should you use?
  - What should you say?
  - How should you say it?
- The following process helps create effective messages:
  - Answer the analysis questions in Figure 1.4.
  - Organize your information to fit your audiences, your purposes, and the context.
  - Make your document visually inviting.
  - Revise your draft to create a friendly, businesslike, positive style.
  - Edit your draft for standard English; double-check names and numbers.
  - Use the response you get to plan future messages.
- Use these six questions to analyze business communication problems:
  1. Who is (are) your audience(s)? What characteristics are relevant to this particular message? If you are writing or speaking to more than one person, how do the people in your audience differ?
  2. What are your purposes in communicating?
  3. What information must your message include?
  4. How can you build support for your position? What reasons or benefits will your audience find convincing?
  5. What objection(s) can you expect your audience to have? What negative elements of your message must you de-emphasize or overcome?

6. What aspects of the total situation may affect audience response? The economy? The time of year? Morale in the organization? The relationship between the audience and communicator? Any special circumstances?

- A solution to a business communication problem must both solve the organization's problem and meet the needs of the writer or speaker, the organization, and the audience.

CHAPTER 1   # Exercises and Problems

1.1   Reviewing the Chapter

1. Why do you need to be able to communicate well? (LO 1)
2. What are some myths about workplace communication? What is the reality for each myth? (LO 1)
3. What are the costs of communication? (LO 2)
4. What are the costs of poor communication? (LO 3)

5. What role do conventions play in business communication? (LO 4)
6. What are the components of a good problem-solving method for business communication opportunities? (LO 5)

1.2   Assessing Your Punctuation and Grammar Skills

To help you see where you need to improve in grammar and punctuation, take the Diagnostic Test, B.1, Appendix B.

1.3   Letters for Discussion—Landscape Plants

Your nursery sells plants not only in your store but also by mail order. Today you've received a letter from Pat Sykes, complaining that the plants (in a $572 order) did not arrive in a satisfactory condition. "All of them were dry and wilted. One came out by the roots when I took it out of the box. Please send me a replacement shipment immediately."

The following letters are possible approaches to answering this complaint. How well does each message meet the needs of the reader, the writer, and the organization? Is the message clear, complete, and correct? Does it save the reader's time? Does it build goodwill?

1.

Dear Sir:

I checked to see what could have caused the defective shipment you received. After ruling out problems in transit, I discovered that your order was packed by a new worker who didn't understand the need to water plants thoroughly before they are shipped. We have fired the worker, so you can be assured that this will not happen again.

Although it will cost our company several hundred dollars, we will send you a replacement shipment.

Let me know if the new shipment arrives safely. We trust that you will not complain again.

2.

Dear Pat:

Sorry we screwed up that order. Sending plants across country is a risky business. Some of them just can't take the strain. (Some days I can't take the strain myself!) We'll send you some more plants sometime next week and we'll credit your account for $572.

3.

Dear Mr. Smith:

I'm sorry you aren't happy with your plants, but it isn't our fault. The box clearly says, "Open and water immediately." If you had done that, the plants would have been fine. And anybody who is going to buy plants should know that a little care is needed. If you pull by the leaves, you will pull the roots out. Since you don't know how to handle plants, I'm sending you a copy of our brochure, "How to Care for Your Plants." Please read it carefully so that you will know how to avoid disappointment in the future.

We look forward to your future orders.

4.

Dear Ms. Sykes:

Your letter of the 5th has come to the attention of the undersigned.

According to your letter, your invoice #47420 arrived in an unsatisfactory condition. Please be advised that it is our policy to make adjustments as per the Terms and Conditions listed on the reverse side of our Acknowledgment of Order. If you will read that document, you will find the following:

> ". . . if you intend to assert any claim against us on this account, you shall make an exception on your receipt to the carrier and shall, within 30 days after the receipt of any such goods, furnish us detailed written information as to any damage."

Your letter of the 5th does not describe the alleged damage in sufficient detail. Furthermore, the delivery receipt contains no indication of any exception. If you expect to receive an adjustment, you must comply with our terms and see that the necessary documents reach the undersigned by the close of the business day on the 20th of the month.

5.

Dear Pat Sykes:

You'll get a replacement shipment of the perennials you ordered next week.

Your plants are watered carefully before shipment and packed in specially designed cardboard containers. But if the weather is unusually warm, or if the truck is delayed, small root balls may dry out. Perhaps this happened with your plants. Plants with small root balls are easier to transplant, so they do better in your yard.

The violas, digitalis, aquilegias, and hostas you ordered are long-blooming perennials that will get even prettier each year. Enjoy your garden!

1.4   Online Messages for Discussion—Responding to Rumors

The Acme Corporation has been planning to acquire Best Products, and Acme employees are worried about how the acquisition will affect them. Ed Zeplin, Acme's human resource manager, has been visiting the Acme chat sites and sees a dramatic rise in the number of messages spreading rumors about layoffs. Most of the rumors are false.

The following messages are possible responses that Ed can post to the chat sides. How well does each message meet the needs of the reader, the writer, and the organization? Is the message clear, complete, and correct? Does it save the reader's time? Does it build goodwill?

1.

It Will Be Great!
Author: L. Ed Zeplin, HR
Date: Tuesday, May 23

I am happy to tell you that the HR news is good. Two months ago, the CEO told me about the merger, and I have been preparing a human resource plan ever since.

I want you to know about this because morale has been bad, and it shouldn't be. You really should wait for the official announcements, and you'll see that the staffing needs will remain strong. My department has been under a lot of pressure, but if you'll be patient, we'll explain everything—the staffing, the compensation.

Our plan should be ready by Monday, and then if you have any questions, just contact your HR rep.

2.

HR Staffing
Author: HR Boss
Date: Tuesday, May 23

The rumors are false. Just ask anyone in HR. There will be no layoffs.

3.

Don't Believe the Rumors
Author: lezeplin@acme.com
Date: Tuesday, May 23

Acme has 475 employees, and Best Products has 132 employees. Our human resource plan for next year calls for 625 employees. If you do the math, you can see that there will be no layoffs. Rather, we will be hiring 20 employees. Of course, as we consolidate operations with Best, there will be some redeployments. However, our plan indicates that we will be able to retain our current staff. All employees are valued at Acme, as our current benefits package testifies.

Our HR plan is based on the best analytic techniques and a business forecast by a top consulting firm. If you're an employee, you should review our business plan, at the Our Goals page on Acme's intranet. Everyone should read Acme's mission statement on our home page, www.acme.com/homepage.html.

4.

Layoff Rumors Do Acme a Disservice
Author: Zeplin in HR
Date: Tuesday, 23 May

If you come here to get your company information, you aren't getting the straight story. The people posting to this discussion board are spreading false rumors, not the truth. If you want to know the truth about Acme, ask the people who have access to the information.

As HR manager, I can assure you we won't be laying off employees after the merger with Best Products. I'm the one who approves the staffing plan, so I should know. If people would ask me, instead of reading the negative, whining lies at this site, they would know the facts, too.

If people really cared about job security, they would be working and exceeding their goals, rather than wasting their time in rumor-mongering on message boards. Hard work: that's the key to success!

5.

The True Story about Lay-Offs
Author: lezeplin@acme.com
Date: Tuesday, 23 May

Whenever there is a merger or acquisition, rumors fly. It's human nature to turn to rumors when a situation seems uncertain. The case of Acme acquiring Best Products is no exception, so I'm not surprised to see rumors about layoffs posted on this message board.

Have no fear! I am working closely with our CEO and with the CEO and human resource manager at Best Products, and we all agree that our current staff is a valuable asset to Acme, to Best, and to our combined companies in the future. We have no plans to lay off any of our valued people. I will continue monitoring this message board and will post messages as I am able to disclose more details about our staffing plans. In the meantime, employees should watch for official information in the company newsletter and on our intranet.

We care about our people! If employees ever have questions about our plans and policies, they should contact me directly.

L. Ed Zeplin, HR Manager

1.5   Discussing Communication Barriers

With a small group, discuss some of the communication barriers you have witnessed in the workplace or classroom. What confuses audiences? What upsets them? What creates ill will? What causes loss of interest? Try to pinpoint exactly how the communication broke down. How closely do the problems you've identified coincide with the content from Chapter 1?

1.6   Identifying Poor Communicators

Almost everyone has come in contact with someone who is a poor communicator. With a small group, discuss some of your experiences with poor communicators either in the workplace or in the classroom. Why was the communicator ineffective? What would have made communication clearer? After your discussion, develop a list of poor communication traits and what can be done to overcome them.

1.7   Discussing Wiio's Laws

Reread the list of Wiio's laws in the sidebar on page 6. With a small group, discuss examples of those laws you have witnessed in
  a.   The workplace
  b.   The classroom
  c.   The news media
  d.   Social networking sites

1.8   Identifying Changing Conventions

This chapter talks about the need to follow conventions, even though it is the nature of conventions to shift with time. What are some changing classroom communication conventions you have observed in your classes? What are some changing communication conventions you have observed at your workplace, or those of your family and friends? With a small group, discuss your examples.

1.9   Understanding the Role of Communication in Your Organization

Interview your work supervisor to learn about the kinds and purposes of communication in your organization. Your questions could include the following:
- What kinds of communication (e.g., memos, e-mail, presentations) are most important in this organization?
- What communications do you create? Are they designed to inform, to persuade, to build goodwill—or to do a combination?
- What communications do you receive? Are they designed to inform, to persuade, to build goodwill—or to do a combination?
- Who are your most important audiences within the organization?
- Who are your most important external audiences?
- What are the challenges of communicating in this organization?
- What kinds of documents and presentations does the organization prefer?

As your instructor directs,
a.   Share your results with a small group of students.
b.   Present your results in a memo to your instructor.
c.   Join with a group of students to make a group presentation to the class.
d.   Post your results online to the class.

1.10   Introducing Yourself to Your Instructor

Write a memo (at least 1½ pages long) introducing yourself to your instructor. Include the following topics:
  Background: Where did you grow up? What have you done in terms of school, extracurricular activities, jobs, and family life?
  Interests: What are you interested in? What do you like to do? What do you like to think about and talk about?
  Academics: What courses have you liked the best in school? Why? What life skills have you gained? How do you hope to use them? What do you hope to gain from this course?
  Achievements: What achievements have given you the greatest personal satisfaction? List at least five. Include things that gave *you* a real sense of accomplishment and pride, whether or not they're the sort of thing you'd list on a résumé.
  Goals: What do you hope to accomplish this term? Where would you like to be professionally and personally five years from now?

Use complete memo format with appropriate headings. (See Appendix A for examples of memo format.) Use a conversational writing style; check your draft to polish the style and edit for mechanical and grammatical correctness. A good memo will enable your instructor to see you as an individual. Use specific details to make your memo vivid and interesting. Remember that one of your purposes is to interest your reader!

1.11   Introducing Yourself to Your Collaborative Writing Group

Write a memo (at least 1½ pages long) introducing yourself to the other students in your collaborative writing group. Include the following topics:

Background: What is your major? What special areas of knowledge do you have? What have you done in terms of school, extracurricular activities, jobs, and family life?

Previous experience in groups: What groups have you worked in before? Are you usually a leader, a follower, or a bit of both? Are you interested in a quality product? In maintaining harmony in the group? In working efficiently? What do you like most about working in groups? What do you like least?

Work and composing style: Do you like to talk out ideas while they're in a rough stage or work them out on paper before you discuss them? Would you rather have a complete outline before you start writing or just a general idea? Do you want to have a detailed schedule of everything that has to be done and who will do it, or would you rather "go with the flow"?

Do you work best under pressure, or do you want to have assignments ready well before the due date?

Areas of expertise: What can you contribute to the group in terms of knowledge and skills? Are you good at brainstorming ideas? Researching? Designing charts? Writing? Editing? Word processing? Managing the flow of work? Maintaining group cohesion?

Goals for collaborative assignments: What do you hope to accomplish this term? Where does this course fit into your priorities?

Use complete memo format with appropriate headings. (See Appendix A for examples of memo format.) Use a conversational writing style; edit your final draft for mechanical and grammatical correctness. A good memo will enable others in your group to see you as an individual. Use details to make your memo vivid and interesting. Remember that one of your purposes is to make your readers look forward to working with you!

1.12   Describing Your Experiences in and Goals for Writing

Write a memo (at least 1½ pages long) to your instructor describing the experiences you've had writing and what you'd like to learn about writing during this course.

Answer several of the following questions:

- What memories do you have of writing? What made writing fun or frightening in the past?

- What have you been taught about writing? List the topics, rules, and advice you remember.

- What kinds of writing have you done in school? How long have the papers been?

- How has your school writing been evaluated? Did the instructor mark or comment on mechanics and grammar? Style? Organization? Logic? Content? Audience analysis and adaptation? Have you gotten extended comments on your papers? Have instructors in different classes had the same standards, or have you changed aspects of your writing for different classes?

- What voluntary writing have you done—journals, poems, stories, essays? Has this writing been just for you, or has some of it been shared or published?

- Have you ever written on a job or in a student or volunteer organization? Have you ever edited other people's writing? What have these experiences led you to think about real-world writing?

- What do you see as your current strengths and weaknesses in writing skills? What skills do you think you'll need in the future? What kinds of writing do you expect to do after you graduate?

Use complete memo format with appropriate headings. (See Appendix A for examples of memo format.) Use a conversational writing style; edit your final draft for mechanical and grammatical correctness.

1.13   All-Weather Case: Presenting to a Community Organization

Doug received an invitation from the Executive Director of the local chapter of Boys and Girls Clubs of America: Would he agree to give a talk on the role of business communication to a special gathering of 1,000 boys and girls? The letter further stated that the Boys and Girls Clubs of America wanted its members to grow up to be responsible young professionals with effective communication skills. Doug knows the Executive Director, and he would like a chance to talk to teenagers, so he e-mails to the Executive Director his acceptance of the invitation.

He sends another e-mail to Caleb, the manager in charge of stakeholder response, who asks Tanner, the executive reporting to him, and Kioni, the student-intern, to prepare Doug's presentation.

"Have you ever talked to your young boy about what you do here?" Doug asks Tanner as he and Kioni sit across from him.

"Um, not really. He doesn't seem interested, to be honest," Tanner says.

"Well, you have to find a way to make it interesting to him. Keep him in mind as you and Kioni work on this presentation," Doug says, looking alternately at Tanner and Kioni. "Kioni, you can think of your younger sister back home." Kioni smiles while nodding her head.

"How long will your presentation be?" Tanner asks, wondering what the PowerPoint font size should be for an audience of 1,000.

"Half-an-hour is all I'll do. Forget about me. I don't think the kids can take it more than that," Doug says. "Any other questions?"

"Not at this stage. We'll keep checking with you," Tanner says, pushing back the chair and turning to leave. Kioni follows him out.

Based on your reading of Chapter 1, brainstorm the following questions for Tanner and Kioni as they mull over their task.

- What is business and administrative communication? Why is it important to a manufacturing company such as All-Weather? Why is it important to Doug and his team in the HR Department?

- Why is poor communication problematic? List possible consequences that Doug and his team in the HR Department might face because of poor communication or lack of communication.

- What are some advantages of improving one's communication skills? What might Doug say to members of his young audience to persuade them to work on improving their communication skills?

- What are some specific stories Doug could use to make his presentation more interesting? Create some likely possibilities.

- In addition to the stories, what else could Doug do to make his presentation more interesting for teenagers?

- How does one approach a communication task? How should Tanner and Kioni approach theirs?

- How does one know if one has communicated effectively? How might Doug know whether his presentation was received with interest?

Adapting Your Message to Your Audience

Chapter Outline

Identifying Your Audiences

Ways to Analyze Your Audience

- Analyzing Individuals
- Analyzing Members of Groups
- Analyzing the Organizational Culture and the Discourse Community

Choosing Channels to Reach Your Audience

Using Audience Analysis to Adapt Your Message

1. How Will the Audience Initially React to the Message?
2. How Much Information Does the Audience Need?
3. What Obstacles Must You Overcome?
4. What Positive Aspects Can You Emphasize?

5. What Are the Audience's Expectations about the Appropriate Language, Content, and Organization of Messages?
6. How Will the Audience Use the Document?

Audience Analysis Works

Audience Benefits

- Characteristics of Good Audience Benefits
- Ways to Identify and Develop Audience Benefits
- Audience Benefits Work

Writing or Speaking to Multiple Audiences with Different Needs

Summary of Key Points

Banking on Multiple Audiences

Bruce Murphy, an executive at KeyBank, is working on a new problem: how to extend banking services to a new audience—people who use banks intermittently or not at all. It is a large group, estimated at 73 million people. Together, they spend an estimated $11 billion dollars in fees at places such as check-cashing outlets, money-wire companies, and paycheck lenders (companies offering cash advances on future paychecks).

However, they are a tough audience. Many of them have a deep distrust of banks or believe banks will not serve them. Murphy also faced another tough audience: bank managers who feared attracting forgeries and other bad checks and thus losing money. One manager actually said, "Are you crazy? These are the very people we're trying to keep out of the bank!"

> *"The bank even has a program to help people with a history of bounced checks to clear their records by paying restitution and taking the financial education class."*

To attract the new customers, KeyBank cashes payroll and government checks for a 1.5% fee, well below the 2.44% which is average for check-cashing outlets. The bank also started offering free financial education classes. In fact, the bank even has a program to help people with a history of bounced checks to clear their records by paying restitution and taking the financial education class.

The program is growing, both among check-cashing clients and branches offering the services, to the satisfaction of both audiences.

What are some other businesses that could expand services to underserved populations? What services would they offer? What problems would they encounter? What audience appeals could they use to attract clients or customers?

Source: Adapted from Ann Carrns, "Banks Court a New Client: The Low-Income Earner: KeyCorp Experiments with Check Cashing," *Wall Street Journal*, March 16, 2007, A1, A14.

Learning Objectives

After studying this chapter, you will know:

1 Ways to analyze different kinds of audiences.

   a. Individuals

   b. Groups

   c. Organizations

2 How to choose channels to reach your audience.

3 How to analyze your audience and adapt your message to it.

4 How to identify and develop audience benefits.

Knowing who you're talking to is fundamental to the success of any message. You need to identify your audiences, understand their motivations, and know how to reach them.

Identifying Your Audiences

The first step in analyzing your audience is to decide who your audience is. Organizational messages have multiple audiences:

1. A **gatekeeper** has the power to stop your message instead of sending it on to other audiences. The gatekeeper therefore controls whether your message even gets to the primary audience. Sometimes the supervisor who assigns the message is the gatekeeper; sometimes the gatekeeper is higher in the organization. In some cases, gatekeepers may exist outside the organization.

2. The **primary audience** decides whether to accept your recommendations or acts on the basis of your message. You must reach the primary audience to fulfill your purposes in any message.

3. The **secondary audience** may be asked to comment on your message or to implement your ideas after they've been approved. Secondary audiences also include lawyers who may use your message—perhaps years later—as evidence of your organization's culture and practices.

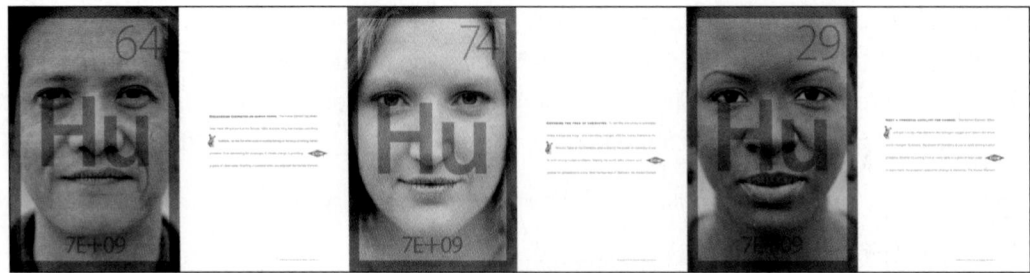

Dow Chemical is aware that an audience is composed of individual people. Their advertising campaign—"The Human Element"—"is intended to make a high-level emotional connection with people and help them see Dow as a responsible and involved citizen of the world," according to Patti Temple Rocks, Dow's Vice President of Global Communications and Reputations.

Source: "Human Element Ad Campaign Jump Starts Reputation Initiative," *Around Dow* 12, no. 6 (July 2006): 1.

4. An **auxiliary audience** may encounter your message but will not have to interact with it. This audience includes the "read-only" people.

5. A **watchdog audience,** though it does not have the power to stop the message and will not act directly on it, has political, social, or economic power. The watchdog pays close attention to the transaction between you and the primary audience and may base future actions on its evaluation of your message.

As the following examples show, one person can be part of two audiences. Frequently, a supervisor is both the primary audience and the gatekeeper.

> Dawn is an assistant account executive in an ad agency. Her boss asks her to write a proposal for a marketing plan for a new product the agency's client is introducing. Her **primary audience** is the executive committee of the client company, who will decide whether to adopt the plan. The **secondary audience** includes the marketing staff of the client company, who will be asked for comments on the plan, as well as the artists, writers, and media buyers who will carry out details of the plan if it is adopted. Her boss, who must approve the plan before it is submitted to the client, is the **gatekeeper.** Her office colleagues who read her plan are her **auxiliary audience.**
>
> Joe works in the information technology department of a large financial institution. He must write a memo explaining a major software change. His boss is the **gatekeeper;** the software users in various departments are the **primary audience.** The **secondary audience** includes the tech people who will be helping the primary audience install and adjust to the new software. The **auxiliary audience** includes department program assistants who forward the memo to appropriate people in each department. A **watchdog audience** is the board of directors.

Ways to Analyze Your Audience

The most important tools in audience analysis are common sense and empathy. **Empathy** is the ability to put yourself in someone else's shoes, to feel with that person. Use what you know about people and about organizations to predict likely responses.

Analyzing Individuals

When you write or speak to people in your own organization and in other organizations you work closely with, you may be able to analyze your audience as individuals. You may already know your audience. You can probably get additional information by talking to members of your audience, talking to people who know your audience, and observing your audience. You may learn that one manager may dislike phone calls, so you will know to write your request in an e-mail. Another manager may have a reputation for denying requests made on a Friday, so you will know to get yours in earlier.

A useful schema for analyzing people is the **Myers-Briggs Type Indicator.**® This instrument uses four pairs of dichotomies to identify ways that people differ.[1] One of these dichotomies is well known: Extroversion-Introversion, measuring how individuals prefer to focus their attention and get energy. Extroverted types are energized by interacting with other people. Introverted types get their energy from within.

The other three dichotomies in Myers-Briggs® typology are Sensing-Intuition, Thinking-Feeling, and Judging-Perceiving. The Sensing-Intuition dichotomy measures the way an individual prefers to take in information. Sensing types gather information through their senses, preferring what is real and tangible. Intuitive types prefer to gather information by looking at the big picture, focusing on the relationships and connections between facts.

A Real Clear Audience

It really pays to know your audience. In 2000 John McIntyre and Tom Bevan pooled $200,000 to launch RealClearPolitics.com, a collection of links to political news stories, blogs, video clips, and polls that focus on US politics. In the past seven years, RealClearPolitics.com has grown into the gold standard for accurately predicting election results and is frequently cited by its primary audience, often bloggers and journalists who have their own wide readership. Consequently, after spending a few thousand on marketing initially, McIntyre and Bevan have gained an average of over a million users a month; in addition, 51 percent of the company was purchased by Forbes Media in November 2007.

Although McIntyre and Bevan's seven-year success at RealClearPolitics has seemed easy, they said that it wasn't: "It requires total vigilance and plenty of sweat equity to make a website good day in and day out." The owners took very few days off. McIntyre and Bevan also suggested that most Internet business ideas are meant for a small group of people, not everyone: "Try to focus on serving a niche of people and serving them as best you can."

Adapted from Liz Wolgemuth, "Politics Junkies Spawn a Real, Clear Success," *US News & World Report*, December 24, 2007, 58.

Reading Levels

One of the most relevant demographic measures for writers is the literacy level of your audience. Unfortunately, even in advanced economies you have to ask how well your audience can read and put information to use. In the United States, the answer may be "not very well."

The National Assessment of Adult Literacy (NAAL), conducted by the US Department of Education, found that 14% of adults had difficulty reading well enough to follow simple instructions (such as when to take medication), 12% struggled to use simple forms (deciding where to sign their name on a form), and 22% had trouble working with numbers (simple addition tasks). NAAL also found that 5% of adults were non-literate—their language skills weren't strong enough to participate in the assessment.

Overall, that translates into 30 million adults in the United States with "below basic" reading and comprehension levels, and another 63 million with only "basic" literacy levels. For business writers, this poses a challenge. When composing a message for a broad audience of employees or customers, you may have to use short sentences, simple words, and clarifying graphics. What other techniques might you use to ensure that audiences with lower literacy levels can understand and use your message?

Adapted from the US Department of Education Institute of Education Sciences National Center for Education Statistics, "National Assessment of Adult Literacy (NAAL)," in *Surveys & Programs: Assessments*, http://nces .ed.gov/naal/ (accessed January 18, 2009).

The Thinking-Feeling dichotomy measures the way an individual makes decisions. Thinking types prefer to use thinking in decision making to consider the logical consequences of a choice or action. Feeling types make decisions based on the impact to people, considering what is important to them and to others involved.

The Judging-Perceiving dichotomy measures how individuals orient themselves to the external world. Judging types like to live in a planned, orderly way, seeking closure. Perceiving types prefer to live in a flexible, spontaneous way, enjoying possibilities.

The descriptors on each of the scales' dichotomies represent a preference, just as we have a preference for using either our right or our left hand to write. If necessary, we can use the opposite style, but we have less practice in it and use it less easily.

You can find your own personality type by taking the Myers-Briggs Type Indicator® instrument at your college's counseling center or student services office. Some businesses administer the Myers-Briggs Type Indicator® instrument to all employees to assist with team building and/or personal growth and development.

As Figure 2.1 suggests, you'll be most persuasive if you play to your audience's strengths. Indeed, many of the general principles of business communication appeal to the types most common among managers. Putting the main point up front satisfies the needs of judging types, and some 75% of US managers are judging. Giving logical reasons satisfies the needs of the nearly 80% of US managers who are thinking types.[2]

Analyzing Members of Groups

In many organizational situations, you'll analyze your audience not as individuals but as members of a group: "taxpayers who must be notified that they owe more income tax," "customers who use our accounting services," or "employees with small children." Focus on what group members have in common. Although generalizations won't be true for all members of the group, generalization is necessary when you must appeal to a large group of people with one message. In some cases, no research is necessary: It's easy to guess

Group membership sometimes gives clues about your audience.

Figure 2.1 Using Myers-Briggs Types in Persuasive Messages

If your audience is	Use this strategy	Because
Introverted type	Write a memo and let the reader think about your proposal before responding.	Introverts prefer to think before they speak. Written documents give them the time they need to think through a proposal carefully.
Extroverted type	Try out your idea orally, in an informal setting.	Extroverts like to think on their feet. They are energized by people; they'd rather talk than write.
Sensing type	Present your reasoning step-by-step. Get all your facts exactly right.	Sensing types usually reach conclusions step-by-step. They want to know why something is important, but they trust their own experience more than someone else's say-so. They're good at facts and expect others to be, too.
Intuitive type	Present the big picture first. Stress the innovative, creative aspects of your proposal.	Intuitive types like solving problems and being creative. They can be impatient with details.
Thinking type	Use logic, not emotion, to persuade. Show that your proposal is fair, even if some people may be hurt by it.	Thinking types make decisions based on logic and abstract principles. They are often uncomfortable with emotion.
Feeling type	Show that your proposal values the people needs of the organization as well as the dollars-and-cents needs of the organization.	Feeling types are very aware of other people and their feelings. They are sympathetic and like harmony.
Perceiving type	Show that you've considered all the alternatives. Ask for a decision by a specific date.	Perceiving types want to be sure they've considered all the options. They may postpone coming to closure.
Judging type	Present your request quickly.	Judging types are comfortable making quick decisions. They like to come to closure so they can move on to something else.

Source: Further Information is available at www.cpp.com where you will find the full range of Introduction to Type® titles along other products that allow you to expand your knowledge and applications of your MBTI® type. Modified and reproduced by special permission of the Publisher, CPP, Inc., Mountain View, CA 94043 from Introduction to Type, 6th Edition by Isabel Briggs Myers. Copyright 1998 by Peter B. Myers and Katharine D. Myers. All rights reserved. Further reproduction is prohibited without the Publisher's written consent.

the attitudes of people who must be told they owe more taxes. In other cases, databases may yield useful information. In still other cases, you may want to do original research.

Databases enable you to map demographic and psychographic profiles of customers or employees. **Demographic characteristics** are measurable features that can be counted objectively: age, sex, race, religion, education level, income, and so on.

Sometimes demographic information is irrelevant; sometimes it's important. Does education matter? Well, the fact that the reader has a degree from Eastern State rather than from Harvard may not matter, but how much the reader knows about accounting may. Does family structure matter? Sometimes. Because almost half of US marriages today are second unions, many involving children, some hotels and resorts are offering newlyweds "familymoon" packages that include baby-sitting, multiple bedrooms, and other family-friendly amenities.[3]

Age certainly matters. Mutual funds are aiming for young investors by lowering the minimum investment to less than the cost of an iPod, and simplifying choices.[4] Nissan is aiming its Pino minicar at young Japanese women, who

Training Generation Y

Cold Stone Creamery uses computer simulations. Nike uses an interactive program called "Sports Knowledge Underground." Cisco Systems developed a computer game.

These companies are part of a growing trend to use technology to attract and train Generation Y, a generation known for its enjoyment of and skill with technology. Because this generation is also known for its short attention span, many of the lessons come in short segments.

Many companies are also using vlogs—video blogs—to show prospective hires what jobs entail. For instance, Ernst & Young gave a video camera to a group of their interns. The resulting three-minute video on the firm's Web site offers an intern's perspective.

What do you think about these training programs? What kind of technology would entice you to a new job? What kind of training would give you negative feelings about a new job?

Adapted from Barbara Rose, "Generation Y: A Learning Experience for Firms," *Chicago Tribune*, March 4, 2007, B1.

Figure 2.2   Some Generational Differences in the Office

	Baby Boomers	Generation X and Y
Birth Dates	Between 1946 and 1964	1964 and on
Work ethic	Long hours in office	Productivity counts, not hours at office
Values	Hard work; consistency; hierarchy; clearly defined roles; serious about work	Work–life balance; flexibility; autonomy, informality; variety of challenges; the workplace can be fun
Preferred channels	Face-to-face, e-mail	Technologies: smartphones, cell phones, social networks
Motivators	Duty to company	Why a task is important; what's in it for them
Communication style	Through channels and hierarchy; accept annual evaluation	Freely offer opinions, both laterally and upward; want great amounts of attention and praise; want faster feedback
Decorum	Follow basic business decorum	May need to be reminded about basic business decorum

Sources: Ron Alsop, "The 'Trophy Kids' Go to Work," *Wall Street Journal*, October 21, 2008, D1, D4; and Piper Fogg, "When Generations Collide," *Chronicle of Higher Education*, July 18, 2008, B18.

tend to be uninterested in cars, by focusing on its accessories—like plush animals, furry seat cushions, star upholstery patterns, and sparkly hubcaps.[5]

One aspect of age that gets much press is the differences between generations in the office. Many older people believe younger workers have a sense of entitlement, that they expect great opportunities and perks without working for them. On the other hand, many younger workers see their older colleagues as rigid and hostile. Figure 2.2 shows some of the frequently mentioned age differences. While awareness of generational differences may help in some communication situations, such lists are also a good place to attach mental warnings against stereotypes. Plenty of baby boomers also like frequent positive feedback, and almost everyone likes a chance to make a difference.

Some cable TV stations are beginning to use demographic data to target ads to specific households. General Motors used demographic characteristics such as age and income to direct ads for luxury cars, foreign-branded cars, and mainstream cars at appropriate households subscribing to a cable TV station. Many large companies have been reluctant to buy ads on cable TV because of the fragmented coverage where no one operator covers the whole United States. Targeted ads may change that reluctance.[6]

As they fight to maintain readers, newspapers also use demographic data. The *Washington Post* has started a free online magazine aimed for a black audience. The magazine will emphasize genealogy to help set it apart from competing Web sites, which focus more on entertainment and lifestyle.[7]

Psychographic characteristics are qualitative rather than quantitative: values, beliefs, goals, and lifestyles. Many marketers use the Values and Life Styles (VALS) profiles developed by the SRI research firm in California. VALS profiles divide US buyers into eight categories according to their primary motivation (ideals, achievement, or self-expression), the amount of resources they have, and the extent to which they innovate. For instance, Strivers are motivated by achievement and are relatively low in resources and innovation. These conspicuous consumers may not have a lot of money, but they do try to be in style. The other VALS categories are called Innovators, Thinkers, Believers, Achievers, Experiencers, Makers, and Survivors.[8] To see where you fit, follow the VALS link from the BAC Web site.

Knowing what your audience finds important allows you to organize information in a way that seems natural to your audience and to choose appeals that the audience will find persuasive. An electric utility increased participation in a conservation program by using VALS to define two target segments and locate the zip codes in which those segments were concentrated. The utility prepared two different mailings, one appealing to each segment, and saw a 25% increase in conservation participation.[9]

Other organizations also use group analysis. Toyota is pushing its expensive hybrid Lexus harder in Japan and Europe than in the United States. While wealthy Japanese look for fuel economy, wealthy American buyers are more interested in performance. The editors of *Grit*, a home gardening magazine, changed the look of the magazine by exchanging its newsprint format for full-color glossy pages in order to appeal to new and younger audiences. Even the content of their articles changed. In addition to articles about crops, animals and small-town life, the magazine began to include topics like organic gardening.[10]

Analyzing the Organizational Culture and the Discourse Community

Be sensitive to the culture in which your audiences work and the discourse community of which they are a part. **Organizational culture** is a set of values, attitudes, and philosophies. An organization's culture is revealed verbally in

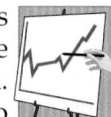

Audience Analysis at the Front Line

Some major businesses are sending their executives out to the front lines for a day or more to increase awareness of both clients' and employees' needs. Such stints are bringing changes to the front lines. A Loews executive who served as a bellhop, pool attendant, and housekeeper at a Florida hotel sweated so much in his polyester uniform that he had both the style and material of the uniforms altered. Executives at DaVita, a firm that runs kidney dialysis centers, learn that patient needs must come first, even before company paperwork.

Other companies which send executives out to be low-level workers include Walt Disney, Continental Airlines, Sysco, and Amazon.com.

What do you think executives learn on the front lines at these companies? Can you think of other companies that would benefit from similar programs for their executives?

Adapted from Joann S. Lublin, "Top Brass Try Life in the Trenches: To Promote Understanding, Firms Require Executives to Perform Entry-Level Jobs," *Wall Street Journal*, June 25, 2007, B1, B3.

Some companies are beginning to accept visible body art and long hair in traditional workplace cultures.

Source: Mielikki Org, "The Tattooed Executive: Body Art Gains Acceptance in Once-Staid Office Settings," *Wall Street Journal*, August 28, 2003, D1.

Whole Foods Values People AND Profits

Since 1980, Whole Foods has been a market leader in organic food. John Mackey, co-founder and CEO, credits his company's success, in part, to its corporate culture. "We have this empowered, decentralized culture, and a high percentage of [store managers] are trying to figure out how to make their stores better, how to improve customer experience. . . . We've got 189 stores. They're all faced with their own unique competitive environments. It's not necessary for me to know everything that's going on everywhere."

Across the country, Mackey empowers his team leaders and store managers to select products and set prices that are right for their unique locations. In order to meet the needs of local customers and to compete with mass-market retailers like Wal-Mart, Whole Foods encourages store managers to customize their product mixes, feature locally produced goods when possible, and aggressively match competitor's prices. The latter task is the trickiest because organic foods are often of higher quality, and more expensive, than nonorganic ones. Mackey acknowledges that most Americans value low prices, but as the population becomes wealthier, he believes that organic foods will penetrate more deeply into American kitchens. Mackey, a vegan, believes that the recent interest in natural and organic foods is "a value system, a belief system. It's penetrating into the mainstream."

Adapted and quoted from Steven Gray, "Natural Benefits," *Wall Street Journal*, December 4, 2006, B1, B3.

the organization's myths, stories, and heroes, as well as in documents such as employee manuals. It is revealed nonverbally in the allocation of space, money, and power. A **discourse community** is a group of people who share assumptions about what channels, formats, and styles to use for communication, what topics to discuss and how to discuss them, and what constitutes evidence.

In an organization that values equality and individualism, you can write directly to the CEO and address him or her as a colleague. In other companies, you'd be expected to follow a chain of command. Some organizations prize short messages; some expect long, thorough documents. Messages that are consistent with the organization's culture have a greater chance of succeeding.

You can begin to analyze an organization's culture by asking the following questions:

- Is the organization tall or flat? Are there lots of levels between the CEO and the lowest worker, or only a few?
- How do people get ahead? Are the organization's rewards based on seniority, education, being well-liked, saving money, or serving customers? Are rewards available only to a few top people, or is everyone expected to succeed?
- Does the organization value diversity or homogeneity? Does it value independence and creativity or being a team player and following orders?
- What stories do people tell? Who are the organization's heroes and villains?
- How important are friendship and sociability? To what extent do workers agree on goals, and how intently do they pursue them?
- How formal are behavior, language, and dress?
- What does the work space look like? Do employees work in offices, cubicles, or large rooms?
- What are the organization's goals? Making money? Serving customers and clients? Advancing knowledge? Contributing to the community?

To analyze an organization's discourse community, ask the following questions:

- What media, formats, and styles are preferred for communication?
- What do people talk about? What topics are not discussed?
- What kind of and how much evidence is needed to be convincing?

Choosing Channels to Reach Your Audience

A communication **channel** is the means by which you convey your message. Communication channels vary in speed, accuracy of transmission, cost, number of messages carried, number of people reached, efficiency, and ability to promote goodwill. Depending on the audience, your purposes, and the situation, one channel may be better than another.

A written message makes it easier to

- Present extensive or complex data.
- Present many specific details.
- Minimize undesirable emotions.

Oral messages make it easier to

- Use emotion to help persuade the audience.
- Focus the audience's attention on specific points.

M&M candies offer a sweet communication channel to organizations.

- Resolve conflicts and build consensus.
- Modify plans.
- Get immediate action or response.

Choosing the right channel can be tricky sometimes. Even in the office, you will have to decide if your message will be more effective as an e-mail, phone call, visit, or sticky note posted on a colleague's computer. In nonstandard situations, choosing a channel can be challenging. If you are the head of a small, nonprofit literacy agency which helps adults learn to read, how do you reach your clients? You cannot afford TV ads, and they cannot read print channels such as flyers. If you are a safety officer for a manufacturer, how do you send out product recall notifications? Who ever files the contact-information cards when they purchase an item? If you are the benefits manager in a large manufacturing plant, how will you get information about your new benefits plan out to the thousand people on the floor? They don't use computers at work and may not have computer access at home.

Businesses are becoming ever more savvy about using the array of channels. Ad money has been moving out of print and TV channels and into online advertising, which is now a $21.4 billion business, and one that is expected to double by 2011.[11] Many companies have interactive Web sites and forums where customers can chat about products. And many consumers aren't waiting to be asked. Compelling and popular advertisements are being created by consumers who upload their own videos about products (e.g., Doritos, iPhone, Converse) on YouTube.[12]

Newspapers are expanding from print to blogs, podcasts, and chatrooms. In fact, Warren Buffet himself warned the *Washington Post,* on whose board he serves, that the paper-only model will no longer work.[13] Even the venerable

No Substitute for Face Time

In the face of globalization and remote video feeds that simultaneously connect workers and clients all around the world, face-to-face meetings are still critical in global business. Culturally, the world is still incredibly diverse, and to make global coalitions, such as launching a Coca-Cola bottling plant in Albania a few years ago, meeting the right people in person was crucial for Coke's CEO.

Another example is MTV in the center of Islamic nations. Would it be possible to enter MTV into the Arabian market without offending the religious institutions of this region? Not without many carefully planned, face-to-face meetings. The chief of MTV Networks International managed to accomplish the establishment of MTV Arabia by convincing the mayor of Mecca that the new station would provide educational opportunities and would not show skin.

Collaborative technologies such as videoconferencing may be convenient and less expensive than frequent flying, but technology simply cannot take the place of physically sitting down with a colleague or client to solve problems and form alliances.

Adapted from Tom Lowry et al., "It's All About the Face-to-Face," *BusinessWeek*, January 28, 2008, 48–51.

Market research firm Claritas, Inc., combines demographic and psychographic data to identify 66 lifestyle segments, including "Young Digerati" (tech-savvy young adults), "Close-In Couples" (older, African-American couples), and "Blue-Chip Blues" (young families with well-paying blue-collar jobs). Both the catchy names and drawings are copyrighted by Claritas, Inc., 2007.

Associated Press gets more of its revenue from broadcasters and Internet companies than it does from US newspapers.[14] In fact, one of the few print channels still thriving is campus newspapers.[15]

The big three TV network newscasts are facing similar problems. In 2007, they lost about 1.2 million viewers and millions of advertising dollars according to Nielsen data. The most sought-after viewer, age 18–49, is not watching the evening news at the dinner hour; in fact, many of them are not even home yet. Instead, the average viewer is 60. In response to the fall in viewership, the networks have reduced their news staff and shifted the subject focus. International coverage, including the war in Iraq, has been cut back. In response to declining viewership, networks are posting news in online stories and videos, as well as blogs.[16]

New channels are appearing everywhere (for more on electronic channels, see Chapter 4):

- IBM is offering Innov8, an interactive video game designed to teach business and IT skills, free to 2,000 universities around the world. One high-tech consulting firm, the Apple Group, predicts one in five of the Global Fortune 500 will be using gaming as a teaching channel by 2012.[17]

- Companies such as Chanel and Ralph Lauren have launched applications for the iPhone that users can download to keep track of style trends, runway shows, and store offerings.[18]

- To attract younger audiences, *Vogue* magazine is helping produce a Web-based reality series about the fashion industry, Model.Live. Viewers will be able to click a link to buy what the models are wearing.[19]

- To reach young men, a difficult market, some US companies such as Coke, Kentucky Fried Chicken, and Electronic Arts are sponsoring an NBA tour.[20]

- Toymaker Mattel's Web site BarbieGirls.com has attracted 11 million users. Mattel also has a game that allows users to design Barbie costumes and host virtual fashion shows.[21]

- Bill Cosby has recorded a hip-hop album to help carry his message of education and self-respect to new audiences. To sell its cleaning products, Clorox put out an album, "The Blue Sky Project: A Clorox Charity Collection." Companies such as Procter & Gamble and Allstate also offer full-length versions of tunes used in their ads. In regions such as the United Kingdom and Asia, original songs featured in ads often become quite popular.[22]

- Paramount Pictures has used widgets to advertise new movies. Widgets are small computer programs that let you install on your desktop or Web page items like clocks, calculators, news updates, and weather information; the items are framed by or placed next to the promotional material.[23]

- Vienna, Austria, is raising money for the main public library with a phone sex hotline. Pay by the minute and you get to hear a famous Austrian actress reading passages from the library's collection of erotic fiction from the 18th through 20th centuries.[24]

Creative channels abound. Ads are appearing on hotel shower curtains, the bellies of pregnant women, airport luggage conveyor belts, grocery checkout conveyors, and toilet stall doors. One company prints ads on cardboard shirt hangers which are distributed free to cleaners. The hangers are touted as a good way to reach male consumers. The US Post Office used shrink wrap to turn selected mail-collection boxes into R2-D2 clones in honor of their Star Wars anniversary stamp.[25]

As consumers become ever more savvy about ways to ignore advertising, one channel that has received publicity is the vivistitial: ads that take advantage of more receptive times in consumers' lives. One much talked about example is the elevator ad. Captivate offers video programming, such as news headlines and weather, in elevators. The programming is not intrusive: screens are not huge and the video does not have sound. Recall of Captivate ads is two to four times higher than that of TV ads.[26]

Channels that are not turning out to be golden are social networks. Although advertising on these sites has grown phenomenally, over 155% in 2007, and amounts to over a billion dollars, results are disappointing. Social networks show some of the lowest response rates on the Web, sometimes as few as 4 in 10,000 viewers. And in an ironic twist, the ads may be a primary cause in the dropping usage of such sites.[27]

Using Audience Analysis to Adapt Your Message

Zeroing in on the right audience with the right message is frequently a formula for success. Mike McNamara, a Texas attorney, aims for the spring break crowd at South Padre Island. His flyer reads, "Got drunk? Got caught? Call Mike. He won't tell your mama!" His Web site includes a picture of him in beach wear with a beer in his hand. Fees for representing someone for a misdemeanor run hundreds of dollars; felony fees run thousands of dollars.[28]

If you know your audience well and if you use words well, much of your audience analysis and adaptation will be unconscious. If you don't know your audience or if the message is very important, take the time to analyze your audience formally and to revise your message with your analysis in mind. The questions in Figure 2.3 will help guide a careful analysis.

As you answer these questions for a specific audience, think about the organizational culture in which the person works. At every point, your audience's reaction is affected not only by his or her personal feelings and preferences but also by the political environment of the organization, the economy, and current events.

Customer Service Channels

"If you think the privacy of your medical information has been compromised, you can file a complaint with the Office for Civil Rights. A brochure distributed by this office tells people they can call and 'ask for a civil-rights or privacy-complaint form.'

"But you can't really ask for anything, because when you call the number, you can't get a person on the line.

"An automated voice thanks you for calling and then breaks the news:

"'We're sorry, a staff person is not able to receive your call. This number is not able to receive messages.'

"Callers are directed to a Web site to file a complaint. Twice. And if you don't have a computer, . . . [t]he voice tells you . . . 'most local libraries have computers available that residents can use to access the Internet at no extra cost.'"*

Is this an ethical way to distribute information? What groups of people does this channel discriminate against? Do you know of other organizations that communicate only through the Web?

*Quoted from "Not Exactly a Model for Customer Service," *Des Moines Register*, August 23, 2008, 14A.

STONE SOUP   BY JAN ELIOT

Mockumentary Advertising

Early in 2008, BMW's ad agency ran a marketing campaign featuring a half-hour mockumentary. The video showed a Bavarian town's attempt to catapult a BMW from a giant ramp to the United States. In addition to the video, the agency developed a Web site for the town and Facebook profiles for several of the characters. For weeks, BMW declined to answer questions about the video in order to keep the debate going about its veracity. The agency says the viral marketing campaign created mostly positive buzz.

How do you feel about such advertising campaigns? Are they ethical? A 2006 blog about a couple traveling in the United States, and that mentioned Wal-Mart stores, was heavily criticized because it did not tell readers that the travelers were fictional and that the blog was connected to Wal-Mart. How was this blog, which received criticism, different from the mockumentary, which received praise?

Adapted from Stephanie Kang, "BMW Ran Risk with Silent Role in Mockumentary," *Wall Street Journal*, June 20, 2008, B5.

1. How Will the Audience Initially React to the Message?

a. Will the audience see this message as important?

Audiences will read and act on messages they see as important to their own careers; they may ignore messages that seem unimportant to them.

When the audience may see your message as unimportant, you need to

- Use a subject line or first paragraph that shows your reader this message is important and relevant.
- Make the action as easy as possible.
- Suggest a realistic deadline for action.
- Keep the message as short as possible.

b. How will the fact that the message is from you affect the audience's reaction?

The audience's experience with you, your organization, and the subject you're writing about shapes the way they respond to this new message. Someone who thinks well of you and your organization will be prepared to receive your

Figure 2.3   Analyzing Your Audience

These questions will help you analyze your audience:

1. How will the audience initially react to the message?
2. How much information does the audience need?
3. What obstacles must you overcome?
4. What positive aspects can you emphasize?
5. What are the audience's expectations about the appropriate language, content, and organization, of messages?
6. How will the audience use the document?

message favorably; someone who thinks poorly of you and the organization will be quick to find fault with what you say and the way you say it.

When your audience has negative feelings about your organization, your position, or you personally, you need to

- Make a special effort to avoid phrases that could seem condescending, arrogant, rude, hostile, or uncaring.
- Use positive emphasis (p. 66) to counteract the natural tendency to sound defensive.
- Develop logic and benefits fully.

2. How Much Information Does the Audience Need?

a. How much does the audience already know about this subject?

It's easy to overestimate the knowledge an audience has. People outside your own immediate unit may not really know what it is you do. Even people who once worked in your unit may have forgotten specific details now that their daily work is in management. People outside your organization won't know how *your* organization does things.

When some of your information is new to the audience, you need to

- Make a special effort to be clear. Define terms, explain concepts, use examples, avoid acronyms.
- Link new information to old information that the audience already knows.
- Use paragraphs and headings to break up new information into related chunks so that the information is easier to digest.
- Test a draft of your document with your reader or a subset of your intended audience to see whether the audience can understand and use what you've written.

b. Does the audience's knowledge need to be updated or corrected?

Our personal experience guides our expectations and actions, but sometimes needs to be corrected. If you're trying to change someone's understanding of something, you need to

- Acknowledge the audience's initial understanding early in the message.
- Use examples, statistics or other evidence to show the need for the change, or to show that the audience's experience is not universal.
- Allow the audience to save face by suggesting that changed circumstances call for new attitudes or action.

c. What aspects of the subject does the audience need to be aware of to appreciate your points?

When the audience must think of background or old information to appreciate your points, you can

- Preface information with "As you know" or "As you may remember" to avoid suggesting that you think the audience does not know what you're saying.
- Put old or obvious information in a subordinate clause.

Retailers Analyze Online Consumers

Ever wonder if you are being watched online? Internet merchants are watching consumer Internet behavior and tastes, then targeting strategies to increase sales. The result is variable pricing, discounts, or free shipping offers based on shopper behavior and demographics.

- Overstock.com Inc. boasts that they can determine the gender and time zone of a consumer in five clicks; these categories then help determine what promotional offers a consumer may receive.
- eBay uses different displays on homepages based on previous view habits and geography.
- Ice.com is testing the results of different offers in different parts of the country.
- Yoox gives frequent customers early notification of discounts and a special site with reduced prices just for them.
- Delightful Deliveries gives customers different discount offers based on the search term they used to find the site. For example, a customer who searches for "gift baskets" may receive a 5% discount while someone who indirectly found the site may receive a free-shipping offer.
- Kiyonna Clothing shows customers different offers based on real-time information about their sessions. For instance, if a customer keeps going back and forth between the checkout page and an item the site often generates a free shipping offer valid only for the day of the Internet shopping event.

Adapted from Jessica E. Vascellaro, "Online Retailers Are Watching You," *Wall Street Journal*, November 28, 2006, D1.

3. What Obstacles Must You Overcome?

a. Is your audience opposed to what you have to say?

People who have already made up their minds are highly resistant to change. When the audience will oppose what you have to say, you need to

- Start your message with any areas of agreement or common ground that you share with your audience.
- Make a special effort to be clear and unambiguous. Points that might be clear to a neutral audience can be misinterpreted by someone opposed to the message.
- Make a special effort to avoid statements that will anger the audience.
- Limit your statement or request to the smallest possible area. If parts of your message could be delivered later, postpone them.
- Show that your solution is the best solution currently available, even though it isn't perfect.

b. Will it be easy for the audience to do as you ask?

Everyone has a set of ideas and habits and a mental self-image. If we're asked to do something that violates any of those, we first have to be persuaded to change our attitudes or habits or self-image—a change we're reluctant to make.

When your request is time-consuming, complicated, or physically or psychologically difficult, you need to

- Make the action as easy as possible.
- Break down complex actions into a list, so the audience can check off each step as it is completed. This list will also help ensure complete responses.
- Show that what you ask is consistent with some aspect of what the audience believes.
- Show how the audience (not just you or your organization) will benefit when the action is completed.

4. What Positive Aspects Can You Emphasize?

a. From the audience's point of view, what are the benefits of your message?

Benefits help persuade the audience that your ideas are good ones. Make the most of the good points inherent in the message you want to convey.

- Put good news first.
- Use audience benefits that go beyond the basic good news.

b. What experiences, interests, goals, and values do you share with the audience?

A sense of solidarity with someone can be an even more powerful reason to agree than the content of the message itself. When everyone in your audience shares the same experiences, interests, goals, and values, you can

- Consider using a vivid anecdote to remind the audience of what you share. The details of the anecdote should be interesting or new; otherwise, you may seem to be lecturing the audience.
- Use a salutation and close that remind the audience of their membership in this formal or informal group.

5. What Are the Audience's Expectations about the Appropriate Language, Content, and Organization of Messages?

a. What style of writing does the audience prefer?

Good writers adapt their style to suit the reader's preferences. A reader who sees contractions as too informal needs a different style from one who sees traditional business writing as too stuffy. As you write,

- Use what you know about your reader to choose a more or less formal, more or less friendly style.
- Use the reader's first name in the salutation only if both of you are comfortable with a first-name basis.

b. Are there hot buttons or "red flag" words that may create an immediate negative response?

You don't have time to convince the audience that a term is broader or more neutral than his or her understanding. When you need agreement or approval, you should

- Avoid terms that carry emotional charges for many people: for example, *criminal, un-American, feminist, fundamentalist, liberal.*
- Use your previous experience with individuals to replace any terms that have particular negative meanings for them.

c. How much detail does the audience want?

A message that does not give the audience the amount of or kind of detail they want may fail. Sometimes you can ask your audience how much detail they want. When you write to people you do not know well, you can

- Provide all the detail they need to understand and act on your message.
- Group chunks of information under headings so that readers can go directly to the parts of the message they find most interesting and relevant.
- Be sure that a shorter-than-usual document covers the essential points; be sure that a longer-than-usual document is free from wordiness and repetition.

d. Does the audience prefer a direct or indirect organization?

Individual personality or cultural background may lead someone to prefer a particular kind of structure. You'll be more effective if you use the structure and organization your audience prefers.

6. How Will the Audience Use the Document?

a. Under what physical conditions will the audience use the document?

Reading a document in a quiet office calls for no special care. But suppose the audience will be reading your message on the train commuting home, or on a ladder as he or she attempts to follow instructions. Then the physical preparation of the document can make it easier or harder to use.

New Cars for Japanese Youth

A 2007 survey by Japan's largest newspaper found that only 25% of Japanese men in their twenties wanted a car. It seems that young Japanese adults are content with using their parents' cars and taking public transportation, thus saving their money for other consumer goods.

To woo these reluctant buyers, Nissan is dreaming up new cars. For Japanese men, who want a car for hanging out with friends, designers are creating a large, touchscreen, interactive display that both passengers and driver can use.

For Japanese women, who want a car that parks easily and removes some of the stress of city driving, designers are creating a "bubble" car that can move sideways to zip into tight parking spaces. The car also has a robot who provides driving directions in a soothing voice.

Although not in production yet, Nissan is hoping that ideas like these will woo back young Japanese adults.

Adapted from John Murphy, "Japan's Young Won't Rally Round the Car: As Youths Forsake Wheels, Designers Try to Make Vehicles Less Stressful, More Convivial," *Wall Street Journal,* February 29, 2008, B1.

Time for Food

To better understand its customers, Domino's visited homes of its patrons and videotaped customers buying and eating pizza. They learned that the primary need of those customers, who wanted quick gratification, was convenience. They also learned that many of the customers still remembered Domino's 30-minute delivery promise, a promise dropped because of legal issues involving accidents with Domino's delivery people.

Capitalizing on this research, Domino's decided to run ads centering around giving customers a gift of time, 30 minutes of time. The humorous ads show people using their time by hanging out with friends or exercising to a video. Fake coupons say they are "good for 30 minutes of video game smack talking."

Aiming at younger consumers, 30 and under, Domino's is relying more heavily on digital ads and clever marketing on the pizza boxes.

Adapted from Janet Adamy, "Will a Twist on an Old Vow Deliver for Domino's Pizza?" *Wall Street Journal*, December 17, 2007, B1, B2.

When the reader will use your document outside an office,

- Use lots of white space.
- Make the document small enough to hold in one hand.
- Number items so the reader can find his or her place after an interruption.

b. Will the audience use the document as a general reference? As a specific guide?

Understanding how your audience will use the document will enable you to choose the best pattern of organization and the best level of detail.

If the document will serve as a general reference,

- Use a specific subject line to aid in filing and retrieval. If the document is online, consider using several keywords to make it easy to find the document in a database search program.
- Use headings within the document so that readers can skim it.
- Give the office as well as the person to contact so that the reader can get in touch with the appropriate person some time from now.
- Spell out details that may be obvious now but might be forgotten in a year.

If the document will be a detailed guide or contain instructions,

- Check to be sure that all the steps are in chronological order.
- Number steps so that readers can easily see which steps they've completed.
- Group steps into five to seven categories if there are many individual steps.
- Put any warnings at the beginning of the document; then repeat them just before the specific step to which they apply.

Audience Analysis Works

Audience analysis is a powerful tool. Amazon.com tracks users' online histories to make suggestions on items they might like. Nintendo believes that much of its success is extending its concept of audience. An important part of its audience is hard-core gamers, a very vocal group—they love to blog. But if Nintendo listened just to them, they would be the only audience Nintendo had. Instead, Nintendo extended its audience by creating the Wii, a new system that the hard-core gamers had not imagined and one that is collecting new users who never imagined owning a system at all.[29] With the introduction of Wii Fit, Nintendo is expanding its audience to more women and even senior citizens.

Match.com has become the largest US online subscription dating site by appealing to singles over 50. Its audience research showed that this group was more likely to pay subscription fees than were younger users. Match.com targets itself as a site for those who want serious relationships, and it has made the site easier to navigate for people who are not Internet-savvy.[30]

Tesco PLC, Britain's largest retailer, is beating Wal-Mart in England by signing up customers for its Clubcard. The card gives customers discounts, and it gives Tesco audience data. When Tesco added Asian herbs and ethnic foods in Indian and Pakistani neighborhoods, the data showed the products were also popular with affluent white customers, so Tesco expanded its roll-out. When customers buy diapers the first time, they get coupons for usual baby products such as wipes and toys. They also get coupons for beer, because the data show that new fathers buy more beer.[31]

Audience Benefits

Use your analysis of your audience to create effective **audience benefits,** advantages that the audience gets by using your services, buying your products, following your policies, or adopting your ideas. In informative messages, benefits give reasons to comply with the information you announce and suggest that the information is good. In persuasive messages, benefits give reasons to act and help overcome audience resistance. Negative messages do not use benefits.

Characteristics of Good Audience Benefits

Good benefits meet four criteria. Each of these criteria suggests a technique for writing good benefits.

1. Adapt benefits to the audience.

When you write to different audiences, you may need to stress different benefits. Suppose that you manufacture a product and want to persuade dealers to carry it. The features you may cite in ads directed toward customers—stylish colors, sleek lines, convenience, durability, good price—won't convince dealers. Shelf space is at a premium, and no dealer carries all the models of all the brands available for any given product. Why should the dealer stock your product? To be persuasive, talk about the features that are benefits from the dealer's point of view: turnover, profit margin, the national advertising campaign that will build customer awareness and interest, the special store displays you offer that will draw attention to the product.

To keep viewers, AOL has sites in such popular categories as sports, health, and news. To attract younger, hipper viewers, it also has created new sites that don't use the AOL name: a technology site (Switched), a hip-hop site (BlackVoices), and a Web trend tracker (Urlesque).[32] Even the Girl Scouts are recognizing the need to adapt to a different audience, one that no longer privileges group activities. The new advertising stresses independence and individuality; new scout topics include time management and online bullying.[33]

2. Stress intrinsic as well as extrinsic motivators.

Intrinsic motivators come automatically from using a product or doing something. **Extrinsic motivators** are "added on." Someone in power decides to give them; they do not necessarily come from using the product or doing the action. Figure 2.4 gives examples of extrinsic and intrinsic motivators for three activities.

Figure 2.4   Extrinsic and Intrinsic Motivators

Activity	Extrinsic motivator	Intrinsic motivator
Making a sale	Getting a commission	Pleasure in convincing someone; pride in using your talents to think of a strategy and execute it
Turning in a suggestion to a company suggestion system	Getting a monetary reward when the suggestion is implemented	Solving a problem at work; making the work environment a little more pleasant
Writing a report that solves an organizational problem	Getting praise, a good performance appraisal, and maybe a raise	Pleasure in having an effect on an organization; pride in using your skills to solve problems; solving the problem itself

Intrinsic motivators or benefits are better than extrinsic motivators for two reasons:

1. There just aren't enough extrinsic motivators for everything you want people to do. You can't give a prize to every customer every time he or she places an order or to every subordinate who does what he or she is supposed to do.
2. Research shows that extrinsic motivators may actually make people *less* satisfied with the products they buy or the procedures they follow.

In a groundbreaking study of professional employees, Frederick Herzberg found that the things people said they liked about their jobs were all intrinsic motivators—pride in achievement, an enjoyment of the work itself, responsibility. Extrinsic motivators—pay, company policy—were sometimes mentioned as things people disliked, but they were never cited as things that motivated or satisfied them. People who made a lot of money still did not mention salary as a good point about the job or the organization.[34] Other motivation experts have found that motivators can vary with employees' ages; for example, young salespeople are more likely to enjoy travel rewards, whereas older salespeople might prefer to remain close to home and family, enjoying cash or merchandise as their rewards for high performance.[35]

Steak 'n Shake restaurant chain wanted to find out what motivated its employees to do their best at work. The company learned that what employees want more than money is respect and the feeling that management listens to them and values their input. Celadon, a trucking company, discovered that addressing drivers by name rather than their truck's number made a big difference in the drivers' satisfaction with the company.[36]

3. Prove benefits with clear logic and explain them in adequate detail.

An audience benefit is a claim or assertion that the audience will benefit if they do something. Convincing the audience, therefore, involves two steps: making sure that the benefit really will occur, and explaining it to the audience.

If the logic behind a claimed benefit is faulty or inaccurate, there's no way to make that particular benefit convincing. Revise the benefit to make it logical.

Faulty logic:	Moving your account information into Excel will save you time.
Analysis:	If you have not used Excel before, in the short run it will probably take you longer to work with your account information using Excel. You may have been pretty good with your old system!
Revised benefit:	Moving your account information into Excel will allow you to prepare your monthly budget pages with a few clicks of a button.

If the logic is sound, making that logic evident to the audience is a matter of providing enough evidence and showing how the evidence proves the claim that there will be a benefit. Always provide enough detail to be vivid and concrete. You'll need more detail in the following situations:

a. The audience may not have thought of the benefit before.
b. The benefit depends on the difference between the long run and the short run.
c. The audience will be hard to persuade, and you need detail to make the benefit vivid and emotionally convincing.

The apparel industry, which is actively seeking a middle-aged and baby boomer audience, is using details to attract them. Jeans makers now have "gentleman's jeans," with a waistband at or near the natural waist and seat and thigh areas that are roomier. Marketers of women's fashions are offering helpful sales

Until recently, Islamic women who wanted to go swimming had a problem. To meet their customers' needs, the Australian company Ahiida now makes hooded full-bodied bathing suits, called Burqinis, for Muslim women who wish to go swimming while still maintaining the Islamic customs of full body coverage.

Source: Lisa Miller, "Belief Watch: Surf's Up!" *Newsweek,* January 29, 2007, 15.

associates and flattering clothes: tops that cover upper arms and pants that are slimming yet comfortable. Their potential market is huge. Women over 35 bought over half the annual $100 billion spent on women's apparel purchases.[37]

4. Phrase benefits in you-attitude.

If benefits aren't in you-attitude (p. 62), they'll sound selfish and won't be as effective as they could be. It doesn't matter how you phrase benefits while you're brainstorming and developing them, but in your final draft, check to be sure that you've used you-attitude.

Lacks you-attitude: We have the lowest prices in town.

You-attitude: At Havlichek Cars, you get the best deal in town.

Ways to Identify and Develop Audience Benefits

Brainstorm lots of benefits—perhaps twice as many as you'll need. Then you can choose the ones that are most effective for your audience, or that you can develop most easily. The first benefit you think of may not be the best.

Sometimes benefits will be easy to think of and to explain. When they are harder to identify or to develop, use the following steps to identify and then develop good benefits:

1. Identify the needs, wants, and feelings that may motivate your audience.
2. Identify the objective features of your product or policy that could meet the needs you've identified.
3. Show how the audience can meet their needs with the features of the policy or product.

Accommodating Audiences

For years Wal-Mart has dominated the retail industry by offering a variety of products at "everyday low prices." But Wal-Mart's strategy of standardization and the resulting economies of scale that helped the company become a retailing giant became an Achilles heel. In trying to be all things to all people, explained Eduardo Castro-Wright, the company's new CEO at the time, "you end up underserving everyone because you don't have an offering that is specific to that customer segment."

To counter slipping sales and make the company even more competitive, Castro-Wright introduced six demographic groups that allowed regional managers to localize their stores' product mix to better suit their customers.

- Stores in Hispanic markets included large farmers-market events offering fresh foods and featured displays for *quinceaneras.*

- Stores in areas with large "empty nest" populations had smaller children's sections and a larger pharmacy area.

- A new urban-style store outside of Chicago quadrupled its display of gospel, rhythm and blues, and hip-hop music and added baby clothes and supplies designed for premature babies to meet the needs of local shoppers.

In addition to localizing its merchandise, Wal-Mart also localized its staff: regional executives, who once lived in company headquarters at Bentonville, AR, were required to live within their regions to better understand their customer base.

Adapted from Ann Zimmerman, "To Boost Sales, Wal-Mart Drops One-Size-Fits-All Approach," *Wall Street Journal,* September 7, 2006, A1.

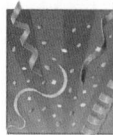

Male Models

1. Identify the needs, wants, and feelings that may motivate your audience.

All of us have basic needs, and most of us supplement those needs with possessions or intangibles we want. We need enough food to satisfy nutritional needs, but we may want our diet to make us look sexy. We need basic shelter, but we may want our homes to be cozy, luxurious, or green. And our needs and wants are strongly influenced by our feelings. We may feel safer in a more expensive car, even though research does not show that car as being safer than cheaper models.

Successful marketers pay attention to the wants and feelings of their audiences. Procter & Gamble increased the market share of Gain detergent, and saw annual sales of over a billion dollars, by focusing on a benefit their audience considered important: the scent. *The Daily Sun*, a South African tabloid, is gaining market share, when other newspapers are losing it, by focusing on stories—soccer, sex, soap operas, local witches, supernatural events like evil flying tortoises—its audience wants to read. This audience, primarily newly enfranchised black Africans, has given the paper an audited paid circulation of over a half million.[38]

The same process works for many organizations. Applied Intellectual Capital had a new process to clean mining waste. It was better and cheaper than other technologies, but mining firms, many of whom see environmental cleanup as a regulatory chore, showed no interest. Then the company realized it had been stressing benefits for the environment rather than the client firm. After stressing how the process could help improve the bottom line, the company got more interest.[39]

2. Identify the objective features of your product or policy that could meet the needs you've identified.

Sometimes just listing the audience's needs makes it obvious which feature meets a given need. Sometimes several features together meet the need. Try to think of all of them.

Suppose that you want to persuade people to come to the restaurant you manage. It's true that everybody needs to eat, but telling people they can satisfy their hunger needs won't persuade them to come to your restaurant rather than going somewhere else or eating at home. Depending on what features your restaurant offered, you could appeal to one or more of the following subgroups:

Subgroup	Features to meet the subgroup's needs
People who work outside the home	A quick lunch; a relaxing place to take clients or colleagues
Parents with small children	High chairs, child-size portions, and things to keep the kids entertained while they wait for their order
People who eat out a lot	Variety both in food and in decor
People on tight budgets	Economical food; a place where they don't need to tip (cafeteria or fast food)
People on special diets	Low-sodium and low-carb dishes; vegetarian food; kosher food
People to whom eating out is part of an evening's entertainment	Music or a floor show; elegant surroundings; reservations so they can get to a show or event after dinner; late hours so they can come to dinner after a show or game

Health insurance policies offer benefits tailored to specific demographics. Younger customers may not get name-brand prescription or maternity coverage, but do get teeth whitening and gym membership discounts. Early retirees may get unlimited office visits, but with a higher co-pay.[40]

Whenever you're communicating with customers or clients about features that are not unique to your organization, it's wise to present both benefits of the features themselves and benefits of dealing with your company. If you talk about the benefits of dining in a relaxed atmosphere but don't mention your own restaurant, people may go somewhere else!

3. Show how the audience can meet their needs with the features of the policy or product.

Features alone rarely motivate people. Instead, link the feature to the audience's needs—and provide details to make the benefit vivid.

Weak: You get quick service.

Better: If you only have an hour for lunch, try our Business Buffet. Within minutes, you can choose from a variety of main dishes, vegetables, and a make-your-own-sandwich-and-salad bar. You'll have a lunch that's as light or filling as you want, with time to enjoy it—and still be back to the office on time.

Audience Benefits Work

Appropriate audience benefits work so well that organizations spend much time and money identifying them and then developing them. Procter & Gamble studies customers' cleaning processes to promote its industrial cleaners. After observing launderers at the Millennium Hotel in Cincinnati, P&G researchers suggested cutting the products used from five to two, thus shortening the hotel's washing machine cycle five to seven minutes and reducing laundry wear on the linens from 4% to 1%. After observing staff at Wendy's, P&G calculated exactly how much product was needed to clean a table and then found a nozzle that would deliver exactly that much in one spritz.[41]

Other organizations are also paying attention to their audience benefits:

- State governments are offering incentives to attract teachers for disciplines experiencing teacher shortages, especially physics, chemistry, and mathematics. Those incentives include scholarships to in-state students who will commit to teaching in the state and payment of student loans after the required years of teaching.[42]

- Hotels study which benefits are worth the money, and which are not. Holiday Inn keeps restaurants and bars in all their hotels, even though they are not money makers, but does not have bellhops. Staybridge Suites cleans less often but has "Sundowner receptions" which give guests a free meal and a chance to socialize.[43]

- Goldstar Events is succeeding where others have failed: they are selling fine-arts performances to the under-40 crowd. How? They are using personalized Web-based marketing to sell discounted tickets to undersold performances. They appeal to this audience with their electronic notifications, online ticket sales, and user reviews.[44]

Remember that audience benefits must be appropriate for the audience before they work. In 2008, Tylenol had a new ad campaign that said, "We put our love into Tylenol." Upset customers who remembered the Tylenol cyanide poisonings wrote in saying they didn't want anyone putting anything into their Tylenol.[45]

Write Your Way into Your New Job

You can learn a bit about your organization's discourse community by listening to people and reading the documents that other people write. But the best way to learn is to write. The feedback you get from your supervisor will show you how to adapt your writing for the particular organization. To make the feedback most useful, categorize the comments and generalize. Are you being asked to provide specific supporting details? To write so that people can understand what you say without having to reread? To use a more or less formal style? To include lots of charts or none at all?

Learning to adapt your content, structure, and style to the organization will make you a more effective writer and a more effective worker. And that means that more often you'll be able to get what you want in the organization.

Playing to a Mixed Audience

MTV Arabia offers viewers popular Western shows like "Cribs" but also has a pop-up that reminds Muslim viewers when it's time for noon prayers. Thus it caters to its dual audiences—Westernized youths seeking more cutting-edge content and traditional Muslims looking for conservative and religious programming. Some even want both.

Executives estimate a potential audience of about 190 million people, 65% of whom are under 25. They plan to edit some of the international music videos to show less skin and "accommodate the local culture."

A different channel, Melody Arabia, features only Arabic songs and is seen as conservative and family-oriented, a classification which attracts more advertisers than racier, more Westernized channels. Advertised goods include head scarves and electronic devices to help Muslims keep track of timing for the five daily prayers.

Adapted from Mariam Fam, "'Cribs' and Calls to Prayer Share Airtime in Mideast," *Wall Street Journal*, November 23, 2007, B1, B2.

Sometimes it is hard to know what your audience wants. A classic example is "feature creep" in electronic goods. Unfortunately, consumers seem to want lots of features in their electronics when they buy them, but then become frustrated trying to use them and return the devices. In the United States, product returns cost $100 billion.[46] Research has shown that over half the wares are in complete working order; consumers just cannot operate them.[47]

Benefits work not only for customers and clients, but also for employees. According to estimates by the International Society for Performance Improvement, US companies spend more than $100 billion annually on employee incentives.[48]

Writing or Speaking to Multiple Audiences with Different Needs

Many business and administrative messages go not to a single person but to a larger audience. When the members of your audience share the same interests and the same level of knowledge, you can use the principles outlined above for individual readers or for members of homogeneous groups. But often different members of the audience have different needs.

Researcher Rachel Spilka has shown that talking to readers both inside and outside the organization helped corporate engineers adapt their documents successfully. Talking to readers and reviewers helped writers involve readers in the planning process, understand the social and political relationships among readers, and negotiate conflicts orally rather than depending solely on the document. These writers were then able to think about content as well as about organization and style, appeal to common grounds (such as reducing

THE McPLAYBOOK

Now That's Fast Food

To pump up business 24/7, McDonald's has sped up its new-product introductions. Here's its secret recipe:

Make it easy to eat

McDonald's does more than half its business at drive-through windows. That means it needs snacks and meals that can be held in one hand while the other is on the steering wheel.

Make it easy to prepare

McDonald's restaurant crews turn over entirely within a year, on average. To maintain consistency amid this churn, tasks must be simple to learn and repeat.

Make it quick

It's called fast food for a reason. McDonald's tests all new products for cooking times so customers don't have to wait even a second longer than absolutely necessary.

Make what the customers want

McDonald's prowls the market for new products and then spends months in carefully monitored field tests to ensure that people will buy its new concoctions.

McDonald's plans menu items to meet the needs and expectations of customers, employees, and franchise owners.

Source: Michael Arndt, "Special Report: McDonald's," Reprinted from the February 5, 2007 issue of *BusinessWeek* by special permission. Copyright © 2007 by The McGraw-Hill Companies, Inc.

waste or increasing productivity) that several readers shared, and reduce the number of revisions needed before documents were approved.[49]

When it is not possible to meet everyone's needs, meet the needs of gate-keepers and decision makers first.

Content and choice of details

- Provide an overview or executive summary for readers who want just the main points.
- In the body of the document, provide enough detail for decision makers and for anyone else who could veto your proposal.
- If the decision makers don't need details that other audiences will want, provide those details in appendices—statistical tabulations, earlier reports, and so forth.

Organization

- Use headings and a table of contents so readers can turn to the portions that interest them.
- Organize your message based on the decision makers' attitudes toward it.

Level of formality

- Avoid personal pronouns. *You* ceases to have a specific meaning when several different audiences use a document.
- If both internal and external audiences will use a document, use a slightly more formal style than you would in an internal document.
- Use a more formal style when you write to international audiences.

Technical level

- In the body of the document, assume the degree of knowledge that decision makers will have.
- Put background and explanatory information under separate headings. Then readers can use the headings and the table of contents to read or skip these sections, as their knowledge dictates.
- If decision makers will have more knowledge than other audiences, provide a glossary of terms. Early in the document, let readers know that the glossary exists.

Summary of Key Points

- The **primary audience** will make a decision or act on the basis of your message. The **secondary audience** may be asked by the primary audience to comment on your message or to implement your ideas after they've been approved. The **auxiliary audience** encounters the message but does not have to interact with it. A **gatekeeper** controls whether the message gets to the primary audience. A **watchdog audience** has political, social, or economic power and may base future actions on its evaluation of your message.
- A communication channel is the means by which you convey your message to your audience.
- The following questions provide a framework for audience analysis:
  1. What will the audience's initial reaction be to the message?
  2. How much information does the audience need?

Localizing Incentive Programs

Incentive programs are employee benefits aimed to reward good work performances. Globalization has complicated such programs, because what works in one country may not work in another.

In the United States, top performers might be rewarded with an expensive luxury item such as a watch. In China or India, a moped might be more appropriate.

Travel awards may also differ. US employees generally prefer unstructured, leisurely vacations, such as those offered by beach resorts. Europeans tend to prefer more adventurous trips, perhaps including a strenuous mountain hike or rafting trip. Many Chinese prefer highly structured tours with carefully planned itineraries.

Religion can also be a factor. Many US employees would appreciate a trip to Las Vegas, with a complimentary bottle of champagne in their room. But many religious people in the Middle East or Asia would not want the gambling or the alcohol.

What are some employee incentives you can name that would be appropriate in one country but not another? What are some ways large firms can work with these differences?

Adapted from Irwin Speizer, "Good Intentions, Lost in Translation," in *Workforce Management*, http://www.workforce.com/archive/feature/24/22/42/index.php(accessed January 18, 2009).

3. What obstacles must you overcome?

4. What positive aspects can you emphasize?

5. What expectations does the audience have about the appropriate language, contents, and organization of messages?

6. How will the audience use the document?

- **Audience benefits** are advantages that the audience gets by using your services, buying your products, following your policies, or adopting your ideas. Benefits can exist for policies and ideas as well as for goods and services.

- Good benefits are adapted to the audience, based on **intrinsic** rather than **extrinsic motivators,** supported by clear logic and explained in adequate detail, and phrased in you-attitude. Extrinsic benefits simply aren't available to reward every desired behavior; further, they reduce the satisfaction in doing something for its own sake.

- To create audience benefits,

  1. Identify the feelings, fears, and needs that may motivate your audience.

  2. Identify the features of your product or policy that could meet the needs you've identified.

  3. Show how the audience can meet their needs with the features of the policy or product.

- When you write to multiple audiences, use the primary audience to determine level of detail, organization, level of formality, and use of technical terms and theory.

CHAPTER 2   # Exercises and Problems

*Go to www.mhhe.com/locker9e for additional Exercises and Problems.

2.1   Reviewing the Chapter

1. Who are the five different audiences your message may need to address? (LO 1)

2. What are some characteristics to consider when analyzing individuals? (LO 1)

3. What are some characteristics to consider when analyzing groups? (LO 1)

4. What are some questions to consider when analyzing organizational culture? (LO 1)

5. What is a discourse community? Why will discourse communities be important in your career? (LO 1)

6. What are standard business communication channels? (LO 2)

7. What kinds of electronic channels seem most useful to you? Why? (LO 2)

8. What are considerations to keep in mind when selecting channels? (LO 2)

9. What are 12 questions to ask when analyzing your audience? (LO 3)

10. What are four characteristics of good audience benefits? (LO 4)

11. What are three ways to identify and develop audience benefits? (LO 4)

12. What are considerations to keep in mind when addressing multiple audiences? (LO 3)

2.2   Reviewing Grammar

Good audience analysis requires careful use of pronouns. Review your skills with pronoun usage by doing grammar exercise B.5, Appendix B.

2.3   Identifying Audiences

In each of the following situations, label the audiences as gatekeeper, primary, secondary, auxiliary, or watchdog:

1. Kent, Carol, and Jose are planning to start a Web site design business. However, before they can get started, they need money. They have developed a business plan and are getting ready to seek funds from financial institutions for starting their small business.

2. Barbara's boss asked her to write a direct mail letter to potential customers about the advantages of becoming a preferred member of their agency's travel club. The letter will go to all customers of the agency who are over 65 years old.

3. Paul works for the mayor's office in a big city. As part of a citywide cost-cutting measure, a blue-ribbon panel has recommended requiring employees who work more than 40 hours in a week to take compensatory time off rather than being paid overtime. The only exceptions will be the police and fire departments. The mayor asks Paul to prepare a proposal for the city council, which will vote on whether to implement the change. Before they vote, council members will hear from (1) citizens, who will have an opportunity to read the proposal and communicate their opinions to the city council; (2) mayors' offices in other cities, who may be asked about their experiences; (3) union representatives, who may be concerned about the reduction in income that will occur if the proposal is implemented; (4) department heads, whose ability to schedule work might be limited if the proposal passes; and (5) the blue-ribbon panel and good-government lobbying groups. Council members come up for reelection in six months.

4. Many customers have written complaint letters to Paws Food Inc. about their pets becoming ill after eating the company's pet foods. The CEO asked Rebecca, who is in charge of public relations, to draft a press release for newspapers notifying customers about the tainted food. The release should also encourage pet owners to avoid feeding their animals canned food until the issue is resolved.

2.4   Choosing a Channel to Reach a Specific Audience

Suppose your organization wants to target a product, service, or program for each of the following audiences. What would be the best channel(s) to reach that group in your city? To what extent would that channel reach all group members?

a. Stay-at-home mothers
b. Vegetarians
c. Full-time students at a university
d. Part-time students at a community college
e. Non-English speakers
f. People who use hearing aids
g. Parents whose children play softball or baseball
h. Attorneys
i. Female owners of small businesses
j. Pet owners

2.5   Identifying and Developing Audience Benefits

Listed here are several things an organization might like its employees to do:

1. Use less paper.
2. Attend a brown-bag lunch to discuss ways to improve products or services.
3. Become more physically fit.
4. Volunteer for community organizations.
5. Ease a new hire's transition into the unit.

As your instructor directs,

a. Identify the motives or needs that might be met by each of the activities.
b. Take each need or motive and develop it as an audience benefit in a full paragraph. Use additional paragraphs for the other needs met by the activity. Remember to use you-attitude!

2.6   Identifying Objections and Audience Benefits

Think of an organization you know something about, and answer the following questions for it:

a. Your organization is thinking about developing a knowledge management system that requires workers to input their knowledge and experience in their job functions into the organizational database. What benefits could the knowledge management system offer your organization? What drawbacks are there? Who would be the easiest to convince? Who would be the hardest?

b.   New telephone software would efficiently replace your organization's long-standing human phone operator who has been a perennial welcoming voice to incoming callers. What objections might people in your organization have to replacing the operator? What benefits might your organization receive? Who would be easiest to convince? Who would be the hardest?

c.   Your organization is thinking of outsourcing one of its primary products to a manufacturer in another country where the product can be made more cost-efficiently. What fears or objections might people have? What benefits might your organization receive? Who would be easiest to convince? Who would be hardest?

As your instructor directs,

a.   Share your answers orally with a small group of students.

b.   Present your answers in an oral presentation to the class.

c.   Write a paragraph developing the best audience benefit you identified. Remember to use you-attitude.

2.7   Addressing Your Audience's Need for Information

"Tell me about yourself."

This may be the most popular opening question of job interviews, but it's also a question that you'll encounter in nearly any social situation when you meet someone new. Although the question may be the same, the answer you give will change based upon the rhetorical situation: the audience, purpose, and context of the question.

For each of the following situations in a–g, ask yourself these questions to help create a good response:

• How will the audience react to your answer? Will the audience see the message as important? What information will you need to include in your answer to keep their attention?

• How will the audience use your answer? Why is the audience asking the question? What information is relevant to the audience and what information can you leave out?

• How much information does the audience need? What information do they already know about you? What level of detail do they need?

• What are the audience's expectations about your answer? What are the appropriate word choices and

tone for your answer? What topics should you avoid (at least for now)?

• What are the physical conditions that will affect your answer? Where are you (e.g., Are you outside, in a noisy room, chatting via IM, on the phone)? How much time do you have to give your response?

Write your response to the statement "Tell me about yourself." Assume that the question is being asked by

a.   A recruiter at a career fair in your university's auditorium.

b.   A recruiter in a job interview in a small interview or conference room.

c.   An attractive male or female at a popular weekend nightspot.

d.   Your instructor on the first day of class.

e.   Your new roommate on your first day in the dormitory.

f.   A new co-worker on your first day at a new job.

g.   A new co-worker on your first day volunteering at your local food pantry.

2.8   Analyzing Individuals

Read about the Myers-Briggs Type Indicator on page 31. On the Web, take one of the free tests similar to the Myers-Briggs. Read about your personality type and consider how accurate the description may be. Print your results.

As your instructor directs,

• Share your results orally with a small group of students and discuss how accurately the Type Indicator describes you. Identify some of the differences among your personality types and consider how the differences would affect efforts to collaborate on projects.

• Identify other students in the classroom with the same combination of personality traits. Create a brief oral presentation to the class that describes your Type Indicator and explains how the pros and cons of your personality will affect group dynamics in collaborative work.

• Write a brief memo to your instructor describing your results, assessing how well the results reflect your personality, and suggesting how your personality traits might affect your work in class and in the workplace.

2.9 Getting Customer Feedback

Smart businesses want to know what their customers and clients are saying about their products and services. Many Web sites can help them do so.

Check some of the common sites for customer comments. Here is a list to get you started:

http://www.amazon.com
http://getsatisfaction.com
http://www.my3cents.com
http://www.ratepoint.com
http://www.suggestionbox.com

http://www.thesqueakywheel.com
http://www.yelp.com

What does each site do?
What are good features of each site?
What are drawbacks?

As your instructor directs,

a. Discuss your findings in a memo to your instructor.
b. Share your findings in small groups.
c. As a group, make a presentation to your classmates.

2.10 Identifying International Audience Benefits

Reread the sidebar on page 42 explaining how Procter & Gamble is marketing its products in developing countries. In small groups, discuss different marketing practices you have become aware of in other countries. How do these practices benefit consumers? How do they benefit store owners?

As your instructor directs,

a. Post your findings electronically to share with the class.
b. Present your findings in a memo to your instructor.
c. Present your findings in an oral presentation to the class.

2.11 Evaluating a New Channel

To combat software piracy, Microsoft tried an unusual communication channel. A new software update turned screens black on computers using pirated software; the update also posted a message to switch to legitimate software copies. The update did not prevent people from using their machines, and they could manually change their wallpaper back to its previous design. But the black screen returned every 60 minutes. Microsoft said there was little protest except in China, where ironically the software piracy problem is greatest.

In small groups, discuss this practice.
- What do you think of this channel?
- Is it ethical?
- Will it help or hurt Microsoft profits in China?

- How do you think receivers of the black screen react?

As your instructor directs,

a. Post your findings electronically to share with the class.
b. Present your findings in a memo to your instructor.
c. Present your findings in an oral presentation to the class.

Source: Loretta Chao and Juliet Ye, "Microsoft Tactic Raises Hackles in China: In Antipiracy Move, Software Update Turns Screens Black and Urges Users to Buy Legal Windows Copies," *Wall Street Journal,* October 23, 2008, B4.

2.12 Announcing a New Employee Benefit

Your company has decided to pay employees for doing charity work. Employees can spend one hour working with a charitable or nonprofit group for every 40 hours they work. As Vice President of Human Resources, you need to announce this new program.

Pick a specific organization you know something about, and answer the following questions about it:

1. What proportion of the employees are already involved in volunteer work?
2. Is community service or "giving back" consistent with the organization's corporate mission?
3. Some employees won't be able or won't want to participate. What is the benefit for them in working for a company that has such a program?

4. Will promoting community participation help the organization attract and retain workers?

As your instructor directs,

a. Present your answers in an oral presentation to the class.
b. Present your answers in a memo to your instructor.
c. Share your answers with a small group of students and write a joint memo reporting the similarities and differences you found.

2.13 Announcing a Tuition Reimbursement Program

Assume that your organization is considering reimbursing workers for tuition and fees for job-related courses. As Director of Education and Training, you will present to company executives a review of pros and cons for the program. To prepare, you have composed a list of questions you know they may have. Pick a specific organization that you know something about, and answer the following questions about it.

1. What do people do on the job? What courses or degrees could help them do their current jobs even better?

2. How much education do people already have? How do they feel about formal schooling?

3. How busy are employees? Will most have time to take classes and study in addition to working 40 hours a week (or more)?

4. Is it realistic to think that people who get more education would get higher salaries? Or is money for increases limited? Is it reasonable to think that most people could be promoted? Or does the organization have many more low-level than high-level jobs?

5. What hassles do people encounter in their daily work? What could be done to alleviate one or more of those hassles? If the work environment were less stressful, how would their lives be easier or more pleasant?

6. How much loyalty do employees have to this particular organization? Is it "just a job," or do they care about the welfare of the organization?

7. How competitive is the job market? How easy is it for the organization to find and retain qualified employees?

8. Is knowledge needed to do the job changing, or is knowledge learned 5 or 10 years ago still up-to-date?

9. How competitive is the economic market? Is this company doing well financially? Can its customers or clients easily go somewhere else? Is it a government agency dependent on tax dollars for funding? What about the current situation makes this an especially good time to hone the skills of the employees you have?

10. Do you support the program? Why or why not?

2.14 Crafting a Memo for a Particular Audience

Your supervisor at a fitness center wants to increase the organization's membership and has asked you to write a letter to the three primary population segments in your town: retirees, college students, and working professionals with families. Using the following fitness benefits your supervisor gave you to help you get started, write a version of a letter targeted at each of the three audiences.

- Become a member with no sign-up fees.
- Attend free nutrition classes to help with weight control and optimal fitness.

- Attend any of our many fitness classes, scheduled for your convenience.
- Enjoy the new indoor/outdoor pool with lap lanes and zero-gravity entrance.
- Use the large selection of free-weights and exercise machines.
- Lose weight and feel your healthiest with a personal trainer, who will guide you toward your fitness goals.

Remember these benefits were just to get you started; you are expected to come up with more on your own.

2.15 Evaluating Audience Benefits

The Federal Centers for Disease Control and Prevention report that 32% of all US adults are obese. Some organizations are starting to address this public concern. For example, Pepsi, which spends more than $1 billion on marketing annually and is one of the biggest manufactures of high-calorie, sugary colas and foods, is now producing alternative snacks.

However, critics question Pepsi's new marketing efforts as a ploy to increase their bottom line. The critics' main objection is that the snacks, although low in fat and sugar, are still "junk food." For example, Baked Cheetos are touted as a healthy alternative for chips, even though a two-ounce serving has 260 calories, only 20 less than a Snickers candy bar.

While it is easy for critics to condemn Pepsi, the organization has demonstrated a desire to benefit consumers by giving $1.7 million for an obesity-prevention program.

In addition, Pepsi was the first major manufacturer to remove trans-fat from its snacks and reduced sugar in 250 products.

What do you think? How ethically is Pepsi acting when they choose to capitalize on consumers' concerns by offering "healthier" snack options? What are their motivations for donating money to an obesity-prevention program? What other products advertise debatable benefits for their consumers?

Work in small groups to discuss the above questions, then present your answers to the class in a short, informal presentation.

Source: Chad Terhune, "Pepsi Sales Force Tries to Push 'Healthier' Snacks in Inner City," *Wall Street Journal*, October 5, 2006, A1. Copyright © 2007 by Dow Jones & Company, Inc. Reproduced with permission of Dow Jones & Company, Inc. via Copyright Clearance Center.

2.16 Analyzing Your Co-Workers

What do your co-workers do? What hassles and challenges do they face? To what extent do their lives outside work affect their responses to work situations? What do your co-workers value? What are their pet peeves? How committed are they to organizational goals? How satisfying do they find their jobs? Are the people you work with quite similar to each other, or do they differ from each other? How?

As your instructor directs,

a. Share your answers orally with a small group of students.

b. Present your answers in an oral presentation to the class.

c. Present your answers in a memo to your instructor.

d. Share your answers with a small group of students and write a joint memo reporting the similarities and differences you found.

2.17 Analyzing the Audiences of Non-Commercial Web Pages

Analyze the implied audiences of two Web pages of two non-commercial organizations with the same purpose (combating hunger, improving health, influencing the political process, etc.). You could pick the home pages of the national organization and a local affiliate, or the home pages of two separate organizations working toward the same general goal.

Answer the following questions:

- Do the pages work equally well for surfers and for people who have reached the page deliberately?
- Possible audiences include current and potential volunteers, donors, clients, and employees. Do the pages provide material for each audience? Is the material useful? Complete? Up-to-date? Does new material encourage people to return?
- What assumptions about audiences do content and visuals suggest?
- Can you think of ways that the pages could better serve their audiences?

As your instructor directs,

a. Share your results orally with a small group of students.

b. Present your results orally to the class.

c. Present your results in a memo to your instructor. Attach copies of the home pages.

d. Share your results with a small group of students, and write a joint memo reporting the similarities and differences you found.

e. Post your results in an e-mail message to the class. Provide links to the two Web pages.

2.18 Analyzing a Discourse Community

Analyze the way a group you are part of uses language. Possible groups include

- Work teams.
- Sports teams.
- Sororities, fraternities, and other social groups.
- Churches, mosques, synagogues, and temples.
- Geographic or ethnic groups.
- Groups of friends.

Questions to ask include the following:

- What specialized terms might not be known to outsiders?
- What topics do members talk or write about? What topics are considered unimportant or improper?
- What channels do members use to convey messages?
- What forms of language do members use to build goodwill? to demonstrate competence or superiority?
- What strategies or kinds of proof are convincing to members?
- What formats, conventions, or rules do members expect messages to follow?
- What are some nonverbal ways members communicate?

As your instructor directs,

a. Share your results orally with a small group of students.

b. Present your results in an oral presentation to the class.

c. Present your results in a memo to your instructor.

d. Share your results with a small group of students, and write a joint memo reporting the similarities and differences you found.

2.19   All-Weather Case: Implementing a Web-Based Performance Appraisal System (Review case introduction on page 18.)

Doug is on the phone with the vice president of marketing, pitching to him the benefits of the new Web-based performance appraisal system that HR wants to implement throughout the company. "It will simplify things for you. More importantly, it will boost your department's performance," Doug says.

The marketing VP leads a department of four managers (residential sales, trade sales, business intelligence, and customer service and installation) and seven executives. The marketing department also controls and directs sales representatives and dealers across the country and internationally.

"What exactly will it do, Doug, that we are unable to do now?" the VP asks.

"Well, let's see," Doug says, browsing the open software on his computer. "The system has a feature called manager's journal, which allows managers to take notes on their subordinates' performance. The system reminds managers and executives of upcoming deadlines to submit appraisals. It provides links to employees' past appraisals, performance goals, and compensation history. It's linked to HR's Web site on the Intranet. Finally, we can customize the system for your department."

"I don't know, Doug," the VP says. "My guys are busy every day increasing revenues and beating the competition. I'd rather they had a simple form to fill out."

"I'm for simplicity, too, but the present system isn't working," Doug says. "Miguel and his team spend a lot of time just organizing the forms. Sometimes, the forms are not there when we need them, and we must get departments and individuals to send them ASAP. Even when forms are there, issues related to promotion and compensation require a lot of going back and forth between dozens of scattered documents, resulting in slower work and more errors."

"I see your point, Doug," the VP says. "Why don't you send Miguel and his team to give us a small presentation on the new system? I'm already on board, but your presentation will help me get others to accept the system as quickly as possible."

"Sure. We will be glad to come and talk," Doug says.

After Doug ends his call, Miguel enters Doug's office. "How soon can we go and talk to them?" Doug asks Miguel, who was brought up-to-date before the phone call.

"I'll find out when they would like us to come," Miguel says.

As Miguel prepares to call the marketing department, Linda is already scouring the administrator's manual accompanying the Web-based performance appraisal system for potential benefits to use.

Based on the information given above and your reading of Chapter 2, perform an audience analysis for Miguel and Linda.

- Begin by determining who their primary and secondary audiences are.

- Next, answer the six "audience-analysis" questions given in the chapter.

- Finally, identify three benefits that meet the criteria of good audience benefits as the chapter explains them.

- To sharpen your analysis, you may want to do a quick Internet research on Web-based performance appraisal systems.

Present your findings in a memo to Miguel and Linda.

Building Goodwill

Chapter Outline

You-Attitude
- How to Create You-Attitude
- You-Attitude beyond the Sentence Level

Positive Emphasis
- How to Create Positive Emphasis
- How to Check Positive Emphasis

Tone, Power, and Politeness

Reducing Bias in Business Communication
- Making Language Nonsexist
- Making Language Nonracist and Nonagist
- Talking about People with Disabilities and Diseases
- Choosing Bias-Free Photos and Illustrations

Summary of Key Points

Truly Friendly Skies

United pilot Denny Flanagan goes out of his way to create goodwill with his passengers and customers. He takes pictures of pets in cargo compartments and shows their owners that the pets are safely onboard. He phones the parents of unaccompanied minors to keep them up-to-date on delays. He hands out his business cards to all passengers, and the lucky ones with his signature on the back get free books, wine, or discount coupons. When his flights are delayed or diverted, he tries to find snacks like McDonald's hamburgers for his passengers. Before some of his delayed flights he is in the passenger lounge using his cellphone to help passengers with their connections.

> *"I just treat everyone like it's the first flight they've ever flown. . . . The customer deserves a good travel experience."*

United recognizes Captain Flanagan as a great ambassador for them. The company supports his efforts by paying for his cards, books, wine, coupons, and delay snacks.

Captain Flanagan says, "I just treat everyone like it's the first flight they've ever flown. . . . The customer deserves a good travel experience."

One of those customers noted, "If other folks in the airline industry had the same attitude, it would go a long way to mitigating some of the negative stuff that has come about in the last four or five years."

What do you think? Would goodwill efforts such as Captain Flanagan's make flying more pleasant for you? Would they overcome the negative effects of a delay? If so, how long a delay?

Learning Objectives

After studying this chapter, you will know how to:

1 Create you-attitude.

2 Create positive emphasis.

3 Improve tone in business communications.

4 Reduce bias in business communications.

Goodwill smooths the challenges of business and administration. Companies have long been aware that treating customers well pays off in more sales and higher profits. Linda Thaler and Robin Koval built The Kaplan Thaler Group into an advertising agency with nearly $1 billion in billings using goodwill, you-attitude, and positive tone.[1] General Motors found that customers who get good service from their dealers are five times more likely to buy another GM car than those who had poor service.[2] Government organizations now realize that they need citizen support—goodwill—to receive funding.

Goodwill is important internally as well as externally. More and more organizations are realizing that treating employees well is financially wise as well as ethically sound. Happy employees create less staff turnover, thus reducing hiring and training costs. A University of Pennsylvania study of 3,000 companies found that investing 10% of revenue on capital improvement boosted company productivity 3.9%, but spending the money on employees increased productivity 8.5%, or more than twice as much.[3]

Some companies put significant money into employee relations. North Shore-LIJ Health System spent about $10 million on training and tuition in 2007 for workers at all levels. That effort helped them achieve an annual retention rate of 96%, in an industry where the average is 88%, and led to better patient care.[4]

You-attitude, positive emphasis, and bias-free language are three ways to help build goodwill. Messages that show you-attitude use the audience's point of view, not the writer's or speaker's. Positive emphasis means focusing on the positive rather than the negative aspects of a situation. Bias-free language does not discriminate against people on the basis of sex, physical condition, race, ethnicity, age, or any other category. All three help you achieve your purposes and make your messages friendlier, more persuasive, more professional, and more humane. They suggest that you care not just about money but also about the needs and interests of your customers, employees, and fellow citizens.

You-Attitude

Putting what you want to say in you-attitude is a crucial step both in thinking about your audience's needs and in communicating your concern to your audience.

How to Create You-Attitude

You-attitude is a style of communication that looks at things from the audience's point of view, emphasizing what the audience wants to know, respecting the audience's intelligence, and protecting the audience's ego.

To apply you-attitude on a sentence level, use the following techniques:

1. **Talk about the audience, not about yourself.**
2. **Refer to the audience's request or order specifically.**
3. **Don't talk about feelings, except to congratulate or offer sympathy.**
4. **In positive situations, use *you* more often than *I*. Use *we* when it includes the audience.**
5. **In negative situations, avoid the word *you*. Protect the audience's ego. Use passive verbs and impersonal expressions to avoid assigning blame.**

Revisions for you-attitude do not change the basic meaning of the sentence. However, revising for you-attitude often makes sentences longer because the revision is more specific and has more information. Long sentences need not be wordy. **Wordiness** means having more words than the meaning requires. We can add information and still keep the writing concise.

1. Talk about the audience, not about yourself.

Your audience wants to know how they benefit or are affected. When you provide this information, you make your message more complete and more interesting.

Lacks you-attitude:	We have negotiated an agreement with Apex Rent-a-Car that gives you a discount on rental cars.
You-attitude:	As a Sunstrand employee, you can now get a 20% discount when you rent a car from Apex.

2. Refer to the customer's request or order specifically.

Refer to the customer's request, order, or policy specifically, not as a generic *your order* or *your policy*. If your customer is an individual or a small business, it's friendly to specify the content of the order. If you're dealing with a company with which you do a great deal of business, give the invoice or purchase order number.

Lacks you-attitude:	Your order . . .
You-attitude (to individual):	The desk chair you ordered . . .
You-attitude (to a large store):	Your invoice #783329 . . .

3. Don't talk about feelings, except to congratulate or offer sympathy.

In most business situations, your feelings are irrelevant and should be omitted.

Lacks you-attitude:	We are happy to extend you a credit line of $10,000.
You-attitude:	You can now charge up to $10,000 on your American Express card.

It *is* appropriate to talk about your own emotions in a message of congratulations or condolence.

You-attitude:	Congratulations on your promotion to district manager! I was really pleased to read about it.

Don't talk about your audience's feelings, either. It's distancing to have others tell us how we feel—especially if they are wrong.

You-Attitude at T-Mobile Applies to Employees Too

Sue Nokes, head of sales and customer service at T-Mobile USA, believes in making her customers happy. She also believes that doing so is easier to do when her 15,000 employees are happy. When Nokes arrived at T-Mobile, absenteeism at call centers averaged 12% daily; turnover was 100 + % annually. Nokes immediately began visiting centers, asking what customers were complaining about and what employees needed improved in their workplace. She then raised salaries, increased training, developed clear performance metrics, and developed rewards—including trips to Hawaii and Las Vegas. Under her leadership, absenteeism has dropped to an annual rate of 3% and attrition to 42%.

Adapted from Jennifer Reingold, "You Got Served," *Fortune*, October 1, 2007, 55–58.

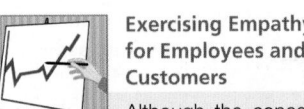

Lacks you-attitude: You'll be happy to hear that Open Grip Walkway Channels meet OSHA requirements.

You-attitude: Open Grip Walkway Channels meet OSHA requirements.

Maybe the audience expects that anything you sell would meet government regulations (OSHA—the Occupational Safety and Health Administration—is a federal agency). The audience may even be disappointed if they expected higher standards. Simply explain the situation or describe a product's features; don't predict the audience's response.

When you have good news, simply give the good news.

Lacks you-attitude: You'll be happy to hear that your scholarship has been renewed.

You-attitude: Congratulations! Your scholarship has been renewed.

4. In positive situations, use *you* more often than *I*. Use *we* when it includes the audience.

Talk about the audience, not you or your company.

Lacks you-attitude: We provide health insurance to all employees.

You-attitude: You receive health insurance as a full-time Procter & Gamble employee.

Most readers are tolerant of the word *I* in e-mail messages, which seem like conversation. But edit paper documents to use *I* rarely if at all. *I* suggests that you're concerned about personal issues, not about the organization's problems, needs, and opportunities. *We* works well when it includes the reader. Avoid *we* if it excludes the reader (as it would in a letter to a customer or supplier or as it might in a memo about what *we* in management want *you* to do).

5. In negative situations, avoid the word *you*. Protect your audience's ego. Use passive verbs and impersonal expressions to avoid assigning blame.

When you report bad news or limitations, use a noun for a group of which your audience is a part instead of *you* so people don't feel that they're singled out for bad news.

Lacks you-attitude: You must get approval from the director before you publish any articles or memoirs based on your work in the agency.

You-attitude: Agency personnel must get approval from the director to publish any articles or memoirs based on their work at the agency.

Use passive verbs and impersonal expressions to avoid blaming people. **Passive verbs** describe the action performed on something, without necessarily saying who did it. (See Chapter 7 for a full discussion of passive verbs.) **Impersonal expressions** omit people and talk only about things. In most cases, active verbs are better. But when your audience is at fault, passive verbs may be useful to avoid assigning blame.

Normally, communication is most lively when it's about people—and most interesting to audiences when it's about them. When you have to report a mistake or bad news, however, you can protect your audience's ego by using an impersonal expression, one in which things, not people, do the acting.

Lacks you-attitude: You made no allowance for inflation in your estimate.

You-attitude (passive):   No allowance for inflation has been made in this estimate.

You-attitude (impersonal):   This estimate makes no allowance for inflation.

Cancer is not who you are—
it's what's happening to you.
So we'll still call each other
and swap stories and
We'll still argue when
and laugh when i'

Hallmark is producing a new line of cards for common situations such as depression or chemotherapy. For example, "Get Well Soon," is not appropriate for someone who is battling cancer. Hallmark has changed the tone of their Journey's Collection to reflect the needs of their dual audiences—buyers and receivers of cards.

Source: David Twiddy, "Hallmark Tackles Real-Life Situations," *Chicago Tribune*, February 19, 2007, sec. Business.

A purist might say that impersonal expressions are illogical: An estimate, for example, is inanimate and can't "make" anything. In the pragmatic world of business writing, however, impersonal expressions help you convey criticism tactfully.

You-Attitude beyond the Sentence Level

Good messages apply you-attitude beyond the sentence level by using content and organization as well as style to build goodwill.

To create goodwill with content,

- Be complete. When you have lots of information to give, consider putting some details in an appendix, which may be read later.
- Anticipate and answer questions your audience is likely to have.
- Show why information your audience didn't ask for is important.
- Show your audience how the subject of your message affects them.

To organize information to build goodwill,

- Put information your audience is most interested in first.
- Arrange information to meet your audience's needs, not yours.
- Use headings and lists so readers can find key points quickly.

Figure 3.1   A Letter Lacking You-Attitude

SIMMONS
STRUCTURAL STEEL

450 INDUSTRIAL PARK
CLEVELAND, OH 44120
(216) 555-4670
FAX: (216) 555-4672

December 11, 2010

Ms. Carol McFarland
Rollins Equipment Corporation
18438 East Night Hawk Way
Phoenix, AZ 85043-7800

Dear Ms. McFarland:

Legalistic

Not you-attitude

We are now ready to issue a check to Rollins Equipment in the amount of
$14,207.02. To receive said check, you will deliver to me a release of the
mechanic's liens in the amount of $14,207.02.   *Sounds dictatorial*

Lacks you-attitude

Focuses on negative

Before we can release the check, we must be satisfied that the release is in the
proper form. We must insist that we be provided with a stamped original of the
lien indicating the document number in the appropriate district court where it
is filed. Also, either the release must be executed by an officer of Rollins
Equipment, or we must be provided with a letter from an officer of Rollins
Equipment authorizing another individual to execute the release.

Hard to read, remember

Please contact the undersigned so that an appointment can be scheduled for
this transaction.   *Jargon*

Sincerely,

Kelly J. Pickett

Kelly J. Pickett

Consider the letter in Figure 3.1. As the red marginal notes indicate, many individual sentences in this letter lack you-attitude. Fixing individual sentences could improve the letter. However, it really needs to be totally rewritten.

Figure 3.2 shows a possible revision of this letter. The revision is clearer, easier to read, and friendlier.

Positive Emphasis

Some negatives are necessary. When you have bad news to give—announcements of layoffs, product defects and recalls, price increases—straightforward negatives build credibility. (See Chapter 15 on how to present bad news.)

Figure 3.2 A Letter Revised to Improve You-Attitude

SIMMONS STRUCTURAL STEEL

450 INDUSTRIAL PARK
CLEVELAND, OH 44120
(216) 555-4670
FAX: (216) 555-4672

December 11, 2010

Ms. Carol McFarland
Rollins Equipment Corporation
18438 East Night Hawk Way
Phoenix, AZ 85043-7800

Dear Ms. McFarland:

Starts with main point from the reader's point of view

Focuses on what reader gets

Let's clear up the lien in the Allen contract.

Rollins will receive a check for $14,207.02 when you give us a release for the mechanic's lien of $14,207.02. To assure us that the release is in the proper form,

List makes it easy to see that reader needs to do two things—and that the second can be done in two ways.

1. Give us a stamped original of the lien indicating the document's district court number, and

2. Either
   a. Have an officer of Rollins Equipment sign the release
      or
   b. Give us a letter from a Rollins officer authorizing someone else to sign the release.

Please call me to tell me which way is best for you. *Emphasizes reader's choice*

Sincerely,

Kelly J. Pickett

Kelly J. Pickett
Extension 5318

Extension number makes it easy for reader to phone.

Sometimes negatives are needed to make people take a problem seriously. In some messages, such as disciplinary notices and negative performance appraisals, one of your purposes is to make the problem clear. Even here, avoid insults or attacks on your audience's integrity or sanity.

Sometimes negatives create a "reverse psychology" that makes people look favorably at your product. German power tool manufacturer Stihl advertises that its chain saws and other tools are *not* sold by chains like Lowe's or Home Depot. Instead, the company emphasizes that its products are sold through independent retailers. While the campaign risks offending potential customers

Defining Allowable Negatives

The Des Moines *Register* issued the following standards for contributors to its electronic forum:

[The Des Moines *Register*'s] updated standards make the distinction between offensive opinion and offensive approach.

. . . We reserve the right to remove comments including these types of specific information or language:

- Libel. In general terms, that means a comment that includes a false statement of fact that actually harms a person's reputation (as opposed to insulting or offending them).

- Sexually explicit or crude sexual comments about someone.

- Threatening statements or statements that suggest violent acts against someone.

- Crude comments about a child.

- Swearing or obscenity.

- Derogatory phrases to define a group of people.

- Nasty name-calling (language such as "moron" and "white trash").

But we will allow opinions some will find offensive.

We will allow conversation that is simply strident in tone.

We will allow criticism of public officials.

We will allow criticism of people who are subjects of stories.

We will allow opinions that some may find offensive about tough social issues around race and sexual orientation, as long as they don't include the kind of specific language described above.

Quoted from Carolyn Washburn, "Inviting Robust Conversation, but Spelling Out a Few Rules," *Des Moines Sunday Register*, April 15, 2007.

by implying that shopping at big box stores means that they don't appreciate quality, Stihl insists that its high-end products are worth the prices that are charged by specialty stores.[5]

But in most situations, it's better to be positive. Researchers Annette N. Shelby and N. Lamar Reinsch, Jr., found that business people responded more positively to positive than to negative language and were more likely to say they would act on a positively worded request.[6] Martin Seligman's research for Met Life found that optimistic salespeople sold 37% more insurance than pessimistic colleagues. As a result, Met Life began hiring optimists even when they failed to meet the company's other criteria. These "unqualified" optimists outsold pessimists 21% in their first year and 57% in the next.[7]

Positive emphasis is a way of looking at things. Is the bottle half empty or half full? You can create positive emphasis with the words, information, organization, and layout you choose. "Part-time" may be a negative phrase for someone seeking full-time employment, but it may also be a positive phrase for college students seeking limited work hours while they pursue their education. It may become even more positive if connected with flexible hours.

How to Create Positive Emphasis

Create positive emphasis by using the following techniques:

1. Avoid negative words and words with negative connotations.
2. Beware of hidden negatives.
3. Focus on what the audience can do rather than on limitations.
4. Justify negative information by giving a reason or linking it to an audience benefit.
5. Put the negative information in the middle and present it compactly.

Choose the technique that produces the clearest, most accurate sentence.

1. Avoid negative words and words with negative connotations.

Figure 3.3 lists some common negative words. If you find one of these words in a draft, try to substitute a more positive word. When you must use a negative, use the *least negative* term that will convey your meaning.

The following examples show how to replace negative words with positive words.

Negative: We have failed to finish taking inventory.

Better: We haven't finished taking inventory.

Still better: We will be finished taking inventory Friday.

Negative: If you can't understand this explanation, feel free to call me.

Better: If you have further questions, just call me.

Still better: Omit the sentence.

Omit double negatives.

Negative: Never fail to back up your documents.

Better: Always back up your documents.

When you must use a negative term, use the least negative word that is accurate.

Negative: Your balance of $835 is delinquent.

Better: Your balance of $835 is past due.

Figure 3.3 Negative Words to Avoid

afraid	error	lacking	trivial
anxious	except	loss	trouble
avoid	fail		wait
bad	fault	**Some mis- words:**	weakness
careless	fear	misfortune	worry
damage	hesitate	missing	wrong
delay	ignorant	mistake	
delinquent	ignore	neglect	**Many un- words:**
deny	impossible	never	unclear
difficulty		no	unfair
	Many in- words:	not	unfortunate
Some dis- words:	inadequate	objection	unfortunately
disapprove	incomplete	problem	unpleasant
dishonest	inconvenient	reject	unreasonable
dissatisfied	insincere	sorry	unreliable
eliminate	injury	terrible	unsure

Getting rid of negatives has the added benefit of making what you write easier to understand. Sentences with three or more negatives are very hard to understand.[8]

2. Beware of **hidden negatives**.

Some words are not negative in themselves but become negative in context. *But* and *however* indicate a shift, so, after a positive statement, they are negative. *I hope* and *I trust that* suggest that you aren't sure. *Patience* may sound like a virtue, but it is a necessary virtue only when things are slow. Even positives about a service or product may backfire if they suggest that in the past the service or product was bad.

Negative: I hope this is the information you wanted. [Implication: I'm not sure.]

Better: Enclosed is a brochure about road repairs scheduled for 2010.

Still better: The brochure contains a list of all roads and bridges scheduled for repair during 2010, specific dates when work will start, and alternate routes.

Negative: Please be patient as we switch to the automated system. [Implication: You can expect problems.]

Better: If you have questions during our transition to the automated system, call Melissa Morgan.

Still better: You'll be able to get information instantly about any house on the market when the automated system is in place. If you have questions during the transition, call Melissa Morgan.

Negative: Now Crispy Crunch tastes better. [Implication: it used to taste terrible.]

Better: Now Crispy Crunch tastes even better.

Removing negatives does not mean being arrogant or pushy.

Negative: I hope that you are satisfied enough to place future orders.

Arrogant: I look forward to receiving all of your future business.

Better: Whenever you need computer chips, a call to Mercury is all it takes for fast service.

When you eliminate negative words, be sure to maintain accuracy. Words that are exact opposites will usually not be accurate. Instead, use specifics to be both positive and accurate.

Negative: The exercycle is not guaranteed for life.

Not true: The exercycle is guaranteed for life.

True: The exercycle is guaranteed for 10 years.

Legal phrases also have negative connotations for most readers and should be avoided whenever possible.

3. Focus on what the audience can do rather than on limitations.

When there are limits, or some options are closed, focus on the alternatives that remain.

Negative: We will not allow you to charge more than $2,000 on your VISA account.

Better: You can charge $2,000 on your new VISA card.

or: Your new VISA card gives you $2,000 in credit that you can use at thousands of stores nationwide.

As you focus on what will happen, check for **you-attitude.** In the last example, "We will allow you to charge $2,000" would be positive, but it lacks you-attitude.

When you have a benefit and a requirement the audience must meet to get the benefit, the sentence is usually more positive if you put the benefit first.

Negative: You will not qualify for the student membership rate of $55 a year unless you are a full-time student.

Better: You get all the benefits of membership for only $55 a year if you're a full-time student.

4. Justify negative information by giving a reason or linking it to an audience benefit.

A reason can help your audience see that the information is necessary; a benefit can suggest that the negative aspect is outweighed by positive factors. Be careful, however, to make the logic behind your reason clear and to leave no loopholes.

Negative: We cannot sell individual marker sets.

Loophole: To keep down packaging costs and to help you save on shipping and handling costs, we sell marker sets in packages of 12.

Suppose the customer says, "I'll pay the extra shipping and handling. Send me six." If you truly sell only in packages of 12, you need to say so:

Better: To keep down packaging costs and to help customers save on shipping and handling costs, we sell marker sets only in packages of 12.

If you link the negative element to a benefit, be sure it is a benefit your audience will acknowledge. Avoid telling people that you're doing things "for their own good." They may have a different notion of what their own good is. You may think you're doing customers a favor by limiting their credit so they don't get in over their heads and go bankrupt. They may think they'd be better off with more credit so they could expand in hopes of making more sales and more profits.

Some stores might say, "Put books you don't want here." But bookseller Joseph Best in Lexington, KY, uses positive emphasis.

Four Ways to Say "Yes" Instead of "No"

"Yes, I want to help."
Even if you have to say no personally, there is usually an alternative yes. By helping to solve someone's problem—say, by referring them to someone who might be able to help them—you keep the positive energy in motion.

"Yes, you can do better."
Rather than say, "This is terrible," it's a lot more motivating to say, "You do such terrific work. I'm not sure this is up to your caliber."

"Yes, I see you."
It only takes a minute to send a thank-you note or respond to an unsolicited résumé.

"Yes, your talents lie elsewhere."
Warren Buffet says that he's never fired anyone. He has just helped them to find the right job.

Quoted from Linda Kaplan Thaler and Robin Koval, *The Power of Nice: How to Conquer the Business World with Kindness* (New York: Currency, 2006), 84–87.

5. Put the negative information in the middle and present it compactly.

Put negatives at the beginning or end only if you want to emphasize the negative. To deemphasize a written negative, put it in the middle of a paragraph rather than in the first or last sentence and in the middle of the message rather than in the first or last paragraphs.

When a letter or memo runs several pages, remember that the bottom of the first page is also a position of emphasis, even if it is in the middle of a paragraph, because of the extra white space of the bottom margin. (The first page gets more attention because it is on top and the reader's eye may catch lines of the message even when he or she isn't consciously reading it; the tops and bottoms of subsequent pages don't get this extra attention.) If possible, avoid placing negative information at the bottom of the first page.

Giving a topic lots of space emphasizes it. Therefore, you can de-emphasize negative information by giving it as little space as possible. Give negative information only once in your message. Don't list negatives with bulleted or numbered lists. These lists take space and emphasize material.

How to Check Positive Emphasis

All five of the strategies listed above help create positive emphasis. However, you should always check to see that the positive emphasis is appropriate, sincere, and realistic.

Goodwill or Greedwill

A recent study by a law professor shows that credit card companies make offers to people fresh out of bankruptcy. In the study of 341 families, almost 100% received credit card offers within a year after completing bankruptcy proceedings, and 87% of those offers mentioned the bankruptcy proceedings. In fact, 20% of the offers came from companies the family had owed before the bankruptcy.

In small groups, discuss whether you think this practice is ethical. Why or why not? What reasons exist for not offering new credit to people who have just gone through bankruptcy? Why might such people need new credit cards?

As you read at the beginning of this section, positive emphasis is not always appropriate. Some bad news is so serious that presenting it with positive tone is insensitive, if not unethical. Layoffs, salary cuts, and product defects are all topics in this category.

Some positive emphasis is so overdone that it seems insincere. The used-car sales rep selling a rusting auto is one stereotype of insincerity. A more common example for most business people is the employee who gushes praise through gritted teeth over your promotion. Most of us have experienced something similar, and we know how easy it is to see through the insincerity.

Positive emphasis can also be so overdone that it clouds the reality of the situation. If your company has two finalists for a sales award, and only one award, the loser does not have second place, which implies a second award. On the other hand, if all sales reps win the same award, top performers will feel unappreciated. Too much praise can also make mediocre employees think they are doing great.

Restraint can help make positive emphasis more effective. Conductor Otto Klemperer was known for not praising his orchestra. One day, pleased with a particularly good rehearsal, he spoke a brusque "good." His stunned musicians broke into spontaneous applause. Klemperer rapped his baton on his music stand to silence them and said, "Not *that* good."[9]

Tone, Power, and Politeness

Tone is the implied attitude of the communicator toward the audience. If the words of a document seem condescending or rude, tone is a problem. Norms for politeness are cultural and generational; they also vary from office to office.

Tone is tricky because it interacts with context and power. Language that is acceptable within one group may be unacceptable if used by someone outside the group. Words that might seem friendly from a superior to a subordinate may seem uppity if used by the subordinate to the superior. Similarly, words that may be neutral among peers may be seen as negative if sent by a superior to subordinate.

Paul Goward, the former police chief of Winter Haven, Florida, discovered this lesson about the connection between power and tone. Goward sent an e-mail to about 80 employees asking "Are You a Jelly Belly?" In the e-mail, he provided 10 reasons why his employees should be in better shape; the reasons ranged from health risks to department image. The e-mail added, "If you are unfit, do yourself and everyone else a favor. . . . See a professional about a proper diet. . . . Stop making excuses. . . . We didn't hire you unfit and we don't want you working unfit." The e-mail so offended employees that Goward was forced to resign.[10]

Using the proper tone with employees can have huge economic impact for a business. A Litigation Trends Survey, based on reports from 310 in-house counsel, found employee lawsuits to be the top litigation concern of corporate lawyers. Disgruntled employees are suing more than ever before, and disputes over wages or hours frequently can be brought as class actions, making them even more expensive.[11]

The desirable tone for business writing is businesslike but not stiff, friendly but not phony, confident but not arrogant, polite but not groveling. The following guidelines will help you achieve the tone you want.

- **Use courtesy titles for people outside your organization whom you don't know well.** Most US organizations use first names for everyone, whatever their age or rank. But many people don't like being called by their first names by people they don't know or by someone much younger. When you talk or write to people outside your organization, use first names only if you've established a personal relationship. If you don't know someone well, use a courtesy title:

Dear Mr. Reynolds:

Dear Ms. Lee:

- **Be aware of the power implications of the words you use.** "Thank you for your cooperation" is generous coming from a superior to a subordinate; it's not appropriate in a message to your superior.

As researchers Margaret Graham and Carol David have found, different ways of asking for action carry different levels of politeness.[12]

Order: (lowest politeness)	Turn in your time card by Monday.
Polite order: (midlevel politeness)	Please turn in your time card by Monday.
Indirect request: (higher politeness)	Time cards should be turned in by Monday.
Question: (highest politeness)	Would you be able to turn in your time card by Monday?

Higher levels of politeness may be unclear. In some cases, a question may seem like a request for information to which it's acceptable to answer, "No, I can't." In other cases, it will be an order, simply phrased in polite terms.

You need more politeness if you're asking for something that will inconvenience the audience and help you more than the person who does the action. Generally, you need less politeness when you're asking for something small, routine, or to the audience's benefit. Some discourse communities, however, prefer that even small requests be made politely.

Lower politeness:	To start the scheduling process, please describe your availability for meetings during the second week of the month.
Higher politeness:	Could you let me know what times you'd be free for a meeting the second week of the month?

Solving an Ethical Dilemma Using Goodwill

Most ethical dilemmas boil down to people, balancing the needs or desires of one constituency against those of another: Management versus staff, stockholders versus customers.

Toro, maker of lawnmowers, faced such a dilemma. One of its popular riding mowers is very hard to overturn, but when it does, it can seriously injure the driver. Toro decided to install roll bars behind the driver's seat on new machines but not raise the price because the bars were added for safety.

Then an even harder issue arose. Shouldn't the same ethical treatment be offered on machines already owned? Those owners would be protected but the cost would adversely affect shareholders.

What would you do? Toro installed the bars for all mowers, new and used, a decision they believed would best serve users and shareholders in the long term.

Adapted from Kevin Cashman. "What Exactly Is Ethics?" in *Leadership: Consulting Cashman*, Forbes.com, http://www.forbes.com/leadership/2007/03/03/leadership-cashman-ethics-leadership-citizen-cx_kc_0305ethics.html(accessed January 17, 2009).

3. Use a general group to which your reader belongs:
    Dear Investor:
    Dear Admissions Committee:

Pronouns

When you refer to a specific person, use the appropriate gender pronouns:

> In his speech, John Jones said that . . .

> In her speech, Judy Jones said that . . .

When you are referring not to a specific person but to anyone who may be in a given job or position, traditional gender pronouns are sexist.

> Sexist: a. Each supervisor must certify that the time sheet for his department is correct.

> Sexist: b. When the nurse fills out the accident report form, she should send one copy to the Central Division Office.

Business communication uses four ways to eliminate sexist generic pronouns: use plurals, use second-person *you,* revise the sentence to omit the pronoun, or use pronoun pairs. Whenever you have a choice of two or more ways to make a phrase or sentence nonsexist, choose the alternative that is the smoothest and least conspicuous.

The following examples use these methods to revise sentences *a* and *b* above.

1. Use plural nouns and pronouns.

    > Nonsexist: a. Supervisors must certify that the time sheets for their departments are correct.

    Note: When you use plural nouns and pronouns, other words in the sentence may need to be made plural too. In the example above, plural supervisors have plural time sheets and departments.

    Avoid mixing singular nouns and plural pronouns.

    > Nonsexist but lacks agreement: b. When the nurse fills out the accident report, they should send one copy to the Central Division Office.

    Since *nurse* is singular, it is incorrect to use the plural *they* to refer to it. The resulting lack of agreement is acceptable orally but is not yet acceptable in writing. Instead, use one of the other ways to make the sentence nonsexist.

2. Use *you.*

    > Nonsexist: a. You must certify that the time sheet for your department is correct.

    > Nonsexist: b. When you fill out an accident report form, send one copy to the Central Division Office.

    You is particularly good for instructions and statements of the responsibilities of someone in a given position.

3. Substitute an article (*a, an,* or *the*) for the pronoun, or revise the sentence so that the pronoun is unnecessary.

    > Nonsexist: a. The supervisor must certify that the time sheet for the department is correct.

    > Nonsexist: b. The nurse will
    >   1. Fill out the accident report form.
    >   2. Send one copy of the form to the Central Division Office.

4. When you must focus on the action of an individual, use pronoun pairs.

    Nonsexist: a. The supervisor must certify that the time sheet for his or her department is correct.

    Nonsexist: b. When the nurse fills out the accident report form, he or she should send one copy to the Central Division Office.

Other words and phrases

If you find any of the terms in the first column in Figure 3.4 in your messages or your company's documents, replace them with terms from the second column.

Not every word containing *man* is sexist. For example, *manager* is not sexist. The word comes from the Latin *manus* meaning *hand*; it has nothing to do with maleness.

Avoid terms that assume that everyone is married or is heterosexual.

    Biased: You and your husband or wife are cordially invited to the dinner.

    Better: You and your guest are cordially invited to the dinner.

Making Language Nonracist and Nonagist

Language is **nonracist** and **nonagist** when it treats all races and ages fairly, avoiding negative stereotypes of any group. Use these guidelines to check for bias in documents you write or edit:

- **Give someone's race or age only if it is relevant to your story.** When you do mention these characteristics, give them for everyone in your story—not just the non-Caucasian, non-young-to-middle-aged adults you mention.

- **Refer to a group by the term it prefers. As preferences change, change your usage.** Fifty years ago, *Negro* was preferred as a more dignified term than *colored* for African Americans. As times changed, *Black* and *African American* replaced it. Surveys in the mid-1990s showed that almost half of blacks aged 40 and older preferred *Black,* but those 18 to 39 preferred *African American.*[14] Currently, the National Association for the Advancement of Colored People (NAACP) uses African American on its Web page.

    Oriental has now been replaced by *Asian.*

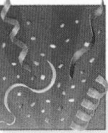

Attempts To Create a Unisex Pronoun

For more than 150 years, people have attempted to coin a unisex pronoun. None of the attempts has been successful.

Date	he or she	his or her	him or her
1850	ne	nis	nim
1884	le	lis	lim
1938	se	sim	sis
1970	ve	vis	ver
1977	e	e's	em
1988	ala	alis	alum

Adapted from Dennis E. Baron, "The Epicene Pronoun: Word That Failed," *American Speech* 56 (1981): 83–97; and Ellen Graham, "Business Bulletin," *Wall Street Journal,* December 29, 1988, A1.

Figure 3.4   Getting Rid of Sexist Terms and Phrases

Instead of	Use	Because
The girl at the front desk	The woman's name or job title: "Ms. Browning," "Rosa," "the receptionist"	Call female employees *women* just as you call male employees *men.* When you talk about a specific woman, use her name, just as you use a man's name to talk about a specific man.
The ladies on our staff	The women on our staff	Use parallel terms for males and females. Therefore, use *ladies* only if you refer to the males on your staff as *gentlemen.* Few businesses do, since social distinctions are rarely at issue.

Manpower
  Manhours
  Manning
	Personnel
	  Hours or worker hours
	  Staffing
		The power in business today comes from both women and men.

Managers and their wives	Managers and their guests	Managers may be female; not everyone is married.

Booming Business

As the 78 million US baby boomers age, more and more companies are making products with adaptations for physical infirmities:

- Appliance control panels with adjustable typefaces and color combinations.

- Ovens, dishwashers, and washer/dryer sets mounted higher so people have to bend over less.

- Sink fixtures with levers instead of knobs, for hands with limited mobility.

- Cell phones with large keys and large numbers on the screen.

Nissan and Ford Motor Companies fit their design engineers with special body suits that mimic aging bodies. The suits have an expanded waist, limited mobility in key joints, and goggles that mimic the effect of cataracts.

Marketing these new features requires a delicate touch, because no one likes to be reminded that their body is failing.

Adopted from Sara Lin, "Designing for the Senior Surge: Makers of Appliances, Bath Fixtures Target Aging Boomer; Cooking for the Forgetful," *Wall Street Journal*, April 25, 2008, W8; Katherine Boehret, "Simple Cells: Basic Phones Put to the Test," *Wall Street Journal*, December 19, 2007, D1; and "Suiting Up to Drive into Aging," *AARP Bulletin*, July–August 2008, 4.

Technology helps blind people contribute fully as members of the workforce. This Braille keyboard allows a computer engineer to key in commands and data. Specialized computer programs such as JAWS can read computer screens out loud.

The term *Latino* is the most acceptable group term to refer to Mexican Americans, Cuban Americans, Puerto Ricans, Dominicans, Brazilianos, and other people with Central and Latin American backgrounds. (*Latina* is the term for an individual woman.) Better still is to refer to the precise group. The differences among various Latino groups are at least as great as the differences among Italian Americans, Irish Americans, Armenian Americans, and others descended from various European groups.

Baby boomers, older people, and *mature customers* are more generally accepted terms than *Senior Citizens* or *Golden Agers.*

- **Avoid terms that suggest that competent people are unusual.** The statement "She is an intelligent purple woman" suggests that the writer expects most purple women to be stupid. "He is an asset to his race" suggests that excellence in the race is rare. "He is a spry 70-year-old" suggests that the writer is amazed that anyone that old can still move.

Talking about People with Disabilities and Diseases

A disability is a physical, mental, sensory, or emotional impairment that interferes with the major tasks of daily living. According to the US Census Bureau, 18% of Americans currently have a disability; of those, about 56% who were 21–64 were employed.[15] The number of people with disabilities will rise as the population ages.

To keep trained workers, more and more companies are making accommodations for disabilties. Companies such as Sylvania, American Express, and General Motors are offering accommodations such as telecommuting, flexible hours, workshift changes, and assignment changes.[16]

- *People-first language* **focuses on the person, not the condition. People-first language** names the person first, then adds the condition. Use it instead of the traditional noun phrases that imply the condition defines the person.

Instead of	Use	Because
The mentally retarded	People with mental retardation	The condition does not define the person or his or her potential.
Cancer patients	People being treated for cancer	

- **Avoid negative terms, unless the audience prefers them.** You-attitude takes precedence over positive emphasis: use the term a group prefers. People who lost their hearing as infants, children, or young adults often prefer to be called *deaf*, or *Deaf* in recognition of Deafness as a culture. But people who lose their hearing as older adults often prefer to be called *hard of hearing*, even when their hearing loss is just as great as that of someone who identifies him- or herself as part of the Deaf culture.

Using the right term requires keeping up with changing preferences. If your target audience is smaller than the whole group, use the term preferred by that audience, even if the group as a whole prefers another term.

Some negative terms, however, are never appropriate. Negative terms such as *afflicted, suffering from,* and *struck down* also suggest an outdated view of any illness as a sign of divine punishment.

Instead of	Use	Because
Confined to a wheelchair	Uses a wheelchair	Wheelchairs enable people to escape confinement.
AIDS victim	Person with AIDS	Someone can have a disease without being victimized by it.
Abnormal	Atypical	People with disabilities are atypical but not necessarily abnormal.

Choosing Bias-Free Photos and Illustrations

When you produce a document with photographs or illustrations, check the visuals for possible bias. Do they show people of both sexes and all races? Is there a sprinkling of various kinds of people (younger and older, people using wheelchairs, etc.)? It's OK to have individual pictures that have just one sex or one race; the photos as a whole do not need to show exactly 50% men and 50% women. But the general impression should suggest that diversity is welcome and normal.

Check relationships and authority figures as well as numbers. If all the men appear in business suits and the women in maids' uniforms, the pictures are sexist even if an equal number of men and women are pictured. If the only nonwhites pictured are factory workers, the photos support racism even when an equal number of people from each race are shown.

Summary of Key Points

- **You-attitude** is a style of communication that looks at things from the audience's point of view, emphasizing what the audience wants to know, respecting the audience's intelligence, and protecting the audience's ego.

1. Talk about the audience, not about yourself.
2. Refer to the audience's request or order specifically.

R-E-S-P-E-C-T

Most major airlines and hotel chains provide disability training to employees. . . . I recognize when someone has been trained—to offer me a Braille menu, use my name when addressing me, or take a moment to orient me to a new environment. What I appreciate even more, though, is . . . simple, common courtesy.

I don't care how many pages in an employee manual somewhere are devoted to . . . the dos and don'ts of interacting with someone who is deaf, blind, or mentally retarded. Among hundreds of experiences in airports and hotels, the one distinction that separates the (mostly) pleasing from the (occasionally) painful in my encounters has been the honest friendliness and respect with which I have or have not been treated.

Ask me where I'd like to sit, whether I need help getting there, and what other kinds of help I need.

Please, assume that I know more about my disability than anyone else ever could.

Respect me as you do any other customer who is paying for the same service, and have the grace to apologize if something does go wrong.

Too many companies, it seems to me, are busy shaking in their boots over the imagined high cost of accommodating people with disabilities when, in many instances, a good old-fashioned refresher course in manners would cover most bases.

Quoted from Deborah Kendrick, "Disabled Resent Being Patronized," *Columbus Dispatch*, July 21, 1996, 3B. Reprinted with permission.

Goodwill Can't Be Bought

Asian multinational companies have encountered problems in merging and acquiring companies in the United States. Scholars speculate that one of the reasons is their inability to create goodwill with the media, activist groups, and politicians. To create goodwill with American companies, Asian businesses are discovering the importance of strategic communication. Goodwill communication practices needed include

1. Targeting audiences: media and corporations.
2. Demonstrating global nature.
3. Building key stakeholder relationships including the government, politicians, unions, employees, local communities, customers, financial analysts, and media of both countries.
4. Outlining benefits to the US economy.
5. Becoming conscious of the culture, concerns, and perceptions of the company and the acquisition.

Adapted from Arun Sudhaman, "When Money Alone Can't Buy Goodwill," *Media*, April 2006, 10A.

3. Don't talk about feelings except to congratulate or offer sympathy.
4. In positive situations, use *you* more often than *I*. Use *we* when it includes the audience.
5. In negative situations, avoid the word *you*. Protect the audience's ego. Use passive verbs and impersonal expressions to avoid assigning blame.

- Apply you-attitude beyond the sentence level by using organization and content as well as style to build goodwill.
- **Positive emphasis** means focusing on the positive rather than the negative aspects of a situation. To create positive emphasis
    1. Avoid negative words and words with negative connotations.
    2. Beware of hidden negatives.
    3. Focus on what the audience can do rather than on limitations.
    4. Justify negative information by giving a reason or linking it to an audience benefit.
    5. Put the negative information in the middle and present it compactly.
- Check to see that your positive emphasis is appropriate, sincere, and clear.
- The desirable tone for business communication is businesslike but not stiff, friendly but not phony, confident but not arrogant, polite but not groveling.
- Bias-free language is fair and friendly; it complies with the law. It includes all members of your audience; it helps sustain goodwill.
- Check to be sure that your language is nonsexist, nonracist, and nonagist.
- Communication should be free from sexism in four areas: job titles, courtesy titles and names, pronouns, and other words and phrases.
- *Ms.* is the nonsexist courtesy title for women. Whether or not you know a woman's marital status, use *Ms. unless* the woman has a professional title or unless you know that she prefers a traditional title.
- Four ways to make pronouns nonsexist are to use plurals, to use *you*, to revise the sentence to omit the pronoun, and to use pronoun pairs.
- When you talk about people with disabilities or diseases, use the term they prefer.
- When you produce newsletters or other documents with photos and illustrations, picture a sampling of the whole population, not just part of it.

CHAPTER 3   Exercises and Problems

Go to www.mhhe.com/locker9e for additional Exercises and Problems.

3.1   Reviewing the Chapter

1. What are five ways to create you-attitude? (LO1)
2. What are five ways to create positive emphasis? (LO2)
3. How can you improve the tone of business messages? (LO3)

4. What are different categories to keep in mind when you are trying to reduce bias in business messages? (LO4)
5. What techniques can you use when you are trying to reduce bias in business messages? (LO4)

3.2 Evaluating the Ethics of Positive Emphasis

The first term in each pair is negative; the second is a positive term that is sometimes substituted for it. Which of the positive terms seem ethical? Which seem unethical? Briefly explain your choices.

cost	investment
second mortgage	home equity loan
tax	user fee
nervousness	adrenaline
problem	challenge
price increase	price change
for-profit hospital	tax-paying hospital
used car	pre-owned car
credit card fees	usage charges

3.3 Eliminating Negative Words and Words with Negative Connotations

Revise each of the following sentences to replace negative words with positive ones. Be sure to keep the meaning of the original sentence.

1. You will lose customer goodwill if you are slow in handling returns and issuing refunds.
2. Do not put any paper in this box that is not recyclable.
3. When you write a report, do not make claims that you cannot support with evidence.
4. Don't drop in without an appointment. Your counselor or case worker may be unavailable.
5. I am anxious to discuss my qualifications in an interview.

3.4 Focusing on the Positive

Revise each of the following sentences to focus on the options that remain, not those that are closed off.

1. Housing applications that arrive December 1 or later cannot be processed.
2. You cannot use flextime unless you have the consent of your supervisor.
3. As a first-year employee, you are not eligible for dental insurance.
4. I will be out of the country October 25 to November 10 and will not be able to meet with you then.
5. You will not get your first magazine for at least four weeks.

3.5 Identifying Hidden Negatives

Identify the hidden negatives in the following sentences and revise to eliminate them. In some cases, you may need to add information to revise the sentence effectively.

1. The seminar will help you become a better manager.
2. Thank you for the confidence you have shown in us by ordering one of our products. It will be shipped to you soon.
3. This publication is designed to explain how your company can start a recycling program.
4. I hope you find the information in this brochure beneficial to you and a valuable reference as you plan your move.
5. In thinking about your role in our group, I remember two occasions where you contributed something.

3.6 Improving You-Attitude and Positive Emphasis

Revise these sentences to improve you-attitude and positive emphasis. Eliminate any awkward phrasing. In some cases, you may need to add information to revise the sentence effectively.

1. You'll be happy to learn that the cost of tuition will not rise next year.
2. Although I was only an intern and didn't actually make presentations to major clients, I was required to prepare PowerPoint slides for the meetings and to answer some of the clients' questions.
3. At DiYanni Homes we have more than 30 plans that we will personalize just for you.
4. Please notify the publisher of the magazine of your change of address as soon as possible to prevent a disruption of subscription service.
5. I'm sorry you were worried. You did not miss the deadline for signing up for a flexible medical spending account.
6. We are in the process of upgrading our Web site. Please bear with us.

7. You will be happy to hear that our cell phone plan does not charge you for incoming calls.

8. The employee discount may only be used for purchases for your own use or for gifts; you may not buy items for resale. To prevent any abuse of the discount privilege, you may be asked to justify your purchase.

9. I apologize for my delay in answering your inquiry. The problem was that I had to check with our suppliers to see whether we could provide the item in the quantity you say you want. We can.

10. If you mailed a check with your order, as you claim, we failed to receive it.

3.7   Eliminating Biased Language

Explain the source of bias in each of the following, and revise to remove the bias.

1. We recommend hiring Jim Ryan and Elizabeth Shuman. Both were very successful summer interns. Jim drafted the report on using rap music in ads, and Elizabeth really improved the looks of the office.

2. All sales associates and their wives are invited to the picnic.

3. Although he is blind, Mr. Morin is an excellent group leader.

4. Unlike many blacks, Yvonne has extensive experience designing Web pages.

5. Chris Renker
   Pacific Perspectives
   6300 West Corondad Blvd.
   Los Angles, CA
   Gentlemen:

6. Enrique Torres has very good people skills for a man.

7. *Parenting 2007* shows you how to persuade your husband to do his share of child care chores.

8. Mr. Paez, Mr. O'Connor, and Tonya will represent our office at the convention.

9. Sue Corcoran celebrates her 50th birthday today. Stop by her cubicle at noon to get a piece of cake and to help us sing "The Old Grey Mare Just Ain't What She Used to Be."

10. Because older customers tend to be really picky, we will need to give a lot of details in our ads.

3.8   Advising a Hasty Subordinate

Three days ago, one of your subordinates forwarded to everyone in the office a bit of e-mail humor he'd received from a friend. Titled "You know you're Southern when . . . ," the message poked fun at Southern speech, attitudes, and lifestyles. Today you get this message from your subordinate:

> Subject: Should I Apologize?
>
> I'm getting flamed left and right because of the Southern message. I thought it was funny, but some people just can't take a joke. So far I've tried not to respond to the flames, figuring that would just make things worse. But now I'm wondering if I should apologize. What do you think?

Answer the message.

3.9   Responding to a Complaint

You're Director of Corporate Communications; the employee newsletter is produced by your office. Today you get this e-mail message from Caroline Huber:

> Subject: Complaint about Sexist Language
>
> The article about the "Help Desk" says that Martina Luna and I "are the key customer service representatives 'manning' the desk." I don't MAN anything! I WORK.

Respond to Caroline. And send a message to your staff, reminding them to edit newsletter stories as well as external documents to replace biased language.

3.16   Evaluating You-Attitude and Positive Emphasis in Brochures

Collect three brochures from organizations on your campus or from businesses in your city. Identify sentences in each brochure that demonstrate (or should demonstrate) you-attitude and positive emphasis.

As your instructor directs,

- Turn in a memo that identifies sentences with good you-attitude and positive emphasis. For sentences that should incorporate you-attitude and/or positive emphasis but did not, include the original sentence and your revision.
- Share your findings with a small group of students. What patterns do you see? How did others revise the problematic sentences you found?

3.17   Evaluating You-Attitude and Positive Emphasis in University Web Sites

As they plan their college visits, many students begin by visiting university Web sites. Imagine you are a high school senior and a prospective student. Go to the "Prospective Students" part of your school's Web site and read about housing, course offerings, and student life. Evaluate the information you find for you-attitude and positive emphasis. Compare the text for prospective students with the text on several sites targeted for current students. Does the tone change? In what ways?

Now visit the Web site of another university. Review the same type of information for prospective students and compare it to that of your own school.

As your instructor directs,

- Share your findings orally with a small group of students.
- Share your findings orally with the class.
- Post your findings in an e-mail to the class.
- Summarize your findings in a memo to your instructor.

3.18   Evaluating You-Attitude and Positive Emphasis at IRS

Reread the IRS sidebar on page 75. Now read their current "Where's My Refund" page on their Web site. What changes have they made? Which version do you like better? Why? Write your answers in a memo to your instructor or classmates.

3.19   Designing for People with Disabilities

Reread the sidebar on page 79. In small groups discuss these questions:

- What are some other products you can think of that could be redesigned for easier use by people with disabilities?
- What themes would you use to advertise these products? Remember that no one likes to be reminded that they are losing physical capacities.
- What are some changes companies should make to their advertising and product information for easier access by people with disabilities?

As your instructor directs, in small groups

- Summarize your discussion in a memo for your instructor.
- Summarize your discussion in a memo for your class list serve.
- Prepare a short presentation for your classmates.

3.20   All-Weather Case: **Revising a "Goodwill Disaster"**

Erin is preparing for an orientation program for a new batch of product engineers joining All-Weather. Mostly mechanical or industrial engineers, these fresh college recruits are bright, as Erin knows, having been thoroughly involved in their selection, but they are also green, especially in their knowledge of customer expectations or market requirements for All-Weather's products. Recently, in a meeting with the vice president of manufacturing, the VP told her, "I want these young engineers to see our products in homes or offices. They have sat in lecture halls a lot, listening to one boring speech after another."

"We'll organize a field visit," Erin replied, thanking the vice president for his help with the orientation program.

After returning to her office, she asks Rudy, the executive reporting to her, to discuss the orientation program with her. Rudy asks Erin if Kioni might join them. "Why not?" answers Erin, as she enters her office.

"Rudy, the vice president of manufacturing wants new product engineers to go on a field visit to see our products in homes or offices," Erin says. "Where do you think we might send them?"

"Huh. This man only wants to increase our work. He should be thankful that—" Rudy begins to say, but Erin waves him to stop.

"That's not how we think in this department, is it?" Erin says, sharply. "Why don't you coordinate with marketing and decide where we could send these engineers? Take Kioni's help; I know she is excited for the orientation program to begin."

"Okey-dokey," Rudy replies, half-throwing his arms up in the air as if to indicate that the whole idea befuddles him.

Erin is by now used to Rudy's antics. Ignoring his gesture, she says, "Also draft a letter to someone requesting this visit." Then, gathering her notes, she leaves for a meeting with Doug, Miguel, and Caleb to discuss the department's action plan for the next quarter.

Around five in the evening when she returns to her office, she finds a typed sheet on her table along with a post-it note signed by Rudy. It's a letter Rudy drafted addressed to a local art gallery that recently installed All-Weather's doors and windows. The letter reads:

Dear Mr. Mason,
Executive Director,
Iconic Art Gallery, St. Paul, MN

You must be glad that you chose All-Weather's energy efficient bow windows, horizontal sliders, and fiberglass doors for your art gallery. As everyone who is anyone knows, we offer the finest quality wood, vinyl, aluminum, steel, and fiberglass composite windows and doors you can find in the US of A. As you also know, our customer service representatives are ready to assist you 24/7 (and more!) with any installation or maintenance needs you may have (even if it's your responsibility or fault, I might add). After doing so much for an important customer such as you, we have a small favor to ask of you, which we're sure you will not deny us. We just hired some new engineers who will join our manufacturing division to continue to make the fine products that we make. Unfortunately, they have never seen how our finished products look outside or inside actual homes or offices. (On a personal note, I confess I don't know what they can learn from one visit to a home or an office.) Our VP (Manufacturing), an asset to All-Weather, says that we should send these engineers out on a field visit. And he should know, shouldn't he, being the VP and all? That is why I'm writing to you (the pleasure is mine, though).

These fresh minds need exposure to actual conditions in actual markets. We think that if they visit your art gallery, they will see how our products are helping you get results your art gallery could never dream of before. If you don't believe me, take a peek inside your exhibits room, whose space seems to have expanded thanks to our bow window that you have installed. I myself remember what a cramped-looking room it was before. No, I'm not asking you to share your admission fees with us, though free exhibition tickets wouldn't hurt (I'm kidding, sir). Also, you should perhaps buy more windows and doors from us (and attract more visitors as a result!). Also, don't forget to mention us favorably to your patrons.

Oh, and by the way, will you please let us know the day and time suitable to you when we might send those engineers to your art gallery? Our orientation program begins in three weeks time. Looking forward to your prompt acceptance of our request (with or without free exhibition tickets).

Sincerely,
Erin
(Manager-HR)

As Erin finishes reading the letter, controlling herself from hyperventilating, she concludes, once again, that she needs to talk to Doug about Rudy. "This guy simply does not get it. Either he hates his job or his communication skills are terrible. Or maybe it's both," she says out loud, knowing that everyone in the office had left. Then, Erin thinks of Kioni. Might she be able to revise Rudy's draft? Erin is loaded with work related to the orientation program and can really use help. She wonders if Kioni assisted Rudy in drafting the letter. The next morning, Erin asks Kioni if she has seen the draft. "No," Kioni replies, "Rudy left soon after we started brainstorming, saying that he would take care of the rest." Erin asks Kioni to revise Rudy's draft.

Questions / tasks to consider:

Based on your reading of Chapter 3, complete the following tasks:

- List problems in Rudy's draft.
- Prepare another list of things that Kioni could do to improve the draft. Be specific in your suggestions. For instance, it's insufficient to say "more you-attitude" or "more politeness." Point to places in the draft where these strategies might be useful. Also, rephrase relevant sentences or paragraphs for more you-attitude or more politeness, whichever is the case.
- What is the primary purpose of the letter? The secondary purpose?
- Revise Rudy's draft for Kioni.

Navigating the Business Communication Environment

Chapter Outline

Technology

- Electronic Tools
- Social Networking
- Information Overload
- Data Security
- Electronic Privacy

Trends in Business Communication

- Focus on Quality and Customers' Needs
- Entrepreneurship
- Diversity
- Globalization and Outsourcing
- Balancing Work and Family
- Teamwork
- Job Flexibility
- Rapid Rate of Change
- Innovation
- Concern for the Environment

Ethics

Corporate Culture

Interpersonal Communication

- Listening
- Conversational Style
- Nonverbal Communication
- Networking

Time Management

- Techniques
- Multitasking

Your First Full-Time Job

Summary of Key Points

Practice Trumps Talent

New research is showing that talent alone is not enough for great success; the more important key is practice. Greatness comes through years of an enormous amount of hard work—also known as practice. Tiger Woods? Began golfing as a toddler, practiced hours every day, and even remade his swing twice. Warren Buffett? Known for his long-standing business discipline and hours spent studying financial records.

Research is producing consistent findings across many disciplines. One of the most interesting findings is that people don't become great without practice, around 10 years or more of it. And not just any kind of practice. Simply going through the motions is not enough; old-timers in many jobs are frequently no better than newcomers. Greatness requires what researchers call "deliberative practice": "activity that's explicitly intended to improve performance, that reaches for objectives just beyond one's level of competence, provides feedback on results, and involves high levels of repetition." Furthermore, elite performers practice every day, including weekends. Findings are consistent in fields as diverse as management, sales, surgery, music, chess, and sports.

So, how do you practice business communication? Many communication skills are available to practice: finding and analyzing data, writing documents, making oral presentations. The key is *how* you practice. Your goal is not just to get it done, but to get better at doing it. Research shows that this new mind-set allows you to process information more deeply and retain it longer. You also need to seek feedback and adjust your performance accordingly. Finally, you need to construct mental models of your work and how all the elements influence each other.

The ultimate finding of this research? You are not held hostage by a Great Dealer of talent cards. You have the power to become successful where you want to (but don't forget the 10 years of hours of daily disciplined practice).

> *"Talent alone is not enough for great success; the more important key is practice."*

Source: Adapted from Geoffrey Colvin, "What It Takes to Be Great," *Fortune,* October 30, 2006, 88–96.

Learning Objectives

After studying this chapter, you will know:

1. How technology is changing business communication.

2. What the trends in business communication are.

3. Why ethics is so important in business communication.

4. How corporate culture impacts the business environment.

5. How to improve interpersonal communication.

6. How to use your time more efficiently.

7. How to succeed at your first full-time job.

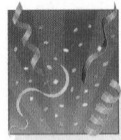

Dilbert May Get You Fired

Catfish Bend Casinos in Burlington, Iowa, fired a seven-year employee for placing a Dilbert cartoon on a company bulletin board. The employee posted the cartoon after the company announced the casino was closing and 170 workers would probably be laid off.

The Dilbert cartoon called decision makers "drunken lemurs" and said they had time but no talent.

The employee, who was identified from security tapes, thought the comic was humorous and might cheer up some of his colleagues. Managers found it insulting misconduct. They then tried to block his unemployment benefits, but the judge sided with the employee, calling the posting "a good-faith error in judgment."

Adapted from Clark Kauffman, "Bosses Check Video, Fire Man Who Put up Comic," *Des Moines Register*, December 19, 2007, 1A, 10A.

In addition to adapting to audiences and building goodwill, business communications are heavily influenced by the environments in which they are created and interpreted. Part of this environment is shaped by the enormous influence of technology. Part is shaped by widespread trends—trends such as globalization or the green movement. Part is shaped by national culture, such as the growing concern about business ethics, and part is shaped by corporate culture. A final part is shaped by individual behaviors, such as those involved in interpersonal communication.

Technology

In this technological age, different forms of media are encompassing all parts of life. For instance, in 2007, the average American spent

- 1,555 hours watching television.
- 974 hours listening to the radio.
- 195 hours using the Internet.
- 86 hours playing video games.

These numbers of hours spent with media are expected to rise significantly in future years.[1]

Technology has even gripped the highest office in the country. President Obama battled with US intelligence agencies to keep his BlackBerry when he took office in January 2009. In fact, he is the first president in the history of our country to use e-mail while in office. If the highest office in the land demands technology, the business world is no exception. When it comes to technology, business continually embraces all forms that help increase productivity and save money. Almost all office employees are expected to know how to navigate through the Web and to use word processing, e-mail, spreadsheet, database, and presentation software.

The following sections—electronic tools, social networking, information overload, data security, and electronic privacy—discuss some key issues of technology use in professional organizations.

Electronic Tools

Businesses are quick to adopt new forms of technology that can enhance the experience of workers and improve the bottom line. New software programs

Technology plays a large role in the changing face of business communication. Tools such as intranets, extranets, faxes, and e-mail have contributed to the efficiency of workplace communication. Meeting rooms are frequently equipped with laptops, pagers, and video-conferencing equipment, making it possible for people to have meetings across continents and time zones.

and devices continually enter the market to help businesses. However, acquiring new technology and helping workers master it entail an enormous capital investment. Learning to use new-generation software and improved hardware takes time and may be especially frustrating for people who were perfectly happy with old software.

Some of the most popular workplace tools that improve productivity are wikis, instant messengers, portable media players, personal digital assistants (PDAs)/smartphones, and telepresences.

Wikis

With the popularity of Web sites like Wikipedia, the business world has been quick to follow suit. Many organizations are using wikis, an online form of content knowledge management, in which users can post information or collaborate on projects. The access to these wikis is limited to employees of the particular organization using them, much like intranets. Employees can use the wikis to bookmark Web pages with a short summary, upload drafts of working documents, or create new entries to the system about workplace practices. Other employees can then quickly search for information using keywords or modify existing uploaded documents.

Wikis are a great way for corporations to create knowledge databases of workplace practices for their particular organization. In addition, Wikis reduce the e-mailing of drafts between employees who are collaborating on a project. As an added bonus, every change made to documents on a wiki can be tracked. Moreover, when employees leave an organization, their job knowledge is still stored on the wiki and can be a valuable resource for new employees.

Instant Messengers

Instant messaging services, like AOL Instant Messenger, Yahoo Messenger, and MSN Messenger, are quickly finding their way into office settings. The advantage of these programs is that they provoke immediate response, faster even than e-mail, which can decrease the time it takes to solve a company issue.

Online Acronyms

E-mail writers often use the following abbreviations. The quick pace of instant messaging has made these even more popular.

ASAP	As soon as possible
BRB	Be right back
BTW	By the way
CU	See you
CWOT	Complete waste of time
EML	E-mail me later
F2F	Face to face
FAQ	Frequently asked questions
GMTA	Great minds think alike
IAE	In any event
IMHO	In my humble opinion
IOW	In other words
LOL	Laughing out loud
NRN	No reply necessary
OTOH	On the other hand
ROTFL	Rolling on the floor laughing
THX	Thanks
TTYL	Talk to you later

For a more complete listing of electronic abbreviations, check out the following Web site: http://searchcrm.techtarget.com/sDefinition/0,,sid11_gci211776,00.html.

A Vision of the Future

Have you ever dreamed about moving objects without using a muscle? Do you wish you could control objects using only your brain?

Thought-conversion technology is the main focus of a company called Emotiv. Right now, the company has advanced the technology to a point where users can move objects with their thoughts in a video game environment. Users wear a wireless headset that contains 16 electrodes that press against the scalp. The device has the capability to measure brain waves and turn thoughts into electronic actions.

Expanded from the science behind EEGs, thought-conversion technology could be the wave of the future. Emotiv doesn't want consumers just to be able to play video games. Eventually, they hope to develop the system so that users can control everything they do on their computer and around the house by mental power.

What implications would a device like this have for the business world? How could it increase productivity? What, if any, drawbacks would there be to a device like this?

Adapted from David H. Freedman, "Reality Bites," *Inc.*, December 2008, 92–99.

Cellular phone technology is spreading worldwide.

Some organizations also believe that IMing fosters better collaboration among employees, particularly those who work from home a few days a week.

When sending an IM, users may think the conversation is lost after they log out or the IM window is closed. Ultimately, that's not the case. For example, Florida Congressman Mark Foley lost his position for holding sexual and inappropriate IM conversations with underage pages. Many businesses monitor all IM conversations with growing frequency. In 2006, at least 2% had fired employees as the result of IM conversations. Some IM service providers are tailoring their products to businesses by offering more tracking capabilities, such as keyword searches of IM conversations.[2]

Portable Media Players

Portable media players (like iPods and MP3 players) feature the ability to broadcast streaming video and audio. Some organizations give employees these devices pre-loaded with recordings of meetings, new product information, or general announcements. These devices help keep employees connected, even when they're not in the office.

Personal Digital Assistants

PDAs, such as Treo, BlackBerry, or Apple iPhone (sometimes called Smartphones or wireless handheld devices), allow users to send and receive e-mail, access Web sites, conduct word processing, learn their next tasks, update a job's status, complete a time sheet, and make telephone calls. Many of these devices also have touch screens or full QWERTY keyboards. Like portable media players, these devices can also broadcast streaming video and audio. With the full functionality of these devices, employees can be connected to their work 24/7.

Telepresence

Telepresence is high-end videoconferencing that uses 50-inch plasma screens and broadcast-quality cameras to create virtual meetings that are almost life-like. These video meetings can occur across different time zones or between different nations instantaneously. However, state-of-the-art telepresence rooms cost anywhere from $150,000 up to $1,000,000. Some of the price is associated with the equipment necessary to create a room, but most of the cost comes from the large amounts of bandwidth required for the conferencing. While the initial price seems high, some organizations, and the makers of these systems, quickly counter that the system will pay for itself within a few months as the amount of national or international travel is greatly reduced. Moreover, meetings never have to be delayed or postponed because of late flights or weather problems. Some estimates suggest that by 2010 tele-presence rooms will see a 22% increase in sales from the $1.15 billion they grossed in 2006.[3]

Social Networking

Following in the footsteps of MySpace and Facebook, larger organizations are adapting social networking tools designed specifically for businesses, such as IBM's BluePages. The software allows employees to post a profile, blog, or useful links which help workers interact on a more personal level. Moreover, employees can share client information, and the social networking tools promote collaboration. The access to the social network is usually limited to an organization's employees.

On IBM's BluePages, 26,000 employees have blogs, on which they post opinions about their work and technology in general. More than 100,000 employees work on 20,000 wikis. Widgets such as polling widgets and rating widgets allow wiki users to quickly rate new features or proposed changes. DogEar allows employees to share useful Web sites and other electronic resources. IBM also owns over 50 islands on Second Life which can be used for training and group discussions.[4]

New social networking sites are on the rise. Here are a few that professionals have been quick to adapt to their business needs:

- LinkedIn—Allows professionals to connect with colleagues, search for new opportunities, post a résumé, and even recruit new employees.
- Xing—Similar features as LinkedIn, but more popular in Europe.
- Orkut—Google's version of Facebook containing many similar options.
- Ning—Allows users to create their own social networking site adapted to their business.
- NetParty—Helps professionals connect online to meet up for happy hour after work.
- Twitter—A microblog that allows users to let their co-workers know what they're doing in 140 characters or less.
- Yammer—Similar to Twitter, but exclusively for updating co-workers about current projects.
- Sermo—Site dedicated exclusively to the medical profession; helps doctors solicit opinions, share information, and improve patient care.

The realm of social networking sites is expanding exponentially. In 2008, an Australian court ruled that a mortgage lender could use Facebook to inform a couple that they lost their home.[5] On the site PatientsLikeMe, consenting participants provide detailed medical histories and discuss side effects of prescribed drugs they're taking. The company then packages this information and sells it to drug and insurance companies, a knowledge transfer which participants believe will help find cures faster. The site can also be used by pharmaceutical companies to invite clinical trial subjects, helping speed up research.[6]

For businesses, the challenge of social networking sites is figuring out how to harness the positives to increase productivity, particularly when dealing with customers. Many smaller firms use social networking sites to establish an identity and relationship with clients.

Another way that businesses are trying to reach customers is through **widgets,** tiny software programs that can be dragged, dropped, and embedded into social networking sites. Building widgets is big business; they cost

Social Networking Connections

"For companies looking to better connect with consumers and build brand loyalty, social networks are increasingly looking like the ideal tool. Users get a forum in which to share information, pictures and videos about themselves and their likes and dislikes—and, companies hope, talk up a product. Companies, in turn, get real-time feedback on trends and products. And they can even bounce off ideas still in the works.

One natural area for social networking seems to be sports. After all, sports and the hottest sports apparel and equipment always get people talking.

The National Hockey League, for instance, has set up a social-networking site, NHL Connect, where hockey fans can create personal profiles, add friends, upload photos, post videos from YouTube, make comments and join chat groups. The site also has NHL news, game schedules and the ability for users to look up other fans based on their favorite teams and players. In addition, the site links to blogs by contributors as well as team blogs for the New York Islanders, Anaheim Ducks and others."

Drawing Customers

Riten Industries makes machine parts for manufacturers. Since standard parts are increasingly made abroad, custom tooling—products made to a customer's specifications—has become a major part of the company's business. However, the company lacked the personnel to follow up on all sales leads received on its Web site.

A new Web site makeover, costing less than $40,000, added a CAD program which allows people to draw the product they want built and then receive a price quote. According to the company's co-owner, the CAD program has "'broken the translation barrier, . . . because everyone [in the engineering field] understands computer-aided design,' regardless of what language they speak."

The close rate for orders based on customer drawings is 80% and has led to an overall revenue increase of 20%.

Adapted from Simona Cover and Raymund Flandez, "Three Strategies to Get Customers to Say 'Yes,'" *Wall Street Journal*, May 29, 2008, B6.

between a few thousand dollars to one hundred thousand dollars or more, depending on the widgets' capabilities.[7] Widgets are changing the way people use the Internet. In the past, people surfed from page to page, but now widgets can bring the power of all those pages into a central location, like a social networking site.[8]

Of course, like all technological tools, social networking sites have some drawbacks. If workers spend too much of their day immersed in social networking sites, how much of their regular work routine is not being completed? Almost a quarter of all US employers block popular social networking sites like MySpace and Facebook, citing data security as the main reason.[9] In addition, once workers post information on social networking sites about themselves, electronic copies of that information are stored indefinitely.

Information Overload

New technology saves time, but it also leads to a new problem: information overload. Workers are becoming overwhelmed with all the information available to them. Cable, e-mail RSS feeds, Web sites, listservs, and blogs increase access to news at all levels, including news in one's professional field. The ease of desktop publishing has increased the flow of newsletters, reports, and flyers—even from individual units within a business. The amount of information is becoming unmanageable:

- A Google search for information on *e-mail* offers close to 7.7 billion entries as of February 2009. A search for *listserv* offers over 15 million.
- 87% of lawyers believe that electronic discovery in court cases is too expensive and causing litigation prices to skyrocket.[10]
- Dupont has a document warehouse with over 200,000 boxes, each box containing about 2,500 pages.[11]
- Chevron processes two million e-mails daily. The company estimates it now has 1,250 terabytes of data, where one terabyte equals the data of one million books.[12]

Some organizations, and even college campuses, experience slowdowns with their networks from file-sharing programs and other online video applications. To solve the issue, organizations are now using "deep packet inspection," which gives IT administrators the power to assign priority to important online material flowing through their networks.[13]

Another way to deal with communication overload is to eliminate the source of the communication. For instance, Sprint Nextel started disconnecting customers who called customer service excessively, which they define as calling an average of 25 times per month.[14]

Perhaps the biggest problem for many employees is the amount of e-mail. The Radicati Group, a technology market research firm, estimates 55 billion e-mails are sent daily (excluding spam).[15] Spam clutters mailboxes—or leads to filters that stop some needed e-mail. Spam also means that many people do not open e-mail if they do not recognize either the sender or the topic.

On a smaller level, workers forward unwanted jokes, pictures, and URLs. Workers who become e-mail addicts, sending too many e-mails with too little content, find that their e-mails are being opened last, if at all. Too many people forward too many messages to uncaring receivers, and the "Reply to All" button is getting a notorious reputation. A study conducted by Basex, another research firm, discovered that more people (31%) labeled normal e-mail as "most disruptive" than did so for spam (27%).[16]

Some software applications and organizations are taking a stand to help employees deal with the approximately 200 e-mails a day that the average worker receives. For instance, software add-ons for e-mail systems can now prioritize messages after analyzing which senders have the most importance.[17] Intel and U.S. Cellular declare e-mail-free Fridays, where employees are encouraged to meet face-to-face, and at PricewaterhouseCoopers employees see a pop-up window that discourages them from sending e-mail on the weekend.[18]

Data Security

As electronic information increases, so do concerns about data theft. Just as individuals take steps—like not providing important identification numbers by e-mail—to prevent identity theft, so do organizations take steps to protect their data. In 2007, an estimated 270 organizations lost customer or employee sensitive information.[19]

Why are people trying to hack into the systems of organizations? It usually comes down to money. Credit card or social security numbers can be sold for $5–$7 dollars each while bank account numbers can bring a hacker up to $400 dollars.[20] Internet security experts also confirm that the economic downturn in 2008 and 2009 actually increased the number of cyber attacks.[21] The hackers take advantage of anxiety during uncertain economic times.

Security measures include bans on electronic devices such as Palm Pilots, BlackBerrys, and MP3 players. Some companies are even disabling extra USB connections to ensure employees cannot attach these devices. Others are performing random checks of laptops to look for unauthorized or unsecured files and using scans of fingerprints, eyes, or faces to limit and track access to specific computers.[22]

With around 30% of organizations providing laptops to their employees, an additional opportunity exists for experiencing data security issues. Millions of laptops are stolen or lost each year; at the end of 2007, 80% of businesses reported that their employees had lost laptops containing sensitive data.[23] Another serious issue causing loss of sensitive data is portable storage devices, commonly called flash drives. While the physical cost to replace these devices is relatively insignificant, the drives themselves can contain sensitive security information.

Electronic Privacy

As organizations respond to growing security concerns, their efforts often encroach on workers' privacy. The division between the two has become increasing complex and blurry. Surveillance does not necessarily stop when employees leave their offices or cars. It can continue to the company parking areas and even employees' personal blogs.

Companies such as Google, Delta Air Lines, and even Burger King have fired workers for content on their personal blogs. Although many workers believe their blogs are protected by the first amendment, the truth is that in most states, companies can fire employees for almost any reason except discrimination.[24]

Organizations are monitoring many different kinds of electronic interactions. According to a 2007 survey by the American Management Association of 304 companies,

- 73% store and review e-mail.
- 66% monitor Internet usage.

As the Old Song Says, "I Got Rhythm"

One of the newest electronic security methods is keystroke authentication. It turns out that your typing pattern, the pressure of your fingers on the keys and your typing speed, is unique. It allows you to prove electronically that you are who you say you are.

Keystroke patterning has a long history. The military began using it over a hundred years ago to identify individual senders of Morse code by their tapping rhythms. As the location of those senders shifted, military trackers got data on enemy movements.

Currently, the biggest users of keystroke patterning are banks and credit unions, who are employing it in addition to standard password authentication. Since identity theft has become such a major problem, banks and credit unions are under a federal mandate to use stronger authentication measures to protect online customers.

Adapted from Kathleen Kingsbury, "Telltale Fingertips: With Biometrics, How You Type Can Allow Websites to Know Who You Are—Or Aren't," *Time Bonus Section*, January 2007, A10.

Identity theft is such a growing concern that some companies make it the main focus of their business.

- 65% block inappropriate Web sites.
- 48% use video surveillance.
- 45% record time spent on phone and numbers dialed.
- 43% store and review computer files.[25]

The same study also showed that 45% track keystrokes (and time spent at the computer).[26] Because of findings from such monitoring, some companies are blocking access to particular Web sites, especially Facebook, MySpace, YouTube, sports and online shopping sites. Many organizations claim that heavy usage of these sites slows down company communications such as file transfers and e-mail. In 2009, Senator Chuck Grassley called for a halt

E-mails, instant messages, telephone calls, and Web searches can all be tracked by your employer and used in lawsuits. You should always observe professional practices while in the workplace.

of funds to the National Science Foundation after a report was released that found that some employees spent up to 20% of their workday looking at porn instead of reviewing grant proposals.[27]

Other surveillance techniques use GPS (global positioning system) chips to monitor locations of company vehicles, as well as arrival and departure times at job sites. Data from Smart Tags on cars, showing exactly when a vehicle was at a particular toll station, are being used in court cases. EZ-Pass, the electronic toll collection system, records are being used in courts as proof of infidelity. Workers may tell their spouses they are in a meeting, but EZ-Pass has a record of where and when their vehicle entered or exited that day.[28] Cell phones give approximate location signals that are accurate enough to help law enforcement officials locate suspects.[29]

New radio frequency (RFID) technology, which incorporates mini-antennas into almost everything sold, is constantly being improved and touted as a way to track consumer habits. Businesses like this technology because they have a better sense of when and how consumers are using the products. On the other hand, consumers are surrendering more of their private lives.[30]

Users of Facebook were outraged about privacy issues in 2007 when the site launched Beacon, a program that alerted friends about shopping purchases and other activities outside Facebook.[31] In 2009, the Federal Trade Commission endorsed industry self-regulation to protect consumer privacy. Web sites and companies that collect consumer data such as searches performed and Web sites visited are to (1) clearly notify consumers that they do so, (2) provide an easy way to opt out, (3) protect the data, and (4) limit its retention.[32]

For many workers, e-mail they thought was private has been the biggest downfall, often exposing lies or crimes. In many instances, the result is usually termination.

- Steven Heyer, former CEO of Starwood Hotels, resigned after sending suggestive e-mails to a younger female employee. Julie Roehm, senior vice president at Wal-Mart, had a similar issue with a male employee.[33]

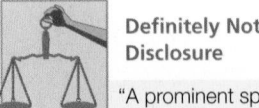

Definitely Not Full Disclosure

"A prominent spine surgeon and researcher at the University of Wisconsin received $19 million in payment over five years from Medtronic Inc., one of the country's largest makers of spinal devices. . . .

"The surgeon . . . received the payments while helping Medtronic develop and promote a number of spinal products. Medtronic's $19 million in payments . . . went 'greatly' beyond what was evident in disclosures he made to the university. . . .

'[During those five years, the surgeon] told the university that he received $20,000 or more from Medtronic. . . . The disclosures conform to school policies, which currently don't require researchers to specify amounts received above $20,000. . . .

"Charles Rosen, a University of California, Irvine, spinal surgeon who is also president of the Association for Medical Ethics, said the Wisconsin disclosure policy is similar to that of many universities and medical societies. He said those policies are insufficient. . . .

"'When you are advocating devices or procedures, it can't be said this is a private matter and that no one should know how much this company is paying me,' he said. 'It should be very public. People should know.'"

Quoted from David Armstrong and Thomas M. Burton, "Medtronic Paid This Researcher More Than $20,000— Much More," *Wall Street Journal*, January 16, 2009. Copyright © 2009 by Dow Jones & Company, Inc. Reproduced with permission of Dow Jones & Company, Inc. via Copyright Clearance Center.

- The Veterans Affairs Department publicly stated there have been fewer than 800 recent suicide attempts by veterans, even though the number stated in an internal e-mail was 12,000.[34]
- Countrywide CEO Angelo Mozilo found himself without a job after he hit "reply all" by mistake and told a customer that their plea for help with a home loan was "disgusting."[35]
- Atul Malhotra, former vice president of Hewlett-Packard, could face 10 years in prison and a $250,000 dollar fine for forwarding a confidential trade secret e-mail from his former employer, IBM.[36]

Companies are not just examining the content of the messages, but also observing when messages are sent. If a worker usually sends e-mails from 9 to 5 and then someone notices that that worker is sending e-mails at 2 AM, red flags definitely go up.

E-mail is not alone, though. With the rise in camera phones and inexpensive video recorders, everyone's privacy is at stake. For instance, in early 2009, Olympic swimmer Michael Phelps lost his sponsorship contract with Kellogg Inc. and was banned from competition for three months by USA Swimming after private pictures surfaced of him smoking from a marijuana bong. Detroit Mayor Kwame Kilpatrick was charged with perjury and forced to resign after text messages he sent were used against him by prosecutors. And even "old" technology can threaten privacy. Illinois Governor Blagojevich was impeached on the basis of taped phone conversations.

However, there is some glimmer of hope for protecting privacy. In July 2008, the US Ninth Circuit Court of Appeals issued a ruling that makes it more difficult for employers to snoop on employees' electronic communications, such as texting, instant messages, and Tweets.[37] In another court case with the European Union, Google agreed to reduce the time it keeps personal search information to only 18 months.[38]

Trends in Business Communication

As the advances in technology show, both business and business communication are constantly changing. Ten trends in business, government, and nonprofit organizations affect business and administrative communication: a focus on quality and customers' needs, entrepreneurship, diversity, globalization and outsourcing, balancing work and family, teamwork, job flexibility, the rapid rate of change, innovation, and concern for the environment.

Focus on Quality and Customers' Needs

After declining during the late 1990s, customer satisfaction among American consumers has been generally on the rise. This trend has a real payoff for businesses; higher levels of the American Customer Satisfaction Index are associated with stronger sales.[39] In an age where unhappy customers can share their experiences with thousands of Web users, focusing on customer satisfaction is vital.

Not only does superior customer service sell, it also increases business performance. A University of Michigan study showed that companies with high customer satisfaction scores outperformed the S&P 500, producing higher stock prices and less volatile stock values and cash flows.[40]

Offering superior customer service doesn't always mean spending extra money. Southwest Airlines customer service agent Sharron Mangone convinced an entire gate area to join in a "biggest hole in the sock" contest while they waited for their plane.[41] To attract patients, hospitals and health care facilities are improving communication, including accurate estimates of wait times and improved explanations of medical procedures, exams, and tests.[42]

Entrepreneurship

Since 1980, the number of businesses in the United States has risen faster than the civilian labor force. The US Census Bureau counted 15 million individual proprietorships (self-employed workers without employees) in 2002.[43]

Some established companies are trying to match the success and growth rate of start-ups by nurturing an entrepreneurial spirit within their organizations. Innovators who work within organizations are sometimes called **intrapreneurs.** A classic article in the *Harvard Business Review* made famous the examples of 3M (where researchers can spend 15 percent of their time on ideas that don't need management approval), Thermo Electron (where managers can "spin out" promising new businesses), and Xerox (where employees write business proposals competing for corporate funds to develop new technologies).[44]

Entrepreneurs have to handle all the communication in the organization: hiring, training, motivating, and evaluating employees; responding to customer complaints; drafting surveys; writing business plans; making presentations to venture capitalists and marketing the product or service.

Diversity

The prevalence of teamwork puts a premium on being able to work with other people—even if they come from different backgrounds.

Women, people of color, and immigrants have always been part of the US workforce. But for most of this country's history, they were relegated to clerical, domestic, or menial jobs. Now, US businesses realize that barriers to promotion hurt the bottom line as well as individuals. Success depends on using the brains and commitment as well as the hands and muscles of every worker.

In the last decade, we have also become aware of other sources of diversity beyond those of gender and race: age, religion, class, regional differences, sexual orientation, physical disabilities. Helping each worker reach his or her potential requires more flexibility from managers as well as more knowledge about intercultural communication. And it's crucial to help workers from different backgrounds understand each other—especially in today's global economy. To learn more about diversity and the workforce, read Chapter 5.

Globalization and Outsourcing

In the global economy, importing and exporting are just a start. More and more companies have offices and factories around the world:

- McDonald's serves food in over 100 countries.[45]
- 3M decided to increase its operations to include China, India, Korea, and Poland.[46]
- UPS delivers packages in India, China, and Japan.[47]
- Coca-Cola receives 80% of its profit outside North America.[48]
- Wal-Mart has 3,000 stores internationally, including ones in Central America, South America, China, and Japan.[49]

The site of the store, factory, or office may not be the site of all the jobs. A data center in Washington can support many workers in India as businesses are outsourcing domestically and globally. **Outsourcing** means going outside

Japanese Companies Woo Former Female Employees

Faced with a looming worker shortage as baby boomers retire, Japanese companies have begun courting their former women employees. Some are accepting former employees' requests to work part-time and offering coaches until the women get back up to speed. Other companies are offering perks to female employees to retain them. Some companies are offering day care centers and coupons for babysitting and house-cleaning services; other companies allow women to work shorter hours or reject overtime work until their youngest child finishes high school.

"'It's not difficult to set up a [female-friendly] system,' says [the] manager of a division promoting women at Mizuho's [one of Japan's major banks] corporate banking unit. 'The hardest part is changing people's mentality. It takes a long time.'"

Adapted and quoted from Miho Inada, "Japanese Companies Woo Women Back to Work," *Wall Street Journal*, July 23, 2007, B1.

McDonald's now serves food in China.

the company for products and services that once were produced by the company's employees. Companies can outsource technology services, customer service, tax services, legal services, accounting services, benefit communications, manufacturing, and marketing. Outsourcing is often a win–win solution: the company saves money or gets better service, and the outsourcers make a profit. In *The World Is Flat,* Thomas Friedman says "the accountant who wants to stay in business in America will be the one who focuses on designing creative, complex strategies. . . . It means having quality-time discussions with clients."[50] He sees the work of the future as customization, innovation, service, and problem solving.[51]

All the challenges of communicating in one culture and country increase exponentially when people communicate across cultures and countries. Succeeding in a global market requires **intercultural competence,** the ability to communicate sensitively with people from other cultures and countries, based on an understanding of cultural differences. To learn more about international communication, see Chapter 5.

Balancing Work and Family

To reduce turnover, respond to a declining labor force, and increase employee satisfaction, companies are trying to be more family friendly by proving flextime, telecommuting, time off for family needs, and extended career breaks for caregiving. The balance of work and family is becoming such a popular topic that the *Wall Street Journal* now runs a regular column called "Work and Family."

At PricewaterhouseCoopers, 36% of employees use flextime and telecommuting; another 10% compress workweeks. Employees can also take up to

Many organizations promote virtual offices, which allow employees to work from home.

Team Communication Saves Lives

Communication breakdowns during patient transfers between units or personnel shifts are the largest source of medical error. The hospital accreditation board is now requiring hospitals to establish standards for transfer communications. To help hospitals, the Institute for Healthcare Improvement is working with hospitals on a communication rubric known as SBAR:

- Situation: describe briefly, get attention.
- Background: offer enough to provide context for the problem.
- Assessment: your assessment of overall condition.
- Recommendation: your specific recommendations.

Kaiser Permanente, the large health care organization, pioneered using the model, which helps doctors and nurses convey the most critical information in just 60 seconds. The model increases communication between doctors who don't want nurses' opinions and nurses who are reluctant to provide their opinions.

One Kaiser physician administrator says, "In almost all serious avoidable episodes of patient harm, communication failure plays a central role. . . . By teaching caregivers new models of 'structured communication,'. . . we can make sure that we are all in the same movie."

Adapted from Laura Landro, "Hospitals Combat Errors at the 'Hand-Off': New Procedures Aim to Reduce Miscues as Nurses and Doctors Transfer Patients to Next Shift," *Wall Street Journal*, June 28, 2006, D1, D2.

five years off to care for children or other family members. The company continues to cover certifications or training, up to $5,000 per year, during that time.[52] At Accenture, employees can work four long days to get Fridays off. The Flexible Transitions program allows employees to take sabbaticals up to two years long while still attending meetings and corporate events if they wish. People on sabbatical have career counselors during their leave.[53]

At times, employees find ways other than physical presence to demonstrate their commitment and enthusiasm for organizational goals. Thanks to technology advances, employees can use laptops, BlackBerrys, e-mail, or cell phones to do work at any time, including weekends and evenings. The downside of this trend is that sometimes work and family life are not so much balanced as blurred. For instance, many employers are giving portable media players to workers for training courses, language lessons, and general organizational announcements to hear on their own time. Some employees are also expected to conduct business 24-hours a day because of different time zones of workplaces. The flexibility of employees is necessary in an age of downsizing and globalization, but it means that families are being impacted.

Teamwork

More and more companies are getting work done through teams. Teamwork brings together people's varying strengths and talents to solve problems and make decisions. Often, teams are cross-functional (drawing from different jobs or functions) or cross-cultural (including people from different nations or cultural groups served by the company).

Teams, including cross-functional teams, helped Sarasota Memorial Hospital resolve major problems with customer and employee satisfaction. For example, team members from the emergency room recorded every step in the process from pulling into the parking lot through decisions about patient care, and then they eliminated unnecessary steps. The ER team worked with the laboratory staff to improve the process of getting test results. At Michelin, the French tire maker, teams bring together people from the United States and

Europe. According to the company's chemical purchasing manager for Europe, the exchange between the two continents helps employees on both sides of the Atlantic understand each other's perspectives and needs.[54]

Increasing emphasis on teamwork is a major reason given by organizations such as AT&T, Intel, Hewlett-Packard, and the US Interior Department for calling telecommuting workers back to the office.[55] To learn more about working in teams, see Chapter 6.

Job Flexibility

In traditional jobs, people did what they were told to do. Now, they do whatever needs to be done, based on the needs of customers, colleagues, and anyone else who depends on their work. They help team members finish individual work; they assist office mates with pressing deadlines. They are resourceful: they know how to find information and solution ideas. They work extra hours when the task demands it. They are ready to change positions and even locations when asked to do so. They need new skill sets even when they don't change jobs.

At Sarasota Memorial Hospital, food service workers do more than bring food to patients; they open containers, resolve problems with meals, help patients read their menus, and adjust orders to meet patients' preferences. This attentiveness not only serves the patients; it is part of a team-spirited approach to patient care that in this case frees nurses to do other work.[56] The experience at Sarasota Memorial is backed up by research suggesting that the most effective workers don't see work as assigned tasks. Instead, they define their own goals based on the needs of customers and clients.[57]

Your parents may have worked for the same company all their lives. You may do that, too, but you have to be prepared to job-hunt throughout your career. That means continuing to learn—keeping up with new technologies, new economic and political realities, new ways of interacting with people.

Rapid Rate of Change

The flexibility required for the modern job market is just one area in which change is defining the workplace. Jobs that are routine can readily be done in other countries at lower cost. Many US jobs have already been subject to such "offshoring," and more are sure to follow. The work that remains in the United States is more likely to be complex work requiring innovation, flexibility, and adaptation to new learning.[58]

As any employee who has watched his or her job shift can testify, change—even change for the better—is stressful. Even when change promises improvements, people have to work to learn new skills, new habits, and new attitudes.

Rapid change means that no college course or executive MBA program can teach you everything you need to know for the rest of your working life. You'll need to stay abreast of professional changes by reading trade journals as well as professional Web sites and blogs, participating in professional listservs, and attending professional events. Take advantage of your company's training courses and materials; volunteer for jobs that will help you gain new skills and knowledge. Pay particular attention to your communication skills; they become even more important as you advance up your career ladder. A survey of 1,400 financial executives found that 75% considered oral, written, and interpersonal skills even more important for finance professionals now than they were just a few years ago.[59]

The skills you learn can stand you in good stead for the rest of your life: critical thinking, computer savvy, problem solving, and the ability to write, to speak, and to work well with other people. It's almost a cliché, but it is still true: the most important knowledge you gain in college is how to learn.

Innovation

As global competition increases, and industrial milieus change ever more quickly, innovation becomes more and more important. *Fortune*'s 2008 list of most admired companies was organized around innovation. Apple, at the top of the list, also got the top marks for innovation.

Many companies rely on all employees for suggestions. 3M sends 9000 employees, in 35 countries, into customers' workplaces to work beside people there and to note problems the company can solve. American Express established a $50 million innovation fund to finance employees' ideas.[60] Google is famous for its 20% rule: technical employees can spend about 20% of their time on projects outside their main job, and even their managers cannot remove that free margin.[61]

Concern for the Environment

As global warming becomes an issue of increasing concern, more and more companies are trying to soften their environmental impact. They do so for a variety of reasons in addition to environmental concerns. Sometimes such awareness saves money; sometimes executives hope it will create favorable publicity for the company. However, many marketing experts say that green advertising is now just standard operating procedure.[62] Environmental activist groups such as Greenpeace and Friends of the Earth go even further. These groups have sharply and publicly criticized some large companies for exaggerating their commitment to the environment.

Fortune's 2007 list of the 20 most admired companies was organized around environmental awareness. The top three companies on it—General Electric, Starbucks, and Toyota—owe a significant part of their growth to strategies and products aimed at helping the environment. United Parcel Service has

Carbon-Emission Reporting

"Carbon-emissions reporting is a laborious undertaking that publicly exposes potentially serious liabilities and risks facing your business—and it's voluntary. So why do it? We explored that question with Alyson Slater, the director of strategy at Global Reporting Initiative, an Amsterdam-based organization that has developed the most widely used framework of reporting principles, guidance, and standard disclosures on environmental, social, and economic performance.

Why should business care about voluntary reporting on carbon emissions?

Today it is very difficult for a company to say that greenhouse gas emissions are not a subject of material interest to stakeholders. . . . More and more investment firms are considering climate change impact as part of a company's risk profile.. . . Failure to disclose can put you at a strategic disadvantage.

How does the reporting process help a company address climate-related risks? . . .

The discipline of sorting out which activities are material to report on and in what depth, and what data will be used to document progress, forces companies to formulate strategies."

Quoted from Christina Bortz, "Conversation: Alyson Slater, Global Reporting Initiative's Director of Strategy, on How Disclosing Emissions Benefits Companies," *Harvard Business Review*, October 2007, 32.

Alternate energy has become a leading environmental issue, bringing both business and good publicity to some companies.

Big Companies Saving the World

American big businesses have recently adopted slogans and behaviors to change their negative image by showing their dedication to help the world. Why? Because customers and employees appreciate the goodwill gestures of large companies benefiting the environment and society.

For example, some of the new slogans include

- Ford   "Better World"
- Wal-Mart   "Change a light. Change the world"
- GE   "Solving some of the world's toughest problems"

Even better than slogans, companies are also modifying some of their behaviors. Starbucks, for example, is buying "fair trade" coffee above market prices to assist poor farmers. Gap and Nike are monitoring global outsourcing manufacturers to ensure good working conditions. Dell and Hewlett-Packard are recycling used computers.

Have you recently heard news about other attempts by big businesses to make the world a better place? To what extent do these goodwill attempts by big companies change your opinion of them? To what extent do they have ulterior motives?

Adapted from Geoff Colvin, "The 500 Gets Religion: Why Big Companies Are in the Business of Solving the World's Woes," in *CNNMoney,* http://money. cnn.com/magazines/fortune/fortune_ archive/2007/04/30/8405462/index. htm (accessed June 15, 2009).

a 1,550 fleet of alternative-fuel delivery trucks. Wal-Mart is cutting back on packaging. Starbucks pays fair market prices to third-world farmers and helps develop ecological farming practices. GE is focusing on sustainable products for green concerns such as wind power, water purification, and pollution monitoring.[63] GE's "ecomagination" initiative expects to have $1.5 billion invested in R&D for cleaner technologies and to be earning at least $20 billion from ecomagination products by 2010.[64]

Ethics

When the Internet stock bubble burst at the beginning of this decade, the plunging stock prices and an overall economic slowdown were accompanied by a wave of news stories about unethical and illegal corporate practices. As investors and consumers heard the accusations of accounting fraud at WorldCom, HealthSouth Corporation, Enron, and Adelphia Communications, many felt distrustful of businesses in general. At other companies, including ImClone and Tyco International, executives were accused of enriching themselves at their companies' expense. Such breaches of financial ethics at the top of a company have tainted, and even destroyed, entire organizations. The public outcry motivated Congress to pass the Sarbanes-Oxley Act, requiring corporations to engage in much more careful control and reporting of their financial activities.[65]

With the official recognition of a serious worldwide recession in the fall of 2008, along with the subprime mortgage debacle, ethics concerns redoubled. Now ethics issues were even more powerfully related to financial concerns as financial giants such as AIG, Bear Sterns, Lehman Brothers, Merrill Lynch, Wachovia, and Washington Mutual had to be bailed out or went bankrupt. Investment banks, corporate officials, rating agencies, all were accused of unethical behavior.

The Ethics Resource Center, America's oldest nonprofit organization devoted to ethical practice, reported in its 2007 *National Business Ethics Survey*®, "More than five years after Enron and other corporate ethics debacles, businesses of all size, type, and ownership show little—if any—meaningful reduction in their enterprise-wide risk of unethical behavior."[66] The report noted that 56% of employees surveyed personally witnessed unethical or illegal behavior; 42% of those witnesses did not report it. The two top reasons for nonreports were fear it would make no difference and fear of retaliation. The riskiest, and most frequent, misconducts included putting one's own interests ahead of those of the organization, lying, abusive behavior, stealing, Internet abuse, discrimination, sexual harassment, and provision of low-quality goods and services.[67]

On the other side of the coin, positive ethical efforts are also getting attention. The United Nations Global Compact, the world's largest corporate effort for global citizenship, focuses on human rights, labor, environment, and anti-corruption measures. More than 4,700 businesses in 120 countries participate.[68] Brazil's Instituto Ethos has 1,300 companies committed to social responsibility.[69] Great Britain's 2006 Companies Act requires public companies to report on social and environmental measures.[70] The U.S. is joining with other nations to successfully battle international bribery.[71]

- GE's chief legal officer for 20 years had an article in the *Harvard Business Review* detailing how GE has tried "to build a culture that fuses high integrity and high performance."[72]
- Bill and Melinda Gates' foundation received double attention when Warren Buffett announced his transfer of billions of dollars to it.
- Google, the "Don't Be Evil" company, has invested over $100 million in Google.org "to use the power of information and technology to address

the global challenges or our age: climate change, poverty and emerging disease."[73]

- The Clinton Global Initiative has brought together hundreds of heads of state and CEOs, who collectively have committed $46 billion. This money has already impacted the lives of 200 million people in 150 countries.[74]

- The (RED) Campaign, through the sale of (RED) products from some of the top brands, is raising millions of dollars for the Global Fund to invest in African AIDS programs.[75]

- Robin Hood, a venture philanthropy, "robs" the rich (its board members cover all costs, so 100% of money donated goes to fund programs) to help the poor in New York City.[76]

At the 2008 World Economic Forum Annual Meeting in Davos, Bill Gates gave a speech calling for "creative capitalism, an approach where governments, businesses, and nonprofits work together to stretch the reach of market forces so that more people can make a profit, or gain recognition, doing work that eases the world's inequities."[77]

Social entrepreneurs, backed by social investors like Gates, are extending the reach of philanthropy. Grameen Bank founder Muhammad Yunus won the 2006 Nobel Peace Prize for his work with microfinance. The bank says it has brought 65% of its 7.5 million clients out of extreme poverty.[78]

Business ethics includes far more than corporate greed, international pacts, and philanthropy, of course. Much of business ethics involves routine practices, and many of these practices involve communication. How can we make our contracts with our clients and suppliers easier to understand? How can we best communicate with our employees during mergers or layoffs? How much should our hospital disclose about our doctors' payments from drug and medical devices companies?

Many basic, daily communication decisions involve an ethics component. Am I including all the information my audience needs? Am I expressing it in ways they will understand? Am I putting it in a format that helps my audience grasp it quickly? Am I including information for all segments of my audience? Am I taking information from other sources accurately? Am I acknowledging my sources? Figure 4.1 lists some of the Web resources that deal with business ethics.

Rule No. 1: Don't Copy Rule 34: Don't Plagiarize

"Do not plagiarize" should have been included in *Unwritten Rules of Management*, the book by William Swanson, CEO of Raytheon. In 2004, Raytheon gave employees free copies of the book, which contained 33 rules. The book quickly became widely read by professionals and executives because of its humorous approach. However, an engineer at Hewlett-Packard discovered that 13 of the rules had been previously published by W. J. King in his 1944 bestseller, *The Unwritten Laws of Engineering*. Further findings uncovered that the additional rules were obtained from Defense Secretary Rumsfeld and humor editorial writer Dave Barry.

Swanson apologized for the mistake, which, he states, began when he asked employees to create a presentation from a file. The presentation was a great hit, which led to the creation of the 33 rules—one for each year he worked for Raytheon. Unfortunately, the rules were not original and the sources were not properly cited.

How can you avoid plagiarism?

Adapted from Lisa Takeuchi Cullen, "Rule No. 1: Don't Copy," *Time*, May 15, 2006, 41.

Figure 4.1   Business Ethics Resources on the Web

- **Business Ethics Resources on the Internet**
  http://www.ethicsweb.ca/resources/business

- **Defense Industry Initiative on Business Ethics and Conduct**
  http://dii.org

- **DePaul University's Institute for Business and Professional Ethics**
  http://commerce.depaul.edu/ethics

- **Ethics Effectiveness Quick Test**
  http://www.ethicsa.com/documents/pdf/EEQT-Short.pdf

- **Ethics in International Business**
  http://library.lib.binghamton.edu/subjects/business/intbuseth.html

- **E-Business Ethics**
  http://www.e-businessethics.com

- **Various Codes of Conduct**
  http://www.ethicsweb.ca/resources/business/codes.html

http://www.ethicsinaction.com/

The Ethics in Action Awards recognize businesses and individuals in British Columbia who are "doing the right thing." Log on to see winners from this year and years past. What services or products that made the list do you use? What components of the winners' organizations contributed to the label "ethical"?

Figure 4.2   Ethical Issues in Business Communications

Manner of conveying the message	Qualities of the message	Larger organizational context of the message
Language, Graphics, and Document Design • Is the message audience-friendly? Does it respect the audience? • Do the words balance the organization's right to present its best case with its responsibility to present its message honestly? • Do graphics help the audience understand? Or are graphics used to distract or confuse? • Does the design of the document make reading easy? Does document design attempt to make readers skip key points? **Tactics Used to Shape Response** • Are the arguments logical? Are they supported with adequate evidence? • Are the emotional appeals used fairly? Do they supplement logic rather than substituting for it? • Does the organizational pattern lead the audience without undue manipulation? • Are the tactics honest? That is, do they avoid deceiving the audience?	• Is the message an ethical one that treats all parties fairly and is sensitive to all stakeholders? • Have interested parties been able to provide input into the decision or message? • Does the audience get all the information it needs to make a good decision? • Is information communicated in a timely way, or is information withheld to reduce the audience's power? • Is information communicated so the audience can grasp it or are data "dumped" without any context?	• How does the organization treat its employees? How do employees treat each other? • How sensitive is the organization to stakeholders such as the people who live near its factories, stores, or offices and to the general public? • Does the organization support employees' efforts to be honest, fair, and ethical? • Do the organization's actions in making products, buying supplies, and marketing goods and services stand up to ethical scrutiny? • Is the organization a good corporate citizen, helpful rather than harmful to the community in which it exists? • Are the organization's products or services a good use of scarce resources?

Small Companies, Large Hearts

Some small companies are building philanthropy into their business models. Hook & Ladder Brewing Company donates a portion of all sales to local firefighters. ColorMe Company, which produces arts and crafts materials for children, gives 10% of earnings to children's charities. The charitable contributions help attract and keep customers and employees and set such companies apart from their competitors.

What do you think of such philanthropic business models? What potential problems do such models have? Do you think the benefits will outweigh the pitfalls?

Adapted from Raymund Flandez, "Small Companies Put Charity into Their Business Plan," *Wall Street Journal*, November 20, 2007, B3.

Figure 4.2 elaborates on ethical components of communication. As it suggests, language, graphics, and document design—basic parts of any business document—can be ethical or manipulative. Persuading and gaining compliance—activities at the heart of business and organizational life—can be done with respect or contempt for customers, co-workers, and subordinates.

Corporate Culture

Another strong influence on the business environment is corporate culture (see Chapter 2 for ways to analyze corporate culture). Corporate cultures vary widely. They range from formal—with individual offices, jackets, and hierarchical lines of command—to informal, with open office space, casual attire, and flat organizational structures.

Google is known for company gyms, pool and ping-pong tables, well-stocked snack rooms, free restaurants, and casual work attire. Ad agency Crispin Porter + Bogusky has a stuffed elephant and a firepole, plus some teepees to use as conference rooms. Personnel get around on bikes and skateboards. Whole Foods features a collaborative environment. Each department, such as meats or vegetables, is a decentralized team, and performance bonuses go to teams, not individuals.[79]

Two companies in the same field may have very different cultures. When Procter & Gamble bought Gillette, they expected a smooth marriage between

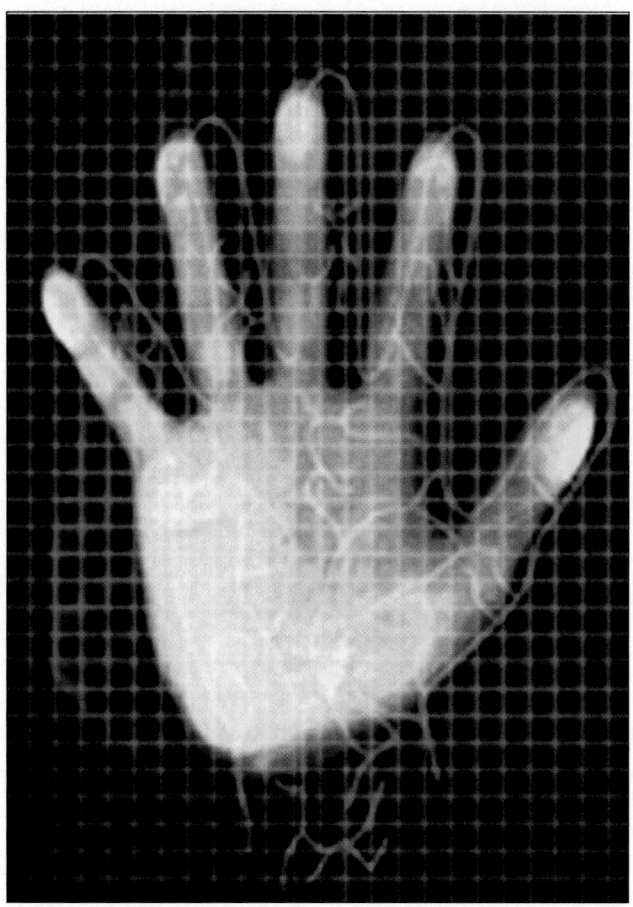

GMAT is now using palm vein scans to eliminate hired test takers. See sidebar on this page.

Business School Ethics

GMAT test scores were canceled for applicants who allegedly supplied or accessed exam questions posted on a Web site. Business schools were notified that these students had prepared improperly for the exam, and the Graduate Management Admission Council, which oversees the exam, obtained a court order to shut down the site, believed to be maintained in China.

The council also announced that it will be requiring GMAT test takers to take a palm vein scan, an infrared picture of the blood vessels in their hands. This new security measure is a new attempt to wipe out proxies—hired brains that take the test for an applicant.

The efforts to cheat continue in business school. Donald McCabe, a Rutgers University professor of management who has studied academic dishonesty for two decades, says that students in business schools cheat more than other students. His findings are backed up by a Duke University study which found that 56% of master's students in business administration cheat, again the highest rate among graduate students.

Adapted from John Hechinger, "Schools Cancel GMAT Scores," *Wall Street Journal*, September 11, 2008, D6; and "The Ethical Mind: A Conversation with Psychologist Howard Gardner," *Harvard Business Review*, March 2007, 51–56.

the world's number one toothbrush, Oral-B, and the world's number two toothpaste, Crest. But cultural differences caused problems. Gillette employees found P&G's culture rigid, its decision making slow. Gillette employees also had to learn P&G's famous acronyms, such as CIB (consumer is boss) and FMOT (first moment of truth, when consumers notice the product). P&G people sent memos, Gillette people called meetings.[80]

In a more voluntary amalgam of corporate cultures, Procter & Gamble has also chosen to temporarily swap employees with Google. Google employees are adopting some of P&G's terminology to aid in work routines; P&G employees are learning online promotional campaigns.[81]

Corporate culture is not just for large companies and professional employees. Small companies develop cultures to attract and keep talented employees. SuperGroupCreativeOmnimedia has 15 employees, who are allowed to pursue their own interests during downtime between client projects. All of them meet twice weekly to discuss both company business and their own projects. These personal projects, in turn, become evidence to clients of staff creativity.[82]

Wise companies also use effective corporate cultures to retain hourly workers. Hotels lose two-thirds of their hourly workers annually, according to hotel survey firm Market Metrix. Each departure costs midrange hotels about $5,000 in lost productivity, recruiting, and training. But Joie de Vivre Hospitality has a turnover rate that is half the industry average. The CEO attributes the low rate to a corporate culture that listens to employees, enacts some of their suggestions, and tries to make work fun. In addition to awards, the company sponsors parties, annual retreats, and regularly scheduled dinners. It also

Bumping the Lamp

"Bumping the lamp" is part of Disney's corporate culture. The phrase refers to a scene in the cartoon movie *Roger Rabbit* in which a character bumps into a lamp and makes it shake. The lamp's shadow shakes, too—a touch of excellence that only a few moviegoers will notice. Bumping the lamp means achieving a level of excellence—whether or not it's noticed.

This emphasis on customer service continues even when families leave a Disney theme park. Every year, 20,000 guests lock their keys in their cars. Cast members, as employees are called, roam the parking lots to help families get into their cars—no phone call to a locksmith, no waiting, no fee.

Adapted from Robert Hiebeler, Thomas B. Kelly, and Charles Ketterman, *Best Practices: Building Your Business with Customer-Focused Solutions* (New York: Simon & Schuster, 1998), 197.

Some employees use exercise balls as desk chairs. The balls require employees to use abdominal and lower back muscles to maintain posture. Employees say they are also fun because they can bounce.

Source: Anjali Athavaley, "The Ball's in Your Cubicle: New Workplace Trend Replaces Office Chairs with Gym Balls," *Wall Street Journal*, February 27, 2007, D1, D3.

offers free classes on subjects such as Microsoft Excel and English as a second language.[83]

International differences also impact corporate culture. Many Asian businesses are conservative: they value face time in the office over telecommuting and group effort over individual initiative. Late nights at the office and even weekend work in the office are expected.[84] On the other hand, some European workers have 35-hour work weeks and six weeks of vacation annually.

Interpersonal Communication

Within the corporate environment, some people are more likely to be successful than others, and one major reason for the variation is interpersonal communication skill. Much important communication takes place in hallways, at the water cooler, and in break rooms. Successful professionals communicate well with different categories of people—co-workers, bosses, clients—in a variety of settings. To do so, they cultivate skills in diverse areas such as listening, conversation, nonverbal communication, and networking. They also practice skills in conflict resolution and teamwork (see Chapter 6 for a discussion of these latter two skills).

These skills are part of what Daniel Goleman has widely popularized as Emotional Intelligence in his books on the subject. He presents much evidence to show that while intelligence and expertise are necessary to climb to the top in organizations, once at the top emotional intelligence, not IQ, predicts the star leaders.[85]

Listening

Listening is crucial to building trust. However, listening on the job may be more difficult than listening in classes. Many classroom lectures are well organized, with signposts and repetition of key points to help hearers follow. But conversations usually wander. A key point about when a report is due may be sandwiched in among statements about other due dates for other projects. Finally, in a classroom you're listening primarily for information. In interchanges with friends and coworkers, you need to listen for feelings, too. Feelings such as being rejected or overworked need to be dealt with as they arise. But you can't deal with a feeling unless you are aware of it.

Listening errors also can result from being distracted by your own emotional response, especially when the topic is controversial. Listeners have to be aware of their emotional responses so that they can clarify the speaker's intent and also allow time for cooling off, if necessary. A "you" attitude is as helpful for listening as it is for writing. Listening is more effective if the listener focuses more on understanding than on formulating a reply. Thinking about your own response too often causes you to miss important information.

Some listening errors also happen because the hearer wasn't paying enough attention to a key point. Be aware of points you need to know and listen for them.

Inattention and emotions can cause listeners to misinterpret a speaker. To reduce listening errors caused by misinterpretation,

Emotional Leaders

According to Kevin S. Groves, a management professor at California State University–Los Angeles, leaders should be selected based on emotional communication ability.

Groves conducted a study with 108 organizational leaders and 325 of their subordinates from various workplace settings. He discovered direct correlations between a leader's emotional communication skills (i.e., facial expressions, direct eye contact, tone of voice, etc.) and being evaluated as effective leaders by their subordinates.

Using "emotional expressivity" as an assessment tool for promotion of managers could improve job performance and the overall productivity of the organization.

Adapted from Kevin S. Groves, "Leader Emotional Expressivity, Visionary Leadership, and Organizational Change," *Leadership & Organizational Development Journal* 27, no. 7 (2006): 566–83.

- Paraphrase what the speaker has said, giving him or her a chance to correct your understanding.
- At the end of the conversation, check your understanding with the other person. Especially check who does what next.
- After the conversation, write down key points that affect deadlines or how work will be evaluated.
- Don't ignore instructions you think are unnecessary. Before you do something else, check with the order giver to see if there is a reason for the instruction.
- Consider the other person's background and experiences. Why is this point important to the speaker? What might he or she mean by it?

Listening to people is an indication that you're taking them seriously. **Acknowledgment responses**—nods, *uh huhs*, smiles, frowns—help carry the message that you're listening. However, remember that listening responses vary in different cultures.

In **active listening,** receivers actively demonstrate that they've understood a speaker by feeding back the literal meaning, the emotional content, or both. These strategies create active responses:

- Paraphrase the content. Feed back the meaning in your own words.
- Identify the feelings you think you hear.
- Ask for information or clarification.
- Offer to help solve the problem. ("What can I do to help?")

Instead of acknowledging what the other person says, many of us immediately respond in a way that analyzes or attempts to solve or dismiss the problem. People with problems need first of all to know that we hear that they're having a rough time. Figure 4.3 lists some of the responses that block communication. Ordering and threatening both tell the other person that the speaker doesn't want to hear what he or she has to say. Preaching attacks the other person. Minimizing the problem suggests the other person's concern is misplaced. It can even attack the other person's competency by suggesting that other people are coping just fine with bigger problems. Even advising shuts off discussion. Giving a quick answer minimizes the pain the person feels and puts him or her down for not seeing (what is to us) the obvious answer. Even if it is a good answer from an objective point of view, the other person may not be ready to hear it. And too often, the off-the-top-of-the-head solution doesn't address the real problem.

Figure 4.3   Blocking Responses versus Active Listening

Blocking response	Possible active response
Ordering, threatening "I don't care how you do it. Just get that report on my desk by Friday."	**Paraphrasing content** "You're saying that you don't have time to finish the report by Friday."
Preaching, criticizing "You should know better than to air the department's problems in a general meeting."	**Mirroring feelings** "It sounds like the department's problems really bother you."
Minimizing the problem "You think *that's* bad. You should see what *I* have to do this week."	**Asking for information or clarification** "What parts of the problem seem most difficult to solve?"
Advising "Well, why don't you try listing everything you have to do and seeing which items are most important?"	**Offering to help solve the problem together** "Is there anything I could do that would help?"

Source: These responses that block communication are based on a list in Thomas Gordon and Judith Gordon Sands, *P.E.T. in Action* (New York: Wyden, 1976), 117–18.

Choose and Listen Wisely

[Jim Collins, author of bestselling business books *Built to Last* and *Good to Great,* suggests that having great people on a team and top executives who will listen to the ideas of these great people contributes to successful businesses.]

[Often,] "the CEO has already made a decision, and his [her] definition of leadership is to get people to participate so that they feel good about the decision he's [she's] already made," [states Collins].

[The problem, however, is that] "you're ignoring people who might know a lot that would be useful in making the decision. You're accepting the idea that because you're in the CEO seat, you somehow know more or you're smarter than everyone else. But what you're really doing is cutting yourself off from hearing options or ideas that might be better. You have to recognize that your position can be a hindrance to getting the best information. And so can your personality."

Quoted from Jerry Useem, "Interview: Jim Collins on Tough Calls," *Fortune,* June 27, 2005, 90–93.

Active listening takes time and energy. Even people who are skilled active listeners can't do it all the time. Active listening can reduce the conflict that results from miscommunication, but it alone cannot reduce the conflict that comes when two people want apparently inconsistent things or when one person wants to change someone else.

Conversational Style

Deborah Tannen, a linguist who specializes in gender discourse, uses the term **conversational style** to denote our conversational patterns and the meaning we give to them: the way we show interest, politeness, appropriateness.[86] Your answers to the following questions reveal your own conversational style:

- How long a pause tells you that it's your turn to speak?
- Do you see interruption as rude? or do you say things while other people are still talking to show that you're interested and to encourage them to say more?
- Do you show interest by asking lots of questions? or do you see questions as intrusive and wait for people to volunteer whatever they have to say?

Tannen concludes that the following features characterize her own conversational style:

Fast rate of speech.

Fast rate of turn-taking.

Persistence—if a turn is not acknowledged, try again.

Preference for personal stories.

Tolerance of, preference for simultaneous speech.

Abrupt topic shifting.

Different conversational styles are not better or worse than each other, but people with different conversational styles may feel uncomfortable without knowing why. A subordinate who talks quickly may be frustrated by a boss who speaks slowly. People who talk more slowly may feel shut out of a conversation with people who talk more quickly. Someone who has learned to make requests directly ("Please pass the salt") may be annoyed by someone who uses indirect requests ("This casserole needs some salt").

In the workplace, conflicts may arise because of differences in conversational style. If people see direct questions as criticizing or accusing, they may see an ordinary question ("Will that report be ready Friday?") as a criticism of their progress. One supervisor might mean the question simply as a request for information. Another supervisor might use the question to mean "I want that report Friday."

Researchers Daniel N. Maltz and Ruth A. Borker believe that differences in conversational style (Figure 4.4) may be responsible for the miscommunication that often occurs in male–female conversations. Certainly conversational style is not the same for all men and for all women, but research has found several common patterns in the US cultures studied so far.[87] For example, researchers have found that women are much more likely to nod and to say *yes* or *mm hmm* than men are.[88] Maltz and Borker hypothesize that to women, these symbols mean simply "I'm listening; go on." Men, on the other hand, may decode these symbols as "I agree" or at least "I follow what you're saying so far." A man who receives nods and *mms* from a woman may feel that she is inconsistent and unpredictable if she then disagrees with him. A woman may feel that a man who doesn't provide any feedback isn't listening to her.

Nonverbal Communication

Nonverbal communication—communication that doesn't use words—takes place all the time. Smiles, frowns, who sits where at a meeting, the size of an office, how long someone keeps a visitor waiting—all these communicate pleasure or anger, friendliness or distance, power and status. Most of the time we are no more conscious of interpreting nonverbal signals than we are conscious of breathing.

Yet nonverbal signals can be misinterpreted just as easily as can verbal symbols (words). And the misunderstandings can be harder to clear up because people may not be aware of the nonverbal cues that led them to assume that they aren't liked, respected, or approved.

Are Interruptions Impolite?

In the dominant US culture, interrupting can seem impolite, especially if a lower-status person interrupts a superior.

Simulated negotiations have measured the interruptions by business people in 10 countries. The following list is ordered by decreasing numbers of interruptions:

Korea
Germany
France
China
Brazil
Russia
Taiwan
Japan
United Kingdom
United States

This list does not mean that US business people are more polite, but rather that how people show politeness differs from culture to culture. Chinese and Italians (who also interrupt frequently) use interruptions to offer help, jointly construct a conversation, and show eagerness to do business—all of which are polite.

Based on Jan M. Ulijn and Xiangling Li, "Is Interrupting Impolite? Some Temporal Aspects of Turn-Taking in Chinese-Western and Other Intercultural Encounters," *Text* 15, no. 4 (1995): 600, 621.

Figure 4.4 Different Conversational Styles

	Debating	Relating
Interpretation of questions	See questions as requests for information.	See questions as way to keep a conversation flowing.
Relation of new comment to what last speaker said	Do not require new comment to relate explicitly to last speaker's comment. Ignoring previous comment is one strategy for taking control.	Expect new comments to acknowledge the last speaker's comment and relate directly to it.
View of aggressiveness	See aggressiveness as one way to organize the flow of conversation.	See aggressiveness as directed at audience personally, as negative, and as disruptive to a conversation.
How topics are defined and changed	Tend to define topics narrowly and shift topics abruptly. Interpret statements about side issues as effort to change the topic.	Tend to define topics gradually, progressively. Interpret statements about side issues as effort to shape, expand, or limit the topic.
Response to someone who shares a problem	Offer advice, solutions.	Offer solidarity, reassurance. Share troubles to establish sense of community.

Sources: Based on Daniel N. Maltz and Ruth A. Borker, "A Cultural Approach to Male-Female Miscommunication," *Language and Social Identity,* ed. John J. Gumperz (Cambridge: Cambridge University Press, 1982), 213; and Deborah Tannen, *Talking from 9 to 5: Women and Men in the Workplace: Language, Sex and Power* (New York: William Morrow, 1995).

Learning about nonverbal language can help us project the image we want to present and make us more aware of the signals we are interpreting. However, even within a single culture, a nonverbal symbol may have more than one meaning.

In the business world, two sets of nonverbal signals are particularly important: spatial cues and body language.

Spatial Cues

In the United States, the size, placement, and privacy of one's office connotes status. Large corner offices have the highest status. An individual office with a door that closes connotes more status than a desk in a common area. Windows also may matter. An office with a window may connote more status than one without.

People who don't know each other well may feel more comfortable with each other if a piece of furniture separates them. For example, a group may work better sitting around a table than just sitting in a circle. Desks can be used as barricades to protect oneself from other people.

Body Language

Posture and body movements provide various signals. In the United States, **open body positions** include leaning forward with uncrossed arms and legs, with the arms away from the body. **Closed** or **defensive body positions** include leaning back, sometimes with both hands behind the head, arms and legs crossed or close together, or hands in pockets. As the labels imply, open positions suggest that people are accepting and open to new ideas. Closed positions suggest that people are physically or psychologically uncomfortable, that they are defending themselves and shutting other people out.

People who cross their arms or legs often claim that they do so only because the position is more comfortable. But notice your own body the next time you're in a perfectly comfortable discussion with a good friend. You'll

(a)   (b)

(a) (left) "THE REAL THING: A real smile involves the whole face, not just the mouth. While muscles pull the corners of the mouth up (1), an involuntary nerve causes the upper eyefold (2) to relax."

(b) (right) "THE SOCIAL SMILE: When faking, the lips are pulled straight across (3). Though this creates cheek folds (4) similar to those of a real smile, the lack of eye crinkles (5) is a dead giveaway."

Quoted from Andy Raskin, "A Face Any Business Can Trust," *Business 2.0* 4, no. 11 (December 2003): 60.

Body language can give big clues about our attitude to office visitors.

"Assertiveness" May Be a Matter of Conversational Style

"Rachel regularly led training groups with a male colleague. He always did all the talking, and she was always angry at him for dominating and not giving her a chance to say anything. . . . He would begin to answer questions from the group while she was still waiting for a slight pause to begin answering. And when she was in the middle of talking, he would jump in—but always when she had paused. So she tried pushing herself to begin answering questions a little sooner than felt polite, and not to leave long pauses when she was talking. The result was that she talked a lot more, and the man was as pleased as she was. Her supervisor complimented her on having become more assertive."

"Whether or not Rachel actually became more assertive is debatable. . . .. [S]he solved her problem with a simple and slight adjustment of her way of speaking, without soul-searching, self-analysis, external intervention, and—most important—without defining herself as having an emotional problem or a personality defect: unassertiveness."

Quoted from Deborah Tannen, *That's Not What I Meant!* (New York: William Morrow, 1986), 177–78.

probably find that you naturally assume open body positions. The fact that so many people in organizational settings adopt closed positions may indicate that many people feel at least slightly uncomfortable in school and on the job.

Some nonverbal communications appear to be made and interpreted unconsciously by many people. Researchers at MIT are showing that when we get excited about something, we have more nervous energy. Another such signal is fluency, or consistency. Consistency in motions (such as in surgery) or tone (speech) tells us who is expert, or at least well practiced. Such signals are hard to fake, which may explain their influence.[89]

Body language is complicated by the fact that nonverbal signs may have more than one meaning. A frown may signal displeasure or concentration. A stiff posture that usually means your co-worker is upset may today just be a sign of sore back muscles.

Misunderstandings are even more common when people communicate with people from other cultures or other countries. Knowing something about other cultures may help you realize that a subordinate who doesn't meet your eye may be showing respect rather than dishonesty. But it's impossible to memorize every meaning that every nonverbal sign has in every culture. And in a multicultural workforce, you may not know whether someone retains the meanings of his or her ancestors or has adopted the dominant US meanings. The best solution is to ask for clarification.

Networking

A much underappreciated skill in the business environment is **networking,** the ability to connect with many different kinds of people. Most of us can relate to the people in our immediate work group, although even there differences in ability to connect impact performance. But true networking is creating connections with still more people. It involves creating connections before they are needed, creating diverse connections in widely spread areas, knowing which people to turn to when you need additional expertise, knowing people outside the company.

Encyclopedia of Ethical Failure

"[Stephen] Epstein, the director of the Pentagon's Standards of Conduct Office, is mounting an ethical cleansing offensive from inside the corridors of power. His weapon of choice is the 'Encyclopedia of Ethical Failure,' a hit parade he publishes on the Internet to regale bureaucrats with tales of shenanigans and shockingly bad judgment that have shot down the careers of fellow public servants across government.

"Take the case of the Customs . . . officer who landed a government helicopter on his daughter's grade-school playground: Despite having a supervisor's ill-considered clearance to fly there, . . . the officer was fired for misusing government property. . . .

"Mr. Epstein combs through the press, legal records and internal government investigation reports for material. . . . He often finds humor in the missteps. Two Veterans Affairs bureaucrats were charged with overbilling the government and receiving kickbacks from a supplier. 'The product? . . . Red tape.'"

Quoted from Jonathan Kapp, "At the Pentagon, an 'Encyclopedia of Ethical Failure': Defense Official Catalogs Bureaucrats' Many Lapses; A Helicopter Visits a School," *Wall Street Journal*, May 14, 2008, A1.

Good networkers know who will help them cut through red tape, who can find an emergency supplier, who will take on extra work in a crisis. Informal conversations, about yesterday's game and Li's photography exhibit as well as what's happening at work, connect them with the **grapevine,** an informal source of company information. Participation in civic, school, religious, and professional organizations connects them to a larger environment. They attend conferences, trade shows, fundraisers, and community events. They use social networking sites such as LinkedIn (see technology section earlier in this chapter for more on electronic networks).

Networking becomes even more important as you climb the corporate ladder. Good managers interact with their employees continually, not just when they need something. They listen to lunchroom conversations; they chat with employees over coffee.

Much research shows that networking is crucial to job success. In *Emotional Intelligence*, Daniel Goleman tells of research in a division at Bell Labs to determine what made the star performers in the division. Everyone in the division had a high academic IQ, which meant that IQ was not a good predictor of job productivity (although academic knowledge and IQ are good predictors of success on earlier career ladder rungs). But networking skill was a good predictor. The stars put effort into developing their network, and they cultivated relationships in that network *before* they were needed.[90]

Goleman identifies three different kinds of workplace networks: conversational (who talks to whom), expertise (who can be turned to for advice), and trust (who can be trusted with sensitive information like gripes). Unsurprisingly, the stars of an organization are often heavily networked in all three varieties.[91]

Time Management

As your work environment becomes more complex, with multiple networks, responsibilities, and projects, good time management becomes crucial. Although much time management advice sounds like common sense, it is amazing the number of people who do not follow it.

Techniques

Probably the most important time management technique is to prioritize the demands on your time, and make sure you spend the majority of your time on the most important demands. If your career success depends on producing reports, news articles, and press releases about company business, then that is what you need to spend the majority of your time doing.

Randy Pausch, in his highly popular video and book *The Last Lecture*, makes this point about prioritizing most eloquently. His lecture is a moving reminder to make time for friends and family. His colleagues noted that he would regularly tell his students they could always make more money later, but they could never make more time.[92]

In *The 7 Habits of Highly Effective People*, Stephen Covey presents a useful time management matrix which sorts activities by urgency and importance; see Figure 4.5. Obviously we should focus our time on important activities, but Covey also advises putting significant time into quadrant II, which he calls the heart of effective management. Quadrant II activities include networking, planning, and preparing.[93]

These are some other common tips for time management:

- Keep lists—both daily and long term. Prioritize items on your list.
- Ask yourself where you want to be in three or five years and work accordingly.

Figure 4.5   Stephen Covey's Time Management Matrix.
Covey advises putting significant time into quadrant II.

	Urgent	Not Urgent
Important	I ACTIVITIES: Crises Pressing problems Deadline-driven projects	II ACTIVITIES: Prevention, PC activities Relationship building Recognizing new opportunities Planning, recreation
Not Important	III ACTIVITIES: Interruptions, some calls Some mail, some reports Some meetings Proximate, pressing matters Popular activities	IV ACTIVITIES: Trivia, busy work Some mail Some phone calls Time wasters Pleasant activities

Source: Stephen R. Covey, *The 7 Habits of Highly Effective People: Restoring the Character* (New York: Free Press, 2004), 150–54. Reprinted with permission of the author.

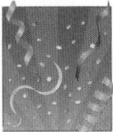

Santa Letters

Even letters to Santa Claus reflect the wider business environment.

During good times, children tend to ask for everything they see. But tougher economic times are reflected in children's letters. The letters talk of grim topics such as lost jobs and homes. They plead for basic necessities—rent money for mom, diapers for the baby, socks and warm clothing for everyone.

The Chicago main post office alone receives over 12,000 letters to Santa. Employees and volunteers sort them by gender and family size, then put them in the lobby where customers can select a child to help. Hundreds do so.

Adapted from Stacy St. Clair, "Letters to Santa Reflect Reality of Grim Economy: Kids' Requests for Toys Are Replaced with Wishes for Pajamas—or Rent Money for Their Parents," *Des Moines Register*, December 11, 2008, 3A.

- Do large, important tasks first, and then fill in around them with smaller tasks.
- Break large tasks into small ones. Remember that you do not always have to work sequentially. If you have been putting off a report because you cannot decide how to write its introduction, start with the conclusions or some other part that is easy for you to write.
- Find blocks of time: put your phone on answering machine, ignore e-mail, avoid the break room, move discretionary meetings. Put these blocks at your most productive time; save e-mail and meetings for less productive times.
- Avoid time sinks: some people, long phone conversations, constant e-mail checks.
- Decide at the end of today's work session what you will do in tomorrow's session, and set yourself up to do it. Find the necessary file; look up the specifications for that proposal.
- At end of week, evaluate what you didn't get done. Should you have done it for promotion, goodwill, ethics?

Multitasking

Many workers believe they can manage some of their time crunch problems by multitasking. Unfortunately, decades of research on the subject show that this is a false belief. It is particularly false when communication tasks are involved.[94] Just think of all the e-mails that get sent to unintended audiences while the writer is multitasking, or all the phone calls for which the caller, busy multitasking, forgets who is being called or why in the short time between dialing and pickup.

Research shows that when we think we are multitasking, we are really switching back and forth between tasks. And there is always a start-up delay involved in returning to a previous task, no matter how brief the delay. These delays may make it faster to do the tasks sequentially, in which case we will

probably do them better, too. In fact, some research shows it can take up to 50% longer to multitask.[95]

When we return to a task following an interruption—either from someone else, like a phone call, or from ourselves, like a visit to FaceBook—it may take us close to half an hour to get back into the original task.[96] Sometimes, we do not get back to the task correctly. Pilots who are interrupted in their preflight checklist may miss an item when they return to it. One crash, in which 153 people died, has been blamed on an error resulting from such an interruption.[97]

Your First Full-Time Job

Just like the step from high school to college, the step from college to your first full-time job brings changes that you must negotiate. The new business environment is exhilarating, with many opportunities, but it also contains pitfalls. As you go to being the new kid on the block yet again, remember all the coping strategies you have developed as a newbie in middle school, high school, and college.

- Reread all your materials on the organization, its competition, and the industry.
- Network with people in the field as well as your new colleagues.
- Talk to recent hires in the organization. Ask them what they found to be helpful advice when they were starting.
- Fit into the corporate culture by being observant. Watch what people wear, how they act, how they talk. Watch how they interact during meetings and in the break room. Look at the kinds of e-mails and letters people send. Discover who people go to when they need help.
- Use your breaks effectively. Stop by the coffee station, water cooler, or break room occasionally to plug into the grapevine.
- Find a successful person who is willing to mentor you. Even better, find a support network.
- Ask lots of questions. It may feel embarrassing, but it will feel even worse to still be ignorant several months down the road.
- Seek early opportunities for feedback. What you hear may not always be pleasant, but it will help you become a valued employee more quickly.
- Learn the jargon, but use it sparingly.
- Be pleasant and polite to everyone, including support personnel.
- Be punctual. Arrive for work and meetings on time.
- Be dependable. Do what you say you will do—and by the deadline.
- Be organized. Take a few minutes to plan your daily work. Keep track of papers and e-mails.
- Be resourceful. Few work projects will come to you with the detailed instructions provided by your professors. Think projects through. Ask for suggestions from trusted colleagues. Have a plan before you go to your boss with questions.
- Use technology professionally. Keep your cell phone on vibrate, or turn it off. Resist the temptation to send text messages during meetings. Don't visit inappropriate Web sites; remember that all computer activity can be tracked.
- Be discreet. Be careful what you say, and where you say it. Above all, be careful what you put in e-mails; remember those company files!

- Go the extra mile. Help out even when you are not asked. Put in extra hours when your help is needed.
- Take advantage of voluntary training opportunities.
- Document your work. Collect facts, figures, and documents. You will need this information for your performance reviews.
- Enjoy yourself. Enthusiasm for your new job and colleagues will have you part of the team in short order.

Summary of Key Points

- Technology is having a major impact on business communications. Hardware such as PDAs and software such as networking tools are enabling workers to be more efficient. The new technologies also raise new concerns about data security and privacy issues.
- Ten trends in business, government, and nonprofit organizations affect business and administrative communication: a focus on quality and customers' needs, entrepreneurship, diversity, globalization and outsourcing, balancing work and family, teamwork, job flexibility, the rapid rate of change, innovation, and concern for the environment.
- The economic news continues to create concern over lapses in business ethics. On the other hand, positive ethical efforts are also increasing.
- Corporate cultures range from informal to formal and impact such widely diverse areas as worker performance and sales.
- Interpersonal communication includes such areas as listening, conversational style, body language, and networking. Its importance in career success is receiving new recognition.
- Time management skills are also crucial to job success. Probably the most important time management technique is to prioritize the demands on your time, and make sure you spend the majority of your time on the most important demands.
- Decades of research on multitasking show that it does not increase job performance and may actually hinder it.

| **CHAPTER 4** | **Exercises and Problems** | *Go to www.mhhe.com/locker9e for additional Exercises and Problems.* |

4.1   Reviewing the Chapter

1. What technology changes are occurring in business? (LO1)
2. What are some electronic privacy issues that could affect you at your workplace? (LO1)
3. What are 10 trends in business communication? What do these trends mean for you? (LO2)
4. What are some positive ethical efforts that are getting attention? (LO3)
5. What are some ethical components of communication? (LO3)
6. What are some elements of corporate culture? How do they affect business? (LO4)
7. What are some ways to improve interpersonal communication? (LO5)
8. What are some communication signals you might receive from specific body language cues? (LO5)
9. What are some ways to manage your time more efficiently? (LO6)
10. What are some tips to help you succeed at your first full-time job? (LO7)

4.2   Describing the Role of Technology Where You Work

Analyze the role of technology in an organization where you—or a friend or family member—have worked.

- What kinds of communication technology do you use most?
- What are some of the newest communication technologies introduced there?
- What kinds of technology upgrades do you wish would be made?
- Are certain kinds of technology used for certain situations? (for instance, are layoffs announced face-to-face or by e-mail?)

- What kinds of data security measures are in force?
- Has anyone there gotten in trouble for misuse of technology?

As your instructor directs,

a.   Share your information in small groups.
b.   Present your group findings to your classmates.
c.   Post your information online for your classmates.

4.3   Following Trends in Business Communication

Pick three of the trends discussed in this chapter and explain how they have impacted business communications in an organization where you—or a friend or family member—have worked.

As your instructor directs,

a.   Share your information in small groups.

b.   Present your group findings to your classmates.
c.   Post your information online for your classmates.

4.4   Analyzing a Trend

The paragraphs on "Concern for the Environment" in this chapter are part of the "Trends" section. Unlike business ethics, environmental concern was not considered to have a significant role in the national culture, partly because so many critics claim the movement is mostly for publicity. Do you agree with this placement? Why or why not?

Write your opinions down in a paragraph or two. In small groups, share your opinions, then take a stand as a group. As a group, write a memo to share with your classmates.

4.5   Making Ethical Choices

Indicate whether you consider each of the following actions ethical, unethical, or a gray area. Which of the actions would you do? Which would you feel uncomfortable doing? Which would you refuse to do?

Discuss your answers with a small group of classmates. In what ways did knowing you would share with a group change your answers?

1.   Taking home office supplies (e.g., pens, markers, calculators, etc.) for personal use.
2.   Inflating your evaluation of a subordinate because you know that only people ranked *excellent* will get pay raises.
3.   Making personal long-distance calls on the company phone.

4.   Writing a feasibility report about a new product and de-emphasizing test results that show it could cause cancer.
5.   Coming in to the office in the evening to use the company's word processor and computer for personal projects.
6.   Designing an ad campaign for a cigarette brand.
7.   Working as an accountant for a company that makes or advertises cigarettes.
8.   Working as a manager in a company that exploits its nonunionized hourly workers.
9.   Writing copy for a company's annual report hiding or minimizing the fact that the company pollutes the environment.

10. "Padding" your expense account by putting on it charges you did not pay for.
11. Writing a subscription letter for a sex magazine that glamorizes rape, violence, and sadism.
12. Doing the taxes of a client who publishes a sex magazine that glamorizes rape, violence, and sadism.
13. Telling a job candidate that the company "usually" grants cost-of-living raises every six months, even though you know that the company is losing money and plans to cancel cost-of-living raises for the next year.
14. Laughing at the racist or sexist jokes a client makes, even though you find them offensive.
15. Reading the *Wall Street Journal* on company time.

4.6   Analyzing Philanthropic Web Sites

Working in small groups, go to the Web sites of some of the large philanthropic organizations such as the Gates Foundation, the (RED) campaign, Google.org, or the Clinton Global Initiative. What commonalities do you see? Which aspects do you like best? If you were a rich multibillionaire who was going to leave a billion dollars to a philanthropy, which one would you choose? Why? Write your findings and answers to these questions in a memo to share with your class.

4.7   Analyzing Pro Bono Work

Pro bono legal work, free legal work for those in need, has long been a law tradition. But now some elite firms are so eager for pro bono work—to boost their image or ranking, to get high-profile cases, and to attract top law students—that they are paying for it. For instance, Lawyers without Borders requires a "donation" of at least $7,500 to work on its cases. But some of those cases are very high profile—such as helping reform Liberia's legal system.*

What do you think of Lawyers without Borders' system of charging law firms to do pro bono work?

What do you think of law firms that do pro bono work just to boost their image or ranking? Does their motivation matter?

When law firms pay to work on high-profile cases, what happens to welfare cases, landlord–tenant disputes, or divorce cases among poorer couples?

Discuss your answers in small groups.

*Source: Ashby Jones, "Law Firms Willing to Pay to Work for Nothing," *Wall Street Journal*, June 19, 2007, B1, B5.

4.8   Analyzing a Letter

Dr. Joseph Biederman, Professor of Psychiatry at Harvard Medical School and Chief of Clinical and Research Programs in Pediatric Psychopharmacology and Adult ADHD, wrote a letter to the editor of the *Wall Street Journal* that appeared December 19, 2008, on page A16. The letter reputes the claim that he had a significant relationship with pharmaceutical manufacturers. Find the letter in your library's electronic copy of the *Wall Street Journal*. (In ProQuest, the letter is listed under the title "I was Doing the Right Thing." Authors of letters to the editor are listed as Anonymous in ProQuest.)

For a memo to your instructor, analyze the letter.

- What was your first impression?
- Is the letter convincing to you?
- What part makes you most sympathetic to the doctor?
- Is there any part that works against the doctor?
- Who are the audiences?
- What is the purpose of the letter?

After you analyze the letter as it is, look up some articles about Dr. Biederman. Three that appeared in the *Wall Street Journal*, including the one referenced in the letter, are

- David Armstrong, "Harvard Researchers Fail To Report Drug Payments," *Wall Street Journal*, June 9, 2008, A2.
- David Armstrong and Alicia Mundy, "J&J Emails Raise Issues of Risperdal Promotion," *Wall Street Journal*, November 25, 2008, B1.
- Jennifer Levitz, "Drug Researcher Agrees to Curb Role," *Wall Street Journal*, December 31, 2008, B3.

Do these articles change your opinion of the letter? Why?

Include both parts of your analysis, of the letter itself and the impact of the articles, in a memo to your instructor.

4.9   Analyzing Corporate Culture

Some businesses are deciding not to hire people with visible body art. Do you think such policies are allowable expressions of corporate culture, or are they a form of discrimination? Discuss your answers in small groups.

4.10   Analyzing Corporate Culture

Go to *Fortune*'s Top 100 Companies to Work For Web site: http://money.cnn.com/magazines/fortune/bestcompanies/

Look up six companies you find interesting. What are unique features of their corporate culture? What features seem to be common with many companies? Which features did you find particularly appealing? Write up your findings in a memo for your instructor.

4.11   Analyzing an Organization's Culture

QuickenLoans.com, the largest online lender, was ranked the second-best company to work for by *Fortune* magazine in 2008. Sticking with "plain vanilla loans" and traditional mortgage financing, QuickenLoans.com avoided being a part of the 2008 subprime mortgage crisis. This organization also encourages its workers to think big and then put those ideas into practice.

- Visit the company's Web site at https://www.quickenloans.com/about/careers.
- What does the question to potential employees, "Are you the DIFF" mean? Why has QuickenLoans.com adopted language that is "anticorporate culture"? What other examples of this attitude can you find on the page?
- Identify a company that you would like to work for or that is well-known in your field of study. Visit the company's Web site and research its corporate culture.
- What information are you able to learn about your target company from its Web site text?

- What types of images does the company use on its Web site? Do these support the information it uses to describe itself and its culture?
- What type of organizational structure does your target company use?
- What other information is available about the culture at your target company?

To find information about a company's culture, refer to fastcompany.com, or businessweek.com. You can also type the company name and "opinion" into a search engine to find unofficial reports of corporate culture.

As your instructor directs,

a. Present your answers in an oral presentation to the class.

b. Present your answers in a memo to your instructor.

c. Share your answers with a small group of students and write a joint memo reporting the similarities and differences you found.

4.12   Analyzing Body Language

Go to a location such as your campus or city library where you can watch people at work and rest. Spend a half hour observing examples of body language around you. Make sure your half hour includes examples of at least one group at work, individuals at work, and individuals relaxing.

- What were some interesting examples of body language you noted?
- What were some common features of body language?

- Did you see any unique body language?
- Could you make assumptions about group relations based on the body language you saw exhibited by members of the group?
- How did the body language of individuals who were relaxing differ from that of the group members?

Write up your findings in a memo for your instructor.

4.13 Analyzing Your Time Management

For two days, write down exactly how you spend your time. Be specific. Don't just say "two hours studying." Instead, note how long you spent on each item of study (e.g., 15 min reviewing underlinings in sociology chapter, 20 min reviewing class notes, an hour and 20 min reading accounting chapter). Include time spent on items such as grooming, eating, talking with friends (both in person and on phone), watching television, and sleeping.

Now analyze your time record. Does anything surprise you? How much time did you spend studying? Is it enough? Did you spend more time studying your most important subjects? Your hardest subjects? Did you spend time on projects that are due later in the term? Did you spend time on health-related items? Do you see items on which you spent too much time? Too little time? Did you spend any time on items that would fit in Covey's quadrant II (see page 115)?

As your instructor directs,

a. Share your findings in small groups.

b. Write up your findings in a memo for your instructor.

4.14 Starting a New Job

Think back to your first weeks on a new job. What were some behaviors that helped you? Did you have a mentor? How did you start networking? If you had those weeks to do over, what would you do differently?

Share your ideas in small groups.

4.15 Analyzing the Business Environment Where You Work

In a memo to your instructor, describe and analyze the business environment at an organization where you have worked. Use this chapter as a guide for content. What aspects of the environment did you like? Dislike? What aspects helped your job performance? What aspects hindered your job performance?

4.16 Introducing *Kaizen* to All-Weather

The three managers in HR, Caleb, Miguel, and Erin, have received the same e-mail note from the secretary in the department:

Doug wants to see you for a meeting at 11 AM in the small conference room. Doug has asked that you bring your deputies along.

The small conference room has enough space for about a dozen people, a projection screen, and a flip chart. Caleb and Tanner, Miguel and Linda, and Erin and Rudy are sitting in pairs around the mahogany table in the room. Kioni has found a chair near the door, behind Erin and Rudy, to get a better view of the screen should there be a presentation.

Doug begins by asking if anyone knows what the term *Kaizen* means. "Of course," Rudy says. "It must be some kind of Buddhist *Zen*. Are we opening offices in East Asia now?" Everyone except Erin laughs.

Doug explains that *Kaizen* is a Japanese strategy focusing on problem solving through teamwork. "We're going to practice *Kaizen* at All-Weather," Doug says, writing the term on the flip chart. Doug explains that he saw the technique being used effectively at a European door and window manufacturer's plant in Denmark.

"But we hardly know what it is," Tanner says, glancing around to see if others feel the same way.

"I'm inviting two management professors from Tokyo's Hitotsubashi University to offer training workshops on *Kaizen*," Doug says, to a round of applause from his team. "Dr. Tanizaki and Dr. Kawabata, they're two of the best experts on the subject," Doug goes on to say, pronouncing the names of the professors slowly and then writing them on the flip chart.

"Doug, can you give us an example of how *Kaizen* might help?" Linda asks, prompting a chorus from the gathered group of her given nickname, "The Practical One."

"Sure, Linda," Doug says. "Let's look at some problems that our products face. Take weatherstrips on doors, for example. Using *Kaizen*, a team consisting of personnel from marketing, manufacturing, and procurement may find a material or a design that is more successful in preventing water or air leakage due to damaged weatherstripping," Doug says, pausing to see if there is a follow-up question from Linda.

"Another example is vinyl claddings on windows. How do we prevent or minimize their discoloration? Again, the problem will probably require a team from manufacturing, marketing, and procurement working together. Not only can *Kaizen* help us with end-product design, it can also help us eliminate wasteful elements in a production process, a financial report, or a sales report. There are many such small but potentially important improvements that *Kaizen* might help us achieve." Linda is more than satisfied with Doug's answer. She admires Doug's ability to listen to a question from a junior employee and answer it as fully as he can.

"Do we introduce *Kaizen* in the entire company at once or start with a few departments?" Tanner asks. Caleb looks at him approvingly.

"What do you all think?" Doug says.

"I think we go ahead and introduce it in every department at the headquarters. After all, once we introduce the concept, our role will be limited to giving support," Caleb says, giving a wink to Miguel who smiles in return.

"I agree," Erin says. "Once there's a discussion here in the headquarters, we'll know how to promote it to plants and field offices." Erin pictures herself taking a plane to Tokyo. She has long wanted to experience *onsen*, Japanese hot spring baths.

"Also, by not promoting it in headquarters, plants, and field offices at the same time, we may not have to put out too many fires at once," Miguel says, using a metaphor for troubleshooting with which the HR Department is all too familiar.

"I agree with you all. My question then is, how do we begin?" Doug asks, sitting down on his chair at last. "Give a presentation? Send a memo, an e-mail, what?"

"I think a memo signed by you will be the best," Caleb says, looking at Erin and Miguel, who seem to concur.

"Go ahead and draft a memo, Caleb," Doug says, standing up.

Everyone except Doug stays behind in the room to help Caleb draft the memo, which will be addressed to All-Weather's president, VPs (Marketing, Manufacturing, Finance, Exports, Procurement, IT), and managers based in the company headquarters and plants. Kioni follows Doug out so he can give her some reading material on *Kaizen* that the group can use in drafting the memo.

Based on the information given above and your reading of Chapter 4, complete the following questions and tasks:

- How does teamwork help organizations? Support your answer with examples from actual organizations you may have worked in or are working in. What communication challenges does teamwork pose? How might one prepare for these challenges in a business communication course?

- In what ways is teamwork connected to other current trends in business and administrative communication that the chapter discusses? For example, video conferencing connects teamwork with technology, diversity, and globalization. Find other examples where current trends in business and administrative communication seem to converge.

- Conduct some Internet or library research on the concept of *Kaizen*. How does this technique help business and other types of organizations? What communication challenges and opportunities does the technique create?

- Help Caleb and the group draft the memo for Doug. Some questions to consider: How will you address its multiple audiences, which include the president, VPs (Marketing, Manufacturing, Finance, Exports, Procurement, IT), and managers based in the company headquarters and plants? What should be the primary purpose of the memo? The secondary purpose? What type of and how much information on *Kaizen* should be included in the memo?

CHAPTER 5

Communicating across Cultures

Chapter Outline

Global Business
- Local Culture Adaptations
- International Career Experience

Diversity in North America

Ways to Look at Culture

Values, Beliefs, and Practices

Nonverbal Communication
- Body Language
- Touch
- Space

- Time
- Other Nonverbal Symbols

Oral Communication
- Understatement and Exaggeration
- Compliments

Writing to International Audiences

Learning More about International Business Communication

Summary of Key Points

Cross-Cultural Collaboration Gone Wrong

Before the merger, the economic benefit of the collaboration was the primary issue, but that changed when the employees from the two companies started working with each other and the cultural differences began to arise. For example, the German workers of Daimler-Benz were used to daily, company-sanctioned beer breaks while the American workers worried that alcohol consumption during work would lead to accidents and legal suits.

In addition, the German professionals were used to a formal, hierarchical structure in the organization and formal business attire. A corporate communications director from Germany observed, "We noticed right away that the American executives were more casually dressed. . . . You would never see anyone here [in the German plant] without a tie on, even if they came in on a Saturday."

Differences in the corporate lifestyle later led to questions as to who got the better end of the deal. US assembly line workers earned more wages per hour than their German counterparts. However, the German workers, who received a six-week annual vacation, fully paid health care and education, and a triennial soul-soothing spa break, undoubtedly had a better benefits package. In addition, while the Daimler plant produced 850,000 vehicles a year with 120,000 employees, Chrysler manufactured 3 million with approximately the same number of employees. These cultural differences eventually overshadowed the positives of this merger.

However, merger companies are usually hesitant to correlate their losses to breakdown in intercultural communication. Studies show that the relation between cultural differences and coordination breakdown is undervalued; when compaines from different cultures face difficulties in their collaborative process, they attribute the loss of productivity to the performance of the other company rather than work on the challenges caused by their cultural differences.

When Daimler-Benz and Chrysler proposed a $36 billion merger in 1998, both parties thought it was a good plan, one that could give them a much-needed economic boost. There was no seeming conflict, no competition between the companies—while Chrysler manufactured cars for the masses, Daimler-Benz catered to the elite population.

The merger was supposed to strengthen each other's place in the automotive market. But in 2007, a third party Cerberus Capital Management bought Daimler-Chrysler for just $7.4 billion. What went wrong?

The cultural differences reflected in the practices of the two companies were a significant factor.

"What went wrong? The cultural differences reflected in the practices of the two companies were a significant factor."

Sources: Associated Press, "A Chronology in the Takeover Saga of Global Automaker DaimlerChrysler AG," *Associated Press Archive,* May 14, 2007; Roberto A. Weber and Colin F. Camerer, "Cultural Conflict and Merger Failure: An Experimental Approach," *Management Science* 49, no. 4 (2003); and Carol Williams, "Steering around Culture Clashes," *Los Angeles Times,* January 17, 1999, C1.

Learning Objectives

After studying this chapter, you will know:

1 Why global business is important.

2 Why diversity is becoming more important.

3 How our values and beliefs affect our responses to other people.

4 How nonverbal communication impacts cross-cultural communications.

5 How to adapt oral communication for cross-cultural communications.

6 How to adapt written communications for international audiences.

Microsoft in China

To succeed in China, Microsoft had to drastically alter its business practices.

Probably the most obvious change was pricing strategy. Microsoft found many Chinese using its expensive software—for free, thanks to pirated versions. Bill Gates argued that if the Chinese were going to pirate software, he wanted it to be Microsoft's. Accepting the piracy turned out to be a smart move; about 90% of China's 120 million PCs use Windows. And Microsoft has dropped the price for legal copies; packages of Windows and Office sell for $3 for Chinese students.

Microsoft also had to learn how to collaborate with the Chinese government instead of fighting it. It offered China the right to substitute some of its own software in the Windows source code so that sensitive political and military offices can install their own cryptography. In return, the government is requiring central and provincial governments to begin using legal software.

Adapted from David Kirkpatrick, "How Microsoft Conquered China," *Fortune*, July 23, 2007, 78–84.

Our values, priorities, and practices are shaped by the culture in which we grow up. Understanding other cultures is crucial if you want to sell your products to other cultures in our country, sell to other countries, manage an international plant or office, or work in this country for a multinational company headquartered in another country.

The successful intercultural communicator is

- Aware of the values, beliefs, and practices in other cultures.
- Sensitive to differences among individuals within a culture.
- Aware that his or her preferred values and behaviors are influenced by culture and are not necessarily "right."
- Sensitive to verbal and nonverbal behavior.
- Flexible and open to change.

The first step in understanding another culture is to realize that it may do things very differently, and that the difference is not bad or inferior. The second step is understanding that people within a single culture differ.

When pushed too far, the kinds of differences summarized in this chapter can turn into stereotypes, which can be just as damaging as ignorance. Psychologists have shown that stereotypes have serious consequences and that they come into play even when we don't want them to. Asking African American students to identify their race before answering questions taken from the Graduate Record Examination, the standardized test used for admission to graduate schools, cut in half the number of items they got right. Similarly, asking students to identify their sex at the beginning of Advanced Placement (AP) calculus tests, used to give high school students college credits, lowered the scores of women. If the sex question were moved to the end of the test, about 5% more women would receive AP credit.[1]

Don't try to memorize the material in this chapter as a rigid set of rules. Instead, use the examples to get a sense for the kinds of things that differ from one culture to another. Test these generalizations against your experience. When in doubt, ask.

Global Business

As we saw in Chapter 4, exports are essential both to the success of individual businesses and to a country's economy as a whole. Most major businesses operate globally, and an increasing share of profits comes from outside the headquarters country:

- McDonald's has restaurants in over 100 countries and earns more than 66% of its income outside the United States.
- 3M has 63% of its sales internationally.
- Procter & Gamble has $20 billion of sales in developing countries.
- Unilever and Colgate-Palmolive have 40% of their business in developing countries.
- Starbucks is expanding into Brazil, Egypt, and Russia, giving it sales in 40 countries. Eventually the company plans to have half its stores outside the United States.
- Wal-Mart's international stores earn "only" 20% of the company's total sales. However, if the international operations were an independent chain, it would be the world's fourth-largest retailer.[2]

Many companies—even service businesses—depend on vendors or operations in other countries. These international operations help companies spend more time with customers, focus more on innovation, and fund projects that otherwise would have been unaffordable. IBM has 43,000 employees in India staffing data centers, call centers, software development, and research. Over a billion dollars of finance and accounting jobs were performed by India's Genpact for Wachovia Corporation. Eli Lilly does 20% of its chemistry work in China and is performing clinical trials in Brazil, Russia, China, and India.[3]

Local Culture Adaptations

As they expand globally, US retailers are catering to local tastes and customs. When expanding to China, Wal-Mart enraged consumers when they sold dead fish and meat packaged in Styrofoam, which shoppers saw as old merchandise. Wal-Mart quickly learned to compensate by leaving meat uncovered and installing fish tanks to sell live fish. They also sell live tortoises and snakes; Johnson's Baby Oil is stocked next to moisturizers containing sheep placenta, a native wrinkle "cure." Wal-Mart lures customers on foot or bikes with free shuttle buses and home deliveries for large items. Perhaps the biggest change is Wal-Mart's acceptance of organized labor in China; in July 2006 it accepted its first union ever into its stores.

Tommy Hilfiger made different changes as it opened its high-end stores in Europe. The company's signature cotton knit sweaters don't sell well in Europe, where men prefer wool sweaters, so Hilfiger began offering lamb's wool sweaters. Underwear packages received more seductive pictures. Baggy jeans, popular in the United States, were replaced with slimmer silhouettes to cater to European tastes.[4]

International Career Experience

When plants, stores, and offices move overseas, people follow—top executives as well migrant workers. After the 2000 dot-com crash, many companies outsourced departments such as software development, data analysis, and research. Now top executives are also being relocated. Cisco Systems, a 50,000-person employer, seeks to locate 20% of senior managers at their Globalization Center in Bangalore, India, by 2010. The executives will represent the best talent from San Jose, California, and Bangalore. IBM currently has 150 executives working and living overseas including 35 in India and 89 in China. At Procter & Gamble, 17 of the top 30 executives have had international assignments. Such assignments give companies a pool of executives with intercultural skills and global awareness.[5]

For their own careers, managers often find they need international experience if they want top-level jobs. A survey of multinational companies by Mercer Human Resource Consulting found that firms were increasing international

Communicating with Subsistence Consumers

Subsistence consumers may earn little money, but they still need to buy necessities. Corporations are learning how best to communicate with them.

Many of them lack basic reading skills, so visual cues are important. Cues such as store layout, package design, and brand logos need to remain consistent for them. Many buy products that look attractive because of packaging colors or pictures. They also tend to buy only brands they recognize by appearance, so changes in colors or visual design have negative impacts.

To better serve these customers, stores need to

- Price products in whole or half numbers, and display these prices graphically— such as a picture of the money needed to buy the product.
- Display pictures of product categories, so shoppers can find the goods they need.
- Train store personnel to form relationships with consumers and offer friendly, individualized assistance.

Adapted from Jose Antonio Rosa, Madhubalan Viswanathan, and Julie A. Ruth, "Emerging Lessons: For Multinational Companies, Understanding the Needs of Poorer Consumers Can Be Profitable and Socially Responsible," *Wall Street Journal*, October 20, 2008, R12.

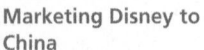

Marketing Disney to China

Only six months after Hong Kong Disneyland opened, Disney officials were scrambling to understand why attendance was so low at the new park. They turned for answers to Chinese travel agents who book tours. Some of these agents believed Disney officials had not tried to understand the local market and Chinese culture.

After the disappointing start at the Hong Kong park, Disney officials were anxious to learn and ready to make changes. Using the travel industry feedback and other market research, Disney developed a new advertising campaign. Original ads had featured an aerial view of the park; new TV spots focused on people and showed guests riding attractions. A new print ad featuring a grandmother, mother, and daughter showed that Disneyland is a place where families can have fun together.

Disney also worked to make visitors more comfortable inside the park. At an attraction offered in three different languages, guests gravitated toward the shortest line—usually the line for English-speaking guests. Now, three separate signs clearly mark which language will be used to communicate with guests in that line. Greater use of Mandarin-speaking guides and materials helps guests better enjoy shows and attractions. Also, additional seating was added in dining areas because Chinese diners take longer to eat than do Americans. Disney is hoping such changes will attract more guests to the Hong Kong park.

Source: Merissa Marr and Geoffrey A. Fowler, "Chinese Lessons for Disney," *Wall Street Journal*, June 12, 2006, B1, B5.

What cultural barriers did Disney need to overcome to help Hong Kong Disneyland succeed? See sidebar on this page.

assignments, and that more of those assignments were going to women. Cross-cultural training for the assignments was provided by 60% of the companies, but once abroad employees generally had to fend for themselves, including finding their own housing.[6]

The executives join a host of migrant workers already abroad. Migrant workers benefit the economies of both host and home countries. The money sent home by expatriate workers, more than $160 billion a year, is far more than the total aid spent by the developed world for developing countries (about $100 billion a year). Thus the money sent home is one of the major drivers of international development. India and China provide one-quarter of the global migrant population, and their contributions are significant. Indian managers and accountants are increasingly running businesses in the Gulf. The Chinese are a particularly strong presence in Africa.[7]

Thomas Friedman, Pulitzer Prize author and *New York Times* columnist, uses the metaphor of a flat world to describe the increasing globalization. In *The World Is Flat: A Brief History of the Twenty-First Century*, he says,

> What the flattening of the world means is that we are now connecting all the knowledge centers on the planet together into a single global network, which—if politics and terrorism do not get in the way—could usher in an amazing era of prosperity, innovation, and collaboration, by companies, communities, and individuals.[8]

Diversity in North America

Even if you stay in the United States and Canada, you'll work with people whose backgrounds differ from yours. Residents of small towns and rural areas may have different notions of friendliness than do people from big cities. Californians may talk and dress differently than people in the Midwest. The cultural icons that resonate for baby boomers may mean little to members of Generation Y. For many workers, local diversity has become as important as international diversity.

The last two decades have seen a growing emphasis on diversity. This diversity comes from many sources:

- Gender.
- Race and ethnicity.
- Regional and national origin.
- Social class.

- Religion.
- Age.
- Sexual orientation.
- Physical ability.

Many young Americans are already multicultural. According to 2005 US census figures, almost 40% of Americans aged 15 to 24 are African American, Latino, Asian, or Native American.[9] Some of them are immigrants or descendants of immigrants. In recent years, the largest numbers of immigrants to the United States have come from Mexico, India, China, Philippines, Cuba, Vietnam, Dominican Republic, and Korea.[10] In 2002 Latinos became the largest minority group in the United States. The US Census Bureau predicts that by 2042, the non-Hispanic white population will be less than 50% of the country's total population.[11] The change is occurring rapidly: in 10% of US counties, whites are already in the minority.[12]

Bilingual Canada has long compared the diversity of its people to a mosaic. But now immigrants from Italy, Greece, and Hong Kong add their voices to the medley of French, English, and Inuit. Radio station CHIN in Toronto broadcasts in 32 languages.[13]

According to 2000 US census figures, about 4.6 million people identified themselves as belonging to more than one race.[14] US Census figures also show that 19.7% of the population nationally and 42.5% in California speak a language other than English at home.[15] In cities such as Los Angeles and San Jose, over half the population speaks a language other than English at home; in El Paso, that percentage is 74.3%.[16]

Faced with these figures, organizations are making special efforts to diversify their workforces. Nike recruits minority students on college campuses and offers them summer internships; Clorox partners with professional organizations like the National Black M.B.A. Association. Microsoft has 44 different diversity advisory councils (DACs). The oldest, BAM—Blacks at Microsoft—has 500 members. Four are for employees with disabilities; still others are for employees from specific international regions. In addition to supporting the group members, DACs help recruit and integrate new employees and help Microsoft adapt their communications and products for diverse segments of the global economy.[17]

These companies are smart; new evidence shows that diversity can improve business. Research analyzing the relationship between diversity levels and business performance of 250 US businesses found a correlation between diversity and business success; companies with high levels of racial and ethic minorities have the highest profits, the highest market shares, and highest number of customers. On the other hand, organizations with low levels of diversity have the lowest profits, the lowest market shares, and the lowest number of customers.[18]

Ways to Look at Culture

Each of us grows up in a **culture** that provides patterns of acceptable behavior and belief. We may not be aware of the most basic features of our own culture until we come into contact with people who do things differently. In India, children might be expected to touch the bare feet of elders to show respect, but in the United States such touching would be inappropriate.[19]

As anthropologist Edward Hall first described, we can categorize cultures as high-context or low-context. In **high-context cultures**, most of the information is inferred from the social relationships of the people and the context of a message; little is explicitly conveyed. Chinese, Japanese, Arabic, and Latin American cultures are high-context. In **low-context cultures**, context is less important; most information is explicitly spelled out. German, Scandinavian, and North American cultures are low-context.

High- and low-context cultures value different kinds of communication and have different attitudes toward oral and written communication. As Figure 5.1 shows, low-context cultures like those of the United States favor direct approaches and may see indirectness as dishonest or manipulative. The written word is seen as more important than oral statements, so contracts are binding

Beyond Stereotypes

Learning about different cultures is important for understanding the different kinds of people we work with. However, leadership coaches Keith Caver and Ancella Livers caution that people are individuals, not just representatives of a cultural group. Based on their work with African American executives and middle managers, Caver and Livers have found that coworkers sometimes treat these individuals first as representatives of black culture, and only second as talented and experienced managers.

As an example, Caver and Livers cite the all-too-common situation of a newly hired black manager who participates in a management development activity. The new manager is prepared to answer questions about her area of business expertise, but the only questions directed toward her are about "diversity." African American clients of Caver and Livers have complained that they are often called upon to interpret the behavior of famous black Americans such as Clarence Thomas or Jesse Jackson, and they wonder whether their white colleagues would feel their race qualifies them to interpret the deeds of famous white Americans.

In this example, stereotypes make well-intentioned efforts at communication offensive. To avoid such offense, consider not only culture, but also people's individual qualities and their roles and experiences. A person who communicates one way in the role of son or daughter may communicate very differently as engineer or client.

Adapted from Keith A. Caver and Ancella B. Livers, "Dear White Boss," *Harvard Business Review* 80, no. 11 (November 2002), 76–81.

Figure 5.1   Views of Communication in High- and Low-Context Cultures

	High-context (Examples: Japan, Saudi Arabia)	Low-context (Examples: Germany, North America)
Preferred communication strategy	Indirectness, politeness, ambiguity	Directness, confrontation, clarity
Reliance on words to communicate	Low	High
Reliance on nonverbal signs to communicate	High	Low
Importance of relationships	High	Low
Importance of written word	Low	High
Agreements made in writing	Not binding	Binding
Agreements made orally	Binding	Not binding
Attention to detail	Low	High

Source: Robert T. Moran, Philip R. Harris, and Sarah V. Moran, *Managing Cultural Differences: Global Leadership Strategies for the 21st Century,* 7th ed. (Boston: Elsevier, 2007), 49–52.

Does the Glass Ceiling Exist?

"The news: Men and women have different views on whether women face a 'glass ceiling' in financial professions, according to a survey of 363 financial executives by *CFO* magazine.

"The numbers: In the survey, 40% of women said they perceive limits to how far women can rise; only 10% of men believe women face a glass ceiling.

"The differences: Two-thirds of women, 66%, said women face one or more obstacles to success in finance, such as a lack of operational experience or an inability to negotiate effectively. But only 38% of men said women face such difficulties. Five times as many women as men said female executives have more trouble gaining the respect and trust of the CEO.

"The background: Few women hold top financial jobs in major U.S. corporations, even though women earn more undergraduate business degrees than men. Just 7% of Fortune 500 companies have female CFOs, according to recruiters Heidrick & Struggles International Inc."

Quoted from Jaclyne Badal, "Surveying the Field: Cracking the Glass Ceiling," *Wall Street Journal,* June 19, 2006, B3.

but promises may be broken. Details matter. Business communication practices in the United States reflect these low-context preferences.

The discussion that follows focuses on national and regional cultures. But business communication is also influenced by the organizational culture and by personal culture, such as gender, race and ethnicity, social class, and so forth. As Figure 5.2 suggests, all of these intersect to determine what kind of communication is needed in a given situation. Sometimes one kind of culture may be more important than another. For example, in a study of aerospace engineers in Europe, Asia, and the United States, researchers found that the similarities of the professional discourse community outweighed differences in national cultures.[20]

Values, Beliefs, and Practices

Values and beliefs, often unconscious, affect our response to people and situations. Most North Americans, for example, value "fairness." "You're not playing fair" is a sharp criticism calling for changed behavior. In some countries, however, people expect certain groups to receive preferential treatment. Many people in the United States value individualism. Other countries may value

Figure 5.2   National Culture, Organizational Culture, and Personal Culture Overlap

Figure 5.3 A Sampling of International Holidays

Holiday	Date	Celebrated in	Commemorates
Chinese New Year (Spring Festival)	January or February (date varies)	Countries with Chinese residents	Beginning of lunar new year
Independence Day	March 6	Ghana	1957 independence from Great Britain
St. Patrick's Day	March 17	Ireland	Ireland's patron saint
Cinco de Mayo	May 5	Mexico	1867 victory over the French
St. Jean-Baptiste Day	June 24	Québec province of Canada	Québec's national holiday
Canada Day	July 1	Canada	1867 proclamation of Canada's status as dominion
Bastille Day	July 14	France	1789 fall of the Bastille prison during the French Revolution
Ramadan	Ninth month of lunar year	Countries with Muslim residents	Atonement; fasting from sunup to sundown
Respect for the Aged Day	September 15	Japan	Respect for elderly relatives and friends
Chun Ben	Last week of September	Cambodia, other Buddhist countries	The dead and actions for one's salvation
Yom Kippur	September or October (dates vary)	Countries with Jewish residents	Day of atonement
Diwali	October or November	Countries with Hindu residents	Festival of lights celebrating renewal of life
Guy Fawkes Day	November 5	England	Capture of Guy Fawkes, who plotted to blow up Parliament
Christmas	December 25	Countries with Christian residents	Birth of Jesus
Boxing Day	December 26	British Commonwealth	Tradition of presenting small boxed gifts to service workers

the group. Japan's traditional culture emphasized the group, but there is evidence that this cultural value is changing.

Religion also affects business communication and business life. Observant Muslims, Jews, and Christians observe days of rest and prayer on Friday, Saturday, and Sunday, respectively. During the holy month of Ramadan, Muslims fast from sunup to sundown; scheduling a business luncheon with a Muslim colleague during Ramadan would be inappropriate. A sampling of international holidays, including Ramadan, appears in Figure 5.3.

Even everyday practices differ from culture to culture. North Americans and Europeans put the family name last; Asians put it first. North American and European printing moves from top to bottom and from left to right; Arabic reads from right to left, but still from top to bottom. The Chinese language is traditionally written using characters signifying ideas, rather than letters signifying sounds. Opening the Internet to Chinese readers has been challenging because of the need to use the Chinese characters. Internet portal Yahoo

HBR on Chinese versus Russian Entrepreneurs

As business opportunities continue to expand in China and Russia, the *Harvard Business Review* offers this summary of the differences between entrepreneurs in the two countries:

- Chinese tend to think concretely and appreciate harmonious and balanced ideas. Russians tend to think abstractly and tolerate contradictory positions.

- Chinese networks tend to be small and close knit: family, friends, and colleagues. Russia's institutional chaos has hastened the formation of new, loosely knit networks.

- Members of Chinese networks exhibit higher levels of trust, Russians lower levels.

Because of these characteristics, Chinese networks are harder to enter than the more fluid Russian networks. However, once you are in, you will be more trusted in a Chinese network than in a Russian one.

However, HBR notes that Americans will always be expected to be different and that trying too hard to fit in will undermine trust.

Adapted from Bat Batjargal, "The Difference between Chinese and Russian Entrepreneurs," *Harvard Business Review* 86, no. 10 (2008): 32.

Living and working in another country require being sensitive to cultural beliefs and practices. The Japanese holiday Shichi-go-san (seven-five-three) is celebrated on November 15th when boys (ages 3 and 5) and girls (ages 3 and 7) are taken by their parents to a Shinto shrine to give thanks for their health and growth, and to pray for their future. Shichi-go-san dates back to ancient times when the families of samurai and noblemen would mark milestones in their children's growth.

gained access to the Chinese market by purchasing Zhou Hongyi's keyword-search firm called 3721 (the name represents ease of use, in the sense of being as easy as "3 times 7 equals 21"). Companies pay 3721 to register their Chinese names as keywords.[21]

In today's electronically connected world, cultural practices can change swiftly. For instance, in China, where age has traditionally been revered, few political or business leaders turn gray, even those who are in their fifties or sixties. Workers are also becoming less group oriented and more individualistic.[22] In such fluid contexts, communication becomes even more important. If you don't know, ask.

Nonverbal Communication

Chapter 4 discussed the significance of nonverbal communication in interpersonal communication. **Nonverbal communication** is also important in intercultural settings. Be aware of usage differences in such areas as body language, touch, space, and time.

Body Language

Just as verbal languages differ, so body languages differ from culture to culture. The Japanese value the ability to sit quietly. They may see the US tendency to fidget and shift as an indication of lack of mental or spiritual balance. Even in North America, interviewers and audiences usually respond negatively to nervous gestures such as fidgeting with a tie or hair or jewelry, tapping a pencil, or swinging a foot.

People use body language to signal such traits as interest, respect, emotional involvement, confidence, and agreement. For example, Americans working in the Middle East are cautioned to avoid pointing their finger at people or showing the soles of their feet when seated. They also need to avoid misreading handholding among Arab men, for whom it is an expression of affection and solidarity.[23]

Eye contact

North American whites see eye contact as a sign of attention; in fact, lack of eye contact is slightly suspect. But in many cultures, dropped eyes are a sign of appropriate deference to a superior. Japanese show respect by lowering their eyes when speaking to superiors. In some Latin American and African

Fast food chains are adapting to international cultures.

MySpace Abroad

As MySpace moves into more countries, it has to vary its approach.

Some places, such as India and parts of Latin America, have relatively slow Internet speeds, so MySpace is developing a version without streaming video and music. Also in India, MySpace is trying to lure Bollywood stars into creating profiles and sharing items with fans.

On the other hand, South Korea has Internet speeds faster than those in the United States. It also has a savvy Web culture, one that loves to blog. The South Korean version of MySpace is more of a blogging service.

In some countries, such as Turkey, social networking is less familiar, so MySpace needs tutorials explaining how to navigate the site and find friends.

In Japan, users were shy about listing personal interests but enjoyed joining fan groups. So MySpace increased the prominence of the groups section.

In China, MySpace needed bulletin boards where thousands could participate, and do so anonymously.

Adapted from Jessica E. Vascellaro, "MySpace Aims for Trickier Markets: In India, Israel, Turkey, Web Speeds and Culture Require Special Touches," *Wall Street Journal*, December 13, 2007, B3; and Geoffrey A. Fowler and Jason Dean, "In China, MySpace May Need to Be 'OurSpace,'" *Wall Street Journal*, February 2, 2007, B1–2.

cultures, such as Nigeria, it is disrespectful for lower-status people to prolong eye contact with their superiors. Similarly, in the United States, staring is considered rude. For the English, however, polite people pay strict attention to speakers and blink their eyes to show understanding. In China, a widening of the eyes shows anger, in the United States—surprise. Among Arab men, eye contact is important; it is considered impolite not to face someone directly.[24] In Muslim countries, women and men are not supposed to have eye contact.

These differences can lead to miscommunication in the multicultural workplace. Superiors may feel that subordinates are being disrespectful when the subordinates are being fully respectful—according to the norms of their culture.

Smiling

The frequency of smiling and the way people interpret smiles may depend on the purpose smiles serve in a particular culture. In the United States, smiling varies from region to region. In Germany, Sweden, and the "less-smiley" US cultures, smiling is more likely to be reserved for close relationships and genuine joy. Frequent smiles in other situations would therefore seem insincere. For other people, including those in Thailand, smiling can be a way to create harmony and make situations pleasant. These people might interpret a lack of smiles to signal a lack of harmony and goodwill. Thais tend to smile in most situations, so the meaning of a smile depends on the context—for example, whether the smiling person is telling a joke or smoothing over difficulties.[25] Greeks may express anger with a smile.[26]

Gestures

US citizens sometimes assume that they can depend on gestures to communicate if language fails. But the meanings of gestures vary widely in different cultures. Kissing is usually an affection gesture in the United States but is a greeting gesture in other countries. In Greece, people may nod their heads to signify *no* and shake their heads to signify *yes*.[27]

Mac and PC's Overseas Adventures

"When Apple Inc. wanted to bring its series of 'Mac vs. PC' ads to international markets, it faced a difficult issue: What's funny in one culture can seem ill-mannered in another.

"In the American ads . . . a nerdy PC guy keeps getting trumped by his hip Mac counterpart, who uses pointed banter that demonstrates how Macs are better. In one recent spot, PC is proudly having a camera taped to his head so he can do video chatting—only to discover that Mac already has a built-in camera. . . .

"But in Japanese culture, where direct-comparison ads have long been frowned upon, it's rude to brag about one's strengths. So for Japanese versions of the ads that rolled out last fall, two local comedians from a troupe called the Rahmens made subtle changes to emphasize that Macs and PCs are not that different. Instead of clothes that cast PC clearly as a nerd and Mac as a hipster, PC wears plain office attire and Mac weekend fashion, highlighting the work/home divide between the devices more than personality differences. . . .

"PC's body language is a big source of the humor in Japan: Mac looks embarrassed when the PC touches his shoulder, or hides behind Mac's legs to avoid viruses. . . .

"The international campaigns reflect a growing move by U.S. companies to refine their ad campaigns for overseas markets."

Quoted from Geoffrey A. Fowler, Brian Steinberg, and Aaron O. Patrick, "Mac and PC's Overseas Adventures: Globalizing Apple's Ads Meant Tweaking Characters, Clothing, Body Language," *Wall Street Journal*, March 1, 2007, B1. Copyright © 2007 by Dow Jones & Company, Inc. Reproduced with permission of Dow Jones & Company, Inc. via Copyright Clearance Center.

HARRY BAUMERT/THE REGISTER
A MULTIPLE-EXPOSURE PHOTOGRAPH IN ONE FRAME

What in the United States could mean "wait" or "hold on" in Nigeria indicates putting on a curse. In India it means "stop" or "enough."

What in the United States illustrates "a small amount," in Japan illustrates the degree of something, as in, "I know little English."

This means "peace" in the United States; it is the same as showing the middle finger in Australia and New Zealand. It can mean the number 2 in many places.

In the United States, this gesture means "well done" or "thumps up," but in Iraq, Iran and Bangladesh it means "up yours."

This refers to the Texas longhorns, but in Norway it salutes the devil; in Argentina it means your wife is cheating on you.

In the United States, this could mean small or contained. In Lebanon it means "wait"; and in Italy, "what the #$%! do you want?"

In India, an open hand wave could be interpreted as a "no."

In some cultures, hands folded as if in prayer means "I'm in deep thought; don't bother me."

An "O" with the thumb and index means "OK" in the U.S., but is an obscenity in Brazil and Germany.

The meanings of gestures vary with cultures.

Source: Mike Kilen, "Watch Your Language: Rude or Polite? Gestures Vary with Cultures," *Des Moines Register*, May 30, 2006, E1–2.

Gestures that mean approval in the United States may have very different meanings in other countries. The "thumbs up" sign, which means "good work" or "go ahead" in the United States and most of western Europe, is a vulgar insult in Iraq, Iran, and Bangladesh. The circle formed with the thumb and first finger that means *OK* in the United States is obscene in Brazil and Germany. In India, the raised middle finger means you need to urinate.[28]

The V-sign is another gesture with multiple meanings. Made with the palm facing out, it was famously used by Churchill during WWII and by the hippies in the 60s and 70s. Made with the palm facing in, it is the equivalent of giving someone the finger in countries such as the United Kingdom, Ireland, and Australia. An American president made interesting headlines when he inadvertently used the V-sign on a visit to Australia.

Touch

Repeated studies have shown that babies need to be touched to grow and thrive and that older people are healthier both mentally and physically if they are touched. But some people are more comfortable with touch than others. Each kind of person may misinterpret the other. A person who dislikes touch may seem unfriendly to someone who's used to touching. A toucher may seem overly familiar to someone who dislikes touch.

Most parts of North America allow opposite-sex couples to hold hands or walk arm-in-arm in public but frown on the same behavior in same-sex couples. People in some other countries have the opposite expectation: male friends or female friends can hold hands or walk arm-in-arm, but it is slightly shocking for an opposite-sex couple to touch in public.

In US business settings, people generally shake hands when they meet, but little other touching is considered appropriate. In Mexico, greetings may involve greater physical contact. Men may embrace one another, and women may kiss one another. In many European settings, business colleagues may shake hands when they encounter one another throughout the day. In countries along the Mediterranean, hugs and shoulder pats are common as well. In some European countries, greetings include light kisses. The typical pattern is to kiss the person's right cheek and then the left (or to kiss the air near the cheek). In Italy this pattern stops with two kisses; Belgians continue for three, and the French for four.[29]

Space

Personal space is the distance people want between themselves and other people in ordinary, nonintimate interchanges. Some research shows that many North Americans, North Europeans, and Asians want a bigger personal space than do many Latin Americans, French, Italians, and Arabs. Even people who prefer lots of personal space are often forced to accept close contact on a crowded elevator or subway, or in a small conference room.

Even within a culture, some people like more personal space than do others. In many cultures, people who are of the same age and sex take less personal space than do mixed-age or mixed-sex groups.

Time

Differences in time zones complicate international phone calls and video conferences. But even more important are different views of time and attitudes toward time. Organizations in the United States—businesses, government, and schools—keep time by the calendar and the clock. Being "on time" is seen as a sign of dependability. Other cultures may keep time by the seasons, the moon, the sun, internal "body clocks," or a personal feeling that "the time is right."

North Americans who believe that "time is money" are often frustrated in negotiations with people who take a much more leisurely approach. Part of the problem is that people in many other cultures want to establish a personal relationship before they decide whether to do business with each other.

The problem is made worse because various cultures mentally measure time differently. Many North Americans measure time in five-minute blocks. Someone who's five minutes late to an appointment or a job interview feels compelled to apologize. If the executive or interviewer is running half an hour late, the caller expects to be told about the likely delay upon arriving. Some people won't be able to wait that long and will need to reschedule their appointments. But in other cultures, half an hour may be the smallest block of time. To someone who mentally measures time in 30-minute blocks, being 45 minutes late is no worse than being 10 minutes late is to someone who is conscious of smaller units.

Different cultures have different lead times for scheduling events. In some countries, you need to schedule important meetings at least two weeks in advance. In other countries, not only are people not booked up so far in advance, but a date two weeks into the future may be forgotten.

Anthropologist Edward Hall distinguishes between **monochronic cultures**, which focus on clock time, and **polychronic cultures**, which focus on relationships.

That's Not What We Meant!

Translating a product's advertising slogan is especially tricky, because the product's benefits have to be packed into just a few words. A poor translation can be embarrassing, as in the following examples:

Kentucky Fried Chicken's slogan in English: *Finger lickin' good.*
Meaning in Chinese translation: *Eat your fingers off.*
Otis Engineering Corporation's slogan: *Completion equipment.*
Meaning in Russian translation: *Equipment for orgasms.*
Parker Pen Company's slogan: *Avoid embarrassment.*
Meaning in Spanish translation: *Avoid pregnancy.*
Perdue Farms' slogan: *It takes a tough man to make a tender chicken.*
Meaning in Spanish translation: *It takes a sexually excited man to make a chicken affectionate.*

Examples quoted from Anton Piëch, "Speaking in Tongues," *Inc.*, June 2003, 50.

https://www.cia.gov/library/publications/the-world-factbook/ and http://countrystudies.us/ respectively.

World Factbook published by the Central Intelligence Agency and *Country Studies* published by the Library of Congress are good starting points for learning about the people of another country. Extensive country-by-country information includes languages spoken and communications technology available.

Thinking Outside the Time Line

To organize a convincing argument, the typical European or North American will develop several points and present a case for them one by one. Negotiating a contract, this person might present a list of terms, such as price, quantity, and delivery date, expecting to discuss each one in turn, moving down the list. This approach seems obvious to a Westerner, because Westerners tend to think sequentially—that is, with ideas moving from a beginning to an end.

The typical Chinese negotiator, in contrast, rarely thinks in terms of a sequence or time line. Rather, the Chinese are more likely to engage in holistic thinking, considering all the details as part of a whole. They want to see a proposal in its full context and are likely to reconsider individual details repeatedly, as part of studying the entire proposal from various angles.

As a result of this difference, Americans negotiating with Chinese often doubt they are making progress. Worse, if they follow a Western-style negotiating strategy, they may make costly concessions. In a negotiation between Tandem Computers and China Telecom, the Tandem sales manager offered to reduce the price by 5 percent in exchange for China Telecom's commitment to sign an order for delivery within one month. The purchasing manager responded that there was no need to rush, but since the price was flexible, the price reduction would be acceptable.

Adapted from John L. Graham and N. Mark Lam, "The Chinese Negotiation," *Harvard Business Review*, October 2003, 82–91.

Eating pizza with chopsticks illustrates how new cultural values interact with native culture to constantly create hybrid cultures.

People in monochronic cultures tend to schedule their time and do one task at a time; people in polychronic cultures tend to want their time unstructured and do multiple tasks at the same time. When US managers feel offended because a Latin American manager also sees other people during "their" appointments, the two kinds of time are in conflict.[30]

Other Nonverbal Symbols

Many other symbols can carry nonverbal meanings: clothing, colors, age, and height, to name a few.

Clothing

In North America, certain styles and colors of clothing are considered more "professional" and more "credible." Some clothing denotes not only status but also occupational group. Cowboy boots, firefighter hats, and judicial robes all may, or may not, signal specific occupations. Tool belts, coveralls, hard hats, and stethoscopes may signal broader occupational groupings.

Colors

Colors can also carry meanings in a culture. Chinese tradition associates red with good fortune. Korean Buddhists use red to announce death. Black is the color of joy in Japan, the color of death in the United States.[31] White is the color of funerals in eastern countries; in the United States it is the color of brides. UPS found its company color working against it when it entered the Spanish market. The brown trucks that distinguish the delivery company's brand in the United States are not a good image in Spain, where hearses are traditionally brown. When UPS realized its mistake, it altered its uniforms and truck colors in Spain, emphasizing the company logo rather than the color brown.[32]

Wal-Mart is one of many companies that have expanded internationally.

Business Card Exchanges

Cultural differences also appear in the process of exchanging business cards.

Russia: Hierarchy is important in eastern Europe, so your card should show status, even though the exchange of cards will probably be casual. Put your title and the founding date of your company on your card.

China: Give and receive cards with both hands. Treat the card with respect: comment on it, then put it in a card case. Do not write on it or shove it in your pocket. You might want to use red and gold, which are lucky colors, on your card.

India: Education is important in India, so your card should show your school, highest degree, and any educational honors. Exchange cards with your right hand.

Adapted from "Business Cards," *BusinessWeek SmallBiz*, June/July 2008, 28.

Age

In the United States, youth is valued. People color their hair and even have face-lifts to look as youthful as possible. In Japan, younger people generally defer to older people. Americans attempting to negotiate in Japan are usually taken more seriously if at least one member of the team is noticeably gray-haired.

Height

Height connotes status in many parts of the world. Executive offices are usually on the top floors; the underlings work below. Even being tall can help a person succeed. A recent study found that white, non-Hispanic males of below-average height earned 10 percent less than males of above-average height. Each additional inch of height was linked to 2.5 percent greater income. Perhaps surprisingly, the measurement that produced this effect was the man's height when he was a teenager. Those who grew later in life did not enjoy the income benefits of greater height. For white women in the study, actual adult height was associated with greater income. The researchers lacked sufficient data on other ethnic groups except to say that there seems to be a height–income effect for black males that resembles the effect for white males.[33]

Oral Communication

Effective oral communication requires cultural understanding. As Figure 5.4 suggests, even an act as specific as a business introduction may differ across cultures. These are general patterns, not absolutes, but they help communicators stay alert for audience preferences.

During business meetings, even words as distinct as *yes* and *no* may cause confusion. In some cultures where saying *no* is considered rude, a *yes* may mean merely "I heard you."

Learning at least a little of the language of the country where you hope to do business will help you in several ways. First, learning the language will give you at least a glimpse into the culture. In English, for example, we say that a clock "runs." The French say *"Il marche"*—literally, "It is walking." Second, learning some of the language will help you manage the daily necessities

Figure 5.4   Cultural Contrasts in Business Introductions

	United States	Japan	Arab countries
Purpose of introduction	Establish status and job identity; network	Establish position in group, build harmony	Establish personal rapport
Image of individual	Independent	Member of group	Part of rich culture
Information	Related to business	Related to company	Personal
Use of language	Informal, friendly; use first name	Little talking	Formal; expression of admiration
Values	Openness, directness, action	Harmony, respect, listening	Religious harmony, hospitality, emotional support

Source: Adapted from Farid Elashmawi and Philip R. Harris, *Multicultural Management 2000: Essential Cultural Insights for Global Business Success* (Houston: Gulf, 1998), 113.

Intercultural Doctors

Latin American medical schools graduate more doctors than they have room for in residency training, while US hospitals and clinics are struggling to serve their Spanish-speaking patients. UCLA has started a program to span the gap.

The program, funded by private foundations, provides prep courses for US licensing exams, hospital observations, and help in applying for a US medical residency. Upon completion of the residency, participants serve three years in a "medically underserved area," usually in a large city or rural area.

The new doctors help eliminate the communication problems that cost millions of dollars in unnecessary tests and emergency room visits and cost patients inaccurate or delayed diagnoses and confusion about medications.

For example, "once" in English means "eleven" in Spanish. Some Spanish-speaking patients have taken "once a day" medicines eleven times; for some medications, this increased dosage could be fatal.

In addition to language fluency, the new doctors grasp cultural nuances, such as herbal medications, that may be relevant.

Adapted from Miriam Jordan, "Pilot Program Aims to Train Spanish-Speaking Doctors," *Wall Street Journal,* December 12, 2007, B1.

of finding food and getting where you need to go while you're there. Finally, in business negotiations, knowing a little of the language gives you more time to think. You'll catch part of the meaning when you hear your counterpart speak; you can begin thinking even before the translation begins.

Frequently you will need good translators when you travel abroad on business. Brief them with the technical terms you'll be using; explain as much of the context of your negotiations as possible. A good translator can also help you interpret nonverbal behavior and negotiating strategies. Some translators can help their clients establish trust and credibility with international businesses.

Understatement and Exaggeration

To understand someone from another culture, you must understand the speaker's conversational style. The British have a reputation for understatement. Someone good enough to play at Wimbledon may say he or she "plays a little tennis." In many contexts, Americans accept exaggeration as a way to express positive thinking. Particularly in advertising, Americans expect some hype. Germans, in contrast, generally see exaggeration as a barrier to clear communication. German customers are likely to be intolerant of claims that seem logically unsupportable. An American writing for a German audience should ensure that any claims are literally true.[34]

Compliments

The kinds of statements that people interpret as compliments and the socially correct ways to respond to compliments also vary among cultures. Statements that seem complimentary in one context may be inappropriate in another. For example, women in business may be uncomfortable if male colleagues or superiors compliment them on their appearance: the comments may suggest that the women are being treated as visual decoration rather than as contributing workers.

Writing to International Audiences

Most cultures are more formal than that of the United States. When you write to international audiences, you may need to use titles, not first names. Avoid contractions, slang, and sports metaphors.

Not: Let's knock these sales figures out of the ballpark.

But: Our goal is to increase sales 7%.

Do write in English unless you're extremely fluent in your reader's language. Be clear, but be adult. Don't write in second-grade English.

Not: We will meet Tuesday. Our meeting room will be Hanscher North. We will start at 9:30 AM.

But: We will meet Tuesday at 9:30 AM in Hanscher North.

The patterns of organization that work for United States audiences may need to be modified in international correspondence. For instance, most North Americans develop an argument linearly; points in a contract such as price, quantity, and delivery date are presented in order, one at a time. However, business people from other cultures may think holistically rather than sequentially, and the business relationship may be far more important than the actual contract, which may not even be considered binding.

In other documents, negative messages may need more buffering and requests may need to be indirect. A junior manager in a financial firm caused hard feelings when he e-mailed a direct question to a colleague at the Manila office: "Were the deal numbers checked against the source?" This question was taken by the employee in Manila as an accusation.[35]

As Figures 5.5 and 5.6 suggest, the style, structure, and strategies that would motivate a US audience may need to be changed for international readers.

> http://www.cyborlink.com/
> http://www.kwintessential.co.uk/
>
> Cyborlink.com and Kwintessential.co.uk provide information on business communication in various countries. On both sites, choose a country to explore and you will get general information on topics such as negotiations, gift giving, personal space, and much more.

Figure 5.5 Cultural Contrasts in Written Persuasive Documents

	United States	Japan	Arab countries
Opening	Request action or get reader's attention	Offer thanks; apologize	Offer personal greetings
Way to persuade	Immediate gain or loss of opportunity	Waiting	Personal connections; future opportunity
Style	Short sentences	Modesty; minimize own standing	Elaborate expressions; many signatures
Closing	Specific request	Desire to maintain harmony	Future relationship, personal greeting
Values	Efficiency; directness; action	Politeness; indirectness; relationship	Status; continuation

Source: Adapted from Farid Elashmawi and Philip R. Harris, *Multicultural Management 2000: Essential Cultural Insights for Global Business Success* (Houston: Gulf, 1998), 139.

Figure 5.6 Cultural Contrasts in Motivation

	United States	Japan	Arab countries
Emotional appeal	Opportunity	Group participation; company success	Religion; nationalism; admiration
Recognition based on	Individual achievement	Group achievement	Individual status; status of class/society
Material rewards	Salary; bonus; profit sharing	Annual bonus; social services; fringe benefits	Gifts for self/family; salary
Threats	Loss of job	Loss of group membership	Demotion, loss of reputation
Values	Competition; risk taking; freedom	Group harmony; belonging	Reputation; family security; religion

Source: Adapted from Farid Elashmawi and Philip R. Harris, *Multicultural Management 2000: Essential Cultural Insights for Global Business Success* (Houston: Gulf, 1998), 169.

Multicultural Diabetes Education

New York City's 11 public hospitals are tailoring diabetes education for different cultures.

The programs start with communications in the patients' native tongues. Handouts come in 11 languages, from Albanian to Urdu. Phone-based translation services allow medical staff to communicate in still more languages. If patients miss their appointments, phone calls and letters in their native language remind them.

Correct portion sizes are illustrated with photos of plates of lamb *korma*, fried plantains, and General Tso's chicken. Cooking classes for Caribbean emigrants demonstrate flavoring rice with fresh herbs and spices rather than tripe or pig snouts. An online guide for Indian foods lists nutritional information for classic dishes such as *roti* (flat bread) and *dal* (bean or pea dishes).

The goal of the program is to make good health care more accessible.

Adapted from Theo Francis, "Treating Diabetes and Understanding Cultures: With Minorities at Risk, Doctors Work to Make Diet Advice Hit Home," *Wall Street Journal*, October 23, 2007, D2.

Relationships become more important, as do politeness strategies. The information in the figures suggests general patterns, not definitive delineations, but such suggestions help communicators look for ways to be more effective. Most writers will benefit from researching a culture before composing messages for people in it.

Response time expectations may also need to be modified. US employees tend to expect fast answers to e-mails. However, other cultures with hierarchical organization structures may need extra response time to allow for approval by superiors. Pressing for a quick response may alienate the people whose help is needed and may result in false promises.[36]

In international business correspondence, list the day before the month:

Not: April 8, 2008

But: 8 April 2008

Spell out the month to avoid confusion.

Business people from Europe and Japan who correspond frequently with North America are beginning to adopt US directness and patterns of organization. Still, it may be safer to modify your message somewhat; it certainly is more courteous.

Learning More about International Business Communication

Learning to communicate with people from different backgrounds shouldn't be a matter of learning rules. Instead, use the examples in this chapter to get a sense for the kinds of factors that differ from one culture to another. Test these generalizations against your experience. Remember that people everywhere have their own personal characteristics. And when in doubt, ask.

You can also learn by seeking out people from other backgrounds and talking with them. Many campuses have centers for international students. Some communities have groups of international business people who meet regularly to discuss their countries. By asking all these people what aspects of the dominant US culture seem strange to them, you'll learn much about what is "right" in their cultures.

Summary of Key Points

- **Culture** provides patterns of acceptable behavior and beliefs.
- The successful intercultural communicator is
  - Aware of the values, beliefs, and practices in other cultures.
  - Sensitive to differences among individuals within a culture.
  - Aware that his or her preferred values and behaviors are influenced by culture and are not necessarily "right."
  - Sensitive to verbal and nonverbal behavior.
  - Flexible and open to change.
- In **high-context cultures**, most of the information is inferred from the context of a message; little is explicitly conveyed. In **low-context cultures**, context is less important; most information is explicitly spelled out.
- **Nonverbal communication** is communication that doesn't use words. Nonverbal communication can include body language, space, time, and other miscellaneous matters such as clothing, colors, age, and height.
- Nonverbal signals can be misinterpreted just as easily as can verbal symbols (words).

- No gesture has a universal meaning across all cultures. Gestures that signify approval in North America may be insults in other countries, and vice versa.
- **Personal space** is the distance someone wants between him- or herself and other people in ordinary, nonintimate interchanges.
- North Americans who believe that "time is money" are often frustrated in negotiations with people who want to establish a personal relationship before they decide whether to do business with each other.
- The patterns of organization that work for North American audiences may need to be modified in international correspondence.

CHAPTER 5   # Exercises and Problems

*Go to www.mhhe.com/locker9e for additional Exercises and Problems.

5.1   Reviewing the Chapter

1. Why is global business important? (LO 1)
2. What are the advantages of receiving an overseas assignment? (LO 1)
3. Why is diversity becoming more important than ever before? (LO 2)
4. What are low-context and high-context cultures? (LO 3)
5. How do our values and beliefs affect our responses to other people? (LO 3)
6. What are some forms of nonverbal communication? What variations would you expect to see in them among people of different cultures? (LO 4)
7. Why do people from monochronic cultures sometimes have trouble with people from polychronic cultures? (LO 4)
8. What are some characteristics of oral communications you should consider when communicating cross-culturally? (LO 5)
9. What are some cautions to consider when writing for international audiences? (LO 6)

5.2   Identifying Sources of Miscommunication

In each of the following situations, identify one or more ways that cultural differences may be leading to miscommunication.

1. Alan is a US sales representative in South America. He makes appointments and is careful to be on time. But the person he's calling on is frequently late. To save time, Alan tries to get right to business. But his hosts want to talk about sightseeing and his family. Even worse, his appointments are interrupted constantly, not only by business phone calls but also by long conversations with other people and even the customers' children who come into the office. Alan's first progress report is very negative. He hasn't yet made a sale. Perhaps South America just isn't the right place to sell his company's products.

2. To help her company establish a presence in Asia, Susan wants to hire a local interpreter who can advise her on business customs. Kana Tomari has superb qualifications on paper. But when Susan tries to probe about her experience, Kana just says, "I will do my best. I will try very hard." She never gives details about any of the previous positions she's held. Susan begins to wonder if the résumé is inflated.

3. Stan wants to negotiate a joint venture with an Asian company. He asks Tung-Sen Lee if the people have enough discretionary income to afford his product. Mr. Lee is silent for a time, and then says, "Your product is good. People in the West must like it." Stan smiles, pleased that Mr. Lee recognizes the quality of his product, and he gives Mr. Lee a contract to sign. Weeks later, Stan still hasn't heard anything. If Asians are going to be so nonresponsive, he wonders if he really should try to do business with them.

4. Elspeth is very proud of her participatory management style. On assignment in India, she is careful not to give orders but to ask for suggestions. But people rarely suggest anything. Even a formal suggestion system doesn't work. And to make matters worse, she doesn't sense the respect and camaraderie of the plant she managed in the United States. Perhaps, she decides gloomily, people in India just aren't ready for a woman boss.

5.3 Interviewing for Cultural Information

Interview a person from an international community about cross-cultural communication. You might want to discuss issues such as these:

- Verbal and nonverbal communication, including body language.
- Tone and organization of professional communications.
- Attitude toward materialism.
- Time awareness differences.
- Concepts of personal space.

Compare the person's responses with your own values and write a memo to your instructor reflecting on the similarities and differences.

5.4 Analyzing Ads

Search for international ads on YouTube using keywords such as "Cell phone ads China" "Domino pizza in India." Compare them to a similar ad created in the Unites States.

- What are some differences you see in the advertisement?
- How do they inform about the cultural values of the commodities shown in the advertisement?

Discuss your findings in small groups. As a group, prepare a short presentation for your classmates.

5.5 Comparing Company Web Pages for Various Countries

Many multinationals have separate Web pages for their operations in various countries. For example, Coca-Cola's pages include pages for Belgium, France, and Japan. Analyze three of the country pages of a company of your choice.

- Is a single template used for pages in different countries, or do the basic designs differ?
- Are different images used in different countries? What do the images suggest?
- If you can read the language, analyze the links. What information is emphasized?
- To what extent are the pages similar? To what extent do they reveal national and cultural differences?

As your instructor directs,

a. Write a memo analyzing the similarities and differences you find. Attach printouts of the pages to your memo.

b. Make an oral presentation to the class. Paste the Web pages into PowerPoint slides.

c. Join with a small group of students to create a group report comparing several companies' Web pages in three specific countries. Attach printouts of the pages.

d. Make a group oral presentation to the class.

5.6 Creating a Web Page

Create a Web page of international information for managers who are planning assignments in another country or who work in this country for a multinational company headquartered in another country.

Assume that this page can be accessed from another of the organization's pages. Offer at least seven links. (More is better.) You may offer information as well as links to other pages with information. At the top of the page, offer an overview of what the page covers. At the bottom of the page, put the creation/update date and your name and e-mail address.

As your instructor directs,

a. Turn in a copy of your page(s). On another page, give the URLs for each link.

b. Write a memo to your instructor (1) identifying the audience for which the page is designed and explaining (2) the search strategies you used to find material on this topic, (3) why you chose the pages and information you've included, and (4) why you chose the layout and graphics you've used.

c. Present your page orally to the class.

Hints:

- Limit your page to just one country or one part of the world.
- You can include some general information about working abroad and culture, but most of your links should be specific to the country or part of the world you focus on.
- Consider some of these topics: history, politics, geography, culture, money, living accommodations, transportation, weather, business practices, and so forth.
- Chunk your links into small groups under headings.

5.7   Comparing International Information

In small groups, find at least four Web sites providing information about a specific international community. Also, if possible, meet with a member of that community and discuss your findings. Do you find any clashing sources of evidence? What do the contradictions tell you about your sources? What do they tell you about that international community in general?

Discuss your findings in small groups. As a group, prepare a short presentation for your classmates.

5.8   Planning an International Trip

Assume that you're going to the capital city of another country on business two months from now. (You pick the country.) Use a search engine to find out

- What holidays will be celebrated in that month.
- What the climate will be.
- What current events are in the news there.
- What key features of business etiquette you might consider.
- What kinds of gifts you should bring to your hosts.
- What sight-seeing you might include.

As your instructor directs,

a. Write a memo to your instructor reporting the information you found.

b. Post a message to the class analyzing the pages. Include the URLs as hotlinks.

c. Make an oral presentation to the class.

d. Join with a small group of students to create a group report on several countries in a region.

e. Make a group oral presentation to the class.

5.9   Evaluating Single-Sex Programs

Although women hold slightly more than half of US managerial positions, they hold far fewer of the top executive positions. To counteract this imbalance, some schools such as Smith College are offering executive-education courses for women only.

Participants, as well as corporations such as Johnson & Johnson and Deloitte & Touche, praise these programs for helping women network and gain confidence. Women can trade strategies for issues such as work/family balance that may be more acute for them than for men.

What do you think of these programs? Are they ethical? Would you feel differently if they were held for men only? Why?

Discuss your opinions in small groups.

Adapted from Erin White, "Female Training Classes Flourish: Executive-Education Tactic Aims to Bolster the Ranks of Women in Management," *Wall Street Journal,* September 25, 2006, B3.

5.10   Recommending a Candidate for an Overseas Position

Your company sells customized computer systems to businesses large and small around the world. The Executive Committee needs to recommend someone to begin a three-year term as Manager of Eastern European Marketing.

As your instructor directs,

a. Write a memo to each of the candidates, specifying the questions you would like each to answer in a final interview.

b. Assume that it is not possible to interview the candidates. Use the information here to write a memo to the CEO recommending a candidate.

c. Write a memo to the CEO recommending the best way to prepare the person chosen for his or her assignment.

d. Write a memo to the CEO recommending a better way to choose candidates for international assignments.

e. Write a memo to your instructor explaining the assumptions you made about the company and the candidates that influenced your recommendation(s).

Information about the candidates:

All the candidates have applied for the position and say they are highly interested in it.

1. **Deborah Gere,** 39, white, single. Employed by the company for eight years in the Indianapolis and New York offices. Currently in the New York office as Assistant Marketing Manager, Eastern United States; successful. University of Indiana MBA. Speaks Russian fluently; has translated for business negotiations that led to the setting up of the Moscow office. Good technical knowledge, acceptable managerial skills, excellent communication skills, good interpersonal skills. Excellent health; excellent emotional stability.

Swims. One child, age 12. Lived in the then–Soviet Union for one year as an exchange student in college; business and personal travel in Europe.

2. **Claude Chabot,** 36, French, single. Employed by the company for 11 years in the Paris and London offices. Currently in the Paris office as Assistant Sales Manager for the European Economic Community; successful. No MBA, but degrees from MIT in the United States and l'Ecole Supérieure de Commerce de Paris. Speaks native French; speaks English and Italian fluently; speaks some German. Good technical knowledge, excellent managerial skills, acceptable communication skills, excellent interpersonal skills. Excellent health, good emotional stability. Plays tennis. No children. French citizen; lived in the United States for two years, in London for five years (one year in college, four years in the London office). Extensive business and personal travel in Europe.

3. **Linda Moss,** 35, African American, married. Employed by the company for 10 years in the Atlanta and Toronto offices. Currently Assistant Manager of Canadian Marketing; very successful. Howard University MBA. Speaks some French.

Good technical knowledge, excellent managerial skills, excellent communication skills, excellent interpersonal skills. Excellent health; excellent emotional stability. Does Jazzercize classes. Husband is an executive at a US company in Detroit; he plans to stay in the States with their children, ages 11 and 9. The couple plans to commute every two to six weeks. Has lived in Toronto for five years; business travel in North America; personal travel in Europe and Latin America.

4. **Steven Hsu,** 42, of Asian American descent, married. Employed by the company for 18 years in the Los Angeles office. Currently Marketing Manager, Western United States; very successful. UCLA MBA. Speaks some Korean. Excellent technical knowledge, excellent managerial skills, good communication skills, excellent interpersonal skills. Good health, excellent emotional stability. Plays golf. Wife is an engineer who plans to do consulting work in eastern Europe. Children ages 8, 5, and 2. Has not lived outside the United States; personal travel in Europe and Asia.

Your committee has received this memo from the CEO.

To: Executive Committee

From: Ed Conzachi *EC*

Subject: Choosing a Manager for the New Eastern European Office

Please write me a memo recommending the best candidate for Manager of East European **Marketing**. In your memo, tell me whom you're choosing and why; also explain why you have rejected the unsuccessful candidates.

This person will be assuming a three-year appointment, with the possibility of reappointment. The company will pay moving and relocation expenses for the manager and his or her family.

The Eastern European division currently is the smallest of the company's international divisions. However, this area is poised for growth. The new manager will supervise the Moscow office and establish branch offices as needed.

The committee has invited comments from everyone in the company. You've received these memos.

To: Executive Committee

From: Robert Osborne, US Marketing Manager *RO*

Subject: Recommendation for Steve Hsu

Steve Hsu would be a great choice to head up the new Moscow office. In the past seven years, Steve has increased sales in the Western Region by 15%—in spite of recessions, earthquakes, and fires. He has a low-key, participative style that brings out the best in subordinates. Moreover, Steve is a brilliant computer programmer. He probably understands our products better than any other marketing or salesperson in the company.

Steve is clearly destined for success in headquarters. This assignment will give him the international experience he needs to move up to the next level of executive success.

To: Executive Committee

From: Becky Exter, Affirmative Action Officer *BE*

Subject: Hiring the New Manager for East European Marketing

Please be sensitive to affirmative action concerns. The company has a very good record of appointing women and minorities to key positions in the United States and Canada; so far our record in our overseas divisions has been less effective.

In part, perhaps, that may stem from a perception that women and minorities will not be accepted in countries less open than our own. But the experience of several multinational firms has been that even exclusionary countries will accept people who have the full backing of their companies. Another concern may be that it will be harder for women to establish a social support system abroad. However, different individuals have different ways of establishing support. To assume that the best candidate for an international assignment is a male with a stay-at-home wife is discriminatory and may deprive our company of the skills of some of its best people.

We have several qualified women and minority candidates. I urge you to consider their credentials carefully.

To: Executive Committee

From: William E. Dortch, Marketing Manager, European Economic Community *WED*

Subject: Recommendation for Debbie Gere

Debbie Gere would be my choice to head the new Moscow office. As you know, I recommended that Europe be divided and that we establish an eastern European division. Of all the people from the States who have worked on the creation of the new division, Debbie is the best. The negotiations were often complex. Debbie's knowledge of the language and culture was invaluable. She's done a good job in the New York office and is ready for wider responsibilities. Eastern Europe is a challenging place, but Debbie can handle the pressure and help us gain the foothold we need.

To: Ed Conzachi, President

From: Pierre Garamond, Sales Representative, European Economic Community *PG*

Subject: Recommendation for Claude Chabot

Claude Chabot would be the best choice for Manager of Eastern European Marketing. He is a superb supervisor, motivating us to the highest level of achievement. He understands the complex legal and cultural nuances of selling our products in Europe as only a native can. He also has the budgeting and managerial skills to oversee the entire marketing effort.

You are aware that the company's record of sending US citizens to head international divisions is not particularly good. European Marketing is an exception, but our records in the Middle East and Japan have been poor. The company would gain stability by appointing Europeans to head European offices, Asians to head Asian offices, and so forth. Such people would do a better job of managing and motivating staffs which will be comprised primarily of nationals in the country where the office is located. Ending the practice of reserving the top jobs for US citizens would also send a message to international employees that we are valued and that we have a future with this company.

To: Executive Committee

From: Elaine Crispell, Manager, Canadian Marketing *EC*

Subject: Recommendation for Linda Moss

Linda Moss has done well as Assistant Manager for the last two and a half years. She is a creative, flexible problem solver. Her productivity is the highest in the office. Though she could be called a "workaholic," she is a warm, caring human being.

As you know, the Canadian division includes French-Speaking Montreal and a large Native Canadian population; furthermore, Toronto is an international and intercultural city. Linda has gained intercultural competence both on a personal and professional level.

Linda has the potential to be our first woman CEO 15 years down the road. She needs more international experience to be competitive at that level. This would be a good opportunity for her, and she would do well for the company.

5.11   Analyzing EEO Statements

Find the EEO statements on the Web of three different companies. Do any of the statements have interesting features? How are the statements similar? How are the statements different?

As your instructor directs,

a.   Present your analysis in a memo to your instructor.

b.   Share your findings in small groups. Using all the group's EEO statements, answer the questions above. Put your analysis in a memo to your instructor, or share your findings orally with the class.

5.12   Researching Diversity at Your School

Research your university's policies and practices regarding diversity. Conduct the following research:

- Locate your university's position statement on diversity for both employment and educational opportunities.
- Find diversity data for your university's student body.
- Gather pictures of the student body you can find from the Internet, brochures, and posters throughout your university.
- Analyze your findings. Do the pictures you find resemble the statistics you find?

As your instructor directs,

a.   Write an e-mail to your instructor explaining your findings, opinions, and conclusions.

b.   Share your results with a small group of students.

c.   Write an e-mail message to the president of the university outlining your opinion on how your university is achieving diversity and what, if anything, needs to be done to improve its efforts.

d.   Make a short oral presentation to the class discussing your findings and conclusions.

5.13   Researching Diversity Programs of Companies

Find three businesses that are successfully globalizing or outsourcing.

- Specify their successes. What actions, behaviors, and policies do they follow to be successful at globalizing and/or outsourcing their organization?
- Note what other organizations can learn from these examples.

Find three businesses that are having problems globalizing or outsourcing.

- Specify their problems. What actions, behaviors, and policies do they follow that are causing the problems?

- Note what other organizations can learn from these examples.

As your instructor directs,

a. Write an e-mail to your instructor explaining your findings, opinions, and conclusions.

b. Share your results with a small group of students.

c. Make a short oral presentation to the class discussing your findings and conclusions.

5.14   All-Weather Case: Welcoming Guests from Japan

Drs. Tanizaki and Kawabata, the two management professors whom Doug invited to conduct workshops on *Kaizen* for All-Weather's employees (see Chapter 4 portion of All-Weather case), are coming to St. Paul, Minnesota, along with their families. The two Japanese professors and their families will be All-Weather's guests for a week before leaving for Washington, DC, and New York en route to Tokyo.

Upon arrival of their flight from Tokyo, Doug and Caleb receive them at the airport and drive them to the hotel, promising to return the next day to discuss preliminary details of the workshops on *Kaizen*.

Once back in the office, Doug receives news of an accident in a production line at the company plant in Cedar Rapids, Iowa. He rushes to Cedar Rapids, asking Caleb to take Tanner in his place for the meeting with the professors. "Call them and let them know I won't be there," Doug tells Caleb before leaving.

Caleb calls Tanner with the news and asks him to inform the professors that Doug will not be able to attend the meeting. He also asks Tanner to do some quick research on Japanese culture and etiquette so as to not make any obvious mistakes at the meeting. Caleb adds that he is also spending some time researching the basics of Japanese culture and etiquette.

On the next day, as Caleb and Tanner drive to the hotel, Caleb asks Tanner whether he informed the professors that Doug will not be there. "Whoa. It slipped out of my mind," Tanner says. Caleb cannot believe his ears. He is about to give a piece of his mind to Tanner but checks himself because he does not want to create unnecessary tension before an important meeting.

The meeting is taking place inside an Asian-style restaurant in the hotel and is hosted by the two professors. The professors extend their hands as Caleb and Tanner approach. Caleb gently shakes Dr. Tanizaki's hand and bows slightly without making a direct eye contact with his host. Tanner, who returns Dr. Kawabata's handshake with a firm handshake of his own, says, *"Moshi moshi,* professor, around here we don't respect soft handshakes." Both Drs. Kawabata and Tanizaki begin to laugh, though they quickly return to their somber selves.

Next, the professors offer their business cards to Caleb and Tanner. Caleb accepts the card with both his hands, briefly reads its contents, and offers his own card to Dr. Tanizaki in the same way he offered his. Tanner takes Dr. Kawabata's card, folds it, and puts it in his wallet. Having forgotten to bring his business cards, he apologizes to Dr. Kawabata, promising to give him a card when he visits All-Weather's headquarters.

Tanner goes on to pat Dr. Kawabata on the back, who smiles at the gesture. Caleb is speechless at how Tanner has been behaving. However, deciding to focus on the meeting, he joins the two professors at a table.

"I must apologize to you for Doug's absence," Caleb says, speaking slowly and leaning forward a little. "We had an accident at our plant site and Doug had to go there."

"Oh, I'm sorry to learn about this," Dr. Tanizaki says, slowly and with a thick Japanese accent. "How did this happen, Mr. Caleb?"

"We're still getting the details," Caleb says, wondering whether it was culturally appropriate to bring up an accident at their first meeting, "but it seems that there was a fire involving one of our extruders."

Caleb spends the next half hour explaining All-Weather's operations and various departments to both professors, who keep nodding and taking notes. Meanwhile, according to prior understanding, Tanner has left the table to buy a gift for the professors and their families.

A few minutes later, Tanner returns with a wrapped box and two flower bouquets. Caleb looks on as Tanner presents the gifts to Drs. Tanizaki and Kawabata. "These are lovely yellow chrysanthemums for your better halves," Tanner says, giving the two plastic-wrapped bouquets to Drs. Tanizaki and Kawabata, who look ill at ease but accept the bouquets while continuing to smile.

Caleb is beginning to regret his decision to follow Doug's advice to bring Tanner along. He knows that Tanner is no jerk, just too much of a product of his own culture. Before leaving for the hotel, Caleb saw Tanner browse through a handbook of common Japanese words with their English equivalents. Having spent a few minutes with the book, Tanner probably felt confident enough to meet with the Japanese professors.

Unfortunately for Caleb, however, Tanner isn't finished yet. He gives the box containing the gift to Dr. Kawabata, insisting that he open the box immediately. Caleb tries to intervene, but Tanner is insistent. Dr. Kawabata opens the box, which contains four coffee mugs bearing All-Weather's logo. "One each for you two and one each for your wives," Tanner announces enthusiastically.

The professors' smiles are even more constrained this time than when they received the bouquets. "Thank you," they whisper weakly.

Shortly afterward, thanking the professors and apologizing to them for any inconvenience, Caleb and Tanner leave the hotel. On their way back, Caleb is angry with Tanner for not learning enough about Japanese culture. Tanner is surprised. "What did I do that was inappropriate?" he asks.

"Everything," Caleb says, quietly.

"I even used a Japanese word," Tanner protests, hinting at the fact that it wasn't Caleb who had done so.

"Yes. I heard you say *moshi moshi,* which means "hello" but only when one speaks on the phone. That's why they laughed," Caleb says, turning his full attention to driving again.

"What else did I do that was inappropriate?" Tanner says, almost pleadingly.

"I'm not going to tell you. Call it your punishment," Caleb says, already thinking of a way to undo the damage caused by Tanner's unintended slights, "but I want you to find that out yourself. Be more prepared the next time we meet them, or I'll have to keep you away from this project."

Complete the following tasks with the help of Internet or library research on Japanese culture and etiquette:

- Find the mistakes that Tanner made in his interaction with the Japanese professors.
- Prepare a memo for Caleb that includes information about some or all of the following aspects of Japanese culture and etiquette:

  - Greeting customs and terms of address.
  - Conversational etiquette and style.
  - Business etiquette.
  - Body language and nonverbal communication.
  - Food habits.
  - Table manners.
  - Significance of different colors.
  - Appropriate gifts.
  - Preferred or popular entertainment or recreational activities for families and children.

Learning Objectives

After studying this chapter, you will know:

1 Different kinds of productive and nonproductive roles in teams.

2 Group decision-making strategies.

3 Characteristics of successful teams.

4 Techniques for resolving conflict.

5 Techniques for making meetings effective.

6 Techniques for collaborative writing.

http://www.team technology.co.uk/

Log on to this Web site to find a wide range of articles and resources about interacting effectively in team settings. More specifically, click on "Team Roles" to find some interactive links to aid in assessing yourself as a team member as well as determining roles of your fellow group members.

Teamwork is crucial to success in an organization. Some teams produce products, provide services, or recommend solutions to problems. Other teams—perhaps in addition to providing a service or recommending a solution—also produce documents.

Interpersonal communication, communication between people, is crucial for good teamwork. It relies heavily on interpersonal skills such as listening and networking. Chapter 4 discusses interpersonal skills vital for good teamwork. Skills in conflict resolution, meeting organization, and collaborative writing also help teamwork. These skills will make you more successful in your job, social groups, community service, and volunteer work. On writing teams, giving careful attention to both teamwork and writing process (see Chapter 7) improves both the final product and members' satisfaction with the team.

Team Interactions

Teams can focus on different dimensions. **Informational dimensions** focus on content: the problem, data, and possible solutions. **Procedural dimensions** focus on method and process. How will the team make decisions? Who will do what? When will assignments be due? **Interpersonal dimensions** focus on people, promoting friendliness, cooperation, and team loyalty.

Different kinds of communication dominate during these stages of the life of a task team: formation, coordination, and formalization.

During **formation,** when members meet and begin to define their task, teams need to develop some sort of social cohesiveness and to develop procedures for meeting and acting. Interpersonal and procedural comments reduce the tension that always exists in a new team. Insistence on information in this first stage can hurt the team's long-term productivity.

Teams are often most effective when they explicitly adopt ground rules. Figure 6.1 lists some of the most common ground rules used by workplace teams.

During formation, conflicts frequently arise when the team defines tasks and procedures. Successful teams clarify what each member is supposed to do. They also set procedures: When and how often will they meet? Will decisions be made by a leader, as is the case with many advisory groups? By consensus or vote? Will the team evaluate individual performances? Will someone keep minutes? Interpersonal communication is needed to resolve the conflict that surfaces during this phase. Successful teams analyze their tasks thoroughly before they begin to search for solutions.

Coordination is the longest phase and the phase during which most of the team's work is done. While procedural and interpersonal comments help

Figure 6.1 Possible Team Ground Rules

- Start team meetings on time; end on time.
- Attend regularly.
- Come to the meeting prepared.
- Leave the meeting with a clear understanding of what each member is to do next.
- Focus comments on the issues.
- Avoid personal attacks.
- Listen to and respect members' opinions.
- Everyone speaks on key issues and procedures.
- Address problems as you become aware of them. If you have a problem with another person, tell that person, not everyone else.
- Do your share of the work.
- Communicate immediately if you think you may not be able to fulfill an agreement.
- Produce your work by the agreed-upon time.

http://www .quintcareers.com/ team_player_quiz_ scoring.html

Log on to QuintCareers.com and take a quiz that gauges how effective you are as a team player.

How did you do? Are you an effective team player? If not, consider the guidelines outlined in this chapter to become a better and more resourceful team member.

maintain direction and friendliness, most of the comments need to deal with information. Good information is essential to good decisions. Successful teams deliberately seek numerous possible solutions. Conflict may occur as the team debates these solutions. Successful teams carefully consider as many solutions as possible before choosing one. They particularly avoid the temptation of going with the first solution that arises.

In **formalization,** the group seeks consensus. The success of this phase determines how well the group's decision will be implemented. In this stage, the group seeks to forget earlier conflicts.

Roles in Teams

Individual members can play multiple roles within teams, and these roles can change during the team's work. Roles can be positive or negative.

Positive roles and actions that help the team achieve its task goals include the following.

- **Seeking information and opinions**—asking questions, identifying gaps in the team's knowledge.
- **Giving information and opinions**—answering questions, providing relevant information.
- **Summarizing**—restating major points, summarizing decisions.
- **Synthesizing**—pulling ideas together, connecting different elements of the team's efforts.
- **Evaluating**—comparing team processes and products to standards and goals.
- **Coordinating**—planning work, giving directions, and fitting together contributions of team members.

Positive roles and actions that help the team build loyalty, resolve conflicts, and function smoothly include the following behaviors (also see the list in Figure 6.2):

- **Encouraging participation**—demonstrating openness and acceptance, recognizing the contributions of members, calling on quieter team members.
- **Relieving tensions**—joking and suggesting breaks and fun activities.
- **Checking feelings**—asking members how they feel about team activities and sharing one's own feelings with others.

Developing Team Cohesiveness

In *The Five Dysfunctions of a Team,* Patrick Lencioni suggests a simple method for helping to establish social cohesiveness in a new team. His low-risk exercise involves having everyone on the team answer a short list of questions about themselves.

The questions, while personal, are not particularly probing, and the group could create the list of questions together. He suggests questions about hometown, number of siblings, a few facts about one's childhood, hobbies, first job, and worst job.

Simply by answering even innocuous questions about themselves, team members begin to relate to each other and see each other as interesting people. This in turn encourages greater empathy and understanding.

Have you tried Lencioni's technique in a team you belonged to? Did it help in team formation? What questions do you think would work best?

Adapted from Patrick Lencioni, *The Five Dysfunctions of a Team: A Leadership Fable* (San Francisco: Jossey-Bass, 2002), 198.

Good Leadership Means the Team Can Survive without You

When CEO Joe Albanese's Naval Reserve unit was called to active duty in the Middle East, he worried that the management team of his construction company would struggle without him. Not so: the company grew 48% while he was away, with revenues of $69 million. That success wasn't because the team didn't need him—early in his deployment, his team consulted him often by phone and videoconference. It was because Albanese had built a team that was resilient enough to take over his duties while he was away, and then transition the responsibility back when he returned.

The team adapted to the "lack" of leadership in three main ways:

- They used technology to overcome the distance between themselves and their leader. Phone and videoconferences allow teams to keep working even when diverse schedules and locations get in the way.

- Each team member took over part of the leadership role, including responsibility for major decisions and building consensus, so that no one team member was burdened with too much extra work.

- The team leader encouraged his team members to lead and supported their decisions—even when he disagreed—to give them the authority they needed to do their work.

A good team doesn't depend on one member to keep everyone working together.

Adapted from Leigh Buchanan, "When Absence Makes the Team Grow Stronger: A CEO Rethinks His Role after a Tour in Iraq," *Inc.*, June 2008, 40–42.

Figure 6.2   The Five Characteristics of an Effective Team

1. They trust one another.
2. They engage in unfiltered conflict around ideas.
3. They commit to decisions and plans of action.
4. They hold one another accountable for delivering against those plans.
5. They focus on the achievement of collective results.

Quoted from Patrick Lencioni, *The Five Dysfunctions of a Team: A Leadership Fable* (San Francisco: Jossey-Bass, 2002), 189–90.

- **Solving interpersonal problems**—opening discussion of interpersonal problems in the team and suggesting ways to solve them.
- **Listening actively**—showing team members that they have been heard and that their ideas are being taken seriously.

Negative roles and actions that hurt the team's product and process include the following:

- **Blocking**—disagreeing with everything that is proposed.
- **Dominating**—trying to run the team by ordering, shutting out others, and insisting on one's own way.
- **Clowning**—making unproductive jokes and diverting the team from the task.
- **Overspeaking**—taking every opportunity to be the first to speak; insisting on personally responding to everyone else's comments.
- **Withdrawing**—being silent in meetings, not contributing, not helping with the work, not attending meetings.

Some actions can be positive or negative depending on how they are used. Active participation by members helps teams move forward, but too much talking from one member blocks contributions from others. Criticizing ideas is necessary if the team is to produce the best solution, but criticizing every idea raised without ever suggesting possible solutions blocks a team. Jokes in moderation can defuse tension and make the team work more fun. Too many jokes or inappropriate jokes can make the team's work more difficult.

Leadership in Teams

You may have noted that "leader" was not one of the roles listed above. Being a leader does *not* mean doing all the work yourself. Indeed, someone who implies that he or she has the best ideas and can do the best work is likely playing the negative roles of blocking and dominating.

Effective teams balance three kinds of leadership, which parallel the three team dimensions:

- Informational leaders generate and evaluate ideas and text.
- Interpersonal leaders monitor the team's process, check people's feelings, and resolve conflicts.
- Procedural leaders set the agenda, make sure that everyone knows what's due for the next meeting, communicate with absent team members, and check to be sure that assignments are carried out.

While it's possible for one person to assume all these responsibilities, in many teams, the three kinds of leadership are taken on by three (or more) different people. Some teams formally or informally rotate or share these responsibilities, so that everyone—and no one—is a leader.

Studies have shown that people who talk a lot, listen effectively, and respond nonverbally to other members of the team are considered to be leaders.[1]

Decision-Making Strategies

Probably the least effective decision-making strategy is to let the person who talks first, last, loudest, or most determine the decision. Most teams instead aim to air different points of view with the objective of identifying the best choice, or at least a choice that seems good enough for the team's purposes. The team discussion considers the pros and cons of each idea. In many teams, someone willingly plays "devil's advocate" to look for possible flaws in an idea. To give ideas a fair hearing, someone should also develop an idea's positive aspects.

After the team has considered alternatives, it needs a method for picking one to implement. Typical selection methods include voting and consensus. Voting is quick but may leave people in the minority unhappy with and uncommitted to the majority's plan. Coming to consensus takes time but usually results in speedier implementation of ideas. Airing preferences early in the process, through polls before meetings and straw votes during meetings, can sometimes help teams establish consensus more quickly. Even in situations where consensus is not possible, good teams ensure everyone's ideas are considered. Most people will agree to support the team's decision, even if it was not their choice, as long as they feel they have been heard.

Business people in different nations have varying preferences about these two methods. An international survey of 15,000 managers and employees found that four-fifths of the Japanese respondents preferred consensus, but a little more than one-third of the Americans did. Other nations in which consensus was preferred included Germany, the Netherlands, Belgium, and France.[2]

Two strategies that are often useful in organizational teams are the standard problem-solving process and dot planning.

The standard problem-solving process has multiple steps:

1. Identify the task or problem. What is the team trying to do?
2. Understand what the team has to deliver, in what form, by what due date. Identify available resources.
3. Gather information, share it with all team members, and examine it critically.
4. Establish criteria. What would the ideal solution include? Which elements of that solution would be part of a less-than-ideal but still acceptable solution? What legal, financial, moral, or other limitations might keep a solution from being implemented?
5. Generate alternate solutions. Brainstorm and record ideas for the next step.
6. Measure the alternatives against the criteria.
7. Choose the best solution.

Dot planning offers a way for large teams to choose priorities quickly. First, the team brainstorms ideas, recording each on pages that are put on the wall. Then each individual gets two strips of three to five adhesive dots in different colors. One color represents high priority, the other lower priority. People then walk up to the pages and stick dots by the points they care most about. Some teams allow only one dot from one person on any one item; others allow someone who is really passionate about an idea to put all of his or her dots

---

Make the Most of Your Brainstorming

Matt Bowen, president of the Aloft Group Inc. marketing and PR agency, has advice on running successful brainstorming meetings:

- Identify a clear, concrete goal before you start. That allows you to establish some boundaries for ideas—about practicality or cost, for example—and helps you keep your brainstorming session focused.

- Let everyone involved in the meeting know what the goal is ahead of time. That gives everyone a chance to have ideas ready when they come to the meeting: if people "prebrainstorm," you can focus your meeting on refining ideas.

- Set limits on meeting size and duration. Bowen recommends limiting a brainstorming meeting to one hour, with no more than five to seven participants. An hour is enough time for a focused discussion, and it's easier for everyone to participate and be heard in a small team.

- Let the ideas flow freely. Bowen recommends practicing active listening skills that encourage people both to share their ideas and to build on each other's ideas.

- Remember that there are no bad ideas: any idea, however impractical, might inspire the best solution, and spending time weeding out weak ideas can stifle creativity.

- Brainstorm with a diverse team. The best ideas come out of teams made up of people with very different perspectives.

Adapted from Kelly K. Spors, "Productive Brainstorms Take the Right Mix of Elements," *Wall Street Journal*, July 24, 2008, B5.

on it. The dots make it easy to see which items the team believes are most and least important.

What happens if your team can't agree, or can't reach consensus? Team-building expert Bob Frisch suggests some strategies for working through a team-decision deadlock. In addition to using standard group techniques (setting clear goals, brainstorming solutions, and weighing the pros and cons of each solution), you should

- Use the current sticking point as the start for a new round of brainstorming. If there are two solutions that your team can't choose between, break the deadlock by brainstorming new solutions that combine the old ones. That will get the team making progress again and get new ideas on the table.
- Instead of rushing to a decision, allow time for team members to consider the options. Sometimes people refuse to compromise in order to avoid making a bad snap decision. Giving your team time to consider the options will take the pressure off. For especially complex decisions, schedule multiple meetings with time in between to do some research and to digest the pros and cons of each solution.
- Allow team members to make their decisions confidentially. People might refuse to state an opinion—or change an opinion—if they feel their opinions and reasoning will be judged negatively by the group. A secret ballot or other confidential form of "discussion" can help break a deadlock by giving team members an opportunity to voice their opinions without being judged or embarrassed.[3]

Feedback Strategies

As soon as the team begins to put its decisions into play, it needs to begin generating and heeding feedback. Sometimes this feedback will be external; it will come from supervisors, suppliers, clients, and customers. It should also, however, come from within the team. Teams frequently evaluate individual team members' performances, team performance, task progress, and team procedures. Feedback should be frequent and regular. Many teams have weekly feedback as well as feedback connected to specific stages of their task. Regular feedback is a good way to keep team members contributing their share of the work in a timely fashion.

One form of feedback that has been gaining popularity with organizations is **360-degree feedback.** This is a form of employee-development assessment in which a team member receives feedback from peers, managers, subordinates, customers, suppliers—from anyone touched by that person's work. Organizations or teams that use this model successfully typically apply it to everyone on the team, including team leaders. Research has shown this method is particularly effective when workers believe they can improve from the feedback. The method is also more effective when the feedback is positive and constructive.[4]

Characteristics of Successful Student Teams

Studies of student teams completing class projects have found that students in successful teams were not necessarily more skilled or more experienced than students in less successful teams. Instead, successful and less successful teams communicated differently.

- Successful teams assign specific tasks, set clear deadlines, and schedule frequent meetings. They also regularly communicate as a team about each member's progress. In less successful teams, members are not sure what they are supposed to be doing or when it is needed. Less successful teams meet less often.

- Successful teams recognize that they have to build trust with each other through goodwill, active listening, and consistent participation. Teams who trust each other tend to work together to solve problems that impact the whole team. Less successful teams expect members to complete their own parts, and fail to bring those parts together into a coherent whole, behaviors which also appear in unsuccessful workplace teams.[5]

- Successful teams recognize the contribution of every team member to the team's success, and take time to acknowledge each member during team meetings. When team members know that their efforts are noticed and appreciated by their peers, they're much more willing to contribute to the team. Less successful teams take individual contributions for granted.

- Successful teams listen carefully to each other and respond to emotions as well as words. Less successful teams pay less attention to what is said and how it is said.

- In successful teams members work more evenly and actively on the project.[6] Successful teams even find ways to use members who don't like working in teams. For example, a student who doesn't want to be a "team player" can be a freelancer for her team, completing assignments by herself and e-mailing them to the team. Less successful teams have a smaller percentage of active members and frequently have some members who do very little on the final project.

- Successful teams make important decisions together. In less successful teams, a subgroup or an individual makes decisions.

- Successful teams listen to criticism and try to improve their performance on the basis of it. In less successful teams, criticism is rationalized.

- Successful teams deal directly with conflicts that emerge; unsuccessful teams try to ignore conflicts.[7]

Research has shown that student teams produce better documents when they disagree over substantive issues of content and document design. The disagreement does not need to be angry: someone can simply say, "Yes, and here's another way we could do it." Deciding among two (or more) alternatives forces the proposer to explain the rationale for an idea. Even when the team adopts the original idea, considering alternatives rather than quickly accepting the first idea produces better writing.[8]

As you no doubt realize, these characteristics of good teams actually apply to most teams, not just student teams. A survey of engineering project teams found that 95% of the team members thought that good communication was the reason for team success, and poor communication the reason for team failures.[9]

Peer Pressure and Groupthink

Teams that never express conflict may be experiencing groupthink. **Groupthink** is the tendency for teams to put such a high premium on agreement that they directly or indirectly punish dissent.

Many people feel so much reluctance to express open disagreement that they will say they agree even when objective circumstances would suggest the first speaker cannot be right. In a series of classic experiments in the 1950s, Solomon Asch showed the influence of peer pressure. People sitting around a table were shown a large card with a line and asked to match it to the line

Break the Routine

Keith McFarland, *Inc.* 500 CEO and author of *The Breakthrough Company: How Everyday Companies Achieve Extraordinary Results*, offers these ideas for getting around groupthink. First, he notes that one of the main functions of a group leader is to identify your team's routine decisions—the ones that people make without thinking—and point them out. It's easy for team members to become so focused on getting the work done that they stop looking for ways to improve, so a team leader with an "outside" perspective can point out groupthink when it starts to happen.

Then, instead of talking about the things you've already accomplished successfully,

- Talk about how you'll meet future goals. When you focus on the future, you encourage people to exchange ideas and advice instead of just acknowledging what's already happened.

- Reflect on things that didn't work out. If you failed to meet a goal, it's not enough to just identify the problem; you need to discuss what happened, why it happened, and what your team needs to do to prevent a repeat.

- Ask people to share what they've learned. The fact that someone met a goal is less interesting than how he or she succeeded, so ask team members to share the secrets of their success. That helps spread good practices, and gets people talking about ways to improve.

Adapted from Keith McFarland, "The Problem with Business as Usual," in *BusinessWeek: Small Biz: Leadership*, http://www.businessweek.com/smallbiz/content/mar2008/sb20080321_755719.htm (accessed February 27, 2009).

Here a Team, There a Team

At ICU Medical, any worker can form a team to tackle any problem he or she wishes. What's more, the CEO has never vetoed a team decision.

Teams elect their own leaders, assign tasks, set meetings and deadlines. Most teams have 5 to 7 people, and 12 to 15 teams generally finish a project each quarter. Teams have changed the company's production process and set up a 401(k) plan.

Serving on a team is voluntary, although some employees with special expertise get invited to join teams frequently. But team participation does not give employees a break from their regular job duties, which still must be performed satisfactorily.

To help teams function smoothly, ICU has a team handbook, created—you guessed it—by yet another team. The 25-page handbook addresses issues like what to do at the first meeting and other frequently asked questions. Teams also must post notes about their meetings on the company intranet, where all employees can offer feedback.

As a final team incentive, ICU rewards successful teams, with the size of the reward reflecting the importance of the project.

Would you like to work at ICU?

Adapted from Erin White, "How a Company Made Everyone a Team Player," *Wall Street Journal*, August 13, 2007, B1.

of the same length on another card. It's a simple test: people normally match the lines correctly almost 100% of the time. However, in the experiment, all but one of the people in the group had been instructed to give false answers for several of the trials. When the group gave an incorrect answer, the focal person accepted the group's judgment 36.8% of the time. When someone else also gave a different answer—even if it was another wrong answer—the focal person accepted the group's judgment only 9% of the time.[10]

The experimenters varied the differences in line lengths, hoping to create a situation in which even the most conforming subjects would trust their own senses. But some people continued to accept the group's judgment, even when one line was seven inches longer than the other.

A classic example of groupthink, and one illustrating the sometimes constraining influence of a powerful team leader, occurred during President Kennedy's administration. The deliberations of Kennedy and his advisers illustrated classic characteristics of groupthink such as premature agreement and suppression of doubts. Kennedy guided the discussions in a way that minimized disagreements. The result was the disastrous decision to launch the Bay of Pigs invasion, whose failure led to the Cuban Missile Crisis. However, Kennedy subsequently analyzed what had gone wrong with the decision process, and he had his advisers do likewise. He used these analyses to change the process for the Cuban Missile Crisis. Although the team again included Kennedy and many of the same advisers, it avoided groupthink. Kennedy ordered the team to question, allowed free-ranging discussions, used separate subteam meetings, and sometimes left the room himself to avoid undue influence of the discussions.[11]

Teams that "go along with the crowd" and suppress conflict ignore the full range of alternatives, seek only information that supports the positions they already favor, and fail to prepare contingency plans to cope with foreseeable setbacks. A business suffering from groupthink may launch a new product that senior executives support but for which there is no demand. Student teams suffering from groupthink turn in inferior documents.

The best correctives to groupthink are to consciously search for additional alternatives, to test one's assumptions against those of a range of other people, and to protect the right of people on a team to disagree. When power roles are a factor, input may need to be anonymous.

Working on Diverse Teams

In any organization, you will work with people whose backgrounds and working styles differ from yours. Residents of small towns and rural areas have different notions of friendliness than do people from big cities. Marketing people tend to have different values and attitudes than researchers or engineers. In addition, differences arise from gender, class, race and ethnicity, religion, age, sexual orientation, and physical ability. Even people who share some of these characteristics are likely to differ in personality type.

These differences affect how people behave on teams and what they expect from teams. For example, in a business negotiation, people from Asia are more likely to see the goal of negotiation as development of a relationship between the parties. In contrast, American negotiators (especially the lawyers on the team) are more likely to see the purpose of a negotiation as producing a signed contract.[12] Such differences are likely to affect what people talk about and how they talk. Some western cultures use direct approaches; other cultures, especially eastern cultures, consider such approaches rude and respond by withholding information.

Other pitfalls of team differences exist. Sometimes people who sense a difference may attribute problems in the team to prejudice, when other factors

Diverse teams can extend the range of group efforts and ideas.

may be responsible. Also, a significant body of research shows that accurate interpretation of emotions in diverse teams is influenced by factors such as gender, nationality, race, and status.[13] On the other hand, another body of research shows that ethnically diverse teams produce more and higher-quality ideas.[14] Research has also found that over time, as team members focus on their task, mission, or profession, cultural differences become less significant than the role of being a team member.[15]

Sometimes the culture to which the team belongs is a distinct asset, uniting strangers in positive ways and giving them strengths to use in high-stakes situations. With their team skills enhanced by the organizational culture, airline crews and emergency teams may perform heroically in a crisis.

Savvy team members play to each other's strengths and devise strategies for dealing with differences. These efforts can benefit the whole team. A study of multicultural teams published in the *Harvard Business Review* found acknowledging cultural gaps openly and cooperatively working through them an ideal strategy for surmounting cultural differences. For example, a US and UK team used their differing approaches to decision making to create a higher-quality decision. The UK members used their slower approach to analyze possible pitfalls, and the US members used their "forge ahead" approach to move the project along. Both sides appreciated the contributions of the other members.[16]

Leading a Team through a Crisis

Being a team leader is challenging enough, but what about leading a team through a high-pressure situation? A crisis puts additional stress on all team members, but especially on the team leader: as the leader, you have to ensure your team remains focused and motivated, even when you're having difficulty being focused and motivated yourself. Try these ideas for leading—or working as a member of—a team under stress:

- Active and empathic listening shows your team members that you're genuinely involved with them and their work. People can be emotional under stress, and nonjudgmental listening can help you understand what your team members are feeling, and why.

- Stay informed about everyone's progress to help you see where you're making progress, where you're falling behind, and why. Instead of letting one team member sink further and further behind, organize the whole team to help him/her. Such rescue efforts build team unity and keep you moving forward.

- Use positive emphasis: instead of dwelling on negative stressors, redirect your team's energy toward future-focused goals.

- Recognize that the whole team is under stress—including you! To help your team through stressful situations you need to deal with your own stress. Better to take time out and work through your own stress than to bottle it up and risk taking out your frustrations on your team members.

Adapted from Emily Thornton, "The New Rules: Managing through a Crisis," *BusinessWeek*, January 19, 2009, 30–34.

Conflict Resolution

Conflicts are going to arise in any group of intelligent people who care about their task. Yet many of us feel so uncomfortable with conflict that we pretend it doesn't exist. However, unacknowledged conflicts rarely go away: they fester, making the next interchange more difficult.

To reduce the number of conflicts in a team,

- Make responsibilities and ground rules clear at the beginning.
- Discuss problems as they arise, rather than letting them fester till people explode.
- Realize that team members are not responsible for each others' happiness.

In spite of these efforts, some conflict is a part of any team's life and that conflict needs to be resolved. When a conflict is emotionally charged, people will need a chance to calm themselves before they can arrive at a well-reasoned solution. Meeting expert John Tropman recommends the "two-meeting rule" for emotional matters: Controversial items should be handled at two different meetings. The first meeting is a chance for everyone to air a point of view about the issue. The second meeting is the one at which the team reaches a decision. The time between the two meetings becomes a cooling-off period.[17]

Figure 6.3 suggests several possible solutions to conflicts that student teams experience. Often the symptom arises from a feeling of not being respected or appreciated by the team. Therefore, many problems can be averted if people advocate for their ideas in a positive way. One way to do this is to devote as much effort to positive observations as possible. Another technique is to state analysis rather than mere opinions. Instead of "I wouldn't read an eight-page brochure," the member of a team could say, "Tests we did a couple of years ago found a better response for two-page brochures. Could we move some of that information to our Web site?" As in this example, an opinion can vary from person to person; stating an opinion does not provide a basis for the team to make a decision. In contrast, analysis provides objective information for the team to consider.[18]

Steps in Conflict Resolution

Dealing successfully with conflict requires attention both to the issues and to people's feelings. The following techniques will help you resolve conflicts constructively.

1. Make sure the people involved really disagree.

Sometimes different conversational styles, differing interpretations of data, or faulty inferences create apparent conflicts when no real disagreement exists.

Someone who asks "Are those data accurate?" may just be asking for source information, not questioning the conclusions the team drew from the data.

Sometimes someone who's under a lot of pressure may explode. But the speaker may just be venting anger and frustration; he or she may not in fact be angry at the person who receives the explosion. One way to find out if a person is just venting is to ask, "Is there something you'd like me to do?"

2. Check to see that everyone's information is correct.

Sometimes people are operating on outdated or incomplete information. People may also act on personal biases or opinions rather than data.

Figure 6.3   Troubleshooting Team Problems

Symptom	Possible solutions
We can't find a time to meet that works for all of us.	a. Find out why people can't meet at certain times. Some reasons suggest their own solutions. For example, if someone has to stay home with small children, perhaps the team could meet at that person's home. b. Assign out-of-class work to "committees" to work on parts of the project. c. Use e-mail to share, discuss, and revise drafts.
One person isn't doing his or her fair share.	a. Find out what is going on. Is the person overcommitted? Does he or she feel unappreciated? Those are different problems you'd solve in different ways. b. Early on, do things to build team loyalty. Get to know each other as writers and as people. Sometimes do something fun together. c. Encourage the person to contribute. "Mary, what do you think?" "Jim, which part of this would you like to draft?" Then find something to praise in the work. "Thanks for getting us started." d. If someone misses a meeting, assign someone else to bring the person up to speed. People who miss meetings for legitimate reasons (job interviews, illness) but don't find out what happened may become less committed to the team. e. Consider whether strict equality is the most important criterion. On a given project, some people may have more knowledge or time than others. Sometimes the best team product results from letting people do different amounts of work. f. Even if you divide up the work, make all decisions as a team: what to write about, which evidence to include, what graphs to use, what revisions to make. People excluded from decisions become less committed to the team.
I seem to be the only one on the team who cares about quality.	a. Find out why other members "don't care." If they received low grades on early assignments, stress that good ideas and attention to detail can raise grades. Perhaps the team should meet with the instructor to discuss what kinds of work will pay the highest dividends. b. Volunteer to do extra work. Sometimes people settle for something that's just OK because they don't have the time or resources to do excellent work. They might be happy for the work to be done—if they don't have to do it. c. Be sure that you're respecting what each person can contribute. Team members sometimes withdraw when one person dominates and suggests that he or she is "better" than other members. d. Fit specific tasks to individual abilities. People generally do better work in areas they see as their strengths. A visual learner who doesn't care about the written report may do an excellent job on the accompanying visuals.
People in the team don't seem willing to disagree. We end up going with the first idea suggested.	a. Brainstorm so you have multiple possibilities to consider. b. After an idea is suggested, have each person on the team suggest a way it could be improved. c. Appoint someone to be a devil's advocate. d. Have each person on the team write a draft. It's likely the drafts will be different, and you'll have several options to mix and match. e. Talk about good ways to offer criticism. Sometimes people don't disagree because they're afraid that other team members won't tolerate disagreement.
One person just criticizes everything.	a. Ask the person to follow up the criticism with a suggestion for improvement. b. Talk about ways to express criticism tactfully. "I think we need to think about x" is more tactful than "You're wrong." c. If the criticism is about ideas and writing (not about people), value it. Ideas and documents need criticism if we are to improve them.

Who Does What

Working successfully on a team depends on being open about preferences, constraints, and skills and then using creative problem-solving techniques.

A person who prefers to outline the whole project in advance may be on a team with someone who expects to do the project at the last minute. Someone who likes to talk out ideas before writing may be on a team with someone who wants to work on a draft in silence and revise it before showing it to anyone. By being honest about your preferences, you make it possible for the team to find a creative solution that builds on what each person can offer.

In one team, Rob wanted to wait to start the project because he was busy with other class work. David and Susan, however, wanted to go ahead now because their schedules would get busier later in the term. A creative solution would be for David and Susan to do most of the work on parts of the project that had to be completed first (such as collecting data and writing the proposal) and for Rob to do work that had to be done later (such as creating tables, revising, editing, proofreading, and making bound copies).

What are your work preferences? What are the preferences of other people on your team? How can you work together to accommodate everyone's schedules and preferences?

3. Discover the needs each person is trying to meet.

Sometimes determining the real needs makes it possible to see a new solution. The **presenting problem** that surfaces as the subject of dissension may or may not be the real problem. For example, a worker who complains about the hours he's putting in may in fact be complaining not about the hours themselves but about not feeling appreciated. A supervisor who complains that the other supervisors don't invite her to meetings may really feel that the other managers don't accept her as a peer. Sometimes people have trouble seeing beyond the presenting problem because they've been taught to suppress their anger, especially toward powerful people. One way to tell whether the presenting problem is the real problem is to ask, "If this were solved, would I be satisfied?" If the answer is *no,* then the problem that presents itself is not the real problem. Solving the presenting problem won't solve the conflict. Keep probing until you get to the real conflict.

4. Search for alternatives.

Sometimes people are locked into conflict because they see too few alternatives. People tend to handle complexity by looking for ways to simplify. In a team, someone makes a suggestion, so the team members discuss it as if it is the only alternative. The team generates more alternatives only if the first one is unacceptable. As a result, the team's choice depends on the order in which team members think of ideas. When a decision is significant, the team needs a formal process to identify alternatives before moving on to a decision. Many teams use brainstorming when they search for alternatives.

5. Repair negative feelings.

Conflict can emerge without anger and without escalating the disagreement, as the next section shows. But if people's feelings have been hurt, the team needs to deal with those feelings to resolve the conflict constructively. Only when people feel respected and taken seriously can they take the next step of trusting others on the team.

Criticism Responses

Conflict is particularly difficult to resolve when someone else criticizes or attacks us directly. When we are criticized, our natural reaction is to defend ourselves—perhaps by counterattacking. The counterattack prompts the critic to defend him- or herself. The conflict escalates; feelings are hurt; issues become muddied and more difficult to resolve.

Just as resolving conflict depends on identifying the needs each person is trying to meet, so dealing with criticism depends on understanding the real concern of the critic. Constructive ways to respond to criticism and get closer to the real concern include paraphrasing, checking for feelings, checking inferences, and buying time with limited agreement.

Paraphrasing

To **paraphrase,** repeat in your own words the verbal content of the critic's message. The purposes of paraphrasing are (1) to be sure that you have heard the critic accurately, (2) to let the critic know what his or her statement means to you, and (3) to communicate that you are taking the critic and his or her feelings seriously.

Criticism: You guys are stonewalling my requests for information.

Paraphrase: You think that we don't give you the information you need.

Checking for feelings

When you check the critic's feelings, you identify the emotions that the critic seems to be expressing verbally or nonverbally. The purposes of checking feelings are to try to understand (1) the critic's emotions, (2) the importance of the criticism for the critic, and (3) the unspoken ideas and feelings that may actually be more important than the voiced criticism.

Criticism: You guys are stonewalling my requests for information.

Feelings check: You sound pretty angry.

Always *ask* the other person if you are right in your perception. Even the best reader of nonverbal cues is sometimes wrong.

Checking for inferences

When you check the inferences you draw from criticism, you identify the implied meaning of the verbal and nonverbal content of the criticism, taking the statement a step further than the words of the critic to try to understand *why* the critic is bothered by the action or attitude under discussion. The purposes of checking inferences are (1) to identify the real (as opposed to the presenting) problem and (2) to communicate the feeling that you care about resolving the conflict.

Criticism: You guys are stonewalling my requests for information.

Inference: Are you saying that you need more information from our team?

Inferences can be faulty. In the above interchange, the critic might respond, "I don't need more information. I just think you should give it to me without my having to file three forms in triplicate every time I want some data."

Buying time with limited agreement

Buying time is a useful strategy for dealing with criticisms that really sting. When you buy time with limited agreement, you avoid escalating the conflict (as an angry statement might do) but also avoid yielding to the critic's point of view. To buy time, restate the part of the criticism you agree to be true. (This is often a fact, rather than the interpretation or evaluation the critic has made of that fact.) *Then let the critic respond, before you say anything else.* The purposes of buying time are (1) to allow you time to think when a criticism really hits home and threatens you, so that you can respond to the criticism rather than simply reacting defensively, and (2) to suggest to the critic that you are trying to hear what he or she is saying.

Criticism: You guys are stonewalling my requests for information.

Limited agreement: It's true that the cost projections you asked for last week still aren't ready.

DO NOT go on to justify or explain. A "Yes, but . . ." statement is not a time-buyer.

You-Attitude in Conflict Resolution

You-attitude means looking at things from the audience's point of view, respecting the audience, and protecting the audience's ego. The *you* statements that many people use when they're angry attack the audience; they do not illustrate you-attitude. Instead, substitute statements about your own feelings. In conflict, *I* statements show good you-attitude!

Lacks you-attitude: You never do your share of the work.

You-attitude: I feel that I'm doing more than my share of the work on this project.

http://www.effective
meetings.com/
sitemap.asp

Log onto
EffectiveMeetings
.com for articles offering
advice about making meetings
effective. What advice offered
in these articles do you think
would be helpful for conducting
meetings with your fellow group
members?

Lacks you-attitude: Even you should be able to run the report through a spelling checker.

You-attitude: I'm not willing to have my name on a report with so many spelling errors. I did lots of the writing, and I don't think I should have to do the proofreading and spell checking, too.

Effective Meetings

Meetings have always taken a large part of the average manager's week. Although e-mail has eliminated some meetings, the increased number of teams means that meetings are even more frequent. As the sidebar on this page suggests, meetings are not always good. Many workers see them as all too often a waste of time, interrupting valuable work.[19] However, meetings can easily be made more effective.

Meetings can have multiple purposes:

- To share information.
- To brainstorm ideas.
- To evaluate ideas.
- To develop plans.
- To make decisions.
- To create a document.
- To motivate members.

Meeting Overload

A recent study by Steven G. Rogelberg from the University of North Carolina at Charlotte confirms what you always believed: too many meetings are bad for you, and for your employer.

Rogelberg distributed surveys to 980 professionals. He found that the more meetings task-oriented employees attended, the less of a positive attitude these employees had about their job and overall well-being. Often these feelings surfaced from these task-oriented employees because they viewed meetings as interruptions to other work they could be completing. On the other hand, for people who had less ambition and motivation about their work, meetings had a positive effect because they provided a structure to their work day.

Are you a goal-oriented person? Do meetings frustrate you?

Adapted from E. Packard, "Meetings Frustrate Task-Oriented Employees, Study Finds," *Monitor on Psychology* 37, no. 6 (June 2006), 10.

When meetings combine two or more purposes, it's useful to make the purposes explicit. For example, in the meeting of a university senate or a company's board of directors, some items are presented for information. Discussion is possible, but the group will not be asked to make a decision. Other items are presented for action; the group will be asked to vote. A business meeting might specify that the first half hour will be time for brainstorming, with the second half hour devoted to evaluation.

Formal meetings are run under strict rules, like the rules of parliamentary procedure summarized in *Robert's Rules of Order*. Motions must be made formally before a topic can be debated. Each point is settled by a vote. **Minutes** record each motion and the vote on it. Formal rules help the meeting run smoothly if the group is very large or if the agenda is very long. **Informal meetings,** which are much more common in the workplace, are run more loosely. Votes may not be taken if most people seem to agree. Minutes may not be kept. Informal meetings are better for team-building and problem solving.

Planning the agenda is the foundation of a good meeting. A good agenda indicates

- A list of items for consideration.
- Whether each item is presented for information, for discussion, or for a decision.
- Who is sponsoring or introducing each item.
- How much time is allotted for each item.

The information on an agenda should be specific enough that participants can come to the meeting prepared with ideas, background information, and any other resources they need for completing each agenda item.

Many groups start their agendas with routine items on which agreement will be easy. Doing so gets the meeting off to a positive start. However, it may also waste the time when people are most attentive. Another approach is to put routine items at the end. If there's a long list of routine items, sometimes you can dispense with them in an omnibus motion. An **omnibus motion** allows a group to approve many items together rather than voting on each separately. A single omnibus motion might cover multiple changes to operational guidelines, or a whole slate of candidates for various offices, or various budget recommendations. It's important to schedule controversial items early in the meeting, when people's energy level is high, and to allow enough time for full discussion. Giving a controversial item only half an hour at the end of the day or evening makes people suspect that the leaders are trying to manipulate them.

Pay attention to people and process as well as to the task at hand. At informal meetings, a good leader observes nonverbal feedback and invites everyone to participate. If conflict seems to be getting out of hand, a leader may want to focus attention on the group process and ways that it could deal with conflict, before getting back to the substantive issues.

If the group doesn't formally vote, the leader should summarize the group's consensus after each point. At the end of the meeting, the leader should summarize all decisions and remind the group who is responsible for implementing or following up on each item. If no other notes are taken, someone should record the decisions and assignments. Long minutes will be most helpful if assignments are set off visually from the narrative.

If you're planning a long meeting, for example, a training session or a conference, recognize that networking is part of the value of the meeting. Allow short breaks at least every two hours and generous breaks twice a day so participants can talk informally to each other. If participants will be strangers, include some social functions so they can get to know each other. If they will have different interests or different levels of knowledge, plan concurrent sessions on different topics or for people with different levels of expertise.

Collaborative Writing

Whatever your career, it is likely that some of the documents you produce will be written with a team. Collaboration is often prompted by one of the following situations:

1. The task is too big or the time is too short for one person to do all the work.
2. No one person has all the knowledge or skills required to do the task.
3. A team representing different perspectives must reach a consensus.
4. The stakes for the task are so high that the organization wants the best efforts of as many people as possible; no one person wants the sole responsibility for the success or failure of the document.

Collaborative writing can be done by two people or by a much larger group. The team can be democratic or run by a leader who makes decisions alone. The team may share or divide responsibility for each stage in the writing process. There are several ways teams commonly divide the work. One person might do the main writing, with others providing feedback. Another approach is to divide the whole project into smaller tasks and to assign each task to a different team member. This approach shares the workload more evenly but is harder to coordinate. Sometimes team members write together simultaneously, discussing and responding to each other's ideas.

Write Meeting Minutes Minutes Later (not Months)

During congressional hearings on the cholesterol drug Vytorin, representatives from Merck and Schering-Plough (the drug's manufacturers) were grilled by lawmakers over a set of meeting minutes.

The minutes were from a meeting held between the drug manufacturers and the outside contractors who had researched the drug's effectiveness. According to the minutes, those consultants had recommended changing the way they evaluated the results of their research to "fudge" the data and make it seem that Vytorin was more effective than it really is. But when they testified before Congress, the researchers claimed that Vytorin's manufacturers had suggested that change in their research process—and that those minutes had been written by Merck employees almost a year after the meeting. In fact, those minutes hadn't been written until after the congressional investigation began—a delay which made it look like Vytorin's manufacturers were "fudging" more than test data.

Meeting minutes serve two main purposes: they preserve a record of what happened and what was decided, and they capture the facts so that if there's a dispute later, it's easier to untangle the truth. In either case, the best practice is to write the minutes right after the meeting, so that everything is still remembered correctly.

Adapted from Alica Mundy and Ron Winslow, "Accuracy of Vytorin Minutes Raises Doubt," *Wall Street Journal*, April 12, 2008, A3.

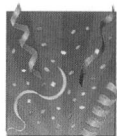

Blue Man Group-Work

The Blue Man Group started in 1988 as a trio of performance artists doing street theater in New York City. Today, Blue Man Group is an entertainment franchise with about 70 Blue Men employed in nine theater shows and two touring concerts worldwide. They fill stadiums, they've founded their own creativity-based preschool, and they've been nominated for a Grammy. How did they do it? Teamwork.

As Matt Goldman, one of the founding Blue Men, notes, "Three is the smallest unit where you can have an outsider." The Blue Man Group uses consensus to create their music, original instruments, and shows—and to run their business. They discuss decisions until they reach a point where all three members can agree. That lets each member bring his/her own unique contributions to the process, while ensuring that the whole team is satisfied with the result. "It takes longer, but we find if you keep talking things through, you reach a better choice."

Working as part of a team is one of the most challenging communication tasks you can face in a professional setting. As a team member, you'll use your audience analysis skills to build goodwill with people inside *and* outside of your team, and your organizational skills to keep both your communication and your work moving smoothly.

Sources: Liz Welch, "How We Did It: The Blue Man Group, from Downtown Performance Art to Global Entertainment Empire," *Inc.*, August 2008, 110–112; and Blue Man Productions, Inc., "Blue Man Group: Blue Man FAQs," in *About: FAQs*, http://www.blueman.com/about/faqs (accessed February 27, 2009).

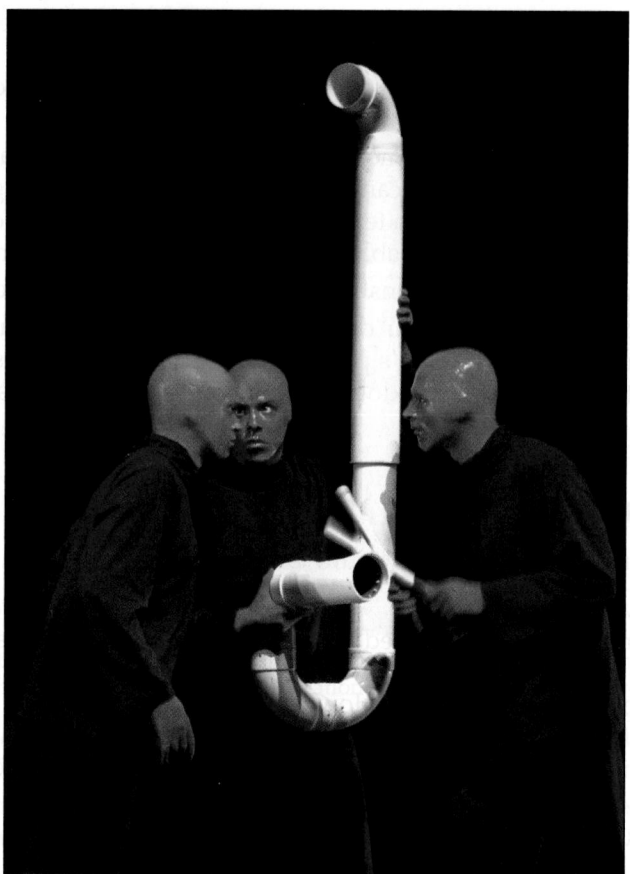

The Blue Man Group uses consensus to create their shows and run their business.

- Have at least one person check the whole document for correctness in grammar, mechanics, and spelling and for consistency in the way that format elements (particularly headings), names, and numbers are handled.
- Run the document through a spell checker.
- Even if you use a computerized spell checker, at least one human being should proofread the document too.

Like any member of the writing team, those handling the editing tasks need to consider how they express their ideas. In many situations, the editor plays the role of diplomat, careful to suggest changes in ways that do not seem to call the writer's abilities into question. Describing the reason for a change is typically more helpful than stating an opinion. Writers are more likely to allow editing of their prose if they know a sentence has a dangling modifier, or a paragraph needs work on parallel structure. Using words like *could* and *should* to modify a direction can add a tone of politeness.

Making the Team Process Work

The information in this chapter can help your team interact effectively, run meetings efficiently, and deal with conflict constructively. The following suggestions apply specifically to writing teams:

- Give yourselves plenty of time to discuss problems and find solutions. Writing a team report may require hours of discussion time in addition to the time individuals spend doing research and writing drafts.

- Take the time to get to know team members and to build team loyalty. Team members will work harder and the final document will be better if the team is important to members.
- Be a responsible team member. Attend all the meetings; carry out your responsibilities on time.
- Be aware that people have different ways of experiencing reality and of expressing themselves.
- Because talking is "looser" than writing, people on a team can think they agree when they don't. Don't assume that because the discussion went smoothly, a draft written by one person will necessarily be acceptable.
- Allow more time at all stages of the writing process than you would if you were writing the document by yourself.

Summary of Key Points

- Effective teams balance information leadership, interpersonal leadership, and procedural team management.
- Successful teams set clear deadlines, schedule frequent meetings, deal directly with conflict, have an inclusive decision-making style, and have a higher proportion of members who worked actively on the project.
- **Groupthink** is the tendency for groups to put such a high premium on agreement that they directly or indirectly punish dissent. The best correctives to groupthink are to consciously search for additional alternatives, to test one's assumptions against those of a range of other people, and to protect the right of each person in the group to disagree.
- To resolve conflicts, first make sure that the people involved really disagree. Next, check to see that everyone's information is correct. Discover the needs each person is trying to meet. The **presenting problem** that surfaces as the subject of dissension may or may not be the real problem. Search for alternatives. Repair negative feelings.
- Constructive ways to respond to criticism include paraphrasing, checking for feelings, checking inferences, and buying time with limited agreement.
- Use statements about your own feelings to own the problem and avoid attacking the audience. In conflict, *I* statements are good you-attitude!
- To make meetings more effective,
  - State the purpose of the meeting at the beginning.
  - Distribute an agenda that indicates whether each item is for information, discussion, or action, and how long each is expected to take.
  - Allow enough time to discuss controversial issues.
  - Pay attention to people and process as well as to the task at hand.
  - If you don't take formal votes, summarize the group's consensus after each point. At the end of the meeting, summarize all decisions and remind the group who is responsible for implementing or following up on each item.
- **Collaborative writing** means working with other writers to produce a single document. Writers producing a joint document need to pay attention not only to the basic steps in the writing process but also to the processes of team formation and conflict resolution. They also need to allow more time than they would for single-authored documents.

CHAPTER 6   # Exercises and Problems

6.1   Reviewing the Chapter

1. What are 10 kinds of productive roles in teams? Which roles do you prefer to play? (LO 1)
2. What are five kinds of nonproductive roles in teams? (LO 1)
3. What are some team decision-making strategies? (LO 2)
4. Name five characteristics of successful teams. (LO 3)
5. What is groupthink? Have you ever experienced it? (LO 2)
6. What are some techniques for resolving conflict? (LO 4)
7. What are some techniques for responding to criticism? (LO 4)
8. What are some techniques for making meetings effective? (LO 5)
9. What are some techniques for collaborative writing? (LO 6)
10. Have you ever been part of a team that wrote a document as a whole group rather than assigning out pieces? If so, how did the process work for your team? (LO 6)

6.2   Brainstorming Ways to Resolve Conflicts

Suggest one or more ways that each of the following teams could deal with the conflict(s) it faces.

1. Mike and Takashi both find writing hard. Elise has been getting better grades than either of them, so they offer to do all the research if she'll organize the document and write, revise, edit, and proofread it. Elise thinks that this method would leave her doing a disproportionate share of the work. Moreover, scheduling the work would be difficult, since she wouldn't know how good their research was until the last minute.
2. Because of their class and work schedules, Lars and Andrea want to hold team meetings from 8 to 10 PM, working later if need be. But Juan's wife works the evening shift, and he needs to be home with his children, two of whom have to be in bed before 8. He wants to meet from 8 to 10 AM, but the others don't want to meet that early.
3. Lynn wants to divide up the work exactly equally, with firm due dates. Marcia is trying to get into medical school. She says she'd rather do the lion's share of the work so that she knows it's good.
4. Jessie's father is terminally ill. This team isn't very important in terms of what's going on in her life, and she knows she may have to miss some team meetings.
5. Sherry is aware that she is the person on her team who always points out the logical flaws in arguments: she's the one who reminds the team that they haven't done all the parts of the assignment. She doesn't want her team to turn in a flawed product, but she wonders whether the other team members see her as too critical.
6. Jim's team missed several questions on their team quiz. Talking to Tae-Suk after class, Jim learns that Tae-Suk knew all the answers. "Why didn't you say anything?" Jim asks angrily. Tae-Suk responds quietly, "Todd said that he knew the answers. I did not want to argue with him. We have to work together, and I do not want anyone to lose face."

6.3   Comparing Meeting Minutes

Have two or more people take minutes of each class or team meeting for a week. Compare the accounts of the same meeting.

- To what extent do they agree on what happened?
- Does one contain information missing in other accounts?
- Do any accounts disagree on a specific fact?
- How do you account for the differences you find?

As your instructor directs,

a. Discuss your findings with your team.
b. Share your team findings orally with the class.
c. Describe and analyze your findings in a memo to your instructor.

6.4   Recommending a Policy on Student Entrepreneurs

Assume that your small team comprises the officers in student government on your campus. You receive this e-mail from the Dean of Students:

> As you know, campus policy says that no student may use campus resources to conduct business-related activities. Students can't conduct business out of dorm rooms or use university e-mail addresses for business. They can't post business Web pages on the university server.
>
> On the other hand, a survey conducted by the Kauffman Center for Entrepreneurial Leadership showed that 7 out of 10 teens want to become entrepreneurs.
>
> Should campus policy be changed to allow students to use dorm rooms and university e-mail addresses for business? (And then what happens when roommates complain and our network can't carry the increased e-mail traffic?) Please recommend what support (if any) should be given to student entrepreneurs.

Your team will be writing a report recommending what (if anything) your campus should do for student entrepreneurs and supporting your recommendation.

Hints:

- Does your campus offer other support for entrepreneurs (courses, a business plan competition, a start-up incubator)? What should be added or expanded?
- Is it realistic to ask alumni for money to fund student start-ups?
- Are campus dorms, e-mail, phone, and delivery services funded by tax dollars? If your school is a public institution, do state or local laws limit business use?

You need to

- Send e-mail messages to team members describing your initial point of view on the issue and discussing the various options.
- Help your team write the report.
- Write a memo to your instructor telling how satisfied you are with
  - The decision your team reached.
  - The process you used to reach it.
  - The document your team produced.

6.5   Recommending a Fair Way to Assign Work around the Holidays

Assume that your team comprises a hospital's Labor-Management Committee. This e-mail arrives from the hospital administrator:

> Subject: Allocating Holiday Hours
>
> It's that time of year again, and we're starting to get requests for time off from every department. We have shifts where every physician and half the nurses want time off. Don't these people realize that we can't close down over a holiday? And what's worse is that some of the shift leads are giving preferential treatment to their friends. The head of the nurses' union has already started complaining to me.
>
> We need a comprehensive, hospital-wide procedure for assigning holiday vacation time that doesn't make us shut down wards. It needs to be flexible, because people like to take a week off around Christmas. But we have to set limits: no more than one-quarter of the staff can take time off at any one time. And those nurses like to swap shifts with each other to arrange their days off into larger blocks, so we need to cover that too.

Write up a policy to keep these people in line. Be sure to throw in the safety concerns and regulatory stuff.

Your team will be performing these tasks:

a. Write a team response recommending a new policy and supporting your recommendations. Include two transmittal e-mails: one to the hospital administrator, and one to the hospital's medical and nursing staff. Take care to address the two audiences' different needs and expectations with good you-attitude and positive emphasis.

b. Create a one-page notice describing your new policy. This notice should be suitable for posting at the duty desk for each ward: that is, in full view of both your employees and your customers (the patients). Create an effective visual design that emphasizes and organizes the text.

You personally need to

- Send e-mail messages to team members describing your initial point of view on the issue and discussing the various options.
- Help your team write the documents.
- Write a memo to your instructor telling how satisfied you are with

  - The decisions your team reached.
  - The process you used to reach them.
  - The documents your team produced.

6.6   Recommending a Dress Policy

Assume that your small team comprises your organization's Labor-Management Committee

This e-mail arrives from the CEO:

In the last 10 years, we became increasingly casual. But changed circumstances seem to call for more formality. Is it time to reinstate a dress policy? If so, what should it be?

Your team will be writing a response recommending the appropriate dress for employees and supporting your recommendation.

Hint:

Agree on an office, factory, store, or other workplace to use for this problem.

You need to

- Send e-mail messages to team members describing your initial point of view on the issue and discussing the various options.
- Help your team write the response.
- Write a memo to your instructor telling how satisfied you are with

  - The decision your team reached.
  - The process you used to reach it.
  - The document your team produced.

6.7   Responding to an Employee Grievance

Assume that your small team comprises the Labor-Management committee at the headquarters of a chain of grocery stores. This e-mail arrives from the vice president for human resources:

As you know, company policy requires that employees smile at customers and make eye contact with them. In the past 9 months, 12 employees have filed grievances over this rule. They say they are being harassed by customers who think they are flirting with them. A produce clerk claims customers have propositioned her and followed her to her car. Another says "Let *me* decide who I am going to say hello to with a big smile." The union wants us to change the policy to let workers *not* make eye contact with customers, and to allow workers to refuse to carry groceries to a customer's car at night. My own feeling is that we want to maintain our image as a friendly store that cares about customers, but that we also don't want to require behavior that leads to harassment. Let's find a creative solution.

Your team will be writing a group response recommending whether to change the policy and supporting your recommendation.

You need to
- Send e-mail messages to team members describing your initial point of view on the issue and discussing the various options.

- Help your team write the response.
- Write a memo to your instructor telling how satisfied you are with
  - The decision your team reached.
  - The process you used to reach it.
  - The document your team produced.

6.8   Answering an Ethics Question

Assume that your team comprises your organization's Ethics Committee. You receive the following anonymous note:

People are routinely using the company letterhead to write letters to members of Congress, senators, and even the president stating their positions on various issues. Making their opinions known is of course their right, but doing so on letterhead stationery implies that they are speaking for the company, which they are not.

I think that the use of letterhead for anything other than official company business should be prohibited.

Your team will be determining the best solution to the problem and then communicating it in a message to all employees.

You need to
- Send e-mail messages to team members describing your initial point of view on the issue and discussing the various options.

- Help your team write the message.
- Write a memo to your instructor telling how satisfied you are with
  - The decision your team reached.
  - The process you used to reach it.
  - The document your team produced.

6.9   Interviewing Workers about Collaborating

Interview someone who works in an organization about his or her on-the-job collaboration activities. Possible questions to ask include the following:
- How often do you work on collaborative projects?
- Do your collaborative projects always include people who are in your immediate office? How often do you collaborate with people via telephone or the Internet?
- How do you begin collaborative projects? What are the first steps you take when working with others?
- How do you handle disagreements?
- What do you do when someone isn't doing their share of the work on a collaborative project?
- What do you do to see every person meets team deadlines?

- How do you handle unexpected problems? Illness? Injury? Broken equipment?
- What advice can you give about effectively collaborating on projects?

As your instructor directs,
a. Share your information with a small team of students in your class.
b. Present your findings orally to the class.
c. Present your findings in a memo to your instructor.
d. Join with other students to present your findings in a team report.

6.10   Writing a Team Action Plan

Before you begin working on a team project, develop a team action plan to establish a framework that will hold your team members accountable for their work.

After reading the project assignment sheet and meeting your team, decide upon answers for the following questions:

- Will you have a team leader? If so, who? Why is that person qualified to be the team leader? What are that person's responsibilities? How will you proceed if the team leader is unable to meet those responsibilities?

- What will be each team member's role? What is each team member's qualification for that role?
- How are you dividing your work? Why did you choose to divide the work the way you did?
- What are the tasks your team needs to accomplish? For each task in the assignment, identify a concrete deliverable (What do you need to hand in?), a concrete measure for success (How will your team decide if you completed that task well?), and a work schedule (When does each task need to be done?)
- How will you resolve disagreements that may arise while working on the project? How will your team make decisions: By majority? By consensus?
- When and where will you hold meetings? Decide whether you can hold meetings if all team members are not present. How will you inform team members of what occurred at meetings if they were not present?
- Define what "absence" means for your team. Are all absences equal? How should a team member who's going to be absent let the team know? How

far in advance does your team need to know about an absence? How many absences from one team member will be too many? What are the consequences of too many absences?

- Create a policy dealing with people who don't attend class during your preparation days or during your presentation; people who don't attend meetings outside class; people who miss deadlines, don't do their work at all or in a timely manner, or who consistently turn in incomplete or poor-quality work. What penalties will you apply? (Some ideas: you might consider loss of points, grade reductions, failure, a team firing, or a team intervention.)
- Will you report problem members to your instructor? If so, at what point? What role do you want your instructor to have in dealing with problem members?

After your team determines and agrees on an action plan, the team's secretary should send your answers in a memo to your instructor, who will keep the document on file in case a problem arises.

6.11   Writing Team Meeting Minutes

As you work in a collaborative team setting, designate a different member to take minutes for each meeting.

As your instructor directs, your minutes should include:

- Name of the team holding the meeting.
- Members who were present.
- Members who were absent.
- Place, time, and date of meeting.
- Work accomplished, and who did it, during the meeting.

- Actions that need to be completed, the person responsible, and the due date.
- Decisions made during the meeting.
- New issues raised at the meeting but not resolved should be recorded for future meetings.
- Signature of acting secretary.

Remember to keep your minutes brief and to the point. When the minutes are complete, e-mail them to your fellow team members and cc: them to your instructor.

6.12   Keeping a Journal about a Team

As you work on a team, keep a journal after each team meeting.

- Who did what?
- What roles did you play in the meeting?
- What decisions were made? How were they made?
- What conflicts arose? How were they handled?
- What strategies could you use to make the next meeting go smoothly?
- Record one observation about each team member.

At the end of the project, analyze your journals. In a memo to your instructor, discuss

- Patterns you see.
- Roles of each team member, including yourself.
- Decision making in your team.
- Conflict resolution in your team.
- Strengths of your team.
- Areas where your team could improve.
- Strengths of the deliverables.
- Areas where the deliverables could be improved.
- Changes you would make in the team and deliverables if you had the project to do over.

6.13   Analyzing the Dynamics of a Team

Analyze the dynamics of a task team of which you are a member. Answer the following questions:

1. Who was the team's leader? How did the leader emerge? Were there any changes in or challenges to the original leader?

2. Describe the contribution each member made to the team and the roles each person played.

3. Did any members of the team officially or unofficially drop out? Did anyone join after the team had begun working? How did you deal with

the loss or addition of a team member, both in terms of getting the work done and in terms of helping people work together?

4. What planning did your team do at the start of the project? Did you stick to the plan or revise it? How did the team decide that revision was necessary?

5. How did your team make decisions? Did you vote? reach decisions by consensus?

6. What problems or conflicts arose? Did the team deal with them openly? To what extent did they interfere with the team's task?

7. Evaluate your team both in terms of its task and in terms of the satisfaction members felt. How did this team compare with other task teams you've been part of? What made it better or worse?

8. What were the strengths of the team? Weaknesses?

9. How did the team's strengths and weaknesses impact the quality of the work produced?

10. If you had the project to do over again, what would you do differently?

As you answer the questions,

- Be honest. You won't lose points for reporting that your team had problems or did something "wrong."

- Show your knowledge of good team dynamics. That is, if your team did something wrong, show that you know what *should* have been done. Similarly, if your team worked well, show that you know *why* it worked well.

- Be specific. Give examples or anecdotes to support your claims.

As your instructor directs,

a. Discuss your answers with the other team members.

b. Present your findings in an individual memo to your instructor.

c. Join with the other team members to write a collaborative memo to your instructor.

6.14 Using Cell Phones as Teamwork Tools

As students, one of the most powerful tools you have for teamwork is your cell phone. A team equipped with cell phones can use them to handle scheduling problems, difficulties finding and meeting at a central location, and team members who don't stay in touch with the group.

As a team, write a proposal to your instructor explaining how you would use cell phones to help you work together to complete a team project. Identify the mobile phone features you'd use and how you'd use them.

Hint:

Be sure that your team's proposal addresses any limitations on mobile phone use.

- Would you want to restrict collaboration to certain times of the day, or block certain times out?

- Would you want to establish a limit on the amount of time per day or month that your team would use your phones to collaborate?

- How could you adapt your recommendations for team members who don't own a mobile phone?

Adapted from Cathie Norris and Elliot Soloway, "Get Cell Phones into Schools," in *Technology: Viewpoint*, http://www.businessweek.com/technology/content/jan2009/tc20090114_741903.htm (accessed February 27, 2009).

6.15 Dealing with a "Saboteur"

It's often said that "there's no *I* in *team*" because on the best teams, everyone works together for the good of the group. What happens when you encounter a team member who believes that "there's a *me* in *team*" and ignores or undermines the team's success in order to achieve personal goals?

Consider this scenario. You're on a team of four students, and you've all been working for the past month to complete a major class project. When you were planning out your project, one team member—let's say Lee—argued with your team's decisions, but agreed to go along with the majority. Lee contributed the bare minimum to your team's work, sat silently during meetings, and when you asked for help overcoming a problem with the project, Lee responded with a shrug, "I told you at the start that I thought this was a bad idea. I guess we're all going to get a failing grade."

Now you're at your last team meeting before the assignment is due. Lee reveals a decision to quit the team and turn in a separate project. Lee doesn't want a grade

that "will suffer from all your 'second-rate' efforts," and tells you that s/he already complained to your instructor about the rest of you.

As your instructor directs,

a. Write a memo to your instructor in which you explain your individual response to this scenario. What would you do? How should your team proceed?

b. Work as a group to establish a working policy that might address this scenario before it happens.

- What policies would you need to protect the group from individual members who are out for themselves?

- What policies would you need to protect team members from having the team take advantage of them?

- What is your instructor's role in your team's policy?

- How would your team evaluate each member's contributions fairly?

Adapted from Bronwyn Fryer, "When Your Colleague Is a Saboteur," *Harvard Business Review* 86, no.11 (2008), 41–52.

6.16   All-Weather Case: Discussing a Personnel Problem

Miguel is contacted by the manufacturing manager at All-Weather's plant at Lincoln, Nebraska. "Son, they gave me your number. I hope I'm talking to the right person because I don't have time to waste," a gruff voice says over the phone. Although not used to being addressed by a familial title despite his young age, Miguel remains his professional self and quickly gathers the details of the problem that the manager is facing.

At the plant, they have a high rate of turnover among crew leads. Deployed at a production line, a crew lead guides operators in lean manufacturing processes while ensuring their safety. Another important contribution that crew leads make is that they can work on every job in a production line. Hence, they can substitute for any absent worker, ensuring unimpeded production.

The plant at Nebraska has been losing these valuable employees at the rate of two every month for the last nine months. As a result, the plant has had to make adjustments on the shop floor, with supervisors sometimes filling in for absent operators in lines without crew leads. To have discussions on the problem, Miguel and Linda are flying to Nebraska.

The plant manufactures vinyl windows and patio doors. Steve, who is the manufacturing manager and in his late 50s, heads the plant, leading a team of three supervisors, each of whom looks after two production lines and 20 operators. Miguel and Linda are greeted by Steve as they arrive at the plant. Linda, visiting a plant for the first time, looks around the huge hangar-like structure with its helmeted employees and complex metal machines.

Discussions begin after a brief presentation by Steve on the turnover problem. He talks about his own experience on the shop floor over the last 20 years and mentions a few details about exit interviews of crew leads who left.

"So, according to your exit interviews, these employees cite low pay as the main reason for leaving," Miguel says, looking at Steve. Linda is disappointed that her young boss, brilliant as he is, once again failed to connect emotionally with his audience before asking pointed questions. He should at least have complimented Steve on his long and outstanding service to the company.

"Yes," Steve says, dryly. "That's the main reason given by at least a dozen of the 20-odd crew leads who have left so far."

"Do we know where these employees go?" Miguel asks, turning his attention to the three supervisors. "I mean in terms of their next job?"

"We hear that many of them have joined Mortensen Windows, a local manufacturer, as production supervisors," one of the supervisors, who wears a pony tail, says.

"But I'm sure they lose on benefits," Miguel says emphatically. "A local company can't match the benefits we provide."

"It doesn't seem logical," the supervisor with the pony tail says, "that they leave for jobs with fewer benefits."

"Yes," another supervisor, who is bald, says. "Why should people who leave citing low pay as the reason go out and join a company that pays even lower?"

"We don't know if they are paid lower," Miguel says, sharply. "What I referred to was the benefit structure."

"Aw, it's the same thing about a local company that you just said," the bald supervisor says, looking at Miguel. "If they can't match us in benefits, they can't match us in pay."

"I'm not sure it's that simple," Miguel says, barely disguising his contempt for the bald supervisor. "They may have a different pay structure."

"So they use the excellent training they receive here to obtain a higher position elsewhere," Linda says, wishing to involve Steve in the discussion, who is sitting quietly, his arms folded across his chest.

"I don't think it's that complicated," Steve says, breaking his silence. "We may need to raise salaries of these workers."

"That may not be necessary," Miguel says dismissively. "I don't think we need an across-the-board pay hike."

"I tell you, sir, if you don't recommend a pay hike, you will see more people leaving," Steve says, the concern in his voice palpable. "We cannot afford a mass exodus."

"Do you all agree with Steve?" Miguel asks, looking at the three supervisors.

"Of course," Steve says, looking a little surprised. "I'm their leader."

"That's not the point," Miguel says, coolly. "All I'm asking is whether all three of your supervisors agree on the need for a general pay hike for all workers on the shop floor."

"We do," the bald supervisor says, quietly.

"Then why have you lost only crew leads, not other workers?" Miguel asks, addressing Steve directly this time, who doesn't answer the question.

"It's only a matter of time before that starts happening too," the bald supervisor says, glad for having an opportunity to fill in for his boss, "especially if we do nothing. The only reason crew leads have left first is that they are more skilled and can more easily find another job."

"There, you just said an important word, 'skilled,' " Miguel says, looking appreciatively at the bald supervisor.

"Yes," the bald supervisor says, pleased at being appreciated in front of his boss. "They're more skilled."

"So why don't you just pay these skilled workers more?" Miguel says, looking at the bald supervisor. "It will keep them from leaving and have an additional effect of motivating other workers who may want to increase their skill-set." Linda has a sense of déjà vu. Her boss has once again impressed her with a brilliant solution to an important problem, but he still hasn't learned how to sell his solution.

"Do you mean creating a pay disparity on the shop floor?" Steve says, angrily. "Are you out of your mind?"

"There's a skills-based pay structure that we can follow for crew leads," Miguel says, looking surprised. "After all, if they have extra skills, why can't we pay them more?"

"Yes," Linda says, trying to defuse the tension between the two men. "It's an effective compensation strategy."

"That may be true," Steve says, in a more dispassionate tone this time, "but I can't risk breaking the bond of brotherhood on the shop floor. These people will not accept it. They will rebel."

"What do you all think, since you're probably closer to these people than Steve is at present?" Miguel asks the three supervisors, who immediately say that Steve is right.

"But how do you know for sure?" Miguel asks, earnestly.

"How many days in your life have you spent on a shop floor?" Steve asks, sharply.

"Steve, you're making me an issue here," Miguel says, spreading his arms in exasperation, "but I'm only here to solve your problem."

"I appreciate that," Steve says, quietly, "but you can't impose your solution on us."

Based on your reading of Chapter 6, analyze the group discussion that you just read.

- What kinds of team leaders do Miguel, Steve, and Linda appear to be?
- How can Miguel and Steve be more effective as leaders?
- What might Miguel have done differently to prevent the discussion from disintegrating into a conflict?

As your instructor directs,

a. Put your opinions in a memo to your instructor.

b. Share your opinions in small groups.

c. As a group, present your opinions to the class.

CHAPTER 7

Planning, Composing, and Revising

Chapter Outline

The Ways Good Writers Write

Activities in the Composing Process

Using Your Time Effectively

Brainstorming, Planning, and Organizing Business Documents

Writing Good Business and Administrative Documents

Half-Truths about Style

- Half-Truth 1: "Write as You Talk."
- Half-Truth 2: "Never Use *I*."
- Half-Truth 3: "Never Use *You*."
- Half-Truth 4: "Never Begin a Sentence with *And* or *But*."
- Half-Truth 5: "Never End a Sentence with a Preposition."
- Half-Truth 6: "Big Words Impress People."

Ten Ways to Make Your Writing Easier to Read

- As You Choose Words
- As You Write and Revise Sentences
- As You Write and Revise Paragraphs

Organizational Preferences for Style

Revising, Editing, and Proofreading

- What to Look for When You Revise
- What to Look for When You Edit
- How to Catch Typos

Getting and Using Feedback

Using Boilerplate

Readability Formulas

Summary of Key Points

I Think I'm Musing My Mind

Roger Ebert's Journal, October 24, 2008

Blind people develop a more acute sense of hearing. Deaf people can better notice events on the periphery, and comprehend the quick movements of lips and sign language. What about people who lose the ability to speak? We expand other ways of communicating. . . .

There is one thing I can do as well as ever. I can write. When I am writing my problems become invisible and I am the same person I always was. All is well. I am as I should be.

After my first stretch in the Rehabilitation Institute of Chicago, I began to write again, a little. After my second, I returned to a nearly normal schedule. This spring during my third rehab, I was able to log onto a wi-fi network and begin writing much more. This year, which has included two major surgeries, I have so far written 170 reviews, 22 Answer Man columns, 28 Great Movie essays (not all yet published), and 37 blog entries.

> *"The Muse visits* during *the process of creation, not before."*

In May, I began to sense a change going on. At first it was subjective. This autumn it has become undeniable. My writing has improved.

By that I don't mean it's objectively better from the reader's point of view. I mean it has expanded within my mind, reaches deeper, emerges more clearly, is more satisfactory. . . .

I take dictation from that place within my mind that knows what to say. I think most good writers do. There is no such thing as waiting for inspiration. The idea of 'diagramming' an essay in advance, as we are taught in school, may be useful to students but is foolishness for any practicing writer. The Muse visits *during* the process of creation, not before. . . .

By losing the ability to speak, I have increased my ability to communicate. I am content.

Ethics and the Writing Process

As you plan a message,

- Be sure you have identified the real audiences and purposes of the message.

- In difficult situations, seek allies in your organization and discuss your options with them.

As you compose,

- Provide accurate and complete information.

- Use reliable sources of material. Document when necessary.

- Warn your readers of limits or dangers in your information.

- Promise only what you can deliver.

As you revise,

- Check to see that your language does not use words that show bias.

- Use feedback to revise text and visuals that your audience may misunderstand.

- Check your sources.

- Assume that no document is confidential. E-mail documents and IMs (instant messages) can be forwarded and printed without your knowledge; both electronic and paper documents, including drafts, can be subpoenaed for court cases.

Skilled performances look easy and effortless. In reality, as every dancer, musician, and athlete knows, they're the products of hard work, hours of practice, attention to detail, and intense concentration. Like skilled performances in other arts, writing rests on a base of work.

The Ways Good Writers Write

No single writing process works for all writers all of the time. However, good writers and poor writers seem to use different processes.[1] Good writers are more likely to

- Realize that the first draft can be revised.
- Write regularly.
- Break big jobs into small chunks.
- Have clear goals focusing on purpose and audience.
- Have several different strategies to choose from.
- Use rules flexibly.
- Wait to edit until after the draft is complete.

The research also shows that good writers differ from poor writers in identifying and analyzing the initial problem more effectively, understanding the task more broadly and deeply, drawing from a wider repertoire of strategies, and seeing patterns more clearly. Good writers also are better at evaluating their own work.

Thinking about the writing process and consciously adopting the processes of good writers will help you become a better writer.

Activities in the Composing Process

Composing can include many activities: planning, brainstorming, gathering, organizing, writing, evaluating, getting feedback, revising, editing, and proofreading. The activities do not have to come in this order. Not every task demands all activities.

Planning

- Analyzing the problem, defining your purposes, and analyzing the audience.
- Brainstorming information to include in the document.
- Gathering the information you need—from the message you're answering, a person, printed sources, or the Web.

- Selecting the points you want to make, and the examples, data, and arguments to support them.
- Choosing a pattern of organization, making an outline, creating a list.

Writing

- Putting words on paper or a screen. Writing can be lists, possible headings, fragmentary notes, stream-of-consciousness writing, incomplete drafts, and ultimately a formal draft.

Revising

- Evaluating your work and measuring it against your goals and the requirements of the situation and audience. The best evaluation results from *re-seeing* your draft as if someone else had written it. Will your audience understand it? Is it complete? Convincing? Friendly?
- Getting feedback from someone else. Is all the necessary information there? Is there too much information? Is your pattern of organization appropriate? Does a revision solve an earlier problem? Are there obvious mistakes?
- Adding, deleting, substituting, or rearranging. Revision can be changes in single words or in large sections of a document.

Editing

- Checking the draft to see that it satisfies the requirements of standard English. Here you'd correct spelling and mechanical errors and check word choice and format. Unlike revision, which can produce major changes in meaning, editing focuses on the surface of writing.
- Proofreading the final copy to see that it's free from typographical errors.

Note the following points about these activities:

- **The activities do not have to come in this order.** Some people may gather data *after* writing a draft when they see that they need more specifics to achieve their purposes.
- **You do not have to finish one activity to start another.** Some writers plan a short section and write it, plan the next short section and write it, and so on through the document. Evaluating what is already written may cause a writer to do more planning or to change the original plan.
- **Most writers do not use all activities for all the documents they write.** You'll use more activities when you write more complex or difficult documents about new subjects or to audiences that are new to you.

Research about what writers really do has destroyed some of the stereotypes we used to have about the writing process. Consider planning. Traditional advice stressed the importance of planning and sometimes advised writers to make formal outlines for everything they wrote. But we know now that not all good documents are based on outlines.

For many workplace writers, pre-writing is not a warm-up activity to get ready to write the "real" document. It's really a series of activities designed to gather and organize information, take notes, brainstorm with colleagues, and plan a document before writing a complete draft. And for many people, these activities do not include outlining. Traditional outlining may lull writers into a false sense of confidence about their material and organization, making it difficult for them to revise their content and structure if they deviate from the outline developed early in the process.[2]

A Professional Writer at Work

When Communication Specialist Roxanne Clemens was asked by a professor to edit an article about meat packing for the World Book Encyclopedia (WBE), she readily agreed to help. As a professional writer, Roxanne saw the project as an opportunity to make technical text accessible to a nontechnical audience. The author did not supply any style guidelines, so Roxanne researched similar articles in the WBE and created her own style guide for the article. Here's how Roxanne describes to the professor her edits to the article:

You may look at this and think, "this is not what I wrote." As you know, the challenge lies in explaining such complex concepts at a 6th-grade level. . . . I based most changes on the examples of WBE entries found on the Internet. Major style choices are the following:

- WBE uses short, concise sentences (almost what we would consider choppy). They use very few compound sentences, so I have broken up compound sentences where I thought the meaning would not be lost.
- Instead of using "however," WBE tends to use two sentences and to start the second sentence with "but."
- WBE uses a terminal comma in a series (e.g. red, white, and blue).

I did some reorganizing at the sentence level. [I also moved] livestock marketing ahead of meat because that's the way the heading reads and it also follows the process of turning animals into meat.

Let me know if you want me to do more or something different to the text.

Adapted and quoted from Roxanne Clemens, e-mail to Donna Kienzler, August 30, 2006.

Overcoming Writer's Block

According to psychologist Robert Boice, who has made a career study of writer's block, these actions help overcome writer's block:

1. **Prepare for writing.** Collect and arrange material. Talk to people; interact with some of your audiences. The more you learn about the company, its culture, and its context, the easier it will be to write—and the better your writing will be.

2. **Practice writing regularly and in moderation.** Try to write almost daily. Keep sessions to a moderate length; Boice suggests an hour to an hour and a half.

3. **Talk positively to yourself:** "I can do this." "If I keep working, ideas will come." "It doesn't have to be perfect; I can make it better later."

4. **Talk to other people about writing.** Value the feedback you get from them. Talking to other people expands your repertoire of strategies and helps you understand your writing community.

Adapted from Robert Boice, *Advice for New Faculty Members: Nihil Nimus* (Boston: Allyn & Bacon, 2000), 111–12.

Not all writing has to be completed in office settings. Some people work better outside, in coffee shops, or from home.

Using Your Time Effectively

To get the best results from the time you have, spend only one-third of your time actually "writing." Spend at least another one-third of your time analyzing the situation and your audience, gathering information, and organizing what you have to say. Spend the final third evaluating what you've said, revising the draft(s) to meet your purposes and the needs of the audience and the organization, editing a late draft to remove any errors in grammar and mechanics, and proofreading the final copy.

Do realize, however, that different writers, documents, and situations may need different time divisions to produce quality communications, especially if documents are produced by teams. Geographic distance will add even more time to the process.

Brainstorming, Planning, and Organizing Business Documents

Spend significant time planning and organizing before you begin to write. The better your ideas are when you start, the fewer drafts you'll need to produce a good document. Start by using the analysis questions from Chapter 1 to identify purpose and audience. Use the strategies described in Chapter 2 to analyze audience and identify benefits. Gather information you can use for your document. Select the points you want to make—and the examples and data to support them.

Sometimes your content will be determined by the situation. Sometimes, even when it's up to you to think of information to include in a report, you'll find it easy to think of ideas. If ideas won't come, try the following techniques:

- **Brainstorming.** Think of all the ideas you can, without judging them. Consciously try to get at least a dozen different ideas before you stop. Good brainstorming depends on generating many ideas.

- **Freewriting.**[3] Make yourself write, without stopping, for 10 minutes or so, even if you must write "I will think of something soon." At the end of 10 minutes, read what you've written, identify the best point in the draft, then set it aside, and write for another 10 uninterrupted minutes. Read this draft, marking anything that's good and should be kept, and then write again for another 10 minutes. By the third session, you will probably produce several sections that are worth keeping—maybe even a complete draft that's ready to be revised.

- **Clustering.**[4] Write your topic in the middle of the page and circle it. Write down the ideas the topic suggests, circling them, too. (The circles are designed to tap into the nonlinear half of your brain.) When you've filled the page, look for patterns or repeated ideas. Use different colored pens to group related ideas. Then use these ideas to develop your content.
- **Talk to your audiences.** As research shows, talking to internal and external audiences helps writers to involve readers in the planning process and to understand the social and political relationships among readers. This preliminary work helps reduce the number of revisions needed before documents are approved.[5]

Thinking about the content, layout, or structure of your document can also give you ideas. For long documents, write out the headings you'll use. For short documents, jot down key points—information to include, objections to answer, benefits to develop. For an oral presentation, a meeting, or a document with lots of visuals, try creating a **storyboard,** with a rectangle representing each page or unit. Draw a box with a visual for each main point. Below the box, write a short caption or label.

Writing Good Business and Administrative Documents

Good business and administrative writing is closer to conversation and less formal than the style of writing that has traditionally earned high marks in college essays and term papers. (See Figure 7.1.)

Writing with Information

Good writers write with information. Michelle Russo writes reports appraising how much a hotel is worth. Gathering information is a big part of her composing process.

She visits the site. She talks to the general manager. She gets occupancy rates, financial statements, and tax forms. She talks to the tax assessor and all the managers of competing hotels. If it's a convention hotel, she talks to the convention bureau and gets the airlines' passenger traffic counts. Gathering all this information takes about four days. When she gets back to the office, she uses databases for even more information.

Adapted from Michelle S. Russo, telephone conversation with Kitty Locker, December 8, 1993.

Figure 7.1   Different Levels of Style

Feature	Conversational style	Good business style	Traditional term paper style
Formality	Highly informal	Conversational; sounds like a real person talking	More formal than conversation would be, but retains a human voice
Use of contractions	Many contractions	OK to use occasional contractions	Few contractions, if any
Pronouns	Uses first- and second-person pronouns	Uses first- and second-person pronouns	First- and second-person pronouns kept to a minimum
Level of friendliness	Friendly	Friendly	No effort to make style friendly
How personal	Personal; refers to specific circumstances of conversation	Personal; may refer to reader by name; refers to specific circumstances of audiences	Impersonal; may generally refer to readers but does not name them or refer to their circumstances
Word choice	Short, simple words; slang	Short, simple words but avoids slang	Many abstract words; scholarly, technical terms
Sentence and paragraph length	Incomplete sentences; no paragraphs	Short sentences and paragraphs	Longer sentences and paragraphs
Grammar	Can be ungrammatical	Uses standard English	Uses more formal standard English
Visual impact	Not applicable	Attention to visual impact of document	No particular attention to visual impact

Most people have several styles of talking, which they vary instinctively depending on the audience. Good writers have several styles, too. An e-mail to your boss complaining about the delays from a supplier will be informal, perhaps even chatty; a letter to the supplier demanding better service will be more formal.

Reports tend to be more formal than letters and memos, since they may be read many years in the future by audiences the writer can barely imagine. Reports tend to avoid contractions, personal pronouns, and second person (since so many people read reports, *you* doesn't have much meaning). See Chapter 19 for more about report style.

Keep the following points in mind as you choose a level of formality for a specific document:

- Use a friendly, informal style to someone you've talked with.
- Avoid contractions, slang, and even minor grammatical lapses in paper documents to people you don't know. Abbreviations are OK in e-mail messages if they're part of the group's culture.
- Pay particular attention to your style when you write to people you fear or when you must give bad news. Research shows our style changes in stressful contexts. We tend to rely on nouns rather than on verbs and deaden our style when we are under stress or feel insecure.[6] Confident people are more direct. Edit your writing so that you sound confident, whether you feel that way or not.

More and more organizations are trying to simplify their communications. Alan Greenspan, former chair of the Federal Reserve, was infamously known for his lack of clarity in communications, but his successor is striving to bring about new clarity in the board's communications (see sidebar on 186). In the financial world, the US Securities and Exchange Commissions's *A Plain English Handbook: How to Create Clear SEC Disclosure Documents* asks for short sentences, everyday words, and active voice. It cautions against legal and highly technical terms.[7]

Of course, the news is full of examples where these efforts have failed. The same negative examples, however, also show the great need for clear, simple style. A major factor in the subprime mortgage disaster was documents written in prose so complex that even experts couldn't understand it. Many homeowners who signed adjustable rate mortgages and subsequently lost their homes claim they did not understand all the consequences of what they were signing. Experts outside the mortgage business agree with the homeowners that the language was too complex for most people to understand.[8]

Communication consultants like Gerard Braud urge clients to simplify their prose. He distinguishes between keeping communication easy to understand and "dumbing it down." Braud warns, "All communication affects [the] bottom line. . . . When a reader, listener, viewer or member of a live audience has to take even a nanosecond to decipher what you are saying because you are making it more complicated than it needs to be, you may lose that person."[9]

Good business style allows for individual variation. Figure 7.2 shows the opening paragraphs from Warren Buffet's letter to shareholders in Berkshire Hathaway's 2008 annual report. Buffett's direct, colorful style suggests integrity and clarity.

Half-Truths about Style

Many generalizations about style are half-truths and must be applied selectively, if at all.

Figure 7.2   Warren Buffett's Letter to Shareholders

BERKSHIRE HATHAWAY INC.

Paragraph 1 uses standard business style

To the Shareholders of Berkshire Hathaway Inc.:

Our *decrease* in net worth during 2008 was $11.5 billion, which reduced the per-share book value of both our Class A and Class B stock by 9.6%. Over the last 44 years (that is, since present management took over) book value has grown from $19 to $70,530, a rate of 20.3% compounded annually.[*]

Colorful metaphor individualizes style.

The table on the preceding page, recording both the 44-year performance of Berkshire's book value and the S&P 500 index, shows that 2008 was the worst year for each. The period was devastating as well for corporate and municipal bonds, real estate and commodities. By yearend investors of all stripes were bloodied and confused, much as if they were small birds that had strayed into a badminton game.

Example from his youth

As the year progressed, a series of life-threatening problems within many of the world's great financial institutions was unveiled. This led to a dysfunctional credit market that in important respects soon turned non-functional. The watchword throughout the country became the creed I saw on restaurant walls when I was young: "In God we trust: all others pay cash."

By the fourth quarter, the credit crisis, coupled with tumbling home and stock prices, had produced a paralyzing fear that engulfed the country. A freefall in business activity ensued, accelerating at a pace that I have never before witnessed. The U.S.—and much of the world—became trapped in a vicious negative-feedback cycle. Fear led to business contraction, and that in turn led to even greater fear.

Poker, medicine, and nursing metaphors

This debilitating spiral has spurred our government to take massive action. In poker terms, the Treasury and the Fed have gone "all in." Economic medicine that was previously meted out by the cupful has recently been dispensed by the barrel. These once-unthinkable dosages will almost certainly bring on unwelcome aftereffects. Their precise nature is anyone's guess, though one likely consequence is an onslaught of inflation. Moreover, major industries have become dependent on Federal assistance, and they will be followed by cities and states bearing mind-boggling requests. Weaning these entities from the public teat will be a political challenge. They won't leave willingly.

Whatever the downsides may be, strong and immediate action by government was essential last year if the financial system was to avoid a total breakdown. Had that occurred, the consequences for every area of our economy would have been cataclysmic. Like it or not, the inhabitants of Wall Street, Main Street and the various Side Streets of America were all in the same boat.

Historical references

Amid this bad news, however, never forget that our country has faced far worse travails in the past. In the 20th century alone, we dealt with two great wars (one of which we initially appeared to be losing); a dozen or so panics and recessions; virulent inflation that led to a 21½% prime rate in 1980; and the Great Depression of the 1930s, when unemployment ranged between 15% and 25% for many years. America has had no shortage of challenges.

Without fail, however, we've overcome them. In the face of those obstacles—and many others—the real standard of living for Americans improved nearly *seven*-fold during the 1900s, while the Dow Jones Industrials rose from 66 to 11,497. Compare the record of this period with the dozens of centuries during which humans secured only tiny gains, if any, in how they lived. Though the path has not been smooth, our economic system has worked extraordinarily well over time. It has unleashed human potential as no other system has, and it will continue to do so. America's best days lie ahead.

---

[*]All per-share figures used in this report apply to Berkshire's A shares. Figures for the B share are 1/30th of those shown for A.

Waren Buffet's letter uses a standard business style personalized with many colorful metaphors.

Source: Berkshire Hathaway, "Warren Buffett's Letter to Berkshire Shareholders," Annual Report 2003, at www.berkshirehathaway.com/. Reproduced from *copyrighted* material with the permission of the author.

To Clarify or Not to Clarify

Former Federal Board Chair Alan Greenspan was known for his lack of clarity. After one speech, a headline in the *Washington Post* read "Greenspan Hints Fed May Cut Interest Rates," while the corresponding headline in the *New York Times* read "Doubt Voiced by Greenspan on a Rate Cut." Even his wife joked that he had to propose twice before she understood what he was saying.

His replacement, Ben Bernanke, has a different style. As he aims for more transparent communications, he is trying to make the Fed clearer about goals for economic growth.

Adapted from Greg Ip, "'Transparent' Vision: New Fed Chairman Hopes to Downplay Impact of His Words," *Wall Street Journal*, September 6, 2006, A1; and Daniel Kadlec, "5 Ways the New Fed Chairman Will Be Different," *Time*, November 7, 2005, 49–50.

Evaluating "Rules" about Writing

Some "rules" are grammatical conventions. For example, standard edited English requires that each sentence have a subject and verb, and that the subject and verb agree. Business writing normally demands standard grammar, but exceptions exist. Promotional materials such as brochures, advertisements, and sales letters may use sentence fragments to mimic the effect of speech.

Other "rules" may be conventions adopted by an organization so that its documents will be consistent. For example, a company might decide to capitalize job titles (e.g., *Production Manager*) even though grammar doesn't require the capitals.

Still other "rules" are attempts to codify "what sounds good." "Never use *I*" and "use big words" are examples of this kind of "rule." To evaluate these "rules," you must consider your audience, purposes, and situation. If you want the effect produced by an impersonal style and polysyllabic words, use them. But use them only when you want the distancing they produce.

Half-Truth 1: "Write as You Talk."

Most of us use a coloquial, conversational style in speech that is too informal for writing. We use slang, incomplete sentences, and even grammatical errors.

Unless our speech is exceptionally fluent, "writing as we talk" can create awkward, repetitive, and badly organized prose. It's OK to write as you talk to produce your first draft, but edit to create a good written style.

Half-Truth 2: "Never Use *I*."

Using *I* too often can make your writing sound self-centered; using it unnecessarily will make your ideas seem tentative. However, when you write about things you've done or said or seen, using *I* is both appropriate and smoother than resorting to awkward passives or phrases like *this writer.*

Half-Truth 3: "Never Use *You*."

Certainly writers should not use *you* in formal reports, as well as other situations where the audience is not known or *you* may sound too informal. But *you* is widely used in situations such as writing to familiar audiences like our office mates, describing audience benefits, and writing sales text.

Half-Truth 4: "Never Begin a Sentence with *And* or *But*."

Beginning a sentence with *and* or *also* makes the idea that follows seem like an afterthought. That's OK when you want the effect of spontaneous speech in a written document, as you may in a sales letter. If you want to sound as though you have thought about what you are saying, put the *also* in the middle of the sentence or use another transition: *moreover, furthermore.*

But tells the reader that you are shifting gears and that the point which follows not only contrasts with but also is more important than the preceding ideas. Presenting such verbal signposts to your reader is important. Beginning a sentence with *but* is fine if doing so makes your paragraph read smoothly.

Half-Truth 5: "Never End a Sentence with a Preposition."

Prepositions are those useful little words that indicate relationships: *with, in, under, to, at.* The prohibition against ending sentences with them is probably based on two facts: (1) The end of a sentence (like the beginning) is a position of emphasis. A preposition may not be worth emphasizing. (2) When readers see a preposition, they expect something to follow it. At the end of a sentence, nothing does.

In job application letters, reports, and important presentations, avoid ending sentences with prepositions. Most other messages are less formal; it's OK to end an occasional sentence with a preposition. Noting exceptions to the rule, Sir Winston Churchill famously scolded an editor who had presumptuously corrected a sentence ending with a preposition, "This is the kind of impertinence up with which I will not put."[10] Analyze your audience and the situation, and use the language that you think will get the best results.

Half-Truth 6: "Big Words Impress People."

Learning an academic discipline requires that you master its vocabulary. After you get out of school, however, no one will ask you to write just to prove that you understand something. Instead, you'll be asked to write or speak to people who need the information you have.

Sometimes you may want the sense of formality or technical expertise that big words create. But much of the time, big words just distance you from your audience and increase the risk of miscommunication. If you feel you need to use big words, make sure you use them correctly. When people misuse big words, they look foolish.

Ten Ways to Make Your Writing Easier to Read

Direct, simple writing is easier to read. One study tested two versions of a memo report. The "high-impact" version had the "bottom line" (the purpose of the report) in the first paragraph, simple sentences in normal word order, active verbs, concrete language, short paragraphs, headings and lists, and first- and second-person pronouns. The high-impact version took 22% less time to read. Readers said they understood the report better, and tests showed that they really did understand it better.[11] Another study showed that high-impact instructions were more likely to be followed.[12]

As You Choose Words

The best word depends on context: the situation, your purposes, your audience, the words you have already used.

1. Use words that are accurate, appropriate, and familiar.

Accurate words mean what you want to say. Appropriate words convey the attitudes you want and fit well with the other words in your document. Familiar words are easy to read and understand.

Sometimes choosing the accurate word is hard. Most of us have word pairs that confuse us. Grammarian Richard Lederer tells Toastmasters that these 10 pairs are the ones you are most likely to see or hear confused.[13]

Affect/Effect	Disinterested/Uninterested
Among/Between	Farther/Further
Amount/Number	Fewer/Less
Compose/Comprise	Imply/Infer
Different from/Different than	Lay/Lie

For help using the pairs correctly, see Appendix B.

Some meanings are negotiated as we interact one-on-one with another person, attempting to communicate. Individuals are likely to have different ideas about value-laden words like *fair* or *empowerment*. The *Wall Street Journal* notes that the Securities and Exchange Commission has upped the ante on the definition of "rich" as it regulates the net worth requirement for those eligible to invest in hedge funds. That definition is important because it often becomes the government's definition of 'rich':

> The SEC . . . says investors need to have investible assets of at least $2.5 million, excluding equity in any homes or businesses, to be eligible to sign on a hedge fund's dotted line. That's a huge jump from the current requirement, which says individuals have to have a net worth of at least $1 million, including the value of primary residences, or an annual income of $200,000 for the previous two years for individuals or $300,000 for couples."[14]

Some word choices have legal implications.

- Confusion about the definition of "wetlands" has reduced these natural resources by more than half.[15]
- Some employees, such as assistant managers in small franchises, are working to be reclassified as nonprofessionals. The word choice affects the workers' paychecks, because under labor laws employers are exempt from paying extra when professionals and administrators work overtime.[16]
- Medicare dropped its opposition to defining obesity as an illness, thus allowing Medicare to cover the payment for some treatments.[17]

Building a Better Style

To improve your style,

- Try telling someone what you really mean. Then write the words.

- Try reading your draft out loud to someone sitting about three feet away—about as far away as you'd sit in casual conversation. If the words sound awkward, they'll seem awkward to a reader, too.

- Ask someone else to read your draft out loud. Readers stumble because the words on the page aren't what they expect to see. The places where that person stumbles are places where your writing can be better.

- Read widely and write a *lot*.

- Use the 10 techniques starting on this page to polish your style.

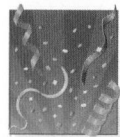

What's in a Name (1): Name that Bandit

For years, the FBI has named serial bank robbers with colorful names. The Time Bandit has everyone in the bank count to 300 before making a move. The Paint-by-Numbers Bandit wears paint-spattered clothes.

The names help characterize robbers and attract media attention, thus resulting in more tips from the public and more arrests.

Some experts, however, warn that the names humanize, even glorify, dangerous criminals while downplaying the threat they pose. How dangerous can the Dr. Seuss Bandit—named after Cat-in-the-Hat headwear—really be? Well, he is a bank robber, and he has robbed 20 banks.

The Clearasil Bandit, named for his severe acne, tried unsuccessfully to sue the FBI for his moniker, which led to severe teasing in prison.

Adapted from Gerry Smith, "Name that Bank Robber: It Takes a Catchy Nickname to Catch a Bandit, FBI Says," *Chicago Tribune*, December 30, 2007, A1.

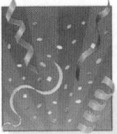

As the last example indicates, some word choices have major health repercussions. Smokers have sued tobacco companies for duping them into believing that "light" cigarettes were less harmful. "Recall," when used in warnings about defective pacemakers and defibrillators, causes patients to ask for replacements, even though the replacement surgery is riskier than the defective device. For this reason, some physician groups prefer "safety advisory" or "safety alert."[18]

Accurate denotations   To be accurate, a word's denotation must match the meaning the writer wishes to convey. Denotation is a word's literal or dictionary meaning. Most common words in English have more than one denotation. The word *pound,* for example, means, or denotes, a unit of weight, a place where stray animals are kept, a unit of money in the old British system, and the verb *to hit.* Coca-Cola spends millions each year to protect its brand names so that *Coke* will denote only that brand and not just any cola drink.

When two people use the same word or phrase to mean, or denote, different things, **bypassing** occurs. For example, a large mail-order drug company notifies clients by e-mail when their prescription renewals get stopped because the doctor has not verified the prescription. Patients are advised to call their doctors and remind them to verify. However, the company's Web site posts a sentence telling clients that the prescription is *being processed.* The drug company means the renewal is in the system, waiting for the doctor's verification. The patients believe the doctor has checked in and the renewal is moving forward. The confusion results in extra phone calls to the company's customer service number, delayed prescriptions, and general customer dissatisfaction.

Problems also arise when writers misuse words.

The western part of Ohio was transferred from Chicago to Cleveland.[19]

(Ohio did not move. Instead, a company moved responsibility for sales in western Ohio.)

Three major associations of property–liability companies are poised to strike out in opposite directions.[20]

(Three different directions can't be opposite each other.)

[Engulf & Devour] has grown dramatically over the past seven years, largely through the purchase of many smaller, desperate companies.[21]

This quote from a corporate news release probably did not intend to be so frank. More likely, the writer relied on a computer's spell checker, which had no way to know it should replace *desperate* with *disparate,* meaning "fundamentally different from one another."

Appropriate connotations   Words are appropriate when their **connotations,** that is, their emotional associations or colorings, convey the attitude you want. A great many words carry connotations of approval or disapproval, disgust or delight. Words in the first column below suggest approval; words in the second column suggest criticism.

Positive word	Negative word
assume	guess
curious	nosy
cautious	fearful
firm	obstinate
flexible	wishy-washy

A supervisor can "tell the truth" about a subordinate's performance and yet write either a positive or a negative performance appraisal, based on the connotations of the words in the appraisal. Consider an employee who pays close attention to details. A positive appraisal might read, "Terry is a meticulous team member who takes care of details that others sometimes ignore." But the same behavior might be described negatively: "Terry is hung up on trivial details."

Advertisers carefully choose words with positive connotations.

- In this youth-conscious society, hearing aids become personal communication assistants.[22]

- A Japanese company producing girdles for men calls its product the "ex walker" and insists that it is exercise wear.[23]

- Expensive cars are never *used;* instead, they're *pre-owned, experienced,* or even *previously adored.*[24]

- Insurers emphasize what you want to *protect* (your home, your car, your life), rather than the losses you are insuring against (fire damage, auto accident, death).

- Credit card companies tell about what you can do with the card (charge a vacation), not the debt, payments, and fees involved.

Words may also connote categories. Some show status. Both *salesperson* and *sales representative* are nonsexist job titles. But the first sounds like a clerk in a store; the second suggests someone selling important items to corporate customers. Some words connote age: *adorable* generally connotes young children, not adults. Other words, such as *handsome* or *pretty,* connote gender.

Connotations change over time. The word *charity* had acquired such negative connotations by the 19th century that people began to use the term *welfare* instead. Now, *welfare* has acquired negative associations. Most states have *public assistance programs* instead.

Ethical implications of word choice   How positively can we present something and still be ethical? *Pressure-treated lumber* sounds acceptable. But naming the material injected under pressure—*arsenic-treated lumber*—may lead the customer to make a different decision. We have the right to package our ideas attractively, but we have the responsibility to give the public or our superiors all the information they need to make decisions.

Word choices have ethical implications in other contexts as well. When scientists refer to 100-year floods, they mean a flood so big that it has a 1% chance of happening in any given year. However, a "1% annual chance flood" is awkward and has not become standard usage. On the other hand, many nonscientists believe a 100-year flood will happen only once every hundred years. After a 100-year flood swamped the Midwest in 1993, many people moved back into flood-prone homes; some even dropped their flood insurance. Unfortunately, both actions left them devastated by a second 100-year flood in 2008.[25]

Perhaps one of the best-known examples of ethical implications deals with the interrogation technique of waterboarding. President Bush's outgoing Attorney General, Michael Mukasey, said waterboarding was not torture; President Obama's Attorney General, Eric Holder, said it was. (Both men agreed that torture is a crime, a distinction that meant people who facilitated torture could be prosecuted.)[26]

Familiar words   Use familiar words, words that are in almost everyone's vocabulary. Use the word that most exactly conveys your meaning, but whenever you can choose between two words that mean the same thing, use the shorter, more common one. Try to use specific, concrete words. They're easier to understand and remember.[27]

A series of long, learned, abstract terms makes writing less interesting, less forceful, and less memorable. When you have something simple to say, use simple words.

Gifts Defined

"[Wal-mart corporate headquarters meeting rooms have] nothing on a wall save a poster labeled 'Gifts and Gratuities.' It reads:

It is our policy that associates of the Company, regardless of their capacity, do not accept for their personal benefits, gratuities, tips, cash, samples, etc., from anyone buying from us or selling to us, or in any way serving our company.

In case anyone misses the point, the poster goes on to define gifts and gratuities as including: tickets to entertainment events, kickbacks in the form of money or merchandise, special discounts, sample merchandise, Christmas gifts, or meals. There is no 'de minimis' rule; even a cup of coffee is forbidden."

What do you think of Wal-mart's definition of "gifts and gratuities"? Is the definition too restrictive? What benefits does it offer employees?

Quoted from Alan Murray, "Wal-Mart's Lesson for Wall Street," *Wall Street Journal,* December 13, 2006, A2.

Menu Word Choice

Some restaurants use humorous names for their dishes so patrons will talk about them to their friends.

- Sticky Fingers RibHouses, a South Carolina–based chain, calls its onion appetizer Git-R-D'onions.
- David Burke at Bloomingdales, New York, offers Angry Roasted Hen-in-Law: a roasted chicken which comes with a knife in its back.
- Spy City Café, next to Washington's Spy Museum, serves Disguise Dogs, hotdogs which come with a selection of 15 toppings ("disguises").

Adapted from Judy Mandell, "Name That Dish: Menu Writing Gets Creative," *USA Weekend*, March 18, 2007, 19.

To change from passive voice to active voice, you must make the agent the new subject. If no agent is specified in the sentence, you must supply one to make the sentence active.

Passive Voice	**Active Voice**
The request was approved by the plant manager.	The plant manager approved the request.
A decision will be made next month. No agent in sentence.	The committee will decide next month..
A letter will be sent informing the customer of the change. No agent in sentence.	[You] Send the customer a letter informing her about the change.

Passive voice has at least three disadvantages:

1. If all the information in the original sentence is retained, passive voice makes the sentence longer. Passive voice takes more time to understand.[29]
2. If the agent is omitted, it's not clear who is responsible for doing the action.
3. Using much passive voice, especially in material that has a lot of big words, can make the writing boring and pompous.

Passive voice is desirable in these situations:

1. Use passive voice to emphasize the object receiving the action, not the agent.

   Your order was shipped November 15.

   The customer's order, not the shipping clerk, is important.
2. Use passive voice to provide coherence within a paragraph. A sentence is easier to read if "old" information comes at the beginning of a sentence. When you have been discussing a topic, use the word again as your subject even if that requires passive voice.

   The bank made several risky loans in the late 1990s. These loans were written off as "uncollectible" in 2001.

   Using *loans* as the subject of the second sentence provides a link between the two sentences, making the paragraph as a whole easier to read.
3. Use passive voice to avoid assigning blame.

   The order was damaged during shipment.

Active voice would require the writer to specify *who* damaged the order. The passive voice is more tactful here.

According to PlainLanguage.gov, changing writing to active voice is the most powerful change that can be made to government documents.[30] But even the self-proclaimed prescriptivist style editor Bill Walsh, a copy chief at the *Washington Post*, admits that sometimes passive voice is necessary—although not as often as many writers think.[31]

4. Use verbs—not nouns—to carry the weight of your sentence.

Put the weight of your sentence in the verb to make your sentences more forceful and up to 25% easier to read.[32] When the verb is a form of the verb *to be*, revise the sentence to use a more forceful verb.

Better: The Payroll

- Termina
- Layoffs
- Recalls
- Transfer
- Promot

7. Use parallel st

Parallel structure pu
and logical form. In
while *note* is an imp
gerunds or both impe

Faulty: Errors can be
errors you und

Parallel: Errors can be
number of err
of the invoice

Also   To check errc

parallel: 1. The numbe

2. The numb
matched.

Note that a list in par
sentence that introdu

Words must also b
niors, seniors, and *ath*
words into nonoverla

Faulty: I interviewed

Parallel: I interviewed
nonathletes.

Parallel structure
smoother, and more
you to tighten your
nate repetition in par

8. Put your read

Use second-person
give your writing m
a single person or to

Figure 7.5   U

These are the
the customer
- Use tracking
- Our products
the software
- The custome
rely on us.

Fai

Weak: The financial advantage of owning this equipment instead of leasing it is 10% after taxes.

Better: Owning this equipment rather than leasing it will save us 10% after taxes.

Nouns ending in *-ment, -ion,* and *-al* often hide verbs.

make an adjustment   adjust
make a payment   pay
make a decision   decide
reach a conclusion   conclude
take into consideration   consider
make a referral   refer
provide assistance   assist

Use verbs to present the information more forcefully.

Weak: We will perform an investigation of the problem.

Better: We will investigate the problem.

Weak: Selection of a program should be based on the client's needs.

Better: Select the program that best fits the client's needs.

5. Eliminate wordiness.

Writing is **wordy** if the same idea can be expressed in fewer words. Unnecessary words increase writing time, bore your reader, and make your meaning more difficult to follow, since the reader must hold all the extra words in mind while trying to understand your meaning. Don Bush, the "friendly editor" columnist for *intercom,* calls wordiness the most obvious fault of technical writing.[33]

Good writing is concise, but it may still be lengthy. Concise writing may be long because it is packed with ideas. In Chapter 3, we saw that revisions to create you-attitude and positive emphasis and to develop benefits were frequently *longer* than the originals because the revision added information not given in the original.

Sometimes you may be able to look at a draft and see immediately how to condense it. When the solution isn't obvious, try the following strategies to condense your writing:

a. Eliminate words that add nothing.

b. Combine sentences to eliminate unnecessary words.

c. Put the meaning of your sentence into the subject and verb to cut the number of words.

You eliminate unnecessary words to save the reader's time, not simply to see how few words you can use. You aren't writing a telegram, so keep the little words that make sentences complete. (Incomplete sentences are fine in lists where all the items are incomplete.)

The following examples show how to use these methods.

a. Eliminate words that add nothing.   Cut words if the idea is already clear from other words in the sentence. Substitute single words for wordy phrases.

Wordy: Keep this information on file for future reference.

Better: Keep this information for reference.

or: File this information.

What's in a
or When Is
Not a Sandv
When It's a

How would you defin
wich? Most of us p
slices of bread with so
filling between them. E
Panera Bread Co.

When Qdoba Me
tried to move into a
center in Massachuse
tried to stop it. The c
clause in its lease th
it from competition by
the shopping center fi
space to another sand
That clause might kee
or Quizno's out, but w
Mexican Grill moved
tried to claim that th
restaurant's burritos
wiches, and thus the
center had violated
ment. To Panera, a
equivalent to bread
with stuffing in bet
sandwich.

Not so, says Mas
Superior Court Juc
Locke. Using testir
chefs as well as a dic
nition, Locke ruled tl
difference is the she
tortilla is not equiva
slices of bread.

Adapted from "Panera
Over Status of Burrito,"
Register, November 12,

7.4   Identifying Words with Multiple Denotations

a. Each of the following words has several denotations. How many can you list without going to a dictionary? How many additional meanings does a good dictionary list?

browser   log
court   table

b. List five words that have multiple denotations.

7.5   Evaluating Connotations

a. Identify the connotations of each of the following metaphors for a multicultural nation.
melting pot
mosaic
tapestry

crazy quilt
garden salad
stew
tributaries

b. Which connotations seem most positive? Why?

7.6   Evaluating the Ethical Implication of Connotations

In each of the following pairs, identify the more favorable term. When is its use justifiable?

1. wasted/sacrificed
2. illegal alien/immigrant
3. friendly fire/enemy attack
4. terminate/fire
5. inaccuracy/lying
6. budget/spending plan
7. feedback/criticism

7.7   Correcting Errors in Denotation and Connotation

Identify and correct the errors in denotation or connotation in the following sentences:

1. In our group, we weeded out the best idea each person had thought of.
2. She is a prudent speculator.
3. The three proposals are diametrically opposed to each other.
4. While he researched companies, he was literally glued to the Web.
5. Our backpacks are hand sewn by one of roughly 16 individuals.

7.8   Using Connotations to Shape Response

Write two sentences to describe each of the following situations. In one sentence, use words with positive connotations; in the other, use negative words.

1. Chris doesn't spend time on small talk.
2. Chris often starts work on a new project without being told to do so.
3. As a supervisor, Chris gives very specific instructions to subordinates.

7.9   Choosing Levels of Formality

Identify the more formal word in each pair. Which term is better for most business documents? Why?

1. adapted to   geared to
2. befuddled   confused
3. assistant   helper
4. pilot project testing the waters
5. cogitate   think

7.10   Eliminating Jargon and Simplifying Language

Revise these sentences to eliminate jargon and to use short, familiar words.

1. When the automobile company announced its strategic downsizing initiative, it offered employees a career alternative enhancement program.

2. Any alterations must be approved during the 30-day period commencing 60 days prior to the expiration date of the agreement.

3. As per your request, the undersigned has obtained estimates of upgrading our computer system. A copy of the estimated cost is attached hereto.

4. Please be advised that this writer is in considerable need of a new computer.

5. Enclosed please find the proposed draft for the employee negative retention plan. In the event that you have alterations which you would like to suggest, forward same to my office at your earliest convenience.

7.11   Changing Verbs from Passive to Active Voice

Identify passive voice in the following sentences and convert it to active voice. In some cases, you may need to add information to do so. You may use different words as long as you retain the basic meaning of the sentence. Remember that imperative verbs are active voice, too.

1. For a customer to apply for benefits, an application must be completed.

2. The cost of delivering financial services is being slashed by computers, the Internet, and toll-free phone lines.

3. When the vacation schedule is finalized it is recommended that it be routed to all supervisors for final approval.

4. As stated in my résumé, I have designed Web pages for three student organizations.

5. Material must not be left on trucks outside the warehouse. Either the trucks must be parked inside the warehouse or the material must be unloaded at the time of receiving the truck.

7.12   Using Strong Verbs

Revise each of the following sentences to replace hidden verbs with action verbs.

1. An understanding of stocks and bonds is important if one wants to invest wisely.

2. We must undertake a calculation of expected revenues and expenses for the next two years.

3. The production of clear and concise documents is the mark of a successful communicator.

4. We hope to make use of the company's Web site to promote the new product line.

5. If you wish to be eligible for the Miller scholarship, you must complete an application by January 31.

6. When you make an evaluation of media buys, take into consideration the demographics of the group seeing the ad.

7. We provide assistance to clients in the process of reaching a decision about the purchase of hardware and software.

7.13   Reducing Wordiness

1. Eliminate words that say nothing. You may use different words.

   a. There are many businesses that are active in community and service work.

   b. The purchase of a new computer will allow us to produce form letters quickly. In addition, return on investment could be calculated for proposed repairs. Another use is that the computer could check databases to make sure that claims are paid only once.

   c. Our decision to enter the South American market has precedence in the past activities of the company.

2. Combine sentences to show how ideas are related and to eliminate unnecessary words.

   a. Some customers are profitable for companies. Other customers actually cost the company money.

   b. If you are unable to come to the session on HMOs, please call the human resources office. You will be able to schedule another time to ask questions you may have about the various options.

   c. Major Japanese firms often have employees who know English well. US companies negotiating with Japanese companies should bring their own interpreters.

7.14   Improving Parallel Structure

Revise each of the following sentences to create parallelism.

1. The orientation session will cover the following information:

   - Company culture will be discussed.
   - How to use the equipment.
   - You will get an overview of key customers' needs.

2. Five criteria for a good Web page are content that serves the various audiences, attention to details, and originality. It is also important to have effective organization and navigation devices. Finally, provide attention to details such as revision date and the Webmaster's address.

3. When you leave a voice-mail message,

   - Summarize your main point in a sentence or two.
   - The name and phone number should be given slowly and distinctly.
   - The speaker should give enough information so that the recipient can act on the message.
   - Tell when you'll be available to receive the recipient's return call.

7.15   Putting Readers in Your Sentences

Revise each of the following sentences to put readers in them. As you revise, use active voice and simple words.

1. Mutual funds can be purchased from banks, brokers, financial planners, or from the fund itself.

2. I would like to take this opportunity to invite you back to Global Wireless. As a previous customer we have outstanding new rate plans to offer you and your family. We invite you to review the rate plans on the attached page and choose the one that best fits your needs. All our customers are important to us.

3. Another aspect of the university is campus life, with an assortment of activities and student groups to participate in and lectures and sports events to attend.

7.16   Editing Sentences to Improve Style

Revise these sentences to make them smoother, less wordy, and easier to read. Eliminate jargon and repetition. Keep the information; you may reword or reorganize it. If the original is not clear, you may need to add information to write a clear revision.

1. There are many different topics that you will read about on a monthly basis once you subscribe to *Inc.*

2. With the new organic fertilizer, you'll see an increase in the quality of your tomatoes and the number grown.

3. New procedure for customer service employees: Please be aware effective immediately, if a customer is requesting a refund of funds applied to their account a front and back copy of the check must be submitted if the transaction is over $500.00. For example, if the customer is requesting $250.00 back, and the total amount of the transaction is $750.00, a front and back copy of the check will be needed to obtain the refund.

4. The county will benefit from implementing flextime.

   - Offices will stay open longer for more business.
   - Staff turnover will be lower.
   - Easier business communication with states in other time zones.
   - Increased employee productivity.

5. There is a seasonality factor in the workload, with the heaviest being immediately prior to quarterly due dates for estimated tax payments.

7.17   Practicing Plain Language

Working with a partner, create three sentences that feature problematic elements that mask meaning.

   - Sentence 1: wordiness and/or euphemisms
   - Sentence 2: jargon from your field of study
   - Sentence 3: words with multiple denotations or connotations

Then exchange your sentences with another team and rewrite their sentences into plain language.

7.18   Using Topic Sentences

Make each of the following paragraphs more readable by opening each paragraph with a topic sentence. You may be able to find a topic sentence in the paragraph and move it to the beginning. In other cases, you'll need to write a new sentence.

1. At Disney World, a lunch put on an expense account is "on the mouse." McDonald's employees "have ketchup in their veins." Business slang flourishes at companies with rich corporate cultures. Memos at Procter & Gamble are called "reco's" because the model P&G memo begins with a recommendation.

2. The first item on the agenda is the hiring for the coming year. George has also asked that we review the agency goals for the next fiscal year. We should cover this early in the meeting since it may affect our hiring preferences. Finally, we need to announce the deadlines for grant proposals, decide which grants to apply for, and set up a committee to draft each proposal.

3. Separate materials that can be recycled from your regular trash. Pass along old clothing, toys, or appliances to someone else who can use them. When you purchase products, choose those with minimal packaging. If you have a yard, put your yard waste and kitchen scraps (excluding meat and fat) in a compost pile. You can reduce the amount of solid waste your household produces in four ways.

7.19   Revising Paragraphs

Revise each paragraph to make it easier to read. Change, rearrange, or delete words and sentences; add any material necessary.

a. Once a new employee is hired, each one has to be trained for a week by one of our supervisors at a cost of $1,000 each which includes the supervisor's time. This amount also includes half of the new employee's salary, since new hires produce only half the normal production per worker for the week. This summer $24,000 was spent in training 24 new employees. Absenteeism increased in the department on the hottest summer days. For every day each worker is absent we lose $200 in lost production. This past summer there was a total of 56 absentee days taken for a total loss of $11,200 in lost production. Turnover and absenteeism were the causes of an unnecessary expenditure of over $35,000 this summer.

b. One service is investments. General financial news and alerts about companies in the customer's portfolio are available. Quicken also provides assistance in finding the best mortgage rate and in providing assistance in making the decision whether to refinance a mortgage. Another service from Quicken is advice for the start and management of a small business. Banking services, such as paying bills and applying for loans, have long been available to Quicken subscribers. The taxpayer can be walked through the tax preparation process by Quicken. Someone considering retirement can use Quicken to ascertain whether the amount being set aside for this purpose is sufficient. Quicken's Web site provides seven services.

7.20   Writing Paragraphs

As your instructor directs, write a paragraph on one or more of the following topics.

a. Discuss your ideal job.
b. Summarize a recent article from a business magazine or newspaper.
c. Explain how technology is affecting the field you plan to enter.
d. Explain why you have or have not decided to work while you attend college.
e. Write a profile of someone who is successful in the field you hope to enter.

As your instructor directs,

a. Label topic sentences, active voice, and parallel structure.
b. Edit a classmate's paragraphs to make the writing even tighter and smoother.

7.21   Identifying Buzzwords and Jargon

This is an actual press release published in the *Des Moines Register* with an article on buzzwords.

> Wal-Mart Stores, Inc., the largest private employer with more than 1.8 million employees and the largest corporate mover of people, selected Capital Relocation Services as the sole source provider for the implementation of its Tier III and Tier IV relocation programs. These two programs account for the vast majority of the company's relocations. Capital was awarded the business following an intensive RFP and due diligence process.
>
> "We're very excited about the synergy that Wal-Mart's selection of Capital brings to both companies," commented Mickey Williams, Capital's CEO. "We are also pleased to welcome to Capital the existing Wal-Mart PMP Relocation team that has been on-site at Wal-Mart's Bentonville headquarters for 14 years. They will continue to serve Wal-Mart and Sam's Club's Associates and will have an active role in the implementation of the new policy."
>
> "What really enabled us to stand out was our focus on the strategic results Wal-Mart was looking for, and connecting that to their relocation program," added Williams. "Additionally, we demonstrated what would need to be done to achieve those results."
>
> Mr. Williams continued, "Several years ago, we realized that traditional relocation solutions weren't enough. The challenge was that relocation management had become a logistics focused straightjacket. The emphasis was on efficiency and not on effectiveness. In a time of unprecedented change, relocation management programs were becoming increasingly inflexible."
>
> "We realized that our continued success required us to stop thinking of ourselves solely as a relocation management company—we had to start thinking and acting as a talent management support company; after all that is the underlying purpose of relocation management in the first place. Wal-Mart's selection of Capital is a big confirmation that our approach is the right one."

Now answer these questions:

1. What is this press release about? What is it saying?

2. Why did Capital Relocation Services get the new contract?

3. Underline the buzzwords and jargon in the press release. What do these words do in the press release?

4. What is the purpose of this press release? Does it meet its purpose? Why or why not?

Write a memo to your instructor evaluating the press release as an effective document.

Source: Larry Ballard, "Decipher a Honcho's Buzzwords, Such as 'Unsiloing,'" *Des Moines Register*, January 21, 2008, 1D.

7.22   Checking Spelling and Grammar Checkers

Each of the following paragraphs contains errors in grammar, spelling, and punctuation. Which errors does your spelling or grammar checker catch? Which errors does it miss? Does it flag as errors any words that are correct?

a.   Answer to an Inquiry

Enclosed are the tow copies you requested of our pamphlet, "Using the Internet to market Your products. The pamphelt walks you through the steps of planning the Home Page (The first page of the Web cite, shows examples of other Web pages we have designed, and provide a questionaire that you can use to analyze audience the audience and purposes.

b.   Performance Appraisal

Most staff accountants complete three audits a month. Ellen has completed 21 audits in this past six months she is our most productive staff accountant. Her technical skills our very good however some clients feel that she could be more tactful in suggesting ways that the clients accounting practices courld be improved.

c.   Brochure

Are you finding that being your own boss crates it's own problems? Take the hassle out of working at home with a VoiceMail Answering System. Its almost as good as having your own secratery.

d.   Presentation Slides

How to Create a Web Résumé

- Omit home adress and phone number
- Use other links only if they help an employer evalaute you.
  - Be Professional.
  - Carefully craft and proof read the phrase on the index apage.

How to Create a Scannable Résumé

- Create a "plain vanilla" document.
- Use include a "Keywords" section. Include personality traits as well sas accomplishments.
- Be specific and quantifyable.

7.23   Revising Documents using "Track Changes"

"Track Changes" is a feature in some word processors that records alterations made to a document. It is particularly useful when you are collaborating with a colleague to create, edit, or revise documents. Track Changes will highlight any text that has been added or deleted to your document but it also allows you to decide, for each change, whether to accept the suggestion or reject it and return to your original text. In addition to Track Changes, many word processors include a comment feature that allows you to ask questions or make suggestions without altering the text itself.

For this exercise, you will electronically exchange a document with one of your classmates. With the Track Changes feature turned on, you will review each other's documents, make comments or ask questions, insert additions, and make deletions to improve the writing, and then revise your work based upon the changes and comments.

As your instructor directs, select the electronic file of the document you created for exercise 7.20 "Writing Paragraphs" or another document that you have created for this class. Exchange this file with your peer review partner.

- Open the file in Microsoft Word.
- In the Tools menu, select Track Changes to turn the feature on.
- Review the document and make suggestions that will help your peer improve the writing. For instance, you can

- Look for accurate, appropriate, and ethical wording as well as instances of unnecessary jargon.
- Look for active voice and concise prose.
- Look for structural issues like topic sentences, tightly written paragraphs, varied sentence structure and length, and focus upon the thesis statement. Suggest where sentences can be combined or where sentences need parallel structure.
- Look for you-attitude.
- Ask questions (using comments) when the text isn't clear or make suggestions to tighten the writing or improve word choices.
- Return the document to its author and open yours to review the changes and comments your partner added to your document.
- For each change, decide whether to Accept or Reject the suggestion.

Continue to revise the document. Then submit a copy of your original version and the revised version to your instructor.

7.24   Valuing drafts

Suppose your state has an open records law, a law that gives citizens broad access to records of communications made by public officials, including records reflecting the development of various decisions and laws. Now suppose your state legislature is considering legislation that would enable government officials to keep drafts secret. Are you for or against the new legislation?

Hints:

1. Why do you think the new legislation is being proposed?
2. What is a draft? Do you want to see brainstorming notes of Senator Doe? Suppose in your state a law is a draft until it has been signed by the governor. Would that fact modify your opinion?
3. Can you think of criteria that would exclude some but not all drafts?

4. Where in the process do you think most of the significant changes are made in policy? Early? Late? Somewhere in-between?
5. When does it become hard to change a policy?
6. Suppose the policy could also be applied to drafts of corporate officials who set company policies with public impact. Now are you for or against the new legislation?

As your instructor directs,

a. Discuss your opinions in small groups.
b. As a group present your opinions to the class.
c. Post your opinions online for your classmates to read.

Adapted from Clark Kauffman, "'Draft' Records Would Be Secret under Proposal: Critics of Changing Iowa Law Say Access Is Needed Even to Preliminary Documents," *Des Moines Register,* March 18, 2008, 1A.

7.25   All-Weather Case: Composing, Revising, Editing, and Proofreading an Environmental Accountability Statement

Doug has asked Caleb to draft All-Weather's environmental accountability statement. After the statement is approved by Doug, it will be vetted by both marketing and manufacturing before being signed by the company's president. Caleb has been typing notes that will go into the drafting of the statement. Right now, his notes read as follows:

All-Weather is commited to protecting the environment for the benefit of future generations in all its activities. We use re-cycled raw materials in our manufacturing processes and operations, 30% in case of wood fiber windows and doors and 20% in vinyl windows and doors. We've limited our green-house gas emisions by locating our plants closer to markets where our products are sold so we don't have to transport our finished products to far-off markets which means lower costs and fuel consumtion for transportation and lower greenhouse gases for the environment. Our doors and windows have received "Energy Star" certification. Some of the ways in which our doors and windows save energy consumtion include, but are not limited to: using low-E glass (energy efficient glazing) for window and door panes, using multiple panes in windows and doors, using gases like argon and krypton between window panes for better insulation, improved weatherstripping in doors. Our products can help builders and architects score points in the Leadership in Energy and Environmental Design (LEED) certification process. Our products have also received better ratings for energy savings by the National Fenestration Rating Council (NFRC). We have reduced energy consumption in our plants and offices by 30% in the last five years. This has been achieved due to both lean manufacturing processes as well as use of energy-efficient products, including light bulbs for example, throughout the company. We bye more than 90% of our wood from forests that are certified by the Forest Stewardship Council (FSC). We also adhere to ISO 14001 in our manufacturing with its requirement of regular environmental audits (once every month).

Tomorrow, Doug wants to see the first complete draft of the statement. Tanner cannot draft the statement because he is busy coordinating *Kaizen* workshops for Drs. Tanizaki and Kawabata (the good-natured Japanese professors have forgiven Tanner for his unintended slights and, on his part, Tanner knows a lot more about Japanese culture and etiquette than he did on that first meeting). So Caleb looks for Kioni instead, who is with her favorite HR Manager, Erin.

"Can you loan Kioni to me for a day?" Caleb asks, smiling.

"Sure, Caleb," Erin says. "Kioni is glad to help."

"Thanks, Erin, for your generosity, as always," Caleb says, bowing his head a little. "Kioni, how're you doing today?"

"I'm fine, sir," Kioni says, smiling politely.

Once inside his office, Caleb prints the notes on the accountability statement that he has typed. He gives the printout to Kioni, asking her to give it a quick reading.

"Awful, isn't it?" Caleb says, referring to the notes. "I need this drafted as a statement on environmental accountability."

"Does it have to be in any particular format?" Kioni asks, remembering her business communication class.

"Oh, a memo will be fine," Caleb says, naming his favorite correspondence medium.

"Any particular writing style?" Kioni asks, knowing by now that there probably were a dozen writing styles in the HR Department alone.

"Um, make it clear and concise. See that it flows well and is logically organized. And, for heaven's sake, don't leave any typos uncorrected," Caleb says, suddenly realizing the minefield of typos his notes are.

"Okay," Kioni says, getting up. "I'll have the draft ready by evening."

"That will be great, Kioni," Caleb says. "You're truly a godsend."

Based on your reading of Chapter 7 and Caleb's notes, help Kioni compose, revise, edit, and proofread the environmental accountability statement in memo format. The memo will go to the vice presidents of marketing and manufacturing; it will be from the vice president of human resources.

Designing Documents

Chapter Outline

The Importance of Effective Design

Design as Part of Your Writing Process(es)

Design and Conventions

Levels of Design

Guidelines for Page Design

1. Use White Space.
2. Use Headings.
3. Limit the Use of Words Set in All Capital Letters.
4. Use No More than Two Fonts in a Single Document.
5. Decide Whether to Justify Margins.
6. Put Important Elements in the Top Left and Lower Right Quadrants.
7. Use a Grid to Unify Graphic Elements.
8. Use Highlighting, Decorative Devices, and Color in Moderation.

Designing Brochures

Designing Web Pages

Testing the Design for Usability

Summary of Key Points

Design at the *Wall Street Journal*

Document design is just about making your work pretty, isn't it? The publishers of the *Wall Street Journal* didn't see it that way. They spent two years researching, creating, and testing designs for the *Journal*'s new look before they unveiled it. After getting advice from their customers in the form of surveys, focus groups, and test marketing, the *Journal*'s publishers chose to redesign their newspaper in specific ways:

- They expanded their use of headings and white space, to make it easier for readers to find articles in the paper and to follow articles from page to page. People are more likely to read, and not skim, if they have clear navigational cues to follow.

- They created a hierarchy, through headline size and story placement, to indicate relative importance of news.

- They changed to a new, narrower paper size that would make the *Journal* more convenient to hold, fold, and read. The more convenient size decreases the time readers spend folding the paper into a manageable shape—which gives them more time to read.

- They added more color to help highlight important topics and help readers find information more easily. They also replaced the *Journal*'s traditional gray shading with soft color pastels, to brighten the paper's overall "look" and make it easier to read text printed in shaded sidebars.

- They also created a new font, named Exchange, for the *Journal*. Exchange was specifically designed to be easy to read, even when printed in a small size, in tight columns, on a narrow page. People are more likely to spend time reading text that's easy on the eyes.

Document design isn't just about making your work "pretty." Everything that you put on the page is a choice: the appearance of a document can guide your readers' attention, build goodwill, and establish rapport with them, just as much as the text on the page can.

> *"Everything that you put on the page is a choice that guides your readers' attention."*

Adapted from L. Gordon Crovitz, "What Is Changing—and What Isn't—in the *Wall Street Journal*," *Wall Street Journal*, December 4, 2006, A17; L. Gordon Crovitz, "What to Expect in Your *Journal*, Starting on Jan. 2," *Wall Street Journal*, December 30–31, 2006, A11; and Mario R. Garcia, "The Relevance of Good Design," *Wall Street Journal*, January 2, 2007, G8.

Learning Objectives

After studying this chapter, you will know:

1   Why document design is important in business communication.

2   The four levels of document design, and how they can help you critique documents.

3   Guidelines for document design.

4   How to design brochures and Web pages.

5   How to do basic usability testing on your documents.

Good Document Design Saves Money, I

Much of the research on document design was done in the 1980s and early 1990s and was accompanied by impressive accounts of organizational savings:

• The British government began reviewing its forms in 1982. After 10 years, it had eliminated 27,000 forms, redesigned 41,000, and saved over $28 million.

• Revising the British lost-baggage form for airline passengers cut a 55% error rate to 3%.

• In Australia, rewriting one legal document saved the Victorian government the equivalent of $400,000 a year in staff salaries.

• In the Netherlands, revising the form for educational grants reduced by two-thirds the number of forms applicants filled out incompletely or incorrectly. The government saved time and money; the applicants got decisions more quickly.

Adapted from Karen Schriver, "Quality in Document Design: Issues and Controversy," *Technical Communication* 40, no. 2 (1993), 250–51.

Good document design saves time and money, reduces legal problems, and builds goodwill. A well-designed document looks inviting, friendly, and easy to read. Effective design also groups ideas visually, making the structure of the document more obvious so the document is easier to read. Easy-to-read documents enhance your credibility and build an image of you as a professional, competent person. Many workplaces expect you to be able to create designs that go beyond the basic templates you'll find in common business software programs.[1] Good design is important not only for reports, Web pages, and newsletters but also for announcements and one–page letters and memos.

The Importance of Effective Design

When document design is poor, both organizations and society suffer. The *Challenger* space shuttle blew up because its O-rings failed in the excessive cold. Poor communication—including charts that hid, rather than emphasized, the data about O-ring performance—contributed to the decision to launch. More recently, after the *Columbia* space shuttle disintegrated during reentry, poor communication was again implicated in NASA's failure to ensure the spacecraft was safe. Mission leaders insisted that engineers had not briefed them on the seriousness of the damage to the shuttle when a piece of foam struck it on takeoff. But after studying transcripts of meetings, Edward R. Tufte, who specializes in visual presentations of evidence, concluded that engineers did offer their concerns and supporting statistics. However, they did so using visuals that obscured the seriousness.[2] In 2000, the badly designed "butterfly ballot" confused enough voters to cloud the outcome of the US presidential election.[3]

Design as Part of Your Writing Process(es)

Design isn't something to "tack on" when you've finished writing. Indeed, the best documents, slides, and screens are created when you think about design at each stage of your writing process(es).

• As you plan, think about your audience. Are they skilled readers? Are they busy? Will they read the document straight through or skip around in it?

• As you write, incorporate lists and headings. Use visuals to convey numerical data clearly and forcefully.

• Get feedback from people who will be using your document. Do they find the document hard to understand? Do they need additional visuals?

• As you revise, check your draft against the guidelines in this chapter.

Design and Conventions

Like all aspects of communication, effective design relies heavily on conventions. These conventions provide a design language. For instance, most graphical interfaces are organized around the desktop metaphor, where we use files, folders, tabs, and trashcans. Commercial Web sites use the metaphor of the shopping cart. We have a mental image of the way brochures, business letters, or business cards are supposed to look.

Conventions may vary by audience, geographic area, industry, company, or even department, but they do exist. Some conventions work well with some audiences but not with others, so careful audience analysis is necessary. The British and Americans prefer serif typefaces; the French and Dutch prefer sans serif. Instruction pictures for office equipment generally show feminine hands using the equipment. Some female readers will relate more readily to the instructions; others will be offended at the implied assumption that only women perform such low-level office jobs.[4]

Conventions also change over time. Résumés used to be typed documents; now most companies ask for electronic ones. Today we rarely use Courier font; we italicize magazine titles rather than underlining them, and we space once rather than twice after periods at ends of sentences.

Conventions also change with new software. The new versions of Word 2007 and Word 2008 broke long-standing Word conventions. The new versions use the font Cambria for headings and Calibri for body text, instead of the traditional Times New Roman. The default spacing has changed from single to 1.5. Time will tell if these new settings become new conventions.

Many Word users were also frustrated at first with the overall interface of the program, because it broke too many conventions at once. Instead of the classic drop-down menus that have been present since early versions of Word, the menus now use a more visual interface, with a small icon representing each task a user wants to perform. For example, if you want to insert a picture, a little picture icon indicates that option. Similarly if you want to do a word count, a little icon with "ABC 123" indicates this option.

Violating conventions is risky: violations may not be interpreted correctly, or they may signal that the author or designer is unreliable or unknowledgeable. Brochures with text that does not fit properly into the folded panels, freehand drawings in a set of installation instructions, or bar charts with garish color designs can destroy the reader's trust.[5]

Levels of Design

Visual communications expert Charles Kostelnick distinguishes four levels of design (see Figure 8.1). These levels give you an organized way to think about the design choices you can make in your own documents, presentations, and visuals. They're also useful when you analyze the documents you encounter in a professional setting: one of the best ways to get ideas for your own document designs is to analyze the design elements in successful documents.

When you look at communication design, look for Kostelnick's four levels:[6]

- Intra—Design choices for individual letters and words. Intra-level design choices include the font and its size you choose; whether you use bold, italics, or color changes to emphasize key words; and the way you use capital letters. The serif font used for body text on this page is an intra-level choice, as is the sans serif font used for headings.

- Inter—Design choices for blocks of text. Inter-level design choices include the ways you use headings, white space, indents, lists, and even text boxes. The headings and bulleted lists that organize information on this page are inter-level choices.

Figure 8.1   Four Levels for Examining Visual Language

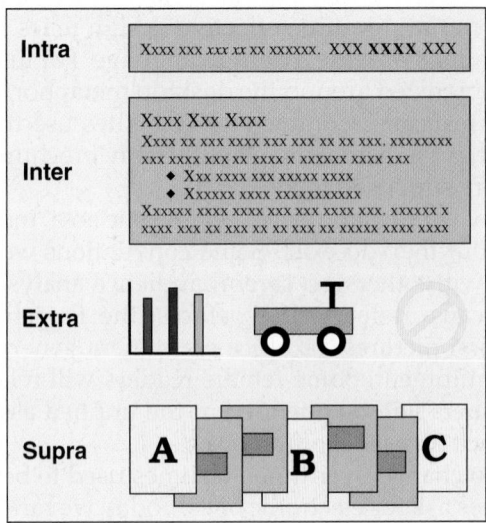

Source: Charles Kostelnick and David Roberts, *Designing Visual Language* (Boston: Allyn & Bacon, 1998), 85. Reprinted by permission of Pearson Education, Inc.

- Extra—Design choices for graphics that go with the text. Extra-level design choices include the way you use pictures, photographs, data displays, charts, and graphs, and the ways in which you emphasize information on those graphics. The figures in this chapter are extra-level design choices.
- Supra—Design choices for entire documents. Supra-level design choices include paper size, headers and footers, and the index and table of contents, as well as color schemes and layout grids that define the look of all sections of a document. The placement of the page numbers in this book, the two-column layout grid on all of the pages in this chapter, and the navigation text in the header on this page are supra-level choices.

The toy safety recall notice in Figure 8.2 illustrates all levels of design. At the intra-level, this notice uses a sans serif font throughout the whole document. Other intra-level elements include the "Safety Recall" in all capital letters and the boldface sentences. Inter-level elements involve the centered text throughout the notice. This choice may not be the best because the sentences that extend for more than one line make the notice difficult to read. Other inter-level elements include chunking text above and below the pictures. The affected/not affected pictures in the middle of the notice are part of the extra-level. These pictures are used to highlight the textual elements that describe the faulty toys. The supra-level includes the size of the paper. Most toy safety recall notices use a standard 8.5" × 11" page size even though the US Consumer Product Safety Commission recommends 11" × 17". Another unifying piece of information on a supra-level that can be found in all safety recall notices is the "post until" date and the "In cooperation with the US Consumer Product Safety Commission" tag. Visually, this information is treated like a page footer, as it can be found on every toy safety recall notice.[7]

Guidelines for Page Design

Use the guidelines in Figure 8.3 to create visually attractive documents.

1. Use White Space.

White space—the empty space on the page—makes material easier to read by emphasizing the material that it separates from the rest of the text. To create white space,

Designing for Baby Boomers

As baby boomers turn 60, many start to lose the ability to see as clearly as they once did. Tiny buttons on cell phones, small typeface on bottles of pills, and even the low lighting in some restaurants all make reading a difficult task. But this baby boomer generation is not bashful when it comes to denouncing issues with poor document design.

As a result, some corporations are trying to help this large population see and function better in our society. For example, Romano's Macaroni Grill supplies reading glasses and large-print menus on request. Target is modifying its labeling on prescription bottles by putting the most important information—patient name, medication, dosage—in large boldface capital letters. Some remote controls and cell phones now have large text and buttons specifically designed for this older audience. Some laundry labels on garments use larger print. Even Microsoft has given users the option to enlarge the size of text on computer screens.

Overall, those companies that are willing to adapt their products to the unique needs of the 77 million baby boomers are more likely to be successful in the future.

Adapted from Katie Hafner, "Their Parents' Eyes," *New York Times,* August 4, 2007, B1.

Figure 8.2   Design Elements in a Toy Safety Recall Notice

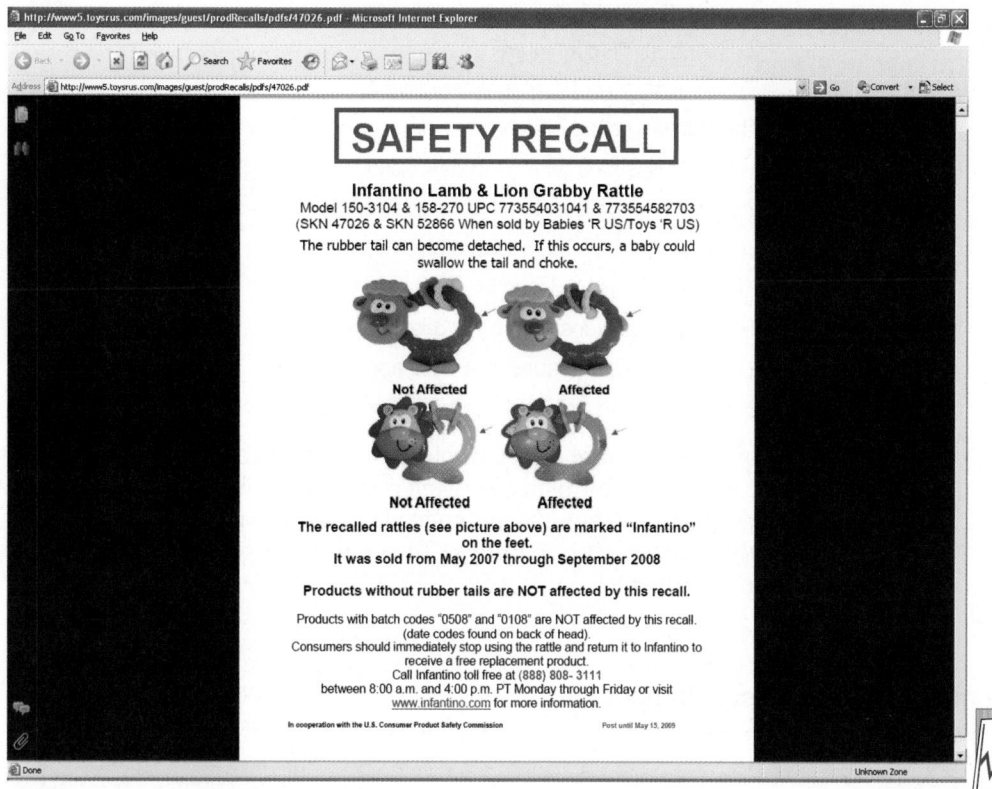

This toy safety recall notice uses all four levels of design.

Source: "Infantino Lamb & Lion Grabby Rattle," in *Toysrus Inc.: Safety: Recalls,* http://www5.toysrus.com/safety/47026
.cfm (accessed March 7, 2009).

Figure 8.3   Guidelines for Page Design

1. Use white space to separate and emphasize points.
2. Use headings to group points and lead the reader through the document.
3. Limit the use of words set in all capital letters.
4. Use no more than two fonts in a single document.
5. Decide whether to justify margins based on the situation and the audience.
6. Put important elements in the top left and lower right quadrants of the page.
7. Use a grid of imaginary columns to unify graphic elements.
8. Use highlighting, decorative devices, and color in moderation.

- Use headings.
- Use a mix of paragraph lengths (most no longer than seven typed lines). It's OK for a paragraph or two to be just one sentence. First and last paragraphs, in particular, should be short.
- Use lists.
  - Use tabs or indents—not spacing—to align items vertically.
  - Use numbered lists when the number or sequence of items is exact.
  - Use **bullets** (large dots or squares like those in this list) when the number and sequence don't matter.

When you use a list, make sure that all of the items in it are parallel (p. 197) and fit into the structure of the sentence that introduces the list.

Good Document Design Saves Money, II

Document design changes are not just cosmetic. Infomap, a communications consulting company, reports these savings among its customers:

- A leading credit card company reduced the average length of phone calls to its customer service center by 60 seconds each after improving the design of its reference materials. This time reduction reduced costs by 20%.
- A leading health care provider redesigned its customer claims manual and saw the number of calls to the help desk decrease by 50%.
- A major government agency struggling with information overload used Information Mapping to create "uniform information architecture" agency wide. Newly trained "mappers" changed over 60,000 pages, and the agency reported over $17 million dollars of cost savings.

Adapted from Information Mapping, in *Expertise,* http://infomap.com/index.cfm/Expertise/Success_Stories (accessed March 6, 2009).

Faulty:	The following suggestions can help employers avoid bias in job interviews:
	1. Base questions on the job description.
	2. Questioning techniques.
	3. Selection and training of interviewers.
Parallel:	The following suggestions can help employers avoid bias in job interviews:
	1. Base questions on the job description.
	2. Ask the same questions of all applicants.
	3. Select and train interviewers carefully.
Also parallel:	Employers can avoid bias in job interviews by
	1. Basing questions on the job description.
	2. Asking the same questions of all applicants.
	3. Selecting and training interviewers carefully.

Figure 8.4 shows an original typed document. In Figure 8.5, the same document has been improved by using shorter paragraphs, lists, and headings. These devices take space. When saving space is essential, it's better to cut the text and keep white space and headings. To see how to set up subheadings, see Figure 19.5 in Chapter 19.

Figure 8.4   A Document with Poor Visual Impact

Full capital letters make title hard to read

MONEY DEDUCTED FROM YOUR WAGES TO PAY CREDITORS

Long para-graph is visually uninviting

When you buy goods on credit, the store will sometimes ask you to sign a Wage Assignment form allowing it to deduct money from your wages if you do not pay your bill. When you buy on credit, you sign a contract agreeing to pay a certain amount each week or month until you have paid all you owe. The Wage Assignment Form is separate. It must contain the name of your present employer, your social security number, the amount of money loaned, the rate of interest, the date when payments are due, and your signature. The words "Wage Assignment" must be printed at the top of the form and also near the line for your signature. Even if you have signed a Wage Assignment agreement, Roysner will not withhold part of your wages unless all of the following conditions are met: 1. You have to be more than forty days late in payment of what you owe; 2. Roysner has to receive a correct statement of the amount you are in default and a copy of the Wage Assignment form; and 3. You and Roysner must receive a notice from the creditor at least twenty days in advance stating that the creditor plans to make a demand on your wages. This twenty-day notice gives you a chance to correct the problems yourself. If these conditions are all met, Roysner must withhold 15% of each paycheck until your bill is paid and give this money to your creditor.

If you think you are not late or that you do not owe the amount stated, you can argue against it by filing a legal document called a "defense." Once you file a defense, Roysner will not withhold any money from you. However, be sure you are right before you file a defense. If you are wrong, you have to pay not only what you owe but also all legal costs for both yourself and the creditor. If you are right, the creditor has to pay all these costs.

Important information is hard to find

Figure 8.5 A Document Revised to Improve Visual Impact

Money Deducted from Your Wages to Pay Creditors

First letter of each main word capitalized—Title split onto two lines

When you buy goods on credit, the store will sometimes ask you to sign a Wage Assignment form allowing it to deduct money from your wages if you do not pay your bill.

Have You Signed a Wage Assignment Form?

Headings divide document into chunks

When you buy on credit, you sign a contract agreeing to pay a certain amount each week or month until you have paid all you owe. The Wage Assignment Form is separate. It must contain

- The name of your present employer,
- Your social security number,
- The amount of money loaned,
- The rate of interest,
- The date when payments are due, and
- Your signature.

List with bullets where order of items doesn't matter

Single-space list when items are short.

The words "Wage Assignment" must be printed at the top of the form and also near the line for your signature.

Headings must be parallel. Here all are questions

When Would Money Be Deducted from Your Wages to Pay a Creditor?

Even if you have signed a Wage Assignment agreement, Roysner will not withhold part of your wages unless all of the following conditions are met:

White space between items emphasizes them

1. You have to be more than 40 days late in payment of what you owe;

2. Roysner has to receive a correct statement of the amount you are in default and a copy of the Wage Assignment form; and

Double-space between items in list when most items are two lines or longer.

Numbered list where number or order of items matter

3. You and Roysner must receive a notice from the creditor at least 20 days in advance stating that the creditor plans to make a demand on your wages. This 20-day notice gives you a chance to correct the problem yourself.

If these conditions are all met, Roysner must withhold fifteen percent (15%) of each paycheck until your bill is paid and give this money to your creditor.

What Should You Do If You Think the Wage Assignment Is Incorrect?

If you think you are not late or that you do not owe the amount stated, you can argue against it by filing a legal document called a "defense." Once you file a defense, Roysner will not withhold any money from you. However, be sure you are right before you file a defense. If you are wrong, you have to pay not only what you owe but also all legal costs for both yourself and the creditor. If you are right, the creditor has to pay all these costs.

What's on the Menu Tonight?

George Rapp is a "menu engineer" who helps restaurants around the world turn their menus into "profitable, user-friendly sales tools." His menus are attractive, full of savory detail, and carefully designed to lead the diner's eye to the high-profit items. Prices are nestled with food descriptions rather than aligned on the edge of the page so that readers can't scan the menu for the cheapest item. Expensive, profitable dishes are placed in the menu's prime real estate, the upper-right-hand corner; cheaper items are harder to locate. The longest, most mouth-watering descriptions are used for the most profitable items.

Adapted from Carolina A. Miranda, "The Menu Magician," *Time*, June 12, 2006, 86.

http://infomap .com/index.cfm/ TheMethod/Demos

Information Mapping uses grids and tables to present complex information in an easy-to-find format. Review some of the online demos on the Information Mapping Web site, and notice how the 'after' documents make strong use of tables, lists, and white space to draw your attention to important points.

Try the fun demo at http://infomap.com/movies/demo.htm to see how they convert time savings to money savings.

2. Use Headings.

Psychological research has shown that our short-term memories can hold only seven plus or minus two bits of information.[8] Only after those bits are processed and put into long-term memory can we assimilate new information. Large amounts of information will be easier to process if they are grouped into three to seven chunks rather than presented as individual items.

Headings are words, short phrases, or short sentences that group points and divide your document into sections. Headings enable your reader to see at a glance how the document is organized, to turn quickly to sections of special interest, and to compare and contrast points more easily. Headings also break up the page, making it look less formidable and more interesting. To use headings effectively,

- Make headings specific.
- Make each heading cover all the material until the next heading.
- Keep headings at any one level parallel.

In a letter or memo, type main headings even with the left margin in bold. Capitalize the first letters of the first word and of other major words; use lowercase for all other letters. (See Figure 8.5 for an example.) In single-spaced text, triple-space between the previous text and the heading; double-space between the heading and the text that follows.

If you need subdivisions under a main heading, again type the heading even with the left margin, but this time put a period after the subhead and begin the paragraph on the same line. Use subheadings only when you have at least two subdivisions under a given main heading.

In a report, you may need more than two levels of headings. Figure 19.5 in Chapter 19 shows levels of headings for reports.

3. Limit the Use of Words Set in All Capital Letters.

We recognize words by their shapes.[9] (See Figure 8.6.) In capitals, all words are rectangular; letters lose the descenders and ascenders that make reading faster and more accurate.[10] In addition, many people interpret text in full capitals as "shouting," especially when that text appears in online documents. In those cases, full capitals might elicit a negative response from your audience. Use full capitals sparingly, if at all.

4. Use No More than Two Fonts in a Single Document.

Fonts are unified styles of type. Each font comes in various sizes and usually in bold and italic. In **fixed** fonts every letter takes the same space; an *i* takes the same space as a *w*. Courier and Prestige Elite are fixed fonts. Most fonts are **proportional** and allow wider letters to take more space than narrower letters. Times Roman, Palatino, Helvetica, and Arial are proportional fonts.

Figure 8.6   Full Capitals Hide the Shape of a Word

Full capitals hide the shape of a word and slow reading 19%.

FULL CAPITALS HIDE THE SHAPE OF A WORD AND SLOW READING 19%.

Figure 8.7   Examples of Different Fonts

This sentence is set in 12-point Times Roman.

This sentence is set in 12-point Arial.

This sentence is set in 12-point New Courier.

This sentence is set in 12-point Lucinda Calligraphy.

This sentence is set in 12-point Broadway.

This sentence is set in 12-point Technical.

Serif fonts have little extensions, called serifs, from the main strokes. (In Figure 8.7, look at the feet on the *r*'s in New Courier and the flick on the top of the *d* in Lucinda.) New Courier, Elite, Times Roman, Palatino, and Lucinda Calligraphy are serif fonts. Helvetica, Arial, Geneva, and Technical are **sans serif** fonts since they lack serifs (*sans* is French for *without*). Sans serif fonts are good for titles and tables.

You should choose the fonts you use carefully, because they shape reader response just as font size does. Research suggests that people respond positively to fonts that fit the genre and purpose of the document. For example, a font like Broadway (see Figure 8.7) is appropriate for a headline in a newsletter, but not for the body text of a memo.[11]

Most business documents use just one font; popular ones are Times Roman, Palatino, Helvetica, or Arial. You can create emphasis and levels of headings by using bold, italics, and different sizes. Bold is easier to read than italics, so use bolding if you need only one method to emphasize text. In a complex document, use bigger type for main headings and slightly smaller type for subheadings and text.

Twelve-point type is ideal for letters, memos, and reports. Smaller type is harder to read, especially for older readers.

If your material will not fit in the available pages, cut it. Putting some sections in tiny type saves space but creates a negative response—a negative response that may extend to the organization that produced the document.

5. Decide Whether to Justify Margins.

Computers allow you to use **full justification** so that type lines up evenly on both the right and left margins. This paragraph you are reading justifies both margins. Margins justified only on the left, sometimes called **ragged right margins,** have lines ending in different places. In this chapter sidebar columns with bullets use ragged right margins.

Use full justification when you

- Can use proportional fonts.
- Want a more formal look.
- Want to use as few pages as possible.

Cultural Differences in Document Design

Cultural differences in document design are based on reading practices and experiences with other documents. Language is one source of these differences. For example, English and other European languages are written in horizontal lines moving from left to right down the page. Hebrew and Arabic languages are read from right to left. This affects where readers of these languages look first when they see a page of text.

People in the United States focus first on the left side of a Web site. Middle Eastern people focus first on the right side, so Web sites in Arabic and Hebrew orient text, links, and graphics from right to left.

Translations also affect the layout of a document. To convey the same message, Spanish and French take up more room than English does. Writing concise text for brochures, packages, and Web pages is more challenging in the wordier languages. The problem is even more complex in designing bilingual or multilingual documents. For example, a company selling in Canada must use both English and French on its packages, and the French type must be printed at least as large as the English. On some products, such as a bottle of medicine or perfume, this requirement leaves little room for fancy graphics.

Adapted from Albert N. Badre, "The Effects of Cross Cultural Interface Design Orientation on World Wide Web User Performance," ftp://ftp.cc.gatech.edu/pub/gvu/tr/2001/01-03.html (accessed March 7, 2009); and Pan Demetrakakes, "Multilingual Labeling Broadens Product Appeal," in *Food and Drug Packaging*, http://www.findarticles.com/p/articles/mi_m0UQX/is_7_67/ai_106423172 (accessed March 7, 2009).

Use ragged right margins when you

- Cannot use a proportional font.
- Want an informal look.
- Want to be able to revise an individual page without reprinting the whole document.
- Use very short line lengths.

6. Put Important Elements in the Top Left and Lower Right Quadrants.

Readers of English start in the upper left-hand corner of the page and read to the right and down. The eye moves in a Z pattern.[12] (See Figure 8.8.) Therefore, the four quadrants of the page carry different visual weights. The top left quadrant, where the eye starts, is the most important; the bottom right quadrant, where the eye ends, is next most important.

7. Use a Grid to Unify Graphic Elements.

For years, graphic designers have used a **grid system** to design pages. In its simplest form, a grid imposes two or three imaginary columns on the page. In more complex grids, these columns can be further subdivided. Then all the graphic elements—text indentations, headings, visuals, and so on—are lined up within the columns. The resulting symmetry creates a more pleasing page and unifies long documents.

Figure 8.9 uses grids to organize a page with visuals and a newsletter page.

8. Use Highlighting, Decorative Devices, and Color in Moderation.

Many word-processing programs have arrows, pointing fingers, and a host of other **dingbats** that you can insert. Clip art packages and presentation software allow you to insert more and larger images into your text. Used in

Figure 8.8   Put Important Elements in the Top Left and Bottom Right Quadrants

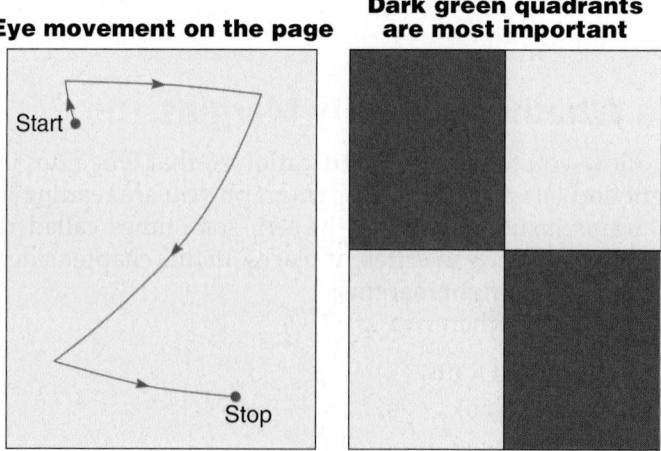

Source: Based on Russel N. Baird, Arthur T. Turnbull, and Duncan McDonald, *The Graphics of Communication: Typography, Layout, Design, Production,* 5th ed. (New York: Holt, Rinehart, and Winston, 1987), 37.

Figure 8.9 Examples of Grids to Design Pages

A page with visuals

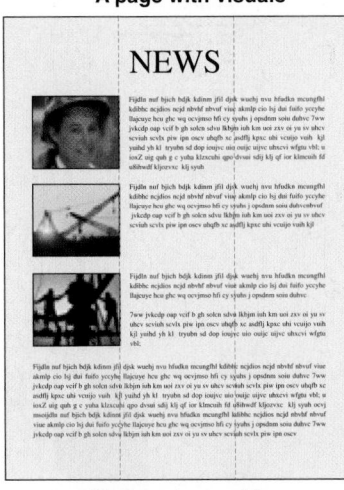

Three-column grid.

A newsletter page

Six-column grid.

moderation, highlighting and decorative devices make pages more interesting. However, don't overdo them. A page or screen that uses every possible high-lighting device just looks busy and hard to read.

Color works well to highlight points. Use color for overviews and main headings, not for small points.[13] Red is appropriate for warnings in North America. Since the connotations of colors vary among cultures, check with experts before you use color with international or multicultural audiences. (For more information on color, see the discussion on page 246.)

Designing Brochures

Designing a good brochure incorporates all elements of document design. To begin, first think about audience and purpose. An "image" brochure designed to promote awareness of your company will have a different look than an "information" brochure telling people how to do something and persuading them to do it.

Use this process to create effective brochures.

1. Determine your objective(s).
2. Identify your target audience(s).
3. Identify a **central selling point:** one overarching benefit the audience will get.
4. Choose the image you want to project. (Clean and clear? Postmodern and hip?)
5. Identify objections and brainstorm ways to deal with them.
6. Draft text to see how much room you need. Do tighten your writing (see Chapter 7). But when you really need more room, use a bigger brochure layout or a series of brochures.
7. Select visuals to accompany text.
8. Experiment with different sizes of paper and layout. Consider how readers will get the brochure—must it fit in a standard rack? Use thumbnail sketches to test layouts.

Figure 8.10   Three Fold Brochure on 8 1/2-by-11-Inch Paper

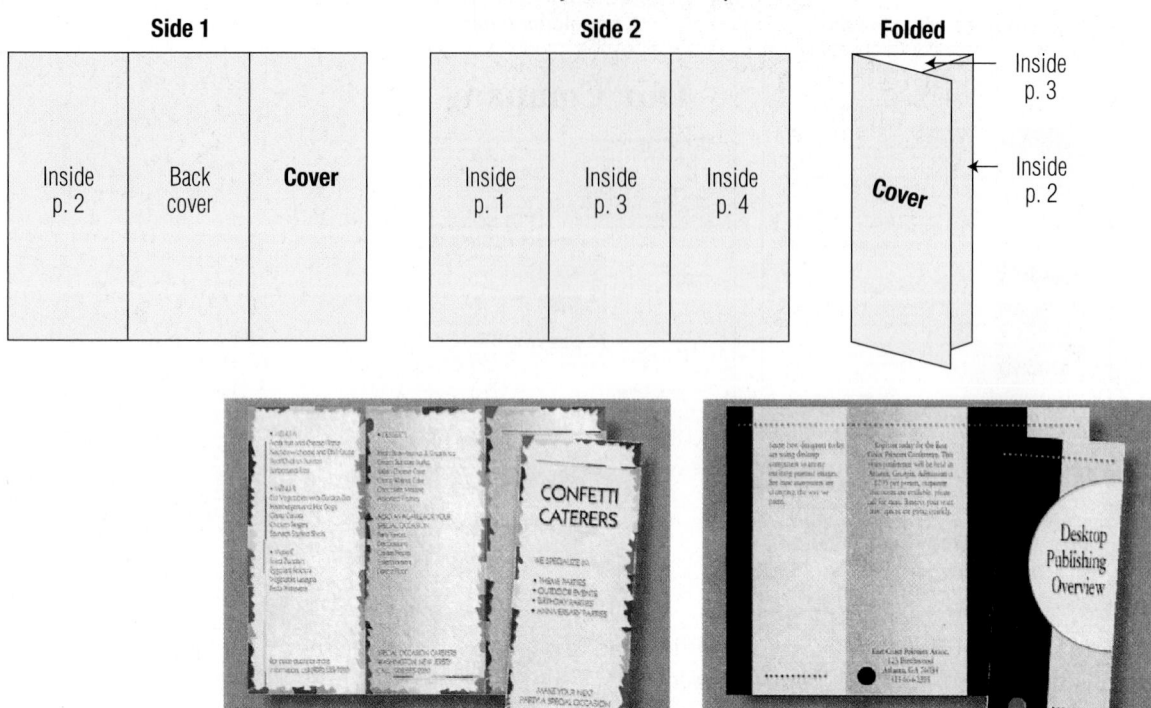

Special stationery is available to use with your laser printer or photocopier to produce brochures.

9. Make every choice—color, font, layout, paper—a conscious one. The three-fold brochure shown in Figure 8.10 is the most common layout, but many other arrangements are possible.

10. Polish the prose and graphics. Use you-attitude and positive emphasis.

Follow these design principles to enhance your brochure:

- Use the cover effectively.
  - Put your central selling point on the cover.
  - Use a visual that tells a story. Remember that the visual has to work for the audience. A photo of a campus landmark may not mean much to an audience thinking about attending a summer program on campus.
- Use a grid to align the elements within the panels. Make sure that the Z pattern emphasizes important points for each spread the reader sees. In a three-fold brochure, the Z pattern needs to work for the cover alone, for inside pages 1 and 2 (as the reader begins to unfold the brochure), and for inside pages 1, 3, and 4 (when the brochure is fully opened).
- Effective brochures not only repeat design elements (headings, small photos) across panels to create a unified look but also contain contrast (between text and visuals, between a larger font for headings and a smaller one for text).
- Use color effectively.
  - Restraint usually works best for informative brochures. To get the effect of color with the least expense, use black print on colored paper.
  - If you use four-color printing, use glossy paper.

http://
colorschemedesigner
.com

Have you ever wondered how color documents might look to a person with color deficiencies? Well, now you can see! This Web site provides the ability to create a color scheme you might incorporate into your professional documents. It also has a drop-down menu that allows you to see how your color creations will be perceived by people with color deficiencies. Since nearly 14.5% of the population has some sort of color deficiency, you should consider how the colors you choose in your designs may affect your audience.

- Make the text visually appealing.
  - Use no more than two fonts—just one may be better.
  - Use proportional fonts.
  - Avoid italic type and underlining, which make text hard to read. To emphasize text, use bold (sparingly).
  - Use small tab indents.
  - Make sure that you have enough white space in your copy. Use lists and headings. Use short paragraphs with extra space between paragraphs.
  - Ragged right margins generally work better with short line lengths.
- If you use a reply coupon, make sure its back side doesn't have crucial information the reader needs to keep.

People are more likely to hold on to brochures if they see something that engages their attention. When you design a brochure:

- Use interesting headlines and selling points by making them informative as well as attention-grabbing, funny, or out-of-the-ordinary.
- Use sidebars with testimonial quotes, examples, or vignettes. Interesting stories can hold your readers' attention.
- Try using an unusual paper size, or try making your brochure look like something else: a postcard, a menu, an insert for a CD jewel box.
- Add something to get your readers involved with your brochure, such as a coupon for a free or discount offer, a quiz, or a puzzle.[14]

Designing Web Pages

Good Web pages have both good content and an interesting design.

Your opening screen is crucial. Not only must it open quickly, but visitors must be able to find what they want quickly. Studies show that users grow impatient after waiting 15 seconds for a page to load, and Jakob Nielsen, a leading Web usability consultant, says users spend less than two minutes figuring out a site before deciding to leave. In addition, first-time visitors tend not to scroll down beyond the first screen of text.[15] To keep visitors around long enough to find (or buy) what they want, make using the first screen extremely easy.

- Provide an introductory statement or graphic orienting the surfing reader to the organization sponsoring the page.
- Offer an overview of the content of your page, with links to take readers to the parts that interest them. Provide navigation bars vertically on the left of the screen or horizontally on the top and bottom. A site index and an internal search engine are valuable tools.
- Make it clear what readers will get if they click on a link.

| Ineffective phrasing: | Employment. Openings and skill levels are determined by each office. |
| Better phrasing: | Employment. Openings listed by skill level and by location. |

Forrester researcher and Web site analyst Bruce Temkin suggests that while Web sites have increased the value they have to offer, the biggest problem now is navigation, especially as sites grow and become more complex. Another common problem is that users often feel they cannot complete an intended task when looking at a Web site's home page.[16]

Making Your Web Page Accessible

Users with hearing impairments need captions for audio material on the Web. Blind users need words, not images. Words can be voiced by a screen reader or translated into Braille text. To make your Web page accessible for people with vision impairments,

- Put a link to a text-only version of the site in the upper-left-hand corner.
- Put navigation links, a site map, and search box at the top of the screen, preferably in the upper-left-hand corner.
- Arrange navigation links alphabetically so that blind users can use a screen reader to jump to the links they want.
- Provide alternative text (an "Alt tag") for all images, applets, and submit buttons.
- Provide a static alternative to flash or animation.
- In hypertext links, use text that makes sense when read alone. A person listening to the audio will not understand "Click here." "Click to order a copy" or "Click for details" offers a better clue.

The Web Accessibility Initiative (www.w3.org) points out that accessible Web sites are easier for a variety of people to use—not just those with obvious impairments.

**http://www.
usableweb.com/**

Usable Web offers
a collection of links
about information architecture,
human factors, user interface
issues, and usable design
specific to the World Wide Web.
Log on to find tips on how to
improve the overall design and
look of your Web site and its
features.

- The best documents are created when you think about design at each stage of the writing process.
  - As you plan, think about the needs of your audience.
  - As you write, incorporate lists, headings, and visuals.
  - Get feedback from people who will be using your document.
  - As you revise, check your draft against the guidelines in this chapter.
- Effective design relies heavily on conventions, which vary by audience.
- The four levels of design help you organize and analyze design choices:
  - Intra—letters and words.
  - Inter—blocks of text.
  - Extra—visuals.
  - Supra—features that serve the entire document.
- These guidelines help writers create visually attractive documents:
  1. Use white space.
  2. Use headings.
  3. Limit the use of words set in all capital letters.
  4. Use no more than two fonts in a single document.
  5. Decide whether to justify margins.
  6. Put important elements in the top left and lower right quadrants.
  7. Use a grid to unify visuals and other graphic elements.
  8. Use highlighting, decorative devices, and color in moderation.
- To design brochures, first think about audience and purpose. Use a consistent design for a series of brochures or for issues of a newsletter.
- Good Web pages have both good content and interesting design.
  - Orient the surfing reader to the organization sponsoring the page.
  - Offer an overview of the content of your page, with links to take readers to the parts that interest them.
  - Make it clear what readers will get if they click on a link.
  - Keep graphics small.
  - Provide visual variety.
- To test a document, observe people reading the document or using it to complete a task.

CHAPTER 8   # Exercises and Problems   *Go to www.mhhe.com/locker9e for additional Exercises and Problems.

8.1   Reviewing the Chapter

1. Why is document design important in business communication? (LO 1)

2. What are the four levels of document design? (LO 2)

3. What are some guidelines for document design? (LO 3)

4. What are some basic guidelines for designing brochures? Web pages? (LO 4)

5. How can you perform basic usability testing on your documents? (LO 5)

8.2 Evaluating Page Designs

Use the guidelines in Chapter 8 to evaluate each of the following page designs. What are their strong points? What could be improved?

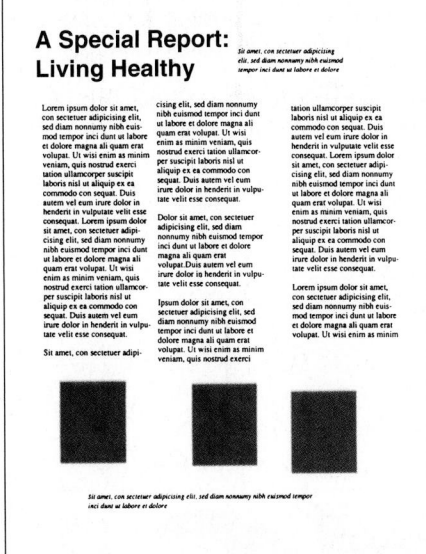

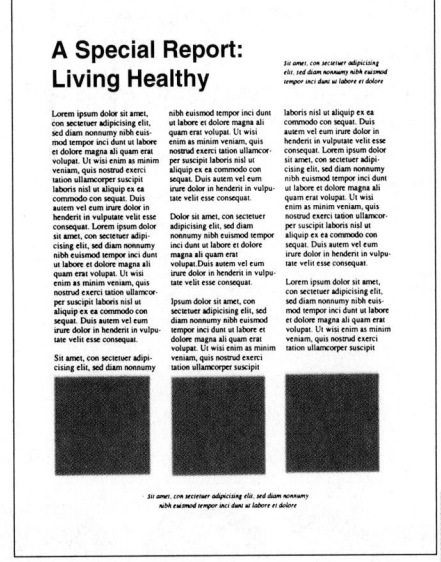

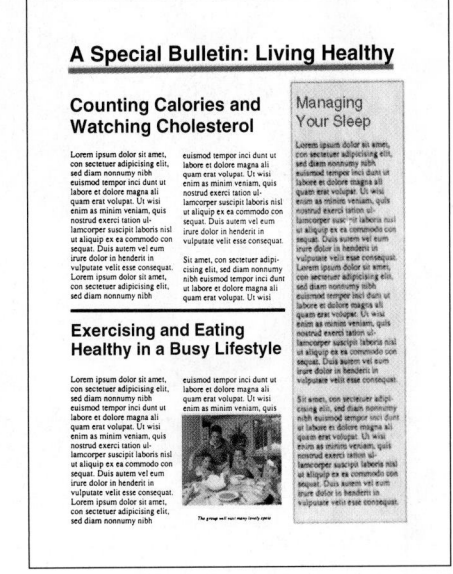

As your instructor directs,

a. Discuss the design elements you see on these sample pages with a small group of classmates.

b. Write a memo to your instructor evaluating the design elements on each of the sample pages. Be sure to address the four levels of design, as well as the guidelines for page and visual design discussed in this chapter.

c. In an oral presentation to the class, explain the process you'd use to redesign one of the sample pages. What design elements would make the page stronger or weaker? What design elements would you change, and how? Given the title of the document, what audience characteristics might your design take into account?

8.3 Recognizing Typefaces

Some companies commission a unique typeface, or wordmark, for their logos. Other companies use a standard font. When a logo is used consistently and frequently, it becomes associated with the organization. Can you name the brands that go with each letter of the alphabet below?

As your instructor directs,

a. Discuss the visual design of these brand visuals with a small group of classmates. What features distinguish them from other, similar brands? What makes them so recognizable?

b. Select one of the brand visuals represented and research it to determine its history. How has the visual changed over time? Write a memo to your instructor evaluating those changes, and identifying some of the design strategies (and business strategies) involved in each change.

Source: "Alphabet Soup," © *Issue: The Journal of Business and Design* 3, no. 2 (Fall 1997): 24–25.

Alphabet Soup You don't always need to see the whole word to recognize the name of the brand. One letter will do. Used effectively, a distinctive logotype becomes the corporate signature. That is why many companies commission the design of a unique typeface, or wordmark, that incorporates clues to their line of business or operating philosophy. Other companies have adopted an off-the-shelf typeface that they have made their own through the use of designated corporate colors, upper or lower case styling, condensed or expanded leading and other techniques. As with any branding tool, a logotype must be used consistently and frequently to work. Test your familiarity with some of the best-known logotypes by naming the brand that goes with each letter in this alphabet.

Source: "Alphabet Soup." Reprinted with permission from © *Issue: The Journal of Business & Design* 3, no. 2 (Fall 1997): 24–25. Published by Corporate Design Foundation and sponsored by Potlatch Corporation.

8.4 Evaluating the Ethics of Design Choices

Indicate whether you consider each of the following actions ethical, unethical, or a gray area. Which of the actions would you do? Which would you feel uncomfortable doing? Which would you refuse to do?

1. Putting the advantages of a proposal in a bulleted list, while discussing the disadvantages in a paragraph.

2. Using a bigger type size so that a résumé visually fills a whole page.

3. Using tiny print and very little white space on a credit card contract to make it less likely that people will read it.

4. Putting important information on the back of what looks like a one-page document.

5. Putting the services that are not covered by your health plan in full caps to make it less likely that people will read the page.

8.5   Using Headings

Reorganize the items in each of the following lists, using appropriate headings. Use bulleted or numbered lists as appropriate.

a. Rules and Procedures for a Tuition Reimbursement Plan

1. You are eligible to be reimbursed if you have been a full-time employee for at least three months.
2. You must apply before the first class meeting.
3. You must earn a "C" or better in the course.
4. You must submit a copy of the approved application, an official grade report, and a receipt for tuition paid to be reimbursed.
5. You can be reimbursed for courses related to your current position or another position in the company, or for courses which are part of a degree related to a current or possible job.
6. Your supervisor must sign the application form.
7. Courses may be at any appropriate level (high school, college, or graduate school).

b. Activities in Starting a New Business

- Getting a loan or venture capital.
- Getting any necessary city or state licenses.
- Determining what you will make, do, or sell.
- Identifying the market for your products or services.
- Pricing your products or services.
- Choosing a location.
- Checking zoning laws that may affect the location.
- Identifying government and university programs for small business development.
- Figuring cash flow.
- Ordering equipment and supplies.
- Selling.
- Advertising and marketing.

8.6   Evaluating Page Designs

1. Collect several documents that you receive as a consumer, a student, or an employee: forms, letters, memos, newsletters, e-mail, announcements, ads, flyers, and reports. Use the guidelines in this chapter to evaluate each of them.
2. Compare these documents in a specific category to the documents produced by competing organizations. Which documents are more effective? Why?

As your instructor directs,

a. Discuss the documents with a small group of classmates.

b. Write a memo to your instructor evaluating three or more of the documents, and comparing them to similar documents produced by competitors. Include originals or photocopies of the documents you discuss in an appendix to your memo.

c. Write a letter to one of the originating organizations, recommending ways it can improve the design of the documents.

d. In an oral presentation to the class, explain what makes one document strong and another one weak.

8.7   Evaluating Web Sites

Compare three Web pages in the same category (for example, shelters for the homeless, organizations, car companies, university departments, food banks). Which page(s) are most effective? Why? What weaknesses do the pages have?

As your instructor directs,

a. Discuss the pages with a small group of classmates.

b. Write a memo to your instructor evaluating the pages. Include URLs of the pages in your memo.

c. In an oral presentation to the class, explain what makes one page good and another one weak.

d. Post your evaluation in an e-mail message to the class. Include the URLs so classmates can click to the pages you discuss.

8.8   Comparing Web Sites

Alexa.com is a Web site that tracks the performance and popularity of other Web sites. In addition to ranking Web sites, the site allows users to input several Web sites and compare their rank and number of page views on a colored graph. The comparisons can range between seven days and a year. Visit the site to see which Web sites currently have the honor of being the top-rated. Where does your organization's or school's Web site rank? How can a tool like this be useful for businesses? What limitations does this tool have?

As your instructor directs,

a. Share your findings with a small group of classmates.

b. Put your findings in a memo to your instructor.

8.9   Creating a Brochure

Create a brochure for a campus, nonprofit, government or business organization. As you work,

- Analyze your intended audience. What are their needs? What factors are most likely to persuade them to read your brochure?
- Choose a story: What's the important information? What idea do you want your audience to take away?
- Make page design choices that create a usable document and generate a positive response from your audience.

- Make visual design choices that enhance and expand on your text without being simply decorative.

As your instructor directs,

a. Write a memo to your instructor explaining your choices for content and design.

b. In an oral presentation to the class, display your brochure and explain your content and design choices.

8.10   Creating a Web Page

Create a Web page for a campus, nonprofit, government or business organization that does not yet have one. As you work,

- Analyze your intended audience. What are their needs? What factors are most likely to persuade them to use this site?
- Choose a story: What's the important information? What action do you want them to take while they're browsing this site?
- Make page design choices that create a usable site and generate a positive response from your audience.

- Make visual design choices that enhance and expand on your text without being distracting.

As your instructor directs,

a. Write a memo to your instructor explaining your choices for content and design.

b. In an oral presentation to the class, display your site and explain your page and visual design choices. Provide the URL, or display images of the site as presentation visuals, so that classmates can evaluate your design as you present it.

8.11   Testing a Document

Ask someone to follow a set of instructions or to fill out a form. (Consider consumer instructions, forms for financial aid, and so forth.)

- Time the person. How long does it take? Is the person able to complete the task?
- Observe the person. Where does he or she pause, reread, seem confused?
- Interview the person. What parts of the document were confusing?

As your instructor directs,

a. Discuss the changes needed with a small group of classmates.

b. Write a memo to your instructor evaluating the document and explaining the changes that are needed. Include the document as an appendix to your memo.

c. Write to the organization that produced the document recommending necessary improvements.

d. In an oral presentation to the class, evaluate the document and explain what changes are needed.

8.12   Improving a Financial Aid Form

You've just joined the financial aid office at your school. The director gives you the following form and asks you to redesign it. The director says:

We need this form to see whether parents have other students in college besides the one requesting aid. Parents are supposed to list all family members that the parents support—themselves, the person here, any other kids in college, and any younger dependent kids.

Half of these forms are filled out incorrectly. Most people just list the student going here; they leave out everyone else.

If something is missing, the computer sends out a letter and a second copy of this form. The whole process starts over. Sometimes we send this form back two or three times before it's right. In the meantime, students' financial aid is delayed—maybe for months. Sometimes things are so late that they can't register for classes, or they have to pay tuition themselves and get reimbursed later.

If so many people are filling out the form wrong, the form itself must be the problem. See what you can do with it. But keep it to a page.

As your instructor directs,

a. Analyze the current form and identify its problems.

b. Revise the form. Add necessary information; reorder information; change the chart to make it easier to fill out.

c. Write a memo to the director of financial aid pointing out the changes you made and why you made them.

Hints:

- Where are people supposed to send the form? What is the phone number of the financial aid office?

Should they need to call the office if the form is clear?

- Does the definition of *half-time* apply to all students or just those taking courses beyond high school?
- Should capital or lowercase letters be used?
- Are the lines big enough to write in?
- What headings or subdivisions within the form would remind people to list all family members whom they support?
- How can you encourage people to return the form promptly?

Please complete the chart below by listing all family members for whom you (the parents) will provide more than half support during the academic year (July 1 through June 30). Include yourselves (the parents), the student, and your dependent children, even if they are not attending college.

EDUCATIONAL INFORMATION, 201_ – 201_

FULL NAME OF FAMILY MEMBER	AGE	RELATIONSHIP OF FAMILY MEMBER TO STUDENT	NAME OF SCHOOL OR COLLEGE THIS SCHOOL YEAR	FULL-TIME	HALF-TIME* OR MORE	LESS THAN HALF-TIME
STUDENT APPLICANT						

*Half-time is defined as 6 credit hours or 12 clock hours a term.

When the information requested is received by our office, processing of your financial aid application will resume.

Please sign and mail this form to the above address as soon as possible. Your signature certifies that this information, and the information on the FAF, is true and complete to the best of your knowledge. If you have any questions, please contact a member of the need analysis staff.

_____   _____

Signature of Parent(s)   Date

8.13 All-Weather Case: Improving Document Design of All-Weather's Safety and Health Policy

After the accident in a production line at Cedar Rapids, Doug wants to review All-Weather's Safety and Health Policy, which was designed about 10 years ago in consultation with Occupational Safety and Health Administration (OSHA) officials. Caleb finds the yellowed document in an old employee manual; surprisingly, the policy has not been posted on HR's Web site on the intranet.

As Caleb realizes quickly after looking at the document for a few seconds, the policy document (given below) is a nightmare in terms of document design, making it difficult to follow and use.

Employee safety and health has always been All-Weather's paramount concern. EVERY PLANT, DEPARTMENT, & OFFICE should take an **inventory of safety and health hazards** it faces including those arising from natural disasters such as hurricanes, storms, flood, earthquake; accidents such as fire, explosion, electric shock, malfunction or mishap involving machinery or equipment, sabotage, employee error or negligence, poor working conditions (slippery surfaces, dimly lit workplace, loose wiring, etc.); health risks such as communicable diseases, lack of sanitation, contamination, defective or not functioning smoke or gas alarms and other safety tools (such as scaffolds, safety belts, barricades, etc.), lack of personal protective clothing and equipment, mishandling or unsafe storage of raw material; and injuries due to workplace stress or violence. EVERY PLANT, DEPARTMENT, & OFFICE should have an emergency plan to respond to the above mentioned safety and health risks. It should also prepare a communication plan that specifies procedures for reporting safety violations and health risks, outlines steps to investigate accidents and health hazards, and lays out in detail the mechanism for warning employees of any hazardous conditions in their workplace. EVERY PLANT, DEPARTMENT, & OFFICE should also have safety and health related meetings and workshops, which will be conducted jointly by HR and the department concerned. The plant, department, and office can also contact **OSHA's COMPLIANCE ASSISTANCE SPECIALISTS (CAS's)** at its local office. EVERY PLANT, DEPARTMENT, & OFFICE should ensure regular inspection of all its facilities as well as safety tools. EVERY PLANT, DEPARTMENT, & OFFICE should reward employees for **exceptional safety and healthful behavior**. EVERY PLANT, DEPARTMENT, & OFFICE should review every change it makes in its work practices from the point of view of employee safety and health. EVERY PLANT, DEPARTMENT, & OFFICE should designate an individual who will be responsible to oversee its efforts in relation to employee safety and health. EVERY PLANT, DEPARTMENT, & OFFICE should maintain records of all employee injuries and sicknesses sustained in the workplace. EVERY PLANT, DEPARTMENT, & OFFICE should review all safety and health violations and each accident fully to make it clear to employees All-Weather's unswerving commitment to employee health and safety. Finally, safety and health in All-Weather concerns **everyone** at All-Weather. Hence, *don't wait* to raise any concern that you might have regarding employee safety and health in our company. *For more information, contact HR.*

Based on your reading of Chapter 8, help Caleb improve the document design of All-Weather's Safety and Health Policy. When you are finished with the revision, write a memo to Doug that explains how you changed the document design and why you made your changes.

Sources: Parts of the document are adapted from U.S. Department of Labor, Occupational Safety and Health Administration, "OSHA FactSheet: Effective Workplace Safety and Health Management Systems," in *OSHA Publications,* http://www.osha.gov/Publications/safety-health-management-systems.pdf (accessed March 7, 2009); and Jonathan F. Hutchings, *OSHA Quick Guide for Residential Builders and Contractors* (New York: Mc-Graw Hill, 1998).

Creating Visuals and Data Displays

Chapter Outline

When to Use Visuals

Guidelines for Visual Design

1. Check the Quality of the Data.
2. Determine the Story You Want to Tell.
3. Choose the Right Visual for the Story.
4. Follow the Conventions for Designing Typical Visuals.
5. Use Color and Decoration with Restraint.
6. Be Sure the Visual Is Accurate and Ethical.

Integrating Visuals in Your Text

Designing Data Displays and Images

- Tables
- Pie Charts
- Bar Charts
- Line Graphs
- Gantt Charts
- Photographs
- Drawings
- Maps
- Dynamic Displays

Summary of Key Points

Visuals of Fallen Heroes

After only a few weeks in office, President Obama reversed a controversial policy dealing with visuals. His administration overturned a policy that prohibited the media from photographing caskets of fallen soldiers returning to the United States. Under the new policy, the families of fallen soldiers have the right to choose whether the media can be present at the Dover Air Force Base in Delaware, where all deceased soldiers are brought.

Former President George H. W. Bush started the policy in 1991 during the Gulf War. Critics suggest the policy was enacted to prevent the public from seeing the horrors of war and the number of people who had died. On the other hand, critics of the new policy argue that allowing the press to be present creates a spectacle out of a private family matter.

Supporters of the new policy believe the photos are a reminder to all Americans of the sacrifices made by our troops and of the high price of freedom.

How ethical do you believe it is to show the final ceremony of fallen soldiers? If you had a family member who died in war, would you want the press to be present when the casket was returned?

"The photos are a reminder to all Americans of the sacrifices made by our troops and of the high price of freedom."

Adapted from Julian E. Barnes, "U.S. to Allow Photos of War Dead's Coffins," in *The Seattle Times: Politics & Government*, http://seattletimes.nwsource.com/html/politics/2008791894_wardead27.html (accessed March 7, 2009).

has to study the labels to get the right picture, the visual is unethical even if the labels are accurate.

Figure 9.4 is distorted by **chartjunk** and dimensionality. In an effort to make the visual interesting, the artist used a picture of a young man (presumably an engineer) rather than simple bars. By using a photograph rather than a bar, the chart implies that all engineers are young, nerdy-looking white men. The photograph also makes it difficult to compare the numbers. The number represented by the tallest figure is not quite 5 times as great as the number represented by the shortest figure, yet the tallest figure takes up 12 times as much space and appears even bigger than that. Two-dimensional figures distort data by multiplying the apparent value by the width as well as by the height—four times for every doubling in value. Three dimensional graphs are especially hard for readers to interpret and should be avoided.[7]

Even simple bar and line graphs may be misleading if part of the scale is missing, or truncated. **Truncated graphs** are most acceptable when the audience knows the basic data set well. For example, graphs of the stock market

Figure 9.4   Chartjunk and Dimensions Distort Data

Source: Adam Lashinsky, "Valley Horror Show: The Incredible Shrinking Engineer," *Fortune,* December 10, 2001, p. 40.

Figure 9.5 Truncated Scales Distort Data

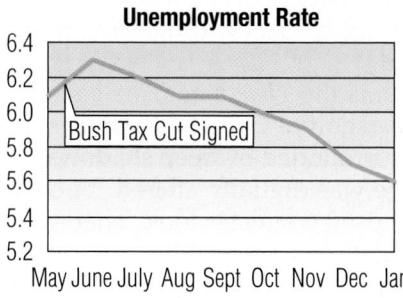

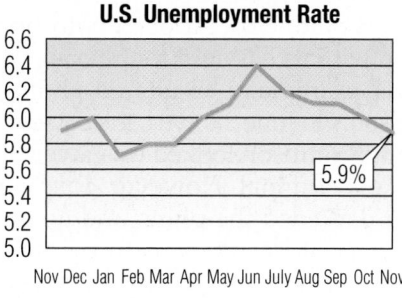

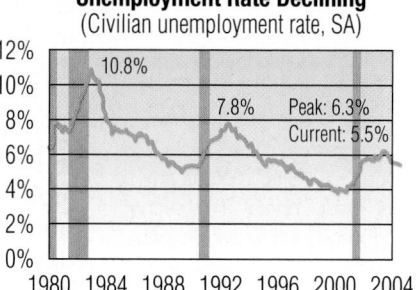

Source: Economy.com

Source: Bureau of Labor Statistics
Gray bars denote recessions

Sources: From Jerry Bowyer, "In Defense of the Unemployment Rate," National Review Online, March 5, 2004, http://article.nationalreview.com/?q=YzNiZGJjYTZI ZDNIYzQzZjUxNzFlMWJkNjBiODlzMmI, Mark Gongloff, "Payroll Growth Disappoints," CNN Money, December 5, 2003, http://money.cnn.com; and Joint Economic Committee, "Charts: Economy," http://jec.senate.gov, last updated August 27, 2004.

almost never start at zero; they are routinely truncated. This omission is acceptable for audiences who follow the market closely.

Since part of the scale is missing in truncated graphs, small changes seem like major ones. Figure 9.5 shows three different truncated graphs of US unemployment data. The first graph shows the trend in unemployment from May 2003 to January 2004. The curve falls from the fifth level of the graph to the second, resembling a 60% decline. But a close look at the numbers shows the decline is from a high of 6.3% to a low of 5.6% (a decline of 11%). The period chosen for the horizontal axis also is truncated. The first graph emphasizes the declining trend in unemployment since a tax cut was enacted in 2003, but the second graph uses the period November 2002–November 2003 to show unemployment wavering around 6%. The graph accompanies a news article about "cautious" employers and unemployment that "edged lower." The truncated scale on the vertical axis again makes the changes appear larger. The third graph takes a longer view (back to 1980) and puts the percentages on a scale starting at zero. On this scale, the changes in the unemployment rate seem less dramatic, and the recent decline looks as if it could be part of a regular pattern that follows recessions (the shaded areas). The graph starting with 1980 shows that the latest ("current") unemployment rate was lower than those after past recessions.[8]

Data can also be distorted when the context is omitted. As Tufte suggests, a drop may be part of a regular cycle, a correction after an atypical increase, or a permanent drop to a new, lower plateau.[9]

To make your data displays more accurate,

- Differentiate between actual and estimated or projected values.
- When you must truncate a scale, do so clearly with a break in the bars or in the background.
- Avoid perspective and three-dimensional graphs.
- Avoid combining graphs with different scales.
- Use images of people carefully in histograms to avoid sexist, racist, or other exclusionary visual statements.

Photographs in particular have received close attention for accuracy and ethics concerns. The doctored Katie Couric photo is a current example (see sidebar on page 250). However, the problem is not new. Photographers have

Absolut-ly Not Political

In a Mexican ad campaign, Absolut Vodka used a map of North America showing Mexico and the United States as being about the same size. The map pictured what the border would look like in an "Absolut World": translate that to be a better world from a Mexican perspective. California, Nevada, Texas, and Utah, plus parts of Arizona, Colorado, New Mexico, and Wyoming were all pictured as part of Mexico, as they would have been without the Mexican–American War.

The ad spread quickly through the Internet. While it appealed to its intended Mexican audience, it riled US audiences—so much so that Absolut issued an apology.

Is the map ethical? Would it offend you? Can you think of other examples where maps have been used for political purposes?

Adapted from "An Absolut Mexico," in *Strange Maps*, http://strangemaps. wordpress.com/?s=absolut+mexico (accessed March 7, 2009).

Slimming Down Couric

Always be careful about altering the appearance of photographs.

Katie Couric has two famous photographs. The first was snapped in May 2006 as an official media photo. The second, supposedly the same photo, appeared in the September 2006 issue of *Watch!*, a magazine with a circulation around 400,000 distributed to CBS affiliates and to passengers on American Airline flights. In the second version Katie Couric dropped around 20 pounds and looked much younger. The magazine article which included the photo advertised Couric's move from NBC's *Today* to CBS's *Evening News*.

When asked about the doctored photo, Couric reportedly said that she liked the original because "there's more of me to love." Media experts suggest that whenever a photo is altered, the public deserves the right to be told about it.

What do you think? What are the ethics of altering photos so that subjects are slimmer and younger looking? How does this altering influence the public's obsession with beauty? How does Couric's photo hinder goodwill between CBS and the public?

Think about the photos you see in the media every day. How many of them have been altered? How would you know? If you wanted to use an altered photo, what steps would you need to take to use it ethically?

Adapted from Buzzle Staff, "Katie Couric Magically Loses Weight in Photo Distributed to Media," in Buzzle.com, http://www.buzzle.com/editorials/9-1-2006-107383.asp (accessed March 7, 2009).

always been able to frame their pictures in ways that cut objects they do not want. Pictures of homes for real estate sales can omit the collapsing garage; shots of collapsed homeless people can omit the image of social workers standing by to give aid. Now Adobe Photoshop has added a new dimension to the discussion with its easy aid for altering photos.

A classic example of an altered photograph is the *Time* magazine cover of O. J. Simpson. On June 27, 1994, the cover of *Time* showed O. J.'s LAPD mug shot. In the photo, Simpson looked unshaven and surrounded by deep shadows: he looked like a criminal. However, *Time*'s image was digitally altered. A computer had darkened the photo and given Simpson a sinister look. That same day, the cover of *Newsweek* featured the original, unaltered photo, and when people saw the two images side-by-side on newsstands, they accused *Time* of biased, unethical journalism.

More recent discussions have involved the use of digital alterations to increase the beauty of ad models to unnatural degrees. You can watch the short video at http://www.campaignforrealbeauty.com/flat4.asp?id=6909 to see an illustration. First the model's looks are greatly enhanced with makeup and hairstyling. But even that gorgeous result is not good enough. The video shows the made-up model having her brows raised and her neck thinned and elongated with digital alterations for her billboard display.

In his discussion of photography ethics, John Long notes that it's easy to think of small changes to photographs as harmless. He argues that any change to the picture is deceptive, because when people see a photo, they assume that it's a true record of a real event. When you change a photo, you use that assumption to deceive.[10]

Integrating Visuals in Your Text

Refer in your text to every visual. Normally the text gives the table or figure number but not the title. Put the visual as soon after your reference as space and page design permit. If the visual must go on another page, tell the reader where to find it:

As Figure 3 shows (page 10), . . .

(See Table 2 on page 14.)

Summarize the main point of a visual *before* you present the visual itself. Then when readers get to it, they'll see it as confirmation of your point.

Weak: Listed below are the results.

Better: As Figure 4 shows, sales doubled in the last decade.

How much discussion a visual needs depends on the audience, the complexity of the visual, and the importance of the point it makes. If the material is new to the audience, you'll need a fuller explanation than if similar material is presented to this audience every week or month. If the visual is complex, you may want to help the reader find key points in it. If the point is important, you'll want to discuss its implications in some detail. In contrast, one sentence about a visual may be enough when the audience is already familiar with the topic and the data, when the visual is simple and well designed, and when the information in the visual is a minor part of your proof.

When you discuss visuals, spell out numbers that fall at the beginning of a sentence. If spelling out the number or year is cumbersome, revise the sentence so that it does not begin with a number.

Forty-five percent of the cost goes to pay wages and salaries.

In 2002, euronotes and coins became legal tender.

Put numbers in parentheses at the end of the clause or sentence to make the sentence easier to read:

Hard to read: As Table 4 shows, teachers participate (54%) in more community service groups than do members of the other occupations surveyed; dentists (20.8%) participate in more service groups than do members of five of the other occupations.

Better: As Table 4 shows, teachers participate in more community service groups than do members of the other occupations surveyed (54%); dentists participate in more service groups than do five of the other occupations (20.8%).

Designing Data Displays and Images

Once you know your story—once you know what you're saying, how you're saying it, and how you want text and visuals to combine to say it—then you're in a position to choose and create visuals. Each type of visual can do different things for you. Here are some of the most common types of visuals (data displays and images), and here's when, where and how they're most effective.

Tables

Use tables only when you want the audience to focus on specific numbers. Graphs convey less specific information but are more memorable. Figure 9.6 illustrates the basic structure of tables. The **boxhead** is the variable whose label is at the top; the **stub** is the variable listed on the side. When constructing tables,

- Use common, understandable units. Round off to simplify the data (e.g., 35% rather than 35.27%; 44.5 million rather than 44,503,276).
- Provide column and row totals or averages when they're relevant.
- Put the items you want readers to compare in columns rather than in rows to facilitate mental subtraction and division.
- When you have many rows, shade alternate rows (or pairs of rows) or double-space after every five rows to help readers line up items accurately.

Showing Trends and Changes

Jerry Atkinson gives his clients not only financial statements but also graphs of key trends. Atkinson is managing director of Atkinson and Company, a 62-employee CPA firm in Albuquerque, New Mexico.

Current-month or -year information isn't enough, he says. Clients need to see trends and changes. And graphs offer an easy way to show that.

Atkinson personalizes the graphs by using the colors of the company being profiled.

Adapted from John von Brachel, "Interpreting Financial Statements: How One Firm Uses the Language of Graphics," *Journal of Accountancy* 180, no. 2 (August 1995), 42–43.

Figure 9.6   Tables Show Exact Values

Visuals That Translate Well

Figure 9.6   Tables Show Exact Values (*continued*)

Top 10 Search Providers for May 2007, Ranked by Searches (U.S.)

Provider	Searches (000)	YOY Growth	Share of Searches
1. Google Search	4,033,277	44.9%	56.3%
2. Yahoo! Search	1,540,949	18.6%	21.5%
3. MSN/Windows Live Search	605,400	0.8%	8.4%
4. AOL Search	381,961	5.1%	5.3%
5. Ask.com Search	142,418	−2.8%	2.0%
6. My Web Search	61,784	N/A	0.9%
7. Comcast Search	34,908	N/A	0.5%
8. EarthLink Search	33,461	21.7%	0.5%
9. BellSouth Search	30,122	N/A	0.4%
10. Dogpile.com Search	26,295	−10.6%	0.4%

Sources: http://www.netratings.com/pr/pr_070620.pdf (accessed March 7, 2009).

Pie Charts

Pie charts force the audience to measure area. However, people can judge position or length (which a bar chart uses) more accurately than they judge area, thus making information in pie charts more difficult for an audience to understand accurately.[11] The data in any pie chart can be put in a bar chart. Therefore, use a pie chart only when you are comparing one segment to the whole. When you are comparing one segment to another segment, use a bar chart, a line graph, or a map—even though the data may be expressed in percentages.

When constructing pie charts,

- Make the chart a perfect circle. Avoid 3D circles; they distort the data.
- Start at 12 o'clock with the largest percentage or the percentage you want to focus on. Go clockwise to each smaller percentage or to each percentage in some other logical order.
- Limit the number of segments to no more than seven. If your data have more divisions, combine the smallest or the least important into a single "miscellaneous" or "other" category.
- Label the segments outside the circle. Internal labels are hard to read.

Bar Charts

Bar charts are easy to interpret because they ask people to compare distance along a common scale, which most people judge accurately. Bar charts are useful in a variety of situations: to compare one item to another, to compare items over time, and to show correlations. Use horizontal bars when your labels are long; when the labels are short, either horizontal or vertical bars will work. When constructing bar charts,

- Order the bars in a logical or chronological order.
- Put the bars close enough together to make comparison easy.
- Label both horizontal and vertical axes.
- Put all labels inside the bars or outside them. When some labels are inside and some are outside, the labels carry the visual weight of longer bars, distorting the data.

- Make all the bars the same width.
- Use different colors for different bars only when their meanings are different: estimates as opposed to known numbers, negative as opposed to positive numbers.
- Avoid using 3D perspective; it makes the values harder to read and can make comparison difficult.

Several varieties of bar charts exist. See Figure 9.7 for examples.

- **Grouped bar charts** allow you to compare either several aspects of each item or several items over time. Group together the items you want to compare. Figure 9.7a shows that sales were highest in the West each year. If we wanted to show how sales had changed in each region, the bars should be grouped by region, not by year.
- **Segmented, subdivided, or stacked bars** sum the components of an item. It's hard to identify the values in specific segments; grouped bar charts are almost always easier to use.
- **Deviation bar charts** identify positive and negative values, or winners and losers.
- **Paired bar charts** show the comparison between two items.
- **Histograms or pictograms** use images to create the bars.

Line Graphs

Line graphs are also easy to interpret. Use line graphs to compare items over time, to show frequency or distribution, and to show possible correlations. When constructing line graphs,

- Label both horizontal and vertical axes. When time is a variable, it is usually put on the horizontal axis.

The Power of the Golden Arches

Company logos have big business implications. In a 2007 taste test with 63 children aged 3 to 5, researchers found that the children preferred food if it came in McDonald's packaging. For example, even though the children were served the same chicken nuggets from McDonald's in two different bags, 59% of children preferred chicken nuggets in the McDonald's packaging; only 23% suggested there was no difference. The same held true for milk with 61% of children preferring the McDonald's cup, fries with 77% preference, and carrots with 54% preference. The researchers also found that the children who lived in houses with more televisions were more likely to prefer McDonald's branded food.

Assuming these results hold true for a larger random sampling of children, what should McDonald's do with this information? What ethical implications exist in this study's results?

Adapted from Nicholas Bakalar, "If It Says McDonald's, Then It Must Be Good," *New York Times*, August 17, 2007, 7.

Figure 9.7   Varieties of Bar Charts

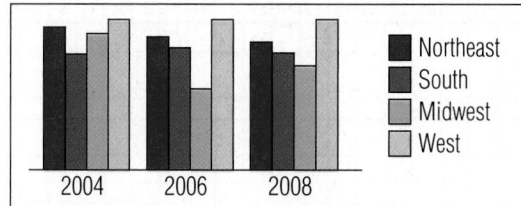

a. Grouped bar charts compare several aspects of each item, or several items over time.

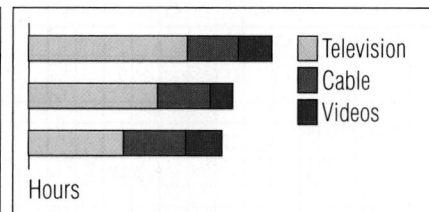

b. Segmented, subdivided, or **stacked bars** sum the components of an item.

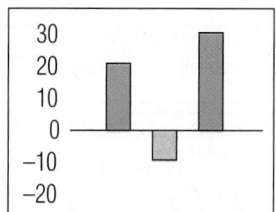

c. Deviation bar charts identify positive and negative values.

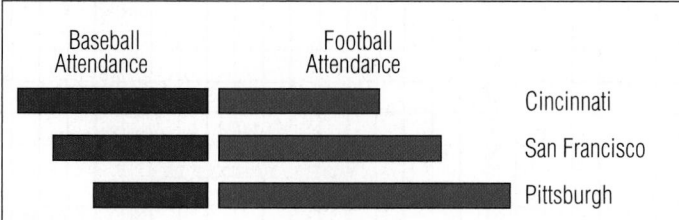

d. Paired bar charts show the comparison between two items.

e. Histograms or **pictograms** use images to create the bars.

Two-Timing Pictures

- Avoid using more than three different lines on one graph. Even three lines may be too many if they cross each other.
- Avoid using perspective. Perspective makes the values harder to read and can make comparison difficult.

Gantt Charts

Gantt charts are bar charts used to show schedules. They're most commonly used in proposals. Figure 9.8 is a Gantt chart for a marketing plan. From the chart, it is easy to see which activities must be completed first in order to finish the total plan on time. When using Gantt charts,

- Color-code bars to indicate work planned and work completed.
- Use a red outline to indicate **critical activities,** which must be completed on time if the project is to be completed by the due date.
- Use diamonds to indicate progress reports, major achievements, or other accomplishments.

Photographs

Photographs convey a sense of authenticity. The photo of a prototype helps convince investors that a product can be manufactured; the photo of a devastated area can suggest the need for government grants or private donations.

You may need to **crop,** or trim, a photo for best results. If someone else is doing the production, mark the places for cropping in the margins of the photo or attach nonsticky paper. Never write or mark on the photo or the negative.

Figure 9.8   Gantt Charts Show the Schedule for Completing a Project

Agenda for Client	Start Date	Finish Date	October Week 1		October Week 2		October Week 3		October Week 4		November Week 5	
Client Kick-Off Meeting	10/09		◆ 10/09									
Determine Client Needs												
Marketing Needs:												
Evaluate in-house market research data	10/10	10/14										
Propose research path	10/14	10/16										
Advertising Needs:												
Review current ads and placements	10/17	10/21										
Bring in Art Department to review	10/25	10/28										
Public Relation Needs:												
Review public perception surveys	10/28	10/29										
Interview Customer Service Dept.	10/29								◆ 10/29			
Develop scope of work and client proposal												
Marketing client rep's material due	10/24						◇ 10/24					
Advertising client rep's material due	10/25						◇ 10/25					
PR client rep's material due	10/28							◇ 10/28				
Team meetings to polish up client proposal	10/25 10/27 10/31	11/01										
Present Client Proposal	11/04										◆ 11/04	
If client accepts, work begins here	11/05										◆ 11/05	

Legend: ▱▱ Need Analysis   ◇▱ Final Review Meetings   ◆ Major Milestones   ◇ Due Dates

A growing problem with photos is that they may be edited or staged, purporting to show something as reality even though it never occurred. See the discussion of ethics and accuracy starting on page 249.

On the other hand, sometimes photos are obviously edited to serve a purpose. The law firm Bingham McCutchen LLP got much publicity from its advertisement, which ran in the *Wall Street Journal* and the *Economist*, showing a grizzly bear holding a human baby between its paws and nuzzling it. The ad's text said, "The best lawyers know how to balance aggression with delicate handling." Even Stephen Colbert poked fun at it, wondering what happened after the photographer's flash went off.[12]

Drawings

The richness of detail in photos makes them less effective than drawings for focusing on details. With a drawing, the artist can provide as much or as little detail as is needed to make the point; different parts of the drawing can show different layers or levels of detail. Drawings are also better for showing structures underground, undersea, or in the atmosphere.

In the drawings in Figure 9.9, no attempt is made to show the details of warehousing and transportation facilities. Such details would distract from

Figure 9.9 Sketches Can Show Processes

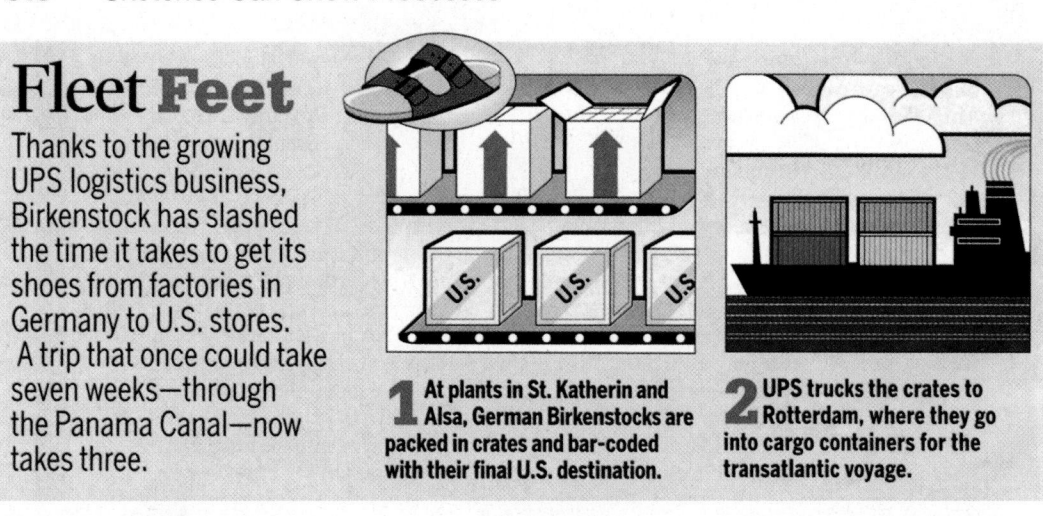

Source: Dean Foust, "Big Brown's New Bag." Reprinted from the July 19, 2004 issue of BusinessWeek by special permission, Copyright © 2004 by The McGraw-Hill Companies, Inc.

the main point. Here, the drawings show how UPS Logistics handles the various activities required to move Birkenstock sandals from the shoe company's German factories to thousands of stores in the United States.

Drawings can also be used to insert creativity into the presentation of information. *Time* magazine used a Seek & Find drawing, like those in magazines asking children to find the hidden items in a picture, to highlight consumer goods whose prices would likely rise as corn is turned into ethanol.[13]

Maps

Use maps to emphasize location or to compare items in different locations. Figure 9.10 shows the prevalence of childhood asthma by state. A map is appropriate because the emphasis is on the distribution of asthma in various regions. Several computer software packages now allow users to generate

Figure 9.10   The State of Childhood Asthma

Current asthma prevalence among children 0–17 years of age, by state, annual average for the period 2001–2005

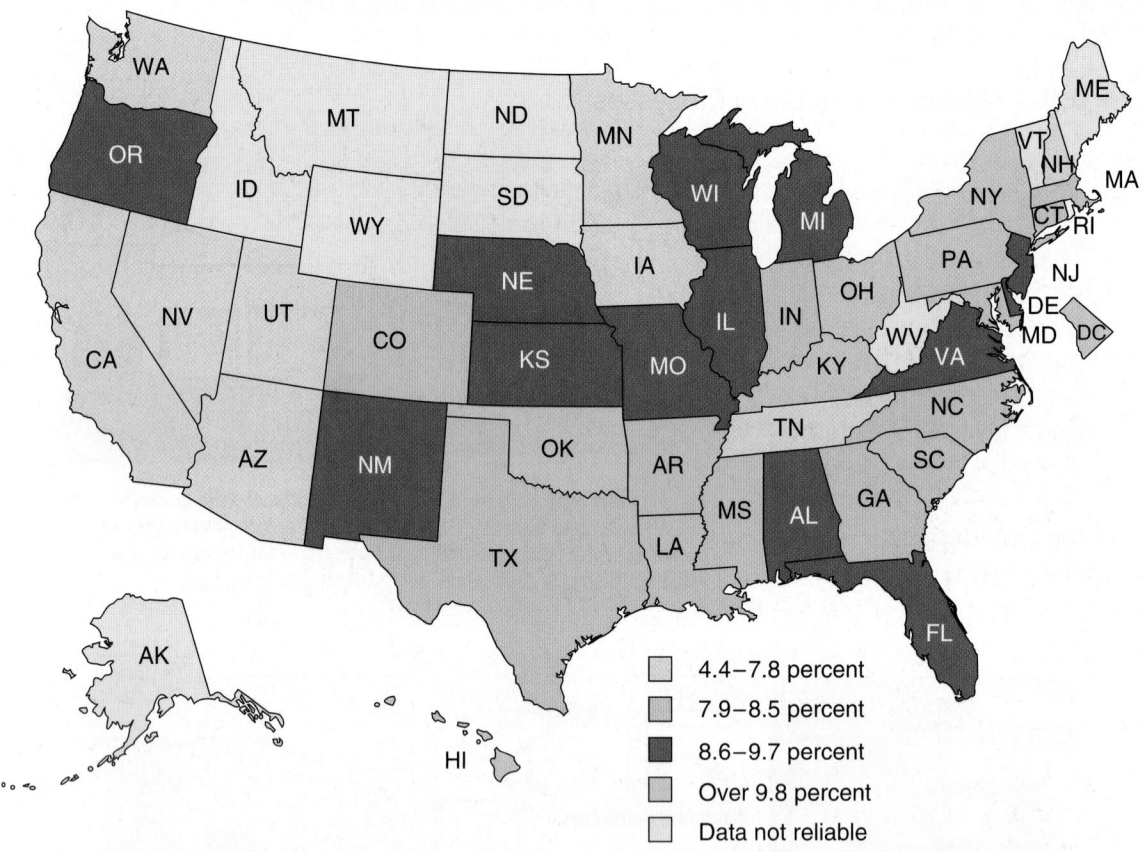

Legend:
- 4.4–7.8 percent
- 7.9–8.5 percent
- 8.6–9.7 percent
- Over 9.8 percent
- Data not reliable

NOTES: Ranges are based on approximate quartiles among states with available estimates. Differences portrayed in this map should be interpreted with caution. The 95 percent confidence intervals for many states overlap. Current asthma prevalence estimates are based on the questions "Has a doctor or other health professional ever told you that (child's name) had asthma?" and "Does (child's name) still have asthma?" Estimates for Delaware, the District of Columbia, Mississippi, Nebraska, Nevada, and New Hampshire have a relative standard error greater than 30 percent and less than or equal to 50 percent and should be interpreted with caution as they do not meet the standard of reliability or precision. The estimates for Alaska, Idaho, Maine, Montana, North Dakota, South Dakota, Vermont, West Virginia, and Wyoming have a relative standard error greater than 50 percent and therefore are not represented in this figure.

SOURCE: CDC/NCHS, National Health Interview Survey.

Source: Lara J. Akinbami, "The State of Childhood Asthma, United States, 1980–2005," in *Advance Data from Vital and Health Statistics* (Hyattsville, MD: National Center for Health Statistics, 2006). (http://www.cdc.gov/nchs/data/ad/ad381.pdf) accessed May 4, 2009.

local, state, national, or global maps, adding color or shadings, and labels. When using maps,

- Label states, provinces, or countries if it's important that people be able to identify levels in areas other than their own.
- Avoid using perspective. Perspective makes the values harder to read and can make comparison difficult.

Dynamic Displays

Online visuals are expanding the possibilities of data displays. Many of these displays are interactive, allowing users to adapt them to personal needs. At BabyNameWizard.com, you can see the popularity of various names over the years, or you can track the popularity of one name. Some displays are animated. At CReSIS, the Center for Remote Sensing of Ice Sheets, you can see the effects of global warming on coastal areas around the world as coasts flood while you watch.[14]

Summary of Key Points

- Visuals help make data meaningful for your audience.
- In the rough draft, use visuals to see that ideas are presented completely and to see what relationships exist. In the final report, use visuals to make points vivid, to emphasize material that the reader might skip, and to present material more compactly and with less repetition than words alone would require.
- You'll use more visuals when you want to show relationships and to persuade, when the information is complex or contains extensive numerical data, and when the audience values visuals.
- Always check the quality of your data.
- Pick data to tell a story, to make a point.
- Visuals are not interchangeable. The best visual depends on the kind of data and the point you want to make with the data.
- Tables are numbers or words arrayed in rows and columns; figures are everything else. Formal visuals have both numbers and titles that indicate what to look for in the visual or why the visual is included and is worth examining.
- Visuals must present data accurately and ethically. **Chartjunk** denotes decorations that at best are irrelevant to the visual and at worst mislead the reader. **Truncated graphs** omit part of the scale and visually mislead readers. Graphs and charts with 3D mislead readers.
- Summarize the main point of a visual before it appears in the text.

CHAPTER 9   Exercises and Problems

Go to www.mhhe.com/locker9e for additional Exercises and Problems.

9.1   Reviewing the Chapter

1. When should you use visuals? (LO 1)
2. What are some specific ways to create effective visuals? (LO 2)
3. What are some concerns that must be addressed to keep your visuals accurate and ethical? (LO 2)
4. What are some guidelines for integrating visuals into your text? (LO 3)
5. What are some guidelines for constructing bar charts? (LO 2)

9.2   Evaluating the Ethics of Design Choices

Indicate whether you consider each of the following actions ethical, unethical, or a gray area. Which of the actions would you do? Which would you feel uncomfortable doing? Which would you refuse to do?

1. Using photos of Hawaiian beaches in advertising for Bermuda tourism, without indicating the location of the beaches.

2. Editing a photo by inserting an image of a young black person into a picture of an all-white group, and using that photo in a recruiting brochure designed to attract minority applicants to a university.

3. Altering people in your photographs so that they look skinnier and younger. (Watch the short video mentioned in the ethics discussion of this chapter.)

4. Modifying real estate photos by changing the physical appearance of houses or stores.

5. Including pictures in restaurant menus that are exaggerated in presentation quality, color appearance, and portion size.

9.3   Evaluating Visuals

Evaluate each of the following visuals.

Is visual's message clear?

Is it the right visual for the story?

Is the visual designed appropriately? Is color, if any, used appropriately?

Is the visual free from chartjunk?

Does the visual distort data or mislead the reader in any way?

In problem 9.3, visuals 1 and 2 are the former and current food pyramids. Which pyramid is clearer? More informative? Which pyramid do you prefer? Why?

1.

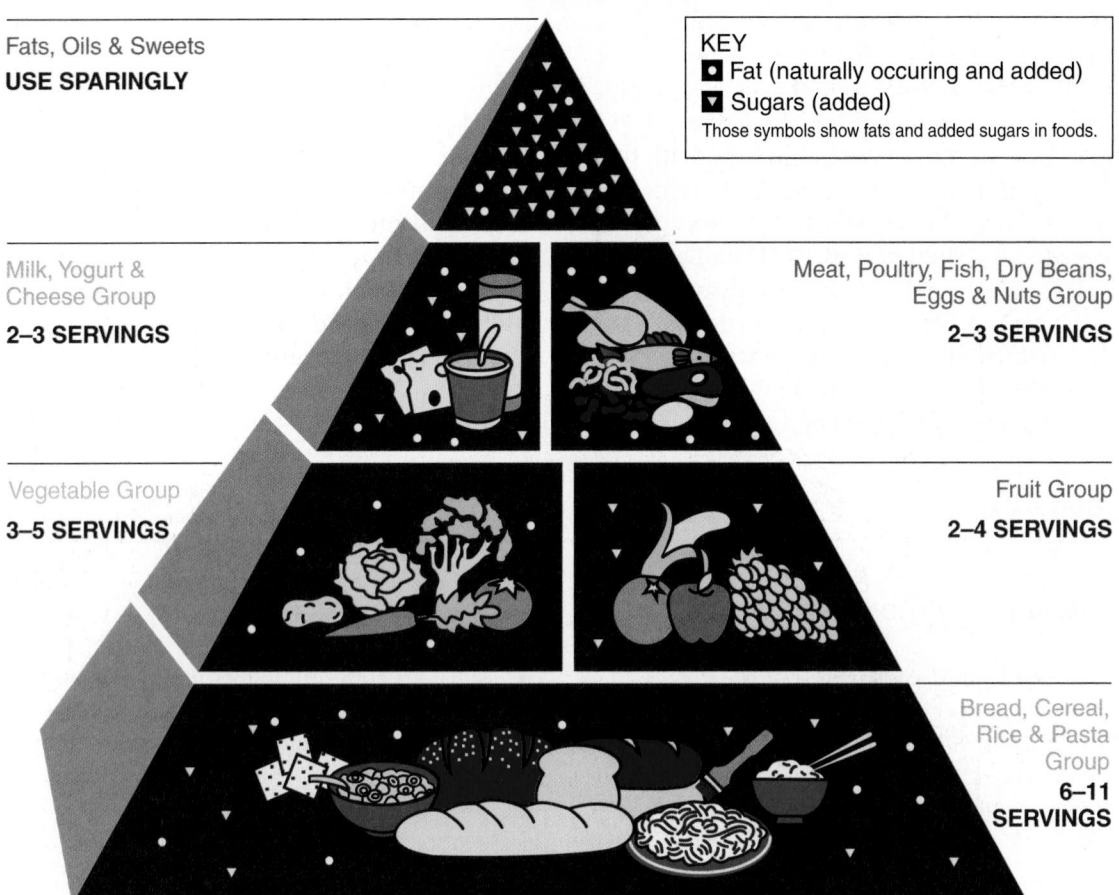

Former food pyramid

Fats, Oils & Sweets
USE SPARINGLY

KEY
■ Fat (naturally occuring and added)
▼ Sugars (added)
Those symbols show fats and added sugars in foods.

Milk, Yogurt & Cheese Group
2–3 SERVINGS

Meat, Poultry, Fish, Dry Beans, Eggs & Nuts Group
2–3 SERVINGS

Vegetable Group
3–5 SERVINGS

Fruit Group
2–4 SERVINGS

Bread, Cereal, Rice & Pasta Group
6–11 SERVINGS

Source: http://www.cnpp.usda.gov/Publications/MyPyramid/OriginalFoodGuidePyramids/FGP/FGPPamphlet.pdf (accessed May 5, 2009)

2.

Anatomy of MyPyramid

One size doesn't fit all

USDA's new MyPyramid symbolizes a personalized approach to healthy eating and physical activity.The symbol has been designed to be simple. It has been developed to remind consumers to make healthy food choices and to be active every day. The different parts of the symbol are described below.

Activity

Activity is represented by the steps and the person climbing them, as a reminder of the importance of daily physical activity.

Moderation

Moderation is represented by the narrowing of each food group from bottom to top. The wider base stands for foods with little or no solid fats or added sugars. These should be selected more often. The narrower top area stands for foods containing more added sugars and solid fats. The more active you are, the more of these foods can fit into your diet.

Personalization

Personalization is shown by the person on the steps, the slogan and the URL. Find the kinds and amounts of food to eat each day at Mypyramid.gov.

Current Food Pyramid

MyPyramid.gov
STEPS TO A HEALTHIER YOU

Proportionality

Proportionality is shown by the different widths of the food group bands. The widths suggest how much food a person should choose from each group. The widths are just a general guide, not exact proportions. Check the Web site for how much is right for you.

Variety

Variety is symbolized by the 6 color bands representing the 5 food groups of the Pyramid and oils. This illustrates that foods from all groups are needed each day for good health.

Gradual Improvement

Gradual improvement is encouraged by the slogan. It suggests that individuals can benefit from taking small steps to improve their diets and lifestyle each day.

USDA U.S. Department of Agriculture
Center for Nutrition Policy
and Promotion
April 2005 CNPP-16

USDA is an equal opportunity provider and employer

| GRAINS | VEGETABLES | FRUITS | OILS | MILK | MEAT& BEANS |

Source: United States Department of Agriculture, "Steps to a Healthier You," in MyPyramid.gov, http://www.mypyramid.gov (accessed May 5, 2009).

3.

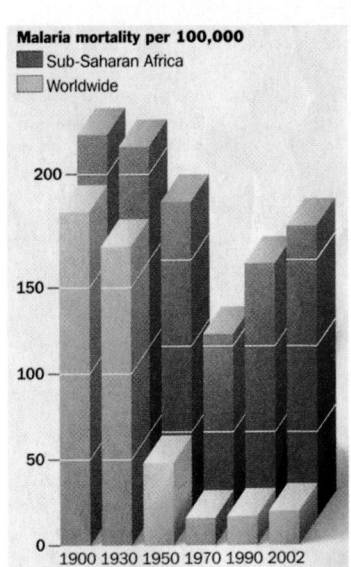

Malaria mortality per 100,000
Sub-Saharan Africa
Worldwide

200 —

150 —

100 —

50 —

0 — 1900 1930 1950 1970 1990 2002

Source: Data provided by World Health Organization.

4.

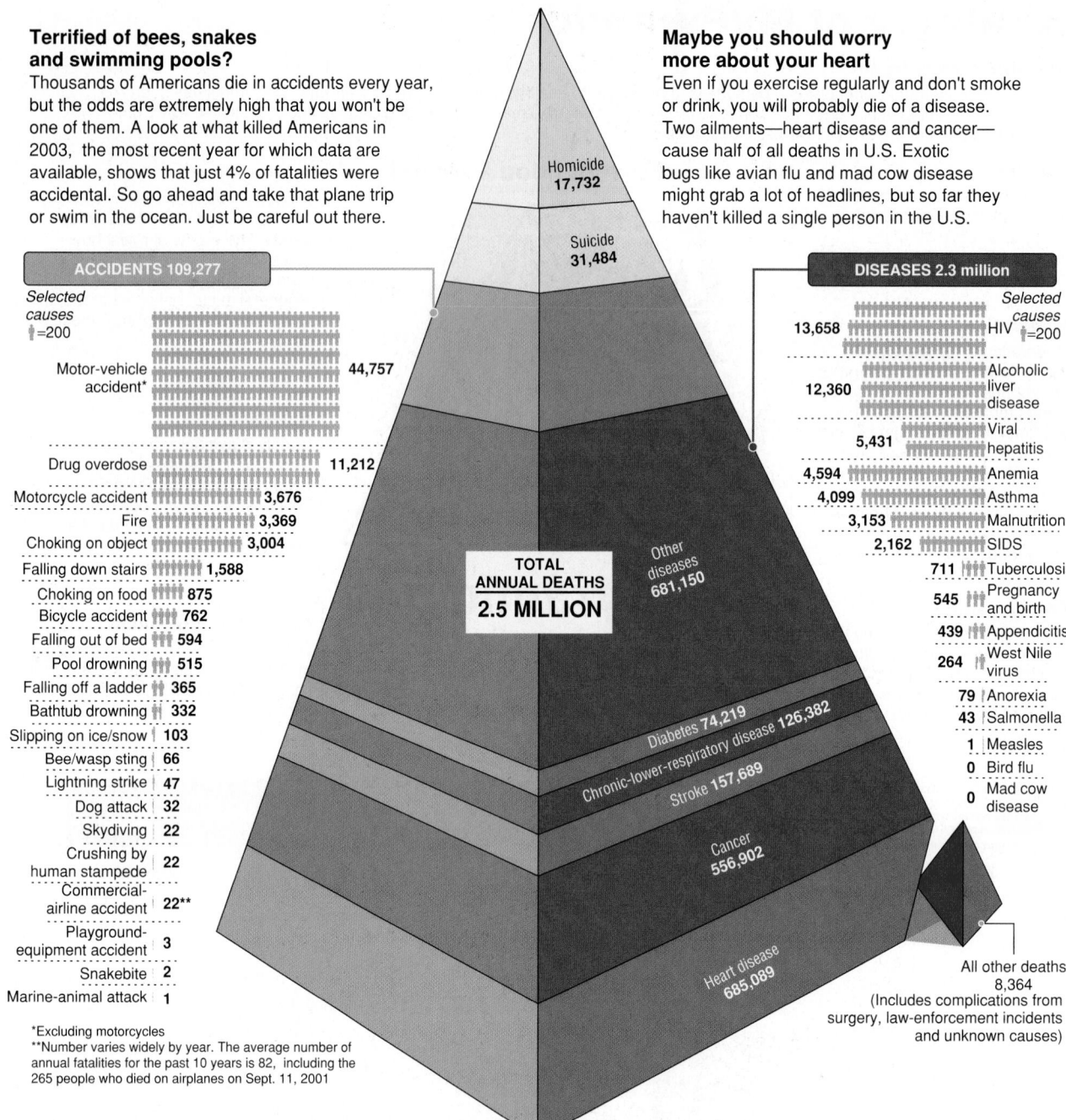

Terrified of bees, snakes and swimming pools?

Thousands of Americans die in accidents every year, but the odds are extremely high that you won't be one of them. A look at what killed Americans in 2003, the most recent year for which data are available, shows that just 4% of fatalities were accidental. So go ahead and take that plane trip or swim in the ocean. Just be careful out there.

Maybe you should worry more about your heart

Even if you exercise regularly and don't smoke or drink, you will probably die of a disease. Two ailments—heart disease and cancer—cause half of all deaths in U.S. Exotic bugs like avian flu and mad cow disease might grab a lot of headlines, but so far they haven't killed a single person in the U.S.

ACCIDENTS 109,277

Selected causes
=200

Motor-vehicle accident*	44,757
Drug overdose	11,212
Motorcycle accident	3,676
Fire	3,369
Choking on object	3,004
Falling down stairs	1,588
Choking on food	875
Bicycle accident	762
Falling out of bed	594
Pool drowning	515
Falling off a ladder	365
Bathtub drowning	332
Slipping on ice/snow	103
Bee/wasp sting	66
Lightning strike	47
Dog attack	32
Skydiving	22
Crushing by human stampede	22
Commercial-airline accident	22**
Playground-equipment accident	3
Snakebite	2
Marine-animal attack	1

*Excluding motorcycles
**Number varies widely by year. The average number of annual fatalities for the past 10 years is 82, including the 265 people who died on airplanes on Sept. 11, 2001

DISEASES 2.3 million

Selected causes
=200

13,658	HIV
12,360	Alcoholic liver disease
5,431	Viral hepatitis
4,594	Anemia
4,099	Asthma
3,153	Malnutrition
2,162	SIDS
711	Tuberculosis
545	Pregnancy and birth
439	Appendicitis
264	West Nile virus
79	Anorexia
43	Salmonella
1	Measles
0	Bird flu
0	Mad cow disease

Homicide **17,732**

Suicide **31,484**

TOTAL ANNUAL DEATHS 2.5 MILLION

Other diseases **681,150**

Diabetes 74,219

Chronic-lower-respiratory disease 126,382

Stroke 157,689

Cancer **556,902**

Heart disease **685,089**

All other deaths 8,364 (Includes complications from surgery, law-enforcement incidents and unknown causes)

Sources: Centers for Disease Control and Prevention; National Transportation Safety Board.

5.

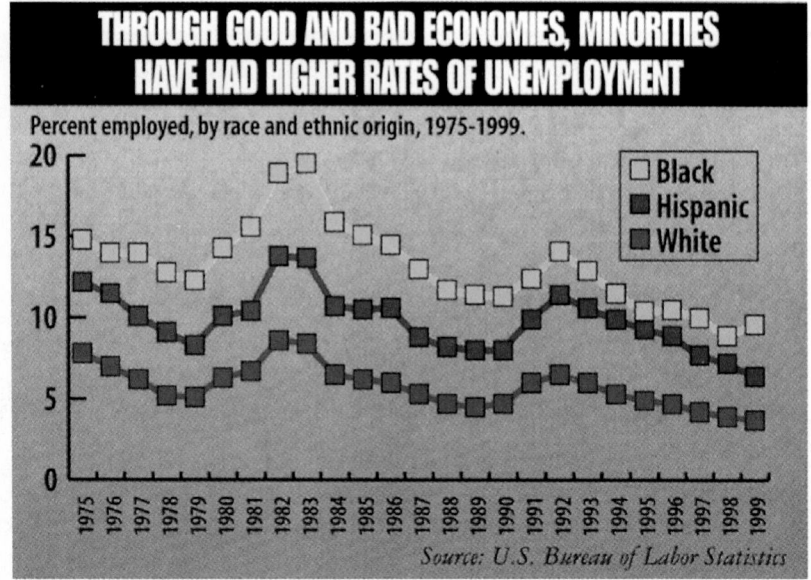

THROUGH GOOD AND BAD ECONOMIES, MINORITIES HAVE HAD HIGHER RATES OF UNEMPLOYMENT

Percent employed, by race and ethnic origin, 1975-1999.

□ Black
■ Hispanic
■ White

Source: U.S. Bureau of Labor Statistics

Source: From American Demographics, June 2000.

6.

Half Full...

Both at home and at work, more and more consumers enjoy broadband access to the Web, which makes online entertainment a better experience (projections, in millions)

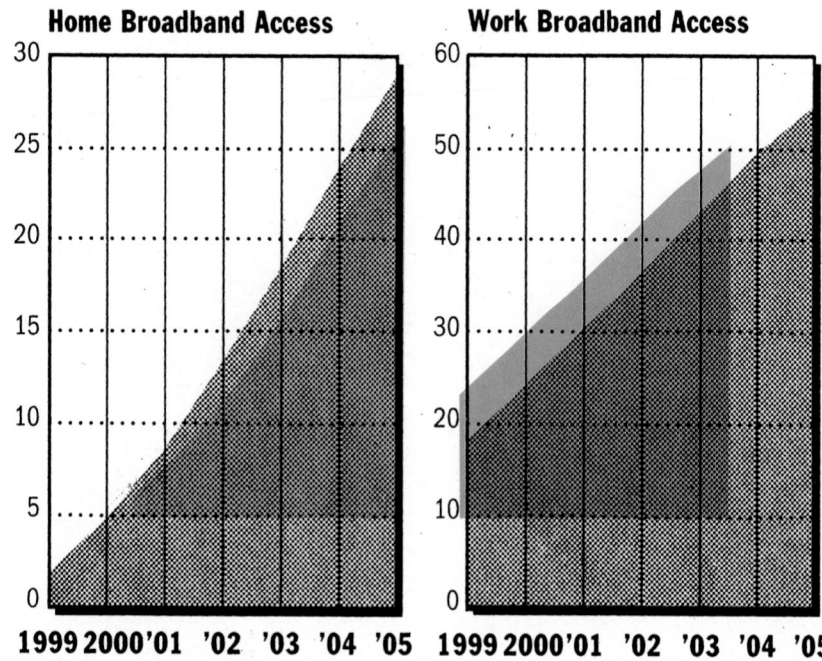

Home Broadband Access

Work Broadband Access

1999 2000 '01   '02   '03   '04   '05   1999 2000 '01   '02   '03   '04   '05

Source: Media Metrix

7.

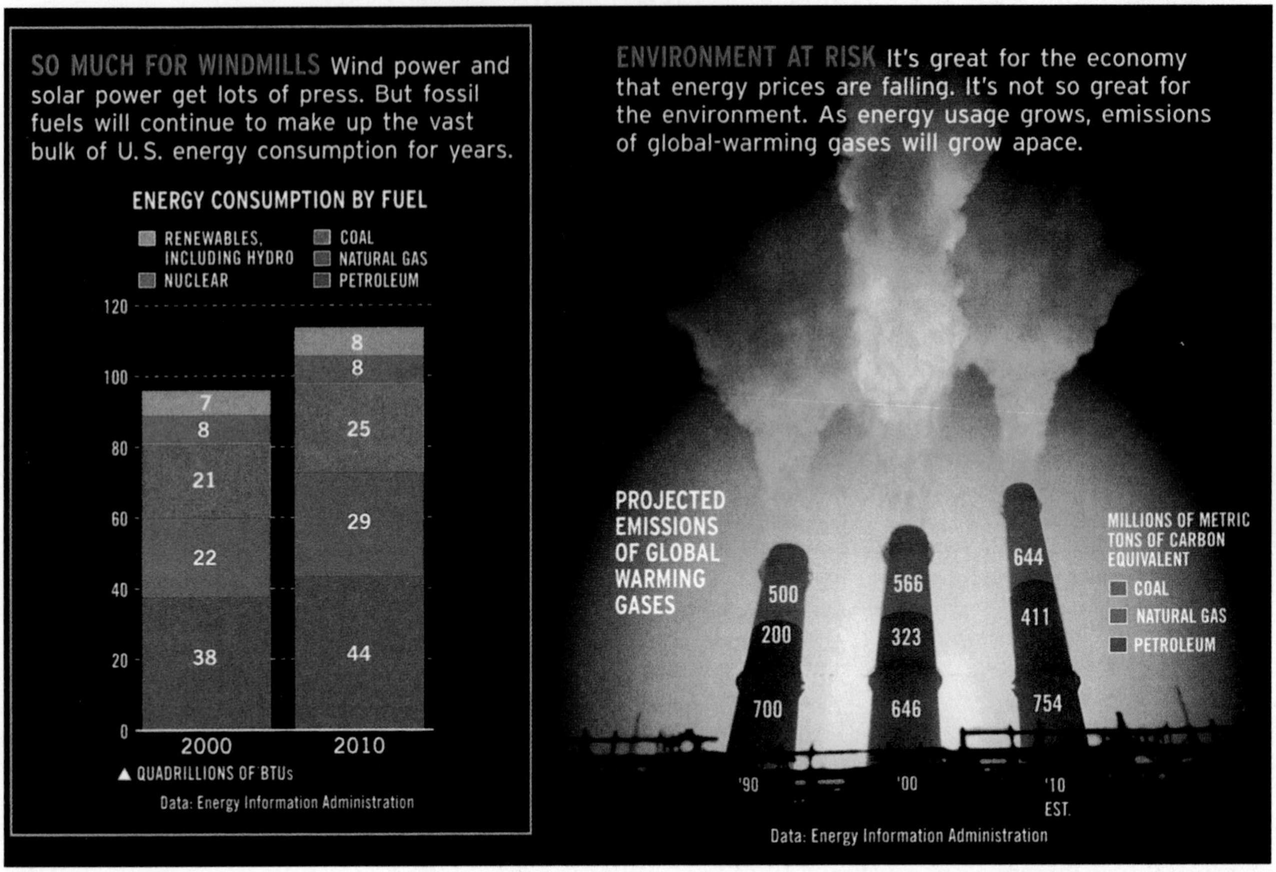

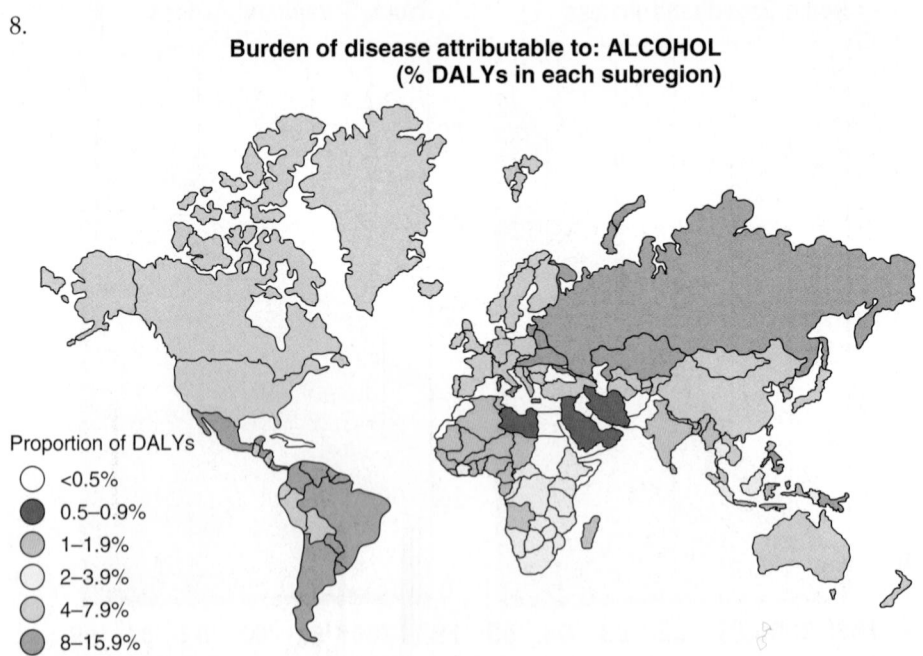

SO MUCH FOR WINDMILLS Wind power and solar power get lots of press. But fossil fuels will continue to make up the vast bulk of U.S. energy consumption for years.

ENERGY CONSUMPTION BY FUEL

- RENEWABLES, INCLUDING HYDRO
- NUCLEAR
- COAL
- NATURAL GAS
- PETROLEUM

2000: 7, 8, 21, 22, 38
2010: 8, 8, 25, 29, 44

▲ QUADRILLIONS OF BTUs

Data: Energy Information Administration

ENVIRONMENT AT RISK It's great for the economy that energy prices are falling. It's not so great for the environment. As energy usage grows, emissions of global-warming gases will grow apace.

PROJECTED EMISSIONS OF GLOBAL WARMING GASES

MILLIONS OF METRIC TONS OF CARBON EQUIVALENT
- COAL
- NATURAL GAS
- PETROLEUM

'90: 500, 200, 700
'00: 566, 323, 646
'10 EST.: 644, 411, 754

Data: Energy Information Administration

Source: Reprinted from the August 27, 2001 issue of BusinessWeek by special permission, Copyright © 2001 by The McGraw-Hill Companies, Inc.

8.

Burden of disease attributable to: ALCOHOL
(% DALYs in each subregion)

Proportion of DALYs
- <0.5%
- 0.5–0.9%
- 1–1.9%
- 2–3.9%
- 4–7.9%
- 8–15.9%

Worldwide alcohol causes 1.8 million deaths (3.2% of total) and 58.3 million (4% of total) of Disability-Adjusted Life Years (DALYs). Unintentional injuries alone account for about one-third of the 1.8 million deaths, while neuro-psychiatric conditions account for close to 40% of the 58.3 million DALYs. The burden is not equally distributed among the countries, as is shown on the map.

Source: World Health Organization, "Alcohol," in *Management of Substance Abuse,* http://www.who.int/substance_abuse/facts/alcohol/en/ (accessed May 5, 2009).

9.6   Interpreting Data

As your instructor directs,

a. Identify at least five stories in one or more of the following data sets.

b. Create visuals for three of the stories.

c. Write a memo to your instructor explaining why you chose these stories and why you chose these visuals to display them.

d. Write a memo to some group that might be interested in your findings, presenting your visuals as part of a short report. Possible groups include career counselors, radio stations, advertising agencies, and Mothers Against Drunk Driving.

e. Brainstorm additional stories you could tell with additional data. Specify the kind of data you would need.

1. Data on tipping.

Tipping Made Easy

The vast majority (74 percent) of Americans tip their waiter or waitress a percentage of the final bill, about 17 percent on average. But 22 percent tip a flat amount instead, $4.67 on average.

	PEOPLE WHO TIP A PERCENTAGE OF THE BILL	AVG. PERCENT	PEOPLE WHO TIP A FLAT AMOUNT	AVG. AMOUNT	PEOPLE WHO DON'T TIP
Waiter or waitress	74%	17%	22%	$4.67	2%
Bartender	20%	16%	48%	$1.85*	18%
Barber, hair stylist, or cosmetician	26%	17%	52%	$4.21	18%
Cab or limousine driver	31%	14%	43%	$5.55	16%
Food delivery person	31%	15%	50%	$2.88	12%
Hotel maid	14%	14%	53%	$8.08**	26%
Skycap or bellhop	N/A	N/A	71%	$3.68***	10%
Masseuse	26%	16%	28%	$7.50	25%
Usher at theatre, sporting events, etc.	5%	13%	17%	$5.26	70%

* for one drink; ** for a two-night stay; *** for two bags
Note: "No Answer/Refused" not shown

Source: Taylor Nelson Sofres Intersearch

Beauty Gets Bucks

While only 11 percent of all Americans say they give a bigger tip to service providers they find attractive, single people are twice as likely to make a habit of it (16 percent) than their married counterparts (8 percent).

PERCENTAGE OF AMERICANS WHO SAY THEY TIP MORE WHEN THEIR SERVICE PROVIDER IS:

	OVERALL	MEN	WOMEN	MARRIED	UNMARRIED	WHITE	BLACK
Older than others who usually do the job	20%	17%	22%	16%	24%	18%	30%
A student	25%	24%	27%	25%	26%	24%	36%
A parent	17%	14%	19%	17%	16%	16%	27%
Attractive	11%	17%	5%	8%	16%	11%	14%
Someone I know	38%	38%	38%	34%	42%	39%	29%
A female	6%	9%	3%	4%	9%	6%	8%
A male	3%	3%	3%	3%	4%	3%	6%
Disabled	33%	34%	32%	33%	34%	32%	47%
A racial minority	3%	3%	3%	2%	4%	2%	9%
Flirtatious	11%	17%	5%	7%	15%	11%	9%

Source: Taylor Nelson Sofres Intersearch

Source: From American Demographics, May 2001.

2.   Alcohol consumption, 1997, 2005, 2006.

Characteristic	Both Sexes			Male			Female		
	1997	2005	2006	1997	2005	2006	1997	2005	2006
Age	Percent current drinkers among all adults								
All persons									
18–44 years	69.4	66.4	65.8	74.8	72.0	71.4	64.2	60.9	60.4
18–24 years	62.2	58.1	59.3	66.7	62.7	64.2	57.7	53.7	54.5
25–44 years	71.6	69.2	68.1	77.2	75.3	73.9	66.1	63.3	62.4
45–64 years	63.3	62.6	61.5	70.8	68.0	67.3	56.2	57.5	56.1
45–54 years	67.1	66.3	64.9	73.8	71.0	69.8	60.7	61.9	60.3
55–64 years	57.3	57.3	56.8	65.8	63.8	63.8	49.4	51.5	50.4
65 years and over	43.4	43.1	43.7	52.7	52.0	54.4	36.6	36.5	35.6
65–74 years	48.6	47.7	48.2	56.7	55.1	58.5	42.0	41.3	39.4
75 years and over	36.6	38.0	38.5	46.7	47.8	48.8	30.2	31.7	31.8
Race									
White only	66.0	64.4	63.8	71.8	69.8	69.4	60.7	59.4	58.6
Black or African American only	47.8	46.4	48.5	56.9	56.2	58.7	40.9	38.8	40.4
American Indian or Alaska Native only	53.9	50.0	52.8	66.1	54.1	57.3	45.2	47.7	48.1
Asian only	45.8	42.9	43.0	60.2	53.5	55.9	31.6	32.4	31.3
Native Hawaiian or Other Pacific Islander only	—	—	—	—	—	—	—	—	—
2 or more races	—	51.6	55.0	—	55.7	59.5	—	48.2	52.9
Hispanic origin and race									
Hispanic or Latino	53.4	50.8	50.5	64.6	61.8	62.6	42.1	39.7	38.2
Mexican	53.0	48.1	49.0	66.9	61.3	61.5	38.9	34.8	35.2
Not Hispanic or Latino	64.1	62.9	62.5	70.2	68.3	68.2	58.7	58.1	57.5
White only	67.5	67.0	66.4	72.7	71.4	70.8	62.9	63.0	62.4
Black or African American only	47.8	46.0	48.4	57.1	55.8	68.8	40.7	38.5	40.3
Geographic region									
Northeast	68.7	69.0	68.5	74.4	74.2	74.5	63.8	64.6	63.6
Midwest	66.8	66.0	65.5	73.0	71.0	70.5	61.1	61.3	60.7
South	56.2	54.2	55.1	63.9	60.3	62.5	49.2	48.8	48.5
West	64.9	61.6	59.6	71.5	69.8	66.8	58.9	53.6	52.8

Source: U.S. Department of Health and Human Services, "Table 68: Alcohol Consumption among Adults 18 Years of Age and Over, by Selected Characteristics: United States, 1997, 2005, and 2006," in *Health, United States, 2007,* http://www.cdc.gov/nchs/data/hus/hus07.pdf#068 (accessed March 7, 2009).

3. Top Celebrities, 2008.

Forbes magazine's Web site provides the full list of 100 top celebrities, explains the methodology, and re-ranks the list on any column. For example, you can click on "pay rank" and get a list ordered by earnings. You can also find lists for other years.

Rank	Name	Pay ($mil)	Web Rank	Press Rank	TV Rank
1	Oprah Winfrey	275	2	5	1
2	Tiger Woods	115	12	1	3
3	Angelina Jolie	14	1	9	15
4	Beyonce Knowles	80	3	32	14
5	David Beckham	50	10	3	18
6	Johnny Depp	72	17	19	36
7	Jay-Z	82	6	43	41
8	The Police	115	15	20	51
9	J. K. Rowling	300	23	27	64
10	Brad Pitt	20	4	8	7
11	Will Smith	80	26	39	32
12	Justin Timberlake	44	5	24	17
13	Steven Spielberg	130	34	23	60
14	Cameron Diaz	50	13	50	45
15	David Letterman	45	42	34	10
16	LeBron James	38	32	13	13
17	Jennifer Aniston	27	21	67	49
18	Michael Jordan	45	38	45	29
19	Kobe Bryant	39	28	18	24
20	Phil Mickelson	45	87	12	23
21	Madonna	40	15	20	67
22	Simon Cowell	72	65	47	40
23	Roger Federer	35	40	2	26
24	Alex Rodriguez	34	51	7	6
25	Jerry Seinfeld	85	79	72	38

Source: Reprinted by permission of Forbes Magazine © 2009 Forbes LLC.

4. Statistics on high school graduates.

a. Curriculum levels completed, by gender

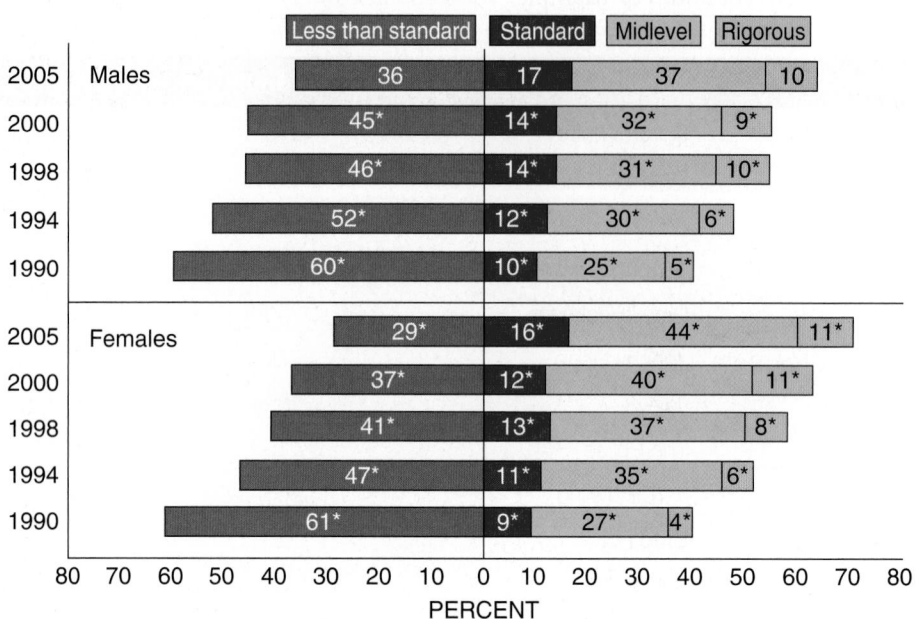

*Significantly different from 2005.
Source: "Curriculum Levels Completed, by Gender," in *U.S. Department of Education, Institute of Education Sciences, National Center for Education Statistics, High School Transcript Study (HSTS), various years, 1990–2005,* http://nationsreportcard.gov/hsts_2005/hs_stu_5b_2.asp (accessed May 5, 2009).

b. Trend in grade point average by gender

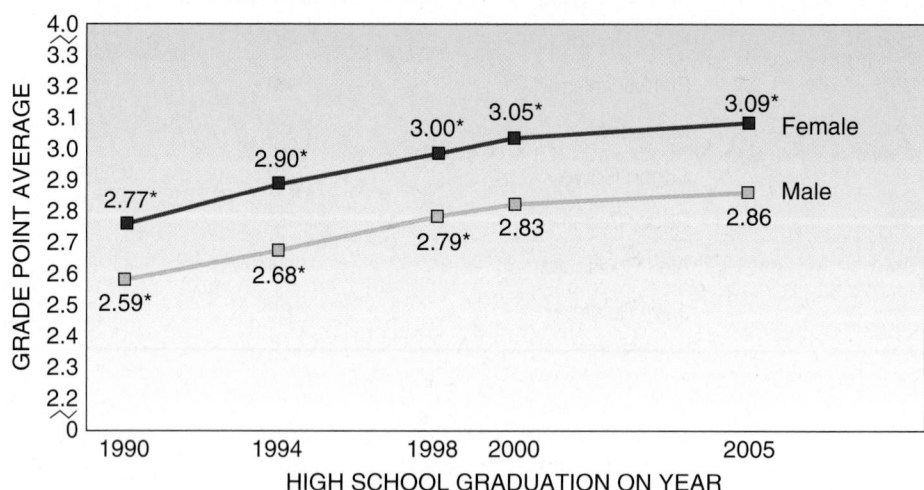

*Significantly different from 2005.
Source: "Trend in Grade Point Average, by Gender," in *U.S. Department of Education, Institute of Education Sciences, National Center for Education Statistics, High School Transcript Study (HSTS), various years, 1990–2005,* http://nationsreportcard.gov/hsts_2005/hs_stu_5b_3.asp (accessed May 5, 2009).

c. Trend in twelfth-grade average NAEP reading scores

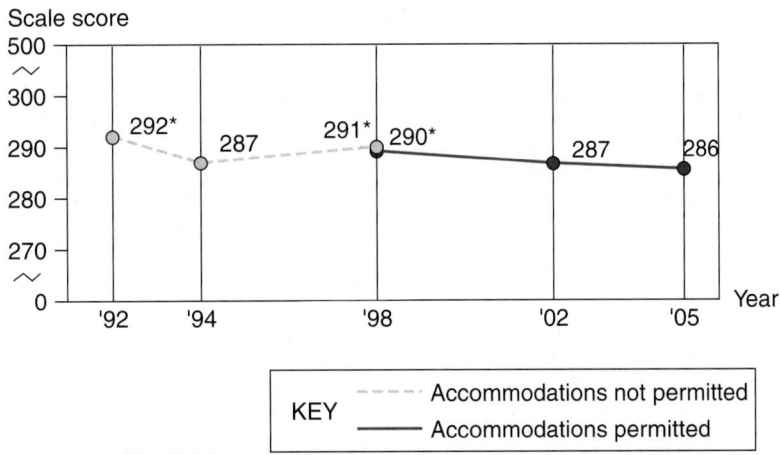

*Significantly different from 2005.
Source: "Trend in Twelfth-Grade Average NAEP Reading Scores," in *U.S. Department of Education, Institute of Education Sciences, National Center for Education Statistics, High School Transcript Study (HSTS), various years, 1990–2005,* http://nationsreportcard.gov/reading_math_grade12_2005/s0202.asp (accessed May 5, 2009).

9.7 Creating Graphs for Two Audiences and Scenarios

"Assume that you work for a local nonprofit organization with the following income expense for 2007 (see Table 1).

Table 1

Income		Expenses	
Description	**$ Amount**	**Description**	**$ Amount**
Government grants	$375,000	Program services	$741,935
Fees for services	$273,467	Administrative costs	$ 88,500
Contributions	$114,763	Miscellaneous	$ 5,230
Special events	$ 58,450		
Sale of products produced by participants in your program	$ 12,468		
Total income	$834,148	Total expenses	$835,665

As directors of the organization, you are responsible for bringing in more money and must present the past year's financial information to two groups of people, described in the following scenarios:

1. Within the community is a core group of consistent contributors who give the same amount each year, although the cost of running your organization continues to go up. You must convince these contributors to give additional funds during your

presentation at the annual fund-raising banquet. You need to create graphic representations of financial data that will convince the contributors of the need for additional funds and that will reassure them the money they have given in the past has been spent wisely.

2. Your organization is eligible for a new grant from a federal government agency. You have to write a

proposal explaining why your organization needs the money and demonstrating that it is fiscally responsible. There is a strict page limit, so you must present financial information concisely but in enough detail to make a strong case."

With a group of two or three peers, as your instructor directs,

a. Create a graphic representation of the financial data for the presentation and the proposal.

b. Write a memo that justifies the choices you made in creating the graphics for the different audiences and situations.

c. Prepare a brief presentation to the class that justifies your choices in creating the graphics.

Quoted from Susan M. Katz, "Creating Appropriate Graphics for Business Situations," *Business Communication Quarterly* 71, no. 1 (March 2008): 71–75. Copyright © 2008 by Sage Publications Inc. Journals. Reproduced with permission of Sage Publications Inc. Journals via Copyright Clearance Center.

9.8   Graphing Data from the Web

Find data on the Web about a topic that interests you. Some sites with data include the following:

Catalyst (women in business)

http://www.catalyst.org/page/64/ browse-research-knowledge

ClickZ (digital marketing)

http://www.clickz.com/showPage.html?page=stats

FEDSTATS (links to 70 US government agencies)

http://www.fedstats.gov/

United Nations Environment Program

http://na.unep.net/

U.S. Congress Joint Economic Committee

http://jec.senate.gov/index .cfm?FuseAction=ChartsData.Home

As your instructor directs,

a. Identify at least five stories in the data.

b. Create visuals for three of the stories.

c. Write a memo to your instructor explaining why you chose these stories and why you chose these visuals to display them.

d. Write a memo to some group which might be interested in your findings, presenting your visuals as part of a short report.

e. Print out the data and include it with a copy of your memo or report.

9.9   Creating a Visual Argument

With a partner, research one of the following topics:

- Having English-only laws in the workplace.
- Introducing new technology into the marketplace.
- Laying off employees during economic downturns.
- Requiring employers to offer insurance plans.
- Banning smoking in the workplace for insurance purposes.
- Hiring/recruiting and diversity in the workplace.
- Current hot business topic.

Then, prepare a four-minute slideshow presentation to share with your peers. The presentation should include only visual elements and contain no words. With the visuals, you should take a stand and present an argument about one of the topics. Recall the guidelines outlined in this chapter about effectively using visuals.

Remember that your presentation needs to be captivating to the audience and effectively convey your purpose. Finally, don't forget to cite all source material.

As your instructor directs,

a. Submit a copy of your slideshow presentation, including both hard and electronic versions.

b. Write a brief memo in which you explain in words the argument you were trying to make.

c. Submit a list of works cited for each of the visuals you used.

9.10   All-Weather Case: Critiquing and Revising Charts Showing Employee Benefits

Doug is to give a presentation to the upper-management team and a few union representatives on the status of employee benefits in All-Weather. Miguel has already given Doug a spreadsheet comparing All-Weather's benefits to those prevalent in private industry as reported by the National Compensation Survey (NCS), 2008, courtesy of the Bureau of Labor Statistics, the U.S. Department of Labor. Miguel uses these numbers as benchmarks because specific numbers related to employee benefits among window and door manufacturers are difficult to obtain. This is what the spreadsheet prepared by Miguel looks like (all categories—except All-Weather, which is fictional—are based on National Compensation Survey, 2008, Bureau of Labor Statistics, US Department of Labor):

	Retirement Benefits		Medical Care		Paid Holidays	
	Private Industry[1]	All-Weather	Private Industry[2]	All-Weather	Private Industry[3]	All-Weather
All employees	61%	72%	71%	78%	77%	78%
Management/professional employees	76%	100%	86%	100%	89%	100%
Service employees	37%	49%	46%	57%	52%	49%
Sales and office employees	65%	75%	71%	80%	81%	90%
Installation, maintenance, and repair employees	67%	55%	83%	65%	93%	65%
Production employees	68%	80%	82%	90%	92%	85%

[1,2,3] Actual numbers reported by the U.S. Department of Labor, Bureau of Labor Statistics, "Employee Benefits in the United States, March 2008," http://www.bls .gov/news.release/pdf/ebs2.pdf, accessed March 7, 2009.

Doug knows he cannot show just the spreadsheet in his presentation. Although he can quickly reduce the spreadsheet to its main points, his colleagues in upper management are too used to charts to let him get away with just showing a table. Doug looks for Kioni, whom everyone in the department admires. However, she has accompanied Erin and the new product engineers on a field visit. Miguel and Linda have gone to Nebraska to sign a contract with the union there. Suddenly Doug spots Rudy, who is turning the pages of a telephone directory. He snaps to attention as Doug approaches.

"How's it going, Rudy?" Doug asks, noticing Rudy's disheveled hair, "Haven't seen you in a while."

"I've been here Doug, on the job," Rudy says, his voice a little trembly.

Doug remembers Erin talking about Rudy a few days back, something to the effect of his increasing absenteeism and late arrivals. However, Doug decides to let Erin take care of Rudy's behavior. Doug needs someone to prepare the charts and Rudy is apparently free.

"Rudy, I have a few charts to make," Doug says, politely. "Why don't you come into my office as soon as you're finished with what you were doing?"

"Oh, I can come now," Rudy says, getting up and following Doug into his office.

After briefly talking about his presentation and explaining the table to Rudy, Doug asks him to prepare charts based on the spreadsheet. "Make them simple to understand and accurate," he says, by way of parting advice.

Rudy nods as he leaves Doug's office.

The next day Rudy returns with the charts. "Here're the charts," he says, apparently pleased with himself.

"Thanks," Doug says, looking up from a report he is reading. "Leave them here and I'll call you if I need you to make changes."

Later, Doug looks at the printouts left by Rudy. The first chart (shown in Figure 1) frustrates Doug because Rudy has chosen an inappropriate type of chart to represent the given data. The second and the third charts (Figures 2 and 3 below) seem right at a first glance, but after looking at them for a few seconds more Doug realizes the problems in the charts.

Figure 1   Retirement Benefits: Private Industry versus All-Weather

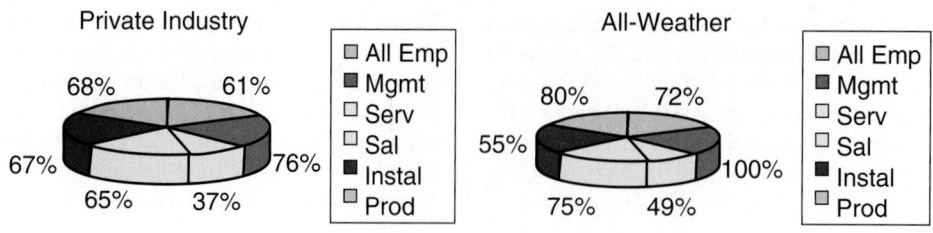

Figure 2   Medical Care: Private Industry versus All-Weather

Figure 3   Paid Holidays: Private Industry versus All-Weather

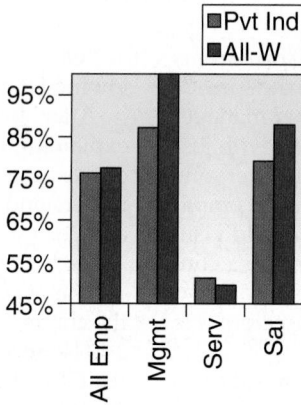

Based on your reading of Chapter 9 and the spreadsheet prepared by Miguel, critique and revise the three charts prepared by Rudy. Before revising the charts, however, identify and list the problems in the three charts. As you look for problems in the charts, look at Miguel's spreadsheet and check whether the numbers reported in the spreadsheet have been accurately and fully depicted in the charts.

Making Oral Presentations

Chapter Outline

Identifying Purposes in Oral Presentations

Comparing Written and Oral Messages

Planning a Strategy for Your Presentation

- Choosing the Kind of Presentation
- Adapting Your Ideas to the Audience
- Planning a Strong Opening and Closing

Planning PowerPoint Slides

- Designing PowerPoint Slides
- Using Figures and Tables
- Using PowerPoint Technology to Involve Your Audience

Choosing Information to Include in a Presentation

- Choosing Data
- Choosing Demonstrations

Organizing Your Information

Delivering an Effective Presentation

- Dealing with Fear
- Using Eye Contact
- Developing a Good Speaking Voice
- Standing and Gesturing
- Using Notes and Visuals

Handling Questions

Making Group Presentations

Summary of Key Points

Comparing Written and Oral Messages

Giving a presentation is in many ways very similar to writing a message. All the chapters up to this point—on using you-attitude and positive emphasis, developing benefits, analyzing your audience, and designing visuals—remain relevant as you plan an oral presentation.

A written message makes it easier to

- Present extensive or complex financial data.
- Present many specific details of a law, policy, or procedure.
- Minimize undesirable emotions.

Oral messages make it easier to

- Use emotion to help persuade the audience.
- Focus the audience's attention on specific points.
- Answer questions, resolve conflicts, and build consensus.
- Modify a proposal that may not be acceptable in its original form.
- Get immediate action or response.

Oral and written messages have many similarities. In both, you should

- Adapt the message to the specific audience.
- Show the audience how they would benefit from the idea, policy, service, or product.
- Overcome any objections the audience may have.
- Use you-attitude and positive emphasis.
- Use visuals to clarify or emphasize material.
- Specify exactly what the audience should do.

Why It's So Hard

"We may grudgingly admit that, like it or not, verbal blunders have the inevitability of gravity. The next question is why? It's because speaking is one of the most complicated human activities that we do, at any age. The average adult English speaker has a vocabulary of around thirty thousand words. . . . Most of us in modern America, apart from the very solitary and the very garrulous, speak anywhere from 7,500 to 22,500 words a day. Grabbing these words, one every four hundred milliseconds on average, and arranging them in sequences that are edited and reviewed for grammar and appropriateness before they're spoken requires a symphony of neurons working quickly and precisely. Pronouncing words in any language requires that your brain coordinate with your body in order to turn the electricity of nerve impulses into waves of sound. So far, scientists have been able to draw only simply models of how the control of language toggles back and forth between the brain and the body.

"Given the speeds involved, why aren't we better equipped to puts units of language in the right order? The problem is that sounds, words, and grammatical items aren't arranged in our brains as though on a library's shelves, with all the items ordered and catalogued by topics and authors. Rather, they're associated with one another in a matrix or a web."

Quoted from Michael Erard, *Um . . . Slips, Stumbles and Verbal Blunders and What They Mean* (New York: Pantheon Books, 2007), 61–62.

Oral presentation skills are a big asset in the business world.

Give the Audience Problems

To meet the challenge of getting and keeping the audience's interest, some speakers are adapting a method used by teachers: problem-based learning. With this technique, students identify a problem and learn principles and methods for solving the problem, often working as a group.

For presentations, speakers apply problem-based learning in various ways:

- They might present the topic in terms of a problem to be solved. For example, if the topic is employee morale, the speaker might describe an employee who feels unappreciated.

- The speaker might ask audience members to work in pairs and brainstorm possible sources of the problem. This activity might last just five minutes, but it gets the audience alert, focused, and involved in the topic.

- The presentation should allow plenty of time for questions. Before replying to a question, the speaker might ask audience members to suggest solutions.

- The presenter should offer resources for further learning after the presentation is over. Motivating participants to continue learning is one of the goals of problem-based learning.

A common thread of the various techniques is that they shift the presenter's role. Not just a deliverer of information, the presenter aims to help the audience learn.

Adapted from Richard T. Kasuya, "Give Your Audience a Problem and They Will Learn," *Presentations* 18, no. 8 (August 2004): 46.

Planning a Strategy for Your Presentation

How will you reach your specific goals with a specific audience?

In all oral presentations, simplify what you want to say. Identify the one idea you want the audience to take home. Simplify your supporting detail so it's easy to follow. Simplify visuals so they can be taken in at a glance. Simplify your words and sentences so they're easy to understand. Researchers at Bell Labs are practicing these techniques. Where once they spent their days on basic research and academic papers, they now are condensing their scientific work into eight-minute PowerPoint presentations for potential corporate partners and venture capital as the Lab's new director seeks to make it profitable.[1]

An oral presentation needs to be simpler than a written message to the same audience. If readers forget a point, they can turn back to it and reread the paragraph. Headings, paragraph indentation, and punctuation provide visual cues to help readers understand the message. Listeners, in contrast, must remember what the speaker says. Whatever they don't remember is lost. Even asking questions requires the audience to remember which points they don't understand.

Analyze your audience for an oral presentation just as you do for a written message. If you'll be speaking to co-workers, talk to them about your topic or proposal to find out what questions or objections they have. For audiences inside the organization, the biggest questions are often practical ones: Will it work? How much will it cost? How long will it take? How will it impact me?

Think about the physical conditions in which you'll be speaking. Will the audience be tired at the end of a long day of listening? Sleepy after a big meal? Will the group be large or small? The more you know about your audience, the better you can adapt your message to them.

Choosing the Kind of Presentation

Choose one of three basic kinds of presentations: monologue, guided discussion, or interactive.

In a **monologue presentation**, the speaker talks without interruption; questions are held until the end of the presentation, at which time the speaker functions as an expert. The speaker plans the presentation in advance and delivers it without deviation. This kind of presentation is the most common in class situations, but it's often boring for the audience. Good delivery skills are crucial, since the audience is comparatively uninvolved.

In a **guided discussion**, the speaker presents the questions or issues that both speaker and audience have agreed on in advance. Rather than functioning as an expert with all the answers, the speaker serves as a facilitator to help the audience tap its own knowledge. This kind of presentation is excellent for

Pepper ... and Salt
THE WALL STREET JOURNAL

"Instead of a story. Can Mommy practice the presentation she has to give tomorrow?"

From The Wall Street Journal, permission by Cartoon Features Syndicate.

presenting the results of consulting projects, when the speaker has specialized knowledge, but the audience must implement the solution if it is to succeed. Guided discussions need more time than monologue presentations, but produce more audience response, more responses involving analysis, and more commitment to the result.

An **interactive presentation** is a conversation, even if the speaker stands up in front of a group and uses charts and overheads. Most sales presentations are interactive presentations. The sales representative uses questions to determine the buyer's needs, probe objections, and gain provisional and then final commitment to the purchase. Even in a memorized sales presentation, the buyer will talk a significant portion of the time. Top salespeople let the buyer do the majority of the talking.

Adapting Your Ideas to the Audience

Measure the message you'd like to send against where your audience is now. If your audience is indifferent, skeptical, or hostile, focus on the part of your message the audience will find most interesting and easiest to accept.

Don't seek a major opinion change in a single oral presentation. If the audience has already decided to hire an advertising agency, then a good presentation can convince them that your agency is the one to hire. But if you're talking to a small business that has always done its own ads, limit your purpose. You may be able to prove that an agency can earn its fees by doing things the owner can't do and by freeing the owner's time for other activities. Only after the audience is receptive should you try to persuade the audience to hire your agency rather than a competitor.

Good presentations adapt their ideas to a particular audience.

Audience Feedback

Just as when you're speaking with someone face-to-face, when you're presenting in front of a group it's important to look for feedback from your audience. Pay attention to body language, and ask your audience questions: the feedback that you get will help you build rapport with your audience so that you can express your message more clearly.

In some settings, such as when you're presenting to a large group, you might use other tools to gather audience feedback. For example, you could build a group discussion into your presentation: give your audience some questions to discuss in small groups, then invite them to share their answers with the room. Give questionnaires to your audience, either before your presentation or during a break. Have a member of your team tabulate audience responses, then build them into the remainder of your talk.

Audience response devices give you another option for getting instant audience feedback. These devices—popular with training departments—allow your audience to respond quickly to multiple-choice or yes/no questions during presentations. Software tabulates the responses as numbers, charts, or graphs for all to see. These devices are particularly good for feedback in situations where people may want anonymity.

Look at the product Web sites of some popular audience response devices:

- www.meridia-interactive.com
- www.optiontechnologies.com
- www.qwizdom.com
- www.turningtechnologies.com

How do these devices compare to each other? How might you use them in your own presentations?

Public Speaking and the Law

When you speak on behalf of a business or group, remember that your presentation doesn't reflect just on you: your public statements can create legal liabilities for both you and your organization. Laws that govern truth in advertising apply to public speech just as they do to public written statements.

Presentations offers useful advice for you if you find yourself in the role of spokesperson:

- Be especially careful to prepare your presentation with accurate information. Don't rely on hearsay for facts and figures: have the actual sources in hand before you create your presentation.

- Don't send different messages to different audiences. It's all right to tailor a message to the needs and expectations of each audience, but don't change the message between groups: doing so is deceptive.

- When in doubt, get advice from experts. Many organizations have legal services available to help you avoid public-disclosure pitfalls. If you have important or sensitive information to share with a public audience, it might be wise to get a legal opinion first.

Look through the news for stories about businesses or organizations that face legal troubles because of information that they did—or didn't—share. What penalties did those businesses face? What happened to the employees involved?

Adapted from Dave Zielinski, "The Speech Trap," *Presentations* 19, no. 8 (2005), 20–25.

Make your ideas relevant to your audience by linking what you have to say to their experiences and interests. Showing your audience that the topic affects them directly is the most effective strategy. When you can't do that, at least link the topic to some everyday experience.

Planning a Strong Opening and Closing

The beginning and the end of a presentation, like the beginning and the end of a written document, are positions of emphasis. Use those key positions to interest the audience and emphasize your key point. You'll sound more natural and more effective if you talk from notes but write out your opener and close in advance and memorize them. (They'll be short: just a sentence or two.)

Consider using one of four common modes for openers: startling statement, narration or anecdote, question, or quotation. The more you can do to personalize your opener for your audience, the better. Recent events are better than things that happened long ago; local events are better than events at a distance; people they know are better than people who are only names.

Startling statement

> Twelve of our customers have canceled orders in the past month.

This presentation to a company's executive committee went on to show that the company's distribution system was inadequate and to recommend a third warehouse located in the Southwest.

Narration or anecdote

When the salespeople for a company that sells storage of backed-up computer data give presentations to clients, they open by telling a story:

> A consultant asked a group of people how many of them had [a backup plan]. One brave soul from a bank raised his hand and said, "I've got a disaster recovery plan—complete and ready to go into action. It's real simple, just one page." And the consultant asked, "A one-page disaster plan? What would you do if your computer center blew up, or flooded, or caught on fire? How could you recover with just a one-page disaster plan?" He said, "Well, it's really very simple. It's a two-step plan. First, I maintain my résumé up-to-date at all times. And second, I store a backup copy off-site."[2]

This anecdote breaks the ice in introducing an uncomfortable subject: the possibility of a company losing valuable data. It uses humor to make major points—that a variety of disasters are possible, many firms are unprepared, and the consequences are great. The client will be more open to listening than if the salespeople started by questioning the client's own planning.

Even better than canned stories are anecdotes that happened to you. The best anecdotes are parables that contain the point of your talk.

Question

Asking the audience to raise their hands or reply to questions gets them actively involved in a presentation. Tony Jeary skillfully uses this technique in sessions devoted to training the audience in presentation skills. He begins by asking the audience members to write down their estimate of the number of presentations they give per week:

"How many of you said one or two?" he asks, raising his hand. A few hands pop up. "Three, four, six, eight?" he asks, walking up the middle of the aisle to the back of the room. Hands start popping up like targets in a shooting gallery. Jeary's Texas drawl accelerates and suddenly the place sounds like a cattle auction. "Do I hear 10? Twelve? Thirteen to the woman in the green shirt! Fifteen to the gentlemen in plaid," he fires, and the room busts out laughing.[3]

Most presenters will not want to take a course in auctioneering, as Jeary did to make his questioning routine more authentic. However, Jeary's approach both engages the audience and makes the point that many jobs involve a multitude of occasions requiring formal and informal presentation skills.

Quotation

According to Towers Perrin, the profits of Fortune 100 companies would be 25% lower if their earnings statements listed the future costs companies are obligated to pay for retirees' health care.

This presentation on options for health care for retired employees urges executives to start now to investigate options to cut the future costs.

Your opener should interest the audience and establish a rapport with them. Some speakers use humor to achieve those goals. However, an inappropriate joke can turn the audience against the speaker. Never use humor that's directed against the audience. For example, the following joke was effective in the context of an oil company executive addressing other industry members about government regulations—and would have been disastrous if told to a group that included environmentalists:

[When regulations slowed the construction of a chemical plant,] I got to feeling a little like Moses crossing the Red Sea with the Egyptians in hot pursuit. When Moses asked God for help, God looked down and said, "I've got some good news and some bad news. The good news is that I'll part the Red Sea, let your people pass through, and then destroy the Egyptians." "That's great," said Moses. "What's the bad news?" God said, "First you have to file an environmental impact statement."[4]

When in doubt about humor, be sure it makes fun of yourself and your own group, not of others.

Humor isn't the only way to set an audience at ease. Smile at your audience before you begin; let them see that you're a real person and a nice one.

Conclusions

The end of your presentation should be as strong as the opener. For your close, you could do one or more of the following:

- Restate your main point.
- Refer to your opener to create a frame for your presentation.
- End with a vivid, positive picture.
- Tell the audience exactly what to do to solve the problem you've discussed.

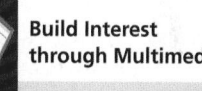

Build Interest through Multimedia

One of the fastest ways to engage your audience is through a multimedia presentation that combines text, images, animation, video, and sound. Though multimedia was once an expensive, time-consuming option, you can now incorporate simple multimedia techniques into your own presentations:

- Add video clips and sound clips to your *PowerPoint* presentations.
- Use a screen-capture program like *Camtasia* to create interactive demonstration movies.
- Create your own animated banner ads and product brochures using *Flash*.
- Convert your printed brochure into a Web site for your clients to visit.

The next time you surf the Internet, pay close attention to your favorite Web sites. What examples of multimedia do you see? How do those sites use multimedia to grab your attention?

Adapted from Guy D. Ball, "Creating Multimedia Presentations for Training," *Intercom*, May 2005, 25–26.

When Mike Powell described his work in science to an audience of nonscientists, he opened and then closed with words about what being a scientist feels like. He opened humorously, saying, "Being a scientist is like doing a jigsaw puzzle . . . in a snowstorm . . . at night . . . when you don't have all the pieces . . . and you don't have the picture you are trying to create." Powell closed by returning to the opening idea of "being a scientist," but he moved from the challenge to the inspiration with this vivid story:

> The final speaker at a medical conference [I] attended . . . walked to the lectern and said, "I am a thirty-two-year-old wife and mother of two. I have AIDS. Please work fast."[5]

When you write out your opener and close, be sure to use oral rather than written style. As you can see in the example close above, oral style uses shorter sentences and shorter, simpler words than writing does. Oral style can even sound a bit choppy when it is read by eye. Oral style uses more personal pronouns, a less varied vocabulary, and more repetition.

http://norvig.com/
Gettysburg/index.htm

Not every speech needs visuals. As Peter Norvig shows, Lincoln's Gettysburg Address is hurt, not helped, by adding bland PowerPoint slides.

Planning PowerPoint Slides

Visuals can give your presentation a professional image and greater impact. One study found that in an informative presentation, multimedia (PowerPoint slides with graphics and animation) produced 5% more learning than overheads made from the slides and 16% more learning than text alone.[6]

Well-designed visuals can serve as an outline for your talk (see Figure 10.1), eliminating the need for additional notes. Visuals can help your audience follow

Figure 10.1 Poorly Formatted Presentation Slides (Top) and Well-Formatted Slides (Bottom)

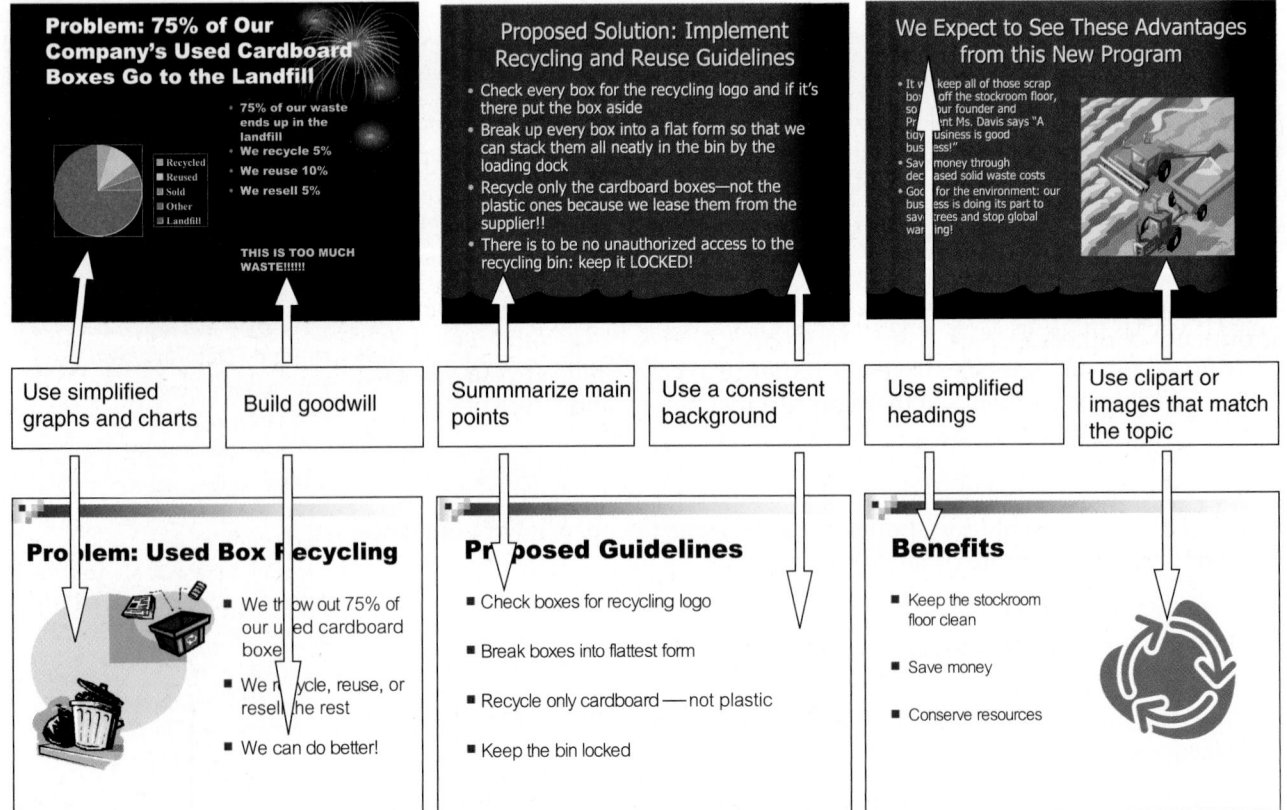

along with you, and help you keep your place as you speak. Your visuals should highlight your main points, not give every detail. Elaborate on your visuals as you talk; most people find it mind-numbing to have slide after slide read to them.

Designing PowerPoint Slides

As you design slides for PowerPoint and other presentation programs, keep the following guidelines in mind:

- Use a consistent background
- Use a big font size: 44 or 50 point for titles, 32 point for subheads, and 28 point for examples. You should be able to read the smallest words easily when you print a handout version of your slides.
- Use bullet-point phrases rather than complete sentences.
- Use clear, concise language.
- Make only three to five points on each slide. If you have more, consider using two slides.
- Customize your slides with your organization's logo, and add visuals: charts, pictures, downloaded Web pages, photos, and drawings.

Use animation to make words and images appear and move during your presentation—but only in ways that help you control information flow and build interest. For example, in a sales presentation for Portola Packaging, a bar graph showing sales growth was redesigned to highlight the company's strong performance: instead of static bars, the graph featured upward-sloping arrows drawn from the initial sales level to the new, higher level. The presenter clicks the mouse once to display the graph title and labels; with the second mouse click, the arrow wipes up, emphasizing the growth pattern.[7] Avoid using animation or sound effects just to be clever; they will distract your audience.

Use **clip art** in your presentations only if the art is really appropriate to your points. Internet sources have made such a wide variety of drawings and photos available that designers really have no excuse for failing to pick images that are both appropriate and visually appealing. Even organizations on tight budgets can find free and low-cost resources, such as the public domain (that is, not copyrighted) collections of the US Fish and Wildlife Service (http://www.fws.gov/digitalmedia) and the National Oceanic and Atmospheric Administration (http://www.photolib.noaa.gov/).

Choose a consistent **template,** or background design, for your entire presentation. Make sure that the template is appropriate for your subject matter and audience. For example, use a globe only if your topic is international business and palm trees only if you're talking about tropical vacations. One problem with PowerPoint is that the basic templates may seem repetitive to people who see lots of presentations made with the program. For an important presentation, you may want to consider customizing the basic template. You can also find many professionally designed free templates online to help lend your presentation a more unique look.

Choose a light **background** if the lights will be off during your presentation and a dark background if the lights will be on. Slides will be easier to read if you use high contrast between the words and backgrounds. See Figure 10.2 for examples of effective and ineffective color combinations.

Using Figures and Tables

Visuals for presentations need to be simpler than visuals the audience reads on paper. For example, to adapt a printed data table for a presentation, you might cut out one or more columns or rows of data, round off the data to simplify them, or replace the chart with a graph or other visual. If you have

New to Admissions: PowerPoint

The University of Chicago Business School took a novel approach to their application process in 2007 when they began asking students to submit PowerPoint presentations in addition to other admission requirements. Since knowing how to create effective slides is crucial for people in business, the inclusion of four slides into the application materials seems almost natural. In fact, Microsoft estimates that 30 million presentations are given per day using their software.

Rose Martinelli, an admissions officer, stated that "we wanted to have a freeform space for students to be able to say what they think is important." The school hopes the new medium will help attract students who can think outside the box, an ability which often bodes well in business.

If you were applying to this school, would you be excited about showing off your presentation skills? What type of material would you include on your slides? What slide design techniques would help you stand out from the pack?

Adapted from Justin Pope, "School Adds PowerPoint for Entrance," *Des Moines Register,* August 8, 2007, D5.

http://www.baruch.cuny.edu/tutorials/powerpoint

Want to sharpen your PowerPoint skills? Try out this tutorial that will help improve your preparation design and delivery the next time you have to deliver a presentation. The site also features pros and cons for using PowerPoint and suggests additional resources.

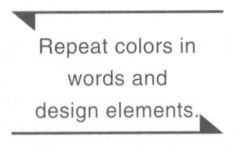
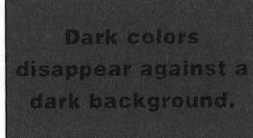
Figure 10.2   Effective and Ineffective Colors for Presentation Slides

Effective

> Use high contrast between words and background.

> Repeat colors in words and design elements.

Ineffective

> Limit the number of bright colors.

> Dark colors disappear against a dark background.

> Light colors disappear against a light background.

many data tables or charts in your presentation, consider including them on a handout for your audience.

Your presentation visuals should include titles, but don't need figure numbers. As you prepare your presentation, be sure to know where each visual is so that you can return to it easily if someone asks about it during the question period. Rather than reading from your slides, or describing visuals to your audience in detail, summarize the story contained on each slide and elaborate on what it means for your audience.

Using PowerPoint Technology to Involve Your Audience

Projected visuals work only if the technology they depend on works. When you give presentations in your own workplace, check the equipment in advance. When you make a presentation in another location or for another organization, arrive early so that you'll have time to not only check the equipment but also track down a service worker if the equipment isn't working. Be prepared with a backup plan to use if you're unable to show your visuals.

Keep in mind how you will use your presentation slides. Most likely, they will provide visual support for an oral presentation in a face-to-face meeting or videoconference. The slides should visually identify the key points of your presentation in a way that allows you to interact with your audience. Your oral presentation should always include more material than the text on your slides. **If the audience can read the entire presentation for themselves, why are you there?**

Consider ways to stimulate your audience's curiosity, invite questions, and build enthusiasm. For instance, instead of saying, "Sales grew 85% with this program," you could show a graph that shows sales declining up to the introduction of the program; invite the audience to consider what this program might do; and finally, after explaining the program, reveal the full sales graph with an animation that highlights the spike using a dramatic magenta line.

Choosing Information to Include in a Presentation

Choose the information that is most interesting to your audience, that answers the questions your audience will have and that is most persuasive for them. Limit your talk to three main points. In a long presentation (20 minutes or more) each main point can have subpoints. Your content will be easier to understand if you clearly show the relationship between each of the main points.

Turning your information into a story also helps. For example, a presentation about a plan to reduce scrap rates on the second shift can begin by setting the scene and defining the problem: Production expenses have cut profits in half. The plot unfolds as the speaker describes the facts that helped her trace the problem to scrap rates on the second shift. The resolution to the story is her group's proposal.

In an informative presentation, link the points you make to the knowledge your audience has. Show the audience members that your information answers their questions, solves their problems, or helps them do their jobs. When you explain the effect of a new law or the techniques for using a new machine, use specific examples that apply to the decisions they make and the work they do. If your content is detailed or complicated, give people a written outline or handouts. The written material both helps the audience keep track of your points during the presentation and serves as a reference after the talk is over.

To be convincing, you must answer the audience's questions and objections.

> Some people think that working women are less reliable than men. But the facts show that women take fewer sick days than men do.

However, don't bring up negatives or inconsistencies unless you're sure that the audience will think of them. If you aren't sure, save your evidence for the question phase. If someone does ask, you'll have the answer.

Choosing Data

As part of choosing what to say, you should determine what data to present, including what to show in visuals. Any data you mention should be necessary for the points you are making. Databases and PowerPoint have given employees direct access to ready-made and easy-to-create slides. The temptation is to overuse them rather than starting with decisions about what the audience needs to know.

Statistics and numbers can be convincing if you present them in ways that are easy to hear. Simplify numbers by reducing them to two significant digits and putting them in a context.

Hard to hear: Our 2010 sales dropped from $12,036,288,000 to $9,124,507,000.

Easy to hear: Our 2010 sales dropped from $12 billion to $9 billion. This is the steepest decline our company has seen in a quarter century.

Double-check your presentation statistics and numbers to ensure they are accurate. Mark Hurd, Chairman and CEO of Hewlett-Packard, gave as the best advice he ever got, "It's hard to look smart with bad numbers."[8]

Choosing Demonstrations

Demonstrations can prove your points dramatically and quickly. During the investigation of the space shuttle *Challenger* disaster, the late physicist Richard Feynman asked for a glass of water. When it came, he put a piece of the space shuttle's O-ring into the cold water. After less than a minute, he took it out and pinched it with a small clamp. The material kept the pinched shape when the clamp came off. The material couldn't return to its original shape.[9] A technical explanation could have made the same point: the O-ring couldn't function in the cold. But the demonstration was fast and easy to understand. It didn't

Sharing the Stage with Visuals

The audience can look at the speaker or the visual, but not both at the same time. An effective speaker directs the audience's attention to the visual and then back to the speaker, rather than trying to compete with the visual.

When Steve Mandel coaches clients on public speaking, he teaches them to use brief silences for visuals, so the audience has time to pay attention. For example, a speaker might say, "I've just talked to you about several problems you might experience. Now I'd like you to see a possible solution." Then the speaker shows the slide without talking for several seconds. This gives the audience time to absorb the contents of the slide. The presenter can regain attention by stepping toward the audience as he or she begins to speak again.

At its sales workshops, Communispond teaches a technique called "think-turn-talk." The presenter stands next to the visual and points to it with an open hand, thinking of what he or she intends to say. Then the presenter turns and makes eye contact with a person in the audience. Finally, the presenter talks. Communispond also teaches presenters to walk toward the audience when giving details from a visual. The connection is between presenter and audience, not presenter and slide.

Adapted from Dave Zielinski, "Perfect Practice," *Presentations* 17, no. 5 (2003): 30–36; and Julia Chang, "Back to School," *Sales and Marketing Management* 156, no. 7 (2004): 28–31.

How Not to Give a Presentation

John R. Brant has some excellent advice on how to give an awful presentation:

- Have a dull opening: If you really want to lose your audience in the first few minutes, read a prepared statement to them from a slide or a handout.

- Bury them in slides: Bore your audience with more slides than they'll be able to remember, or speed through your slides so quickly that your PowerPoint turns into a blur.

- Use the wrong humor: Make everyone uncomfortable with self-deprecating humor.

- Show them your back: Demonstrate how disconnected you are with your audience by turning your back to them, and avoid the possibility of rapport-building eye contact by looking at the screen instead of at your audience.

Think about the uninspiring presentations you've seen from other students, or even from your instructors. What could the presenters have done to improve their work and gain your interest?

Adapted from John R. Brandt, "Missing the (Power) Point," *Industry Week*, January 2007, 48.

require that the audience follow complex chemical or mathematical formulas. In an oral presentation, seeing is believing.

Demonstrations are an effective way to teach a process and to show what a product can do for the audience. Hewlett-Packard has developed a series of presentations that show consumers how to use its products for applications that may be unfamiliar. In one presentation, demonstrators teach how to use an HP computer to prepare digital photographs. A specialist showed how to restore a 50-year-old photograph of a football team. When she was done, she commented that the picture included her father, who had died two years earlier, and she planned to give the restored photo to her mother. The personal information made her presentation memorable and brought home the value of learning the skill she was teaching.[10]

Demonstrations can also help people remember your points. Dieticians had long known that coconut oil, used on movie popcorn, was bad for you. But no one seemed to care. Until, that is, the folks at the Center for Science in the Public Interest (CSPI) took up the cause. They called a press conference to announce that a medium movie popcorn (and who eats just a medium?) had more saturated fat than a bacon-and-eggs breakfast, a Big Mac and fries lunch, and a steak dinner with all the trimmings—combined. They provided the full buffet for TV cameras. The story played on all the major networks as well as the front pages of many newspapers. Even better, people remembered the story and popcorn sales plunged.[11]

In their book *Made to Stick: Why Some Ideas Survive and Others Die*, Chip Heath and Dan Heath say that ideas are remembered—and have lasting impact on people's opinions and behavior—when they have six characteristics:

1. **Simplicity:** they are short but filled with meaning: both demonstrations above could be comprehended in seconds.
2. **Unexpectedness:** they have some novelty for us: a bag of movie popcorn is worse than a whole day's meals of fatty foods.
3. **Concreteness:** the ideas must be explained with psychological description (see page 487) or in terms of human actions.
4. **Credibility:** ideas have to carry their own credibility if they do not come from an acknowledged expert. In both demonstrations above, people could see the effects for themselves.
5. **Emotions:** the ideas must make people feel some emotion, and it has to be the right emotion. Antismoking campaigns for teenagers have not been successful using fear, but they have had some success using resentment at the duplicity of cigarette companies.
6. **Stories:** the ideas have to tell stories.

The Heaths call the combination of these six factors stickiness. And the concept really works. Amounts of saturated fats are not exciting ideas, but CSPI changed movie popcorn with its demonstration.[12]

Organizing Your Information

Most presentations use a direct pattern of organization, even when the goal is to persuade a reluctant audience. In a business setting, the audience is in a hurry and knows that you want to persuade them. Be honest about your goal, and then prove that your goal meets the audience's needs too.

In a persuasive presentation, start with your strongest point, your best reason. If time permits, give other reasons as well and respond to possible objections. Put your weakest point in the middle so that you can end on a strong note.

Often one of five standard patterns of organization will work:

- **Chronological.** Start with the past, move to the present, and end by looking ahead. This pattern works best when the history helps show a problem's complexity or magnitude, or when the chronology moves people to an obvious solution.

- **Problem–causes–solution.** Explain the symptoms of the problem, identify its causes, and suggest a solution. This pattern works best when the audience will find your solution easy to accept.

- **Excluding alternatives.** Explain the symptoms of the problem. Explain the obvious solutions first and show why they won't solve the problem. End by discussing a solution that will work. This pattern may be necessary when the audience will find the solution hard to accept.

- **Pro–con.** Give all the reasons in favor of something, then those against it. This pattern works well when you want the audience to see the weaknesses in its position.

- **1–2–3.** Discuss three aspects of a topic. This pattern works well to organize short informative briefings. "Today I'll review our sales, production, and profits for the last quarter."

Make your organization clear to your audience. Written documents can be reread; they can use headings, paragraphs, lists, and indentations to signal levels of detail. In a presentation, you have to provide explicit clues to the structure of your discourse.

Early in your talk—perhaps immediately after your opener—provide an overview of the main points you will make.

> First, I'd like to talk about who the homeless in Columbus are. Second, I'll talk about the services The Open Shelter provides. Finally, I'll talk about what you—either individually or as a group—can do to help.

An overview provides a mental peg that hearers can hang each point on. It also can prevent someone from missing what you are saying because he or she wonders why you aren't covering a major point that you've saved for later.

Offer a clear signpost as you come to each new point. A **signpost** is an explicit statement of the point you have reached. Choose wording that fits your style. The following statements are four different ways that a speaker could use to introduce the last of three points:

> Now we come to the third point: what you can do as a group or as individuals to help homeless people in Columbus.

> So much for what we're doing. Now let's talk about what you can do to help.

> You may be wondering, what can I do to help?

> As you can see, the Shelter is trying to do many things. We could do more things with your help.

Part of an effective presentation is its setting. Do you think this outdoor setting helps or hinders the presentation?

Delivering an Effective Presentation

Audiences want the sense that you're talking directly to them and that you care that they understand and are interested. They'll forgive you if you get tangled up in a sentence and end it ungrammatically. They won't forgive you if you seem to have a "canned" talk that you're going to deliver no matter who the audience is or how they respond. You can convey a sense of caring to your audience by making direct eye contact with them and by using a conversational style.

Dealing with Fear

Feeling nervous is normal: about 70% of people rank giving a public speech as their greatest fear.[13] But you can harness that nervous energy to help you do your best work. As various trainers have noted, you don't need to get rid of your butterflies. All you need to do is make them fly in formation.

To calm your nerves before you give an oral presentation,

- Be prepared. Analyze your audience, organize your thoughts, prepare visual aids, practice your opener and close, check out the arrangements.
- Use only the amount of caffeine you normally use. More or less may make you jumpy.
- Avoid alcoholic beverages.
- Relabel your nerves. Instead of saying, "I'm scared," try saying, "My adrenaline is up." Adrenaline sharpens our reflexes and helps us do our best.

Just before your presentation,

- Consciously contract and then relax your muscles, starting with your feet and calves and going up to your shoulders, arms, and hands.
- Take several deep breaths from your diaphragm.

During your presentation,

- Pause and look at the audience before you begin speaking.
- Concentrate on communicating, not your feelings.
- Use body energy in strong gestures and movement.

New software is being developed to help nervous speakers improve their delivery. For example, the "Presentation Sensei" uses a microphone and camera, plus speech- and image-processing techniques, to provide feedback on eye contact, speaking rate, and timing.[14]

Using Eye Contact

Look directly at the people you're talking to. In one study, observers were more than twice as likely to notice and comment on poor presentation features, like poor eye contact, than good features, and tended to describe speakers with poor eye contact as disinterested, unprofessional, and poorly prepared.[15] In another study, subjects rated speakers who made more eye contact and longer eye contact as being friendlier and more engaged than speakers who had poor eye contact—especially when speakers combined good eye contact with friendly facial expressions.[16]

The point in making eye contact is to establish one-on-one contact with the individual members of your audience. People want to feel that you're talking to them. Looking directly at individuals also enables you to be more conscious of feedback from the audience, so that you can modify your approach if necessary.

Michael Campbell, author of *Bulletproof Presentations*, suggests some techniques to improve eye contact. Make eye contact before you start speaking. With each person, make eye contact for about five seconds. Then look at someone else for about five seconds. If you can, pick a few friendly faces in different parts of the room, so that you feel encouraged. Without the five-second eye contact, your gaze will appear to be roving aimlessly around the room. If you are reading notes or a speech, pause while you read, and then make eye contact while you speak.[17]

Developing a Good Speaking Voice

People will enjoy your presentation more if your voice is easy to listen to. To find out what your voice sounds like, tape-record it. Listen to your voice qualities and delivery.

Voice Qualities

Tone of voice refers to the rising or falling inflection that tells you whether a group of words is a question or a statement, whether the speaker is uncertain or confident, whether a statement is sincere or sarcastic.

When tone of voice and the meaning of words conflict, people "believe" the tone of voice. If you respond to your friends' "How are you?" with the words "I'm dying, and you?" most of your friends will reply "Fine." If the tone of your voice is cheerful, they may not hear the content of the words.

Pitch measures whether a voice uses sounds that are low or high. Low-pitched voices are usually perceived as being more authoritative, sexier, and more pleasant to listen to than are high-pitched voices. Most voices go up in pitch when the speaker is angry or excited; some people raise pitch when they increase volume. Women whose normal speaking voices are high may need to practice projecting their voices to avoid becoming shrill when they speak to large groups.

Stress is the emphasis given to one or more words in a sentence. As the following example shows, emphasizing different words can change the meaning.

I'll give you a raise.

[Implication, depending on pitch and speed: "Another supervisor wouldn't" or "I have the power to determine your salary."]

Deep Voice Politics

"[Political candidates'] vocal chords—as much as the substance of their words—can influence who becomes the next president, claim the people who study, measure, and coach the human voice.

"'Voice matters—it's what sells,' says John Daly, a University of Texas communications professor who has written a book about persuasion. University of California at Los Angeles psychology professor Albert Mehrabian even claims to have quantified how important a voice is. When we are deciding whether we like the person delivering a message, tone of voice accounts for 38% of our opinion, body language for 55%, and the actual words for just 7%, his studies suggest."

Do you believe that your impressions of public speakers are shaped by vocal tones?

Quoted from June Kronholz, "Talk Is Cheap in Politics, but a Deep Voice Helps," *Wall Street Journal*, November 3, 2007, A1.

LIE through the Q&A

Communication consultant Michael Sheehan argues that the question-and-answer session after a presentation is no time to relax. He asserts that presenters should remain on the offense throughout this part of a presentation, always be ready for the unexpected, and practice as much as possible beforehand.

He also offers a short acronym to help speakers: LIE. The "L" stands for *listening* to the entire question before answering. The "I" stands for the ability to *identify* whether a succinct or more in-depth answer will be best. And finally, the "E" stands for *enhance*. Sheehan suggests that speakers should enhance their answers by leaving the audience with something memorable such as a metaphor or anecdote.

Adapted from Julia Kirby and Michael Sheehan, "Stay on the Q&A Offensive," *Harvard Business Review* 85, no. 4 (2007): 25.

ways to consider that matter. The way you just mentioned—and a way that starts from a slightly different base." Then Senator Simon would politely explain his point of view. This kind of response respects the questioner by leaving room for more than one viewpoint.[19]

Occasionally someone will ask a question that is really designed to state the speaker's own position. Respond to the question if you want to. Another option is to say, "I'm not sure what you're asking," or even, "That's a clear statement of your position. Let's move to the next question now." If someone asks about something that you already explained in your presentation, simply answer the question without embarrassing the questioner. No audience will understand and remember 100% of what you say.

If you don't know the answer to a question, say so. If your purpose is to inform, write down the question so that you can look up the answer before the next session. If it's a question to which you think there is no answer, ask if anyone in the room knows. When no one does, your "ignorance" is vindicated. If an expert is in the room, you may want to refer questions of fact to him or her. Answer questions of interpretation yourself.

At the end of the question period, take two minutes to summarize your main point once more. (This can be a restatement of your close.) Questions may or may not focus on the key point of your talk. Take advantage of having the floor to repeat your message briefly and forcefully.

Making Group Presentations

Plan carefully to involve as many members of the group as possible in speaking roles.

The easiest way to make a group presentation is to outline the presentation and then divide the topics, giving one to each group member. Another member can be responsible for the opener and the close. During the question period, each member answers questions that relate to his or her topic.

In this kind of divided presentation, be sure to

- Plan transitions.
- Enforce time limits strictly.
- Coordinate your visuals so that the presentation seems a coherent whole.
- Practice the presentation as a group at least once; more is better.

Some group presentations are even more fully integrated: the group writes a very detailed outline, chooses points and examples, and creates visuals together. Then, within each point, voices trade off. This presentation is effective because each voice speaks only a minute or two before a new voice comes in. However, it works only when all group members know the subject well and when the group plans carefully and practices extensively.

Whatever form of group presentation you use, be sure to introduce each member of the team to the audience and to pay close attention to each other. If other members of the team seem uninterested in the speaker, the audience gets the sense that that speaker isn't worth listening to.

Summary of Key Points

- **Informative presentations** inform or teach the audience. **Persuasive presentations** motivate the audience to act or to believe. **Goodwill presentations** entertain and validate the audience. Most oral presentations have more than one purpose.

- A written message makes it easier to present extensive or complex information and to minimize undesirable emotions. Oral messages make it easier to use emotion, to focus the audience's attention, to answer questions and resolve conflicts quickly, to modify a proposal that may not be acceptable in its original form, and to get immediate action or response.

- In both oral and written messages, you should
  - Adapt the message to the specific audience.
  - Show the audience how they benefit from the idea, policy, service, or product.
  - Overcome any objections the audience may have.
  - Use you-attitude and positive emphasis.
  - Use visuals to clarify or emphasize material.
  - Specify exactly what the audience should do.

- An oral presentation needs to be simpler than a written message to the same audience.

- In a **monologue presentation,** the speaker plans the presentation in advance and delivers it without deviation. In a **guided discussion,** the speaker presents the questions or issues that both speaker and audience have agreed on in advance. Rather than functioning as an expert with all the answers, the speaker serves as a facilitator to help the audience tap its own knowledge. An **interactive presentation** is a conversation using questions to determine needs, probe objections, and gain provisional and then final commitment to the objective.

- Adapt your message to your audience's beliefs, experiences, and interests.

- Use the beginning and end of the presentation to interest the audience and emphasize your key point.

- Use visuals to seem more prepared, more interesting, and more persuasive.

- Limit your talk to three main points. Early in your talk—perhaps immediately after your opener—provide an overview of the main points you will make. Offer a clear signpost as you come to each new point. A **signpost** is an explicit statement of the point you have reached.

- To calm your nerves as you prepare to give an oral presentation,
  - Be prepared. Analyze your audience, organize your thoughts, prepare visual aids, practice your opener and close, check out the arrangements.
  - Use only the amount of caffeine you normally use. Avoid alcoholic beverages.
  - Relabel your nerves. Instead of saying, "I'm scared," try saying, "My adrenaline is up." Adrenaline sharpens our reflexes and helps us do our best.

- During your presentation,
  - Pause and look at the audience before you begin speaking.
  - Concentrate on communicating, not your feelings.
  - Use body energy in strong gestures and movement.

- Convey a sense of caring to your audience by making direct eye contact with them and by using a conversational style.

- Treat questions as opportunities to give more detailed information than you had time to give in your presentation. Link your answers to the points you made in your presentation.

- Repeat the question before you answer it if the audience may not have heard it or if you want more time to think. Rephrase hostile or biased questions before you answer them.

Giving Feedback

Getting feedback from peers is one important part of preparing a presentation, and speakers can't get good feedback without peers who can give good feedback.

Too often peers comment just on simple things, like word choice or body posture, but the most important feedback is frequently about content. Help the speaker adapt their material to the audience by asking questions about the people they expect to address. Also, summarize the presenter's message as you understand it, and repeat it back. Doing so can help your presenter see where they need to clarify.

No one likes to be criticized, so phrase your critiques in positive terms. Point out changes or suggestions that will make their presentation better, and if you can, back up your advice with tips from professionals.

Think about the way you prepare your own presentations. Do you practice them in front of an audience? What kind of feedback do you get? How could you encourage a practice audience to give you more helpful advice?

Adapted from Kinley Levack, "Talking Head to Rock Star: How You Can Turn Your Top Executives into Polished Presenters," *Successful Meetings* 55, no.13 (December 2006): 28–33.

CHAPTER 10   # Exercises and Problems

10.1   Reviewing the Chapter

1. What are four major components of planning effective presentations? (LO 1)
2. What are four different kinds of presentation openers you can use? (LO 1)
3. Name 10 guidelines for creating effective visuals. (LO 1)
4. What are some major criteria for choosing the information for your presentation? (LO 2)

5. Provide a suitable topic for each of the five common patterns of organization for presentations. (LO 2)
6. What are some ways to deal with the common fear of public speaking? Which ways would work for you? (LO 3)
7. List some pointers for effectively handling questions during presentations. (LO 4)

10.2   Analyzing Openers and Closes

The following openers and closes came from class presentations on information interviews.

- Does each opener make you interested in hearing the rest of the presentation?
- Does each opener provide a transition to the overview?
- Does the close end the presentation in a satisfying way?

a. Opener: I interviewed Mark Perry at AT&T.

    Close: Well, that's my report.

b. Opener: How many of you know what you want to do when you graduate?

    Close: So, if you like numbers and want to travel, think about being a CPA. Ernst & Young can take you all over the world.

c. Opener: You don't have to know anything about computer programming to get a job as a technical writer at CompuServe.

    Close: After talking to Raj, I decided technical writing isn't for me. But it is a good career if you work well under pressure and like learning new things all the time.

d. Opener: My report is about what it's like to work in an advertising agency.

    Middle: They keep really tight security; I had to wear a badge and be escorted to Susan's desk.

    Close: Susan gave me samples of the agency's ads and even a sample of a new soft drink she's developing a campaign for. But she didn't let me keep the badge.

10.3   Developing Points of Interest

One of the keys to preparing an engaging presentation is finding interesting points to share with your audience, either in the form of personal anecdotes to create rapport and build goodwill, or in the form of interesting facts and figures to establish your ethos as a presenter. For each of the following topics, prepare one personal anecdote based on your own experience, and research one interesting fact to share with your audience.

1. Why people need to plan.
2. Dealing with change.
3. The importance of lifelong learning.

4. The importance of effective communication.
5. The value of good customer service.
6. The value of listening.

As your instructor directs,

a. Share your points of interest with a small group of students, and critique each other's work.
b. Turn in your stories in a memo to your instructor.
c. Make a short (1–2 minute) oral presentation featuring your story and fact(s) for one of the assignment topics.

10.4   Evaluating PowerPoint Slides

Evaluate the following drafts of PowerPoint slides.

- Are the slides' background appropriate for the topic?
- Do the slides use words or phrases rather than complete sentences?

- Is the font big enough to read from a distance?
- Is the art relevant and appropriate?
- Is each slide free from errors?

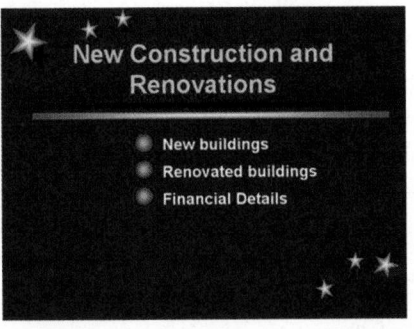

a(1)

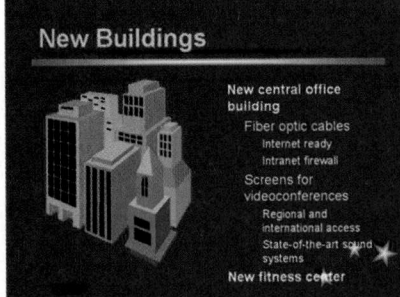

a(2)

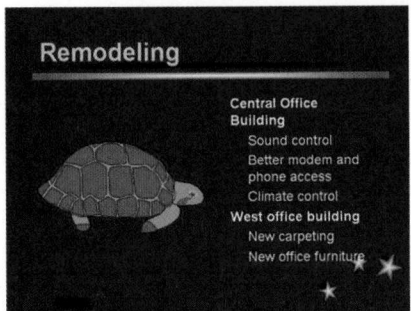

a(3)

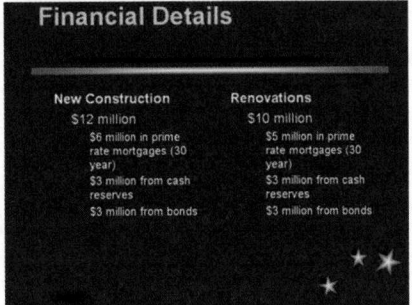

a(4)

b(1)

b(2)

b(3)

b(4)

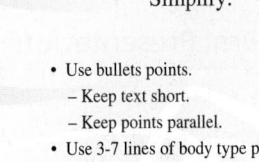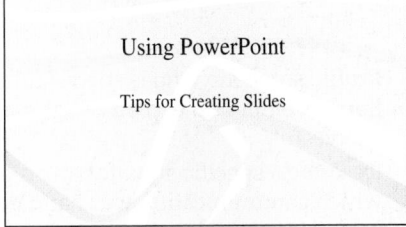

c(1)

c(2)

c(3)

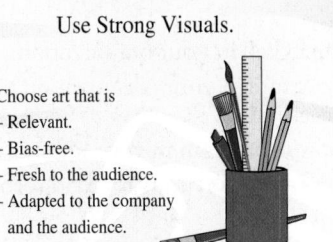

c(4)

10.5   Evaluating Speakers

Attend a lecture or public presentation on your campus. While the speaker is presenting, don't focus on the content of the message. Instead, focus only on his/her speaking ability and take notes. Pay attention to the speaker's abilities to deal with fear, use eye contact with the audience, and project a clear speaking voice. In addition, notice how the speaker stands and gestures, uses notes and visuals, and handles questions.

As your instructor directs,

a. Deliver your findings to the rest of the class in a short 2–4 minute presentation.

b. Write a memo to your instructor that discusses the presenter's speaking abilities, and how, if at all, they can be improved.

10.6   Evaluating the Way a Speaker Handles Questions

Listen to a speaker talking about a controversial subject. (Go to a talk on campus or in town, or watch a speaker on a TV show like *Face the Nation* or *60 Minutes*.) Observe the way he or she handles questions.

- About how many questions does the speaker answer?
- What is the format for asking and answering questions?
- Are the answers clear? responsive to the question? something that could be quoted without embarrassing the speaker and the organization he or she represents?
- How does the speaker handle hostile questions? Does the speaker avoid getting angry? Does the speaker retain control of the meeting? How?

- If some questions were not answered well, what (if anything) could the speaker have done to leave a better impression?
- Did the answers leave the audience with a more or less positive impression of the speaker? Why?

As your instructor directs,

a. Share your evaluation with a small group of students.

b. Present your evaluation formally to the class.

c. Summarize your evaluation in a memo to your instructor.

10.7   Presenting the News

Research a hot business communication topic from the news (ethics, the economy, job layoffs, toy safety recalls, etc.). Find at least 3–5 sources for your topic. Then, make a short (2–3 minute) presentation where you share your findings with the class. Your presentation should invoke some effective communication strategies you learned in this course by discussing how the situation could have been handled more effectively.

As your instructor directs,

a. Deliver your presentation to the class.

b. Turn in a listing of your sources in APA or MLA format.

c. Write a memo to your instructor that discusses the situation and explains how business communication principles would have helped improve the situation.

10.8   Making a Short Oral Presentation

As your instructor directs,

Make a short (3–5 minute) presentation with PowerPoint slides on one of the following topics:

1. Explain how what you've learned in classes, in campus activities, or at work will be useful to the employer who hires you after graduation.
2. Describe your boss's management style.
3. Describe how your co-workers employ teamwork on the job.
4. Explain a "best-practice" in your organization.
5. Explain what a new hire in your organization needs to know to be successful.
6. Tell your boss about a problem in your unit.
7. Make a presentation to raise funds for a nonprofit organization.

8. Profile someone who is successful in the field you hope to enter and explain what makes him or her successful.
9. Describe a specific situation in an organization in which communication was handled well or badly.
10. Explain one of the challenges (e.g., technology, ethics, international competition) that the field you plan to enter is facing.
11. Profile a company that you would like to work for and explain why you think it would make a good employer.
12. Share the results of an information interview.
13. Share some advice for students currently on the job market.
14. Explain your job interview strategy.

10.9   Making a Longer Oral Presentation

As your instructor directs,

Make a 5- to 12-minute presentation on one of the following. Use visuals to make your talk effective.

1. Persuade your supervisor to make a change that will benefit the organization.
2. Persuade your organization to make a change that will improve the organization's image in the community.
3. Describe the communication process of a person you've interviewed who is working in the field you plan to enter.
4. Evaluate a business document.
5. Evaluate the design of a corporate Web page.
6. Present a Web page you have designed.
7. Analyze rejection letters that students on your campus have received.
8. Persuade an organization on your campus to make a change.
9. Analyze international messages that your workplace has created or received.
10. Present the results of a survey you conduct.
11. Research an organization you would like to work for.
12. Persuade classmates to donate time or money to a charitable organization.

10.10   Watching Yourself

One of the best ways to improve your presentation skills is to watch yourself present. After you have prepared a presentation on one of the topics listed in exercise 10.8 or 10.9, check out a video camera from your school's media resource center and record your presentation. You should then review your presentation, noting what you did well and what you could improve.

As your instructor directs,

a. Write a two-page memo that discusses your strengths and weaknesses as a presenter. Address how you could improve your weaknesses.
b. Prepare a brief (two-minute) oral summation for your peers about your strengths and weaknesses.
c. Record the presentation a second time to see if you have improved some of your weaknesses.

10.11   Making a Group Oral Presentation

As your instructor directs,

Make an 8- to 12-minute presentation on one of the following. Use visuals to make your talk effective.

1. Explain the role of communication in one or more organizations.
2. Create and present a fund-raising strategy for a nonprofit organization.
3. Report on the nonverbal customs of another country.
4. Report on the written communication styles of another country.
5. Report on the business outlook of another country.
6. Analyze print business materials of an organization and present your findings to the class.
7. Interview the employees of an organization about their teamwork strategies and present the information to the class.
8. Interview an employee about his/her routine communication practices and present your findings to the class.

10.12   Evaluating Oral Presentations

Evaluate an oral presentation given by a classmate or a speaker on your campus. Use the following categories:

Strategy

1. Choosing an effective kind of presentation for the situation.
2. Adapting ideas to audience's beliefs, experiences, and interests.
3. Using a strong opening and close.
4. Using visual aids or other devices to involve audience.

Content

5. Providing a clear, unifying purpose.
6. Using specific, vivid supporting material and language.
7. Providing rebuttals to counterclaims or objections.

Organization

8. Providing an overview of main points.
9. Signposting main points in body of talk.
10. Providing adequate transitions between points and speakers.

Visuals

11. Using an appropriate design or template.
12. Using standard edited English.
13. Being creative.

Delivery

14. Making direct eye contact with audience.
15. Using voice effectively.
16. Using gestures effectively.

17. Handling questions effectively.
18. Positioning (not blocking screen)

As your instructor directs,

a. Fill out a form indicating your evaluation in each of the areas.
b. Share your evaluation orally with the speaker.
c. Write a memo to the speaker evaluating the presentation. Send a copy of your memo to your instructor.

10.13   Evaluating Team Presentations

Evaluate team presentations using the following questions:

1. How thoroughly were all group members involved?
2. Did members of the team introduce themselves or each other?
3. Did team members seem interested in what their teammates said?
4. How well was the material organized?
5. How well did the material hold your interest?
6. How clear did the material seem to you?
7. How effective were the visuals?

8. How well did the team handle questions?
9. What could be done to improve the presentation?
10. What were the strong points of the presentation?

As your instructor directs,

a. Fill out a form indicating your evaluation in each of the areas.
b. Share your evaluation orally with the team.
c. Write a memo to the team evaluating the presentation. Send a copy of your memo to your instructor.

10.14   All-Weather Case: Preparing and Presenting All-Weather's Values Statement

All-Weather's president has asked Doug to prepare a values statement for the company. "I don't want this statement to be just printed, laminated, framed, and hung in an office, or included in an employee manual to be only occasionally noticed," the president says, answering Doug's question about what kind of statement he was looking for. "I want this statement to be fully understood, appreciated, and internalized by our employees."

"Shouldn't marketing be doing this, Mark?" Doug says, reminding Mark Chambers, his boss and All-Weather's president, of his former department when he was VP of marketing.

"No, Doug, I believe that it's HR's call," Mark says, pausing a moment, "because HR has a better pulse on the values of all our employees. However, I do have five keywords around which I want the statement to be built. They are efficiency, strength, beauty, perfection, and unity. To give you an example of how these words could be combined for a values statement, we might say, for example, that I see All-Weather as an energy-efficient company that builds strong and beautiful products through perfect application of human and material resources and unity across different functions and departments."

"There, that's a good one right there," Doug says, trying to mentally repeat the statement coined by Mark.

"It's too lengthy and a bit pedantic, Doug," Mark says, looking at the writing pad on which he has scribbled the statement. "I want a values statement that our employees can instantly relate to and remember. It need not be, probably should not be, a long sentence. It could take the form of a visual, along with a caption; or it could cleverly employ metaphors as words and images. Whatever form it takes, let the values statement be a crisp, creative, and memorable reminder of what we as a company believe in."

"That's some task, Mark," Doug says, feeling delighted at having been chosen to work on the statement yet putting the company's interests first. "Shouldn't we be turning to professionals?"

"Good point, Doug," Mark says, appreciating Doug's sentiments, "but they wouldn't understand us as well as we understand ourselves."

"I see your point," Doug says, getting up. "We'll do our best."

"I'm confident of that," Mark says, shaking Doug's hand.

After returning to his office, Doug summons Caleb, Erin, and Miguel to discuss how to go about preparing the company's values statement. The three managers propose that two of their deputies—Tanner and Linda—work on the task together, a recommendation that Doug approves. It's also decided that Tanner and Linda will give a Power-Point presentation (or some other form of presentation that they think is suitable) displaying the values statement.

Based on your reading of Chapter 10, information presented above, and your knowledge of All-Weather, help Tanner and Linda prepare All-Weather's values statement. Feel free to be creative with visuals and metaphors as you prepare the values statement. Then, prepare a brief presentation that communicates the statement to All-Weather's employees. You may use PowerPoint or some other presentation strategy that you think effectively communicates the statement.

Building Résumés

Chapter Outline

A Time Line for Job Hunting

Evaluating Your Strengths and Interests

Using the Internet in Your Job Search

How Employers Use Résumés

Guidelines for Résumés

- Length
- Emphasis
- Details
- Writing Style
- Layout and Design

Kinds of Résumés

What to Include in a Résumé

- Name and Contact Information
- Career Objective
- Summary of Qualifications
- Education
- Honors and Awards
- Experience
- Other Skills
- Activities
- Portfolio

References

What Not to Include in a Résumé

Dealing with Difficulties

- "All My Experience Is in My Family's Business."
- "I've Been Out of the Job Market for a While."
- "I Want to Change Fields."
- "I Was Fired."
- "I Was Laid Off."
- "I Don't Have Any Experience."

Electronic Résumés

- Creating a Scannable Résumé
- Using Keywords
- Sending Your Résumé Electronically
- Posting Your Résumé on the Web

A Caution about Blogs and Social Networking Sites

Honesty

Summary of Key Points

Cooking Up a Job

The catch phrases "Bam" and "Kick it up a notch!" are now familiar among cooking fans and conjure images of a famous chef adding dashes of garlic and essence. Emeril Lagasse, chef, restauranteur, and television personality, has created a unique niche for himself in the food world through sheer creativity and astute entrepreneurship. But he also has good "ingredients" for finding the right job.

Have the right ingredients for success: When Emeril replaced Paul Prudhomme as executive chef of the famed New Orleans restaurant Commander's Palace, Ella Brennan, the co-owner of the restaurant, asked what he thought of the kitchen. He replied, "Smells just like my mom's kitchen!" His sense of humor, enthusiasm, integrity, and energy got him the job and made him one of the youngest executive chefs in the food industry at the age of 23!

Believe in your choices: Cooking was not Emeril's only forte; he was also good at music. In fact his musical talents gained him a full scholarship to the New England Conservatory. However, when making a choice between free education and an expensive college experience, Emeril followed his heart and chose cooking. He faced severe opposition from his family, but he stuck to his resolve.

Turn a challenge into your advantage: "Life just doesn't hand you things. You have to go out there and make things happen. . .that's the exciting part," says Emeril. When his acting stint in *How to Boil Water* did not work out, he decided to just be himself and hosted *EmerilLive* and *Essence of Emeril*, which led him to celebrity status.

"His sense of humor, enthusiasm, integrity, and energy got him the job."

Make a profession out of passion: Emeril's success hinges on his passion for cooking. He recalls his childhood, "Our family revolved around the kitchen and eating and cooking together. It was then that I learned how happy food can make people." This observation—food can make people happy—became his guiding principle.

Source: Marcia Layton Turner, *Emeril: Inside the Amazing Success of Today's Most Popular Chef* (Hoboken, NJ: John Wiley, 2004).

Learning Objectives

After studying this chapter, you will know how to:

1   Prepare a detailed time line for your job search.

2   Prepare a résumé that makes you look attractive to employers.

3   Deal with common difficulties that arise during job searches.

4   Handle the online portion of job searches.

5   Keep your résumé honest.

A **résumé** is a persuasive summary of your qualifications for employment. If you're on the job market, having a résumé is a basic step in the job hunt. When you're employed, having an up-to-date résumé makes it easier to take advantage of opportunities that may come up for an even better job. If you're several years away from job hunting, preparing a résumé now will help you become more conscious of what to do in the next two or three years to make yourself an attractive candidate.

This chapter covers paper, Web, and scannable résumés. Job application letters (sometimes called cover letters) are discussed in Chapter 12. Chapter 13 discusses interviews and communications after the interview. All three chapters focus on job hunting in the United States. Conventions, expectations, and criteria differ from culture to culture: different norms apply in different countries.

All job communications should be tailored to your unique qualifications and the specifications of the job you want. Adopt the wording or layout of an example if it's relevant to your own situation, but don't be locked into the forms in this book. You've got different strengths; your résumé will be different, too.

A Time Line for Job Hunting

Many employers consider the way you do your job hunt to be evidence of the way you will work for them. Therefore, you should start preparing yourself several years ahead of your formal applications. Informal preparation for job hunting should start soon after you arrive on campus. Check out the services of your college placement and advising offices. Join extracurricular organizations on campus and in the community to increase your knowledge and provide a network for learning about jobs. Find a job that gives you experience. Note which courses you like—and why you like them. If you like thinking and learning about a subject, you're more likely to enjoy a job in that field. Select course projects and paper topics that will help you prepare for a job—and look good on your résumé.

Once you have selected a major, start reading job ads, particularly those posted on your professional organization's Web site. What kinds of jobs are available? Do you need to change your course selections to better fit them? What kinds of extras are employers seeking? Do they want communication skills? Spreadsheet familiarity? Extra statistics courses? International experience? Learn this information early while you still have time to add to the knowledge and skill sets you are acquiring. Attend job seminars and job fairs. Join your professional association and its listserv.

Formal preparation for job hunting should begin a full year *before you begin interviewing*. Enroll for the services of your campus placement office. Ask friends who are on the job market about their experiences in interviews; find out what kinds of job offers they get. Check into the possibility of getting an internship or a co-op job that will give you relevant experience before you interview.

The year you interview, register with your Placement Office early. An active job search takes significant chunks of time, so plan accordingly. If you plan to graduate in the spring, prepare your résumé and plan your interview strategy early in the fall. Initial campus interviews occur from October to February for May or June graduation. In January or February, write to any organization you'd like to work for that hasn't interviewed on campus. From February to April, you're likely to visit one or more offices for a second interview.

Try to have a job offer lined up *before* you get the degree. People who don't need jobs immediately are more confident in interviews and usually get better job offers. If you have to job-hunt after graduation, plan to spend at least 30 hours a week on your job search. The time will pay off in a better job that you find more quickly.

Evaluating Your Strengths and Interests

A self-assessment is the first step in producing a good résumé. Each person could do several jobs happily. Richard Bolles, a nationally recognized expert in career advising for over a third of a century and author of the *What Color Is Your Parachute* books, says most people who don't find a job they like fail because they lack information about themselves.[1] Personality and aptitude tests can tell you what your strengths are, but they won't say, "You should be a ———." You'll still need to answer questions like these:

- What skills and strengths do you have?
- What achievements have given you the most satisfaction? *Why* did you enjoy them?
- What work conditions do you like? Would you rather have firm deadlines or a flexible schedule? Do you prefer working independently or with other people? Do you prefer specific instructions and standards for evaluation or freedom and uncertainty? How comfortable are you with pressure? How much challenge do you want?
- What kind of work/life balance do you want? Are you willing to take work home? To work weekends? To travel? How important is money to you? Prestige? Time to spend with family and friends?
- How fast do you want to move up? Are you willing to pay your dues for several years before you are promoted?
- Where do you want to live? What features in terms of weather, geography, cultural and social life do you see as ideal?
- Is it important to you that your work achieve certain purposes or values, or do you see work as just a way to make a living? Are the organization's culture and ethical standards important to you?

Once you know what is most important to you, analyze the job market to see where you could find what you want. For example, Peter's greatest interest is athletics, but he isn't good enough for the pros. Studying the job market might suggest several alternatives. He could teach sports and physical fitness as a high school coach or a corporate fitness director. He could cover sports for a newspaper, a magazine, or a TV station. He could go into management or sales for a professional sports team, a health club, or a company that sells

What Employers Want, I

You can increase your odds of getting an interview by understanding what hiring managers are thinking while they evaluate your résumé. The following are questions managers ask themselves:

Can this applicant fill the needs of the company? Your résumé should stress all of your most relevant skills and experience which match the position opening. Rather than submitting a generic résumé for every position you apply for, create a customized résumé based on your review of the job opening.

Will this applicant stay with the company long-term? Managers seek employees who are most likely to stay with a company long-term because the hiring process is long, difficult, and costly. The cost of replacing an employee averages $13,355 according to a study conducted by the Employment Policy Foundation. To avoid costly turnover, managers look at your résumé to see if you have a stable work history.

Will this applicant be professional? Your résumé represents your ability to communicate. Unfortunately, managers will eliminate résumés for the slightest problems since they may receive hundreds of résumés for one position. Make sure your résumé is easy to follow and does not contain typos or grammatical mistakes.

Employers are also looking for your dedication to your profession. To illustrate your professional interests, include related professional associations that you have joined, certificates you possess, or professional seminars you have taken.

Adapted from Robert Half International, "What Employers Think When They Read Your Résumé," in *Career Advice: Job Search*, http://www.careerbuilder.com/Article/CB-427-Cover-Letters-and-Resumes-What-Employers-Think-When-They-Read-Your-R%c3%a9sum%c3%a9/ (accessed March 13, 2009).

What Employers Want, II

Careerbuilder.com asked hiring managers what the top five attributes are when they hire new graduates.

1. **Relevant experience:** Managers look for a candidate's ability to make his/her job experience relevant to the company—and find this ability lacking. Most managers say they view volunteer activities as relevant experience.

2. **Professionalism during the interview:** Managers want to see candidates who dress professionally, who have researched the company, and who are prepared to answer standard interview questions.

3. **Fit within the company culture:** Managers want candidates whose personalities and work styles fit well.

4. **Education:** Managers consider the school, degree, major, GPA, and relevant courses.

5. **Enthusiasm:** Managers want candidates who are clearly interested in the job and show the energy they would bring to their work.

Adapted from Laura Morsch, "Five Must-Haves for New Grads," in *Advice & Resources: Articles,* http://careerbuilder.com/Article/CB-418-Job-Search-Five-Must-Haves-for-New-Grads/ (accessed March 13, 2009).

sports equipment. Each possibility will require somewhat different training and course selection, underscoring the need for Peter to begin considering his job search process early in his college career.

Using the Internet in Your Job Search

As the Internet gains in importance for finding information, it becomes a crucial tool for job seekers as well as employers. According to a survey of over 3,000 hirers cited in the *Wall Street Journal,* more employers intend to increase their hiring budget in 2009 for online recruitment sites than for any other recruitment tool.[2]

Probably the most common use of the Internet for job candidates is to search for openings. In addition to popular sites like Monster and CareerBuilder, job candidates typically check electronic listings in local newspapers and professional societies. However, you do need to be careful when responding to online ads. Some of them turn out to be pitches from career or financial services firms, or even phishing ads—ploys from identity thieves seeking your personal information.

Phishing ads often look like real postings; many have company names and logos nearly identical to those of real employers. People behind phishing ads may even e-mail job candidates to build up trust. Even the *Wall Street Journal* is warning its readers to be careful. Privacy experts caution job candidates to be particularly careful with job postings that lack details about the hiring company or job description, and ads that list a large salary range.[3]

In addition to searching for ads, every job candidate should check the Internet for information about writing résumés and application letters, researching specific companies and jobs, and preparing for interviews. Many comprehensive sites give detailed information that will help you produce more effective documents and be a better-prepared job candidate.

As you search the Web, remember that not all sites are current and accurate. In particular, be careful of .com sites: some are good, others are not. Check your school's career site for help. Check the sites of other schools: Stanford and Berkeley have particularly excellent career sites. And even good sources can have advice that is bad for you. When advice conflicts—and it will—choose the advice which is best for you. Figure 11.1 lists some of the best sites.

Figure 11.1　Comprehensive Web Job Sites Covering the Entire Job Search Process

America's Job Bank	Monster.com
www.jobbankinfo.org	www.monster.com
Campus Career Center	MonsterTrak
www.campuscareercenter.com	www.monstertrak.monster.com
CareerBuilder	Quintessential Careers
www.careerbuilder.com	www.quintcareers.com
College Central	The Riley Guide
www.collegecentral.com	www.rileyguide.com
College Grad Job Hunter	The Rockport Institute
www.collegegrad.com	www.rockportinstitute.com
The Five O'Clock Club	Spherion Career Center
www.fiveoclockclub.com	www.spherion.com/corporate/ret-registered.jsp
JobHuntersBible.com (Dick Bolles)	Snag a Job
www.jobhuntersbible.com	www.snagajob.com
JobStar Central	
http://jobstar.org	

Figure 11.2   Employers Rate the Importance of Specific Qualities/Skills

Quality/Skill	Rating
Communication skills	4.6
Strong work ethic	4.6
Teamwork skills	4.5
Initiative	4.4
Interpersonal skills	4.4
Problem-solving skills	4.4
Analytical skills	4.3
Flexibility/adaptability	4.2
Computer skills	4.1
Technical skills	4.1
Detail-oriented	4.0
Organizational skills	4.0

(5-point-scale where 1 = not important; 2 = not very important; 3 = somewhat important; 4 = very important; and 5 = extremely important)

Source: Chart from Andrea Koncz, "'Perfect' Job Candidate Pairs Communication Skills with Strong Work Ethic," in *National Association of Colleges and Employers: Press Releases,* http://www.naceweb.org/press/display .asp?year=&prid=270#1.

Play Safe

Before posting your job application online, you should verify the site is safe. Here are some criteria:

1. **Have you heard of the site?** If not, be careful. Look for online reviews of the site.

2. **Does it ask you to register before you can search for jobs?** This is a big red flag. Try a different site.

3. **Does it have a comprehensive privacy policy?** Read the policy to see if they sell or rent your information. Putting up your job packet on a nonprivate forum could affect your identity in the future. Do not assume the site is protected if it has a privacy seal—check if the seal is valid and click it to make sure the link opens a Web page from the privacy seal's domain.

4. **Can you limit access to your personal contact information?** Good sites allow you to protect this information.

5. **Does it let you delete your résumé after you get a job?** Safe Web sites should allow you to delete your documents or make them inactive while you are not conducting a job search. You don't want your new boss to think you are still on the job market for an even better position.

Adapted from Susan Joyce, "15 Critical Criteria for Choosing the Best Job Site for You," in *Job-Hunt: Job Search Advice,* http://www.job-hunt. org/choosing.shtml (accessed on March 20, 2009).

A relatively new use of the Internet for job searchers in online job fairs. At online fairs, you can browse through virtual booths, leave your résumé at promising ones, and sometimes even apply on the spot, all without leaving your home. Other advantages of online job fairs are their wide geographic and 24-hour access.

How Employers Use Résumés

Understanding how employers use résumés will help you create a résumé that works for you.

1. **Employers use résumés to decide whom to interview.** See Figure 11.2. (The major exceptions are on-campus interviews, where the campus placement office has policies that determine who meets with the interviewer.) Since résumés are used to screen out applicants, omit anything that may create a negative impression.

2. **Résumés are scanned or skimmed.** At many companies, résumés are scanned electronically. Only résumés that match keywords are skimmed by a human being. A human may give a résumé 3 to 30 seconds before deciding to keep or toss it. You must design your résumé to pass both the "scan test" and the "skim test" by emphasizing crucial qualifications.

3. **Employers assume that your letter and résumé represent your best work.** Neatness, accuracy, and freedom from typographical errors are essential.

4. **Interviewers usually reread your résumé before the interview to refresh their memories.** Be ready to offer fuller details about everything on your résumé.

5. **After an employer has chosen an applicant, he or she submits the applicant's résumé to people in the organization who must approve the appointment.** These people may have different backgrounds and areas of expertise. Spell out acronyms. Explain awards, Greek-letter honor societies, unusual job titles, or organizations that may be unfamiliar to the reader.

What Employers Want, III

According to the National Association of Colleges and Employers' Job Outlook 2009 Survey of almost 1,200 organizations, employers want it all in a tight employment market.

• Almost 70% screen candidates by GPA, with a 3.0 being the cutoff.

• Among skills and attributes, employers seek communication and teamwork skills, as well as initiative and a strong work ethic. They also look for evidence of leadership experience.

• Relevant work experience is desired by over three-quarters of employers. They also consider internships and co-op assignments.

Although this list is certainly not new, in a tight market employers can find people who demonstrate all the desired qualities.

How do you measure up?

Adapted from Andrea Koncz, "Employers Cite Qualities, Attributes of 'Perfect' Job Candidate," in *National Association of Colleges and Employers: Press Releases*, http://www.naceweb.org/press/display.asp?year=2009&prid=295 (accessed March 13, 2009).

Guidelines for Résumés

Writing a résumé is not an exact science. What makes your friend look good does not necessarily help you. If your skills are in great demand, you can violate every guideline here and still get a good job. But when you must compete against many applicants, these guidelines will help you look as good on paper as you are in person.

Length

A one-page résumé is sufficient, but do fill the page. Less than a full page suggests that you do not have very much to say for yourself.

If you have more good material than will fit on one page, use a second page. It is a myth that all résumés must fit on one page. According to surveys conducted by international staffing firm Accountemps of managers at the 1,000 largest companies in this country, approval of the one-page résumé is dropping. Ten years ago only 28% said one page was the ideal length; now the percentage has dropped to 7%.[4] An experiment that mailed one- or two-page résumés to recruiters at major accounting firms showed that even readers who said they preferred short résumés were more likely to want to interview the candidate with the longer résumé.[5] The longer résumé gives managers a better picture of how you will fit in.

If you do use more than one page, the second page should have at least 10 to 12 lines. Use a second sheet of paper; do not print on the back of the first page. Leave less important information for the second page. Put your name and "Page 2" on the page. If the pages are separated, you want the reader to know whom the qualifications belong to and that the second page is not your whole résumé.

Emphasis

Emphasize the things you've done that (a) are most relevant to the position for which you're applying, (b) show your superiority to other applicants, and (c) are recent.

Show that you're qualified by giving relevant details on course projects, activities, and jobs where you've done similar work. Be brief about low-level jobs that simply show dependability. To prove that you're the best candidate for the job, emphasize items that set you apart from other applicants: promotions, honors, achievements, experience with computers or other relevant equipment, foreign languages, and so on.

If you're getting a two-year or a four-year degree, you should generally omit high school jobs, activities, and honors unless they are particularly relevant to a specific job, you need them to show geographic flexibility, or you need them to fill the page. Focus on achievements in the last three to five years. Whatever your age at the time you write a résumé, you want to suggest that you are now the best you've ever been.

Include full-time work after high school before you entered college and work during college to support yourself or to earn expenses. If the jobs you held then were low-level ones, present them briefly or combine them:

> 2006–10 Part-time and full-time jobs to finance education

You can emphasize material by putting it at the top or the bottom of a page, by giving it more space, and by setting it off with white space. The beginning and end—of a document, a page, a list—are positions of emphasis. When you have a choice (e.g., in a list of job duties), put less important material in the middle, not at the end, to avoid the impression of "fading out." You can also emphasize material by presenting it in a vertical list, by using informative headings, and by providing details.

Details

Details provide evidence to support your claims, convince the reader, and separate you from other applicants. Numbers make good details. Tell how many people you trained or supervised, how much money you budgeted or raised. Describe the interesting aspects of the job you did.

Too vague: Sales Manager, *The Daily Collegian*, University Park, PA, 2008–10. Supervised staff; promoted ad sales.

Good details: Sales Manager, *The Daily Collegian*, University Park, PA, 2008–10. Supervised 22-member sales staff; helped recruit, interview, and select staff; assigned duties and scheduled work; recommended best performers for promotion. Motivated staff to increase paid ad inches 10% over previous year's sales.

Omit details that add nothing to a title, that are less impressive than the title alone, or that suggest a faulty sense of priorities (e.g., listing hours per week spent filing). Either use strong details or just give the office or job title without any details.

Writing Style

Without sacrificing content, be as concise as possible.

Wordy: Member, Meat Judging Team, 2006–07

Member, Meat Judging Team, 2007–08

Member, Meat Judging Team, 2008–09

Captain, Meat Judging Team, 2009–10

Tight: Meat Judging Team, 2006–10; Captain 2009–10

Wordy: Performed foundation load calculations

Tight: Calculated foundation loads

Résumés normally use phrases and sentence fragments. Complete sentences are acceptable if they are the briefest way to present information. To save space and to avoid sounding arrogant, never use *I* in a résumé. *Me* and *my* are acceptable if they are unavoidable or if using them reduces wordiness.

Verbs or gerunds (the *-ing* form of verbs) create a more dynamic image of you than do nouns, so use them on résumés that will be read by people. (Rules for scannable résumés to be read by computers come later in this chapter.) In the following revisions of job responsibilities, nouns, verbs, and gerunds are in bold type:

Nouns: Chair, Income Tax Assistance Committee, Winnipeg, MB, 2009–10. Responsibilities: **recruitment** of volunteers; flyer **design, writing,** and **distribution** for **promotion** of program; **speeches** to various community groups and nursing homes to advertise the service.

Verbs: Chair, Income Tax Assistance Committee, Winnipeg, MB, 2009–10. **Recruited** volunteers for the program. **Designed, wrote,** and **distributed** a flyer to

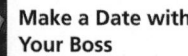
promote the program; **spoke** to various community groups and nursing homes to advertise the service.

Gerunds: Chair, Income Tax Assistance Committee, Winnipeg, MB, 2009–10. Responsibilities included **recruiting** volunteers for the program; **designing, writing,** and **distributing** a flyer to promote the program; and **speaking** to various community groups and nursing homes to advertise the service.

Note that the items in the list must be in parallel structure (p. 197).

Layout and Design

Do not use résumé templates that come with word-processing software. Many employers see so many résumés from these templates that they learn to recognize—and discount— them. Web sites, such as those in Figure 11.1, also offer templates. If you choose to use one, make sure it emphasizes your strongest points. Check for unintended white space: Is the space for experience larger than you filled with your details?

Almost certainly, you can create a better résumé by adapting a basic style you like to your own unique qualifications. Experiment with layout, fonts, and spacing to get an attractive résumé. Consider creating a letterhead that you use for both your résumé and your application letter.

One of the major decisions you will make is how to treat your headings. Do you want them on the left margin, with text immediately below them, as in Figure 11.3? Do you want them alone in the left column, with text in a column to the right, as in Figure 11.5? Would you like them boxed, as in Figure 11.6? Generally, people with more text on their résumés use the first or third option. Putting headings in their own column on the left takes space and thus helps spread a thinner list of accomplishments over the page. But be careful not to make the heading column too wide, or it will make your résumé look unbalanced and empty.

Work with fonts, bullets, and spacing to highlight your information. Do be careful, however, not to make your résumé look "busy" by using too many fonts. Generally three fonts should be the top limit, and you should avoid unusual fonts. Keep fonts readable by using at least 10-point type for large fonts such as Arial and 11-point for smaller fonts such as Times New Roman. Use enough white space to group items and make your résumé easy to read, but not so much that you look as if you're padding.

Use color sparingly, if at all. Colored text and shaded boxes can prevent accurate scanning. Similarly, white 8½- by 11-inch paper is standard, but do use a good-quality paper.

All of these guidelines are much more flexible for people in creative fields such as advertising and design.

Kinds of Résumés

Two basic categories of résumés are chronological and skills. A **chronological résumé** summarizes what you did in a time line (starting with the most recent events, and going backward in **reverse chronology**). It emphasizes degrees, job titles, and dates. It is the traditional résumé format. Figures 11.3 and 11.6 show chronological résumés.

Use a chronological résumé when

- Your education and experience are a logical preparation for the position for which you're applying.
- You have impressive job titles, offices, or honors.

Figure 11.3   A Community College Chronological Résumé to Use for Career Fairs and Internships

Abhishek Ankit
aankit@mcc.edu

Vary font sizes. Use larger size for name and main headings.

Campus Address
1524 Main Street
Boone, IA 50036
515-432-1997

Using both addresses ensures continuous contact information.

Permanent Address
2526 Prairie Lane
Omaha, NE 68235
402-442-7793

Education
Midwest Community College, Des Moines, IA
AA in Financial Management, June 2010
GPA: 3.0/4.0 *Give your grade average if it's 3.0 or higher.*

Summary of Qualifications
Use keywords employers might seek.

- Self-motivated, detail-minded, results-oriented
- Consistently successful track record in sales
- Effectively developed and operated entrepreneurial business

List 3–7 qualifications.

Sales Experience
Financial Sales Representative, ABC Inc., Des Moines, IA, February 2008 – present
- Establish client base
- Develop investment strategy plans for clients
- Research and recommend specific investments

Other Experience
Entrepreneur, A-Plus T-Shirt Company, Omaha, NE, September 2006 – January 2008

One way to handle self-employment.

- Created a saleable product (graphic T-shirts)
- Secured financial support
- Located a manufacturer
- Supervised production
- Sold T-shirts to high school students
- Realized a substantial profit to pay for college expenses

Cook, Hamburger Shack, Omaha, NE, Summers 2005–2006
- Learned sales strategies
- Ensured customer satisfaction
- Worked cooperatively with a team of 25

Collector and Repair Worker, ACN, Inc., Omaha, NE, Summers 2003–2004
- Collected and counted approximately $10,000 a day *Specify large sums of money.*
- Worked with technicians troubleshooting and repairing coin mechanisms

Other Skills
Computer: Outlook, HTML, Excel, Dreamweaver, Frontpage, GoLive
Language: Fluent in Spanish *Many employers appreciate a second language.*

Unconventional Job Searches

In tough economic times, the traditional job search of application, résumé, and maybe a prayer doesn't work. Tough times require different approaches.

Dick Gaither, founder of Job Search Training Systems, recommends some unconventional search techniques:

- "Churchgoers should leave business cards in the pews on Sunday and ask to address the congregation, he says. 'People in church are helpers by nature.'"

- "To identify employers who may be preparing to hire, Mr. Gaither recommends talking to bank officers about recent loans, government agencies about employers moving into the area, and construction workers on commercial projects. 'If you're there first, you win,' he says."

- "He urges workers to research prospective employers, and not just via the Internet. 'Go to bars where people who do the job you want hang out,' he says."

What do you think of these suggestions? Do they all seem ethical to you? Would you try them?

Bullets quoted from Cari Tuna, "Hard Truths for Hard Times," *Wall Street Journal*, February 10, 2009, D1.

A **skills résumé,** also called a functional résumé, emphasizes the skills you've used, rather than the job in which you used them or the date of the experience. Figure 11.5 shows a skills résumés. Use a skills résumé when

- Your education and experience are not the usual route to the position for which you're applying.
- You're changing fields.
- You want to combine experience from paid jobs, activities, volunteer work, and courses to show the extent of your experience in administration, finance, public speaking, and so on.

The two kinds differ in what information is included and how that information is organized. You may assume that the advice in this chapter applies to both kinds of résumés unless there is an explicit statement that the two kinds of résumés would handle a category differently.

What to Include in a Résumé

Although the résumé is a factual document, its purpose is to persuade. In a job application form or an application for graduate or professional school, you answer every question even if the answer is not to your credit. In a résumé, you cannot lie, but you can omit some information that does not work in your favor.

Résumés commonly contain the following information. The categories marked with an asterisk are essential.

*Name and Contact Information

Career Objective

Summary of Qualifications

*Education

Honors and Awards

A résumé is your most important document at career fairs.

*Experience

Other skills

Activities

Portfolio

You may choose other titles for these categories and add categories that are relevant for your qualifications, such as computer skills or foreign languages.

Education and Experience always stand as separate categories, even if you have only one item under each head. Combine other headings so that you have at least two long or three short items under each heading. For example, if you're in one honor society and two social clubs, and on one athletic team, combine them all under Activities and Honors.

If you have more than seven items under a heading, consider using subheadings. For example, a student who had a great many activities might divide them into Campus Activities and Community Service.

Put your strongest categories near the top and at the bottom of the first page. If you have impressive work experience, you might want to put that category first and Education second.

Name and Contact Information

Use your full name, even if everyone calls you by a nickname. You may use an initial rather than spelling out your first or middle name. Put your name in big type.

If you use only one address, consider centering it under your name. If you use two addresses (office and home, campus and permanent, until____ /after____) set them up side by side to balance the page visually. Place a comma after the city and before the state. Use either post office (two-letter, full caps, no period) abbreviations for the state or spell out the state name, but do be consistent throughout your résumé.

Urbana, IL 61801

Wheaton, Illinois 60187

Provide an e-mail address. Some job candidates set up a new e-mail address just for job hunting. Your e-mail address should look professional; avoid sexy, childish, or illicit addresses.

Give a complete phone number, including the area code. Some job candidates give both home and cell phone numbers. Do provide a phone number where you can be reached during the day. Employers usually call during business hours to schedule interviews and make job offers. Do not give lab or dorm phone numbers unless you are sure someone there will take an accurate message for you at all times. Also, be sure that all answering machines have a professional-sounding message.

Career Objective

Career objective statements should sound like the job descriptions an employer might use in a job listing. Keep your statement brief—two lines at most. Tell what you want to do, what level of responsibility you want to hold. The best career objectives are targeted to a specific job at a specific company.

Ineffective career objective: To offer a company my excellent academic foundation in hospital technology and my outstanding skills in oral and written communication

Better career objective: Hospital and medical sales for Rand Medical requiring experience with state-of-the-art equipment

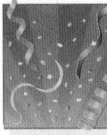

Résumé Blunders

Job site CareerBuilders .com recently asked pollsters Harris Interactive to survey hiring managers and find out the wackiest resume items they've seen lately. Out of 2,627 responses, here are the top ten:

A job candidate . . .

1. . . . attached a letter from her mother.

2. . . . used pale blue paper with teddy bears printed around the border.

3. . . . explained a three-month gap in employment by saying that he was getting over the death of his cat.

4. . . . specified that his availability to work Fridays, Saturdays or Sundays is limited because the weekends are 'drinking time.'

5. . . . included a picture of herself in a cheerleading uniform.

6. . . . drew a picture of a car on the outside of the envelope and said the car would be a gift to the hiring manager.

7. . . . listed hobbies that included sitting on a levee at night watching alligators.

8. . . . mentioned the fact that her sister had once won a strawberry-eating contest.

9. . . . stated that he works well in the nude.

10. . . . explained an arrest record by stating, 'We stole a pig, but it was a really small pig.'

Quoted from Anne Fisher, "10 Dumbest Résumé Blunders," April 26, 2007, Fortune.com. Copyright © 2007 Time Inc. All rights reserved.

Good career objectives are hard to write. If you talk about entry-level work, you won't sound ambitious; if you talk about where you hope to be in 5 or 10 years, you won't sound as though you're willing to do entry-level work. When you're applying for a job that is a natural outgrowth of your education and experience, you may omit this category and specify the job you want in your cover letter.

Often you can avoid writing a career objective statement by putting the job title or field under your name:

| Joan Larson Ooyen | Terence Edward Garvey | David R. Lunde |
| Marketing | Technical Writer | Corporate Fitness Director |

Note that you can use the field you're in even if you're a new college graduate. To use a job title, you should have some relevant work experience.

If you use a separate heading for a career objective, put it immediately after your address, before the first major heading (see Figure 11.5). The résumé in Figure 11.6 combines the Career Objective with the Summary of Qualifications section. The résumé in Figure 11.3 does not use a Career Objective because it is being used for various jobs offered at a career fair. If you were particularly interested in several jobs there, you would make targeted résumés for those companies.

Summary of Qualifications

A section summarizing the candidate's qualifications seems to have first appeared with scannable résumés, where its keywords helped increase the number of matches a résumé produced. But the section proved useful for human readers as well and now is a standard part of most résumés. The best summaries show your knowledge of the specialized terminology of your field and offer specific, quantifiable achievements.

Weak: Staff accountant

Better: Experience with accounts payable, accounts receivable, audits, and month end closings. Prepared monthly financial reports.

Weak: Presentation skills

Better: Gave 20 individual and 7 team presentations to groups ranging from 5 to 100 people.

Education

Education can be your first major category if you've just earned (or are about to earn) a degree, if you have a degree that is essential or desirable for the position you're seeking, or if you can present the information briefly. Put your Education section later if you need all of page 1 for another category or if you lack a degree that other applicants may have (see Figure 11.5).

Under Education, provide information about your undergraduate and graduate degrees, including the location of institutions and the year you received or expect your degree.

Use the same format for all schools. List your degrees in reverse chronological order (most recent first).

Master of Accounting Science, May 2010, Arizona State University, Tempe, AZ
Bachelor of Arts in Finance, May 2008, New Mexico State University, Las Cruces, NM

BS in Industrial Engineering, May 2010, Iowa State University, Ames, IA
AS in Business Administration, May 2008, Des Moines Area Community College, Ankeny, IA

When you're getting a four-year degree, include community college only if it will interest employers, such as by showing an area of expertise different from that of your major. You may want to include your minor and any graduate courses you have taken. Include study abroad, even if you didn't earn college credits. If you got a certificate for international study, give the name and explain the significance of the certificate. Highlight proficiency in foreign or computer languages by using a separate category.

To punctuate your degrees, do not space between letters and periods:

A.S. in Office Administration

B.S. in Accounting

Ed.D. in Business Education

Current usage also permits you to omit the periods:

MBA

PhD in Finance

Be consistent with the usage you choose.

Professional certifications can be listed under Education or in a separate category.

If your GPA is good, include it. Because grade point systems vary, specify what your GPA is based on: "3.4/4.0" means 3.4 on a 4.0 scale. If your GPA is under 3.0 on a 4.0 scale, use words rather than numbers: "B– average." If your GPA isn't impressive, calculate your average in your major and your average for your last 60 hours. If these are higher than your overall GPA, consider using them. The National Association of Colleges and Employers, in its Job Outlook 2007 survey, found that 66% of employers do screen job applicants by GPA.[6] If you leave your GPA off your résumé, most employers will automatically assume that it is below a 3.0. If yours is, you will need to rely on internships, work experience, and skills acquired in activities to make yourself an attractive job candidate.

After giving the basic information (degree, field of study, date, school, city, state) about your degree, you may wish to list courses, using short descriptive titles rather than course numbers. Use a subhead like "Courses Related to Major" or "Courses Related to Financial Management" that will allow you to list all the courses (including psychology, speech, and business communication) that will help you in the job for which you're applying. Don't say "Relevant Courses," as that implies your other courses were irrelevant.

Résumé Advice on the Web

The sites listed in Figure 11.1 give advice about résumés. In addition, specialized résumé sites exist. The following are worth checking:

Yana Parker's Damn Good Résumé Guide

http://www.damngood.com/jobseekers/tips.html

Before-and-After Examples of Résumés

http://www.eresumeiq.com/feature.html

Rebecca Smith's Résumés and Resources

http://www.eresumes.com

Quintessential Careers (Dr. Randall Hansen)

http://www.quintcareers.com/resume_samples.html

Bachelor of Science in Management, May 2010, Illinois State University, Normal, IL
GPA: 3.8/4.0

Courses Related to Management:

Personnel Administration	Business Decision Making
Finance	International Business
Management I and II	Marketing
Accounting I and II	Legal Environment of Business
Business Report Writing	Business Speaking

Listing courses is an unobtrusive way to fill a page. You may also want to list courses or the number of hours in various subjects if you've taken an unusual combination of courses that uniquely qualify you for the position for which you're applying.

Paying for school expenses just with loans is generally not considered noteworthy.

Formats for setting up Experience

There are two basic ways to set up the Experience section of your résumé. In **indented format**, items that are logically equivalent begin at the same space, with carryover lines indented. Indented format emphasizes job titles. It provides work information in this order:

Job title, name of organization, city, state, dates. Other information.

> **Experience**
>
> **Engineering Assistant,** Sohio Chemical Company, Lima, Ohio, Summers 2009 and 2010.
>
> - Tested wastewater effluents for compliance with Federal EPA standards
> - Helped chemists design a test to analyze groundwater quality and seepage around landfills
> - Presented weekly oral and written progress reports to Director of Research and Development
>
> **Animal Caretaker,** Animalcare, Worthington, Ohio, Summers 2006–2008.

Two-margin or **block format** emphasizes *when* you worked, so it is appropriate if you've held only low-level jobs. Don't use two-margin format if your work history has gaps or if you've worked as an intern or held another job directly relevant to the position you're applying for.

> **EXPERIENCE**
>
> | | |
> |---|---|
> | Summers, 2008–10 | Repair worker, Bryant Heating and Cooling, Providence, RI |
> | 2008–09 | Library Clerk, Boston University Library, Boston, MA. Part-time during school year |
> | 2006–08 | Food Service Worker, Boston University, Boston, MA. Part-time during school year |
> | Summer, 2007 | Delivery person, Domino's Pizza, Providence, RI |

Use a hyphen to join inclusive dates:

March-August, 2010 (or write out March to August, 2010)
2007–2010
2009–10

If you use numbers for dates, do not space before or after the slash:

10/08-5/09

Skills résumés

Skills résumés stress the skills you have acquired rather than specific jobs you have held. They show employers that you do have the desired skill set even if you lack the traditional employment background. They allow you to include skills acquired from activities and course projects in addition to jobs. On the other hand, they are also a clue to employers that you do lack that traditional background, or that you have gaps in your job history, so you will need to make your skill set convincing.

In a skills résumé, the heading of your main section usually changes from "Experience" to "Skills." Within the section, the subheadings will be replaced with the skills used in the job you are applying for, rather than the title or the dates of the jobs you've held (as in a chronological résumé). For entries under each skill, combine experience from paid jobs, unpaid work, classes, activities, and community service.

Use headings that reflect the jargon of the job for which you're applying: *logistics* rather than *planning* for a technical job; *procurement* rather than *purchasing* for a job with the military. Figure 11.5 shows a skills résumé for someone who is changing fields.

A job description can give you ideas for headings. Possible headings and subheadings for skills résumés include

Administration	**Communication**
Budgeting	Conducting Meetings
Coordinating	Editing
Evaluating	Fund-Raising
Implementing	Interviewing
Negotiating	Negotiating
Planning	Persuading
Scheduling	Presenting
Solving Problems	Proposal Writing
Supervising	Report Writing

Many jobs require a mix of skills. Try to include the skills that you know will be needed in the job you want. You need at least three subheadings in a skills résumé; six or seven is not uncommon. Give enough detail under each subheading so the reader will know what you did. Put the most important category from the reader's point of view first.

In a skills résumé, list your paid jobs under Work History or Employment Record near the end of the résumé (see Figure 11.5). List only job title, employer, city, state, and dates. Omit details that you have already used under Skills.

Other Skills

You may want a brief section in a chronological résumé where you highlight skills not apparent in your work history. These skills may include items such as foreign languages or programming languages. You might want to list software you have used or training on expensive equipment (electron microscopes, NMR machines). As always on your résumé, be completely honest: "four years of high school German," or "elementary speaking knowledge of Spanish." Any knowledge of a foreign language is a plus. It means that a company desiring a second language in its employees would not have to start from scratch in training you. See Figure 11.6 for an example.

Activities

Employers may be interested in your activities if you're a new college graduate because they can demonstrate leadership roles, management abilities, and social skills as well as the ability to juggle a schedule. If you've worked for several years after college or have an advanced degree (MBA, JD), you can omit Activities and include Professional Activities and Affiliations or

Figure 11.5   A Skills Résumé for Someone Changing Fields

Sophia Barber
www.ukansas.edu/~Barber1278/home.htm

If you have a professional Web page, include its URL.

266 Van Buren Drive
Lawrence, KS 66044
barber@ukansas.edu
785-897-1534 (home)
785-842-4242 (cell)

Objective   To contribute my enthusiasm for writing as a Technical Writer at PDF
Productions

Job objective includes the position and name of the company.

Skills   Computer

Largest section on skills résumé, allows you to combine experiences from work and class.

- Designed a Web page using Dreamweaver
  www.lawrenceanimalshelter.com
- Used a variety of Macintosh and PC platform programs and languages:

Aspects (online discussion forum)	Storyspace
Dreamweaver	GoLive
PageMaker	HTML
XML	InDesign CS2

Specify computer programs you know well.

Design and Writing

Use parallel structure for bulleted lists.

- Designed a quarterly newsletter for local animal shelter
- Developed professional brochures
- Wrote a variety of professional documents: letters, memos, and reports
- Edited internal documents and promotional materials
- Proofread seven student research papers as a tutor

Organization and Administration

- Coordinated program schedules
- Developed work schedules for five employees
- Led a ten-member team in planning and implementing sorority
  philanthropy program
- Created cataloging system for specimens
- Ordered and handled supplies, including live specimens

**Employment
History**

Condensed to make room for skills.

Technical Writer, Lawrence Animal Shelter, Lawrence, KS, 2008–present
Undergraduate Lab Assistant, Department of Biology, University of
    Kansas, Lawrence, KS, 2008–present
Tutor, University of Kansas, Lawrence, KS, 2008–2009

Uses reverse chronology.

Education   Bachelor of Science, May 2010
University of Kansas, Lawrence, KS
Major: Animal Ecology
Minor: Chemistry
GPA: 3.4/4.0

Give minor when it can be helpful.

Honors   Phi Kappa Phi Honor Society
Alpha Lambda Delta Honor Society, Ecology Honorary
Dean's List, 2007 to present
Raymond Hamilton Scholarship, 2009–2010
    ($5,000 to a top ecology student in Kansas)

Explain honors your reader may not know.

End with strong items at the bottom of your page, a position of emphasis.

Community and Public Service. If you went straight from college to graduate school but have an unusually strong record demonstrating relevant skills, include this category even if all the entries are from your undergraduate days.

Include the following kinds of items under Activities:

- Volunteer work. Include important committees, leadership roles, communication activities, and financial and personnel responsibilities.

- Membership in organized student activities. Include important subcommittees, leadership roles. Include minor offices only if they're directly related to the job for which you're applying or if they show growing responsibility (you held a minor office one year, a bigger office the following year). Include so-called major offices (e.g., vice president) even if you did very little. Provide descriptive details if (but only if) they help the reader realize how much you did and the importance of your work, or if they demonstrate usable job skills.

- Membership in professional associations. Many of them have special low membership fees for students, so you should join one or more.

- Participation in varsity, intramural, or independent athletics. However, don't list so many sports that you appear not to have had adequate time to study.

- Social clubs, if you held a major leadership role or if social skills are important for the job for which you're applying.

As you list activities, add details that will be relevant for your job. Did you handle a six-figure budget for your Greek organization? Plan all the road trips for your soccer club? Coordinate all the publicity for the campus blood drive? Design the posters for homecoming? Major leadership, financial, and creative roles and accomplishments may look more impressive if they're listed under Experience instead of under Activities.

Portfolio

If you have samples of your work available, you may want to end your résumé by stating "Portfolio (or writing samples) available on request."

References

References are generally no longer included on résumés. Nor do you say "References Available on Request," since no job applicant is going to refuse to supply references. However, you will probably be asked for references at some point in your application process, so it is wise to be prepared.

You will need at least three, usually no more than five, never more than six. As a college student or a new graduate, include at least one professor and at least one employer or adviser—someone who can comment on your work habits and leadership skills. If you're changing jobs, include your current superior. For a skills résumé, choose references who can testify to your abilities in the most important skills areas. Omit personal or character references, who cannot talk about your work. Don't use relatives, friends, or roommates, even if you've worked for them, because everyone will believe they are biased in your favor.

Always ask permission to use the person as a reference. Instead of the vague "May I list you as a reference?" use, "Can you speak specifically about my work?" Jog the person's memory by taking along copies of work you did for him or her and a copy of your current résumé. Tell the person what

What to Know about Job References

Many job reference myths exist that may undermine your job search:

Myth: I don't have to mention a job that didn't work out, especially if I worked there only a short while.

Fact: Employers can check jobs through Social Security, and they will believe the worst of omissions.

Myth: Companies are not legally allowed to give damaging information about applicants.

Fact: Although many companies have formal policies of providing only bare-bones data, many employees within those organizations still engage in providing additional, negative information about applicants. Voice tone, or mentioning that you may not be eligible for rehire, may speak volumes.

Myth: References do not matter once you are hired.

Fact: References may still be checked after you are hired and can be used for grounds for termination.

Myth: If you sue an employer, that information may not be disclosed.

Fact: Employers indirectly release negative information by stating such things as, "Please hold while I discuss with our legal department what we are allowed to say about this applicant."

Myth: References are not needed after you have a job.

Fact: Stay in contact with your references. You never know when you may want to change jobs.

Adapted from Anne Fisher, "The Seven Deadly Myths of Job References," in *CNNMoney.com: Fortune: Commentary: Ask Annie,* http://money.cnn.com/2005/10/25/news/economy/annie/fortune_annie102505/index.htm (accessed March 9, 2009).

Figure 11.6 A Two-Page Chronological Résumé

Uses a little more formatting than the other résumés. Goes well with architecture degree.

Maria Sanchez

sanchez@unl.edu ▪ 1535 Mission Way ▪ Lincoln, NE 68501 ▪ 402.975.6992

Summary of Qualifications for Architect Position at Da Vinci

- Two architecture internships
- International experience in study abroad program
- Managed $100,000 budget
- Fluent in Spanish and Italian   *Note language facility.*
- Proficient in AutoCAD

Education

2005–2010

Bachelor of Arts Degree
University of Nebraska–Lincoln, NE

- Major: Architecture
- Major GPA: 3.4/4.0

Course lists are good if you have unusual ones or ones that show you are particularly well-prepared.

Design Coursework

Renaissance Design	Conceptual Design	Principles of Construction
Medieval Design	History of Design	Building Structures
Postmodern Design	Theory of Landscape Structures	Architectural Aesthetics

Professional Experience

June 2008–Present

Architecture Intern
Cutting Edge Architecture Firm–Lincoln, NE

- Conduct safety site surveys for four residential areas
- Research code requirements and prepare survey reports
- Prepare remodeling drawings using AutoCAD 2007 to remedy concerns
- Collaborate with various organizations and professionals to complete reports

Use present tense when you are doing the job now.

Sept. 2007–Dec. 2007

Study Abroad Participant
Nebraska Study Abroad Program–Turin and Rome, Italy

- Studied the varied architecture of Italy
- Participated in artistic and cultural traditions of Italy
- Engaged in intensive language learning of Italian

Use past tense for jobs that are over.

June 2007–Sept. 2007

Architecture Intern
Debalt Architects–Minneapolis, MN

- Generated construction drawings and details
- Created designs using AutoCAD 2006
- Developed and maintained client relationships

Figure 11.6 *Continued*

Maria Sanchez

sanchez@unl.edu
Page 2

If you use two pages, be sure to put your name, e-mail, and "Page 2" on the second page.

April 2005–Sept. 2006 **Publicist/Laborer**
Harman Contractors–Lincoln, NE

- Installed fixtures in new residential homes
- Filled cracks with plaster and sanded patches
- Finished painted work surfaces
- Designed publicity brochures and business cards

Leadership Experience

May 2007–Present **Assistant Director of Volunteer Recruitment**
Habitat for Humanity–Lincoln, NE

- Supervise four office volunteers
- Publicize volunteer opportunities to local community and university
- Develop a recruitment action plan

Sept. 2009–Present **President**
Chi Omega Sorority–U of Nebraska–Lincoln, NE

- Oversee operation of 65 member sorority
- Call and preside over all executive meetings
- Manage $100,000 annual budget

Quantify your experiences where possible.

Volunteer Experience

June 2008 **Swimming Official**
Special Olympics Semi-National Games–Lincoln, NE

- Encouraged athletes while timing relays
- Promoted positive environment

Other Skills

AutoCAD 2007
Sketch-up
Adobe Photoshop, Illustrator, and InDesign CS2
Fluent in Spanish and Italian

Affiliations

American Institute of Architecture Students
Interfraternity Council
Intramural Council

Keep lists of extras short. Focus them to appeal to employers.

Portfolio Available at Password Protected Web Site

One way to make your professional work available to interested employers.

Should I Create a Video Résumé?

What is a video résumé?

Job hunters post short videos as part of their job applications through services such as YouTube and Google video.

Who uses video résumés?

Anyone can. Currently, most video résumés are produced by applicants interested in entertainment and media, but job seekers in other industries are starting to use video postings.

Are there risks?

Yes, embarrassment. One Yale student applying for an international investment-banking job made national news when his video became a YouTube favorite. He did not get the job.

What are the benefits to employers?

Employers get an opportunity to screen applicants before asking for an interview. This may save an employer from conducting an interview.

If you decide to create a video posting, you may want to consider these tips for your video résumé:

1. Be brief and concise. Your video should be less than three minutes.

2. Be prepared. Avoid reading a script. You should be conversational and natural in your presentation.

3. Tailor the video to the specific employer and position.

4. Be careful where you post your video. Remember anyone can watch it.

5. Be professional. Post a video that is clear, audible, and free from background noise.

Adapted from Anjali Athavaley, "Posting Your Résumé on YouTube: Young Job Hunters Try Using Video Clips to Stand Out; The Risk of Humiliation," *Wall Street Journal,* December 6, 2006, D1.

Third, try to learn from the experience. You'll be a much more attractive job candidate if you can show that you've learned from the experience—whether your lesson is improved work habits or that you need to choose a job where you can do work you can point to with pride.

Fourth, collect evidence showing that earlier in your career you were a good worker. This evidence could include references from earlier employers, good performance evaluations, and a portfolio of good work.

Some common strategies may also give you some help for references. You should check with the Human Resources Department to see what the company's reference policy is. Some companies now give no references other than verification of job title and work dates. Others do not give references for employees who worked only a short time.[9] Another option is to ask someone other than your former boss for a reference. Could you ask a supplier or vendor? A different department head?

A different tactic is suggested by Phil Elder, an interviewer for an insurance company. He suggests calling the person who fired you and saying something like this: "Look, I know you weren't pleased with the job I did at _____. I'm applying for a job at _____ now and the personnel director may call you to ask about me. Would you be willing to give me the chance to get this job so that I can try to do things right this time?" All but the hardest of heart, says Elder, will give you one more chance. You won't get a glowing reference, but neither will the statement be so damning that no one is willing to hire you.[10]

Above all, be honest. Do not lie about your termination at an interview or on a job application. The application usually requires you to sign a statement that the information you are providing is true and that false statements can be grounds for dismissal.

"I Was Laid Off."

In times of large layoffs, this is not an overwhelming obstacle. You do not need to point out the layoff in your application materials; the end date of your last employment will make the point for you. Instead, use your documents to highlight your strengths.

Do be prepared to be asked about the layoff in an interview. Why were you laid off when other employees were retained? It helps if you can truthfully give a neutral explanation: the accounting work was outsourced; our entire lab was closed; the company laid off everyone who had worked fewer than five years. Be sure you do not express bitterness or self-pity; neither emotion will help you get your new job. On the other hand, do not be overly grateful for an interview; such excess shows a lack of self-confidence.

"I Don't Have Any Experience."

If you have a year or more before you job hunt, you can get experience in several ways:

*   Take a fast-food job—and keep it. If you do well, you'll be promoted to a supervisor within a year. Use every opportunity to learn about the management and financial aspects of the business.

*   Sign on with agencies that handle temporary workers. As an added bonus, some of these jobs become permanent.

*   Join a volunteer organization that interests you. If you work hard, you'll quickly get an opportunity to do more: manage a budget, write fundraising materials, and supervise other volunteers.

*   Freelance. Design brochures, create Web pages, do tax returns for small businesses. Use your skills—for free, if you have to at first.

- Write. Create a portfolio of ads, instructions, or whatever documents are relevant for the field you want to enter. Ask a professional—an instructor, a local business person, someone from a professional organization—to critique them. Volunteer your services to local fund-raising organizations and small businesses.

If you're on the job market now, think carefully about what you've really done. Complete sentences using the action verbs in Figure 11.4. Think about what you've done in courses, in volunteer work, in unpaid activities. Especially focus on skills in problem solving, critical thinking, teamwork, and communication. Solving a problem for a hypothetical firm in an accounting class, thinking critically about a report problem in business communication, working with a group in a marketing class, and communicating with people at the senior center where you volunteer are experience, even if no one paid you.

If you're not actually looking for a job but just need to create a résumé for this course, ask your instructor whether you may assume that you're a senior and add the things you hope to do between now and your senior year.

Electronic Résumés

According to a study by Taleo Research, 94% of the top 500 US corporations solicit electronic résumés and use software to sort them and make matches with jobs.[11] Pat Kendall, president of the National Résumé Writers' Association, says over 80% of résumés are searched for keywords.[12] Electronic searches mean that you will need electronic résumés in addition to your print résumé.

Many companies give specific directions for how they want their electronic résumés. Check company Web sites and be sure to follow directions exactly.

Creating a Scannable Résumé

To increase the chances that your résumé is scanned correctly,

- Use a standard typeface such as Helvetica, Futura, Arial, Times New Roman, and Palatino.
- Use 12-point type.
- Use a ragged right margin rather than full justification. Scanners can't always handle the extra spaces between words and letters that full justification creates.
- Don't italicize or underline words—even titles of books or newspapers that grammatically require such treatment.
- Don't bold text. You can use full caps for major headings if you wish, but don't overdo them.
- Don't use bullets or tabs. You can replace them with keyboard characters such as asterisks, hyphens, or spaces if you wish.
- Print your résumé on a high-quality printer.
- Use standard size 8½ × 11 white or a very light color paper. Use high-quality paper.
- Don't fold or staple your pages.
- Mail paper copies flat in a page-sized envelope.

Using Keywords

Electronic résumés need to use **keywords**—words and phrases the employer will have the computer seek. Keywords are frequently nouns or

Résumé Blasting

Résumé blasting is the process of distributing your résumé to dozens, hundreds, or thousands of résumé sites and databases. Résumé blasting services typically cost between $49 to $199, depending on the type of service and distribution you choose.

ResumeDoctor.com surveyed over 5,000 recruiters and hiring managers about online job postings. Top complaints were

1. Large numbers of irrelevant responses (92%). Most participants indicated that they receive hundreds of responses per online job posting.
2. Résumés not matching the job description (71%).
3. Job candidates "blasting out" résumés (63%).

Adapted from Pat Kendall, "Marketing Your Résumé on the Net," http://www.jumpstartyourjobsearch.com/marketing.html (accessed July 3, 2009); and "The Truth About 'Résumé Blasting," in *ResumeDoctor.com Resource Center*, http://resumedoctor.com/ResourceCenter.htm (accessed March 9, 2009).

Beware of Spam Filters

Employers are using filters to keep out spam and damaging computer viruses. Unfortunately, legitimate e-mails, including résumés, are also getting blocked. Applicants who send résumés with an e-mail may be rejected by spam filters for various reasons such as "foul" language (B.S.) or overused phrases (*responsible for* or *duties included*).

What can you do to avoid spam filters?

- Avoid acronyms or titles that may be considered "foul" language.
- Watch overusing words or phrases.
- Avoid words like *free, extend, unbelievable, opportunity, trial, mortgage*.
- Avoid using colored backgrounds.
- Be careful of using all capitals, exclamation points, or dollar amounts in subject lines.

What preventative steps can you take to avoid being caught by spam filters?

- Set your personal spam filter to high; then send your résumé to your own e-mail account
- Send your résumé to a spam checker.

Adapted from "Good Grief What Next—Spam-Friendly Résumés!" in Gayle's Blog (The Official Top Margin Blog), http://www.topmargin.com/blog/?p=16 (accessed March 13, 2009); and Susan P. Joyce, "Keep Your E-Mail (and Résumé) out of the Spam Filters," in *Online Job Search Guide: Articles*, http://www.job-hunt.org/article_antispam.shtml (accessed March 12, 2009).

templates unless you are asked to do so; they will rarely present you as well as the layout you have designed for yourself.

For safety reasons, use your e-mail address as contact information instead of your address and phone number. Make sure your e-mail address looks professional; you should not be HotLips@Yahoo.com. To foil identity thieves, some Web consultants also recommend that you remove all dates from your résumé, and that you replace employer names with generic descriptions (state-wide information technology company). Identity thieves can take information directly from online résumés, or they can call employers and, claiming to be conducting background checks, get additional information. They then use the information to apply for credit cards and loans in the job seeker's name.[15]

Since many databases sort résumés by submission date, renew your résumé by making small changes to it at least every two weeks. If you don't get any response to your résumé after a month or two, post it on a different site.

When you have your new job, remove your résumé from all sites. Your new employer will probably take a dim view of finding your résumé on job sites. In fact, new employees have been fired for such lapses. With all the private e-mail accounts available, it is virtually impossible to block your online résumé from people at your current place of employment.

If you post your résumé on your personal Web site, be sure that all the links go to professional-looking pages, such as documents you have created. Now is not the time to link to pictures of you partying. Also, make sure the first screen includes a current job objective and Summary of Qualifications. One study found that résumés on personal Web sites were particularly useful for self-employed workers, for whom they attracted clients.[16]

A Caution about Blogs and Social Networking Sites

Many employers routinely Google job candidates, and many report they are totally turned off by what they find—especially on personal blogs and Web pages and social networking sites such as Facebook and MySpace. If you have a personal blog, Web page, or other electronic presence, check sites carefully before you go on the job market.

- Remove any unprofessional material such as pictures of you at your computer with a beer in your hand or descriptions of your last party.
- Remove negative comments about current or past employers and teachers. People who spread dirt in one context will probably do so in others, and no one wants to hire such people.
- Remove political and social rants. While thoughtful, supported opinions can show both education and logic, emotional or extreme statements will turn off most employers.
- Remove any personal information that will embarrass you on the job. If you blog about romance novels, but don't want to be teased about your choice in literature on your new job, make ruthless cuts on your blog.
- Check your blog for writing aptitude. Many employers will consider your blog an extended writing sample. If yours is full of grammatical and spelling errors, obviously you are not a good writer.

Even if you take your blog off-line while you are job searching, employers may still find it in cached data on search engines. The best advice is to plan ahead and post nothing unprofessional on the Web.

Honesty

Be absolutely honest on your résumé—and in the rest of your job search. Just ask Marilee Jones, former Dean of Admissions at Massachusetts Institute of Technology (MIT). In 1979, when she applied for an admissions job at MIT, her résumé listed bachelor's and master's degrees from Rensselaer Polytechnic Institute. In reality, she attended there only one year as a part-time student. By 1997, when she was promoted to the deanship, she did not have the courage to correct her résumé. In April 2007, she was forced to resign, even though she was a nationally recognized leader in admissions, after an anonymous tip.[17]

According to the Society for Human Resource Management, 96% of all businesses now conduct some kind of background check on job applicants.[18] Even graduate schools, particularly business schools, are checking applicants.[19]

A 2008 survey of over 3,000 hirers conducted for CareerBuilder reported that 49% had caught lies on résumés. Background checks on job candidates can include a credit check, legal and criminal records, complete employment history, and academic credentials. Such checks turn up some incredible whoppers. Résumés have been found using someone else's photo, listing degrees from nonexistent schools, listing fake Mensa memberships, and even claiming a false connection to the Kennedy clan.[20]

You can omit some material on your résumé, because obviously you cannot include everything about your life to date. For instance, it's still ethical to omit a low GPA, although most employers will assume it is very low indeed to be omitted. But what you do include must be absolutely honest.

Some of the most frequent inaccuracies on résumés are inflated job titles and incorrect dates of employment. While these data are easy to fudge, they are also easy to catch in background checks. It is also possible that some of these particular inaccuracies come from careless records kept by job candidates. Do you remember the exact job title of that first job you held as a sophomore in high school? Keep careful records of your employment history!

If employers do an employment history check, and many do, they will have a complete work history for you. They will be able to spot inaccurate company names and work dates. If you left a company off your résumé, they may wonder why; some may assume your performance at that company was not satisfactory.

Other areas where résumés are commonly inaccurate are

- Degrees: many people conveniently forget they were a few hours short of a degree.
- GPAs: inflating one's grade point seems to be a big temptation.
- Honors: people list memberships in fake honoraries, or fake memberships in real honoraries.
- Fake employers.
- Job duties: many people inflate them.
- Salary increases.
- Fake addresses: people create these to have the "local" advantage.
- Fake contact information: this information frequently leads to family members or friends who will give fake referrals.
- Technical abilities.
- Language proficiency.

Résumé Lies Lead to Termination

Listed below are high-level professionals who learned the hard way that eventually employers will discover discrepancies on résumés.

- Dave Edmondson, former chief executive of RadioShack, resigned after lying about having a college degree.

- Joseph Ellis, Pulitzer Prize–winning historian, falsely told students that he had fought in the Vietnam War. In response, Mount Holyoke College suspended him for one year without pay.

- Jeffrey Papows, former president of IBM's Lotus unit, quit over discrepancies in his military and educational record.

- Gregory Probert, president of Herbalife, lost his job over a fake master's degree.

- Sam Box, president of Tetra Tech, was demoted for not having earned his claimed bachelor's degree.

- James DeHoniesto left his job as CIO of Cabot Microelectronics after his listed bachelor's degree was found to be false.

Have you checked your résumé to make sure you have not inflated your credentials?

Adapted from Keith J. Winstein and Daniel Golden, "MIT Admissions Dean Lied on Résumé in 1979, Quits," *Wall Street Journal*, April 27, 2007, B1; and Cari Tuna and Keith J Winstein, "Economy Promises to Fuel Résumé Fraud: Practices Vary for Vetting Prospective Employees, but Executives Usually Face Tougher Background Checks," *Wall Street Journal*, November 17, 2008, B4.

All dishonesty on a résumé is dangerous, keeping you from being hired if discovered early, and causing you to be fired if discovered later. However, the last two bullets listed above are particular dangerous because your chances are good of being asked at an interview to demonstrate your listed proficiencies.

Summary of Key Points

- Informal preparation for job hunting should start soon after you arrive on campus. Formal preparation for job hunting should begin a full year before you begin interviewing. The year you interview, register with your placement office early.

- Employers skim résumés to decide whom to interview. Employers assume that the letter and résumé represent your best work. Interviewers normally reread the résumé before the interview. After the search committee has chosen an applicant, it submits the résumé to people in the organization who must approve the appointment.

- A résumé must fill at least one page. Use two pages if you have extensive activities and experience.

- Emphasize information that is relevant to the job you want, is recent (last three years), and shows your superiority to other applicants.

- To emphasize key points, put them in headings, list them vertically, and provide details.

- Résumés use sentence fragments punctuated like complete sentences. Items in the résumé must be concise and parallel. Verbs and gerunds create a dynamic image of you.

- A **chronological résumé** summarizes what you did in a time line (starting with the most recent events, and going backward in **reverse chronology**). It emphasizes degrees, job titles, and dates. Use a chronological résumé when
  - Your education and experience are a logical preparation for the position for which you're applying.
  - You have impressive job titles, offices, or honors.

- A **skills résumé** emphasizes the skills you've used, rather than the job in which or the date when you used them. Use a skills résumé when
  - Your education and experience are not the usual route to the position for which you're applying.
  - You're changing fields.
  - You want to combine experience from paid jobs, activities, volunteer work, and courses to show the extent of your experience in administration, finance, speaking, etc.
  - Your recent work history may create the wrong impression (e.g., it has gaps, shows a demotion, shows job-hopping, etc.).

- Résumés contain the applicant's contact information, education, and experience. Career objectives, summary of qualifications, honors and awards, other skills, activities, and a portfolio reference may also be included.

- Many résumés are now sent electronically and are posted on the Internet or the organization's Web site.

- Remove any unprofessional material from your personal Web page, blog, and social networking sites.

- Always be completely honest in your résumé and job search.

CHAPTER 11 # Exercises and Problems

11.1 Reviewing the Chapter

1. What should you do soon after starting college to prepare for your job search? (LO 1)
2. What should you do a full year before your job search? (LO 1)
3. How can you use writing components such as emphasis and details to help set yourself apart from other candidates? (LO 2)
4. What are factors you should consider when preparing your contact information? (LO 2)
5. Why are career objectives hard to write? (LO 2)
6. What are keywords? How do you use them in your summary of qualifications? In electronic résumés? (LO 2)
7. What kinds of details make your experience look most attractive to potential employers? (LO 2)
8. How can activities help make you look attractive to potential employers? (LO 2)
9. What can you do to help get the best references possible? (LO 2)
10. Pick one of the common problems job hunters may face and explain how you would deal with it if it happened to you during your career. (LO 3)
11. What are some basic guidelines of e-mail job-hunting etiquette? (LO 4)
12. What safety precautions do you need to take when you post your résumé online? (LO 4)
13. What roles are blogs and Facebook pages playing in the job search? (LO 4)
14. Why is it more important now than ever before to be completely honest on your résumé? (LO 5)

11.2 Reviewing Grammar

Most résumés use lists, and items in lists need to have parallel structure. Polish your knowledge of parallel structure by revising the sentences in Exercise B.7, Appendix B.

11.3 Analyzing Your Accomplishments

List the 10 achievements that give you the most personal satisfaction. These could be things that other people wouldn't notice. They can be accomplishments you've achieved recently or things you did years ago.

Answer the following questions for each accomplishment:

1. What skills or knowledge did you use?
2. What personal traits did you exhibit?
3. What about this accomplishment makes it personally satisfying to you?

As your instructor directs,

a. Share your answers with a small group of other students.
b. Summarize your answers in a memo to your instructor.
c. Present your answers orally to the class.

11.4 Remembering What You've Done

Use the following list to jog your memory about what you've done. For each item, give three or four details as well as a general statement.

Describe a time when you

1. Used facts and figures to gain agreement on an important point.
2. Identified a problem that a group or organization faced and developed a plan for solving the problem.
3. Made a presentation or a speech to a group.
4. Won the goodwill of people whose continued support was necessary for the success of some long-term project or activity.
5. Interested other people in something that was important to you and persuaded them to take the actions you wanted.
6. Helped a group deal constructively with conflict.
7. Demonstrated creativity.
8. Took a project from start to finish.
9. Created an opportunity for yourself in a job or volunteer position.
10. Used good judgment and logic in solving a problem.

As your instructor directs,

a. Identify which job(s) each detail is relevant for.
b. Identify which details would work well on a résumé.
c. Identify which details, further developed, would work well in a job letter.

11.5   Developing Action Statements

Use 10 of the verbs from Figure 11.4 to write action statements describing what you've done in paid or volunteer work, in classes, in extracurricular activities, or in community service.

11.6   Evaluating Career Objective Statements

The following career objective statements are not effective. What is wrong with each statement as it stands? Which statements could be revised to be satisfactory? Which should be dropped?

1. To use my acquired knowledge of accounting to eventually own my own business.
2. A progressively responsible position as a MARKETING MANAGER where education and ability would have valuable application and lead to advancement.
3. To work with people responsibly and creatively, helping them develop personal and professional skills.
4. A position in international marketing which makes use of my specialization in marketing and my knowledge of foreign markets.
5. To bring Faith, Hope, and Charity to the American workplace.
6. To succeed in sales.
7. To design and maintain Web pages.

11.7   Deciding How Much Detail to Use

In each of the following situations, how detailed should the applicant be? Why?

1. Ron Oliver has been steadily employed for the last six years while getting his college degree, but the jobs have been low-level ones, whose prime benefit was that they paid well and fit around his class schedule.
2. Adrienne Barcus was an assistant department manager at a clothing boutique. As assistant manager, she was authorized to approve checks in the absence of the manager. Her other duties were ringing up sales, cleaning the area, and helping mark items for sales.
3. Lois Heilman has been a clerk-typist in the Alumni Office. As part of her job, she developed a schedule for mailings to alumni, set up a merge system, and wrote two of the letters that go out to alumni. The merge system she set up has cut in half the time needed to produce letters.
4. As a co-op student, Stanley Greene spends every other term in a paid job. He now has six semesters of job experience in television broadcasting. During his last co-op he was the assistant producer for a daily "morning magazine" show.

11.8   Evaluating Web Résumés

Evaluate five résumés you find on the Web. Many schools of business have places where students can post résumés online. You may find other résumés on job boards (see the list in Figure 11.1).

As your instructor directs,

a. Share your results with a small group of students.
b. Write an e-mail message analyzing what works and what doesn't. Provide URLs or links to the pages you discuss.
c. Write a memo analyzing what works and what doesn't. Attach printouts of each page you discuss.
d. Join with a small group of students to analyze the pages.
e. Make a short oral presentation to the class discussing the best (or worst) page you found.

11.9   Writing Job Search Goals

Write a list of goals and tasks you need to accomplish for a successful job search. Which ones are crucial? What steps do you need to start taking now to accomplish these goals and tasks? Make a tentative time line for the steps.

11.10   Writing a Job Description

Write a job description for your "dream position." Include the following:

- Position title
- Position description including tasks, special requirements
- Location
- Work hours
- Working conditions (for example, office space, scheduling, amount of supervision)
- Company culture

- Pay
- Experience and education requirements
- Personal competencies (for example, ability to communicate, work in teams, problem solve, etc.).
- Amount of travel

- Social, political, and ethical issues that may be involved

In small groups, share your descriptions. Did you get some ideas from the dream jobs of other students?

11.11   Performing a Needs Analysis

Identify a specific job posting you are interested in and list its requirements. Analyze the needs of the job and identify your personal strengths and qualifications to obtain it.

As your instructor directs,

a. Work on incorporating your list into a résumé.

b. Compose bullet entries for each qualification using action verbs.

c. Identify areas in which you still need to improve. Brainstorm a list of ways in which you can achieve what you need.

11.12   Researching a Job Ad

For a specific job ad online, list job requirements and keywords. Search online for the corporation that has posted the job. Look up the corporation's mission and objectives pages and look for repeating keywords and hot buttons. Find correlations between the job posting and the company's objectives.

As your instructor directs,

a. Share your findings with a group and discuss how the given job posting correlates to the company's overall mission and needs.

b. Identify one such case from your group and present it to the class.

11.13   Editing a Résumé

Below are a job ad and a résumé applying for that job. Using the information you have about Jennifer's two jobs (given below the résumé), critique Jennifer's résumé. Her job letter is Exercise 12.17, if you wish to look at it, too.

Redo her résumé to improve it. Then write a memo to your instructor discussing the strengths and weaknesses of the résumé and explaining why you made the changes you did.

Account Manager

Location: Aurora, IL
Job Category: Business/Strategic Management
Career Level: Entry-Level Manager (Manager/Supervisor of Staff)

Quantum National is the market leader in providing research, sales and marketing, health care policy consulting, and health information management services to the health care industry. Quantum has more than 20,000 employees worldwide and offices in 15 countries in Central and South America. Medical Innovation Communications, a division of Quantum National, currently has an opportunity for an Account Manager in our Aurora, IL, office. Medical Innovation Communications provides comprehensive product commercialization at all stages of product development: from phase 2, through national and international product launches to ongoing support.

The Account Manager has global responsibility for managing the client's marketing communications programs, assuring that the client's objectives are met in terms of program quality and on-time delivery.

Responsibilities include:

- Day-to-day client contact to identify and translate marketing objectives into strategic medical communications/education programs.
- Develop proposals, budgets, estimates of job cost, and profitability.
- Lead a team of Project Managers and Marketing Associates through guidance, delegation, and follow-up; and significant interaction with the client.
- Work with New Business Development Teams to develop proposals, budgets, and presenting company capabilities/business pitches to clients.
- Schedule the workflow of a 30-person demonstration and marketing team.

Requirements:

- Bachelors degree.
- Ability to define and respond to client needs, working effectively under tight deadlines.
- Proven client management experience.
- Proven team management experience.
- Superior written and spoken communication skills.

E-mail applications and résumés to pattersj@micquant.com, and direct inquiries to J. Pattersen.

Jennifer Stanton	8523 8th Street	125 A S. 27th Ave
wildechilde@gmail.com	Ames, IA 50011	Omaha, NE 68101
cell: 515-668-9011	515-311-8243	402-772-5106

Objective
To get a job as an account manager.

Education
Iowa State University, Ames, IA—Business
May 2009, maybe December 2009
Minor: Botany
Cumulative GPA: 2.63 / 4.0

Mid-Plains Community College, North Platte, NE—Associate of Arts
May 2005

Bryan High School, Omaha, NE
May 2002

Work Experience
May 2008–August 2008—Summer Internship at FirstWest Insurance, Des Moines, IA

- Worked with a senior account manager to oversee some medical and EAP accounts.
- Made her phone calls to customers.
- Organized meetings with customers.
- I had to write some training "how-to's" for the new billing database.

1995–2007—*Worked in family business*
Worked weekends and summers in my parents' used-book store.

Skills
Microsoft Office
Fluent in Spanish

When you ask, Jennifer tells you about her two jobs:

> At her internship this summer, the person she worked with was pretty much an absentee supervisor: Jennifer had to do all the work alone (and she's still a little bitter about that). Her department managed five Employee Assistance Provider accounts with a total of about 36,000 individual policy holders in five midwestern states. She had to set up and maintain work schedules for 12 employees, and manage the expense reports for the entire group. Four of those employees traveled a lot, so there were lots of expense reports to manage; there were so many that Jennifer had to revise the department's budget twice. She spent about four hours of every day returning customer phone calls and linking customers up on conference calls with her department's employees. And those training how-to's? That turned into a 20 page how-to manual, which she wrote up and then had FirstWest's IT department turn into a Web site for the department to use.
>
> Her parents' family bookstore in Omaha is actually a franchise of a national chain of aftermarket bookstores: Booktopia. The store generates about $450,000 in gross sales per year, and stocks about 100,000 titles (not counting Internet sales and special orders); it employs 5 full-time and 17 part-time employees. In addition to filling in as a floor clerk, stocker, and cashier—all jobs that put her customer-service, cash-handling, and "people skills" to the test—Jennifer has been handling all of the paperwork between the store and the Booktopia corporate office. (Her parents are great salespeople but they're not good at paying attention to details. That's created friction between them and the corporate office.) That paperwork includes all of the store's quarterly and yearly budget, staffing, and marketing reports since 1999.

Note: This exercise was written by Matthew Search.

11.14   Creating a Web or Paper Portfolio

Create a Web or paper portfolio highlighting your professional and academic accomplishments. Include course projects, workplace samples, and other documents that support your professional accomplishments and goals.

11.15   Preparing a Résumé

Write a résumé that you could use in your job search.

As your instructor directs,

a. Write a résumé for the field in which you hope to find a job.

b. Write two different résumés for two different job paths you are interested in pursuing. Write a memo to your instructor explaining the differences.

c. Adapt your résumé to a specific company you hope to work for. Write a memo to your instructor explaining the specific adaptations you make and why.

d. Write a résumé for the dream job you developed in Exercise 11.10.

11.16   Critiquing Your Résumé, I

Answer the following overview questions for your résumé:

1. Exactly what position are you applying for? How did you choose the position?

2. What are your concerns with applying for this position?

3. What could the concerns of your audience be with your application? How did you try to address these concerns?

4. How do you think the audience will perceive your résumé? Explain.

5. Does your résumé target your employer and position specifically?

Answer the following questions on your design choices:

1. Does the page look balanced?

2. Does the résumé look original or based on a template?

3. Does the length of your résumé fit your situation and position?

4. Does your résumé include clear headings, bullets, and white space?

5. Do you use fonts appropriate for the career level and industry?

6. Do you use consistent font sizes and spacing throughout the document?

7. Does the design reflect your personality and your career ambitions?

Answer the following questions on the content of your résumé.

1. Are the résumé sections clearly, correctly, and consistently labeled?

2. Does the order of the headings highlight your strongest qualifications?

3. Is the work history listed from most recent to past positions?

4. Do you omit high school information? If not, explain your choice.

5. Do you provide details for your best qualifications?

6. Do you use numbers to support your accomplishments?

7. Is the information provided relevant to the position?

8. Does the information support your claim that you are qualified and the best person for this position?

9. Does the information flow logically and easily?

10. Do your bulleted lists use parallel structure?

11. Do you avoid grammar, punctuation, and spelling errors?

Variation: Review a class member's résumé using the same questions.

11.17 Critiquing Your Résumé, II

Rate your résumé using the résumé checklist in the page 322 sidebar. Write a one-page memo to your instructor stating how you believe your résumé rates. Explain and support your position.

11.18 All-Weather Case: Analyzing Job Applicants Based on Their Résumés

Erin is reviewing applications for the position of Cost Accountant to be based at All-Weather's plant in Cedar Rapids, Iowa. She has received 12 applications for the position. As she picks up the first two résumés (given below), she sees in them a few problems right away (like most HR executives, Erin detests typos). Suddenly a thought strikes her. Why not ask Kioni, who is reading an old departmental report, to go through the résumés, preparing a list of their strengths and weaknesses? Not only will the exercise help Kioni get used to something she herself might do in the future, but Kioni's going through the résumés will also offer Erin another perspective on these applicants.

As always, Kioni jumps at the chance to do what she likes to call "real" work. Based on your reading of Chapter 11, the following job description for the position, and the two résumés below, help Kioni analyze the two applicants for the position. What are their strengths and weaknesses as highlighted by their résumés? Which of the two candidates would you select? Why?

Job description for Cost Accountant

The position of Cost Accountant is responsible for budgeting, reviewing, analyzing, controlling, and forecasting costs involving different cost centers throughout the production process, including raw material procurement, inventory management, manufacturing, warehousing, and shipping. Other responsibilities include analyzing G/L reports; ensuring compliance with Generally Accepted Accounting Principles (GAPP) and Cost Accounting Standards (CAS); conducting breakeven (BE), contribution margin, and variance analyses; and preparing periodic reports for upper management. The position requires a bachelor's degree in accounting. A certification in management accounting from the Institute of Management Accountants (IMA) will be a plus. The position also requires a minimum of two years of work experience in cost accounting at a manufacturing company.

STAN GOLDBERG

1010, Buck St., Fairfax, VA
Stanberg@bestwebsite.com

OBJECTIVE

Cost Accountant position in which I can effectively utilize my skills in budgeting, accounting, costing, forecasting, reporting, and teamworking

EXPERIENCE

2005–2006   Abacus Engineering   Portland, OR.

Cost Accounting Trainee

- Calculated cost variance for different cost centers.
- Prepared quarterly budget reports
- Coodinated with employees at different levels for data collection

2007-till date   Bourke Winodws   Fairfax, VA

Costing Manager

- Monitored 12 cost centers
- Implemented policies that reduced costs by 25%
- Supervised a staff of three, including one cost accountant.
- I also produced multiple G/L reports for the production department as well as upper management

EDUCATION

2001-2005   Edward Young University, Perry, OH

- B.A., accounting.
- Currently pursuing CMA of Institute of Management Accounting

INTERESTS

Country music, computers, fishing, golf

Jamal Robinson

1212 S. E. Avenue, Earl, PA
(111) 112-1121-jr8@pearlnews.com

Qualification Summary

Skills in controling and reucing costs, experience with GAAP and CAS, skills in cost analyses, project management, CMA (IMA), member of the Financial Management Association International, well-versd with ERP software

Education

- Certification in Management Accounting

  Graduation- 2007

  Institute of Management Accountants

- True Blue University, Roald, PA

  Graduation- 2006

  Degree- Bachelor of Sciences (BS)

  Major- Accounting, G.P.A. 3.55

Experience

Silverstein Windows and Doors, Earl, PA   2007-Till date

Cost Accountant

- Estimate, review, budget, analyze, and forecast direct / indirect and variable and fixed costs for all stages of production
- Work on the ERP system to genrate reports and data sheets giving cost analyses
- Suggested a procedure in a contract that saved the company $35,000
- Worked with the Marketing Department on the costing / pricing of lower-priced vinyl casement windows

Achievements

- Volunteered more than 100 hours for the Habitat for Humnity Award 2005-2006
- Visted door and widow manufacturing plants in Argentina, Belgium, and Japan
- Received the best employee of the month award at Silverstein Windows and Doors
- Wrote articles for *Financial Control Weekly,* a publication of Costing Professionals Association

References

Available upon requestAdvice for Johnny Bunko

Writing Job Application Letters

Chapter Outline

How Job Letters Differ from Résumés

How to Find Out about Employers and Jobs

- Using the Internet
- Taking an Internship
- Tapping into the Hidden Job Market
  - Networking
  - Information interviews
  - Referral interviews

Content and Organization for Job Application Letters

- How to Organize Solicited Letters
- How to Organize Prospecting Letters
- First Paragraphs of Solicited Letters
- First Paragraphs of Prospecting Letters
- Showing a Knowledge of the Position and the Company

- Showing What Separates You from Other Applicants
- The Last Paragraph

E-Mail Application Letters

Creating a Professional Image

- Writing Style
- Positive Emphasis
- You-Attitude
- Paragraph Length and Unity
- Letter Length
- Editing and Proofreading
- Follow-Up

Application Essays

Summary of Key Points

Get the Most out of Internships

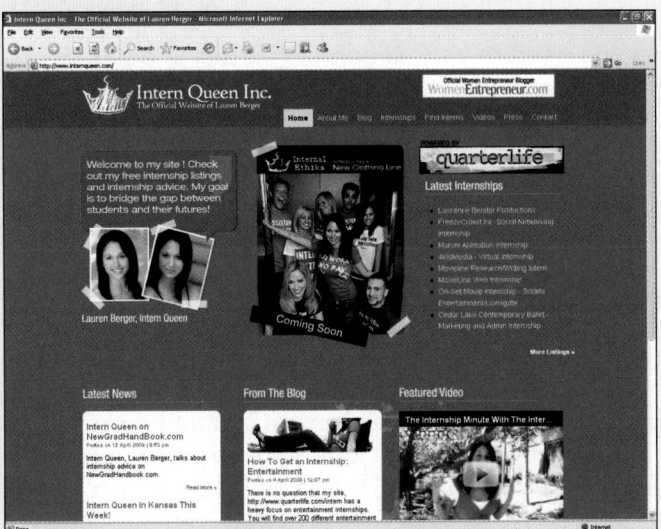

After bagging 15 internships during four years of college, Lauren Berger has earned the title of "The Intern Queen." Berger's internships include ones at a variety of entertainment, publication, and public relations firms, such as Fox, MTV, NBC, and BWR Public Relations.

In 2006, Berger established Intern Queen, Inc., a media lifestyle company, where she has created a network forum for aspiring interns and her own line of intern fashion wear. According to Berger, "The intern is not just one who works for free—an intern is a lifestyle. It describes your average 17–25-year-old who is just starting to figure things out for themselves."

Here are her top five tips for interns:

• Set Real Goals: Make your goals clear to your supervisor as early as possible; it could be as simple as saying that you would like to learn how to write a press release.

"Follow through on small details."

• Get Coffee Skills: Bizarre, but true. Most interns might be asked to make coffee or use the copy machines. Being unable to perform basic functions on their machines may make you look inexperienced.

• Stay Focused: Follow through on small details like being on time, dressing professionally, and avoiding personal calls or Internet surfing. Most of the time supervisors notice if the intern is slacking from work; doing so might prevent you from getting bigger projects and better experience.

• Know Your Place: Remember you are not an employee, so you might not enjoy the perks of one.

• Keep in Touch: Keep in touch with people where you interned. You can do that by sending notes twice a year. Informing them of your current activities and contact information makes it more likely they will recommend you for new job opportunities and keeps your network active and growing.

Source: Lauren Berger, "Intern Queen Inc.," © 2009. Reprinted with permission.

Learning Objectives

After studying this chapter, you will know how to:

1   Find the information you need to write a good job letter to a specific employer.

2   Write a job letter that makes you look attractive to employers.

Dream Jobs

Two different surveys of over 6,000 employees found that nearly 85% said they were not in their dream jobs. In the 2007 survey, having fun at work was the most important characteristic of a dream job (39%); making a difference in the world was second (17%). In the 2008 survey, 90% wanted a job that would allow them to make a difference; 35% would even accept a pay cut to help others.

Among the professionals, police and firefighters were the most likely to believe they held dream jobs (35%), followed by teachers (32%), real estate professionals (28%), and engineers (25%). Those least likely to believe they held dream jobs were workers in hotel and food services (9%), manufacturing (9%), and retail (10%).

What is your dream job?

Adapted from Richard Castellini, "Your Dream Job Search Begins Now," in *Advice & Resources*, http://www.careerbuilder.com/Article/CB-794-Job-Search-Your-Dream-Job-Search-Begins-Now/?ArticleID=794&cbRecursionCnt=1&cbsid=32d2909b4eb34343bd7b346ef330ee1e-290517324-VT-4 (accessed March 16, 2009); and "National 'Dream Jobs' Survey Reveals Four out of Five US Workers Are Still Searching for Their Dream Jobs," in *Press Release*, January 25, 2007, http://www.careerbuilder.com/share/aboutus/pressreleasesdetail.aspx?id=pr347&sd=1/25/2007&ed=12/31/2007&cbRecursionCnt=2&cbsid=04858cf9c8e64c09b8b152bd60578865-290415313-JG-5 (accessed March 16, 2009).

The purpose of a job application letter is to get an interview. If you get a job through interviews arranged by your campus placement office or through contacts, you may not need to write a letter. Similarly, if you apply electronically through a company's Web site, a letter may not be part of the materials you submit. However, if you want to work for an organization that isn't interviewing on campus, or later when you change jobs, you may need a letter. A survey conducted by Robert Half International, the world's largest specialized staffing firm, found 86% of executives said cover letters were still valuable components of job applications in the electronic age.[1]

Job letters are frequently seen as evidence of your written communication skills, so you want to do your best work in them. Flaws in your letter may well be seen as predicting shoddy job performance in the future.

How Job Letters Differ from Résumés

The job application letter accompanies your résumé and serves as its cover letter. Make the most of your letter; it is your chance to showcase the features that set you apart from the crowd. Here you bring to life the facts presented in your vita; here you can show some personality (don't overdo it). The cover letter is your opportunity to "sell" yourself into an interview.

Although résumés and job letters overlap somewhat, they differ in various ways:

- A résumé is adapted to a position. The letter is adapted to the needs of a particular organization.

- The résumé summarizes all your qualifications. The letter expands your best qualifications to show how you can help the organization meet its needs, how you differ from other applicants, and how much knowledge of the organization you possess.

- The résumé avoids controversial material. The job letter can explain in a positive way situations such as career changes or gaps in employment history.

- The résumé uses short, parallel phrases and sentence fragments. The letter uses complete sentences in well-written paragraphs.

How to Find Out about Employers and Jobs

To adapt your letter to a specific organization, you need information both about the employer and about the job itself. You'll need to know

- **The name and address of the person who should receive the letter.** To get this information, check the ad, call the organization, check its Web site, or check with your job search contacts. An advantage of calling is that you can find out what courtesy title (p. 74) the individual prefers and get current information.

Figure 12.1 Web Sources for Facts about Companies

Company Facts

http://www.jobbankinfo.org/

http://careernet.4jobs.com/

http://www.employmentspot.com/

http://www.financialjobs.com/

http://www.job-hunt.org/

http://www.jobweb.com/

http://www.wetfeet.com/

http://www.forbes.com/

http://www.talentzoo.com/website/
  content/

http://efinancialcareers.com/

http://www.irin.com/cgi-bin/main.cgi

http://metamoney.com/w100/

http://www.hoovers.com/free/

http://www.corporateinformation.com/

http://www.vault.com/

http://www.stockmarketyellowpages
  .com/

http://www.prars.com/

http://money.cnn.com/

http://www.inc.com/inc5000/

http://www.bbb.org/

http://allstocks.com/links/

http://www.nypl.org/research/sibl/company/
  c2index.htm

http://www.lib.berkeley.edu/BUSI/

Salary Calculators

http://www.careerjournal.com/

http://salaryexpert.com/

http://www.indeed.com/salary

http://www.payscale.com/

- **What the organization does, and some facts about it.** Knowing the organization's larger goals enables you to show how your specific work will help the company meet its goals. Useful facts can include market share, new products or promotions, the kind of computer or manufacturing equipment it uses, plans for growth or downsizing, competitive position, challenges the organization faces, the corporate culture (p. 108), and so forth.

The Web sites listed in Figure 12.1 provide a wide range of information. More specific information about companies can be found on their Web sites. To get specific financial data (and to see how the organization presents itself to the public), get the company's annual report from your library or the Web. (Note: Only companies whose stock is publicly traded are required to issue annual reports. In this day of mergers and buyouts, many companies are owned by other companies. The parent company may be the only one to issue an annual report.) Recruiting notebooks at your campus placement office may provide information about training programs and career paths for new hires. To learn about new products, plans for growth, or solutions to industry challenges, read business newspapers such as the *Wall Street Journal*, business magazines such as *Fortune, BusinessWeek,* or *Forbes,* and trade journals.

- **What the job itself involves.** Campus placement offices and Web listings often have fuller job descriptions than appear in ads. Talk to friends who have graduated recently to learn what their jobs involve. Conduct information interviews to learn more about opportunities that interest you.

Using the Internet

As Figure 12.2 shows, many job listings are on the Web. Even better, the Web can be a fast way to learn about the company you hope to join. Check professional listservs and electronic bulletin boards. Employers sometimes post specialized jobs on them, and they're always a good way to get information about the industry you hope to enter.

The Value of an Internship

Vault's Internship Survey found that 82% of the responding students said completing an internship was "extremely important" for their careers. In fact, 53% of students were completing two or more internships by the summer after graduation. Students found their internships from college career centers and on-campus recruiting efforts (43%), networking connections (28%), and cold calling (9%). For 64% of the students, internships led to full-time work offers from the companies where they interned.

Internships can be lucrative. According to the survey, 64% of the students were paid. Dollar amounts provided to the students ranged from $10/hr to $2,600/week for 10 weeks. Students also mentioned such perks as a company car, free lunches, and tickets to concerts and sporting events.

What steps should you take to start finding your internship?

Adapted from Vault.com, "More Students Interning This Summer, Says New Vault Survey," in *Job Advice: Internships: News & Research*, http://www.vault.com/nr/newsmain.jsp?nr_page=3&ch_id=322&article_id=27063890 (accessed March 11, 2009).

Figure 12.2   Job Listings on the Web

Job listings

America's Job Bank
www.jobbankinfo.org

CareerBuilder.com
www.careerbuilder.com

Careers.org
www.careers.org

EmploymentGuide.com
www.employmentguide.com

Federal Jobs Career Central
www.fedjobs.com

Indeed.com
www.indeed.com

Monster.com
www.monster.com

MonsterTrak
www.monstertrak.monster.com

Yahoo.com
www.hotjobs.yahoo.com

Job listings from the *Chicago Tribune, Detroit News, Los Angeles Times, Miami Herald, Philadelphia Inquirer, San Jose Mercury News*, and other city newspaper's Web sites.

Taking an Internship

Internships are becoming increasingly important as ways to find out about professions, employers, and jobs. Many companies use their internships to find full-time employees. Even if your internship does not lead to a full-time job, it can still give you valuable insight into the profession, as well as contacts you can use in your job search. An increasingly important side benefit is the work you do in your internship, which can become some of the best items in your professional portfolio.

Tapping into the Hidden Job Market

Many jobs are never advertised—and the number rises the higher on the job ladder you go. In fact, some authorities put the percentage of jobs that are not advertised as high as 80%.[2] Many new jobs come not from responding to an ad but from networking with personal contacts. Some of these jobs are created especially for a specific person. These unadvertised jobs are called the **hidden job market**. Information and referral interviews are two organized methods of networking.

Networking

Networking is using your connections with other people to help you achieve a goal—in this case, getting a job. To network most effectively, you need to spread a big net. Rather than having just a few close friends and family members helping you, you need to share your job search with a large group of your acquaintances: people at your gym, students in Chess Club with you, former classmates, people at your religious institution, friends of friends, your social networking sites. Ask people if they know of jobs. Ask your contacts for the names of people who already have the kind of job you want; follow up to get up-to-date information from someone on the "inside." If you are interested in a particular company, ask if people know anyone who works there.

Networking will also help you when you are actually applying. As noted in Chapter 11, employers value references from their own employees; such references set you apart from the hundreds of other applicants. It does not matter if the person who knows you works in an entry-level job. That's probably where you will be, too, so that person's opinion is relevant.

Information interviews

In an **information interview** you talk to someone who works in the area you hope to enter to find out what the day-to-day work involves and how you can best prepare to enter that field. An information interview can let you know whether or not you'd like the job, give you specific information that you can use to present yourself effectively in your résumé and application letter, and create a good image of you in the mind of the interviewer. If you present yourself positively, the interviewer may remember you when openings arise.

In an information interview, you might ask the following questions:

- How did you get started in this field?
- What have you been working on today?
- How do you spend your typical day?
- Have your duties changed a lot since you first started working here?
- What do you like best about your job? What do you like least?
- What do you think the future holds for this kind of work?
- What courses, activities, or jobs would you recommend as preparation for this kind of work?

To set up an information interview, you can phone or write an e-mail like the one in Figure 12.3. If you do e-mail, phone the following week to set up a specific time.

Referral interviews

Referral interviews are interviews you schedule to learn about current job opportunities in your field. Sometimes an interview that starts out as an information interview turns into a referral interview.

A referral interview should give you information about the opportunities currently available in the area you're interested in, refer you to other people who can tell you about job opportunities, and enable the interviewer to see that you could make a contribution to his or her organization. Therefore, the goal of a referral interview is to put you face-to-face with someone who has the power to hire you: the president of a small company, the division vice president or branch manager of a big company, the director of the local office of a state or federal agency.

Start by scheduling interviews with people you know who may know something about that field—professors, co-workers, neighbors, friends, former classmates. Use your alumni Web site to get the names and phone numbers of alumni who now work where you would like to work. Talk to them to get advice about improving your résumé and about general job-hunting strategy, but also to get referrals to other people. In fact, go into the interview with the names of people you'd like to talk to. If the interviewer doesn't suggest anyone, say, "Do you think it would be a good idea for me to talk to——?"

Armed with a referral from someone you both know, you can call people with hiring power, and say, "So-and-so suggested I talk with you about job-hunting strategy." Even when you talk to the person who could create a job for you, you *do not ask for a job.* But to give you advice about your résumé, the person has to look at it. If there's a match between what you can do and what the organization needs, that person has the power to create a position for you.

Many business people are cynical about information and referral interviewing; they know the real purpose of such interviews, and they resent the time needed. Therefore you need to prepare carefully for these interviews. Prepare a list of good questions; know something about the general field or industry; research the specific company.

Always follow up information and referral interviews with personal thank-you letters. Use specifics to show that you paid attention during the interview, and enclose a copy of your revised résumé.

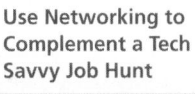

Use Networking to Complement a Tech Savvy Job Hunt

While you may be tech savvy in your job searching, recruiting experts stress the importance of traditional social networking. Recruiters complain that young candidates rely too much on technology, so much that they fail to use enough verbal communication to get a job. According to Jenny Hudak, VP–Director of Talent Management for the strategy group at Leo Burnett, Chicago, "the biggest component of recruiting is the personal, human part of it." Brad Karsh, founder of JobBound, estimates that two out of three people still get jobs by networking, and new candidates must tap this potential more. A few simple steps to ensure effective social networking include these:

- Make sure you include your telephone number on your résumé in case employers want to make that quick call.
- Attend job fairs and professional conferences where you have a better chance of meeting recruiters face-to-face.
- Join professional communities and attend their events , local and national, to build your circle of contacts.

Adapted from Emily Bryson York, "Tech Savvy Is No Replacement for Networking," *Advertising Age,* November 5, 2007, 36.

Figure 12.3 E-mail Requesting an Information Interview

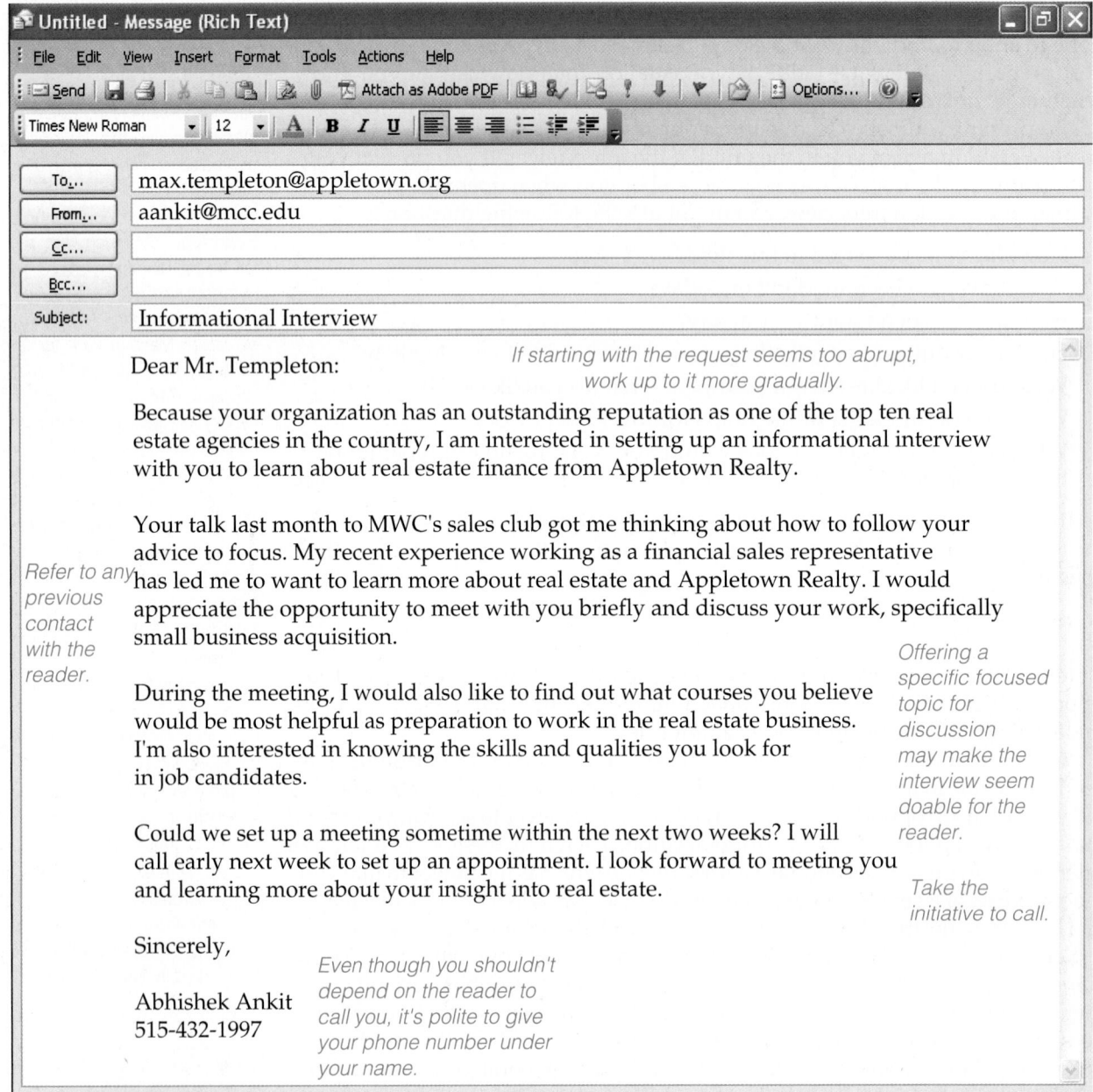

Content and Organization for Job Application Letters

Job letters help show employers why they should interview you instead of other—sometimes hundreds of others—qualified applicants. In your letter, focus on

- Your qualifications to meet major requirements of the job.
- Points that separate you from other applicants.
- Points that show your knowledge of the organization.
- Qualities that every employer is likely to value: the ability to write and speak effectively, to solve problems, to work well with people.

Two different hiring situations call for two different kinds of application letters. Write a **solicited letter** when you know that the company is hiring: you've seen an ad, you've been advised to apply by a professor or friend, you've read in a trade publication that the company is expanding. This situation is similar to a direct request in persuasion (p. 477): you can indicate immediately that you are applying for the position. Sometimes, however, the advertised positions may not be what you want, or you may want to work for an organization that has not announced openings in your area. Then you write a **prospecting letter**. (The metaphor is drawn from prospecting for gold.) The prospecting letter is like a problem-solving persuasive message (p. 479).

Prospecting letters help you tap into the hidden job market. In some cases, your prospecting letter may arrive at a company that has decided to hire but has not yet announced the job. In other cases, companies create positions to get a good person who is on the market. Even in a hiring freeze, jobs are sometimes created for specific individuals.

In both solicited and prospecting letters you should

- Address the letter to a specific person (a must for a prospecting letter).
- Indicate the specific position for which you're applying.
- Be specific about your qualifications.
- Show what separates you from other applicants.
- Show a knowledge of the company and the position.
- Refer to your résumé (which you would enclose with the letter).
- Ask for an interview.

The following discussion follows the job letter from beginning to end. The two kinds of letters are discussed separately where they differ and together where they are the same. Letters for internships follow the same patterns: use a solicited letter to apply for an internship that has been advertised and a prospecting letter to create an internship with a company that has not announced one.

http://www.intel.com

Many Web sites give you all the information you need to write a good job letter. Intel's home page has links to jobs, current Intel news, and global responsibility. Follow links on "About Intel" to information on products or health care; that page also links to the annual report. Both the home page and "pressroom" give information about recent achievements. "Investor relations" has financial information.

How to Organize Solicited Letters

When you know the company is hiring, use the pattern of organization in Figure 12.4. A sample solicited letter for a graduating senior is shown in Figure 12.5. A solicited letter following up from a career fair and requesting an internship is shown in Figure 12.8.

Figure 12.4 How to Organize a Solicited Job Application Letter

1. State that you're applying for the job (phrase the job title as your source phrased it). Tell where you learned about the job (ad, referral, etc.). Include any reference number mentioned in the ad. Briefly show that you have the major qualifications required by the ad: a college degree, professional certification, job experience, etc. Summarize your other qualifications briefly in the same order in which you plan to discuss them in the letter.

2. Develop your major qualifications in detail. Be specific about what you've done; relate your achievements to the work you'd be doing in this new job.

3. Develop your other qualifications, even if the ad doesn't ask for them. Show what separates you from the other applicants who will also answer the ad. Demonstrate your knowledge of the organization.

4. Ask for an interview; tell when you'll be available to be interviewed and to begin work. End on a positive, forward-looking note.

Figure 12.5 A Solicited Letter from a Graduating Senior

Maria Sanchez

sanchez@unl.edu ▪ 1535 Mission Way ▪ Lincoln, NE 68501 ▪ 402.975.6992

February 5, 2010

Ms. Catherine Thomas
DaVinci Designs
2285 Michigan Avenue
Chicago, IL 67214

Use the countesy title
the reader prefers.

Dear Ms. Thomas:

Tell where you learned about the job.
If the job has a reference number, provide it.

In paragraph 1, show you have the qualifications the ad lists.

I wish to apply for your Architect position announced on DaVinci Designs' Web site (A6782). This spring I will graduate from the University of Nebraska–Lincoln with a BA in Architecture and an emphasis in design. DaVinci's focus on international design and superior level of excellence are particularly attractive to me. My unique mix of architecture internships, senior design project, and international study make me an ideal candidate.

This summary sentence forecasts the structure of the rest of the letter.

Shows enthusiasm for the profession and picks up on the teamwork emphasis in the job ad.

While I always knew I enjoyed architecture, I realized my love for it the past two summers as I interned at Debalt in Minneapolis and Cutting Edge in Lincoln. Every single day I couldn't wait to go to work. Moreover, I would often be so immersed in a project that I would stay late to finish it. These internships also taught me the value of collaborating with fellow workers. Prior to my summer work, I had no idea just how much collaboration really goes on in an architecture firm. I can bring the lessons I learned about teamwork to DaVinci Design to help create the best projects.

Evidence of communication skills is a plus for almost any job.

Completing the senior design project, a redesign of Lincoln's main street, taught me the patience needed to carry a design through all planning stages. Moreover, the one-hour presentation I gave about my project to the design faculty at Nebraska helped increase my public speaking skills. I was well prepared for the presentation by monthly design critiques in my courses, where I had to present my work and then modify it on the basis of feedback I received. These skills will be beneficial as I interact and explain ideas to clients of DaVinci.

Many college courses provide concrete experiences.

Relates what she has done to what she could do for the company.

Maria found out about DaVinci's international design emphasis from reading the company Web site.

Studying abroad in Italy honed my understanding of classical architecture. It's one thing to read about architecture in books; it's something entirely different to experience it firsthand. In addition, everywhere I traveled, I was also struck by the stylish women's fashion, which influenced my perception of and sparked creativity for design. Your firm can benefit from this international experience as I contribute ideas while working on international accounts.

During the week of March 13–17, I will be in the Chicago area and would be available for an interview. I would appreciate the opportunity to meet you and discuss the position. Your company has an excellent reputation for customer satisfaction, and I know that the combination of my experience and motivation to excel will make me an asset to your design department.

Sincerely,

Maria Sanchez

Figure 12.6 How to Organize a Prospecting Letter

1. Catch the reader's interest.
2. Create a bridge between the attention-getter and your qualifications. Focus on what you know and can do. Since the employer is not planning to hire, he or she won't be impressed with the fact that you're graduating. Summarize your qualifications briefly in the same order in which you plan to discuss them in the letter. This summary sentence or paragraph then covers everything you will talk about and serves as an organizing device for your letter.
3. Develop your strong points in detail. Be specific. Relate what you've done in the past to what you could do for this company. Show that you know something about the company. Identify the specific niche you want to fill.
4. Ask for an interview and tell when you'll be available for interviews. (Don't tell when you can begin work.) End on a positive, forward-looking note.

Passion

[Lucinda B. Watson, career counselor and author of *How They Achieved: Stories of Personal Achievement and Business Success*, transcribes in her book an interview with Ted Bell, the former Vice Chairman and Worldwide Creative Director of Young and Rubicam. An excerpt:]

"My advice to young people is to just be passionate about whatever it is you do. Be the most passionate person in the room. Not the smartest or the cleverest, but the most passionate. Total passion. Say thank you. Say please. Don't take credit, take the blame. Do all that stuff, that's good. But if you are the most passionate person, you'll probably win. Care more about it than anybody and you'll be the one that wins. People love that. People gravitate toward that."

Quoted from Lucinda Watson, *How They Achieved: Stories of Personal Achievement and Business Success* (New York: John Wiley, 2001), 66.

How to Organize Prospecting Letters

When you don't have any evidence that the company is hiring, you cannot use the pattern for solicited letters. Instead, use the pattern of organization in Figure 12.6. A sample prospecting letter for a student desiring to change fields is shown in Figure 12.7.

First Paragraphs of Solicited Letters

When you know that the firm is hiring, announcing that you are applying for a specific position enables the firm to route your letter to the appropriate person, thus speeding consideration of your application. Identify where you learned about the job: "the position of junior accountant announced in Sunday's *Dispatch*," "William Paquette, our placement director, told me that you are looking for. . . ."

Note how the following paragraph picks up several of the characteristics of the ad:

Ad: Business Education Instructor at Shelby Adult Education. Candidate must possess a Bachelor's degree in Business Education. Will be responsible for providing in-house training to business and government leaders. . . . Candidate should have at least one year teaching experience.

Letter: I am applying for your position in Business Education that is posted on your school Web site. In December, I will receive a Bachelor of Science degree from North Carolina A & T University in Business Education. My work has given me two years' experience teaching word processing and computer accounting courses to adults plus leadership skills developed in the North Carolina National Guard.

Your **summary sentence** or **paragraph** covers everything you will talk about and serves as an organizing device for your letter.

Through my education, I have a good background in standard accounting principles and procedures and a working knowledge of some of the special accounting practices of the oil industry. This working knowledge is enhanced by practical experience in the oil fields: I have pumped, tailed rods, and worked as a roustabout.

My business experience, familiarity with DeVilbiss equipment, and communication skills qualify me to be an effective part of the sales staff at DeVilbiss.

Figure 12.7   A Prospecting Letter from a Career Changer

Sophia Barber
www.ukansas.edu/~Barber1278/home.htm

266 Van Buren Drive
Lawrence, KS 66044
barber@ukansas.edu
785-897-1534 (home)
785-842-4242 (cell)

Sophia uses a "letterhead" that hamonizes with her résumé. (see Figure 11.5)

March 2, 2010

Mr. Pete Jenkins
PDF Productions
3232 White Castle Road
Minneapolis, MN 85434

Dear Mr. Jenkins:

In a prospecting letter, open with a sentence which (1) will seem interesting and true to the reader and (2) provides a natural bridge to talking about yourself.

The Wall Street Journal says that PDF Productions is expanding operations into Kansas, Minnesota, and Nebraska. My experience in technical writing, design, and computers would be an asset to your expanding organization.

Shows knowledge of the organization.

Briefly shows a variety of technical writing and computer skills.

While working at a local animal shelter, I used my technical writing skills to create a Web site that allows users to easily access information. To improve the Web site, I conducted usability tests which provided useful feedback that I incorporated to modify the overall design. In addition, I was also responsible for writing and editing the shelter's monthly newsletter, which was distributed to roughly 1,200 "Friends of the Shelter." I have extensive computer and design skills, which I am anxious to put to use for PDF Productions.

Relates what she's done to what she could do for this company.

Coursework has also prepared me well for technical writing. I have written technical material on a variety of levels ranging from publicity flyers for the animal shelter to scientific reports for upper-level science courses. My coursework in statistics has shown me how to work with data and present it accurately for various audiences. Because of my scientific background, I also have a strong vocabulary in both life sciences and chemistry. This background will help me get up to speed quickly with clients such as ChemPro and Biostage. My background in science has also taught me just how important specific details can be.

Shows how her coursework is an asset.

Names specific clients, showing more knowledge of company.

In May, I will complete my degree from the University of Kansas and will be most interested in making a significant contribution to PDF Productions. I am available every Monday, Wednesday, and Friday for an interview (785-897-1534). I look forward to talking with you about technical writing I can do for PDF Productions.

Sincerely,

Sophia Barber

Sophia Barber

Figure 12.8 Letter Following Up from a Career Fair and Requesting an Internship

Abhishek Ankit
aankit@mcc.edu

Campus Address	**Permanent Address**	*Letterhead matches his résumé.*
1524 Main Street	2526 Prairie Lane	
Boone, 1A 50036	Omaha, NE 68235	
515-232-5718	402-442-7793	

January 23, 2010

Mr. Ron Pascel, HR Department
Prime Financial
Prime Park Place
Des Moines, IA 50023

Dear Mr. Pascel:

Uses his contact immediately.

Mary Randi at the Midwest Community College Career Fair suggested I send you my résumé for the Sales Advisor internship. My education combined with my past work experiences makes me a strong candidate for Prime Financial.

Shows he has been getting full value from his schooling.

While working toward my Associate of Arts degree in Financial Management from Midwest Community College, I have learned the value of fiscal responsibility. For example, in my social financial planning course, I developed a strategic plan to eliminate credit card debt for a one-income household with two children. Moreover, in my business communication course, I improved my oral communication ability so that I could effectively communicate my plans to potential clients. This ability will be an asset to Prime Financial as the organization works to maintain the strong relationship with the community and small business owners that Ms. Randi informed me about.

Refers to knowledge gained at career fair.

Paragraphs 2 and 3 show he has skills he can use immediately as an intern.

My financial education, combined with my previous work experiences in sales, will allow me to thoroughly analyze investment opportunities and establish a strong client base for Prime Financial. For example, I started the A-Plus T-Shirt Company that sold graphic T-shirts to high school students; it had a routine client base of over 150 customers. From managing this business, I know what it takes to be reliable and responsive to customer needs. I am looking forward to learning new approaches from Prime Financial's internship, particularly new ways to work with small businesses.

Provides details about his sales experience to interest his reader.

With my education and experience, I can provide the innovative and competitive edge necessary to be part of your team. I would welcome an interview to discuss your internship and the contributions I could make at Prime Financial.

Sincerely,

Abhishek Ankit

First Paragraphs of Prospecting Letters

In a prospecting letter, asking for a job in the first paragraph is dangerous: unless the company plans to hire but has not yet announced openings, the reader is likely to throw the letter away. Instead, catch the reader's interest. Then in the second paragraph you can shift the focus to your skills and experience, showing how they can be useful to the employer and specifying the job you are seeking.

Here are some effective first and second paragraphs that provide a transition to the writer's discussion of his or her qualifications:

- First two paragraphs of a letter to the Director of Publications of Standard Oil:

> If scarcity of resources makes us use them more carefully, perhaps it would be a good idea to ration words. If people used them more carefully, internal communications specialists like you would have fewer headaches because communications jobs would be done right the first time.

> For the last six years I have worked on improving my communications skills, learning to use words more carefully and effectively. I have taught business communication at a major university, worked for two newspapers, completed a Master's degree in English, and would like to contribute my skills to your internal communications staff.

- First two paragraphs of a letter applying to be a computer programmer for an insurance company:

> As you know, merging a poorly written letter with a database of customers just sends out bad letters more quickly. But you also know how hard it is to find people who can both program computers and write well.

> My education and training have given me this useful combination. I'd like to put my associate's degree in computer technology and my business experience writing to customers to work in State Farm's service approach to insurance.

  Notice how the second paragraph provides a transition to a discussion of qualifications.

- Questions work well only if the answers aren't obvious. The computer programmer above should *not* ask this question:

> Do you think that training competent and motivated personnel is a serious concern in the nuclear power industry?

If the reader says *yes,* the question will seem dumb. If the reader says *no,* the student has destroyed his or her common ground. The computer programmer, however, could pose this question:

> How often do you see a programmer with both strong programming skills and good communication skills?

This question would give him or her an easy transition into paragraphs about his/her programming and communication skills.

Showing a Knowledge of the Position and the Company

If you could substitute another inside address and salutation and send out the letter without any further changes, it isn't specific enough. A job application letter is basically a claim that you could do a specific job for a particular company. Use your knowledge of the position and the company to choose relevant evidence from what you've done to support your claims that you could help the company. (See Figures 12.5 and 12.7.)

The following paragraphs show the writer's knowledge of the company.

- A letter to PricewaterhouseCoopers's Minneapolis office uses information the student learned in a referral interview with a partner in an accounting firm. Because the reader will know that Herr Wollner is a partner in the Berlin office, the student does not need to identify him.

> While I was studying in Berlin last spring, I had the opportunity to discuss accounting methods for multinational clients of PricewaterhouseCoopers with Herr Fritz Wollner. We also talked about communication among PricewaterhouseCoopers's international offices.
>
> Herr Wollner mentioned that the increasing flow of accounting information between the European offices—especially those located in Germany, Switzerland, and Austria— and the US offices of PricewaterhouseCoopers makes accurate translations essential. My fluency in German enables me to translate accurately; and my study of communication problems in Speech Communication, Business and Professional Speaking, and Business and Technical Writing will help me see where messages might be misunderstood and choose words which are more likely to communicate clearly.

- A letter to KMPG uses information the student learned in a summer job.

> As an assistant accountant for Pacific Bell during this past summer, I worked with its computerized billing and record-keeping system, BARK. I had the opportunity to help the controller revise portions of the system, particularly the procedures for handling delinquent accounts. When the KMPG audit team reviewed Pacific Bell's transactions completed for July, I had the opportunity to observe your System 2170. Several courses in computer science allow me to appreciate the simplicity of your system and its objective of reducing audit work, time, and costs.

One or two specific details about the company usually are enough to demonstrate your knowledge. Be sure to use the knowledge, not just repeat it.

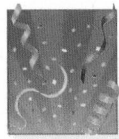

Wacky Cover Letters I

[Vault, an employer research company, asked employers to share the most ridiculous thing they ever saw in a cover letter. One amazing response:]

"I once had a candidate submit her resume for an entry level position. In her cover letter, she said that if she was not offered an entry level position, she would like to ask for a corporate donation from our company. She stated that she had quit her job, was a single mom of 2 children and could use the money to maintain her current standard of living and attend the local community college to get a degree. She then requested that all checks be bank certified!"—Staffing specialist, technology company.

Quoted from Vault.com, "What's the Most Ridiculous Thing You've Ever Seen on a Résumé or Cover Letter?': EmployerVault Question of the Week," in *EmployerVault: Recruiting: Hot Topics,* http://www.vault.com/nr/newsmain.jsp?nr_page=3&ch_id=400&article_id=5853753&cat_id=1083 (accessed March 11, 2009).

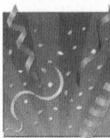

Wacky Cover Letters II

[More amazing cover letters from Vault:]

- "I recently received a resume and cover letter typed on note book paper, holes and fringe included!"—Recruiter, technology consulting firm

- "I received a resume via email and the link took me to the applicant's web home page. I clicked on the link, and a photo appeared of the applicant jumping off a cliff into the sea . . . NAKED!"—HR Manager, major metropolitan area public library system

- "A candidate explained that he wanted to get into the IT field, but his description of his previous job assisting with autopsies went a bit too far, he graphically explained his work in detail, parts and all!"—IT Recruiter, hi tech firm

- "Greetings: The voices repeat the phrase almost daily in a low whisper. 'Go the distance.' The voices follow me everywhere I go. When I discuss my passion for working with Microsoft software and tools, many of my colleagues, friends and family members tell me to listen to the voices. Just like Kevin Costner's character in the hit movie 'Field of Dreams,' I too have a calling. My mission is to reach even higher."—Recruiter, hi tech firm

Quoted from Vault.com, "'What's the Most Ridiculous Thing You've Ever Seen on a Résumé or Cover Letter?': EmployerVault Question of the Week," in *EmployerVault: Recruiting: Hot Topics*, http://www.vault.com/nr/newsmain.jsp?nr_page=3&ch_id=400&article_id=5853753&cat_id=1083 (accessed March 11, 2009).

Never present the information as though it will be news to the reader. After all, the reader works for the company and presumably knows much more about it than you do.

Showing What Separates You from Other Applicants

Your knowledge of the company can separate you from other applicants. You can also use coursework, an understanding of the field, and experience in jobs and extracurricular events to show that you're unique. Stress your accomplishments, not your job responsibilities. Be specific but concise; usually three to five sentences will enable you to give enough specific supporting details.

This student uses both coursework and summer jobs to set herself apart from other applicants. Her research told her Monsanto had recently adopted new accounting methods for fluctuations in foreign currencies. Therefore, she mentions relevant simulations from her coursework.

> My college courses have taught me the essential accounting skills required to contribute to the growth of Monsanto. In two courses in international accounting, I compiled simulated accounting statements of hypothetical multinational firms in countries experiencing different rates of currency devaluation. Through these classes, I acquired the skills needed to work with the daily fluctuations of exchange rates and at the same time formulate an accurate and favorable representation of Monsanto.
>
> Both my summer jobs and my coursework prepare me to do extensive record keeping as well as numerous internal and external communications. As Office Manager for the steamboat *Julia Belle Swain*, I was in charge of most of the bookkeeping and letter writing for the company. I kept accurate records for each workday, and I often entered over 100 transactions in a single day. In business and technical writing I learned how to write persuasive letters and memos and how to present extensive data in reports in a simplified style that is clear and easy to understand.

In your résumé, you may list activities, offices, and courses. In your letter, give more detail about what you did and show how those experiences will help you contribute to the employer's organization more quickly.

When you discuss your strengths, don't exaggerate. No employer will believe that a new graduate has a "comprehensive" knowledge of a field. Indeed, most employers believe that six months to a year of on-the-job training is necessary before most new hires are really earning their pay. Specifics about what you've done will make your claims about what you can do more believable and ground them in reality.

The Last Paragraph

In the last paragraph, indicate when you'd be available for an interview. If you're free anytime, you can say so. But it's likely that you have responsibilities in class and work. If you'd have to go out of town, there may be only certain days of the week or certain weeks that you could leave town for several days. Use a sentence that fits your situation.

> November 5–10 I'll be attending the Oregon Forestry Association's annual meeting and will be available for interviews then.

Any Monday or Friday I could come to Memphis for an interview.

Should you wait for the employer to call you, or should you call the employer to request an interview? In a solicited letter, it's safe to wait to be contacted: you know the employer wants to hire someone, and if your letter and résumé show that you're one of the top applicants, you'll get an interview. In a prospecting letter, call the employer. Because the employer is not planning to hire, you'll get a higher percentage of interviews if you're assertive.

If you're writing a prospecting letter to a firm that's more than a few hours away by car, say that you'll be in the area the week of such-and-such and could stop by for an interview. Companies pay for follow-up visits, but not for first interviews. A company may be reluctant to ask you to make an expensive trip when it isn't yet sure it wants to hire you.

End the letter on a positive note that suggests you look forward to the interview and that you see yourself as a person who has something to contribute, not as someone who just needs a job.

I look forward to discussing with you ways in which I could contribute to The Limited's continued growth.

Do not end your letter with a variation of the tired cliché "Please do not hesitate to contact me." Why do you think they would hesitate? Using an overworked ending dumps you right back in the pool with all the other applicants.

Oh yes, one more thing. Don't forget to sign your letter—with blue or black ink—legibly.

E-Mail Application Letters

Some Web ads give you a street address to submit applications but say "e-mail preferred." Other ads just give an e-mail address. It is becoming more likely all the time that you will e-mail some of your applications.

If your application is solicited, you can paste your traditional letter into your e-mail. If your application is prospecting, you need a shorter letter that will catch the reader's attention within the first screen (see Figure 12.9). Your first paragraph is crucial; use it to hook the reader.

Some sources are starting to recommend a shorter letter for both situations, but many caution that you need to include enough information to make you seem to be the person for the job instead of other numerous applicants. Frequently that is hard to do in one screen.

When you submit an e-mail letter with an attached résumé,

- Include your name as part of the subject line.
- Put the job number or title for which you're applying in the first paragraph.
- Prepare your letter in a word-processing program. Use a spell checker to make it easier to edit and proof the document; then paste it into the e-mail.
- Use standard business letter features: salutation, standard closing, double-spacing between paragraphs.

Figure 12.9   An E-mail with Application Letter and Résumé

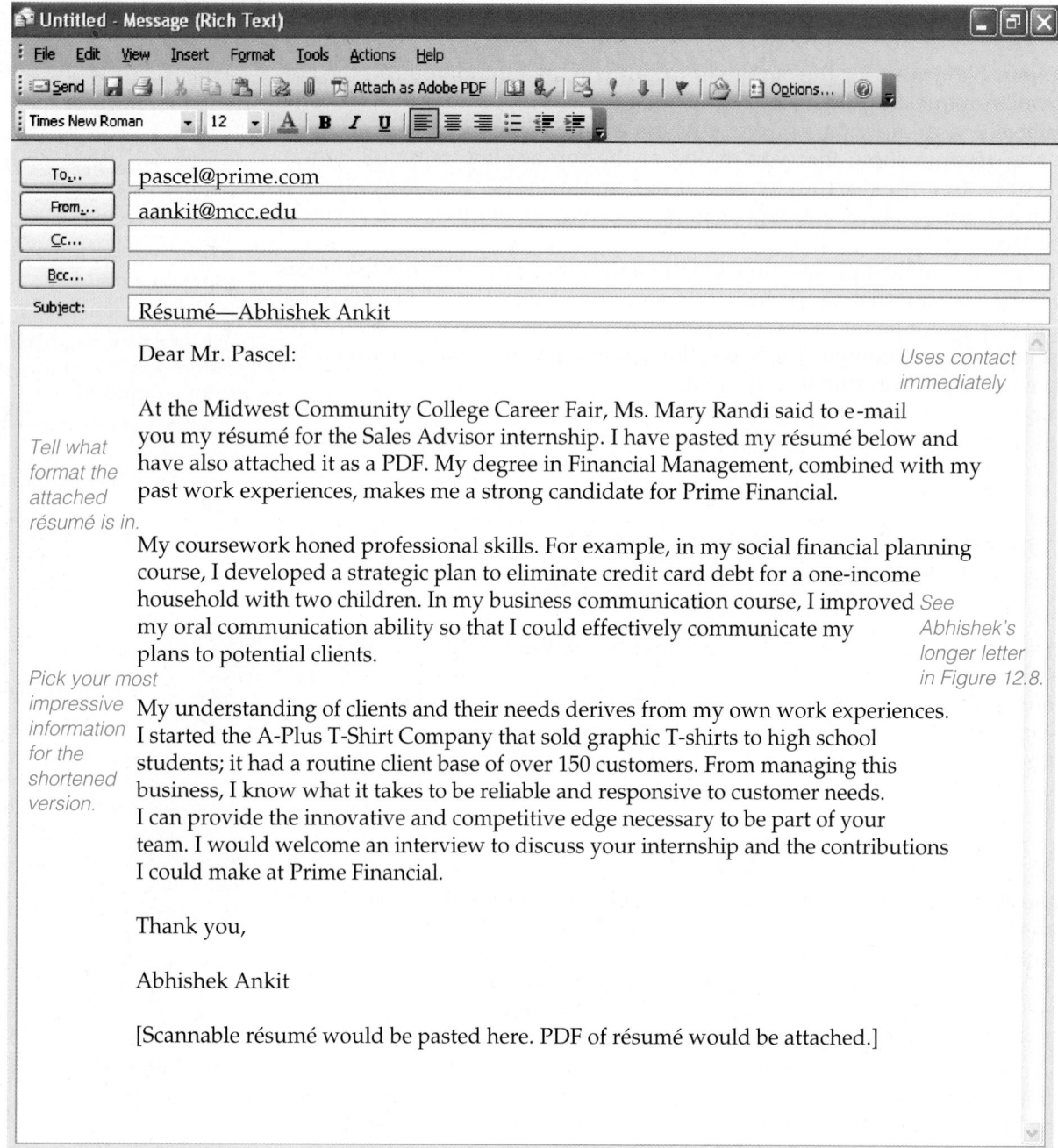

- Keep line length to a maximum of 65 characters, including spaces, so receivers won't get a strange mixture of long and short lines.
- Don't send anything in all capital letters.
- Don't use smiley faces or other emoticons.
- Put your name at the end of the message.

Follow all guidelines posted by the company. Do not add attachments unless you know doing so is OK. Test your letter by sending it to a friend; have your friend recheck it for appearance and correctness.

Since yo
number of

Under n
Courses
My resp

In partic
preposition

As my r
In my cc
As a sun
While I ₁

Paragra

Keep your
or five type
long parag
When y
subject. If
graphs.
Use topi
look organi

Letter L

Have at lea
be persuas
that you ar
Without
you're usin
use slightly
on the page
If you ha
as you have
gives you r
about your
ers don't w
and *if* the ;
dentials the
shorter lett

Editing

Be sure you
the work yo
ing errors ₁
mer). In fac
example, R
Killian & C
their Web ;
Night-befo₁

Creating a Professional Image

Every employer wants businesslike employees who understand professionalism. To make your application letter professional,

- Create your letter in a word-processing program so you can use features such as spell check. Use a standard font such as Times New Roman, Arial, or Helvetica in 12-point type.
- Address your letter to a specific person. If the reader is a woman, call the office to find out what courtesy title she prefers.
- Don't mention relatives' names. It's OK to use names of other people if the reader knows those people and thinks well of them, if they think well of you and will say good things about you, and if you have permission to use their names.
- Omit personal information not related to the job.
- Unless you're applying for a creative job in advertising, use a conservative style: few contractions; no sentence fragments, clichés, or slang.
- Edit the letter carefully and proof it several times to make sure it's perfect. Errors suggest that you're careless or inept. Double-check the spelling of the receiver's name.
- Print on the same paper (both color and weight) you used for your résumé. Envelopes should match, too.
- Use a computer to print the envelope address.

Writing Style

Use a smooth, concise writing style (p. 197). Use the technical jargon of the field to show your training, but avoid businessese and stuffy words like *utilize, commence,* and *transpire* (for *happen*). Use a lively, energetic style that makes you sound like a real person.

Avoid words that can be interpreted sexually. A model letter distributed by the placement office at a midwestern university included the following sentence:

I have been active in campus activities and have enjoyed good relations with my classmates and professors.

One young woman incorporated this sentence in a letter she mailed. The recipient circled the sentence and then passed the letter around the office (and did not invite the woman for an interview). That's not the kind of attention you want your letter to get!

Positive Emphasis

Be positive. Don't plead ("Please give me a chance") or apologize ("I cannot promise that I am substantially different from the lot"). Most negatives should be omitted from the letter.

Avoid word choices with negative connotations (p. 66). Note how the following revisions make the writer sound more confident.

Negative: I have learned an excessive amount about writing through courses in journalism and advertising.

Positive: Courses in journalism and advertising have taught me to recognize and to write good copy. My profile of a professor was published in the campus newspaper; I earned an "A + " on my direct mail campaign for the American Dental Association to persuade young adults to see their dentist more often.

You(r) Attitude Matters

If you find getting a job difficult, your attitude may be the reason. Here are four common career-blocking attitudes and responses to them:

Attitude: I deserve a good job because I went to school for four years.

Response: Employers are looking for who is best for a job, not who "deserves" a job.

Attitude: I am open to any job. I have no idea what I want to do.

Response: Employers want workers who are focused.

Attitude: I don't have experience because no one will give me a chance.

Response: Employers do not employ people to give them a "chance." Employers are concerned with what an applicant can do for them.

Attitude: I am so down on myself that it's hard to keep looking for a job.

Response: Get professional help, because this attitude is poisonous to your life as well as your career.

Adapted from Peter Vogt. "Self-Defeating Attitudes Will Stop Your Job Search Cold," in *MonsterTRAK Career Advice Archives: Job Hunt,* http://www.monstertrak.com/career-guide/career-planning/self-defeating-attitudes-1 (accessed March 15, 2009).

Gimme Gimmicks—Maybe Not

Although the temptation to make your job package stand out may be strong, remember that most gimmicks are resounding failures. These are some that failed:

- Delivering the package by homing pigeon.
- Delivering the package in a gorilla suit.
- Delivering a cut up résumé piece by piece inside Russian stacking dolls.
- E-mailing hirers jokes or goofy photos to stay on the radar.

If you are in a creative profession like advertising or marketing, a gimmick carefully chosen for a particular audience *may* work. Even here, you need to exercise great judgment. It may be far better to show creativity by offering a link to your professional blog or e-portfolio.

Adapted from Sarah E. Needleman, "In Quest to Stand Out, Take Care with Gimmicks," *Wall Street Journal*, July 3, 2007, A10.

Check your content one last time to ensure that everything presents you as a hard-working professional. Make sure you are not revealing any frustration with the job search process in your content or diction. Check your tone to see that it is positive about your previous experiences and yourself. Don't beg or show too much gratitude for commonplaces such as reading your letter (thank you so much for considering my application).

Follow-Up

Follow up with the employer once if you hear nothing after two or three weeks. It is also OK to ask once after one week if e-mail materials were received. If your job letter was prospecting, it is fine to follow up two or three times. Do not make a pest of yourself, however, by calling or e-mailing too often; doing so could eliminate you from further consideration.

Application Essays

Some jobs and internships, and many scholarship and graduate school applications, ask for an application essay. In a sense, this essay is an extended cover letter, but one written in an essay format rather than letter format. It will detail your strengths for the job/internship/scholarship/graduate school slot and show why you should be chosen instead of other applicants.

The essay offers you a chance to expand on your best points in more detail than does a cover letter. In so doing, you need to capture your readers' attention and show that you are exceptional. Frequently this means you need to put some of your personality into your essay. Here you can spell out with more interesting details skills you have already acquired from previous experiences and will bring to the new job or internship. Here you can elaborate on your academic achievements so you seem worthy of a scholarship or able to thrive in the rigors of graduate school. You can also expand more on general skills such as communication, problem solving, and teamwork. Show that you are capable, hard working, and interesting.

The essay also gives you room to include content that you would not put in a cover letter. For instance, you might want to include an anecdote that shows something about you as a developing professional (hint: make it interesting but not melodramatic). Or you might talk some about future goals. How did you arrive at these goals? How would this internship advance your career goals? Why do you want to go to graduate school? What do you want to do after the internship, scholarship, or graduate career is over? Be careful when giving goals for job application essays. You do not want your goals to make the job seem like a quick stepping-stone to better opportunities.

Remember to use the good writing techniques you have learned in this course and your other communication classes.

- Follow the directions, especially word and page limits, precisely. If the essay is to respond to a question, make sure it answers the question.

- Have a focal point for your essay, a unifying theme. This will help prevent you from merely listing accomplishments (your résumé did that).

- Start your essay with an interesting paragraph to catch attention. Do not summarize your essay, or your reader may go no further.

- Remember your audience. Show what you can do for this company, or why you want to go to this particular graduate school. But most of all, show what's in it for them if they accept you.

- Use vivid details in the body of the essay. They don't have to be wildly creative for a job essay; showing how you cut production time for the department newsletter by 15% will be interesting to your reader if the job is a good fit for you.
- Use some unique details. If your sentence could be used in many other applications, it is not showing why *you* should get the internship/job/scholarship/graduate school slot.
- Avoid unsupported generalities and clichés.
- Use topic sentences at the beginnings your paragraphs. Remember these essays are frequently read quickly.
- Let your word choice reveal your personal voice. Since the essay is about you, it's fine to use some first person. Avoid thesaurus diction.
- End with a strong concluding paragraph. Remember, this is their last impression of you. Do not waste it on a boring summary of a one-page essay.

Summary of Key Points

- Résumés differ from letters of application in the following ways:
  - A résumé is adapted to a position. The letter is adapted to the needs of a particular organization.
  - The résumé summarizes all your qualifications. The letter expands your best qualifications to show how you can help the organization meet its needs, how you differ from other applicants, and that you have some knowledge of the organization.
  - The résumé avoids controversial material. The letter can explain in positive ways situations such as gaps in employment history.
  - The résumé uses short, parallel phrases and sentence fragments. The letter uses complete sentences in well-written paragraphs.
- Use the Internet, annual reports, recruiting literature, business periodicals, trade journals, and internships to get information about employers and jobs to use in your letter.
- **Networking** and information and referral interviews can help you tap into the **hidden job market**—jobs that are not advertised. In an **information interview** you find out what the day-to-day work involves and how you can best prepare to enter that field. **Referral interviews** are interviews you schedule to learn about current job opportunities in your field.
- When you know that a company is hiring, send a **solicited job letter.** When you want a job with a company that has not announced openings, send a **prospecting job letter.** In both letters, you should
  - Address the letter to a specific person.
  - Indicate the specific position for which you're applying.
  - Be specific about your qualifications.
  - Show what separates you from other applicants.
  - Show a knowledge of the company and the position.
  - Refer to your résumé (which you would enclose with the letter).
  - Ask for an interview.
- Use your knowledge of the company, your coursework, your understanding of the field, and your experience in jobs and extracurricular activities to show that you're unique.

- Don't repeat information that the reader already knows; don't seem to be lecturing the reader on his or her business.
- Use positive emphasis to sound confident. Use you-attitude by supporting general claims with specific examples and by relating what you've done to what the employer needs.
- Have at least three paragraphs in your letter. Most job letters are only one page.
- Application essays give you a chance to expand on your best points and show your personality.

CHAPTER 12   Exercises and Problems

12.1   Reviewing the Chapter

1. What are four ways that job letters differ from résumés? (LO 2)

2. What are four ways to research specific employers? (LO 1)

3. What is the difference between information and referral interviews? (LO 1)

4. What are the differences between solicited and prospecting letters? (LO 2)

5. What are five tips for writing a job letter that makes you look attractive to employers? (LO 2)

6. What are 10 ways to create a professional image with your letter? (LO 2)

12.2   Reviewing Grammar

As you have read, it is crucial that your job letter be error-free. One common error in job letters, and one that spell-checking programs will not catch, is confusing word pairs like *affect/effect*. Practice choosing the correct word with Exercises B.12, B.13, and B.14 in Appendix B.

12.3   Analyzing First Paragraphs of Prospecting Letters

All of the following are first paragraphs in prospecting letters written by new college graduates. Evaluate the paragraphs on these criteria:

- Is the paragraph likely to interest readers and motivate them to read the rest of the letter?
- Does the paragraph have some content that the student can use to create a transition to talking about his or her qualifications?
- Does the paragraph avoid asking for a job?

1. For the past two and one-half years I have been studying turf management. On August 1, I will graduate from —— University with a BA in Ornamental Horticulture. The type of job I will seek will deal with golf course maintenance as an assistant superintendent.

2. Ann Gibbs suggested that I contact you.

3. Each year, the Christmas shopping rush makes more work for everyone at Nordstrom's, especially for the Credit Department. While working for Nordstrom's Credit Department for three Christmas and summer vacations, the Christmas sales increase is just one of the credit situations I became aware of.

4. Whether to plate a two-inch eyebolt with cadmium for a tough, brilliant shine or with zinc for a rust-resistant, less expensive finish is a tough question. But similar questions must be answered daily by your salespeople. With my experience in the electroplating industry, I can contribute greatly to your constant need of getting customers.

5. What a set of tractors! The new 9430 and 9630 diesels are just what is needed by today's farmer with his ever-increasing acreage. John Deere has truly done it again.

6. Prudential Insurance Company did much to help my college career as the sponsor of my National Merit Scholarship. Now I think I can give something back to Prudential. I'd like to put my education, including a BS degree in finance from —— University, to work in your investment department.

7. Since the beginning of Delta Electric Construction Co. in 1993, the size and profits have grown steadily. My father, being a stockholder and vice president, often discusses company dealings with me.

Although the company has prospered, I understand there have been a few problems of mismanagement. I feel with my present and future qualifications, I could help ease these problems.

12.4 Improving You-Attitude and Positive Emphasis in Job Letters

Revise each of these sentences to improve you-attitude and positive emphasis. You may need to add information.

1. I understand that your company has had problems due to the mistranslation of documents during international ad campaigns.

2. Included in my résumé are the courses in Finance that earned me a fairly attractive grade average.

3. I am looking for a position that gives me a chance to advance quickly.

4. Although short on experience, I am long on effort and enthusiasm.

5. I have been with the company from its beginning to its present unfortunate state of bankruptcy.

12.5 Evaluating Rough Drafts

Evaluate the following drafts. What parts should be omitted? What needs to be changed or added? What parts would benefit from specific supporting details?

1.

Dear_____:

There is more to a buyer's job than buying the merchandise. And a clothing buyer in particular has much to consider.

Even though something may be in style, customers may not want to buy it. Buyers should therefore be aware of what customers want and how much they are willing to pay.

In the buying field, request letters, thank-you letters, and persuasive letters are frequently written.

My interest in the retail field inspired me to read The Gap's annual report. I saw that a new store is being built. An interview would give us a chance to discuss how I could contribute to this new store. Please call me to schedule an interview.

Sincerely,

2.

Dear Sir or Madam:

I am taking the direct approach of a personnel letter. I believe you will under stand my true value in the areas of practical knowledge and promotional capabilities.

I am interested in a staff position with Darden in relation to trying to improve the operations and moral of the Olive Garden Restaurants, which I think that I am capable of doing. Please take a minute not to read my résumé (enclosed) and call to schedule an interview.

Sincerely,

3.

> Dear_____:
>
> I would like to apply for the opening you announced for an Assistant Golf Course Superintendent. I have the qualifications you are asking for.
>
> Every year the Superintendent must go before the greens committee to defend its budget requests. To prepare myself to do this, I took courses in accounting, business and administrative writing, and speech.
>
> I have done the operations necessary to maintain the greens properly.
>
> I look forward to talking with you about this position.
>
> Sincerely,

12.6 Gathering Information about an Industry

Use six recent issues of a trade journal to report on three or four trends, developments, or issues that are important in an industry.

As your instructor directs,

a. Share your findings with a small group of other students.

b. Summarize your findings in a memo to your instructor. Include a discussion of how you could use this information in your job letter and résumé.

c. Present your findings to the class.

d. Join with a small group of other students to write a report summarizing the results of this research.

12.7 Gathering Information about Companies in Your Career Field

Use five different Web sites, such as those listed in Figure 12.1, to investigate three companies in your career field. Look at salary guides for your level of qualifications, product/service information, news articles about the companies, mission/vision statements, main competitors, annual reports, and financial reports.

As your instructor directs,

a. Share your findings with a small group of other students.

b. Summarize your findings in a memo to your instructor. Include a discussion of how you could use this information in your job letter and résumé.

c. Present your findings to the class.

d. Join with a small group of other students to write a report summarizing the results of this research.

12.8 Gathering Information about a Specific Organization

Gather information about a specific organization, using several of the following methods:

- Check the organization's Web site.
- Read the company's annual report.
- Pick up relevant information at the Chamber of Commerce.
- Read articles in trade publications and the *Wall Street Journal* or that mention the organization (check the indexes).
- Read recruiting literature provided by the company.

As your instructor directs,

a. Share your findings with a small group of other students.

b. Summarize your findings in a memo to your instructor. Include a discussion of how you could use this information in your job letter and résumé:

c. Present your findings orally to the class.

d. Write a paragraph for a job letter using (directly or indirectly) the information you found.

12.9   Conducting an Information Interview

Interview someone working in a field you're interested in. Use the questions listed on page 345 or the shorter list here:

- How did you get started in this field?
- What do you like about your job?
- What do you dislike about your job?
- What courses and jobs would you recommend as preparation for this field?

As your instructor directs,

a. Share the results of your interview with a small group of other students.

b. Write up your interview in a memo to your instructor. Include a discussion of how you could use this information in your job letter and résumé.

c. Present the results of your interview orally to the class.

d. Write to the interviewee thanking him or her for taking the time to talk to you.

12.10   Networking

a. Write to a friend who is already in the workforce, asking about one or more of the following topics:

- Are any jobs in your field available in your friend's organization? If so, what?
- If a job is available, can your friend provide information beyond the job listing that will help you write a more detailed, persuasive letter? (Specify the kind of information you'd like to have.)
- Can your friend suggest people in other organizations who might be useful to you in your job search? (Specify any organizations in which you're especially interested.)

b. List possible networking contacts from your co-workers, classmates, fraternity/sorority members, friends, family friends, former employers and co-workers, neighbors, faculty members, and local business people. Who would be the most valuable source of information for you? Who would you feel most comfortable contacting?

12.11   Writing a Solicited Letter

Write a letter of application in response to an announced opening for a full-time job (not an internship) you would like.

   Turn in a copy of the listing. If you use option (a) below, your listing will be a copy. If you choose option (b), you will write the listing.

a. Respond to an ad in a newspaper, in a professional journal, in the placement office, or on the Web. Use an ad that specifies the company, not a blind ad. Be sure that you are fully qualified for the job.

b. If you have already worked somewhere, assume that your employer is asking you to apply for full-time work after graduation. Be sure to write a fully persuasive letter.

12.12   Writing a Prospecting Letter

Pick a company you'd like to work for and apply for a specific position that is not being advertised. The position can be one that already exists or one that you would create if you could to match your unique blend of talents.

   Address your letter to the person with the power to create a job for you: the president of a small company, or the area vice president or branch manager of a large company.

   Create a job description; give your instructor a copy of it with your letter.

12.13 Critiquing a Job Letter

After you have written your job letter for Exercise 12.11 or 12.12, bring it to class and share it with a classmate.

- Read your cover letter aloud to your classmate noting any changes you would like to make and any areas that may not sound appropriate.

- Have your classmate reread your job letter and make suggestions to enhance it.
- Swap letters and go through the exercise again.

Write a memo to your instructor discussing the changes you will make to your job letter on the basis of this exercise.

12.14 Writing a Rhetorical Analysis of Your Job Letter

a. Examine the job letter you wrote for Exercise 12.11 or 12.12 and answer the following questions in a memo to your instructor:

- Who is your audience? Identify them beyond their name. What will they be looking for?
- How did you consider this audience when selecting information and the level of detail to use? What information did you exclude? How did you shape the information about you to address your audience's needs?
- How did you organize your information for this audience?

- How did you adapt your tone and style for this audience? How did you balance your need to promote yourself without bragging? Where did you use you-attitude, positive tone, and goodwill?
- How did you show knowledge of the company and the position without telling your audience what they already know?

b. Review a class member's cover letter using the same questions.

12.15 Applying Electronically

Write an e-mail application letter with a résumé in the text of the message.

12.16 Applying at Intel

Using the Intel sidebar on page 347, research possible jobs at Intel. Pick the one most appropriate for you and write an electronic job letter to Intel.

12.17 Editing a Cover Letter

In Chapter 11, Exercise 11.13, you critiqued the résumé of Jennifer Stanton. Below is her cover letter. Using the information about Jennifer from Exercise 11.13, redo her letter to improve it. Then write a memo to your instructor discussing the strengths and weaknesses of the letter and explaining why you made the changes you did.

From: wildechilde@gmail.com

To: pattersj@micquant.com

Date: 13 February, 2009

Re: Job!

Dear Ms. Patterson:

My name is Jennifer Stanton and I really want to work with you at Quantum National! Your job looks a whole lot like the one I had at my internship this past summer, so I'm pretty sure I'd be great at it.

I can't start until this Summer, because I'm finishing up my degree at Iowa State. I'm currently working on a degree in Buisness Management, so I'd be a great manager at your business. The one thing I've learned for sure in college is how to balance deadlines to get everything done on time. I've had a few classes where we had to work in teams, and I've been the team leader every time: once I step in, people just want to follow where I lead.

I think my work experience is exactly what you're looking for, too. At my internship last summer, I was basically unsupervised, so I had to learn fast! I managed cliet and department needs, I did the budgets—twice!—and I worked with a sales and marketing team to put together client information packages. I also did the scheduling for the team the whole time, which was my supervisor's job but she delegated it to me, because I am trustworthy. I also worked for years at my family's bookstore, which shows I can hold down a job.

Like I said, I'm really interested in this job. I think that this would be a great place to start my career, and I know I can do the job! Give me a call on my cell when you decide who you're interviewing!

Thanks,

Jennifer Stanton

12.18   All-Weather Case: Reviewing Cover Letters

All-Weather invited applications for the position of Sales Representative (Residential Sales). To be based in Nebraska, this person will be mainly responsible for sales of All-Weather's vinyl windows in local markets, including single- and double-hung windows and casement windows. All-Weather's marketing department has identified five market segments in the state in which increased construction of low-cost housing offers opportunities for further market penetration. The job description for the position reads as follows:

The Sales Representative (Residential Sales) will be responsible for successful market penetration of identified market segments. Specifically, the duties include achieving targeted sales, conducting product demonstrations, contacting customers and other stakeholders, gathering market intelligence, preparing market and sales reports, communicating with internal customers, coordinating between customers and the Service and Installation Group, participating in meetings of trade associations and government agencies, attending company training events, and performing other duties assigned by managers. The ideal candidate will be someone with a BS degree, preferably with a technical major. Additionally, the candidate must have at least one year of sales experience, preferably in industrial products. Candidates with experience in brand marketing will also be considered. Among skills for the job, the candidate must possess computer skills, PR and communication skills, teamwork skills, and the ability to perform basic mathematical computations.

All-Weather has received six applications for the position. Erin and the marketing manager are reviewing the applications. The first two applications belong to Antonio Ramirez and Michelle Chang. Both candidates have excellent résumés highlighting their very different backgrounds. Antonio sells PVC resin for a petrochemicals company based in Texas. An account representative with a local advertising agency, Michelle is an energetic member of a team that has handled a number of brands. After going through Antonio's and Michelle's résumés, Erin and the marketing manager agree that they will need to look carefully at the candidates' cover letters (Figures 1 and 2 below) to be able to rank their applications. Help Erin and her marketing colleague evaluate the two cover letters by listing their strengths and weaknesses in light of the job description given above.

Figure 1   Antonio Ramirez's Cover Letter

Antonio Ramirez aramirez@bestmail.com 164 Beet St. Houston, TX

October 12, 2008
Ms. Erin Lenhardt
1210 Polaroid Av.
St. Paul, MN

Dear Ms. Lenhardt:

Please consider this letter as my application for the post of Sales Representative (Residential Sales). I learned about your job from the journal *Plastics US* (September issue). I have a bachelor's degree in chemistry from the University of Austin, Texas, and have two years of experience selling PVC resin.

The last two years I have been a Sales Executive in Goodman Petrochemicals in Houston, TX. My responsibilities include selling Goodman's PVC resin to Houston-based PVC processors of rigid and flexible applicatons.

As you suggest in your advertisement, my degree in chemistry will help me explain to customers the important technical attributes of your vinyl windows. My focus during my bachelor's degree was inorganic chemistry, especially hydrocarbons and its practical applications. Apart from my coursework, I also interned at Bright Fenestration Products in Austin, TX.

I look forward to discussing my experience and interst in your organization with you in a face-to-face interview. I'm available for the interview anytime in the next two weeks at a day's notice. I'm confident I will meet—and exceed—all your expetations for this important front line position.

Sincerely,

Antonio Ramirez

Figure 2   Michelle Chang's Cover Letter

Michelle Chang
4334, Sunset Boulevard, Lincoln, NE
mchang@myemail.com

October 14, 2008
Ms. Erin Lenhardt
HR Manager
1210 Polaroid Av.
St. Paul, MN

Dear Ms. Lenhardt:

I wish to apply for the position of Sales Representative (Residential Sales) advertised through Monster.com. After acquiring a bachelor's degree in design, I joined Albatross Advertising in November, 2006, as a trainee in the Accounts Department. Currently, I'm an Account Representative handling three of our most promising brands: *LiteWait* vacuum cleaners, Nebraska Furniture Mart, and Chimney Rock Art Gallery.

My bachelor's degree in design with a major in community and regional planning not only familiarized me with demands of buildings and landscapes in our 21st century living but also acquainted me with concepts of media and design. I joined Albatross because I wanted to see if my education has equipped me to inform, persuade, and help customers with regard to products and brands.

During my nearly two-year tenure at Albatross as Account Representative, I have created and given insightful presentations to clients. As a result of my performance, the agency has entrusted me with three of its most promising accounts, the ones that I mention above.

I would be delighted at an opportunity for a personal interview to further make my case for the job. You can contact me at my e-mail address mentioned above.

Sincerely,

Michelle Chang

Learning Objectives

After studying this chapter, you will know:

1 What kinds of interviews you may encounter.

2 What preparations to make before you start interviewing.

3 What to do during an interview.

4 How to answer common interview questions.

5 What to do after an interview.

"Best" Hires

Fortune magazine offers these tips to increase your chances for a job at one of its "100 Best Companies to Work For."

Know someone at the company; most of these companies rely on employee referrals.

Emphasize your volunteer work; these companies support community outreach.

Be ready for multiple interviews, as many as 15.

Put your inner storyteller to work; you will be asked how you handled various work scenarios.

Do more research about the company than your rivals do.

Be a team player (one manager actually counts the number of times candidates say "I").

Show your willingness to build your career in that company; most are looking for long-term employees.

Show a passion for learning and growing at that company.

Adapted from Anne Fisher, "How to Get Hired by a 'Best' Company," *Fortune*, February 4, 2008, 96.

Job interviews are scary, even when you've prepared thoroughly. But when you are prepared, you can harness the adrenaline to work for you, so that you put your best foot forward and get the job you want. The best way to prepare is to know as much as possible about the process and the employer.

21st Century Interviews

Interviews remain an important part of the hiring process. A survey of 600 managers found that they overwhelmingly preferred evaluating job candidates in person, either by interviews (38%) or temporary work performance (38%). Only 6% chose the résumé and cover letter.[1]

Interviews are changing, however, as employers respond to interviewees who are prepared to answer the standard questions. Today, many employers expect you to

- Be more assertive. Many employers expect you to call them to arrange interviews.
- Follow instructions to the letter. The owner of a delivery company tells candidates to phone at a precise hour. Failing to do so means that the person couldn't be trusted to deliver packages on time.[2]
- Participate in many interviews. Candidates may have one or more interviews by phone, computer, or video before they have an office interview.
- Take one or more tests, including drug tests, psychological tests, aptitude tests, computer simulations, and essay exams where you're asked to explain what you'd do in a specific situation.
- Be approved by the team you'll be joining. In companies with self-managed work teams, the team has a say in who is hired.
- Provide—at the interview or right after it—a sample of the work you're applying to do. You may be asked to write a memo or a proposal, calculate a budget on a spreadsheet, write computer code, or make a presentation.

All the phoning required in 21st-century interviews places a special emphasis on phone skills. Be polite to everyone with whom you speak, including administrative assistants and secretaries. Find out the person's name on your first call and use it on subsequent calls. Be considerate: "Thank you for being so patient. Can you tell me when a better time might be to try to reach Ms. X? I'll try again on [date]." Sometimes, if you call after 5 PM, executives answer their own phones since clerical staff have gone home. However, some of them resent interruptions at that time, so be particularly well prepared and focused.

If you get someone's voice mail, leave a concise message—complete with your name and phone number. Give the phone number slowly so it can be jotted down. Keep your voice pleasant. If you get voice mail repeatedly, call the main company number to speak with a receptionist. Ask whether the person you're trying to reach is in the building. If he or she is on the road, ask when the person is due in.

Interview Strategy

Develop an overall strategy based on your answers to these three questions:

1. **What about yourself do you want the interviewer to know?** Pick two to five points that represent your strengths for that particular job and that show how you will add value to the organization. These facts are frequently character traits (such as enthusiasm), achievements and experiences that qualify you for the job and separate you from other applicants, or unique abilities such as fluency in Spanish. For each strength, think of a specific accomplishment to support it. For instance, be ready to give an example to prove that you're hardworking. Be ready to show how you helped an organization save money or serve customers better.

   Then at the interview, listen to every question to see if you could make one of your key points as part of your answer. If the questions don't allow you to make your points, bring them up at the end of the interview.

2. **What disadvantages or weaknesses do you need to minimize?** Expect that you may be asked to explain weaknesses or apparent weaknesses in your record such as lack of experience, so–so grades, and gaps in your record.

   Plan how to deal with these issues if they arise. Decide if you want to bring them up yourself, particularly disadvantages or weaknesses that are easily discoverable. If you bring them up, you can plan the best context for them during the interview. Many students, for example, have been able to get good jobs after flunking out of school by explaining that the experience was a turning point in their lives and pointing out that when they returned to school they maintained a B or better grade point average. Although it is illegal to ask questions about marital status, married candidates with spouses who are able to move easily sometimes volunteer that information: "My husband is a dentist and is willing to relocate if the company wants to transfer me." See the suggestions later in this chapter under "Answering Traditional Interview Questions" and "Behavioral and Situational Interviews."

3. **What do you need to know about the job and the organization to decide whether or not you want to accept this job if it is offered to you?** Plan *in advance* the criteria on which you will base your decision (you can always change the criteria). Use "Deciding Which Offer to Accept" below to plan questions to elicit the information you'll need to rank each offer.

Interview Preparation

Preparing for your interviews can help you to feel more confident and make a better impression.

Final Research

Research the company interviewing you. Read their Web pages, company newsletters, annual reports. Read about them in trade journals and newspapers. Do a Google search. Ask your professors, classmates, friends, family, and co-workers about them. If possible, find out who will interview you and research them, too.

Also research salaries for the job: What is average? What is the range? Use Web tools like indeed.com/salary or salary.com to find salary information by job title and location.

Travel Planning

If your interview is not on campus, make sure you can find the building and the closest parking. Plan how much time you will need to get there. Leave time margins for stressors such as traffic jams or broken elevators. If you are fortunate enough to be flown to an interview, don't schedule too tightly. Allow for flight delays and cancellations. Plan how you will get from the airport to the interview site. Take enough cash and credit cards to cover emergencies.

Attire

The outfit you wear to an interview should meet your interviewer's expectations. The most conservative choice is the traditional dark business suit with a light blouse or shirt, plus tie shoes with matching dark socks for men and close-toed pumps with nude, unpatterned hose for women. Although this outfit is probably still the most common choice, you cannot count on it being the right choice.

For campus interviews, you should follow the dress code of your campus career center.

For office interviews, you should show that you understand the organization's culture. Try to find out from your career contacts what is considered appropriate attire. Some interviewers do not mind if you ask them what you should wear to the interview. (Others do mind, so be careful. They believe it means you have not done your homework.)

Paul Capelli, former public relations executive at Amazon.com and now vice president of public relations at CNBC, suggests that applicants find out what employees wear "and notch it up one step":

> If the dress is jeans and a T-shirt, wear slacks and an open collar shirt . . . If it's slacks and an open collar shirt, throw on a sport coat. If it's a sport coat, throw on a suit. At least match it and go one step up.[3]

Choose comfortable shoes. You may do a fair amount of walking during an onsite interview. Check your heels to make sure they aren't run down; make sure your shoes are shined.

Make conservative choices. Have your hair cut or styled conservatively. Jewelry and makeup should be understated; face jewelry, such as eyebrow and nose studs, should be removed. If possible, cover tattoos. Personal hygiene must be impeccable, with close attention paid to fingernails and breath. Make sure your clothes are clean and pressed. Avoid cologne and perfumed aftershave lotions.

What Not to Wear at an Interview

CareerBuilder.com surveyed hiring professionals to discover the top fashion mistakes interviewees make:

1. Too-short skirts
2. Overly bright or vividly patterned clothing
3. Wrinkled or stained clothing
4. Poorly fitted clothing
5. Socks that are too short, or don't go with the shoes
6. Patterned hosiery or bare legs
7. Scuffed or inappropriate footwear, including sneakers, stilettos, sandals, and open-toed shoes
8. Extra buttons or tags attached to a new suit
9. Earrings on men; multiple sets of earrings on women
10. Visible tattoos, tongue jewelry, facial piercings
11. Heavy makeup
12. Long or bright fingernails
13. Unnatural hair colors or styles
14. Strong aftershaves, perfumes, or colognes
15. Backpacks, fanny packs, or purses (use a briefcase)
16. Sunglasses on top of your head or headphones around your neck

Adapted from "What Not to Wear to an Interview: Top 20 Wardrobe Malfunctions," in *Advice & Resources: Career Resources: Getting Hired*, http://www.careerbuilder.com/Article/CB-462-Getting-Hired-What-Not-to-Wear-to-an-Interview/ (accessed March 19, 2009).

You can wear a wide range of apparel to interviews. Find out what is appropriate—and inappropriate—for each interview. Which of these outfits would you wear?

Professional Materials

Take extra copies of your résumé. If your campus placement office has already given the interviewer a data sheet, present the résumé at the beginning of the interview: "I thought you might like a little more information about me."

Take something to write on and something to write with. It's OK to carry a small notepad with the questions you want to ask on it.

Take copies of your work or a portfolio: an engineering design, a copy of a memo you wrote on a job or in a business writing class, an article you wrote for the campus paper. You don't need to present these unless the interview calls for them, but they can be very effective: "Yes, I have done a media plan. Here's a copy of a plan I put together in my advertising seminar last year. We had a fixed budget and used real figures for cost and rating points, just as I'd do if I joined Foote, Cone & Belding."

Take the names, addresses, and phone numbers of references. Take complete details about your work history and education, including dates and street addresses, in case you're asked to fill out an application form.

Career Fair Advice

Stanford University's Career Development Center offers the following tips for career fairs:

1. Prepare for the Career Fair. Answer the following questions before you attend:
   - What organizations are attending?
   - How will the employers be organized at the event?
   - What is the starting and ending time?
   - What attire is appropriate?

2. Prepare a résumé to hand out to potential employers. However, if you do not have a résumé, you can still attend the fair to gather information.

3. Set up a plan: Make a prioritized list of organizations you want to visit. However, be open to interesting organizations you run across at the fair.

4. Create a one-minute presentation to give to potential employers outlining your background and qualifications which will meet the organization's needs.

5. Bring questions to ask.

6. Bring a pen and notepad to stay organized during the fair.

7. Thank employers at the fair for materials you are given.

8. Collect business cards and write a fact on the back to remember when you write a thank you.

9. Write a thank-you note to those organizations you wish to pursue.

Adapted from Stanford University Career Development Center, "Before the Career Fair," in *Prepare for the Job Search: Career Fair Preparation*, http://cardinalcareers.stanford.edu/jobsearch/cfprep/before.htm (accessed March 9, 2009).

If you can afford it, buy a briefcase in which to carry these items. At this point in your life, an inexpensive vinyl briefcase is acceptable. Women should let the briefcase replace a purse.

Interview Channels

Interviews use other channels in addition to the popular office setting. As a college student, you may well find yourself being interviewed on campus. You may also find you have a phone or video conference, as more and more companies use technology to keep hiring costs in check. Most of the interview advice in this chapter applies to all settings, but some channels do have unique particulars you should consider.

Campus Interviews

Most campus career offices have written protocols and expectations for campus interviews arranged through them. Be sure to follow these expectations so that you look informed.

However, because campus interviewers will see so many students who are all following the same protocols, it is important that you have good details and professional stories about your work to help you stand out from the crowd. Focus on three to four selling points you most want the interviewer to remember about you. If you have a choice, do not schedule your interview late in the day when interviewers are getting tired.

Phone Interviews

Some organizations use phone interviews to narrow the list of candidates they bring in for office visits. Phone interviews give you some advantages. Obviously, you do not have to dress up for them, or find an office. You can use all the materials you want as you speak. You can also take all the notes you want, although copious note-taking will probably impact your speaking quality, and you certainly don't want the sound of keyboard clicking to be heard by your interviewer.

On the other hand, phone interviews obviously deny you the important component of visual feedback. To compensate for this loss, you can ask your interviewer for verbal feedback (e.g., Is this sufficient detail? Would you like more on this topic?).

Although you always want to speak distinctly at an interview, doing so is even more crucial for a phone interview. And speech experts recommend that you smile, lean forward, and even gesture, although no one can see you. Such activities add warmth to your words. Be sure to eliminate all background noise such as music or TV. Finally, just as you did for a campus interview, focus on three to four selling points you most want the interviewer to remember about you.

Video Interviews

Video interviews are becoming more common. You may experience two different kinds. In one, the organization sends you a list of questions and you prepare a video which you send back to them. In the other, the organization conducts live interviews using videoconferencing equipment.

If you are preparing a video,

- Practice your answers so you are fluent. You don't want to stumble over your responses, but you also don't want to sound like you have memorized the answers.

- Be thorough. Since the employer can't ask follow-up questions, you want to consider what those questions could be and then be sure to answer them.

   If you are participating in a videoconference,

- Do a practice video of yourself ahead of time. Listen to your pronunciation and voice qualities. Watch your video with the sound turned off: check your posture, gestures, facial expressions, and clothing. Do you have nervous mannerisms you need to control?
- During the actual interview, keep your answers under two minutes. Then ask if interviewers want more information. People are generally more reluctant to interrupt a speaker in another location, and body language cues are limited, so ask for feedback ("Would you like to hear about that?").

Interview Practice

Rehearse everything you can: Put on the clothes you'll wear and practice entering a room, shaking hands, sitting down, and answering questions. Ask a friend to interview you. Saying answers out loud is surprisingly harder than saying them in your head. If your department or career center offers practice interviews, take advantage of them.

Some campuses have videotaping facilities so that you can watch your own sample interview. Videotaping is particularly valuable if you can do it at least twice, so you can modify behavior the second time and check the tape to see whether the modification works.

Interview Etiquette: Deteriorating?

Vault.com surveyed 675 employers and employees on their opinions about interview etiquette. The study found that 80% of the employers indicated that interviewing manners have deteriorated over the last two years.

Here are some other interesting results about employers that you may want to keep in mind during your next interview:

- 95% would disqualify a candidate for making a cell phone call.
- 86.3% would disqualify a candidate for accepting a cell phone call.
- 77.1% would disqualify a candidate for exhibiting poor hygiene.
- 60.3 % would disqualify a candidate for bringing a child to the interview.
- 9.7% would disqualify a candidate for arriving more than 30 minutes early.

Adapted from "Vault.com's Interview Manners Survey," in *Surveys*, Vault.com, http://www.vault.com/surveys/manners/mannersresults.jsp?results=1&image=employer (accessed March 19, 2009).

Phil blows his interview before even sitting down.

you won't work with people or give speeches in your first job, you'll need those skills later in your career, so don't use them for this question.) End your answer with a positive that *is* related to the job:

> [For a creative job in advertising:] I don't like accounting. I know it's important, but I don't like it. I even hire someone to do my taxes. I'm much more interested in being creative and working with people, which is why I find this position interesting.

> [For a job in administration:] I don't like selling products. I hated selling cookies when I was a Girl Scout. I'd much rather work with ideas—and I really like selling the ideas that I believe in.

> [For a job in architecture:] I hate fund-raising. It always seemed to me if people wanted to give, they would anyway. I'd much rather have something to offer people which will help them solve their own problems and meet their own needs.

b.   Discuss a weakness that you are working to improve:

> In the past, I wasn't a good writer. But last term I took a course in business writing that taught me how to organize my ideas and how to revise. I may never win a Pulitzer Prize, but now I can write effective reports and memos.

c.   Describe advice you received, and how that advice helped your career.

> The professor for whom I was an undergraduate assistant pointed out to me that people respond well to liberal praise, and that I was not liberal with mine. As I have worked on providing more positive feedback, I have become a better manager.

16. **What are your career goals? Where do you want to be in five years? Ten years?**   This question is frequently a test to see if you fit with this company. Are your goals ones that can be met at this company? Or will the company have the expense of training you only to see you move on promptly to another company?

17. **Why are you looking for another job?**   Do not answer this with a negative—"My boss didn't like me," "I didn't like the work"—even if the negative is true. Stress the new opportunities you're looking for in a new job, not why you want to get away from your old one: "I want more opportunity to work with clients."

    Also be careful of hidden negatives: "I couldn't use all my abilities in my last job" sounds like you are complaining. It also suggests that you don't take the initiative to find new challenges. If you are looking for a job with a bigger salary, it is better to use other points when answering this question.

    If you were fired, say so. There are various acceptable ways to explain why you were fired:

a.   It wasn't a good match. Add what you now know you need in a job, and ask what the employer can offer in this area.

b. You and your supervisor had a personality conflict. Make sure you show that this was an isolated incident, and that you normally get along well with people.

c. You made mistakes, but you've learned from them and are now ready to work well. Be ready to offer a specific anecdote proving that you have indeed changed.

18. **Why do you have a gap in your employment history?** Answer briefly and positively; do not apologize for family decisions.

> I cared for an ill family member. Because of the time it took, it wasn't fair to an employer to start a new job.

> I stayed home with my children while they were young. Now that they are both in school, I can devote myself to top performance in your company.

If you were laid off, be prepared to explain why you were one of the people let go. It helps if you can truthfully say that all new employees with less than three years' experience at the firm were laid off, or that legal services were outsourced, or that the entire training department was disbanded. Be careful you do not display bitter, angry feelings; they will not help you get a new job. It may help you to realize that in tight economies, being laid off is not an issue for many interviewers.

19. **What questions do you have?** This question gives you a chance to cover things the interviewer hasn't brought up; it also gives the interviewer a sense of your priorities and values. Almost all interviewers will ask you for questions, and it is crucial that you have some. A lack of questions will probably be interpreted as a lack of interest in the company and a lack of preparation for the interview. These are some questions you might want to ask:

- What do you like best about working for this company?
- What would I be doing on a day-to-day basis?
- What's the top challenge I would face in this job?
- What kind of training program do you have?
- How do you evaluate employees? How often do you review them?
- Where would you expect a new trainee (banker, staff accountant) to be three years from now? Five years? Ten years?
- What happened to the last person who had this job?
- How are interest rates (new products from competitors, imports, demographic trends, government regulations, etc.) affecting your company? Questions like these show that you care enough to do your homework and that you are aware of current events.
- How would you describe the company's culture?
- This sounds like a great job. What are the drawbacks?

Do not ask these questions:

- Questions about information you can easily find (and should have found) on the company's Web site.
- Questions that indicate dissatisfaction with the job for which you are being interviewed (How soon can I get promoted?).
- Questions about salary and benefits (wait until you have a job offer).

Handling Improper Interview Questions

If you are asked an improper question, you have several options:

- **You can answer the question.** However, you may not get hired if you give the "wrong" answer.

- **You can refuse to answer the question.** Doing so is within your rights, but it will make you look uncooperative or confrontational, so again you may not get hired.

- **You can look for the intent behind the question and provide an answer related to the job.** For example, it is illegal to ask you what country you are from. You could respond, however, by saying that you are authorized to work in the United States. If you are asked who will care for your children when you have to work late on an urgent project, you could answer that you can meet the work schedule a good performance requires.

Do be careful. Legal and illegal questions may look similar. It is legal to ask if you are over 18, illegal to ask how old you are. It is legal to ask what languages you speak (if that talent is relevant for the job), illegal to ask what your native language is.

Also be careful of variants of illegal questions. Asking when you graduated from high school gives the interviewer a pretty good idea of your age.

Adapted from "Illegal Interview Questions," in *USAToday, Careers and Workplace,* http://www.usatoday.com/careers/resources/interviewillegal.htm#more (accessed July 5, 2009).

STAR: An Interviewing Technique

"One strategy for preparing for behavioral interviews is to use the STAR Technique, as outlined below. (This technique is also referred to as the SAR and PAR techniques.)

Situation or Task

Describe the situation that you were in or the task that you needed to accomplish. You must describe a specific event or situation, not a generalized description of what you have done in the past. Be sure to give enough detail for the interviewer to understand. This situation can be from a previous job, from a volunteer experience, or any relevant event.

Action You Took

Describe the action you took and be sure to keep the focus on you. Even if you are discussing a group project or effort, describe what you did—not the efforts of the team. Don't tell what you might do, tell what you did.

Results You Achieved

What happened? How did the event end? What did you accomplish? What did you learn?"

Quoted from Randall Hansen, "STAR Interviewing Response Technique for Success in Behavioral Job Interviews," in *Quintessential Interviewing Resources*, Quintessential Careers, http://www.quintcareers.com/STAR_interviewing.html (accessed March 9, 2009).

Stress interviews can use physical conditions and people placement to see how candidates respond to uncomfortable situations. You have the option to change some uncomfortable conditions, such as lights shining in your eyes.

deliberate answers. In another possibility, a single interviewer may probe every weak spot in your record and ask questions that elicit negatives. If you get questions that put you on the defensive, rephrase them in less inflammatory terms, if necessary, and then treat them as requests for information.

Q: Why did you major in physical education? That sounds like a pretty Mickey Mouse major.

A: Are you wondering whether I have the academic preparation for this job? I started out in physical education because I've always loved team sports. I learned that I couldn't graduate in four years if I officially switched my major to business administration because the requirements were different in the two programs. But I do have 21 hours in business administration and 9 hours in accounting. And my sports experience gives me practical training in teamwork, motivating people, and management.

Respond assertively. The candidates who survive are those who stand up for themselves and who explain why indeed they *are* worth hiring.

Sometimes the stress comes in the form of unusual questions: Why are manhole covers round? How many tennis balls would fit inside a school bus? If you were a cookie/car/animal, what kind would you be? If you could be any character from a book, who would you be? How you handle the question will be as important as your answer, maybe more important. Can you think creatively under pressure?

Silence can also create stress. One woman walked into her scheduled interview to find a male interviewer with his feet up on the desk. He said, "It's been a long day. I'm tired and I want to go home. You have five minutes to sell yourself." Since she had planned the points she wanted to be sure interviewers knew, she was able to do this. "Your recruiting brochure said that you're looking for someone with a major in accounting and a minor in finance. As you may remember from my résumé, I'm majoring in accounting and have had 12 hours in finance. I've also served as treasurer of a local campaign committee and have worked as a volunteer tax preparer through the Accounting Club." When she finished, the interviewer told her it was a test: "I wanted to see how you'd handle it."

Group Interviews

In group interviews, sometimes called "cattle calls," multiple candidates are interviewed at a time. While many interview tips still apply to these interviews, successful candidates will also practice other techniques. Researching the job and company becomes even more important, because your time to show how you fit the job will be so limited. Have a two-minute summary of your education and experience that shows how you fit this job. Practice it ahead of time so you can share it during the interview.

Arrive early so you have time to meet as many interviewers and interviewees as possible. Get business cards from the interviewers if you can. This pre-interview time may be part of the test, so make the most of it.

During the interview, listen carefully to both interviewers and interviewees. Make eye contact with both groups as well. Participate in the discussion, and look engaged even when you aren't. Watch your body language (see Chapter 4) so you don't give off unintended signals.

Some group interviews are organized around tasks. The group may be asked to solve a problem. Another scenario is that the group will be split into teams, with each team performing a task and then presenting to the whole group. Remember that your participation in these activities is being watched. You will be judged on skills such as communication, persuasion, leadership, organization, planning, analysis, and problem-solving. Do you help move the action forward? Are you too assertive? Too shy? Do you praise the contributions of others? Do you help the group achieve consensus? Are you knowledgeable?

Many group interviews particularly test how you interact with other people. Talking too much may work against you. Making an effort to help quiet people enter the discussion may work in your favor. Connecting your comments to previous comments shows you are a good listener as well as a team player. Be careful not to get caught up in a combative situation.

At the end of the interview, thank each interviewer. Follow up with a written thank you to each interviewer.

Final Steps for a Successful Job Search

What you do after the interview can determine whether you get the job. Many companies expect applicants to follow up on their interviews within a week. If they don't, the company assumes that they wouldn't follow up with clients.

If the employer sends you an e-mail query, answer it promptly. You're being judged not only on what you say but on how quickly you repond. Have your list of references (see page 321) and samples of your work ready to send promptly if requested to do so.

Interview Bloopers

A recent survey asked executives for the most embarrassing interview moments they had encountered. Here are some examples.

- "The candidate sent his sister to interview in his place."

- "The person was dancing during the interview. He kept saying things like, 'I love life!' and 'Oh yeah!'"

- "The candidate stopped the interview and asked me if I had a cigarette."

- "We had one person who walked out of an interview into a glass door—and the glass shattered."

- "The candidate got his companies confused and repeatedly mentioned the strengths of a competing firm, thinking that's who he was interviewing with."

- "A guy called me by the wrong name during the entire interview."

- "We're a retail company, and when we asked the candidate why she wanted to work for us, she said she didn't want to work in retail anymore."

- "An interviewee put his bubble gum in his hand, forgot about it, and then shook my hand."

- "A candidate fell asleep during the interview."

Adapted from Robert Half International, "Dancing, Smoking, Sleeping and Other Bad Interview Moves: Survey Reveals Most Embarrassing Job Interview Blunders," in *OfficeTeam: About Us: Press Room: May 28, 2008,* http://www.officeteam.com/PressRoom?id=2260 (accessed March 19, 2009).

Following Up with Phone Calls and Written Messages

After a first interview, make follow-up phone calls to show enthusiasm for the job, to reinforce positives from the first interview, to overcome any negatives, and to provide information to persuade the interviewer to hire you.

A thank-you note, written within 24 hours of an interview, is essential. Some companies consider the thank-you note to be as important as the cover letter. The note should

- Thank the interviewer for useful information and any helpful action.
- Remind the interviewer of what he or she liked in you.
- Use the jargon of the company and refer to specific things you learned during your interview or saw during your visit.
- Be enthusiastic about the position.
- Refer to the next move, whether you'll wait to hear from the employer or whether you want to call to learn about the status of your application.

If the note is for a site visit, thank your hosts for their hospitality. In the postscript, mention enclosed receipts for your expenses.

Be sure your thank-you is well written and error free. Double-check the spelling of all names. The note can be an e-mail, but many employers are still impressed by paper thank-you notes. In either case, do not use text messaging abbreviations or emoticons.

Figure 13.2 is an example of a follow-up letter after a site visit.

Negotiating for Salary and Benefits

The best time to negotiate for salary and benefits is after you have the job offer. Try to delay discussing salary early in the interview process, when you're still competing against other applicants.

Prepare for salary negotiations by finding out what the going rate is for the kind of work you hope to do. Cultivate friends who are now in the workforce to find out what they're making. Ask the campus placement office for figures on what last year's graduates got. Check trade journals and the Web.

This research is crucial. In one study, male students expected salaries in their first jobs that were 14% higher than the salaries female students expected. More than twice as many men as women expected to receive signing bonuses. Men were 16% more likely to expect annual bonuses, and the bonuses men expected were 16% higher than the bonuses women expected.[7] Knowing what a job is worth will give you the confidence to negotiate more effectively.

The best way to get more money is to convince the employer that you're worth it. During the interview process, show that you can do what the competition can't.

After you have the offer, you can begin negotiating salary and benefits. You're in the strongest position when (1) you've done your homework and know what the usual salary and benefits are and (2) you can walk away from this offer if it doesn't meet your needs. Avoid naming a specific salary. Don't say you can't accept less. Instead, say you would find it difficult to accept the job under the terms first offered.

Remember that you're negotiating a package, not just a starting salary. A company that truly can't pay any more money now might be able to review you for promotion sooner than usual, or pay your moving costs, or give you a better job title. Some companies offer fringe benefits that may compensate for lower taxable income: use of a company car, reimbursements for education, child care or elder care subsidies, or help in finding a job for your spouse or partner. And think about your career, not just the initial salary. Sometimes a

Figure 13.2   Follow-Up Letter after an Office Visit

405 West College, Apt. 201   *Single-space your address and the date*
Thibodaux, LA 70301   *when you don't use letterhead.*
April 2, 2010

Mr. Robert Land, Account Manager
Sive Associates
378 Norman Boulevard
Cincinnati, OH 48528

Dear Mr. Land:

After visiting Sive Associates last week, I'm even more sure that writing direct mail is the career for me.

Refers to things she saw and learned during the interview.

I've always been able to brainstorm ideas, but sometimes, when I had to focus on one idea for a class project, I wasn't sure which idea was best. It was fascinating to see how you make direct mail scientific as well as creative by testing each new creative package against the control. I can understand how pleased Linda Hayes was when she learned that her new package for *Smithsonian* beat the control.

Seeing Kelly, Luke, and Gene collaborating on the Sesame Street package gave me some sense of the tight deadlines you're under. As you know, I've learned to meet deadlines, not only for my class assignments, but also in working on Nicholls' newspaper. The award I won for my feature on the primary election suggests that my quality holds up even when the deadline is tight!

Reminds interviewer of her strong points.

Thank you for your hospitality while I was in Cincinnati. You and your wife made my stay very pleasant. I especially appreciate the time the two of you took to help me find information about apartments that are accessible to wheelchairs. Cincinnati seems like a very livable city.

I'm excited about a career in direct mail and about the (possibility) of joining Sive Associates. I look forward to hearing from you soon!

Be positive, not pushy. She doesn't assume she has the job.

Refers to what will happen next.

Sincerely,

Gina Focasio

Gina Focasio
(504) 555-2948

Writer's phone number.

Puts request for reimbursement in P.S. to de-emphasize it; focuses on the job, not the cost of the trip.

P.S. My expenses totaled $454. Enclosed are receipts for my plane fare from New Orleans to Cincinnati ($367), the taxi to the airport in Cincinnati ($30), and the bus from Thibodaux to New Orleans ($57).

Encl.: Receipts for Expenses

Crazy Job-Seeking Stunts

In the struggle to land the perfect job, some job seekers will do almost anything to get noticed and secure a position. A survey conducted by CareerBuilder.com discovered some of the most unconventional methods experienced by hiring managers as candidates attempted to get a job. The following are some of the most bizarre and ones you probably want to avoid:

- Used an official celebrity fan site as a portfolio accomplishment
- Sent a nude photo to the hiring manager
- Performed a stand-up comedy routine
- Waited for the hiring manager at his car
- Dressed as a cat
- Wore a tuxedo
- Brought coffee for the entire office
- Asked the interviewer to dinner
- Provided Yankee tickets for the interviewer
- Provided a baby gift for a pregnant interviewer

Keep in mind, the goal of an interview is to be remembered in a positive way!

Adapted from Rosemary Haefner, "Weirdest Job Seeker Stunts," in *Advice & Resources Articles: Job Search,* http://careerbuilder.com/Article/CB-263-Job-Search-Weirdest-Job-Seeker-Stunts/ (accessed March 19, 2009).

low-paying job at a company that will provide superb experience will do more for your career (and your long-term earning prospects) than a high salary now with no room to grow.

Work toward a compromise. You want the employer to be happy that you're coming on board and to feel that you've behaved maturely and professionally.

Deciding Which Offer to Accept

The problem with choosing among job offers is that you're comparing apples and oranges. The job with the most interesting work pays peanuts. The job that pays best is in a city where you don't want to live. The secret of professional happiness is taking a job where the positives are things you want and the negatives are things that don't matter as much to you.

To choose among job offers, you need to know what is truly important to *you*. Start by answering questions like the following:

- Are you willing to work after hours? To take work home? To travel? How important is money to you? Prestige? Time to spend with family and friends?

- Would you rather have firm deadlines or a flexible schedule? Do you prefer working alone or with other people? Do you prefer specific instructions and standards for evaluation or freedom and uncertainty? How comfortable are you with pressure? How much variety and challenge do you want?

- What kinds of opportunities for training and advancement are you seeking?

- Where do you want to live? What features in terms of weather, geography, cultural and social life do you see as ideal?

- Is it important to you that your work achieve certain purposes or values, or do you see work as "just a way to make a living"? Are the organization's culture and ethical standards ones you find comfortable? Will you be able to do work you can point to with pride?

No job is perfect but some jobs will fulfill more of your major criteria than will others.

Some employers offer jobs at the end of the office visit. In other cases, you may wait for weeks or even months to hear. Employers may offer jobs orally. You must say something in response immediately, so it's good to plan some strategies in advance.

If your first offer is not from your first choice, express your pleasure at being offered the job, but do not accept it on the phone. "That's great! I assume I have two weeks to let you know?" Then *call* the other companies you're interested in. Explain, "I've just gotten a job offer, but I'd rather work for you. Can you tell me what the status of my application is?" Nobody will put that information in writing, but almost everyone will tell you over the phone. With this information, you're in a better position to decide whether to accept the original offer.

Companies routinely give applicants two weeks to accept or reject offers. Some students have been successful in getting those two weeks extended to several weeks or even months. Certainly if you cannot decide by the deadline, it is worth asking for more time: The worst the company can do is say *no*. If you do try to keep a company hanging for a long time, be prepared for weekly phone calls asking you if you've decided yet.

Make your acceptance contingent upon a written job offer confirming the terms. That letter should spell out not only salary but also fringe benefits and any special provisions you have negotiated. If something is missing, call the interviewer for clarification: "You said that I'd be reviewed for a promotion and higher salary in six months, but that isn't in the letter." Even well-intentioned people can forget oral promises. You have more power to resolve misunderstandings now than you will after six months or a year on the job. Furthermore, the person who made you the promise may no longer be with the company a year later.

When you've accepted one job, let the other places you visited know that you're no longer interested. Then they can go to their second choices. If you're second on someone else's list, you'll appreciate other candidates' removing themselves so the way is clear for you.

Summary of Key Points

- Develop an overall strategy based on your answers to these three questions:
    1. What two to five facts about yourself do you want the interviewer to know?
    2. What disadvantages or weaknesses do you need to overcome or minimize?
    3. What do you need to know about the job and the organization to decide whether or not you want to accept this job if it is offered to you?
- Check on dress expectations before the interview.
- Rehearse everything you can. In particular, practice answers to common questions. Ask a friend to interview you. If your campus has practice interviews or videotaping facilities, use them so that you can evaluate and modify your interview behavior.
- Bring an extra copy of your résumé, something to write on and write with, and copies of your work to the interview.
- Record the name of the interviewer, tips the interviewer gave you, what the interviewer liked about you, answers to your questions about the company, and when you'll hear from the company.
- Successful applicants know what they want to do, use the company name in the interview, have researched the company in advance, back up claims with specifics, use appropriate technical jargon, ask specific questions, and talk more of the time.
- **Behavioral interviews** ask the applicant to describe actual behaviors, rather than plans or general principles. To answer a behavioral question, describe the situation, tell what you did, and tell what happened. Think about the implications of what you did and be ready to talk about what you'd do the next time or if the situation were slightly different.
- **Situational interviews** put you in a situation that allows the interviewer to see whether you have the qualities the company is seeking.
- **Stress interviews** deliberately create physical or psychological stress. Change the conditions that create physical stress. Meet psychological stress by rephrasing questions in less inflammatory terms and treating them as requests for information.
- Use follow-up phone calls and written messages to reinforce positives from the first interview, and to provide information to persuade the interviewer to hire you.
- The best time to negotiate for salary and benefits is after you have the job offer.
- If your first offer isn't from your first choice, call the other companies you're interested in to ask the status of your application.

Job Seekers Make the Most Mistakes at Interviews

Successfully completing an interview is no easy task suggests a survey conducted by Robert Half Finance & Accounting, a financial recruitment service. The survey asked 1,400 chief financial officers to list the area in which job applicants make the most mistakes. According to the study, employers believe that job applicants make more mistakes during interviews than any other time in the hiring process.

Respondents cast their votes this way:

Interview	32%
Résumé	21%
Cover letter	9%
Reference checks	9%
Interview follow-up	7%
Screening call	6%
Other	2%
Don't know	14%

Interview mistakes frequently occur as a result of "not knowing enough about the company or position, displaying a bad attitude or inquiring about compensation prematurely," according to Max Messmer, Chairman of Robert Half Finance & Accounting and author of *Managing Your Career for Dummies.*

What steps can you take to better prepare yourself for an interview?

Adapted from Robert Half Finance & Accounting, "Tell Me about Yourself," in *Press Room: 2005,* http://www.roberthalffinance.com/PressRoom?id=1577 (accessed March 19, 2009).

CHAPTER 13   ## Exercises and Problems

13.1   Reviewing the Chapter

1. Name four interview channels. What special considerations do you have to make for them? (LO 1)
2. What are three special kinds of interviews you may encounter? What are tips to succeed in them? (LO 1)
3. What preparations should you make before an interview? (LO 2)
4. What are some behavior tips you should keep in mind during an interview? (LO 3)
5. What should you accomplish in the close of an interview? (LO 3)
6. What are some common interview questions? What are effective answers for you? (LO 4)
7. What do you need to do after an interview? (LO 5)
8. When do you negotiate for salary? Why? (LO 5)

13.2   Interviewing Job Hunters

Talk to students at your school who are interviewing for jobs this term. Possible questions to ask them include the following:

- What field are you in? How good is the job market in that field this year?
- How long is the first interview with a company, usually?
- What questions have you been asked at job interviews? Were you asked any stress or sexist questions? Any really oddball questions?
- What answers seemed to go over well? What answers bombed?
- At an office visit or plant trip, how many people did you talk to? What were their job titles?
- Were you asked to take any tests (skills, physical, drugs)?

- How long did you have to wait after a first interview to learn whether you were being invited for an office visit? How long after an office visit did it take to learn whether you were being offered a job? How much time did the company give you to decide?
- What advice would you have for someone who will be interviewing next term or next year?

As your instructor directs,

a. Summarize your findings in a memo to your instructor.
b. Report your findings orally to the class.
c. Join with a small group of students to write a group report describing the results of your survey.

13.3   Interviewing an Interviewer

Talk to someone who regularly interviews candidates for entry-level jobs. Possible questions to ask include the following:

- How long have you been interviewing for your organization? Does everyone on the management ladder at your company do some interviewing, or do people specialize in it?
- Do you follow a set structure for interviews? What are some of the standard questions you ask?
- What are you looking for? How important are (1) good grades, (2) leadership roles in extracurricular groups, or (3) relevant work experience? What advice would you give to someone who lacks one or more of these?
- What are the things you see students do that create a poor impression? Think about the worst candidate you've interviewed. What did he or she do (or not do) to create such a negative impression?

- What are the things that make a good impression? Recall the best student you've ever interviewed. Why did he or she impress you so much?
- How does your employer evaluate and reward your success as an interviewer?
- What advice would you have for someone who still has a year or so before the job hunt begins?

As your instructor directs,

a. Summarize your findings in a memo to your instructor.
b. Report your findings orally to the class.
c. Join with a small group of students to write a group report describing the results of your survey.
d. Write to the interviewer thanking him or her for taking the time to talk to you.

13.4   Analyzing a Video Interview

Analyze a video clip of an interview session.

As your instructor directs,

1. In groups of four, search on a video-based Web site such as Google video or YouTube for terms such as "interview" or "student interview."
2. Watch a video clip of an interview and note the strengths and weaknesses of the interviewee.

3. Discuss your observations with your group and explain why you considered certain responses as strengths and weaknesses.
4. Share your video and analysis with your class.

13.5   Preparing an Interview Strategy

Prepare your interview strategy.

1. List two to five things about yourself that you want the interviewer to know before you leave the interview.
2. Identify any weaknesses or apparent weaknesses in your record and plan ways to explain them or minimize them.
3. List the points you need to learn about an employer to decide whether to accept an office visit or plant trip.

As your instructor directs,

a. Share your strategy with a small group of other students.
b. Describe your strategy in a memo to your instructor.
c. Present your strategy orally to the class.

13.6   Preparing Questions to Ask Employers

Prepare a list of questions to ask at job interviews.

1. Prepare a list of three to five general questions that apply to most employers in your field.
2. Prepare two to five specific questions for the three companies you are most interested in.

As your instructor directs,

a. Share the questions with a small group of other students.
b. List the questions in a memo to your instructor.
c. Present your questions orally to the class.

13.7   Preparing Answers to Questions You May Be Asked

Prepare answers to each of the interview questions listed in this chapter and to any other questions that you know are likely to be asked of job hunters in your field or on your campus.

As your instructor directs,

a. Write down the answers to your questions and turn them in.
b. Conduct mini-interviews in a small group of students. In the group, let student A be the interviewer and ask five questions from the list. Student B will play the job candidate and answer the questions, using real information about student B's field and qualifications.

Student C will evaluate the content of the answer. Student D will observe the nonverbal behavior of the interviewer (A); student E will observe the nonverbal behavior of the interviewee (B).

After the mini-interview, let students C, D, and E share their observations and recommend ways that B could be even more effective. Then switch roles. Let another student be the interviewer and ask five questions of another interviewee, while new observers note content and nonverbal behavior. Continue the process until everyone in the group has had a chance to be "interviewed."

13.8   Writing a Follow-Up Message after an Onsite Visit

Write a follow-up e-mail message or letter after an office visit or plant trip. Thank your hosts for their hospitality; relate your strong points to things you learned about the company during the visit; allay any negatives that may remain; be enthusiastic about the company; and submit receipts for your expenses so you can be reimbursed.

13.9   Clarifying the Terms of a Job Offer

Last week, you got a job offer from your first choice company, and you accepted it over the phone. Today, the written confirmation arrived. The letter specifies the starting salary and fringe benefits you had negotiated. However, during the office visit, you were promised a 5% raise in six months. The job offer says nothing about the raise. You do want the job, but you want it on the terms you thought you had negotiated.

Write to your contact at the company, Damon Winters.

13.10   Researching a Geographic Area

Research a geographic area where you would like to work. Investigate the cost of living, industrial growth in the area, weather and climate, and attractions in the area you could visit. The local Chamber of Commerce is a good place to start your research.

As your instructor directs,

a. Share your findings with a small group of other students.

b. Describe your findings in a memo to your instructor.

c. Present your findings orally to the class.

13.11   All-Weather Case: Interviewing Candidates for the Position of Process Engineer

Doug and Erin are interviewing the two short-listed candidates for the position of process engineer at All-Weather's Camden, IL, plant. The plant manufactures fiberglass composite exterior doors.

The job involves monitoring the production process with the goal of improving efficiency and cost control using techniques and skills such as JIT, PFMEA, Auto-CAD, Inventor, Microsoft Project, etc. The process engineer needs to take a hands-on approach in working with shift engineers as well as the operators; he or she will report to the manufacturing manager and give quarterly recommendations to management about cost reduction and efficiency improvement. Among soft skills necessary for the job, the advertisement stated that applicants should be motivated, driven, creative, and excellent communicators.

Both Doug and Erin are big believers in behavioral interviews. "Resumes can be padded and cover letters ghostwritten," Doug likes to say, "but it is difficult to wing it face-to-face, especially when people questioning you are experienced professionals." Erin has seen too many résumés and cover letters to disagree with Doug's belief; besides, she respects Doug's judgment.

The first candidate to be interviewed is Ryan Sullivan, who holds a bachelor's degree in mechanical engineering from Illinois Institute of Technology, Chicago. He has previously worked as a production engineer trainee in Glendale Windows and Doors in Pleasant City, Kansas. The last two years, Ryan has been working in a technology consulting firm that advises clients on production process improvement and cost control.

The second candidate to be interviewed is Ashley Brewer, who holds an MS in mechanical engineering from the University of Illinois at Urbana–Champaign. She has four years of work experience as a consultant in an operations management consulting firm that advises clients on all aspects of operations, including production, supply chain management (transportation, procurement, inventory management), and information technology. However, Ashley has never worked on the factory floor.

"Wish we could combine Ryan and Ashley," Erin says, finishing her scan of the two candidates' applications.

"Do you mean we should take them both?" Doug asks.

"No. I mean having a candidate who has both the factory floor and the consulting experiences," Erin says, explaining herself.

Just then, the HR secretary announces Mr. Ryan Sullivan. Both Doug and Erin straighten themselves, ready to greet their candidate.

Doug also likes to say, "You don't get a second chance to make the first impression." Ryan Sullivan is wearing a sport coat with elbow patches.

After a few preliminary questions, Doug asks Ryan to tell him about the most challenging project on which he has worked, either during his traineeship with Glendale Windows and Doors or in his stint with the consulting firm. "That's easy," Ryan snaps back. "It would have to be my experience working as part of a six-member team advising a midsized automotive parts company on environmental standards of ISO 17025."

"You realize," Doug says, hiding his disappointment, "that our products already have the best environmental certifications, including LEED and ENERGY STAR."

"Yes. I know," Ryan replies, smiling. "However, I can help your company maintain the tough standards that surely follow these certifications."

"Can you help us in any other area besides the environmental issues?" Doug asks, forcing himself not to be led by preconceived notions.

"Yes, I can," Ryan replies, again before Doug finishes his sentence. "I can help your company with safety matters. In my experience at Glendale, I helped set up a system of checking out safety equipment that ensured that everyone on the factory floor was safe."

"Yes. Safety is very important," Doug says, remembering All-Weather's recently revised Safety and Health Policy and his proposal to management to hire a manager in HR solely responsible for safety.

After Ryan leaves, Doug discusses his observations with Erin. Both agree that Ryan did not display an adequate knowledge of the job for which he had come to interview. They also hope that Ashley will be a better candidate because Erin has worked on this job selection for the past three months. Should the position remain unfilled, she may have to start from scratch.

Ashley walks in with a briefcase in her hand. She is wearing a black suit and looks thoroughly professional. Erin wonders, however, whether Ashley would fit in All-Weather's no-frills culture. After Ashley has answered the initial ice-breaking questions, Doug asks Ashley the same question that he put to Ryan: "What was your most challenging assignment?"

Ashley considers the question for a moment. Then she gives her reply, "It was leading a process audit for a pipe manufacturing company. I had to critically analyze every step in the process, along with its costs and implications for the throughput. I worked with engineers and the lowest levels of workers to understand the process, including intricacies of mixers and extruders. One year after our recommendations were implemented, the company reported a 25% increase in production and a 15% reduction in costs."

Both Doug and Erin are impressed with the answer. However, they withhold judgment.

Erin asks the next question, "I noticed when you came in that you looked very professionally dressed. Do you think you can interact with workers on the factory floor dressed in this manner?"

"Of course not," Ashley replies, softening her words with a polite smile. "When I will be on the factory floor, which I know I will be, I will wear work clothes that will not intimidate anyone, I can assure you."

"One more thing," Doug says, looking a bit uncomfortable. "We don't yet have many women employees working in our plants. Do you think you will be comfortable in an environment that is predominantly male?"

"I'd prefer to work in a more gender-balanced environment," Ashley says, keeping her voice free of emotion. "However, I'm first a professional, then a woman, so I can adapt, especially in a company that I'm excited to work for."

After Ashley leaves, Doug and Erin confer about the two candidates. While Ashley is clearly the superior candidate, Doug is still unsure whether she is up to the factory floor experience. He tells Erin that doing a plant audit for a few weeks is one thing, but working on factory floor every day for eight hours is another. Erin disagrees. She believes that Ashley is a quick learner and knows what is required of the job, unlike Ryan. However, Erin does not belabor the point much, because she knows that Doug has to attend a meeting. She reminds herself to write an e-mail to Doug later in the evening outlining reasons why Ashley should be selected.

Based on your reading of Chapter 13, first discuss the following questions:

- What aspects of preparing for the interview does the case highlight?
- Are Doug and Erin correct about the importance of behavioral interviews? What other interviewing methods might they have used?
- What are some other questions they might have asked at the interview?

Then, take up Erin's task and write an e-mail addressed to Doug discussing the following points:

- Analysis of both the candidates as seen from their interview performance.
- Your recommendation on the candidate who deserves to be chosen and the reasons supporting your decision (Note: you can also recommend not selecting either candidate, but you must explain why).

CHAPTER

14

Sharing Informative and Positive Messages

Chapter Outline

Information Overload

Common Media

- Face-to-Face Contacts
- Phone Calls
- Instant Messages and Text Messaging
- E-Mails, Letters, and Paper Memos

Organizing Informative and Positive Messages

Subject Lines for Informative and Positive Messages

- Making Subject Lines Specific
- Making Subject Lines Concise
- Making Subject Lines Appropriate for the Pattern of Organization
- Pointers for E-Mail Subject Lines

Managing the Information in Your Messages

Using Benefits in Informative and Positive Messages

Ending Informative and Positive Messages

Humor in Informative Messages

Varieties of Informative and Positive Messages

- Transmittals
- Summaries
- Thank-You and Positive Feedback Notes
- Positive Responses to Complaints

Solving a Sample Problem

- Problem
- Analysis of the Problem
- Discussion of the Sample Solutions

Summary of Key Points

Information for Healthy Eating

To help consumers make better choices in the grocery store and fight the alarming rates of obesity in the country, some supermarket chains are creating informational signage displayed near healthy foods. These signs help consumers quickly understand that the products have met federal guidelines. Since some consumers have difficulty understanding the labels required by the US Food and Drug Administration, the informational labeling system of supermarkets helps simplify choices between similar products.

Stop & Shop and Giant Food have introduced the "Healthy Ideas" system, which provides labels on over 3,000 nutritious foods sold in their stores. Similarly, Price Chopper and HyVee supermarkets started the "NuVal" system, which rates the nutritional value of foods on a scale of 1 to 100. Another system, the "Guiding Stars," has been used in Hannaford Bros. supermarkets since 2006. This system gives stars to foods in three categories: good, better, and best.

> *"The "NuVal" system . . . rates the nutritional value of foods on a scale of 1 to 100."*

While these informational message systems are a step in a right direction, nutritionists warn that portion control and comprehension of the FDA's labels are still important in maintaining a healthy diet.

Source: Timothy W. Martin, "Grocers Launch Labels to Identify Healthy Foods," *Wall Street Journal,* January 2, 2009, A4.

Learning Objectives

After studying this chapter, you will know:

1 When to use common business media.

2 How to use the chosen channel effectively.

3 How to write letters and memos.

4 How to compose some of the common varieties of informative and positive messages.

Welcome News

Many companies like to maintain ties with customers by sending out a regular newsletter via e-mail. Customers welcome this type of communication only if it is truly interesting and easy to read.

There are many newsletter services that do much of the work for you such as www.myemma.com or www.constantcontact.com. Here are a few pointers for publishing an effective newsletter:

- Be relevant. Limit the newsletter to information the readers can actually use.

- Be brief. Give something of value in less than one minute.

- Be consistent. Set up a regular schedule for the newsletters, but not more than every two weeks.

- Be intriguing. Use headlines that help readers understand the content of articles clearly.

- Be considerate. Send the newsletter only to people who have subscribed. Set yourself apart from spammers by making it easy to unsubscribe and avoiding subject lines that filter into spam (i.e., "free" or "$$$").

Adapted from Rhonda Abrams, "E-mail Newsletters an Easy, Effective Tool," *Des Moines Register*, July, 21, 2008, 1D, 4D.

Business messages must meet the needs of the sender (and the sender's organization), be sensitive to the audience, and accurately reflect the topic being discussed. Informative and positive messages are the bread-and-butter messages in organizations.

When we need to convey information to which the receiver's basic reaction will be neutral, the message is **informative.** If we convey information to which the receiver's reaction will be positive, the message is a **positive or good news message.** Neither message immediately asks the receiver to do anything. You usually do want to build positive attitudes toward the information you are presenting, so in that sense, even an informative message has a persuasive element. Chapter 15 will discuss messages where the receiver will respond negatively; Chapter 16 will discuss messages where you want the receiver to change beliefs or behavior.

Informative and positive messages include acceptances; positive answers to requests; information about meetings, procedures, products, services, or options; announcements of policy changes that are neutral or positive; and changes that are to the receiver's advantage.

Even a simple informative or good news message usually has several purposes:

Primary purposes:

To give information or good news to the receiver or to reassure the receiver.
To have the receiver view the information positively.

Secondary purposes:

To build a good image of the sender.
To build a good image of the sender's organization.
To cement a good relationship between the sender and the receiver.
To deemphasize any negative elements.
To reduce or eliminate future messages on the same subject.

Informative and positive messages are not necessarily short. Instead, the length of a message depends on your purposes, the audience's needs, and the complexity of the situation.

Information Overload

Although obviously some business communications must be longer, one of the realities of communication today is information overload. As Chapter 4 noted, technology enables other people to bombard us with junk mail, sales calls, spam, and other advertisements. The flood of e-mail has overwhelmed some people and even caused some to stop responding altogether. Venture capitalist Fred Wilson announced on his blog that he was "so far behind on his e-mail he was declaring [e-mail] bankruptcy." Recording artist Moby followed a similar path when in September he informed all his e-mail contacts that he was taking a break from e-mail until the end of the year.[1]

On another level, even more routine communications are becoming overwhelming. With fast and cheap e-mails, plus the genuine belief in more transparent business procedures, businesses send more announcements of events, procedures, policies, services, and employee news. Departments send newsletters. Employees send announcements of and best wishes for births, birthdays, weddings, and promotions. Customers send comments about products, service, policies, and advertisements. According to marketing research firm Radicati Group, the average number of corporate e-mails sent and received per person per day is 156. They also predict that within two years, workers will spend 41% of their day managing e-mail.[2]

With this flood of information, you need to protect your communication reputation. You do not want to be the person whose e-mails or voice-mail messages are opened last because they take so long to get to the point, or even worse, the person whose messages are rarely opened at all because you send so many that aren't important or necessary.

One research study on e-mail overload found that length was not the problem: most e-mails in the study were short, four lines or less. Rather, the study found three factors that contributed to the perception of e-mail overload. The first, unstable requests, included requests that got refined in the process of e-mail correspondence and frequently morphed into requests for more work. The second, pressure to respond, included requests for information within hours. People in the study noted that they were never away from their e-mail, and that these requests could come any time. The third factor, delegation of tasks and shifting interactants, included tasks that were indirectly delegated (Could anyone get me the figures on X for the noon meeting?) or that recipients of the group e-mail then gave to their own subordinates.[3]

An e-mail survey found yet another factor in overload: inappropriate e-mails. This group included jokes, personal information, and non-job-related e-mails, as well as e-mails that were unnecessarily long, trivial, and irrelevant.[4] However, another study found that as people became more comfortable working together on projects, their e-mails became more informal and personal and included such content as family commitments and personal health information. As their relationships developed, they also became more tolerant of spelling and grammar errors. When outsiders joined the project, however, e-mails went back to a formal, correct level.[5]

Common Media

In the office, most informative and positive communications are made through six channels: face-to-face contacts, phone calls, instant messages and text messaging, e-mails, letters, and paper memos. Many people have personal preferences that need to be recognized. They may keep up with their e-mail but avoid listening to voice-mail messages; they may enjoy drop-in visitors but think instant messages are silly. Similarly, some channels seem better fitted for some situations than others.

Face-to-Face Contacts

Some businesses are encouraging their employees to write fewer e-mails and visit each other's offices to conduct business.[6] Visits are a good choice when

- You know a colleague welcomes your visits.
- You are building a business relationship with a person.
- A real-time connection saves multiple phone calls or e-mails (e.g., setting a meeting agenda).

Phone Answering Machine Pet Peeves

- Callback numbers that are mumbled or given too quickly.
- Messages longer than 30 seconds.
- Messages that require serious note taking (when an e-mail would have been better).
- Too much or too little information.
- Demands to contact people without saying why.
- Messages expecting an immediate response.
- Angry messages.

Cell Phone Etiquette

If you must use your cell phone in public, obey these guidelines to avoid annoying those around you and to keep yourself safe.

1. Safety—Use your cell phone while driving only if you have a hands-free device.
2. Volume—Speak softly. Eliminate loud and annoying ring tones.
3. Proximity—Try to remain 10–20 feet away from people.
4. Privacy—Avoid talking about business in public spaces.
5. Tone—Maintain a civil tone. Save emotional conversations for private places.
6. Location—Pick spots where a cell phone conversation won't be distracting.
7. Timing—Do not answer your phone if it would be rude (i.e., while ordering food, entering a restaurant, or joining a meeting).

Adapted from "Mobile Phone Etiquette," in *Etiquette*, http://phoney business.com/etiquette.html (accessed March 27, 2009).

- Your business requires dialogue or negotiation.
- You need something immediately (like a signature).
- Discretion is vital and you do not want to leave a paper trail.
- The situation is complex enough that you want as many visual and aural cues as possible.

Use these tips for effective face-to-face contact:

- Ensure the timing is convenient for the recipient.
- If you are discussing something complex, have appropriate documents in hand.
- Don't usurp their space. Don't put your papers on top of their desk or table without their permission.
- Look for "time to go" signs. Some people have a limited tolerance for small talk, especially when they are hard at work on a task.

Phone Calls

Phone calls provide fewer contextual cues than face-to-face visits, but more cues than electronic or paper messages. Phone calls are a good choice when

- Tone of voice is important.
- A real-time connection saves multiple phone calls or e-mails (e.g., setting a meeting time).
- You need something immediately (like an OK).
- You do not want to leave a paper trail (but remember that phone records are easily obtained, as we all know from Hewlett-Packard's use of board member phone records).

Use these tips for effective phone calls:

- Ensure the timing is convenient for the recipient; promptly return calls to your answering machine.
- Speak clearly, especially when giving your name and phone number (even more important when leaving your name and phone number on an answering machine).
- Use an information hook: I am calling about. . . .
- Keep the call short and cordial. If you need to leave a message, keep it brief: 1–2 sentences.
- Focus on the call; do not do other work. Most people can tell if you are reading e-mail or Web pages while talking to them, and they get the message that their concern is not important to you.

Instant Messages and Text Messaging

Formerly limited primarily to students, instant messages and text messaging are beginning to gain acceptance in the business world. However, you will probably find more enthusiasm for them among your younger colleagues. But not always! In many cities around the nation, police are encouraging 20-somethings to send text messages identifying criminals or alerting police about a crime that might happen.[7] Health care companies are using text messaging to send out health information. Even 2008 US presidential hopefuls used text messages to encourage voter support.

Many parents have been initiated to these messages by their children. Because they are less intrusive than phone calls or visits, these messages are good for running commentary or questions on tasks you and your colleagues are working on simultaneously. Even here, audience is important. Some people will not recognize common abbreviations; others will not appreciate ones like OMG (oh my God). Remember that like e-mails, these messages can be saved, forwarded, and printed. They too leave a paper trail.

E-Mails, Letters, and Paper Memos

When people think of business communications, many think of e-mails, letters, and paper memos. Letters go to someone outside your organization; paper memos go to someone in your organization; e-mails can go anywhere. Today most memos are sent as e-mails rather than paper documents. A study by Rogen International reports that executives spend at least two hours a day on e-mail.[8]

E-mails, letters, and memos use different formats. The most common formats are illustrated in Appendix A. The simplified letter format is very similar to memo format: it uses a subject line and omits the salutation and the complimentary close. Thus, it is a good choice when you don't know the reader's name.

The differences in audience and format are the only differences among these documents. All of these messages can be long or short, depending on how much you have to say and how complicated the situation is. All of these messages can be informal when you write to someone you know well, or more formal when you write to someone you don't know, to several audiences, or for the record. All of these messages can be simple responses that you can dash off in 15 minutes; they can also take hours of analysis and revision when you're facing a new situation or when the stakes are high.

E-mails are commonly used for these purposes:

- To accomplish routine, noncontroversial business activities (setting up meetings/appointments, reminders, notices, quick updates, information sharing).
- To save time: many people can look through 60–100 e-mails an hour.
- To save money: one e-mail can go to many people, including global teams.
- To allow readers to deal with messages at their convenience, when timing is not crucial.
- To communicate accurately.
- To provide readers with details for reference (meetings).
- To create a paper trail.

E-mails do not work well for some purposes. Negative critiques and bad news generally have better outcomes when delivered in person. Sarcasm and irony are too frequently misinterpreted to be safely used. Similarly, avoid passing on gossip in your e-mails. The chances of having your gossip forwarded with your name attached are just too great.

Many people read their e-mails very quickly. They may read for only a few seconds or lines to decide if the e-mail is pertinent. Value your readers' time: Put the most important information in the first sentence. If your e-mail is more than one screen long, use headings and enumeration to help draw readers to successive screens.

Another factor in e-mail miscommunication is the lack of nonverbal cues. Many of the billions of e-mails sent daily contain intentional and unintentional emotions that can cause misinterpretation of information. One study showing this misinterpretation found that study participants believed they could accurately convey emotions in e-mail but doubted the abilities of their co-workers to do so.[9]

Remember that e-mails are public documents and may be widely forwarded. Save lowercase and instant message abbreviations for friends, if you use them at all. Never put anything in an e-mail that would embarrass you or harm your career if your employer, colleague, parent, or child saw it. Examples abound of public and corporate officials forced to resign because of misbehaviors documented in e-mails they sent to others. But the senders don't have to be officials to cause corporate trouble.

E-Mail Pet

- Missing or vague subject lines.
- Copying everyone rather than just the people that might find the information useful/interesting.
- Too much information/too little information.
- Too many instant messaging acronyms.
- Lack of capitalization and punctuation.
- Long messages without headings or bullets.
- Delayed response e-mails that don't include the original message. Sometimes readers have no idea what the e-mails are responding about.
- Writers who send a general request to multiple people, creating confusion about who is responsible for handling the request.
- People who expect an immediate answer.
- People who never respond to queries.
- People who don't read their e-mail carefully enough to absorb a simple message.
- People who send too many unimportant e-mails.
- Superfluous images and attachments.
- Flaming.

Doctors and E-mail

"Suzanne Kreuziger is a nurse who uses e-mail almost exclusively to communicate with friends. But when she tries to send a message to her doctor, she hits a firewall. The barrier is her doctor's own reluctance to talk to patients through e-mail. . . .

"Kreuziger's experience is shared by most Americans: They want the convenience of e-mail for non-urgent medical issues, but fewer than a third of U.S. doctors use e-mail to communicate with patients, recent surveys found.

"Doctors have their reasons for not hitting the reply button more often. Some worry that doing so will increase their workload, and in most cases, insurers don't reimburse physicians for e-mail consultations. Others fear hackers could compromise patient privacy.

"There are also concerns that patients will send urgent messages that don't get answered promptly. And any snafu raises the specter of legal liability.

"A survey conducted last year by Manhattan Research found that only 31 percent of doctors e-mailed their patients in the first quarter of 2007."

Quoted from "Most Doctors Refrain from Using E-Mail," *Associated Press*, April 23, 2008. Reprinted with permission of The YGS Group.

- An employee e-mail arranging for a group to leave work early and go drinking at a topless bar was used as evidence of poor oversight in a product-contamination lawsuit against the company.[10]
- An American employee responded to a request for floor mats from an American GI in Iraq by saying "We would NEVER ship to Iraq. If you were sensible, you and your troops would pull out of Iraq." The e-mail quickly circulated on the Internet, getting the employee fired and the business boycotted.[11]
- Starbucks had a different e-mail problem. An e-mail coupon for a free grande iced beverage was sent to some Atlanta employees to forward to family and friends. The coupon made its way to the Web, where it became an Internet star. It spread so widely that Starbucks stopped honoring the coupon.[12]

Marketing research firm Radicati found that 6% of employees sent company information they shouldn't have to someone through e-mail.[13]

Organizing Informative and Positive Messages

The patterns of organization in this chapter and others follow standard conventions of business. The patterns will work for many of the writing situations most people in business, nonprofits, and government face. Using the appropriate pattern can help you compose more quickly, create a better final product, and demonstrate you know the conventions. However, the patterns should never be used blindly. You must always consider whether your audience, purpose, and context would be better served with a different organization. If you decide to use a pattern:

- Be sure you understand the rationale behind each pattern so that you can modify the pattern when necessary.
- Realize not every message that uses the basic pattern will have all the elements listed.
- Realize sometimes you can present several elements in one paragraph; sometimes you'll need several paragraphs for just one element.

Figure 14.1 shows how to organize informative and positive messages. Figures 14.2 and 14.3 illustrate two ways that the basic pattern can be applied.

Figure 14.1   How to Organize Informative and Positive Messages

1. **Start with good news or the most important information.** Summarize the main points. If the audience has already raised the issue, make it clear that you're responding.

2. **Give details, clarification, background.** Answer all the questions your audience is likely to have; provide all the information necessary to achieve your purposes. If you are asking or answering multiple questions, number them. Enumeration increases your chances of giving or receiving all the necessary information. Present details in the order of importance to the reader or in some other logical order.

3. **Present any negative elements—as positively as possible.** A policy may have limits; information may be incomplete; the audience may have to satisfy requirements to get a discount or benefit. Make these negatives clear, but present them as positively as possible.

4. **Explain any benefits.** Most informative messages need benefits. Show that the policy or procedure helps your audience, not just the company. Give enough detail to make the benefits clear and convincing. In letters, you may want to give benefits of dealing with your company as well as benefits of the product or policy.

    In a good news message, it's often possible to combine a short benefit with a goodwill ending.

5. **Use a goodwill ending: positive, personal, and forward-looking.** Shifting your emphasis away from the message to the specific audience suggests that serving the audience is your real concern.

Figure 14.2   A Positive Letter

eBusCompanyToday

P.O. Box 12345
Tampa, FL   33660
813-555-5555

June 17, 2010

Dear Ms. Locker:

Main point presented as good news — We're excited to share some great news! *eBusCompanyToday* has merged with another business magazine, *High-Tech Business News*. This merged publication will be called *High-Tech Business News* and will continue to be edited and published by the *eBusCompanyToday* staff.

Details focus on benefits to the reader — The "new" *High-Tech Business News* is a great tool for navigating today's relentlessly changing marketplace, particularly as it's driven by the Internet and other technologies. It reports on the most innovative business practices and the people behind them; delivers surprising, useful insights; and explains how to put them to work. Please be assured that you will continue to receive the same great editorial coverage that you've come to expect from *eBusCompanyToday*.

You will receive the "new" *High-Tech Business News* in about 4 weeks, starting with the combined August/September issue. If you already subscribe to *High-Tech Business News*, your subscription will be extended accordingly. And if you'd rather not receive this publication, please call 1-800-555-5555 within the next 3 weeks. — *Option to cancel is offered but not emphasized*

Positive, personal, forward-looking ending — Thank you for your continued loyalty to *eBusCompanyToday*; we're confident that you will enjoy reading *High-Tech Business News* every month.

Sincerely,

Alan Schmidt

Alan Schmidt, Editor and President

High-Tech Business News is published monthly except for two issues combined periodically into one and occasional extra, expanded or premium issues.

Figure 14.3   A Positive Memo, Sent to Chamber of Commerce Employees and Members

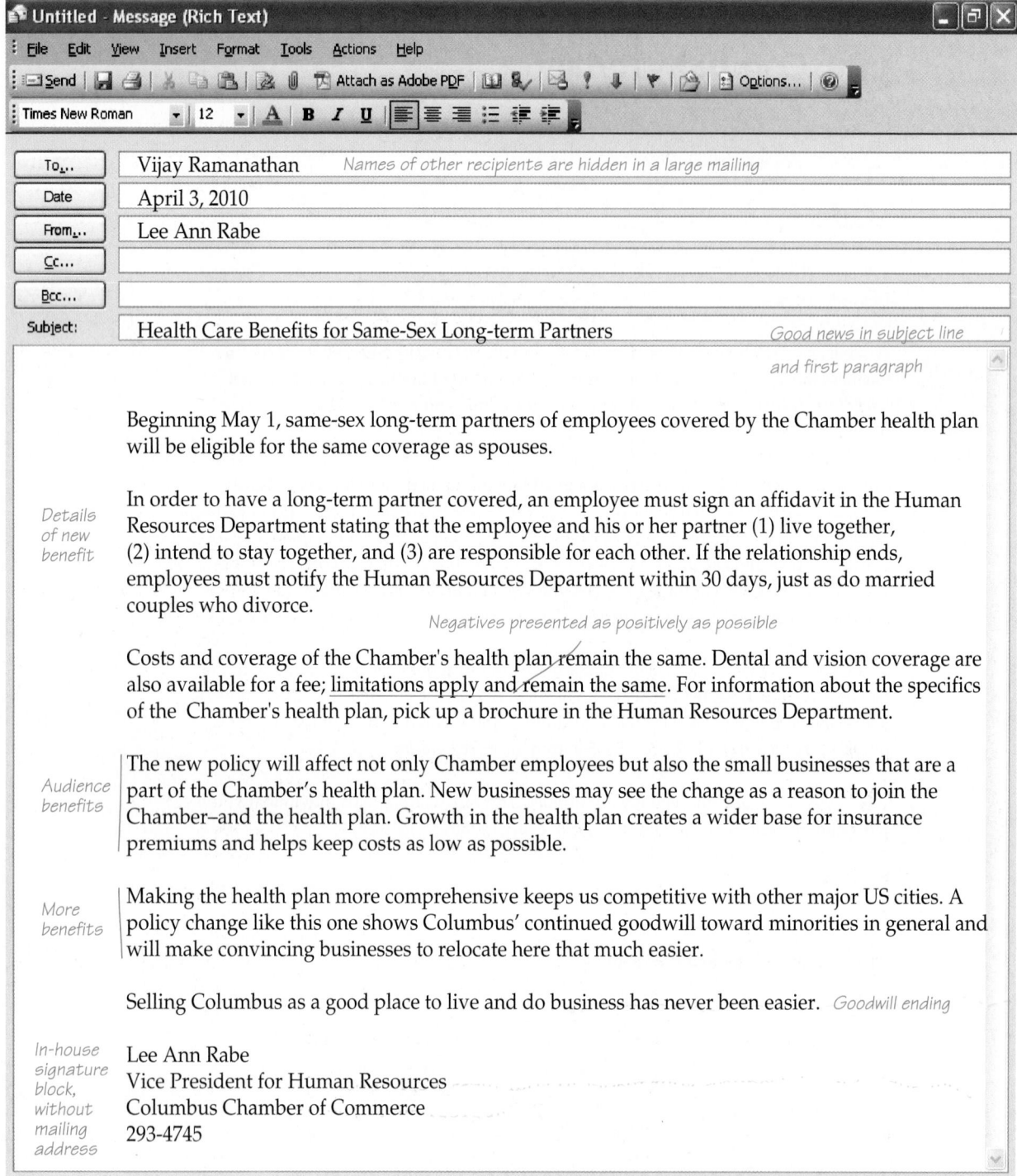

The letter in Figure 14.2 announces a change in a magazine's ownership. Rather than telling subscribers that their magazine has been acquired, which sounds negative, the first two paragraphs describe the change as a merger that will give subscribers greater benefits from the combined magazine. Paragraph 3 provides details about how the arrangement will work, along with a way to opt out. A possible negative is that readers who already have subscriptions to both magazines will now receive only one. The company addresses this situation positively by extending the subscription to the jointly published magazine. The goodwill ending has all the desired characteristics: it is positive ("we're confident"), personal ("your continued loyalty"), and forward-looking ("you will enjoy").

The memo in Figure 14.3 announces a new employee benefit. The first paragraph summarizes the policy. Paragraphs 2–3 give details. Negative elements are stated as positively as possible. The last section of the memo gives benefits and a goodwill ending.

Subject Lines for Informative and Positive Messages

A **subject line** is the title of a document. It aids in filing and retrieving the document, tells readers why they need to read the document, and provides a framework in which to set what you're about to say. Subject lines are standard in memos and e-mails. Letters are not required to have subject lines (see Appendix A, Formats for Letters, Memos, and E-Mail Messages).

A good subject line meets three criteria: it is specific, concise, and appropriate to the kind of message (positive, negative, persuasive).

Making Subject Lines Specific

The subject line needs to be specific enough to differentiate that message from others on the same subject, but broad enough to cover everything in the message.

| Too general: | Training Sessions |
| Better: | Dates for 2008 Training Sessions |

Making Subject Lines Concise

Most subject lines are relatively short. MailerMailer, a Web-based e-mail management service, found that e-mails whose subject lines were 35 characters or fewer were significantly more likely to be opened by readers than subject lines with more than 35 characters.[14]

| Wordy: | Survey of Student Preferences in Regards to Various Pizza Factors |
| Better: | Students' Pizza Preferences |

If you can't make the subject both specific and short, be specific.

Making Subject Lines Appropriate for the Pattern of Organization

Since your subject line introduces your reader to your message, it must satisfy the psychological demands of the situation; it must be appropriate to your purposes and to the immediate response you expect from your reader. In general, do the same thing in your subject line that you would do in the first paragraph.

When you have good news for the reader, build goodwill by highlighting it in the subject line. When your information is neutral, summarize it concisely for the subject line.

Subject: Discount on Rental Cars Effective January 2

Starting January 2, as an employee of Amalgamated Industries you can get a 15% discount on cars you rent for business or personal use from Roadway Rent-a-Car.

Subject: Update on Arrangements for Videoconference with France

In the last month, we have chosen the participants and developed a tentative agenda for the videoconference with France scheduled for March 21.

Pointers for E-Mail Subject Lines

Many people skim through large lists of e-mails daily, so subject lines in e-mails are even more important than those in letters and memos. Subject lines must be specific, concise, and catchy. In these days of spam, some e-mail users get so many messages that they don't bother reading messages if they don't recognize the sender or if the subject doesn't catch their interest. Create a subject line that will help your e-mail get read:

- Use important information in the subject line. Many people delete blanks and generic tags such as "hello," "your message," "thank you," and "next meeting," if they don't recognize the sender, especially now that so much spam has common business tags.
- Put good news in the subject line.
- Name drop to make a connection: Lee Pizer gave me your name.
- Make e-mail sound easy to deal with: Two Short Travel Questions.

The following subject lines would be acceptable for informative and good news e-mail messages:

Travel Plans for Sales Meeting
Your Proposal Accepted
Reduced Prices during February
Your Funding Request Approved

When you reply to a message, check to see that the automatic subject line "Re: [subject line of message to which you are responding]" is still appropriate. If it isn't, you may want to create a new subject line. And if a series of messages arises, you probably need a new subject line. "Re: Re: Re: Re: Question" is not an effective subject line.

Managing the Information in Your Messages

Information control is important. You want to give your audience the information they need, but you don't want to overwhelm them with information. Sometimes you will have good reasons for not providing all the information they want.

When you are the person in the know, it is easy to overestimate how much your audience knows. As a patient seeking medical treatment, you understand how much you would appreciate being told how long the wait is. When you leave a medical facility, you know how difficult it is to remember accurately those complicated instructions given to you orally by a doctor or nurse. Unfortunately, most of the huge medical industry seems to be just discovering these facts now. Medical offices are beginning to communicate waiting times and send patients home with written instructions for self-care and follow-up visits.

But, of course, information management is not always that simple. Pharmaceutical companies struggle with how much information to provide about their drugs. In 2004, the FDA publicized an analysis showing that young people on antidepressants had a 2% risk of suicidal thoughts. There were no actual suicides reported in the studies, just suicidal thoughts. Nevertheless, the FDA put a Black Box warning—the strongest possible warning—on antidepressants. Parents and physicians began backing away from the medications. Use of SSRI (selective serotonin reuptake inhibitors) medications in young people declined 14%, and suicides increased 18% among young people the first year of the warnings.[15]

Sometimes pharmaceutical companies, and other organizations, get in trouble because their information management withholds information that others—shareholders, regulators, customers, etc.—believe should be revealed. Glaxo-SmithKline was sued by shareholders and patients for not fully disclosing the risks of its diabetes drug Avandia. Merck faced similar lawsuits for its painkiller Vioxx. Both drugs were linked to an increased risk of heart attacks.[16] In a different venue, responding to donor desires for more transparency about how charities spend their money, the IRS revised the charities' annual tax form to require more information. This form must be made available on request.[17]

Other concerns about managing information are more prosaic. If you send out regularly scheduled messages on the same topic, such as monthly updates of training seminars, try to develop a system that lets people know immediately what is new. Use color for new or changed entries. Put new material at the top.

If your e-mail is long (more than one screen), use headings and bullets so readers can find the information they need. If you are answering multiple questions, use numbers.

If you send messages with an attachment, put the most vital information in the e-mail too. Don't make readers open an attachment merely to find out the time or location of a meeting.

Check your message for accuracy and completeness. Remember all the e-mails you receive about meetings that forget to include the time, place, or date, and don't let your e-mails fall in that incomplete category. Make a special effort to ensure that promised attachments really are attached. Be particularly careful with the last messages you send for the day or the week, when haste can cause errors.

Using Benefits in Informative and Positive Messages

Not all informative and positive messages need benefits. You don't need benefits when

- Presenting factual information only.
- The audience's attitude toward the information doesn't matter.
- Stressing benefits may make the audience sound selfish.
- The benefits are so obvious that to restate them insults the audience's intelligence.

You do need benefits when

- Presenting policies.
- Shaping your audience's attitudes toward the information or toward your organization.
- Stressing benefits presents the audience's motives positively.
- Some of the benefits may not be obvious.

Benefits are hardest to develop when you are announcing policies. The organization probably decided to adopt the policy because it appeared to help

Revealing Information

"Orthopedic surgeon Joseph Zuckerman recently started giving his patients some additional information before they undergo surgery. It is a letter revealing that Dr. Zuckerman is one of the designers of the artificial shoulder the patient is about to receive and that he is paid royalties from the implant manufacturer—Exatech Inc. of Gainesville, Fla. As is standard, Dr. Zuckerman doesn't collect any royalties on the shoulders he installs himself, but the surgeon nonetheless thought his patients should know of his financial relationship with the maker.

"'There should be a discussion between physicians and patients about financial involvements,' says Dr. Zuckerman, chairman of orthopedic surgery at NYU Hospital for Joint Diseases. . . .

"Dr. Zuckerman is unusual. Many physicians don't volunteer information about financial relationships that might bear on treatment decisions. At the same time, patients often find the discussion of a doctor's financial connections to be awkward and one they are reluctant to initiate."

What do you think? Should doctors disclose their financial ties? Should patients take greater responsibility by asking informative questions about financial ties when being treated?

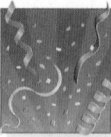

the organization; the people who made the decision may not have thought at all about whether it would help or hurt employees. Yet benefits are most essential in this kind of message so employees see the reason for the change and support it.

When you present benefits, be sure to present advantages *to the audience.* Most new policies help the organization in some way, but few workers will see their own interests as identical with these of the organization. Employees' benefits need to be spelled out, as do those of customers. To save money, an organization may change health care providers, but the notice to employees should spell out new benefits for employees and their families. Airlines announced their new check-in kiosks to customers as a way to avoid lines and save travelers' time.

To develop benefits for informative and positive messages, use the steps suggested in Chapter 2. Be sure to think about benefits that come from the activity or policy itself, in addition to any financial benefits. Does a policy improve customers' experience or the hours employees spend at work?

Ending Informative and Positive Messages

Ending a letter or memo gracefully can be a problem in short informative and positive messages. In a one-page memo where you have omitted details and proof, you can tell readers where to get more information. In long messages, you can summarize your basic point. In a short message containing all the information readers need, either write a goodwill paragraph that refers directly to the reader or the reader's organization, or just stop. In many short e-mails, just stopping is the best choice.

Goodwill endings should focus on the business relationship you share with your reader rather than on the reader's hobbies, family, or personal life. Use a paragraph that shows you see your reader as an individual. Possibilities include complimenting the reader for a job well done, describing a benefit, or looking forward to something positive that relates to the subject of the message.

> Thanks so much for sending those two extra sales tables. They were just what I needed for Section IV of the report.

When you write to one person, a good last paragraph fits that person so specifically that it would not work if you sent the same basic message to someone else or even to a person with the same title in another organization. When you write to someone who represents an organization, the last paragraph can refer to your company's relationship to the reader's organization. When you write to a group (for example, to "All Employees"), your ending should apply to the whole group.

> Remember that the deadline for enrolling in this new benefit plan is January 31.

Some writers end every message with a standard invitation:

> If you have questions, please do not hesitate to ask.

That sentence implies both that your message did not answer all questions, and that readers will hesitate to contact you. Both implications are negative. But revising the line to say "feel free to call" is rarely a good idea. People in business aren't shrinking violets; they will call if they need help. Don't make more work for yourself by inviting calls to clarify simple messages. Simply omit this sentence.

Humor in Informative Messages

Some writers use humor to ensure their messages are read. Humor is a risky tool because of its tendency to rile some people. However, if you know your audience well, humor may help ensure that they read and remember your messages.

If you decide to use humor, these precautions will help keep it useful.

- Do not direct it against other people, even if you believe they will never see your message. The Internet abounds with proof that such certainties are false. In particular, never aim humor against a specific group of people.
- Political, religious, and sexual humor should always be avoided; it is against discrimination policies in many businesses.
- Use restraint with your humor; a little levity goes a long way.

Used with care, however, humor in carefully chosen situations can help your communications. An information technology person sent the following e-mail in his small, nonprofit organization:[18]

> My set of screw driver tips is missing. I may well have loaned them to someone, perhaps weeks ago. If you have them, please return them to me. I use them when someone reports that they have a screw loose.

He got his tips back promptly. Because he has a reputation for clever e-mails, people regularly read his messages.

Varieties of Informative and Positive Messages

Many messages can be informative, negative, or persuasive depending on what you have to say. A transmittal, for example, can be positive when you're sending glowing sales figures or persuasive when you want the reader to act on the information. A performance appraisal is positive when you evaluate someone who's doing superbly, negative when you want to compile a record to justify firing someone, and persuasive when you want to motivate a satisfactory worker to continue to improve. Each of these messages is discussed in the chapter of the pattern it uses most frequently. However, in some cases you will need to use a pattern from a different chapter.

Transmittals

When you send someone something, you frequently need to attach a memo or letter of transmittal explaining what you're sending. A transmittal can be as simple as a small yellow Post-it™ note with "FYI" ("for your information") written on it, or it can be a separate typed document.

Organize a memo or letter of transmittal in this order:

1. Tell the reader what you're sending.
2. Summarize the main point(s) of the document.
3. Indicate any special circumstances or information that would help the reader understand the document. Is it a draft? Is it a partial document that will be completed later?
4. Tell the reader what will happen next. Will you do something? Do you want a response? If you do want the reader to act, specify exactly what you want the reader to do and give a deadline.

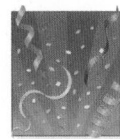

April Fool's Hoaxes: Famous (Mis)Information

"[In 1996] the Taco Bell Corp. announced that it had bought the Liberty Bell and was renaming it the Taco Liberty Bell. Hundreds of outraged citizens called the National Historic Park in Philadelphia where the bell was housed to express their anger.

"[In 1998] Burger King published a full page advertisement in *USA Today* announcing the introduction of a new item to their menu: a 'Left-Handed Whopper' specially designed for the 32 million left-handed Americans. According to the advertisement, the new whopper included the same ingredients as the original Whopper (lettuce, tomato, hamburger patty, etc.), but all the condiments were rotated 180 degrees for the benefit of their left-handed customers. The following day Burger King issued a follow-up release revealing that although the Left-Handed Whopper was a hoax, thousands of customers had gone into restaurants to request the new sandwich. Simultaneously, according to the press release, 'many others requested their own "right-handed" version.'"

What benefits did these companies gain from their hoaxes? How could this misinformation backfire?

Hoaxes quoted from "The Top 100 April Fool's Day Hoaxes of All Time," http://www.museumofhoaxes.com/hoax/aprilfool/ (accessed March 26, 2009).

Turkey Talk

In 1980, Butterball, a nationwide distributor of turkeys, started the "Turkey Talk-Line," in which operators answer calls from customers with questions about preparing turkeys. The operators have to graduate from Butterball University, where they learn to prepare turkeys many different ways. At each call station, operators are also prepared with a four-inch binder containing turkey information.

Approximately 10,000 calls come in on Thanksgiving Day. In a given year, the center receives approximately 100,000 calls with turkey questions. The questions cover thawing turkeys in a snow bank because of lack of refrigerator space, thawing it in bathtubs where kids put soap bubbles on it, or even cooking a turkey on a grill that was lined with kitty litter.

How useful do you believe this informative service is to customers? How does this open line of communication help Butterball improve its business?

Adapted from Jenny Mero, "Turkey Talker," *Fortune*, November 27, 2006, 70.

Frequently transmittals have important secondary purposes. Consider the writer's purpose in Figure 14.4, a transmittal from a lawyer to her client. The primary purpose of this transmittal is to give the client a chance to affirm that his story and the lawyer's understanding of it are correct. If there's anything wrong, the lawyer wants to know *before* she files the brief. But an important secondary purpose is to build goodwill: "I'm working on your case; I'm earning my fee." The greatest number of complaints officially lodged against lawyers are for the lawyer's neglect—or what the client perceives as neglect—of the client's case.

Summaries

You may be asked to summarize a conversation, a document, or an outside meeting for colleagues or superiors. (Minutes of an internal meeting are usually more detailed. See Chapter 6 for advice on writing minutes of meetings.)

In a summary of a conversation for internal use, identify the people who were present, the topic of discussion, decisions made, and who does what next.

To summarize a document, start with the main point. Then go on to give supporting evidence or details. In some cases, your audience may also want you to evaluate the document. Should others in the company read this report? Should someone in the company write a letter to the editor responding to this newspaper article?

When you visit a client or go to a conference, you may be asked to share your findings and impressions with other people in your organization. Chronological accounts are the easiest to write but the least useful for the reader. Your company doesn't need a blow-by-blow account of what you did; it needs to know what *it* should do as a result of the meeting.

Summarize a visit with a client or customer in this way:

1. Put the main point from your organization's point of view—the action to be taken, the perceptions to be changed—in the first paragraph.
2. Provide an **umbrella paragraph** to cover and foreshadow the points you will make in the report.

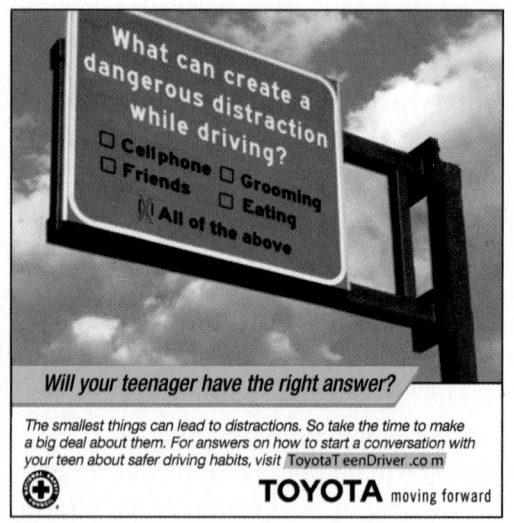

In 2006, Toyota launched an ad campaign to encourage safe driving among teenagers, who hold the highest rate for being in an accident. In the ads, Toyota attempts to inform the public about safety issues of driving recklessly, while also appealing to the viewers' emotions.

Source: Toyota Advertisements, *Wall Street Journal*, October 4, 2006, A1, and September 27, 2006, A1.

Figure 14.4   A Transmittal

DREW & Associates

100 Barkley Plaza • Denver, CO 80210 • 303.555.4783 • Fax 303.555.4784

October 8, 2010

Mr. Charles Gibney
Personnel Manager
Roydon Interiors
146 East State Street
Denver, CO 80202

Dear Mr. Gibney:

Paragraph one tells reader what is enclosed and summarizes main points.

Here is a copy of the brief we intend to file with the Tenth Circuit Court in support of our position that the sex discrimination charge against Roydon Interiors should be dropped.

Will you please examine it carefully to make sure that the facts it contains are correct? If you have changes to suggest, please call my office by October 22nd, so that we can file the brief by October 24th.

Sincerely,

Last paragraph asks for action by a specific date.

Diana Drew

Diana Drew

---

3. Provide necessary detail to support your conclusions and cover each point. Use lists and headings to make the structure of the document clear.

In the following example, the revised first paragraph summarizes the sales representative's conclusions after a call on a prospective client:
   Original:

On October 10th, Rick Patel and I made a joint call on Consolidated Tool Works. The discussion was held in a conference room, with the following people present:

1. Kyle McCloskey (Vice President and General Manager)
2. Bill Petrakis (Manufacturing Engineer)
3. Garett Lee (Process Engineering Supervisor)
4. Courtney Mansor-Green (Project Engineer)

Electronic Feedback

In an attempt to boost business and promote discussion of products and services, small businesses are increasingly adding customer reviews to their Web sites. These reviews offer consumers a chance to weigh in on their experiences with a product or service. Over time, this review process has been shown to promote repeat and loyal business because consumers are more likely to trust word of mouth reviews than more traditional avenues of marketing.

A survey conducted by Forrester Research found that 71% of adults online (22 and over) and 81% of youth online (ages 13–21) use customer product ratings. The reviews not only help a small business know what's good about its organization, they also provide direct feedback on what could be improved or changed with a product or service.

Adapted from Kelly K. Spors, "How Are We Doing? Small Companies Find It Pays to Ask Customers That Question," *Wall Street Journal*, November 13, 2006, R9.

Revised:

> Consolidated Tool Works is an excellent prospect for purchasing a Matrix-Churchill grinding machine. To get the order, we should
>
> 1. Set up a visit for CTW personnel to see the Matrix-Churchill machine in Kansas City;
> 2. Guarantee 60-day delivery if the order is placed by the end of the quarter; and
> 3. Extend credit terms to CTW.

Thank-You and Positive Feedback Notes

We all like to feel appreciated. Stress reduction expert Richard Carlson always recommended liberal applications of positive feedback in his popular books and lectures. As he reminded his audiences, employees who feel appreciated are happier and work harder and better than those who feel taken for granted.[19]

Praising or congratulating people can cement good feelings between you and them and enhance your own visibility.

> Congratulations, Sam, on winning the Miller sales award. I bet winning that huge Lawson contract didn't hurt any!

Make your praise sound sincere by offering specifics and avoiding language that might seem condescending or patronizing. For example, think how silly it would sound to praise an employee for completing basic job requirements or to gush that one's mentor has superior knowledge. In contrast, thanks for a kind deed and congratulations or praise on completing a difficult task are rewarding in almost any situation.

Sending a **thank-you note** will make people more willing to help you again in the future. Thank-you letters can be short but must be prompt. They need to be specific to sound sincere.

> Chris, thank you for the extra-short turnaround time. You were a major reason we made the deadline.

Personal Touch

"E-mails are fine, but if you really want to thank a customer for his [or her] business, write a short note instead. Businesspeople get so few handwritten notes these days that your thank you is sure to stand out."

Quoted from "Networking Tip," *Sales & Marketing Management*, May 2004, 64.

Most thank-you notes are e-mails now, so handwritten ones stand out.

If you make it a habit to watch for opportunities to offer thanks and congratulations, you may be pleasantly surprised at the number of people who are extending themselves. Lawrence Fish, chief executive of Citizens Bank, tries to write a note of thanks or congratulations to one member of his team every day. During his six-year term, Douglas Conant, Chief Executive of Campbell, sent over 16,000 handwritten thank-you notes to employees ranging from top executives to hourly workers. Linden Labs, a San Francisco virtual reality firm, has a "Love Machine" that allows employees to send other employees a note of thanks. These notes are tracked in a database, which is accessed during performance reviews.[20] As Kenneth Blanchard and Spencer Johnson, authors of the business best seller *The One Minute Manager*, note, "People who feel good about themselves produce good results."[21]

Dear Professor Carlton,

Thank you for all your help this semester. My writing skills have improved greatly as have my organizational skills. The extra time you gave me really paid off. I've already had three job interviews due to the job packet I prepared for your course. I will miss your funny dog stories!!! Thanks again for everything!

Pat
Robbins

Thank-you notes can be written on standard business stationery, using standard formats. But one student noticed that his professor really liked dogs and told funny dog stories in class. So the student found a dog card for a thank-you note.

Positive Responses to Complaints

Complaining customers expect organizations to show that they are listening and want to resolve the problem. When you grant a customer's request for an adjusted price, discount, replacement, or other benefit to resolve a complaint, do so in the very first sentence.

Your Visa bill for a night's lodging has been adjusted to $63. Next month a credit of $37 will appear on your bill to reimburse you for the extra amount you were originally asked to pay.

Don't talk about your own process in making the decision. Don't say anything that sounds grudging. Give the reason for the original mistake only if it reflects credit on the company. (In most cases, it doesn't, so the reason should be omitted.)

Bad Words

Ruth King, who coaches building contractors, has advice for employees who handle customer complaints. When a customer complains, King says, avoid using the following words in your reply:

- **We're busy.** These words focus on your organization; you should focus on the customer. State the earliest possible time you can give your attention to the problem.

- **No.** When a customer is angry, the word *no* is like "gasoline on a fire." Instead, offer reasonable alternatives to choose from.

- **We can't.** These words are as infuriating as *no*. Again, specify what you *can* offer.

- **It's our policy.** Writing about the organization's policy takes the focus off the customer and is yet another way to say what you will not do. Customers aren't interested in policies, and they are likely to ask that the policy be changed or waived. Focus on alternatives that are available.

Adapted from Ruth King, "Five Things You Should Never Say to Customers," *Journal of Light Construction* 22, no. 1 (2003): 10.

Solving a Sample Problem

Workplace problems are richer and less well defined than textbook problems and cases. But even textbook problems require analysis before you begin to write. Before you tackle the assignments for this chapter, examine the following problem. See how the analysis questions from Chapter 1 probe the basic points required for a solution. Study the two sample solutions to see what makes one unacceptable and the other one good. Note the recommendations for revision that could make the good solution excellent. The checklist at the end of the chapter (p. 419) can help you evaluate a draft.

Problem

At Interstate Fidelity Insurance (IFI) there is often a time lag between receiving a payment from a customer and recording it on the computer. Sometimes, while the payment is in line to be processed, the computer sends out additional notices: past-due notices or collection letters. Customers are frightened or angry and write or call asking for an explanation. In most cases, if they just waited a little while, the situation would be straightened out. But policyholders are afraid that they'll be without insurance because the company thinks the bill has not been paid.

IFI doesn't have the time to check each individual situation to see if the check did arrive and has been processed. It wants you to write a letter that will persuade customers to wait. If something is wrong and the payment never reached IFI, IFI would send a legal notice to that effect saying the policy would be canceled by a certain date (which the notice would specify) at least 30 days after the date on the original premium bill. Continuing customers always get this legal notice as a third chance (after the original bill and the past-due notice).

Prepare a form letter that can go out to every policyholder who claims to have paid a premium for automobile insurance and resents getting a past-due notice. The letter should reassure readers and build goodwill for IFI.

Analysis of the Problem

1. Who is (are) your audience(s)? What characteristics are relevant to this particular message? If you are communicating with more than one person, how do the audiences differ?

   Automobile insurance customers who say they've paid but have still received a past-due notice. They're afraid they're no longer insured. Since it's a form letter, different readers will have different situations: in some cases payments did arrive late, in some cases the company made a mistake, in some the reader never paid (check was lost in mail, unsigned, bounced, etc.).

2. What are your purposes in writing?

   To reassure readers that they're covered for 30 days. To inform them that they can assume everything is OK *unless* they receive a second notice. To avoid further correspondence on this subject. To build goodwill for IFI: (a) we don't want to suggest IFI is error-prone or too cheap to hire enough people to do the necessary work; (b) we don't want readers to switch companies; (c) we do want readers to buy from IFI when they're ready for more insurance.

3. What information must your message include?

   Readers are still insured. We cannot say whether their checks have now been processed (company doesn't want to check individual accounts). Their insurance will be canceled if they do not pay after receiving the second past-due notice (the legal notice).

4. How can you build support for your position? What reasons or benefits will your audience find convincing?

We provide personal service to policyholders. We offer policies to meet all their needs. Both of these points would need specifics to be interesting and convincing.

5. What objection(s) can you expect your audience(s) to have? What negative elements of your message must you deemphasize or overcome?

    We are slow in processing payments. We don't know if the checks have been processed. We will cancel policies if their checks don't arrive.

6. What aspects of the total situation may affect audience response? The economy? The time of year? Morale in the organization? The relationship between the communicator and audience? Any special circumstances?

    The insurance business is highly competitive—other companies offer similar rates and policies. The customer could get a similar policy for about the same money from someone else. The economy is making money tight, so customers will want to keep insurance costs low. Yet the fact that prices are steady or rising means that the value of what they own is higher—they need insurance more than ever.

    Many insurance companies are refusing to renew policies (car, liability, home). These refusals to renew have gotten lots of publicity, and many people have heard horror stories about companies and individuals whose insurance has been canceled or not renewed after a small number of claims. Readers don't feel very kindly toward insurance companies.

    People need car insurance. If they have an accident and aren't covered, they not only have to bear the costs of that accident alone but also (depending on state law) may need to place as much as $50,000 in a state escrow account to cover future accidents. They have a legitimate worry.

Discussion of the Sample Solutions

The solution in Figure 14.5 is unacceptable. The red marginal comments show problem spots. Since this is a form letter, we cannot tell customers we have

---

One Tablespoon or Two?

The Internet has provided a means for information on just about any subject to be at your fingertips. For example, chefs are now communicating over the Internet to provide cooking tips to families just like yours. These chefs communicate through IM, e-mail, or chat boards—some services for free and some for a cost. This instant access to consumers provides just one more way chefs and restaurateurs can promote their businesses. Check out some of these sites from the following list and determine how effective they are at delivering informative messages:

- http://www.chefsline.com
- http://www.chefs.com
- http://www.cheftalk.com
- http://www.chefjoanna.com

Adapted from Yuliya Cherrnova, "Soggy Stuffing, Dry Turkey? Now You Can IM a Chef," *Wall Street Journal,* November 22, 2006, D1.

Figure 14.5 An Unacceptable Solution to the Sample Problem

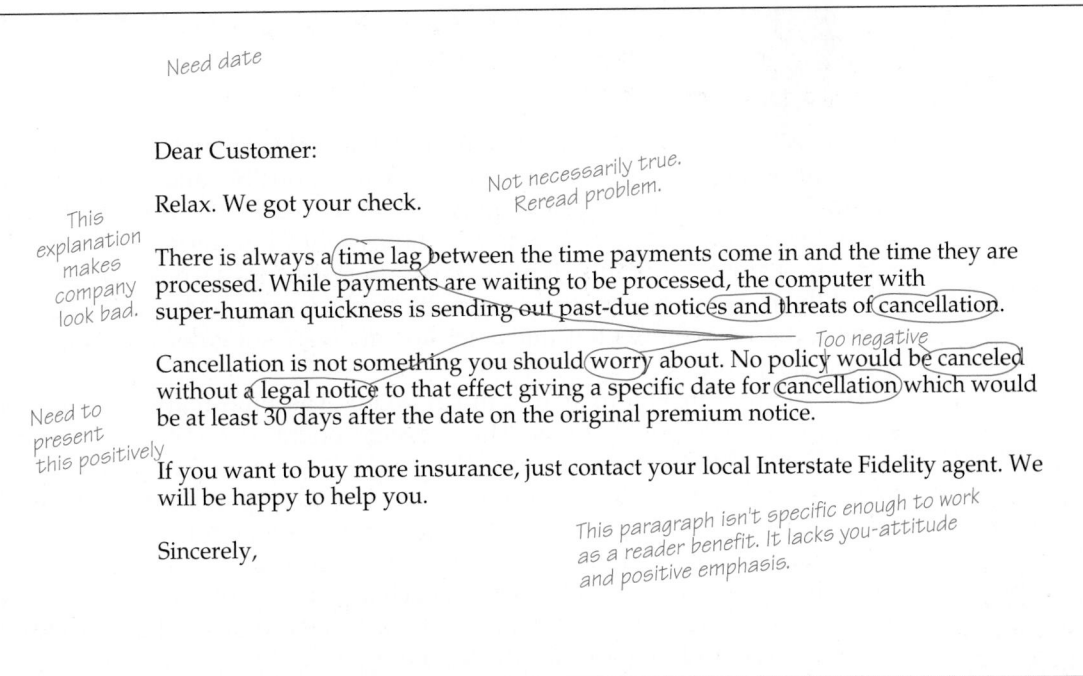

Figure 14.6   A Good Solution to the Sample Problem

Need date

Dear Customer: *Better: use computer to personalize. Put in name and address of a specific reader*

Your auto insurance is still in effect.   *Good ¶ 1. True for all readers*

Good to treat notice as information, tell reader what to do if it arrives

Past-due notices are mailed out if the payment has not been processed within three days after the due date. This may happen if a check is delayed in the mail or arrives without a signature or account number. When your check arrives with all the necessary information, it is promptly credited to your account.   *Good you-attitude*

Even if a check is lost in the mail and never reaches us, you still have a 30-day grace period. If you do get a second notice, you'll know that we still have not received your check. To keep your insurance in force, just stop payment on the first check and send a second one.

Benefits of using IFI

IFI is always checking to ensure that you get any discounts you're eligible for: multicar, accident-free record, good student. If you have a claim, your agent finds quality repair shops quickly, whatever car you drive. You get a check quickly—usually within 3 working days—without having to visit dealer after dealer for time-consuming estimates.   *Too negative*

Better to put in agent's name, phone number

Need to add benefits of insuring with IFI

Today, your home and possessions are worth more than ever. You can protect them with Interstate Fidelity's homeowners' and renters' policies. Let your local agent show you how easy it is to give yourself full protection. If you need a special rider to insure a personal computer, jewelry, a coin or gun collection, or a fine antique, you can get that from IFI, too.   *Good specifics*

Whatever your insurance needs—auto, home, life, or health—one call to IFI can do it all.

Sincerely,   *Acceptable ending*

http://www.thecoca-colacompany.com/heritage/stories/index.html

Stories are powerful ways to inform, teach, and persuade. Coca-Cola is one of several companies posting customer stories on its Web site. Log on to read some of the stories or submit your own memory involving Coca-Cola.

While reading the stories, consider how these positive messages help the organization build goodwill with its consumers. Why are these stories powerful? Out of all the mail Coca-Cola receives, why do you think these particular stories were chosen to appear on their Web site? Furthermore, why do you think interactive sites like these build brand loyalty with customers?

their checks; in some cases, we may not. The letter is far too negative. The explanation in paragraph 2 makes IFI look irresponsible and uncaring. Paragraph 3 is far too negative. Paragraph 4 is too vague; there are no benefits; the ending sounds selfish. A major weakness with the solution is that it lifts phrases straight out of the problem; the writer does not seem to have thought about the problem or about the words he or she is using. Measuring the draft against the answers to the questions for analysis suggests that this writer should start over.

The solution in Figure 14.6 is much better. The blue marginal comments show the letter's good points. The message opens strongly with the good news that is true for all audiences. Paragraph 2 explains IFI's policy in more positive terms. The negative information is buried in paragraph 3 and is presented positively: the notice is information, not a threat; the 30-day extension is a "grace period." Telling the reader now what to do if a second notice arrives eliminates the need for a second exchange of letters. Paragraph 4 offers benefits for being insured by IFI. Paragraph 5 promotes other policies the company sells and prepares for the last paragraph.

As the red comments indicate, this good solution could be improved by personalizing the salutation and by including the name and number of the local agent. Computers could make both of those insertions easily. This good letter could be made excellent by revising paragraph 4 so that it doesn't end on a negative note and by using more benefits. For instance, can agents advise clients of the best policies for them? Does IFI offer good service—quick, friendly, nonpressured—that could be stressed? Are agents well trained? All of these might yield ideas for additional benefits.

You—A Most Important Subject

On the job, one of the most important subjects you can communicate about is your own performance. Make sure your boss knows what you are doing. You don't have to brag; simply noting your accomplishments is usually enough, because many employees do not take the time to do so.

Remember that raises are based not on the hard work you actually do, but the hard work your boss knows about. Furthermore, bosses count the work they want done, which is not always the work employees emphasize.

Provide your boss with paper copies of your work; CC him/her on major e-mails, if appropriate. Have 30-second blurbs ready for times when you and your boss are alone in the elevator or break room: "We got the McCluskey contract ready a day early" or "the new G7 database is going to IT tomorrow."

✔ *Checklist* 　 Checklist for Informative and Positive Messages

☐ In positive messages, does the subject line give the good news? In either message, is the subject line specific enough to differentiate this message from others on the same subject?

☐ Does the first paragraph summarize the information or good news? If the information is too complex to fit into a single paragraph, does the paragraph list the basic parts of the policy or information in the order in which the memo discusses them?

☐ Is all the information given in the message? What information is needed will vary depending on the message, but information about dates, places, times, and anything related to money usually needs to be included. When in doubt, ask!

☐ In messages announcing policies, is there at least one benefit for each segment of the audience? Are all benefits ones that seem likely to occur in this organization?

☐ Is each benefit developed, showing that the benefit will come from the policy and why the benefit matters to this audience? Do the benefits build on the specific circumstances of the audience?

☐ Does the message end with a positive paragraph—preferably one that is specific to the readers, not a general one that could fit any organization or policy?

And, for all messages, not just informative and positive ones,

☐ Does the message use you-attitude and positive emphasis?

☐ Is the tone friendly?

☐ Is the style easy to read?

☐ Is the visual design of the message inviting?

☐ Is the format correct?

☐ Does the message use standard grammar? Is it free from typos?

Originality in a positive or informative message may come from

- Creating good headings, lists, and visual impact.
- Developing benefits.
- Thinking about audiences; giving details that answer their questions and make it easier for them to understand and follow the policy.

Summary of Key Points

- Good communicators need to thoughtfully select one of the six most common modes of office communications: face-to-face contact, phone calls, instant messages and text messaging, letters, e-mails, and paper memos.

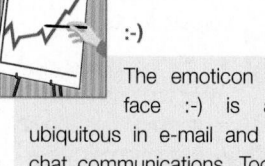

:-)

The emoticon smiley face :-) is almost ubiquitous in e-mail and online chat communications. Today, of course, the symbol has made great advancements with most e-mail programs and even some word-processing programs automatically changing :-) into 🙂.

Believe it or not, the :-) has been around for over 25 years. A Carnegie Mellon University professor, Scott Fahlman, was the first to use the colon, hyphen, and parenthesis combination. He posted the three keystrokes on an online bulletin board at 11:44 AM on September 19, 1982, during a discussion of online humor.

Does the :-) really help to convey humor in an otherwise nonverbal electronic medium? Think about other popular emoticons; will :-) remain a mainstay in electronic communication? Can you think of other emoticons that could eventually replace it? Will emoticons become obsolete as society creates new ways to express emotion within electronic media?

Adapted from Daniel Lovering, "Simple :-) Endures for 25 Years as Online Emblem of Emotion," *Des Moines Register*, September 19, 2007.

- Informative and positive messages normally use the following pattern of organization:

    1. Start with good news or the most important information; summarize the main points.

    2. Give details, clarification, background.

    3. Present any negative elements—as positively as possible.

    4. Explain any benefits.

    5. Use a goodwill ending: positive, personal, and forward-looking.

- A **subject line** is the title of a document. A good subject line meets three criteria: it's specific; it's reasonably short; and it's adapted to the kind of message (positive, negative, persuasive). If you can't make the subject both specific and short, be specific.

- The subject line for an informative or positive message should highlight any good news and summarize the information concisely.

- Good messages provide the necessary information without overwhelming their audience.

- Use benefits in informative and positive messages when you want to shape your audience's attitudes toward the information or toward your organization.

- **Goodwill endings** should focus on the business relationship you share with your audience or the audience's organization. The last paragraph of a message to a group should apply to the whole group.

- Humor is a risky tool. Use it carefully in written messages, and only when you and your audience know each other well.

- Use the analysis questions listed in Chapter 1 to probe the basic points needed for successful informative and positive messages.

CHAPTER 14   Exercises and Problems   *Go to www.mhhe.com/locker9e for additional Exercises and Problems.*

14.1   Reviewing the Chapter

1. What are the multiple purposes of informative and good news messages? (LO 1)

2. How does information overload impact your communications? (LO 1)

3. When do you use face-to-face contacts? Phone calls? Instant messages? Letters? Memos and e-mails? (LO 1)

4. What are some tips for effectively using face-to-face contacts? Phone calls? Instant messages? Letters? Memos and e-mails? (LO 2)

5. How do you organize informative and positive letters and memos/e-mails? (LO 3)

6. What are some concerns to consider when choosing and ordering the information in your message? (LO 3)

7. What are tips for composing some of the common varieties of informative and positive messages? (LO 4)

14.2   Reviewing Grammar

Good letters and e-mails need correct grammar. Practice yours by doing the exercises from Appendix B on correcting sentence errors (B.8) and editing for grammar and usage (B.9).

14.3   Critiquing a Letter—Economic Stimulus Payment Notice

The following letter was sent to more than 130 million households after the US Congress passed a stimulus package in early 2008. Read the letter and then critique it in small groups. Here are some questions to get you started:

1. What is the purpose of this letter?
2. How well does this letter inform the audience of its purpose?
3. Does the letter violate any of the guidelines for constructing informational messages you read about in this chapter? If so, which ones?
4. What kind of impression is given to readers by the document design choices?

Write a memo to your instructor summarizing your group discussion.

IRS
Department of the Treasury
Internal Revenue Service
Notice 1377 (February 2008)
Catalog Number 51255B
www.irs.gov

Economic Stimulus Payment Notice

Dear Taxpayer:

We are pleased to inform you that the United States Congress passed and President George W. Bush signed into law the Economic Stimulus Act of 2008, which provides for economic stimulus payments to be made to over 130 million American households. Under this new law, you may be entitled to a payment of up to $600 ($1,200 if filing a joint return), plus additional amount for each qualifying child.

We are sending this notice to let you know that based on this new law the IRS will begin sending the one-time payments starting in May. To receive a payment in 2008, individuals who qualify will not have to do anything more than file a 2007 tax return. The IRS will determine eligibility, figure the amount, and send the payment. This payment should not be confused with any 2007 income tax refund that is owed to you by the federal government. Income tax refunds for 2007 will be made separately from this one-time payment.

For individuals who normally do not have to file a tax return, the new law provides for payments to individuals who have a total of $3,000 or more in earned income, Social Security benefits, and/or certain veterans' payments. Those individuals should file a tax return for 2007 to receive a payment in 2008.

Individuals who qualify may receive as much as $600 ($1,200 if married filing jointly). Even if you pay no income tax but have a total of $3,000 or more in earned income, Social Security benefits, and/or certain veterans' payments, you may receive a payment of $300 ($600 if married filing jointly).

In addition, individuals eligible for payments may also receive an additional amount of $300 for each child qualifying for the child tax credit.

For taxpayers with adjusted gross income (AGI) of more than $75,000 (or more than $150,000 if married filing jointly), the payment will be reduced or phased out completely.

To qualify for the payment, an individual, spouse, and any qualifying child must have a valid Social Security number. In addition, individuals cannot receive a payment if they can be claimed as a dependent of another taxpayer or they filled a 2007 Form 1040NR, 1040NR-EZ, 1040-PR, or 1040-SS.

All individuals receiving payments will receive a notice and additional information shortly before the payment is made. In the meantime, for additional information, please visit the IRS website at *www.irs.gov*.

Source: Internal Revenue Service, "Economic Stimulus Payment Notice," in *Notice 1377 (February 2008) Catalog Number 51255B,* http://www.irs.gov/pub/irs-utl/economic_stimulus_payment_notice.pdf (accessed March 27, 2009).

14.4   Introducing a Suggestion System—Memos for Discussion

Your organization has decided to institute a suggestion system. Employees on hourly pay scales will be asked to submit suggestions. (Managers and other employees on salary are not eligible for this program; they are supposed to be continually suggesting ways to improve things as part of their regular jobs.) If the evaluating committee thinks that the suggestion will save money, the employee will receive 10% of the first year's estimated annual savings. If the suggestion won't save money but will improve work conditions, service, or morale, the employee will get a check for $50.

The following memos are possible approaches. How well does each message meet the criteria in the checklist for informative and positive messages?

1.

Subject: Suggestion System (SS)

I want to introduce you to the Suggestion System (SS). This program enables the production worker to offer ideas about improving his job description, working conditions, and general company procedures. The plan can operate as a finely tuned machine, with great ideas as its product.

Operation will begin October 1. Once a week, a designate of SS will collect the ideas and turn them over to the SS Committee. This committee will evaluate and judge the proposed changes.

Only employees listed as factory workers are eligible. This excludes foremen and the rest of supervisory personnel. Awards are as follows:

1. $50 awards will be given to those ideas judged operational. These are awarded monthly.
2. There will be grand prizes given for the best suggestions over the six-month span.

Ideas are judged on feasibility, originality, operational simplicity, and degree of benefit to the worker and company. Evaluation made by the SS Committee is final. Your questions should be channeled to my office.

2.

Subject: Establishment of Suggestion System

We announce the establishment of a Suggestion System. This new program is designed to provide a means for hourly employees to submit suggestions to company management concerning operations and safety. The program will also provide an award system to compensate nonmanagement employees for implemented suggestions.

Here is how the program will work: beginning October 1, suggestions can be submitted by hourly workers to the company on Form 292, which will be furnished to all plants and their departments by October 1st. On the form, the submitting employee should include the suggestion, his or her name, and the department number. The form can be deposited in a suggestion drop box, which will be located near the personnel office in each plant.

Any suggestion dealing with the improvement of operations, safety, working conditions, or morale is eligible for consideration. The award structure for the program will be as follows:

1. For an implemented suggestion which improves safety or efficiency with no associated monetary benefits or cost reduction: $50.00.
2. For an implemented suggestion which makes or saves the company money: 10% of the first year's estimated annual savings or additional revenue.

It is hoped that we will have a good initial and continuous response from all hourly employees. This year, we are out to try to cut production costs, and this program may be the vehicle through which we will realize new savings and increased revenues. New ideas which can truly increase operational efficiency or cut safety problems will make the company a nicer place for all employees. A safer work environment is a better work environment. If department operations can be made more efficient, this will eventually make everyone's job just a little easier, and give that department and its employees a sense of pride.

3.

Subject: New Employee Suggestion System

Beginning October 1, all of you who are hourly employees of Video Adventures will be able to get cash awards when your suggestions for improving the company are implemented.

Ideas about any aspect of Video Adventures are eligible: streamlining behind-the-counter operations, handling schedule problems, increasing the life of videotapes.

- If your idea cuts costs or increases income (e.g., increasing membership sales, increasing the number of movie rentals per customer), you'll receive 10% of the first year's estimated annual savings.
- If the idea doesn't save money but does improve service, work conditions, or morale, you'll receive a check for $50.

To submit a suggestion, just pick up a form from your manager. On the form, explain your suggestion, describe briefly how it could be implemented, and show how it will affect Video Adventures. Return the completed form in the new suggestion box behind the back counter. Suggestions will be evaluated at the end of each month. Turn in as many ideas as you like!

Think about ways to solve the problems you face every day. Can we speed up the check-in process? Cut paperwork? Give customers faster service? Increase the percentage of customers who bring back their tapes on time? As you serve people at the counter, ask them what they'd like to see at Video Adventures.

Your ideas will keep Video Adventures competitive. Ten years ago, Video Adventures was the only video store on the west side of town. Now there are six other video stores within a two-mile radius. Efficiency, creativity, and service can keep Video Adventures ahead.

Employees whose ideas are implemented will be recognized in the regional Video Adventures newsletter. The award will also be a nice accomplishment to add to any college application or résumé. By suggesting ways to improve Video Adventures, you'll demonstrate your creativity and problem-solving abilities. And you'll be able to share the credit for keeping Video Adventures' reputation as the best video store in town.

14.5   Saying Yes to a Subordinate—E-Mails for Discussion

Today, you get this request from a subordinate.

> Subject: Request for Leave
>
> You know that I've been feeling burned out. I've decided that I want to take a three-month leave of absence this summer to travel abroad. I've got five weeks of vacation time saved up; I would take the rest as unpaid leave. Just guarantee that my job will be waiting when I come back!

You decide to grant the request. The following messages are possible responses. How well does each message meet the criteria in the checklist for informative and positive messages?

1.
> Subject: Re: Request for Leave
>
> I highly recommend Italy. Spend a full week in Florence, if you can. Be sure to visit the Brancacci Chapel—it's been restored, and the frescoes are breathtaking. And I can give you the names of some great restaurants. You may never want to come back!

2.
> Subject: Your Request for Leave
>
> As you know, we are in a very competitive position right now. Your job is important, and there is no one who can easily replace you. However, because you are a valued employee, I will permit you to take the leave you request, as long as you train a replacement before you leave.

3.
> Subject: Your Request for Leave Granted
>
> Yes, you may take a three-month leave of absence next summer using your five weeks of accumulated vacation time and taking the rest as unpaid leave. And yes, your job will be waiting for you when you return!
>
> I'm appointing Garrick to take over your duties while you're gone. Talk with him to determine how much training time he'll need, and let me know when the training is scheduled.
>
> Have a great summer! Let us know every now and then how you're doing!

14.6   Managing Overdraft Information

Banks make billions of dollars from overdraft fees. They maintain that the overdraft service allows customers to make vital purchases even when their account is empty.

On the other side, many customers are furious at how the current system allows them to rack up hundreds of dollars in overdraft fees without knowing they are doing so. Many of them claim they did not know they had overdraft service until they saw the fees. They want to be alerted when a purchase will result in an overdraft. They also object to the bank practice of processing a large purchase before several small ones that occurred at almost the same time, so that each small purchase gets an overdraft fee that it would not have gotten if the large purchase had been processed last.

In small groups, discuss how much overdraft information should be shared. Here are some questions to get you started:

- For what groups are overdraft services a benefit?
- Which groups do such services hurt most?

- Should people be automatically enrolled in such services, as is now the case for most customers?
- Should banks notify customers that they are about to incur an overdraft fee? How would third-party processors affect such notifications?

Write a memo to your instructor summarizing your group's discussion.

Source: Kelly Evans, "Consumers Vent on Overdraft Fees," *Wall Street Journal,* March 26, 2009, D2.

14.7 Offering Restaurant Nutrition Information

The Food and Drug Administration wants restaurants to provide more nutritional information, including calorie counts of offerings, so that customers can make more nutritious choices. You own a restaurant and are considering whether or not you should change your menu to comply. On the one hand, you know obesity is a national problem, and you might be able to attract health-conscious customers if you change your menu. On the other hand, the large majority of your customers do not seem to be counting calories. Their favorites on your menu are the comfort food selections such as fried chicken, mashed potatoes, pies, and cakes. Furthermore, it would cost you between $11,500 and $46,000 for a lab to test your menu items and provide nutritional content and calorie counts. In small groups, discuss whether or not your restaurant will comply. What are some compromises you can think of? Write a memo to your instructor summarizing your group's conclusions.

Adapted from Janet Adamy, "Restaurants Urged to Stress Nutrition: FDA-Funded Report Seeks Focus on Healthful Foods and More Data on Calories," *Wall Street Journal,* May 31, 2006, D4.

14.8 Revising a Letter

You work for a credit card company and asked your assistant to draft a letter to new customers who have recently opened an account. The purpose of the letter is to inform clients of the services available to them, persuade them to use the services, and build goodwill.

Subject: Credit Card

Dear Sir or Madame,

This letter will let you know about our organization and what we can do for you. We believe that you will like using our services, as we offer many convenient ones.

Before we tell you about the great services we have to offer, we want to let you know how glad we our to have you as a new customer. We got out of our way to make sure you get the best benefits. 2% back on grocery purchases, no annual fee, and reward dollars—who could ask for anything more?! Shop, Shop, Shop and the rewards will pile up. Go online to sign up for rewards so you don't lose out. While your there, don't forget to enroll in e-mail alerts to remind you of upcoming due dates.

We have been helping clients for almost a quarter of a century and are happy your apart of the family. Like a family member who just drops in, you get to chose your payment due date. Now how's that for convenience!

Thank you for joining our service. We look forward to continuing our business relationship with you.

Sincerely,

This draft definitely needs some work. It lacks you-attitude and needs attention to the organization. Moreover, the new services are not clearly explained, and there are many mechanical errors.

As your instructor directs,

a. Write a memo to your subordinate, explaining what revisions are necessary.

b. Revise the letter.

14.16   Announcing a New Employee Benefit

Your company has decided to pay employees for doing charity work. Employees can spend 1 hour working with a charitable on nonprofit group for every 40 they work. Employees will be paid for this hour, so their salaries will not fall. People who choose not to participate will work and be paid for the same number of hours as before. Supervisors are responsible for ensuring that essential business services are covered during business hours. Any employee who will be away during regular business hours (either to volunteer or to take off an hour in compensation for volunteering off-shift or on a weekend) will need to clear the planned absence with his or her supervisor. Your office is collecting a list of organizations that would welcome volunteers. People can work with an organized group or do something informal (such as tutoring at a local school or coaching kids at a local playground). People can volunteer 1 hour every week, 2 hours every other week, or a half-day each month. Volunteer hours cannot be banked from one month to the next; they must be used each month. The program starts January 1 (or June 1). The various groups that people work with will be featured in company publications.

As Vice President of Human Resources, write a memo to all employees announcing this new program.

Hints:

- Pick a business, government, or nonprofit organization that you know something about.
- What proportion of your employees are already involved in volunteer work?
- Is community service or "giving back" consistent with your corporate mission?
- Some employees won't be able or won't want to participate. What is the benefit for them in working for a company that has such a program?
- Will promoting community participation help your organization attract and retain workers?

14.17   Writing a Company Newsletter

Today your boss decided that your organization might be able to maintain better relations with customers and shareholders if your company sent a monthly newsletter by e-mail.

As your instructor directs:

a. Investigate newsletters of two or three organizations. Look for conventional features included in each one.

b. Summarize what seem to be the most and least effective features in a memo to your instructor.

c. Create a one- or two-page newsletter as the boss has requested. Include information that would be useful for customers and shareholders.

Hints:

- Choose a business, government, or nonprofit organization that you know something about.
- Consider what type of information would be most appealing to your audiences.
- Use the tips found in the newsletter sidebar in this chapter to write your newsletter.
- Design your newsletter using strategies from Chapter 8: Designing Documents.

14.18   Announcing an Employee Fitness Center

Your company is ready to open an employee fitness center with on-site aerobics and yoga classes, exercycles, tread mills, and weight machines. The center will be open 6 AM to 10 PM daily; at least one qualified instructor will be on duty at all times. Employees get first preference; if there is extra room, clients, spouses, and children may also use the facilities. Locker rooms and showers will also be available.

Your company hopes that the fitness center will help out-of-shape employees get the exercise they need to be more productive. Other companies have saved between $2.30 and $10.10 for every $1.00 spent on wellness programs. The savings come from lower claims on medical insurance, less absenteeism, and greater productivity.

Write the memo announcing the center.

Hints:

- Who pays the medical insurance for employees? If the employer pays, then savings from healthier employees will pay for the center. If another payment plan is in effect, you'll need a different explanation for the company's decision to open the fitness center.
- Stress benefits apart from the company's saving money. How can easier access to exercise help employees? What do they do? How can exercise reduce stress, improve strength, help employees manage chronic illnesses such as diabetes and high blood pressure, and increase productivity at work?
- What kind of record does the company have of helping employees be healthy? Is the fitness center

a departure for the company, or does the company have a history of company sports teams, stop-smoking clinics, and the like?

- What is the company's competitive position? If the company is struggling, you'll need to convince readers that the fitness center is a good use of scarce funds. If the company is doing well, show how having fit employees can make people even more productive.
- Stress fun as a benefit. How can access to the center make employees' lives more enjoyable?

14.19 Announcing New Smoking Policy

During a recent board meeting, your organization's officers decided to respond to complaints from workers and clients about smokers who gather outside the main entrance to your office building. Complaints ranged from the effects of secondhand smoke to the message the smokers shed on the organization's image to outside clients who need to enter the building. The board decided that smoking will be allowed only in a designated area at the far end of the parking lot. Smokers can no longer congregate near the building's main entrance.

As vice president, write a memo to all employees announcing the immediate change in the smoking policy.

In addition, write a memo to your instructor that analyzes your rhetorical situation (context, audiences, and purposes) and the ethical decisions you had to make to construct this memo.

Hints:

- Pick a business, government, or nonprofit organization that you know something about.
- What benefits can you stress to employees about the new policy?
- Some employees, particularly those who smoke, may be disgruntled with the new policy. What benefits can you stress for them and how will you overcome their negative feelings?

14.20 Providing Information to Job Applicants

Your company is in a prime vacation spot, and as personnel manager you get many letters from students asking about summer jobs. Company policy is to send everyone an application for employment, a list of the jobs you expect to have open that summer with the rate of pay for each, a description of benefits for seasonal employees, and an interview schedule. Candidates must come for an interview at their own expense and should call to schedule a time in advance. Competition is keen: Only a small percentage of those interviewed will be hired.

Write a form letter to students who've written to you asking about summer jobs. Give them the basic information about the hiring procedure and tell them what to do next. Be realistic about their chances, but maintain their interest in working for you.

14.21 Announcing a Premium Holiday

Rather than paying fees to an insurer, your company is self-insured. That is, you set aside corporate funds to pay for medical bills. If claims are light, the company saves money.

Employees pay a monthly fee for part of the amount of their health insurance. However, with one month to go in the fiscal year, you have more than enough set aside to cover possible costs. You're going to pass along some of the savings to employees (who, by staying healthy, have kept medical costs down). Next month will be a "premium holiday." You will not deduct the monthly premium from employees' checks. As a result, they will have a slightly higher take-home pay next month. The holiday is just for one month; after it, the premium for health insurance will again be deducted each month.

Write a memo to all employees.

14.22 Announcing a Tuition Reimbursement Program

Your organization has decided to encourage employees to take courses by reimbursing each eligible employee a maximum of $3,500 in tuition and fees during any one calendar year. Anyone who wants to participate in the program must apply before the first class meeting; the application must be signed by the employee's immediate supervisor. The Office of Human Resources will evaluate applications. That office has application forms; it also has catalogs from nearby schools and colleges.

The only courses employees may choose are those either related to the employee's current position (or to a position in the company that the employee might hold someday) or part of a job-related degree program. Again, the degree may be one that would help the employee's current position or that would qualify him or her for a promotion or transfer in the organization.

Only tuition and fees are covered, not books or supplies. People whose applications are approved will be reimbursed when they have completed the course with a grade of C or better. An employee cannot be reimbursed until he or she submits a copy of the approved application, an official grade report, and a statement of the tuition paid. If someone is eligible for other financial aid (scholarship, veterans benefits), the company will pay tuition costs not covered by that aid as long as the employee does not receive more than $3,500 and as long as the total tuition reimbursement does not exceed the actual cost of tuition and fees.

Part-time employees are not eligible; full-time employees must work at the company a year before they can apply to participate in the program. Courses may be at any appropriate level (high school, college, or graduate). However, the Internal Revenue Service currently requires workers to pay tax on any reimbursement for

graduate programs. Undergraduate and basic education reimbursements of $5,250 a year are not taxed.

As Director of Human Resources, write a memo to all employees explaining this new benefit.

Hints:

- Pick an organization you know something about. What do its employees do? What courses or degrees might help them do their jobs better?
- How much education do employees already have? How do they feel about formal schooling?
- The information in the problem is presented in a confusing order. Put related items together.
- The problem stresses the limits of the policy. Without changing the provisions, present them positively.
- How will having a better educated workforce help the organization? Think about the challenges the organization faces, its competitive environment, and so forth.

14.23 Summarizing Negative Feedback

Today, your in-basket contains this message from your boss:

> As you know, I'm leaving tomorrow for a vacation in New Zealand. While I'm gone, will you please scan the Internet each day for negative customer feedback and summarize any chat room threads that are relevant to our business? I'd like your summary in hard copy on my desk when I return.

As your instructor directs,

a. Choose one to three "anticorporate activism" Web sites or customer feedback Web sites where people discuss your company. (In a search engine, key in the company name and "customer opinion," or visit sites that specialize in this type of feedback—for example, PlanetFeedback, NetComplaints, eComplaints, or ePinions.) Scan the sites until you find three to five relevant chat room postings or threads for the company you have chosen.

b. Summarize the articles in a memo.

c. Compare summaries with a small group of students. Do summaries for different organizations focus on similar issues?

d. Present one of your summaries to the class.

Hints:

- Pick an organization you know something about. If the organization is large, focus on one division or department.
- Provide an overview to let your boss know whether the articles you've summarized are on a single topic or on several topics.
- Show how each posting or thread relates to the organization.
- Give the full citation (see Chapter 17) so that it's easy to track down postings if the boss wants to see the original.

14.24 Summarizing Information

Summarize one or more of the following:

1. An article from a recent edition of *BusinessWeek* or *Harvard Business Review*.

2. A tip from Jakob Nielsen's Alertboxes, http://www.alertbox.com.

3. An article about college, career development, or job searching from Quintessential Careers, http://www.quintcareers.com/articles.html.

4. Online information about options for recycling or donating used, outdated computers.

5. Options for consolidating student loans and other finances (visit http://www.finaid.org/loans/consolidation.phtml).

6. An article or Web page assigned by your instructor.

As your instructor directs,

a. Write a summary of no more than 100 words.

b. Write a 250- to 300-word summary.

c. Write a one-page summary.

d. In a small group compare your summaries. How did the content of the summaries vary? How do you account for any differences?

14.25   Writing a Thank-You Letter

Write a thank-you letter to someone who has helped you achieve your goals.

As your instructor directs,

a. Turn in a copy of the letter.

b. Mail the letter to the person who helped you.

c. Write a memo to your instructor explaining the situation and choices you made in writing the thank-you letter.

14.26   Analyzing the Ethics of Confidentiality Statements

The information contained in this electronic message is confidential information intended for the use of the individual entity named above. If the reader of this message is not the intended recipient, or an employee responsible for delivering this electronic message to the intended recipient, you are hereby notified that any dissemination or copying of this communication is strictly prohibited. If this message contains non-public personal information about any customer of the sender or intended recipient, you are further prohibited under penalty of law from using or disclosing the information to any third party by provisions of the Gramm-Leach-Biley Act.

The above text is routinely attached to organizational e-mail correspondences. Using the Internet, research laws surrounding confidentiality statements in e-mail messages. Have there been many legal cases involving confidentiality statements that were attached to e-mails? What exactly does the law say about e-mail confidentiality statements? Consider your personal stance on these confidentiality statements. Have you ever received an e-mail with such a statement? Did you treat it differently than other e-mail correspondences? How effective do you think the confidentiality statements are when the medium in which these appear can be forwarded to multiple recipients with the click of the mouse?

As your instructor directs,

a. Write a memo to your instructor that discusses your answers to these questions.

b. Prepare a brief presentation of your findings for the class.

14.27   All-Weather Case: Communicating about the Lilly Ledbetter Fair Pay Act

Miguel has just finished reading the text of the Lilly Ledbetter Fair Pay Act of 2009. He is discussing the act's various provisions with the legal team of All-Weather when Doug walks into his office.

"Do we need to work on any issues related to the act?" Doug asks, shaking the hands of the three members of the legal team.

"Mostly I don't think so, Doug," Miguel says, glancing at the copy of the act on his table. "We have our act in order. The pay differential that we have between the two genders is minimal, if any. In an odd sense, I think we have an advantage in not having too many female employees working, something we need to work on, of course."

"I agree," Doug says, closing his eyes for a moment. "Make sure that you send out a communication nonetheless, explaining what the act means, particularly to our female employees."

"I'm on it, Doug," Miguel says.

"See to it that Linda approves of the draft before it reaches me," Doug says.

After some more discussion with the legal team, Miguel sits down to draft the memo. Regardless of Doug's parting banter, Miguel trusts Linda's writing skills and seldom fails to involve her in writing and other assignments. Later in the afternoon, when Linda sees a letterhead on her desk, she knows it's the memo that Miguel drafted.

To: All Employees

From: Miguel Diaz, Manager (HR)

Subject: Implications of the Lilly Ledbetter Fair Pay Act, 2009, for All-Weather's Employees

Date: March 29, 2009

Recently, the president signed into law the Lilly Ledbetter Fair Pay Act, 2009. The act overturns a 2007 Supreme Court verdict that imposed a time limit on lawsuits female employees could file over discrimination in salary and benefits. Effective immediately, managers in all departments need to first consult with HR before offering any additional (over and above the company compensation structure) salary and benefits to employees. This precaution will avoid any possible lawsuits related to compensation matters under the new act. We will also review the compensation structure of our female employees at all levels. While legal experts and HR professionals are still debating the full extent of the act's implications, the act allows female employees to legally challenge discrimination in salary and benefits at any time during or after their employment.

In this regard, we additionally request departmental managers to carefully keep their performance appraisals (including old paper forms) with respect to all employees but especially those related to our women employees.

At All-Weather, we are largely unaffected by the act because our company has always believed in pay parity between genders. Consequently, women employees have comparable compensation and promotion benefits to those enjoyed by their male counterparts. If you have additional questions about the act, feel free to swing by the HR or call me or Linda at 8734. Bottom line: nothing changes except the two things I have asked the departmental managers to follow.

Sources: Some of the information contained in the draft memo is based on these sources: Joanne Sammer, "Adjusting to the Ledbetter Pay Law," in *HR Disciplines: Compensation: Articles,* http://moss07.shrm.org/hrdisciplines/compensation/Articles/Pages/AdjustingtotheLedbetterPayLaw.aspx (accessed March 29, 2009); and Allen Smith, "Ledbetter Act Adds Lengthy To-Do List for HR," in *Legal Issues: Federal Resources: Pages,* http://moss07.shrm.org/LegalIssues/FederalResources/Pages/Ledbetter ActoDoListforHR.aspx (accessed March 29, 2009).

Linda knows that Miguel is a brilliant HR strategist; however, she also knows (and sometimes tells her boss) that he is not the best communicator. He often comes across as high-handed and abrupt, both in his oral and written communications, when Linda knows full well there isn't an arrogant bone in his body. Miguel is also less than effective in organizing messages, something Linda has had to consistently help him with. She often tells her boss that he is a "zigzag" thinker.

As Linda thinks about how to improve the draft memo, she remembers Kioni has been spending a week with Miguel and Linda to learn about compensation issues. She decides to ask Kioni to read the draft and offer suggestions for improvement. The draft will help provide Kioni with an insight into an actual internal communication issue; it will also provide Linda with another perspective.

Based on your reading of Chapter 14, take on Kioni's task and analyze Miguel's draft. Specifically, consider the following issues discussed in the chapter:

- Organization of informative and positive messages.
- The role of benefits in informative and positive messages.
- You-attitude and tone of the message.
- Subject line and ending.
- Level and amount of information given.

On the basis of your analysis of Miguel's draft, rewrite the memo. Also, write an e-mail to Linda offering her your suggestions to improve the draft and giving reasons for the changes.

Delivering Negative Messages

Chapter Outline

Organizing Negative Messages

The Parts of a Negative Message

Apologies

Tone in Negative Messages

Alternative Strategies
for Negative Situations

Varieties of Negative Messages

Solving a Sample Problem

Summary of Key Points

Learning Objectives

After studying this chapter, you will know:

1 Different ways to organize negative messages.

2 Ways to construct the different parts of negative messages.

3 How to improve the tone of negative messages.

4 Ways to construct different kinds of negative messages.

Online Reviews Matter

With ever-increasing options for customers to praise a great service or, in many cases, broadcast a negative experience on Web sites like Yelp, Citysearch, InsiderPages, and Yahoo Local, small businesses need to be proactive with their online reputations.

Experts suggest small business owners should routinely check the reviews their establishments receive. If there are many negative opinions, small business owners should take two steps. First, contact the critics to obtain information and to correct the situation as best they can. Second, determine whether the online reviewers address real problems within the organization and correct them if they do.

Peggy Borgman, a spa owner in California, was shocked at the low quality of her online reviews. To improve the rating, she encourages her happy customers to go online and leave a review after a visit to the spa. She also contacts unhappy customers to understand exactly why they had a poor experience and tries to correct the situation. In just a few months, Borgman's efforts changed her 2½ star rating to 4. Good customer service is always key, even online.

Adapted from Riva Richmond, "Look Who's Talking: It's Tempting to Dismiss Online Reviews of Your Business. Tempting, but Not Smart." *Wall Street Journal*, June 25, 2007, R4.

In a **negative message,** the basic information we have to convey is negative; we expect the audience to be disappointed or angry. Some jobs entail conveying more negative messages than others. Customer service representatives, employee relations personnel, and insurance agents all have to say no on a regular basis.

Negative communications such as refusals, rejections, recalls, and apologies are hard to compose. Yet they are so important. Good ones restore corporate reputations as well as customer and employee goodwill. Bad ones can lead to lawsuits. Corporate officers can be promoted or fired on the basis of a negative communication. Employees reporting negative situations (whistle-blowing) are frequently penalized; one study found the percentage being penalized to be 82%. In spite of the penalties, the study found that 19% of corporate fraud was uncovered by employees.[1]

Negative messages are a vital part of business and administrative communication. A medical study found that cardiac care units with nurses with negative attitudes had a death rate four times higher than that of comparable units.[2] One Silicon Valley company calculated the costs of negative communications from a sales person known for negative interpersonal skills and e-mails. Their costs included managerial time, HR time, anger management training and counseling, among others, and came to $160,000 for just one year. The company also deducted 60% of that cost from the employee's bonus. A British study estimated the costs of bullying in firms with 1,000 employees to be about $2 million a year per firm.[3]

The other side of the coin, and a classic illustration of how to handle negatives, is the Tylenol case. When Johnson and Johnson learned that seven people in the Chicago area had died from cyanide-laced Tylenol capsules, they immediately communicated their knowledge. They ordered the entire supply withdrawn from store shelves, and they offered to replace Tylenol capsules in people's homes with tablets. This decision cost the company tens of millions of dollars. But it was the right decision. When Tylenol was released again several months later in new, tamper-resistant containers, it recovered its market share. The company's forthright communications of the situation confirmed its integrity.[4] This chapter will follow the Tylenol path and look at some of the preferred ways to convey negative messages.

Negative messages include rejections and refusals, announcements of policy changes that do not benefit the audience, requests the audience will see as insulting or intrusive, negative performance appraisals, disciplinary notices, and product recalls or notices of defects.

A negative message always has several purposes:

Primary purposes:

- To give the audience the bad news.
- To have the audience read, understand, and accept the message.
- To maintain as much goodwill as possible.

Secondary purposes:

- To maintain, as much as possible, a good image of the communicator and the communicator's organization.
- To reduce or eliminate future communication on the same subject so the message doesn't create more work for the sender.

In many negative situations, the communicator and audience will continue to deal with each other. Even when further interaction is unlikely (for example, when a company rejects a job applicant or refuses to renew a customer's insurance), the firm wants anything the audience may say about the company to be positive or neutral rather than negative.

Some messages that at first appear to be negative can be structured to create a positive feeling: a decision that may be negative in the short term may be shown to be a positive one in the long term; or the communication of a problem can be directly connected to an effective solution.

Even when it is not possible to make the audience happy with the news we must convey, we still want the audience to feel that

- They have been taken seriously.
- Our decision is fair and reasonable.
- If they were in our shoes, they would make the same decision.

Organizing Negative Messages

The best way to organize a negative message depends on your audience and on the severity of the negative information. This chapter presents several possible patterns and connects them with their most likely contexts. But you will always need to consider your particular situation when choosing an organizing pattern.

Giving Bad News to Clients and Customers

When you must give bad news to clients and customers, you need to be clear, but you also need to maintain goodwill. Compromises or alternatives can help you achieve both goals. See the first column in Figure 15.1 for a way to organize these messages.

Figure 15.2 illustrates another basic pattern for negative messages. This letter omits the reason for the policy change, probably because the change benefits the company, not the customer. Putting the bad news first (though pairing it immediately with an alternative) makes it more likely that the recipient will read the letter. If this letter seemed to be just a routine renewal, or if it opened with the good news that the premium was lower, few recipients would read the letter carefully, and many would not read it at all. Then, if they had accidents and found that their coverage was reduced, they'd blame the company for not communicating clearly. Emphasizing the negative here is both good ethics and good business.

JetBlue

On February 14, 2007, JetBlue attempted to continue operations during an ice storm. They boarded passengers and rolled planes to runways for de-icing, betting that planes would be able to take off as the storm subsided.

Other planes were subsequently parked at terminal gates, preventing JetBlue planes from returning to the gates to unload passengers. Hundreds of passengers were held aboard planes, some for as long as 11 hours. Thousands more passengers and mounds of baggage were stranded at the terminal.

JetBlue's problems were exacerbated by the company's poor communication:

- Posting delays for flights instead of cancellations kept passengers waiting for hours.
- Passengers stranded on planes reported they were not given information about their status because the flight crews were not being informed.
- The JetBlue phone number was overloaded. Callers experienced lengthy holds, and many could not get through at all.
- The airline's computer system and crew-scheduling software were inadequate for the task of scheduling crews after the storm, slowing the return to full service.

JetBlue publicly apologized and offered refunds, free flight vouchers, and penalty-free rebooking. Besides the damage to the company's reputation, estimated costs to JetBlue included $14 million in customer refunds, $16 million in vouchers, and $4 million in staff overtime.

Sources: Allan Sloan, with Temma Ehrenfeld, "Skies Were Cloudy before Jet Blew It," *Newsweek*, March 5, 2007, 26; and Jesus Sanchez and Alana Semuels, "JetBlue Struggles to Get Past Last Week's Fiasco," *Chicago Tribune*, February 19, 2007.

Figure 15.1   How to Organize Negative Messages

Negative messages to clients and customers	Negative messages to superiors	Negative messages to peers and subordinates
1. **When you have a reason that the audience will understand and accept, give the reason before the refusal.** A good reason prepares the audience to expect the refusal.	1. **Describe the problem.** Tell what's wrong, clearly and unemotionally.	1. **Describe the problem.** Tell what's wrong, clearly and unemotionally.
2. **Give the negative information or refusal just once, clearly.** Inconspicuous refusals can be missed altogether, making it necessary to say *no* a second time.	2. **Tell how it happened.** Provide the background. What underlying factors led to this specific problem?	2. **Present an alternative or compromise, if one is available.** An alternative not only gives the audience another way to get what they want but also suggests that you care about them and helping them meet their needs.
3. **Present an alternative or compromise, if one is available.** An alternative not only gives the audience another way to get what they want but also suggests that you care about them and helping them meet their needs.	3. **Describe the options for fixing it.** If one option is clearly best, you may need to discuss only one. But if your superiors will think of other options, or if different people will judge the options differently, describe all the options, giving their advantages and disadvantages.	3. **If possible, ask for input or action.** People in the audience may be able to suggest solutions. And workers who help make a decision are far more likely to accept the consequences.
4. **End with a positive, forward-looking statement.**	4. **Recommend a solution and ask for action.** Ask for approval so that you can make the necessary changes to fix the problem.	

Giving Bad News to Superiors

Your superior expects you to solve minor problems by yourself. But sometimes, solving a problem requires more authority or resources than you have. When you give bad news to a superior, also recommend a way to deal with the problem. Turn the negative message into a persuasive one. See the middle column in Figure 15.1.

Giving Bad News to Peers and Subordinates

When passing along serious bad news to peers and subordinates, many people use the organization suggested in the last column in Figure 15.1.

No serious negative (such as being downsized or laid off) should come as a complete surprise, nor should it be delivered by e-mail. Researchers Timmerman and Harrison note that managers may be inclined to use electronic forms of communication to deliver bad news, but they should resist the temptation in most situations. Their study outlines four factors that should be considered when choosing a medium for delivering bad news: the severity of the message, the complexity of the explanation, the type of explanation, and the relationship between the superior and subordinates. Timmerman and Harrison suggest managers must always juggle the efficiency of delivering the message with its impact on receivers. Typically, managers who deliver bad news in face-to-face settings are more appreciated and accepted by employees.[5]

Managers can prepare for possible negatives by giving full information as it becomes available. It is also possible to let the people who will be affected by a decision participate in setting the criteria. Someone who has bought into

Figure 15.2 A Negative Letter

Vickers
Insurance Company

3373 Forbes Avenue
Rosemont, PA 19010
(215) 572-0100

Negative information highlighted so reader won't ignore message

**Liability Coverage
Is Being Discontinued—
Here's How to Replace It!**

Negative

Alternative

Dear Policyholder:

Negative

When your auto insurance is renewed, it will no longer include liability coverage unless you select the new Assurance Plan. Here's why.

Liability coverage is being discontinued. It, and the part of the premium which paid for it, will be dropped from all policies when they are renewed.

Positive information underlined for emphasis

This change could leave a gap in your protection. But you can replace the old Liability Coverage with Vickers' new Assurance Plan.

No reason is given. The change probably benefits the company rather than the reader, so it is omitted.

Alternative

With the new Assurance Plan, you receive benefits for litigation or awards arising from an accident—regardless of who's at fault. The cost for the Assurance Plan at any level is based on the ages of drivers, where you live, your driving record, and other factors. If these change before your policy is renewed, the cost of your Assurance Plan may also change. The actual cost will be listed in your renewal statement.

To sign up for the Assurance Plan, just check the level of coverage you want on the enclosed form and return it in the postage-paid envelope within 14 days. You'll be assured of the coverage you select.

Forward-looking ending emphasizes reader's choice

Sincerely,

C. J. Morgan

C. J. Morgan
President

Alternative

P.S. The Assurance Plan protects you against possible legal costs arising from an accident. Sign up for the plan today and receive full coverage from Vickers.

the criteria for retaining workers is more likely to accept decisions using such criteria. And in some cases, the synergism of groups may make possible ideas that management didn't think of or rejected as "unacceptable." Some workplaces incorporate employee suggestion systems to help reduce excess costs and improve organizational effectiveness.

When the bad news is less serious, as in Figure 15.3, try using the pattern in the first column of Figure 15.1 unless your knowledge of the audience suggests that another pattern will be more effective. The audience's reaction is influenced by the following factors:

- Do you and the audience have a good relationship?
- Does the organization treat people well?
- Has the audience been warned of possible negatives?
- Has the audience bought into the criteria for the decision?
- Do communications after the negative decision build goodwill?

Some organizations use "open book management," which provides employees with financial information of the organization in the hopes that open communication will foster ideas to improve productivity and cut costs. For example, Springfield Manufacturing, which was financially suffering, used

Figure 15.3   A Negative Memo to Subordinates

FIRST BANK
Great Plains, Nebraska

Memo

Date: January 10, 2010
To: All Employees
From: Floyd E. Mattson   *FEM*

Subject: Group Dental Insurance

First Bank is always seeking to provide employees with a competitive benefits package that meets their needs.

Reason given before negative

In response to many requests, the Human Resource Deparment solicited bids for expanded dental coverage. As this time none of the responses from insurers serving our area are affordable for us. We continue to negotiate, but with costs rising at 20% per year, success seems unlikely. Other banks in the area are in a similar situation, so our current benefits

Positive

package matches or exceeds what they offer.

Alternatives

First Bank continues to offer enrollment in an employee-funded group plan with ABC Dental. The coverage includes 37 dentists in our county and pays 50 percent of allowable fees. Many of our employees have found this coverage helpful. Employees also may use their medical savings account for dental care. Consider one of these options for the present,

Positive close

and First Bank will continue to investigate new opportunities for expanded coverage.

this approach to reduce a $3 million dollar debt and improve the state of the organization and lives of employees.[6]

The Parts of a Negative Message

This section provides more information about wording each part of a negative message.

Subject Lines

Many negative messages put the topic, but not the specific negative, in the subject line.

> Subject: Status of Conversion Table Program

Other negative message subject lines focus on solving the problem.

> Subject: Improving Our Subscription Letter

Use a negative subject line in messages when you think readers may ignore what they believe is a routine message. Also use a negative subject line when the reader needs the information to make a decision or to act.

> Subject: Elevator to Be Out Friday, June 17

Many people do not read all their messages, and a neutral subject line may lead them to ignore the message.

Buffers

Traditionally, textbooks recommended that negative messages open with buffers. A **buffer** is a neutral or positive statement that allows you to delay the negative. Recent research suggests that buffers do not make readers respond more positively,[7] and good buffers are very hard to write. However, in special situations, you may want to use a buffer.

To be effective, a buffer must put the reader in a good frame of mind, not give the bad news but not imply a positive answer either, and provide a natural transition to the body of the letter. The kinds of statements most often used as buffers are good news, facts and chronologies of events, references to enclosures, thanks, and statements of principle.

1. **Start with any good news or positive elements the letter contains.**

> Starting Thursday, June 26, you'll have access to your money 24 hours a day at First National Bank.

Letter announcing that the drive-up windows will be closed for two days while automatic teller machines are installed

2. **State a fact or provide a chronology of events.**

> As a result of the new graduated dues schedule—determined by vote of the Delegate Assembly last December and subsequently endorsed by the Executive Council—members are now asked to establish their own dues rate and to calculate the total amount of their remittance.

Do You Have a Bad Boss?

A study from Florida State University's College of Business found that many employees think they have a bad boss. More than 700 workers in various fields were asked how their bosses treat them. The study cites these findings:

- 39% of workers said their supervisor failed to keep promises.
- 37% said their supervisor failed to give credit when due.
- 31% said their supervisor gave them the "silent treatment" in the past year.
- 27% said their supervisor made negative comments about them to other employees or managers.
- 23% said their supervisors blamed others to cover up mistakes or to minimize embarrassment.

Employees who are not happy with their work environment are less productive, less concerned with the overall well-being of the organization, and more likely to look for other employment. The study recommends that workers stay optimistic in negative employment situations, since supervisor-subordinate relationships typically have a high turnover rate.

Adapted and quoted from Brent Kallestad, "2 in 5 Bosses Don't Keep Word, Florida State University Survey Shows," *Associated Press Archive*, January 1, 2007.

Medical Students Learn How To Deliver Bad News

Oncologists, doctors who specialize in treating cancer, have one of the toughest jobs when it comes to delivering bad news. These doctors often inform patients that they have a difficult battle to face or that there is almost no hope and death may be imminent.

Recently, some medical schools have begun to insist that medical students learn how to deliver bad news to patients, particularly those suffering from cancer. These medical programs are adding classes where students can learn to give the negative news not only through verbal but also nonverbal forms of communication. Some studies suggest that the manner in which bad news is presented to a patient has significant effects on their overall health. "Patients are more satisfied, better retain information about their disease, and cope and adjust better with the illness when physicians have good communication skills," says Dr. Walter Baile.

Overall, the new emphasis on approaches to delivering bad news is a trend in medicine that puts patients and their needs first. Approximately 29 medical schools reported in 2007 that they teach their graduates the importance of presenting bad news. Some of these schools use role playing with patient-actors. The medical students have to inform the actors of an unwanted diagnosis and appropriately deal with the actor's response.

Adapted and quoted from Dawn Sagario, "Doctors Learn to Convey Facts in Appropriate, Thoughtful Way," *Des Moines Register*, October 17, 2006, E1, E2.

Announcement of a new dues structure that will raise most members' dues

3. Refer to enclosures in the letter.

> Enclosed is a new sticker for your car. You may pick up additional ones in the office if needed.

Letter announcing increase in parking rental rates

4. Thank the reader for something he or she has done.

> Thank you for scheduling appointments for me with so many senior people at First National Bank. My visit there March 14 was very informative.

Letter refusing a job offer

5. State a general principle.

> Good drivers should pay substantially less for their auto insurance. The Good Driver Plan was created to reward good drivers (those with five-year accident-free records) with our lowest available rates. A change in the plan, effective January 1, will help keep those rates low.

Letter announcing that the company will now count traffic tickets, not just accidents, in calculating insurance rates—a change that will raise many people's premiums

Some audiences will feel betrayed by messages whose positive openers delay the central negative point. Therefore, use a buffer only when the audience (individually or culturally) values harmony or when the buffer serves another purpose. For example, when you must thank the reader somewhere in the letter, putting the "thank you" in the first paragraph allows you to start on a positive note.

Buffers are hard to write. Even if you think the reader would prefer to be let down easily, use a buffer only when you can write a good one.

Reasons

Research shows that audiences who described themselves as "totally surprised" by negative news had many more negative feelings and described their feelings as being stronger than did those who expected the negative.[8] A clear and convincing reason prepares the audience for the negative, resulting in people who more easily accept it.

The following reason is inadequate.

Weak reason: The goal of the Knoxville CHARGE-ALL Center is to provide our customers faster, more personalized service. Since you now live outside the Knoxville CHARGE-ALL service area, we can no longer offer you the advantages of a local CHARGE-ALL Center.

If the reader says, "I don't care if my bills are slow and impersonal," will the company let the reader keep the card? No. The real reason for the negative is that the bank's franchise allows it to have cardholders only in a given geographic region.

Real reason: Each local CHARGE-ALL center is permitted to offer accounts to customers in a several-state area. The Knoxville CHARGE-ALL center serves customers east of the Mississippi. You can continue to use your current card until it expires. When that happens, you'll need to open an account with a CHARGE-ALL center that serves Texas.

Don't hide behind "company policy": your audience will assume the policy is designed to benefit you at their expense. If possible, show how your audience benefits from the policy. If they do not benefit, don't mention policy at all.

Weak reason: I cannot write an insurance policy for you because company policy does not allow me to do so.

Better reason: Gorham insures cars only when they are normally garaged at night. Standard insurance policies cover a wider variety of risks and charge higher fees. Limiting the policies we write gives Gorham customers the lowest possible rates for auto insurance.

Avoid saying that you *cannot* do something. Most negative messages exist because the communicator or company has chosen certain policies or cutoff points. In the example above, the company could choose to insure a wider variety of customers if it wanted to do so.

Often you as a middle manager will enforce policies that you did not design and announce decisions that you did not make. Don't pass the buck by saying, "This was a terrible decision." Carelessly criticizing your superiors is never a good idea.

If you have several reasons for saying *no*, use only those that are strong and watertight. If you give five reasons and readers dismiss two of them, readers may feel that they've won and should get the request.

Weak reason: You cannot store large bulky items in the dormitory over the summer because moving them into and out of storage would tie up the stairs and the elevators just at the busiest times when people are moving in and out.

Way to dismiss the reason: We'll move large items before or after the two days when most people are moving in or out.

If you do not have a good reason, omit the reason rather than use a weak one. Even if you have a strong reason, omit it if it makes the company look bad.

Reason that hurts company: Our company is not hiring at the present time because profits are down. In fact, the downturn has prompted top management to reduce the salaried staff by 5% just this month, with perhaps more reductions to come.

Better: Our company does not have any openings now.

Refusals

Deemphasize the refusal by putting it in the same paragraph as the reason, rather than in a paragraph by itself.

Sometimes you may be able to imply the refusal rather than stating it directly.

Direct refusal: You cannot get insurance for just one month.

Implied refusal: The shortest term for an insurance policy is six months.

Be sure the implication is crystal clear. Any message can be misunderstood, but an optimistic or desperate reader is particularly unlikely to understand a

Waiting Impacts Business

The longer customers wait, the more annoyed they can become. A team of marketing professors examined the waiting experiences of 844 customers in banking and hair-cutting industries. The researchers identified five pieces of advice that affect how customers respond to waiting.

1. Give customers a focus other than the wait: If customers are doing something, they are less focused on how long the wait lasts.

2. Try to reduce anxiety of waiting: Providing wait estimates or music can help reduce customer anxiety.

3. Show fairness in waiting: If customers are waiting, they don't want to see (or perceive) other people getting special treatment.

4. Create a relaxed environment: Make sure seating, temperatures, and noise levels are all appropriate when customers wait.

5. Support regular customers.

Adapted from Laura Pieper, "The Waiting Game: ISU Professor Researches What Makes the Wait Easier," *Ames Tribune*, January 30, 2008, B6.

negative message. One of your purposes in a negative message is to close the door on the subject. You do not want to have to send a second message saying that the real answer is *no*.

Alternatives

Giving your audience an alternative or a compromise, if one is available, is a good idea for several reasons:

- It offers the audience another way to get what they want.
- It suggests that you really care about your audience and about helping to meet their needs.
- It enables your audience to reestablish the psychological freedom you limited when you said *no*.
- It allows you to end on a positive note and to present yourself and your organization as positive, friendly, and helpful.

When you give an alternative, give your audience all the information they need to act on it, but don't take the necessary steps. Let your audience decide whether to try the alternative.

Negative messages limit your audience's freedom. People may respond to a limitation of freedom by asserting their freedom in some other arena. Sharon and Jack Brehm calls this phenomenon **psychological reactance.**[9] Psychological reactance is at work when a customer who has been denied credit no longer buys even on a cash basis, a subordinate who has been passed over for a promotion gets back at the company by deliberately doing a poor job, or someone who has been laid off sabotages the company's computers.

An alternative allows your audience to react in a way that doesn't hurt you. By letting your audience decide for themselves whether they want the alternative, you allow them to reestablish their sense of psychological freedom.

The specific alternative will vary depending on the circumstances. In Figure 15.4, the company suggests using a different part. In different circumstances, the writer might offer different alternatives.

Endings

If you have a good alternative, refer to it in your ending: "If you can use A515 grade 70, please let me know."

The best endings look positively to the future.

> Wherever you have your account, you'll continue to get all the service you've learned to expect from CHARGE-ALL, and the convenience of charging items at over a million stores, restaurants, and hotels in the United States and abroad—and in Knoxville, too, whenever you come back to visit!

Letter refusing to continue charge account for a customer who has moved

Avoid endings that seem insincere.

> We are happy to have been of service, and should we be able to assist you in the future, please contact us.

This ending lacks you-attitude and would not be good even in a positive message. In a situation where the company has just refused to help, it's likely to sound sarcastic.

Figure 15.4 A Refusal with an Alternative

Steel Fabrication

"Serving the needs of America since 1890"
1800 Olney Avenue • Philadelphia, PA 19140 • 215•555•7800 • Fax: 215•555•9803

April 27, 2010

Mr. H. J. Moody
Canton Corporation
2407 North Avenue
Kearney, NE 68847

Subject: Bid Number 5853, Part Number D-40040

Dear Mr. Moody:

Buffer Thank you for requesting our quotation on your Part No. D-40040.

Reason Your blueprints call for flame-cut rings 1/2" thick A516 grade 70. To use that grade, we'd have to grind down from 1" thick material. However, if you can use A515 grade 70, which we stock in 1/2" thick, you can cut the price by more than half.

Quantity	Description	Gross Weight	Price/Each
75	Rings Drawing D-40040, A516 Grade 70 1" thick x 6" O.D. x 2.8" I.D. ground to .5" thick.	12 lbs.	$15.08
75	Rings Drawing D-40040, A515 Grade 70 1/2" thick x 6" O.D. x 2.8" I.D.	6 lbs.	$6.91

Alternative (Depending on circumstances, different alternatives may exist.)

If you can use A515 grade 70, please let me know.

Leaves decision up to reader to re-establish psychological freedom

Sincerely,

Valerie Prynne
Valerie Prynne

VP:wc

Apologies

Apologies seem to be in the news frequently. Southwest Airlines CEO offered an apology to customers and safety regulators for poor maintenance measures in an effort to restore a tarnished reputation.[10] Jet Blue's apology for poor storm decisions is described in the sidebar on page 437, and the *Los Angeles Times'* apology is the chapter opener "In the News."

Baby Face to the Rescue

Schwinn needed a new product line to attract sophisticated cyclists. This apology for its old, boring line moves quickly to a discussion of its new technology. By evoking an experience every cyclist has had, the headline also suggests that falling is a minor event.

Not all negative messages, however, need to include apologies. In business documents, apologize only when you are at fault. If you need to apologize, do it early, briefly, and sincerely. Do so only once, early in the message. Do not dwell on the bad things that have happened. The reader already knows this negative information. Instead, focus on what you have done to correct the situation.

- **No explicit apology is necessary if the error is small and if you are correcting the mistake.**

  Negative: We're sorry we got the nutrition facts wrong in the recipe.

  Better: You're right. We're glad you made us aware of this. The correct amounts are 2 grams of fat and 4 grams of protein.

- **Do not apologize when you are not at fault.** The phrase "I'm sorry" is generally interpreted to mean the sorry person is accepting blame or responsibility. When you have done everything you can and when a delay or problem is due to circumstances beyond your control, you aren't at fault and don't need to apologize. It may, however, be appropriate to include an explanation so the reader knows you weren't negligent. In the previous example acknowledging an error, the writer might indicate the source of the error (such as a reference book or a government Web site). If the news is bad, put the explanation first. If you have good news for the reader, put it before your explanation.

Negative:	I'm sorry that I could not answer your question sooner. I had to wait until the sales figures for the second quarter were in.
Better (neutral or bad news):	We needed the sales figures for the second quarter to answer your question. Now that they're in, I can tell you that. . . .
Better (good news):	The new advertising campaign is a success. The sales figures for the second quarter are finally in, and they show that. . . .

  If the delay or problem is long or large, it is good you-attitude to ask the reader whether he or she wants to confirm the original plan or make different arrangements.

This cereal box mocks the accelerating trend for apologies in the workplace.

Source: The Denver Post and The Flip Side Staff, "Eating Crow," *Columbus Dispatch,* September 8, 2004, F8.

Disgruntled Customer with a Hammer

Providing good customer service should be a goal of any business. When it's not, customers get angry and can exert their frustrations in negative ways.

In Bristow, Virginia, Mona Shaw, a 75-year-old woman who wanted phone, Internet, and cable service installed, vented her frustrations with Comcast by going to their office and smashing a keyboard, monitor, and telephone . . . with a hammer.

She claims her frustration was the result of poor customer service. She waited for an installation technician who showed up two days late. Once there, he never finished the job. To top things off, two days later Comcast cut all her services. The tipping point came when she waited two hours to talk to a Comcast manager before being informed he had left for the day.

For her brash response, Shaw received a fine and three-month suspended sentence. She is also forbidden to go near the Comcast office. She eventually got her phone, Internet, and cable working, but with different providers.

Adapted from "Woman, 75, Fined for Smashing Comcast Office with Hammer in Customer Service Dispute," *Associated Press Archive,* October 19, 2007.

Negative:	I'm sorry that the chairs will not be ready by August 25 as promised.
Better:	Because of a strike against the manufacturer, the desk chairs you ordered will not be ready until November. Do you want to keep that order, or would you like to look at the models available from other suppliers?

Sometimes you will be in a fortunate position where you can pair your apology with an appropriate benefit. When the Hallmark Flowers Web site stopped taking orders the week before Mother's Day, Hallmark sent an e-mail asking customers to try again and offering free shipping for a day.[11] When Apple sharply cut the price on the iPhone a few months after it came on the market, Steve Jobs offered an apology to earlier buyers and provided them with a $100 Apple store credit. Many airlines now have computer programs that generate apology letters for customers on flights with lengthy delays or other major problems; the letters frequently offer additional frequent-flyer miles or discount vouchers for future trips.[12]

Sincere apologies go hand in hand with efforts to rectify the problem.

Tone in Negative Messages

Tone—the implied attitude of the author toward the reader and the subject—is particularly important when you want readers to feel that you have taken their requests seriously. Check your draft carefully for positive emphasis and you-attitude (see Chapter 3), both at the level of individual words and at the level of ideas. In many situations, empathizing with your audience will help you create a more humane message.

Workplace Violence

© Randy Glasbergen. Reprinted with permission.

Figure 15.5 lists some of the words and phrases to avoid in negative messages. Figure 3.3 in Chapter 3 suggests more negative words to avoid.

Even the physical appearance and timing of a message can convey tone. An obvious form rejection letter suggests that the writer has not given much consideration to the reader's application. An immediate negative suggests that the rejection didn't need any thought. A negative delivered just before a major holiday seems especially unfeeling.

Alternative Strategies for Negative Situations

Whenever you face a negative situation, consider recasting it as a positive or persuasive message. Southwest Airlines, the low-cost airline, is famous for saying no to its customers. It says no to such common perks as reserve seats, meals, and interairline baggage transfers. But it recasts all those negatives into its two biggest positives, low-cost fares and conveniently scheduled frequent flights.[13]

Figure 15.5   Avoid These Phrases in Negative Messages

Phrase	Because
I am afraid that we cannot	You aren't fearful. Don't hide behind empty phrases.
I am sorry that we are unable	You probably *are able* to grant the request; you simply choose not to. If you are so sorry about saying *no*, why don't you change your policy and say *yes*?
I am sure you will agree that	Don't assume that you can read the reader's mind.
Unfortunately	*Unfortunately* is negative in itself. It also signals that a refusal is coming.

Recasting the Situation as a Positive Message

If the negative information will directly lead to a benefit that you know readers want, use the pattern of organization for informative and positive messages:

Situation: Your airline has been mailing out quarterly statements of frequent-flier miles earned. To save money, you are going to stop mailing statements and ask customers to look up that information at your Web site.

Negative: Important Notice: This is your last Preferred Passenger paper statement.

Positive emphasis: New, convenient online statements will replace this quarterly mailing. Now you can get up-to-the-minute statements of your miles earned. Choose e-mail updates or round-the-clock access to your statement at our Web site, www.aaaair.com. It's faster, easier, and more convenient.

Recasting the Situation as a Persuasive Message

Often a negative situation can be recast as a persuasive message. If your organization has a problem, ask readers to help solve it. A solution that workers have created will be much easier to implement.

When the Association for Business Communication raised dues, the Executive Director wrote a persuasive letter urging members to send in renewals early so they could beat the increase. The letter shared some of the qualities of any persuasive letter: using an attention-getting opener, offsetting the negative by setting it against the benefits of membership, telling the reader what to do, and ending with a picture of the benefit the reader received by acting. More recent increases, however, have been announced directly.

If you are criticizing someone, your real purpose may be to persuade the reader to act differently. Chapter 16 offers patterns for problem-solving persuasive messages.

After an alligator escaped from his cage at the Los Angeles Zoo, a spokesperson recast the negative situation as a positive by telling reporters that the escape proved the alligator was smart and healthy.

Source: Justin Scheck and Ben Worthen, "When Animals Go AWOL, Zoos Try to Tame Bad PR," *Wall Street Journal,* January 1, 2008, A1, A10.

International Firing

"When doing business in another country, it is often easy to assume that things there are the same as in your country. . . . It is wise to know the proper way to dismiss an employee when working with other cultures. This is a difficult task to perform in a familiar territory but it is especially tricky when one is in a foreign country and does not always fully understand the local culture. An American manager stationed in Indonesia reportedly discovered this when he tried to fire an oil-rig employee. Rather than notifying the employee privately of this dismissal, the manager publicly told the timekeeper to send the man 'packing.' In Indonesia, this public dismissal was considered unacceptable 'loss of face' which offended both the dismissed man and his friends. So, rather than leave quietly, the man grabbed fire axes and ran after the American manager. Reportedly, the American was barely rescued in time. Obviously, it is dangerous to ignore local management practices and customs!"

Quoted from David A. Ricks, *Blunders in International Business*, 4th ed. (Malden, MA: Blackwell Publishing, 2006), 105.

Varieties of Negative Messages

One of the most common negative messages is the claim. Three of the most difficult kinds of negative messages to write are rejections and refusals, disciplinary notices and negative performance appraisals, and layoffs and firings.

Claims and Complaints

Claims and complaint messages are needed when something has gone wrong: you didn't get the files you needed in time for the report; the supplier didn't send enough parts; the copy machine breaks down daily. Many claims and complaints are handled well with a quick phone call or office visit, but sometimes you will need a paper trail. United Airlines took a new approach to responding to complaints when they stopped their customer relations phone service at the end of April 2009. Now, complaint responses are handled by United representatives through e-mail and letters. The company believes customers will get a better quality of feedback.[14]

When writing a claim or complaint, you generally will use a direct organization: put a clear statement of the problem in the first sentence. An indirect approach, such as starting with a buffer, may be interpreted as a weak claim.

Give supporting facts—what went wrong, the extent of the damage. Give identifiers such as invoice numbers, warranty codes, and order dates. If this is a claim, specify what is necessary to set things right (be realistic!). Avoid anger and sarcasm; they will only lessen your chances of a favorable settlement. In particular, avoid saying you will never use the company, service, machine again. Such a statement may eliminate your audience's will to rectify the problem. See Figure 15.6 for the *Wall Street Journal*'s suggestions for e-mail claims to airlines.

Rejections and Refusals

A lot of consumers are angry these days, and organizations should be responsive to their complaints. In a recent study on customer rage by Customer Care Measurement and Consulting Firm, 70% of consumers report having bad customer-service experiences that left them "upset" or "extremely upset." Furthermore, 46% of consumers said they were dissatisfied with how a company handled their complaint. Most said they told their friends and family about their bad experience. This kind of bad publicity is risky in an Internet economy.[15]

When you refuse requests from people outside your organization, try to give an alternative if one is available. For example, you may not be able to replace for free an automotive water pump that no longer is on warranty. But

Figure 15.6   Airline Complaint Tips

These tips can improve your chances of a favorable response from an airline:

- Ask for the compensation you want.
- Be realistic. You will not get compensation for a routine delay.
- Be direct and short. Do provide flight, reservation, and frequent-flyer numbers.
- Don't threaten. Particularly don't say you will never fly with them again.
- Write to Customer Service. Your complaint will eventually end up there no matter where you send it.

Source: Scott McCartney, "What Airlines Do When You Complain," *Wall Street Journal*, March 20, 2007, D1.

you may be able to offer your customer a rebuilt one that is much less expensive than a new pump.

Politeness and length help. In two different studies, job applicants preferred rejection letters that said something specific about their good qualities, that phrased the refusal indirectly, that offered a clear explanation of the procedures for making a hiring decision, that offered an alternative (such as another position the applicant might be qualified for), and that were longer.[16] Furthermore, businesses that follow this pattern of organization for rejection letters will retain applicants who still view the organization favorably, who will recommend the organization to others interested in applying there, and who will not file lawsuits.[17]

Double-check the words in a refusal to be sure the reason can't backfire if it is applied to other contexts. The statement that a plant is too dangerous for a group tour could be used as evidence against the company in a worker's compensation claim.[18] Similarly, writing resignation letters for a variety of reasons—leaving a job, opting out of a fellowship—can be a delicate practice and can have serious future implications. Many readers will see the letter as a statement that their organization is not good enough. The best letters try to neutralize these feelings. A negative and poorly worded resignation letter can impact your chances for receiving a positive recommendation or reference in the future.

When you refuse requests within your organization, use your knowledge of the organization's culture and of the specific individual to craft your message. Some organizations share more negative information than others. Some individuals prefer a direct no; others may find a direct negative insulting. The sample problem at the end of this chapter is a refusal to someone within the company.

Disciplinary Notices and Negative Performance Appraisals

Performance appraisals, discussed in detail in Chapter 16, will be positive when they are designed to help a basically good employee improve. But when an employee violates company policy or fails to improve after repeated negative appraisals, the company may discipline the employee or build a dossier to support firing him or her.

Present disciplinary notices and negative performance appraisals directly, with no buffer. A buffer might encourage the recipient to minimize the message's importance—and might even become evidence in a court case that the employee had not been told to shape up "or else." Cite quantifiable observations of the employee's behavior, rather than generalizations or inferences based on it.

Weak: Lee is apathetic about work.

Better: Lee was absent 15 days and late by one hour 6 days in the quarter beginning January 1.

Weak: Vasu is careless with her written documents.

Better: Vasu had multiple spelling errors in her last three client letters; a fourth letter omitted the date of the mandatory federal training seminar.

Not all disciplinary notices are as formal as performance appraisals. Blanchard and Johnson, of *One Minute Manager* fame, present what they call the One Minute Reprimand. Much of the effectiveness of these reprimands comes from the fact that supervisors tell their employees from the beginning, before any reprimands are needed, that there will be explicit communication about both positive and negative performances. The reprimand itself is to

Open Communication Should Be Key Value

Mattress Discounters had to file for Chapter 11 bankruptcy to restructure the organization. Even though the news was bad and the employees were worried, the organization's management wanted to retain employees to ensure continued sales. To do so, they adopted an open communication policy with all employees about the negative news.

In fact, before filing for bankruptcy, the management made sure the payroll would still go through. The CEO and president held a companywide conference call with all employees so that they were informed of the organization's intentions and future. They also reassured employees, who work mostly by commission, they should not have to feel any financial strain.

Throughout the reorganization, the company also adopted a values implementation planning committee. This committee started an employee recognition program and developed a value forum. As a result of the open communication throughout the dark times, Mattress Discounters retained its qualified workforce, dropped the percent of employee turnover from 90% to 27% in only a few years, and attracted new talent because of its communication practices.

Adapted from "Communications and Values Can Help Organizations Succeed—Even in Tough Times," *HR Focus*, December 2007, 7, 10.

come immediately after negative behavior and specify exactly what is wrong. It distinguishes between positive feelings for the employee and negative feelings for his or her performance in the specific situation.[19]

Layoffs and Firings

If a company is in financial trouble, management needs to communicate the problem clearly. Sharing information and enlisting everyone's help in finding solutions may make it possible to save jobs. Sharing information also means that layoff notices, if they become necessary, will be a formality; they should not be new information to employees.

Give the employee an honest reason for the layoff or firing. Based on guidance from your organization's human resource experts, state the reasons in a way that is clear but does not expose the organization to legal liabilities.

Show empathy for affected employees; think about how you would feel if you were losing your job. Show how the company will help them with severance pay and other aid, such as job search advice. Remember that many studies show that layoffs may temporarily help the bottom line, but they rarely provide long-term savings. They also hurt the productivity of remaining employees.[20]

Firings for unsatisfactory performance have always been a part of business. Now, however, as technology blurs the line between work and home, firings are also happening for personal reasons, even if the behavior is not tied to work and occurs off-site. The CEO of HBO was asked to resign after he was accused of assaulting his girlfriend in a parking lot. Kaiser Aluminum's CFO had to resign because of a personal relationship with another employee, as did Boeing's former president and CEO Harry Stonecipher.[21]

Information about layoffs and firings is normally delivered orally but accompanied by a written statement explaining severance pay or unemployment benefits that may be available. RadioShack made negative headlines when it fired 400 employees with a two-sentence e-mail.[22]

Solving a Sample Problem

Solving negative problems requires careful analysis. The checklist at the end of the chapter can help you evaluate your draft.

Problem

You're Director of Employee Benefits for a Fortune 500 company. Today, you received the following memo:

> From: Michelle Jagtiani
> Subject: Getting My Retirement Benefits
>
> Next Friday will be my last day here. I am leaving [name of company] to take a position at another firm.
>
> Please process a check for my retirement benefits, including both the deductions from my salary and the company's contributions for the last six and a half years. I would like to receive the check by next Friday if possible.

You have bad news for Michelle. Although the company does contribute an amount to the retirement fund equal to the amount deducted for retirement from the employee's paycheck, employees who leave with less than seven years of employment get only their own contributions. Michelle will get back only the money that has been deducted from her own pay, plus 4½% interest compounded quarterly. Her payments and interest come to just over $17,200; the amount could be higher depending on the amount of her last paycheck, which will include compensation for any unused vacation days and sick leave. Furthermore, since the amounts deducted were not considered taxable income, she will have to pay income tax on the money she will receive.

You cannot process the check until after her resignation is effective, so you will mail it to her. You have her home address on file; if she's moving, she needs to let you know where to send the check. Processing the check may take two to three weeks.

Write a memo to Michelle.

Analysis of the Problem

Use the analysis questions in the first chapter to help you solve the problem.

1. Who is (are) your audience(s)? What characteristics are relevant to this particular message? If you are writing to more than one person, how do the people in your audience differ?

   Michelle Jagtiani. Unless she's a personal friend, I probably wouldn't know why she's leaving and where she's going.

   There's a lot I don't know. She may or may not know much about taxes; she may or may not be able to take advantage of tax-reduction strategies. I can't assume the answers because I wouldn't have them in real life.

2. What are your purposes in communicating?

   To tell her that she will get only her own contributions, plus 4½% interest compounded quarterly; that the check will be mailed to her home address two to three weeks after her last day on the job; and that the money will be taxable as income.

   To build goodwill so that she feels that she has been treated fairly and consistently. To minimize negative feelings she may have.

   To close the door on this subject.

3. What information must your message include?

   When the check will come. The facts that her check will be based on her contributions, not the employer's, and that the money will be taxable income. How lump-sum retirement benefits are calculated. The fact that we have her current address on file but need a new address if she's moving.

4. How can you build support for your position? What reasons or benefits will your audience find convincing?

   Giving the amount currently in her account may make her feel that she is getting a significant sum of money. Suggesting someone who can give free tax advice (if the company offers this as a fringe benefit) reminds her of the benefits of working with the company. Wishing her luck with her new job is a nice touch.

5. What objection(s) can you expect your audience(s) to have? What negative elements of your message must you deemphasize or overcome?

   She is getting about half the amount she expected, since she gets no matching funds. She might have been able to earn more than 4½% interest if she had invested the money in the stock market. Depending on her

www.useit.com/
alertbox/20000123
.html

General guidelines for saying no can be applied to specific situations. Computer expert Jakob Neilsen explains how to tell users that your Web site can't do what they want. Neilsen suggests telling users "no" upfront when your Web site cannot do something. Otherwise, users will spend too much time looking for the desired feature, and in the process will develop negative feelings for the site.

He also suggests if your site cannot meet a user's needs, that you direct them to another site that will. This referral builds goodwill and will make your site the starting point for the customer's next search. If an item will be available reasonably soon, you can allow customers to preorder or provide their e-mail for notification when the product or service becomes available. Log onto Neilsen's site and read the rest of his advice for telling users no. Can you think of other ways to tell Web site users no that Neilsen hasn't suggested?

personal tax situation she may pay more tax on the money as a lump sum than would have been due had she paid it each year as she earned the money.

6. What aspects of the total situation may affect audience response? The economy? The time of year? Morale in the organization? The relationship between the audience and the communicator? Any special circumstances?

   Since this is right after taxes are due, she may be particularly interested in the tax advice. With the weak economy, she may have been counting on the extra money. On the other hand, most people take another job to get more money, so maybe she is too. I don't know for sure. Since she and I don't know each other, I don't know about her special circumstances.

Discussion of the Sample Solutions

The solution in Figure 15.7 is not acceptable. The subject line gives a bald negative with no reason or alternative. The first sentence has a condescending tone that is particularly offensive in negative messages; it also focuses on what

Figure 15.7   An Unacceptable Solution to the Sample Problem

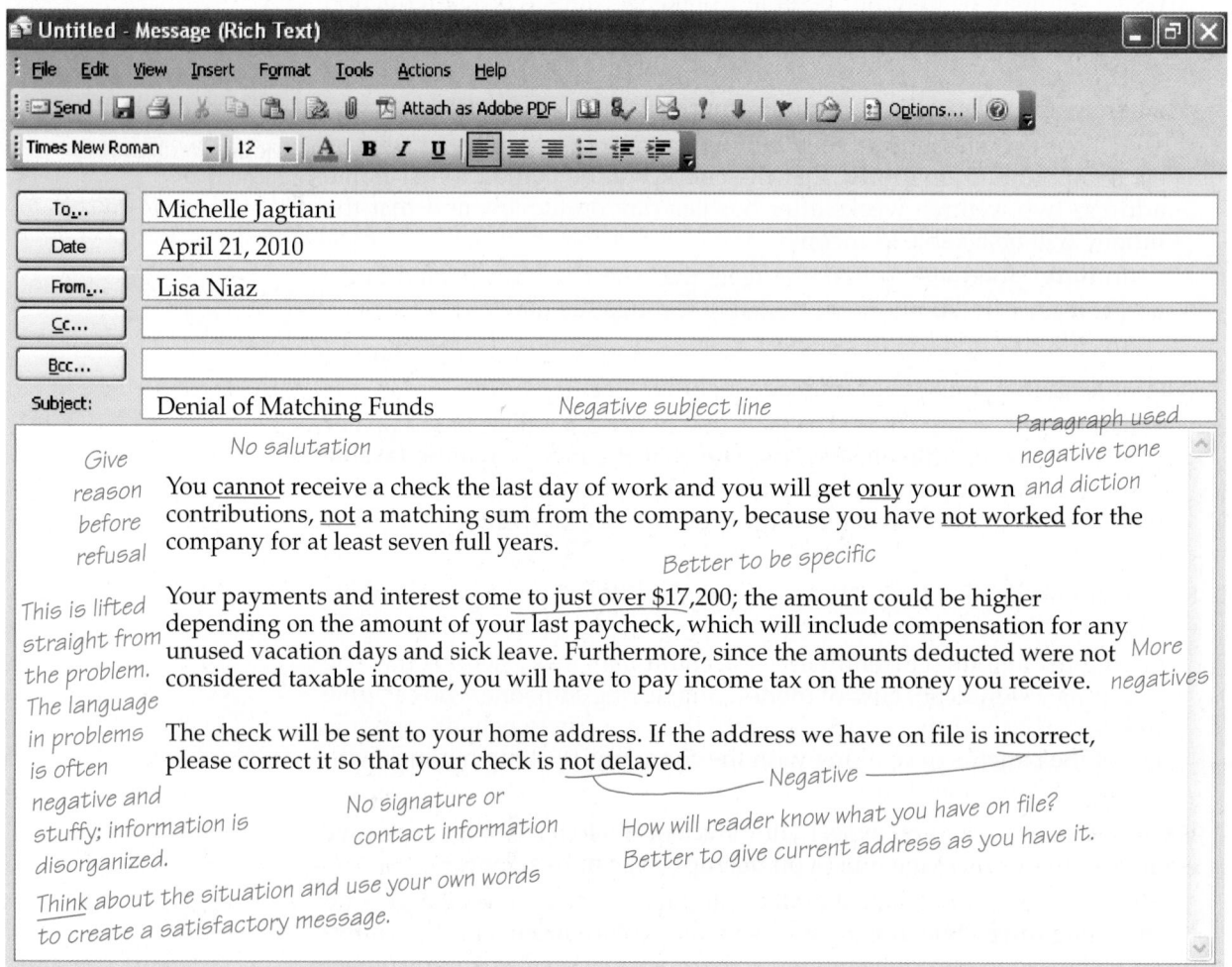

Figure 15.8   A Good Solution to the Sample Problem

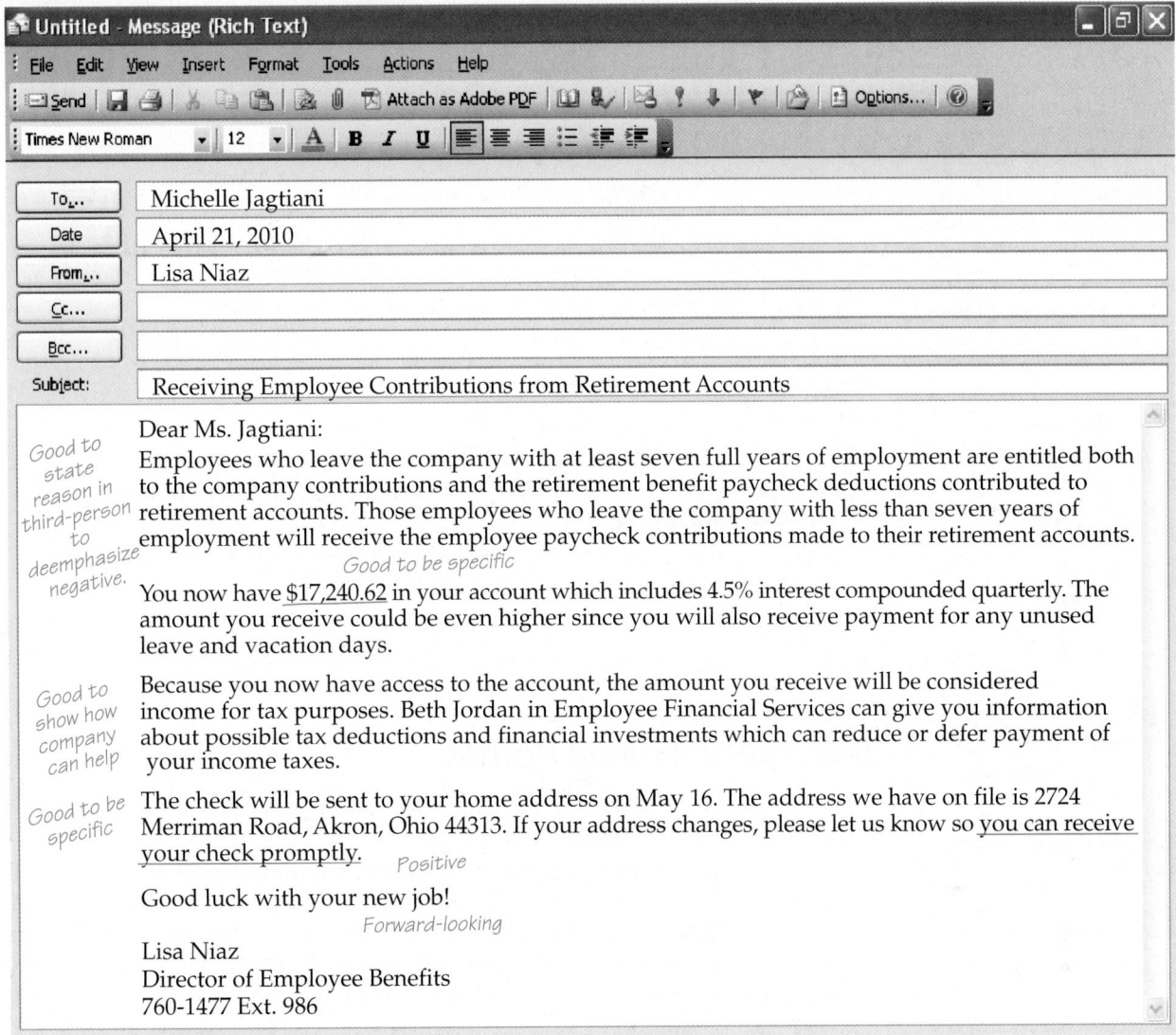

is being taken away rather than what remains. Paragraph 2 lacks you-attitude and is vague. The memo ends with a negative. There is nothing anywhere in the memo to build goodwill.

The solution in Figure 15.8, in contrast, is very good. The policy serves as a buffer and explanation. The negative is stated clearly but is buried in the paragraph to avoid overemphasizing it. Paragraph 2 emphasizes the positive by specifying the amount in the account and the fact that the sum might be even higher.

Paragraph 3 contains the additional negative information that the amount will be taxable but offers the alternative that it may be possible to reduce taxes. The writer builds goodwill by suggesting a specific person the reader could contact.

Paragraph 4 tells the reader what address is in the company files (Michelle may not know whether the files are up-to-date), asks that she update it if necessary, and ends with the reader's concern: getting her check promptly.

The final paragraph ends on a positive note. This generalized goodwill is appropriate when the writer does not know the reader well.

Effective Negative Letters

Researcher Catherine Schryer asked writers at an insurance company to evaluate the firm's letters denying claims. She found four differences between the letters judged effective and the letters judged ineffective:

- Good letters were easier to read. Poor letters contained more jargon; longer words and sentences; and stiff, awkward phrasing.

- Good letters gave fuller reasons for the rejection. Poor letters often used boilerplate and did not explain terms.

- Good letters were less likely to talk about the reader's emotions ("angry," "disappointed").

- Good letters were more likely to portray the writer and reader as active agents.

Adapted from Catherine Schryer, "Walking a Fine Line: Writing Negative Letters in an Insurance Company," *Journal of Business and Technical Communication* 14 (October 2000): 445–97.

✓ *Checklist* ▌Negative Messages

- ☐ Is the subject line appropriate?
- ☐ Is the organization and content appropriate for the audience?
- ☐ If a buffer is used, does it avoid suggesting either a positive or a negative response?
- ☐ Is the reason, if it is given, presented before the refusal? Is the reason watertight, with no loopholes?
- ☐ Is the negative information clear?
- ☐ Is an alternative given if a good one is available? Does the message provide all the information needed to act on the alternative but leave the choice up to the audience?
- ☐ Does the last paragraph avoid repeating the negative information?
- ☐ Is tone acceptable—not defensive, but not cold, preachy, or arrogant either?

Originality in a negative message may come from

- ☐ An effective buffer, if one is appropriate.
- ☐ A clear, complete statement of the reason for the refusal.
- ☐ A good alternative, clearly presented, which shows that you're thinking about what the audience really needs.
- ☐ Adding details that show you're thinking about a specific organization and the specific people in that organization.

Summary of Key Points

- In a negative message, the basic information is negative; we expect the audience to be disappointed or angry.

- A good negative message conveys the negative information clearly while maintaining as much goodwill as possible. The goal is to make the audience feel that they have been taken seriously, that the decision is fair and reasonable, and that they would have made the same decision. A secondary purpose is to reduce or eliminate future communication on the same subject.

- The best way to organize negative messages depends on the particular audiences and situations involved. Figure 15.1 suggests possible organizations.

- A **buffer** is a neutral or positive statement that allows you to delay the negative message. Buffers must put the audience in a good frame of mind, not give the bad news but not imply a positive answer either, and provide a natural transition to the body of the message. Use a buffer only when the audience values harmony or when the buffer serves a purpose in addition to simply delaying the negative.

- A good reason prepares the audience for the negative and must be watertight. Give several reasons only if all are watertight and are of comparable importance. Omit the reason for the refusal entirely if it is weak or if it makes your organization look bad. Do not hide behind company policy.

- Make the refusal crystal clear.

- Giving the audience an alternative or a compromise

  - Offers the audience another way to get what they want.

  - Suggests that you really care about the audience and about helping to meet their needs.

  - Allows you to end on a positive note and to present yourself and your organization as positive, friendly, and helpful.

- When you give an alternative, give the audience all the information they need to act on it, but don't take the necessary steps for them. Letting the audience decide whether to try the alternative allows the audience to reestablish a sense of psychological freedom.
- Many negative situations can be redefined as informative, positive, or persuasive messages.

CHAPTER 15	**Exercises and Problems**	*Go to www.mhhe.com/locker9e for additional Exercises and Problems.*

15.1   Reviewing the Chapter

1. What are the reasons behind the patterns of organization for negative messages in different situations (Figure 15.1)? (LO 1)
2. What are the parts of negative messages? How may those parts be changed for different contexts? (LO 2)
3. When should you not use a buffer? (LO 2)
4. When should you not apologize? (LO 2)
5. What are some ways you can maintain a caring tone in negative messages? (LO 3)
6. What are some different varieties of negative messages? What are some examples from the chapter text and sidebars? (LO 4)

15.2   Reviewing Grammar

Negative news is frequently placed in dependent clauses to help de-emphasize it. Unfortunately, some dependent clauses and phrases are dangling or misplaced modifiers.

Do the exercise from Appendix B on improving modifiers (B.6) to help you learn to recognize this error.

15.3   Letters for Discussion—Credit Refusal

As director of customer service at C'est Bon, an upscale furniture store, you manage the store's credit. Today you are going to reject an application from Frank Steele. Although his income is fairly high, his last two payments on his college loans were late, and he has three bank credit cards, all charged to the upper limit, on which he's made just the minimum payment for the last three months.

The following letters are possible approaches to giving him the news. How well does each message meet the criteria in the checklist for negative messages?

1.

Dear Mr. Steele:

Your request to have a C'est Bon charge account shows that you are a discriminating shopper. C'est Bon sells the finest merchandise available.

Although your income is acceptable, records indicate that you carry the maximum allowable balances on three bank credit cards. Moreover, two recent payments on your student loans have not been made in a timely fashion. If you were given a C'est Bon charge account, and if you charged a large amount on it, you might have difficulty paying the bill, particularly if you had other unforeseen expenses (car repair, moving, medical emergency) or if your income dropped suddenly. If you were unable to repay, with your other debt you would be in serious difficulty. We would not want you to be in such a situation, nor would you yourself desire it.

Please reapply in six months.

Sincerely,

2.

Dear Frank:

No, you can't have a C'est Bon credit card—at least not right now. Get your financial house in order and try again.

Fortunately for you, there's an alternative. Put what you want on layaway. The furniture you want will be held for you, and paying a bit each week or month will be good self-discipline.

Enjoy your C'est Bon furniture!

Sincerely,

3.

Dear Mr. Steele:

Over the years, we've found that the best credit risks are people who pay their bills promptly. Since two of your student loan payments have been late, we won't extend store credit to you right now. Come back with a record of six months of on-time payments of all bills, and you'll get a different answer.

You might like to put the furniture you want on layaway. A $50 deposit holds any item you want. You have six months to pay, and you save interest charges.

You might also want to take advantage of one of our Saturday Seminars. On the first Saturday of each month at 11 AM, our associates explain one topic related to furniture and interior decorating. Upcoming topics are

How to Wallpaper a Room	February 5
Drapery Options	March 6
Persian Carpets	April 1

Sincerely,

15.4   E-Mails for Discussion—Saying *No* to a Colleague

A colleague in another state agency has e-mailed you asking if you would like to use the payroll software her agency developed. You wouldn't. Switching to a new program would take a lot of time, and what you have works well for you.

The following messages are possible approaches to giving her the news. How well does each message meet the criteria in the checklist for negative messages?

1.

Subject: Re: Use Our Software?

No.

2.

Subject: Re: Use Our Software?

Thanks for telling me about the payroll software your team developed. What we have works well for us. Like every other agency, we're operating on a bare-bones budget, and no one here wants to put time (that we really don't have) into learning a new program. So we'll say, no, thanks!

3.

> Subject: Re: Use Our Software?
>
> The payroll software your team developed sounds very good.
>
> I might like to use it, but the people here are computer phobic. They HATE learning new programs. So, being a good little computer support person, I soldier on with the current stuff. (And people wonder why state government is SO INEFFICIENT! Boy, the stories I could tell!)
>
> Anyway, thanks for the offer. Keep me posted on the next development—maybe it will be something so obviously superior that even the Neanderthals here can see its advantages!

15.5 Revising a Negative Message

Rewrite the following negative message:

> Dear Madam:
>
> Unfortunately, because you have not paid your account for the last three months, we have absolutely NO CHOICE but to turn off your heat soon. We know that winter is upon us and it's a horrible time to be without heat, but you really brought this on yourself.
>
> Next time, we recommend PAYING your bills ON TIME.
>
> If you get us your outstanding payments soon, you can keep your heat.
>
> As always, we appreciate your business and value you as our customer.
>
> Sincerely,
>
> WarmHomes Customer Service Team

15.6 Notifying Baby Boomers about Housing Rules

Erin and TJ Bouda are baby boomers who live in a 55-plus Clearwater, Florida, housing development run by WaterBlue Homeowners Association. They have lived in their current house for five years and plan to live the rest of their lives in this home.

A few months ago, the Boudas started raising their three-year-old grandson, Riley, because his mother has a substance abuse problem and his father is deceased. Unfortunately, WaterBlue Homeowners Association has a policy that prohibits children under 18 years of age as permanent residents. Two neighbors of the Boudas have already complained about Riley.

Take on the role of the homeowners association and write to the Boudas telling them that their grandson has to leave (which is not an option) or that they have to give up their home. As you write, be sure to consider the audience and the effect your letter will have on them.

Hints:
- What reasons besides "policy" can you offer the Boudas to help them understand the situation?
- What help can you offer them?
- Are there any alternatives that you can offer?

Source: Blair S. Walker, "Painful Choice between Home and Family," *AARP Bulletin*, May 2007, 6.

15.7   Notifying Seniors That They May Not Graduate

State University asks students to file an application to graduate one term before they actually plan to graduate. The application lists the courses the student has already had and those he or she will take in the last two terms. Your office reviews the lists to see that the student will meet the requirements for total number of hours, hours in the major, and general education requirements. Some students have forgotten a requirement or not taken enough courses and cannot graduate unless they take more courses than those they have listed.

As your instructor directs,

Write form e-mail messages to the following audiences. Leave blanks for the proposed date of graduation and specific information that must be merged into the message:

a.   Students who have not taken enough total hours.

b.   Students who have not fulfilled all the requirements for their majors.

c.   Students who are missing one or more general education courses.

d.   Advisers of students who do not meet the requirements for graduation.

15.8   Correcting a Mistake

Today, as you reviewed some cost figures, you realized they didn't fit with the last monthly report you filed. You had pulled the numbers together from several sources, and you're not sure what happened. Maybe you miscopied, or didn't save the final version after you'd checked all the numbers. But whatever the cause, you've found errors in three categories. You gave your boss the following totals:

Personnel	$2,843,490
Office supplies	$43,500
Telephone	$186,240

E-mail your boss to correct the information.

As your instructor directs,

Write e-mail messages for the following situations:

a.   The correct numbers are

Personnel	$2,845,490
Office supplies	$34,500
Telephone	$186,420

b.   The correct numbers are

Personnel	$2,845,490
Office supplies	$84,500
Telephone	$468,240

Variations for each situation:

1.   Your boss has been out of the office; you know she hasn't seen the data yet.

2.   Your boss gave a report to the executive committee this morning using your data.

Hints:

- How serious is the mistake in each situation?
- In which situations, if any, should you apologize?
- Should you give the reason for the mistake? Why or why not?
- How do your options vary depending on whether your job title gives you responsibility for numbers and accounting?

15.9   Refusing to Pay an Out-of-Network Bill

Your employees' health insurance allows them to choose from one of three health maintenance organizations (HMOs). Once employees have selected an HMO, they must get all medical care (except for out-of-state emergency care) from the HMO. Employees receive a listing of the doctors and hospitals affiliated with each HMO when they join the company and pick an HMO and again each October when they have a one-month "open enrollment period" to change to another of the three HMOs if they choose.

As Director of Employee Benefits, you've received an angry e-mail from Alvin Reineke. Alvin had just received a statement from his HMO stating that it would not pay for the costs of his hernia operation two months ago at St. Catherine's Hospital in your city. Alvin is furious: one of the reasons he accepted a job with your company six months ago was its excellent health care coverage. He feels the company lied to him and should pay for his (rather large) hospital bill since the HMO refuses to do so.

The HMO which Alvin had selected uses two hospitals, but not St. Catherine's. When Alvin joined the company six months ago, he (like all new employees) received a thick booklet explaining the HMO options. Perhaps he did not take the time to read it carefully. But that's not your fault. Alvin can change plans during the next open enrollment, but even if he switched to an

HMO that included St. Catherine's, that HMO wouldn't pay for surgery performed before he joined that HMO.

Write an e-mail message to Alvin giving him the bad news.

Hints:

- What tone should you use? Should you be sympathetic? Should you remind him that this is his own fault?

- Is there any help you can give Alvin (e.g., information about credit-union short-term loans or even information about negotiating payment terms with the hospital)?
- What can you do to make Alvin feel that the company has not lied to him?

15.10 Announcing a Reduction in Benefits

In years past, your company has had a generous health insurance policy, fully funded by the employer. Employees pay only a $10 copayment for doctor visits and a $6 copayment for prescriptions. However, the cost of health insurance has risen much faster than the company's other expenses and much faster than the prices your company can charge its customers. Most other companies now expect their employees to contribute part of the cost of their health insurance through payroll deductions, and management has determined that your company must begin doing the same. For a group insurance policy similar to the one employees have received in the past, they will now have to pay $50 per month, and the copayment for doctor visits will rise to $15 per visit. The coverage for prescriptions will vary, with the $6 copayment

applying only to generic drugs. For brand-name drugs, employees will have to pay more.

As your instructor directs,

Write an e-mail message to the employees of

a. A large advertising agency in a big city. The agency's billings have fallen 30% in the last six months, and 10% of the staff have already been laid off.

b. A manufacturing company. The company is still making a profit, but just barely. Unless the company saves money, layoffs may be necessary.

c. A successful service business. The business is doing well, but most of the employees earn only the minimum wage. They do not own stock in the company.

15.11 Complaining about the Dead

You are traveling on a first-class flight from New Dehli to London. When you wake, you find the corpse of a woman, who died in the economy section of the airplane, sitting next to you. After flagging down the flight attendant, you're told the crew moved the woman who died so her family could have some privacy to grieve. They could not put the body in the aisle or the attendant station for safety reasons. Needless to say, you're appalled by the situation.

As your instructor directs,

- Write a complaint letter to the airline.
- Write an apology letter from the perspective of the airline who has just received your complaint.

Source: Jennifer Quinn, "Passenger Dies on International Flight, Body Moved to First-Class Cabin," *Associated Press Archive*, March 19, 2007.

15.12 E-Mailing Bad News about Lab Hours

You're the administrator of your university's computer labs. Many students have asked for longer lab hours, and you presented the request to your superiors. However, you've just been informed that, beginning next term, the hours for the computer labs are being reduced. The labs

will open one hour later each morning as a cost-saving measure.

Write an e-mail message, including subject line, to all students, informing them of this change.

15.13   Telling Employees to Remove Personal Web Sites

You're Director of Management and Information Systems (MIS) in your organization. At your monthly briefing for management, a vice president complained that some employees have posted personal Web pages on the company's Web server.

"It looks really unprofessional to have stuff about cats and children and musical instruments. How can people do this?"

You took the question literally. "Well, some people have authorization to post material—price changes, job listings, marketing information. Someone who has authorization could put up anything."

Another manager said, "I don't think it's so terrible—after all, there aren't any links from our official pages to these personal pages."

A third person said, "But we're paying for what's posted—so we pay for server space and connect time. Maybe it's not much right now, but as more and more people become Web-literate, the number of people putting up unauthorized pages could spread. We should put a stop to this now."

The vice president agreed. "The Web site is carefully designed to present an image of our organization.

Personal pages are dangerous. Can you imagine the flak we'd get if someone posted links to pornography?"

You said, "I don't think that's very likely. If it did happen, as system administrator, I could remove the page."

The third speaker said, "I think we should remove all the pages. Having any at all suggests that our people have so much extra time that they're playing on the Web. That suggests that our prices are too high and may make some people worry about quality. In fact, I think that we need a new policy prohibiting personal pages on the company's Web server. And any pages that are already up should be removed."

A majority of the managers agreed and told you to write a message to all employees. Create an e-mail message to tell employees that you will remove the personal pages already posted and that no more will be allowed.

Hint:

- Suggest other ways that people can post personal Web pages.
- Give only reasons that are watertight and make the company look good.

15.14   Refusing to Waive a Fee

As the Licensing Program Coordinator for your school, you evaluate proposals from vendors who want to make or sell merchandise with the school's name, logo, or mascot. If you find the product acceptable, the vendor pays a $250 licensing fee and then 6.5% of the wholesale cost of the merchandise manufactured (whether or not it is sold). The licensing fee helps to support the cost of your

office; the 6.5% royalty goes into a student scholarship fund. At well-known universities or those with loyal students and alumni, the funds from such a program can add up to hundreds of thousands of dollars a year.

On your desk today is a proposal from a current student, Meg Winston.

I want to silk-screen and sell T-shirts printed with the name of the school, the mascot, and the words "We're Number One!" (A copy of the design I propose is enclosed.) I ask that you waive the $250 licensing fee you normally require and limit the 6.5% royalty only to those T-shirts actually sold, not to all those made.

I am putting myself through school by using student loans and working 30 hours a week. I just don't have $250. In my marketing class, we've done feasibility analyses, and I've determined that the shirts can be sold if the price is low enough. I hope to market these shirts in an independent study project with Professor Doulin, building on my marketing project earlier this term. However, my calculations show that I cannot price the shirts competitively if just one shirt must bear the 6.5% royalty for all the shirts produced in a batch. I will of course pay the 6.5% royalty on all shirts sold and not returned. I will produce the shirts in small batches (50–100 at a time). I am willing to donate any manufactured but unsold shirts to the athletic program so that you will know I'm not holding out on you.

By waiving this fee, you will show that this school really wants to help students get practical experience in business, as the catalog states. I will work hard to promote these shirts by getting the school president, the coaches, and campus leaders to endorse them, pointing out that the money goes to the scholarship fund. The shirts themselves will promote school loyalty, both now and later when we're alumni who can contribute to our alma mater.

I look forward to receiving the "go-ahead" to market these shirts.

The design and product are acceptable under your guidelines. However, you've always enforced the fee structure across the board, and you see no reason to make an exception now. Whether the person trying to sell merchandise is a student or not doesn't matter; your policy is designed to see that the school benefits whenever it is used to sell something. Students aren't the only ones whose cash flow is limited; many businesses would find it easier to get into the potentially lucrative business of selling clothing, school supplies, and other items with the school name or logo if they got the same deal Meg is asking for. (The policy also lets the school control the kinds of items on which its name appears.) Just last week, your office confiscated about 400 T-shirts and shorts made by a company that had used the school name on them without permission; the company has paid the school $7,500 in damages.

Write a letter to Meg rejecting her special requests. She can get a license to produce the T-shirts, but only if she pays the $250 licensing fee and the royalty on all shirts made.

15.15 Correcting Misinformation

You're the director of the city's Division of Water. Your mail today contains this letter:

> When we bought our pool, the salesman told us that you would give us a discount on the water bill when we fill the pool. Please start the discount immediately. I tried to call you three times and got nothing but busy signals.
>
> Sincerely,
>
> *Larry Shadburn-Butler*
>
> Larry Shadburn-Butler

The salesperson was wrong. You don't provide discounts for pools (or anything else). At current rates, filling a pool with a garden hose costs from $8.83 (for a 1,800-gallon pool) to $124.67 (for 26,000 gallons) in the city. Filling a pool from any other water source would cost more. Rates are 30% higher in the suburbs and 50% higher in unincorporated rural areas. And you don't have enough people to answer phones. You tried a voicemail system but eliminated it when you found people didn't have time to process all the messages that were left. But the city budget doesn't allow you to hire more people.

As your instructor directs,

a. Write a letter to Mr. Shadburn-Butler.
b. Write a letter to all the stores that sell swimming pools, urging them to stop giving customers misinformation.
c. Write a notice for the one-page newsletter that you include with quarterly water bills. Assume that you can have half a page for your information.

15.16 Analyzing Job Rejection Letters

1. Here are three rejections letters to an applicant who applied for an accounting position.

Letter 1

We realize that the application process for the accounting position at AlphaBank required a substantial amount of thought, time, and effort on your part. Therefore, we would like to express our sincere appreciation for your willingness to participate in the search process.

The task of selecting a final candidate was difficult and challenging due to the quality of the applicant pool. We regret to inform you that we selected another candidate who we believe will best meet the needs of AlphaBank.

We thank your for your interest in employment at AlphaBank and extend our best wishes as you pursue your professional goals.

Letter 2

Thank you for your interest in the accounting position at AlphaBank. I'm sorry to inform you that you were not one of the finalists. The position has now been filled.

The search committee and I wish you the best in your future employment searches.

Letter 3

Thank you for your interest in the accounting position at AlphaBank.

I'm sorry to inform you that the search committee has decided to offer the position to another candidate. This was an extremely difficult decision for us to make. We were all impressed with your résumé and credentials.

Again, thank you for your interest in AlphaBank.

Analyze these three job rejection letters by answering the following questions:

- Do these letters use buffers? If so, how effective are they?
- What reasons do the letters give, if any?
- Does the letter attempt to build goodwill with the audience? If yes, how so?
- Do any of the letters offer an alternative?
- How do you think recipients will react to each of the letters? Which (if any) are more preferable?

As your instructor directs,
a. Discuss your findings in a small group.
b. Present your findings orally to the class.
c. Present your findings in a memo to your instructor.

2. Collect job rejection letters mailed to seniors on your campus. Analyze the letters, answering the following questions:

- Do these letters use buffers? If so, how effective are they?
- What reasons do the letters give, if any?
- Do the letters attempt to build goodwill with the audience? If yes, how so?
- Do any of the letters offer an alternative?
- How do you think recipients will react to each of the letters? Which (if any) are more preferable?

As your instructor directs,
a. Discuss your finding in a small group.
b. Present your findings orally to the class.
c. Present your findings in a memo to your instructor.
d. Join with other students to write a report based on your findings.

15.17 Creating Equal Work Distribution

You noticed recently that Clare, the woman who works next to you at a call center, takes extended lunches and makes a lot of personal phone calls. As the result of her phone calls and breaks, you and your co-workers complete more work throughout the day. After discussing the situation with a close friend, you decide you are going to tell the boss about her behavior.

As your instructor directs,

- Write a memo or e-mail to your boss in which you discuss Clare's behavior and ask for a resolution.
- Partner up with a classmate and role-play the situation of telling the boss. One of you is the employee and one of you is the boss.

- Partner up with a classmate and role-play the situation of confronting Clare. One of you is the employee and one of you is Clare.

Hints:

- How can you deliver the negative news without sounding like a tattletale?
- How can you make the situation seem severe enough so that your boss takes action?

15.18 Turning Down a Faithful Client

You are Midas Investment Services' specialist in estate planning. You give talks to various groups during the year about estate planning. You ask nonprofit groups (churches, etc.) just to reimburse your expenses; you charge for-profit groups a fee plus expenses. These fees augment your income nicely, and the talks also are marvelous exposure for you and your company.

Every February for the last five years, Gardner Manufacturing Company has hired you to conduct an eight-hour workshop (two hours every Monday night for four weeks) on retirement and estate planning for its employees who are over 60 or who are thinking of taking early retirement. These workshops are popular and have generated clients for your company. The session last February went smoothly, as you have come to expect.

Today, out of the blue, you got a letter from Hope Goldberger, Director of Employee Benefits at Gardner, asking you to conduct the workshops every Tuesday evening *next* month at your usual fee. She didn't say whether this is an extra series or whether this will replace next February's series.

You can't do it. Your spouse, a microbiologist, is giving an invited paper at an international conference in Paris next month and the two of you are taking your children, ages 13 and 9, on a three-week trip to Europe. (You've made arrangements with school authorities to have the kids miss three weeks of classes.) You've been looking forward to and planning the trip for the last eight months.

Unfortunately, Midas Investment Services is a small group, and the only other person who knows anything about estate planning is a terrible speaker. You could suggest a friend at another financial management company, but you don't want Gardner to turn to someone else permanently; you enjoy doing the workshops and find them a good way to get leads.

Write the letter to Ms. Goldberger.

15.19 Pacifying Customers

Macy's, a New York–based department store and financer of the annual Macy's Thanksgiving Day Parade, launched a nationwide takeover of many long-standing department stores, such as Marshall Field's, Kauffmann's, and Meier & Frank. Beyond the name change, shoppers really began to notice when Macy's changed some long-standing holiday traditions.

For example in Portland, Oregon, the annual parade was shorter and the Santa Land monorail, a family tradition at Meier & Frank, was not in operation. In Chicago customers were disgruntled with losing their long-time Marshall Field's store; some customers refused to shop there during the holiday season. In fact, a survey by Deloitte & Touche suggested that 41% of Chicagoans were unhappy with the name change. Macy's is in a bind. Clearly, they want to keep loyal customers.

Take on the role of the Macy's Communication Department and write to angry Meier & Frank customers.

Hints:

- Remember to always maintain goodwill by analyzing how the audience feels about the situation.
- Point out the advantages of having a historically and nationally known department store take over smaller, less-known department stores.
- Keep in mind the monorail is only down for one year during the store renovation.

- Macy's also plans to add to the parade next year by including new inflatable characters for the kids and electrically powering the floats.

Based on Venessa O'Connell, "Macy's Brands the Holidays: As Marshall Field's, Kaufmann's, Others Take Chain's Name, Department Stores Try to Maintain Local Shoppers' Loyalty," *Wall Street Journal,* November 22, 2006, B1, B2.

15.20   Sending Negative Messages to Real Audiences

As your instructor directs, write a negative letter that responds to one of the following scenarios:

- Write a letter to the owner of a restaurant where you received poor service.
- Write a letter to a company whose product unsatisfactorily met your expectations or needs.
- Identify a current political topic on which you disagree with your congressional representative. Write a letter that outlines your views for him/her and calls for change.
- Identify a television advertisement with which you disagree. Write a letter to the company explaining

your position and request that the advertisement be altered or taken off the air.

Hints:

- For all of these scenarios, your main goal should be to promote change.
- Express your complaint as positively as possible.
- Remember to consider your audience's needs; how can you build support for your position?

15.21   Getting Information from a Co-worker

Your boss has been pressuring you because you are weeks late turning in a termination report. However, you cannot begin your section of the report until your colleague, Matt Churetta, finishes his section. Right now, he is the problem. Here is a series of e-mail exchanges between you and Matt:

7/25/2010

Matt,

The boss wants the termination report now. Send over your section as soon as you finish.

Thanks,

Matt's reply:

7/31/2010

My apologies about the report,

On another note, I'm waiting to see my oncology surgeon to see what the course of treatment will be for the esophageal cancer. I will keep you posted on the process.

Please let me know if there is anything else coming up.

Thanks,

8/15/2010

Matt,

I had no idea that you are dealing with esophageal cancer. Definitely keep me posted on your condition. Best wishes as you work through your treatment.

I need your section of the termination report as soon as you finish it. The boss has been waiting patiently for the finished version.

Thanks,

Matt's reply:

8/26/2010

Report is coming along. The last two weeks have been difficult dealing with all the tests, doctors' appointments, etc. I will beat this deal!!!

Take Care,

It is now September, and over a month has passed from the termination report's original due date. While you are sympathetic to Matt's situation, the boss is demanding the finished report.

As your instructor directs,

a. Write an e-mail to Matt telling him you have to have his portion of the report as soon as possible. You are concerned for your job security, as well as his, if this report is not finalized soon.

b. Write a memo to your boss explaining the situation.

c. Write a memo to your instructor that focuses on the ethical choices you had to make while constructing the two messages.

15.22   All-Weather Case: Communicating Layoffs

Doug, Caleb, and Tanner are huddled in the small conference room to discuss what none of them (including Doug) has ever had to face before: layoffs. Erin, whose duties include terminations, would have been present too but is away on an important business meeting. Doug has asked the secretary to block any visitors or calls for the duration of the meeting. The blinds in the room are drawn, hiding the view of Walnut Street below. In situations demanding serious thinking, Doug likes to focus on the "internal world," as he is fond of saying.

Because of reduced home construction business, All-Weather is facing its first quarter of losses year-to-year. Sales are especially bad for the New Construction aluminum windows that are manufactured at All-Weather's plant in Long Prairies, Minnesota. The ongoing production costs at the plant are no longer sustainable because of the nearly 80% reduction in the demand for New Construction windows. Estimates indicate that the plant has been losing money at the rate of half a million dollars every month.

The plant is run by a manufacturing manager, 3 shift engineers, and 20 operators. Doug and his team have completed a detailed evaluation of these employees, and their conclusion is that only one of them deserves to be relocated to All-Weather's other plants. This employee, an operator, was one of the earliest to join the company. He was moved to Long Prairies, Minnesota, only a year ago and has also been a whistle-blower regarding the dereliction of quality and safety norms in the plant.

The manufacturing manager and the 3 shift engineers, along with the other 19 operators, have added to the adverse effects of an already declining demand by producing products that are below All-Weather's quality standards. This deterioration in quality has not gone unnoticed; local consumer protection agencies and builders associations have protested against the plant's manufacturing practices. However, the 23 employees in question have been with All-Weather for an average of five years, making the task of firing them difficult.

"How do we go about doing this?" Doug asks, wringing his hands. "That it's not a three- or four-figure layoff does not make it any easier."

"We'll have to talk to them first," Caleb says, checking the calendar on his Blackberry, "before we send them a layoff notice."

"See that we follow the WARN Act in all respects," Doug says, referring to the Worker Adjustment and Retraining Notification (WARN) Act,[*] 1989, which stipulates giving an advance notice of two months before laying off employees.

The next day, Caleb and Tanner drive to the Long Prairies plant. They hold a meeting of all the employees and break the news. The manufacturing manager walks out. The three engineers remain in the room but do nothing to help Caleb as he faces angry questions and accusations from the operators. Caleb has not yet told the one operator, whom Doug and he have decided to relocate, the news that he wouldn't be losing his job; however, this operator too joins the other 19 in demanding to know why a company like All-Weather cannot protect these jobs regardless of the state of the economy. Caleb listens to everyone and promises to get back after further deliberations.

Back in the headquarters, Doug, Caleb, and Tanner sit down again. Doug has also spoken with the VP of Manufacturing in the meanwhile. "Gentlemen, how do you think we should proceed?" Doug asks, this time in a more

determined voice, knowing that he has to go through with this no matter how unpleasant the task. The costs of running the plant are substantial and cannot be tolerated in view of the first-ever quarterly loss All-Weather has suffered. Besides, Doug does not want to set a bad precedent by relocating these 23 employees despite their poor performance which has cost the company dearly.

"Let us issue them the notice without further delay," Tanner says, looking at Caleb.

"No. I think we owe them one more meeting," Caleb says, quietly. "This time here in the headquarters."

"But Caleb we can't—," Tanner begins to say but is waved off by Doug.

"Caleb is right," Doug says, standing up, "but it's a risk because they may not be satisfied with the second meeting."

"I believe it's a risk we must take," Caleb says, walking up to the flip chart in the room and writing on it the following: *Issue the notice first, then have the meeting.* "I think what we need to do," he begins to explain, "is first to communicate clearly to them that they will lose their jobs, then offer to help."

"Sounds like the path of least resistance," Doug says.

Caleb asks Tanner to draft the layoff notice, a memo on All-Weather's letterhead that will be signed by Doug. Here is the draft that Tanner has prepared to show Caleb, though he has a feeling that the draft needs improvement and that he may have to revisit it before Caleb reads it:

[*] The information about the WARN Act is taken from http://www.doleta .gov/programs/factsht/warn.htm.

To: All Employees, Long Prairies Plant, MN

From: VP (HR)

Subject: Layoffs

Date: April 15, 2010

As was discussed during our recent visit to your plant, we are forced to close your plant immediately due to continuing heavy losses. Consequently, your job with the company will end on June 30, 2010. The only exception will be Mr. J. L. Broder, who will be transferred to a suitable plant within the company. We're making this exception because he was among the first to join the company and has taken steps to voice his concerns with your plant even though he only recently joined your team. In other words, we believe we cannot fault him for what has happened, which we believe was largely the doing of all the others of you who work in the plant.

Your plant has cost the company nearly $3.5 million. We can no longer sustain these kinds of losses in view of the sagging economy and our first-ever recorded loss in the first quarter. The product your plant makes is also no longer in demand; its demand has declined by as much as 80%. We don't know for sure when the demand will rise again. Even if it reaches its old levels some day, we cannot in those hopes alone carry on the burden of a loss-making plant for an indefinite period of time. Sorry, but the fittest survive in this or any other industry.

To make your departure as easy as possible on you and your families, we invite you for a personal meeting and counseling to the HR Department at headquarters.

Both the VP of HR and the VP of Manufacturing will talk to you in spite of their very busy schedules. You can also ask them for any help you need, though we cannot promise anything. Once again, we're sorry that you have to leave, but we hope we will part company without much fuss. Have a great day.

Based on of your reading of chapter 15, analyze Tanner's draft. To help with your analysis, refer to the checklist for negative messages included at the end of the chapter. Does the draft effectively address a negative situation such as a layoff? Does it strike the right tone with its audience of upset employees? Based on your analysis of the draft, work in groups to revise Tanner's draft.

Crafting Persuasive Messages

Chapter Outline

Analyzing Persuasive Situations
1. What Do You Want People to Do?
2. What Objections, If Any, Will the Audience Have?
3. How Strong Is Your Case?
4. What Kind of Persuasion Is Best for the Organization and the Culture?

Choosing a Persuasive Strategy

Why Threats Are Less Effective than Persuasion

Making Persuasive Direct Requests

Writing Persuasive Problem-Solving Messages
- Subject Lines for Problem-Solving Messages
- Developing a Common Ground
- Dealing with Objections
- Offering a Reason for the Audience to Act Promptly

- Building Emotional Appeal
- Putting It All Together

Tone in Persuasive Messages

Varieties of Persuasive Messages
- Performance Appraisals
- Letters of Recommendation

Sales and Fund-Raising Messages
- Organizing a Sales or Fund-Raising Message
- Strategy in Sales Messages and Fund-Raising Appeals
- Writing Style

Solving a Sample Problem
- Problem
- Analysis of the Problem
- Discussion of the Sample Solutions

Summary of Key Points

Super Ads for the Super Bowl

Since 2007, Frito-Lay has purchased air time during the Super Bowl to run Doritos ads that are created by people who know that product well: their customers. The Doritos marketing team asked fans of the brand to create their own ads and submit them online, for a chance to see their ad on air during the big game. They then asked other fans to choose which ad would air. Other brands, including the National Football League, also solicited fan ideas for in-game ads.

This approach uses powerful persuasive techniques. By involving their customers as authors and judges, Frito-Lay builds common ground with their audience: they foster the idea that they and their customers are partners, linked by the product. The campaign also encourages customers to picture themselves enjoying the product, then to share that vision with others.

As Jon Fine, a columnist for *BusinessWeek*, observed, ad executives are skeptical of this marketing strategy. He quotes one advertiser who maintains that "We are pros, and although it looks easy to create advertising, it isn't." That's true. The best persuasive messages look and sound natural and effortless, but in reality, sales and persuasive messages are some of the most challenging kinds of business communication you can attempt. These messages require careful attention to audience and purpose, and a thorough knowledge of your subject. What will move your audience? What actions do you want your audience to take, and how willing will they be to take those actions? How can you ethically share—or adapt—the information you possess to persuade your audience?

> "When you persuade, you not only provide information, establish credibility, and build goodwill: to be successful, you also have to motivate someone to change beliefs or take action."

When you persuade, you not only provide information, establish credibility, and build goodwill: to be successful, you also have to motivate someone to change beliefs or take action. Persuasive and sales messages combine all of the techniques of good professional communication. They also give you the opportunity to employ visual design, creativity, and most important—as Doritos' fans did—your knowledge and enthusiasm.

Sources: Jon Fine, "What Makes 'Citizen Ads' Work," *BusinessWeek,* February 19, 2007, 24; and Frito-Lay North America Inc., "Doritos® Presents: CRASH THE SUPERBOWL," http://www.crashthesuperbowl.com/ (accessed April 5, 2009).

Learning Objectives

After studying this chapter, you will know how to:

1 Analyze a persuasive situation.

2 Identify basic persuasive strategies.

3 Write persuasive direct requests.

4 Write persuasive problem-solving messages.

5 Write sales and fund-raising messages.

6 Use rational and emotional appeals to support persuasive messages.

Persuasion for Peace

As reported in *The Economist*, the government of Indonesia is taking a new approach toward reducing violence from radical Islamic groups. Instead of relying on Muslim clerics or the police to convince young Muslims to renounce violence, as the leaders of other Muslim countries do, they're giving the task to people with a unique perspective on terrorism: former terrorists.

The Indonesian government found that the young Muslim men who turn to terrorist groups as an outlet for their religious and political beliefs also do not trust the government or moderate religious leaders. However, terrorists who've given up violence as part of their philosophy can reach that audience. They come from the same background, they share the same religious beliefs, and they understand the reasons why radical Muslims turn to violence. That common ground enables them to make a connection where other persuasive messages fail.

While some question the program's ability to reduce violence, others note one important success: the program has opened up a dialog between police and would-be terrorists. That gives the police a better understanding of people who are prepared to commit violence in support of extremist views, which helps them stop violence before it begins.

Adapted from "Preachers to the Converted," *The Economist*, December 15, 2007, 71.

Persuasion is almost universal in good business communications. If you are giving people information, you are persuading them to consider it good information, or to remember it, or even to use it. If you are giving people negative news, you are trying to persuade them to accept it. But some messages seem more obviously persuasive to us than others. Employees try to persuade their supervisors to institute flex hours or casual Fridays; supervisors try to persuade workers to keep more accurate records, thus reducing time spent correcting errors; or to follow healthier lifestyles, thus reducing health benefit costs. You may find yourself persuading your colleagues to accept your ideas, your staff to work overtime on a rush project, and your boss to give you a raise.

Whether you're selling safety equipment or ideas, effective persuasion is based on accurate logic, effective emotional appeal, and credibility or trust. Reasons have to be ones the audience finds important; emotional appeal is based on values the audience cares about; credibility is in the eye of the beholder.

Persuasive messages include requests, proposals and recommendations, sales and fund-raising messages, job application letters, and efforts to change people's behavior, such as collection letters, criticisms or performance appraisals where you want the subordinate to improve behavior, and public-service ads designed to reduce drunk driving, drug use, and so on. Reports are persuasive messages if they recommend action.

This chapter gives general guidelines for persuasive messages. Chapter 18 discusses proposals; reports are the subject of Chapter 19. Chapter 12 covers job application letters.

All persuasive messages have several purposes:

Primary purpose:
- To have the audience act or change beliefs.

Secondary purposes:
- To build a good image of the communicator.
- To build a good image of the communicator's organization.
- To cement a good relationship between the communicator and audience.
- To overcome any objections that might prevent or delay action.
- To reduce or eliminate future communication on the same subject so the message doesn't create more work for the communicator.

Analyzing Persuasive Situations

Choose a persuasive strategy based on your answers to four questions. Use these questions to analyze persuasive situations:

CARE's Web site presents a complex persuasive argument that poverty can be eased for millions of people.

Source: CARE USA Communications and Marketing Department., "CARE USA 2008 Annual Report," in *Newsroom: Publications: Annual Reports,* http://www.care.org/newsroom/publications/annualreports/index.asp?s_src= 170960110000&s_subsrc= (accessed April 4, 2009).

1. What do you want people to do?
2. What objections, if any, will the audience have?
3. How strong is your case?
4. What kind of persuasion is best for the organization and the culture?

1. What Do You Want People to Do?

Identify the specific action you want and the person who has the power to do it. If your goal requires several steps, specify what you want your audience to do *now.* For instance, your immediate goal may be to have people come to a meeting or let you make a presentation, even though your long-term goal is a major sale or a change in policy.

Tempest in a Water Glass

Everyone needs water, so how much persuasion does it take to sell it? As the *Wall Street Journal* reported, there's a lot of persuasion involved in the water business—and some controversy as well.

Bottled water is big business in France: French citizens consume 145 liters per person per year, compared to 85 liters a year for Americans. When the public water companies that serve Paris ran advertisements promoting tap water over bottled with the slogan "Which brand delivers excellent water to your house all year round?" the major bottled water companies responded in kind. Their ad featured a toilet bowl and the catchphrase "I don't drink the water I use to flush."

Think about the persuasive techniques involved in the two ad campaigns. What psychological descriptions of their target audience do the ads employ? How do you think the Parisian Water Works ought to respond to the bottled water ads?

Adapted from David Gauthier-Villars, "Water Fight in France Takes a Dirty Turn," *Wall Street Journal,* February 1, 2007, B7.

Put It in Writing

Raymond Dreyfack credits his writing skills for his successful career at Faberge Perfumes. As he worked in supervisory and management jobs, he kept his eye open for opportunities to solve problems and improve performance. Then, when he had an idea, he wrote a memo to his boss.

Why a memo? The written format forced Dreyfack to organize his initial idea clearly and concisely. Editing memos trained Dreyfack to consider whether his messages reflected the reader's interests and viewpoints. The written format also gave Dreyfack's boss time to consider the idea and reflect on its merits. (If you spring an idea on your boss in the hallway, he or she might find it easier to blurt out a *no* than to give the idea fair consideration.)

Adapted from Raymond Dreyfack, "The Write Way to Jump-Start Your Career," *Supervision* 65, no. 4 (April 2004): 13–15.

2. What Objections, If Any, Will the Audience Have?

If you're asking for something that requires little time, money, or physical effort and for an action that's part of the person's regular duties, the audience is likely to have few objections.

Often, however, you'll encounter some resistance. People may be busy and have what they feel are more important things to do. They may have other uses for their time and money. To be persuasive, you need to show your audience that your proposal meets their needs; you need to overcome any objections.

The easiest way to learn about objections your audience may have is to ask. Particularly when you want to persuade people in your own organization or your own town, talk to knowledgeable people. Phrase your questions nondefensively, in a way that doesn't lock people into taking a stand on an issue: "What concerns would you have about a proposal to do *x?*" "Who makes a decision about *y?*" "What do you like best about [the supplier or practice you want to change]?" Ask follow-up questions to be sure you understand: "Would you be likely to stay with your current supplier if you could get a lower price from someone else? Why?"

People are likely to be most aware of and willing to share objective concerns such as time and money. They will be less willing to tell you that their real objection is emotional. People have a **vested interest** in something if they benefit directly from keeping things as they are. People who are in power have a vested interest in retaining the system that gives them their power. Someone who designed a system has a vested interest in protecting that system from criticism. To admit that the system has faults is to admit that the designer made mistakes. In such cases, you'll need to probe to find out what the real reasons are.

Whether your audience is inside or outside your organization, they will find it easier to say *yes* when you ask for something that is consistent with the person's self-image. A manager, for example, is likely to have the self-image of being a careful decision maker who considers the company's best interests.

3. How Strong Is Your Case?

The strength of your case is based on three aspects of persuasion: argument, credibility, and emotional appeal.

Argument refers to the reasons or logic you offer. Sometimes you may be able to prove conclusively that your solution is best. Sometimes your reasons may not be as strong, the benefits may not be as certain, and obstacles may be difficult or impossible to overcome. For example, suppose that you wanted to persuade your organization to offer a tuition reimbursement plan for employees. You'd have a strong argument if you could show that tuition reimbursement would improve the performance of marginal workers or that reimbursement would be an attractive recruiting tool in a tight job market. However, if dozens of fully qualified workers apply for every opening you have, your argument would be weaker. The program might be nice for workers, but you'd have a hard job proving that it would help the company.

Credibility is the audience's response to you as the source of the message. Credibility in the workplace has three sources: expertise, image, and relationships.[1] Citing experts can make your argument more credible. In some organizations, workers build credibility by getting assigned to high-profile teams. You build credibility by your track record. The more reliable you've been in the past, the more likely people are to trust you now.

We are also more likely to trust people we know. That's one reason that new CEOs make a point of visiting as many branch offices as they can. Building a relationship with someone—even if the relationship is based on an outside interest, like sports or children—makes it easier for that person to see you as an individual and to trust you.

When you don't yet have the credibility that comes from being an expert or being powerful, build credibility by the language and strategy you use:

- **Be factual.** Don't exaggerate. If you can test your idea ahead of time, do so, and report the results. Facts about your test are more convincing than opinions about your idea.

- **Be specific.** If you say "X is better," show in detail *how* it is better. Show the audience exactly where the savings or other benefits come from so that it's clear that the proposal really is as good as you say it is.

- **Be reliable.** If you suspect that a project will take longer to complete, cost more money, or be less effective than you originally thought, tell your audience *immediately.* Negotiate a new schedule that you can meet.

Emotional appeal means making the audience *want* to do what you ask. People don't make decisions—even business decisions—based on logic alone. As John Kotter and Holger Rathgeber, authors of the popular business book *Our Iceberg Is Melting,* found, "feelings often trump thinking."[2] Jonah Lehrer, author of *How We Decide,* goes a step further. He offers research that shows people make better decisions—ones that satisfy them better—about large purchases such as a couch when they followed their emotions: "The process of thinking requires feeling, for feelings are what let us understand all the information that we can't directly comprehend. Reason without emotion is impotent."[3]

De Tijd, a Belgian business newspaper, won a European Marketing Council award for its emotional appeal to get human resource managers to use its pension brochure. Every manager who published a job ad in the newspaper received a handwritten letter from Cyriel, age 84, applying for the position. The message on the last page of Cyriel's application read, "Save your employees from having to do like Cyriel: to look for a job when they retire. Offer your employees our brochure." Sales of the brochure increased 24%.[4]

4. What Kind of Persuasion Is Best for the Organization and the Culture?

A strategy that works in one organization may not work somewhere else. One corporate culture may value no-holds-barred aggressiveness. In another organization with different cultural values, an employee who used a hard-sell strategy for a request would antagonize people.

Organizational culture (p. 35) isn't written down; it's learned by imitation and observation. What style do high-level people in your organization use? When you show a draft to your boss, are you told to tone down your statements or to make them stronger? Role models and advice are two ways organizations communicate their culture to newcomers.

Different kinds of persuasion also work for different social cultures. In North Carolina, police are using a new combination to persuade drug dealers to shut down. The combination includes iron-clad cases against the dealers, but also pressure from loved ones—mothers, grandmothers, mentors—along with a second chance. Texas used a famous antilitter campaign based on the slogan "Don't Mess with Texas." Research showed the typical Texas litterer was 18–35, male, a pickup driver, and a lover of sports and country music. He did not respond to authority (Don't litter) or cute owls (Give a hoot; don't pollute). Instead, the campaign aimed to convince this target audience that people like him did not pollute. Ads featured Texan athletes and musicians making the point that Texans don't litter. The campaign was enormously successful: during its first five years, Texas roadside litter decreased 72% and roadside cans 81%.[5]

Persuasion through the Press

When you're communicating with your customers and investors, there's one audience you can't ignore: the press.

It can be hard for smaller businesses to reach analysts and investors with a persuasive message, because there is so much competition for attention. In that case, an active campaign of creative press releases can get a small business "on the radar," and in front of investors' eyes.

Smaller companies usually only come to the attention of the press when something goes wrong—bad news sells. In that case, actively work with the press to buffer any negative news with a positive and persuasive message.

When you're looking for ways to persuade a target audience, it always pays to remember that you will have multiple audiences in any situation. Some of those audiences—like the press—can be useful gatekeeper audiences who can help you get your message in front of your primary audience.

Adapted from Gregory Miller, "How to Talk to Investors—through the Press," *Harvard Business Review* 86, no. 1 (January 2008), 26.

Different cultures also have different preferences for gaining compliance. In one study, students who were native speakers of American English judged direct statements ("Do this"; "I want you to do this") clearer and more effective than questions ("Could you do this?") or hints ("This is needed"). Students who were native speakers of Korean, in contrast, judged direct statements to be *least* effective. In the Korean culture, the clearer a request is, the ruder and therefore less effective it is.[6] Another study notes that communicators from countries such as China, Japan, and Korea prefer to establish personal relationships before they address business issues. They also show modesty and humility, debasing their egos in favor of collective relationships and disdaining personal profit.[7]

Microsoft's MSN Latino, a Spanish-language Web site, is marketing to second-generation Latinos. New research has shown that they respond well to advertisements in Spanish and to cultural cues (music, family, food). However, they're also more likely to shop or research online (which suggests combining media for maximum persuasive value), and often respond well to advertisements that mix English and Spanish (because they often mix both languages in their own communication).[8]

Choosing a Persuasive Strategy

If your organization prefers a specific approach, use it. If your organization has no preference, or if you do not know your audience's preference, use the following guidelines to help you choose a strategy. These guidelines work in many cases but not all. You always need to consider your audience and situation before choosing your persuasive strategy.

- Use the **direct request pattern** when
  - The audience will do as you ask without any resistance,
  - You need responses only from people who will find it easy to do as you ask, or
  - The audience may not read all of the message.
- Use the **problem-solving pattern** when the audience may resist doing as you ask and you expect logic to be more important than emotion in the decision.
- Use the **sales pattern** when the audience may resist doing as you ask and you expect emotion to be more important than logic in the decision.

Why Threats Are Less Effective than Persuasion

Sometimes people think they will be able to mandate change by ordering or threatening subordinates. Real managers disagree. Research shows that managers use threats only for obligatory duties such as coming to work on time. For more creative duties—like being part of a team or thinking of ways to save the company money—good managers persuade. Persuasion not only keeps the lines of communication open, it fosters better working relationships and makes future discussions go more smoothly.[9]

When you set out to advocate change, consider the motivators that might convince people to change. A survey found that salespeople in the United States and United Kingdom are most motivated by the potential to earn large incomes. (In other countries, primary motivators included ability to use one's talents, the stimulation and challenge of the job, and freedom from routine.)[10]

Threats are even less effective in trying to persuade people whose salaries you don't pay.

A **threat** is a statement—explicit or implied—that someone will be punished if he or she does (or doesn't do) something. Various reasons explain why threats don't work:

1. **Threats don't produce permanent change.** Many people obey the speed limit only when a marked police car is in sight.

2. **Threats won't necessarily produce the action you want.** If you punish whistleblowers, you may stop hearing about problems you could be solving—hardly the response you'd want!

3. **Threats may make people abandon an action—even in situations where it would be appropriate.** Criticizing workers for talking on the way to the water cooler may reduce their overall business communications with each other.

4. **Threats produce tension.** People who feel threatened put their energies into ego defense rather than into productive work.

5. **People dislike and avoid anyone who threatens them.** A supervisor who is disliked will find it harder to enlist cooperation and support on the next issue that arises.

6. **Threats can provoke counteraggression.** Getting back at a boss can run the gamut from complaints to work slowdowns to sabotage.

In *The Tipping Point,* Malcolm Gladwell describes classic fear experiments conducted at Yale University. The point of the experiments was to get students to go to the health center for tetanus shots. Students were given high-fear or low-fear versions of booklets explaining why they should get the shots. The high-fear booklet included gruesome pictures and text; the low-fear booklet did not. As you might predict, more of the students reading the high-fear booklet said they would get the shots than those reading the low-fear version. But only 3% of students in either group actually did so. However, one small change upped the percentage to 28% (evenly spread across both groups). That change was including a campus map with the health center circled and the times shots were available listed. The map shifted the persuasion from abstract material about the dangers of tetanus to practical, personal advice.[11]

Making Persuasive Direct Requests

When you expect quick agreement, you can generally save your audience's time by presenting the request directly (see Figure 16.1). Also use the direct request pattern for busy people who do not read all the messages they receive and in organizations whose cultures favor putting the request first.

Direct *and* Persuasive

Supervisors typically use direct requests as their persuasive strategy with employees. This pattern makes sense because the message is clear and employees consider their role in the company to include following their supervisor's directions. Even so, supervisors can be more persuasive if they follow these guidelines when making requests:

- Explain requests completely, even if the explanation includes bad news.

- If possible, when directing employees to correct a problem, give them some latitude in how to solve it. People are more committed to a solution they feel is their own.

- Be honest. If a task will be difficult, don't try to make it sound easy. Emphasize benefits without exaggerating them.

- When a request involves a significant change, allow time for employees to get used to the idea. Give information ahead of the change.

- Use a tone that is quiet and assertive, rather than demanding and aggressive.

- Recognize that if a request sounds difficult, employees may feel afraid or angry. Allow time for emotions to drain before countering objections rationally.

Adapted from W. H. Weiss, "Using Persuasion Successfully," *Supervision* 64, no. 1 (2003): 3–6.

Figure 16.1 How to Organize a Persuasive Direct Request

1. **Consider asking immediately for the information or service you want.** Delay the request if it seems too abrupt or if you have several purposes in the message.

2. **Give your audience all the information they will need to act on your request.** Number your questions or set them off with bullets so readers can check to see that all have been answered.

3. **Ask for the action you want.** Do you want a check? A replacement? A catalog? Answers to your questions? If you need an answer by a certain time, say so. If possible, show why the time limit is necessary.

In written direct requests, put the request, the topic of the request, or a question in the subject line.

> Subject: Request for Updated Software
>
> My copy of HomeNet does not accept the nicknames for Gmail accounts.

> Subject: Status of Account #3548-003
>
> Please get me the following information about account #3548-003.

> Subject: Do We Need an Additional Training Session in October?
>
> The two training sessions scheduled for October will each accommodate 20 people. Last month, you said that 57 new staff accountants had been hired. Should we schedule an additional training session in October? Or can the new hires wait until the next regularly scheduled session in February?

Figure 16.2 illustrates a direct request. Note that a direct request does not contain benefits and does not need to overcome objections: it simply asks for what is needed.

Figure 16.2   A Direct Request

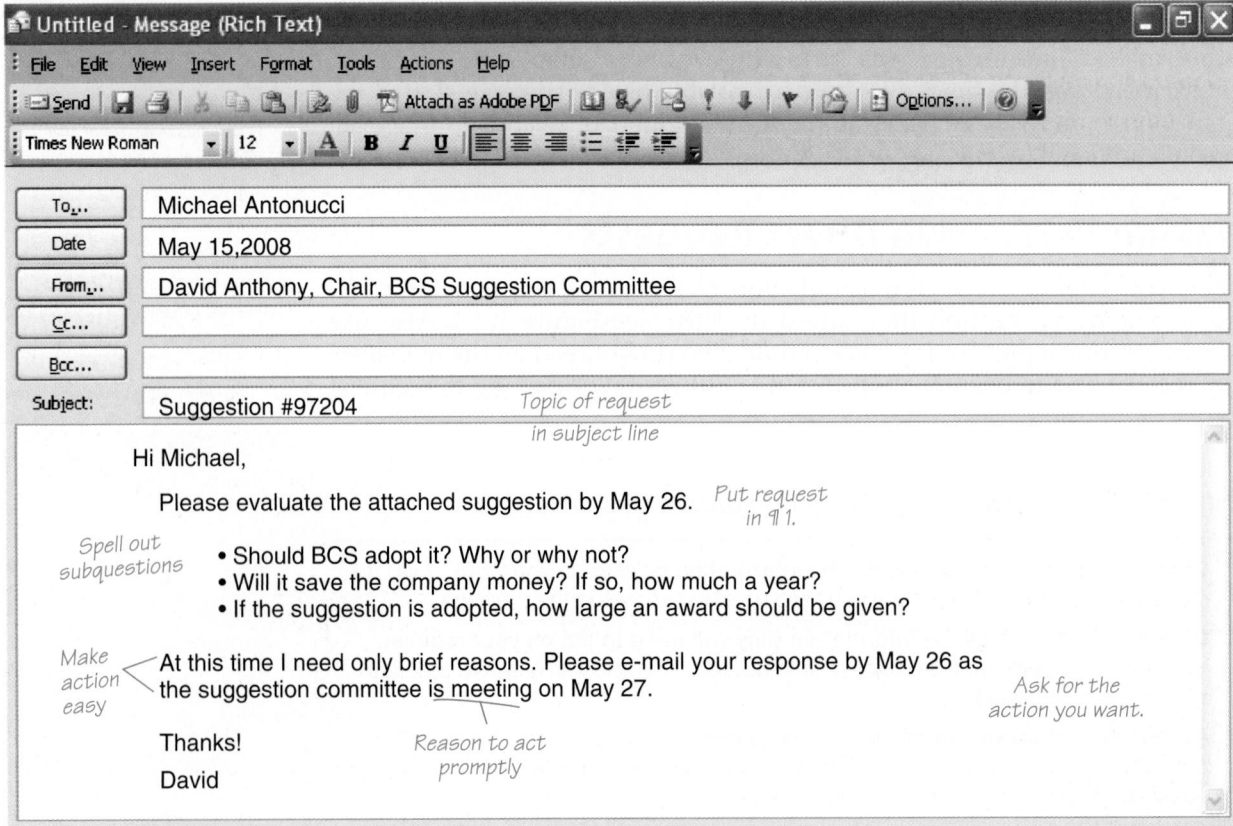

Direct requests should be clear. Don't make people guess what you want.

| Indirect request: | Is there a newer version of the 2003 *Chicago Manual of Style*? |
| Direct request: | If there is a newer version of the 2003 *Chicago Manual of Style*, please send it to me. |

In a claim, a message asking for correction or compensation for goods or services, explain the circumstances so that the reader knows what happened. Be sure to include all the relevant details: date of purchase, model or invoice number, and so on.

In more complicated direct requests, anticipate possible responses. Suppose you're asking for information about equipment meeting certain specifications. Explain which criteria are most important so that the reader can recommend an alternative if no single product meets all your needs. You may also want to tell the reader what your price constraints are and ask whether the item is in stock or must be special-ordered.

During the 2008 recession, the Campaign for a Commercial-Free Childhood urged parents to write to toy manufacturers asking them to suspend advertising toys to children during the holiday season. The CCFC offered parents a sample letter, one which put the request in the first sentence. Anticipating strong reactions from toy manufacturers, the CCFC pointed out that it is wrong to make children expect toys that their parents cannot afford. The letter offered the alternative of advertising the toys to parents, who of course buy the toys, rather than to children. (See Exercise 16.29 for more details and the text of the sample letter.)[12]

Writing Persuasive Problem-Solving Messages

Generally, you will use an indirect approach and the problem-solving pattern of organization (see Figure 16.3) when you expect resistance from your audience but can show that doing what you want will solve a problem you and your audience share. This pattern allows you to disarm opposition by showing all the reasons in favor of your position before you give your audience a chance to say *no*.

The message in Figure 16.4 uses the problem-solving pattern of organization. Benefits can be brief in this kind of message since the biggest benefit comes from solving the problem.

Figure 16.3   How to Organize a Persuasive Problem-Solving Message

1. **Catch the audience's interest by mentioning a common ground.** Show that your message will be interesting or beneficial. You may want to catch attention with a negative (which you will go on to show can be solved).

2. **Define the problem you both share (which your request will solve).** Present the problem objectively: don't assign blame or mention personalities. Be specific about the cost in money, time, lost goodwill, and so on. You have to convince people that *something* has to be done before you can convince them that your solution is the best one.

3. **Explain the solution to the problem.** If you know that the audience will favor another solution, start with that solution and show why it won't work before you present your solution.

   Present your solution without using the words *I* or *my*. Don't let personalities enter the picture; don't let the audience think they should say *no* just because you've had other requests accepted recently.

4. **Show that any negative elements (cost, time, etc.) are outweighed by the advantages.**

5. **Summarize any additional benefits of the solution.** The main benefit—solving the problem—can be presented briefly since you described the problem in detail. However, if there are any additional benefits, mention them.

6. **Ask for the action you want.** Often your audience will authorize or approve something; other people will implement the action. Give your audience a reason to act promptly, perhaps offering a new benefit. ("By buying now, we can avoid the next quarter's price hikes.")

Figure 16.4 A Problem-Solving Persuasive Message

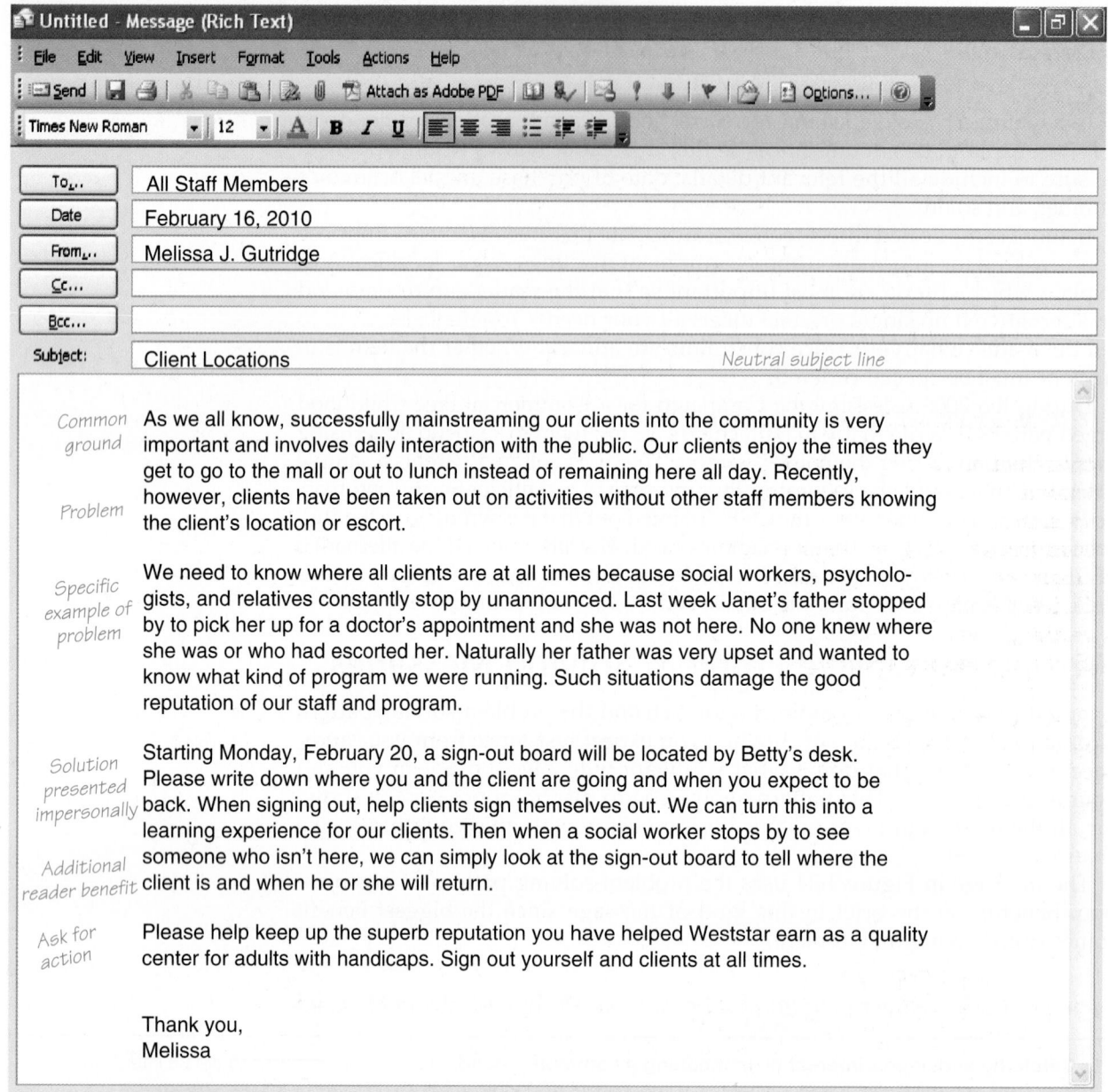

Subject Lines for Problem-Solving Messages

When you have a reluctant audience, putting the request in the subject line just gets a quick *no* before you've had a chance to give all your arguments. One option is to use a neutral subject line. In the following examples, the first is the most neutral. The remaining two increasingly reveal the writer's preference.

Subject: A Proposal to Change the Formula for Calculating Retirees' Benefits

Subject: Arguments for Expanding the Marysville Plant

Subject: Why Cassano's Should Close Its West Side Store

Another option is to use common ground or a benefit—something that shows the audience that this message will help them.

> Subject: Reducing Energy Costs in the Louisville Office
>
> Energy costs in our Louisville office have risen 12% in the last three years, even though the cost of gas has fallen and the cost of electricity has risen only 5%.

Although your first paragraph may be negative in a problem-solving message, your subject line should be neutral or positive.

Developing a Common Ground

A common ground avoids the me-against-you of some persuasive situations and suggests that both you and your audience have a mutual interest in solving the problems you face. To find a common ground, we analyze the audience; understand their biases, objections, and needs; and identify with them to find common goals. This analysis could be carried out in a cold, manipulative way. It should, however, be based on a respect for and sensitivity to the audience's position.

Audiences are highly sensitive to manipulation. No matter how much you disagree with your audience, respect their intelligence. Try to understand why they believe or do something and why they may object to your position. If you can understand your audiences' initial positions, you'll be more effective—and you won't alienate your audience by talking down to them.

The best common grounds are specific. Often a negative—a problem the audience will want to solve—makes a good common ground.

Vague common ground:	This program has had some difficulty finding enough individuals to volunteer their services for the children. As a result, we are sometimes unable to provide the one-on-one mentoring that is our goal.
Improved specific common ground:	On five Sundays in the last three months, we've had too few volunteers to provide one-on-one mentoring. Last Sunday, we had just two college students to take eight children to the Museum of Science and Industry.

Generalizations are likely to bore the audience. Instead, use the idea behind the generalization to focus on something the audience cares about.

Vague common ground:	We all want this plant to be profitable.
Improved specific common ground:	We forfeited a possible $1,860,000 in profits last month due to a 17% drop in productivity.

In your common ground, emphasize the parts of your proposal that fit with what your audience already does or believes. Some HMOs are trying to improve patients' health (and cut the costs of providing care for them) by reaching out to individual patients and persuading them to take medications, get needed tests, and manage chronic conditions. Often, they first have to overcome patients' belief that HMOs want to limit their access to care. They do so by emphasizing the patients' needs and health.

❡ Use audience analysis to evaluate possible common grounds. Suppose you want to install a system to play background music in a factory. To persuade management to pay for the system, a possible common ground would be increasing productivity. However, to persuade the union to pay for the system, you'd need a different common ground. Workers would see productivity

From Full Time to Part Time

Many employees dream about working fewer hours or even cutting back to part-time work. But managers agree that most employees ask their boss the wrong way. Too often employees focus on why *they* want part-time work; managers want to hear about advantages and disadvantages for the company.

You might use these persuasive arguments to convince your employer to let you work fewer hours:

- Demonstrate that you understand and appreciate corporate policies on part-time work.
- Stress that your dedication to your work won't fade when you start working fewer hours.
- Agree to be reached outside the office if your colleagues need you.
- Present a plan detailing how the rest of your work will get done.
- Suggest a trial period to show your plan will work.
- Above all, treat the situation as a persuasive message: develop a common ground with your employer, anticipate objections, and suggest solutions.

Adapted from Erin White, "Build a Case before Asking to Work Less," *Wall Street Journal*, October 24, 2006, B7.

The series of which this letter is a part sells season tickets to the Atlanta Ballet by focusing on the people who work to create the season. Each letter quotes a different member of the company. The opening quote is used on the envelope over a picture of the ballerina and as an opener for the letter. The letters encourage readers to see the artists as individuals, to appreciate their hard work, and to share their excitement about each performance.

Body

The body of the message provides the logical and emotional links that move the audience from their first flicker of interest to the action that is wanted. A good body answers the audience's questions, overcomes their objections, and involves them emotionally.

All this takes space. One of the industry truisms is "The more you tell, the more you sell." Tests show that longer letters bring in more new customers or new donors than do shorter letters. A four-page letter is considered ideal for mailings to new customers or donors.

Can short letters work? Yes, when you're writing to old customers or when the mailing is supported by other media. One study showed that a one-page letter was just as effective as a two-page letter in persuading recent purchasers of a product to buy a service contract.[27] E-mail direct mail is also short—generally just one screen. The Direct Marketing Association says a postcard is the mailing most likely to be read.[28] The shortest message on record may be the two-word postcard that a fishing lake resort sent its customers: "They're biting!"

Content for the body of the message can include

- Information the audience will find useful even if they do not buy or give.
- Stories about how the product was developed or what the organization has done.
- Stories about people who have used the product or who need the organization's help.
- Word pictures of people enjoying the benefits offered.

Because consumers are more likely to choose or favor the familiar, linking your sales message to the things people do or use every day is a good way to increase your message's perceived importance. Of course, that requires that you do a good job of audience analysis up front. Stanford University researchers showed that children given chicken nuggets and French fries preferred the taste of the food in McDonald's packaging, even though all the food came from the same source. The familiarity effect works on adults, too. In another study, adults tasting the same peanut butter from three different jars preferred the spread from the jar with a name brand label.[29]

Costs are generally mentioned near the end of the body and are connected to specific benefits. Sometimes costs are broken down to monthly, weekly, or daily amounts: "For less than the cost of a cup of coffee a day, you can help see that Eren is no longer hungry."

Action Close

The action close in the message must do four things:

1. **Tell the audience what to do:** Specify the action you want. Avoid *if* ("If you'd like to try . . . ") and *why not* ("Why not send in a check?"). They lack positive emphasis and encourage your audience to say *no*.
2. **Make the action sound easy:** "Fill in the information on the reply card and mail it today." If you provide an envelope and pay postage, say so.

3. **Offer a reason for acting promptly.** People who think they are convinced but wait to act are less likely to buy or contribute. Reasons for acting promptly are easy to identify when a product is seasonal or there is a genuine limit on the offer—time limit, price rise scheduled, limited supply, and so on. Sometimes you can offer a premium or a discount if the your audience acts quickly. When these conditions do not exist, remind readers that the sooner they get the product, the sooner they can benefit from it; the sooner they contribute funds, the sooner their dollars can go to work to solve the problem.

4. **End with a positive picture** of the audience enjoying the product (in a sales message) or of the audience's money working to solve the problem (in a fund-raising message). The last sentence should never be a selfish request for money.

The action close can also remind people of central selling points, and mention when the customer will get the product.

Using a P.S.

In a direct mail letter or e-mail, the postscript, or P.S., occupies a position of emphasis by being the final part of the message. Direct mail often uses a deliberate P.S. after the signature block. It may restate the central selling point or some other point the letter makes, preferably in different words so that it won't sound repetitive when the reader reads the letter through from start to finish.

Here are four of the many kinds of effective P.S.'s.

- Reason to act promptly:

> P.S. Once I finish the limited harvest, that's it! I do not store any SpringSweet Onions for late orders. I will ship all orders on a first-come, first-served basis and when they are gone they are gone. Drop your order in the mail today . . . or give me a call toll free at 800-531-7470! (In Texas: 800-292-5437)

Sales letter for Frank Lewis Alamo Fruit

- Description of a premium the reader receives for giving:

> P.S. And . . . we'll be pleased to send you—as a new member—the exquisite, full-color Sierra Club Wilderness Calendar. It's our gift . . . absolutely FREE to you . . . to show our thanks for your membership at this critical time.

Fund-raising letter for Sierra Club

- Reference to another part of the package:

> P.S. Photographs may be better than words, but they still don't do justice to this model. Please keep in mind as you review the enclosed brochure that your SSJ will look even better when you can see it firsthand in your own home.

Sales letter for the Danbury Mint's model of the Duesenberg SSJ

- Restatement of central selling point:

> P.S. It is not easy to be a hungry child in the Third World. If your parents' crops fail or if your parents cannot find work, there are no food stamps . . . no free government-provided cafeteria lunches.
>
> Millions of hungry schoolchildren will be depending on CARE this fall. Your gift today will ensure that we will be there—that CARE won't let them down.

Fund-raising letter for CARE

Provoke Them to Act Promptly

One way to drive sales in a downturn—even when customers might not want to buy—is to show your customers that your products are a solution to a potentially expensive problem. Here's how:

- Lodge your provocation. Begin the meeting by raising a critical issue that the target company is under pressure to resolve, and do so in an original manner. You cannot afford to play it safe. If you aren't clear and passionate about your message, the executive may think you are wasting his or her time.

- Capture reaction to the provocation. If there is no reaction, retreat with dignity. If the reaction is negative, explore it for deeper understanding, seeking common ground. If the reaction is positive, move on.

- Discuss war stories. Describe the experiences of similar companies that either have faced or are facing the problem. Such stories reinforce its importance and demonstrate that you are knowledgeable about it and are bringing a new solution to the table. They also make the executive feel safe in acknowledging that the problem exists in his or her organization.

- Offer to conduct a short diagnostic study.

What kinds of audience might respond well to this approach? What persuasive techniques might you use to augment your message?

Bulleted items quoted from Philip Lay, Todd Hewlin, and Geoffrey Moore, "In a Downturn, Provoke Your Customers," *Harvard Business Review* 87, no. 3 (2009): 54.

Strategy in Sales Messages and Fund-Raising Appeals

In both sales messages and fund-raising appeals, the basic strategy is to help your audience see themselves using your products/services or participating in the goals of your charity. Too often, communicators stress the new features of their gadgets, rather than picturing the audience using it, or the statistics about their cause, rather than stories about people helping that cause.

Sales Messages

The basic strategy in sales messages is satisfying a need. Your message must remind people of the need your product meets, prove that the product will satisfy that need, show why your product is better than similar products, and make people *want* to have the product. Use psychological description (p. 487) to show people how the product will help them. Details about how the product is made can carry the message of quality. Testimonials from other buyers can help persuade people that the product works. In fact, sales trainer and best-seller business author Jeffrey Gitomer cites customer testimonials as one of the best ways to overcome price resistance.[30]

Generally, the price is not mentioned until the last fourth of the message, after the content makes the audience *want* the product.

You can make the price more palatable with the following techniques:

1. **Link the price to the benefit the product provides.** "Your piece of history is just $39.95."

2. **Link the price to benefits your company offers.** "You can reach our customer service agents 24/7."

3. **Show how much the product costs each day, each week, or each month.** "You can have all this for less than the cost of a cup of coffee a day." Make sure that the amount seems small and that you've convinced people that they'll use this product sufficiently.

4. **Allow customers to charge sales or pay in installments.** Your bookkeeping costs will rise, and some sales may be uncollectible, but the total number of sales will increase.

Fund-Raising Appeals

In a fund-raising appeal, the basic emotional strategy is **vicarious participation.** By donating money, people participate vicariously in work they are not able to do personally. This strategy affects the pronouns you use. Throughout the appeal, use *we* to talk about your group. However, at the end, talk about what *you* the audience will be doing. End positively, with a picture of the audience's dollars helping to solve the problem.

Fund-raising appeals require some extra strategy. To achieve both your primary and secondary purposes, you must give a great deal of information. This information (1) helps to persuade people; (2) gives supporters evidence to use in conversations with others; and (3) gives people who are not yet supporters evidence that may make them see the group as worthwhile, even if they do not give money now.

In your close, in addition to asking for money, suggest other ways people can help: doing volunteer work, scheduling a meeting on the subject, writing letters to Congress or the leaders of other countries, and so on. By suggesting other ways to participate, you not only involve your audience but also avoid one of the traps of fund-raising appeals: sounding as though you are interested in your audience only for the money they can give.

Deciding How Much to Ask For

Most messages to new donors suggest a range of amounts, from $50 or $100 (for employed people) up to perhaps double what you *really* expect to get from a single donor. A second strategy is to ask for a small, set amount that nearly everyone can afford ($15 or $25).

One of the several reasons people give for not contributing is that a gift of $25 or $100 seems too small to matter. It's not. Small gifts are important both in themselves and to establish a habit of giving. The American Heart Association recently determined that first-time donors responding to direct mail give an average of $21.84 and give $40.62 over a lifetime. But multiplied by the 7.6 million donors who respond to the AHA's mailings, the total giving is large. Also, over $20 million of the money that the AHA receives from estate settlements after a person's death comes from people who have a relationship as direct-mail donors.[31]

You can increase the size of gifts by using the following techniques:

1. **Link the gift to what it will buy.** Tell how much money it costs to buy a brick, a hymnal, or a stained glass window for a church; a book or journal subscription for a college library; a meal for a hungry child. Linking amounts to specific gifts helps the audience feel involved and often motivates them to give more: instead of saying, "I'll write a check for $25," the person may say, "I'd like to give a _____" and write a check to cover it.

2. **Offer a premium for giving.** Public TV and radio stations have used this ploy with great success, offering books, CDs, DVDs, umbrellas, and carryall bags for gifts at a certain level. The best premiums are things that people both want and will use or display, so that the organization will get further publicity when other people see the premium.

3. **Ask for a monthly pledge.** People on modest budgets could give $15 or $25 a month; more prosperous people could give $100 a month or more. These repeat gifts not only bring in more money than the donors could give in a single check but also become part of the base of loyal supporters, which is essential to the continued success of any organization that raises funds.

Annual appeals to past donors often use the amount of the last donation as the lowest suggested gift, with other gifts 25%, 50%, or even 100% higher.

Always send a thank-you message to people who respond to your appeal, whatever the size of their gifts. By telling about the group's recent work, a thank-you message can help reinforce donors' commitment to your cause.

Logical Proof in Fund-Raising Messages

The body of a fund-raising message must prove that (1) the problem deserves attention, (2) the problem can be solved or at least alleviated, (3) your organization is helping to solve or alleviate it, (4) private funds are needed, and (5) your organization will use the funds wisely.

1. The problem deserves attention. No one can support every cause. Show why your audience should care about solving this problem.

If your problem is life-threatening, give some statistics: Tell how many people are killed in the United States every year by drunk drivers, or how many children in the world go to bed hungry every night. Also tell about one individual who is affected.

If your problem is not life-threatening, show that the problem threatens some goal or principle your audience find important. For example, a fund-raising

Donating to Operating Expenses?

Wouldn't you want to make sure that your charitable donations went to support worthwhile causes, rather than overhead expenses within a nonprofit organization? Many people do, and so look for nonprofits that either limit their spending on overhead or can guarantee that gifts will go toward specific programs, not overhead.

However, even nonprofit organizations have bills to pay. As the *Wall Street Journal* reports, some nonprofits are challenged with the tasks of soliciting donations while convincing donors that money spent on overhead is still money well spent. One solution? Some nonprofits ask for donations specifically to cover their operating expenses by asking for money to support their teams or their business plans.

Philanthropy advisers suggest that donors also consider how effectively the charity uses its money. Some organizations that spend 70% of their funds on their core mission do a better job than those who spend 80%.

The very best way to judge a charity? Be one of their volunteers.

How would asking for a donation to pay for a nonprofit's overhead be different than asking for donations to support a worthy cause? What persuasive strategies could you use to make that request?

Adapted from Rachel Emma Silverman and Sally Beatty, "Save the Children (but Pay the Bills, Too)," *Wall Street Journal*, December 26, 2006, D1, D2.

www.habitat.org

Habitat for Humanity's Web site provides information for potential and current donors, volunteers, and clients.

Enclosures In Fund-Raising Letters

Fund-raising letters sometimes use inexpensive enclosures to add interest and help carry the message.

Brochures are inexpensive, particularly if you photocopy them. Mailings to alumni have included "Why I Teach at Earlham" (featuring three professors) and letters from students who have received scholarships.

Seeds don't cost much. Mailings from both Care and the New Forests Fund include four or five seeds of the leucaena, a subtropical tree that can grow 20 feet in a year. Its leaves feed cattle; its wood provides firewood or building materials; its roots reduce soil erosion. (Indeed, the enclosure easily becomes the theme for the letter.)

Reprints of newspaper or magazine articles about the organization or the problem it is working to solve add interest and credibility. Pictures of people the organization is helping build emotional appeal.

Major campaigns may budget for enclosures: pictures of buildings, CDs of oral history interviews, and maps of areas served.

letter to boosters of a high school swim team showed that team members' chances of setting records were reduced because timers relied on stopwatches. The letter showed that automatic timing equipment was accurate and produced faster times, since the timer's reaction time was no longer included in the time recorded.

2. The problem can be solved or alleviated.   People will not give money if they see the problem as hopeless—why throw money away? Sometimes you can reason by analogy. Cures have been found for other deadly diseases, so it's reasonable to hope that research can find a cure for cancer and AIDS. Sometimes you can show that short-term or partial solutions exist. For example, UNICEF shows how simple changes—oral rehydration, immunization, and breast feeding—could save the lives of millions of children. These solutions don't affect the underlying causes of poverty, but they do keep children alive while we work on long-term solutions.

3. Your organization is helping to solve or alleviate the problem.   Prove that your organization is effective. Be specific. Talk about your successes in the past. Your past success helps readers believe that you can accomplish your goals.

This is one of the specifics the CARE Web site gives about CARE's poverty relief program:

> Poverty is not having access to clean drinking water or adequate sanitation systems. Last year, CARE helped 3 million people in 34 countries gain access to clean water and sanitation, reducing time spent gathering water and illness caused by poor hygiene.[32]

4. Private funds are needed to accomplish your group's goals.   We all have the tendency to think that taxes, or foundations, or church collections yield enough to pay for medical research or basic human aid. If your group does get some tax or foundation money, show why more money is needed. If the organization helps people who might be expected to pay for the service, show why they cannot pay, or why they cannot pay enough to cover the full cost. If some of the funds have been raised by the people who will benefit, make that clear.

5. Your organization will use the funds wisely.   Prove that the money goes to the cause, not just to the cost of fund-raising. This point is becoming increasingly important as stories become more common of "charities" that give little money to their mission. One study of 80 professional fund-raisers serving over 500 charities found the median percentage of proceeds going to the charity was 24%; only five charities received more than 75%. In fact, one fund-raising company charged charities more money than the company raised.[33]

Emotional Appeal in Fund-Raising Messages

Emotional appeal is needed to make people pull out their checkbooks. How strong should emotional appeal be? A mild appeal is unlikely to sway anyone who is not already committed, but your audience will feel manipulated by appeals they find too strong and reject them. Audience analysis may help you decide how much emotional appeal to use. If you don't know your audience well, use the strongest emotional appeal *you* feel comfortable with.

Catalogs are still an excellent way for companies to build customer interest and persuade customers to buy—even if the sales are made at the company's Web site.

The Changing Role of Catalogs

If sales from mass-mailer catalogs have been declining in recent years, replaced by e-commerce sales through web sites, isn't it time to retire paper catalogs? Not necessarily: catalogs are still an excellent way for companies to build customer interest and persuade customers to make purchases—even if those purchases are online.

Catalogs can be an integral part of a company's marketing plan:

- Instead of showing a company's entire stock, a good catalog will save space (and costs!) by listing a representative sampling. The idea is to attract the widest possible range of customers, with the widest possible interests.

- Good catalogs increase customer involvement with the products, either by providing them with a shopping experience "in hand" or by directing them to an interactive web site.

Think about the catalogs that you receive in the mail. How do you use them? What would you need to see in a catalog to convince you to visit its web site or a physical store?

Adapted from Louise Lee, "Catalogs, Catalogs, Everywhere," *Business-Week*, December 4, 2006, 32–34.

Emotional appeal is created by specifics. It is hard to care about, or even to imagine, a million people; it is easier to care about one specific person. Details and quotes help us see that person as real. According to Bobby Dean, director of donor services for Cal Farley's Boys Ranch and Affiliates, the Texas provider of residential care for at-risk youths emphasizes stories about the children it has helped. Its mailings to donors include stories about the children's successes—and sometimes their setbacks, too, which make the stories more realistic. In ongoing correspondence, Cal Farley's brings donors up to date about the progress these now-grown-up people make in their lives. Similarly, in its work for children's hospitals, Newport Creative Communications has found that stories about patients are the most effective appeal in its fund-raising letters. Newport vice president Stephen Power reports that the effectiveness of an appeal was especially critical in the aftermath of the September 2001 terrorist attacks, when donations flowed heavily to the Red Cross and New York City charities, leaving many local nonprofits underfunded.[34]

Sample Fund-Raising Letter

The letter from Run for Congo Women (Figure 16.8), a sample letter for volunteers to use, capitalizes on personal connections. The sender, who will be known to the receiver, shares what she is doing to support the cause and invites her friends both to support her effort and to make their own effort.

The bulleted list calls attention to the problem, the appalling conditions in the DR Congo, which many readers may not know about. It then shows how the organization can help alleviate conditions for some women. The approach is particularly effective because it shows how money raised can lead to sustained improvement.

The letter could be improved by using some standard fund-raising techniques. For instance, it could separate out the desired action for supporting the run from other possible actions, and it could eliminate some of the "I" pronouns in the last four paragraphs. What other improvements would you make to the letter?

Figure 16.8   A Fund-Raising Letter

*Picture serves
to grab interest*

Sample Fundraising Letter

Dear Friend,   *Clichéd opening lacks you-attitude*

I am writing to ask for your help.

Almost no one knows (because the press rarely reports on it) that:

Gripping details

- More than 5,000,000 people have died in DR Congo since 1998 as a result of what has been called "Africa's First World War."
- 45.5% of those deaths have occurred in children under 5.
- Women regularly endure savage gang rapes, torture and mutilation, forced cannibalism, being forced to watch family members brutally murdered, and are held as sex slaves by militias.
- Women who survive have no means of supporting their surviving children, which accounts for the staggering death rate among small children.

This bullet needs parallel structure

An expert recently reported that conditions for women in DR Congo are the worst she has ever seen anywhere. (Reuters. July 30, 2007.)

Reputable support for claims

Yet there are very real, simple things we can do to save lives and help women to regain a foothold for life for themselves and their surviving children. Women for Women International, an award winning non-profit, operates a year long sponsorship program that provides these women with direct cash aid; healing group work with other women who share similar experiences; training in how to operate a small business; literacy training; rights awareness training, and seed money to start a business when they complete the program.

Paragraph shows situation is not hopeless; individuals can take actions that help.

I will be taking part in Run for Congo Women on {date} in {city} to raise awareness about Congo and enough money to sponsor one woman for every mile that I run.

I plan to {run / walk} {5} miles.

Too many first-person pronouns in closing section.

I would love to have your support. If you can do only one thing, please sign up to sponsor a woman for a year. It only costs $27 in monthly payments +$30 initiation fee. Flat donations are welcome if you cannot become a sponsor at this time.

Cost broken down into doable sums.

I will be hosting a gathering at my home to share more about Congo (we need to know about this) and my run on _____ at _____. I hope you will come. Please invite your friends, or consider having a gathering at your home where I could speak. Our simple efforts have a huge impact for women and children in Congo. To a mother who has nothing, sponsorship provides a lifeline by providing her the means to support her children. Please pass on this email to anyone and everyone you think might be interested.

Good emotional appeal in close

Take care,
{Emily}

Writing Style

Direct mail is the one kind of business writing where elegance and beauty of language matter; in every other kind, elegance is welcome but efficiency is all that finally counts. Direct mail imitates the word choice and rhythm of conversation. The best sales, fund-raising, and promotional writing is closer to the language of poetry than to that of academia: it shimmers with images, it echoes with sound, it vibrates with energy.

Many of the things that make writing vivid and entertaining *add* words because they add specifics or evoke an emotional response. Individual sentences should flow smoothly. The passage as a whole may be fun to read precisely because of the details and images that "could have been left out."

1. Make Your Writing Interesting.

If the style is long-winded and boring, the reader will stop reading. Eliminating wordiness is crucial. You've already seen ways to tighten your writing in Chapter 7. Direct mail goes further, breaking some of the rules of grammar. In the following examples, note how sentence fragments and ellipses (spaced dots) are used in parallel structure to move the reader along:

> Dear Member-elect:
>
> If you still believe that there are nine planets in our solar system . . . that wine doesn't breathe . . . and that you'd recognize a Neanderthal man on sight if one sat next to you on the bus . . . check your score. There aren't. It does. You wouldn't.

Subscription letter for *Natural History*

2. Use Psychological Description.

Psychological description (p. 487) means describing your product or service with vivid sensory details. In a sales letter, you can use psychological description to create a scenario so readers can picture themselves using your product or service and enjoying its benefits. You can also use psychological description to describe the problem your product or service will solve.

A *Bon Appétit* subscription letter uses psychological description in its opener and in the P.S., creating a frame for the sales letter:

> Dear Reader:
>
> First, fill a pitcher with ice.
> Now pour in a bottle of ordinary red wine, a quarter cup of brandy, and a small bottle of Club soda.
> Sweeten to taste with a quarter to half cup of sugar, garnish with slices of apple, lemon, and orange. . . .
> . . . then *move your chair to a warm, sunny spot.* You've just made yourself Sangria—one of the great glories of Spain, and the perfect thing to sit back with and sip while you consider this invitation. . . .
>
> . . .
> P.S. One more thing before you finish your Sangria. . . .

It's hard to imagine any reader really stopping to follow the recipe before finishing the letter, but the scenario is so vivid that one can imagine the sunshine even on a cold, gray day.

Humiliation for Debt Collection

Humiliation is becoming a major persuader in Spain, a country with an overwhelmed legal system. Since the courts can't help, many companies believe the only way to collect debt is to shame debtors in front of their neighbors. It is particularly persuasive in this country where one's honor and public image are so important.

Debt collection companies are becoming ingenious in creating humiliation. Collectors arrive at homes dressed as bull fighters, Zorro, Franciscan friars, or even the Pink Panther. The Scottish Collector threatens to send a Scottish bagpipe player to debtors' homes. Sometimes they phone the neighbors.

One collection agency acquired the guest list for a lavish but unpaid wedding reception. They began calling guests and charging them for the food they ate. Needless to say, the debtors paid their bill.

What do you think about this collection method? Do you agree with U.S. law which prohibits it?

Adapted from Thomas Catan, "Spain's Showy Debt Collectors Wear a Tux, Collect the Bucks: Their Goal: Publicly Humiliate Non-Payers; Seeing the Pink Panther at the Door," *Wall Street Journal*, October 11, 2008, A1.

Face-to-face Persuasion

When you present your persuasive messages in a spoken, face-to-face format, remember that your interpersonal interactions are an important part of your message. A recent study of successful retail salespeople identified some strong techniques you can use when you're speaking persuasively:

- Use their name. People respond well when you show that you care enough about them to use their name.

- Show your interest. Build goodwill and rapport by asking about, noticing, and remembering details about your audience's history and preferences.

- Identify mutual interests. Turn your persuasive pitch into a conversation by inviting stories from your audience and sharing your own in return.

- Be polite and honest. Many people react to persuasive messages by being on guard against potential dishonesty. Demonstrate your respect for your audience by backing up your claims with evidence: show them, don't tell them, and invite them to judge for themselves.

- Give—and seek—information. Take the pressure off your persuasive message by changing it into an informative message instead of sales. Build rapport by inviting your audience to share their knowledge with you.

Adapted from Dwayne D. Gremler and Kevin P. Gwinner, "Rapport-Building Behaviors Used by Retail Employees," *Journal of Retailing* 84, no. 3 (2008): 308–24.

3. Make Your Letter Sound Like a Letter, Not an Ad.

Maintain the image of one person writing to one other person that is the foundation of all letters. Use an informal style with short words and sentences, and even slang.

You can also create a **persona**—the character who allegedly writes the letter—to make the letter interesting and keep us reading. Use the rhythms of speech, vivid images, and conversational words to create the effect that the author is a "character."

The following opening creates a persona who fits the product:

Dear Friend:

There's no use trying. I've tried and tried to tell people about my fish. But I wasn't rigged out to be a letter writer, and I can't do it. I can close-haul a sail with the best of them. I know how to pick out the best fish of the catch, I know just which fish will make the tastiest mouthfuls, but I'll never learn the knack of writing a letter that will tell people why my kind of fish—fresh-caught prime-grades, right off the fishing boats with the deep-sea tang still in it—is lots better than the ordinary store kind.

Sales letter, Frank Davis Fish Company

This letter, with its "Aw, shucks, I can't sell" persona, with language designed to make you see an unassuming fisherman ("rigged out," "close-haul"), was written by a professional advertiser.[35]

Solving a Sample Problem

Little things add up to big issues, especially where workplace quality of life is at stake.

Problem

FirstWest Insurance's regional office has 300 employees, all working the same 8-to-5 shift. Many of them schedule their lunch break during the noon hour, and that's where the problem started: there was only one microwave in the canteen. People had to wait up to 30 minutes to heat their lunches. As Director of Human Resources, you implemented lunch shifts to break the gridlock. That program failed: people were used to their schedules and resisted the change. In your second attempt, you convinced FirstWest's Operations Vice President to approve a purchase order for a second microwave oven.

Now there's a new problem: fish. FirstWest recently recruited five new employees. They're from the Philippines, and fish is a prominent part of their diet. Each afternoon, they take lunch together and reheat their meals—often containing fish—and each afternoon, the air conditioning system in your closed-air building sends the aroma of spiced fish wafting through the whole office.

Other employees have complained bitterly about the "foul odor." You've spoken to the new employees, and while they're embarrassed by the complaints, they see no reason to change. After all, they're just as disgusted by the smell of cooking beef: why haven't you asked the American employees not to reheat hamburger? And having just purchased a second oven, you know that management won't pay $1,000 for a new microwave with a filter system that will eliminate the odors. It's time to set a microwave-use policy.

Analysis of the Problem

Use the problem analysis questions in the first chapter to think through the problem.

1. Who is (are) your audience(s)? What characteristics are relevant to this particular message? If you are communicating to more than one audience, how do they differ?

> You'll be addressing all of the employees at this location. That's a broad audience, but they have certain characteristics in common, at least regarding this topic. They're all on a similar lunch schedule, and many of them use the canteen and the microwaves. They've also responded poorly to a previous attempt to change their lunch habits.

2. What are your purposes in writing?

> To help eliminate cooking odors. To solve a minor issue before it begins to impact morale.

3. What information must your message include?

> The effects of the present situation. The available options and their costs (in money, and also in time, effort, and responsibility).

4. How can you build support for your position? What reasons or benefits will your audience find convincing?

> Improving the workplace environment—and eliminating a minor but persistent irritation—should improve morale. While expensive solutions exist, this is a matter that can, and should, be solved with cooperative behaviors.

5. What objection(s) can you expect your audience to have? What negative elements of your message must you de-emphasize or overcome?

> Many members of your audience won't see this as their problem: only the new employees are doing something objectionable. The new employees will react poorly to being singled out.

6. What aspects of the total situation may affect the response? The economy? The time of year? Morale in the organization? The relationship between the reader and the writer? Any special circumstances?

> This issue is a minor one, and it may be difficult to get people to take it seriously. The easy solution—mandating what the new employees are allowed to bring for lunch—is discriminatory. For budgetary reasons, company management will not invest in a third (and much more expensive) microwave for the canteen.

Discussion of the Sample Solutions

The solution shown in Figure 16.9 is unacceptable. By formatting the communication as a notice designed to be posted in the canteen, the author invites the audience to publicly embarrass their co-workers: a form of threat. The subject line displays the author's biases in a way that discourages further discussion on the topic and eliminates the possibility of a broader consensus for any solution to the problem. The author uses emotional appeals to place blame on a small segment of the audience, but the lack of logical observations

The "Default" Choice Is Yes

Have you ever been presented with an online form that had response boxes prechecked for you? One way to sidestep your customers' objections is to provide them with default responses: choices they can make that encourage an easy, objection-free response. Here are some common types of defaults:

- **Benign** default choices give customers a range of responses that you've chosen for them: you present a sample of the best or most likely responses ("Press one for English, para Espanol oprima numero dos").

- **Persistent** default choices use the customer's last response to the same situation as their current response (such as a billing form which assumes that your billing address is the same as your mailing address).

- **Smart** default choices use what you know about past customer behavior to suggest current choices that they're likely to agree with (such as retailer Web sites that offer a list of other products you may be interested in based on what you've selected already).

- **Forced** defaults are selections your customers must make in order to access a product or service (such as the licensing agreement for most software packages).

These defaults offer quick, convenient ways to encourage customers to respond in predictable ways. They can also allow you to constrain your customers' choices. What ethical concerns do you need to consider before you use defaults in your persuasive messages?

Adapted from Daniel G. Goldstein et al., "Nudge Your Customers toward Better Choices," *Harvard Business Review* 86, no. 12 (December 2008): 99–105.

Ethics and Direct Mail

Deception in direct mail is all too easy to find.

Some mailers have sent "checks" to readers. But the "check" can only be applied toward the purchase of the item the letter is selling.

Some mailings now have yellow Post-it notes with "handwritten" notes signed with initials or a first name only—to suggest that the mailing is from a personal friend.

One letter offers a "free" membership "valued at $675" (note the passive—who's doing the valuing?) but charges—up front—$157 for "maintenance fees."

Such deception has no place in well-written direct mail.

Play before You Pay

For video game companies, one of the most persuasive "messages" is the playable demo. Many game developers make trial versions of their games available for download on the Internet, or on trial-version DVDs, so that potential customers can experience the graphics and gameplay first-hand. Downloadable game demos are abridged versions of a full game; they compare to song clips that let consumers sample music before they buy.

These demos generate real sales. According to research conducted by Microsoft through their Xbox Live online service, about 40% of users who download a game demo will play the final version of the game, which they will likely buy.

What other Internet or online services might benefit from the same sales model? How might you convince a skeptical boss to try this kind of promotion?

Adapted from Nick Wingfield, "Downloadable Game Demos Get Test," *Wall Street Journal,* August 23, 2006, B3.

Figure 16.9   An Unacceptable Solution to the Sample Problem

or arguments (and the presence of clip art and emoticons) undermines the author's seriousness. The demand to stop cooking food with strong smells is vague: does this include pizza? popcorn? The author concludes with a threat, again eliminating the possibility of consensus-based actions.

✓ *Checklist*   Checklist for Direct Requests

☐ If the message is a memo, does the subject line indicate the request? Is the subject line specific enough to differentiate this message from others on the same subject?

☐ Does the first paragraph summarize the request or the specific topic of the message?

☐ Does the message give all of the relevant information? Is there enough detail?

☐ Does the message answer questions or overcome objections that readers may have without introducing unnecessary negatives?

☐ Does the closing tell the reader exactly what to do? Does it give a deadline if one exists and a reason for acting promptly?

Originality in a direct request may come from

☐ Good lists and visual impact.

☐ Thinking about readers and giving details that answer their questions, overcome any objections, and make it easier for them to do as you ask.

☐ Adding details that show you're thinking about a specific organization and the specific people in that organization.

Figure 16.10   A Good Solution to the Sample Problem

Date: November 15, 2011

To: FirstWest Grand Harbor Co-Workers

From: Arnold M. Morgan, Human Resources Director *AMM*

Subject: Canteen Microwave Policies   *Neutral subject line*

Creates common ground
We all notice when someone uses the microwaves in the first-floor canteen to reheat strong-smelling food. These odors are distracting—whether they're the scent of burned popcorn, a fish lunch, or fresh-baked brownies—and none of us need any extra distractions in our busy days! Let's work together to "clear the air."

Cause of problem
How is it that we all smell food cooking in the first-floor canteen? Our building has a closed-air ventilation system: it's good for the environment and it saves on heating and cooling costs by recirculating air throughout the building. It also circulates any odors in the air. That's why we can smell food from the first-floor canteen down in the basement archives and up in the third-floor conference rooms: we're all sharing the same air.

We're all sharing the same microwaves, too. Due to popular demand, we recently purchased a second microwave to relieve crowding at lunchtime. We've looked into purchasing a third microwave—an odor-eliminating, air-filtration microwave—but that would cost $1,000, plus $20/month for filters. That seems expensive, especially since there are simple things each of us can do to reduce problems with odors.

Easy solutions to problem
- **Use containers with lids** when you heat up your food. Not only will this help contain any odors, it will reduce the mess in the microwaves.

- **Clean up any mess you make** when you cook. If you cook something with a strong odor—or something that spatters!—take a minute when you're done and wipe the oven down with a damp paper towel.

- **Stay with your food** while it's cooking. When food overcooks or burns, it smells more strongly, so watching your food and removing it from the oven before it overcooks is the easiest way to avoid creating a distracting smell.

We work together as a team every day to serve our customers and succeed as an organization. Please take a little time to use the microwaves responsibly, and help us make sure that the only smell in our workplace is success!

ends on positive note

The second solution, shown in Figure 16.10, is a more effective persuasive message. The author recognizes that this persuasive situation centers on goodwill, and begins with a neutral subject line (as a more directed subject could detract from goodwill). The opening paragraph creates common ground by describing the problem in terms of group experience, rather than by assigning blame. It includes fish odors in with pleasant odors (brownies) and suggests that the memo's purpose is to propose a consensus-based solution.

The problem is spelled out in detail, balancing the emotional, goodwill-centered problem with rational arguments based on process and cost. The solution is presented as small, easily accommodated, changes. The memo ends by linking cooperation with the audience benefit of group participation and identity.

✓ *Checklist* **Checklist for Problem-Solving Persuasive Messages**

- ☐ If the message is a memo, does the subject line indicate the writer's purpose or offer a benefit? Does the subject line avoid making the request?
- ☐ Does the first sentence interest the audience?
- ☐ Is the problem presented as a joint problem both communicator and audience have an interest in solving, rather than as something the audience is being asked to do for the communicator?
- ☐ Does the message give all of the relevant information? Is there enough detail?
- ☐ Does the message overcome objections that the audience may have?
- ☐ Does the message avoid phrases that sound dictatorial, condescending, or arrogant?
- ☐ Does the closing tell the audience exactly what to do? Does it give a deadline if one exists and a reason for acting promptly?

Originality in a problem-solving persuasive message may come from

- ☐ A good subject line and common ground.
- ☐ A clear and convincing description of the problem.
- ☐ Thinking about the audience and giving details that answer their questions, overcome objections, and make it easier for them to do as you ask.
- ☐ Adding details that show you're thinking about a specific organization and the specific people in that organization.

Summary of Key Points

- The primary purpose in a persuasive message is to have the audience act. Secondary purposes are to overcome any objections that might prevent or delay action, to build a good image of the communicator and the communicator's organization, to cement a good relationship between the communicator and audience, and to reduce or eliminate future communication on the same subject.

- **Credibility** is the audience's response to you as the source of the message. You can build credibility by being factual, specific, and reliable.

- Use the persuasive strategy your organization prefers.

- Use the **direct request pattern** when the audience will do as you ask without any resistance. Also use the direct request pattern for busy readers in your own organization who do not read all the messages they receive. See Figure 16.1.

- Use the **problem-solving pattern** when the audience may resist doing what you ask and you expect logic to be more important than emotion in the decision. See Figure 16.3.

- Use the **sales pattern** when the audience may resist doing as you ask and you expect emotion to be more important than logic in the decision. See Figure 16.10.

- Use one or more of the following strategies to counter objections that you cannot eliminate:
  - Specify how much time and/or money is required.

- Put the time and/or money in the context of the benefits they bring.
- Show that money spent now will save money in the long run.
- Show that doing as you ask will benefit some group the audience identifies with or some cause the audience supports.
- Show the audience that the sacrifice is necessary to achieve a larger, more important goal to which they are committed.
- Show that the advantages as a group outnumber or outweigh the disadvantages as a group.
- Turn the disadvantage into an opportunity.

- Threats don't produce permanent change. They won't necessarily produce the action you want, they may make people abandon an action entirely (even in situations where abandoning would not be appropriate), and they produce tension. People dislike and avoid anyone who threatens them. Threats can provoke counteraggression.

- To encourage people to act promptly, set a deadline. Show that the time limit is real, that acting now will save time or money, or that delaying action will cost more.

- Build emotional appeal with stories and psychological description.

- Performance appraisals should cite specific observations, not inferences. They should contain specific suggestions for improvement and identify the two or three areas that the worker should emphasize in the next month or quarter.

- Letters of recommendation must be specific and tell how well and how long you've known the person.

- A good opener makes readers want to read persuasion messages and provides a reasonable transition to the body of the message. Four modes for openers are questions, narration, startling statements, and quotations. A good body answers the audience's questions, overcomes their objections, and involves them emotionally. A good action close tells people what to do, makes the action sound easy, gives them a reason for acting promptly, and ends with a benefit or a picture of their contribution helping to solve the problem.

- In a fund-raising appeal, the basic strategy is vicarious participation. By donating money, people participate vicariously in work they are not able to do personally.

- The primary purpose in a fund-raising appeal is to get money. An important secondary purpose is to build support for the cause so that people who are not persuaded to give will still have favorable attitudes toward the group and will be sympathetic when they hear about it again.

Get Involved

Getting involved with nonprofit work is a great opportunity to give back to your community while developing your professional and communication skills. Here are some online resources to get you started:

- networkforgood.org
- change.org
- dosomething.org
- firstgiving.org
- donorschoose.org
- kiva.org
- opportunity.org
- accion.org

CHAPTER 16   # Exercises and Problems

Go to www.mhhe.com/locker9e for additional Exercises and Problems.

16.1   Reviewing the Chapter

1. What are four questions you should answer when analyzing persuasive situations? Which question do you think is the most important? Why? (LO 1)

2. What are three basic persuasive strategies? In what kinds of situations is each preferred? (LO 2)

3. Why aren't threats effective persuasion tools? (LO 2)

4. How do you start the body of persuasive direct requests? Why? (LO 3)

5. How do you organize persuasive problem-solving messages? (LO 4)

6. How do you develop a common ground with your audience? (LO 4)

7. What are 10 ways to deal with objections? (LO 4 and LO 6)

8. What are ways to build emotional appeal? (LO 4 and LO 6)

9. What are four good beginnings for sales and fund-raising messages? (LO 5)

10. What are ways to de-emphasize costs or donation requests? (LO 5)

11. What kinds of rational evidence should you use to support your persuasion? (LO 6)

12. What kinds of emotional appeals should you use to support your persuasion? (LO 6)

16.2   Reviewing Grammar

Persuasion uses lots of pronouns. Correct the sentences in Exercise B.4, Appendix B, to practice making pronouns agree with their nouns, as well as practicing subject–verb agreement.

16.3   Writing Psychological Description

For one or more of the following groups, write two or three paragraphs of psychological description that could be used in a brochure, news release, or direct mail message directed to members of that group.

1. Having a personal trainer.

    Audiences: Professional athletes.
    Busy managers.
    Someone trying to lose weight.
    Someone making a major lifestyle change after a heart attack.

2. Volunteering time to a local charity event (you pick the charity) as part of a team from your workplace.

    Audiences: Your workplace colleagues
    Your boss
    Finance department
    PR department

3. Using vending machines newly installed in school cafeterias and stocked with healthful snacks, such as yogurt, raisins, carrots with dip, and all-natural juices.

    Audiences: High school students
    Parents
    High school faculty

4. Attending a fantasy sports camp (you pick the sport), playing with and against retired players who provide coaching and advice.

5. Attending a health spa where clients get low-fat and low-carb meals, massages, beauty treatments, and guidance in nutrition and exercise.

Hints:

- For this assignment, you can combine benefits or programs as if a single source offered them all.
- Add specific details about particular sports, activities, and so on, as material for your description.
- Be sure to use vivid details and sense impressions.
- Phrase your benefits with you-attitude.

16.4   Evaluating Subject Lines

Evaluate the following subject lines. Is one subject line in each group clearly best? Or does the "best" line depend on company culture, whether the message is a paper memo or an e-mail message, or on some other factor?

1. Subject: Request
    Subject: Why I Need a New Computer
    Subject: Increasing My Productivity

2. Subject: Who Wants Extra Hours?
    Subject: Holiday Work Schedule
    Subject: Working Extra Hours During the Holiday Season

3. Subject: Student Mentors
    Subject: Can You Be an E-Mail Mentor?
    Subject: Volunteers Needed

4. Subject: More Wine and Cheese
    Subject: Today's Reception for Japanese Visitors
    Subject: Reminder

5. Subject: Reducing Absenteeism
    Subject: Opening a Day Care Center for Sick Children of Employees
    Subject: Why We Need Expanded Day Care Facilities

16.5   Evaluating P.S.'s

Evaluate the following P.S.'s. Will they motivate readers to read the whole messages if readers turn to them first? Do they create a strong ending for those who have already read the message?

1. P.S. It only takes <u>one</u> night's stay in a hotel you read about here, <u>one</u> discounted flight, <u>one</u> budget-priced cruise, or <u>one</u> low-cost car rental to make mailing back your Subscription Certificate well worth it.

An Open Letter to <u>All</u> Airline Customers:

Our country is facing a possible sharp economic downturn because of skyrocketing oil and fuel prices, but by pulling together, we can all do something to help now.

For airlines, ultra-expensive fuel means thousands of lost jobs and severe reductions in air service to both large and small communities. To the broader economy, oil prices mean slower activity and widespread economic pain. This pain can be alleviated, and that is why we are taking the extraordinary step of writing this joint letter to our customers.

Since high oil prices are partly a response to normal market forces, the nation needs to focus on increased energy supplies and conservation. However, there is another side to this story because normal market forces are being dangerously amplified by poorly regulated market speculation.

Twenty years ago, 21 percent of oil contracts were purchased by speculators who trade oil on paper with no intention of ever taking delivery. Today, oil speculators purchase 66 percent of all oil futures contracts, and that reflects just the transactions that are known. Speculators buy up large amounts of oil and then sell it to each other again and again. A barrel of oil may trade 20-plus times before it is delivered and used; the price goes up with each trade and consumers pick up the final tab. Some market experts estimate that current prices reflect as much as $30 to $60 per barrel in unnecessary speculative costs.

Over seventy years ago, Congress established regulations to control excessive, largely unchecked market speculation and manipulation. However, over the past two decades, these regulatory limits have been weakened or removed. We believe that restoring and enforcing these limits, along with several other modest measures, will provide more disclosure, transparency and sound market oversight. Together, these reforms will help cool the over-heated oil market and permit the economy to prosper.

The nation needs to pull together to reform the oil markets and solve this growing problem.

We need your help. Get more information and contact Congress by visiting www.StopOilSpeculationNow.com.

Robert Fornaro
Chairman, President and CEO
AirTran Airways

Bill Ayer
Chairman, President and CEO
Alaska Airlines, Inc.

Gerard J. Arpey
Chairman, President and CEO
American Airlines, Inc.

Lawrence W. Kellner
Chairman and CEO
Continental Airlines, Inc.

Richard Anderson
CEO
Delta Airlines, Inc.

Mark B. Dunkerley
President and CEO
Hawaiian Airlines, Inc.

Dave Barger
CEO
JetBlue Airways Corporation

Timothy E. Hoeksema
Chairman, President and CEO
Midwest Airlines

Douglas M. Steenland
President and CEO
Northwest Airlines, Inc.

Gary Kelly
Chairman and CEO
Southwest Airlines Co.

Glenn F. Tilton
Chairman, President and CEO
United Airlines, Inc.

Douglas Parker
Chairman and CEO
US Airways Group, Inc.

S.O.S. NOW
www.StopOilSpeculationNow.com

4. What common ground does it use?
5. What emotional appeals does it use?
6. How does the letter deal with objections?
7. Does the letter convince you to contact Congress? Why or why not?
8. How could the letter be improved?

As your instructor directs,

a. As a group, share your analysis with the class in a five-minute presentation.

b. As an individual, write a detailed analysis of the letter for your instructor.

Source: An Open Letter to All Airline Customers from www.StopOilSpeculationNow.com.

16.12 Asking for More Time and/or Resources

Today, this message from your boss shows up in your e-mail inbox:

> Subject: Want Climate Report
>
> This request has come down from the CEO. I'm delegating it to you. See me a couple of days before the board meeting—the 4th of next month—so we can go over your presentation.
>
> I want a report on the climate for underrepresented groups in our organization. A presentation at the last board of directors' meeting showed that while we do a good job of hiring women and minorities, few of them rise to the top. The directors suspect that our climate may not be supportive and want information on it. Please prepare a presentation for the next meeting. You'll have 15 minutes.

Making a presentation to the company's board of directors can really help your career. But preparing a good presentation and report will take time. You can look at exit reports filed by Human Resources when people leave the company, but you'll also need to interview people—lots of people. And you're already working 60 hours a week on three major projects, one of which is behind schedule. Can one of the projects wait? Can someone else take one of the projects? Can you get some help? Should you do just enough to get by? Ask your boss for advice—in a way that makes you look like a committed employee, not a shirker.

16.13 Persuading Employees Not to Share Files

Your computer network has been experiencing slowdowns, and an investigation has uncovered the reason. A number of employees have been using the system to download and share songs and vacation photos. You are concerned because the bulky files clog the network, and downloading files opens the network to computer viruses and worms. In addition, management does not want employees to spend work time and resources on personal matters. Finally, free downloads of songs are often illegal, and management is worried that a recording firm might sue the company for failing to prevent employees from violating its copyrights.

As Director of Management Information Systems (MIS), you want to persuade employees to stop sharing files unrelated to work. You are launching a policy of regularly scanning the system for violations, but you prefer that employees voluntarily use the system properly. Violations are hard to detect, and increasing scanning in an effort to achieve system security is likely to cause resentment as an intrusion into employees' privacy.

Write an e-mail message to all employees, urging them to refrain from downloading and sharing personal files.

16.14 Not Doing What the Boss Asked

Today, you get this e-mail message:

> To: All Unit Managers
>
> Subject: Cutting Costs
>
> Please submit five ideas for cutting costs in your unit. I will choose the best ideas and implement them immediately.

You think your boss's strategy is wrong. Cutting costs will be easier if people buy into the decision rather than being handed orders. Instead of gathering ideas by e-mail, the boss should call a meeting so that people can brainstorm, teaching each other why specific strategies will or won't be easy for their units to implement.

Reply to your boss's e-mail request. Instead of suggesting specific ways to cut costs, persuade the boss to have a meeting where everyone can have input and be part of the decision.

16.15   Convincing a Member to Become Active Again

In every organization, one of the ongoing problems is convincing inactive members to become active again. Sometimes members become inactive because of short-term pressures. Sometimes they are offended by something the organization has done or not done. Sometimes they fall through the cracks and are not included in events. Whatever the reason, once they've become less active, it's psychologically easy for them to drop out entirely. Persuading these members to become active again is important. Because they once supported the organization, it may be easier to persuade them than to seek new members. And if they remain disenchanted with the organization, they may convince other people that the organization has little to offer.

As your instructor directs,

a.   Write to someone you know well, urging him or her to become active in the organization again.

b.   Write notes for a phone conversation or meeting with your friend.

c.   Join with a small group of students to write a form letter to go to inactive members in an organization.

d.   Write a memo to your instructor explaining your audience analysis and your choice of strategy and appeals.

Hints:

- Pick a campus, professional, civic, social, or religious organization you know well.
- Be specific about what the organization is doing now, how readers can benefit from it, and why the organization needs them.
- If your audience objects to specific things the organization has done or not done, respond to these concerns in your message. Did a misunderstanding occur? Is change already under way? Is change possible if enough people (like your audience, perhaps) work for it?
- What are your audience's priorities? Can you show that this organization will help your audience meet its needs?

16.16   Handling a Sticky Recommendation

As a supervisor in a state agency, you have a dilemma. You received this e-mail message today:

From: John Inoye, Director of Personnel, Department of Taxation

Subject: Need Recommendation for Peggy Chafez

Peggy Chafez has applied for a position in the Department of Taxation. On the basis of her application and interview, she is the leading candidate. However, before I offer the job to her, I need a letter of recommendation from her current supervisor.

Could you please let me have your evaluation within a week? We want to fill the position as quickly as possible.

Peggy has worked in your office for 10 years. She designed, writes, and edits a monthly statewide newsletter that your office puts out; she designed and maintains the department Web site. Her designs are creative; she's a very hard worker; she seems to know a lot about computers.

However, Peggy is in many ways an unsatisfactory staff member. Her standards are so high that most people find her intimidating. Some find her abrasive. People have complained to you that she's only interested in her own work; she seems to resent requests to help other people with projects. And yet both the newsletter and the Web page are projects that need frequent interaction. She's out of the office a lot. Some of that is required by her job (she takes the newsletters to the post office, for example), but some people don't like the fact that she's out of the office so much. They also complain that she doesn't return voice-mail and e-mail messages.

You think managing your office would be a lot smoother if Peggy weren't there. You can't fire her: state employees' jobs are secure once they get past the initial six-month probationary period. Because of budget constraints, you can hire new employees only if vacancies are created by resignations. You feel that it would be pretty easy to find someone better.

If you recommend that John Inoye hire Peggy, you will be able to hire someone you want. If you recommend that John hire someone else, you may be stuck with Peggy for a long time.

As your instructor directs,

a.   Write an e-mail message to John Inoye.

b.   Write a memo to your instructor listing the choices you've made and justifying your approach.

Hints:

- Polarization may make this dilemma more difficult than it needs to be. What are your options? Consciously look for more than two.
- Is it possible to select facts or to use connotations so that you are truthful but still encourage John

to hire Peggy? Is it ethical? Is it certain that John would find Peggy's work as unsatisfactory as you do? If you write a strong recommendation and Peggy doesn't do well at the new job, will your credibility suffer? Why is your credibility important?

16.17   Persuading Tenants to Follow the Rules

As resident manager of a large apartment complex, you receive free rent in return for collecting rents, doing simple maintenance, and enforcing the complex's rules. You find the following notice in the files:

> Some of you are failing to keep any kind of standard of sanitation code, resulting in the unnecessary cost on our part to hire exterminators to rid the building of roaches.
>
> Our leases state breach of contract in the event that you are not observing your responsibility to keep your apartment clean.
>
> We are in the process of making arrangements for an extermination company to rid those apartments that are experiencing problems. Get in touch with the manager no later than 10 PM Monday to make arrangements for your apartment to be sprayed. It is a fast, odorless operation. You are also required to put your garbage in plastic bags. Do not put loose garbage or garbage in paper bags in the dumpster, as this leads to rodent or roach problems.
>
> Should we in the course of providing extermination service to the building find that your apartment is a source of roaches, then you will be held liable for the cost incurred to rid your apartment of them.

The message is horrible. The notice lacks you-attitude, and it seems to threaten anyone who asks to have his or her apartment sprayed.

The annual spraying scheduled for your complex is coming up. Under the lease, you have the right to enter apartments once a year to spray. However, for spraying to be fully effective, residents must empty the cabinets, remove kitchen drawers, and put all food in the refrigerator. People and pets need to leave the apartment for about 15 minutes while the exterminator sprays.

Tell residents about the spraying. Persuade them to prepare their apartments to get the most benefit from it,

and persuade them to dispose of food waste quickly and properly so that the bugs don't come back.

Hints:

- What objections may people have to having their apartments sprayed for bugs?
- Why don't people already take garbage out promptly and wrap it in plastic? How can you persuade them to change their behavior?
- Analyze your audience. Are most tenants students, working people, or retirees? What tone would be most effective for this group?

16.18   Evaluating the Persuasion on Social Networking Sites

Some companies, nonprofit organizations, and government agencies use public community sites such as MySpace.com, Facebook.com, and YouTube.com as advertising venues. In addition to purchasing traditional ads, they create and maintain "personal" profiles, media, and other resources designed to market to the people who use those sites.

As your instructor directs,

a.   Log on to MySpace.com, Facebook.com, or YouTube.com and locate an example of this type of

advertising. Evaluate the persuasive strategies that the advertisements employ. Then compose an e-mail to the organization that's maintaining the ad and suggest improvements to their message. Be sure to identify any ethical challenges you see in their message, and recommend ways for them to improve.

b.   Write a memo to your instructor describing the process you used to make your recommendations. Be sure to describe and evaluate the response you receive to your e-mail.

Hints:

- You can find this type of marketing on MySpace or YouTube by searching for profiles, blogs, channels, and other media that reference current films, advertising campaigns, or political campaigns.
- Who is the target audience for the ad? Write to the people who have listed this ad as "friends" or who have left comments on it. Collect their opinions to provide data for your evaluations, and to provide evidence for your recommendations.
- Examine other persuasive messages linked to the ads you find. For example, if you find a MySpace page for a character from a movie, look up the official movie site, the trailer, and advertising related to the film.

16.19 Asking an Instructor for a Letter of Recommendation

You're ready for the job market, transfer to a four-year college, or graduate school, and you need letters of recommendation.

As your instructor directs,

a. Assume that you've orally asked an instructor for a recommendation, and he or she has agreed to write one. "Why don't you write up something to remind me of what you've done in the class? Tell me what else you've done, too. And tell me what they're looking for. Be sure to tell me when the letter needs to be in and to whom it goes."

b. Assume that you've been unable to talk with the instructor whose recommendation you want. When you call, no one answers the phone; you stopped by once and no one was in. Write asking for a letter of recommendation.

c. Assume that the instructor is no longer on campus. Write him or her a letter asking for a recommendation.

Hints:

- Be detailed about what the organization is seeking and the points you'd like the instructor to mention.
- How well will this instructor remember you? How much detail about your performance in his or her class do you need to provide?
- Specify the name and address of the person to whom the letter should be written; specify when the letter is due. If there's an intermediate due date (for example, if you must sign the outside of the envelope to submit the recommendation to law school), say so.

16.20 Writing a Performance Appraisal for a Member of a Collaborative Group

During your collaborative writing group meetings, keep a log of events. Record specific observations of both effective and ineffective things that group members do. Then evaluate the performance of the other members of your group. (If there are two or more other people, write a separate appraisal for each of them.)

In your first paragraph, summarize your evaluation. Then in the body of your memo, give the specific details that led to your evaluation by answering the following questions:

- What specifically did the person do in terms of the task? Brainstorm ideas? Analyze the information? Draft the text? Suggest revisions in parts drafted by others? Format the document or create visuals? Revise? Edit? Proofread? (In most cases, several people will have done each of these activities together. Don't overstate what any one person did.) What was the quality of the person's work?
- What did the person contribute to the group process? Did he or she help schedule the work? Raise or resolve conflicts? Make other group members feel valued and included? Promote group cohesion? What roles did the person play in the group?

Support your generalizations with specific observations. The more observations you have and the more detailed they are, the better your appraisal will be.

As your instructor directs,

a. Write a midterm performance appraisal for one or more members of your collaborative group. In each appraisal, identify the two or three things the person should try to improve during the second half of the term.

b. Write a performance appraisal for one or more members of your collaborative group at the end of the term. Identify and justify the grade you think each person should receive for the portion of the grade based on group process.

c. Give a copy of your appraisal to the person about whom it is written.

16.21 Evaluating Sales and Fund-Raising Messages

Collect the sales and fund-raising messages that come to you, your co-workers, landlord, neighbors, or family. Use the following questions to evaluate each package:

- What mode does the opener use? Is it related to the rest of the message? How good is the opener?
- What central selling point or common ground does the message use?
- What kinds of proof does the message use? Is the logic valid? What questions or objections are not answered?

- How does the message create emotional appeal?
- Is the style effective?
- Does the close tell people what to do, make action easy, give a reason for acting promptly, and end with a positive picture?
- Does the message use a P.S.? How good is it?
- Is the message visually attractive? Why or why not?
- What other items besides the letter or e-mail are in the package?

As your instructor directs,

a. Share your analysis of one or more messages with a small group of your classmates.

b. Analyze one message in a presentation to the class. Make a copy of the message to use as a visual aid in your presentation.

c. Analyze one message in a memo to your instructor. Provide a copy of the message along with your memo.

d. With several other students, write a group memo or report analyzing one part of the message (e.g., openers) or one kind of letter (e.g., political messages, organizations fighting hunger, etc.). Use at least 10 messages for your analysis if you look at only one part; use at least 6 messages if you analyze one kind of message. Provide copies as an appendix to your report.

16.22   Writing a Fund-Raising Appeal

Write a 2½- to 4-page letter to raise money from *new donors* for an organization you support. You must use a real organization, but it does not actually have to be conducting a fund-raising drive now. Assume that your letter would have a reply card and postage-paid envelope. You do NOT have to write these, but DO refer to them in your letter.

  Options for organizations include

- Tax-deductible charitable organizations—religious organizations; hospitals; groups working to feed, clothe, and house poor people.
- Lobbying groups—Mothers Against Drunk Driving, the National Abortion Rights Action League, the National Rifle Association, groups working against nuclear weapons, etc.
- Groups raising money to fight a disease or fund research.
- Colleges trying to raise money for endowments, buildings, scholarships, faculty salaries.

  For this assignment, you may also use groups which do not regularly have fund-raising drives but which may have special needs. Perhaps a school needs new uniforms for its band. Perhaps a sorority or fraternity house needs repairs, remodeling, or expansion.

16.23   Combining Charitable Giving with Marketing

When Crate & Barrel, the upscale furniture retailer, set out to support education with donations, they didn't just give money to needy schools. Instead, they sent out coupons in their mailers, inviting their customers to use www.DonorsChoose.org to decide how and where Crate & Barrel would donate its money. Their customers responded enthusiastically to the program—and to Crate & Barrel.

  Write a letter to a local business or organization recommending a similar program that combines charitable giving with a marketing opportunity. Detail the benefits to the organization, the benefits to the organization(s) receiving funds, and the process(es) by which they could ensure their customers' involvement.

Hints:

- Talk to a representative from the business you're targeting to find out what types of charitable giving they currently support.

- Look at targetable donation sites such as www.DonorsChoose.org, www.Kiva.org, www.ModestNeeds.org, and www.GlobalGiving.org for ideas about the types of charitable projects that your proposed program might fund.
- It might be easier to persuade businesses to support causes close to home. So, ask locally: many charities and nonprofits maintain lists to those Web sites of worthwhile causes in your local community.

This exercise based on Emily Steel, "Novel Program Blends Charity and Marketing," *Wall Street Journal,* December 20, 2006, B1, B5.

16.24   Planning a Game or Contest

Many companies are using games and contests to solve problems in an enjoyable way. One company promised to give everyone $30 a month extra if they got the error rate below 0.5%. The rate improved immediately. After several successful months, the incentive went to $40 a month for getting it under 0.3% and finally to $50 a month for getting it under 0.2%. Another company offered workers two "well hours" if they got in by 7 AM every day for a month. An accounting and financial-services company divided its employees into two teams. The one that got the most referrals and new accounts received a meal prepared and served by the losing team (the firm paid for the food). Games are best when the people who will play them create them. Games need to make business sense and give rewards to many people, not just a few. Rewards should be small.

Think of a game or contest that could improve productivity or quality in your classroom, on campus, or in a workplace you know well.

As your instructor directs,

a.   Write a message to persuade your instructor, boss, or other decision maker to authorize the game or contest.

b.   Write a message announcing the game or contest and persuading people to participate in it.

Source: Based on John Case, *The Open-Book Experience: Lessons from Over 100 Companies Who Successfully Transformed Themselves* (Reading, MA: Addison-Wesley, 1998), 129–201.

16.25   Asking to Telecommute

You need to relocate to another city, where the company you work for does not have a branch office. You would prefer to remain working at this company, so telecommuting would be an ideal situation. Write a proposal in memo format to persuade your employer to allow you to work from a remote location.

Hints:

• Establish common ground: you want to stay, and many firms would rather allow an employee to telecommute than risk losing a valued team member.

• Point out potential benefits to your employer: you may save the company money on office resources, extend their usual business hours, or provide customer service to a remote location.

• Provide for oversight: outline a framework for evaluating your performance and participating on team projects, and perhaps offer a trial period.

Adapted from Sue Shellenbarger, "Work & Family Mailbox," *Wall Street Journal*, February 14, 2008, D2.

16.26   Calling in a Favor

Last month, your co-worker Mike asked you for a favor: he needed to take an afternoon off to look after one of his children, but he didn't have any vacation or leave time left. Your supervisor had authorized him to take the time off as long as he could get someone else to cover his client meetings for him. You agreed, and spent the day covering for him.

Now you're in the same position: you need to take a morning off, and your supervisor wants you to convince someone to cover for you. You'll be missing a conference call with a client that cannot be rescheduled, and which will take an hour. Mike is the obvious choice—he knows the client, and he owes you a favor—but you know that he's very busy and might object to taking on more work. Write a short memo or e-mail to Mike asking him to return the favor and cover for you.

Hints:

• Your informal relationship with Mike allows you to exchange favors. It also means that you can use more informal language and tone in your e-mail. (Not too informal, though: any e-mail can be forwarded.)

• Be sure to build common ground and goodwill as part of your opening.

• Mike may object to taking on more work. What other objections might he raise? Be sure to address those objections in your e-mail.

Adapted from Jared Sandberg, "People Can't Resist Doing a Big Favor—Or Asking for One," *Wall Street Journal*, December 18, 2007, B1.

16.27   Creating a Healthy Snackfood Alley

You work in a friendly environment where people like to bring in treats to share with their co-workers. They

do it so often that there's an area in your workplace that people jokingly call "Snackfood Alley," lined with donuts, candy, chips, pretzels, soda, and other not-too-healthy fare.

Write a memo, suitable for distributing to a wide audience at your workplace, to convince your co-workers to make the switch to healthy snacks. Build common ground, offset any negatives with benefits, and provide concrete suggestions for future actions. Be sure to build

and maintain goodwill: people contribute to Snackfood Alley to be friendly, and may interpret your request as a complaint.

Adapted from Nanci Bompey, "Employees Follow Crumbs toward Healthful Choices," *Des Moines Register,* March 17, 2008, 2D.

16.28   Recostuming Happy Halloween

Your team has been put in charge of organizing your company's Halloween event. Employees may come to work dressed in a costume. During the lunch hour, you'll hold a costume contest with prizes for the most original costumes (and a prize for the department or team with the highest rate of participation), followed by a party for your staff members. Last year's party was a big hit: about 30% of your employees dressed up, and you anticipate that the number will be higher this year.

However, last year there were a number of (moderately) racy and (somewhat) tasteless costumes, and some complaints about those costumes. The team who organized last year's Halloween ignored those complaints "because we're all adults here, and we can all take a joke." Well, this year, we *won't* all be adults: your company is also sponsoring a trick-or-treat event for kids from 10 local foster homes. Immediately following the costume contest and lunch, there will be dozens of (supervised) kids, ages 2–8, going office-to-office for candy. Your Human Resources department has provided

the candy and treats, but it's up to you to make sure that the costume contest is kid-friendly.

As your instructor directs:

- Write a memo, suitable for distributing to all staff, which establishes guidelines for participating in the costume contest and persuades your co-workers to comply.

- Create a sign, suitable for posting in the common areas of your workplace, that establishes your costume guidelines and invites your co-workers to participate in the event.

Hints:

- Adults are more likely to comply with a policy decision when they understand the rationale behind that decision. Be sure to communicate your decision process as well as your guidelines.

- Choose a persuasive message format, create common ground and goodwill, and use creativity in both your language and your visual design.

16.29   Campaigning against Holiday Toy Ads

Discussions on pages 479 and 488 outlined the campaign of CCFC (Campaign for a Commercial-Free Childhood) against holiday toy ads directed at children.

This is the sample letter to toy manufacturers from parents suggested by CCFC:

I am writing to urge you to suspend all advertising to children this holiday season. With the global economic crisis intensifying, many families will have to scale back their holiday shopping this year. It's wrong to create unrealistic expectations in children or to foment family stress by encouraging kids to lobby for gifts that their parents may not be able to afford.

I understand the need to create awareness of your products. I urge you to do that by advertising directly to parents instead of enlisting children as lobbyists for their holiday gifts. Since it's parents, not children, who can truly understand their family's financial situation in these difficult times, it is more important than ever that you respect their authority as gatekeepers. Please target parents instead of children with your holiday advertising.

Source: Judge Baker Children's Center and Campaign for a Commercial-Free Childhood, "Tell Toy Companies: Target Parents, Not Kids, with Holiday Ads," in *CCFC Guide to Commercial-Free Holidays,* http://salsa.democracyinaction.org/o/621/t/6914/campaign.jsp?campaign_KEY=26139 (accessed April 5, 2009). Reprinted with permission of Judge Baker Children's Center, Boston, MA.

This is the letter to toy manufacturers from the CCFC:

Campaign for a Commercial-Free Childhood
c/o Judge Baker Children's Center
53 Parker Hill Avenue, Boston, MA 02120-3225
Phone: 617-278-4172• Fax: 617-232-7343
Email: CCFC@JBCC.Harvard.edu
Website: www.commercialfreechildhood.org

PLEASE NOTE: This letter was sent to 24 companies, not just Mattel. A complete list can be found at: www.commercialfreechildhood.org/actions/holidaymarketers.htm

October 27, 2008

CCFC
STEERING COMMITTEE:

Enola Aird, JD

Kathy Bowman, EdS

Nancy Carlsson-Paige, EdD

Allen Kanner, PhD

Tim Kasser, PhD

Joe Kelly

Velma LaPoint, PhD

Diane Levin, PhD

Karen Lewis

Alex Molnar, PhD

Alvin F. Poussaint, MD

Michele Simon, JD, MPH

Mr. Robert Eckert
Chief Executive Officer, Mattel
333 Continental Boulevard
El Segundo, CA 90245

Dear Mr. Eckert:

As families struggle to cope with the global economic crisis, we are writing to urge you to suspend all holiday marketing aimed at children. With fears of a recession or even a depression intensifying, Americans routinely list the economy as their number one concern. There is little doubt that many parents will have to scale back their holiday purchases significantly and experts predict that parents will spend less money on toys and gifts for children this holiday season. [1] Under normal circumstances it is unfair to bypass parents and target children directly with marketing, but with an uncertain future and budgets tighter than ever, it is particularly egregious to foment family conflict by advertising toys and games directly to kids that their parents may not be able to afford.

Research demonstrates that children's exposure to advertising is linked to the things they ask their parents to buy and family stress. [2] Using advertising to encourage children to nag for products may be good for sales, but it creates considerable family conflict. Even in normal times, buying holiday gifts causes financial strain for many families. A 2005 poll found that approximately one-third of Americans took more than three months to pay off their holiday credit card debt and 14% carried credit card debt into the next holiday season. [3]

Early reports indicate that spending on advertising to children will not reflect the current economic downturn. To date, spending forecasts for forth quarter television advertising on children's television have not been affected. [4] If parents are cutting their purchases back this holiday season while commercial pressures on children remain at record levels, the burden on families will be tremendous.

As you know, children are more vulnerable to advertising than adults. Seductive advertising designed explicitly to exploit their vulnerabilities will create unrealistic expectations in kids too young to understand the economic crises and will make parenting in these uncertain times even more difficult. **We understand the need to create awareness of your products. We urge you to do that by advertising directly to parents instead of enlisting children as lobbyists for their holiday gifts.** Since it's parents, not children, who can truly understand their family's financial situation in these difficult times, it is more important than ever that you respect their authority as gatekeepers: Target parents instead of children this holiday season.

Please note that we are sending this letter to CEO's of all the leading toy and game manufacturers and will be happy to offer public praise for any company that puts America's families first by suspending their holiday advertising to children. We would also welcome the opportunity to discuss this matter with you further.

Sincerely,

Susan Linn, Ed.D.

---

[1] Anderson, M. (2008, Oct 8). Holiday spending on toys expected to be less. *The Associated Press.* Accessed October 17, 2008 from http://www.thenewstribune.com/1031/v-lite/story/502479.html.
[2] Buijen, M. & Valkenburg (2003). The effects of television advertising on materialism, parent–child conflict, and unhappiness: A review of research. *Applied Developmental Psychology*, 24, 437–456.
[3] Center for a New American Dream (2005). Hot Holiday Gift for Kids This Year? — A Piggy Bank, Say Fed Up Americans. Accessed October 17, 2008 from http://www.newdream.org/holiday/poll05.php.
[4] Freidman, W. (2008, Oct 13). So Far, Kids' TV Saved from Ad Hits. *MediaPost's Media Daily News.* Accessed October 17, 2008 from http://www.mediapost.com/publications/?fa=Articles.showArticle&art_aid=92573.

Source: Susan Linn and Alvin Poussaint, "Campaign for a Commercial-Free Childhood," in *Judge Baker Children's Center,* http://www.commercialfreechildhood.org/actions/lettertoceo.pdf (accessed April 5, 2009). Reprinted with permission of Judge Baker Children's Center, Boston, MA.

This is the response from the TIA (Toy Industry Association):

Toy Industry Association's Statement

The Toy Industry Association notes with interest, but begs to disagree with, the Campaign for a Commercial-Free Childhood's suggestion that marketing of toys be focused this year on parents and not on children.

We believe parents should know what their children want and are perfectly capable of deciding, as they have always done, how to fit satisfaction of those desires into the family budget. Children are a vital part of the gift selection process and should not be removed from it.

We offer several thoughts to guide families through the gift buying process:

- Children have their own ideas about what appeals to them and parents are not necessarily going to know, without their children's input, if a new toy is going to excite them. We have faith in parents' ability to hear from their children what they would like and then make a decision as to what, and how much, to give them.
- In fact, most parents and grandparents appreciate knowing which items are on their child's wish lists before they go out to purchase a gift for them, as it makes shopping easier. If children are not aware of what is new and available, how will they be able to tell their families what their preferences are?
- Parents do a pretty good job of budgeting and making purchase decisions. While there is certainly greater economic disturbance going on now, families have always faced different levels of economic well-being and have managed to tailor their spending to their means.

Toy Industry Association, Inc.

Source: Judge Baker Children's Center and Campaign for a Commercial-Free Childhood, "Toy Industry Responds to CCFC Members," in *CCFC Guide to Commercial-Free Holidays,* http://www.commercialfreechildhood.org/actions/holidaymarketersrespond.htm (accessed April 7, 2009). Reprinted with permission of Judge Baker Children's Center, Boston, MA.

This is the statement on the Web site of the TIA:

TIA Statement on Marketing to Children

TIA Position Statement for Holiday Season 2008

The Toy Industry Association and its members are proud of the toys and games we produce and their role in play, which is an important, life-shaping experience in the growth of a child. We believe it is appropriate to market toys and games both to children and to their parents, so long as it is done responsibly.

Ultimately, TIA and its members understand that a parent or primary caregiver knows his or her child best. Our research confirms that parents agree that they should be involved in all aspects of their child's life, including the child's television viewing, computer time, and purchasing decisions.

The toy industry believes firmly in self-regulation and is committed to follow best practices in marketing to our consumers, as reflected in various national codes and industry guidelines. These include the Children's Advertising Review Unit of the Council of Better Business Bureaus (of which TIA is a long-standing member) in the United States and the codes of the International Chamber of Commerce and local self-regulatory codes internationally. We are actively involved with various self-regulatory organizations in continually reviewing and improving those guidelines as needed.

Children are the reason our industry exists. We are parents ourselves and we treat all children with the same care and respect.

Source: Toy Industry Association Inc., "TIA Statement on Marketing to Children: TIA Position Statement for Holiday Season 2008," in *Industry Statements,* http://www.toyassociation. org/AM/Template.cfm?Section=Industry-Statements&TEMPLATE=/CM/HTMLDisplay .cfmCONTENTID=1474 (accessed April 5, 2009).

In small groups, discuss these four documents. Here are some questions to get you started:

1. Do the openers grab your attention? Why or why not?
2. What persuasive strategies do they use?
3. What arguments do they use? How do they build credibility?
4. What common ground do they use?
5. What emotional appeals do they use?
6. How do they deal with objections?
7. What are the differences between the TIA response to CCFC and the TIA's statement on its own Web site?
8. Do the documents convince you? Why or why not? Which document is the most persuasive?
9. How could these documents be improved?

As your instructor directs,

a. As a group, share your analyses with the class in a five-minute presentation.
b. Prepare three documents for your instructor.
   - Write a detailed analysis of one of the documents.
   - On the basis of that analysis, rewrite the document.
   - Write a memo explaining the changes you made and why you kept some of the original document (if you did).

16.30 All-Weather Case: Persuading Employees of the Value of Cross-Cultural Training

Just a week after the second meeting with the employees of the Long Prairies plant, Caleb received news of another employee relations crisis. Two operators at the company's plant in Cedar Rapids, Iowa, had an altercation in which one, Randy Murray, a Caucasian, assaulted the other, Jose Gutierrez, a Hispanic immigrant from El Salvador. Fortunately, the assault did not result in injury to either of the employees involved; nonetheless, charges were filed against Murray, who was issued a notice of temporary suspension without pay with a warning of certain termination should he be involved in any further misconduct.

The altercation began when Mr. Murray called Mr. Gutierrez a "wetback," a derogatory term often used for illegal immigrants entering the United States from its southern border. While the incident was still being investigated, the manager of the plant lost no time in calling for a meeting of all employees. At the meeting, the 15 Caucasian operators and the 7 Hispanic operators traded charges and countercharges, dividing into two camps. The Caucasian group accused the Hispanic group of being "ungrateful" to their new home, and the Hispanic group called the other group intolerant.

A similar incident had occurred at the Nebraska plant four months ago when a Native American employee accused a shift engineer of ethnic discrimination. The last time All-Weather provided cross-cultural sensitivity training to its employees was when Hispanic employees first began to work at the company's plants over two years ago.

As Doug, Caleb, and Tanner finish reading the critical incident report sent by the manager of the Cedar Rapids plant, Caleb asks Tanner, "What do you think? Do we need to have the cultural sensitivity training again?"

Tanner hasn't forgotten his cultural gaffes with the two Japanese professors. He declares his resounding support for the training.

However, Doug is not so sure. "I think we need to think this over," he says, somewhat slowly, as if mulling his words. "We haven't had any other incidents in the plants, and no cultural problems have ever occurred at any of our offices."

"I disagree, Doug" Caleb says, respectfully. "I think it's good to be proactive in this matter. Simply because it hasn't happened too many times is no guarantee that it would not happen in the future, especially considering our increasingly diverse workforce."

"You're right," Doug says, matter-of-factly. "Go ahead. But the training shouldn't be seen as something that we're trying to force on anyone."

Caleb arranges a teleconference with the four plant managers (all except the manager of the Long Prairies plant, which is closing its operations) to ask for their input on the type of training that should be offered.

"I don't know," says Steve, manager at the Lincoln, Nebraska, plant, "my engineers and operators alike feel that the sensitivity training is just an exercise in PC."

"The effect of such training wears off quickly," the manager at the Camden, Illinois, plant says.

"My employees will likely feel that they're the target of the training because of the incident that just occurred," the manager of the Cedar Rapids plant warns, even though he himself wrote that he would like some kind of training.

The fourth manager is positive about the need for training, but he wants the training to be more comprehensive and include leadership training. "We have to teach some of our employees that the 21st century world is different from the 20th century world."

Next, Caleb asks Tanner to send an e-mail to All-Weather's 32 U.S. offices (international offices will be covered at a later date) requesting their input on the cross-cultural training. Seventeen offices respond; the reaction is mixed. However, the majority of the offices feel that the day-long training is not useful. They would like the training only if it can help them improve the working relationships among their employees. Most offices feel that the present one-day training format is inadequate—and far too theoretical—to achieve this objective. Some even feel that the whole cross-cultural training is passé and puts unnecessary pressure on employees to conform to politically correct standards of behavior. This group believes that cultural stereotypes are not meant to be taken seriously and that any attempt to fight them only ends up reinforcing them. A few offices have straightforwardly called cross-cultural training a waste of company time and resources in view of the first-ever quarterly loss that All-Weather has suffered.

Caleb shakes his head after reading some of these e-mails, saying, as if addressing the sender through the screen, "Walk one day in the shoes of a victim of these stereotypes, pal."

On the question of what to include in such training, the responses range from cultural awareness, respect for colleagues, and improved written communication, to leadership training, listening skills, and nonverbal communication. On the question of whether different levels of employees need different types of training, the majority believes a common session for everyone, along with topical sessions for different levels of employees, will be the most effective training format.

Caleb decides that the training will be offered both on location as well as through videoconferencing. Since the two incidents involving cultural problems occurred at the Lincoln, Nebraska, and the Cedar Rapids, Iowa, plants, Caleb decides to begin the cross-cultural sensitivity training at these two plants. Both he and Tanner will visit the plants to conduct the training, which will last two work days.

To begin designing the training program, Caleb asks Tanner to come up with a brief list of books and Web sites on cross-cultural training that can help provide the material for the training. By the next afternoon, Tanner is ready with his list, which includes the following:

- Paul B. Pedersen and Daniel Hernandez, *Decisional Dialogues in a Cultural Context: Structured Exercises* (Thousand Oaks, CA: Sage Publications, 1997).

- *Diversity in the Workplace: Human Resources Initiatives,* ed. Susan E. Jackson and Associates (New York: Guilford Press, 1992).

- Tracy Novinger, *Intercultural Communication: A Practical Guide* (Austin, TX: University of Texas Press, 2001).

- Brooks Peterson, *Cultural Intelligence: A Guide to Working with People from Other Cultures* (Yarmouth, ME: Intercultural Press, 2004).

- Conflict Research Consortium, "General Information about Communication Problems," in *International Online Training Program on Intractable Conflict,* http://www.colorado.edu/conflict/peace/ problem/commprob.htm (accessed April 5, 2009).

- ITIM International, "Geert Hofstede™ Cultural Dimensions," in *Hofstede Resource Pages,* http:// www.geert-hofstede.com/geert_hofstede_resources .shtml (accessed April 5, 2009).

Caleb also asks Tanner to draft a memo—a transmittal to accompany a brochure outlining the training program—addressed to the managers of the Lincoln, Nebraska, and the Cedar Rapids, Iowa, plants, announcing the two-day cross-cultural training program for their employees beginning on the second Monday of the next month. "Make the memo engaging and persuasive. I want them to have an open mind about the training," Caleb says, by way of parting advice to Tanner.

Based on your reading of Chapter 16 and the details provided in the case, draft a persuasive memo for Tanner. You may consult one or more of the sources mentioned in Tanner's list to make your memo more persuasive by mentioning some of the possible topics to be included in the training program (note: you may discuss and finalize the details of the training program as a group).

Learning Objectives

After studying this chapter, you will know how to:

1 Define report problems.

2 Employ different research strategies.

3 Use and document sources.

Reports depend on research. The research may be as simple as pulling up data with a computer program or as complicated as calling many different people, conducting focus groups and surveys, or even planning and conducting experiments. Care in planning, proposing, and researching reports is needed to produce reliable data.

In writing any report, there are five basic steps:

1. Define the problem.
2. Gather the necessary data and information.
3. Analyze the data and information.
4. Organize the information.
5. Write the report.

After reviewing the varieties of reports, this chapter focuses on the first two steps. Chapter 19 discusses the last three steps.

Varieties of Reports

Many kinds of documents are called *reports*. In some organizations, a report is a long document or one that contains numerical data. In others, one- and two-page memos are called *reports*. In still others, *reports* consist of PowerPoint slides delivered orally or printed and bound together. A short report to a client may use letter format. **Formal reports** contain formal elements such as a title page, a transmittal, a table of contents, and a list of illustrations. **Informal reports** may be letters and memos or even computer printouts of production or sales figures. But all reports, whatever their length or degree of formality, provide the information that people in organizations need to make plans and solve problems.

Reports can provide just information, both information and analysis alone, or information and analysis to support a recommendation (see Figure 17.1). Reports can be called **information reports** if they collect data for the reader, **analytical reports** if they interpret data but do not recommend action, and **recommendation reports** if they recommend action or a solution.

The following reports can be information, analytical, or recommendation reports, depending on what they provide:

- *Accident reports* can simply list the nature and causes of accidents in a factory or office. These reports can also analyze the data and recommend ways to make conditions safer.
- *Credit reports* can simply summarize an applicant's income and other credit obligations. These reports can also evaluate the applicant's collateral and creditworthiness and recommend whether or not to provide credit.
- *Progress and interim reports* can simply record the work done so far and the work remaining on a project. These reports can also analyze the

Figure 17.1 Three Levels of Reports

Reports can provide

Information only

- **Sales reports** (sales figures for the week or month).
- **Quarterly reports** (figures showing a plant's productivity and profits for the quarter).

Information plus analysis

- **Annual reports** (financial data and an organization's accomplishments during the past year).
- **Audit reports** (interpretations of the facts revealed during an audit).
- **Make-good or pay-back reports** (calculations of the point at which a new capital investment will pay for itself).

Information plus analysis plus a recommendation

- **Recommendation reports** evaluate two or more alternatives and recommend which alternative the organization should choose.
- **Feasibility reports** evaluate a proposed action and show whether or not it will work.
- **Justification reports** justify the need for a purchase, an investment, a new personnel line, or a change in procedure.
- **Problem-solving reports** identify the causes of an organizational problem and recommend a solution.

Always the Same, Always Different

Jane Garrard, the vice president for investor and media relations at Tupperware Brands Corporation is responsible for producing an earnings release statement for the company Web site every quarter. Every quarter that task requires the same steps. She gathers facts and data about Tupperware's business and earnings; summarizes that information for Tupperware's shareholders and investors; produces the tables, graphs, and balance sheets that are part of the standard earnings release "boilerplate," or template; and circulates the document for review. That's a *writing* process, and it's the same every quarter.

But it's also a *communication* process, one that's different every quarter. Every quarter brings different numbers, different directions for the company, different market conditions with different investor expectations. Every quarter, it's a new message, requiring a new approach and new interpretations. Garrard and her team must decide the best ways to balance their responsibility to Tupperware's customers with regulatory requirements and company interests. They have to interpret the data, analyze their audience, consult with their co-workers, and then compose an earnings release statement that meets everyone's goals. That's a challenging job.

Adapted from Assaf Kadem, "Facts and Interpretation," *Communication World*, December 2006, 30.

quality of the work and recommend that a project be stopped, continued, or restructured.

- *Trip reports* can simply share what the author learned at a conference or during a visit to a customer or supplier. These reports can also recommend action based on that information.
- *Closure reports* can simply document the causes of a failure or possible products that are not economically or technically feasible under current conditions. They can also recommend action to prevent such failures in the future.

The Report Production Process

When you write a report, you know the actual writing will take a significant chunk of time. But you should also plan to spend significant time analyzing your data, revising drafts, and preparing visuals and slides.

When you write a report for a class project, plan to complete at least one-fourth of your research before you write the proposal. Begin analyzing your data as you collect it; prepare your list of sources and drafts of visuals as you go along. Start writing your first draft before the research is completed. An early draft can help clarify where you need more research. Save at least one-fourth of your time at the end of the project to think and write after all your data are collected. For a collaborative report, you'll need even more time to write and revise.

Up-front planning helps you use your time efficiently. Start by thinking about the whole report process. Talk to your readers to understand how much detail and formality they want. Look at reports that were produced earlier (sample reports in this text are in Chapter 19). List all the parts of the report you'll need to prepare. Then articulate—to yourself or your team members—the purposes,

Research for Developing Countries

Procter & Gamble researchers found that 60% of shoppers at tiny stores in developing countries already know what they want, so they do not spend time browsing. But they do gaze at the cashier's area for 5 seconds as they wait for their purchase or change. So P&G is thinking of ways to persuade store owners to put more P&G products in these areas.

Because running water is in short supply for many low-income Mexican consumers, P&G researchers developed a fabric softener that, when added to the laundry load along with the detergent, can eliminate a rinse cycle in the kinds of washing machines being used.

To keep prices down for these customers, P&G employs "reverse engineering." It starts with the price consumers can afford for the product and then adjusts features and manufacturing accordingly. To hold down the cost of a detergent used for hand washing clothes, P&G used fewer enzymes. The result was a cheaper product, and one that was gentler on the hands than the regular detergent.

Adapted from Ellen Byron, "P&G's Global Target: Shelves of Tiny Stores: It Woos Poor Women Buying Single Portions; Mexico's 'Hot Zones,'" *Wall Street Journal*, July 16, 2007, A1.

audiences, and generic constraints for each part. The fuller idea you have of the final product when you start, the fewer drafts you'll need to write and the better your final product will be.

Report Topics

Good reports grow out of real problems: disjunctions between reality and the ideal, choices that must be made. When you write a report as part of your job, the organization may define the topic. To think of problems for class reports, think about problems that face your college or university; housing units on campus; social, religious, and professional groups on campus and in your city; local businesses; and city, county, state, and federal governments and their agencies. Read your campus and local papers and newsmagazines; read the news on the Internet, watch it on TV, or listen to it on National Public Radio.

A good report problem in business or administration meets the following criteria:

1. The problem is
   - Real.
   - Important enough to be worth solving.
   - Narrow but challenging.
2. The audience for the report is
   - Real.
   - Able to implement the recommended action.
3. The data, evidence, and facts are
   - Sufficient to document the severity of the problem.
   - Sufficient to prove that the recommendation will solve the problem.
   - Available to *you*.
   - Comprehensible to *you*.

Often problems need to be narrowed. For example, "improving the college experiences of international students studying in the United States" is far too broad. First, choose one college or university. Second, identify the specific problem. Do you want to increase the social interaction between US and international students? Help international students find housing? Increase the number of ethnic grocery stores and restaurants? Third, identify the specific audience that would have the power to implement your recommendations. Depending on the specific topic, the audience might be the Office of International Studies, the residence hall counselors, a service organization on campus or in town, a store, or a group of investors.

Some problems are more easily researched than others. If you have easy access to the Chinese Student Association, you can survey them about their experiences at the local Chinese grocery. However, if you want to recommend ways to keep the Chinese grocery in business, but you do not have access to their financial records, you will have a much more difficult time solving the problem. Even if you have access, if the records are written in Chinese, you will have problems unless you read the language or have a willing translator.

Pick a problem you can solve in the time available. Six months of full-time (and overtime) work and a team of colleagues might allow you to look at all the ways to make a store more profitable. If you're doing a report in 6 to 12 weeks for a class that is only one of your responsibilities, limit the topic. Depending on your interests and knowledge, you could choose to examine the prices and brands carried, its inventory procedures, its overhead costs, its layout and decor, or its advertising budget.

Hasbro does extensive research to keep developing games people will play.

How you define the problem shapes the solutions you find. For example, suppose that a manufacturer of frozen foods isn't making money. If the problem is defined as a marketing problem, the researcher may analyze the product's price, image, advertising, and position in the market. But perhaps the problem is really that overhead costs are too high due to poor inventory management, or that an inadequate distribution system doesn't get the product to its target market. Defining the problem accurately is essential to finding an effective solution.

Once you've defined your problem, you're ready to write a purpose statement. The purpose statement goes both in your proposal and in your final report. A good **purpose statement** makes three things clear:

- The organizational problem or conflict.
- The specific technical questions that must be answered to solve the problem.
- The rhetorical purpose (to explain, to recommend, to request, to propose) the report is designed to achieve.

The following purpose statement has all three elements:

> Current management methods keep the elk population within the carrying capacity of the habitat but require frequent human intervention. Both wildlife conservation specialists and the public would prefer methods that controlled the elk population naturally. This report will compare the current short-term management techniques (hunting, trapping and transporting, and winter feeding) with two long-term management techniques, habitat modification and the reintroduction of predators. The purpose of this report is to recommend which techniques or combination of techniques would best satisfy the needs of conservationists, hunters, and the public.

Report audience: The superintendent of Yellowstone National Park

To write a good purpose statement, you must understand the basic problem and have some idea of the questions that your report will answer. Note, however, that you can (and should) write the purpose statement before researching the specific alternatives the report will discuss.

Research and Innovation: Fun and Games at Hasbro

On Fridays, employees at Hasbro spend their lunchtime playing board games and thinking about ways to update games or create new ones. The Friday games are just one of the creative approaches to research and innovation used at the company that manufactures some of America's best-known board games, such as Monopoly, Scrabble, Sorry, and Clue.

In the world of board games, continuous innovation is necessary to fit games to changing consumer lifestyles and preferences. Hasbro invests in extensive market research, such as conducting online surveys, observing children and adults playing games in the company's Game-Works lab, and talking with people about how they want to spend leisure time.

In response to information obtained through these strategies, Hasbro has modified several of its traditional games.

- To accommodate consumers' tight schedules, Hasbro developed "express" versions of Monopoly, Sorry, and Scrabble that can be completed within 20 minutes.

- To address consumers' desire for more balanced lives, The Game of Life now includes life experience, education, and family life as elements of a successful life, rather than basing success only on making the most money.

- Based on 3 million votes cast in an online survey, a revised version of Monopoly replaces Boardwalk with Times Square and Pacific Avenue with Las Vegas Boulevard.

- To attract customers who enjoy using technology to play games, game designers developed electronic versions of games.

Adapted from Carol Hymowitz, "All Companies Need Innovation: Hasbro Finds a New Magic," *Wall Street Journal*, February 26, 2007, B1.

Research Strategies for Reports

Research for a report may be as simple as getting a computer printout of sales for the last month; it may involve finding published material or surveying or interviewing people. **Secondary research** retrieves information that someone else gathered. Library research and online searches are the best known kinds of secondary research. **Primary research** gathers new information. Surveys, interviews, and observations are common methods for gathering new information for business reports.

Finding Information Online and in Print

You can save time and money by checking online and published sources of data before you gather new information. Many college and university libraries provide

- Workshops on research techniques.
- Handouts explaining how to use printed and computer-based sources.
- Free or inexpensive access to computer databases.
- Research librarians who can help you find and use sources.

Categories of sources that may be useful include

- Specialized encyclopedias for introductions to a topic.
- Indexes to find articles. Most permit searches by keyword, by author, and often by company name.
- Abstracts for brief descriptions or summaries of articles. Sometimes the abstract will be all you'll need; almost always, you can tell from the abstract whether an article is useful for your needs.
- Citation indexes to find materials that cite previous research. Citation indexes thus enable you to use an older reference to find newer articles on the topic. The *Social Sciences Citation Index* is the most useful for researching business topics.

Good research uses multiple media and sources.

PARDON MY PLANET

© Vic Lee, King Features Syndicate.

- Newspapers for information about recent events.
- US Census reports, for a variety of business and demographic information.

To use a computer database efficiently, identify the concepts you're interested in and choose keywords that will help you find relevant sources. **Keywords** are the terms that the computer searches for. If you're not sure what terms to use, check the ABI/Inform Thesaurus for synonyms and the hierarchies in which information is arranged in various databases.

Specific commands allow you to narrow your search. For example, to study the effect of the minimum wage on employment in the restaurant industry, you might use a Boolean search (see Figure 17.2):

(minimum wage) and(restaurant or fast food) and
(employment rate or unemployment).

This descriptor would give you the titles of articles that treat all three of the topics in parentheses. Without *and,* you'd get articles that discuss the minimum wage in general, articles about every aspect of *restaurants,* and every article that refers to *unemployment,* even though many of these would not be relevant to your topic. The *or* descriptor calls up articles that use the term *fast food* or the term *restaurant.* Many Web search engines, including AltaVista and Google, allow you to specify words that cannot appear in a source.

Many words can appear in related forms. To catch all of them, use the database's **wild card** or **truncated code** for shortened terms and root words. To find this feature and others, go to the Advanced Search screen for the search engine

Figure 17.2 Example of a Boolean Search

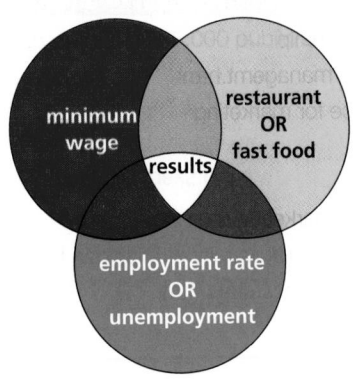

Web Searching: Insider Information

"You want to know how fast an F-16 flies, but your search engine spits back details on camera shutter speeds. To save yourself these detours, take a page from the book of Sergey Brin, co-founder of the search-engine Google: Think more like a programmer and ask yourself: What words do I want to come back in my response?

"When Mr. Brin, who watches his waistline, wants to know how much protein is in a serving of chicken breast, he doesn't just type in 'chicken breast' and 'protein.' He adds the word 'grams.'

"Another of his winnowing tricks is to use the minus sign. To ensure that a search for 'dolphins' doesn't bring up a slew of references to the Miami Dolphins football team, for instance, type dolphin -miami. (A space must be added before the minus sign, and the minus sign must go directly before the word to be removed.)

"Mr. Brin has another secret. For local addresses and phone numbers, he uses Yahoo."

Quoted from "Tricks of the Trade: Web Searching with a Pro," *Wall Street Journal,* June 5, 2002, D1. Copyright © 2002 by Dow Jones & Company, Inc. Reproduced with permission of Dow Jones & Company, Inc. via Copyright Clearance Center.

Watch Your Language

In two decades of writing and using surveys, psychologist Palmer Morrel-Samuels has seen that the wording of a survey question can affect responses. For example, the connotation of a phrase can unintentionally skew the way people react to a question. He recalls a survey that a maker of photographic equipment used to learn about the leadership skills of its managers. A question asked employees whether their manager "takes bold strides" and "has a strong grasp" of complicated issues. Male managers tended to outscore female managers. Morrel-Samuels noted that, in a literal sense, males on average take longer strides and have more muscle strength than females. The company changed the wording of the survey. "Has a strong grasp of complex problems" became "discusses complex problems with precision and clarity." After this change, the difference in ratings of female and male managers disappeared. Employees apparently stopped mixing images of size and strength into their ratings of intellectual insight.

Another word-related bias is that respondents tend to agree more than disagree with statements. If a survey about managers asks employees whether their manager is fair, ethical, intelligent, knowledgeable, and so on, they are likely to assign all of these qualities to the manager—and to agree more and more as the survey goes along. To correct for this, some questions should be worded to generate the opposite response. For example, a statement about ethics can be balanced by a statement about corruption, and a statement about fairness can be balanced by a statement about bias or stereotypes.

Adapted from Palmer Morrel-Samuels, "Getting the Truth into Workplace Surveys," *Harvard Business Review* 80, No. 2 (February 2002): 111–18.

phones and car accidents that all cite the same Toronto study, you have one source, not five. Choose the most complete for your project.

Many students start their research with Wikipedia. If you are one of them, you are not alone. Wikipedia is the largest, most popular encyclopedia ever. It has over 10 million articles in 253 languages and is one of the top five Web sites.[1] So, while it may be acceptable as a starting place, be aware that many instructors and other professionals do not accept Wikipedia—or any encyclopedia, frequently—as an authoritative source. These are some of their reasons:

- Many remember the beginnings of Wikipedia when it was full of errors.
- Because not all entries are written by experts on the topic, some entries still contain errors.
- Wikipedia makes the news when pranksters maliciously alter entries.
- Thanks to WikiScanner, some editors have been shown to have self-interest. For instance, Diebold deleted paragraphs criticizing its electronic voting machines, and PepsiCo deleted paragraphs on negative health effects in the Pepsi entry.[2]
- Because Wikipedia is constantly changing, information you cite may be changed or eliminated if someone goes to check it.

Designing Questions for Surveys and Interviews

A **survey** questions a large group of people, called **respondents** or **subjects.** The easiest way to ask many questions is to create a **questionnaire,** a written list of questions that people fill out. An **interview** is a structured conversation with someone who will be able to give you useful information. Organizations use surveys and interviews to research both internal issues such as employee satisfaction and external issues such as customer satisfaction. Responding to anger over huge executive pay packages as the recession continued, biotechnology firm Amgen surveyed shareholders about its compensation plan. The survey was a 10-question online survey.[3] Figure 17.4 shows some of the mistakes and best practices in marketing survey research.

Figure 17.4   Marketing Research Mistakes and Best Practices

Mistakes	Best Practices
Focusing on current customers (blinds you to new market opportunities)	Identifying the most valuable customers, the ones who spend the most in your business
Basing strategy on public information (reports from industry associations and investment firms, reports designed to avoid giving any one user an advantage)	Using a market panel, "a sweeping, detailed and continuing survey of a large, carefully selected group of consumers who reflect a statistically reliable sample of a much larger market"
Relying on qualitative research (focus groups, interviews) without balancing it with quantitative data	Examining in detail where you stand against competitors
Using a piecemeal approach (narrow, one-time studies, frequently undertaken by competing divisions within a company)	Tracking your performance over time

Source: Calvin P. Duncan, Constance M. O'Hare, and John M. Matthews, "Raising Your Market IQ," *Wall Street Journal,* December 1, 2007, R4. Copyright © 2004 by Dow Jones & Company, Inc. Reproduced with permission of Dow Jones & Company, Inc. via Copyright Clearance Center.

Characteristics of Good Survey Questions

Surveys and interviews can be useful only if the questions are well designed. Good questions have these characteristics:

1. They ask only one thing.
2. They are phrased neutrally.
3. They avoid making assumptions about the respondent.
4. They mean the same thing to different people.

At a telecommunications firm, a survey asked employees to rate their manager's performance at "hiring staff and setting compensation." Although both tasks are part of the discipline of human resource management, they are different activities. A manager might do a better job of hiring than of setting pay levels, or vice versa. The survey gave respondents—and the company using the survey—no way to distinguish performance on each task.[4]

Phrase questions in a way that won't bias the response. In the political sphere, for example, opinions about rights for homosexuals vary according to the way questions are asked. More Americans oppose "allowing gays and lesbians to marry legally" than oppose "legal agreements giving many of the same rights as marriage." With regard to homosexual relations, the number of people who say such behavior should be "illegal" is greater than the number who say "consenting adults engaged in homosexual activities in private should be prosecuted for a crime."[5]

The order in which questions are asked may matter. Asking about the economy—and its impact on families—before asking about the President will lower opinions of the President during bad economic times; the opposite is true for good economic times.[6]

Avoid questions that make assumptions about your subjects. The question "Does your wife have a job outside the home?" assumes that your respondent is a married man.

Use words that mean the same thing to you and to the respondents. If a question can be interpreted in more than one way, it will be. Words like *often* and *important* mean different things to different people. When a consulting firm called Employee Motivation and Performance Assessment helped Duke Energy assess the leadership skills of its managers, an early draft of the employee survey asked employees to rate how well their manager "understands the business and the marketplace." How would employees know what is in the manager's mind? Each respondent would have to determine what is reasonable evidence of a manager's understanding. The question was rephrased to identify behavior the employees could observe: "resolves complaints from customers quickly and thoroughly." The wording is still subjective ("quickly and thoroughly"), but at least all employees will be measuring the same category of behavior.[7]

Even questions that call for objective information can be confusing. For example, consider the owner of a small business confronted with the question "How many employees do you have?" Does the number include the owner as well as subordinates? Does it include both full- and part-time employees? Does it include people who have been hired but who haven't yet started work, or someone who is leaving at the end of the month? A better wording would be

How many full-time employees were on your payroll the week of May 16?

http://www
.publicagenda.org/
pages/20-questions-
journalists-should-
ask-about-poll-results

Public Agenda provides 20 questions to ask about poll results. Questions include
- Who did the poll and who paid for it?
- How many people were surveyed and how were they chosen?
- How was the survey done?
- What questions were asked?

http://www
.galluppoll.com

Designing survey questions is an important and difficult part of getting valid results. For examples of surveys, including information about their design, visit the Gallup Poll pages of the Gallup Organization's Web site. The Web site also includes videos of Gallup's survey work. Some videos discuss the results of particular polls; some also talk about the poll's audience and purpose, important factors in a survey's design. Watch several videos and examine several polls for the ways in which audience and purpose shape the questions in the survey.

Figure 17.6   Questionnaire for a Student Report Using Survey Research

An interesting title can help.

In your introductory ¶,
① *tell how to return the survey*
② *tell how the information will be used*

Survey: Why Do Students Attend Athletic Events?

The purpose of this survey is to determine why students attend sports events, and what might increase attendance. All information is to be used solely for a student research paper. Please return completed surveys to Elizabeth or Vicki at the Union help desk. Thank you for your assistance!

Start with easy–to–answer questions

1. Gender (Please circle one)   M   F

2. What is your class year? (Please circle)   1   2   3   4   Grad   Other

3. How do you feel about women's sports? (Please circle)

The words below each number anchor responses, while still allowing you to average the data.

1	2	3	4	5
I enjoy watching women's sports		I'll watch, but it doesn't really matter		Women's sports are boring/ I'd rather watch men's sports

Seeing a response in a survey can make respondents more willing to admit to feelings they may be embarrassed to volunteer.

4. Do you like to attend MSU men's basketball games? (Please circle)
   Y   N

5. How often do you attend MSU women's basketball games? (Please circle)

1	2	3	4	5
All/most games	Few games a season	Once a season	Less than once a year	Never

6. If you do not attend all of the women's basketball games, why not? (Please check all that apply. If you attend all the games, skip to #7.)

__I've never thought to go.
__I don't like basketball.
__I don't like sporting events.
__The team isn't good enough.
__My friends are not interested in going.
__I want to go, I just haven't had the opportunity.
__The tickets cost too much ($5).
__Other (please specify) _____

Think about factors that affect the problem you're studying, and write survey questions to get information about them.

7. To what extent would each of the following make you more likely to attend an MSU women's basketball game? (please rank all)

1	2	3
Much more likely to attend	Possibley more likely	No effect

__Increased awareness on campus (fliers, chalking on the Oval, more articles in the *Gazette*)
__Marketing to students (give-aways, days for residence halls or fraternities/sororities)
__Student loyalty program (awarding points towards free tickets, clothing, food for attending games)
__Education (pocket guide explaining the rules of the game provided at the gate)
__Other (please specify) _____

Thank you!
Please return this survey to Elizabeth or Vicki at the Union help desk.

Repeat where to turn in or mail completed surveys.

Conducting Surveys and Interviews

Face-to-face surveys are convenient when you are surveying a fairly small number of people in a specific location. In a face-to-face survey, the interviewer's sex, race, and nonverbal cues can bias results. Most people prefer not to say things they think their audience will dislike. For that reason, women will be more likely to agree that sexual harassment is a problem if the interviewer is also a woman. Members of a minority group are more likely to admit that they suffer discrimination if the interviewer is a member of the same minority.

Telephone surveys are popular because they can be closely supervised. Interviewers can read the questions from a computer screen and key in answers as the respondent gives them. The results can then be available just a few minutes after the last call is completed.

Phone surveys also have limitations. First, they reach only people who have phones and thus underrepresent some groups such as poor people. Answering machines, caller ID, and cell phones also make phone surveys more difficult. Since a survey based on a phone book would exclude people with unlisted numbers, professional survey-takers use automatic random-digit dialing.

To increase the response rate for a phone survey, call at a time respondents will find convenient. Avoid calling between 5 and 7 PM, a time when many families have dinner.

Mail surveys can reach anyone who has an address. Some people may be more willing to fill out an anonymous questionnaire than to give sensitive information to a stranger over the phone. However, mail surveys are not effective for respondents who don't read and write well. Further, it may be more difficult to get a response from someone who doesn't care about the survey or who sees the mailing as junk mail. Over the phone, the interviewer can try to persuade the subject to participate.

Online surveys deliver questions over the Internet. The researcher can contact respondents with e-mail containing a link to a Web page with the survey or can ask people by mail or in person to log on and visit the Web site with the survey. Another alternative is to post a survey on a Web site and invite the site's visitors to complete the survey. This approach does not generate a random sample, so the results probably do not reflect the opinions of the entire population. Interactive technology makes it easy to use branching questions; the survey can automatically send respondents to the next question on a branch. However, many people worry about the privacy of online surveys, so they may be reluctant to participate. Researchers have found that a lower percentage of people are willing to complete online surveys than other kinds. To encourage participation, researchers should make online surveys as short as possible. Few people are likely to bother finishing a 32-screen survey, as one bank discovered.[8]

A major concern with any kind of survey is the **response rate,** the percentage of people who respond. People who refuse to answer may differ from those who respond, and you need information from both groups to be able to generalize to the whole population. Low response rates pose a major problem, especially for phone surveys. Answering machines and caller ID are commonly used to screen incoming calls resulting in decreased response rates.

Widespread use of cell phones in recent years has also negatively affected the ability of telephone surveyors to contact potential respondents.[9] Federal figures show that 3 out of 10 households either have no landline phone or rarely answer it. People in the latter category often rely so heavily on their cell phones that they assume calls on the landline are

And the Survey Says . . .

Increasingly, companies use surveys to measure their customer's satisfaction with their products or services. But are they really using that data? A survey by Bain & Company of 362 companies and their customers has revealed a discrepancy between the companies' and consumers' perceptions of customer satisfaction. The survey found that while 80% of the companies thought they were providing a "superior" consumer experience, only 8% of the customers described their experience that way.

Unfortunately, an even wider disconnect exists between measuring customer satisfaction and changing corporate business practices to achieve it. Getting data is one thing. But, circulating the findings and making sure the findings are put to use is another. So, when you go to the work of collecting data, make sure that you also make the data work for you.

Adapted from Christopher Meyer and Andre Schwager, "Understanding Customer Experience," *Harvard Business Review* 85, no. 2 (February 2007): 116–26.

Online Polling: Pros and Cons

Many polls used to be conducted by phone. In the last few years, however, companies have turned to online market research. The advantages are obvious: consumers can take online surveys at their convenience, and researchers can ask questions that are uncomfortable to ask in person ("How often do you bathe?"). Additionally, online research can cover numerous respondents and is faster and cheaper.

However, companies such as P&G doubt the reliability of online market research, which critics say is not based on random sampling. As an example, P&G cited the case of an online market research company that described a concept as attractive but in a poll a week later found it "below average." Jon Krosnick, a Stanford professor, says that "drawing hard conclusions from online polls can be like making an automobile out of soft plastic."

On the other side, Benjamin Malbon of the ad agency Bartle Bogle Hegarty believes that online research can be beneficial if it researches a specific target audience, such as housewives or people who like tennis. Such research need not be totally representative, he states.

Despite skepticism, online market research is likely to stay and become more reliable. Knowledge Networks, a market research company, has found a happy medium between the rigors of random sampling and the convenience of online research. It first telephones randomly selected respondents, then asks them to take the online survey.

Adapted from Burt Helm, "Online Polls: How Good Are They?" in *BusinessWeek: Marketing*, http://www.businessweek.com/magazine/content/08_24/b4088086641658.htm (accessed April 10, 2009).

telephone solicitors or surveys and thus do not answer. People who have only cell phones are young, less affluent, unmarried, and less likely to own their home.[10] These figures show that phone surveys that are land-line only, as is true for most, may have significant biases built into their samples.

The problem of nonresponse has increased dramatically in recent years. The University of Michigan's Survey of Consumer Attitudes experienced only a small drop in response rate between 1979–1996, from 72% to 67%. But the deterioration in response rate has accelerated since then, and in 2003 the response rate had dropped to 48%.[11]

According to figures that researchers have reported to the Marketing Research Association, the response rate for door-to-door surveys was 53%, and the response rate for face-to-face surveys in malls and other central locations was 38%. The response rate for Web surveys averaged 34%.[12] To get as high a response rate as possible, good researchers follow up, contacting nonrespondents at least once and preferably twice to try to persuade them to participate in the survey. Sometimes money or other rewards are used to induce people to participate.

Selecting a sample for surveys and interviews

To keep research costs reasonable, usually only a sample of the total population is polled. How that sample is chosen and the attempts made to get responses from nonrespondents will determine whether you can infer that what is true of your sample is also true of the population as a whole.

A **sample** is a subset of the population. The **sampling units** are those actually sampled. Frequently, the sampling unit is an individual. If a list of individuals is not available then a household can be the sampling unit. The list of all sampling units is the **sampling frame.** For interviews, this could be a list of all addresses, or for companies a list of all Fortune 500 CEOs.[13] The **population** is the group you want to make statements about. Depending on the purpose of your research, your population might be all Fortune 1000 companies, all business students at your college, or all consumers of tea in the mid-Atlantic states.

A **convenience sample** is a group of subjects who are easy to get: students who walk through the union, people at a shopping mall, workers in your own unit. Convenience samples are useful for a rough pretest of a questionnaire and may be acceptable for some class research projects. However, you cannot generalize from a convenience sample to a larger group.

A purposive or **judgment sample** is a group of people whose views seem useful. Someone interested in surveying the kinds of writing done on campus might ask each department for the name of a faculty member who cared about writing, and then send surveys to those people.

In a **random sample,** each person in the population theoretically has an equal chance of being chosen. When people say they did something *randomly* they often mean *without conscious bias.* However, unconscious bias exists. Someone passing out surveys in front of the library will be more likely to approach people who seem friendly and less likely to ask people who seem intimidating, in a hurry, much older or younger, or of a different race, class, or sex. True random samples rely on random digit tables, published in statistics texts and books such as *A Million Random Digits.* An online random number table site can be found at http://ts.nist.gov/WeightsandMeasures/upload/AppendB-HB133-05-Z.pdf. Computers can also be programmed to generate random numbers.

Speedo conducted extensive research before launching its new LZR Racer Speedo, which enabled many swimmers to break records at the Beijing Olympics.

Source: Christopher Rhodes and Hiroko Tabuchi, "Olympic Swimmers Race to Get Well Suited," *Wall Street Journal,* June 12, 2008, B8.

If you take a true random sample, you can generalize your findings to the whole population from which your sample comes. Consider, for example, a random phone survey that shows 65% of respondents approve of a presidential policy. Measures of variability should always be attached to survey-derived estimates like this one. Typically, a confidence interval provides this measure of variability. Using the confidence interval, we might conclude it is likely that between 58% and 72% of the population approve of the presidential policy when the confidence interval is $\pm$ 7%. The accuracy range is based on the size of the sample and the expected variation within the population. Statistics texts tell you how to calculate these measures of variability.

Do not confuse sample size with randomness. A classic example is the 1936 Literary Digest poll which predicted Republican Alf Landon would beat Democrat incumbent President Franklin Roosevelt. Literary Digest sent out 10 million ballots to its magazine subscribers as well as people who owned cars and telephones, all of whom in 1936 were richer than the average voter—and more Republican.[14]

Many people mistakenly believe any survey provides information about the general population. One survey with a biased sample that got much publicity involved "sexting." "One in five teenagers electronically share nude or seminude photos of themselves" declared the news stories. However, the sample for the survey came from a teenage research panel formed by phone and online recruiting, plus recruiting from existing panel members. This sample included many electronically savvy users, users who would be comfortable sending pictures electronically. So the survey showed the

Ethical Issues in Interviewing

If you're trying to get sensitive information, interviewees may give useful information when the interview is "over" and the tape recorder has been turned off. Is it ethical to use that information?

If you're interviewing a hostile or very reluctant interviewee, you may get more information if you agree with everything you can legitimately agree to, and keep silent on the rest. Is it ethical to imply acceptance even when you know you'll criticize the interviewee's ideas in your report?

Most people would say that whatever public figures say is fair game: they're supposed to know enough to defend themselves. Do you agree?

Many people would say that different rules apply when you'll cite someone by name than when you'll use the information as background or use a pseudonym so that the interviewee cannot be identified. Do you agree?

As a practical matter, if someone feels you've misrepresented him or her, that person will be less willing to talk to you in the future. But quite apart from practical considerations, interview strategies raise ethical issues as well.

figures were true for this panel (and even there, the numbers were raised by responses from 18- and 19-year-old panelists, a group less inhibited than younger teens and more likely to respond), but because the panel is not a representative sample, no conclusions should be drawn about a wider population.[15]

Conducting research interviews

Schedule interviews in advance; tell the interviewee about how long you expect the interview to take. A survey of technical writers (who get much of their information from interviews) found that the best times to interview subject matter experts are Tuesdays, Wednesdays, and Thursday mornings.[16] People are frequently swamped on Mondays and looking forward to the weekend, or trying to finish their week's work on Fridays.

Interviews can be structured or unstructured. In a **structured interview,** the interviewer uses a detailed list of questions to guide the interview. Indeed, a structured interview may use a questionnaire just as a survey does.

In an **unstructured interview,** the interviewer has three or four main questions. Other questions build on what the interviewee says. To prepare for an unstructured interview, learn as much as possible about the interviewee and the topic. Go into the interview with three or four main topics you want to cover.

Interviewers sometimes use closed questions to start the interview and set the interviewee at ease. The strength of an interview, however, is getting at a person's attitudes, feelings, and experiences. Situational questions let you probe what someone would do in a specific circumstance. Hypothetical questions that ask people to imagine what they would do generally yield less reliable answers than questions about **critical incidents** or key past events.

Hypothetical question:	What would you say if you had to tell an employee that his or her performance was unsatisfactory?
Critical incident question:	You've probably been in a situation where someone who was working with you wasn't carrying his or her share of the work. What did you do the last time that happened?

A **mirror question** paraphrases the content of the last answer: "So you confronted him directly?" "You think that this product costs too much?" Mirror questions are used both to check that the interviewer understands what the interviewee has said and to prompt the interviewee to continue talking. **Probes** follow up an original question to get at specific aspects of a topic:

Question:	What do you think about the fees for campus parking?
Probes:	Would you be willing to pay more for a reserved space? How much more? Should the fines for vehicles parked illegally be increased? Do you think fees should be based on income?

Probes are not used in any definite order. Instead, they are used to keep the interviewee talking, to get at aspects of a subject that the interviewee has not yet mentioned, and to probe more deeply into points that the interviewee brings up.

If you read questions to subjects in a structured interview, use fewer options than you might in a written questionnaire.

I'm going to read a list of factors that someone might look for in choosing a restaurant. After I read each factor, please tell me whether that factor is Very Important to you, Somewhat Important to you, or Not Important to you.

If the interviewee hesitates, reread the scale.

Always tape the interview. Test your equipment ahead of time to make sure it works. If you think your interviewee may be reluctant to speak on tape, take along two tapes and two recorders; offer to give one tape to the interviewee.

Pulitzer Prize winner Nan Robertson offers the following advice to interviewers[17]:

- Do your homework. Learn about the subject and the person before the interview.
- To set a nervous interviewee at ease, start with nuts-and-bolts questions, even if you already know the answers.
- Save controversial questions for the end. You'll have everything else you need, and the trust built up in the interview makes an answer more likely.
- Go into an interview with three or four major questions. Listen to what the interviewee says and let the conversation flow naturally.
- At the end of the interview, ask for office and home telephone numbers in case you need to ask an additional question when you write up the interview.

Well-done interviews can yield surprising results. When the owners of Kiwi shoe polish interviewed people about what they wanted in shoe care products, they learned that shiny shoes were far down on the list. What people cared most about was how fresh and comfortable their shoes were on the inside. So Kiwi developed a new line of products, including "fresh'ins" (thin, lightly scented shoe inserts) and "smiling feet" (cushioning and nonslip pads and strips).[18]

Using Focus Groups

A **focus group,** yet another form of qualitative research, is a small group of people convened to provide a more detailed look into some area of interest—a product, service, process, concept, and so on. Because the group setting allows members to build on each other's comments, carefully chosen focus groups can provide detailed feedback; they can illuminate underlying attitudes and emotions relevant to particular behaviors.

Focus groups also have some problems. The first is the increasing use of professional respondents drawn from databases, a practice usually driven by cost and time limitations. The *Association for Qualitative Research Newsletter* labeled these respondents as a leading industry problem.[19] In order to get findings that are consistent among focus groups, the groups must accurately represent the target population. A second problem with focus groups is that such groups sometimes aim to please rather than offering their own evaluations.

An updated version of the focus group is the online network. Del Monte, for instance, has an online community, called "I Love My Dog," of 400 hand-picked dog enthusiasts that it can query about dog products. These networks, first cultivated as research tools by technology and video game companies, are

Nokia's Global Research

Nokia is working to add new customers in emerging markets. To do so, their researchers spend time with people around the world to understand communication behaviors. Other researchers look at both long- and short-term trends for colors, surface textures, and user choices.

One key finding was that in rural areas, mobile phones are shared by families or even villages. Therefore, Nokia designed new phones that are sturdy enough to withstand usage from different people: they have a special grip area that makes them easier to hold in hot climates and seamless keypads to keep out dust. Address books allow each user to save his or her own contacts and numbers separately.

The phones also have a demo mode so people with limited or no experience can quickly learn how to use the phones.

Adapted from Nandini Lakshman, "Nokia's Global Design Sense," in *Inside Innovation*, http://www.businessweek.com/print/innovate/content/aug2007/id20070810_686743.htm (accessed April 10, 2009).

being employed by various producers of consumer products and services. The networks are often cheaper and more effective than traditional focus groups because they have broader participation and allow for deeper and ongoing probing. Companies can use them for polls, real-time chats with actual consumers, and product trials.[20]

Observing Customers and Users

Answers to surveys and interviews may differ from actual behavior—sometimes greatly. To get more accurate consumer information, many marketers observe users. For example, one problem with asking consumers about their television-watching behavior is that they sometimes underreport the number of hours they watch and the degree to which they watch programs they aren't proud of liking. Researchers have tried to develop a variety of measurement methods that collect viewing data automatically. Arbitron introduced the Portable People Meter (PPM), which receives an inaudible electronic signal from radio stations and broadcast and cable TV stations. Consumers simply carry the PPM, and it records their media exposure. One of the first results showed that consumers listened to radio more than they had indicated in diaries.[21] Nielsen Media Research has added commercial viewings to its famous TV show numbers; advertisers are naturally anxious to know how many people actually watch commercials instead of leaving to get a snack or fast-forwarding through them on digital video recorders.[22] Nielsen has also started tracking college students' viewing, installing its people meters in commons areas such as dorms. The new data boosted ratings for some shows, such as *Grey's Anatomy* and *America's Next Top Model*, by more than 35%.[23]

Observation can tell marketers more about customers than the customers can put into words themselves. Intuit, a leader in observation studies, sends employees to visit customers and watch how they use Intuit products such as QuickBooks. Watching small businesses struggle with QuickBooks Pro told the company of the need for a new product, QuickBooks Simple Start.[24] Nokia sends researchers to various countries to learn about local tastes in mobile phones. They have learned that in India the phone is a status symbol and therefore must have the right style and project the proper image. In China and

Kroger has researched customer shopping patterns to help increase sales.
Source: Aili McConnon, "Grocers: A Shift toward Thrift," *BusinessWeek,* August 25/September 1, 2008, 72, 73.

Africa, on the other hand, price is paramount.[25] See the sidebar on this page for more about Nokia's research.

Observation can also be used for gathering in-house information such as how efficiently production systems operate and how well employees serve customers. Many businesses use "mystery shoppers." For instance, McDonald's has used mystery shoppers to check cleanliness, customer service, and food quality. The company posts store-by-store results online, giving store operators an incentive and the information they need to improve quality on measures where they are slipping or lagging behind the region's performance.[26]

Even health care facilities use mystery shoppers. After they give their reports, the most common changes are improved estimates of waiting times and better explanations of medical procedures. So many organizations use mystery shoppers that there is a Mystery Shopping Providers Association; it reported $600 million revenue for the industry in 2004.[27]

Observation is often combined with other techniques to get the most information. *Think-aloud protocols* ask users to voice their thoughts as they use a document or product: "First I'll try. . . ." These protocols are tape-recorded and later analyzed to understand how users approach a document or product. *Interruption interviews* interrupt users to ask them what's happening. For example, a company testing a draft of computer instructions might interrupt a user to ask, "What are you trying to do now? Tell me why you did that." *Discourse-based interviews* ask questions based on documents that the interviewee has written: "You said that the process is too complicated. Tell me what you mean by that."

Source Citation and Documentation

In a good report, sources are cited and documented smoothly and unobtrusively. **Citation** means attributing an idea or fact to its source *in the body of the report:* "According to the 2000 Census . . ." "Jane Bryant Quinn argues that. . . ." Citing sources demonstrates your honesty and enhances your credibility. **Documentation** means providing the bibliographic information readers would need to go back to the original source. The two usual means of documentation are notes and lists of references.

Failure to document and cite sources is **plagiarism,** the passing off of the words or ideas of others as one's own. Plagiarism can lead to nasty consequences. The news regularly showcases examples of people who have been fired or sued for plagiarism. Now that curious people can type sentences into Google and find the sources, plagiarism is easier than ever to catch.

Note that citation and documentation are used in addition to quotation marks. If you use the source's exact words, you'll use the name of the person you're citing and quotation marks in the body of the report; you'll indicate the source in parentheses and a list of references or in a footnote or endnote. If you put the source's idea into your own words, or if you condense or synthesize information, you don't need quotation marks, but you still need to tell whose idea it is and where you found it. See Figures 17.7 and 17.8 for examples of quoting and paraphrasing.

Long quotations (four typed lines or more) are used sparingly in business reports. Since many readers skip quotes, always summarize the main point of the quotation in a single sentence before the quotation itself. End the sentence with a colon, not a period, since it introduces the quote. Indent long quotations on the left and right to set them off from your text. Indented quotations do not

Looking with the Customers' Eyes

IDEO, a design firm based in Palo Alto, California, uses observational research to design work processes that improve the customer's experience. IDEO requires its clients to participate in the research so that they can see how it feels to be one of their own customers. Clients may try using the company's product or go on shopping trips, or they may quietly observe customers. Following an initial observation phase, IDEO works with clients to use the observation data for brainstorming. IDEO then prepares and tests prototypes of the redesigned service, refines the ideas, and puts the revisions into action.

IDEO helped Kaiser Permanente revise its long-term growth plan to be more focused on clients' experiences with the health system. Working in teams with nurses, doctors, and managers from Kaiser, IDEO employees observed patients and occasionally role-played patient experiences. They saw that the check-in process was annoying, and waiting rooms were uncomfortable. Many of the patients arrived with a relative or friend for support, but they were often not allowed to remain together. Sitting alone in examination rooms was unpleasant and unnerving.

Based on these observations, Kaiser realized that it needed to focus more on improving patient experiences than on the original plan of modernizing buildings. The company created more comfortable areas in which patients could wait with family and friends, as well as examination rooms large enough to accommodate two people in addition to the patient. Instructions on where to go were made clearer as well.

Adapted from Bruce Nussbaum, "The Power of Design," *BusinessWeek*, May 17, 2004, 86.

Figure 17.7   Report Paragraphs with APA Documentation

Headings and paragraph numbers help readers find material in a Web site without page numbers. If the source does not number the paragraphs, number the paragraphs yourself under each heading.

Square brackets indicate a change from the original to make the quote fit into the structure of your sentence.

Because source is adequately identified in text, no parenthetical source citation is needed.

Basic APA citation: Place author and date in parentheses; separate with a comma, Use page numbers only for a direct quote.

Social media can be defined as "technology facilitated dialogue among individuals or groups, such as blogs, microblogs, forums, wikis," and other unofficial forms of electronic communication (Cone, 2008, What is social media? ¶. 1). In a 2008 study on social media, Cone found that 39% of Americans reported using social media Web sites at least once a week; 30% reported using them two or more times a week. Additionally, the study found that 34% believed that companies should have a presence on social media Web sites and use their presence to interact with their customers. Fifty-one percent of users believed that companies should be present on these Web sites but interact only if customers ask them to do so (Cone). "While the ultimate measure [of most companies' marketing efforts] is sales, social media expands that because of its focus on influencers," says Simon Salt (2009, p. 20), the CEO of Inc-Slingers, a marketing communication firm. For example, he says "cable provider Comcast utilizes social media to monitor existing customer issues. . . . Known on Twitter as @comcastcares, it quickly developed a reputation for engaging its customer base" (p. 20).   *Use page number for direct quote. Author's name already in text, so not repeated here.*

The Cone study also found that 25% of users of social media Web sites reported interacting with companies at least once a week. When asked what kind of role companies should play on these Web sites, 43% said giving virtual customer service, 41% said soliciting customer feedback. Among some of the most popular social media Web sites are Facebook, My Space, Twitter, Blogger, and Digg.

Twitter, a microblogging Web site, asks its users a simple question: "What are you doing?" Users can post their own updates and follow others' updates. Twitter has grown at a breathtaking pace in the last few months. It registered a whopping 600% increase in traffic in the 12 months leading up to November 2008. It is estimated that the microblogging Web site has approximately 3 million registered account holders from across the globe (Salt, 2009). A message or post on Twitter, known as a "tweet," cannot be more than 140 characters long. Companies and organizations are increasingly taking to Twitter.

Visible Technologies, a Seattle-based market research firm, helps companies search for valuable market information from a virtual pool of millions of tweets. Some of the firm's clients include Hormel Foods and Panasonic. The computer manufacturer Dell, another customer, asks its customer representatives to interact with customers on Twitter. Recently, the company announced that it increased its sales by $500,000 through the use of Twitter (Baker, 2008, Promotional Tweets, para. 1). Zappos.com, an online shoe seller, encourages its employees to use Twitter to communicate about subjects as wide-ranging as politics to marketing plans (Vascellaro, 2008).

Numbers at the beginning of sentences must be written out.

This citation for a direct quote uses only year and page number ("p." before number) since author is identified in sentence.

Ellipses (three spaced dots) indicate some material has been omitted. An extra dot serves as the period of the sentence.

No need to provide a citation for facts that are general or common knowledge.

Date of publication (year month day) for a weekly source.

Use URL of a specific Web page; do not put period after URL. Break long URLs after a /

Source by a corporate author.

Only initials for all names except last.

List all works (but only those works) cited in the text. List sources alphabetically.

References

Baker, S. (2008 May 15). Why Twitter matters. *BusinessWeek* Retrieved April 15, 2009, from http://www.businessweek.com/technology/content/may2008/tc20080514_269697.htm

Cone. (2008). 2008 business in social media study [Fact sheet]. Retrieved April 15, 2009 from http://www.coneinc.com /stuff /contentmgr/ files/0/26ff8eb1d1a9371210502558013fe2a6/files / 2008_business_in_social_media_fact_sheet.pdf

Salt, S. (2009, February 15). Track your success. *Marketing News, 43*, 20.

Vascellaro, J. (2008, October 27). Twitter goes mainstream. *Wall Street Journal*, p. R3.

Article titles use sentence capitalization and no quotation marks.

Retrieval date is month day, year.

Italicize volume number.

Don't abbreviate month.

Figure 17.8   Report Paragraphs with MLA Documentation

Do not list page or paragraph numbers if the source is unnumbered.

Square brackets indicate a change from the original to make the quote fit into the structure of your sentence.

Ellipses (three spaced dots) indicate some material has been omitted. An extra dot serves as the period of the sentence.

Because source is identified in text and has no page numbers, no citation is needed.

Basic MLA citation: author and page number. Give page number for facts as well as quotes. No comma or "p." between author and number.

Social media can be defined as "technology facilitated dialogue among individuals or groups, such as blogs, microblogs, forums, wikis" and other unofficial forms of electronic communication (Cone). In a 2008 study on social media, Cone found that 39% of Americans reported using social media Web sites at least once a week; 30% reported using them two or more times a week. Additionally, the study found that 34% believed that companies should have a presence on social media Web sites and use their presence to interact with their customers. Fifty-one percent of users believed that companies should be present on these Web sites but interact only if customers ask them to do so (Cone). "While the ultimate measure [of most companies' marketing efforts] is sales, social media expands that because of its focus on influencers," says Simon Salt, the CEO of Inc-Slingers, a marketing communication firm (20). For example, he says "cable provider Comcast utilizes social media to monitor existing customer issues. . . . Known on Twitter as @comcastcares, it quickly developed a reputation for engaging its customer base" (20).

Numbers at the beginnings of sentences must be written out.

No "p." before page number; use only page number since author identified in sentence.

Use page number (no "p.") for direct quote. Author's name is already in text, so is not repeated here.

The Cone study also found that 25% of users of social media Web sites reported interacting with companies at least once a week. When asked what kind of role companies should play on these Web sites, 43% said giving virtual customer service, 41% said soliciting customer feedback. Among some of the most popular social media Web sites are Facebook, MySpace, Twitter, Blogger, and Digg.

No need to provide a citation for facts that are general or common knowledge.

Twitter, a microblogging Web site, asks its users a simple question: "What are you doing?" Users can post their own updates and follow others' updates. Twitter has grown at a breathtaking pace in the last few months. It registered a whopping 600% increase in traffic in the 12 months leading up to November 2008. It is estimated that the micro-blogging Web site has approximately 3 million registered account holders from across the globe (Salt 20). A message or post on Twitter, known as a "tweet," cannot be more than 140 characters long. Companies and organizations are increasingly taking to Twitter.

Visible Technologies, a Seattle-based market research firm, helps companies search for valuable market information from a virtual pool of millions of tweets. Some of the firm's clients include Hormel Foods and Panasonic. The computer manufacturer Dell, another customer, asks its customer representatives to interact with customers on Twitter. Recently, the company announced that it increased its sales by $500,000 through the use of Twitter (Baker). Zappos.com, an online shoe seller, encourages its employees to use Twitter to communicate, about subjects as wide-ranging as politics to marketing plans (Vascellaro R3).

Do not list headings or paragraph numbers if the source is unnumbered.

Article titles use title capitalization and quotation marks.

Date of publication: day month (abbreviated) year.

Source by a corporate author.

All names typed as they appear in the source.

Abbreviate months with five of more letters.

Works Cited

List all works (but only those works) cited in the text. List sources alphabetically.

Baker, Stephen. "Why Twitter Matters." *BusinessWeek.* 15 May 2008. Web. 2 Apr. 2009.

Type of source (Print or Web).

Date you visited site: day month year. Abbreviate months.

Cone. "2008 Business in Social Media Study." 2008. Web. 2 Apr. 2009 <http://www.coneinc.com/stuff/contentmgr/files/0/26ff8eb1d1a9371210502558013fe2a6/files/2008_business_in_social_media_fact_sheet.pdf>.

Salt, Simon. "Track Your Success." *Marketing News.* 2 Apr. 2009: 20 Print.

Vascellaro, Jessica. "Twitter Goes Mainstream." *Wall Street Journal.* 27 Oct. 2008: R3. Print.

Volume and issue number not listed for weekly magazines.

URL in angle brackets; period after angle brackets. Break long URLs after a slash. URLs are only given for sites that may be difficult to find otherwise.

Figure 17.9 APA Format for Sources Used Most Often in Reports

APA internal documentation gives the author's last name and the date of the work in parentheses in the text. A comma separates the author's name from the date (Salt, 2009). The page number is given only for direct quotations or in cases where the reader may need help to find the location: (Salt, 2009, p. 20). If the author's name is used in the sentence, only the date is given in parentheses (see Figure 17.7). A list of references gives the full bibliographic citation, arranging the entries alphabetically by the first author's last name.

In titles of articles and books capitalize only (1) first word, (2) first word of subtitle, (3) proper nouns.

In the examples below, headings in green identify the kind of work being referenced. The green headings are not part of the actual citation itself.

Capitalize all major words in title of journal, magazine, or newspaper.

Put authors' last names first. Use only initials for first and middle names.

Note comma after initial, use of ampersand, period after parenthesis.

No quotation marks around title of article.

Article in a Periodical
Kangasharju, H., & Nikko, T. (2009). Emotions in organizations: Joint laughter in workplace meetings. *The Journal of Business Communication*, *46*, 100–119.

Give complete page numbers. No "pp." when journal has a volume number

Volume number is italicized. Provide issue number in parentheses only if each issue begins with page 1.

Date is year, month day

Article in a Newspaper
Siegel, L. (2009, January 24). The hidden state of culture. *The Wall Street Journal*, pp. W3, W5.

Use "p." for single page,"pp." for multiple pages.

Separate discontinuous pages with a comma and a space.

Author and editor names use initials for first and middle names.

Article in an Edited book
Belknap, J., Hartman, J. L., & Lippen, V. L. (2010). Misdemeanor domestic violence cases in the courts: A detailed description of the cases. In V. Garcia & J. Clifford (Eds.), *Female victims of crime: Reality reconsidered* (pp. 259–278). Upper Saddle River, NJ: Prentice Hall.

Put editors before book title.

Editors' names have last names last.

Ampersands join names of coauthors, coeditors.

Give state abbreviation when city is not well known.

Use full page numbers for article.

Publication date: year, month day.

Article from a Publication on the Web
O'Rourke, M. (2008, June 5). Death of a saleswoman: How Hillary Clinton lost me—and a generation of young voters. *Slate*. Retrieved December 3, 2008, from http://www.slate.com/id/2192827/

Retrieval date: Month date, year.

No punctuation after URL

Book
Miller, K. (2008). *Organizational communication: Approaches and processes*. Florence, KY: Cengage Learning.

(Continued)

Figure 17.9 APA Format for Sources Used Most Often in Reports (Concluded)

Indicates organization authoring document also published it.

Book or Pamphlet with a Corporate Author
Royal Institute of British Architects. (2008). *Architect's job book.* [London:]

Author.

Put in brackets information known to you but not printed in document.

E-mail Message
[Identify e-mail messages in the text as personal communications. Give name of author

and as specific a date as possible. Do not list in References.]

Abbreviate and use periods.

Government Document Available on the Web from the GPO Access Database
U.S. Government Accountability Office. (2007, May.) *Aviation security: Foreign*

airport assessments and air carrier inspections help enhance security but oversight of

these efforts can be strengthened. (Publication No. GAO-07-729). Retrieved April 9,

2009, from Government Accountability Office Reports Online via GPO Access:

http://frwebgate.access.gpo.gov/cgi-bin/getdoc.cgi?dbname=gao&docid=f:d07729.pdf

Abbreviate Government Printing Office

Interview Conducted by the Researcher
[Identify interviews in the text as personal communications. Give name of interviewee

and as specific a date as possible. Do not list in References.]

Italicize titles of stand-alone works. An article that is part of a larger work is put in Roman type and quotation marks.

Break long URLs after a slash. No period after URL

n.d. if no date is given
Web site
Berry, T. (n.d.). *Getting started on your business plan.* Retrieved April 9, 2009, from

http://articles.bplans.com/writing-a-business-plan/getting-started-on-your-business-plan

need quotation marks; the indentation shows the reader that the passage is a quote.

To make a quotation fit the grammar of your report, you may need to change one or two words. Sometimes you may want to add a few words to explain something in the longer original. In both cases, use square brackets to indicate words that are your replacements or additions. Omit any words in the original source that are not essential for your purposes. Use ellipses (spaced dots) to indicate where your omissions are. See Figures 17.7 and 17.8 for examples.

Document every fact and idea that you take from a source except facts that are common knowledge. Historical dates and facts are considered common knowledge. Generalizations are considered common knowledge ("More and more women are entering the workforce") even though specific statements

Figure 17.10 MLA Format for Sources Used Most Often in Reports

MLA internal documentation gives the author's last name and page number in parentheses in the text for facts as well as for quotations. Unlike APA, the year is not given, no comma separates the name and page number, and the abbreviation "p." is not used: (Salt 20). If the author's name is used in the sentence, only the page number is given in parentheses (see Figure 17.8). A list of Works Cited gives the full bibliographic citation, arranging the entries alphabetically by the first author's last name. Note that the Works Cited list gives the medium (e.g., Web, Print). URLs for Web sources are given only when the item may be hard to find otherwise.

In the examples below, headings in green identify the kind of work being referenced. The green headings are not part of the actual citation itself.

Use authors' full names as printed in source. First name first for second author

Put quotation marks around title of article

Capitalize all major words in titles of articles, books, journals, magazines, and newspapers

Article in a Periodical
Kangasharju, Helena and Tuija Nikko. "Emotions in Organizations: Joint Laughter in Workplace Meetings." *The Journal of Business Communication* 46.1 (2009): 100–19. Print.

Omit "1" in "119"

Entries designated as Print or Web

Use both volume and issue number

Omit introductory articles (e.g. "The") for newspapers and journals.

Article in a Newspaper
Siegel, Lee. "The Hidden State of Culture." *Wall Street Journal* 29 Jan. 2009: W3+. Print.

Plus sign indicates article skips one or more pages before continuing

Date given as day month (abbreviated) year

Give authors', editors' full names as printed in the source. All but first author have last name last.

Article in an Edited book
Belknap, Joanne, Jennifer L. Hartman, and Victoria L. Lippen. "Misdemeanor Domestic Violence Cases in the Courts: A Detailed Description of the Cases." *Female Victims of Crime: Reality Reconsidered*. Ed. Vanessa Garcia and Janice Clifford. Upper Saddle River: Prentice Hall, 2010. 259–78. Print.

Put book title before editors' names.

Join editors' names with "and."

City of publication but not state

Omit "2" from "278" in article page numbers.

Article from a Publication on the Web
O'Rourke, Meghan. "Death of a Saleswoman: How Hillary Clinton Lost Me—and a Generation of Young Voters." *Slate*. Washingtonpost.Newsweek Interactive Co. LLC, 5 June 2008. Web. 9 Apr. 2009.

Publication date

Access date

URLS are only given for sites that may be difficult to find.

Publisher or sponsor of site.

Book
Miller, Katherine. *Organizational Communication: Approaches and Processes*. Florence: Cengage Learning, 2008. Print.

Date after city and publisher

(Continued)

Figure 17.10   MLA Format for Sources Used Most Often in Reports (Concluded)

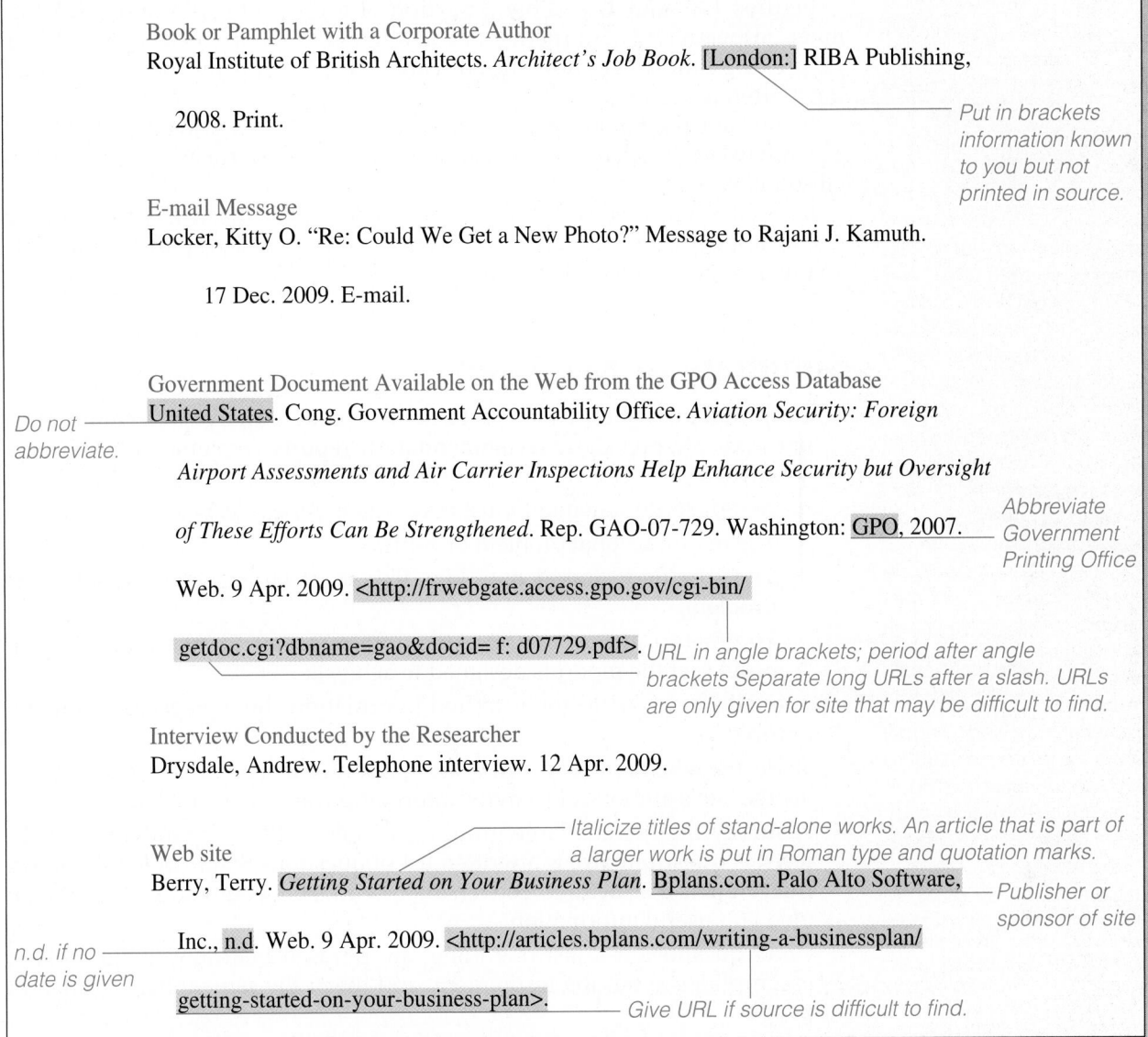

about the same topic (such as the percentage of women in the workforce in 1975 and in 2000) would require documentation.

The three most widely used formats for footnotes, endnotes, and bibliographies in reports are those of the American Psychological Association (APA), the Modern Language Association (MLA), and the University of Chicago *Manual of Style* format, which this book uses. **Internal documentation** provides in parentheses in the text the source where the reference was found. For MLA format, the source is indicated by the author's last name (if that isn't already in the sentence), or by the last name plus the date of the work if you're using two or more works by the same author, or if the dates of the works are important. MLA internal documentation also provides the page number. For APA format, the source is indicated by the author's last name plus the year, unless those items are already in the text. APA format gives page numbers only for quotes or in cases where readers may need help to find the exact location. The

Tools to Assess Internal Organizational Communication

The Communication Satisfaction Questionnaire (CSQ) and Critical Incident Technique (CIT) are research tools for assessing the communication climate within organizations. While CSQ consists of Likert-scale–type questions on topics such as informal communication and relationships with superiors and subordinates, CIT is an open-ended and qualitative exploration of positive and negative communication incidents as employees perceive them.

Using these two techniques, researchers performed a communication audit of three institutions. The results showed that the two techniques, though different, produced similar findings. The researchers also concluded that CSQ was an effective technique in assessing overall communication climate of organizations, including impact of communication training on employees' performance. Perhaps an even more important conclusion of the study was that CSQ needed to be employed along with qualitative research techniques such as CIT and focus groups to get a more reliable picture of organizational communication.

Adapted from K. Zwizje-Koning and M. de Jong, "Evaluating the Communication Satisfaction Questionnaire as a Communication Audit Tool," *Management Communication Quarterly* 20, no. 3 (2007): 261–82.

full bibliographical citation appears in a list of references or works cited at the end of the report.

Figures 17.7 and 17.8 show a portion of a report in APA and MLA formats, respectively, with the list of references (APA) or works cited (MLA). Figures 17.9 and 17.10 show the APA and MLA formats for the sources used most often in reports.

If you have used many sources that you have not cited, you may want to list separately both works cited and works consulted. The term *bibliography* covers all sources on a topic.

If you use a printed source that is not readily available, consider including it as an appendix in your report. For example, you could copy an ad or include an organization's promotional brochure.

Summary of Key Points

- **Information reports** collect data for the reader; **analytical reports** present and interpret data; **recommendation reports** recommend action or a solution.

- A good purpose statement must make three things clear:
  - The organizational problem or conflict.
  - The specific technical questions that must be answered to solve the problem.
  - The rhetorical purpose (to explain, to recommend, to request, to propose) that the report is designed to achieve.

- Use indexes and directories to find information about a specific company or topic.

- To decide whether to use a Web site as a source in a research project, evaluate the site's authors, objectivity, information, and revision date.

- A **survey** questions a large group of people, called **respondents** or **subjects**. A **questionnaire** is a written list of questions that people fill out. An **interview** is a structured conversation with someone who will be able to give you useful information.

- Good questions ask just one thing, are phrased neutrally, avoid making assumptions about the respondent, and mean the same thing to different people.

- **Closed questions** have a limited number of possible responses. **Open questions** do not lock the subject into any sort of response. **Branching questions** direct different respondents to different parts of the questionnaire based on their answers to earlier questions. A **mirror question** paraphrases the content of the last answer. **Probes** follow up an original question to get at specific aspects of a topic.

- A **convenience sample** is a group of subjects who are easy to get. A **judgment sample** is a group of people whose views seem useful. In a **random sample,** each person in the population theoretically has an equal chance of being chosen. A sample is random only if a formal, approved random sampling method is used. Otherwise, unconscious bias can exist.

- **Citation** means attributing an idea or fact to its source in the body of the report. **Documentation** means providing the bibliographic information readers would need to go back to the original source.

Exercises and Problems

17.1   Reviewing the Chapter

1. What are some criteria for defining report problems? (LO 1)
2. What are four criteria for evaluating Web sources? (LO 2)
3. What are some criteria for good survey questions? (LO 2)
4. What is a random sample? (LO 2)
5. Choose either APA or MLA. For that format, write a References entry or Works Cited entry for a book, journal article, and Web site. (LO 3)

17.2   Reviewing Grammar

Reports use lots of numbers. Test your knowledge about writing numbers by doing Exercise B.10 in Appendix B.

17.3   Defining Report Problems

In small groups, turn the following topics into specific report problems. The first topic has been converted into a specific report problem for your reference.

1. Global warming or climate change ("Alternative Energy in Iowa")
2. Globalization
3. Marketing to younger audiences
4. Social networking Web sites
5. Entrepreneurship
6. Career planning
7. Customer service
8. Credit card debt
9. Campus-based organizations
10. Research and innovation

17.4   Identifying the Weaknesses in Problem Statements

Identify the weaknesses in the following problem statements.

- Is the problem narrow enough?
- Can a solution be found in a semester or quarter?
- What organization could implement any recommendations to solve the problem?
- Could the topic be limited or refocused to yield an acceptable problem statement?

1. One possible report topic I would like to investigate would be the differences in women's intercollegiate sports in our athletic conference.
2. How to market products effectively to college students.
3. Should Web banners be part of a company's advertising?
4. How can US and Canadian students get jobs in Europe?
5. We want to explore ways our company can help raise funds for the Open Shelter. We will investigate whether collecting and recycling glass, aluminum, and paper products will raise enough money to help.
6. How can XYZ University better serve students from traditionally underrepresented groups?
7. What are the best investments for the next year?

17.5   Writing a Preliminary Purpose Statement

Answer the following questions about a topic on which you could write a formal report.

As your instructor directs,

a. Be prepared to answer the questions orally in a conference.
b. Bring written answers to a conference.
c. Submit written answers in class.
d. Give your instructor a photocopy of your statement after it is approved.

1. What problem will you investigate or solve?
   a. What is the name of the organization facing the problem?
   b. What is the technical problem or difficulty?
   c. Why is it important to the organization that this problem be solved?
   d. What solution or action might you recommend to solve the problem?
   e. List the name and title of the person in the organization who would have the power to accept or reject your recommendation.
2. Will this report use information from other classes or from work experiences? If so, give the name and topic of the class and/or briefly describe the job. If you will need additional information (that you have not already gotten from other classes or from a job), how do you expect to find it?
3. List the name, title, and business phone number of a professor who can testify to your ability to handle the expertise needed for this report.
4. List the name, title, and business phone number of someone in the organization who can testify that you have access to enough information about that organization to write this report.

17.6   Choosing Research Strategies

For each of the following reports, indicate the kinds of research that might be useful. If a survey is called for, indicate the most efficient kind of sample to use.
a. How can XYZ store increase sales?
b. What is it like to live and work in [name of country]?
c. Should our organization have a dress code?
d. Is it feasible to start a monthly newsletter for students in your major?
e. How can we best market to mature adults?
f. Can compensation programs increase productivity?
g. What skills are in demand in our area? Of these, which could the local community college offer courses in?

17.7   Evaluating Web Sites

Choose five Web sites that are possible resources for a report. Evaluate them on the credibility and trustworthiness of their information. Consider the following questions and compare and contrast your findings.

- What person or organization sponsors the site? What credentials do the authors have?
- Does the site give evidence to support its claims? Does it give both sides of controversial issues?
- Is the tone professional?
- How complete is the information? What is it based on?
- How current is the information?

Based on your findings, which sites are best for your report and why?

As your instructor directs,
a. Write a memo to your instructor summarizing your results.
b. Share your results with a small group of students.
c. Present your results to the class in an oral presentation.

17.8   Choosing Samples for Surveys and Interviews

For the following topics, indicate the types of sample(s) you would use in collecting survey data and in conducting interviews.
a. How can your school save money to limit tuition increases?
b. How can your favorite school organization attract more student members?
c. How can your school improve communication with international students?
d. How should your school deal with hate speech?
e. How can instructors at your school improve their electronic presentations for students?

17.9 Evaluating Survey Questions

Evaluate each of the following questions. Are they acceptable as they stand? If not, how can they be improved?

a. Survey of clerical workers:

Do you work for the government? ☐
or the private sector? ☐

b. Questionnaire on grocery purchases:

1. Do you *usually* shop at the same grocery store?
    a. Yes
    b. No
2. Do you use credit cards to purchase items at your grocery store?
    a. Yes
    b. No
3. How much is your average grocery bill?
    a. Under $25
    b. $25–50
    c. $50–100
    d. $100–150
    e. Over $150

c. Survey on technology:

1. Would you generally welcome any technological advancement that allowed information to be sent and received more quickly and in greater quantities than ever before?
2. Do you think that all people should have free access to all information, or do you think that information should somehow be regulated and monitored?

d. Survey on job skills:

How important are the following skills for getting and keeping a professional-level job in US business and industry today?

	Low				High
Ability to communicate	1	2	3	4	5
Leadership ability	1	2	3	4	5
Public presentation skills	1	2	3	4	5
Selling ability	1	2	3	4	5
Teamwork capability	1	2	3	4	5
Writing ability	1	2	3	4	5

17.10 Designing Questions for an Interview or Survey

Submit either a one- to three-page questionnaire or questions for a 20- to 30-minute interview AND the information listed below for the method you choose.

Questionnaire

1. Purpose(s), goal(s).
2. Subjects (who, why, how many).
3. How and where to be distributed.
4. Any changes in type size, paper color, etc., from submitted copy.
5. Rationale for order of questions, kinds of questions, wording of questions.
6. References, if building on questionnaires by other authors.

Interview

1. Purpose(s), goal(s).
2. Subjects (who, and why).
3. Proposed site, length of interview.
4. Rationale for order of questions, kinds of questions, wording of questions, choice of branching or follow-up questions.
5. References, if building on questions devised by others.

As your instructor directs,

a. Create questions for a survey on one of the following topics:

- Survey students on your campus about their knowledge of and interest in the programs and activities sponsored by a student organization.
- Survey workers at a company about what they like and dislike about their jobs.
- Survey people in your community about their willingness to pay more to buy products using recycled materials and to buy products that are packaged with a minimum of waste.
- Survey two groups on a topic that interests you.

b. Create questions for an interview on one of the following topics:

- Interview an international student about the forms of greetings and farewells, topics of small talk, forms of politeness, festivals and holidays, meals at home, size of families, and roles of family members in his or her country.
- Interview a TV producer about what styles and colors work best for people appearing on TV.
- Interview a worker about an ethical dilemma he or she faced on the job, what the worker did and why, and how the company responded.
- Interview the owner of a small business about problems the business has, what strategies the owner has already used to increase sales and

- What can you tell about the company's financial situation from the report?
- What role do visuals play in the report? What image do they portray for the company? How do the visuals help establish credibility for the report? What do they imply about power distribution in the company?
- Does the report deal with any ethical issues?

As your instructor directs,

a. Write a memo to your instructor comparing and contrasting the two reports according to your analysis answers. Explain which report you find more effective and why.

b. Share your results orally with a small group of students.

c. Present your results to the class.

17.17　All-Weather Case: Evaluating the Cross-Cultural Training Program

Caleb is designing the new cross-cultural training program. Two years ago, when All-Weather had its first cross-cultural training program, the one-day program was videotaped but no evaluation of the program was done, resulting in Caleb's having to spend a week this time just to gather the employees' feedback on the earlier training program. Many of the employees who had taken the training found it hard to remember anything about the training program after two years.

Caleb and his team could not find concrete evidence of what worked and what did not work in the training two years ago. Caleb watched several videotaped sessions of the earlier training, but watching the tapes of more than three dozen sessions was out of the question because of the time involved. Had the program been evaluated, the final evaluative/recommendation report would have given quick and succinct information about the effectiveness of the program.

Because Tanner is busy working on the finer details of the training program for two plants (Lincoln, Nebraska, and Cedar Rapids, Iowa), Caleb asks his colleagues Erin and Miguel to temporarily loan him the services of their deputies, Rudy and Linda. He also asks for Kioni's help. She is excited to be involved in what she sees as a "major" project during her internship. Erin has a slight hesitation in offering Rudy's services given his past attitude. However, Rudy has improved in his behavior of late, though his work continues to be mediocre.

Giving Rudy, Linda, and Kioni each a copy of the proposed agenda for the cross-cultural training program, Caleb asks them to work on a process that can usefully evaluate the on-site training (such as for the two plants) as well as, with some modifications, training given through videoconferencing. The results of the evaluation will be compiled into a recommendation report to be used to design future training programs on cross-cultural issues.

"So what do we do?" Rudy asks, breaking into a grin. "Come up with a questionnaire?"

"You may," Caleb says, ignoring Rudy's unseemly grin. "But you will have to do much more than that. You will suggest how and when to evaluate the training program. Do we want to evaluate each training session, or do we want to wait for all the training sessions to be over and then evaluate them all together? Do we interview participants? Give out a questionnaire to the trainees? Observe them as they're receiving the training? Or do we

do all of these things? How do we evaluate on-site training versus the training given through videoconferencing?"

"That's easy," Rudy says excitedly. "Let's do everything and see what works."

"Hmm," Caleb says, politely. "We must have reasons for why we choose a certain method or a combination of methods. Linda, what do you think?"

"I think it would be best," Linda says, looking at Rudy and Kioni, "if we read and discussed the training agenda first. Then we will have a better understanding."

"Absolutely," Kioni agrees. "We need to know about the program if we're to design a plan evaluating it."

"Of course, you do," Caleb says, in an apologetic tone. "Here is the tentative agenda of the two-day training program that Tanner has prepared."

Day 1

9:00–10:15: Cultural Intelligence: Many World Views: Presentation and group discussion

10:30–12:00: Roleplaying a News Story: Individual presentation

12:00–1:00: Lunch break

1:15–2:45: Hofstede's Cultural Dimensions: Presentation

3:00–4:15: Nonverbal Communication: Exercises

Day 2

9:00–10:15: Diversity Management at All-Weather: Presentation

10:30–12:00: United States, Mexico, and Latin America: Cultural Issues: Guest speakers

12:00–1:00: Lunch break

1:15–3:00: Two workshops:

1. Managing Diversity: Cases—for engineers and managers

2. Leadership in the 21st Century: Cases—all employees

3:15–4:15: Benefits of Working Together: Open forum

Rudy is the first to speak when he, Linda, and Kioni discuss the agenda. "I think we should interview all the participants. Just go up to them and record their instant reaction," he says.

"Do you think it will yield meaningful results, though?" Linda says, keeping her tone even and respectful.

a noncompetitive
can still be enorm
$1 billion proposal

Proposal Que

To write a good p
hope to solve and
proposal must ans

- **What problem**
  lem and the or
  it, even if you b
  Sometimes yo
  management r
  that your prop

- **Why does the**
  health, or soci
  predicted cons

- **How are you g**
  that a solution
  investigate. Ex
  tive and desira

- **Can you do t**
  knowledge, m
  larger projects
  data, personne

- **Why should**
  should do the
  the work. Wh
  direct and ind

- **When will yo**
  when each ph

- **How much w**
  for items such
  unique expens
  fees? Pay bene

- **What exactly**
  produce; deve

Since proposal
ing documents, ge
if the proposal w
safeguard your p
products at the sp

Proposal Sty

Good proposals
ence may not be
data analysis pr
tific studies may
language your re
questions your
with data and ot
make sure you in

"Why not observe them instead?" Kioni says, leaning forward.

"Smart idea," Linda says, noting it down. "How do we observe them? I mean how do we observe participants in videoconferencing sessions?"

"Well, we can still see how they're reacting, hear the moderator's comments," Kioni says, remembering a videoconference she sat in on in the HR Department that used the Polycom technology. "Besides, observation will be just one of the methods we will use."

"Why should we use more methods when one will do fine," Rudy says, looking at Linda, whose face remains expressionless.

"What methods can we use to evaluate the on-site training?" Linda says, checking off an item in her writing pad.

"We can give out questionnaires," Rudy says, in an uncharacteristically modest tone.

"I agree," Kioni says.

"What about interviews?" Linda says, stealing a look at her wristwatch. "I think Rudy spoke about this."

"I think we can interview a select group of participants in every session using purposive sampling or something," Kioni says, a little sheepishly, conscious of the fact that she was reciting the information out of a book on qualitative research methods.

"You mean find the people you want to interview according to a design you have in mind," Linda says, making a note in her writing pad.

"Yes," Kioni replies, looking at Rudy, who seems to have dozed off.

"Let's get this started," Linda says. "Rudy, would you like to work on the questionnaire by yourself? Kioni and I can take up the drafting of the evaluation plan."

"That's perfect, Linda," Rudy says, looking a little embarrassed.

On the basis of your reading of Chapter 17 and the details given in the case, discuss the evaluation plan Linda and Kioni should prepare. What research methods should they use in evaluating the cross-cultural training program, both one that is offered on-site and one that is offered through videoconferencing? Do you agree with Kioni that they should use more than one method of primary research (interviews, survey, observation), or do you agree with Rudy that using just one method, a survey, is all that is needed?

After one reminder from Linda, Rudy's draft questionnaire (see below) to evaluate the cross-cultural training program is ready.

1. How would you rate the training that you just received?
   a. Very good
   b. Good
   c. Average
   d. Poor
   e. Very poor
   f. Not helpful
2. Which session did you like the most? (Pick any two)
   a. Cultural Intelligence
   b. Roleplaying a News Story
   c. Hofstede's dimensions

---

   d. Nonverbal communication
   e. Diversity topics
   f. Guest speakers
   g. Open forum
3. Did the training cover everything?
   a. Yes
   b. No
   c. No opinion
4. Was the training enough?
   a. Yes
   b. No
   c. Maybe
5. Did the training address your real concerns about cultural issues?
   a. Yes
   b. No
   c. Can't say
6. Can you rank the following in the order in which you found it less boring?
   a. Presentation
   b. Exercises
   c. Group discussions
   d. Guest speakers
7. Name one thing that made you laugh, was funny, about the training.
8. Name one thing that was the most boring.
9. Your gender
   a. Male
   b. Female
10. Your ethnicity
    a. White
    b. Hispanic
    c. Puerto Rican
    d. Native American
    e. African American
11. Your age
    a. 20–30
    b. 30–40
    c. 40–50
    d. 50–60
    e. 60–70

THANK YOU FOR YR RESPONSE

Linda is shocked to see the draft questionnaire that Rudy has prepared. She starts looking at her schedule to find some time to meet with Rudy and Kioni to work on revising the questionnaire.

Review Rudy's draft questionnaire and suggest revisions that need to be made. Also, offer suggestions on how the questionnaire should be administered: through telephone, through e-mail, as a handout, or through a Web site (such as, for example, www.surveymonkey.com). Justify your chosen method of administering the questionnaire.

564

Under each heading, the group could discuss the tasks it has completed and those that remain.

Task progress reports are appropriate for large projects with distinct topics or projects.

Recommendation Progress Reports

Recommendation progress reports recommend action: increasing the funding or allotted time for a project, changing its direction, canceling a project that isn't working out. When the recommendation will be easy for the reader to accept, use the direct request pattern of organization from Chapter 16 (p. 477). If the recommendation is likely to meet strong resistance, the problem-solving pattern (p. 479) may be more effective.

Summary of Key Points

- A proposal must answer the following questions:
  - What problem are you going to solve?
  - Why does the problem need to be solved now?
  - How are you going to solve it?
  - Can you do the work?
  - Why should you be the one to do it?
  - When will you complete the work?
  - How much will you charge?
  - What exactly will you provide for us?
- In a proposal for a class research project, prove that your problem is the right size, that you understand it, that your method will give you the information you need to solve the problem, that you have the knowledge and resources, and that you can produce the report by the deadline.
- In a project budget, ask for everything you will need to do a good job. Research current cost figures so yours are in line.
- Business plans need to pay particular attention to market potential and financial forecasts.
- In a proposal for funding, stress the needs your project will meet. Show how your project will help fulfill the goals of the organization you are asking for funds.
- Progress reports may be organized by chronology, by task, or to support a recommendation.
- Use positive emphasis in progress reports to create an image of yourself as a capable, confident worker.

Figure 18.1

CHAPTER 18   Exercises and Problems

18.1   Reviewing the Chapter

1. What are six questions a good proposal should answer? (LO 1)

2. What are some guidelines for preparing a budget for a proposal? (LO 2)

3. What are the differences between chronological and task progress reports? (LO 3)

18.2 Writing a Proposal for a Student Report

Write a proposal to your instructor to do the research for a formal or informal report.

The headings and the questions in the section titled "Proposals for Class Research Projects" are your RFP; be sure to answer every question and to use the headings exactly as stated in the RFP. Exception: where alternate heads are listed, you may choose one, combine the two ("Qualifications and Facilities"), or treat them as separate headings in separate categories.

18.3 Proposing a Change

No organization is perfect, especially when it comes to communication. Propose a change that would improve communication within your organization. The change can be specific to your unit or can apply to the whole organization; it can relate to how important information is distributed, who has access to important information, how information is accessed, or any other change in communication practices that you see as having a benefit. Direct your proposal to the person or committee with the power to authorize the change.

18.4 Proposing to Undertake a Research Project

Pick a project you would like to study whose results could be used by your organization. Write a proposal to your supervisor requesting time away from other duties to do the research. Show how your research (whatever its outcome) will be useful to the organization.

18.5 Writing a Proposal for Funding for a Nonprofit Group

Pick a nonprofit group you care about. Examples include professional organizations, a charitable group, a community organization, or your own college or university.

As your instructor directs,

a. Check the Web or a directory of foundations to find one that makes grants to groups like yours. Brainstorm a list of businesses that might be willing to give money for specific projects. Check to see whether state or national levels of your organization make grants to local chapters.

b. Write a proposal to obtain funds for a special project your group could undertake if it had the money. Address your proposal to a specific organization.

c. Write a proposal to obtain operating funds or money to buy something your group would like to have. Address your proposal to a specific organization.

18.6 Writing a Sales Proposal

Pick a project that you could do for a local company or government office. Examples include

- Creating a brochure or Web page.
- Revising form letters.
- Conducting a training program.
- Writing a newsletter or an annual report.
- Developing a marketing plan.
- Providing plant care, catering, or janitorial services.

Write a proposal specifying what you could do and providing a detailed budget and work schedule.

As your instructor directs,

a. Phone someone in the organization to talk about its needs and what you could offer.

b. Write an individual proposal.

c. Join with other students in the class to create a group proposal.

d. Present your proposal orally.

18.7 Presenting a Stockholder Proposal

Visit the Web sites of the following companies and locate their latest proxy statements or reports. These are generally linked from the "about us/company information-investor relations" or "investors" pages. Find shareholder proposals under the heading "proposals requiring your vote," "stockholder proposals," or "shareholder proposals."

- Ford Motor Company
- Citigroup
- AT&T

- J. P. Morgan Chase & Co.
- Southwest Airlines
- Home Depot
- Procter & Gamble
- Boeing
- Google
- Dow Chemical

As a group, select one proposal, and the management response following it, and give an oral presentation answering these questions:

1. What is the problem discussed in the proposal?

2. What is the rationale given for the urgency to solve the problem?

3. How does the proposal seek to solve it?

4. What benefits does the proposal mention that will accrue from the solution?

5. What is the management response to the proposal and what are the reasons given for the response? Does the management response strike you as justified? Why or why not?

Hint: it may help you to do some research on the topic of the proposal.

18.8   Writing a Progress Report to Your Superior

Describe the progress you have made this week or this month on projects you have been assigned. You may describe progress you have made individually, or progress your unit has made as a team.

18.9   Writing a Progress Report

Write a memo to your instructor summarizing your progress on your report.

In the introductory paragraph, summarize your progress in terms of your schedule and your goals. Under a heading titled *Work Completed,* list what you have already done. (This is a chance to toot your own horn: if you have solved problems creatively, say so. You can also describe obstacles you've encountered that you have not yet solved.) Under *Work to Be Completed,* list what you still have to do. If you are more than two days behind the schedule you submitted with your proposal, include a revised schedule, listing the completion dates for the activities that remain.

18.10   Writing a Progress Report for a Group Report

Write a memo to your instructor summarizing your group's progress.

In the introductory paragraph, summarize the group's progress in terms of its goals and its schedule, your own progress on the tasks for which you are responsible, and your feelings about the group's work thus far.

Under a heading titled *Work Completed,* list what has already been done. Be most specific about what you yourself have done. Describe briefly the chronology of group activities: number, time, and length of meetings; topics discussed and decisions made at meetings.

If you have solved problems creatively, say so. You can also describe obstacles you've encountered that you have not yet solved. In this section, you can also comment on problems that the group has faced and whether or not they've been solved. You can comment on things that have gone well and have contributed to the smooth functioning of the group.

Under *Work to Be Completed,* list what you personally and other group members still have to do. Indicate the schedule for completing the work.

18.11   All-Weather Case: Inviting Proposals for the Revision of the Employee Handbook

Doug wants to revise All-Weather's Employee Handbook, which was prepared in the early 1990s but has not been revised since, although new policies have been announced as amendments. Of late, Doug has seen a steady rise in the number of inquiries from offices and plants about employee-related policies and issues. All three managers, Caleb, Erin, and Miguel, have had to deal with these inquiries. Recently, at a meeting with the vice presidents of manufacturing and finance, Doug heard about varying interpretations of some policies in the handbook among different levels of employees. Doug wants the handbook to be revised before these problems become even bigger.

As Doug is rifling through the pages of the handbook, Miguel enters Doug's office.

"You wanted to talk, Doug?" Miguel asks, pulling up a chair.

"Yes. I want you to oversee the revision of the Employee Handbook," Doug says, closing the handbook and spreading his arms.

"Doug, I'm sorry to come across as less than enthusiastic, but I'm loaded with work, as you know," Miguel says, somewhat apologetically.

"I know," Doug says, sympathetically. "But Erin and Caleb just can't do it, with the layoffs, cross-cultural training, and everything else that they have on their plates. Besides, we all know your aptitude for policy details."

"We can outsource this, Doug," Miguel says, picking up the handbook from the table.

"You mean offshoring?" Doug asks. "Because that might require us to edit and proofread the document."

"No. I mean awarding a contract to a US-based writing agency or a consultant," Miguel says, remembering the communication and report-writing problems he encountered in offshoring a part of compensation analysis.

"All right," Doug says. "How's the cost analysis looking?"

"I'm still working on it," Miguel says, getting up. "Let's see where we can cut costs without hurting."

By the next evening, Miguel has prepared an RFP (see below) to invite proposals to revise All-Weather's Employee Handbook, to be placed on All-Weather's Web site as well as the Web site of the Society for Human Resource Management (SHRM) of which both Miguel and All-Weather as a company are members:

RFP for Revising the Employee Handbook of a Midwestern Windows and Doors Manufacturer

All-Weather is a midwestern windows and door manufacturer having 32 offices and five plants across the US and six offices internationally. We employ almost 900 personnel in the US and 180 personnel outside the US. Our products include vinyl, wood, aluminum, steel, and fiberglass composite windows and doors. They are certified by the American Architectural Manufacturers Association (AAMA) and the Window and Door Manufacturers Association (WDMA).

The Task: Revising our Employee Handbook (last revised in 1993)
The contents of the handbook include the following:

- Introductory messages by the chairman and the VP (HR)
- Company mission and values statements
- Job Categories
- New Employee Orientation
- Performance Reviews
- Promotions and Transfers
- Compensation and Benefits
- Holidays
- Personal and Sick Leave
- Leave of Absence
- Retirement
- Occupational Health
- Confidential information
- Fire and Safety
- Disciplinary Action
- Grievance Reviews

The proposal must be submitted online. Please read the rules and conditions before submitting the proposal. You can also view a copy of the existing handbook in pdf and html formats. Your proposal must include a clear statement of the problem, a detailed exposition of your methods, time line, benefits, budget, qualifications, and tangibles.

Based on your reading of Chapter 18 and the details given in the case, draft a proposal to revise All-Weather's Employee Handbook. You can draft the proposal as an individual consultant or assume that you head or work for a consulting agency.

Analyzing Information and Writing Reports

Chapter Outline

Using Your Time Efficiently

Analyzing Data and Information for Reports

- Identifying the Source of the Data
- Analyzing Numbers
- Analyzing Words
- Analyzing Patterns
- Checking Your Logic

Choosing Information for Reports

Organizing Information in Reports

- Basic Patterns for Organizing Information
- Specific Varieties of Reports

Presenting Information Effectively in Reports

1. Use Clear, Engaging Writing.
2. Keep Repetition to a Minimum.

3. Introduce Sources and Visuals.
4. Use Forecasting, Transitions, Topic Sentences, and Headings.

Writing Formal Reports

- Title Page
- Letter or Memo of Transmittal
- Table of Contents
- List of Illustrations
- Executive Summary
- Introduction
- Background or History
- Body
- Conclusions and Recommendations

Summary of Key Points

Inadequate or Misleading Financial Reporting

In September 2008, Lehman Brothers, a global financial services company, declared bankruptcy after the US Federal Reserve Bank refused to bail it out. The event became a symbol of the global economic crisis that saw banks and financial institutions fail across the globe. The financial crisis once again raised questions about how companies disclose and report financial information.

Paul Miller, professor of accounting at the University of Colorado, believes that companies must respect the concerns and needs of their investors the same way they have learned to respect the concerns and needs of their customers, employees, and suppliers. He points out that companies often deliberately provide inadequate or misleading information in their financial reports, creating avoidable risks for investors.

As examples of areas that are subject to inadequate or misleading financial reporting, Professor Miller points out the treatment of "off-the-balance sheet financing" and "pension fund accounting."

Experts like Kenneth Scott, Stanford University law professor and senior research fellow at the Hoover Institution, are calling for electronic financial reporting into a central database.

Numbers reveal important information vital to business decision making. However, numbers can also be used to hide crucial information. Should companies provide detailed narratives (not just footnotes) explaining items on their financial statements? What do you think?

> *"The financial crisis once again raised questions about how companies disclose and report financial information."*

Source: David Bogoslaw, "How to Fix Financial Reporting," in *BusinessWeek: Investing,* http://www.businessweek.com/investor/content/nov2008/pi2008119_257282.htm (accessed April 12, 2009).

Learning Objectives

After studying this chapter, you will know:

1   Ways to analyze data, information, and logic.

2   How to choose information for reports.

3   Different ways to organize reports.

4   How to present information effectively in reports.

5   How to prepare the different components of formal reports.

Careful analysis, smooth writing, and effective document design work together to make effective reports, whether you're writing a 2½-page memo report or a 250-page formal report complete with all the report components.

Chapter 17 covered the first two steps in writing a report:

1. Define the problem.
2. Gather the necessary data and information.

This chapter covers the last three steps:

1. Analyze the data and information.
2. Organize the information.
3. Write the report.

Using Your Time Efficiently

To use your time efficiently, think about the parts of the report before you begin writing. Much of the introduction can come from your proposal, with only minor revisions. You can write six sections even before you've finished your research: Purpose, Scope, Assumptions, Methods, Criteria, and Definitions.

Mock up tables and figures early. Since they provide information on which you will base your arguments or explanations, it is important to arrange data logically and plan how you will use them in the report. As you tally and analyze the data, prepare your figures and tables, and a complete list of references. The background reading for your proposal can form the first draft of your list of references. Save a copy of your questionnaire or interview questions to use as an appendix. You can print appendixes before the final report is ready if you number their pages separately. Appendix A pages would be A-1, A-2, and so forth; Appendix B pages would be B-1, B-2, and so forth.

You can write the title page and the transmittal as soon as you know what your recommendation will be.

After you've analyzed your data, write the body, the conclusions and recommendations, and the executive summary. Prepare a draft of the table of contents and the list of illustrations.

When you write a long report, list all the sections (headings) that your report will have. Mark those that are most important to your reader and your logic, and spend most of your time on them. Write the important sections early. That way, you won't spend all your time on Background or History of the Problem. Instead, you'll get to the meat of your report.

Analyzing Data and Information for Reports

Good reports begin with good data. Analyzing the data you have gathered is essential to produce the tight logic needed for a good report. Analyze your data with healthy skepticism. Check to see that they correspond with expectations or other existing data. If they don't, check for well-supported explanations of the difference.

Spreadsheets can be particularly troublesome. Cell results derived by formulas can be subtly, or grossly, wrong by incorrectly defining ranges, for example. It is easy to generate results that are impossible, such as sums that exceed known totals. Always have an estimate of the result of a calculation. Using spreadsheets, you can easily be wrong by a factor of 10, 100, or 1,000. Results produced by this kind of error are wrong at best, and can be ludicrous and embarrassing. One study found that 30% of spreadsheets had errors, such as misplaced decimal points, transposed digits, and wrong signs, built into their rules.[1] Some of these errors are enormous. Former accounting giant Arthur Andersen made a $644 million one on a NASA audit.[2]

Try to keep ball-park figures, estimates of what the numbers should be, in mind as you look at numerical data. Question surprises before accepting them.

Analyzing data can be hard even for experts. New techniques continually appear, allowing experts to challenge earlier conclusions. One example is the Number Needed to Treat (NNT), a new measure of drug effectiveness developed within the past 20 years. Most clinical trials answer the question, "Will patients on this drug do better than those taking a placebo?" For statins, drugs to reduce high cholesterol, the answer is yes: you may see 30% fewer heart attacks, depending on the particular trial. Sounds great, yes? But how many of those people would have had heart attacks in the first place? If the number is very small, 30% fewer isn't much of a decrease, particularly considering the cost of statins and possible side effects including liver damage. The NNT asks, "How many people have to take this drug to avoid one heart attack?" For statins, the answer is about 50, much different odds and more food for thought for America's aging population as it decides whether or not to take more prescriptions.[3]

Numerous studies exist in scholarly journals challenging the data-based conclusions of earlier articles. One example is the fate of unmarried, college-educated women over 30. A famous *Newsweek* cover story, "Too Late for Prince Charming?" reported the Yale and Harvard study that suggested such women had only a 20% chance of finding husbands, and only a 2.6% chance by the time they reached 40. Twenty years later an economist at the University of Washington examined 30 years of census data. Her figures for the decade of the original study showed that women aged 40–44 with advanced degrees were only 25% less likely to be married than comparably aged women with just high school diplomas. By 2000, those women with postcollege education were slightly more likely to be married than those who had finished only high school.[4]

Identifying the Source of the Data

Check to be sure that your data come from a reliable source. Use the strategies outlined in Chapter 17 to evaluate Web sources (p. 534). When the source has a vested interest (p. 474) in the results, scrutinize the data with special care. To analyze a company's financial prospects, use independent information as well as the company's annual report and press releases.

Drug and medical device companies, and the researchers funded by them, keep appearing in the news with reports of undue influence. Duke University

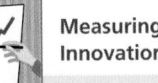

Measuring Innovation

It is commonly accepted wisdom that one measure of a company's innovation is the number of patents it commands. In recent years, however, research has shown that companies increasingly use patents as a defensive strategy rather than a strategy for innovation.

A Boston University study found that software companies with more patents actually reduced their research and development expenditure vis-à-vis sales. Additionally, with companies vying for patents for the smallest addition to product features, patents may be a dubious measure of innovation.

Compared to patents themselves, patent citations, or the references to a company's patent by patents of other companies, may be a better metric of innovation. A high number of patent citations may show that the company's patent truly represents innovation and may be licensed for a fee or royalties. Companies such as Procter & Gamble have adopted this strategy.

Recent studies on patents also show a growing trend of acquiring patents on design or form of products rather than their technical aspects. Companies such as Samsung Electronics and Nike have earned a name for themselves for innovation by acquiring patents based on product design.

Adapted from Jena McGregor, "Are Patents the Measure of Innovation?" in *BusinessWeek: Innovation: May 4, 2007*, http://www.businessweek .com/innovate/content/may2007/ id20070504_323562.htm (accessed April 12, 2009).

Getting the Right Data

Surveys are often used to measure consumer satisfaction, asking people to rate products and services. However, does high customer satisfaction also mean that the quality of the product or service is also high? In a recent study, medical researchers found no correlation between patient satisfaction and the quality of the care received. Those patients that rated the quality of their care as 10 (on a scale of 1 to 10) were no more likely to have received better care than those who gave it a 5.

This example shows some of the thorny issues associated with surveys. First, because surveys are easy to get and report, they are popular. But people who respond to surveys tend to be those who are satisfied with the product or service. In addition, relying on survey data can exclude other important findings. As in the case in medical research, customer satisfaction can mean something very different than the quality of medical care received.

Given these complexities, how can surveys be used effectively?

Adapted from David Wessel, "In Health Care, Consumer Theory Falls Flat," *Wall Street Journal*, September 7, 2006, A2.

researchers checked 746 studies of heart stents published in one year in medical journals. They found that 83% of the papers did not disclose whether authors were paid consultants for companies, even though many journals require that information. Even worse, 72% of the papers did not say who funded the research.[5] A study in the prestigious *New England Journal of Medicine* noted that positive studies of antidepressant trials got published and negative ones did not: "According to the published literature, it appeared that 94% of the trials conducted were positive. By contrast, the FDA analysis showed that 51% were positive."[6]

If your report is based upon secondary data from library and online research, look at the sample, the sample size, and the exact wording of questions to see what the data actually measure. (See Chapter 17 for more information on sampling and surveying.) Does the sample have a built-in bias? A survey of city library users may uncover information about users, but it may not find what keeps other people away from the library.

For many kinds of research, a large sample is important for giving significant results. Nielsen Media Research collects about 2 million television viewing diaries annually to gather viewing data. The large numbers also allow it to provide viewing information for local stations and their advertisers.[7]

A survey that has been the target of much questioning in the press is the one behind the annual college rankings of *US News & World Report*. Critics charge that the rankings are based far too heavily on opinion (peer evaluations from other schools), uncorroborated data supplied by the schools themselves, and irrelevant data (such as rates of alumni giving). Critics also charge schools with gaming the system through practices such as heavy solicitation of students who have almost no chance of being accepted (low acceptance rates help schools' rankings).[8]

Identify exactly what the data measure. When advertisers began to place messages on the Internet, they soon realized that they had a measurement problem. The tools they used to measure viewer response counted the number of people who clicked on an ad that delivered them to the advertiser's Web site. In most cases, of course, advertisers want more than Web site visitors; they want people to buy from the company. Now more sophisticated tools can keep track of the percentage of people who click on the ad and then make a purchase at the company's Web site. Advertisers can use this information to test different versions of their advertising, so they use only the most profitable versions. At the same time, the companies that sell online advertising complain that these measures are unfair because they hold Internet advertising to a higher standard. Other media, such as magazines and television, merely estimate the number of people who see an ad, not the percentage who make a purchase.[9]

Identify the assumptions used in analyzing the data. When Nielsen Media Research estimates the number of people who view television stations, it must make a number of assumptions. The company has to determine how well its People Meter actually tracks whether people are watching, and it has to make decisions about how to count groups that are hard to measure. Nielsen has reported that 18- to 34-year-old males are watching less television, in part because they spend more time with videogames and DVDs. However, television networks complained that the company was underreporting this group's hours for a variety of reasons. For example, Nielsen was not counting young people who leave for college, and its sample did not include homes with TiVo or other personal video recorders (devices that make measurement more difficult). Because of such differences, the networks, Nielsen, and advertisers disagree about whether young men are losing interest in television programming.[10] Nielsen continually refines the ways it collects data. Since its original

Sharp uses what it calls "academic marketing" to sell air purifiers in Japan. Ads in Japanese newspapers and magazines provide data, diagrams, and charts in support of Sharp's plasmacluster technology.

Source: Daisuke Wakabayashi, "Using 'Academic Marketing' to Sell Air Purifiers," *Wall Street Journal*, December 26, 2008, B4.

Sun and Statistics

Recent research suggests that patients with low levels of vitamin D, which can be gained from moderate exposure to the sun, have higher risks of cancer, heart disease, and autoimmune disorders.

The Indoor Tanning Association quickly jumped at this new finding. They used their interpretation of the statistics about low vitamin D levels as a way to promote indoor tanning, suggesting that UV rays can prevent cancer.

The medical community was outraged at the ITA's twisted approach to the statistics. Doctor Lichtenfeld of the American Cancer Society suggested that UV ray promotion was "like recommending smoking to reduce stress." The ITA advertisements failed to suggest there were any downsides to tanning, such as the link between prolonged exposure to UV rays and melanoma. They also omitted that the tanner the skin, the longer it takes to absorb vitamin D.

How ethical is the ITA's use of research statistics? Would you be more likely to tan indoors if you saw one of their advertisements?

Adapted from Pat Wingert, "Teens, Tans, and Truth," *Newsweek*, May 19, 2008, 42–43.

report on young men, for instance, it has started measures to track college students' viewing. Those efforts have increased ratings for some shows by more then 35%.[11]

Analyzing Numbers

Many reports analyze numbers—either numbers from databases and sources or numbers from a survey you have conducted. The numerical information, properly analyzed, can make a clear case in support of a recommendation. Suppose, for example, you are trying to make your company's Web site easier to use. In your report, you might want to include numbers from Jakob Nielsen that using Web sites is 206% harder for people with disabilities and 122% harder for elderly people.[12] These numbers are striking because they are large and because they are quite different. They make the case that some groups are having great difficulty with Web sites; if your company cares about serving these groups, it would be worthwhile to find out how to make your company's Web site easier for them to use. Also, depending on your team's objectives, you might decide to focus more on people with disabilities (because they have much more difficulty) or to focus more on elderly computer users (because they are a larger part of the population). The next steps would include finding out why these groups have trouble and how to make your company's Web site more user friendly. (The Web Accessibility Initiative provides excellent material on how to make Web sites accessible to the disabled: http://www.w3.org/WAI/intro/accessibility.php)

Recognize that even authorities can differ on the numbers they offer, or on the interpretations of the same data sets. Researchers from the United Nations and Johns Hopkins University differed on their estimates of Iraqi deaths in

Getting the Data Right

A 2006 report by Johns Hopkins University claimed that 655,000 Iraqis had died in the war in Iraq, a figure that diverged wildly from other estimates—sometimes more than 1,000%. The Hopkins figure is 500% more than that of the United Nations. Such a difference from other reports calls into question the accuracy of the Hopkins report.

To understand why the figure is so much higher than other research reports, it is important to consider how the data were gathered. The Hopkins researchers used cluster sampling for interviews, a methodology that makes sense given the country's war-zone status. Researchers randomly selected neighborhoods and then conducted door-to-door interviews with "clusters" of individuals from within those neighborhoods. Such a technique saves time and money and is common in research within developing countries.

But the key to this kind of technique is to use enough cluster points. A lack of cluster points can mean that the population sampled isn't representative of the population in Iraq. The Hopkins researchers did not use enough cluster points. In addition, the Hopkins researchers didn't gather demographic data from their participants for comparison to census data. Doing so would have added to the believability of their results.

Getting the data right is important because numbers can have a significant impact on decisions and policies. In terms of casualties, the decisions made based on the numbers reported have an impact on millions of Iraqis and Americans.

Adapted from Stephen E. Moore, "655,000 War Dead?" *Wall Street Journal*, October 18, 2006, A20.

the war by 500% (see sidebar on this page).[13] The cover story of the January 4, 2008, *National Journal* was an explanation of how the two estimates could vary so wildly (research design and execution flaws; sampling error; lack of transparency with the data).[14] You will be best able to judge the quality of data if you know how it was collected.

In their books, *The Tipping Point* and *Freakonomics*, Malcolm Gladwell and Steven D. Levitt and Stephen J. Dubner reach different conclusions about the data on dropping crime rates for New York City. Gladwell attributes the drop to the crackdown by the new police chief on even minor crimes such as graffiti and public drunkenness. Levitt and Dubner first explain why the cause was not a crackdown on crime (the years don't match well; other cities also experienced the drop) and attribute it to the legalization of abortion (at the time of the crime drop the first wave of children born after Roe v. Wade was hitting late teen years and thus prime crime time; that group was short on the category most likely to become criminal: unwanted children). They also provide corroborating evidence from other countries.[15]

If you've conducted a survey, your first step in analyzing your numbers is to transfer the responses on the survey form into numbers. For some categories, you'll assign numbers arbitrarily. For example, you might record men as 1 and women as 2—or vice versa. Such assignments don't matter, as long as you're consistent throughout your project. In these cases, you can report the number and percentage of men and women who responded to your survey, but you can't do anything else with the numbers.

When you have numbers for salaries or other figures, start by figuring the average (or mean), the median, and the range. The **average** or **mean** is calculated by adding up all the figures and dividing by the number of samples. The **mode** is the number that occurs most often. The **median** is the number that is exactly in the middle. When you have an odd number of observations, the median will be the middle number. When you have an even number, the median will be the average of the two numbers in the center. The **range** is the difference between the high and low figures for that variable.

Averages are particularly susceptible to a single extreme figure. In 2007, three different surveys reported the average cost of a wedding at nearly $30,000. Many articles picked up that figure because weddings are big business. However, the median cost in those three surveys was only about $15,000. And even that is probably on the high side, since the samples were convenience samples for a big wedding Web site, a bride magazine, and a maker of wedding invitations.[16]

Figure 19.1 shows the raw data that a student recorded in a report evaluating a hospital's emergency room procedures. To analyze the data, we could rearrange them, listing them from low to high (see Figure 19.2). The average waiting time is 26.6 minutes, but the median (the middle number) is only 22.

Finding the average takes a few more steps when you have different kinds of data. For example, it's common to ask respondents whether they find a feature "very important," "somewhat important," or "not important." You might code "very important" as "3," "somewhat important" as "2," and "not important" as "1." To find the average in this kind of data,

1. For each response, multiply the code ("1," "2," or "3") by the number of people who gave that response.
2. Add up the figures.
3. Divide by the total number of people responding to the question.

Figure 19.1   Raw Data from Observations for a Report

Amount of time (rounded off to the nearest minute) that patients wait in the emergency room before being examined in triage.

Patient	Wait	Patient	Wait	Patient	Wait
1	12	6	17	11	19
2	17	7	35	12	31
3	15	8	12	13	41
4	22	9	54	14	23
5	35	10	50	15	17

Figure 19.2   Rearranging Data to Find the Average (Mean), Mode, and Median

12, 12   Average: 26.6 minutes
15   Median: 22 minutes
17, 17, 17   Mode: 17 minutes
19   Range: 12 – 54 minutes
22
23
31
35, 35
41
50
54

For example, suppose you have the following data after selecting a random sample and surveying 50 people about the features they want in a proposed apartment complex:

	Very important (coded as "3")	Somewhat important (coded as "2")	Not important (coded as "1")
Party house	26	12	13
Extra parking for guests	26	23	1

Following step 1, to get the average for "party house," multiply $3 \times 26 = 78$; $2 \times 12 = 24$; and $1 \times 13 = 13$. Then add $78 + 24 + 13 = 115$. Divide by the number of people answering the question and you get the average for that factor: 115 divided by $50 = 2.3$. Repeat the process for the next factor, "extra parking": $3 \times 26 = 78$; $2 \times 23 = 46$; $1 \times 1 = 1$. Adding $78 + 46 + 1 = 125$; dividing by $50 = 2.5$.

The average then gives an easy way to compare various features. If the party house averages 2.3 while extra parking for guests is 2.5, you know that your respondents would find extra parking more important than a party house. (Whether the difference is significant or not is a statistics question.) You can now arrange the factors in order of importance:

Charity Data

Many people believe they "know" "facts" and figures that are not so. When you encounter these false beliefs, you need to be sure you provide reliable data to counteract them. One area subject to common misperceptions is charity donations. Below are some common myths paired with realities.

Myth: Most charitable giving goes to help the needy. Reality: Less than one-third of individually donated money to nonprofits goes to the economically disadvantaged. And only 8% provides basic needs like food and shelter.

Myth: The wealthy look after those in need. Reality: Only about a quarter of their donations go to the poor, and only 4% to basic needs.

Myth: Religious donations go to those in need. Reality: Less than one-fifth of money donated goes to the poor.

Myth: Americans give generously to international causes. Reality: Only 8% of US individual donations support any international cause whatsoever.

Adapted from Sheryl Sandberg [board member of Google.org, Google's philanthropic arm], "The Charity Gap," *Wall Street Journal*, April 4, 2007, A15.

Measure What Matters

Adapted from Frederick F. Reichheld, "The One Number You Need to Grow," *Harvard Business Review* 81, no. 12 (December 2003): 46–54.

Table 4. "How Important Is Each Factor to You in Choosing an Apartment?"

$n = 50$; $3 = $ "Very Important"

Extra parking for guests	2.5
Party house	2.3
Pool	2.2
Convenient to bus line	2.0

Often it's useful to simplify numerical data: rounding it off, combining similar elements. Then you can see that one number is about 2½ times another. Charting it can also help you see patterns in your data. (See Chapter 9 for a full discussion of charts as a way of analyzing and presenting numerical data.) Look at the raw data as well as at percentages. For example, a 50% increase in shoplifting incidents sounds alarming. An increase from two to three shoplifting incidents sounds less so but is the same data stated differently.

Both numbers and words require interpretation and context to have meaning. Consider the data collected by the Department of Transportation's National Highway Traffic Safety Administration (NHTSA). For each year, the NHTSA gathers and reports statistics on the number of motor vehicle accident fatalities, breaking down the data by type of accident, type of vehicle, and state. In 2003 the agency determined that 42,643 people died in traffic accidents in the United States. When the data were ready, the NHTSA news release proclaimed, "DOT Announces Historic Low Highway Fatality Rate in 2003." The release quoted Transportation Secretary Norman Mineta as saying, "America's roads are safer than ever." The "historic low" was a rate of 1.48 per 100 million vehicle miles traveled, the first time that rate had been less than 1.5 since the NHTSA began gathering the data. A columnist for the *Wall Street Journal* acknowledged the good news but observed that the rate of decline was just 0.8%. The NHTSA news release emphasized reasons for the decline in fatalities (more seat belt use and stiffer drunk-driving laws), whereas the *Wall Street Journal* highlighted reasons for the small size of the decline (the popularity of SUVs and pickups, whose fatality rates are declining but are higher than those for passenger cars).[17]

The same numbers can be presented in different ways to create very different impressions. In the case of the NHTSA data, the *Kansas City Star* and *Time* magazine prepared articles emphasizing not the overall decline in fatalities, but the difference between the fatality rates observed for passenger cars and SUVs. Both articles mentioned that people are "11% more likely to die" in a crash if they are driving an SUV rather than an automobile. A story in *Forbes* magazine, however, called SUVs "slightly more dangerous" but focused on additional data comparing various types of crashes. The *Forbes* article emphasized that in crashes between a light truck and a passenger car, if someone died, that person usually was an occupant of the car. The article listed the number of deaths recorded in each type of crash but not the percentage of fatalities (13%) in crashes between cars and light trucks.[18] In each of these examples, the publication used the same data to reach a conclusion that is more dramatic than a decline in fatalities of less than 1%.

A common myth associated with numbers is that numbers are more objective than words: "numbers don't lie." But as the above examples show, numbers can be subject to widely varying interpretation.

Analyzing Words

If your data include words, try to find out what the words mean to the people who said them or responded to them. An effort to measure the effectiveness of four TV commercials in Australia asked whether each commercial "encourages me to try/buy the brand product." The question is ambiguous. Some consumers might think the researcher wants to know whether the ad is obviously a sales pitch. (Is the ad "encouraging me to buy" or just trying to make me feel good?) Others might think the question is asking about how effective the ad is in persuading the consumer. (Did the ad succeed at encouraging me, or did it fail?) This question therefore might measure either the commercials' content or their ability to persuade, depending on how people interpret the words.[19]

Also try to measure words against numbers. A study of annual reports in the United Kingdom from 1965 to 2004 found a large increase (375%) in narrative information and noted that accounting narratives were being used to manage impressions of annual performance.[20]

Analyzing Patterns

Patterns can help you draw meaning from your data. If you have library sources, on which points do experts agree? Which disagreements can be explained by early theories or numbers that have now changed? Which disagreements are the result of different interpretations of the same data? Which are the result of having different values and criteria? In your interviews and surveys, what patterns do you see?

- Have things changed over time?
- Does geography account for differences?
- Do demographics such as gender, age, or income account for differences?
- What similarities do you see?
- What differences do you see?
- What confirms your hunches?
- What surprises you?

Many descriptions of sales trends are descriptions of patterns derived from data.

Checking Your Logic

State accurately what your data show. For example, suppose that you've asked people who use computers if they could be as productive without them and the overwhelming majority say *no*. This finding shows that people *believe* that computers make them more productive, but it does not prove that they in fact are more productive.

Be sure you are clear about definitions on which data are based. For instance, China and the United States are jockeying for first place in number of Internet users. Different sources give different results, and one reason is that they are defining "Internet user" in different ways: Is a user anyone who has access to the Internet at home, school, or work? What about a four-year-old child who has access to the Internet through her family but does not use it? Is anyone who has used the Internet only once in the past six months a user?[21]

Don't confuse causation with correlation. *Causation* means that one thing causes or produces another. *Correlation* means that two things happening at the same time are positively or negatively related. One might cause the other,

Facts, Spin, and Annual Reports

In 2005, the US Securities and Exchange Commission (SEC) started legal action against the former CEO and CFO of Kmart Corporation, because the Management's Discussion and Analysis (MD&A) portion of Kmart's 2001 annual report was misleading to stockholders. The report explained an increase in inventory on "seasonal fluctuations" (a natural part of doing business that stockholders wouldn't question) when the increase was really caused by one executive's poor decisions (which would reflect badly on the company). Did Kmart's CEO and CFO actually write that report themselves? Probably not, but they signed off on the information and certified it as factual, so the SEC found them liable for the lies.

Kmart wasn't the only corporation whose annual report has come under heavy scrutiny: in the post-Enron business world, the SEC now watches corporate annual reports more closely than ever. The result? Many US companies have replaced descriptive, easy-to-read MD&A sections with simple "10-K" statements: tables of financial data taken directly from the Form 10-K that all publicly held US companies must file with the SEC. These new MD&A's are factual and detailed, with no spin and no misleading information, but they don't provide much actual information about the companies' economic realities.

A good annual report should do both: it should combine hard data with the explanations and details that are necessary for readers to understand the numbers.

Adapted from Amy Borrus, "The SEC: Cracking Down on Spin," *Business-Week*, September 26, 2005, 94–97.

Tapping into the Research Experts

but both might be caused by a third. For instance, consider a study that shows pulling all-nighters hurts grades: students who pull all-nighters get lower grades than those who do not pull all-nighters. But maybe it is not the all-nighter causing the poor grades; maybe students who need all-nighters are weaker students to begin with.

Correlation and causation are easy to confuse, but the difference is important. The Census Bureau publishes figures showing that greater education levels are associated with greater incomes. A widely held assumption is that more education causes greater earnings. But might people from richer backgrounds seek more education? Or might some third factor, such as intelligence, lead to both greater education and higher income?[22]

Some spurious correlations are amusing. The *Wall Street Journal* reported with tongue in cheek the Tiger Woods phenomenon. During the 11 years of 1997–2008, the April bond market performed positively when Woods won the Masters golf tournament, and negatively when he did not.[23]

Consciously search for at least three possible causes for each phenomenon you've observed and at least three possible solutions for each problem. The more possibilities you brainstorm, the more likely you are to find good options. In your report, discuss in detail only the possibilities that will occur to readers and that you think are the real reasons and the best solutions.

When you have identified causes of the problem or the best solutions, check these ideas against reality. Can you find support in references or in numbers? Can you answer claims of people who interpret the data in other ways?

Make the nature of your evidence clear to your reader. Do you have observations that you yourself have made? Or do you have inferences based on observations or data collected by others? Old data may not be good guides to future action.

If you can't prove the claim you originally hoped to make, modify your conclusions to fit your data. Even when your market test is a failure or your experiment disproves your hypothesis, you can still write a useful report.

- Identify changes that might yield a different result. For example, selling the product at a lower price might enable the company to sell enough units.
- Divide the discussion to show what part of the test succeeded.
- Discuss circumstances that may have affected the results.

As employees become buried in paperwork, it becomes even more important to select carefully and interpret clearly the information to be included in reports.

- Summarize your negative findings in progress reports to let readers down gradually and to give them a chance to modify the research design.
- Remember that negative results aren't always disappointing to the audience. For example, the people who commissioned a feasibility report may be relieved to have an impartial outsider confirm their suspicions that a project isn't feasible.

Choosing Information for Reports

Don't put information in reports just because you have it or just because it took you a long time to find it. Instead, choose the information that your reader needs to make a decision. NASA received widespread criticism over the way it released results from an $11.3 million federal air safety study. NASA published 16,208 pages of findings with no guide to understanding them. Critics maintain the lapse was deliberate because the data contained hundreds of cases of pilot error.[24]

If you know your readers well, you may know what their priorities are. For example, the supervisor of a call center knows that management will be looking for certain kinds of performance data, including costs, workload handled and forecast, and customer satisfaction. To write regular reports, the supervisor would set up a format in which it is easy to see how well the center is doing in each of these areas. Using the same format month after month simplifies the reader's task. Presenting the actual performance alongside objectives helps managers focus on major successes and failures. The supervisor also would highlight and explain any unusual data, such as an unexpected surge in volume or a one-time expense.[25]

If you don't know your readers, you may be able to get a sense of what is important by showing them a tentative table of contents (a list of your headings) and asking, "Have I included everything?" When you cannot contact an external audience, show your draft to colleagues and superiors in your organization.

How much information you need to include depends on whether your audience is likely to be supportive, neutral, or skeptical. If your audience is likely to be pleased with your research, you can present your findings directly. If your audience will not be pleased, you will need to explain your thinking in a persuasive way and provide substantial evidence.

You must also decide whether to put information in the body of the report or in appendixes. Put material in the body of the report if it is crucial to your proof, if your most significant readers will want to see it there, or if it is short. (Something less than half a page won't interrupt the reader.) Frequently decision makers want your analysis of the data in the report body rather than the actual data itself. Supporting data that will be examined later by specialists such as accountants, lawyers, and engineers are generally put in an appendix.

Anything that a careful reader will want but that is not crucial to your proof can go in an appendix. Appendixes can include

- A copy of a survey questionnaire or interview questions.
- A tally of responses to each question in a survey.
- A copy of responses to open-ended questions in a survey.
- A transcript of an interview.
- Computer printouts.
- Complex tables and visuals.
- Technical data.
- Previous reports on the same subject.

Tell Them a Story

To persuade people, tell them a story or anecdote that proves your point.

Experiments with both high school teachers and quantitatively trained MBA students show that people are more likely to believe a point and more likely to be committed to it when points were made by examples, stories, and case studies. Stories alone were more effective than a combination of stories and statistics; the combination was more effective than statistics alone. In another experiment, attitude changes lasted longer when the audience had read stories than when they had only read numbers. Research suggests that stories are more persuasive because people remember them.

In many cases, you'll need to provide statistics or numbers to convince the careful reader that your anecdote is a representative example. But give the story first. It's more persuasive.

Adapted from Dean C. Kazoleas, "A Comparison of the Persuasive Effectiveness of Qualitative versus Quantitative Evidence," *Communication Quarterly* 41, no. 1 (Winter 1993): 40–50; and Joanne Martin and Melanie E. Powers, "Truth of Corporate Propaganda," in *Organizational Symbolism*, ed. Louis R. Pondy, et al. (Greenwich, CT: JAI Press, 1983), 97–107.

Organizing Information in Reports

Most sets of data can be organized in several logical ways. Choose the way that makes your information easiest for the reader to understand and use. If you were compiling a directory of all the employees at your plant, for example, alphabetizing by last name would be far more useful than listing people by height, social security number, or length of service with the company, although those organizing principles might make sense in other lists for other purposes.

In one company, a young employee comparing the economics of two proposed manufacturing processes gave his logic and his calculations in full before getting to his conclusion. But his superiors didn't want to wade through eight single-spaced pages; they wanted his recommendation up front.[26]

The following three guidelines will help you choose the arrangement that will be the most useful for your audience:

1. **Process your information before you present it to your audience.** The order in which you became aware of information usually is not the best order to present it to your audience.
2. **When you have lots of information, group it into three to seven categories.** The average person's short-term memory can hold only seven chunks, though the chunks can be of any size.[27] By grouping your information into seven categories (or fewer), you make your report easier to comprehend.
3. **Work with the audience's expectations, not against them.** Introduce ideas in the overview in the order in which you will discuss them.

Basic Patterns for Organizing Information

Eight basic patterns for organizing information are particularly useful in reports:

1. Comparison/contrast.
2. Problem-solution.
3. Elimination of alternatives.
4. SWOT analysis.
5. General to particular or particular to general.
6. Geographic or spatial.
7. Functional.
8. Chronological.

Any of these patterns can be used for a whole report or for only part of it.

1. Comparison/contrast

Many reports use comparison/contrast sections within a larger report pattern. Comparison/contrast can also be the purpose of the whole report. Feasibility studies usually use this pattern. You can focus either on the alternatives you are evaluating or on the criteria you use. See Figure 19.3 for examples of these two patterns in a report.

Focus on the alternatives when

- One alternative is clearly superior.
- The criteria are hard to separate.
- The reader will intuitively grasp the alternative as a whole rather than as the sum of its parts.

Figure 19.3 Two Ways to Organize a Comparison/Contrast Report

Focus on alternatives	
Alternative A	Opening a New Store on Campus
Criterion 1	Cost of Renting Space
Criterion 2	Proximity to Target Market
Criterion 3	Competition from Similar Stores
Alternative B	Opening a New Store in the Suburban Mall
Criterion 1	Cost of Renting Space
Criterion 2	Proximity to Target Market
Criterion 3	Competition from Similar Stores
Focus on criteria	
Criterion 1	Cost of Renting Space for the New Store
Alternative A	Cost of Campus Locations
Alternative B	Cost of Locations in the Suburban Mall
Criterion 2	Proximity to Target Market
Alternative A	Proximity on Campus
Alternative B	Proximity in the Suburban Mall
Criterion 3	Competition from Similar Stores
Alternative A	Competing Stores on Campus
Alternative B	Competing Stores in the Suburban Mall

Focus on the criteria when

- The superiority of one alternative to another depends on the relative weight assigned to various criteria. Perhaps Alternative A is best if we are most concerned about Criterion 1, cost, but worst if we are most concerned about Criterion 2, proximity to target market.
- The criteria are easy to separate.
- The reader wants to compare and contrast the options independently of your recommendation.

A variation of the comparison/contrast pattern is the **pro-and-con pattern.** In this pattern, under each specific heading, give the arguments for and against that alternative. A report recommending new plantings for a university quadrangle uses the pro-and-con pattern:

Advantages of Monocropping
   High Productivity
   Visual Symmetry
Disadvantages of Monocropping
   Danger of Pest Exploitation
   Visual Monotony

This pattern is least effective when you want to deemphasize the disadvantages of a proposed solution, for it does not permit you to bury the disadvantages between neutral or positive material.

2. Problem-solution

Identify the problem; explain its background or history; discuss its extent and seriousness; identify its causes. Discuss the factors (criteria) that affect the decision. Analyze the advantages and disadvantages of possible solutions. Conclusions and recommendation can go either first or last, depending on the preferences of your reader. This pattern works well when the reader is neutral.

A report recommending ways to eliminate solidification of a granular bleach during production uses the problem-solution pattern:

> Recommended Reformulation for Vibe Bleach
> Problems in Maintaining Vibe's Granular Structure
>   Solidification during Storage and Transportation
>   Customer Complaints about "Blocks" of Vibe in Boxes
> Why Vibe Bleach "Cakes"
>   Vibe's Formula
>   The Manufacturing Process
>   The Chemical Process of Solidification
> Modifications Needed to Keep Vibe Flowing Freely

3. Elimination of alternatives

After discussing the problem and its causes, discuss the *impractical* solutions first, showing why they will not work. End with the most practical solution. This pattern works well when the solutions the reader is likely to favor will not work, while the solution you recommend is likely to be perceived as expensive, intrusive, or radical.

A report on toy commercials, "The Effect of TV Ads on Children," eliminates alternatives:

> Alternative Solutions to Problems in TV Toy Ads
>   Leave Ads Unchanged
>   Mandate School Units on Advertising
>   Ask the Industry to Regulate Itself
>   Give FCC Authority to Regulate TV Ads Directed at Children

4. SWOT Analysis

A **SWOT analysis** is frequently used to evaluate a proposed project, expansion, or new venture. The analysis discusses **S**trengths, **W**eaknesses, **O**pportunities, and **T**hreats of the proposed action. Strengths and weaknesses are usually factors within the organization; opportunities and threats are usually factors external to the organization.

A report recommending an in-house training department uses a SWOT analysis to support its recommendation:

> Advantages of In-House Training
> Disadvantages of In-House Training
> Competitor Training Businesses
> Opportunities for Training Expansion

This report switches the order of threats (Competitor Training Businesses) and opportunities in order to end with positive information.

5. General to particular or particular to general

General to particular starts with the problem as it affects the organization or as it manifests itself in general and then moves to a discussion of the parts of the problem and solutions to each of these parts. Particular to general starts with the problem as the audience defines it and moves to larger issues of which the problem is a part. Both are good patterns when you need to redefine the reader's perception of the problem to solve it effectively.

The directors of a student volunteer organization, VIP, have defined their problem as "not enough volunteers." After studying the subject, the writer is convinced that problems in training, supervision, and campus awareness are responsible for both a high dropout rate and a low recruitment rate. The general-to-particular pattern helps the audience see the problem in a new way:

Why VIP Needs More Volunteers
Why Some VIP Volunteers Drop Out
    Inadequate Training
    Inadequate Supervision
    Feeling That VIP Requires Too Much Time
    Feeling That the Work Is Too Emotionally Demanding
Why Some Students Do Not Volunteer
    Feeling That VIP Requires Too Much Time
    Feeling That the Work Is Too Emotionally Demanding
    Preference for Volunteering with Another Organization
    Lack of Knowledge about VIP Opportunities
How VIP Volunteers Are Currently Trained and Supervised
Time Demands on VIP Volunteers
Emotional Demands on VIP Volunteers
Ways to Increase Volunteer Commitment and Motivation
    Improving Training and Supervision
    Improving the Flexibility of Volunteers' Hours
    Providing Emotional Support to Volunteers
    Providing More Information about Community Needs and VIP Services

6. Geographic or spatial

In a geographic or spatial pattern, you discuss problems and solutions by units according to their physical arrangement. Move from office to office, building to building, factory to factory, state to state, region to region, etc.

A sales report uses a geographic pattern of organization:

Sales Have Risen in the European Community
Sales Are Flat in Eastern Europe
Sales Have Fallen Sharply in the Middle East
Sales Are Off to a Strong Start in Africa
Sales Have Risen Slightly in Asia
Sales Have Fallen Slightly in South America
Sales Are Steady in North America

Annual Reports

Report Watch posts annual lists of the best annual reports. They also post tips for creating good annual reports:

- Start with an eye-catching, interest-grabbing cover.
- Live up to the cover's promise in the body of the report.
- Don't just give a 10-K or 20-F.
- Offer a longer-term, strategic view in addition to information about the past year.
- Use a clear, readable style.

Adapted from Report Watch, "Report Essentials," in *Report Essentials*, http://www.reportwatch.net/report-essentials/ (accessed April 11, 2009).

7. Functional

In functional patterns, discuss the problems and solutions of each functional unit. For example, a small business might organize a report to its venture capitalists by the categories of research, production, and marketing. A government report might divide data into the different functions an agency performed, taking each in turn:

> Major Accomplishments FY 10
>   Regulation
>   Education
>   Research
>   International coordination

8. Chronological

A chronological report records events in the order in which they happened or are planned to happen. Many progress reports are organized chronologically:

> Work Completed in October
> Work Planned for November

If you choose this pattern, be sure you do not let the chronology obscure significant points or trends.

Specific Varieties of Reports

Informative, recommendation, and justification reports will be more successful when you work with the readers' expectations for that kind of report.

Informative and closure reports

Informative and **closure reports** summarize completed work or research that does not result in action or recommendation.

Informative reports often include the following elements:

- Introductory paragraph summarizing the problems or successes of the project.
- Purpose and scope section(s) giving the purpose of the report and indicating what aspects of the topic it covers.
- Chronological account of how the problem was discovered, what was done, and what the results were.
- Concluding paragraph with suggestions for later action. In a recommendation report, the recommendations would be based on proof. In contrast, the suggestions in a closure or informative report are not proved in detail.

Figure 19.4 presents this kind of informative closure report.

Closure reports also allow a firm to document the alternatives it has considered before choosing a final design.

Recommendation reports

Recommendation reports evaluate two or more alternatives and recommend one of them. (Doing nothing or delaying action can be one of the alternatives.)

Figure 19.4   An Informative Memo Report Describing How a Company Solved a Problem

March 14, 2010

To: Kitty O. Locker

From: Sara A. Ratterman *SAR*   *Informal short reports use letter or memo format.*

First paragraph summarizes main points.   Subject: Recycling at Bike Nashbar

Two months ago, Bike Nashbar began recycling its corrugated cardboard boxes. The program was easy to implement and actually saves the company a little money compared to our previous garbage pickup.

Purpose and scope of report.   In this report, I will explain how and why Bike Nashbar's program was initiated, how the program works and what it costs, and why other businesses should consider similar programs.

Bold or underline headings.

The Problem of Too Many Boxes and Not Enough Space in Bike Nashbar

Cause of problem.   Every week, Bike Nashbar receives about 40 large cardboard boxes containing bicycles and other merchandise. As many boxes as possible would be stuffed into the trash bin behind the building, which also had to accommodate all the other solid waste the shop produces. Boxes that didn't fit in the trash bin ended up lying around the shop, blocking doorways, and taking up space needed for customers' bikes. The trash bin was emptied only once a week, and by that time, even more boxes would have arrived.

Triple space before heading.

The Importance of Recycling Cardboard Rather than Throwing It Away

Double space after heading.

Arranging for more trash bins or more frequent pickups would have solved the immediate problem at Bike Nashbar but would have done nothing to solve the problem created by throwing away so much trash in the first place.

Double space between paragraphs within heading.

Further seriousness of problem.   According to David Crogen, sales representative for Waste Management, Inc., 75% of all solid waste in Columbus goes to landfills. The amount of trash the city collects has increased 150% in the last five years. Columbus's landfill is almost full. In an effort to encourage people and businesses to recycle, the cost of dumping trash in the landfill is doubling from $4.90 a cubic yard to $9.90 a cubic yard next week. Next January, the price will increase again, to $12.95 a cubic yard. Crogen believes that the amount of trash can be reduced by cooperation between the landfill and the power plant and by recycling.

How Bike Nashbar Started Recycling Cardboard   *Capitalize first letter of major words in heading.*

Solution.   Waste Management, Inc., is the country's largest waste processor. After reading an article about how committed Waste Management, Inc., is to waste reduction and recycling, I decided to see whether Waste Management could recycle our boxes. Corrugated cardboard (which is what Bike Nashbar's boxes are made of) is almost 100% recyclable, so we seemed to be a good candidate for recycling.

(Continued)

Figure 19.4   An Informative Memo Report Describing How a Company Solved a Problem *(Continued)*

Kitty O. Locker   *Reader's name,*
March 14, 2010   *date,*
Page 2   *page number.*

To get the service started, I met with a friendly sales rep, David Crogen, that same afternoon to discuss the service.

Waste Management, Inc., took care of all the details. Two days later, Bike Nashbar was recycling its cardboard.

How the Service Works and What It Costs   *Talking heads tell reader what to expect in each section.*

Details of solution. Waste Management took away our existing 8-cubic-yard garbage bin and replaced it with two 4-yard bins. One of these bins is white and has "cardboard only" printed on the outside; the other is brown and is for all other solid waste. The bins are emptied once a week, with the cardboard going to the recycling plant and the solid waste going to the landfill or power plant.

Double space between paragraphs. Since Bike Nashbar was already paying more than $60 a week for garbage pickup, our basic cost stayed the same. (Waste Management can absorb the extra overhead only if the current charge is at least $60 a week.) The cost is divided 80/20 between the two bins: 80% of the cost pays for the bin that goes to the landfill and power plant; 20% covers the cardboard pickup. Bike Nashbar actually receives $5.00 for each ton of cardboard it recycles.

Each employee at Bike Nashbar is responsible for putting all the boxes he or she opens in the recycling bin. Employees must follow these rules:

- The cardboard must have the word "corrugated" printed on it, along with the universal recycling symbol.

Indented lists provide visual variety.

- The boxes must be broken down to their flattest form. If they aren't, they won't all fit in the bin and Waste Management would be picking up air when it could pick up solid cardboard. The more boxes that are picked up, the more money that will be made.

- No other waste except corrugated cardboard can be put in the recycling bin. Other materials could break the recycling machinery or contaminate the new cardboard.

- The recycling bin is to be kept locked with a padlock provided by Waste Management so that vagrants don't steal the cardboard and lose money for Waste Management and Bike Nashbar.

Figure 19.4   An Informative Memo Report Describing How a Company Solved a Problem
(Concluded)

Kitty O. Locker
March 14, 2010
Page 3

Dis-
advantages
of
solution.

Minor Problems with Running the Recycling Program

The only problems we've encountered have been minor ones of violating the rules. Sometimes employees at the shop forget to flatten boxes, and air instead of cardboard gets picked up. Sometimes people forget to lock the recycling bin. When the bin is left unlocked, people do steal the cardboard, and plastic cups and other solid waste get dumped in the cardboard bin. I've posted signs where the key to the bin hangs, reminding employees to empty and fold boxes and relock the bin after putting cardboard in it. I hope this will turn things around and these problems will be solved.

Advantages of the Recycling Program

Advantages
of
solution.

The program is a great success. Now when boxes arrive, they are unloaded, broken down, and disposed of quickly. It is a great relief to get the boxes out of our way, and knowing that we are making a contribution to saving our environment builds pride in ourselves and Bike Nashbar.

Our company depends on a clean, safe environment for people to ride their bikes in. Now we have become part of the solution. By choosing to recycle and reduce the amount of solid waste our company generates, we can save money while gaining a reputation as a socially responsible business.

Why Other Companies Should Adopt Similar Programs

Argues
that her
company's
experience
is relevant
to other
companies.

Businesses and institutions in Franklin County currently recycle less than 4% of the solid waste they produce. David Crogen tells me he has over 8,000 clients in Columbus alone, and he acquires new ones every day. Many of these businesses can recycle a large portion of their solid waste at no additional cost. Depending on what they recycle, they may even get a little money back.

The environmental and economic benefits of recycling as part of a comprehensive waste reduction program are numerous. Recycling helps preserve our environment. We can use the same materials over and over again, saving natural resources such as trees, fuel, and metals and decreasing the amount of solid waste in landfills. By conserving natural resources, recycling helps the U.S. become less dependent on imported raw materials. Crogen predicts that Columbus will be on a 100% recycling system by the year 2020. I strongly hope that his prediction will come true and the future may start to look a little brighter.

Recommendation reports normally open by explaining the decision to be made, listing the alternatives, and explaining the criteria. In the body of the report, each alternative will be evaluated according to the criteria using one of the two comparison/contrast patterns. Discussing each alternative separately is better when one alternative is clearly superior, when the criteria interact, or when each alternative is indivisible. If the choice depends on

The Importance of Annual Reports

A survey, conducted by WithumSmith & Brown and MGT Design Inc., found that the annual report is the most important publication that a company produces. To understand the value of annual reports, the survey asked individual investors, portfolio managers, and securities analysts (the primary audiences for annual reports) about the ways that they read and use the reports to make decisions.

Here are some of their findings:

- 75% said the annual report is the most important publication that a company produces.

- 79% said the annual report is an important tool for investment decisions.

- 66% prefer photos and/or illustrations in annual reports.

- 90% said that important concerns facing the industry, such as environment issues and corporate governance, should be addressed in the report.

- 81% prefer a print version over electronic versions. Respondents said the print documents were easier to read, highlight, annotate, and file.

Taken together, these findings suggest that the annual report is an important communication for organizations and well worth the time spent creating it.

Adapted from Kirk Holderbaum, "Survey Reveals Importance of Corporate Annual Reports," http://www.withum.com/fileSave\Commerce_Kirk_0207.pdf (accessed April 11, 2009).

the weight given to each criterion, you may want to discuss each alternative under each criterion.

Whether your recommendation should come at the beginning or the end of the report depends on your reader and the culture of your organization. Most readers want the "bottom line" up front. However, if the reader will find your recommendation hard to accept, you may want to delay your recommendation until the end of the report when you have given all your evidence.

Justification reports

Justification reports justify a purchase, investment, hiring, or change in policy. If your organization has a standard format for justification reports, follow that format. If you can choose your headings and organization, use this pattern when your proposal will be easy for your reader to accept:

1. **Indicate what you're asking for and why it's needed.**   Since the reader has not asked for the report, you must link your request to the organization's goals.
2. **Briefly give the background of the problem or need.**
3. **Explain each of the possible solutions.**   For each, give the cost and the advantages and disadvantages.
4. **Summarize the action needed to implement your recommendation.**   If several people will be involved, indicate who will do what and how long each step will take.
5. **Ask for the action you want.**

If the reader will be reluctant to grant your request, use this variation of the problem-solving pattern described in Chapter 16 (p. 479):

1. **Describe the organizational problem (which your request will solve).** Use specific examples to prove the seriousness of the problem.
2. **Show why easier or less expensive solutions will not solve the problem.**
3. **Present your solution impersonally.**
4. **Show that the disadvantages of your solution are outweighed by the advantages.**
5. **Summarize the action needed to implement your recommendation.**   If several people will be involved, indicate who will do what and how long each step will take.
6. **Ask for the action you want.**

How much detail you need to give in a justification report depends on the corporate culture and on your reader's knowledge of and attitude toward your recommendation. Many organizations expect justification reports to be short—only one or two pages. Other organizations may expect longer reports with much more detailed budgets and a full discussion of the problem and each possible solution.

Presenting Information Effectively in Reports

The advice about style in Chapter 7 also applies to reports, with three exceptions:

1. **Use a fairly formal style, without contractions or slang.**
2. **Avoid the word *you*.**   In a document with multiple audiences, it will not be clear who *you* is. Instead, use the company name.

3. **Include in the report all the definitions and documents needed to understand the recommendations.** The multiple audiences for reports include readers who may consult the document months or years from now; they will not share your special knowledge. Explain acronyms and abbreviations the first time they appear. Explain as much of the history or background of the problem as necessary. Add as appendixes previous documents on which you are building.

The following points apply to any kind of writing, but they are particularly important in reports:

1. Use clear, engaging writing.
2. Keep repetition to a minimum.
3. Introduce sources and visuals.
4. Use forecasting, transitions, topic sentences, and headings to make your organization clear to your reader.

Let's look at each of these principles as they apply to reports.

1. Use Clear, Engaging Writing.

Most people want to be able to read a report quickly while still absorbing its important points. You can help them do this by using accurate diction. Not-quite-right word choices are particularly damaging in reports, which may be skimmed by readers who know very little about the subject. Occasionally you can simply substitute a word:

Incorrect:	With these recommendations, we can overcome the solutions to our problem.
Correct:	With these recommendations, we can overcome our problem.
Also correct:	With these recommendations, we can solve our problem.

Sometimes you'll need to completely recast the sentence.

Incorrect:	The first problem with the incentive program is that middle managers do not use good interpersonal skills in implementing it. For example, the hotel chef openly ridicules the program. As a result, the kitchen staff fear being mocked if they participate in the program.
Better:	The first problem with the incentive program is that some middle managers undercut it. For example, the hotel chef openly ridicules the program. As a result, the kitchen staff fear being mocked if they participate in the program.

A strong writing style is especially important when you are preparing a report that relies on a wealth of statistics. Most people have difficulty absorbing number after number. To help your readers, use text to highlight the message you want the statistics to convey. Examples and action-oriented details keep the reader engaged. An example that has this level of clarity is the 2004 report of the US government's commission investigating the terrorist attacks of September 11, 2001. The report was praised for its clear narrative, sense of drama, rich detail, and precise language. The commission's executive director, Philip D. Zelikow, said the report was intentionally made readable because the commission's leadership wanted people to read and act on it.[28]

2. Keep Repetition to a Minimum.

Some repetition in reports is legitimate. The conclusion restates points made in the body of the report; the recommendations appear in the transmittal, the

Who Did What?

The passive verbs and impersonal constructions in US reports of coal mine disasters ("coal dust was permitted to accumulate" and "an accident occurred") suggest that accidents are inevitable. Who permitted the coal dust to accumulate? What could have been done to prevent the accumulation? Mine disaster reports contain sentences like the following: "The . . . fatality occurred when the victim proceeded into an area . . . before the roof was supported." *Why* did the man who was killed go into the area? Had a supervisor checked to see that the roof was supported? Who ordered what?

British reports of mine disasters, in contrast, focus on people and what they did to limit the damage from the disaster. Perhaps as a result, British mines have a much lower incidence of disasters than do US coal mines.

Adapted from Beverly A. Sauer, "Sense and Sensibility in Technical Documentation: How Feminist Interpretation Strategies Can Save Lives in the Nation's Mines," *Journal of Business and Technical Communication* 7 (January 1993): 63–83.

Legal Liability and Report Drafts

During civil litigation (such as a tort case charging that a product has injured a user), rough drafts may be important to establish the state of mind and intent of a document's drafters.

To protect the company, one lawyer recommends labeling all but the final draft "Preliminary Draft: Subject to Change." That way, if there's ever a lawsuit, the company will be able to argue that only the final report, not the drafts, should be used as evidence.

Adapted from Elizabeth McCord, "'But What You Really Meant Was . . . Multiple Drafts and Legal Liability," paper presented at the Association for Business Communication Midwest Regional Conference, Akron, OH, April 3–5, 1991.

abstract or executive summary, and in the recommendations sections of the report. However, repetitive references to earlier material ("As we have already seen") may indicate that the document needs to be reorganized. Read the document through at a single sitting to make sure that any repetition serves a useful purpose.

3. Introduce Sources and Visuals.

The first time you cite an author's work, use his or her full name as it appears on the work: "Thomas L. Friedman points out. . . . " In subsequent citations, use only the last name: "Friedman shows. . . . " Use active rather than passive verbs.

The verb you use indicates your attitude toward the source. *Says* and *writes* are neutral. *Points out, shows, suggests, discovers,* and *notes* suggest that you agree with the source. Words such as *claims, argues, contends, believes,* and *alleges* distance you from the source. At a minimum, they suggest that you know that not everyone agrees with the source; they are also appropriate to report the views of someone with whom you disagree.

The report text should refer to all visuals:

As Table 1 shows, . . .
See Figure 4.

4. Use Forecasting, Transitions, Topic Sentences, and Headings.

Forecasts are overviews that tell the reader what you will discuss in a section or in the entire report. Make your forecast easy to read by telling the reader how many points there are and using bullets or numbers (either words or figures). In the following example, the first sentence in the revised paragraph tells the reader to look for four points; the numbers separate the four points clearly. This overview paragraph also makes a contract with readers, who now expect to read about tax benefits first and employee benefits last.

Paragraph without numbers:	Employee stock ownership programs (ESOPs) have several advantages. They provide tax benefits for the company. ESOPs also create tax benefits for employees and for lenders. They provide a defense against takeovers. In some organizations, productivity increases because workers now have a financial stake in the company's profits. ESOPs are an attractive employee benefit and help the company hire and retain good employees.
Revised paragraph with numbers:	Employee stock ownership programs (ESOPs) provide four benefits. First, ESOPs provide tax benefits for the company, its employees, and lenders to the plan. Second, ESOPs help create a defense against takeovers. Third, ESOPs may increase productivity by giving workers a financial stake in the company's profits. Fourth, as an attractive employee benefit, ESOPs help the company hire and retain good employees.

Transitions are words, phrases, or sentences that tell readers whether the discussion is continuing on the same point or shifting points.

There are economic advantages, too.

(Tells the reader that we are still discussing advantages but that we have now moved to economic advantages.)

An alternative to this plan is . . .

(Tells reader that a second option follows.)

The second factor . . .

(Tells reader that the discussion of the first factor is finished.)

These advantages, however, are found only in A, not in B or C.

(Prepares reader for a shift from A to B and C.)

A **topic sentence** introduces or summarizes the main idea of a paragraph. Readers who skim reports can follow your ideas more easily if each paragraph begins with a topic sentence.

Hard to read (no topic sentence):	Another main use of ice is to keep the fish fresh. Each of the seven kinds of fish served at the restaurant requires one gallon twice a day, for a total of 14 gallons. An additional 6 gallons a day are required for the salad bar.
Better (begins with topic sentence):	Twenty gallons of ice a day are needed to keep food fresh. Of this, the biggest portion (14 gallons) is used to keep the fish fresh. Each of the seven kinds of fish served at the restaurant requires one gallon twice a day. An additional 6 gallons a day are required for the salad bar.

Headings (see Chapter 8, p. 224) are single words, short phrases, or complete sentences that indicate the topic in each section. A heading must cover all of the material under it until the next heading. For example, *Cost of Tuition* cannot include the cost of books or of room and board; *College Costs* could include all costs. You can have just one paragraph under a heading or several pages. If you do have several pages between headings you may want to consider using subheadings. Use subheadings only when you have two or more divisions within a main heading.

Topic headings focus on the structure of the report. As you can see from the following example, topic headings give very little information.

Topic headings are vague.

Recommendation

Problem

    Situation 1

    Situation 2

Causes of the Problem

    Background

    Cause 1

    Cause 2

Recommended Solution

Talking heads, in contrast, tell the reader what to expect. Talking heads, like those in the examples in this chapter, provide an overview of each section and of the entire report.

Talking heads are specific.

Recommended Reformulation for Vibe Bleach

Problems in Maintaining Vibe's Granular Structure

   Solidification during Storage and Transportation

   Customer Complaints about "Blocks" of Vibe in Boxes

Why Vibe Bleach "Cakes"

  Vibe's Formula

  The Manufacturing Process

  The Chemical Process of Solidification

Modifications Needed to Keep Vibe Flowing Freely

Headings must be parallel (p. 197); that is, they must use the same grammatical structure. Subheads must be parallel to each other but do not necessarily have to be parallel to subheads under other headings.

Not parallel:	Are Students Aware of VIP?
	Current Awareness among Undergraduate Students
	Graduate Students
	Ways to Increase Volunteer Commitment and Motivation
	We Must Improve Training and Supervision
	Can We Make Volunteers' Hours More Flexible?
	Providing Emotional Support to Volunteers
	Provide More Information about Community Needs and VIP Services
Parallel:	Campus Awareness of VIP
	Current Awareness among Undergraduate Students
	Current Awareness among Graduate Students
	Ways to Increase Volunteer Commitment and Motivation
	Improving Training and Supervision
	Improving the Flexibility of Volunteers' Hours
	Providing Emotional Support to Volunteers
	Providing More Information about Community Needs and VIP Services

In a very complicated report, you may need up to three levels of headings. Figure 19.5 illustrates one way to set up headings. Follow these standard conventions for headings:

- Although the figure shows only one example of each level of headings, in an actual report you would not use a subheading unless you had at least two subsections under the next higher heading.
- Whatever the format for headings, avoid having a subhead come immediately after a heading. Instead, some text should follow the main heading before the subheading. (If you have nothing else to say, give an overview of the division.)
- Avoid having a heading or subheading all by itself at the bottom of the page. Instead, have at least one line (preferably two) of type. If there isn't room for a line of type under it, put the heading on the next page.
- Don't use a heading as the antecedent for a pronoun. Instead, repeat the noun.

Figure 19.5 Setting Up Headings in a Single-Spaced Document

Center the title; use bold and a bigger font. **Typing Titles and Headings for Reports** *14-point type.*

For the title of a report, use a bold font two point sizes bigger than the largest size in the body of the report. You may want to use an even bigger size or a different font to create an attractive title page. Capitalize the first word and all major words of the title.

Heading for main divisions

Two empty spaces (triple space)

Typing Headings for Reports *12-point type.*

One empty space (double space)

12-point type for body text

Center main headings, capitalize the first and all major words, and use bold. In single-spaced text, leave two empty spaces before main headings and one after. Also leave an extra space between paragraphs. You may also want to use main headings that are one point size bigger than the body text.

This example provides just one example of each level of heading. However, in a real document, use headings only when you have at least two of them in the document. In a report, you'll have several.

Two empty spaces (triple space)

Typing Subheadings *Bold; left margin*

One empty space

Most reports use subheadings under some main headings. Use subheadings only if you have at least two of them under a given heading. It is OK to use subheadings in some sections and not in others. Normally you'll have several paragraphs under a subheading, but it's OK to have just one paragraph under some subheadings.

12-point type

Subheadings in a report use the same format as headings in letters and memos. Bold subheadings and set them at the left margin. Capitalize the first word and major words. Leave two empty spaces before the subheading and one empty space after it, before the first paragraph under the subheading. Use the same size font as the body paragraphs.

One empty space (normal paragraph spacing)

Period after heading

Typing Further Subdivisions. For a very long report, you may need further subdivisions under a subheading. Bold the further subdivision, capitalizing the first word and major words, and end the phrase with a period. Begin the text on the same line. Use normal spacing between paragraphs. Further subdivide a subheading only if you have at least two such subdivisions under a given subheading. It is OK to use divisions under some subheadings and not under others.

Writing Formal Reports

Formal reports are distinguished from informal letter and memo reports by their length and by their components. A full formal report may contain the following components (see Figures 19.6 and 19.7):

Cover

Title Page

Letter or Memo of Transmittal

Table of Contents

List of Illustrations

Executive Summary

Report Body

Introduction (Orients the reader to the report. Usually has subheadings for Purpose and Scope; depending on the situation, may also have Limitations, Assumptions, Methods, Criteria, and Definitions.)

Figure 19.6   The Components in a Report Can Vary

More formal ←	→	Less formal
Cover	Title Page	Introduction
Title Page	Table of Contents	Body
Transmittal	Executive Summary	Conclusions
Table of Contents	Body	Recommendations
List of Illustrations	Introduction	
Executive Summary	Body	
Body	Conclusions	
Introduction	Recommendations	
Body		
Conclusions		
Recommendations		
References/Works Cited		
Appendixes		
Questionnaires		
Interviews		
Computer Printouts		
Related Documents		

Background or History of the Problem (Orients the reader to the topic of the report. Serves as a record for later readers of the report.)

Body (Presents and interprets data in words and visuals. Analyzes causes of the problem and evaluates possible solutions. Specific headings will depend on the topic of the report.)

Conclusions (Summarizes main points of report.)

Recommendations (Recommends actions to solve the problem. May be combined with Conclusions; may be put at beginning of body rather than at the end.)

Notes, References, or Works Cited (Documents sources cited in the report.)

Appendixes (Provides additional materials that the careful reader may want: transcripts of interviews, copies of questionnaires, tallies of all the questions, complex tables, computer printouts, previous reports.)

As Figure 19.6 shows, not every formal report necessarily has all these components. In addition, some organizations call for additional components or arrange these components in a different order. As you read each section below, you may want to turn to the corresponding pages of the long report in Figure 19.7 to see how the component is set up and how it relates to the total report.

Title Page

The title page of a report usually contains four items: the title of the report, the person or organization for whom the report is prepared, the person or group who prepared the report, and the release date. Some title pages also contain a brief summary or abstract of the contents of the report; some title pages contain decorative artwork.

Figure 19.7 A Formal Report

Viva Panera!

Center all text on the title page.

Use a large font size for the main title.

Expanding Panera into Chile

Use a slightly smaller font size for the subheading.

Prepared for

No punctuation.

The rest of the document should use 12-point font size.

Mr. Ronald M. Shaich, CEO
Panera Bread Company
Richmond Heights, MO 63117

Name of reader, job title, organization, city, state, and zip code.

Prepared by

No punctuation.

JOABA Consulting
April Hoffmeyer
Betsy Hertz
Andrea Keeney
Jessica Oney
Omar Romero
Iowa State University
Ames, IA 50011

Name of writer(s), organization, city, state, and zip code.

April 17, 2010

Date report is released.

(Continued)

Figure 19.7   A Formal Report *(Continued)*

This student group designed their own letterhead, assuming they were doing this report as consultants.

JOABA Consulting
131 Ross Hall
Ames, IA 50011

This letter uses block format.

April 17, 2010

Mr. Ronald M. Shaich, CEO
Panera Bread Company
6710 Clayton Road
Richmond Heights, MO 63117

In paragraph 1, release the report. Note when and by whom the report was authorized. Note report's purpose.

Dear Mr. Shaich:

Here you will find the report you requested in March including information on the feasibility of expanding a Panera Bread facility into Chile and our recommendations for a plan of action.

During the market analysis, our team considered and researched various macro environment factors including location, customs and behaviors, politics, economics and laws, and market possibilities and competition. Our findings show that Chile is an attractive market to invest in, and we recommend it as a location into which Panera Bread should expand. The research conducted about your business and Chile's consumer market leads us to recommend opening a corporate-owned facility in the capital city of Santiago.

Give recommendations or thesis of report.

Santiago is already home to many successful American franchises, and to stay competitive with these franchises, we suggest you expand into this market. With the use of appropriate marketing campaigns and employment of locals with management experience, your business has the potential to penetrate the market in Santiago.

Note sources that were helpful.

The analysis in this report came from several helpful resources. The U.S. Commercial Services, the Central Intelligence Agency's *World Factbook*, and the Santiago Chamber of Commerce were all very helpful and cooperative in answering our questions.

Thank reader for the opportunity to do the research.

Thank you for allowing us to conduct this research. We have learned about Panera, the country of Chile, and the international business environment. If you have any questions, please contact our firm at any time (515-294-4100; joaba@gmail.com). Answering additional questions is included in the initial fee at no additional cost. We look forward to working with you in the future.

Offer to answer questions about the report.

Sincerely,

April Hoffmeyer
JOABA Team Leader

Center page number at the bottom of the page. Use a lowercase Roman numeral for initial pages of report.

i

Figure 19.7 A Formal Report *(Continued)*

Main headings are parallel, as are subheadings within a section.

Table of contents does not list itself.

Table of Contents

Letter of Transmittal.. i

Executive Summary... iii

Introduction.. 1
    Purpose and Scope.. 1
    Assumptions.. 1
    Methods... 1
    Limitations.. 1
    Criteria.. 1

Location.. 2

Chilean Customs and Behaviors... 2
    Food Preferences.. 2
    Eating Times... 3
    Family Life.. 3
    Greetings and Address... 3
    Body Language... 4
    Religion.. 4

Chilean Politics... 4
    Presidential Power.. 4
    Trade Agreements... 4

Chilean Economics and Legal Concerns... 5
    Economic Growth.. 5
    Currency and GDP... 6
    Imports.. 6
    Franchising... 7

Market Possibilities and Competitors.. 7

Conclusions and Recommendations... 8

References.. 9

Capitalize first letter of each major word in headings.

Indentions show level of heading at a glance.

Use lowercase Roman numerals for initial pages.

Introduction begins on page I.

Line up right margin (justify).

Add a "List of Illustrations" at the bottom of the page or on a separate page if the report has graphs and other visuals.

Figures and tables are numbered independently, so you could have both a Figure 1 and a Table 1.

List of Illustrations

Figure 1   Economic Growth in Chile: 2000–2005.. 5

Figure 2   Franchising Ownership.. 7

(Continued)

Figure 19.7   A Formal Report *(Continued)*

Viva Panera!

Expanding Panera into Chile

Report title.

Many audiences read only the Executive Summary, not the report. Include enough information to give readers the key points you make.

Executive Summary

Start with recommendation or thesis.

To remain competitive with an ever-expanding market, Panera should expand into Santiago, Chile's capital. Santiago is home to approximately 5.6 million people and is one of the most modern cities in South America because of its buildings, subway system, and green areas. Santiago is already home to many American franchises, several direct competitors of Panera, and remaining competitive with these chains would be beneficial to Panera.

Our research shows expanding into Chile is likely to be a profitable decision for several reasons. First, the country's foods are similar to those of Panera's and would not require extensive menu changes. Second, the current economic situation is among the most stable in South America, and with an unemployment rate of 8%, there will likely be workers to fill positions at the restaurant. Third, the political situation and lack of legal barriers in Chile is beneficial to foreign-run businesses.

Provide brief support for recommendation.

To ensure a successful expansion, JOABA recommends the following:

1. **Expand into one location in Santiago, Chile.** Opening one store in this large city will introduce the restaurant into the Chilean culture with minimal risk. The locals will have the opportunity to show their acceptance or rejection of Panera through their patronage.
   - Start a company-owned store (as opposed to a franchise).
   - Open the store with both an American and a Chilean manager so the American can train the Chilean in the business to ensure Panera's identity is maintained.
   - Hire local people in Santiago as employees.

2. **Evaluate the success and expansion feasibility at the end of a 12-month period.**
   - Survey locals in the area for their feedback on the restaurant.
   - Explore additional places in Santiago to expand to (if expansion is the result of the evaluation).

3. **After three years, investigate selling the company-owned stores to managers to transition the stores into franchises.**
   - Evaluate the success of the stores based on sales and community response.
   - Research the economic feasibility of this change of ownership.

Language in Executive Summary can come from report. Make sure any repeated language is well-written!

The Abstract or Executive Summary contains the logic skeleton of the report: the recommendation(s) and supporting evidence.

iii

Figure 19.7   A Formal Report *(Continued)*

A running header is optional.
Viva Panera!: Expanding Panera into Chile   1

Introduction   *Center main headings.*

To stay competitive in the global market, Panera Bread has asked us to explore expanding into Chile. In order to make a wise and well-researched proposal, JOABA Consulting has researched Chilean data to see if Panera would be potentially prosperous and successful there.

"Purpose" and "Scope" can be separate sections if either is long.

Purpose and Scope

Panera has experienced recent success and is growing rapidly within the United States. To stay competitive in the global market, they must look to expand into other countries. The purpose of this research is to determine if and to what extent Panera should expand into Chile.

Topics in "Scope" section should match those in the report.

Tell what you discuss and how thoroughly you discuss each topic.   This report will cover several topics about Chile including location, customs and behaviors, politics, economics and laws, and market possibilities and competition. Throughout this report, we do not discuss topics dealing with the internal intricacies of Panera Bread Company. We also do not include any on-site research from local Chilean people.   *Give topics in the order in which you'll discuss them.*

List any relevant topics you do not discuss.

Assumptions   *Assumptions cannot be proved. But if they are wrong, the report's recommendation*

Our recommendation is based on the assumption that Panera's expansion process will be similar to that of other American competitors who have successfully opened stores in Chile. We are also assuming that Chile's political outlook will remain stable and its economic situation will remain healthy.   *may no longer be valid.*

If you collected original data (surveys, interviews, or observations), tell how you chose whom to study, what kind of sample you used, and when you collected the information. This report does not use original data; it just provides a brief discussion of significant sources.

Methods

The information from this report came from newspapers, library books, and online sources. We have found the U.S. Commercial Services, the Central Intelligence Agency's *World Factbook*, and Kwintessential Language and Cultural Specialists Web sites to be extremely useful resources for exploring this expansion possibility.

Limitations   *If your report has limitations, state them.*

This research was limited to materials available via the Internet and from our university's library. In addition, only one of the five JOABA group members is a business major, and the other group members are somewhat unfamiliar with this type of business analysis. Time constraints have limited the possibility of an exhaustive search for information regarding the expansion of Panera Bread into Chile. Moreover, our group would have greatly benefited by actually traveling to Chile for on-location research.

Criteria

This section outlines the criteria used to make the overall recommendation.   JOABA Consulting established criteria, which we used during our investigation of Chile. These criteria included the location, customs, politics, economic climate and legal issues, market

---

(Continued)

Figure 19.7   A Formal Report *(Continued)*

Viva Panera!: Expanding Panera into Chile   2

possibilities and competition. At least four of these five criteria needed to be favorable for us to give a positive recommendation.

Triple space before headings and double space below them.

Location

While Chile offers many possible cities for Panera's expansion, we believe that Santiago would be the most profitable. Santiago, the capital of Chile and home to approximately 5.6 million people, is one of the most modern cities of South America because of its buildings, subway system, and green areas (Central Intelligence Agency, 2009). Expanding Panera Bread into Santiago would be ideal because of the large market.

It's ok to have subheadings under some headings and not others.

Begin most paragraphs with topic sentences.

Moreover, Santiago ranked first on AméricaEconomía's list of the *Best Cities for Doing Business in Latin America* . The study looked at the costs and benefits of different locations and was based on the recommendations of international consulting firms. Santiago was found to add the most value to a business and to offer the best combination of quality of life, business potential, and professional development. The ranking also points out the city's attention to transportation infrastructure, showing that it benefits both commuters and business visitors (Chile Foreign Investment Committee, 2008). In 2008, Santiago was ranked second behind São Paulo, Brazil.

The continued high ranking of Santiago reinforces it as one of the best cities for doing business in Latin America, and supports our belief that Santiago would make a great city in which Panera could expand.

Not every idea needs a source. Here, general population figures are readily available.

Chilean Customs and Behaviors

Panera must have a deep understanding of the approximately 16 million Chilean people if it is to effectively adapt products to its new audience. Panera representatives, who would implement the plan, must appreciate and respect Chilean customs and behavioral norms so they do not send negative and offensive signals to the Chilean people.

In order to ensure a smooth expansion effort for Panera, we have researched food preferences, eating times, family life, greetings and address, body language, and religion. The following information presents the results of this research and can serve as a guide to understanding some of the customs and behaviors of Chilean people.

List subtopics in the order in which they are discussed.

Food Preferences

Use subheadings only when you have two or more sections.

Chilean cuisine boasts a wide range of tastes, which vary from region to region. Seafood dishes are popular, including the use of eel, bass, scallops, clams and other shellfish. Although many assume Chilean food to be hot, spiciness is a rarity in this country. Chano en piedra and pebre are two common spices used in Chilean cooking. Chano en piedra is made by grinding tomato, garlic and onions with a stone. Pebre is made from tomatoes, onions, chili, coriander, and chives. Main dishes are commonly made from beef, chicken or pork and lots of vegetables (Woodward Chile, 2007).

Figure 19.7   A Formal Report *(Continued)*

Viva Panera!: Expanding Panera into Chile   3

Sandwiches and breads are also popular in Chile. Both cold and grilled sandwiches are served for the smaller meals during the day. The type of sandwiches eaten ranges from ham and chicken deli meat to hamburgers and hotdogs, usually topped with vegetables, especially tomatoes and avocados. Breads are also served at smaller meals. Pan amasado is a homemade bread and sopaipilla is a deep fried flat bread made using pumpkin and flour (Woodward Chile, 2007).

Period goes outside of the parenthesis.

Many Chilean dishes correspond with Panera's menu. The popularity of vegetables suggests salads would work well. Sandwiches are well-liked in Chile both grilled and cold, often with deli meats. Panera could easily adapt their menu for the Chilean people by blending traditional Panera flavors with common Chilean flavors. Soups and stews are common in Chile and could also be adapted for a menu in Chile. A Panera in Chile could also offer more seafood because of its popularity and availability. Panera's traditional coffees and teas would fit in to the culture and could be served, especially during the *once* meal.

Eating Times
In Chile, most people customarily eat four meals a day. Breakfast is a small meal consisting of fresh bread with jelly or manjar (a caramel-like spread). Lunch is the largest meal of the day, having several courses, usually a cazuela soup or stew, a main dish, and a vegetable side dish, often beans. Once (pronounced own-say) is served in the afternoon between 4:00 and 7:00 PM. It includes bread or a sandwich served with coffee or tea. Dinner is a smaller meal than lunch and is typically served late evening (Rawlinson, n.d.).

Use author's name in parentheses when it isn't in the sentence introducing quote.

Family Life
Chilean life is family-centered, and people spend a lot of time with their extended family and distant relatives. Large family gatherings are common, and Panera restaurants in Chile would have to cater to the needs of large groups for such events. Family is also important in the business world, as many businesses in Chile are run by a single family (Nicol, 2008). A Panera franchise could potentially be owned and operated by a single family.

Greetings and Address
People in Chile are traditional as well as friendly. When greeting someone new, a firm handshake and good eye contact are usually expected. If a man is greeting a friend or family member, he would give them a hug, while a woman would kiss them on the cheek (Kwintessential Cross-Cultural Solutions, 2006). When engaged in conversation, Chileans speak close to one another and usually maintain eye contact. Common conversational topics are family and children (Nicol, 2008).

Addressing people by the proper name is important to build goodwill with people in business. In Chile, it is common for people to have two surnames, one from both the mother and the father. Most of the time the father's name is first and that is what most people will go by (San Marcos Church, 2002).

(Continued)

Figure 19.7   A Formal Report *(Continued)*

Body Language

Body language is also important to keep in mind when interacting with someone from Chile. Hitting one's fist into the other hand is usually considered obscene. Holding one's fist to the same height as one's head is a sign of communism. In addition, a hand palm-up with fingers spread out signals you think something is stupid. Moreover, yawns should always be covered or stifled (Nicol, 2008). At meals, hands should always be above the table, with wrists resting on the edge of the table. Serving wine with the left hand is sometimes seen as disrespectful. (Kwintessential, 2006).

After 1st reference to it, corporate author can be shortened.

Religion

Roman Catholicism is the predominant religion in Chile for 89% of the population (Central Intelligence, 2009). The religion is integrated into the society, as it is taught in most public schools and is the reason for most public holidays. Even many of the country's laws are influenced by Catholic beliefs. For example, because of the Church's disbelief in divorce, it was illegal until 2004 (Kwintessential, 2006). The religion of Chile would affect Panera's business, particularly during the Lenten season, because Catholics change their diet by refraining from eating meat on Fridays. The Catholic religion also affects holidays for the customers, as well as the employees.

Chilean Politics

Headings must cover everything under that heading until next one.

To comprehend the importance of the current political stability, Panera must understand some recent Chilean political history. Specifically, it should know about presidential power and trade agreements.

Capitalize all main words of headings and subheadings.

Presidential Power

In 1973, Augusto Pinochet led a military coup and declared himself president. His regime hurt the country and its economy, closing down the Chilean Parliament and banning all political and trade union activity. Pinochet was overthrown in 1990 and democracy was finally restored to Chile (Franklin, 2004).

Chile is currently a republic with seven primary political parties, which are grouped into two main groups (Central Intelligence, 2009). The Concertación coalition has been in power since the end of Pinochet's rule. In January 2006, the first female president in Chile's history, Michelle Bachelet, was elected. Bachelet is the fourth consecutive head of state from the center-left Concertación coalition (Chile Foreign, 2008).

Trade Agreements

In addition to the positive political environment, the country is also taking positive steps to improve its stability through relations with other countries. The U.S. Chile Free Trade Agreement (FTA) has expanded U.S–Chilean trade ties, and relations between the U.S. and Chile are the best they have ever been (U.S. Commercial Service, *Franchising*, 2009).

Figure 19.7 A Formal Report *(Continued)*

Viva Panera!: Expanding Panera into Chile   5

The two governments regularly discuss issues of mutual concern including multilateral diplomacy, security, culture, and science. The strong relationship between the governments shows the political stability of Chile. The U.S. Embassy in Santiago will also be available to assist Panera through its involvement in strengthening the relationship between the two countries (U.S. Commercial Service, *Franchising*, 2009).

Chilean Economics and Legal Concerns

We believe that Panera should know characteristics of the Chilean economy and legal concerns before expanding. Ideally, Panera wants a stable economy before expanding there because economic instability might affect Panera's success. The local currency and its stability should be taken into account when considering how to price our products. The GDP per capita is also important because it is an indicator of the average income of an average citizen. Our analysis of Chile's economy shows us that Chile is well suited for the expansion of Panera Bread into its market because of its stable and growing economy and its willingness to allow foreign investment and free trade.

Refer to Figure in text before you show it. Tell what point it makes.

Economic Growth

By the end of 1999, exports and economic activity had begun to recover from the low growth levels seen for much of the '90s. By 2000, economic growth increased to 4.5%. However, growth once again dropped in 2001 to 3.4% and to 2.2% in 2002 as seen in Figure 1. The drop occurred largely because of low global growth, and the devaluation of the Argentine peso (Chile Foreign, 2008).

Label both axes. See Chapter 9 for more information on creating graphs and visuals.

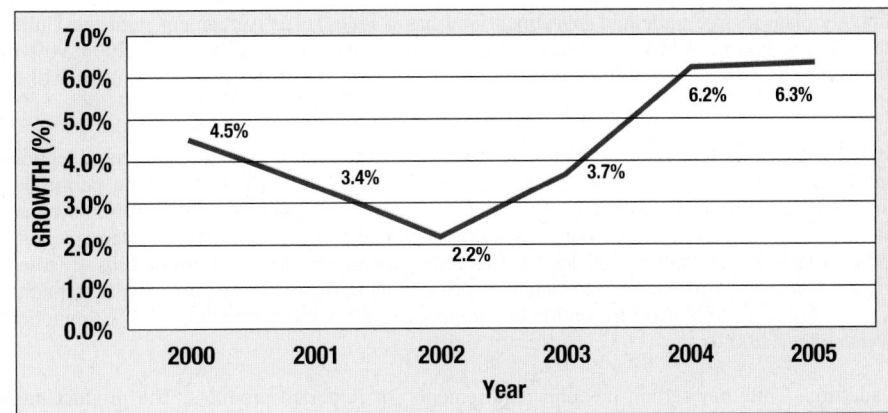

Figure 1. Recent economic growth rates in Chile (Data from Chile Foreign, 2008).

Number Figures and Tables independently.

Figure captions need to be descriptive. Cite source of data.

(Continued)

Figure 19.7 A Formal Report *(Continued)*

However, in 2003, Chile's economy began a recovery resulting in growth of 3.7% and increasing to 6.2% and 6.3% in 2004 and 2005, respectively, while Chile maintained a low rate of inflation (Chile Foreign, 2008). Over the last few years, GDP growth can be attributed to record high copper prices, solid export earnings, and increased foreign investment. The growth in GDP has reduced inflation but unemployment remains high at 7.0% (Central Intelligence, 2009), which indicates a large labor pool.

Currency and GDP

The currency of Chile is the Chilean peso (CPL), and the current exchange rate between the U.S. dollar and the Chilean peso is $1 to 514.90 CPL. In recent years, the Chilean peso has strengthened significantly against the U.S. dollar and has remained stable. This can be attributed to the growing GDP of the country and increased trade with other countries (Central Intelligence, 2009). The stable currency will make Panera's expansion more favorable.

In 2005, the GDP was $180.6 billion, with a GDP per capita of approximately $11,300. In 2005, Chile had a current account balance of $309 million and external debt of $44.8 billion. As of 2002, Chile has not received economic aid from the IMF, the World Bank, or another country (Central Intelligence, 2009). Chile serves as an economic model for the rest of Latin America with its continued economic growth and is expected to continue growing into 2009 (Chile Foreign, 2008).

Imports

The country's largest import partners are Argentina, United States, Brazil, and China. Chile is relatively open to free trade and investment and has a Free Trade Agreement with the United States. When the U.S.–Chile Free Trade Agreement came into effect in January 1, 2004, 90% of tariffs on U.S. exports were eliminated. By 2015, all trade between the two countries will be duty-free.

Typically, Chile has few barriers to imports. However, in the case of agriculture, some exceptions apply. If Panera is going to import processed food products, it will have to obtain permission from the Health Service Officer at the port of entry, who will take samples and perform necessary tests. Upon importation, there is some necessary documentation that will have to accompany the products. This documentation includes commercial invoices, certificates of origin, bills of lading, freight insurance and packing lists. Franchises are subject to regular trade laws. The withholding tax on royalties is 35% and all imports are subject to 19% value-added tax (U.S. Commerical Service, *Made*, 2009).

In addition, Chile has certain labeling requirements for imported products. The product must display the country of origin before being sold. Packaged goods must be marked with the quality, purity, ingredients, and the net weight or measure. The labeling must also be in Spanish and measurements should use the metric system. Foreign firms in Chile are allowed the same protection and operate under the same conditions as local firms. Trademarks, patents, industrial designs, models, and copyrights are protected in Chile under the Paris Convention because Chile belongs to the World Intellectual Property Organization. Trademark stockpiling is rather common in Chile, so U.S. companies are encouraged to register their trademarks as soon as possible (U.S. Commerical Service, *Made*, 2009).

Figure 19.7 A Formal Report *(Continued)*

Viva Panera!: Expanding Panera into Chile   7

This legal analysis provides Panera with a synopsis of the opportunities and restrictions available to the company when considering doing business in Chile. These legal restrictions will need to be followed if opening a facility in Chile so that any legal risk between the business and consumers or the government can be avoided.

Franchising

Chile offers attractive opportunities for new franchises, something that bodes well for the advancement of Panera (U.S. Commercial Service, *Franchising*, 2009). The current franchise fee of a Panera store is $35,000 plus royalties of 4–5% of annual sales (Panera Bread, 2009). Because of this high startup cost, the Panera facility that would open in Chile would be company owned. After an evaluation of the success of the initial restaurant, the facility could change from being company owned to becoming a franchise with opportunities to expand in numbers of franchises.

Refer to figure before it appears in report.

Market Possibilities and Competitors

Panera also needs to be aware of the Chilean market possibilities and current competitors, now there are about 50 franchise businesses operating in Chile with over 914 locations. As seen below in Figure 2, U.S.-run franchise operations account for 55% of the total Chilean markets mostly because of technology, convenience, and marketing strategies borrowed from the U.S.

Be sure to proofread for errors such as incorrect words and comma splices.

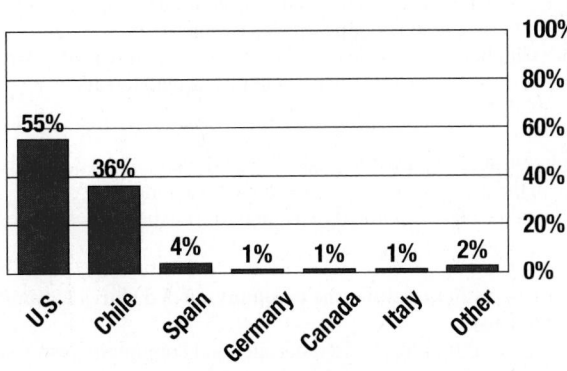

Number Figures consecutively throughout the report.

Figure 2. The current franchise ownership in Santiago, Chile (USCS, *Franchising*, 2009)

Note that spelling checkers would not catch this mistake.

American restaurant franchises currently present are Domino's Pizza, Kentucky Friend Chicken, Pizza Hut, Burger King, Dunkin Donuts, Bennigans, Chuck E. Cheese, TGI Fridays, Taco Bell, McDonald's, and Ruby Tuesday. The local franchise competitors are Schop Dog,

(Continued)

Figure 19.7 A Formal Report *(Continued)*

Viva Panera!: Expanding Panera into Chile   8

Lomito'n, and Doggis, all fast food restaurants, and Tavelli. These local competitors are in direct competition with American-based franchises, especially in Santiago. This competition most likely will be positive for Panera because of the market awareness created by the competitors.

However, it should be noted that full service restaurants are listed among the best commercial opportunities because in general, they can compete with the inadequate amount of restaurants present (U.S. Commercial Service, *Franchising*, 2009). Some café- and bakery- style restaurants, such as Tavelli, have done extremely well in Santiago. The marketability and the success of Tavelli in Chile is a key indicator that Panera could do the same (Lonely Planet, 2009).

Moreover, other foreign restaurants have done equally well. For example, Doggendorf is a family run German bakery in Santiago. The franchise began as a doughnut shop, and has now expanded into a larger commercial operation of four family owned and run bakeries (Yahoo, 2009). The fact that Chileans have accepted this foreign bakery is a good indicator that Panera would also be well-accepted.

Conclusions repeat points made in the report. Recommendations are actions the readers should take.

Some companies ask for Conclusions and Recommendations at the beginning of the report.

Conclusions and Recommendations

Chile's unique culture and customs, progressive politics, and efficient business management along with its growing economy lead JOABA Consulting to believe the Chilean market is ready for a new franchise. Therefore, we recommend that Panera should expand into Chile. We recommend the following process to ensure a successful expansion:

1. **Expand into one location in Santiago, Chile.** Opening one store in this large city will introduce the restaurant into the Chilean culture with minimal risk. The locals will have the opportunity to show their acceptance or rejection of Panera through their patronage.
   - Start a company-owned store (as opposed to a franchise).
   - Open the store with both an American and a Chilean manager so the American can train the Chilean in the business to ensure Panera's identity is maintained.
   - Hire local people in Santiago as employees.

Numbering points makes it easier for readers to follow and discuss them.

2. **Evaluate the success and expansion feasibility at the end of a 12-month period.**
   - Survey locals in the area for their feedback on the restaurant.
   - Explore additional places in Santiago to expand to (if expansion is the result of the evaluation).

Make sure all items in a list are parallel.

3. **After three years, investigate selling the company-owned stores to managers to transition the stores into franchises.**
   - Evaluate the success of the stores based on sales and community response.
   - Research the economic feasibility of this change of ownership.

Because many readers turn to the "Recommendations" first, provide enough information so that the reason is clear all by itself. The ideas in this section must be logical extensions of the points made and supported in the body of the report.

Figure 19.7 A Formal Report *(Concluded)*

Viva Panera!: Expanding Panera into Chile   9

References   *This report uses APA citation style.*

Central Intelligence Agency. (2009). *The world factbook: Chile*. Retrieved March 15, 2009, from
    https://www.cia.gov/library/publications/the-world-factbook/geos/ci.html

Chile Foreign Investment Committee. (2008). *Business environment*. Retrieved March 20, 2009, from
    http://www.cinver.cl/english/clima/inversion_reconocido.asp

Franklin, J. (2004, November 15). Chile identified 35,000 victims of Pinochet. *The Guardian*. Retrieved
    March 22, 2009, from http:// www.guardian.co.uk/chile/story/0,13755,1351421,00.html

Kwintessential Cross-Cultural Solutions. (2006). *Chile—Language, culture, customs and etiquette*.
    Retrieved March 22, 2009, from http://www.kwintessential.co.uk/
    resources/global-etiquette/chile.html

Lonely Planet. (2009). *Santiago—Place to eat: Tavelli café*. Retrieved March 31, 2009, from
    http://www.lonelyplanet.com/worldguide/chile-and-easter-island/santiago/
    where-to-eat/1000300106?list=true

Nicol, J. (2008). *Chile*. International Business Center. Retrieved March 31, 2009, from
    http://www.cyborlink.com/besite/chile.htm

Panera Bread. (2009). *Franchise information overview*. Retrieved March 15, 2009, from
    http://www.panerabread.com/about/franchise/

Rawlinson, J. (n.d.). *Chilean food*. Pepe's Chile. Retrieved March 30, 2009, from
    http://www.joeskitchen.com/chile/culture/food.htm

San Marcos Church. (2002). *Chile: Culture and customs*. Retrieved March 31, 2009, from
    http://www.sanmarcoschurch.cl/fr_culture.html

U.S. Commercial Service. (2009). *Franchising*. U.S. Department of State. Retrieved March 15, 2009,
    from http://www.buyusa.gov/chile/en/121.html#3

U.S. Commercial Service. (2009). *Made in USA, sold in Chile*. U.S. Department of State.
    Retrieved March 17,2009, from http://www.buyusa.gov/chile/en/

Woodword Chile. (2007). *Typical Chilean food*. Retrieved March 17, 2009, from
    http://www.woodward.cl/chilefood.htm

Yahoo U.K. & Ireland Travel. (2009). *Doggendorf—details*. Retrieved April 1, 2009, from
    http:// uk.holidaysguide.yahoo.com/p-travelguide-33211-action-describe-
    doggendorf_santiago-i

Compare this list of sources with those in the proposal. Notice how the authors had to adjust the list as they completed the research.

List all the printed and online sources cited in your report. Do not list sources you used for background but did not cite.

The title of the report should be as informative as possible. Like subject lines, report titles are straightforward.

Poor title: New Plant Site

Better title: Eugene, Oregon, Site for the New Kemco Plant

Large organizations that issue many reports may use two-part titles to make it easier to search for reports electronically. For example, US government report titles first give the agency sponsoring the report, then the title of that particular report.

> Small Business Administration: Management Practices Have Improved for the Women's Business Center Program

In many cases, the title will state the recommendation in the report: "Why the United Nations Should Establish a Seed Bank." However, the title should omit recommendations when

- The reader will find the recommendations hard to accept.
- Putting all the recommendations in the title would make it too long.
- The report does not offer recommendations.

If the title does not contain the recommendation, it normally indicates what problem the report tries to solve or the topic the report discusses.

Eliminate any unnecessary words:

Wordy: Report of a Study on Ways to Market Life Insurance to Urban Professional People Who Are in Their Mid-40s

Better: Marketing Life Insurance to the Mid-40s Urban Professional

The identification of the receiver of the report normally includes the name of the person who will make a decision based on the report, his or her job title, the organization's name, and its location (city, state, and zip code). Government reports often omit the person's name and simply give the organization that authorized the report.

If the report is prepared primarily by one person, the *Prepared by* section will have that person's name, his or her title, the organization, and its location (city, state, and zip code). In internal reports, the organization and location are usually omitted if the report writer works at the headquarters office.

If several people write the report, government reports normally list all their names, using a separate sheet of paper if the group working on the report is large. Practices in business differ. In some organizations, all the names are listed; in others, the division to which they belong is listed; in still others, the name of the chair of the group appears.

The **release date,** the date the report will be released to the public, is usually the date the report is scheduled for discussion by the decision makers. The report is frequently due four to six weeks before the release date so that the decision makers can review the report before the meeting.

If you have the facilities and the time, try using type variations, color, and artwork to create a visually attractive and impressive title page. However, a plain typed page is acceptable. The format in Figure 19.7 will enable you to create an acceptable typed title page.

Letter or Memo of Transmittal

Use a letter of transmittal if you are not a regular employee of the organization for which you prepare the report; use a memo if you are a regular employee.

The transmittal has several purposes: to transmit the report, to orient the reader to the report, and to build a good image of the report and of the writer. An informal writing style is appropriate for a transmittal even when the style in the report is more formal. A professional transmittal helps you create a good image of yourself and enhances your credibility. Personal statements are appropriate in the transmittal, even though they would not be acceptable in the report itself.

Organize the transmittal in this way:

1. **Transmit the report.**   Tell when and by whom it was authorized and the purpose it was to fulfill.

2. **Summarize your conclusions and recommendations.**   If the recommendations will be easy for the reader to accept, put them early in the transmittal. If they will be difficult, summarize the findings and conclusions before the recommendations.

3. **Mention any points of special interest in the report. Show how you surmounted minor problems you encountered in your investigation. Thank people who helped you.**   These optional items can build goodwill and enhance your credibility.

4. **Point out additional research that is necessary, if any.**   Sometimes your recommendation cannot be implemented until further work is done. If you'd be interested in doing that research, or if you'd like to implement the recommendations, say so.

5. **Thank the reader for the opportunity to do the work and offer to answer questions.**   Provide contact information. Even if the report has not been fun to do, expressing satisfaction in doing the project is expected. Saying that you'll answer questions about the report is a way of saying that you won't charge the reader your normal hourly fee to answer questions (one more reason to make the report clear!).

The letter of transmittal on page i of Figure 19.7 uses this pattern of organization.

Table of Contents

In the table of contents, list the headings exactly as they appear in the body of the report. If the report is less than 25 pages, you'll probably list all the levels of headings. In a very long report, pick a level and put all the headings at that level and above in the table of contents.

Page ii of Figure 19.7 shows the table of contents.

List of Illustrations

A list of illustrations enables readers to refer to your visuals.

Report visuals comprise both tables and figures. *Tables* are words or numbers arranged in rows and columns. *Figures* are everything else: bar graphs, pie charts, flow charts, maps, drawings, photographs, computer printouts, and so on. Tables and figures may be numbered independently, so you may have both a Table 1 and a Figure 1. In a report with maps and graphs but no other visuals, the visuals are sometimes called Map 1 and Graph 1. Whatever you call the illustrations, list them in the order in which they appear in the report; give the name of each visual as well as its number.

See Chapter 9 for information about how to design and label visuals.

Executive Summary of a Government Plan

On February 18, 2009, the Obama administration announced a "Homeowner Affordability and Stability" plan to counter the home mortgage crisis. The executive summary of the plan—given to the press—included the following:

- First, a statement of background, which included bullet points listing the effects of the crisis (for example, that nearly 6 million households will face foreclosure), and ending with the purpose of the plan (that the plan will help nearly 7 to 9 million families to "restructure" their mortgages to avoid foreclosure).

- Then, the two main components of the plan ("affordability" and "stability") together with their subcomponents (a few subcomponents are given below as examples):

  - "Affordability"

    - "Enabling refinancing"

    - "Reducing monthly payments"

  - "Stability"

    - "Helping homeowners stay in their homes"

    - "Not aiding speculators"

    - "Protecting neighborhoods"

The summary provided numbers and, where appropriate, examples to inform and explain the plan. A busy reader—or one who wanted to know the broad contours of the plan without going through its nuts and bolts—would likely benefit from reading the summary before deciding whether to read the whole plan.

Adapted from "Homeowner Affordability and Stability Plan Executive Summary," in *BusinessWeek: Top News: February 18, 2009,* http://www.business week.com/bwdaily/dnflash/content/feb2009/db20090218_403370.htm (accessed April 12, 2009).

Executive Summary

An **executive summary** or **abstract** tells the reader what the document is about. It summarizes the recommendation of the report and the reasons for the recommendation or describes the topics the report discusses and indicates the depth of the discussion. It should be clear even to people who will read only the abstract.

A good abstract is easy to read, concise, and clear. Edit your abstract carefully to tighten your writing and eliminate any unnecessary words.

Wordy: The report describes two types of business jargon, *businessese* and *reverse gobbledygook.* It gives many examples of each of these and points out how their use can be harmful.

Tight: The report describes and illustrates two harmful types of business jargon, *businessese* and *reverse gobbledygook.*

Abstracts generally use a more formal style than other forms of business writing. Avoid contractions and colloquialisms. Try to avoid using the second-person *you.* Because reports may have many different readers, *you* may become inaccurate. It's OK to use exactly the same words in the abstract and the report.

Summary abstracts present the logic skeleton of the report: the thesis or recommendation and its proof. Use a summary abstract to give the most useful information in the shortest space.

> To market life insurance to mid-40s urban professionals, Interstate Fidelity Insurance should advertise in upscale publications and use direct mail.
>
> Network TV and radio are not cost-efficient for reaching this market. This group comprises a small percentage of the prime-time network TV audience and a minority of most radio station listeners. They tend to discard newspapers and general-interest magazines quickly, but many of them keep upscale periodicals for months or years. Magazines with high percentages of readers in this group include *Architectural Digest, Bon Appetit, BusinessWeek, Forbes, Golf Digest, Metropolitan Home, Southern Living,* and *Smithsonian.*
>
> Any advertising campaign needs to overcome this group's feeling that they already have the insurance they need. One way to do this would be to encourage them to check the coverage their employers provide and to calculate the cost of their children's expenses through college graduation. Insurance plans that provide savings and tax benefits as well as death benefits might also be appealing.

One way to start composing an abstract is to write a sentence outline. A **sentence outline** not only uses complete sentences rather than words or phrases but also contains the thesis sentence or recommendation and the evidence that proves that point. Combine the sentences into paragraphs, adding transitions if necessary, and you'll have your abstract.

Descriptive abstracts indicate what topics the report covers and how deeply it goes into each topic, but they do not summarize what the report says about each topic. Phrases that describe the report ("this report covers," "it includes," "it summarizes," "it concludes") are marks of a descriptive abstract. An additional mark of a descriptive abstract is that the reader can't tell what the report says about the topics it covers.

> This report recommends ways Interstate Fidelity Insurance could market insurance to mid-40s urban professionals. It examines demographic and psychographic profiles of the target market. Survey results are used to show attitudes toward insurance. The report suggests some appeals that might be successful with this market.

Introduction

The **Introduction** of the report always contains a statement of purpose and scope and may include all the parts in the following list.

- **Purpose.** The purpose statement (p. 531) identifies the problem the report addresses, the technical investigations it summarizes, and the rhetorical purpose (to explain, to recommend).
- **Scope.** The scope statement identifies how broad an area the report surveys. For example, Company XYZ is losing money on its line of computers. Does the report investigate the quality of the computers? The advertising campaign? The cost of manufacturing? The demand for computers? A scope statement allows the reader to evaluate the report on appropriate grounds.
- **Assumptions.** Assumptions in a report are like assumptions in geometry: statements whose truth you assume, and which you use to prove your final point. If they are wrong, the conclusion will be wrong too.

  For example, to plan cars that will be built five years from now, an automobile manufacturer commissions a report on young adults' attitudes toward cars. The recommendations would be based on assumptions both about gas prices and about the economy. If gas prices radically rose or fell, the kinds of cars young adults wanted would change. If there were a major recession, people wouldn't be able to buy new cars.

  Almost all reports require assumptions. A good report spells out its assumptions so that readers can make decisions more confidently.
- **Methods.** If you conducted surveys, focus groups, or interviews, you need to tell how you chose your subjects, and how, when, and where they were interviewed. If the discussion of your methodology is more than a paragraph or two, you should probably make it a separate section in the body of the report rather than including it in the introduction. Reports based on scientific experiments usually put the methods section in the body of the report, not in the Introduction.

  If your report is based solely on library or online research, provide a brief description of significant sources. See Chapter 17 on how to cite and document sources.
- **Limitations.** Limitations make your recommendations less valid or valid only under certain conditions. Limitations usually arise because time or money constraints haven't permitted full research. For example, a campus pizza restaurant considering expanding its menu may ask for a report but not have enough money to take a random sample of students and townspeople. Without a random sample, the writer cannot generalize from the sample to the larger population.

  Many recommendations are valid only for a limited time. For instance, a campus store wants to know what kinds of clothing will appeal to college men. The recommendations will remain in force only for a short time: Three years from now, styles and tastes may have changed, and the clothes that would sell best now may no longer be in demand.
- **Criteria.** The criteria section outlines the factors or standards that you are considering and the relative importance of each. If a company is choosing a city for a new office, is the cost of office space more or less important than the availability of skilled workers? Check with your audience before you write the draft to make sure that your criteria match those of your readers.
- **Definitions.** Many reports define key terms in the introduction. For instance, a report on unauthorized Internet use by employees might

Life and Death Data

"The 'value of a statistical life' is $6.9 million in today's dollars, the Environmental Protection Agency reckoned in May—a drop of nearly $1 million from just five years ago. . . .

"The devaluation has real consequences. When drawing up regulations, government agencies put a value on human life and then weigh the costs versus the lifesaving benefits of a proposed rule.

"Consider, for example, a hypothetical regulation that costs $18 billion to enforce but will prevent 2,500 deaths. At $7.8 million per person (the old figure), the lifesaving benefits outweigh the costs. But at $6.9 million per person, the rule costs more than the lives it saves, so it may not be adopted. . . .

"The EPA figure is not based on people's earning capacity, or potential contributions to society, or how much they are loved and needed—factors used in wrongful-death lawsuits.

"Instead, economists calculate the value based on what people are willing to pay to avoid certain risks, and on how much extra employers pay their workers to take on additional risks. Most of the data is drawn from payroll statistics; some comes from opinion surveys."

Quoted from Seth Borenstein, "Life Worth Less Now than in 2003, EPA Officials Say," Associated Press, July 11, 2008. Reprinted with permission of The YGS Group.

define what is meant by "unauthorized use." A report on the corporate dress code might define such codes broadly to include general appearance, so it could include items such as tattoos, facial piercings, and general cleanliness. Also, if you know that some members of your primary, secondary, or intermediate audience will not understand technical terms, define them. If you have only a few definitions, you can put them in the Introduction. If you have many terms to define, put a **glossary** in an appendix. Refer to it in the Introduction so that readers know that you've provided it.

Background or History

Formal reports usually have a section that gives the background of the situation or the history of the problem. Even though the current audience for the report probably knows the situation, reports are filed and consulted years later. These later audiences will probably not know the background, although it may be crucial for understanding the options that are possible.

In some cases, the history section may cover many years. For example, a report recommending that a US hotel chain open hotels in Romania may give the history of that country for at least several decades. In other cases, the background section is much briefer, covering only a few years or even just the immediate situation.

The purpose of most reports is rarely to provide a history of the problem. Do not let the background section achieve undue length.

Body

The body of the report is usually its longest section. Here you analyze causes of the problem and offer possible solutions. Here you present your argument with all its evidence and data. Data that are necessary to follow the argument are included with appropriate visuals and explanatory text. Extended data sets, such as large tables and long questionnaires, are generally placed in appendices. It is particularly important in the body that you use headings, forecasting statements, and topic sentences to help lead your readers through the text. Readers will also appreciate clear, concise, and engaging prose. Remember to cite your sources (see Chapter 17) and to refer in the text to all visuals and appendices.

Conclusions and Recommendations

Conclusions summarize points you have made in the body of the report; **Recommendations** are action items that would solve or ameliorate the problem. These sections are often combined if they are short: *Conclusions and Recommendations.* No new information should be included in this section.

Many readers turn to the recommendations section first; some organizations ask that recommendations be presented early in the report. Number the recommendations to make it easy for people to discuss them. If the recommendations will seem difficult or controversial, give a brief paragraph of rationale after each recommendation. If they'll be easy for the audience to accept, you can simply list them without comments or reasons. The recommendations will also be in the executive summary and perhaps in the title and the transmittal.

Summary of Key Points

* Good reports begin with good data. Make sure your data come from reliable sources.
* Analyze report numbers and text for accuracy and logic.
* Choose an appropriate organizational pattern for your information and purposes. The most common patterns are comparison/contrast, problem-solving, elimination of alternatives, SWOT analysis, general to particular, particular to general, geographic or spatial, functional, and chronological.
* Reports use the same style as other business documents, with three exceptions:
  1. Reports use a more formal style, without contractions or slang, than do many letters and memos.
  2. Reports rarely use the word *you*.
  3. Reports should include all the definitions and documents needed to understand the recommendations.
* To create good report style,
  1. Use clear, engaging writing.
  2. Keep repetition to a minimum.
  3. Introduce all sources and visuals.
  4. Use forecasting, transitions, topic sentences, and headings.
* **Headings** are single words short phrases, or complete sentences that describe all of the material under them until the next heading. **Talking heads** tell the reader what to expect in each section.
* Headings must use the same grammatical structure. Subheads under a heading must be parallel to each other but do not necessarily have to be parallel to subheads under other headings.
* The title page of a report usually contains four items: the title of the report, whom the report is prepared for, whom it is prepared by, and the date.
* If the report is 25 pages or less, list all the headings in the table of contents. In a long report, pick a level and put all the headings at that level and above in the contents.
* Organize the transmittal in this way:
  1. Release the report.
  2. Summarize your conclusions and recommendations.
  3. Mention any points of special interest in the report. Show how you surmounted minor problems you encountered in your investigation. Thank people who helped you.
  4. Point out additional research that is necessary, if any.
  5. Thank the reader for the opportunity to do the work and offer to answer questions.
* **Summary abstracts** present the logic skeleton of the article: the thesis or recommendation and its proof. **Descriptive abstracts** indicate what topics the article covers and how deeply it goes into each topic, but do not summarize what the article says about each topic.
* A good abstract or executive summary is easy to read, concise, and clear. A good abstract can be understood by itself, without the report or references.
* The **Introduction** of the report always contains a statement of purpose and scope. The **Purpose** statement identifies the organizational problem the report addresses, the technical investigations it summarizes, and the rhetorical purpose (to explain, to recommend). The **Scope** statement identifies

Analyzing Numbers

"True story. One of the Big Three Detroit Automakers put together a customer relationship management (CRM) system that helped it decide which cars to manufacture based on what was going on in dealers' lots. It worked great.

Well, except for one catch. According to Eric Almquist, VP at Mercer Management Consulting, the company's marketing team had just created sales incentives to get rid of a lot of lime-green cars, which no one wanted. As consumers snapped up the special deals on the cars, the CRM software noticed the surge of sales in lime-green cars and instructed the factory to produce more. The automaker lost millions of dollars before it caught the error."

Quoted from Brian Caulfield, "Facing Up to CRM," *Business 2.0*, August/September 2001, 149.

how broad an area the report surveys. The introduction may also include **Limitations,** problems or factors that limit the validity of your recommendations; **Assumptions,** statements whose truth you assume, and which you use to prove your final point; **Methods,** an explanation of how you gathered your data; **Criteria** used to weigh the factors in the decision; and **Definitions** of terms readers may not know.

- A **Background** or **History** section is usually included because reports are filed and may be consulted years later by people who no longer remember the original circumstances.

- The **Body** of the report, usually the longest section, analyzes causes of the problem and offers possible solutions. It presents your argument with all evidence and data.

- **Conclusions** summarize points made in the body of the report; **Recommendations** are action items that would solve or ameliorate the problem. These sections are often combined if they are short.

CHAPTER 19   Exercises and Problems

19.1   Reviewing the Chapter

1. What are some criteria to check to ensure you have quality data? (LO 1)
2. What kinds of patterns should you look for in your data and text? (LO 1)
3. What are some guidelines for choosing information for reports? (LO 2)
4. Name seven basic patterns for organizing reports. For four of them, explain when they would be particularly effective or ineffective. (LO 3)
5. What are three ways that style in reports differs from conventional business communication style? (LO 4)
6. Name four good writing principles that are particularly important in reports. (LO 4)

7. How do you introduce sources in the text of the report? (LO 4)
8. Why should reports try to have a topic sentence at the beginning of each paragraph? (LO 4)
9. What are the characteristics of an effective report title? (LO 5)
10. What goes in the letter of transmittal? (LO 5)
11. What is the difference between summary and descriptive abstracts? (LO 5)
12. What goes in the introduction of a report? (LO 5)
13. What is the difference between conclusions and recommendations? (LO 5)

19.2   Identifying Assumptions and Limitations

Indicate whether each of the following would be an assumption or a limitation in a formal report.

a. Report on Ways to Encourage More Students to Join XYZ Organization
1. I surveyed a judgment sample rather than a random sample.
2. These recommendations are based on the attitudes of current students. Presumably, students in the next several years will have the same attitudes and interests.

b. Report on the Feasibility of Building Hilton Hotels in Romania
1. This report is based on the expectation that the country will be politically stable.
2. All of my information is based on library research. The most recent articles were

published two months ago; much of the information was published a year ago or more. Therefore some of my information may be out of date.

c. Report on Car-Buying Preferences of Young Adults
1. These recommendations may change if the cost of gasoline increases dramatically or if there is another deep recession.
2. This report is based on a survey of adults ages 20 to 24 in California, Texas, Illinois, Ontario, and Massachusetts.
3. These preferences are based on the cars now available. If a major technical or styling innovation occurs, preferences may change.

19.3 Revising an Executive Summary

The following Executive Summary is poorly organized and too long. Rearrange information to make it more effective. Cut information that does not belong in the summary. You may use different words as you revise.

> In this report I will discuss the communication problems which exist at Rolling Meadows Golf Club. The problems discussed will deal with channels of communication. The areas which are causing problems are internal. Radios would solve these internal problems.
>
> Taking a 15-minute drive on a golf cart in order to find the superintendent is a common occurrence. Starters and rangers need to keep in touch with the clubhouse to maintain a smooth flow of players around the course. The rangers have expressed an interest in being able to call the clubhouse for advice and support.
>
> Purchasing two-channel FM radios with private channels would provide three advantages. First, radios would make the golf course safer by providing a means of notifying someone in the event of an emergency. Second, radios would make the staff more efficient by providing a faster channel of communication. Third, radios would enable clubhouse personnel to keep in touch with the superintendent, the rangers, and the starters.
>
> During the week, radios can be carried by the superintendent, the golf pro, and another course worker. On weekends and during tournaments, one radio will be used by the golf professional. The other two will be used by one starter and one ranger. Three radios is the minimum needed to meet basic communication needs. A fourth radio would provide more flexibility for busy weekends and during tournaments.
>
> Tekk T-20 radios can be purchased from Page-Com for $129 each. These radios have the range and options needed for use on the golf course. Radios are durable and easy to service. It is possible that another brand might be even less expensive.
>
> Rolling Meadows Golf Club should purchase four radios. They will cost under $600 and can be paid for from the current equipment budget.

19.4 Analyzing a Report Introduction

The following paragraphs form the introduction in Ford Motor Company's 2007–2008 sustainability report (accessible at http://www.ford.com/doc/sr07-ford-sustainability.pdf). The "I" in the first sentence belongs to Alan Mulally, the President and CEO of the company.

Analyze this introduction based on the discussion of report introductions given in the chapter. For example, where in the three paragraphs do you see the report's purpose, scope, assumptions, and so forth? How can you improve this introduction? Discuss in small groups.

> I am convinced that our vision makes sense from a business point of view as well as an ethical one. Climate change may be the first sustainability issue to fundamentally reshape our business, but it will not be the last. How we anticipate and respond to issues like human rights, the mobility divide, resource scarcity and poverty will determine our future success.
>
> For example, urbanization, congestion, high fuel prices and other trends are putting safe, affordable transportation out of reach for many people around the world. We view this as an enormous opportunity and are leading the implementation of a prototype program to provide smart, innovative urban mobility solutions.

Our progress in addressing climate change, mobility and our other material sustainability issues is summarized below. I believe that our approach to sustainability will be one of the most important factors in both our short-term financial recovery and our long-term success. I hope that what you read in this report demonstrates that we are on the right track.

19.5 Comparing Report Formats

Locate five business or organizational reports (or white papers as they're sometimes called) on the Internet. A good online collection of organizational reports is the Web site of the Council on Library and Information Resources (CLIR) accessible at http://www.clir.org/pubs/reports/reports.html. Additionally, you can find reports linked from the Web sites of the Fortune 500 organizations, or you can search for them on Google using keywords such as "reports," "business reports," "company reports," or "organizational reports."

The reports you find could be about the organizations' environmental sustainability efforts, their products, or any other aspect of their operations.

Compare the organization (the reports' contents or the way they're structured) of the five reports you select. What similarities and differences do yo u see in the formatting of all these reports? Make a table of your findings. Discuss your findings in small groups.

19.6 Comparing Style in Annual Reports

Locate two annual reports on the Internet. A good source is Report Watch, http://www.reportwatch.net/ Compare the style of the two reports. Here are some questions to get you started:

1. How do they use visuals to keep attention?
2. What differences do you see in the letters from the CEOs?
3. How do they present number-heavy information? Do they rely mainly on tables and graphs? Do they give prose summaries?
4. Is the writing easy to understand?
5. Do you see places where negative information is given a positive spin?

6. Is one report easier to understand than the other? Why?
7. Is one report more interesting than the other? Why?
8. Is one report more convincing than the other? Why?

As your instructor directs,
a. Work in small groups to do your comparison. Share your findings in a five-minute oral presentation to the class.
b. Work in small groups to do your comparison. Share your findings in a memo posted on the class Web site.
c. Work individually to do your comparison. Share your findings in a memo to your instructor.

19.7 Analyzing Data and Information

Every year, *Business Ethics* magazine releases its annual survey of the "100 Best Corporate Citizens." The survey measures a company's social responsibility to the environment and to their community and employees.

Go to the Web site http://www.business-ethics.com/BE100_all and analyze the data and information used to create their list. Consider the following questions:
- Do the data come from a reliable source? Does the source have a vested interest in the results?
- What do the data actually measure?

- Are there any assumptions or limitations that need to be considered when analyzing these numbers?

As your instructor directs,
- Write a memo to your instructor summarizing your analysis.
- Share your analysis orally with a small group of students.
- Present your analysis to the class.

19.8 Evaluating a Report from Your Workplace

Consider the following aspects of a report from your workplace:
- Content. How much information is included? How is it presented?

- Emphasis. What points are emphasized? What points are deemphasized? What verbal and visual techniques are used to highlight or minimize information?

- Visuals and layout. Are visuals used effectively? Are they accurate and free from chartjunk? What image do the pictures and visuals create? Are color and white space used effectively? (See Chapter 9 on visuals.)

As your instructor directs,

a. Write a memo to your instructor analyzing the report.

b. Join with a small group of students to compare and contrast several reports. Present your evaluation in an informal group report.

c. Present your evaluation orally to the class.

19.9   Analyzing and Writing Reports

Reread the sidebar about the Pew Internet and American Life Project at http://www.pewinternet.org/ on page 608. Go to the Web site and browse through the reports. Select a report and answer the following questions:

- Who is the report's audience?
- What is its purpose?
- How were the data collected?
- What did the data collection measure?
- Why was the data collection important?

Given your analysis of the report's audience, purpose, and data collection, consider the strategies used in the report to convey the information. Answer these questions:

- What tone did the writer adopt?

- How was the report organized and designed to meet the needs of the audience?
- What language choices did the writer make?

Finally, examine the press releases that are written about the report (the press releases for each report are included as links) for the ways the information in the report is adapted for a different audience and purpose. How do the content, organization, tone, and language choices differ from those of the original report? Do you see any ethical issues involved in condensing the report into a press release?

As your instructor directs,

- Write a report of your findings to your instructor.
- Present your findings to the class using presentation software.

19.10   Preparing an Information Report

Visit the Web site of the Global Reporting Initiative (http://www.globalreporting.org/Home), a group of analysts from various industries and professions that is committed to advancing the cause of socially responsible reporting by organizations. Prepare an information report, either as a memo to your instructor or as a PowerPoint presentation for the class, describing the organization, the people behind it, their guidelines, their work, and their impact on the corporate world.

19.11   Recommending Action

Write a report recommending an action that your unit or organization should take. Possibilities include

- Buying more equipment for your department.
- Hiring an additional worker for your department.
- Making your organization more family-friendly.
- Making a change that will make the organization more efficient.
- Making changes to improve accessibility for customers or employees with disabilities.

Address your report to the person who would have the power to approve your recommendation.

As your instructor directs,

a. Create a document or presentation to achieve the goal.

b. Write a memo to your instructor describing the situation at your workplace and explaining your rhetorical choices (medium, strategy, tone, wording, graphics or document design, and so forth).

19.12   Writing a Recommendation Report

Write a report evaluating two or more alternatives. Possible topics include the following:

1. Should students in your major start a monthly newsletter?

2. Should your student organization write an annual report? Would doing so help the next year's officers?

3. Should your student organization create a wiki, blog, or newsletter to facilitate communication with a constituency?
4. Should your workplace create a newsletter to communicate internally?
5. Should a local restaurant open another branch? Where should it be?

In designing your study, identify the alternatives, define your criteria for selecting one option over others, carefully evaluate each alternative, and recommend the best course of action.

19.13 Writing an Informative or Closure Report

Write an informative report on one of the following topics.

1. What should a US manager know about dealing with workers from _____ [you fill in the country or culture]? What factors do and do not motivate people in this group? How do they show respect and deference? Are they used to a strong hierarchy or to an egalitarian setting? Do they normally do one thing at once or many things? How important is clock time and being on time? What factors lead them to respect someone? Age? Experience? Education? Technical knowledge? Wealth? Or what? What conflicts or miscommunications may arise between workers from this culture and other workers due to cultural differences? Are people from this culture similar in these beliefs and behaviors, or is there lots of variation?

2. What benefits do companies offer? To get information, check the Web pages of three companies in the same industry. Information about benefits is usually on the page about working for the company.

3. Describe an ethical dilemma encountered by workers in a specific organization. What is the background of the situation? What competing loyalties exist? In the past, how have workers responded? How has the organization responded? Have whistle-blowers been rewarded or punished? What could the organization do to foster ethical behavior?

4. Describe a problem or challenge encountered by an organization where you've worked. Describe the problem, show why it needed to be solved, tell who did what to try to solve it, and tell how successful the efforts were. Possibilities include

   • How the organization is implementing work teams, downsizing, or changing organizational culture.
   • How the organization uses e-mail or voice mail.
   • How the organization uses telecommuting.
   • How managers deal with stress, make ethical choices, or evaluate subordinates.
   • How the organization is responding to changing US demographics, the Americans with Disabilities Act, or international competition and opportunities.

19.14 Writing a Consultant's Report—Restaurant Tipping

Your consulting company has been asked to conduct a report for Diamond Enterprises, which runs three national chains: FishStix, The Bar-B-Q Pit, and Morrie's. All are medium-priced, family-friendly restaurants. The CEO is thinking of replacing optional tips with a 15% service fee automatically added to bills.

You read articles in trade journals, surveyed a random sample of 200 workers in each of the chains, and conducted an e-mail survey of the 136 restaurant managers. Here are your findings:

1. Trade journals point out that the Internal Revenue Service (IRS) audits restaurants if it thinks that servers underreport tips. Dealing with an audit is time-consuming and often results in the restaurant's having to pay penalties and interest.

2. Only one Morrie's restaurant has actually been audited by the IRS. Management was able to convince the IRS that servers were reporting tips accurately. No penalty was assessed. Management spent $1,000 on CPA and legal fees and spent over 80 hours of management time gathering data and participating in the audit.

3. Restaurants in Europe already add a service fee (usually 15%) to the bill. Patrons can add more if they choose. Local custom determines whether tips are expected and how much they should be. In Germany, for example, it is more usual to round up the bill (from 27 € to 30 €, for example) than to figure a percentage.

4. If the restaurant collected a service fee, it could use the income to raise wages for cooks and hosts and pay for other benefits, such as health insurance, rather than giving all the money to servers and bussers.

5. Morrie's servers tend to be under 25 years of age. FishStix employs more servers over 25, who are doing this for a living. The Bar-B-Q Pit servers are students in college towns.

6. In all three chains, servers oppose the idea. Employees other than servers generally support it.

	Retain tips	Change to service fee added to bill	Don't care
FishStix servers ($n = 115$)	90%	7%	3%
Bar-B-Q servers ($n = 73$)	95%	0%	5%
Morrie's servers ($n = 93$)	85%	15%	0%
Morrie's nonservers ($n = 65$)	25%	70%	5%
FishStix nonservers ($n = 46$)	32%	32%	37%
Bar-B-Q nonservers ($n = 43$)	56%	20%	25%

(Numbers do not add up to 100% due to rounding.)

7. Servers said that it was important to go home with money in their pockets (92%), that their expertise increased food sales and should be rewarded (67%), and that if a service fee replaced tips they would be likely to look for another job (45%). Some (17%) thought that if the manager distributed service-fee income, favoritism rather than the quality of work would govern how much tip income they got. Most (72%) thought that customers would not add anything beyond the 15% service fee, and many (66%) thought that total tip income would decrease and their own portion of that income would decrease (90%).

8. Managers generally support the change.

	Retain tips	Change to service fee added to bill	Don't care
FishStix managers ($n = 44$)	20%	80%	0%
Bar-B-Q managers ($n = 13$)	33%	67%	0%
Morrie's managers ($n = 58$)	55%	45%	0%

9. Comments from managers include: "It isn't fair for a cook with eight years of experience to make only $12 an hour while a server can make $25 an hour in just a couple of months," and "I could have my pick of employees if I offered health insurance."

10. Morale at Bar-B-Q seems low. This is seen in part in the low response rate to the survey.

11. In a tight employment market, some restaurants might lose good servers if they made the change. However, hiring cooks and other nonservers would be easier.

12. The current computer systems in place can handle figuring and recording the service fee. Since bills are printed by computer, an additional line could be added. Allocating the service-fee income could take extra managerial time, especially at first.

Write the report.

19.15 Writing a Library Research Report

Write a library research report.

As your instructor directs,

Turn in the following documents:

a. The approved proposal.

b. Two copies of the report, including

Cover.

Title Page.

Letter or Memo of Transmittal.

Table of Contents.

List of Illustrations.

Executive Summary or Abstract.

Body (Introduction, all information, recommendations). Your instructor may specify a minimum length, a minimum number or kind of sources, and a minimum number of visuals.

References or Works Cited.

c. Your notes and at least one preliminary draft.

Choose one of the following topics.

1. **Selling to College Students.** Your car dealership is located in a university town, but the manager doubts that selling cars to college students will be profitable. You agree that college incomes are low to nonexistent, but you see some students driving late-model cars. Recommend to the dealership's manager whether to begin marketing to college students, suggesting some tactics that would be effective.

2. **Advertising on the Internet.** You work on a team developing a marketing plan to sell high-end sunglasses. Your boss is reluctant to spend money for online advertising because she has heard that the money is mostly wasted. Also, she associates the ads with spam, which she detests. Recommend whether the company should devote some of its advertising budget to online ads. Include samples of online advertising that supports your recommendation.

3. **Improving Job Interview Questions.** Turnover among the sales force has been high, and your boss believes the problem is that your company has been hiring the wrong people. You are part of a team investigating the problem, and your assignment is to evaluate the questions used in job interviews. Human resource personnel use tried-and-true questions like "What is your greatest strength?" and "What is your greatest weakness?" The sales manager has some creative alternatives, such as asking candidates to solve logic puzzles and seeing how they perform under stress by taking frequent

phone calls during the interview. You are to evaluate the current interviewing approaches and propose changes that would improve hiring decisions.

4. **Selling to Wal-Mart.**   Your company has a reputation for making high-quality lamps and ceiling fans sold in specialty stores. Although the company has been profitable, it could grow much faster if it sold through Wal-Mart. Your boss is excited about her recent discussions with that retailer, but she has heard from associates that Wal-Mart can be a demanding customer. She asked you to find out if there is a downside to selling through Wal-Mart and, if so, whether manufacturers can afford to say no to a business deal with the retail giant.

5. **Making College Affordable.**   The senator you work for is concerned about fast-rising costs of a college education. Students say they cannot afford their tuition bills. Colleges say they are making all the cuts they can without compromising the quality of education. In order to propose a bill that would help make college affordable for those who are qualified to attend, the senator has asked you to research alternatives for easing the problem. Recommend one or two measures the senator could include in a bill for the Senate to vote on.

6. With your instructor's permission, investigate a topic of your choice.

19.16   Writing a Recommendation Report

Write an individual or a group report.

As your instructor directs,

Turn in the following documents:

1. The approved proposal.
2. Two copies of the report, including
   Cover.
   Title Page.
   Letter or Memo of Transmittal.
   Table of Contents.
   List of Illustrations.
   Executive Summary or Abstract.
   Body (Introduction, all information, recommendations). Your instructor may specify a minimum length, a minimum number or kind of sources, and a minimum number of visuals.
   Appendixes if useful or relevant.
3. Your notes and at least one preliminary draft.

Pick one of the following topics.

1. **Improving Customer Service.**   Many customers find that service is getting poorer and workers are getting ruder. Evaluate the service in a local store, restaurant, or other organization. Are customers made to feel comfortable? Is workers' communication helpful, friendly, and respectful? Are workers knowledgeable about products and services? Do they sell them effectively? Write a report analyzing the quality of service and recommending what the organization should do to improve.

2. **Recommending Courses for the Local Community College.**   Businesses want to be able to send workers to local community colleges to upgrade their skills; community colleges want to prepare students to enter the local workforce. What skills are in demand in your community? What courses at what levels should the local community college offer?

3. **Improving Sales and Profits.**   Recommend ways a small business in your community can increase sales and profits. Focus on one or more of the following: the products or services it offers, its advertising, its decor, its location, its accounting methods, its cash management, or any other aspect that may be keeping the company from achieving its potential. Address your report to the owner of the business.

4. **Increasing Student Involvement.**   How could an organization on campus persuade more of the students who are eligible to join or to become active in its programs? Do students know that it exists? Is it offering programs that interest students? Is it retaining current members? What changes should the organization make? Address your report to the officers of the organization.

5. **Evaluating a Potential Employer.**   What training is available to new employees? How soon is the average entry-level person promoted? How much travel and weekend work are expected? Is there a "busy season," or is the workload consistent year-round? What fringe benefits are offered? What is the corporate culture? Is the climate nonracist and nonsexist? How strong is the company economically? How is it likely to be affected by current economic, demographic, and political trends? Address your report to the Placement Office on campus; recommend whether it should encourage students to work at this company.

6. With your instructor's permission, choose your own topic.

19.17   All-Weather Case: Writing a Recommendation Report

The cross-cultural training program has recently ended (see All-Weather case in Chapters 16–17). There were a dozen on-site sessions and about twice that number of sessions given through videoconferencing. Linda, Rudy, and Kioni gathered evaluations of the sessions: over two dozen interviews, 20 observation reports, and 180 returned questionnaires.

While Caleb supervised the collection of data, Doug asked Erin to supervise the analysis of the results of the evaluation and the preparation of a recommendation report that can be used to improve future cross-cultural training programs.

Linda, Rudy, and Kioni have begun transcribing the interviews and analyzing the questionnaires as well as the observation reports. The three of them meet with Erin to discuss some of the preliminary findings (briefly summarized below) of the evaluation (based on the analysis of a half-dozen interview transcripts, 10 observation reports, and 110 questionnaires).

A: Questionnaires ($n = 110$)

- Rating of the training program (25% respondents said very useful, 35% said useful, 25% said average, and 15% said poor)
- Most preferred topics (the respondents could select multiple responses):
  - Role-playing a News Event (79.6%)
  - US, Mexico, and Latin America: Cultural Issues: Guest speakers (67.5%)
  - Managing Diversity: Cases for engineers and managers (62%)
  - Benefits of Working Together: Open forum (58.5%)
- Least-preferred topics (the respondents could select multiple responses):
  - Nonverbal Communication: Exercises (81.2%)
  - Leadership in the 21st Century: Cases—all employees (71.5%)
  - Hofstede's Cultural Dimensions: Presentation (70.5%)
  - Multicultural Intelligence: Presentation and group discussion (66.5%)
- Most-preferred training formats (the respondents could select multiple responses):
  - Exercises (e.g., "Role-playing"): 75%
  - Guest speakers (69.5%)
  - Open forum (66%)
  - Cases (60%)
- Least-preferred training formats:
  - Presentations (73%)
  - Group discussions after presentations (67.5%)

B: Interviews (6) and Observation Reports (10)

Interview responses and observations appear to support the findings revealed in the questionnaires. For example, an operator mentioned that the "Role-playing a News Event" exercise made him "walk in the shoes of the person in the incident." This, he went on to say, made him realize for the first time what it meant to be born and raised in a culture different from his own.

Both a manufacturing manager and a marketing manager found discussions of diversity cases exciting and enlightening. "The cases made me see assumptions that I used to make every time I dealt with someone from a different culture, which often resulted in things I had not intended to convey," the marketing manager said.

Referring to guest speakers who talked about the US, Mexico, and Latin American cultural issues, an engineer said that the knowledge gained through the session will help her interact better with her Hispanic operators and crew leads.

However, many interviewees also vented criticism of some topics of the training program. Referring to the presentation on Hofstede's Cultural Dimensions, a finance assistant said that it made her sleep. A residential sales representative expressed dissatisfaction with nonverbal communication exercises, stating that they "were basic and poorly executed." An operator said he thought he learned "nothing new" from the leadership cases that might help him improve his leadership skills.

Similarly, observation reports also noted livelier audience reactions for the "Role-playing a News Event" exercise and during lectures by guest speakers. Conversely, the reports noted that the audience participation and response fell significantly during nonverbal communication exercises and the leadership cases.

Based on your reading of Chapter 19 and the details given in the case, answer the following questions in groups:

- On the basis of the data presented here, how would you best organize the information in the report so that it is most useful to the HR Department in helping improve its future cross-cultural training programs (see the section "Basic Patterns for Organizing Information" in the chapter)? Provide reasons for your organizational choices.
- What are some of the challenges and opportunities in analyzing and presenting the primary data given in the case? Be specific in your response.

Prepare an outline of the recommendation report for Erin and her team (see the chapter for information on the typical contents of formal reports).

Figure A.1   Comparing and Contrasting Letter Formats

	Block	**Modified block**	**Simplified**
Date and signature block	Lined up at left margin	Lined up ½ or ⅔ of the way over to the right	Lined up at left margin
Paragraph indentation	None	Optional	None
Salutation and complimentary close	Yes	Yes	None
Subject line	Optional	Rare	Yes
Lists, if any	Indented	Indented	At left margin
Writer's typed name	Upper- and lowercase	Upper- and lowercase	Full capital letters
Paragraph spacing	Single-spaced, double-space between	Single-spaced, double-space between	Single-spaced, double-space between

- When you have good news, put it in the subject line.
- When your information is neutral, summarize it concisely in the subject line.
- When your information is negative, use a negative subject line if the reader may not read the message or needs the information to act. Otherwise, use a neutral subject line.
- When you have a request that will be easy for the reader to grant, put either the subject of the request or a direct question in the subject line.
- When you must persuade a reluctant reader, use a common ground, a benefit, or a neutral subject line.

For examples of subject lines in each of these situations, see Chapters 14, 15, and 16.

A **reference line** refers the reader to the number used on the previous correspondence this letter replies to, or the order or invoice number this letter is about. Very large organizations, like the IRS, use numbers on every piece of correspondence they send out so that it is possible to find quickly the earlier document to which an incoming letter refers.

All three formats can use headings, lists, and indented sections for emphasis.

Each of the three formats has advantages. Both block and simplified can be typed quickly since everything is lined up at the left margin. Block format is the format most frequently used for business letters; readers expect it. Modified block format creates a visually attractive page by moving the date and signature block over into what would otherwise be empty white space. Modified block is also a traditional format; readers are comfortable with it.

The examples of the three formats in Figures A.2–A.4 show one-page letters on company letterhead. **Letterhead** is preprinted stationery with the organization's name, logo, address, and phone number. Figure A.5 shows how to set up modified block format when you do not have letterhead. (It is also acceptable to use block format without letterhead.)

When your letter runs two or more pages, use a heading on the second page to identify it. Using the reader's name helps the writer, who may be printing out many letters at a time, to make sure the right second page gets in the envelope. The two most common formats are shown in Figures A.6, A.7, A.8,

Figure A.2   Block Format on Letterhead

*Line up
everything
at left
margin*

Northwest Hardware Warehouse

100 Freeway Exchange   Provo, UT 84610   (801) 555-4683   www.northwesthardware.com

1–6 spaces depending on length of letter

June 20, 2011

1"–1½"

Mr. James E. Murphy, Accounts Payable   *Title could be on a separate line*
Salt Lake Equipment Rentals
5600 Wasatch Boulevard
Salt Lake City, Utah 84121 ← *zip code on same line*

*Use first
name in
salutation
if you'd
use it on
the phone*

Dear Jim: *Colon in mixed punctuation*

The following items totaling $393.09 are still open on your account.   ¶ *1 never has a heading*

Invoice #01R-784391 *Bold or underline heading*

After the bill for this invoice arrived on May 14, you wrote saying that the material had not been   *¾"–1"*
delivered to you. On May 29, our Claims Department sent you a copy of the delivery receipt signed
by an employee of Salt Lake Equipment. You have had proof of delivery for over three weeks, but
your payment has not yet arrived.
                                                          Single space paragraphs
                                                          Double-space between paragraphs (one blank space)
Please send a check for $78.42.

                          *Triple space before a
                          heading (2 blank spaces);
                          double space after the heading*
Voucher #59351

*Do not
indent
paragraphs*

The reference line on your voucher #59351, dated June 16, indicates that it is the gross payment for
invoice #01G-002345. However, the voucher was only for $1171.25, while the invoice amount was
$1246.37. Please send a check for $75.12 to clear this item.

Voucher #55032

Voucher #55032, dated June 16, subtracts a credit for $239.55 from the amount due. Our records do
not show that any credit is due on this voucher. Please send either an explanation or a check to
cover the $239.55 immediately.

Total Amount Due   *Headings are optional in letters*

Please send a check for $393.09 to cover these three items and to bring your account up to date.
                    1–2 spaces
Sincerely,

2–4 spaces

Neil Hutchinson
Credit Representative

cc: Joan Stottlemyer, Credit Manager

*Leave bottom margin of 6 spaces—
more if letter is short*

Figure A.3   Modified Block Format on Letterhead

Bay City Information Systems
151 Bayview Road • San Francisco, CA 81153 • (650) 405-7849 • www.baycity.com

2–6 spaces

September 15, 2011
Line up date with signature block
½ or ⅔ of the way over to the right

1–4 spaces

1"–1½"

Ms. Mary E. Arcas
Personnel Director
Cyclops Communication Technologies
1050 South Sierra Bonita Avenue
Los Angeles, CA 90019 *Zip code on same line*

Dear Ms. Arcas: *Colon in mixed punctuation*

¾"–1"

Indenting ¶ is optional in modified block

Let me respond to your request for an evaluation of Colleen Kangas. Colleen was hired as a clerk-typist by Bay City Information Systems on April 4, 2009, and was promoted to Administrative Assistant on August 1, 2010. At her review in June, I recommended that she be promoted again. She is an intelligent young woman with good work habits and a good knowledge of computer software.

Single-space paragraphs

As an Adminstrative Assistant, Colleen not only handles routine duties such as processing time cards, ordering supplies, and entering data, but also screens calls for two marketing specialists, answers basic questions about Bay City Information Systems, compiles the statistics I need for my monthly reports, and investigates special assignments for me. In the past eight months, she has investigated freight charges, inventoried department hardware, and transferred files to CD-Roms. I need only to give her general directions: she has a knack for tracking down information quickly and summarizing it accurately.

Double-space between paragraphs (one blank line)

Although the department's workload has increased during the year, Colleen manages her time so that everything gets done on schedule. She is consistently poised and friendly under pressure. Her willingness to work overtime on occasion is particularly remarkable considering that she has been going to college part-time ever since she joined our firm.

At Bay City Information Systems, Colleen uses Microsoft Word and Access software. She tells me that she has also used PowerPoint in her college classes.

If Colleen were staying in San Francisco, we would want to keep her. She has the potential either to become an Executive Secretary or to move into line or staff work, especially once she completes her degree. I recommend her highly.

1–2 spaces

Headings are optional in letters

Sincerely, *Comma in mixed punctuation*

2–4 spaces

Jeanne Cederlind
Jeanne Cederlind
Vice President, Marketing
jeanne_c@baycity.com

Line up signature block with date

1–4 spaces

Encl.: Evaluation Form for Colleen Kangas

Leave at least 6 spaces at bottom of page—more if letter is short

Figure A.4   Simplified Format on Letterhead

McFarlane
HOSPITAL
Memorial

1500 Main Street   Iowa City, IA 52232   (319) 555-3113

Line up everything at left margin

↕ *2–4 spaces*

August 24, 2011

↕ *1–4 spaces*

←→ *1"–1½"*

Melinda Hamilton
Medical Services Division
Health Management Services, Inc.
4333 Edgewood Road, NE
Cedar Rapids, IA 52401

Triple space (two blank spaces)   *Subject line in full capital letters*

REQUEST FOR INFORMATION ABOUT COMPUTER SYSTEMS

← *No salutation*

We're interested in upgrading our computer system and would like to talk to one of your marketing representatives to see what would best meet our needs. We will use the following criteria to choose a system:

1.   Ability to use our current software and data files.

Double space (one blank space) between items in list if any items are more than one line long

2.   Price, prorated on a three-year expected life.

3.   Ability to provide auxiliary services, e.g., controlling inventory of drugs and supplies, monitoring patients' vital signs, and processing insurance forms more quickly.

4.   Freedom from downtime.

Triple space (two blank spaces) between list, next paragraph

Do not indent paragraphs

McFarlane Memorial Hospital has 50 beds for acute care and 75 beds for long-term care. In the next five years, we expect the number of beds to remain the same while outpatient care and emergency room care increase.

Could we meet the first or the third week in September? We are eager to have the new system installed by Christmas if possible.

Please call me to schedule an appointment.

Headings are optional in letters

No close.

HUGH PORTERFIELD   *Writer's name in full capital letters*
Controller

↕ *1–4 spaces*

Encl.:   Specifications of Current System
         Databases Currently in Use

cc: Rene Seaburg

↕ *Leave 6 spaces at bottom of page—more if letter is short*

Figure A.5   Modified Block Format without Letterhead

6–12 spaces

Single space   11408 Brussels Avenue NE
Albuquerque, NM 87111
November 5, 2011

1″–1½″

1–6 spaces

Mr. Tom Miller, President
Miller Office Supplies Corporation
P.O. Box 2900
Lincolnshire, IL 60197-2900

Subject: Invoice No. 664907, 10/29/11   *Subject line is optional in block & modified block*

Dear Mr. Miller:

Indenting paragraphs is optional in modified block   My wife, Caroline Lehman, ordered and received the briefcase listed on page 71 of your catalog (881-CD-L-9Q-4). The catalog said that the Leatherizer, 881-P-4, was free. On the order blank she indicated that she did want the Leatherizer and marked "Free" in the space for price. Nevertheless, the bill charged us for the Leatherizer.   *¾″–1″*

Please remove the $8.19 charge for the Leatherizer from our bill. The total bill was for $112.53, and with the $8.19 deducted, I assume the correct amount for the bill should be $104.34. I have enclosed a check for $104.34.

Please confirm that the charge has been removed and that our account for this order is now paid in full.

Sincerely,

2–4 spaces

William T. Mozing

1–4 spaces

Encl.: Check for $104.34   *Line up signature block with date* and below. Note even when the signature block is on the second page, it is still lined up with the date.

Reader's Name
Date
Page Number

or

Reader's Name	Page Number	Date

When a letter runs two or more pages, use letterhead only for page 1. (See Figures A.6, A.7, and A.8.) For the remaining pages, use plain paper that matches the letterhead in weight, texture, and color.

Set side margins of 1 inch to $1\frac{1}{2}$ inches on the left and $\frac{3}{4}$ inch to 1 inch on the right. If you are right justifying, use the 1 inch margin. If your letterhead extends all the way across the top of the page, set your margins even with the ends of the letterhead for the most visually pleasing page. The top margin should be three to six lines under the letterhead, or 2 inches down from the top of the page if you aren't using letterhead. If your letter is very short, you may want to use bigger side and top margins so that the letter is centered on the page.

The **inside address** gives the reader's name, title (if appropriate), and address: always double check to see the name is spelled correctly. To eliminate typing the reader's name and address on an envelope, some organizations use envelopes with cut-outs or windows so that the inside address on the letter shows through and can be used for delivery. If your organization does this, adjust your margins, if necessary, so that the whole inside address is visible.

Many letters are accompanied by other documents. Whatever these documents may be—a multipage report or a two-line note—they are called **enclosures,** since they are enclosed in the envelope. The writer should refer to the enclosures in the body of the letter: "As you can see from my résumé, . . . " The enclosure notation (Encl.:) at the bottom of the letter lists the enclosures. (See Figures A.3, A.4, and A.5.)

Sometimes you write to one person but send copies of your letter to other people. If you want the reader to know that other people are getting copies, list their names on the last page. The abbreviation *cc* originally meant *carbon copy* but now means *computer copy*. Other acceptable abbreviations include *pc* for *photocopy* or simply *c* for *copy*. You can also send copies to other people without telling the reader. Such copies are called **blind copies.** Blind copies are not mentioned on the original; they are listed on the copy saved for the file with the abbreviation *bcc* preceding the names of people getting these copies.

Formats for Envelopes

Business envelopes need to put the reader's name and address in the area that is picked up by the Post Office's Optical Character Readers (OCRs). Use side margins of at least 1 inch. Your bottom margin must be at least $\frac{5}{8}$ inch but no bigger than $2\frac{1}{4}$ inches.

Most businesses use envelopes that already have the return address printed in the upper left-hand corner. When you don't have printed envelopes, type

Figure A.6   Second Page of a Two-Page Letter, Block Format

State
University

4300 Gateway Boulevard
Midland, TX

August 11, 2011

1"–1½ "

Ms. Stephanie Voght
Stephen F. Austin High School
1200 Southwest Blvd.
San Antonio, TX 78214

↕ 1 – 2 spaces

Dear Ms. Voght: *Colon in mixed punctuation.*

Enclosed are 100 brochures about State University to distribute to your students. The brochures describe the academic programs and financial aid available. When you need additional brochures, just let me know.

¾"–1"

Videotape about State University

You may also want to show your students the videotape "Life at State University." This

---

*Plain paper
for page 2.*

↕ ½"–1"

Center

Stephanie Voght ← *Reader's
name*   2   August 11, 2011

*Also OK to line up page number and
date at left under reader's name.*

campus life, including football and basketball games, fraternities and sororities, clubs and organizations, and opportunities for volunteer work. The tape stresses the diversity of the student body and the very different lifestyles that are available at State.

*Triple-space before
each new heading (two blank spaces).*

Scheduling the Videotape   *Bold or underline headings.*

*Same
margins
as p 1.*

To schedule your free showing, just fill out the enclosed card with your first, second, and third choices for dates, and return it in the stamped, self-addressed envelope. Dates are reserved in the order that requests arrive. Send in your request early to increase the chances of getting the date you want.

"Life at State University" will be on its way to give your high school students a preview of the college experience.

1–2 spaces ↕

Sincerely,   *Comma in mixed punctuation.*

*2–4
spaces ↕*

Michael L. Mahler

Michael L. Mahler
Director of Admissions

*Headings are
optional in
letters.*

↕ 1–4 spaces

Encl.: Brochures, Reservation Form

cc: R. J. Holland, School Superintendent
    Jose Lavilla, President, PTS Association

Figure A.7   Second Page of a Two-Page Letter, Modified Block Format

1500 Summit Avenue   (612) 555-1002
Minneapolis, MN   Fax (612) 555-4032
                      www.glenarvon.biz

↕ 1–4 spaces

November 5, 2010

Line up date with signature block.

Mr. Roger B. Castino
Castino Floors and Carpets
418 E. North Street
Brockton, MA 02410

Indenting paragraphs is optional in modified block.

Dear Mr. Castino:

Welcome to the team of Glenarvon Carpet dealers!

Your first shipment of Glenarvon samples should reach you within ten days. The samples include

---

↕ ½"–1"

Plain paper for page 2   Mr. Roger B. Castino ← *Reader's name*

Center

2

November 5, 2010

territory . In addition, as a dealer you receive

- Sales kit highlighting product features
- Samples to distribute to customers
- Advertising copy to run in local newspapers
- Display units to place in your store.

Indent or center list to emphasize it.

The Annual Sales Meeting each January keeps you up-to-date on new products while you get to know other dealers and Glenarvon executives and relax at a resort hotel.

Use same margins as p 1.

Make your reservations now for Monterey January 10-13 for your first Glenarvon Sales Meeting!

2–4 spaces

Cordially,

Barbara S. Charbonneau (signature)

Barbara S. Charbonneau
Vice President, Marketing

Line up signature block with date in heading and on p1.

↕ 1–4 spaces

Encl.: Organization Chart
        Product List
        National Advertising Campaigns in 2009
            1–4 spaces
cc: Nancy Magill, Northeast Sales Manager
     Edward Spaulding, Sales Representative
        ↕ 6 spaces – more if second page isn't a full page.

Figure A.8   Second Page of a Two-Page Letter, Simplified Format

ptions
for Living

115 State Street
Ames, IA 50014
515-292-8756
www.optionsforliving.org

1–4 spaces

January 20, 2010

1–2 spaces

Gary Sammons, Editor
Southeastern Home Magazine
253 North Lake Street
Newport News, VA 23612

Triple-space (two blank spaces)   *Subject line in full caps*

MATERIAL FOR YOUR STORY ON HOMES FOR PEOPLE WITH DISABILITIES

No salutation

Apartments and houses can easily be designed to accommodate people with disabilities. From the outside, the building is indistinguishable from conventional housing. But the modifications inside permit people who use wheelchairs or whose sight or hearing is impaired to do everyday things like shower, cook, and do laundry.

½"–1"   *Plain paper for page 2*

Gary Sammons   ← *Reader's name*
January 20, 2010
Page 2

Everything lined up at left margin   in hallways and showers and adjustable cabinets that can be raised or lowered. Cardinal says that the adaptations can run from a few dollars to $5000, depending on what the customer selects.

Same margins as page 1   The Builders Association of Virginia will install many features at no extra cost: 36-inch doorways—eight inches wider than standard—to accommodate wheelchairs and extra wiring for electronic items for people whose sight or hearing is impaired.

If you'd like pictures to accompany your story, just let me know.

No close   MARILYN TILLOTSON   *Writer's name in full caps*
Executive Director

Encl.: Blueprints for Housing for People with Disabilities

cc: Douglas Stringfellow, President, BASF
     Thomas R. Galliher, President, Cardinal Industries

at least 6 spaces—more if page 2 is not a full page

your name (optional), your street address, and your city, state, and zip code in the upper left-hand corner. Since the OCR doesn't need this information to route your letter, exact margins don't matter. Use whatever is convenient and looks good to you.

Formats for Memos

Memos omit both the salutation and the close entirely. Memos rarely use indented paragraphs. Subject lines are required; headings are optional but useful in memos a full page or longer. Each heading must cover all the information until the next heading. Never use a separate heading for the first paragraph.

Figure A.9 illustrates the standard memo format typed on a plain sheet of paper. Note that the first letters of the date, reader's name, writer's name, and subject phrase are lined up vertically. Note also that memos are usually initialed by the To/From block. Initialing tells the reader that you have proofread the memo and prevents someone sending out your name on a memo you did not in fact write.

Some organizations have special letterhead for memos. (See Figure A.10.)

Some organizations alter the order of items in the Date/To/From/Subject block. Some organizations ask employees to sign memos rather than simply initialing them. The signature goes below the last line of the memo and prevents anyone from adding unauthorized information.

If the memo runs two pages or more, set up the second and subsequent pages in one of the following ways (see Figure A.11):

Brief Subject Line
Date
Page Number

or

Brief Subject Line	Page Number	Date

Formats for E-Mail Messages

E-mail programs prompt you to supply the various parts of the memo format. See Chapters 14, 15, and 16 for information about designing e-mail subject lines. "Cc:" denotes computer copies; the recipient will see that these people are getting the message. "Bcc:" denotes blind computer copies; the recipient does not see the names of these people. Most e-mail programs also allow you to attach documents from other programs, thus e-mails have attachments rather than enclosures. The computer program supplies the date and time automatically.

Some aspects of e-mail format are still evolving. In particular, some writers treat e-mail messages as if they were informal letters; some treat them as memos. Even though the e-mail screen has a "To" line (as do memos), some writers still use an informal salutation, as in Figure A.12. The writer in Figure A.12 ends the message with a signature block. Signature blocks are particularly useful for e-mail recipients outside the organization who may not know your title or contact information. You can store a signature block in the e-mail program and set the program to insert the signature block automatically.

Figure A.9   Memo Format (on plain paper)

*Everything
lined up at left*   *Plain paper*

                          Line up
              Date: |October 7, 2011

Double space   To: |Annette T. Califero
(one blank space)
              From: |Kyle B. Abrams **KBA** *Writer's initials added in ink*

   1″–1½″
 ←————→ Subject: |A Low-Cost Way to Reduce Energy Use *Capitalize first letter of each
                                                          major word in subject line*

No   As you requested, I've investigated low-cost ways to reduce our energy use. Reducing   *¾″–1″*
heading   the building temperature on weekends is a change that we could make immediately,   ←————→
for ¶ 1   that would cost nothing, and that would cut our energy use by about 6%.

                  Triple space before each new heading (two blank spaces)

The Energy Savings from a Lower Weekend Temperature *Bold or underline headings*

Single space   Lowering the temperature from 68° to 60° from 8 p.m. Friday evening to 4 a.m.
paragraphs;   Monday morning could cut our total consumption by 6%. It is not feasible to lower the
double-space   temperature on weeknights because a great many staff members work late; the cleaning
between   crew also is on duty from 6 p.m. to midnight. Turning the temperature down for only
paragraphs   four hours would not result in a significant heat saving.
(one blank
space)
                 Turning the heat back up at 4 a.m. will allow the building temperature to be back to 68°
                 by 9 a.m. Our furnace already has computerized controls which can be set to
                 automatically lower and raise the temperature.

                  Triple space (two blank spaces)

How a Lower Temperature Would Affect Employees *Capitalize first letter of
                                                     each major word of heading*

Do not   A survey of employees shows that only 7 people use the building every weekend or
indent   almost every weekend. Eighteen percent of our staff have worked at least one weekend
paragraphs   day in the last two months; 52% say they "occasionally" come in on weekends.

                 People who come in for an hour or less on weekends could cope with the lower
                 temperature just by wearing warm clothes. However, most people would find 60° too
                 cool for extended work. Employees who work regularly on weekends might want to
                 install space heaters.

Action Needed to Implement the Change

                 Would you also like me to check into the cost of buying a dozen portable space
                 heaters? Providing them would allow us to choose units that our wiring can handle and
                 would be a nice gesture towards employees who give up their weekends to work. I
                 could have a report to you in two weeks.

                 We can begin saving energy immediately. Just authorize the lower temperature, and I'll
                 see that the controls are reset for this weekend.

                  *Memos are initialed by
                  To/From/Subject block — no signature usually*   *Headings are optional in memos*

Figure A.10   Memo Format (on memo letterhead)

Kimball,
Walls, and
Morganstern

aligned vertically

Date: March 15, 2010   *Line up horizontally with printed Date/To/From/Subject*

To: Annette T. Califero

From: Kyle B. Abrams *KBA*   *Writer's initials added in ink*

Subject: The Effectiveness of Reducing Building Temperatures on Weekends

Capitalize first letter of each major word in subject line

Triple space (two blank spaces)

Reducing the building temperature to 60° on weekends has cut energy use by 4% compared to last year's use from December to February and has saved our firm $22,000.

This savings is particularly remarkable when you consider that this winter has been colder than last year's, so that more heat would be needed to maintain the same temperature.

$\frac{3}{4}" - 1"$

Fewer people have worked weekends during the past three months than during the preceding three months, but snow and bad driving conditions may have had more to do with keeping people home than the fear of being cold. Five of the 12 space heaters we bought have been checked out on an average weekend. On one weekend, all 12 were in use and some people shared their offices so that everyone could be in a room with a space heater.

Fully 92% of our employees support the lower temperature. I recommend that we continue turning down the heat on weekends through the remainder of the heating season and that we resume the practice when the heat is turned on next fall.

Headings are optional in memos

In contrast, the writer in Figure A.13 omits both the salutation and his name. When you send a message to an individual or a group you have set up, the "From:" line will have your name and e-mail address.

If you post a message to a listserv, be sure to give at least your name and e-mail address at the end of your message, as some list-servs strip out identifying information when they process messages.

When you hit "reply," the e-mail program automatically uses "Re:" (Latin for *about*) and the previous subject line. The original message is set off, usually with one or more vertical lines in the left margin or with carats (see Figure A.14). You may want to change the subject line to make it more appropriate for your message.

Use short line lengths in your e-mail message. If the line lengths are too long, they'll produce awkward line breaks, as in Figure A.14.

Figure A.11   Second Page of Two-Page Memo

1"–1½ "

February 18, 2011

To: Dorothy N. Blasingham

Double-
space   From: Roger L. Trout **R.L.T.** *Writer's initials added in ink*
(one blank space)

                                                                    Capitalize first letter of all
          Subject: Request for Third-Quarter Computer Training Sessions *major words in subject line*

                        Triple space (two blank spaces)

¶ 1 never
has a   Could you please run advanced training sessions on using Excel in April and May and   *¾"–1"*
heading   basic training sessions for new hires in June?

                  Triple-space before a heading (two blank spaces)

Advanced Sessions on Excel
          Bold or underline headings

Double-   Once the tax season is over, Jose Cisneros wants to have his first- and second-year people take
space   your advanced course on Excel. Plan on about 45-50 people in three sessions. The
between   people in the course already use Excel for basic spreadsheets but need to learn the fine
paragraphs points of macros and charting.
(one blank space)

          If possible, it would be most convenient to have the sessions run for four afternoons rather

Plain paper   *½"–1"*
for page 2   *Brief*
          Dorothy N. Blasingham ←— *subject line or*   2 *Page*   February 18, 2011
                                    reader's name   *number*

                                                                    Also OK to line up page number,
                                                                    date at left under reader's name

Same margins before the summer vacation season begins.
as p 1.

          Orientation for New Hires   *Capitalize first letter of all*
                                          major words in heading

          With a total of 16 full-time and 34 part-time people being hired either for summer or
          permanent work, we'll need at least two and perhaps three orientation sessions. We'd like to
          hold these the first, second, and third weeks in June. By May 1, we should know how many
          people will be in each training session.

          Would you be free to conduct training sessions on how to use our computers on June 9, June
          16, and June 23? If we need only two dates, we'll use June 9 and June 16, but please block off
          the 23rd too in case we need a third session.

                  Triple-space before a heading (two blank spaces)

          Request for Confirmation

          Let me know whether you're free on these dates in June, and which dates you'd prefer. If you'll
          let me know by February 25, we can get information out to participants in plenty of time
          for the sessions.

          Thanks!   *Headings are optional*
                                                                    in memos

                  Memos are initialed by
                  To/From/Subject block

Figure A.12 A Basic E-Mail Message (direct request)

Untitled - Message (Rich Text)

File Edit View Insert Format Tools Actions Help

Send | Attach as Adobe PDF | Options...

Times New Roman 12

To... larenzor@artemis.com

From... Sacha Zevchik <zevchik.2@acme.com> *System puts in writer's name and e-mail address.*

Subject: Please Protect Computers

Cc...

Bcc...

Attached:

Roger-- *Some writers use an informal salutation to make the message friendlier.*

No need to indent paragraphs.

Just a reminder: when your workers install the ceiling insulation next week, be sure to have them put plastic sheeting over the desks and computers to protect them from sawdust, insulation, and debris.

Thanks!

Sacha Zevchik
Administrative Assistant
Voice: 630-555-1000 ext. 117
Fax: 630-555-2391
E-Mail: zevchik.2@acme.com

The writer creates the signature block once, then can use it automatically. Some e-mail programs permit you to store several signature blocks with different levels of formality.

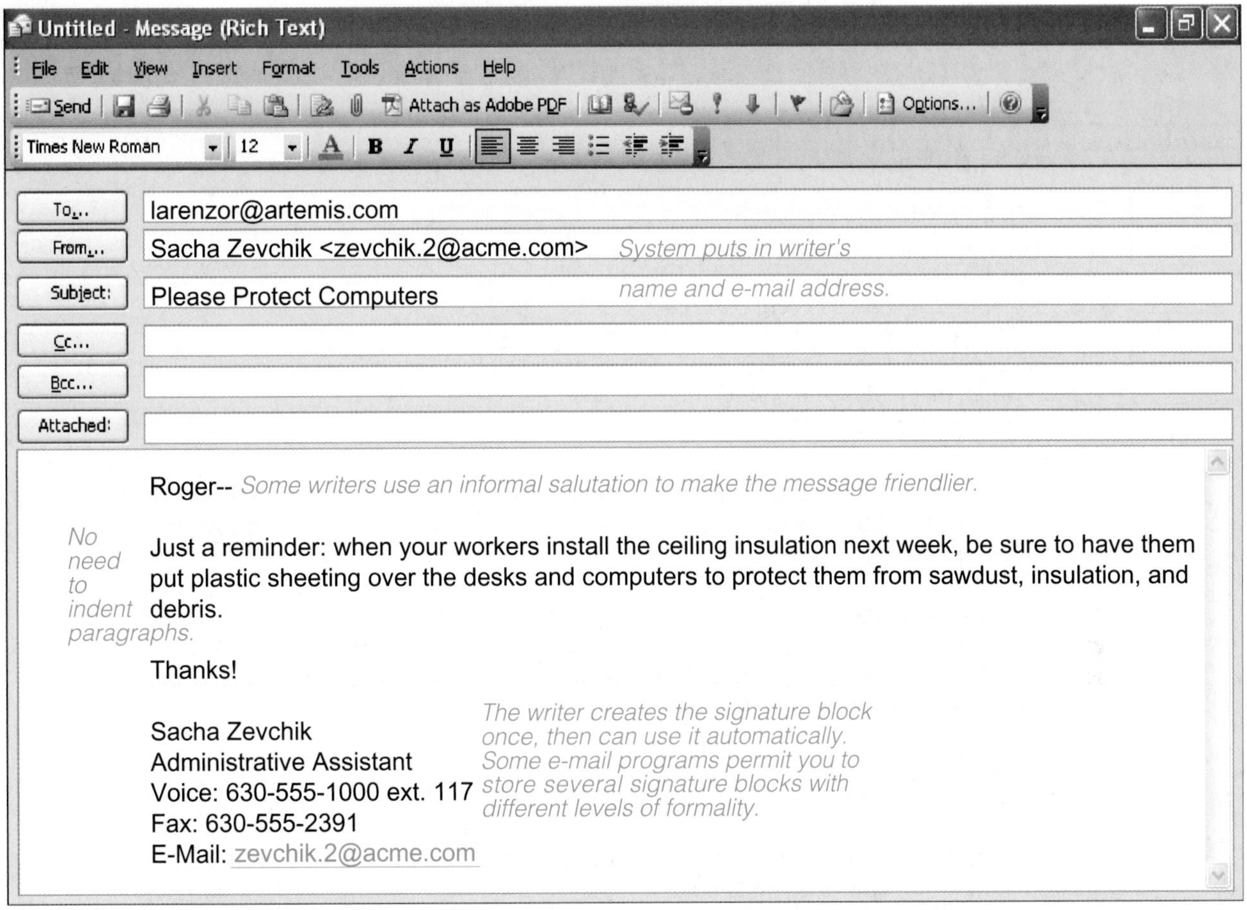

Figure A.13 An E-Mail Message with an Attachment (direct request)

Untitled - Message (Rich Text)

File Edit View Insert Format Tools Actions Help

Send | Attach as Adobe PDF | Options...

Times New Roman 12

To... TAC <tac@acme.com>

From... Keith Lee <lee.526@acme.com>

Subject: Please Comment on Draft

E-mail programs allow you to create "nicknames" or "aliases" for individuals and names for groups. "TAC" sends messages to everyone on the "Technology Advisory Committee"

Cc...

Bcc...

Attached: D:\comm\personalcomputer.draft

When you use the "attach" icon, the path on your computer is inserted.

Attached is the current draft on personally-owned computers that people bring into the office.

c:\attachments\personalcomputer.draft

Many e-mail programs support hyperlinks. Readers can click here (the path where the message is stored on the recipient's computer) to go to the document.

Please send me any changes by 10 a.m. Thursday—I'll collate them and bring them to our meeting Thursday afternoon.

This writer omits salutation and signature block.

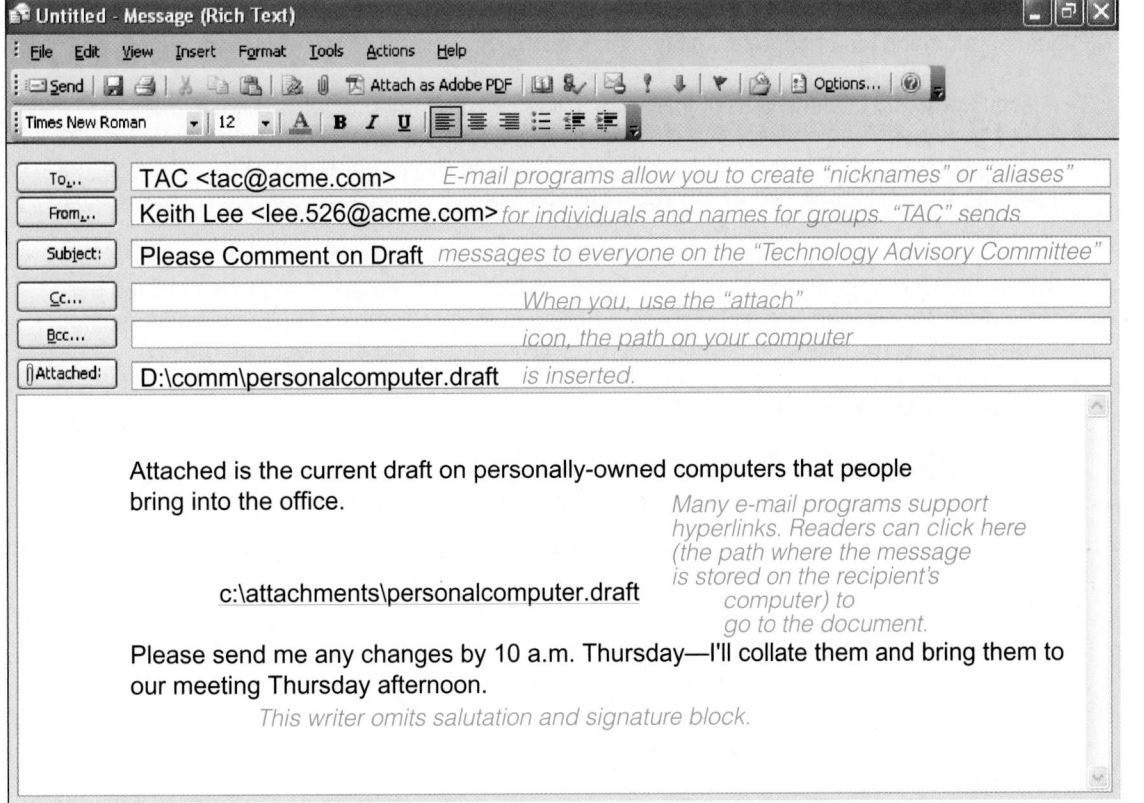

Figure A.14 An E-Mail Reply with Copies (response to a complaint)

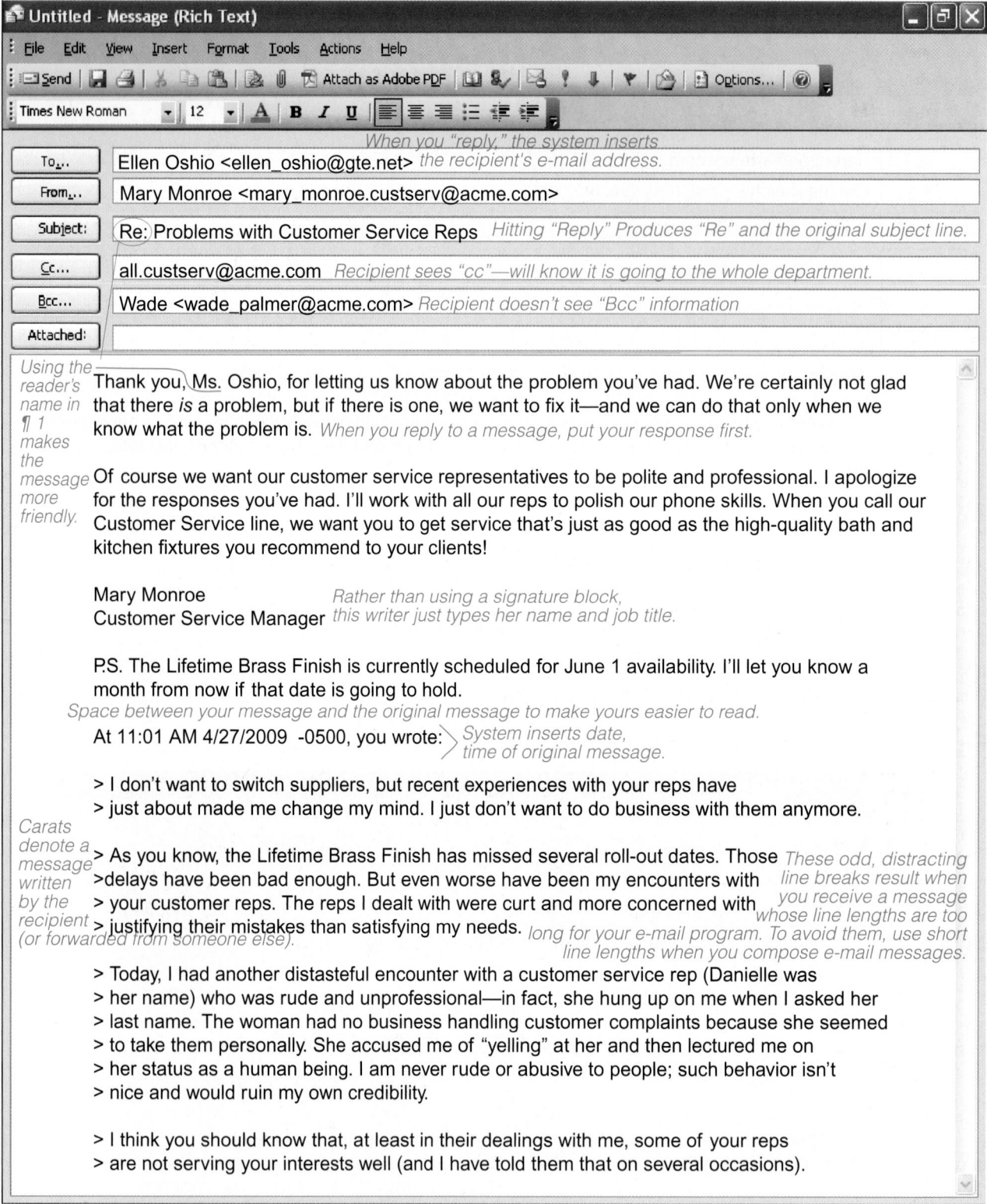

State and Province Abbreviations

States with names of more than five letters are frequently abbreviated in letters and memos. The Post Office abbreviations use two capital letters with no punctuation. See Figure A.15.

Figure A.15 Post Office Abbreviations for States, Territories, and Provinces

State name	Post Office abbreviation	State name	Post Office abbreviation
Alabama	AL	Missouri	MO
Alaska	AK	Montana	MT
Arizona	AZ	Nebraska	NE
Arkansas	AR	Nevada	NV
California	CA	New Hampshire	NH
Colorado	CO	New Jersey	NJ
Connecticut	CT	New Mexico	NM
Delaware	DE	New York	NY
District of Columbia	DC	North Carolina	NC
Florida	FL	North Dakota	ND
Georgia	GA	Ohio	OH
Hawaii	HI	Oklahoma	OK
Idaho	ID	Oregon	OR
Illinois	IL	Pennsylvania	PA
Indiana	IN	Rhode Island	RI
Iowa	IA	South Carolina	SC
Kansas	KS	South Dakota	SD
Kentucky	KY	Tennessee	TN
Louisiana	LA	Texas	TX
Maine	ME	Utah	UT
Maryland	MD	Vermont	VT
Massachusetts	MA	Virginia	VA
Michigan	MI	Washington	WA
Minnesota	MN	West Virginia	WV
Mississippi	MS	Wisconsin	WI
		Wyoming	WY

Territory name	Post Office abbreviation	Province name	Post Office abbreviation
Guam	GU	Alberta	AB
Puerto Rico	PR	British Columbia	BC
Virgin Islands	VI	Manitoba	MB
		New Brunswick	NB
		Newfoundland and Labrador	NL
		Northwest Territories	NT
		Nova Scotia	NS
		Nunavut	NU
		Ontario	ON
		Prince Edward Island	PE
		Quebec	QC
		Saskatchewan	SK
		Yukon Territory	YT

Banished Words

Correct grammar and spelling are basic ways to signal careful, intelligent writing. Another fundamental is to choose words and phrases that say what you mean. Out of habit or carelessness, however, writers may sprinkle their work with meaningless words.

To highlight the problem, Lake Superior State University each January announces its "List of Words Banished from the Queen's English for Mis-Use, Over-Use and General Uselessness." A sample from their lists:

- *Captured alive*—If someone is dead, it's too late to capture him or her.

- *Place stamp here* (on a return envelope)—This phrase states the obvious. Mail requires postage; we know where to put the stamp, don't we?

- *On the ground* (in news broadcasts)—With the exception of the occasional report from a helicopter or battleship, where else would the reporter be?

- *It is what it is*—This phrase says nothing.

- *Now playing in theaters* (in movie advertisements)— Where else do we expect first-run movies to play?

- *Drug deal gone bad*—Are drug deals ever good?

Based on Lake Superior State University, "List of Banished Words," http://www.lssu.edu/banished/archived_lists.php (accessed July 24, 2009).

Correct: Here is the booklet you asked for.

Correct: There are the blueprints I wanted.

Note that some words that end in *s* are considered to be singular and require singular verbs.

Correct: A series of meetings is planned.

When a situation doesn't seem to fit the rules, or when following a rule produces an awkward sentence, revise the sentence to avoid the problem.

Problematic: The Plant Manager in addition to the sales representative (was, were?) pleased with the new system.

Better: The Plant Manager and the sales representative were pleased with the new system.

Problematic: None of us (is, are?) perfect.

Better: All of us have faults.

Errors in **noun–pronoun agreement** occur if a pronoun is of a different number or person than the word it refers to.

Incorrect: All drivers of leased automobiles are billed $300 if damages to his automobile are caused by a collision.

Correct: All drivers of leased automobiles are billed $300 if damages to their automobiles are caused by collisions.

Incorrect: A manager has only yourself to blame if things go wrong.

Correct: As a manager, you have only yourself to blame if things go wrong.

The following words require a singular verb and pronoun:

everybody	neither
each	nobody
either	a person
everyone	

Correct: Everyone should bring his or her copy of the manual to the next session on changes in the law.

If the pronoun pairs necessary to avoid sexism seem cumbersome, avoid the terms in this list. Instead, use words that take plural pronouns or use second-person *you*.

Each pronoun must refer to a specific word. If a pronoun does not refer to a specific term, add a word to correct the error.

Incorrect: We will open three new stores in the suburbs. This will bring us closer to our customers.

Correct: We will open three new stores in the suburbs. This strategy will bring us closer to our customers.

Hint: Make sure *this* and *it* refer to a specific noun in the previous sentence. If either refers to an idea, add a noun ("this strategy") to make the sentence grammatically correct.

Use *who* and *whom* to refer to people and *which* to refer to objects. *That* can refer to anything: people, animals, organizations, and objects.

Correct: The new Executive Director, who moved here from Boston, is already making friends.

Figure B.1 The Case of the Personal Pronoun

	Nominative (subject of clause)	Possessive	Objective	Reflexive/ intensive
Singular				
1st person	I	my, mine	me	myself
2nd person	you	your, yours	you	yourself
3rd person	he/she/it	his/her(s)/its	him/her/it	himself/herself/itself
	one/who	one's/whose	one/whom	oneself/(no form)
Plural				
1st person	we	our, ours	us	ourselves
2nd person	you	your, yours	you	yourselves
3rd person	they	their, theirs	them	themselves

Correct: The information which she wants will be available tomorrow.

Correct: This confirms the price that I quoted you this morning.

Case

Case refers to the grammatical role a noun or pronoun plays in a sentence. Figure B.1 identifies the case of each personal pronoun.

Use **nominative case** pronouns for the subject of a clause.

Correct: Shannon Weaver and I talked to the customer, who was interested in learning more about integrated software.

Use **possessive case** pronouns to show who or what something belongs to.

Correct: Microsoft Office will exactly meet her needs.

Use **objective case** pronouns as objects of verbs or prepositions.

Correct: When you send in the quote, thank her for the courtesy she showed Shannon and me.

Hint: Use *whom* when *him* would fit grammatically in the same place in your sentence.

To (who/whom) do you intend to give this report?

You intend to give this report to him.

Whom is correct.

Have we decided (who, whom?) will take notes?

Have we decided he will take notes?

Who is correct.

Use **reflexive** pronouns to refer to or emphasize a noun or pronoun that has already appeared in the sentence.

Correct: I myself think the call was a very productive one.

Do not use reflexive pronouns as subjects of clauses or as objects of verbs or propositions.

The Errors That Bother People in Organizations

Professor Maxine Hairston constructed a questionnaire with 65 sentences, each with one grammatical error. The administrators, executives, and business people who responded were most bothered by the following:

- Wrong verb forms ("he brung his secretary with him")
- Double negatives
- Objective pronoun used for subject of sentence ("Him and Richards were the last ones hired.")
- Sentence fragments
- Run-on sentences
- Failure to capitalize proper names
- "Would of" for "would have"
- Lack of subject–verb agreement
- Comma between verb and complement ("Cox cannot predict, that street crime will diminish.")
- Lack of parallelism
- Adverb errors ("He treats his men bad.")
- "Set" for "sit"

They also disliked
- Errors in word meaning
- Dangling modifiers
- "I" as objective pronoun ("The army moved my husband and I")
- Not setting off interrupters (e.g., "However") with commas
- Tense switching
- Plural modifiers with singular nouns.

Based on Maxine Hairston, "Not All Errors Are Created Equal: Nonacademic Readers in the Professions Respond to Lapses in Usage," *College English* 43, no. 8 (December 1981), 794–806.

The Fumblerules of Grammar

1. Avoid run-on sentences they are hard to read.
2. A writer must not shift your point of view.
3. Verbs has to agree with their subjects.
4. No sentence fragments.
5. Reserve the apostrophe for it's proper use and omit it when its not needed.
6. Proofread carefully to see if you any words out.
7. Avoid commas, that are unnecessary.
8. Steer clear of incorrect forms of verbs that have snuck in the language.
9. In statements involving two word phrases make an all out effort to use hyphens.
10. Last but not least, avoid clichés like the plague; seek viable alternatives.

Quoted from William Safire, "On Language: The Fumblerules of Grammar," *New York Times Magazine*, November 11, 1979, 16; and "On Language: Fumblerule Follow-up," *New York Times Magazine*, November 25, 1979, 14.

Incorrect:	Elaine and myself will follow up on this order.
Correct:	Elaine and I will follow up on this order.
Incorrect:	He gave the order to Dan and myself.
Correct:	He gave the order to Dan and me.

Note that the first-person pronoun comes after names or pronouns that refer to other people.

Dangling Modifier

A **modifier** is a word or phrase that gives more information about the subject, verb, or object in a clause. A **dangling modifier** refers to a word that is not actually in the sentence. The solution is to reword the modifier so that it is grammatically correct.

Incorrect:	Confirming our conversation, the truck will leave Monday. [The speaker is doing the confirming. But the speaker isn't in the sentence.]
Incorrect:	At the age of eight, I began teaching my children about American business. [This sentence says that the author was eight when he or she had children who could understand business.]

Correct a dangling modifier in one of these ways:

- Recast the modifier as a subordinate clause.

Correct:	As I told you, the truck will leave Monday.
Correct:	When they were eight, I began teaching my children about American business.

- Revise the main clause so its subject or object can be modified by the now-dangling phrase.

Correct:	Confirming our conversation, I have scheduled the truck to leave Monday.
Correct:	At the age of eight, my children began learning about American business.

Hint: Whenever you use a verb or adjective that ends in *-ing,* make sure it modifies the grammatical subject of your sentence. If it doesn't, reword the sentence.

Misplaced Modifier

A **misplaced modifier** appears to modify another element of the sentence than the writer intended.

Incorrect:	Customers who complain often alert us to changes we need to make. [Does the sentence mean that customers must complain frequently to teach us something? Or is the meaning that frequently we learn from complaints?]

Correct a misplaced modifier by moving it closer to the word it modifies or by adding punctuation to clarify your meaning. If a modifier modifies the whole sentence, use it as an introductory phrase or clause; follow it with a comma.

Correct:	Often, customers who complain alert us to changes we need to make.

Parallel Structure

Items in a series or list must have the same grammatical structure.

Not parallel: In the second month of your internship, you will

1. Learn how to resolve customers' complaints.

2. Supervision of desk staff.

3. Interns will help plan store displays.

Parallel: In the second month of your internship, you will

1. Learn how to resolve customers' complaints.

2. Supervise desk staff.

3. Plan store displays.

Also parallel: Duties in the second month of your internship include resolving customers' complaints, supervising desk staff, and planning store displays.

Hint: When you have two or three items in a list (whether the list is horizontal or vertical) make sure the items are in the same grammatical form. Put lists vertically to make them easier to see.

Predication Errors

The predicate of a sentence must fit grammatically and logically with the subject. Make sure that the verb describes the action done by or done to the subject.

Incorrect: Our goals should begin immediately.

Correct: Implementing our goals should begin immediately.

In sentences using *is* and other linking verbs, the complement must be a noun, an adjective, or a noun clause.

Incorrect: The reason for this change is because the SEC now requires fuller disclosure.

Correct: The reason for this change is that the SEC now requires fuller disclosure.

Understanding Punctuation

Punctuation marks are road signs to help readers predict what comes next. (See Figure B.2.)

When you move from the subject to the verb, you're going in a straight line; no comma is needed. When you end an introductory phrase or clause, the comma tells readers the introduction is over and you're turning to the main clause. When words interrupt the main clause, like this, commas tell the reader when to turn off the main clause for a short side route and when to return.

Anguished English

Richard Lederer recorded the following howlers:

- CEMETERY ALLOWS PEOPLE TO BE BURIED BY THEIR PETS.
- KICKING BABY CONSIDERED TO BE HEALTHY.
- DIRECTOR OF TRUMAN LIBRARY KNOWS NEWSMAN'S PROBLEMS—HE WAS ONE.
- MAN FOUND BEATEN, ROBBED BY POLICE.

Quoted from Richard Lederer, *More Anguished English* (New York: Delacorte Press, 1993), 166–67.

Figure B.2   What Punctuation Tells the Reader

Mark	Tells the reader
Period	We're stopping.
Semicolon	What comes next is closely related to what I just said.
Colon	What comes next is an example of what I just said.
Dash	What comes next is a dramatic example of or a shift from what I just said.
Comma	What comes next is a slight turn, but we're going in the same basic direction.

What Bothers Your Boss?

Most bosses care deeply about only a few points of grammar. Find out which errors are your supervisor's pet peeves, and avoid them.

Any living language changes. New usages appear first in speaking. Here are four issues on which experts currently disagree:

1. Plural pronouns to refer to *everybody, everyone,* and *each.* Standard grammar says these words require singular pronouns.

2. Split infinitives. An infinitive is the form of a verb that contains *to: to understand.* An infinitive is split when another word separates the *to* from the rest of an infinitive: *to easily understand.*

3. *Hopefully* to mean *I hope that. Hopefully* means "in a hopeful manner." However, a speaker who says "Hopefully, the rain will stop" is talking about the speaker's hope, not the rain's.

4. *Verbal* to mean *oral. Verbal* means "using words." Both writing and speaking are verbal communication. Nonverbal communication (for example, body language) does not use words.

Ask your instructor and your boss whether they are willing to accept the less formal usage. When you write to someone you don't know, use standard grammar and usage.

Some people have been told to put commas where they'd take breaths. That's bad advice. How often you'd take a breath depends on how big your lung capacity is, how fast and loud you're speaking, and how much emphasis you want. Commas aren't breaths. Instead, like other punctuation, they're road signs.

Punctuating Sentences

A sentence contains at least one main clause. A **main** or **independent clause** is a complete statement. A **subordinate** or **dependent clause** contains both a subject and a verb but is not a complete statement and cannot stand by itself. A phrase is a group of words that does not contain both a subject and a verb.

Main clauses

Your order will arrive Thursday.

He dreaded talking to his supplier.

I plan to enroll for summer school classes.

Subordinate clauses

if you place your order by Monday

because he was afraid the product would be out of stock

since I want to graduate next spring

Phrases

With our current schedule

As a result

After talking to my advisor

A clause with one of the following words will be subordinate:

after	if
although, though	when, whenever
because, since	while, as
before, until	

Using the correct punctuation will enable you to avoid three major sentence errors: comma splices, run-on sentences, and sentence fragments.

Comma Splices

A **comma splice** or **comma fault** occurs when two main clauses are joined only by a comma (instead of by a comma and a coordinating conjunction).

Incorrect: The contest will start in June, the date has not been set.

Correct a comma splice in one of the following ways:

*   If the ideas are closely related, use a semicolon rather than a comma. If they aren't closely related, start a new sentence.

    Correct: The contest will start in June; the exact date has not been set.

*   Add a coordinating conjunction.

    Correct: The contest will start in June, but the exact date has not been set.

*   Subordinate one of the clauses.

    Correct: Although the contest will start in June, the exact date has not been set.

Remember that you cannot use just a comma with the following transitions:

however   nevertheless

therefore   moreover

Instead, either use a semicolon to separate the clauses or start a new sentence.

Incorrect: Computerized grammar checkers do not catch every error, however, they may be useful as a first check before an editor reads the material.

Correct: Computerized grammar checkers do not catch every error. However, they may be useful as a first check before an editor reads the material.

Run-on Sentences

A **run-on sentence** strings together several main clauses using *and, but, or, so*, and *for*. Run-on sentences and comma splices are "mirror faults." A comma splice *uses only* the comma and omits the coordinating conjunction, while a run-on sentence uses *only* the conjunction and omits the comma. Correct a short run-on sentence by adding a comma. Separate a long run-on sentence into two or more sentences. Consider subordinating one or more of the clauses.

Incorrect: We will end up with a much smaller markup but they use a lot of this material so the volume would be high so try to sell them on fast delivery and tell them our quality is very high.

Correct: Although we will end up with a much smaller markup, volume would be high since they use a lot of this material. Try to sell them on fast delivery and high quality.

Fused Sentences

A **fused sentence** results when two sentences or more are *fused*, or joined with neither punctuation nor conjunctions. To fix the error, add the punctuation, add punctuation and a conjunction, or subordinate one of the clauses.

Incorrect: The advantages of Intranets are clear the challenge is persuading employees to share information.

Correct: The advantages of Intranets are clear; the challenge is persuading employees to share information.

Also correct: Although the advantages of Intranets are clear, the challenge is persuading employees to share information.

Sentence Fragments

In a **sentence fragment,** a group of words that is not a complete sentence is punctuated as if it were a complete sentence.

Incorrect: Observing these people, I have learned two things about the program. The time it takes. The rewards it brings.

To fix a sentence fragment, either add whatever parts of the sentence are missing or incorporate the fragment into the sentence before it or after it.

The Most Common Errors in First-Year Composition Papers

A survey of hundreds of student papers found that the following errors were most common:

1. No comma after introductory element
2. Vague pronoun reference
3. No comma in compound sentence
4. Wrong word
5. No comma in nonrestrictive clause
6. Wrong/missing inflected endings
7. Wrong or missing preposition
8. Comma splice
9. Possessive apostrophe error
10. Tense shift
11. Unnecessary shift in person
12. Sentence fragment
13. Wrong tense or verb form
14. Subject–verb agreement error
15. Lack of comma in series
16. Pronoun agreement error
17. Unnecessary comma with restrictive clause
18. Run-on or fused sentence
19. Dangling or misplaced modifier
20. Its/it's error

Based on Robert J. Connors and Andrea A. Lunsford, "Frequency of Formal Errors in Current College Writing, or Ma and Pa Kettle Do Research," *College Composition and Communication* 39, no. 4 (December 1988), 403.

Correct: Observing these people, I have learned that the program is time-consuming but rewarding.

Remember that clauses with the following words are not complete sentences. Join them to a main clause.

after	if
although, though	when, whenever
because, since	while, as
before, until	

Incorrect: We need to buy a new computer system. Because our current system is obsolete.

Correct: We need to buy a new computer system because our current system is obsolete.

Punctuation within Sentences

The good business and administrative writer knows how to use the following punctuation marks: apostrophes, colons, commas, dashes, hyphens, parentheses, periods, and semicolons.

Apostrophe

1.   Use an apostrophe in a contraction to indicate that a letter or symbol has been omitted.

We're trying to renegotiate the contract.

The '90s were years of restructuring for our company.

2.   To indicate possession, add an apostrophe and an *s* to the word.

The corporation's home office is in Houston, Texas.

Apostrophes to indicate possession are especially essential when one noun in a comparison is omitted.

This year's sales will be higher than last year's.

When a word already ends in an *s*, add only an apostrophe to make it possessive.

The meeting will be held at New Orleans' convention center.

With many terms, the placement of the apostrophe indicates whether the noun is singular or plural.

Incorrect: The program should increase the participant's knowledge. [Implies that only one participant is in the program.]

Correct: The program should increase the participants' knowledge. [Many participants are in the program.]

Hint: Use "of" in the sentence to see where the apostrophe goes.

The figures of last year = last year's figures

The needs of our customers = our customers' needs

Note that possessive pronouns (e.g., *his, ours*) usually do not have apostrophes. The only exception is *one's*.

Pity the Apostrophe

The apostrophe is so often misused that in England John Richards founded the Apostrophe Protection Society. The society's Web site, www.apostrophe.fisnet.co.uk, summarizes the basic rules for using apostrophes in English. The entertaining part of the Web site is its examples, photos of signs that have abused apostrophes in many ways, including overuse and omission. Here are some examples:

• In a banquet hall's brochure: "The Ultimate Attraction for all sorts of Function's ranging from, Fair's, Carnival's, Bon Fire Display's, Music Concert's, Party's, Ball's, Corporate Function's and even Wedding's" (and that's just what the ideas range *from; imagine what they range to!*).

• By a parking lot: "Resident's and Visitor's Only" (meaning something belonging to one resident and one visitor).

• By a school parking lot: "Reserved for Principals Office" (a sign that will not enhance the school's reputation).

• In a set of contest rules: "The judges decision is final." (Writer couldn't decide where to put the apostrophe, so he or she didn't try.)

• At a government office building: "Disabled Access (All Depts's) via Dep. of Social Security" (trying all punctuation possibilities at once).

Based on John Richards, Apostrophe Protection Society Web site, home page and examples, www.apostrophe.org.uk (accessed July 24, 2009).

The company needs the goodwill of its stockholders.

His promotion was announced yesterday.

One's greatest asset is the willingness to work hard.

3. Do not use an apostrophe to make plurals.

Incorrect: Use the folder's above the cabinet to file these documents.

Correct: Use the folders above the cabinet to file these documents.

Colon

1. Use a colon to separate a main clause and a list that explains the last element in the clause. The items in the list are specific examples of the word that appears immediately before the colon.

Please order the following supplies:

Printer cartridges

Computer paper (20-lb. white bond)

Bond paper (25-lb., white, 25% cotton)

Company letterhead

Company envelopes

When the list is presented vertically, capitalize the first letter of each item in the list. When the list is run in with the sentence, you don't need to capitalize the first letter after the colon.

Please order the following supplies: printer cartridges, computer paper (20-lb. white bond), bond paper (25-lb., white, 25% cotton), company letterhead, and company envelopes.

Do not use a colon when the list is grammatically part of the main clause.

Incorrect: The rooms will have coordinated decors in natural colors such as: eggplant, moss, and mushroom.

Correct: The rooms will have coordinated decors in natural colors such as eggplant, moss, and mushroom.

Also correct: The rooms will have coordinated decors in a variety of natural colors: eggplant, moss, and mushroom.

If the list is presented vertically, some authorities suggest introducing the list with a colon even though the words preceding the colon are not a complete sentence.

2. Use a colon to join two independent clauses when the second clause explains or restates the first clause.

Selling is simple: give people the service they need, and they'll come back with more orders.

Comma

1. Use commas to separate the main clause from an introductory clause, the reader's name, or words that interrupt the main clause. Note that commas both precede and follow the interrupting information.

R. J. Garcia, the new Sales Manager, comes to us from the Des Moines office.

The History of Punctuation

WHENWRITING BEGANTHERE WERENOBREAKS BETWEENWORDS

In inscriptions on monuments in ancient Greece, breaks were chosen to create balance and proportion.

WHENWRITI
NGBEGANTH
EREWERENO
BREAKSBET
WEENWORDS

In the third century bce, Aristophanes added a dot high in the line (like this •), after a complete thought, or *periodos*. For part of a complete thought, or *colon,* he used a dot on the line (like this •). For a comma, or subdivision of a colon, he used a dot halfway up (like this •).

The monks in the Middle Ages substituted a strong slash for the midway dot. As time went on, the strong slash was shortened and acquired a curl—becoming our comma today.

Based on Lionel Casson, "howandwhy punctuationevercametobeinvented," *Smithsonian* 19, no. 7 (October 1988), 216.

A **nonrestrictive** (nonessential) **clause** gives extra information that is not needed to identify the noun it modifies. Because nonrestrictive clauses give extra information, they need extra commas.

Sue Decker, who wants to advance in the organization, has signed up for the company training program in sales techniques.

Do not use commas to set off information that restricts the meaning of a noun or pronoun. **Restrictive clauses** give essential, not extra, information.

Anyone who wants to advance in the organization should take advantage of on-the-job training.

The clause "who wants to advance in the organization" restricts the meaning of the pronoun *anyone*.

Do not use commas to separate the subject from the verb, even if you would take a breath after a long subject.

Incorrect: Laws requiring registration of anyone collecting $5,000 or more on behalf of another person, apply to schools and private individuals as well to charitable groups and professional fund-raisers.

Correct: Laws requiring registration of anyone collecting $5,000 or more on behalf of another person □ apply to schools and private individuals as well to charitable groups and professional fund-raisers.

2. Use a comma, with a conjunction, after the first clause in a compound sentence.

This policy eliminates all sick-leave credit of the employee at the time of retirement, and payment will be made only once to any individual.

Do not use commas to join independent clauses without a conjunction. Doing so produces comma splices.

3. Use commas to separate items in a series. Using a comma before the *and* or *or* is not required by some authorities, but using a comma always adds clarity. The comma is essential if any of the items in the series themselves contain the word *and*.

The company pays the full cost of hospitalization insurance for eligible employees, spouses, and unmarried dependent children under age 23.

Dash

Use dashes to emphasize a break in thought.

Ryertex comes in 30 grades—each with a special use.

To type a dash, use two hyphens with no space before or after.

Hyphen

1. Use a hyphen to indicate that a word has been divided between two lines.

Attach the original receipts for lodging, meals, tips, transportation, and registration fees.

Divide words at syllable breaks. If you aren't sure where the syllables divide, look up the word in a dictionary. When a word has several syllables, divide it after a vowel or between two consonants. Don't divide words of one syllable (e.g., *used*); don't divide a two-syllable word if one of the syllables is only one letter long (e.g., *acre*).

2. Use hyphens to join two or more words used as a single adjective.

Order five 10- or 12-foot lengths.

The computer-prepared income and expense statements will be ready next Friday.

The hyphen prevents misreading. In the first example, five lengths are needed, not lengths of 5, 10, or 12 feet. In the second example, without the hyphen, the reader might think that *computer* was the subject and *prepared* was the verb.

Spell-Checker's Errors

The *Dallas Morning News* raised hackles in the computer industry . . . when an editor accidentally accepted all of a spell-checker's alternate spellings in a technology article that appeared in print—changing chip maker Intel into "Until" and Microsoft into "Microvolts."

Quoted from Joan E. Rigdon, "Microsoft Word's Spell-Checker Gets Failing Grade in Computerese," *Wall Street Journal*, November 15, 1995, B1.

Parentheses

1. Use parentheses to set off words, phrases, or sentences used to explain or comment on the main idea.

For the thinnest Ryertex (.015″) only a single layer of the base material may be used, while the thickest (10″) may contain over 600 greatly compressed layers of fabric or paper. By varying the fabric used (cotton, asbestos, glass, or nylon) or the type of paper, and by changing the kind of resin (phenolic, melamine, silicone, or epoxy), we can produce 30 different grades.

Any additional punctuation goes outside the second parenthesis when the punctuation applies to the whole sentence. It goes inside when it applies only to the words in the parentheses.

Please check the invoice to see if credit should be issued. (A copy of the invoice is attached.)

2. Use parentheses for the citations in a text. See Chapter 19 for examples.

Period

1. Use a period at the end of a sentence. Space once before the next sentence.

2. Use a period after some abbreviations. When a period is used with a person's initials, leave one space after the period before the next letter or word. In other abbreviations, no space is necessary.

R. J. Tebeaux has been named Vice President for Marketing.

The U.S. division plans to hire 300 new M.B.A.s in the next year.

The trend is to reduce the use of punctuation. It would also be correct to write

The US division plans to hire 300 new MBAs in the next year.

Semicolon

1. Use semicolons to join two independent clauses when they are closely related.

We'll do our best to fill your order promptly; however, we cannot guarantee a delivery date.

Using a semicolon suggests that the two ideas are very closely connected. Using a period and a new sentence is also correct but implies nothing about how closely related the two sentences are.

2. Use semicolons to separate items in a series when the items themselves contain commas.

International Punctuation

Cultures differ in their use of punctuation marks. US writers put periods and commas inside closing quotation marks; writers in England put them outside the quotation marks. Spanish writers also put sentence-ending punctuation outside. Also, in some regions Spanish writers use angled quotation marks: << and >>. Angled quotation marks also are the norm in French writing.

In dialogue, French and Spanish writers traditionally signal a change of speakers by starting with a dash.

Chinese and Japanese use different punctuation marks with their writing systems. For example, a period is a small circle, set near the base line, and quotation marks are 90-degree angles that appear at the upper left and lower right. Because the characters cannot be italicized as Roman letters can, Chinese and Japanese use book title marks and chapter marks.

Some languages use accents as well as punctuation marks. Accents identify how a letter is to be pronounced, and they affect the meaning of a word. Sametz Blackstone Associates, a consulting firm, was wise to have a native speaker check a translation into Spanish. The proofreader caught a missing tilde (~). Without the tilde, the Spanish version didn't say "celebrating 35 years"; it said "celebrating 35 anuses."

Based on Complete Translation Services, "A History of Punctuation," http://www.completetranslation.com, (accessed September 20, 2004; and Mark Lasswell, "Lost in Translation," *Business 2.0*, 5, no. 7 (August 2004): 68.

The final choices for the new plant are El Paso, Texas; Albuquerque, New Mexico; Salt Lake City, Utah; Eureka, California; and Eugene, Oregon.

Hospital benefits are also provided for certain specialized care services such as diagnostic admissions directed toward a definite disease or injury; normal maternity delivery, Caesarean section delivery, or complications of pregnancy; and in-patient admissions for dental procedures necessary to safeguard the patient's life or health.

Hint: A semicolon could be replaced by a period and a capital letter. It has a sentence on both sides.

Special Punctuation Marks

Quotation marks, square brackets, ellipses, and underlining are necessary when you use quoted material.

Quotation Marks

1. Use quotation marks around the names of brochures, pamphlets, and magazine articles.

    Enclosed are 30 copies of our pamphlet "Saving Energy."

    You'll find articles like "How to Improve Your Golf Game" and "Can You Keep Your Eye on the Ball?" in every issue.

    In US punctuation, periods and commas go inside quotation marks. Colons and semicolons go outside. Question marks go inside if they are part of the material being quoted.

2. Use quotation marks around words to indicate that you think the term is misleading.

    These "pro-business" policies actually increase corporate taxes.

3. Use quotation marks around words that you are discussing as words.

    Forty percent of the respondents answered "yes" to the first question.

    Use "Ms." as a courtesy title for a woman unless you know she prefers another title.

    It is also acceptable to italicize words instead of using quotation marks.

4. Use quotation marks around words or sentences that you quote from someone else.

    "The Fog Index," says its inventor, Robert Gunning, is "an effective warning system against drifting into needless complexity."

Square Brackets

Use square brackets to add your own additions to or changes in quoted material.

Senator Smith's statement:	"These measures will create a deficit."
Your use of Smith's statement:	According to Senator Smith, "These measures [in the new tax bill] will create a deficit."

The square brackets show that Smith did not say these words; you add them to make the quote make sense in your document.

Ellipses

Ellipses are spaced dots. In typing, use three spaced periods for an ellipsis. When an ellipsis comes at the end of a sentence, use a dot immediately after the last letter of the sentence for a period. Then add three spaced dots, with another space after the last dot.

1. Use ellipses to indicate that one or more words have been omitted in the middle of quoted material. You do not need ellipses at the beginning or end of a quote.

   The Wall Street Journal notes that Japanese magazines and newspapers include advertisements for a "$2.1 million home in New York's posh Riverdale section . . . 185 acres of farmland [and] . . . luxury condos on Manhattan's Upper East Side."

2. In advertising and direct mail, use ellipses to imply the pace of spoken comments.

   If you've ever wanted to live on a tropical island . . . cruise to the Bahamas . . . or live in a castle in Spain . . .

   . . . you can make your dreams come true with Vacations Extraordinaire.

Underlining and Italics

1. Underline or italicize the names of newspapers, magazines, and books.

The Wall Street Journal	*The Wall Street Journal*
Fortune	*Fortune*
The Wealth of Nations	*The Wealth of Nations*

   Titles of brochures and pamphlets are put in quotation marks.

2. Underline or italicize words to emphasize them.

   Here's a bulletin that gives you, in handy chart form, workable data on over 50 different types of tubing and pipe.

   You may also use bold to emphasize words. Bold type is better than either underlining or italics because it is easier to read.

Writing Numbers and Dates

Spell out **numbers** from one to nine. Use figures for numbers 10 and over in most cases. Always use figures for amounts of money (The new office costs $1.7 million). Large numbers frequently use a combination of numbers and words (More than 20 million people are affected by this new federal regulation).

Spell out any number that appears at the beginning of a sentence. If spelling it out is impractical, revise the sentence so that it does not begin with a number.

Fifty students filled out the survey.

In 2002, euro notes and coins entered circulation.

When two numbers follow each other, spell out the smaller number and use figures for the larger number.

In **dates,** use figures for the day and year. The month is normally spelled out. Be sure to spell out the month in international business communication. American usage puts the month first, so that *1/10/10* means *January 10, 2010.* European usage puts the day first, so that *1/10/10* means *October 1, 2010.* Modern punctuation uses a comma before the year only when you give both the month and the day of the month:

May 1, 2010

but

Summers 2007–10

August 2010

Fall 2009

No punctuation is needed in military or European usage, which puts the day of the month first: 13 July 2009. Do not space before or after the slash used to separate parts of the date: 10/05–5/09.

Use a hyphen to join inclusive dates.

March–August 2010 (**or write out:** March to August 2010)

'08–'09

1999–2001

Note that you do not need to repeat the century in the date that follows the hyphen: 2008–09.

Words That Are Often Confused

Here's a list of words that are frequently confused. Master them, and you'll be well on the way to using words correctly.

1. accede/exceed
    accede: to yield
    exceed: to go beyond, surpass
    I accede to your demand that we not exceed the budget.
2. accept/except
    accept: to receive; to agree to
    except: to leave out or exclude; but
    I accept your proposal except for point 3.
3. access/excess
    access: the right to use; admission to
    excess: surplus
    As supply clerk, he had access to any excess materials.
4. adapt/adopt
    adapt: adjust
    adopt: to take as one's own
    She would adapt her ideas so people would adopt them.
5. advice/advise
    advice: (noun) counsel
    advise: (verb) to give counsel or advice to someone
    I asked him to advise me, but I didn't like the advice I got.
6. affect/effect
    affect: (verb) to influence or modify
    effect: (verb) to produce or cause; (noun) result
    He hoped that his argument would affect his boss's decision, but so far as he could see, it had no effect.
    The tax relief effected some improvement for the citizens whose incomes had been affected by inflation.

7. affluent/effluent

affluent: (adjective) rich, possessing in abundance

effluent: (noun) something that flows out

> Affluent companies can afford the cost of removing pollutants from the effluents their factories produce.

8. a lot/allot

a lot: many (informal)

allot: divide or give to

> A lot of players signed up for this year's draft. We allotted one first-round draft choice to each team.

9. among/between

among: (use with more than two choices)

between: (use with only two choices)

> This year the differences between the two candidates for president are unusually clear.
>
> I don't see any major differences among the candidates for city council.

10. amount/number

amount: (use with concepts or items that can be measured but that cannot be counted individually)

number: (use when items can be counted individually)

> It's a mistake to try to gauge the amount of interest he has by the number of questions he asks.

11. attributed/contributed

attributed: was said to be caused by

contributed: gave something to

> The rain probably contributed to the accident, but the police officer attributed the accident to driver error.

12. cite/sight/site

cite: (verb) to quote

sight: (noun) vision, something to be seen

site: (noun) location, place where a building is or will be built

> She cited the old story of the building inspector who was depressed by the very sight of the site for the new factory.

13. complement/compliment

complement: (verb) to complete, finish; (noun) something that completes

compliment: (verb) to praise; (noun) praise

> The compliment she gave me complemented my happiness.

14. compose/comprise

compose: make up, create

comprise: consist of, be made up of, be composed of

> The city council is composed of 12 members. Each district comprises an area 50 blocks square.

15. confuse/complicate/exacerbate

confuse: to bewilder

complicate: to make more complex or detailed

exacerbate: to make worse

> Because I missed the first 20 minutes of the movie, I didn't understand what was going on. The complicated plot exacerbated my confusion.

The Knead for Approve Reed Her with a Spell Chequer

"Who wood have guest The Spell Chequer would super seed The assent of the editor Who was once a mane figure? . . . Once, awl sought his council; Now nun prophet from him. How suite the job was; It was all sew fine. . . . Never once was he board As he edited each claws, Going strait to his deer work Where he'd in cyst on clarity. Now he's holy unacceptable, Useless and knot kneaded. . . . This is know miner issue, Fore he cannot urn a wage. Two this he takes a fence, Butt nose naught watt too due. He's wade each option Of jobs he mite dew, But nothing peaks his interest Like making pros clear. Sum will see him silly For being sew upset, But doesn't good righting Go beyond the write spelling?"

Quoted from Jeff Lovill, "On the Uselessness of an Editor in the Presents of a Spell Chequer," *Technical Communication* 35, no. 4 (1988), 267; and Edward M. Chilton, "Various Comments on 4Q88," *Technical Communication* 36, no. 2 (1989), 173.

16. dependant/dependent

    dependant: (noun) someone for whom one is financially responsible
    dependent: (adjective) relying on someone else

    > IRS regulations don't let us count our 25-year-old son as a dependant, but he is still financially dependent on us.

17. describe/prescribe

    describe: list the features of something, tell what something looks like
    prescribe: specify the features something must contain

    > The law prescribes the priorities for making repairs. This report describes our plans to comply with the law.

18. different from/different than

    Almost always *different from* (try changing the adjective *different* to the verb *differs*)

    > Bob's job description is different from mine.

    The most common exception is the indirect comparison.

    > Susan has a different attitude than you and I [*do* is implied].

19. discreet/discrete

    discreet: tactful, careful not to reveal secrets
    discrete: separate, distinct

    > I have known him to be discreet on two discrete occasions.

20. disinterested/uninterested

    Disinterested: impartial

    Uninterested: unconcerned

    > Because our boss is uninterested in office spats, she makes a disinterested referee.

21. elicit/illicit

    elicit: (verb) to draw out

    illicit: (adjective) not permitted, unlawful

    > The reporter could elicit no information from the senator about his illicit love affair.

22. eminent/immanent/imminent

    eminent: distinguished

    immanent: existing in the mind or consciousness

    imminent: about to happen

    > The eminent doctor believed that death was imminent. The eminent minister believed that God was immanent.

23. farther/further

    Farther: use for physical difference

    Further: use for metaphoric difference; also use for *additional* or *additionally*

    > As I traveled farther from the destruction at the plant, I pondered the further evidence of sabotage presented to me today.

24. fewer/less

    fewer: (use for objects that can be counted individually)

    less: (use for objects that can be measured but not counted individually)

    > There is less sand in this bucket; there are probably fewer grains of sand, too.

25. forward/foreword

    forward: ahead

foreword: preface, introduction

    The author looked forward to writing the foreword to the book.

26. good/well

good: (adjective, used to modify nouns; as a noun, means something that is good)

well: (adverb, used to modify verbs, adjectives, and other adverbs)

    Her words "Good work!" told him that he was doing well.

    He spent a great deal of time doing volunteer work because he believed that doing good was just as important as doing well.

27. i.e./e.g.

i.e.: (*id est*—that is) introduces a restatement or explanation of the preceding word or phrase

e.g.: (*exempli gratia*—for the sake of an example; for example) introduces one or more examples

    Although he had never studied Latin, he rarely made a mistake in using Latin abbreviations, e.g., i.e., and etc., because he associated each with a mnemonic device (i.e., a word or image used to help one remember something). He remembered *i.e.* as *in effect,* pretended that *e.g.* meant *example given,* and used *etc.* only when *examples to continue* would fit.

28. imply/infer

imply: suggest, put an idea into someone's head

infer: deduce, get an idea out from something

    She implied that an announcement would be made soon. I inferred from her smile that it would be an announcement of her promotion.

29. it's/its

it's: it is, it has

its: belonging to it

    It's clear that a company must satisfy its customers to stay in business.

30. lectern/podium

lectern: raised stand with a slanted top that holds a manuscript for a reader or notes for a speaker

podium: platform for a speaker or conductor to stand on

    I left my notes on the lectern when I left the podium at the end of my talk.

31. lie/lay

lie: to recline; to tell a falsehood (never takes an object)

lay: to put an object on something (always takes an object)

    He was laying the papers on the desk when I came in, but they aren't lying there now.

32. loose/lose

loose: not tight

lose: to have something disappear

    If I lose weight, this suit will be loose.

33. moral/morale

moral: (adjective) virtuous, good; (noun: morals) ethics, sense of right and wrong

morale: (noun) spirit, attitude, mental outlook

    Studies have shown that coed dormitories improve student morale without harming student morals.

34. objective/rationale

objective: goal

rationale: reason, justification

> The objective of the meeting was to explain the rationale behind the decision.

35. personal/personnel

personal: individual, to be used by one person

personnel: staff, employees

> All personnel will get personal computers by the end of the year.

36. possible/possibly

possible: (adjective) something that can be done

possibly: (adverb) perhaps

> It is possible that we will be able to hire this spring. We can choose from possibly the best graduating class in the past five years.

37. precede/proceed

precede: (verb) to go before

proceed: (verb) to continue; (noun: proceeds) money

> Raising the money must precede spending it. Only after we obtain the funds can we proceed to spend the proceeds.

38. principal/principle

principal: (adjective) main; (noun) person in charge; money lent out at interest

principle: (noun) basic truth or rule, code of conduct

> *The Prince,* Machiavelli's principal work, describes his principles for ruling a state.

39. quiet/quite

quiet: not noisy

quite: very

> It was quite difficult to find a quiet spot anywhere near the floor of the stock exchange.

40. regulate/relegate

regulate: control

relegate: put (usually in an inferior position)

> If the federal government regulates the size of lettering on country road signs, we may as well relegate the current signs to the garbage bin.

41. respectfully/respectively

respectfully: with respect

respectively: to each in the order listed

> When I was introduced to the queen, the prime minister, and the court jester, I bowed respectfully, shook hands politely, and winked, respectively.

42. role/roll

role: part in a play or script, function (in a group)

roll: (noun) list of students, voters, or other members; round piece of bread; (verb) move by turning over and over

> While the teacher called the roll, George—in his role as class clown—threw a roll he had saved from lunch.

43. simple/simplistic

   simple: not complicated

   simplistic: watered down, oversimplified

   She was able to explain the proposal in simple terms without making the explanation sound simplistic.

44. stationary/stationery

   stationary: not moving, fixed

   stationery: paper

   During the earthquake, even the stationery was not stationary.

45. their/there/they're

   their: belonging to them

   there: in that place

   they're: they are

   There are plans, designed to their specifications, for the house they're building.

46. to/too/two

   to: (preposition) function word indicating proximity, purpose, time, etc.

   too: (adverb) also, very, excessively

   two: (adjective) the number 2

   The formula is too secret to entrust to two people.

47. unique/unusual

   unique: sole, only, alone

   unusual: not common

   I believed that I was unique in my ability to memorize long strings of numbers until I consulted *Guinness World Records* and found that I was merely unusual: someone else had equaled my feat in 1993.

48. verbal/oral

   verbal: using words

   oral: spoken, not written

   His verbal skills were uneven: his oral communication was excellent, but he didn't write well. His sensitivity to nonverbal cues was acute: he could tell what kind of day I had just by looking at my face.

   Hint: Oral comes from the Latin word for mouth, *os*. Think of Oral-B Toothbrushes: for the mouth. Verbal comes from the Latin word for word, *verba*. Nonverbal language is language that does not use words (e.g., body language, gestures).

49. whether/weather

   whether: (conjunction) used to introduce possible alternatives

   weather: (noun) state of the atmosphere: wet or dry, hot or cold, calm or storm

   We will have to see what the weather is before we decide whether to hold the picnic indoors or out.

50. your/you're

   your: belonging to you

   you're: you are

   You're the top candidate for promotion in your division.

Proofreading Symbols

Use the proofreading symbols in Figure B.3 to make corrections on paper copies. Figure B.4 shows how the symbols can be used to correct a typed text.

Figure B.3   Proofreading Symbols

ℓ	delete	⌐	move to left
ℓ	insert a letter	⌐	move to right
¶	start a new paragraph here	⌐	move up
(stet)	stet (leave as it was before the marked change)	⌐	move down
(tr) ⌐	transpose (reverse)	#	leave a space
(lc)	lower case (don't capitalize)	⌒	close up
≡	capitalize	//	align vertically

Figure B.4   Marked Text

We could cut our travel bill by reimbursing employees only for the cost of a budget hotel or motel room.

A recent article from *The Wall Street Journal* suggests that many low-cost hotles and motels are tring to appeal to business travelers. chains that are actively competing for the business market include

Motel 6
Hampton Inns
    Fairfield Inns
Econologde
Super 8

Comfort Inn
Travelodge.

To attract business travelers, some budget chains now offer free local phone calls, free in-room movies, free continental breakfasts, and free Computer hookups.

By staying in a budget hotel, the business travelers can save at least $10 to $20 a night--often much more. For a company whose employees travel frequently, the savings can be considerable. Last year Megacorp reimbursed employees for a total of 4,392 nights in hotels. If each employee had stayed in a budget hotel, our expenses for travel would be $44,000 to $88,000 lower. Budget hotels would not be appropriate for sales meetings since they lack photocopying facilities or meeting rooms. However, we could and should use budget hotels and motels for ordinary on-the-road travel.

APPENDIX B   # Exercises and Problems

B.1   Diagnostic Test on Punctuation and Grammar

Identify and correct the errors in the following passages.

a.

Company's are finding it to their advantage to cultivate their suppliers. Partnerships between a company and it's suppliers can yield hefty payoffs for both company and supplier. One example is Bailey Controls an Ohio headquartered company. Bailey make control systems for big factories. They treat suppliers almost like departments of their own company. When a Bailey employee passes a laser scanner over a bins bar code the supplier is instantly alerted to send more parts.

b.

Entrepreneur Trip Hawkins appears in Japanese ads for the video game system his company designed. "It plugs into the future! he says in one ad, in a cameo spliced into shots of U.S kids playing the games. Hawkins is one of several US celebrieties and business people whom plug products on Japanese TV. Jodie Foster, harrison ford, and Charlie Sheen adverstises canned coffee beer and cigarettes respectively.

c.

Mid size firms employing between 100 and 1000 peopole represent only 4% of companies in the U.S.; but create 33% of all new jobs. One observe attributes their success to their being small enough to take advantage of economic opportunity's agilely, but big enough to have access to credit and to operate on a national or even international scale. The biggest hiring area for midsize company's is wholesale and retail sales (38% of jobs), construction (20% of jobs, manufacturing (19% of jobs), and services (18 of jobs).

B.2   Providing Punctuation

Provide the necessary punctuation in the following sentences. Note that not every box requires punctuation.

1. The system □ s □ user □ friendly design □ provides screen displays of work codes □ rates □ and client information.

2. Many other factors also shape the organization □ s □ image □ advertising □ brochures □ proposals □ stationery □ calling cards □ etc.

3. Charlotte Ford □ author of □ Charlotte Ford □ s □ Book of Modern Manners □□ says □□ Try to mention specifics of the conversation to fix the interview permanently in the interviewer □ s □ mind and be sure to mail the letter the same day □ before the hiring decision is made □□

4. What are your room rates □ and charges for food service □

5. We will need accommodations for 150 people □ five meeting rooms □ one large room and four small ones □ □ coffee served during morning and afternoon breaks □ and lunches and dinners.

6. The Operational Readiness Inspection □ which occurs once every three years □ is a realistic exercise □ which evaluates the National Guard □ s □ ability to mobilize □ deploy □ and fight.

7. Most computer packages will calculate three different sets of percentages □ row percentages □ column percentages □ and table percentages □

8. In today □ s □ economy □ it □ s almost impossible for a firm to extend credit beyond it □ s regular terms.

9. The Department of Transportation does not have statutory authority to grant easements □ however □ we do have authority to lease unused areas of highway right □ of □ way.

10. The program has two goals □ to identify employees with promise □ and to see that they get the training they need to advance.

B.3   Providing Punctuation

Provide the necessary punctuation in the following sentences. Note that not every box requires punctuation.

1. Office work □□ especially at your desk □□ can create back □ shoulder □ neck □ or wrist strain.
2. I searched for □ vacation □ and □ vacation planning □ on Google and Alta Vista.
3. I suggest putting a bulletin board in the rear hallway □ and posting all the interviewer □ s □ photos on it.
4. Analyzing audiences is the same for marketing and writing □ you have to identify who the audiences are □ understand how to motivate them □ and choose the best channel to reach them.
5. The more you know about your audience □□ who they are □ what they buy □ where they shop □□ the more relevant and effective you can make your ad.
6. The city already has five □ two □ hundred □ bed hospitals.
7. Students run the whole organization □ and are advised by a board of directors from the community.
8. The company is working on three team □ related issues □ interaction □ leadership □ and team size.
9. I would be interested in working on the committee □ however □ I have decided to do less community work so that I have more time to spend with my family.
10. □ You can create you own future □□ says Frank Montaño □□ You have to think about it □ crystallize it in writing □ and be willing to work at it □ We teach a lot of goal □ setting and planning in our training sessions □□

B.4   Creating Agreement

Revise the following sentences to correct errors in noun–pronoun and subject–verb agreement.

1. If there's any tickets left, they'll be $17 at the door.
2. A team of people from marketing, finance, and production are preparing the proposal.
3. Image type and resolution varies among clip art packages.
4. Your health and the health of your family is very important to us.
5. If a group member doesn't complete their assigned work, it slows the whole project down.
6. Baker & Baker was offended by the ad agency's sloppy proposal, and they withdrew their account from the firm.
7. To get out of debt you need to cut up your credit cards, which is hard to do.
8. Contests are fun for employees and creates sales incentives.
9. The higher the position a person has, the more professional their image should be.
10. A new employee should try to read verbal and nonverbal signals to see which aspects of your job are most important.

B.5   Correcting Case Errors

Revise the following sentences to correct errors in pronoun case.

1. I didn't appreciate him assuming that he would be the group's leader.
2. Myself and Jim made the presentation.
3. Employees which lack experience in dealing with people from other cultures could benefit from seminars in intercultural communication.
4. Chandra drew the graphs after her and I discussed the ideas for them.
5. Please give your revisions to Cindy, Tyrone, or myself by noon Friday.
6. Let's keep this disagreement between you and I.

B.6   Improving Modifiers

Revise the following sentences to correct dangling and misplaced modifiers.

1. Originally a group of four, one member dropped out after the first meeting due to a death in the family.
2. Examining the data, it is apparent that most of our sales are to people on the northwest side of the city.
3. As a busy professional, we know that you will want to take advantage of this special offer.
4. Often documents end up in files that aren't especially good.
5. By making an early reservation, it will give us more time to coordinate our trucks to better serve you.

B.7   Creating Parallel Structure

Revise the following sentences to create parallel structure.

1. To narrow a Web search,
   - Put quotation marks around a phrase when you want an exact term.
   - Many search engines have wild cards (usually an asterisk) to find plurals and other forms of a word.
   - Reading the instructions on the search engine itself can teach you advanced search techniques.
2. Men drink more alcoholic beverages than women.
3. Each issue of *Hospice Care* has articles from four different perspectives: legislative, health care, hospice administrators, and inspirational authors.
4. The university is one of the largest employers in the community, brings in substantial business, and the cultural impact is also big.

5. These three tools can help competitive people be better negotiators:
   1. Think win–win.
   2. It's important to ask enough questions to find out the other person's priorities, rather than jumping on the first advantage you find.
   3. Protect the other person's self-esteem.
6. These three questions can help cooperative people be better negotiators:
   1. Can you developing a specific alternative to use if negotiation fails?
   2. Don't focus on the bottom line. Spend time thinking about what you want and why you need it.
   3. Saying "You'll have to do better than that because . . . " can help you resist the temptation to say "yes" too quickly.

B.8   Correcting Sentence Errors

Revise the following sentences to correct comma splices, run-on sentences, fused sentences, and sentence fragments.

1. Members of the group are all experienced presenters, most have had little or no experience using PowerPoint.
2. Proofread the letter carefully and check for proper business format because errors undercut your ability to sell yourself so take advantage of your opportunity to make a good first impression.
3. Some documents need just one pass others need multiple revisions.
4. Videoconferencing can be frustrating. Simply because little time is available for casual conversation.
5. Entrepreneurs face two main obstacles. Limited cash. Lack of business experience.

6. The margin on pet supplies is very thin and the company can't make money selling just dog food and the real profit is in extras like neon-colored leashes, so you put the dog food in the back so people have to walk by everything else to get to it.
7. The company's profits jumped 15%. Although its revenues fell 3%.
8. The new budget will hurt small businesses it imposes extra fees it raises the interest rates small businesses must pay.
9. Our phones are constantly being used. Not just for business calls but also for personal calls.
10. Businesses are trying to cut travel costs, executives are taking fewer trips and flying out of alternate airports to save money.

B.9   Editing for Grammar and Usage

Revise the following sentences to eliminate errors in grammar and usage.

1. The number of students surveyed that worked more than 20 hours a week were 60%.
2. Not everyone is promoted after six months some people might remain in the training program a year before being moved to a permanent assignment.
3. The present solutions that has been suggested are not adequate.
4. At times while typing and editing, the text on your screen may not look correct.
5. All employees are asked to cut back on energy waste by the manager.
6. The benefits of an online catalog are
   1. We will be able to keep records up-to-date;

2. Broad access to the catalog system from any networked terminal on campus;
3. The consolidation of the main catalog and the catalogs in the departmental and branch libraries;
4. Cost savings.
7. You can take advantage of several banking services. Such as automatic withdrawal of a house or car payment and direct deposit of your pay check.
8. As a freshman, business administration was intriguing to me.
9. Thank you for the help you gave Joanne Jackson and myself.
10. I know from my business experience that good communication among people and departments are essential in running a successful corporation.

B.10   Writing Numbers

Revise the following sentences to correct errors in writing numbers.

1. 60% percent of the respondents hope to hold internships before they graduate.
2. 1992 marked the formal beginning of the European Economic Community.
3. In the year two thousand, twenty percent of the H-1B visas for immigrants with high-tech skills went to Indians.
4. More than 70,000,000 working Americans lack an employer-sponsored retirement plan.
5. The company's sales have risen to $16 million but it lost five million dollars.

B.11   Using Plurals and Possessives

Choose the right word for each sentence.

1. Many Canadian (companies, company's) are competing effectively in the global market.
2. We can move your (families, family's) furniture safely and efficiently.
3. The (managers', manager's) ability to listen is just as important as his or her technical knowledge.
4. A (memos, memo's) style can build goodwill.
5. (Social workers, social worker's) should tell clients about services available in the community.
6. The (companies, company's) benefits plan should be checked periodically to make sure it continues to serve the needs of employees.
7. Information about the new community makes the (families, family's) move easier.
8. The (managers, manager's) all have open-door policies.
9. (Memos, memo's) are sent to other workers in the same organization.
10. Burnout affects a (social workers', social worker's) productivity as well as his or her morale.

B.12   Choosing the Right Word

Choose the right word for each sentence.

1. Exercise is (good, well) for patients who have had open-heart surgery.
2. This response is atypical, but it is not (unique, unusual).
3. The personnel department continues its (roll, role) of compiling reports for the federal government.
4. The Accounting Club expects (its, it's) members to come to meetings and participate in activities.
5. Part of the fun of any vacation is (cite, sight, site)-seeing.
6. The (lectern, podium) was too high for the short speaker.
7. The (residence, residents) of the complex have asked for more parking spaces.
8. Please order more letterhead (stationary, stationery).
9. The closing of the plant will (affect, effect) house prices in the area.
10. Better communication (among, between) design and production could enable us to produce products more efficiently.

B.13   Choosing the Right Word

Choose the right word for each sentence.

1. The audit revealed a small (amount, number) of errors.
2. Diet beverages have (fewer, less) calories than regular drinks.
3. In her speech, she (implied, inferred) that the vote would be close.
4. We need to redesign the stand so that the catalog is eye-level instead of (laying, lying) on the desk.
5. (Their, There, They're) is some evidence that (their, there, they're) thinking of changing (their, there, they're) policy.
6. The settlement isn't yet in writing; if one side wanted to back out of the (oral, verbal) agreement, it could.
7. In (affect, effect), we're creating a new department.
8. The firm will be hiring new (personal, personnel) in three departments this year.
9. Several customers have asked that we carry more campus merchandise, (i.e., e.g.,) pillows and mugs with the college seal.
10. We have investigated all of the possible solutions (accept, except) adding a turning lane.

B.14   Choosing the Right Word

Choose the right word for each sentence.

1. The author (cites, sights, sites) four reasons for computer phobia.
2. The error was (do, due) to inexperience.
3. (Your, You're) doing a good job motivating (your, you're) subordinates.
4. One of the basic (principals, principles) of business communication is "Consider the reader."
5. I (implied, inferred) from the article that interest rates would go up.
6. Working papers generally are (composed, comprised) of working trial balance, assembly sheets, adjusting entries, audit schedules, and audit memos.
7. Eliminating time clocks will improve employee (moral, morale).
8. The (principal, principle) variable is the trigger price mechanism.
9. (Its, It's) (to, too, two) soon (to, too, two) tell whether the conversion (to, too, two) computerized billing will save as much time as we hope.
10. Formal training programs (complement, compliment) on-the-job opportunities for professional growth.

B.15   Tracking Your Own Mechanical Errors

Analyze the mechanical errors (grammar, punctuation, word use, and typos) in each of your papers.

- How many different errors are marked on each paper?
- Which three errors do you make most often?
- Is the number of errors constant in each paper, or does the number increase or decrease during the term?

As your instructor directs,

a. Correct each of the mechanical errors in one or more papers.

b. Deliberately write two new sentences in which you make each of your three most common errors. Then write the correct version of each sentence.

c. Write a memo to your instructor discussing your increasing mastery of mechanical correctness during the semester or quarter.

d. Briefly explain to the class how to avoid one kind of error in grammar, punctuation, or word use.

A

abstract   A summary of a report, specifying the recommendations and the reasons for them. Also called an executive summary.

acknowledgment responses   Nods, smiles, frowns, and words that let a speaker know you are listening.

active listening   Feeding back the literal meaning or the emotional content or both so that the speaker knows that the listener has heard and understood.

active voice   A verb that describes the action done by the grammatical subject of the sentence.

adjustment   A positive response to a claim letter. If the company agrees to grant a refund, the amount due will be adjusted.

alliteration   A sound pattern occurring when several words begin with the same sound.

alternating pattern (of organization)   Discussing the alternatives first as they relate to the first criterion, then as they relate to the second criterion, and so on: ABC, ABC, ABC. Compare *divided pattern*.

analytical report   A report that interprets information.

argument   The reasons or logic offered to persuade the audience.

assumptions   Statements that are not proved in a report, but on which the recommendations are based.

audience benefits   Benefits or advantages that the audience gets by using the communicator's services, buying the communicator's products, following the communicator's policies, or adopting the communicator's ideas. Audience benefits can exist for policies and ideas as well as for goods and services.

auxiliary audience   People who may encounter your message but will not have to interact with it. This audience includes "read only" people.

average   See *mean*.

B

bar chart   A visual consisting of parallel bars or rectangles that represent specific sets of data.

behavioral interviews   Job interviews that ask candidates to describe actual behaviors they have used in the past in specific situations.

bias-free language   Language that does not discriminate against people on the basis of sex, physical condition, race, age, or any other category.

blind ads   Job listings that do not list the company's name.

blind copies   Copies sent to other recipients that are not listed on the original letter, memo or e-mail.

block format   In letters, a format in which inside address, date, and signature block are lined up at the left margin; paragraphs are not indented. In résumés, a format in which dates are listed in one column and job titles and descriptions in another.

blocking   Disagreeing with every idea that is proposed.

body language   Nonverbal communication conveyed by posture and movement, eye contact, facial expressions, and gestures.

boilerplate   Language from a previous document that a writer includes in a new document. Writers use boilerplate both to save time and energy and to use language that has already been approved by the organization's legal staff.

boxhead   Used in tables, the boxhead is the variable whose label is at the top.

brainstorming   A method of generating ideas by recording everything people in a group think of, without judging or evaluating the ideas.

branching question   Question that sends respondents who answer differently to different parts of the questionnaire. Allows respondents to answer only those questions that are relevant to their experience.

bridge (in prospecting job letters)   A sentence that connects the attention-getter to the body of a letter.

brochure   Leaflet (often part of a direct mailing) that gives more information about a product or organization.

buffer   A neutral or positive statement designed to allow the writer to delay, or buffer, the negative message.

build goodwill   To create a good image of yourself and of your organization—the kind of image that makes people want to do business with you.

bullets   Small circles (filled or open) or squares that set off items in a list. When you are giving examples, but the number is not exact and the order does not matter, use bullets to set off items.

business plan   A document written to raise capital for a new business venture or to outline future actions for an established business.

businessese   A kind of jargon including unnecessary words. Some words were common 200–300 years ago but are no longer part of spoken English. Some have never been used outside of business writing. All of these terms should be omitted.

buying time with limited agreement   Agreeing with the small part of a criticism that one does accept as true.

bypassing   Miscommunication that occurs when two people use the same language to mean different things.

C

case   The grammatical role a noun or pronoun plays in a sentence. The nominative case is used for the subject of a clause, the possessive to show who or what something belongs to, the objective case for the object of a verb or a preposition.

central selling point   A strong audience benefit, big enough to motivate people by itself, but also serving as an umbrella to cover other benefits and to unify the message.

channel   The physical means by which a message is sent. Written channels include e-mails memos, letters, and billboards. Oral channels include phone calls, speeches, and face-to-face conversations.

channel overload   The inability of a channel to carry effectively all the messages that are being sent.

chartjunk   Decoration that is irrelevant to a visual and that may be misleading.

checking for feelings   Identifying the emotions that the previous speaker seemed to be expressing verbally or nonverbally.

checking for inferences   Trying to identify the unspoken content or feelings implied by what the previous speaker has actually said.

chronological résumé   A résumé that lists what you did in a dated order, starting with the most recent events and going backward in reverse chronology.

citation   Attributing a quotation or other idea to a source in the body of the report.

claim   The part of an argument that the speaker or writer wants the audience to agree with.

claim letter   A letter seeking a replacement or refund.

clip art   Predrawn images that you can import into your documents.

close   The ending of a document.

closed body position   Includes keeping the arms and legs crossed and close to the body. Suggests physical and psychological discomfort, defending oneself, and shutting the other person out. Also called a defensive body position.

closed question   Question with a limited number of possible responses.

closure report   A report summarizing completed work that does not result in new action or a recommendation.

clowning   Making unproductive jokes and diverting the group from its task.

cluster sample   A sample of subjects at each of a random sample of locations. This method is usually faster and cheaper than random sampling when face-to-face interviews are required.

clustering   A method of thinking up ideas by writing the central topic in the middle of the page, circling it, writing down the ideas that topic suggests, and circling them.

cognitive dissonance   A theory which posits that it is psychologically uncomfortable to hold two ideas that are dissonant or conflicting. The theory of cognitive dissonance explains that people will resolve dissonance by deciding that one of the ideas is less important, by rejecting one of the ideas, or by constructing a third idea that has room for both of the conflicting ideas.

cold list   A list used in marketing of people with no prior connection to your group.

collaborative writing   Working with other writers to produce a single document.

collection letter   A letter asking a customer to pay for goods and services received.

collection series   A series of letters asking customers to pay for goods and services they have already received. Early letters in the series assume that the reader intends to pay but final letters threaten legal action if the bill is not paid.

comma splice or comma fault   Using a comma to join two independent clauses. To correct, use a semicolon, use a comma with a conjunction, subordinate one of the clauses, or use a period and start a new sentence.

common ground   Values and goals that the communicator and audience share.

communication channel   The means by which you convey your message.

communication theory   A theory explaining what happens when we communicate and where miscommunication can occur.

complaint letter   A letter that challenges a policy or tries to get a decision changed.

complex sentence   Sentence with one main clause and one or more subordinate clauses.

complimentary close   The words after the body of the letter and before the signature. *Sincerely* and *Yours truly* are the most commonly used complimentary closes in business letters.

compound sentence   Sentence with two main clauses joined by a comma and conjunction.

conclusions   Section of a report that restates the main points.

conflict resolution   Strategies for getting at the real issue, keeping discussion open, and minimizing hurt feelings so that people can find a solution that seems good to everyone involved.

connotations   The emotional colorings or associations that accompany a word.

contact letter   Letter written to keep in touch with a customer or donor.

convenience sample   A group of subjects to whom the researcher has easy access; not a random sample.

conventions   Widely accepted practices.

conversational style   Conversational patterns such as speed and volume of speaking, pauses between speakers, whether questions are direct or indirect. When different speakers assign different meanings to a specific pattern, miscommunication results.

coordination   The second stage in the life of a task group, when the group finds, organizes, and interprets information and examines alternatives and assumptions. This is the longest of the stages.

counterclaim   A statement whose truth would negate the truth of the main claim.

credibility   Ability to come across to the audience as believable.

criteria   The standards used to evaluate or weigh the factors in a decision.

critical activities (in a schedule)   Activities that must be done on time if a project is to be completed by its due date.

critical incident   An important event that illustrates behavior or a history.

crop   To trim a photograph to fit a specific space, typically to delete visual information that is unnecessary or unwanted.

culture   The unconscious patterns of behavior and beliefs that are common to a people, nation, or organization.

cutaway drawings   Line drawings that depict the hidden or interior portions of an object.

cycling   The process of sending a document from writer to superior to writer to yet another superior for several rounds of revisions before the document is approved.

D

dangling modifier   A phrase that modifies a word that is not actually in a sentence. To correct a dangling modifier, recast the modifier as a subordinate clause or revise the sentence so its subject or object can be modified by the dangling phrase.

decode   To extract meaning from symbols.

decorative visual   A visual that makes the speaker's points more memorable but that does not convey numerical data.

defensive body position   See *closed body position*.

demographic characteristics   Measurable features of an audience that can be counted objectively: age, education level, income, etc.

denotation   A word's literal or "dictionary" meaning. Most common words in English have more than one denotation. Context usually makes it clear which of several meanings is appropriate.

dependent clause   See *subordinate clause*.

descriptive abstract   A listing of the topics an article or report covers that does not summarize what is said about each topic.

deviation bar charts   Bar charts that identify positive and negative values, or winners and losers.

dingbats   Small symbols such as arrows, pointing fingers, and so forth that are part of a typeface.

direct mail   A form of direct marketing that asks for an order, inquiry, or contribution directly from the reader.

direct mail package   The outer envelope of a direct mail letter and everything that goes in it: the letter, brochures, samples, secondary letters, reply card, and reply envelope.

direct marketing   All advertisements that ask for an order, inquiry, or contribution directly from the audience. Includes direct mail, catalogs, telemarketing (telephone sales), and newspaper and TV ads with 800 numbers to place an order.

direct request pattern   A pattern of organization that makes the request directly in the first paragraph.

discourse community   A group of people who share assumptions about what channels, formats, and styles to use for communication, what topics to discuss and how to discuss them, and what constitutes evidence.

divided pattern (of organization)   Discussing each alternative completely, through all criteria, before going on to the next alternative: AAA, BBB, CCC. Compare *alternating pattern*.

document design   The process of writing, organizing, and laying out a document so that it can be easily used by the intended audience.

documentation   Providing full bibliographic information so that interested readers can go to the original source of material used in a report.

dominating (in groups)   Trying to run a group by ordering, shutting out others, and insisting on one's own way.

dot chart   A chart that shows correlations or other large data sets. Dot charts have labeled horizontal and vertical axes.

dot planning   A way for large groups to set priorities; involves assigning colored dots to ideas.

E

editing   Checking the draft to see that it satisfies the requirements of good English and the principles of business writing. Unlike revision, which can produce major changes in meaning, editing focuses on the surface of writing.

ego-involvement   The emotional commitment that people have to their positions.

elimination of alternatives   A pattern of organization for reports that discusses the problem and its causes, the impractical solutions and their weaknesses, and finally the solution the writer favors.

ellipses   Spaced dots used in reports to indicate that words have been omitted from quoted material and in direct mail to give the effect of pauses in speech.

emotional appeal   A persuasive technique that uses the audience's emotions to make them want to do what the writer or speaker asks.

empathy   The ability to put oneself in someone else's shoes, to feel with that person.

enclosure   A document that accompanies a letter.

enunciate   To voice all the sounds of each word while speaking.

evaluating   Measuring something, such as a document draft or a group decision, against your goals and the requirements of the situation and audience.

evidence   Data the audience already accepts.

exaggeration   Making something sound bigger or more important than it really is.

executive summary   See *abstract*.

expectancy theory   A theory that argues that motivation is based on the expectation of being rewarded for performance and the importance of the reward.

external audiences   Audiences who are not part of the writer's organization.

external documents   Documents that go to people in another organization.

external report   Report written by a consultant for an organization of which he or she is not a permanent employee.

extranets   Web pages for customers and suppliers.

extrinsic motivators   Benefits that are "added on"; they are not a necessary part of the product or action.

eye contact   Looking another person directly in the eye.

F

feasibility report   A report that evaluates a proposed action and shows whether or not it will work.

feedback   The receiver's response to a message.

figure   Any visual that is not a table.

five Ws and H   Questions that must be answered early in a press release: who, what, when, where, why, and how.

fixed font   A typeface in which each letter has the same width on the page. Sometimes called *typewriter typeface*.

flaming   Sending out an angry e-mail message before thinking about the implications of venting one's anger.

focus groups   Small groups who come in to talk with a skilled leader about a potential product or process.

font A unified style of type. Fonts come in various sizes.

forecast An overview statement that tells the audience what you will discuss in a section or an entire report.

form letter A prewritten, fill-in-the-blank letter designed to fit standard situations.

formal meetings Meetings run under strict rules, like the rules of parliamentary procedure summarized in *Robert's Rules of Order.*

formal report A report containing formal elements such as a title page, a transmittal, a table of contents, and an abstract.

formalization The third and last stage in the life of a task group, when the group makes its decision and seeks consensus.

format The parts of a document and the way they are arranged on a page.

formation The first stage in the life of a task group, when members choose a leader and define the problem they must solve.

freewriting A kind of writing uninhibited by any constraints. Freewriting may be useful in overcoming writer's block, among other things.

frozen evaluation An assessment that does not take into account the possibility of change.

full justification Making both right and left margins of a text even, as opposed to having a ragged right margin.

fused sentence The result when two or more sentences are joined without punctuation or conjunctions.

G

Gantt charts Bar charts used to show schedules. Gantt charts are most commonly used in proposals.

gatekeeper The audience with the power to decide whether your message is sent on to other audiences.

gathering data Physically getting the background data you need. It can include informal and formal research or simply getting the letter to which you're responding.

general semantics The study of the ways behavior is influenced by the words and other symbols used to communicate.

gerund The *-ing* form of a verb; grammatically, it is a verb used as a noun.

getting feedback Asking someone else to evaluate your work. Feedback is useful at every stage of the writing process, not just during composition of the final draft.

glossary A list of terms used in a document with their definitions.

good appeal An appeal in direct marketing that offers believable descriptions of benefits, links the benefits of the product or service to a need or desire that motivates the audience and makes the audience act.

goodwill The value of a business beyond its tangible assets, including its reputation and patronage. Also, a favorable condition and overall atmosphere of trust that can be fostered between parties conducting business.

goodwill ending Shift of emphasis away from the message to the reader. A goodwill ending is positive, personal, and forward-looking and suggests that serving the reader is the real concern.

goodwill presentation A presentation that entertains and validates the audience.

grammar checker Software program that flags errors or doubtful usage.

grapevine An organization's informal informational network that carries gossip and rumors as well as accurate information.

grid system A means of designing layout by imposing columns on a page and lining up graphic elements within the columns.

ground rules Procedural rules adopted by groups to make meetings and processes run smoothly.

grouped bar chart A bar chart that allows the viewer to compare several aspects of each item or several items over time.

groupthink The tendency for a group to reward agreement and directly or indirectly punish dissent.

guided discussion A presentation in which the speaker presents the questions or issues that both speaker and audience have agreed on in advance. Instead of functioning as an expert with all the answers, the speaker serves as a facilitator to help the audience tap its own knowledge.

H

headings Words or short phrases that group points and divide your letter, memo, e-mail or report into sections.

hearing Perceiving sounds. (Not the same thing as listening.)

hidden job market Jobs that are never advertised but that may be available or may be created for the right candidate.

hidden negatives Words that are not negative in themselves, but become negative in context.

high-context culture A culture in which most information is inferred from the context, rather than being spelled out explicitly in words.

histogram A bar chart using pictures, asterisks, or points to represent a unit of the data.

I

impersonal expression A sentence that attributes actions to inanimate objects, designed to avoid placing blame on a reader.

indented format A format for résumés in which items that are logically equivalent begin at the same horizontal space, with carryover lines indented.

independent clause See *main clause.*

infinitive The form of the verb that is preceded by *to.*

informal meetings Loosely run meetings in which votes are not taken on every point.

informal report A report using letter or memo format.

information interview   An interview in which you talk to someone who works in the area you hope to enter to find out what the day-to-day work involves and how you can best prepare to enter that field.

information overload   A condition in which a person cannot process all the messages he or she receives.

information report   A report that collects data for the reader but does not recommend action.

informational dimensions   Dimensions of group work focusing on the problem, data, and possible solutions.

informative message   Message giving information to which the reader's basic reaction will be neutral.

informative presentation   A presentation that informs or teaches the audience.

informative report   A report that provides information.

inside address   The reader's name and address; put below the date and above the salutation in most letter formats.

interactive presentation   A presentation that is a conversation between the speaker and the audience.

intercultural competence   The ability to communicate sensitively with people from other cultures and countries, based on an understanding of cultural differences.

internal audiences   Audiences in the communicator's organization.

internal document   Document written for other employees in the same organization.

internal documentation   Providing information about a source in the text itself rather than in footnotes or endnotes.

internal report   Reports written by employees for use only in their organization.

interpersonal communication   Communication between people.

interpersonal dimensions   In a group, efforts promoting friendliness, cooperation, and group loyalty.

interview   Structured conversation with someone who is able to give you useful information.

intranet   A Web page just for employees.

intrapreneurs   Innovators who work within organizations.

intrinsic motivators   Benefits that come automatically from using a product or doing something.

introduction   The part of a report that states the purpose and scope of the report. The introduction may also include limitations, assumptions, methods, criteria, and definitions.

J

jargon   There are two kinds of jargon. The first kind is the specialized terminology of a technical field. The second is businessese, outdated words that do not have technical meanings and are not used in other forms of English.

judgment   See *opinion.*

judgment sample   A group of subjects whose views seem useful.

justification report   Report that justifies the need for a purchase, an investment, a new personnel line, or a change in procedure.

justified margins   Margins that end evenly on both sides of the page.

K

keywords   Words used in (1) a résumé to summarize areas of expertise, qualifications, and (2) an article or report to describe the content. Keywords facilitate computer searches.

L

letter   Short document using block, modified, or simplified letter format that goes to readers outside your organization.

letterhead   Stationery with the organization's name, logo, address, and telephone number printed on the page.

limitations   Problems or factors that constrain the validity of the recommendations of a report.

line graph   A visual consisting of lines that show trends or allow the viewer to interpolate values between the observed values.

low-context culture   A culture in which most information is conveyed explicitly in words rather than being inferred from context.

M

main clause   A group of words that can stand by itself as a complete sentence. Also called an independent clause.

Maslow's hierarchy of needs   Five levels of human need posited by Abraham H. Maslow. They include physical needs, the need for safety and security, for love and belonging, for esteem and recognition, and for self-actualization.

mean   The average of a group of numbers. Found by dividing the sum of a set of figures by the number of figures.

median   The middle number in a ranked set of numbers.

memo   Document using memo format sent to readers in your organization.

methods section   The section of a report or survey describing how the data were gathered.

minutes   Records of a meeting, listing the items discussed, the results of votes, and the persons responsible for carrying out follow-up steps.

mirror question   Question that paraphrases the content of the answer an interviewee gave to the last question.

misplaced modifier   A word or phrase that appears to modify another element of the sentence than the writer intended.

mixed punctuation   Using a colon after the salutation and a comma after the complimentary close in a letter.

mode   The most frequent number in a set of numbers.

modified block format   A letter format in which the inside address, date, and signature block are lined up with each other one-half or two-thirds of the way over on the page.

modifier   A word or phrase giving more information about another word in a sentence.

monochronic culture   Culture in which people do only one important activity at a time.

monologue presentation   A presentation in which the speaker talks without interruption. The presentation is planned and is delivered without deviation.

multiple graphs Three or more simple stories told by graphs juxtaposed to create a more powerful story.

Myers-Briggs Type Indicator A scale that categorizes people on four dimensions: introvert-extravert; sensing-intuitive; thinking-feeling; and perceiving-judging.

N

negative message A message in which basic information conveyed is negative; the reader is expected to be disappointed or angry.

networking Using your connections with other people to help you achieve a goal.

neutral subject line A subject line that does not give away the writer's stance on an issue.

noise Any physical or psychological interference in a message.

nominative case The grammatical form used for the subject of a clause. *I, we, he, she,* and *they* are nominative pronouns.

nonagist Refers to words, images, or behaviors that do not discriminate against people on the basis of age.

nonracist Refers to words, images, or behaviors that do not discriminate against people on the basis of race.

nonrestrictive clause A clause giving extra but unessential information about a noun or pronoun. Because the information is extra, commas separate the clause from the word it modifies.

nonsexist language Language that treats both sexes neutrally, that does not make assumptions about the proper gender for a job, and that does not imply that one sex is superior to or takes precedence over the other.

nonverbal communication Communication that does not use words.

normal interview A job interview with mostly expected questions.

noun–pronoun agreement Having a pronoun be the same number (singular or plural) and the same person (first, second, or third) as the noun it refers to.

O

objective case The grammatical form used for the object of a verb or preposition. *Me, us, him, her,* and *them* are objective pronouns.

omnibus motion A motion that allows a group to vote on several related items in a single vote. Saves time in formal meetings with long agendas.

open body position Includes keeping the arms and legs uncrossed and away from the body. Suggests physical and psychological comfort and openness.

open punctuation Using no punctuation after the salutation and the complimentary close.

open question Question with an unlimited number of possible responses.

opinion A statement that can never be verified, since it includes terms that cannot be measured objectively. Also called a judgment.

organization (in messages) The order in which ideas are arranged.

organizational culture The values, attitudes, and philosophies shared by people in an organization that shape its behaviors and reward structure.

outsourcing Going outside the company for products and services that once were made by the company's employees.

P

package The outer envelope and everything that goes in it in a direct mailing.

paired bar chart A bar chart that shows the correlation between two items.

parallel structure Using the same grammatical and logical form for words, phrases, clauses, and ideas in a series.

paraphrase To repeat in your own words the verbal content of another communication.

passive voice A verb that describes action done to the grammatical subject of the sentence.

people-first language Language that names the person first, then the condition: "people with mental retardation." Used to avoid implying that the condition defines the person's potential.

performance appraisals Supervisors' written evaluations of their subordinates' work.

persona The "author" or character who allegedly writes a document; the voice that a communicator assumes in creating a message.

personal space The distance someone wants between him- or herself and other people in ordinary, nonintimate interchanges.

personalized A message that is adapted to the individual reader by including the reader's name and address and perhaps other information.

persuade To motivate and convince the audience to act or change a belief.

persuasive presentation A presentation that motivates the audience to act or to believe.

pie chart A circular chart whose sections represent percentages of a given quantity.

pitch The highness or lowness of a sound.

plagiarism Passing off the words or ideas of others as one's own.

planning All the thinking done about a subject and the means of achieving your purposes. Planning takes place not only when devising strategies for the document as a whole, but also when generating "miniplans" that govern sentences or paragraphs.

polarization A logical fallacy that argues there are only two possible positions, one of which is clearly unacceptable.

polychronic culture Culture in which people do several things at once.

population The group a researcher wants to make statements about.

positive emphasis Focusing on the positive rather than the negative aspects of a situation.

positive or good news message Message to which the reader's reaction will be positive.

possessive case The grammatical form used to indicate possession or ownership. *My, our, his, hers, its,* and *their* are possessive pronouns.

post office abbreviations Two-letter abbreviations for states and provinces.

prepositions Words that indicate relationships, for example, *with, in, under, at.*

presenting problem The problem that surfaces as the subject of discord. The presenting problem is often not the real problem.

primary audience The audience who will make a decision or act on the basis of a message.

primary research Research that gathers new information.

pro-and-con pattern A pattern of organization that presents all the arguments for an alternative and then all the arguments against it.

probe question A follow-up question designed to get more information about an answer or to get at specific aspects of a topic.

problem-solving pattern A pattern of organization that describes a problem before offering a solution to the problem.

procedural dimensions Dimensions of group work focusing on methods: how the group makes decisions, who does what, when assignments are due.

process of writing What people actually do when they write: planning, gathering, writing, evaluating, getting feedback, revising, editing, and proofreading.

progress report A statement of the work done during a period of time and the work proposed for the next period.

proofreading Checking the final copy to see that it's free from typographical errors.

proportional font A font in which some letters are wider than other letters (for example, *w* is wider than *i*).

proposal Document that suggests a method and personnel for finding information or solving a problem.

prospecting letter A job application letter written to a company that has not announced openings but where you'd like to work.

psychographic characteristics Human characteristics that are qualitative rather than quantitative: values, beliefs, goals, and lifestyles.

psychological description Description of a product or service in terms of audience benefits.

psychological reactance Phenomenon occurring when a person reacts to a negative message by asserting freedom in some other arena.

purpose statement The statement in a proposal or a report specifying the organizational problem, the technical questions that must be answered to solve the problem, and the rhetorical purpose of the report (to explain, to recommend, to request, to propose).

Q

questionnaire List of questions for people to answer in a survey.

R

ragged right margins Margins that do not end evenly on the right side of the page.

random sample A sample for which each member of the population has an equal chance of being chosen.

recommendation report A report that evaluates two or more possible alternatives and recommends one of them. Doing nothing is always one alternative.

recommendations Section of a report that specifies items for action.

reference line A *subject line* that refers the reader to another document (usually a numbered one, such as an invoice).

referral interview Interviews you schedule to learn about current job opportunities in your field and to get referrals to other people who may have the power to create a job for you. Useful for tapping into unadvertised jobs and the hidden job market.

reflexive pronoun Refers to or emphasizes a noun or pronoun that has already appeared in the sentence. *Myself, herself,* and *themselves* are reflexive pronouns.

release date Date a report will be made available to the public.

reply card A card or form designed to make it easy for the reader to respond to a direct mail letter. A good reply card repeats the central selling point, basic product information, and price.

request for proposal (RFP) A statement of the service or product that an agency wants; an invitation for proposals to provide that service or product.

respondents The people who fill out a questionnaire; also called subjects.

response rate The percentage of subjects receiving a questionnaire who answer the questions.

restrictive clause A clause limiting or restricting the meaning of a noun or pronoun. Because its information is essential, no commas separate the clause from the word it restricts.

résumé A persuasive summary of your qualifications for employment.

résumé blasting Posting your résumé widely—usually by the hundreds—on the Web.

reverse chronology Starting with the most recent events, such as job or degree, and going backward in time. Pattern of organization used for chronological résumés.

revising Making changes in the draft: adding, deleting, substituting, or rearranging. Revision can be changes in single words, but more often it means major additions, deletions, or substitutions, as the writer measures the draft against purpose and audience and reshapes the document to make it more effective.

RFP See *request for proposal.*

rhetorical purpose The effect the writer or speaker hopes to have on the audience (to inform, to persuade, to build goodwill).

rhythm The repetition of a pattern of accented and unaccented syllables.

rival hypotheses Alternate explanations for observed results.

rule of three The rule noting a preference for three short parallel examples and explaining that the last will receive the most emphasis.

run-on sentence A sentence containing two or more main clauses strung together with *and, but, or, so,* or *for.*

S

sales pattern A pattern of persuasion that consists of an attention getting opener, a body with reasons and details, and an action close.

salutation The greeting in a letter: "Dear Ms. Smith."

sample *(in marketing)* A product provided to the audience to whet their appetite for more.

sample *(in research)* The portion of the population a researcher actually studies.

sampling frame The list of all possible sampling units.

sampling units Those items/people actually sampled.

sans serif Literally, *without serifs.* Typeface whose letters lack bases or flicks. Helvetica and Geneva are examples of sans serif typefaces.

saves the reader's time The result of a message whose style, organization, and visual impact help the reader to read, understand, and act on the information as quickly as possible.

schematic diagrams Line drawings of objects and their parts.

scope statement A statement in a proposal or report specifying the subjects the report covers and how broadly or deeply it covers them.

secondary audience The audience who may be asked by the primary audience to comment on a message or to implement ideas after they've been approved.

secondary research Research retrieving data someone else gathered. Includes library research.

segmented, subdivided, or stacked bars Bars in a bar chart that sum components of an item.

semantics or general semantics The study of the ways behavior is influenced by the words and other symbols used to communicate.

sentence fragment Words that are not a complete sentence but that are punctuated as if they were a complete sentence.

sentence outline An outline using complete sentences. It contains the thesis or recommendation plus all supporting points.

serif The little extensions from the main strokes on letters. Times Roman and Courier are examples of serif typefaces.

signpost An explicit statement of the place that a speaker or writer has reached: "Now we come to the third point."

simple sentence Sentence with one main clause.

simplified format A letter format that omits the salutation and complimentary close and lines everything up at the left margin.

situational interviews Job interviews in which candidates are asked to describe what they would do in specific hypothetical situations.

skills résumé A résumé organized around the skills you've used, rather than the date or the job in which you used them.

solicited letter A job letter written when you know that the company is hiring.

spot visuals Informal visuals that are inserted directly into text. Spot visuals do not have numbers or titles.

stereotyping Putting similar people or events into a single category, even though significant differences exist.

storyboard A visual representation of the structure of a document, with a rectangle representing each page or unit. An alternative to outlining as a method of organizing material.

strategy A plan for reaching your specific goals with a specific audience.

stratified random sample A sample generated by first dividing the sample into subgroups in the population and then taking a random sample for each subgroup.

stress (in a communication) Emphasis given to one or more words in a sentence, or one or more ideas in a message.

stress interview A job interview that deliberately puts the applicant under stress, physical or psychological. Here it's important to change the conditions that create physical stress and to meet psychological stress by rephrasing questions in less inflammatory terms and treating them as requests for information.

structured interview An interview that follows a detailed list of questions prepared in advance.

stub The variable listed on the side in a table.

subject line The title of the document, used to file and retrieve the document. A subject line tells readers why they need to read the document and provides a framework in which to set what you're about to say.

subjects The people studied in an experiment, focus group, or survey.

subordinate clause A group of words containing a subject and a verb but that cannot stand by itself as a complete sentence. Also called a dependent clause.

summarizing Restating and relating major points, pulling ideas together.

summary abstract The logic skeleton of an article or report, containing the thesis or recommendation and its proof.

summary sentence or paragraph A sentence or paragraph listing in order the topics that following sentences or paragraphs will discuss.

survey A method of getting information from a group of people.

SWOT analysis A method of evaluating a proposed action that examines both internal factors (Strengths, Weaknesses) and external factors (Opportunities, Threats).

T

table Numbers or words arrayed in rows and columns.

talking heads Headings that are detailed enough to provide an overview of the material in the sections they introduce.

template A design or format that serves as a pattern.

10-K report   A report filed with the Securities and Exchange Commission summarizing the firm's financial performance.

thank-you note   A note thanking someone for helping you.

threat   A statement, explicit or implied, that someone will be punished if he or she does or doesn't do something.

360-degree feedback   A form of assessment in which an employee receives feedback from peers, managers, subordinates, customers, and suppliers.

tone   The implied attitude of the author toward the reader and the subject.

tone of voice   The rising or falling inflection that indicates whether a group of words is a question or a statement, whether the speaker is uncertain or confident, whether a statement is sincere or sarcastic.

topic heading   A heading that focuses on the structure of a report. Topic headings give little information.

topic outline   An outline listing the main points and the subpoints under each main point. A topic outline is the basis for the table of contents of a report.

topic sentence   A sentence that introduces or summarizes the main idea in a paragraph.

transmit   To send a message.

transitions   Words, phrases, or sentences that show the connections between ideas.

transmittal   A message explaining why something is being sent.

truncated code   Symbols such as asterisks that turn up other forms of a keyword in a computer search.

truncated graphs   Graphs with part of the scale missing.

two-margin format   A format for résumés in which dates are listed in one column and job titles and descriptions in another. This format emphasizes work history.

U

umbrella sentence or paragraph   A sentence or paragraph listing in order the topics that following sentences or paragraphs will discuss.

understatement   Downplaying or minimizing the size or features of something.

unity   Using only one idea or topic in a paragraph or other piece of writing.

unjustified margins   Margins that do not end evenly on the right side of the page.

unstructured interview   An interview based on three or four main questions prepared in advance and other questions that build on what the interviewee says.

usability testing   Testing a document with users to see that it functions as desired.

V

venting   Expressing pent-up negative emotions.

verbal communication   Communication that uses words; may be either oral or written.

vested interest   The emotional stake readers have in something if they benefit from maintaining or influencing conditions or actions.

vicarious participation   An emotional strategy in fundraising letters based on the idea that by donating money, readers participate in work they are not able to do personally.

visual impact   The visual "first impression" you get when you look at a page.

volume   The loudness or softness of a voice or other sound.

W

watchdog audience   An audience that has political, social, or economic power and that may base future actions on its evaluation of your message.

white space   The empty space on the page. White space emphasizes material that it separates from the rest of the text.

widget   A software program that can be dropped into social networking sites and other places.

wild card   Symbols such as asterisks that turn up other forms of a keyword in a computer search. See also *truncated code*.

withdrawing   Being silent, not contributing, not helping with the work, not attending meetings.

wordiness   Taking more words than necessary to express an idea.

works cited   The sources specifically referred to in a report.

works consulted   Sources read during the research for a report but not mentioned specifically in the report.

Y

you-attitude   A style of communicating that looks at things from the audience's point of view, emphasizes what the audience wants to know, respects the audience's intelligence, and protects the audience's ego. Using *you* generally increases you-attitude in positive situations. In negative situations or conflict, avoid *you* since that word will attack the audience.

Chapter 1

1. National Association of Colleges and Employers, "Employers Cite Communication Skills, Honesty/Integrity as Key for Job Candidates," in *News for Media Professionals*, http://www.naceweb.org/press/display.asp?year=2007&prid=254 (accessed January 15, 2009).

2. Peter Coy, "The Future of Work," *BusinessWeek*, March 22, 2004, 50.

3. The National Commission on Writing for America's Families, Schools, and Colleges, "Writing: A Ticket to Work . . . Or a Ticket Out: A Survey of Business Leaders," in *College Board* (2004), 7–8.

4. Anne Fisher, "The High Cost of Living and Not Writing Well," *Fortune*, December 7, 1998, 244.

5. Jeffrey Gitomer, *Jeffrey Gitomer's Little Black Book of Connections: 6.5 Assets for Networking Your Way to Rich Relationships* (Austin, TX: Bard Press, 2006), 128–31.

6. Peter D. Hart Research Associate, Inc., *How Should Colleges Assess and Improve Student Learning? Employers' Views on the Accountability Challenge: A Survey of Employers Conducted on Behalf of The Association of American Colleges and Universities* (Washington, DC: The Association of American Colleges and Universities, 2008), 3.

7. The Conference Board et al., "Are They Really Ready to Work? Employers' Perspectives on the Basic Knowledge and Applied Skills of New Entrants to the 21st Century U.S. Workforce," in *Publications: Research Reports*, http://www.conference-board.org/pdf_free/BED-06-workforce.pdf (accessed January 19, 2009).

8. Tom DeMint, "So You Want to Be Promoted," *Fire Engineering* 159, no. 7 (2006); Karen M. Kroll, "Mapping Your Career," *PM Network* 19, no. 11 (2005): 28; and Jeff Snyder, "Recruiter: What It Takes," *Security* 43, no. 11 (2006): 70.

9. Devlin Barrett, "Rebate Alert Draws Flack—Money Could Be Better Spent, Democrats Say," *Houston Chronicle*, March 8, 2008, 2.

10. Claudia MonPere McIsaac and Mary Ann Aschauer, "Proposal Writing at Atherton Jordan, Inc.: An Ethnographic Study," *Management Communication Quarterly* 3 (1990): 535.

11. Xerox Corporation, "Case Studies," in *Home: Document Outsourcing*, http://www.consulting.xerox.com/case-studies/enus.html (accessed January 16, 2009).

12. Eric Krell, "The Unintended Word," *HRMagazine* 51, no. 8 (2006): 52.

13. Alex Cassini, "Not So Cheap After All: Email Storage Costs Continue to Grow," *Docume.nt* [sic] 12, no. 4 (2004): 31; and Pui-Wing Tam, "Cutting Files Down to Size: New Approaches Tackle Surplus of Data," *Wall Street Journal*, May 8, 2007, B4.

14. Manuel E. Sosa, Steven D. Eppinger, and Craig M. Rowles, "Are Your Engineers Talking to One Another When They Should?" *Harvard Business Review* 85, no. 11 (2007): 133–42.

15. The National Commission on Writing for America's Families, Schools, and Colleges, "A Powerful Message from State Government," in *College Board* (2005), 26.

16. The National Commission on Writing for America's Families, Schools, and Colleges, "Writing: A Ticket to Work . . . Or a Ticket Out: A Survey of Business Leaders," 29.

17. Michael Lewis, "The End of Wall Street's Boom," in *Home: News & Markets: National News*, http://www.portfolio.com/news-markets/national-news/portfolio/2008/11/11/The-End-of-Wall-Streets-Boom (accessed January 16, 2009).

18. Janet Adamy, "Advertising: Will a Twist on an Old Vow Deliver for Domino's Pizza?" *Wall Street Journal*, December 17, 2007, B1.

19. Stephen Baker, "A Painful Lesson: E-mail Is Forever," *BusinessWeek*, March 21, 2005, 36; Gary McWilliams, "Walmart Details Roehm Firing," *Wall Street Journal*, March 21, 2007, B11; and Peter Waldman and Don Clark, "California Charges Dunn, 4 Others in H-P Scandal; Action Sends Strong Message to Business about Privacy; Precedents for the Web Age?" *Wall Street Journal*, October 5, 2006, A1.

20. Elizabeth A. McCord, "The Business Writer, the Law, and Routine Business Communication: A Legal and Rhetorical Analysis," *Journal of Business and Technical Communication* 5, no. 3 (1991): 173–99.

Chapter 2

1. Isabel Briggs Myers, *Introduction to Type* (Palo Alto, CA: Consulting Psychologists Press, 1980). The material in this section follows Myers' paper.

2. Isabel Briggs Myers and Mary H. McCaulley, *Manual: A Guide to the Development and Use of the Myers-Briggs Type Indicator* (Palo Alto, CA: Consulting Psychologists Press, 1985), 248, 251.

3. Jeffrey Zaslow, "Moving On: After a Honeymoon, a Conceptionmoon?" *Wall Street Journal*, November 11, 2006, D2.

4. Eleanor Laise, "Fund Firms Lower Bar for Younger Investors: Wall Street Unveils Slew of Products with 20-Something Slant; 'My Whatever Plan' Cuts Minimums but Limits Choices," *Wall Street Journal*, July 17, 2007, D1.

5. Amy Chozick, "Nissan's Pitch for Mini-Car: Accessorize It: Pino Is Secondary in Spots That Woo Young Women," *Wall Street Journal*, March 30, 2007, B3.

6. Stephanie Kang and Vishesh Kumar, "TV Learning Importance of Targeting," *Wall Street Journal*, April 4, 2008, B4.

7. Richard Perez-Pena, "Washington Post Starts an Online Magazine for Blacks: Harvard Professor Is Editor in Chief," *New York Times*, January 28, 2008, C3.

8. SRI Consulting Business Intelligence (SRIC-BI), "Global Leader in Psychological Consumer Segmentation Announces System Enhancements to Anticipate the Evolving Marketplace," in *Press Release 18 November 2002*, http://www.sric-bi.com/press/2002-11-18.shtml (accessed January 18, 2009).

9. SRI Consulting Business Intelligence, "Representative VALS™ Projects," in *VALS™ Survey*, http://www.sric-bi.com/VALS/projects.shtml (accessed January 18, 2009).

10. Amy Chozick, "Toyota Tempers Sales View of Lexus Hybrid in U.S.," *Wall Street Journal*, May 19, 2007, A6; and Joseph Weber, "Giving Some Glamour to Grit," *BusinessWeek*, September 18, 2006, 12.

11. Josh Quittner and Jessi Hempel, "The Battle for Your Social Circle," *Fortune*, November 26, 2007, 30.

12. Rob Walker, "Amateur Hour, Web Style," *Fast Company*, October 2007, 87.

13. Marc Gunther, "Hard News," *Fortune*, August 6, 2007, 82.

14. Russell Adams, "New-Media Focus Splits Associated Press," *Wall Street Journal*, June 26, 2008, B3.

15. Tyler Hill, "Big Papers on Campus," *BusinessWeek*, July 9 & 16, 2007, 12.

16. Brian Steinberg, "The End of Network News As We Know It?" *Advertising Age* 79, no. 17 (2008): 12.

17. Julie Moran Alterio, "Whiz Kids Swap Joysticks for Business Learning Tool: New Video Game Teaches Skills to Students and Young Professionals," *Des Moines Register*, December 3, 2007, 2D.

18. Eric Wilson, "Collections Packed into an iPhone," *New York Times,* August 28, 2008, 4.

19. Rachel Dodes, "Vogue Models a New Reality Series," *Wall Street Journal,* July 7, 2008, B1.

20. Aaron O. Patrick, "NBA Tour Courts Europe's Young Men: U.S. Sponsors Hope Superstars Will Appeal to an Elusive Group," *Wall Street Journal,* August 10, 2007, B3.

21. Nicholas Casey, "As Barbie Sales Slow, Mattel Looks to Simplify Its Iconic Line," *Wall Street Journal,* April 22, 2008, B3.

22. Stephanie Kang, "Magic of Clorox Sells for a Song," *Wall Street Journal,* March 28, 2008, B4; and "Meet the Newest Rap Recording Artist," *Des Moines Register,* April 16, 2008, 2A.

23. Emily Steel, "Web-Page Clocks and Other 'Widgets' Anchor New Internet Strategy," *Wall Street Journal,* November 21, 2006, B4.

24. "Steamy Hot Line Raises Pulses, Library Funds," *Des Moines Register,* May 9, 2007, 4A.

25. Corey Dade, "R2-D2 Gets Top Billing in Postal Service Promotion," *Wall Street Journal,* March 16, 2007, B3; Laura Petrecca, "Product Placement—You Can't Escape It," *USA Today,* October 11, 2006, 1B; Suzanne Vranica, "Hanger Ads Ensure Message Gets Home," *Wall Street Journal,* March 12, 2007, B4; and Elizabeth Woyke, "A Marriage of Conveyance," *BusinessWeek,* October 30, 2006, 16.

26. Jeffery F. Rayport, "Where Is Advertising Going? Into 'Stitials,'" *Harvard Business Review* 86, no. 5 (2008): 18–19.

27. Spencer E. Ante and Catherine Holahan, "Generation MySpace Is Getting Fed Up," *BusinessWeek,* February 18, 2008, 54–55.

28. Susan Warren, "Spring Break Is a Legal Specialty for Ben Bollinger," *Wall Street Journal,* March 17, 2007, A2.

29. Lev Grossman, "A Game for All Ages," *Time,* May 15, 2006, 39.

30. Sara Silver, "How Match.com Found Love among Boomers: Dating Site Prospers Targeting Older Singles," *Wall Street Journal,* January 27, 2007, A1.

31. Cecilie Rohwedder, "Store of Knowledge: No. 1 Retailer in Britain Uses 'Clubcard' to Thwart Wal-Mart: Data from Loyalty Program Help Tesco Tailor Products As It Resists U.S. Invader," *Wall Street Journal,* June 6, 2006, A1.

32. Emily Steel, "AOL's Web Sites Show Gains in Traffic," *Wall Street Journal,* April 25, 2008, B1.

33. Ellen Byron, "Girl Scouts Seek an Image Makeover: Green Skirts Are Out as Organization Faces a 'Nonjoiner' Society," *Wall Street Journal,* March 25, 2008, B5.

34. Frederick Herzberg, "One More Time: How Do You Motivate Employees?" *Harvard Business Review,* September–October, 1987, 109–20.

35. Diane Cadrain, "Cash vs. Noncash Rewards," *HRMagazine,* April, 2003, 82–83; and Jennifer Gilbert, "Motivating through the Ages," *Sales & Marketing Management,* November, 2003, 31–40.

36. John Ketzenberger, "Respect, Not Money, Priceless in Cutting Turnover," *Des Moines Register,* November 20, 2006, 3D.

37. Teri Agins, "Over-40 Finds a Muse," *Wall Street Journal,* December 6, 2008, W4; and Ray A. Smith, "Jean Therapy for Older Guys: As Men's Sales Sag, Makers Court the Over-40 Crowd; Roomier 'Gentleman's Jeans,'" *Wall Street Journal,* July 21, 2007, P7.

38. Ellen Byron, "How P&G Led Also-Ran to Sweet Smell of Success: By Focusing on Fragrance, Gain Detergent Developed a Billion-Dollar Following," *Wall Street Journal,* September 4, 2007, B2; and David Wessel, "Paper Chase: South Africa's Sun Targets New Class: Tabloid Melds Sex, Soccer with Tales from Townships; Report on Flying Tortoise," *Wall Street Journal,* August 17, 2007, A1.

39. Phred Dvorak, "Eureka: Inventor Finds Bottom Line Seals the Deal: Entrepreneur Looks Past Gee-Whiz Technology to Focus on Client Profit," *Wall Street Journal,* August 20, 2007, B3.

40. M. P. McQueen, "Health Insurers Target the Individual Market," *Wall Street Journal,* August 21, 2007, D1.

41. Ellen Byron, "Aiming to Clean Up, P&G Courts Business Customers," *Wall Street Journal,* January 26, 2007, B1.

42. Anne Marie Chaker, "Amid Shortage, States Scramble to Hire Teachers; New Laws Offer Incentives to Lure More People into the Profession," *Wall Street Journal,* August 17, 2006, D1.

43. Ryan Chittum, "Price Points: Good Customer Service Costs Money. Some Expenses Are Worth It—and Some Aren't," *Wall Street Journal,* October 30, 2006, R7.

44. Terry Teachout, "What Young Audiences Want: Has Goldstar Events Cracked the Code?" *Wall Street Journal,* June 23, 2007, 16.

45. Richard M. Smith, "Stay True to Your Brand: Ad Guru Rance Crain Says the Rules Are Eternal," *Newsweek,* May 5, 2008, E18.

46. James Surowiecki, "The Financial Page Feature Presentation," *The New Yorker,* May 28, 2007, 28.

47. Reuters, "Scientist: Complexity Causes 50% of Product Returns," in *Computerworld.com: Today's Top Stories,* http://www.computerworld.com/hardwaretopics/hardware/story/0,10801,109254,00.html (accessed January 18, 2009).

48. Irwin Speizer, "Good Intentions, Lost in Translation," in *Workforce Management,* http://www.workforce.com/archive/feature/24/22/42/index.php (accessed January 18, 2009).

49. Rachel Spilka, "Orality and Literacy in the Workplace: Process- and Text-Based Strategies for Multiple Audience Adaptation," *Journal of Business and Technical Communication* 4, no. 1 (1990): 44–67.

Chapter 3

1. Linda Kaplan Thaler and Robin Koval, *The Power of Nice: How to Conquer the Business World with Kindness* (New York: Currency, 2006), 3.

2. David Welch, "Looser Rules, Happier Clients," *BusinessWeek,* March 5, 2007, 62.

3. John A. Byrne, "How to Lead Now: Getting Extraordinary Performance When You Can't Pay for It," *Fast Company,* August, 2003, 65.

4. Barbara Kiviat, "The Rage to Engage: Giving Attention to Workers Can Pay Off as Much as Pay," *Time,* April 28, 2008, Global 10.

5. Timothy Aeppel, "Too Good for Lowe's and Home Depot?" *Wall Street Journal,* July 24, 2006, B1, B6.

6. Annette N. Shelby and N. Lamar Reinsch, "Positive Emphasis and You-Attitude: An Empirical Study," *Journal of Business Communication* 32, no. 4 (1995): 303–27.

7. Martin E. P. Seligman, *Learned Optimism: How to Change Your Mind and Your Life,* 2nd ed. (New York: Pocket Books, 1998), 96–107.

8. Mark A. Sherman, "Adjectival Negation and the Comprehension of Multiply Negated Sentences," *Journal of Verbal Learning and Verbal Behavior* 15 (1976): 143–57.

9. Jeffrey Zaslow, "In Praise of Less Praise," *Wall Street Journal,* May 3, 2007, D1.

10. Associated Press, "Florida Police Chief Ousted After 'Jelly Bellies' Memo Telling Cops to Get Fit," in *Fox News.Com: Home,* http://www.foxnews.com/story/0,2933,226808,00.html (accessed January 17, 2009).

11. Stephen C. Dillard, "Litigation Nation," *Wall Street Journal,* November 25, 2006, A9.

12. Margaret Baker Graham and Carol David, "Power and Politeness: Administrative Writing in an 'Organized Anarchy,'" *Journal of Business and Technical Communication* 10, no. 1 (1996): 5–27.

13. Priscilla S. Rogers and Song-Mei Lee-Wong, "Reconceptualizing Politeness to Accommodate Dynamic Tensions in Subordinate-to Superior Reporting," *Journal of Business and Technical Communication* 17, no. 4 (2003): 379–412.

14. Brad Edmondson, "What Do You Call a Dark-Skinned Person?" *American Demographics,* October 1993, 9.

15. Robert Bernstein, "More Than 50 Million Americans Report Some Level of Disability," in *US Census Bureau: Newsroom: Releases: Aging Population, Children, Miscellaneous,* http://www.census.gov/Press-Release/www/releases/archives/aging_population/006809.html (accessed January 16, 2009).

16. M. P. McQueen, "Workplace Disabilities Are on the Rise: Employers Devise Strategies to Accommodate Growing Ranks of Employees Impaired by Age, Obesity and Disease," *Wall Street Journal,* May 1, 2007, D1.

Chapter 4

1. Stephen Ohlemacher, "Media Compete with Breathing for American's Time," *Des Moines Register,* December 15, 2006, D1.

2. Amol Sharma and Jessica E. Vascellaro, "Those IMs Aren't as Private as You Think," *Wall Street Journal,* October 4, 2006, D1, D2.

3. William M. Bulkeley, "Better Virtual Meetings: With Pricey Cameras, Plasma Screens, 'Telepresence' Replaces Video-Conferencing," *Wall Street Journal,* September 28, 2006, B1, B5.

4. William M. Bulkeley, "Playing Well with Others: How IBM's Employees Have Taken Social Networking to an Unusual Level," *Wall Street Journal,* June 18, 2007, R10.

5. "Australian Court OKs Using Facebook to Serve Papers," *Des Moines Register,* December 18, 2008, 18A.

6. Catherine Arnst, "Can Patients Cure Health Care?" *BusinessWeek,* December 15, 2008, 58–61.

7. Carline Waxler, "Social Misfits," *Fast Company,* November 2008, 160.

8. "Little Widgets, Big Ad Dollars?" *Fortune,* August 20, 2007, 14.

9. Larry Ballard, "Get off Networks, Get Back to Work," *Des Moines Register,* September 8, 2008, 1D.

10. Gary Fields, "Digital Data Drive Up Legal Costs," *Wall Street Journal,* September 6, 2008, A3.

11. Peter Engardio, "Let's Offshore the Lawyers," *BusinessWeek,* September 18, 2006, 42.

12. Pui-Wing Tam, "Cutting Files Down to Size: New Approaches Tackle Surplus of Data," *Wall Street Journal,* May 8, 2007, B4.

13. Bobby White, "A Question of Priorities: Faced with Clogged Networks, Companies and College Campuses Get More Sophisticated about Which Online Material Gets in First," *Wall Street Journal,* July 30, 2007, R7.

14. Samar Srivastava, "Sprint Drops Clients over Excessive Inquiries," *Wall Street Journal,* July 7, 2007, A3.

15. Jared Sandberg, "Employees Forsake Dreaded Email for the Beloved Phone," *Wall Street Journal,* September 26, 2006, B1.

16. Sandberg, "Employees Forsake Dreaded Email for the Beloved Phone," B1.

17. Robert Scoble, "Reengineer Your Inbox: Six Tools to Help Tackle Overflowing E-mail with Assembly-Line Efficiency," *Fast Company,* February 2009, 50.

18. Michelle Kessler, "Swamped by E-mail, Some Take a Day Off or Delete: Various Employers Now Encourage Face-to-Face Communication on Fridays," *Des Moines Register,* October 15, 2007, 2D; and Jena McGregor, "Can't It Wait Till Monday?" *BusinessWeek,* May 19, 2008, 54.

19. Ben Worthen, "Beyond the Firewall: As a New Breed of Professional Hacker Emerges, Companies Are Finding New Tools to Protect Their Networks," *Wall Street Journal,* December 11, 2007, R4.

20. Worthen, "Beyond the Firewall: As a New Breed of Professional Hacker Emerges, Companies are Finding New Tools to Protect Their Networks," R4.

21. M. P. McQueen, "The Menace in the Machines: Cyber-Scams on the Uptick in Downturn," *Wall Street Journal,* January 29, 2009, D1.

22. Stephanie Armour, "Employers Look Closely at What Workers Do on Job: Companies Get More Vigilant as Technology Increases Their Risks," *USA Today,* November 8, 2006, 2B; and M. P. McQueen, "Laptop Lockdown: Companies Start Holding Employees Responsible for Security of Portable Devices They Use for Work," *Wall Street Journal,* June 28, 2006, D1.

23. Ben Charny, "Catching Hold of Computers Set Free: Businesses Devise Ways to Guard, Manage Laptops That Have Left the Office," *Wall Street Journal,* December 18, 2007, B4.

24. Armour, "Employers Look Closely at What Workers Do on Job: Companies Get More Vigilant as Technology Increases Their Risks," 2B; M. P. McQueen, "Workers' Terminations for Computer Misuse Rise," *Wall Street Journal,* July 15, 2006, B4; and "Burger King Fires Workers over Blogs," *Wall Street Journal,* May 14, 2008, A18.

25. American Management Association, "2007 Electronic Monitoring & Surveillance Survey," in *Survey Summaries,* http://www.amanet.org/research/survey-summaries.htm (accessed February 13, 2009).

26. American Management Association, "2007 Electronic Monitoring & Surveillance Survey," in *Survey Summaries.*

27. Andie Coller, "Grassley Launches Porn Inquiry," in *Politico.com,* http://www.politico.com/news/stories/0109/18070.html (accessed February 13, 2009).

28. Chris Newmarker, "On the Off-Ramp to Adultery, There's No Fooling EZ-Pass," *Des Moines Register,* August 12, 2007, 8A.

29. Roger Cheng, "I Can See You: Small Businesses and Local Governments Are Finding It's Easier Than Ever to Track Their Employees," *Wall Street Journal,* November 11, 2006, R6; and Ellen Nakashima, "Enjoying Technology's Conveniences But Not Escaping Its Watchful Eyes," *Washington Post,* January 16, 2007, A01.

30. Todd Lewan, "As Tracking Technology Evolves, How Much Will Remain Personal?" *Des Moines Register,* January 27, 2008, 1AA.

31. Randall Rothenberg, "Facebook's Flop," *Wall Street Journal,* December 14, 2007, A21.

32. Emily Steel and Jessica E. Vascellaro, "FTC Backs Web-Ad Self-Regulation: Agency Lays Out Principles for Protecting the Privacy of 'Targeted' Users," *Wall Street Journal,* February 13, 2009, B7.

33. "E-Mail May Be Hazardous to Your Career," *Fortune,* May 14, 2007, 24.

34. Les Blumenthal, "Senator: VA Lying about Suicides," *Des Moines Register,* April 24, 2008, 10A.

35. Penelope Patsuris, "21 Dumbest Moments in Business 2008," in *CnnMoney.com,* http://money.cnn.com/galleries/2008/fortune/0812/gallery.dumbest_moments_2009.fortune/5.html (accessed February 13, 2009).

36. Justin Scheck and Lauren Pollock, "Former H-P Executive Pleads Guilty: Malhotra Could Get Jail Time for Stealing IBM Trade Secrets," *Wall Street Journal*, July 14, 2008, B8.

37. Jennifer Ordonez, "They Can't Hide Their Pryin' Eyes," *Newsweek*, July 7/14, 2007, 22.

38. Anne Jolis and Peppi Kiviniemi, "Google to Trim Hold on Data: In Deference to EU, Information to Be Kept for a Short Period," *Wall Street Journal*, June 13, 2007, B5.

39. Claes Fornell, "Customer Satisfaction at an All-Time High; Home Depot Makes U-Turn, Best Buy Gains; MetLife Rebounds," in *American Customer Satisfaction Index*, http://www.theacsi.org/index.php?option=com_content&task=view&id=168&Itemid=162 (accessed January 16, 2009).

40. Christopher W. Hart, "Beating the Market with Customer Satisfaction," *Harvard Business Review* 85, no. 3 (2007): 30–32.

41. "June 2000 Star of the Month," in *Careers: Star of the Month*, http://www.southwest.com/careers/stars/star_June00.html (accessed July 12, 2001).

42. Shirley S. Wang, "Health Care Taps 'Mystery Shoppers': To Improve Service, Hospitals and Doctors Hire Spies to Pose as Patients and Report Back," *Wall Street Journal*, August 8, 2006, D1.

43. Mike Bergman, "Nation Adds 2.2 Million Nonemployer Businesses over Five-Year Period," in *Releases: Economic Census*, http://www.census.gov/Press-Release/www/releases/archives/economic_census/001814.html (accessed January 16, 2009).

44. L. D. DeSimone et al., "How Can Big Companies Keep the Entrepreneurial Spirit Alive?" *Harvard Business Review*, November–December (1995): 183–92.

45. McDonald's Corporation, "About McDonald's," in *mcdonalds.com: Corporate McDonald's: About McDonald's*, http://www.mcdonalds.com/corp/about.html (accessed February 1, 2009).

46. Michael Mandel, "What Spending Slowdown? Forget Those Antiquated Government Statistics. U.S. Corporate Investment Is Booming—Just Take a Look Overseas," *BusinessWeek*, April 23, 2007, 30; and Robyn Meredith and Suzanne Hoppough, "Why Globalization Is Good," *Forbes* 179, no. 8 (2007): 64–68.

47. Bruce Stanley, "UPS Battles Traffic Jams to Gain Ground in India," *Wall Street Journal*, January 25, 2008, B1.

48. Betsy McKay and Anjali Cordeiro, "Coke Warns of Challenges from Stronger Dollar," *Wall Street Journal*, February 13, 2009, B3.

49. "Wal-Mart Is Looking East: Retailer Creates Post to Explore Expansion into Russia, Elsewhere," *Wall Street Journal*, April 15, 2008, B9.

50. Thomas L. Friedman, *The World Is Flat: A Brief History of the Twenty-First Century*, updated and expanded ed. (New York: Farrar, Straus, and Giroux, 2006), 14.

51. Friedman, *The World Is Flat*, 86.

52. Working Mother Media Inc., "PricewaterhouseCoopers," in *2008 Working Mother 100 Best Companies*, http://www.workingmother.com/web?service=direct/1/ViewTopListingPage/dlinkDetails2&sp=564&sp=3214 (accessed February 1, 2009).

53. Working Mother Media Inc., "Accenture," in *2008 Working Mother 100 Best Companies*, http://www.workingmother.com/web;jsessionid=8DE7CCB41F585263B4C0A BEBCF2E3AE9?service=direct/1/ViewTopListingPage/dlinkDetails&sp=481&sp=3214 (accessed February 1, 2009).

54. Christine Uber Grosse, "Managing Communication within Virtual Intercultural Teams," *Business Communication Quarterly* (2002): 22 (17); and Linda H. Heuring, "Patients First," *HRMagazine*, July 2003, 67–68.

55. Sue Shellenbarger, "Some Companies Rethink the Telecommuting Trend," *Wall Street Journal*, February 28, 2008, D1.

56. Heuring, "Patients First," 67–68.

57. Jörgen Sandberg, "Understanding Competence at Work," *Harvard Business Review*, March 2001, 24–28.

58. Peter Coy, "The Future of Work," *BusinessWeek*, March 22, 2004, 50; Kerry A. Dolan and Robyn Meredith, "A Tale of Two Cities," *Forbes*, April 12, 2004, 94–102; and Jennifer Reingold, "Into Thin Air," *Fast Company*, April 2004, 76–82.

59. Max Messmer, "Soft Skills Are Key to Advancing Your Career," *Business Credit* 109, no. 4 (2007): 34.

60. Anne Fisher, "America's Most Admired Companies," *Fortune*, March 17, 2008, 65–67.

61. "How Google Fuels Its Idea Factory," *BusinessWeek*, May 12, 2008, 54–55.

62. Betsy McKay and Suzanne Vranica, "Firms Use Earth Day to Show Their Green Side," *Wall Street Journal*, April 22, 2008, B7.

63. Anne Fisher, "America's Most Admired Companies," *Fortune*, March 19, 2007, 88–92.

64. "A Change in Climate," *Economist*, January 19, 2008, 14–20.

65. Nanette Byrnes et al., "Reform: Who's Making the Grade: A Performance Review for CEOs, Boards, Analysts, and Others," *BusinessWeek*, September 22, 2003, 80; and "On Trial; This Year, the Wheels of Justice May Catch Up to Some Movers and Shakers," *BusinessWeek*, January 12, 2004, 80.

66. See page 15 of the "ERC's 2007 National Business Ethics Survey," in *Ethics Resource Center: Research: NBES Overview*, http://www.ethics.org/research/nbes.asp (accessed February 1, 2009).

67. See pages 15–22 of "ERC's 2007 National Business Ethics Survey."

68. "United Nations Global Compact Participants " in *Home: Participants & Other Stakeholders*, http://www.unglobalcompact.org/ParticipantsAndStakeholders/index.html (accessed February 1, 2009).

69. "Going Global," *Economist*, January 19, 2008, 20–21.

70. "Just Good Business," *Economist*, January 19, 2008, 3–6.

71. Russell Gold and David Crawford, "U.S., Other Nations Step Up Bribery Battle: Prosecutions Climb on Tougher Laws Aimed at Businesses," *Wall Street Journal*, September 12, 2008, B1.

72. Ben W. Heineman, Jr., "Avoiding Integrity Land M!ines [sic]," *Harvard Business Review*, April 2007, 102.

73. "Grants and Investments," in *google.org: projects*, http://www.google.org/projects.html (accessed February 1, 2009); and "Searching for Solutions," in *google.org*, http://www.google.org/index.html (accessed February 1, 2009).

74. Clinton Global Initiative, "About CGI," in *Clinton Global Initiative: About Us*, http://www.clintonglobalinitiative.org/NETCOMMUNITY/Page.aspx?pid=2358&srcid=2356 (accessed February 1, 2009).

75. The Persuaders LLC, "FAQs " in *(PRODUCT) RED: Learn: About (RED): FAQ: Frequently Asked Questions about (RED)*, http://www.joinred.com/Learn/AboutRed/FAQs.aspx (accessed February 1, 2009).

76. Robin Hood Foundation, "Robin Hood: Targeting Poverty in New York City," in *Robin Hood: Home*, http://www.robinhood.org/ (accessed February 1, 2009); and Andy Serwer, "The Legend of Robin Hood," *Fortune*, September 18, 2006, 103–14.

77. Microsoft Corporation, "Bill Gates: World Economic Forum 2008," in *PressPass: Information for Journalists*, http://www.

microsoft.com/Presspass/exec/billg/speeches/2008/
01-24WEFDavos.mspx (accessed February 1, 2009).

78. Steve Hamm, "Capitalism with a Human Face: Social Entrepreneurs Tackle the World's Problems in the Face of a Global Downturn," *BusinessWeek,* December 8, 2008, 50.

79. "Being Bogusky," *Wall Street Journal,* May 19, 2007, P7; Tamara J. Erickson and Linda Gratton, "What It Means to Work Here," *Harvard Business Review,* 85, no. 3 (2007): 107; and Samuel Greengard, "Sun's Shining Example," *Workforce Management* 84, no. 3 (2005): 48.

80. Ellen Byron, "Merger Challenge: Unite Toothbrush, Toothpaste: P&G and Gillette Find Creating Synergy Can Be Harder Than It Looks," *Wall Street Journal,* April 24, 2007, A1.

81. Ellen Byron, "A New Odd Couple: Google, P&G Swap Workers to Spur Innovation," *Wall Street Journal,* November 19, 2008, A1.

82. Simona Covel, "Tapping the Creativity of Downtime: Web-Design Firm Uses Projects Employees Pursue in Their Spare Time at Work to Help Win New Business," *Wall Street Journal,* July 24, 2008, B5.

83. Phred Dvorak, "Hotelier Finds Happiness Keeps Staff Checked In," *Wall Street Journal,* December 17, 2007, B3.

84. Moon Ihlwan and Kenji Hall, "New Tech, Old Habits: Despite World-Class IT Networks, Japanese and Korean Workers Are Still Chained to Their Desks," *BusinessWeek,* March 26, 2007, 48–49.

85. Daniel Goleman, *Emotional Intelligence: The Tenth Aniversary Edition* (New York: Bantam, 2005), xiv–xv.

86. Deborah Tannen, *That's Not What I Meant!* (New York: William Morrow, 1986).

87. Daniel N. Maltz and Ruth A. Borker, "A Cultural Approach to Male-Female Miscommunication," in *Language and Social Identity,* ed. John J. Gumperz (Cambridge: Cambridge University Press, 1982), 202.

88. Marie Helweg-Larson et al., "To Nod or Not to Nod: An Observational Study of Nonverbal Communication and Status in Female and Male College Students," *Psychology of Women Quarterly* 28, no. 4 (2004): 358–61.

89. Alex "Sandy" Pentland, "The Power of Nonverbal Communication," *Wall Street Journal,* October 20, 2008, R2.

90. Goleman, *Emotional Intelligence: The Tenth Anniversary Edition,* 161–62.

91. Goleman, *Emotional Intelligence: The Tenth Aniversary Edition,* 162.

92. Jessica Hodgins, "'You Can't Make More Time': Randy Pausch's Heartfelt Views on Using Time to the Fullest," *BusinessWeek,* September 1, 2008, 71.

93. Stephen R. Covey, *The 7 Habits of Highly Effective People: Restoring the Character* (New York: Free Press, 2004), 150–54.

94. Jared Sandberg, "Yes, Sell All My Stocks. No, the 3:15 from JFK. And Get Me Mr. Sister," *Wall Street Journal,* September 12, 2006, B1.

95. Toddi Gutner, "Beat the Clock: E-mails, Faxes, Phone Calls, Oh My. Here's How to Get It All Done," *BusinessWeek SmallBiz,* February/March, 2008, 58.

96. Maggie Jackson, "May We Have Your Attention, Please?" *BusinessWeek,* June 23, 2008, 56.

97. Sharon Begley, "Will the BlackBerry Sink the Presidency?" *Newsweek,* February 16, 2009, 37.

Chapter 5

1. Sharon Begley, "Studies Take Measure of How Stereotyping Alters Performance," *Wall Street Journal,* February 23, 2007, B1; and Claude Steele and Joshua Aronson, "Stereotype Threat and Intellectual Test Performance of African Americans," *Journal of Personality and Social Psychology* 69, no. 5 (1995): 797–811.

2. Ellen Byron, "P&G's Global Target: Shelves of Tiny Stores: It Woos Poor Women Buying Single Portions; Mexico's 'Hot Zones,'" *Wall Street Journal,* July 16, 2007, A1; "Financial Facts—Year-End 2006," in *Our Company: Company Information: 3M Facts,* http://solutions.3m.com/wps/portal/3M/en_US/our/company/information/financialfacts (accessed July 27, 2009); "Google's International Revenue Outstrips US for First Time," in *News,* http://www.mediaweek.co.uk/news/832812/Googles-internationalrevenue-outstrips-US-first-time/ (accessed July 27, 2009); Geraldo Samor, Cecilie Rohwedder, and Ann Zimmerman, "Innocents Abroad? Wal-Mart's Global Sales Rise as It Learns from Mistakes; No More Ice Skates in Mexico," *Wall Street Journal,* May 16, 2006, B1; "Give Me a Double Shot of Starbucks Nostalgia," in March 3, 2007: Talking Business, http://select.nytimes.com/2007/03/03/business/03nocera.html?scp=1&sq=Starbucks%20Wants%2040,000%20Stores%20Worldwide,%20up%20from%2030,000%20Goal&st=cse (accessed July 27, 2009); and Daniel Workman, "McDonald's Global Sales: Big Mac's International Revenues Sizzle in 2006," in *World Affairs: International Trade: International Trade Leaders: Articles,* http://internationaltrade.suite101.com/article.cfm/mcdonalds_global_sales (accessed July 27, 2009).

3. Pete Engardio, "The Future of Outsourcing," *BusinessWeek,* January 30, 2006, 50–58; and Steve Hamm, "Big Blue Shift," *BusinessWeek,* June 5, 2006, 108.

4. Teri Agins, "For U.S. Fashion Firms, a Global Makeover: Tommy Hilfiger Finds Assimilating in Europe Requires a New Look," *Wall Street Journal,* February 2, 2007, A1, A17; Keith Naughton, "The Great Wal-Mart of China," *Newsweek,* October 30, 2006, 50; and Samor, Rohwedder, and Zimmerman, "Innocents Abroad?," B1.

5. Rachel Konrad, "Cisco Shifts Senior Executives to India's Tech Hub," in *Redmond Report: News,* http://redmondmag.com/news/article.asp?editorialsid=8091 (accessed July 27, 2009).

6. Mark Larson, "More Employees Go Abroad as International Operations Grow," in *Feature,* http://www.workforce.com/section/09/feature/24/41/22/index_printer.html (accessed July 27, 2009).

7. David Loyn, "Migrants 'Shape Globalised World,'" in *BBC News: Special Reports,* http://news.bbc.co.uk/2/hi/in_depth/6183803.stm (accessed July 27, 2009).

8. Thomas L. Friedman, *The World Is Flat: A Brief History of the Twenty-first Century,* Updated and Expanded ed. (New York: Farrar, Straus and Giroux, 2006), 8.

9. U.S. Census Bureau, "Statistical Abstract of the United States, Table 15: Resident Population by Race, Hispanic Origin, and Single Years of Age: 2005," http://www.census.gov/prod/2006pubs/07statab/pop.pdf (accessed July 27, 2009).

10. U.S. Census Bureau, "Statistical Abstract of the United States, Table 10: Immigrants Admitted by State and Leading Country of Birth: 2005," http://www.census.gov/prod/2006pubs/07statab/pop.pdf (accessed July 27, 2009).

11. Conor Dougherty, "Whites to Lose Majority Status in U.S. by 2042," *Wall Street Journal,* August 14, 2008, A3.

12. Stephen Ohlemacher, "Whites Are Now in Minority in 10 Percent of U.S. Counties," *Des Moines Register,* August 9, 2007, 3A.

13. Larson, "More Employees Go Abroad as International Operations Grow."

14. U.S. Census Bureau, "Statistical Abstract of the United States, Table 15: Resident Population by Race, Hispanic Origin, and Single Years of Age: 2005."

15. U.S. Census Bureau, "Statistical Abstract of the United States: Table 53: Language Spoken at Home by State: 2006," http://www.census.gov/prod/2008pubs/09statab/pop.pdf (accessed February 15, 2009).

16. U.S. Census Bureau, "Statistical Abstract of the United States: Table 54: Language Spoken at Home—25 Largest Cities: 2006," http://www.census.gov/prod/2008pubs/09statab/pop.pdf (accessed February 15, 2009).

17. Julie Bennett, "West Coast Makes Diversity a Corporate Imperative," *Wall Street Journal,* January 30, 2007, B9.

18. Shankar Vedantam, "In Boardrooms, Courtrooms, Diversity Makes Difference," *Cincinnati Post,* January 15, 2007, B2.

19. Abhijit Rao, e-mail message to author, February 15, 2009.

20. John Webb and Michael Keene, "The Impact of Discourse Communities on International Professional Communication," in *Exploring the Rhetoric of International Professional Communication: An Agenda for Teachers and Researchers,* eds. Carl R. Lovitt and Dixie Goswami (Amityville, NY: Baywood, 1999), 81–109.

21. Russell Flannery, "As Easy as $3 \times 7 = 21$," *Forbes* 173, no. 13 (2004): 110.

22. Kathryn King–Metters and Ricard Metters, "Misunderstanding the Chinese Worker: Western Impressions Are Dated—and Probably Wrong," *Wall Street Journal,* July 7, 2008, R11; and Jason Leow, "Chinese Bigwigs Are Quick to Reach for the Hair Color: Politicians and Executives Look for Youth in a Bottle of Black Dye on the Sly," *Wall Street Journal,* December 11, 2007, A1, A24.

23. Robert T. Moran, Philip R. Harris, and Sarah V. Moran, *Managing Cultural Differences: Global Leadership Strategies for the 21st Century,* 7th ed. (Boston: Elsevier, 2007), 341–42.

24. Moran, Harris, and Moran, *Managing Cultural Differences,* 64.

25. Martin J. Gannon, *Understanding Global Cultures: Metaphorical Journeys through 23 Nations,* 2nd ed. (Thousand Oaks, CA: Sage, 2001), 32; and Moran, Harris, and Moran, *Managing Cultural Differences,* 484.

26. Moran, Harris, and Moran, *Managing Cultural Differences,* 579.

27. Moran, Harris, and Moran, *Managing Cultural Differences,* 579.

28. Mike Kilen, "Watch Your Language: Rude or Polite? Gestures Vary with Cultures," *Des Moines Register,* May 30, 2006, E1–2.

29. Gannon, *Understanding Global Cultures,* 13.

30. Edward Twitchell Hall, *Hidden Differences: Doing Business with the Japanese* (Garden City, NY: Anchor–Doubleday, 1987), 25.

31. Moran, Harris, and Moran, *Managing Cultural Differences,* 445, 78.

32. Malcolm Fleschner, "Worldwide Winner," *Selling Power,* November–December 2001, 54–61.

33. Ira Carnahan, "Presidential Timber Tends to Be Tall," in *Leadership: Compensation: Business in the Beltway,* http://www.forbes.com/compensation/2004/05/19/cz_ic_0519beltway.html (accessed July 27, 2009).

34. Craig Storti, *Old World, New World: Bridging Cultural Differences: Britain, France, Germany, and the U.S.* (Yarmouth, ME: Intercultural Press, 2001), 209.

35. Nick Easen, "Don't Send the Wrong Message," *Business 2.0,* August 2005, 102.

36. Easen, "Don't Send the Wrong Message," 102.

Chapter 6

1. Kevin S. Groves, "Leader Emotional Expressivity, Visionary Leadership, and Organizational Change," *Leadership & Organizational Development Journal* 27, no. 7 (2006): 566–83; Ajay Mehra et al., "Distributed Leadership in Teams: The Network of Leadership Perceptions and Team Performance," *The Leadership Quarterly* 17, no. 3 (2006): 232–45; and Kenneth David Stand, "Examining Effective and Ineffective Transformational Project Leadership," *Team Performance Management* 11, no. 3/4 (2005): 68–103.

2. Jeswald W. Salacuse, *The Global Negotiator: Making, Managing, and Mending Deals around the World in the Twenty-First Century* (New York: Palgrave Macmillan, 2003), 92.

3. Bob Frisch, "When Teams Can't Decide," *Harvard Business Review* 86, no. 11 (2008): 121–26.

4. Caroline Bailey and Michelle Austin, "360 Degree Feedback and Developmental Outcomes: The Role of Feedback Characteristics, Self-Efficacy and Importance of Feedback Dimensions to Focal Managers' Current Role," *International Journal of Selection and Assessment* 14, no. 1 (2006): 51–66.

5. Kimberly Merriman, "Low-Trust Teams Prefer Individualized Pay," *Harvard Business Review* 86, no. 11 (2008): 32.

6. Sari Lindblom–Ylanne, Heikki Pihlajamaki, and Toomas Kotkas, "What Makes a Student Group Successful? Student–Student and Student–Teacher Interaction in a Problem-Based Learning Environment," *Learning Environments Research* 6, no. 1 (2003): 59–76.

7. Karen A. Jehn and Elizabeth A. Mannix, "The Dynamic Nature of Conflict: A Longitudinal Study of Intragroup Conflict and Group Performance," *Academy of Management Journal* 44, no. 2 (2001): 238–51.

8. Rebecca E. Burnett, "Conflict in Collaborative Decision Making," in *Professional Communication: The Social Perspective,* eds. Nancy Roundy Blyler and Charlotte Thralls (Newbury Park, CA: Sage, 1993), 144–62; and Rebecca E. Burnett, "Productive and Unproductive Conflict in Collaboration," in *Making Thinking Visible: Writing, Collaborative Planning, and Classroom Inquiry,* eds. Linda Flower et al. (Urbana, IL: NCTE, 1994), 239–44.

9. Sue Dyer, "The Root Causes of Poor Communication," *Cost Engineering* 48, no. 6 (2006): 8–10.

10. Solomon F. Asch, "Opinions and Social Pressure," *Scientific American* 193, no. 5 (1955): 31–35. For a review of more recent literature on groupthink, see Marc D. Street, "Groupthink: An Examination of Theoretical Issues, Implications, and Future Research Suggestions," *Small Group Research* 28, no. 1 (1997): 72–93.

11. Jared Diamond, *Collapse: How Societies Choose to Fail or Succeed* (New York: Penguin Books, 2005), 439.

12. Francesca Bariela–Chiappini et al., "Five Perspectives on Intercultural Business Communication," *Business Communication Quarterly* 66, no. 3 (2003): 73–96.

13. Ursula Hess and Pierre Philippot, *Group Dynamics and Emotional Expression* (New York: Cambridge University Press, 2007).

14. Kristina B. Dahlin, Laurie R. Weingart, and Pamela J. Hinds, "Team Diversity and Information Use," *Academy of Management Journal* 68, no. 6 (2005): 1107–23; Susannah B. F. Paletz et al., "Ethnic Composition and Its Differential Impact on Group Processes in Diverse Teams," *Small Group Research* 35, no. 2 (2004): 128–57; and Leisa D. Sargent and Christina Sue-Chan, "Does Diversity Affect Efficacy? The Intervening Role of Cohesion and Task Interdependence," *Small Group Research* 32, no. 4 (2001): 426–50.

15. Salacuse, *The Global Negotiator,* 96–97.

16. Jeanne Brett, Kristin Behfar, and Mary C. Kern, "Managing Multicultural Teams," *Harvard Business Review* 84, no. 11 (2006): 84–91.

17. John E. Tropman, *Making Meetings Work,* 2nd ed. (Thousand Oaks, CA: Sage, 2003), 28.

18. Seth Godin, "How to Give Feedback," *Fast Company,* March 2004, 103.

19. E. Packard, "Meetings Frustrate Task-Oriented Employees, Study Finds," *Monitor on Psychology* 37, no. 6 (2006): 10.

20. Burnett, "Productive and Unproductive Conflict in Collaboration," 239–44.

21. Kitty O. Locker, "What Makes a Collaborative Writing Team Successful? A Case Study of Lawyers and Social Service Workers in a State Agency," in *New Visions in Collaborative Writing,* ed. Janis Forman (Portsmouth, NJ: Boynton, 1991), 37–52.

22. Lisa Ede and Andrea Lunsford, *Singular Texts/Plural Authors: Perspectives on Collaborative Writing* (Carbondale, IL: Southern Illinois Press, 1990), 66.

Chapter 7

1. See especially Linda Flower and John R. Hayes, "The Cognition of Discovery: Defining a Rhetorical Problem," *College Composition and Communication* 31, no. 1 (February 1980): 21–32; Mike Rose, *Writer's Block: The Cognitive Dimension,* Published for Conference on College Composition and Communication, 1984; and the essays in two collections: Charles R. Cooper and Lee Odell, *Research on Composing: Points of Departure,* Urbana, IL: National Council of Teachers of English (1978); and Mike Rose, ed., *When a Writer Can't Write: Studies in Writer's Block and Other Composing-Process Problems* (New York: Guilford Press, 1985).

2. Elizabeth Blackburn–Brockmann, "Prewriting, Planning, and Professional Communication," *English Journal* 91 no. 2 (2001): 51–53; and Mark Torrance, Glyn V. Thomas, and Elizabeth J. Robinson, "Individual Differences in Undergraduate Essay-Writing Strategies: A Longitudinal Study," *Higher Education* 39 no. 2 (2000): 181–200.

3. Peter Elbow, *Writing with Power: Techniques for Mastering the Writing Process* (New York: Oxford University Press, 1981), 15–20.

4. See Gabriela Lusser Rico, *Writing the Natural Way* (Los Angeles: J. P. Tarcher, 1983), 10.

5. Rachel Spilka, "Orality and Literacy in the Workplace: Process- and Text-Based Strategies for Multiple Audience Adaptation," *Journal of Business and Technical Communication* 4, no. 1 (January 1990): 44–67.

6. Robert L. Brown, Jr., and Carl G. Herndl, "An Ethnographic Study of Corporate Writing: Job Status as Reflected in Written Text," in *Functional Approaches to Writing: A Research Perspective,* ed. Barbara Couture (Norwood, NJ: Ablex, 1986), 16–19, 22–23.

7. U.S. Secretaries and Exchange Commission Office of Investor Education and Assistance, *A Plain English Handbook: How to Create Clear SEC Disclosure Documents* (Washington, DC: 1998).

8. Eleanor Laise, "Some Consumers Say Wall Street Failed Them," *Wall Street Journal,* November 28, 2008, B1.

9. Gerard Braud, "What Does That Mean?" *Communication World* 24, no. 1 (2007): 34.

10. Richard Lederer and Richard Dowis, *Sleeping Dogs Don't Lay: Practical Advice for the Grammatically Challenged,* 1st ed. (New York: St. Martin's Press, 1999), 91–92.

11. James Suchan and Robert Colucci, "An Analysis of Communication Efficiency between High-Impact and Bureaucratic Written Communication," *Management Communication Quarterly* 2, no. 4 (1989): 464–73.

12. Hilvard G. Rogers and F. William Brown, "The Impact of Writing Style on Compliance with Instructions," *Journal of Technical Writing and Communication* 23, no. 1 (1993): 53–71.

13. Richard Lederer, "The Terrible Ten," *Toastmaster,* July 2003, 28–29.

14. Robert Frank, "The Wealth Report: Millionaires Need Not Apply; SEC and Others Rewrite the Definition of 'Rich'; The Haves and Have-Mores," *Wall Street Journal,* March 16, 2007, W2.

15. Geoff Mullins, "With Wetlands, Words Matter," *Ames Tribune,* April 3, 2008, A4.

16. Arlene Weintraub, "Revenge of the Overworked Nerds," *BusinessWeek,* December 8, 2003, 41.

17. Peter Conrad, *The Medicalization of Society: On the Transformation of Human Conditions into Treatable Disorders* (Baltimore: The Johns Hopkins University Press, 2007).

18. Chad Bray and Anjali Cordeiro, "Tobacco Firms Score Victory as Class-Action Suit Is Denied," *Wall Street Journal,* April 4, 2008, B3; and "FDA May Rephrase Pacemaker Warnings," *Wall Street Journal,* September 29, 2006, A8.

19. Interoffice memo in a steel company.

20. Quoted by Emery Hutchison, "Things My Mother Never Taught Me about Writing," *Journal of Organizational Communications* (1972): 20.

21. Mary Newton Bruder, *Much Ado about a Lot: How to Mind Your Manners in Print and in Person* (New York: Hyperion, 2000), 51.

22. Melinda Beck, "Getting an Earful: Testing a Tiny, Pricey Hearing Aid," *Wall Street Journal,* January 29, 2008, D1.

23. Miho Inada, "Is a Girdle Just for Men a Stretch? Japanese Company Calls Product 'Exercise Wear,' Says It Tones Muscles," *Wall Street Journal,* December 28, 2007, A8.

24. Jaguar ad, *Wall Street Journal,* September 29, 2000, A20.

25. Betsy Taylor, "Experts: Flood Terms Can Deceive," *Des Moines Register,* July 1, 2008, 9A.

26. Evan Perez, "Mukasey Cites Risk in Using Term 'Torture,'" *Wall Street Journal,* January 17, 2009, A2.

27. Richard C. Anderson, "Concretization and Sentence Learning," *Journal of Educational Psychology* 66, no. 2 (1974): 179–83.

28. Ben Worthen, "Oracle's Hot New Offering: Corporate Technobabble," *Wall Street Journal,* February 12, 2008, B4.

29. Pamela Layton and Adrian J. Simpson, "Deep Structure in Sentence Comprehension," *Journal of Verbal Learning and Verbal Behavior* 14 (1975); and Harris B. Savin and Ellen Perchonock, "Grammatical Structure and the Immediate Recall of English Sentences," *Journal of Verbal Learning and Verbal Behavior* 4 (1965): 348–53.

30. Federal Aviation Administration and Web Content Management Working Group of the Interagency Committee on Government Information, "How To/Tools: Checklist," in *PlainLanguage.gov: Improving Communication from the Federal Government to the Public,* http://www.plainlanguage.gov/howto/quickreference/checklist.cfm (accessed January 20, 2009).

31. Bill Walsh, *The Elephants of Style: A Trunkload of Tips on the Big Issues and Gray Areas of Contemporary American English* (New York: McGraw-Hill, 2004), 68.

32. Lloyd Bostian and Ann C. Thering, "Scientists: Can They Read What They Write?" *Journal of Technical Writing and Communication* 17 (1987): 417–27; E. B. Coleman, "The Comprehensibility of Several Grammatical Transformations," *Journal of Applied Psychology* 48, no. 3 (1964): 186–90; and Keith Rayner, "Visual Attention in Reading: Eye Movements Reflect Cognitive Processes," *Memory and Cognition* 5 (1977): 443–48.

33. Don Bush, "The Most Obvious Fault in Technical Writing," *Intercom*, July/August, 2003, 50.

34. Thomas N. Huckin, "A Cognitive Approach to Readability," in *New Essays in Technical and Scientific Communication: Research, Theory, Practice*, eds. Paul V. Anderson, R. John Brockmann, and Carolyn R. Miller (Farmingdale, NY: Baywood, 1983), 93–98.

35. James Suchan and Ronald Dulek, "A Reassessment of Clarity in Written Managerial Communications," *Management Communication Quarterly* 4, no. 1 (1990): 93–97.

36. Doris Kearns Goodwin, *Team of Rivals: The Political Genius of Abraham Lincoln* (New York: Simon & Schuster, 2005), 583–87.

37. "Law Typo Allows Children to Marry." *Des Moines Register*, August 18, 2007, 8A.

38. Ben Levisohn, "Write On, Dood," *BusinessWeek*, August 4, 2008, 16.

39. Lynne Truss, *Eats, Shoots & Leaves: The Zero Tolerance Approach to Punctuation* (New York: Gotham Books, 2003), 9–10.

40. Bill Walsh, *Lapsing into a Comma: A Curmudgeon's Guide to the Many Things that Can Go Wrong in Print—and How to Avoid Them* (Lincolnwood, IL: Contemporary Books, 2000), 1.

41. Judith Cape Craig, "The Missing Link between School and Work: Knowing the Demands of the Workplace," *English Journal* 91 no. 2 (2001): 46–50.

42. Dianna Booher, "Cutting Paperwork in the Corporate Culture," *New York: Facts on File Publications* (1986), 23.

43. Susan D. Kleimann, "The Complexity of Workplace Review," *Technical Communication* 38, no. 4 (1991): 520–26.

44. Glenn J. Broadhead and Richard C. Freed, *The Variables of Composition: Process and Product in a Business Setting*, Conference on College Composition and Communication Studies in Writing and Rhetoric (Carbondale, IL: Southern Illinois University Press, 1986), 57.

45. Janice C. Redish and Jack Selzer, "The Place of Readability Formulas in Technical Communication," *Technical Communication* 32, no. 4 (1985): 46–52.

Chapter 8

1. Eva R. Brumberger, "Visual Rhetoric in the Curriculum: Pedagogy for a Multimodal Workplace," *Business Communication Quarterly* 68, no. 3 (2005): 318–19.

2. Edward Tufte, *Beautiful Evidence* (Cheshire, CT: Graphics Press, 2006), 153–55.

3. Bruce Tognazzini, "The Butterfly Ballot: Anatomy of a Disaster," in *NN/g Home: Ask Tog: Columns*, http://www.asktog.com/columns/042ButterflyBallot.html (accessed March 7, 2009).

4. Charles Kostelnick and Michael Hassett, *Shaping Information: The Rhetoric of Visual Conventions* (Carbondale, IL: Southern Illinois University Press, 2003), 92, 94.

5. Kostelnick and Hassett, *Shaping Information*, 206–07.

6. Charles Kostelnick and David Roberts, *Designing Visual Language* (Boston: Allyn & Bacon, 1998), 85–87.

7. Christopher Toth, *Child's Play: Investigating the Genre of Toy Safety Recall Notices* (Iowa State University, 2009), 52–61.

8. George A. Miller, "The Magical Number Seven, Plus or Minus Two: Some Limits on Our Capacity for Processing Information," *Psychological Review* 63, no. 2 (1956): 81–97.

9. Jerry E. Bishop, "Word Processing: Research on Stroke Victims Yields Clues to the Brain's Capacity to Create Language," *Wall Street Journal*, October 12, 1993, A6; and Anne Meyer and David H. Rose, *Learning to Read in the Computer Age*, ed. Jeanne S. Chall, Reading Research to Practice (Cambridge, MA: Brookline Books, 1998), 4–6.

10. Karen A. Schriver, *Dynamics in Document Design* (New York: John Wiley & Sons, 1997), 274.

11. Jo Mackiewicz, "What Technical Writing Students Should Know about Typeface Personality," *Journal of Technical Writing and Communication* 34 no. 1–2 (2004): 113–31.

12. Russell N. Baird, Arthur T. Turnbull, and Duncan McDonald, *The Graphics of Communication: Typography, Layout, Design, Production*, 5th ed. (New York: Holt, Rinehart & Winston, 1987), 37.

13. Elizabeth Keyes, "Typography, Color, and Information Structure," *Technical Communication* 40, no. 4 (November 1993): 652; and Joseph Koncelik, "Design, Aging, Ethics, and the Law," Paper presented in Columbus, OH, May 6, 1993.

14. Judy Gregory, "Social Issues Infotainment: Using Emotion and Entertainment to Attract Readers' Attention in Social Issues Leaflets," *Information Design Journal* 11, no. 1 (2002–2003): 67–81.

15. Reid Goldsborough, "Substance, Not Style, Draws Hits," in *Philadelphia Inquirer: Personal Computing*, http://findarticles.com/p/articles/mi_kmtpi/is_200405/ai_kepm472154 (accessed March 7, 2009).

16. Lee Gomes, "Good Site, Bad Site: Evolving Web Design," *Wall Street Journal*, June 12, 2007, B3.

17. Jakob Nielsen, "F-Shaped Pattern for Reading Web Content," in *Jakob Nielsen's Alertbox: April 17, 2006*, http://www.useit.com/alertbox/reading_pattern.html (accessed March 7, 2009).

18. Harald Weinreich et al., "Not Quite the Average: An Empirical Study of Web Use," *ACM Transactions on the Web* 2, no. 1 (2008): 18.

19. Kostelnick and Hassett, *Shaping Information*, 160.

20. Jakob Nielsen, "Top Ten Mistakes in Web Design," in *Jacob Nielsen's Alertbox: Top 10 Design Mistakes*, http://www.useit.com/alertbox/9605.html (accessed March 7, 2009); and Emily Steel, "Neglected Banner Ads Get a Second Life," *Wall Street Journal*, June 20, 2007, B4.

21. "Corporate News: Target Settles with Blind Group on Web Access," *Wall Street Journal*, August 28, 2008, B4; and Lauren Pollock, "iTunes Eases Access for Blind," *Wall Street Journal*, September 29, 2008, B5.

22. Jakob Nielsen, "Why You Only Need to Test with 5 Users," in *Alertbox*, www.useit.com/alertbox/20000319.html (accessed March 7, 2009).

23. Jakob Nielsen, "Usability 101: Introduction to Usability," in *Jakob Nielsen's Alertbox: Usability 101: Definition and Fundamentals: What, Why, How*, http://www.useit.com/alertbox/20030825.html (accessed March 7, 2009).

Chapter 9

1. SmartMoney.com, "Market Map 1000," in *SmartMoney: Tools*, http://www.smartmoney.com/marketmap/ (accessed March 9, 2009); and Stephen H. Wildstrom, "A Picture Is Worth 1,000 Charts," *BusinessWeek*, January 20, 2003, 20.

2. Monica M. Clark, "Nielsen's 'People Meters' Go Top 10: Atlanta Debut Is Milestone for Device That's Redefining Local TV Audiences' Image," *Wall Street Journal*, June 30, 2006, B2.

3. Gerald J. Alred, Charles T. Brusaw, and Walter E. Oliu, *The Business Writer's Handbook*, 8th ed. (New York: St. Martin's Press, 2006), 248–50; William Horton, "The Almost Universal Language: Graphics for International Documents," *Technical Communication* 40, no. 4 (1993): 687; Thyra Rauch, "IBM Visual Interface Design," *The STC Usability PIC Newsletter*, January, 1996, 3; and L. G. Thorell and W. J. Smith,

Using Computer Color Effectively: An Illustrated Reference (Englewood Cliffs, NJ: Prentice Hall, 1990), 12–13.

4. Eric Kenly and Mark Beach, *Getting It Printed: How to Work with Printers and Graphic Imaging Services to Assure Quality, Stay on Schedule, and Control Costs,* 4th ed. (Cincinnati, OH: HOW Design Books, 2004), 68.

5. Miles A. Kimball and Ann R. Hawkins, *Document Design: A Guide for Technical Communicators* (Boston: Bedford/St. Martins, 2008), 253.

6. *The Chicago Manual of Style,* 15th ed. (Chicago: University of Chicago Press, 2003); and Edward R. Tufte, *The Visual Display of Quantitative Information,* 2nd ed. (Cheshire, CT: Graphics Press, 2001), 107–21.

7. Charles Kostelnick, "The Visual Rhetoric of Data Displays: The Conundrum of Clarity," *IEEE Transactions on Professional Communication* 51, no. 1 (2008): 116–30.

8. Jerry Bowyer, "In Defense of the Unemployment Rate," in *National Review Online: BuzzCharts: Financial,* http://article.nationalreview.com/?q=YzNiZGJjYTZlZDNlYzQzZjUxNzFlMWJkNjBiODIzMmI= (accessed March 7, 2009); Joint Economic Committee, "Charts: Economy," in, Charts & Data http://jec.senate.gov (accessed March 7, 2009); and Mark Gongloff, "Payroll Growth Disappoints," in *CNN Money,* http://money.cnn.com/2003/12/05/news/economy/jobs/index.htm (accessed March 7, 2009).

9. Tufte, *The Visual Display of Quantitative Information,* 74–75.

10. John Long, "Ethics in the Age of Digital Photography," in *National Press Photographers Association: Educational Workshops,* http://www.nppa.org/professional_development/self-training_resources/eadp_report/index.html (accessed March 7, 2009).

11. Rebecca E. Burnett, *Technical Communication,* 6th ed. (Boston: Thomson–Wadsworth, 2005), 426.

12. Peter Lattman, "Bingham Generates Buzz with Bear of an Ad Campaign," *Wall Street Journal,* December 26, 2007, B2.

13. Lon Tweeten, "Seek & Find," *Time,* June 25, 2007, 64.

14. Kostelnick, "The Visual Rhetoric of Data Displays: The Conundrum of Clarity," 116–30.

Chapter 10

1. Sara Silver, "With Its Future Now Uncertain, Bell Labs Turns to Commerce: Storied Font of Basic Research Gets More Practical Focus Amid Worry over a Merger," *Wall Street Journal,* August 21, 2006, A1.

2. G. Michael Campbell, *Bulletproof Presentations* (Franklin Lakes, NJ: Career Press, 2003), 66–67.

3. Julie Hill, "The Attention Deficit," *Presentations* 17, no. 10 (2003): 26.

4. Campbell, *Bulletproof Presentations,* 65.

5. Patricia Fripp, "Want Your Audiences to Remember What You Say? Learn the Importance of Clear Structure," in *Articles: Public Speaking and Presentation Skills Articles,* http://frippandassociates.com/art.clearstructure_faa.html (accessed March 21, 2009).

6. Tad Simmons, "Multimedia or Bust," *Presentations,* February 2000, 44, 48–50.

7. Julie Terberg, "Presentation Visuals Should Complement a Company's Printed Materials," *Presentations* 17, no. 1 (2003): 26–27.

8. Jon Birger et al., "The Best Advice I Ever Got," *Fortune,* May 12, 2008, 70.

9. Andy Rooney, "World Has Lost Mental Magician," *The Columbus Dispatch,* February 22, 1988, 7A.

10. Jennifer Saranow, "Show, Don't Tell: Microsoft and H-P Are Heading to Retail Outlets to Overcome a Big Impediment to Sales: Ignorance," *Wall Street Journal,* March 22, 2004, R-9.

11. Chip Heath and Dan Heath, *Made to Stick: Why Some Ideas Survive and Others Die* (New York: Random House, 2007), 7.

12. Heath and Heath, *Made to Stick,* 16–18.

13. Simmons, "Multimedia or Bust." 44, 48–50

14. Kazutaka Kurihara et al., "Presentation Sensei: A Presentation Training System Using Speech and Image Processing" (paper presented at the Proceedings of the 9th International Conference on Multimodal Interfaces, 2007), 358–65.

15. Ann Burnett and Diane M. Badzinski, "Judge Nonverbal Communication on Trial: Do Mock Trial Jurors Notice?" *Journal of Communication* 55, no. 2 (2005): 209–24.

16. Judee K. Burgoon, Thomas Birk, and Michael Pfau, "Nonverbal Behaviors, Persuasion, and Credibility," *Human Communication Research* 17, no. 1 (1990): 140–69.

17. Campbell, *Bulletproof Presentations,* 44–45, 126–27.

18. Michael Waldholz, "Lab Notes," *Wall Street Journal,* March 19, 1991, B1; and Dave Zielinski, "Perfect Practice," *Presentations* 17, no. 5 (2003): 30–36.

19. Campbell, *Bulletproof Presentations,* 122.

Chapter 11

1. Richard Nelson Bolles, *What Color Is Your Parachute? A Practical Manual for Job-Hunters and Career-Changers* (Berkeley: Ten Speed Press, 2007), 209.

2. Dana Mattioli, "Who's Reading Online Résumés? Identity Crooks," *Wall Street Journal,* October 17, 2006, B9.

3. Sarah E. Needleman, "It Isn't Always a Job behind an Online Job Posting: Employment Ads on the Web Can Lead You to Marketing Pitches, or Worse: Ways to See Which Ones Are Sincere," *Wall Street Journal,* February 17, 2009, B14.

4. Anne Fisher, "Does a Résumé Have to Be One Page Long?" in *CNNMoney.com: Fortune: Commentary: Ask Annie,* http://money.cnn.com/2007/03/28/news/economy/resume.fortune/index.htm?postversion=2007032911 (accessed March 10, 2009).

5. Elizabeth Blackburn–Brockman and Kelly Belanger, "One Page or Two? A National Study of CPA Recruiters' Preferences for Résumé Length," *The Journal of Business Communication* 38 (2001): 29–45.

6. David Koeppel, "Those Low Grades in College May Haunt Your Job Search," *New York Times,* December 31, 2006, 1.

7. Anjali Athavaley, "Job References You Can't Control," *Wall Street Journal,* September 27, 2007, D1.

8. Sue Shellenbarger, "Turning Stay-at-Home Skills into Career-Track Assets," *Wall Street Journal,* March 8, 2007, D1.

9. Roni Noland, "It's Not a Disaster if Your Old Boss Won't Provide a Reference," *Boston Globe,* March 8, 2009, 5.

10. Phil Elder, "The Trade Secrets of Employment Interviews" (paper presented at the Association for Business Communication Midwest Convention, Kansas City, MO, May 2, 1987).

11. Douglas MacMillan, "The Art of the Online Résumé: How to Get Yours Past Electronic Filters That Cull the Herd of Applicants," *BusinessWeek,* May 7, 2007, 86.

12. Katharine Hansen, "Quintessential Careers: Tapping the Power of Keywords to Enhance Your Résumé's Effectiveness," in *Words to Get Hired By: The Jobseeker's Quintessential Lexicon of Powerful Words and Phrases for Résumés and Cover Letters,* http://www.quintcareers.com/printable/resume_keywords.html (accessed March 10, 2009).

13. "Nearly Half of Employers Have Caught a Lie on a Résumé, CareerBuilder.com Survey Shows," in *Share: About*

Us: Press Release: July 30, 2008, http://www.careerbuilder. com/share/aboutus/pressreleasesdetail.aspx?id= pr448&sd=7/30/2008&ed=7/30/2099 (accessed March 13, 2009).

14. Sarah E. Needleman, "Recruiters Are On to Résumé Tricks: Thanks to Technology Advances, Some Sneakier Tactics of Job Hunters No Longer Work," *The Globe and Mail (Canada),* May 9, 2007, C7.

15. Mattioli, "Who's Reading Online Résumés? Identity Crooks," B9.

16. John B. Killoran, "Self-Published Web Résumés: Their Purposes and Their Genre Systems," *Journal of Business and Technical Communication* 20, no. 4 (2006): 425–59.

17. Keith J. Winstein and Daniel Golden, "MIT Admissions Dean Lied on Résumé in 1979, Quits," *Wall Street Journal,* April 27, 2007, B1.

18. Lisa Takeuchi Cullen, "Getting Wise to Lies," *Time,* May 1, 2006, 59.

19. Jon Weinbach, "The Admissions Police," *Wall Street Journal,* April 6, 2007, W1, W10.

20. ". . . And I Invented Velcro," *BusinessWeek,* August 4, 2008; "Nearly Half of Employers Have Caught a Lie on a Résumé, CareerBuilder.com Survey Shows"; and Cari Tuna and Keith J Winstein, "Economy Promises to Fuel Résumé Fraud: Practices Vary for Vetting Prospective Employees, but Executives Usually Face Tougher Background Checks," *Wall Street Journal,* November 17, 2008, B4.

Chapter 12

1. Max Messmer, "Cover Letter Still Important in Online Age," *Pittsburgh Post–Gazette,* August 10, 2008, J1.

2. Katharine Hansen and Randall Hansen, "The Basics of a Dynamic Cover Letter," in *Cover Letter Resources for Job-Seekers,* http://www.quintcareers.com/cover_letter_ basics.html (accessed May 29, 2007).

Chapter 13

1. "The Personal Connection: Survey Shows That in Hiring Process, There's No Substitute for Being There," in *Accountemps: Press Releases: September 11, 2008,* http://www. accountemps.com/PressRoom?id=2318 (accessed March 19, 2009).

2. Thomas Petzinger, Jr., "Lewis Roland's Knack for Finding Truckers Keeps Firm Rolling," *Wall Street Journal,* December 1, 1995, B1.

3. Rachel Emma Silverman, "Choosing the Appropriate Clothes Adds to Stress of the Job Interview," in *Wall Street Journal: Careers: Career Strategies: Managing Your Career,* http://online.wsj.com/article/SB987460110121095208. html (accessed March 19, 2009).

4. Victoria Knight, "Personality Tests as Hiring Tools," in *Wall Street Journal: Business,* http://online.wsj.com/article/ SB114237811535098217.html (accessed March 19, 2009).

5. Dana Mattioli, "Sober Thought: How to Mix Work, Alcohol: Taking Cues from Bosses and Clients Can Keep Parties or Meals under Control," *Wall Street Journal,* December 5, 2006, B10.

6. Geoff Smart and Randy Street, *Who: The A Method for Hiring* (New York: Ballantine, 2008), 121.

7. Rachel Emma Silverman, "Great Expectations," *Wall Street Journal,* July 25, 2000, B10.

Chapter 14

1. Mike Musgrove, "Some E-Mail Recipients Say, 'Enough!'" *Washington Post,* May 26, 2007, A1.

2. Rebecca Buckman, "Email's Friendly Fire," *Wall Street Journal,* November 27, 2007, B1.

3. Gail Fann Thomas and Cynthia L. King, "Reconceptualizing E-Mail Overload," *Journal of Business and Technical Communication* 20, no. 3 (2006): 252–87.

4. David Dawley and William Anthony, "User Perceptions of E-Mail at Work," *Journal of Business and Technical Communication* 17, no. 2 (2003): 170–200.

5. Cristina Zucchermaglio and Alessandra Talamo, "The Development of a Virtual Community of Practices Using Electronic Mail and Communicative Genres," *Journal of Business and Technical Communication* 17, no. 3 (2003): 259–84.

6. Diane Brady, "*!#?@ the E-Mail. Can We Talk?" *BusinessWeek,* December 4, 2006, 109.

7. Mitch Stacy, "Police Hope Youths Use Texting to Send Tips," *Des Moines Register,* July, 8, 2008, 3AA.

8. Gail Fann Thomas and Cynthia L King, "Reconceptualizing E-Mail Overload," 253.

9. Kristin Byron, "Carrying Too Heavy a Load? The Communication and Miscommunication of Emotion by E-Mail," *Academy of Management Review* 33, no. 2 (2008): 309–27.

10. Jane Larson, "Be Careful with Business E-Mail Content," *Des Moines Register,* January 21, 2008, 2D.

11. Dinesh Ramde, "Anti-War E-Mail to Soldier Stirs Furor," *Des Moines Register,* January 24, 2007, 5A.

12. Laura Gunderson, "Coupon Isn't Worth Beans at Starbucks," *The Oregonian,* August 31, 2006.

13. Nicholas Hoover, "More E-mail, More Problems," *InformationWeek,* January 22, 2007, 43–47.

14. MailerMailer LLC, "Email Marketing Metrics Report: November 2008," in *Email Marketing Metrics,* http://image hosting.mailermailer.com/email-marketing-metrics-2008h1.pdf (accessed March 17, 2009).

15. Gilbert Ross, "Black Box Backfire," *Wall Street Journal,* April 21, 2007, A8.

16. Jeanne Whalen, "Shareholders Sue Glaxo over Avandia Disclosure," *Wall Street Journal,* June 13, 2007, D7.

17. Mike Spector, "New IRS Rules Help Donors Vet Charities: Revised Tax Form Will Make Nonprofits Reveal More about How They Spend," *Wall Street Journal,* May 29, 2008, D1.

18. Bob Mills, e-mail message to author.

19. Richard Carlson, *Don't Sweat the Small Stuff at Work: Simple Ways to Minimize Stress and Conflict While Bringing Out the Best in Yourself and Others* (New York: Hyperion, 1998), 266.

20. "Lighting a Fire under Campbell," *BusinessWeek,* December 4, 2006, 96; Alison Overholt, "Power Up the People," *Fast Company,* January, 2003, 50; and Philip Rosedale and Michael Fitzgerald, "How I Did It: Philip Rosedale," *Inc.,* February, 2007, 85.

21. Kenneth Blanchard and Spencer Johnson, *The One Minute Manager* (New York: William Morrow, 1982), 19.

Chapter 15

1. Ben Levisohn, "Getting More Workers to Whistle," *BusinessWeek,* January 28, 2008, 18.

2. Daniel Goleman, Richard Boyatzis, and Anni McKee, *Primal Leadership: Learning to Lead with Emotional Intelligence* (Boston: Harvard Business School Press, 2002), 16.

3. Robert I. Sutton, *The No Asshole Rule: Building a Civilized Workplace and Surviving One That Isn't* (New York: Warner Business Books, 2007), 45–48.

4. William Ury, *The Power of a Positive No: How to Say No and Still Get to Yes* (New York: Bantam Books, 2007), 41–42.

5. Peter D. Timmerman and Wayne Harrison, "The Discretionary Use of Electronic Media: Four Considerations for

Bad News Bearers," *Journal of Business Communication* 42, no. 4 (2005): 379–89.

6. Holly Dolezalek, "Opening Up the Books," *Training,* April 2006, 44.

7. Kitty O. Locker, "Factors in Reader Responses to Negative Letters: Experimental Evidence for Changing What We Teach," *Journal of Business and Technical Communication* 13, no. 1 (January 1999): 21.

8. Locker, "Factors in Reader Responses to Negative Letters: Experimental Evidence for Changing What We Teach," 25–26.

9. Sharon S. Brehm and Jack W. Brehm, *Psychological Reactance: A Theory of Freedom and Control* (New York: Academic Press, 1981), 3.

10. Melanie Trottman and Andy Pasztor, "Southwest Airlines CEO Apologizes for Lapses," *Wall Street Journal,* March 14, 2008, B1.

11. hallmark@update.hallmark.com, e-mail message to author, May 8, 2007.

12. Scott McCartney, "What Airlines Do When You Complain," *Wall Street Journal,* March 20, 2007, D1; and Nick Wingfield, "Steve Jobs Offers Rare Apology Credit for iPhone," *Wall Street Journal,* September 7, 2007, B1.

13. Ury, *The Power of a Positive No: How to Say No and Still Get to Yes,* 19.

14. "United Airlines to Unplug Number of Complaints," *Wall Street Journal,* February 11, 2009, D6.

15. Knowledge @W. P. Carey, "Customer Rage: It's Not Always about the Money," in *Marketing and Services Leadership,* http://knowledge.wpcarey.asu.edu/article.cfm?articleid=1143&specialid=27 (accessed March 30, 2009).

16. Stephen W. Gilliland et al., "Improving Applicants' Reactions to Rejection Letters: An Application of Fairness Theory," *Personnel Psychology* 54, no. 3 (2001): 669–704; and Robert E. Ployhart, Karen Holcombe Ehrhart, and Seth C. Hayes, "Using Attributions to Understand the Effects of Explanations on Applicant Reactions: Are Reactions Consistent with the Covariation Principle?" *Journal of Applied Social Psychology* 35, no. 2 (2005): 259–96.

17. John P. Hausknecht, David V. Day, and Scott C. Thomas, "Applicant Reactions to Selection Procedures: An Updated Model and Meta-analysis," *Personnel Psychology* 57, no. 3 (2004): 639–84.

18. Elizabeth A. McCord, "The Business Writer, the Law, and Routine Business Communication: A Legal and Rhetorical Analysis," *Journal of Business and Technical Communication* 5, no. 2 (1991): 183.

19. Kenneth Blanchard and Spencer Johnson, *The One Minute Manager* (New York: William Morrow, 1982), 59.

20. Carol Hymowitz, "Though Now Routine, Bosses Still Stumble During Layoff Process," *Wall Street Journal,* June 25, 2007, B1.

21. Carol Hymowitz, "Personal Boundaries Shrink as Companies Punish Bad Behavior," *Wall Street Journal,* June 18, 2007, B1.

22. Tara Weiss, "You've Got Mail: You're Fired," in *Leadership: Management Mistakes,* http://www.forbes.com/2006/08/31/leadership-radio-shack-management-cx_tw_0831layoffs.html (accessed March 29, 2009).

Chapter 16

1. Jay A. Conger, "The Necessary Art of Persuasion," *Harvard Business Review* 76, no. 3 (May–June 1998): 88.

2. John Kotter and Holger Rathgeber, *Our Iceberg Is Melting: Changing and Succeeding under Any Conditions* (New York: St. Martin's Press, 2005), 140.

3. Jonah Lehrer, *How We Decide* (New York: Houghton Mifflin Harcourt, 2009), 26, 235.

4. EACA Promotional Marketing Council, "Cyriel (84) Needs a Job," in *European Awards 2006: The Media,* http://www.adforum.com/affiliates/creative_archive/2006/AW888891_PMC/reel_detail2.asp?ID=6684218&TDI=VD16Kqqetr&PAGE=1&bShop=&awcat=&ob=intlevel&awid= (accessed March 18, 2009).

5. Chip Heath and Dan Heath, *Made to Stick: Why Some Ideas Survive and Others Die* (New York: Random House, 2007), 195–98; and Mark Schoofs, "Novel Police Tactic Puts Drug Markets out of Business: Confronted by the Evidence, Dealers in High Point, N.C., Succumb to Pressure," *Wall Street Journal,* September 27, 2006, A1, A16.

6. Min-Sun Kim and Steven R. Wilson, "A Cross-Cultural Comparison of Implicit Theories of Requesting," *Communication Monographs* 61, no. 3 (September 1994): 210–35; and K. Yoon, C. H. Kim, and M. S. Kim, "A Cross-Cultural Comparison of the Effects of Source Credibility on Attitudes and Behavioral Intentions," *Mass Communication and Society* 1, no. 3&4 (1998): 153–73.

7. Daniel D. Ding, "An Indirect Style in Business Communication," *Journal of Business and Technical Communication* 20, no. 1 (2006): 87–100.

8. Stephanie Kang, "Pitches to Hispanics Get More Nuanced," *Wall Street Journal,* January 8, 2008, B7.

9. E. L. Fink et al., "The Semantics of Social Influence: Threats vs. Persuasion," *Communication Monographs* 70, no. 4 (2003): 295–316.

10. G. W. Dudley, J. F. Tanner, and C. A. Fletcher, "What Motivates UK Salespeople to Sell? New University Study Shows Sales Motivation Differs by Country," *PR Newswire,* February 11, 2004.

11. Malcolm Gladwell, *The Tipping Point: How Little Things Can Make a Big Difference* (New York: Little, Brown and Company, 2002), 96–98.

12. Judge Baker Children's Center and Campaign for a Commercial-Free Childhood, "Tell Toy Companies: Target Parents, Not Kids, with Holiday Ads," in *CCFC Guide to Commercial-Free Holidays,* http://salsa.democracyinaction.org/o/621/t/6914/campaign.jsp?campaign_KEY=26139 (accessed April 5, 2009).

13. Ray Considine and Murray Raphael, *The Great Brain Robbery* (Los Angeles: Rosebud Books, 1980), 95–96.

14. Phred Dvorak, "How Understanding the 'Why' of Decisions Matters," *Wall Street Journal,* March 19, 2007, B3.

15. Heath and Heath, *Made to Stick: Why Some Ideas Survive and Others Die,* 165–68.

16. Used Cardboard Boxes, "The Cheapest, Easiest, and Most Earth-Friendly Way to Get Boxes for Packing, Moving, Shipping and Storage," in *Our Company: About Us,* http://www.usedcardboardboxes.com/static_page.php?id=1 (accessed April 5, 2009).

17. Martin Lindstrom, *Buyology: Truth and Lies about Why We Buy* (New York: Doubleday, 2008), 133–34.

18. "Around the World," *Washington Post,* March 27, 2009, A14.

19. Brian Steinberg, "Kraft Vies for Eyes—and Noses: Ad Play in People Magazine Uses Some Scented Spots to Tickle Readers' Fancy," *Wall Street Journal,* November 13, 2006, B5.

20. Susan Linn and Alvin Poussaint, "Campaign for a Commercial-Free Childhood," in *Judge Baker Children's Center,* http://www.commercialfreechildhood.org/actions/lettertoceo.pdf (accessed April 5, 2009).

21. Samuel A. Culbert, "Get Rid of the Performance Review! It Destroys Morale, Kills Teamwork and Hurts the Bottom

Line. And That's Just for Starters," *Wall Street Journal,* October 20, 2008, R4; and Jared Sandberg, "Performance Reviews Need Some Work, Don't Meet Potential," *Wall Street Journal,* November 20, 2007, B1.

22. Jeffrey Zaslow, "The Most-Praised Generation Goes to Work," *Wall Street Journal,* April 20, 2007, W1, W7.

23. Erin White, "For Relevance, Firms Revamp Worker Reviews," *Wall Street Journal,* July 17, 2006, B1, B5.

24. Steve Salerno, "As Seen on TV: But Wait . . . There's More!," *Wall Street Journal,* March 25, 2009, A11.

25. Robert Guth, "How Microsoft Is Learning to Love Online Advertising," *Wall Street Journal,* November 16, 2006, A1; and Brian Steinberg, "Philips Bets Magazine Readers Need a Reprieve," *Wall Street Journal,* August 1, 2006, B2.

26. Ken Magill, "E-mail Tops in ROI," in *DM Disciplines: Email,* http://directmag.com/disciplines/email/market-ing_email_tops_roi/ (accessed March 18, 2009).

27. John D. Beard, David L. Williams, and J. Patrick Kelly, "The Long versus the Short Letter: A Large Sample Study of a Direct-Mail Campaign," *Journal of Direct Marketing* 4, no. 12 (Winter 1990): 13–20.

28. "How To Launch a Direct-Mail Campaign," *BusinessWeek SmallBiz,* August/September 2008, 28.

29. Barbara Kiviat, "Why We Buy: Consumers Tend to Go with What (Little) They Know," *Time,* August 27, 2007, 50–51.

30. Jeffrey Gitomer, *Little Red Book of Sales Answers: 99.5 Real World Answers That Make Sense, Make Sales, and Make Money* (Upper Saddle River, NJ: Prentice Hall, 2005), 112.

31. Beth Negus Viveiros, "Gifts for Life," *Direct,* July (2004): 9.

32. "How CARE Is Fighting Poverty," in *Home, Campaigns, Poverty Solutions from CARE,* http://www.care.org/cam-paigns/poverty.asp?s_src=170960110000&s_subsrc= (accessed April 5, 2009).

33. Lee Rood, "Little Raised over Phone Goes to Charity," *Des Moines Register,* December 14, 2008, 1A.

34. "Reading Is Fundamental: Stealing the Best Ideas from Leading Fundraisers," *Non-Profit Times* 16, no. 22 (2002): 1–5.

35. Maxwell Sackheim, *My First Sixty-Five Years in Advertising* (Blue Ridge Summit, PA: Tab Books, 1975), 97–100.

Chapter 17

1. L. Gordon Crovitz, "Wikipedia's Old-Fashioned Revolution," *Wall Street Journal,* April 6, 2009, A13.

2. Katie Hafner, "Seeing Corporate Fingerprints in Wikipedia Edits," in *The New York Times: Technology,* http://www.nytimes.com/2007/08/19/technology/19wikipedia.html?_r=1 (accessed April 10, 2009).

3. Phred Dvorak, "Companies Seek Shareholder Input on Pay Practices: Amid Anger over Compensation Packages, Executives and Directors Look for New Ways to Appease Investors," *Wall Street Journal,* April 6, 2009, B4.

4. Palmer Morrel-Samuels, "Getting the Truth into Workplace Surveys," *Harvard Business Review* 80, no. 2 (2002): 111–18.

5. See, for example, Public Agenda, "Many Who Say Homosexual Relations Should Be Illegal Change Their Minds When Told It Could Mean That Consenting Adults Could Be Prosecuted for Activities in Their Own Homes," in *Charts,* http://www.publicagenda.org/charts/many-who-say-homosexual-relations-should-be-illegal-change-their-minds-when-told-it-could-mean-consenting-adults (accessed April 10, 2009); and Public Agenda, "Now Online—Just the Facts on Gay Rights,"

in *Press Releases,* http://www.publicagenda.org/press-releases/now-online-just-facts-gay-rights (accessed April 10, 2009).

6. Public Agenda, "20 Questions Journalists Should Ask about Poll Results," in *Articles & Speeches,* http://www.publicagenda.org/pages/20-questions-journalists-should-ask-about-poll-results (accessed April 10, 2009).

7. Morrel-Samuels, "Getting the Truth into Workplace Surveys," 116.

8. Palmer Morrel-Samuels, "Web Surveys' Hidden Hazards," *Harvard Business Review* 81, no. 7 (2003): 16–17; and Jakob Nielsen, "Keep Online Surveys Short," in *Alertbox,* http://www.useit.com/alertbox/20040202.html (accessed March 18, 2009).

9. J. Michael Brick et al., "Cell Phone Survey Feasibility in the U.S.: Sampling and Calling Cell Numbers versus Landline Numbers," *Public Opinion Quarterly* 71, no. 1 (Spring 2007): 36.

10. Alan Fram, "Cell Phones Only," *Associated Press Archive,* May 14, 2008.

11. Richard Curtin, Stanley Presser, and Eleanor Singer, "Changes in Telephone Survey Nonreponse over the Past Quarter Century," *Public Opinion Research Quarterly* 69, no. 1 (2005): 87–98.

12. Council for Marketing and Opinion Research, "Recommendations to Improve Respondent Cooperation," in *CMOR: Respondent Cooperation: Tools of the Trade,* http://www.cmor.org/rc/tools.cfm (accessed March 18, 2009).

13. Sharon L. Lohr, *Sampling: Design and Analysis* (Pacific Grove, CA: Duxbury Press, 1999), 3.

14. Cynthia Crossen, "Fiasco in 1936 Survey Brought 'Science' to Election Polling," *Wall Street Journal,* October 2, 2006, B1.

15. Carl Bialik, "Which Is Epidemic–Sexting or Worrying about It? Cyberpolls, Relying on Skewed Samples of Techno-Teen, Aren't Always Worth the Paper They're Not Printed On," *Wall Street Journal,* April 8, 2009, A9.

16. Earl E. McDowell, Bridget Mrolza, and Emmy Reppe, "An Investigation of the Interviewing Practices of Technical Writers in Their World of Work," in *Interviewing Practices for Technical Writers,* ed. Earl E. McDowell (Amityville, NY: Baywood Publishing, 1991), 207.

17. Thomas Hunter, "Pulitzer Winner Discusses Interviewing," *IABC Communication World,* April 1985, 13–14.

18. Julie Jargon, "Kiwi Goes beyond Shine in Effort to Step Up Sales," *Wall Street Journal,* December 20, 2007, B1.

19. Peter Noel Murray, "Focus Groups Are Valid When Done Right," *Marketing News,* September 1, 2006, 21, 25.

20. Emily Steel, "The New Focus Groups: Online Networks: Proprietary Panels Help Consumer Companies Shape Products, Ads," *Wall Street Journal,* January 14, 2008, B6.

21. Louise Witt, "Inside Intent," *American Demographics* 26, no. 2 (2004): 34.

22. Suzanne Vranica, "Upfront Deal Turns the Corner; NBC Universal Pact Uses New System Covering Ads Watched via DVR," *Wall Street Journal,* June 14, 2007, B5.

23. Emily Steel, "TV Networks Launch Big Campus Push; New Nielsen System Makes College Students Coveted-Ratings Draw," *Wall Street Journal,* March 5, 2007, B3.

24. Christopher Meyer and Andre Schwager, "Understanding Customer Experience," *Harvard Business Review* 85, no. 2 (2007): 116–26.

25. Nandini Lakshman, "Nokia's Global Design Sense," in *Inside Innovation,* http://www.businessweek.com/print/

innovate/content/aug2007/id20070810_686743.htm (accessed April 10, 2009).

26. Daniel Kruger, "You Want Data with That?" *Forbes* 173, no. 6 (2004): 58.

27. Shirley S. Wang, "Health Care Taps 'Mystery Shoppers'; To Improve Service, Hospitals and Doctors Hire Spies to Pose as Patients and Report Back," *Wall Street Journal*, August 8, 2006, D1.

Chapter 18

1. For a useful taxonomy of proposals, see Richard C. Freed and David D. Roberts, "The Nature, Classification, and Generic Structure of Proposals," *Journal of Technical Writing and Communication* 19, no. 4 (1989): 317–51.

2. Dana Topousis, "Fact Sheet: National Science Foundation," in *News*, http://www.nsf.gov/news/news_summ. jsp?cntn_id=100595 (accessed April 11, 2009); and Elias A. Zerhouni, "FY 2009 Director's Budget Request Statement," in *Home: About NIH: Director: Budget Requests*, http://www.nih.gov/about/director/budgetrequest/ fy2009directorssenatebudgetrequest.htm (accessed April 11, 2009).

3. Julianne Pepitone, "Census Bureau Submits $1B Job Creation Proposal: Agency Received Funds through the Stimulus Measure," in *News: Economy: Census Stimulus*, http:// money.cnn.com/2009/04/10/news/economy/census_ stimulus/index.htm (accessed April 11, 2009).

4. Susan J. Wells, "Merging Compensation Strategies," *HRMagazine* 49, no. 5 (2004): 66.

5. Wells, "Merging Compensation Strategies," 66.

6. Todd Dorman, "No Double-Space? No Grant for You: Preschool Grants Tossed for Failing to Double-Space on Application," *Ames Tribune*, September 12, 2007, B1.

7. Laura K. Grove, "Finding Funding: Writing Winning Proposals for Research Funds," *Technical Communication* 51 (2004): 25–33.

8. Christine Peterson Barabas, *Technical Writing in a Corporate Culture: A Study of the Nature of Information* (Norwood, NJ: Ablex Publishing, 1990), 327.

Chapter 19

1. Michael Schrage, "Take the Lazy Way Out? That's Far Too Much Work," *Fortune*, February 5, 2001, 212.

2. Patty Reinert, "Andersen Reportedly Missed $644 Million Error in NASA Audit," *Houston Chronicle*, January 30, 2002, 15A.

3. Michael D. Lemonick, "Medicine's Secret Stat," *Time*, February 26, 2007, 54.

4. Jeffrey Zaslow, "An Iconic Report 20 Years Later: Many of Those Women Married After All," *Wall Street Journal*, May 25, 2006, D1.

5. Arlene Weintraub, "What the Doctors Aren't Disclosing: A New Study Shows How Authors of Medical Journal Articles Flout Rules on Revealing Conflicts of Interest," *BusinessWeek*, May 26, 2008, 32.

6. Erick H. Turner et al., "Selective Publication of Antidepressant Trials and Its Influence on Apparent Efficacy," *New England Journal of Medicine* 358, no. 3 (2008): 252.

7. Nielsen Media Research, "Our Measurement Techniques," in *Inside TV Ratings: Meters & Diaries*, http:// www.nielsenmedia.com/nc/portal/site/Public/menuit em.55dc65b4a7d5adff3f65936147a062a0/?vgnextoid=096 047f8b5264010VgnVCM100000880a260aRCRD (accessed April 7, 2009).

8. "United States: The Ladder of Fame; College Education," *The Economist*, August 26, 2006, 35.

9. Mylene Mangalindan, "Web Ads on the Rebound," *Wall Street Journal*, August 25, 2003, B1, B6; and Michael Totty, "At Last, a Way to Measure Ads," *Wall Street Journal*, June 16, 2003, R4.

10. Mangalindan, "Web Ads on the Rebound"; and Tracie Rozhon, "Networks Criticize Report on Male Viewers," *New York Times*, November 26, 2003, 8.

11. Emily Steel, "Networks Launch Big Campus Push; New Nielsen System Makes College Students Coveted-Ratings Draw," *Wall Street Journal*, March 5, 2007, B3.

12. Jakob Nielsen, "Risks of Quantitative Studies," in *Alertbox*, http://www.useit.com/alertbox/20040301.html (accessed April 7, 2009).

13. Stephen E. Moore, "655,000 War Dead?" *Wall Street Journal*, October 18, 2006, A20.

14. Neil Munro and Carl M. Cannon, "Data Bomb," in *National Journal: News Features: Cover Story*, http://news.national- aljournal.com/articles/databomb/index.htm (accessed April 12, 2009).

15. Malcolm Gladwell, *The Tipping Point: How Little Things Can Make a Big Difference* (New York: Little, Brown, 2002), 146; and Steven D. Levitt and Stephen J. Dubner, *Freakonomics: A Rogue Economist Explores the Hidden Side of Everything* (New York: William Morrow, 2005), 119–41.

16. Carl Bialik, "Weddings Are Not the Budget Drains Some Surveys Suggest," *Wall Street Journal*, August 24, 2007, B1.

17. U.S. Department of Transportation, "DOT Announces Historic Low Highway Fatality Rate in 2003," in *In the News: 2004 Press Releases: August 10*, http://www.nhtsa.dot.gov/ portal/site/nhtsa/template.MAXIMIZE/menuitem.f2217 bee37fb302f6d7c121046108a0c/?javax.portlet.tpst=1e5153 1b2220b0f8ea14201046108a0c_ws_MX&javax.portlet.prp_ 1e51531b2220b0f8ea14201046108a0c_viewID=detail_view &itemID=79f433612d89ff00VgnVCM1000002c567798RCR D&pressReleaseYearSelect=2004 (accessed April 7, 2009); and Joseph B. White, "A Turbulent Transition for SUVs: Safety Reports on SUVs and Fuel Laws Paint a Puzzling Picture for Consumers," in *Life & Style: Autos: Eyes on the Road*, http://online.wsj.com/article/0,SB109242124890391151- search,00.html?collection=autowire (accessed April 7, 2009).

18. Dan Ackman, "SUVs Deadly to Car Drivers," in *Business: Autos: August 20, 2004*, http://www.forbes.com/2004/ 08/20/cx_da_0820suv.html (accessed April 7, 2009); Daren Fonda, "The Shrinking SUV," *Time*, August 30, 2004, 65; and Danny Hakim, "Safety Gap Grows Wider between SUVs and Cars," *New York Times*, August 17, 2004, Business/Financial Desk 1.

19. Byron Sharp, "Comparative Quackery," *New Zealand Marketing Magazine*, June 2004.

20. Vivien Beattie, Alpa Dhanani, and Michael John Jones, "Longitudinal Perspective Investigating Presentational Change in U.K. Annual Reports," *Journal of Business Communication* 45, no. 2 (2008): 186, 95.

21. Carl Bialik, "Numbers Show China Beats U.S. in Net Use, but Which Numbers?" *Wall Street Journal*, March 28, 2008, B1.

22. Nielsen, "Risks of Quantitative Studies"; and Dan Seligman, "The Story They All Got Wrong," *Forbes* 170, no. 11 (November 25, 2002): 124.

23. "Tiger Effect? Not This Year," *Wall Street Journal*, April 15, 2008, B6.

24. "NASA Releases Information on Federal Survey of Pilots," *Des Moines Register*, January 1, 2008, 2A.

25. Brad Cleveland, "Reporting Call Center Activity," *Call Center* 16, no. 12 (December 1, 2003): 36.

26. James Paradis, David Dobrin, and Richard Miller, "Writing at Exxon ITD: Notes on the Writing Environment of an R&D Organization," in *Writing in Nonacademic Settings* (New York: Guilford, 1985), 300–2.

27. George A. Miller, "The Magical Number Seven, Plus or Minus Two: Some Limits on Our Capacity for Processing Information," *Psychological Review* 63, no. 2 (1956): 81–97.

28. Christopher Marquis, "Reports on Attacks Are Gripping, Not Dry," *New York Times,* June 20, 2004, 27.

Chapter 1

Page 3, U.S. Coast Guard photograph by Petty Officer 2nd Class NyxoLyno Cangemi
Page 6, The McGraw-Hill Companies, Inc./Jill Braaten, photographer
Page 11, AP Images/NASA/JPL/Caltech

Chapter 2

Page 29, Courtesy of KeyBank
Page 30, Courtesy of the Dow Chemical Company
Page 32, JOHN KUNTZ/The Plain Dealer/Landov
Page 35, © LWA-Dann Tardif/Corbis
Page 37, MY M&M'S ® is a registered trademark of Mars, Incorporated and its affiliates. This trademark is used with permission. Mars, Incorporated is not associated with McGraw-Hill Higher Education. Advertisement printed with permission of Mars, Incorporated.
Page 47, © Anoek De Groot/AFP/Getty Images

Chapter 3

Page 61, © George Rose/Getty Images
Page 65, AP Images/Orlin Wagner
Page 71, Kitty O. Locker, by permission of Joseph-Beth Booksellers
Page 78, AP Images/Bill Sikes

Chapter 4

Page 89, © David Cannon/Getty Images
Page 91, © Digital Vision/Getty Images
Page 92, © Angelo Cavalli/Getty Images/The Image Bank
Page 96, Courtesy of McAfee.com
Page 97, © Shuji Kobayashi/Getty Images/Stone
Page 100, © Tim Graham/Getty Images
Page 101, © Jose Luis Pelaez, Inc./Corbis
Page 103, Doug Sherman/Geofile
Page 107, Courtesy of Fujitsu Computer Products of America, Inc.
Page 108, © Kelvin Murray/Getty Images/Stone
Page 112, © Jeff Sciortino Photography
Page 112, © Jeff Sciortino Photography
Page 113, © Keith Brofsky/Getty Images

Chapter 5

Page 125, © Bill Pugliano/Getty Images
Page 128, © Matt Stroshane/epa/Corbis
Page 132, © Toru Yamanaka/AFP/Getty Images
Page 133, © Matthew Ashton/Alamy
Page 134, Photo by Harry Baumert, Copyright 2006, The Des Moines Register and Tribune Company. Reprinted with permission.
Page 136, © PCL/Alamy
Page 137, AP Images/Eugene Hoshiko

Chapter 6

Page 151, Khaled Fazaa/AFP/Getty Images
Page 159, © Ryan McVay/Getty Images
Page 166, © Bettmann/CORBIS,
Page 168, Photo by David Hawe © Blue Man Productions, Inc.

Chapter 7

Page 179, © Jesse Grant/WireImage/Getty Images
Page 182, © The McGraw-Hill Companies, Inc./Lars A. Niki

Chapter 8

Page 217, McGraw-Hill Companies Inc, Jill Braaten, photographer

Chapter 9

Page 241, Thememoryhole.org via Getty Images
Page 247, © EVARISTO SA/AFP/Getty Images
Page 248, © Getty Images (3)

Chapter 10

Page 275, AP Images/Lenny Ignelzi
Page 277, The McGraw-Hill Companies, Mark Dierker photographer.
Page 288, © Thinkstock/PunchStock

Chapter 11

Page 301, © Logan Fazio/FilmMagic/Getty Images
Page 310, © Mark Ralston/AFP/Getty Images

Chapter 12

Page 341, Lauren Berger, Intern Queen, Inc., © 2009. Reprinted with permission.

Chapter 13

Page 371, © Chip Somodevilla/Getty Images
Page 375, (top left) Rubberball Productions
Page 375, (top middle) © Jack Hollingsworth/Getty Images/Photodisc
Page 375, (top right) © imagewerks/Getty Images
Page 375, (bottom left) © Jurgen Reisch/Getty Images/Digital Vision
Page 375, (bottom middle) Digital Vision
Page 375, (bottom right) © C. Borland/PhotoLink/Getty Images
Page 386, Copyrights © Danny Turner. All rights reserved.
Page 388, © Hans Neleman/zefa/Corbis

Chapter 14

Page 399, AP Images/Candice Choi
Page 412, Courtesy of Toyota Motor North America, Inc.
Page 415, No credit needed

Chapter 15

Page 435, © Vince Bucci/Getty Images for NAACP
Page 446, Courtesy, Schwinn Bicycle
Page 447, Reprinted with permission of the Columbus Dispatch
Page 449, AP Images/Nick Ut

Chapter 16

Page 471, The McGraw-Hill Companies, Mark Dierker photographer.
Page 485, www.savedaruf.org. Reprinted with permission of © Olivier Jobard/SIPA Press
Page 486, Courtesy of the Advertising Council, Inc.
Page 501, The McGraw-Hill Companies, Mark Dierker photographer.

Chapter 17

Page 527, © SHAUN CURRY/AFP/Getty Images
Page 531, McGraw-Hill Companies Inc, Jill Braaten, photographer
Page 532, © PhotoAlto
Page 543, © Junko Kimura/Getty Images
Page 546, AP Images/David Kohl

Chapter 18

Page 563, © Banana Stock Ltd.

A

Abboud, Lelia, 486
Abrams, Rhonda, 400
Adam, Christine, 16
Adams, John, 166
Adamy, Janet, 44, 425
Airoldi, Donna M., 387
Akinbami, Lara J., 256
Albanese, Joe, 153, 154
Alquist, Eric, 627
Alred, Gerald J., 252
Alsop, Ron, 34
Anson, Chris M., 15
Arden, Mary Dawne, 379
Armstrong, David, 98, 409
Arndt, Michael, 50
Asch, Solomon, 157
Athavaley, Anjali, 108, 324
Atkinson, Jerry, 251

B

Badal, Jaclyne, 130
Badre, Albert N., 225
Baile, Walter, 442
Baird, Russel N., 226
Bakalar, Nicholas, 253
Ball, Guy D., 281
Ballard, Larry, 212
Barabas, Christine, 574
Barnes, Julian E., 241
Baron, Dennis E., 77
Batjargal, Bat, 132
Bauder, David, 74
Beatty, Sally, 499
Beaudette, Marie, 72
Beavan, Tom, 31
Beck, Catherine, 571–572
Beck, Marla Malcolm, 508
Bee, Samantha, 74
Bell, Ted, 349
Berger, Lauren, 341
Bernanke, Ben, 186
Bernhard, Tara Siegel, 592
Berry, Drew, 202
Best, Joseph, 71
Best, Robert O., 4
Birks, David A., 450
Blair, John G., 70
Blanchard, Kenneth, 414, 451, 489
Blodgett, Henry M., 10
Blundell, William E., 10
Bodenberg, Thomas M., 626
Boehret, Katherine, 78
Bogoslaw, David, 583
Boice, Robert, 182
Bolles, Richard, 303
Bompey, Nancy, 520
Borenstein, Seth, 626
Borgman, Peggy, 436
Borker, Ruth A., 111
Borrus, Amy, 591
Bortz, Christina, 103
Boston, Bruce O., 672
Bowen, Matt, 155
Bowyer, Jerry, 249
Box, Sam, 329

Bradley, Allen, 195
Brant, John R., 286
Braud, Gerard, 184
Brehm, Jack, 444
Brehm, Sharon, 444
Brennan, Ella, 301
Brin, Sergey, 533
Brusaw, Charles T., 252
Buchanan, Leigh, 153–154
Buffett, Warren, 37, 89, 104, 184–185
Burke, Lisa A., 284
Burns, Enid, 263–264
Burton, Thomas M., 98
Bush, Don, 193
Bush, George H. W., 241
Bush, George W., 189, 245
Byron, Ellen, 42, 530

C

Camerer, Colin F., 125
Campbell, Michael, 289
Capell, Perri, 4
Capelli, Paul, 374
Carlson, Richard, 414
Carms, Ann, 29
Case, John, 519
Cashman, Kevin, 73
Casson, Lionel, 663
Castellini, Richard, 341–342
Castro-Wright, Eduardo, 47
Catan, Thomas, 503
Caulfield, Brian, 627
Caver, Keith A., 129
Chabon, Michael, 201
Chaker, Anne Marie, 315
Chang, Julia, 285
Chao, Loretta, 55
Chernova, Yuliya, 417
Chilton, Edward M., 669
Christensen, John, 17
Churchill, Winston, 134, 186
Clemens, Roxanne, 181
Clements, Jonathan, 493
Coher, Adam, 486
Colbert, Stephen, 255
Collins, Jim, 110
Colvin, Geoffrey, 89, 104
Combs, Sean, 435
Conant, Douglas, 414
Connors, Robert J., 661
Cosby, Bill, 39
Couric, Katie, 74, 249–250
Cover, Simona, 94
Covey, Stephen, 114–115
Crosen, Cynthia, 166
Crovitz, L. Gordon, 217
Cullen, Lisa Takeuchi, 105

D

Dahl, Cheryl, 83
Daly, John, 289
David, Carol, 73
Davis, Bob, 485
de Jong, M., 554
Deal, Justen, 408

Dean, Bobby, 501
Dean, Jason, 133
DeBruicker, John, 352
DeHoniesto, James, 329
Delaney, Kevin J., 244
Demetrakakes, Pan, 225
Domeyer, Diane, 322–323
Dowling, Daisy Wademan, 490
Dreyfack, Raymond, 474
Dubner, Stephen J., 588
Dulek, Ronald, 199
Duncan, Calvin P., 536
Dunn, Patricia, 10
Dvorak, Phred, 151, 314

E

Ebert, Roger, 179
Eccleston, Jennifer, 74
Echikson, William, 486
Ede, Lisa, 166
Edmondson, Dave, 329
Ehrenfeld, Temma, 437
Elashmawi, Farid, 138–139
Eliot, Jan, 40
Ellis, Joseph, 329
Emery, David, 535
Epstein, Stephen, 114
Erard, Michael, 277

F

Fahlman, Scott, 420
Fam, Mariam, 50
Farrell, Greg, 572
Fernandez, Bob, 448
Feynman, Richard, 285
Fieg, John P., 70
Fine, Jon, 471
Fish, Lawrence, 414
Fisher, Anne, 166, 311, 319, 371–372
Flanagan, Denny, 61
Flandez, Raymund, 94, 106
Flesher, Jared, 326
Foley, Mark, 10, 92
Forsberg, L. Lee, 15
Foust, Dean, 255
Fowler, Geoffrey A., 128, 133–134
Francis, Theo, 140
Franklin, Benjamin, 166
Freed, Richard C., 564
Freed, Shervin, 564
Freedman, Aviva, 16
Freedman, David H., 92, 243
Friedman, Thomas, 100, 128
Frisch, Bob, 156
Fryer, Bronwyn, 175

G

Gaither, Dick, 310
Gallo, Carmine, 275
Galloni, Alessandra, 485
Garcia, Mario R., 217
Gardner, Margaret, 494
Garrard, Jane, 529
Gates, Bill, 104–105, 126
Gates, Melinda, 104

Gauthier-Villars, David, 473
Gitomer, Jeffrey, 5, 498
Gladwell, Malcolm, 476–477, 588
Glasbergen, Rancy, 448
Golden, Daniel, 329
Goldman, Matt, 168
Goldstein, Daniel G., 505
Goleman, Daniel, 108, 114
Gongloff, Mark, 249
Gordon, Thomas, 110
Gorman, Christine, 259
Gorman, James, 184
Goward, Paul, 72–73
Graham, Ellen, 77
Graham, John L., 136
Graham, Margaret, 73
Grassley, Chuck, 96
Gray, Steven, 36
Green, David, 289–290
Greenspan, Alan, 184, 186
Gremler, Dwayne D., 504
Groves, Kevin S., 109
Gumperz, John J., 111
Gwinner, Kevin P., 504

H

Haefner, Rosemary, 392
Hafner, Katie, 220
Hairston, Maxine, 657
Hall, Edward, 129, 135
Hansen, Randall, 388
Harrington, Richard J., 527
Harris, Phillip R., 130, 138–139
Harrison, Wayne, 438
Hartley, James, 539
Heath, Chip, 286, 485
Heath, Dan, 286, 485
Hechinger, John, 107
Helm, Burt, 476, 483, 542
Herzberg, Frederick, 46
Hewlin, Todd, 497
Heyer, Steven, 97
Hiebeler, Robert, 108
Hill, Julie, 291
Holder, Eric, 189
Holderbaum, Kirk, 602
Holstein, William J., 563
Hongyi, Zhou, 132
Horowitz, Adam, 203
Hudak, Jenny, 345
Hurd, Mark, 285
Hutchings, Jonathan F., 238
Hymowitz, Carol, 76, 201, 531

I

Imus, Don, 74
Inada, Miho, 100
Ip, Greg, 186

J

James, Judi, 380
James, Karen E., 284
Jansing, Chris, 74
Jeary, Tony, 280–281
Jefferson, Thomas, 166

Jereb, Barry, 195
Jobs, Steve, 447
Johar, Gita, 446
Johnson, John H., 12
Johnson, Linda A., 247
Johnson, Patt, 188
Johnson, Spencer, 414, 451, 489
Jones, Ashby, 119
Jones, Marilee, 329
Jordan, Miriam, 138
Joyce, Susan, 305, 328

K

Kadem, Assaf, 529
Kadiec, Daniel, 186
Kallestad, Brent, 441
Kang, Stephanie, 40, 69
Kapner, Suzanne, 532
Kapp, Jonathan, 114
Karsh, Brad, 345
Kasuya, Richard T., 278
Katz, Susan M., 270
Kauffman, Clark, 90, 213
Kazaleas, Dean C., 593
Kelly, Thomas B., 108
Kendall, Pat, 325
Kendrick, Deborah, 79
Kennedy, John F., 158
Ketterman, Charles, 108
Kienzler, Donna, 181
Kilpatrick, Kwame, 10, 98
King, Ruth, 416
King, W. J., 105
Kingsbury, Kathleen, 95
Kinzie, Susan, 512
Kirby, Julia, 292
Kirkpatrick, David, 126
Klein, Mike, 134
Klemperer, Otto, 72
Kluger, Jeffrey, 260
Knight, Rebecca, 378
Koncz, Andrea, 305–306
Kostelnick, Charles, 218–220
Kotter, John, 475
Koval, Robin, 62, 71
Kreuziger, Suzanne, 404
Kronholz, June, 203–204, 289
Krosnick, Jon, 542
Kushner, David, 45

L

Lagasse, Emeril, 301
Lakshman, Nandini, 546
Lam, N. Mark, 136
Landro, Laura, 101, 246
LaRouche, Janice, 622
Lashinsky, Adam, 248
Lasswell, Mark, 666
Lavinsky, Dave, 576
Lay, Philip, 497
Lederer, Richard, 187, 659, 667
Lee, Louise, 501
Legasse, Emeril, 301
Lehrer, Jonah, 475
Leighton, Ronald, 197
Lencioni, Patrick, 153–154

Levack, Kinley, 293
Levitt, Steven D., 588
Li, Xiangling, 111
Lin, Sara, 78
Lincoln, Abraham, 200, 282
Lindstrom, Martin, 486
Linn, Susan, 521
Livers, Ancella B., 129
Locke, Jeffrey, 196
Locker, Kitty, 183
Lockyer, Bill, 205
Long, John, 250
Lovering, Daniel, 420
Lovill, Jeff, 669
Lowry, Tom, 38
Lublin, Joann S., 35, 37
Lundin, Stephen C., 17
Lunsford, Andrea A., 166, 661
Lutz, Bill, 184

M

Mackey, John, 36
Malbon, Benjamin, 542
Malhotra, Atul, 98
Maltz, Daniel N., 111
Mandel, Steve, 285
Mandell, Judy, 192
Mangalindan, Mylene, 496
Mangone, Sharron, 98
Marr, Merissa, 128, 482
Martin, Joanne, 593
Martin, Timothy W., 399
Martinelli, Rose, 283
Matthews, John M., 536
Mattioli, Dana, 314
McCabe, Donald, 107
McCarthy, Ryan, 245
McCartney, Scott, 61, 450
McConnon, Aili, 546
McCord, Elizabeth, 604
McDonald, Duncan, 226
McFarland, Keith, 155, 157
McGregor, Jena, 64, 585
McIntyre, John, 31
McNamara, Mike, 39
Mehrabian, Albert, 289
Mero, Jenny, 412
Messmer, Max, 393
Meyer, Christopher, 541
Mieskowski, Katherine, 287
Miller, Amy, 386
Miller, Gregory, 475
Miller, Lisa, 47
Miller, Paul, 583
Miller, Stephen, 46
Mineta, Norman, 590
Miranda, Carolina A., 224
Moby, 400
Moore, Geoffrey, 497
Moore, Stephen E., 588
Moran, Robert T., 130
Moran, Sarah V., 130
Morel-Samels, Palmer, 536
Morsch, Laura, 304
Mozilo, Angelo, 98
Mukasey, Michael, 189

Mulally, Alan, 629
Mundy, Alica, 165
Murphy, Bruce, 29
Murphy, John, 43
Murphy, Tom, 193
Murray, Alan, 189
Myers, Isabel Briggs, 33

N

Nathan, John, 598
Needleman, Sarah E., 360
Neilsen, Jakob, 452
Nicholson, Rob, 151
Nielsen, Jakob, 229–231, 453
Nolan, Katherine, 246
Norris, Cathie, 175
Norvig, Peter, 282
Nussbaum, Bruce, 547

O

Obama, Barack, 90, 241, 623
O'Dell, Walden, 201
O'Hare, Constance M., 536
Oliu, Walter E., 252
Orey, Michael, 446
Org, Mielkki, 35

P

Packard, E., 164
Papows, Jeffrey, 329
Patrick, Aaron O., 134
Paul, Harry, 17
Pausch, Randy, 114
Pessin, Jaime Levy, 184
Phelps, Michael, 98
Piéch, Anton, 135
Pieper, Laura, 443
Pitzi, Mary Jo, 203
Pollock, Ted, 198
Pondy, Louis R., 593
Pope, Justin, 283
Poussaint, Alvin, 521
Powell, Mike, 282
Power, Stephen, 501
Powers, Melanie E., 593
Price, Carol, 315
Probert, Gregory, 329
Prudhomme, Paul, 301

Q

Quattrone, Frank, 10
Quinn, Jennifer, 461
Quinn, Stephen, 532

R

Rand, David, 378
Rapp, George, 224
Raskin, Andy, 112
Rathgeber, Holger, 475
Read, Madlen, 383
Redish, Janice C., 204–205
Reed-Woodward, Marcia A., 326
Reeves, Scott, 359, 379
Reichheld, Frederick F., 590

Reinsch, N. Lamar, Jr., 68
Rhodes, Christopher, 543
Richards, John, 662
Richmond, Riva, 436
Ricks, David A., 450
Rigdon, Joan E., 166, 665
Roberts, David, 220
Robertson, Nan, 545
Robinette, Scott, 489
Rocks, Patti Temple, 30
Roehm, Julie, 10, 97
Rogelberg, Steven G., 164
Rogers, Gary, 74
Romano, Joseph D., 564
Roosevelt, Franklin D., 543
Rosa, Jose Antonio, 127
Rose, Barbara, 34
Rosen, Charles, 98
Rossi, Lisa, 200
Rundle, Rhonda L., 408
Russo, Michelle S., 183
Ruth, Julie A., 127

S

Safire, William, 658
Sagario, Dawn, 442
Sammer, Joanne, 432
Sanchez, Jesus, 437
Sandberg, Jared, 519
Sandberg, Sheryl, 589
Sands, Judith Gordon, 110
Saranow, Jennifer, 96
Sauer, Patrick J., 566
Schechner, Sam, 201
Scheck, Julian, 449
Schriver, Karen, 218
Schryer, Catherine, 456
Schwager, Andre, 541
Scott, James Calvert, 197
Scott, Kenneth, 583
Search, Matthew, 335
Seligman, Martin, 68
Selzer, Jack, 205
Semuels, Alana, 437
Shakur, Tupac, 435
Shaw, Mona, 447
Sheehan, Michael, 292
Shelby, Annette N., 68
Shellenbarger, Sue, 519
Sheng, Ellen, 93
Silverman, Rachel Emma, 499
Simon, Paul, 291–292
Simpson, O. J., 250
Singletary, Michelle, 452
Slater, Alyson, 103
Slayter, Mary, 308
Sloan, Allan, 437
Sloate, Laura, 166
Smart, Geoff, 386
Smith, Allen, 432
Smith, Gerry, 187
Smith, Ray A., 48
Soloway, Elliot, 175
Speizer, Irwin, 51
Spencer, Jane, 248

Spilka, Rachel, 50
Spors, Kelly K., 155, 414
St. Clair, Stacy, 115
Steel, Emily, 498, 518
Steinberg, Brian, 134
Steinberg, Edwin R., 195
Stewart, Julia, 490
Stonecipher, Harry, 10, 452
Street, Randy, 386
Stross, Randall, 8
Sturgeon, Julie, 315–316
Suchan, James, 199
Sudhaman, Arun, 80
Swanson, William, 105

T

Tabuchi, Hiroko, 543
Takesh, Sarah, 566
Tan, Chreyl Tu-Lien, 508
Tannen, Deborah, 110–111, 113
Temkin, Bruce, 229
Terhune, Chad, 56
Thaler, Linda Kaplan, 62, 71
Thornton, Emily, 160
Timmerman, Peter D., 438
Tjan, Anthony K., 527
Tonnesen, Gretchen, 352
Tropman, John, 160
Truss, Lynne, 202
Tufte, Edward R., 218, 247, 249
Tumbull, Arthur T., 226
Tuna, Cari, 310, 329
Turnbull, Arthur T., 226
Turner, Marcia Layton, 301
Twiddy, David, 65

U

Ulijn, Jan M., 111
Useem, Jerry, 110

V

Vascellaro, Jessica E., 41, 133
Vella, Matt, 159
Viswanathan, Madhubalan, 127
Vogt, Peter, 357
von Brachel, John, 251
Vranica, Suzanne, 116

W

Wakabayashi, Daisuke, 587
Walker, Blair S., 459
Walsh, Bill, 194, 202
Washburn, Carolyn, 68
Waterman, Robert H., 534
Watson, Lucinda, 349
Waugh, Barbara, 287
Weber, Roberto A., 125
Weiss, W. H., 476–477
Welch, Liz, 168
Wessel, David, 484, 586
White, Erin, 143, 158, 167, 481
Wiio, Osmo A., 6
Wildstrom, Stephen H., 205
Williams, Carol, 125

Wilson, Fred, 400
Wingert, Pat, 587
Wingfield, Nick, 506
Winslow, Ron, 165
Winstein, Keith J., 329
Witt, Alex, 74
Wolgermuth, Liz, 31
Womack, Sean, 10

Woods, Tiger, 89, 592
Worthen, Ben, 230, 449
Woyke, Elizabeth, 596

Y

Ye, Juliet, 55, 248
York, Emily Bryson, 345
Yunus, Muhammad, 105

Z

Zaslow, Jeffrey, 444
Zelikow, Philip D., 603
Zielinski, Dave, 280, 285
Ziff, William B., Jr., 46
Zimmerman, Ann, 47
Zuckerman, Joseph, 409
Zwizje-Koning, K., 554

A

Absolut Vodka, 249
Accenture, 101
Ad Council, 486
Adelphia Communications, 104
Ahiida, 47
AIG, 104
Allstate Insurance Company, 39
Aloft Group Inc., 155
Alumni Athlete Network, 352
Amazon.com, 35, 44, 374
America Cancer Society, 493
American Airlines, 250
American Cancer Society, 587
American Demographics, 261, 265
American Express, 78, 103, 493
American Heart Association, 499
American Management Association, 95
Amy's Ice Cream Stores, 386
Anaheim Ducks, 93
AOL, 8, 45, 91, 535
Apostrophe Protection Society, 662
Appalachian Voices, 244
Apple Computer, 134, 447
Apple Group, 38
Applied Developmental Psychology, 488
Applied Intellectual Capital, 48
Arbitron, 546
Arthur Andersen, 585
Associated Press, 38, 488
Association of American Colleges and
    Universities, 5
Association for Business Communication, 448
Association for Medical Ethics, 98
*Association for Qualitative Research
    Newsletter*, 545
AT&T, 102
Atkinson and Company, 251

B

Bain & Company, 541
Banc of America Investment Services, 184
Bank of America, 184, 205, 254, 476, 490
Bartle Bogle Hegarty, 542
Basex, 94
Bass Pro Shops, 496
Bear Stearns, 104
Bell Atlantic, 571–572
Bell Labs, 114, 278
Berkeley Career Center, 322
Berkshire Hathaway, 184–185
Best Buy, 69, 188
Bingham McCutchen LLP, 255
Birkenstock, 256
Blue Man Group, 168
BMW, 40
Boeing, 10, 452
Boker, 534
Bon Appétit, 503
Boston University, 585
Bridgestone, 8, 116
Brookstone, Inc., 496
Bureau of Labor Statistics, 448
Burger King, 95, 411
BusinessWeek, 262, 471, 476
BWR Public Relations, 341

C

Cabela's, 64
Cabot Microelectronics, 329
Cal Farley's Boys Ranch and Affiliates, 501
California State University—Los Angeles, 109
Campaign for a Commercial-Free
    Childhood (CCFC), 479, 488, 521–522
Campbell's, 414
Care, 500
CARE USA, 473
CareerBuilder, 304, 311, 326–327, 329, 374, 392
Carnegie Mellon University, 420, 485
Carnival Cruise, 69
Catfish Bend Casinos, 90
CBS, 74, 250
Celadon, 46
Center for Science in the Public Interest
    (CSPI), 286
Central Intelligence Agency, 135
Cerberus Capital Management, 125
Chanel, 38
Chevron, 8, 94
China Telecom, 136
Chrysler, 125
Cisco Systems, 34, 127
CitiBank, 493
Citizens Bank, 414
Citysearch, 436
Claritas, Inc., 38
Clorox, 39, 129
CNBC, 374
CNN, 74
Coca-Cola, 38, 99, 188, 247, 418
Cold Stone Creamery, 34
Colgate-Palmolive, 127
ColorMe Company, 106
Columbia Business School, 446
Columbia University, 289
Columbus Dispatch, 79, 447
Comcast, 8, 447
Commander's Palace, 301
Communispond, 285
Continental Airlines, 35
Countrywide, 98
Craigslist, 308
Crate & Barrel, 498
Credit Suisse First Boston, 10
Crispin Porter + Bogusky, 106
Crossroads Foundation, 485
Customer Care Measurement and
    Consulting Firm, 450
Cyborlink.com, 139

D

Daily Sun, The, 48
Daimler-Benz, 125
Daimler Chrysler, 205
Dale Carnegie & Associates, 289–290
Dallas Morning News, 665
Dartmouth, 596
Davita, 35
Delightful Deliveries, 41
Dell, 104, 254
Delta Air Lines, 95
Denny's, 116
Denver Post, 447

Des Moines Register, 39, 68, 115, 134, 442
Diebold, 201
DineEquity, 490
Direct Marketing Association, 493, 496
Disney, 108, 128
Domini Social Investments, 563
Domino's, 10, 44
DonorsChoose, 498
Dow Chemical, 30
Dow Jones & Company, 408–409, 536
Duke University, 107, 585
Dupont, 94

E

Earthlink, 590
eBay, 41
Economist, 255, 472
EffectiveMeetings.com, 164
Electronic Arts, 38
Eli Lilly, 127
Emotiv, 92
Employment Policy Foundation, 303
Enron, 10, 104
Enterprise Rent-A-Car, 590
Environmental Protection Agency, 626
Ernst & Young, 34
Ethics Resource Center, 104
European Marketing Council, 475
Exatech Inc., 409
ExecuNet, 326
Exxon, 563

F

Faberge Perfumes, 474
Facebook, 93–94, 96–97, 116, 322, 326, 328
Federal Bureau of Investigation (FBI), 187, 435
Federal Deposit Insurance Corp., 476
Federal Reserve, 184, 186, 583
Federal Trade Commission, 97
FEMA, 3
Florida State University, College of
    Business, 440
Foote, Cone & Belding, 374
Forbes, 267, 359
Ford Motor Company, 8, 78, 104, 243, 629
Forrester Research, 229–230, 414
Fortune, 103, 372
Foundation Center, 573
Four Seasons Hotels, 64
Fox News, 74, 341
France Telecom, 486
Friends of the Earth, 103
Frito-Lay, 471

G

Gallup Organization, 537
Gap, 104
General Electric, 103–104, 116, 315, 380
General Motors, 34, 62, 78, 243
Genpact, 127
Giant Food, 399
Gillette, 106–107
Girl Scouts, 45
Glaxo-SmithKline, 409
Goldstar Events, 49
Goodyear, 486

Google, 94–95, 98, 103–104, 106–107, 244, 315, 326, 328, 374, 533, 589, 592
Graduate Management Admission Council, 107
Grameen Bank, 105
Greenpeace, 103
Grit, 35
Growthink, 576
GTE, 571–572

H

Habitat for Humanity, 493, 500
Hallmark, 65, 447, 535
Hannaford Bros., 399
Harvard Business Review, 99, 103, 132, 490, 497, 505
Harvard University, 352, 585
Hasbro, 531
HBO, 452
HealthConnect, 408
HealthSouth Corporation, 104
Heidrick & Struggles International Inc., 130
Herbalife, 329
Hewlett-Packard, 10, 98, 102, 104–105, 247, 285–287
Home Depot, 67, 167, 563
Honda, 203
Hook & Ladder Brewing Company, 106
Hoover Institution, 583
HyVee Supermarkets, 399

I

IBM, 38, 93, 98, 127, 151, 247, 329
Ice.com, 41
ICU Medical, 158
IDEO, 547
ImClone, 104
Indoor Tanning Association, 587
InnoCentive, 484
InsiderPages, 436
Institute for Healthcare Improvement, 101
Instituto Ethos, 104
Intel, 95, 102, 347
InterContinental Hotel Groups, 8
Intern Queen, Inc., 341
Internal Revenue Service, 7, 75, 198, 409, 421
International Society for Performance Improvement, 50
Interstate Fidelity Insurance (IFI), 416
Intuit, 546

J

Jesuit Volunteer Corps, 315
JetBlue, 437, 445
Job Search Training Systems, 310
JobBound, 345
Jobster, 322
Johns Hopkins University, 587–588
Johnson & Johnson, 49, 127, 436
Joie de Vivre Hospitality, 107
Journal of the American Academy of Dermatology, 383
Journal of Consumer Research, 446
JP Morgan Chase & Co., 352

K

Kaiser Aluminum, 452
Kaiser Permanente, 101, 408, 547

Kansas City Star, 590
Kaplan Thaler Group, 62
Kellogg Inc., 98
Kentucky Fried Chicken, 38, 135
KeyBank, 29, 254
KidSmart, 566
Killian & Company, 359
Kiwi, 545
Kiyonna Clothing, 41
Kmart, 591
KMPG, 353
Knowledge Networks, 542
Kraft, 488
Kroger, 546
Kwintessential.co.uk, 139

L

Lake Superior State University, 656
Land's End, 490
Lehman Brothers, 104, 583
Leo Burnett, 345
Library of Congress, 135
Linden Labs, 414
LinkedIn, 93, 114, 322
Literary Digest, 543
Litigation Trends Survey, 73
Loews, 35
Los Angeles Police Department, 250
Los Angeles Times, 408, 435, 445
Los Angeles Zoo, 449
Lowe's, 67
Loyola University–Chicago, 596

M

Manhattan Research, 404
Maritz, 476
Market Meterix, 107
Massachusetts Institute of Technology, 113, 329
Match.com, 44
Mattel's, 38
Mattress Discounters, 451
McAfee, 96
McCarter & English LLP, 202
McDonald's, 50, 61, 99–100, 127, 253, 496, 547
McLellan Marketing Group, 188
Medicare, 187
Medtronic, Inc., 98
Mercer Human Resource Consulting, 127
Mercer Management Consulting, 627
Merck, 165, 409
Merrill Lynch, 10, 104
MetLife, 68, 254
MGT Design Inc., 602
Miami Dolphins, 533
Michelin, 101, 486
Michigan Lawsuit Abuse Watch, 410
Microsoft, 91, 108, 126, 129, 205, 220, 246, 476, 506, 535
Millennium Hotel, 49
Mizuho, 100
Monsanto, 354
Monster, 304, 308, 327, 357
Morgan Stanley, 184
Mother, 37

Motion Picture Association of America, 205
Mount Holyoke College, 329
MSNBC, 74
MTV, 38, 50, 341
MySpace, 93–94, 96, 133, 322, 328
Mystery Shopping Providers Association, 547

N

NASA, 9, 11, 218, 585, 593
National Association of Colleges and Employers, 306
National Basketball Association (NBA), 38
National Commission on Writing, 4, 8
National Federation of the Blind, 231
National Football League, 471
National Guard, 3
National Highway Traffic Safety Administration, 203
National Historic Park, 411
National Hockey League, 93
National Journal, 588
National Oceanic and Atmospheric Administration, 283
National Résumé Writers' Association, 325
National Science Foundation, 97
Naval Reserve, 153
NBC, 8, 250, 341
Netflix, 484
New England Conservatory, 301
New England Journal of Medicine, 586
New Forests Fund, 500
New York Islanders, 93
New York Presbyterian Hospital, 495
New York Times, 186, 202, 658
Newport Creative Communications, 501
Newsweek, 250, 585
Nielsen Media Research, 38, 243, 546, 586
Nike, 34, 104, 129, 585
Nintendo, 44
Nissan, 33, 43, 78
Nokia, 546
North Shore–LIJ Health System, 62
Northwest Airlines, 452
Nynex Corporation, 571–572
NYU Hospital for Joint Diseases, 409

O

Occupational Safety and Health Administration, 64, 238
Office for Civil Rights, 39
OfficeTeam, 322
Otis Engineering Corporation, 135
Overstock.com Inc., 41

P

Pacific Bell, 573
Panera Bread Co., 196
Paramount Pictures, 39
Parker Pen Company, 135
Peace Corps, 315
PepsiCo., 532
Perdue Farms, 135
PETA, 167, 487
Petco Animal Supplies, 496
Pew Internet & American Life Project, 608
Pfizer, 254

Philadelphia Inquirer, 448
Philanthropic Research Inc., 573
Portola Packaging, 283
Price Chopper, 399
PricewaterhouseCoopers, 95, 100, 353
Princeton University, 352
Procter & Gamble, 39, 42, 48–49,
   106–107, 127, 530, 542, 585
Psychology Today, 493
Public Agenda, 537

Q

Qdoba Mexican Grill, 196
QuintCareers.com, 153
Quizno's, 196

R

Radicati Group, 94, 401, 404
RadioShack, 329, 452
Ralph Lauren, 38
Raytheon, 105
RealClearPolitics.com, 31
RealMatch, 308
Red Cross, 501
Rehabilitation Institute of Chicago, 179
Rensselaer Polytech Institute, 329
Report Watch, 597
Republican National Committee, 493
ResumeDoctor.com, 325
Riten Industries, 94
Robert Half Finance & Accounting, 393
Robert Half International, 259, 303, 312,
   342, 359, 389
Rock and Roll Hall of Fame, 245
Rogen International, 403
Romano's Macaroni Grill, 220
Run for Congo Women, 501–502
Rutgers University, 74, 107
Ryerson Tull, 6

S

SABMiller, 486
Sametz Blackstone Associates, 666
Samsung Electronics, 585
Sanford University, 376
Sarasota Memorial Hospital, 101–102
Saturday Evening Post, 46
Save the Children, 485
Schering-Plough, 165
Schwinn, 446
SCO Group, 205
Scooter Store Inc., 490
Securities America Inc., 378
Securities and Exchange Commission, 184,
   187, 591, 596
Servision Inc., 247
Sharp, 587
Shering-Plough, 165
Sisters of St. Dominic, 563
Smart Tags, 97
Smith Barney, 184
Society for Human Resource
   Management, 329
Southwest Airlines, 98, 448, 590
Speedo, 543
Springfield Manufacturing, 440
Sprint Nextel, 94

SRI, 34
Stanford Graduate School of Business, 314
Stanford University, 304, 496, 583
Staples, Inc., 496
Starbucks, 103–104, 127, 245, 404
Starwood Hotels, 97
Staybridge Suites, 49
Steak 'n Shake, 46
Stihl, 67–68
Stop & Shop, 399
Subway, 196
SuperGroupCreativeOmnimedia, 107
Survey for Human Resource
   Management, 379
Sylvania, 78
Sysco, 35

T

T-Mobile USA, 63
Taco Bell Corp., 411
Tandem Computers, 136
Target, 532
Teach for America, 315
Tesco PLC, 44
Tetra Tech, 329
Texas Children's Hospital, 490
Thermo Electron, 99
Thomson Reuters, 527
3M, 99, 103, 127, 598
Time, 46, 250, 256, 590
Time-Life Books, 493
Toastmasters, 187
Tommy Hilfiger, 127
Toro, 73
Towers Perrin, 281
Toy Industry Association, 523
Toyota, 35, 103, 412
Toys 'R Us, 221
Tuck School of Business, 314, 596
Tupperware Brands Corporation, 529
Tyco International, 104

U

U-Haul, 167
UNICEF, 500
Unilever, 127
United Airlines, 61
United Nations, 104, 587–588
United Parcel Service, 99, 103, 136, 256
U.S. Cellular, 95
U.S. Census Bureau, 78, 99, 129, 592
U.S. Consumer Product Safety
   Commission, 220
U.S. Department of Agriculture, 259
U.S. Department of Education, 32, 268–269
U.S. Department of Health and Human
   Services, 266, 573
U.S. Department of Labor, 271
U.S. Department of Transportation's
   National Highway Traffic Safety
   Administration (NHTSA), 590
U.S. Department of Treasury, 75
U.S. Fish and Wildlife Service, 283
U.S. Food and Drug Administration, 399,
   408–409, 586
U.S. House of Representatives, 3
U.S. Interior Department, 102

U.S. Naval Academy, 18
U.S. Navy, 199
U.S. Post Office, 39
U.S. Small Business Administration, 573
University of Calgary, 8
University of California at Berkeley, 304
University of California at Irvine, 98
University of California at Los Angeles,
   138, 289
University of Chicago Business School, 283
University of Colorado, 583
University of Michigan, 98
University of North Carolina at Charlotte, 164
University of Pennsylvania, 62
University of Texas, 289, 566
University of Washington, 585
University of Wisconsin, 98
UNUMProvident, 4
Urban Legends, 535
US News & World Report, 586
USA Today, 411
USAA, 64

V

Vault, 353–354
Vault.com, 344, 377
Verizon, 571
Veterans Affairs Department, 98
Virgin Group, 245
Vogue, 38

W

Wachovia Corporation, 104, 127
Wachovia Securities, 184
Wal-Mart, 10, 36, 40, 42, 44, 47, 97, 99, 104,
   127, 137, 167, 189, 483, 532
Wall Street Journal, 4, 16, 43, 69, 77, 100,
   127, 143, 190, 217, 255, 261, 304, 444,
   450, 473, 481, 486, 493, 499, 508, 533,
   586–590, 592, 665
Walt Disney, 35
Washington Mutual, 104, 254, 476
Washington Post, 34, 37, 186, 194
Watch!, 250
Wells Fargo, 127
Wendy's, 49
Whirlpool corporation, 490
Whole Foods Market, 36, 106, 371
WithumSmith & Brown, 602
Witness.org, 45
World Book Encyclopedia (WBE), 181
World Health Organization, 262
WorldCom, 104
WorldTeach, 315

X

X-Prize Foundation, 484
Xerox, 99

Y

Yahoo, 91, 96, 436
Yale, 585
Yankelovich Partners, 494
Yelp, 436
YGS Group, 404
Yoox, 41
Young and Rubicam, 349
YouTube, 45, 96, 324

A

a lot/allot, 669
Abstracts, 623–624
accede/exceed, 668
accept/except, 668
access/excess, 668
Accident reports, 528
Accuracy of visuals, 247–250
Accurate words, 187
Acknowledgment responses, 109
Acronyms, 190
Action close, 496–497
Action verbs, for résumés, 315
Active listening, 109
  acknowledgment responses, 109
  blocking responses vs., 110
Active voice, 191–192
Activities on résumé, 317–319
adapt/adopt, 668
Administrative documents, 183–184
advice/advise, 668
affect/effect, 187, 668
affluent/effluent, 669
Agendas, 164
Agreement, 655–657
  noun-pronoun, 656
  subject-verb, 655
Alternatives
  elimination of alternatives pattern, 596
  negative messages, 444
American Psychological Association (APA)
  format, 548, 550–551
among/between, 187, 669
amount/number, 187, 669
Analytical reports, 528
and/but, 186
Anecdotes, 280, 494
Annual reports, 529, 597, 602
APA (American Psychological Association)
  format, 548, 550–551
Apologies, 445–447
Apostrophes, 662–663
Appendixes, 593
Application essays, 360–361
Appropriate words, 187
Argument, 474
Assumptions, formal report, 625
Attire, 374–377
Attitude; *see* You-attitude
attributed/contributed, 669
Audience
  adapting your message for, 39–44, 279–280
  auxiliary audience, 31
  for business communications, 14–15, 183
  choosing channels to reach, 36–39
  class research project, 566
  demographic characteristics of, 33
  document use, 43–44
  expectations of, 43
  external, 6
  gatekeeper, 30
  identification of, 30–31
  individual/members of groups, 31–35, 40
  information needed, 41
  initial reaction to message, 40–41
  internal/external audience, 6
  knowledge of, 41
  motivations for, 48
  obstacles to overcome, 42
  oral presentations, 279–280
  primary audience, 30
  questions from, 291–292
  reason to act promptly, 484–485
  secondary audience, 30
  watchdog audience, 31
  writing for international, 138–139
Audience analysis, 44
Audience benefits, 45–50
  characteristics of, 45–47
  extrinsic/extrinsic motivators, 45–46
  identifying and developing of, 47–49
  logic of, 46–47
  you-attitude, 47
Auxiliary audience, 31
Average, 588–589

B

Baby boomers, 34, 220
Background or history section, 283
  formal report, 626
Bad news; *see* Negative messages
Bar charts, 245, 252–253
  deviation, 253
  grouped bar charts, 253
  histograms/pictograms, 253
  paired bar charts, 253
  segmented, subdivided, stacked, 253
  varieties of, 253
bc (blind copies), 407
Behavioral interviews, 386–388
Beliefs, 130–132
Bias-free language, 74
Bias-free photos/illustrations, 79
Bibliography, 554
Blind copies (bc), 643
Block format, 316, 637–639, 644
Blocking responses, 110
Blogs/bloggers, 95, 328
Body of formal report, 626
Body language, 112–113; *see also* Nonverbal
  communication
  closed/defensive body positions, 112
  eye contact, 132–133
  gestures, 133–134
  job interviews, 379
  open body positions, 112
  smiling, 133
Body of message, 496
Boilerplate, 204
Boxhead, 251
Brainstorming, 14, 47, 483
  business documents, 182
  team meetings, 155
Branching questions, 539
Brochures, design of, 227–229
Budget sections, 574
Buffers, 441
  negative messages, 441–442
Building goodwill; *see* Goodwill
Bulletproof Presentations (Campbell), 289

Bullets, 221
Business attire, 374–377
Business cards, 137
Business communications, 4–5; *see also*
  Organizational writing; Visuals
  analyzing situations for, 13
  audiences for, 14–15
  bias-free documents, 74–77
  brainstorming for, 14, 182
  building support for position, 15
  channel for, 13
  clarity of, 12
  completeness of, 12
  content of, 13
  conventions of, 12
  correctness of, 12
  cost of poor communication, 8–11
  criteria for effective messages, 12
  culture and, 130
  diversity, 99
  editing of, 17
  entrepreneurship, 99
  environmental concerns, 103–104
  ethical issues in, 106
  factoring in total situation, 15
  feedback on, 17
  globalization and outsourcing, 99–100
  good business style, 187
  goodwill and, 12
  information to include, 15
  innovation in, 103
  international business communication,
    140
  job flexibility, 102
  knowledge for, 14
  nonsexist language, 74–77
  objections and negative elements, 15
  organization of, 16, 182–183
  organizational context of, 13
  planning of, 182–183
  problem solving strategies for, 13–14
  professional image for, 357–360
  for promotability and success, 4–5
  purpose of, 15
  quality and customers' needs, 98–99
  questions for analysis, 14–16
  rate of change in, 102–103
  reader's time and, 112
  revising a draft, 16
  style of, 183
  teamwork, 101–102
  trends in, 98–104
  visual attractiveness of, 16
  work-family balance, 100–101
  you-attitude, 16
Business documents; *see* Reports
Business ethics resources, 105
Business introductions, 138
Business jargon, 190–191
Business plans, 572–573, 576
  budget and costs sections, 574
Business style, 183
Businessese, 190
but, 186
Bypassing, 188

C

c (copy), 643
Campus interviews, 376
Capital letters, 224
Carbon/computer copy (*cc*), 407, 643
Career fairs, 376
Career objective statements, 311–312
Case, 657–658
Catalogs, 501
Causation, 591–592
cc (carbon/computer copy), 407, 643
Cell phone etiquette, 402
Central selling point, 227
Channel, 36
Chartjunk, 247–248
Charts
    bar charts, 245, 252–253
    pie charts, 245, 252
Chronological organization, 287, 598
Chronological progress reports, 576–577
Chronological résumé, 308–309, 320–321
Citation, 547
cite/sight/site, 669
Claims, 450
Class research projects
    audience, 566
    call to action, 567
    feasibility, 566
    methods/procedure, 567
    problem definition, 566
    proposals for, 566–571
    qualifications/facilities/resources, 567
    topics to investigate, 567
    work schedule, 567
Clauses
    dependent, 660
    nonrestrictive (nonessential) clause, 664
    subordinate, 660
Clip art, 247, 283
Closed (defensive) body positions, 112
Closed questions, 538
Closing (concluding) statement, 281–282
    action close, 496–497
Closure reports, 529, 598
Clothing, 136
Clustering, 183
Collaborative writing, 165–169
    composing drafts for, 167
    editing and proofreading, 167–168
    making process work, 168–169
    planning work and document, 166–167
    revising document, 167
Colon, 659, 663
Color, 136, 226–227, 246–247
    common connotations in Western
        culture, 246
    presentation slides, 284
Columbia disaster, 9
Comma, 659, 661, 663–664
Comma fault, 660
Comma splices, 660
Common media, 401–404
    e-mails, letters, and paper memos,
        403–404
    face-to-face contacts, 401–402

    instant messages/text messaging, 402–403
    phone calls, 402
Communication; *see also* Business
      communications
    benefits of improving, 11
    cost of, 6–11
    cross-cultural, 132–137
    forms of, 4
    in high- and low-context cultures, 130
    Hurricane Katrina disaster, 3, 8
    internal/external audiences, 6
    international business communication, 140
    interpersonal communication, 108–113, 152
    on the job, 6, 102–103
    legal consequences of, 10–11
    nonverbal communication, 4, 111–113,
        132–137
    poor communication costs, 8–11
Communication ability, promotability
    and, 4–5
Communication channel, 36
Communication Satisfaction Questionnaire
    (CSQ), 553
Comparison/contrast pattern, 594–595
Competitive proposals, 564
Complaints, 450
    positive responses to, 415
complement/compliment, 669
Complex sentences, 195
Complimentary closes, 637
Compliments, 138
compose/comprise, 187, 669
Composing process
    activities in, 180–181
    editing, 181
    planning, 180–181
    revising, 181
    writing, 181
Compound sentences, 195
Computer copy (cc), 407, 643
Computer use; *see* Internet; Web pages
Concluding statement, 281–282
Conclusions, formal report, 626
Conflict resolution
    empathy in, 31
    presenting problem, 162
    responding to criticism, 162–163
    steps in, 160–162
    in teams, 160–164
    troubleshooting team problems, 161
    you-attitude in, 163–163
confuse/complicate/exacerbate, 669
Connotations, 188–189
Convenience sample, 542
Conventions, 12–13, 219, 246
Conversational styles, 110–111, 113, 183
Coordination of teams, 152
Copy (c), 643
Corporate culture, 106–108, 343; *see also*
    Organizational culture
Corporate philanthropy, 106
Correlation, 591–592
Correspondence; *see* E-mail; Letters
Costs of poor communication, 8–11
    legal problems, 10–11
    lost goodwill, 9–10

    wasted efforts, 9
    wasted time, 9
Costs sections, 574
Courtesy titles and names, 73–76, 342
Cover letters; *see* Job application letters
Credibility, 474–475
Credit reports, 528
Criteria, formal report, 625
Critical activities, 254
Critical incidents, 544, 554
Criticism
    buying time strategy, 163
    feelings/inferences, 163
    paraphrasing of, 162
    responding to, 162–163
Cross-cultural training, 128
Cross-functional teams, 101
Cultural differences
    body language, 132–134
    business introductions, 138
    colors, 136, 246–247
    eye contact, 132–133
    gestures, 133–134
    global business and, 125–127
    international career experience, 127–128
    local culture adaptations, 127
    nonverbal communication, 132–137
    nonverbal symbols, 136–137
    oral communication, 137–138
    personal space, 135
    persuasive messages, 475–476
    in smiling, 133
    successful communication, 132–137
    in time, 135–136
    in touch, 134–135
    translating advertising slogans, 135
    values, beliefs, and practices, 130–132
    visuals and, 252
    in workplace, 99, 128–129, 158–159
    writing to international audiences,
        138–140
Culture, 129–130; *see also* Diversity;
    Organizational culture
    high-context, 129–130
    low-context, 129–130
    monochronic, 135–136
    polychronic, 135–136
    values, beliefs, and practices, 130–132
Customer service, 8, 39
Customers
    negative messages to, 437–438
    observations of, 546–547
Customers' needs, 98–99
Cycling, 7, 204

D

Dangling modifier, 658
Dash, 659, 664
Data displays and images, 251–257
    bar charts, 252–253
    drawings, 255–256
    dynamic displays, 257
    Gantt charts, 254
    line graphs, 253–254
    maps, 256–257

photographs, 254–255
pie charts, 252
tables, 251–252
Data and information
    analyzing numbers, 587–590
    analyzing patterns, 591
    analyzing for reports, 585–593
    analyzing words, 591
    checking logic in, 591–593
    correlation/causation, 591–592
    identifying source of, 585–587
    mean, median, range, 588–589
    for oral presentations, 25
    quality for visuals, 243, 249
Data security, 95
Databases, 33
Dates, 667
Decision-making strategies, 155–156
    dot planning, 155–156
    problem-solving process, 155
Decorative devices, 226–227, 246
Defensive body positions, 112
Definitions, for formal report, 625–626
Delivery of oral presentation, 290
Demographic characteristics, 33
Demonstrations, 285–286
Denotation, 188
dependant/dependent, 670
Dependent clause, 660
describe/prescribe, 670
Descriptive abstracts, 624
Design, 217; *see also* Page design guidelines
    brochures, 227–229
    business communication, 16
    conventions, 219
    cultural differences in, 225
    extra-design, 220
    importance of, 218
    inter-design, 219
    intra-design, 219
    levels of, 219–220
    page design guidelines, 220–227
    as part of writing process, 218
    résumés, 308
    scannable résumé, 325
    supra-design, 220
    usability testing, 231
    visual design guidelines, 243–250
    Web pages, 229–231
Design elements
    capital letters, 224
    fonts, 224–225
    grid and graphic elements, 226
    headings, 224
    highlighting and color, 226–227
    margins, 225–226
    placement of important elements, 226
    white space, 220–221
Deviation bar charts, 253
different from/different than, 187, 670
Dingbats, 226
Direct marketing, 49
Direct requests, 476–479
    checklist for, 506
    example of, 478

organization of, 477
    subject line for, 478
Disabilities and disease, 78–79
Disciplinary notices, 451
Discourse-based interviews, 547
Discourse community, 36
discreet/discrete, 670
disinterested/uninterested, 187, 670
Diversity, 99, 128–129; *see also* Cultural differences; Culture
    in North America, 128–129
    working on diverse teams, 158–159
    in workplace, 99, 128–129
Document cycling processes, 7, 204
Document design; *see* Design
Documentation, 547
Dot chart, 245
Dot planning, 155–156
Double negatives, 68–69
Drafts; *see also* Revision
    checklist for, 205
    of collaborative writing, 167
    visuals in, 242
Drawings, 255–256
Dynamic displays (online visuals), 257

E

E-mail, 4, 10
    common uses for, 403
    electronic privacy, 95–98
    format for messages, 647, 651–652
    information overload, 94–95, 275, 400
    job application letters, 355–356
    legal implications of, 10–11
    newsletters, 400
    online acronyms, 91
    résumés via, 325–328
    storage costs for, 8
    subject lines for, 408
Eats, Shoots & Leaves (Truss), 202
Editing, 181, 200–202
    of collaborative documents, 167–168
    job application letters, 359–360
    typos, 202–203
Education on résumé, 312–313
Electronic privacy, 95–98
Electronic résumés, 325–328
    blogs/social networking sites, 328
    creating a scannable résumé, 325
    keywords for, 325–326
    safety for, 305, 328
    sending electronically, 327
    spam filters and, 328
    Web posting of, 327–328
Electronic tools, 90–93
    instant messengers, 91–92
    personal digital assistants, 92
    portable media players, 92
    telepresence, 92
    Wikis, 91
elicit/illicit, 670
Elimination of alternatives pattern, 596
Ellipses, 667
eminent/immanent/imminent, 670

Emoticons, 420
Emotional appeals, 475, 485–488
    in fund-raising messages, 500–501
Emotional Intelligence (Goleman), 108, 114
Empathy, 31
Enclosures, 643
Entrepreneurship, 99
Enunciation, 290
Envelopes, formatting of, 643, 647
Environmental impacts, 103–104
Ethics, 104–106, 114
    in interviewing, 544
    unethical sales pitch, 493
    word choice implications, 189
    writing process and, 180
Exaggeration, 138
Excluding alternatives, 287
Executive summary, formal reports, 573, 623–624
Experience on résumé, 314–317
    formats for, 316
    skills résumé, 316–317
    what to include, 314–315
External audiences, 6
External documents, examples of, 7
Extrinsic motivators, 45–46
Eye contact
    cultural differences in, 132–133
    during oral presentations, 289

F

Face-to-face contacts, 401–402
Face-to-face meetings, 38
Face-to-face surveys, 541
Familiar words, 187, 189–190
Family-work balance, 100–101
farther/further, 187, 670
Fear of public speaking, 288–289
Feasibility reports, 529, 566
Feedback, 17, 279
    electronic feedback, 414
    improving your document, 204
    strategies for, 156
Feedback notes, 414
fewer/less, 187, 670
Firings, 450, 452
First full-time job, 116–117
Fish: A Remarkable Way to Boost Morale and Improve Results (Lundin, Paul, and Christensen), 17
Fixed fonts, 224
Fleisch Reading Ease Scale, 205
Focus groups, 545–546
Follow-up phone call/letter, 389–391
    sample letter, 351
Fonts, 224–225
Forecasts, 604
Form letter, 5
Formal meetings, 164
Formal reports, 528, 607–626
    assumptions, 625
    background/history, 626
    body, 626
    components of, 607–608

Formal reports—*Cont.*
conclusions/recommendations, 62
criteria, 625
definitions, 625
example of, 609–621
executive summary, 623–624
introduction, 625–626
letter/memo of transmittal, 622–623
limitations, 625
list of illustrations, 623
methods, 625
purpose, 625
release date, 622
scope, 625
table of contents, 623
title page, 608, 622
Formalization of teams, 153
Format
experience on résumé, 316
for letters, 637–643
Formation of teams, 152
forward/foreword, 670
Freewriting, 182
Full justification, 225
Functional patterns, 598
Functional résumé, 310, 316–317
Fund-raising appeals; *see* Sales and fund-raising messages
Funding proposals, 572–573
Fused sentences, 661

G

Gantt charts, 245, 254
Gatekeeper, 30–31
General to particular pattern, 597
Generational differences, 34
Geographic or spatial pattern, 597
Gestures/gesturing, 133–134, 290–291
Global business, 126–128
international career experience, 127–128
local cultural adaptations, 127
Global positioning system (GPS), 97
Global teams, 151
Globalization, 99–100
Good news messages; *see* Positive messages
good/well, 671
Goodwill, 62; *see also* You-attitude
to create with content, 65–66, 80
effective messages and, 12
poor communication losses, 9–10
Goodwill endings, 410
Goodwill presentations, 276; *see also* Oral presentations
Grammar, 655–659
agreement, 655–657
case, 657–658
comma splices, 660
dangling modifiers, 658
fused sentences, 661
misplaced modifiers, 658
parallel structure, 197, 658–659
predication errors, 659
run-on sentences, 661
Grapevine, 114
Graphs; *see also* Data displays and images
line, 245
truncated, 248–249

Grid system, 226–227
Group(s); *see also* Collaborative writing; Teams
analyzing members of, 32–35
focus groups, 545–546
leadership in, 154–155, 160
peer pressure in, 157–158
Group interviews, 389
Group leadership, 154–155, 160
Group presentations, 292; *see also* Oral presentations
Grouped bar charts, 253
Grouped visuals, 244
Groupthink, 157–158
Guided discussion, 278
Gunning Fox Index, 205

H

Headings, 224, 604–607
Height, 137
Hidden job market, 344
Hidden negatives, 69–70
High-context cultures, 129–130
Highlighting, 226
Histograms, 253
History, formal report, 626
Honors and awards on résumé, 314
Hot buttons, 43
Humor, 281, 411
Hurricane Katrina disaster and FEMA, 3, 8
Hyphen, 664–665

I

I use of, 186
Identity theft, 96
i.e./e.g., 671
Illustrations, as bias-free, 79
Images; *see* Data displays and images
Impersonal expressions, 64
imply/infer, 187, 671
Independent clause, 660
Individuals
analysis of, 31–32
generational differences, 34
Inferences, 163
Informal meetings, 164
Informal reports, 528; *see also* Reports
Information
analyzing for reports, 585
in business communications, 15
chronological, 598
comparison/contrast, 594–595
elimination of alternatives, 596
functional, 598
general to particular, 597
geographic or spatial, 597
negative information, 70–71
online/print research, 532–534
organization for presentations, 286–287
problem-solution, 596
for reports, 593–602
SWOT analysis, 596–597
Information interview, 345–346
Information management, 408–409
Information overload, 94–95, 275, 400
Information reports, 528
Informational dimensions, 152

Informative messages
benefits in, 409–410
checklist for, 419
ending of, 410–411
humor in, 411
organization of, 404–407
subject lines for, 407
summaries, 412–413
transmittals, 411–412
varieties of, 411–415
Informative presentations, 276; *see also* Oral presentations
Informative reports, 598–601
Innovation, 103
Inside address, 643
Instant messages (IMs), 91–92, 402–403
Interactive presentation, 279
Intercultural communicator, 126
Intercultural competence, 100
Interim reports, 528
Internal audiences, 6
Internal documents, 553
examples of, 7
International audience, writing to, 138–140
International business communication, 140
International career experience, 127–128
International punctuation, 666
International teams, 151
Internet; *see also* Web research
company research via, 343–344
job search using, 304–305, 344
online testimonials, 496
Internships, 303, 341, 344
Interpersonal communication, 108–113, 152
conversational style, 110–111
listening, 108–110
networking, 113–114
nonverbal communication, 111–113
teamwork and, 152
Interpersonal dimensions, 152
Interruption interviews, 547
Interviews, 372–373, 536, 541–542; *see also* Job interviews
behavioral interviews, 386–388
campus interviews, 376
communication behaviors of successful, 381
customs for, 378–380
ethical issues in, 544
follow-up to, 389–391
group interviews, 389
information interviews, 345
kinds of, 386–389
phone interview, 376
practice for, 377
referral interviews, 345
research interviews, 544–545
sample selection for, 542–544
situational interviews, 387
strategy for, 373
stress interviews, 387–389
traditional questions/answers, 380–386
video interviews, 376–377
Intrinsic motivators, 45–46
Introduction of formal report, 625
Italics, 667
it's/its, 671

J

Jargon, 190–191
Job application essays, 360–361
Job application letters
   content and organization of, 346–355
   e-mail application letters, 355–356
   editing and proofreading, 359–360
   follow-up to, 360
   knowledge of position/company,
     353–354
   last paragraph, 354–355
   length of, 359
   paragraph length and unity, 359
   positive emphasis, 357–358
   professional image in, 357–360
   prospecting letter, 349–350, 352
   purpose of, 342
   researching position/company, 342–345
   résumés vs., 342
   solicited letter, 347–349
   standing out in, 354
   writing style in, 357
   you-attitude, 358–359
Job flexibility, 102
Job hunting, 302–303, 310; *see also*
   Résumés
   accepting an offer, 392–393
   blogs/social networking sites, 328
   follow-up letters and calls, 389–390
   hidden job market and, 344–345
   information interviews, 345–346
   Internet and, 304–305, 308
   networking, 344–345
   preparation for, 302–303
   referral interviews, 345
   researching employers and jobs,
     342–345
Job interviews, 371–393
   attire for, 374–377
   behavior during, 378–379
   behavioral interviews, 386–387
   checklist for, 380
   current expectations for, 372–373
   customs of, 378–380
   final research for, 374
   follow-up for, 389–391
   group interviews, 389
   illegal/improper interview questions,
     385–386
   interview channels, 376–377
   kinds of, 386–389
   negotiating for salary/benefits, 390–392
   note-taking, 379–380
   practice for, 377
   preparation for, 373–376
   professional materials, 375–376
   segments of (opening, body, and
     close), 380
   situational interviews, 387
   strategy for, 373
   stress interviews, 387–389
   traditional questions/answers, 380–386
   travel planning for, 374
Job references, 319–322
Job titles, 74
Judgment sample, 542
Justification reports, 529, 602

K

Keystroke authentication, 95
Keywords, 325–326, 533

L

Language
   bias-free, 74–77
   goodwill and, 9
   nonagist, 77–78
   nonracist, 77–78
   nonsexist language, 74–77
   people-first language, 78–79
Last Lecture, The (Pausch), 114
lay/lie, 187
Layoffs, 452
Leadership, in teams, 154–155, 160
lectern/podium, 671
Legal phrases, 70
Letter of transmittal, 622–623
Letterhead, 638
Letters, 403–403, 637; *see also* Job application
     letters; Sales and fund-raising messages
   block format for, 637–639, 644
   comparing/contracting formats, 638
   courtesy titles and names, 73–76, 342
   enclosures, 643
   format for, 637–643
   inside address, 643
   modified block format for, 637–638,
     640, 645
   recommendation letters, 491
   second pages for, 644–646
   simplified format, 637–638, 641, 646
lie/lay, 671
Limitations, formal report, 625
Line graphs, 245, 253–254
List of illustrations, formal reports, 623
Listening
   acknowledgment responses, 109
   active listening, 109–110
   blocking responses vs., 110
   good listeners, practices of, 109
   importance of, 108–110
Literacy, 32
Local cultural adaptations, 127
loose/lose, 671
Low-context cultures, 129–130

M

Mail surveys, 541
Main clause, 660
Make-good reports, 529
Maps, 256–257
Margins, 225–226
Mars Climate Orbiter communication errors, 11
Mean, 588–589
Median, 588–589
Meetings, 164–165
   agendas for, 164
   corporate annual meetings, 167
   effectiveness of, 164–165
   formal meetings, 164
   informal meetings, 164
   minutes for, 164–165
   omnibus motion, 165
   purposes of, 164
   two-meeting rule, 160

Memo of transmittal, formal reports,
     622–623
Memos, 637
   example of, 648
   format for, 647–648
   informative memo report, 599–601
   page two of, 650
   positive memo (example), 406
Messages; *see also* E-mail; Negative
     messages; Persuasive messages;
     Positive messages
   audience analysis and, 39–40
   criteria for effective, 12
   initial reaction to, 40
   managing information in, 408–409
Methods, formal report, 625
Mirror questions, 544
Misplaced modifier, 658
Mixed punctuation, 637
MLA (Modern Language Association)
     format, 549, 552–554
Mode, 588–589
Modern Language Association (MLA)
     format, 549, 552–554
Modified block format, 637–638, 640, 642, 645
Modifier, 658
Monochronic cultures, 135–136
Monologue presentation, 278
moral/morale, 671
Ms., 75
Multimedia presentation, 281
Multitasking, 115–116
Myers-Briggs Type Indicator, 31–33
Mystery shoppers, 547

N

Narration, 280, 494
National Commission on Writing, 4, 8
Negative messages, 13, 436–437
   alternative strategies for, 448–449
   apologies, 445–447
   bad news, 74, 437–441
   buffers, 441–442
   checklist for, 456
   claims and complaints, 450
   common ground, 481–482
   disciplinary notices, 451–452
   layoffs and firings, 450, 452
   online reviews, 436
   organization of, 437–441
   parts of, 441–444
   peers and subordinates, 438–450
   performance appraisals, 451–452
   phrases to avoid, 448
   primary/secondary purposes of, 437
   reasons in, 442–443
   recasting as persuasive message, 449
   recasting as positive message, 449
   refusals, 443–444
   rejection and refusals, 450–451
   reverse psychology, 67
   sample problem, 452–455
   subject line for, 441
   superiors, 438
   tone in, 447–448
   varieties of, 450–452
   words to avoid, 69

Negative words, 68–69
  hidden negatives, 69–70
  legal phrases, 70
  words to avoid, 69
Networking, 113–114, 344
Nominative case, 657
Nonagist language, 77–78
Noncompetitive proposals, 564
Nonracist language, 77–78
Nonrestrictive (nonessential) clause, 664
Nonsexist language, 74–77
  courtesy titles and names, 74–76
  examples of, 77
  job titles, 74
  pronouns, 76–77
  words and phrases, 77
Nonverbal communication, 4, 111–113,
    132–137
  age, 137
  body language, 112–113, 132–134
  clothing, 136
  colors, 136
  height, 137
  other symbols, 136–137
  space, 135
  spatial cues, 112
  time, 135–136
  touch, 134–135
Note-taking during job interviews, 379–380
Notes, 291
Noun-pronoun agreement, 656
Numbers, 667–668
  analyzing numbers, 587–590

O

Objections
  identifying and overcoming, 15
  in persuasive messages, 482–484
Objective case, 657
objective/rationale, 672
Observing customers and users, 546–547
Offshoring, 102
Omnibus motion, 165
1-2-3 organization, 287
Online acronyms, 91
Online information, 532–534
Online surveys, 541–542
Online visuals, 257
Open body positions, 112
Open questions, 538
Opening statements, 280–282
  narration or anecdote, 280, 494
  question, 280–281, 494
  quotation, 281, 495–496
  sales or fund-raising message, 493
  startling statements, 280, 495
Optical Character Readers (OCRs), 643
Oral communication; *see* Verbal
  communication
Oral messages, 277
Oral presentations, 275; *see also*
  PowerPoint slides
  adapting ideas to audience, 279–280
  choosing kind of, 278–279
  coping with interruptions, 291
  data choice, 285

delivering effective, 275, 288–291
  demonstrations for, 285–286
  eye contact, 289
  fear of public speaking, 288–289
  feedback from peers, 293
  goodwill presentations, 276
  group presentations, 292
  information to include, 284–286
  informative presentations, 276
  multiple audiences, 50–51
  notes and visuals, 291
  openers/closers, planning, 280–282
  organization of information, 286–287
  persuasive presentations, 276
  purposes of, 276
  questions from audience, 291–292
  speaking voice, 289–290
  spokesperson role, 280
  standing and gesturing, 290–291
  strategy for, 278–282
  visuals for, 291
  written vs. oral messages, 277
Organization
  of business documents, 182–183
  chronological, 287
  of direct requests, 477
  excluding alternatives, 287
  of information in reports, 594–602
  of informative/positive messages,
    404–407
  of job application letters, 346–355
  of negative messages, 437–440
  one-two-three, 287
  of oral presentations, 286–287
  pro-con, 287
  problem-causes-solution, 287
  of problem-solving messages, 479–488
  sales or fund-raising message, 493
Organizational culture, 35
  analysis of, 35–36
  discourse community, 36
  effect on business communication, 13
  persuasive messages and, 475–476
  writing styles and, 199
Organizational writing
  to build goodwill, 6
  external documents (examples), 7
  to inform, 6
  internal documents (examples), 8
  to persuade, 6
  three basic purposes of, 6
Other focusing, 12
Outsourcing, 99–100

P

Page design guidelines, 220–227
  capital letters, 224
  fonts, 224–225
  graphic elements, 226
  grid system, 226–227
  headings, 224
  highlighting and color, 226–227
  margins, 225–226
  placement of important elements, 226
  for résumés, 308
  right quadrants, 226

  visual impact, 223
  white space, 220–223
Paired bar charts, 253
Panel interviews, 371
Paper memos, 403–403
Paragraphs
  job application letters, 359
  summary, 349
  topic sentences for, 198–199
  transitions to link ideas, 199
  umbrella paragraph, 412
  unity in, 359
Parallel structure, 197–198, 606, 658–659
Paraphrase, 162
Parentheses, 665
Particular to general pattern, 597
Passive verbs, 64
Passive voice, 191–192
Patterns, 591
Pay-back reports, 529
Peer pressure, 157–158
People with disabilities and diseases,
    78–79
People-first language, 78–79
Performance appraisals, 489–491
  example of, 492
  negative, 451
Periods, 659, 665
Persona, 504
Personal digital assistants (PDAs), 92
Personal pronoun, 657
Personal space, 135
personal/personnel, 672
Personality tests, 33
Persuasive messages, 471–472; *see also*
  Sales and fund-raising messages
  analyzing situations for, 472–476
  argument, 474
  building common ground in, 481–482
  credibility, 474–475
  dealing with objections, 482–484
  direct requests, 476–479
  emotional appeal in, 485–488
  face-to-face persuasion, 504
  identifying specific actions, 473–474
  letters of recommendation, 491
  Myers-Briggs types in, 33
  objections, identifying and
    overcoming, 474
  organizational/cultural values in,
    475–476
  performance appraisals, 489–491
  primary/secondary purposes of, 472
  problem-solving messages, 476, 479–481
  reason to act promptly, 484–485
  recasting negatives as, 449
  solving a sample problem, 504–506
  strategy for, 476
  strength of case, 474–475
  threats vs., 476–477
  tone in, 489
  varieties of, 489–491
Persuasive presentations, 276; *see also* Oral
  presentations
Phone calls, 402
Phone interviews, 376

Photographs, 254–255
  altered photos, 250
  as bias-free, 79
Phrases, 660
Pictograms, 253
Pie charts, 245, 252
Pitch, 289
Plagiarism, 105, 201, 547
Planning; *see also* Revision; Writing
  business documents, 182–183
  collaborative writing, 166–167
  composing process, 180–182
  dot planning, 155–156
Politeness, 72–73
Polychronic cultures, 135–136
Population, 542
Portable media players, 92
Portable People Meter (PPM), 546
Portfolio, 319
Positive emphasis, 66–68, 71–72
  creation of, 68–71
  job application letters, 357–358
  tone, power, and politeness, 72–74
Positive feedback notes, 414
Positive messages, 400
  benefits in, 409–410
  checklist for, 419
  common media, 401–404
  ending for, 410–411
  managing information in, 408–409
  organization of, 404–407
  positive feedback notes, 414
  positive letter (example), 405
  positive memo (example), 406
  primary/secondary purposes of, 400
  problem solving example, 416–419
  recasting negatives as, 449
  responses to complaints, 415
  subject lines for, 407
  thank-you notes, 414
  varieties of, 411–415
  you-attitude, 65
Possessive case, 657
possible/possibly, 672
Post office abbreviations, 653
Postscript (P.S.), 497
Power, 72–73
  tone and, 73
PowerPoint slides, 4, 242, 278, 291, 528
  audience involvement with, 284
  background for, 283
  clip art, 283
  colors for, 284
  design of, 281, 283
  figures and tables, 283–284
  planning for, 282–284
  template, 283
Practices, 130–132
precede/proceed, 672
Predication errors, 659
Prepositions, 186
Presentations; *see* Oral presentations; Visuals
Presenting problem, 162
Primary audience, 30–31
Primary research, 532
principal/principle, 672

Pro-and-con pattern, 287, 595
Probes, 544
Problem-causes-solution, 287
Problem-solution pattern, 596
Problem-solving persuasive messages, 476, 479–488
  checklist for, 508
  dealing with objections, 482–484
  developing common ground, 481–482
  emotional appeal, 485–488
  example of, 480
  organization of, 479
  reasons to act promptly, 484–485
  subject line for, 480–481
Problem-solving process, 155
Problem-solving reports, 529
Procedural dimensions, 152
Progress reports, 528, 564, 574–578
  chronological, 576–577
  political uses of, 578
  recommendation progress reports, 578
  task progress reports, 576–578
Pronouns
  eliminating sexist language, 76–77
  intensive, 657
  nominative, 657
  noun-pronoun agreement, 656
  objective, 657
  personal, 657
  possessive, 657
  reflective, 657
Proofreading, 17–18, 181, 200, 203
  collaborative documents, 168–169
  job application letters, 359–360
  marked text (example), 674
  résumé, 323
Proofreading symbols, 655, 673–674
Proportional fonts, 224
Proposals, 564–574
  for action, 571–572
  budget and costs, 574
  business plans/funding proposals, 572–573
  class research projects, 566–571
  questions for, 565
  requests for proposals (RFPs), 566
  sales proposals, 572
  situation, proposal, final report, 564
  style for, 565–566
  writing of, 564–574
Prospecting letters, 347
  career change (example), 350
  first paragraphs of, 352–353
  organization of, 349
Province abbreviations, 653
Psychographic characteristics, 34, 38
Psychological description, 487, 503
Punctuation, 659–666
  apostrophe, 662–663
  colon, 659, 663
  commas, 659, 663–664
  dashes, 659, 664
  ellipses, 667
  hyphens, 664–665
  international punctuation, 666
  italics, 667

  parentheses, 665
  periods, 659
  quotation marks, 666
  semicolons, 659, 665–666
  square brackets, 666
  underlining, 667
Purpose, of business communication, 15
Purpose statement, 531
  formal report, 625

Q

Qualifications on résumé, 312
Quality focus, 98–99
Quarterly reports, 529
Questionnaires, 536, 540
Questions
  branching, 539
  closed/open, 538
  oral presentations, 291–292
  proposal questions, 565
  in sales and fund-raising messages, 494
  to start oral presentations, 280–281
  survey questions, 537–538
quiet/quite, 672
Quotation marks, 666
Quotations, 281, 495

R

Radio frequency (RFID) technology, 97
Ragged right margins, 225
Random sample, 542
Range, 588
Readability formulas, 205
Recommendation letters, 491
Recommendation progress reports, 576
Recommendation reports, 528–529, 598–602
Recommendations, formal report, 626
Red flag words, 43
Reference line, 638
References, 319–322
Referral interviews, 345
Reflective pronouns, 657
Refusals, 443–444, 450
regulate/relegate, 672
Rejections, 450
Release date, 622
Reports, 184, 528; *see also* Formal reports; Progress reports
  analyzing data/information for, 585–593
  basic steps in, 528
  clear, engaging writing in, 603
  closure reports, 598
  criteria for, 530
  efficient time management, 584
  forecasting, 604
  headings in, 604–605
  information for, 593
  informative reports, 598
  justification reports, 602
  keeping repetition minimal, 603–604
  levels of, 529
  presenting information effectively in, 602–606
  production process for, 529–530
  purpose statement, 531
  recommendation reports, 598–602

Reports, 184, 528;
  source citation and
    documentation, 547–554
  talking heads, 605–606
  topic sentences/headings in, 604–605
  topics, 530–531
  transitions in, 604–605
  varieties of, 528–529, 598–602
Requests for proposals (RFPs), 566
Research interviews, 544–545
Research strategies, 532–547; *see also* Class
  research projects
  evaluating Web sources, 534–536
  focus groups, 545–546
  mistakes and best practices, 536
  observing customers and users,
    546–547
  online/print information, 532–534
  primary research, 532
  research interviews, 544–545
  secondary research, 532
  surveys and interviews, 536–544
respectfully/respectively, 672
Respondents, 536
Response rate, 541
Restrictive clause, 664
Résumé blasting, 325, 327
Résumés, 302; *see also* Electronic résumés;
  Job hunting
  action verbs for, 315
  activities and other skills, 317–319
  attracting attention to, 303–304, 306
  career objective, 311–312
  checklist for, 322
  chronological résumé, 308–309
  details on, 307
  education, 312–313
  electronic résumés, 325–328
  emphasis in, 306–307
  essential information for, 310–311
  experience, 314–316
  guidelines for, 306–308
  honesty on, 329–330
  honors and awards, 314
  how employers use, 305
  job application letters vs., 342
  kinds of, 308–310
  layout and design, 308
  length of, 306
  name and contact information, 311
  portfolio, 319
  references, 319–322
  scan test/skim test, 305
  self-assessment for, 303–304
  skills (functional) résumé, 310, 316–317
  special problems/situations, 323–325
  summary of qualifications, 312
  video résumé, 324
  Web resources for, 313, 315
  what not to include, 322
  writing style, 307–308
Reverse chronology résumé, 308
Reverse psychology, 67
Revision, 181, 200–201; *see also* Writing
  checklist for, 203
  for clarity, 191–192

of collaborative documents, 167
  strategy for, 200–201
Right quadrants, 226
Robert's Rules of Order, 164
role/roll, 672
Run-on-sentences, 661

S

Sales and fund-raising messages, 476, 491–502
  action close, 496–497
  body of letter, 496
  emotional appeal in, 500–501
  fund-raising appeals, 498
  logical proof in, 499–500
  monetary requests, 499
  narration, stories, anecdotes, 494–495
  organization of, 493
  primary purpose, 493
  questions in, 494
  quotations, 495
  sales messages, 498
  sample letter, 501–502
  secondary purpose, 493
  startling statements, 495
  strategy in, 498–501
  unethical sales pitches, 493
  using a P.S., 497
  writing style, 503–504
Sales messages; *see* Sales and fund-raising
  messages
Sales pattern, 476
Sales proposals, 572
Sales reports, 529
Salutation, 637
Sample, 542
Sampling frame, 542
Sampling units, 542
Sans serif fonts, 225
Sarbanes-Oxley Act, 104
SBAR (situation, background, assessment,
  recommendation) model, 101
Scan test, 305
Scannable résumé, 325
Scope, formal report, 625
Secondary audience, 30–31
Secondary research, 532
Segmented bars, 253
Semicolon, 659, 661, 665
Sentence outline, 624
Sentences
  complex, 195
  compound, 185
  fused, 661
  grouping words into chunks in, 196
  including readers in, 197–198
  length and structure, 195–197
  parallel structure, 197
  punctuation of, 660–666
  run-on, 661
  sentence fragments, 661–662
  simple, 195
  subordinate clauses, 660
  topic sentences, 198–199
Serif fonts, 225
7 Habits of Highly Effective People, The
  (Covey), 114

Signpost, 287
Simple sentences, 195
simple/simplistic, 673
Simplified format, 637–638, 641, 646
Situational interviews, 387
Six-column grid, 227
Sketches, 255
Skills résumé, 310, 316–318
Skim test, 305
Slides; *see* PowerPoint slides; Visuals
Smiling, 133
Social networking sites, 93–94, 328
Solicited letters, 347
  example of, 348
  first paragraph of, 349
  organization of, 347–348
Source citation, 547–554
Sources, 604
Space, 135
Spam/spam filters, 94, 328
Spatial cues, 112
Spatial pattern, 597
Speaking voice, 289–290
  delivery, 290
  voice qualities, 289–290
Spelling, 672
Spokespersons, 280
Spot visuals, 246
Square brackets, 666
Stacked bar charts, 253
Standing and gesturing, 290–291
STAR interviewing technique, 388
State and province abbreviations, 653
stationary/stationery, 673
Storyboard, 183
Stress, 289
Stress interviews, 387–389
Structured interview, 544
Stub, 251
Student reports; *see* Class research projects
Student teams, characteristics of
  successful, 156–157
Study abroad programs, 355
Style
  conversational style, 183
  different levels of, 183
  generalizations about, 184–187
  good business style, 183
  improvement of, 187
  job application letters, 357
  organizational preferences for, 199
  for proposals, 565–566
  for résumés, 307–308
  traditional term paper, 183
Subdivided bar charts, 253
Subject, 195
Subject lines, 637
  as appropriate for organization, 407
  as concise, 407
  for e-mail messages, 408
  for informative/positive messages, 407
  negative messages, 441
  as specific, 407
Subject-verb agreement, 655
Subjects, 536
Subordinate clauses, 660

Summaries, 412–414
Summary abstracts, 624
Summary sentence, 349
Surveys, 541–544
  characteristics of good questions, 537–538
  designing questions for, 526–540
  face-to-face surveys, 541
  mail surveys, 541
  online surveys, 541–542
  response rates, 541
  samples for, 542–544
  telephone surveys, 541
  wording of questions for, 536
SWOT (strengths, weaknesses, opportunities, and threats) analysis, 596–598

T

Table of contents, 623
Tables, 245–246, 251–252
Talking heads, 605
Task progress reports, 576–578
Teams; *see also* Collaborative writing
  characteristics of successful, 154, 156–157
  conflict resolution, 160–164
  coordination of, 152
  criticism responses, 162–163
  decision-making strategies, 155–156
  diverse teams, 158–159
  effective meetings, 164–165
  feedback strategies, 156
  formation of, 152
  global teams, 151
  ground rules for, 152–153
  interaction of, 152–154
  leadership in, 154–155, 160
  making process work, 168–169
  peer pressure and groupthink, 157–158
  roles in, 153–154
  statistics on, 159
  troubleshooting problems of, 161
Teamwork, 101–102
Technical jargon, 190
Technology, 90–98
  data security, 95
  electronic privacy, 95–98
  electronic tools, 90–93
  information overload, 94–95
  social networking, 93–94
Telephone surveys, 541
Telepresence, 92–93
Template, 283
Term paper style, 183
Text messaging, 402–403
Thank-you letters/notes, 414
their/there/they're, 673
Think-aloud protocols, 547
Threats, 476–477
Three-column grid, 227
360-degree feedback, 156, 490
Time, 135–136
  monochronic cultures, 135–136
  polychronic cultures, 135–136
Time management, 114–116, 182
  Covey's matrix, 115

multitasking, 115–116
for report writing, 584
techniques for, 114–115
writing process, 182
Title page, 608, 622
to/too/two, 673
Tone, 72–73
  goodwill and, 9
  guidelines for, 73
  negative messages, 447–448
  persuasive messages, 489
  power implications, 73
Tone of voice, 289
Topic headings, 605
Topic sentences, 198–199, 604–605
Touch, 134–135
Trademarks, 245
Transitions, 199, 604–605
  transition words and phrases, 200
Transmittals, 411–413
Trip reports, 529
Truncated code, 533
Truncated graphs, 248–249
Two-margin format, 316
Two-meeting rule, 160
Typos, 202–203

U

Umbrella paragraph, 412
Underlining, 667
Understatement, 138
unique/unusual, 673
University of Chicago *Manual of Style,* 553
Unstructured interview, 544
Usability testing, 229, 231

V

Values, 130–132
Values and Life Styles (VALS), 34–35
Verbal communication, 4, 137–138
  compliments, 138
  cultural understanding and, 137–138
  understatement and exaggeration, 138
verbal/oral, 673
Verbs, 195
Vested interest, 474
Video interviews, 376–377
Video résumé, 324
Visuals, 4, 220, 241–242; *see also* PowerPoint slides
  accuracy of, 247–250
  bar charts, 245, 252–253
  chartjunk, 247–248
  choosing type of, 245
  clip art, 247
  color and decoration in, 246–247
  conventions for, 246
  cultural difference and, 252
  data displays and images, 251–257, 285
  dot chart, 245
  drawings, 255–256
  dynamic displays, 257
  ethical use of information in, 247–250
  Gantt charts, 245, 254
  grouped visuals, 244
  guidelines for design, 243–250

integration into text, 250–251
line graphs, 245, 253–254
maps, 256–256
online visuals, 257
oral presentations, 291
photographs, 250, 254–255
pie charts, 245, 252
quality of data, 243
in reports, 604
in rough drafts, 242
spot visuals, 246
stories told by, 243–244
tables, 245–246, 251–252
use of, 242–243
Vocabulary, 186
Voice qualities, 289–290
  pitch, 289
  stress, 289–290
  tone of voice, 289

W

Watchdog audience, 31
Web pages
  accessibility of, 229
  blogging, 95, 328
  design of, 229–231
  F-shaped pattern, 230
  posting résumé on, 327–328
Web research, 532–534
  business ethics resources, 105
  company information, 343
  evaluating Web sources, 534–536
  job sites, 304–305, 308
  news sites, 535
  reference collections, 535
  sources for, 534–535
  subject matter directories, 534
  U.S. government information, 535
What Color is Your Parachute (Bolles), 303
Whether/weather, 673
White space, 220
Widgets, 93–94
Wikipedia, 536
Wikis, 91
Wild card, 533
Wordiness, 63
Words
  accurate, 10, 187
  analysis of, 591
  appropriate, 187
  bypassing, 188
  choosing, 187–190
  confusing words, 668–673
  connotations, 188–189
  denotations of, 188
  eliminating wordiness, 193–195
  ethical implications of, 189
  familiar, 187, 189–190
  jargon, 190–191
  legal implications of, 187
  nonsexist language, 77–78
  positive/negative words, 188
  sentence length and structure, 195–197
  transition, 200
  use of verbs not nouns, 192–193
  value-laden words, 187

Wordy writing, 193
Work-family balance, 100–101
Workplace flexibility, 102
World Is Flat: A Brief History of the Twenty-First Century, The (Friedman), 100, 128
Writer's block, 182
Writing, 5, 181; *see also* Collaborative writing
   active vs. passive voice, 191–192
   bias-free documents, 74, 79
   business and administrative documents, 183–184
   conventions in, 186
   design as part of, 218
   direct mail, 503–504
   easier to read writing, 187–199
   eliminate wordiness, 193–195
   ethics and, 180
   good business style, 187
   importance of, 5
   integrating visual in text, 250–251
   to international audience, 139–140, 197
   job application letters, 357
   for multiple audiences, 50–51
   paragraphs and topic sentences, 198–199
   parellelism in, 197–198, 606, 658–659
   progress reports, 574–578
   time management for, 182
   use of verbs, 192–193
   ways good writers write, 180
   word choice, 187–190
   writer's block, 182
   written vs. oral messages, 277
Writing teams; *see* Collaborative writing

Y

you, 186
You-attitude, 16, 62–66, 70
   audience benefits and, 47
   beyond the sentence level, 65–66
   in conflict resolution, 163–164
   creation of, 62–63
   feelings and, 63–64
   job application letters, 358–358
   in negative situations, 64–65
   in positive situations, 65
your/you're, 673

Z

Z pattern, 226, 228